FIFTH EDITION

ASSESSMENT OF READING AND WRITING DIFFICULTIES

An Interactive Approach

Marjorie Y. Lipson
University of Vermont, Burlington, Professor Emerita

Karen K. Wixson
University of North Carolina at Greensboro

PEARSON

Boston   Columbus   Indianapolis   New York   San Francisco   Upper Saddle River

Amsterdam   Cape Town   Dubai   London   Madrid   Milan   Munich   Paris   Montréal   Toronto

Delhi   Mexico City   São Paulo   Sydney   Hong Kong   Seoul   Singapore   Taipei   Tokyo

Vice President, Editor in Chief, Teacher Education: *Aurora Martínez Ramos*
Editor: *Kathryn Boice*
Editorial Assistant: *Michelle Hochberg*
Senior Marketing Manager: *Krista Clark*
Production Editor: *Paula Carroll*
Editorial Production Service: *Element LLC*
Manufacturing Buyer: *Megan Cochran*
Electronic Composition: *Element LLC*
Interior Design: *Element LLC*
Cover Designer: *Jodi Notowitz*
Cover Image: *mojito.mak[dog]gmail[dot]com/Shutterstock.com*

10 9 8 7 6 5 4 3 2 1

ISBN-10: 0-13-299300-7
ISBN-13: 978-0-13-299300-5

Contents

SECTION THREE   Evaluating the Context   143

5   Evaluating the Instructional Environment/Context *coauthored with Nancy DeFrance*   **145**

CONTENTS   **vii**

SECTION FOUR   Evaluating the Learner: Looking More Closely   299

7 Assessing Young Readers and Writers   301

Understanding the Foundations of Literacy   301
Background   301
The Language Foundations of Literacy   302
Oral Language and Its Relationship to Reading and Writing   309
The Contextual and Experiential Foundations of Literacy   314
The Development of Written Language   324

Strategies and Tools for Assessing the Foundations of Literacy   327
Assessment of Early Language and Literacy   327
Observing Spontaneous Use of Knowledge and Skill   329
Structured Interviews and Observations   345
Structured Writing Assessments   353
Using Stories to Assess Emergent Abilities   356
Standardized Tests of Early Language and Literacy   358

Diagnostic Evidence of Emergent Literacy: The Case of Kyle   370

Chapter Summary   374

8 Structured Inventories and Benchmark and Progress Monitoring Assessments   376

Understanding Structured Inventories and Assessments   376

Strategies and Tools for Structured Assessment   378
Informal Reading Inventories   378
Interpreting Results from an IRI: Issues and an Example   396
Contemporary Innovations on the IRI Format   401
Oral Reading Fluency   412
Tests of Word Recognition and Phonics Decoding   417
Spelling Assessments   425
Assessing Written Language   429
Periodic Benchmark Assessment   435

Diagnostic Evidence from Structured Inventories and Benchmark Assessments   438
Tha'm   438
Kyle   438

Chapter Summary   439

Preface

This text, like the previous editions, is based on an interactive view of ability and disability. Since we first planned and wrote this text, the field has changed significantly in its treatment of reading and writing and in its awareness of the importance of assessing and teaching struggling readers and writers. We are encouraged that some ideas we have espoused for more than twenty years are more visible today. For example, it is now well-accepted practice to use information about students' instructional program and their success in high-quality first instruction as diagnostic and evaluative indicators. Indeed, the emerging framework for identifying students with learning disabilities—response to intervention (RTI), which we discuss throughout this edition—is premised on the idea that we must monitor students' progress and achievement in relation to their initial (core) instruction and also subsequent intervention attempts. Similarly, virtually every educator has some appreciation for the importance of continuous assessment to monitor students' performance and the impact of instruction, and there has been a resurgence of interest in dynamic assessment/diagnostic teaching.

At the same time, some issues that we addressed in the very first edition continue to cause concern. For example, large-scale assessments have begun to re-exert significant influence on decision making to the exclusion of ongoing, more authentic assessments. Although these tools are important, educators should remember to employ multiple measures as they consider student progress and to consider formative assessments as they examine whether a specific literacy program is benefitting groups and individuals. Similarly, the nature of these assessments must be considered with great care. We address these and other concerns throughout the text.

The more careful and extensive discussion of language acquisition, vocabulary development, and early literacy, as well as greater attention to English language learners, that were implemented in the fourth edition are retained in this edition. Additionally, we have continued to focus attention toward adolescent literacy. Finally, information about the RTI process has been tightened and embedded in a more thorough discussion of its role in the assessment-instruction process. We have, of course, updated the information throughout the book.

NEW TO THIS EDITION

While retaining these elements from earlier editions, there are a number of dramatic changes in this fifth edition. Two of these are especially notable: (1) a reorientation of the assessment-instruction process and (2) a focus on assessment.

First, we have reoriented the assessment-instruction process to more closely reflect the contexts and processes of contemporary school settings. Assessment is no longer the purview of specialists only, and differentiation and intervention start in the classroom, not waiting for a comprehensive diagnostic workup. Thus, we start the process in the classroom, where teachers use a wide range of available data to understand groups of students and to identify students who may be at risk for reading difficulties. Chapters 5 and 6 continue to focus on evaluating contextual factors such as methods, materials, and resources. These components are even more critical today because they may be used as part of the assessment consideration for identifying students for specific learning disability. In any event, as we continue through the book, we move from the use of every-pupil data to identify students who are struggling, to progress monitoring data that can refine our information about individual students, to diagnostic information that can inform our instruction/intervention for specific students. Throughout, we use case examples to bring the issues and practices into sharp focus. The case examples of both Kyle and Tha'm are threaded throughout the book, but you will meet other students as well, including Jackson in Chapter 3 and Yasmin, Lionel, and Simon in Chapter 10. These students capture most of the types of reading and/or writing difficulties that educators are likely to encounter.

We continue to believe that the interactive view of reading and writing offers a productive alternative to the deficit view that still dominates textbooks on reading and writing disability. Deficit models suggest that the cause of reading or writing difficulties lies entirely within the reader. Instructional programs based on a deficit model focus primarily on the "search for pathology" within the reader (Sarason & Doris, 1979). In contrast, an interactive view suggests that reading or writing disability is a relative concept, not a static state, and that the difficulty often lies in the match between the learner and the conditions of the learning situation. Extensive research has generated converging evidence to strengthen this perspective (Jenkins et al., 2003; Spear-Swerling & Sternberg, 1998), and additional research suggests strongly that all but a small proportion of struggling readers can learn to read and write well (Scanlon, Anderson, & Sweeney, 2010; Torgesen et al., 2001; Vellutino et al., 1996).

Consistent with an interactive perspective, this text focuses on the process of evaluating the existing match between the learner and the instructional context and identifying an optimal match. The content of this text also reflects our belief that the most important factor in effective assessment and instruction is the knowledge and expertise of the teacher. Accordingly, the first section of the text presents background information regarding reading, writing, and disability.

Section One, Theory into Practice, contains two chapters that provide the knowledge base for using the remainder of the text. In Chapter 1, "Perspectives on Reading and Writing Ability," we describe a historical view and several theoretical views of reading and writing. We also discuss legal and political perspectives on reading and writing and examine the legal and social roots of special education. In this chapter, also, we introduce concepts related to RTI as part of the most recent IDEA reauthorization. Chapter 2, "An Interactive View of Reading and Writing," details this view, providing a comprehensive picture of the various elements of skilled performance and the factors that influence it.

Section Two, Getting Started with the Assessment-Instruction Process, contains two chapters. In Chapter 3, "Reading and Writing Ability and the Assessment-Instruction Process," we consider different types and purposes of assessment and provide an overview of the assessment-instruction process that is used to guide the remainder of the text.

The case study of Jackson serves as an example. The remaining chapters are organized in a manner that parallels elements of the assessment-instruction process described in Chapter 3. In Chapter 4, "Getting Started," we use data from a classroom to demonstrate how data can be used to understand groups of students and identify students who may be at risk for reading difficulties. As well, we address important statistical concepts and provide a detailed description of the characteristics and types of tests that are commonly associated with assessment in reading and writing. Examples of screening, monitoring, and diagnostic tests are described and evaluated..

Section Three, Evaluating the Context, contains two chapters on evaluating the reading/writing context. Chapter 5, "Evaluating the Instructional Environment/Context," is the first of these two chapters. It considers how the overall classroom setting and instructional practices (including instructional goals such as the Common Core State Standards, methods, routines, and assessments) may influence reading and writing performance and provides tools for evaluating these aspects of the context. Chapter 6, "Instructional Resources," describes how reading and writing performance can be affected by these factors and provides additional tools and strategies for assessing the context.

The next three chapters are contained in **Section Four, Evaluating the Learner: Looking More Closely**. Chapter 7, "Assessing Young Readers and Writers," is devoted to an understanding of the language basis for literacy and the assessment and instruction of early literacy concepts, including phonological awareness. Chapter 8, "Structured Inventories and Benchmark Assessments and Progress Monitoring," provides an in-depth discussion of issues and practices in using information reading inventories (IRIs) and other more systematic assessment tools that are typically used for progress monitoring and/or screening. In Chapter 9, "Formative and Diagnostic Assessment," we focus on continuous methods of assessing decoding and word recognition, fluency, comprehension, and writing. These tools, more formative and diagnostic in nature, can provide critical information about individual students.

Section Five, Interactions: Assessment as Inquiry, consists of a single chapter, Chapter 10, "Interactive Decision Making," which emphasizes the juncture where assessment and instruction come together. Here we describe steps in the assessment-instruction process that involve evaluating the match between the learner and the context, reflecting on and generating hypotheses about the source of interference with learning, and identifying an optimal instructional match. We provide extensive discussion of dynamic assessment and diagnostic teaching and multiple examples of how this type of assessment may inform our instruction and intervention. We also reexamine progress monitoring and its pivotal role in continuing to improve instruction and intervention for struggling readers and writers. Finally, this chapter ends with a list of evidence-based instruction and intervention approaches that can be used in working with students whose reading/writing difficulties are more clearly evident as the result of our assessment-instruction process.

New! CourseSmart eBook and Other eBook Options Available

CourseSmart is an exciting new choice for purchasing this book. As an alternative to purchasing the printed book, you may purchase an electronic version of the same content via CourseSmart for reading on PC, Mac, as well as Android devices, iPad, iPhone, and iPod

Touch with CourseSmart Apps. With a CourseSmart eBook, readers can search the text, make notes online, and bookmark important passages for later review. For more information or to purchase access to the CourseSmart eBook, visit http://www.coursesmart.com. Also look for availability of this book on a number of other eBook devices and platforms.

MyEducationLab

MyEducationLab¨ Proven to engage students, provide trusted content, and improve results, Pearson MyLabs have helped over 8 million registered students reach true understanding in their courses. MyEducationLab engages students with real-life teaching situations through dynamic videos, case studies and student artifacts. Student progress is assessed, and a personalized study plan is created based on the student's unique results. Automatic grading and reporting keeps educators informed to quickly address gaps and improve student performance. All of the activities and exercises in MyEducationLab are built around essential learning outcomes for teachers and are mapped to professional teaching standards.

In Preparing Teachers for a Changing World, Linda Darling-Hammond and her colleagues point out that grounding teacher education in real classrooms—among real teachers and students and among actual examples of students' and teachers' work—is an important, and perhaps even an essential, part of training teachers for the complexities of teaching in today's classrooms.

In the MyEducationLab for this course you will find the following features and resources.

Study Plan Specific to Your Text

MyEducationLab gives students the opportunity to test themselves on key concepts and skills, track their own progress through the course, and access personalized Study Plan activities.

The customized Study Plan—with enriching activities—is generated based on students' results of a pretest. Study Plans tag incorrect questions from the pretest to the appropriate textbook learning outcome, helping students focus on the topics they need help with. Personalized Study Plan activities may include eBook reading assignments, and review, practice and enrichment activities.

After students complete the enrichment activities, they take a posttest to see the concepts they've mastered or the areas where they may need extra help. MyEducationLab then reports the Study Plan results to the instructor. Based on these reports, the instructor can adapt course material to suit the needs of individual students or the entire class.

Connection to National Standards

Now it is easier than ever to see how coursework is connected to national standards. Each topic, activity and exercise on MyEducationLab lists intended learning outcomes connected to the either the Common Core State Standards for Language arts or the IRA Standards for Reading Professionals.

Assignments and Activities

Designed to enhance your understanding of concepts covered in class, these assignable exercises show concepts in action (through videos, cases, and/or student and teacher artifacts). They help you deepen content knowledge and synthesize and apply concepts and strategies you read about in the book. (Correct answers for these assignments are available to the instructor only.)

Building Teaching Skills and Dispositions

These unique learning units help users practice and strengthen skills that are essential to effective teaching. After presenting the steps involved in a core teaching process, you are given an opportunity to practice applying this skill via videos, student and teacher artifacts, and/or case studies of authentic classrooms. Providing multiple opportunities to practice a single teaching concept, each activity encourages a deeper understanding and application of concepts, as well as the use of critical thinking skills. After practice, students take a quiz that is reported to the instructor gradebook.

Lesson Plan Builder

The Lesson Plan Builder is an effective and easy-to-use tool that you can use to create, update, and share quality lesson plans. The software also makes it easy to integrate state content standards into any lesson plan.

IRIS Center Resources

The IRIS Center at Vanderbilt University (http://iris.peabody.vanderbilt.edu), funded by the U.S. Department of Education's Office of Special Education Programs (OSEP), develops training enhancement materials for preservice and practicing teachers. The Center works with experts from across the country to create challenge-based interactive modules, case study units, and podcasts that provide research-validated information about working with students in inclusive settings. In your MyEducationLab course we have integrated this content where appropriate.

A+RISE Activities

A+RISE activities provide practice in targeting instruction. A+RISE®, developed by three-time Teacher of the Year and administrator, Evelyn Arroyo, provides quick, research-based strategies that get to the "how" of targeting instruction and making content accessible for all students, including English language learners.

A+RISE® Standards2Strategy™ is an innovative and interactive online resource that offers new teachers in grades K-12 just in time, research-based instructional strategies that:

- Meet the linguistic needs of ELLs as they learn content
- Differentiate instruction for all grades and abilities

- Offer reading and writing techniques, cooperative learning, use of linguistic and nonlinguistic representations, scaffolding, teacher modeling, higher order thinking, and alternative classroom ELL assessment
- Provide support to help teachers be effective through the integration of listening, speaking, reading, and writing along with the content curriculum
- Improve student achievement
- Are aligned to Common Core Elementary Language Arts standards (for the literacy strategies) and to English language proficiency standards in WIDA, Texas, California, and Florida.

Course Resources

The Course Resources section of MyEducationLab is designed to help you put together an effective lesson plan, prepare for and begin your career, navigate your first year of teaching, and understand key educational standards, policies, and laws. It includes the following:

- The Preparing a Portfolio module provides guidelines for creating a high-quality teaching portfolio.

Beginning Your Career offers tips, advice, and other valuable information on:

- Resume Writing and Interviewing: Includes expert advice on how to write impressive resumes and prepare for job interviews.
- Your First Year of Teaching: Provides practical tips to set up a first classroom, manage student behavior, and more easily organize for instruction and assessment.
- Law and Public Policies: Details specific directives and requirements you need to understand under the No Child Left Behind Act and the Individuals with Disabilities Education Improvement Act of 2004.

Acknowledgments

The Certification and Licensure section is designed to help you pass your licensure exam by giving you access to state test requirements, overviews of what tests cover, and sample test items.

The Certification and Licensure section includes the following:

- State Certification Test Requirements: Here, you can click on a state and will then be taken to a list of state certification tests.
- You can click on the Licensure Exams you need to take to find:
  - basic information about each test;
  - descriptions of what is covered on each test; and
  - sample test questions with explanations of correct answers.
- National Evaluation Series™ by Pearson: Here, students can see the tests in the NES, learn what is covered on each exam, and access sample test items with descriptions and rationales of correct answers. You can also purchase interactive

online tutorials developed by Pearson Evaluation Systems and the Pearson Teacher Education and Development group.

■ ETS Online Praxis Tutorials: Here you can purchase interactive online tutorials developed by ETS and by the Pearson Teacher Education and Development group.

Tutorials are available for the Praxis I exams and for select Praxis II exams.
Visit www.myeducationlab.com for a demonstration of this exciting new online teaching resource.

ACKNOWLEDGMENTS

We would like to acknowledge our appreciation to the many people who provided advice, encouragement, and assistance in the development of this text. First, we acknowledge a new contributor to this edition. Nancy DeFrance, professor at Grand Valley State University, revised Chapters 5 and 6 and provided insightful reaction to other chapters as well. We also gratefully acknowledge the thoughtful critiques offered by our reviewers. Their careful reading and clear insights improved this edition. Any failure to implement their helpful suggestions rests entirely with us. We would like to thank Jane Kanfer, Amber Jenkins, and the entire faculty and administration at Milton Elementary School, whose efforts to transform their assessment-instruction practices have resulted in such dramatic benefits for so many students. They are truly changing children's lives. We thank also Pam Chomsky-Higgins, for her special assistance in facilitating the work with Tha'm, and Julie Graham and Stefanie Hockenbury, who provided information that lead to the case discussion of Jackson. We are indebted to Molly McClasky for providing an inspiring teaching model and to Alysia Backman for conducting and writing the case study of Susie. We also thank Kyle and Tha'm and their parents for allowing us to share in the excitement of learning to read, and the educators at Essex Elementary School and John F. Kennedy Elementary School for their professional commitment to literacy development. Finally, we would like to acknowledge the special contribution of the students in our graduate and undergraduate courses who offered us feedback and ideas based on the original text.

We are grateful to the many individuals who have communicated with us about earlier versions of the text and hope that this revision keeps alive the dialogue. We look forward to our readers' responses to the challenges presented in this text.

Marjorie Y. Lipson
Karen K. Wixson

Theory into Practice

*I*n the first section of this book, we provide a theoretical foundation and rationale for the remainder of the text. This section contains three chapters. In Chapter 1, we describe various conceptualizations of reading and writing. We use available theory and research to advance an interactive perspective on reading and writing that lays the foundation for the assessment and instruction process described in the book. In the final part of this chapter, we describe the legal and political aspects of special education and disability and implications for instruction.

In Chapter 2, we discuss the component skills and strategies required to succeed in reading and writing tasks. This chapter may be a review for some students taking a graduate course in assessment and instruction, but the information is essential for teachers and specialists to make sound decisions during assessment and to plan appropriate instruction. In addition, we discuss in detail how learner factors, text factors, and contextual factors interact to influence student performance in reading and writing.

CHAPTER 1

Perspectives on Reading and Writing Ability

*C*oncerns about reading and writing instruction—and the number of children who are failing to learn—often dominate both public and professional conversation about education. Too often, these issues and what to do about them are argued from personal experience. One person favors a particular approach because it worked for her daughter. Others argue for a different approach because they themselves feel more comfortable with certain practices. Teachers, however, need to base their decisions on a broad base of data, looking for patterns and evidence of efficacy for many students. Sound decision making comes from a combination of personal experience and years of practice, along with information from empirical research, formal case studies, and structured observations.

Good teaching always involves adapting instruction to the needs of specific individuals or groups of students. Such essential adaptations are especially important when we are concerned, as we are in this text, with students who are not learning to read and write easily and well. These students require thoughtfully planned and executed instruction, fitted to their particular needs. What is needed for one "disabled" or struggling learner may be quite different from what is required for another to succeed.

How can we decide what to change, how do we need to adapt existing practice, and how can we help these students who have failed to learn when given exposure to the usual and customary instruction? To make decisions, teachers need to consider theories of learning and teaching, both scholarly and practical. As J. Dewey (1946, 1998) indicated, if you don't know where you're going, any road will take you there, but those who teach without theories may follow the road that leads nowhere. In reality, all teachers have some sort of theory, whether they realize it or not. Sometimes called "teacher beliefs" (Anders & Evans, 1994) and sometimes "perspective" (Gutiérrez-Clellen, Pena, & Quinn, 1995), teachers' theories about reading and writing are extremely important, because the particular theory a teacher holds determines, at least in part, what that teacher does in the name of reading and writing instruction. In fact, Robinson (1998) suggested that teachers generally hold "problem-solving-based theories." In other words, they ignore some sources of data (e.g., some types of research) if the data do not address the problems they face or the settings in which they work.

In this chapter, we describe the ways in which existing views of reading and writing have influenced both assessment and instruction over the years and provide information that will help you refine your own theories of reading and writing. In addition, we trace the legal and political roots of programs designed to address the needs of students with reading and writing difficulties. These various perspectives help teachers reflect on their existing knowledge and beliefs, setting the stage for a more extensive discussion in Chapter 2 of an interactive view of reading and writing.

UNDERSTANDING READING AND WRITING

In this section, we describe the historical contexts in which reading and writing came to be viewed separately in education in the United States. This is followed by a discussion of more-recent cognitive and social perspectives that have resulted in added integration of reading and writing in educational theory and practice.

Historical Perspectives on Reading and Writing

The field of literacy education as we know it today began as reading instruction in the public school at the primary grade levels. Public schooling was seen as a way to provide a growing population with the foundations of good citizenship, and reading was the way for students to acquire common moral and political principles. The first public schools of the mid-nineteenth century gave instruction in reading brief biblical passages and other moral-istic texts; later, primers offered secular patriotic readings with questions and answers for students to copy and recite (Clifford, 1984; Squire, 1991).

Writing at that time was considered less important than oral communication, because most citizens of the new nation had no need to write except to sign their names. Like reading, writing was thought to be a simple matter—a way to put into print words that would otherwise be spoken. All students needed to know for that simple translation was handwriting and spelling (Clifford, 1984; Russell, 1991).

After the Civil War, the growing commercial and professional class was divided into many separate communities. These communities were linked more by written texts—such as memos, reports, professional literature, and administrative records—than by geography or social class (Russell, 1991). The new professionals demanded that schools provide their children an education that would prepare them for roles in government, commerce, and the growing professions. The purposes for school literacy instruction expanded to serve the general population as well as the college-bound elite (Katz, 1987; Russell, 1991).

In 1894 a committee composed of university professors, professionals, and business-men issued the Report of the Committee of Ten on public high schools. The report called for greater emphasis on English literature, because literature was seen as a vehicle for transmitting common values and "uplifting" ordinary citizens (Applebee, 1974). Following this report, a National Conference on College Entrance Requirements produced a list of core readings—a literary canon that dominated the entire high school English curriculum for decades (Applebee, 1974).

The Committee of Ten also set standards for written expression that were accepted throughout the country (Heath, 1991; Russell, 1991). As a result, schools and other public institutions began emphasizing standard English in writing as well as speaking; correct spelling and grammar thus became a focus of instruction. Classroom writing activities typically consisted of copying texts, underlining, circling, and supplying one-word responses (Clifford, 1989; North, 1987). Graded reading books that matched children's age and ability level, first printed in 1836, became the norm by the late 1800s and established the pattern for the basal reading series still used today (Squire, 1991).

From the mid-1800s through the first decades of the twentieth century, a progressive philosophy of education gained influence among educators. The foremost progressive philosopher of education, John Dewey, advocated a public school system that functioned neither to preserve privileged traditions nor to prepare students for prevailing social conditions, but rather to improve students' lives and create a society whose benefits accrued to all citizens (Applebee, 1974; Cremin, 1989). Dewey rejected the literary canon and instead recommended curriculum materials that had relevance to students. He promoted cooperation and group work in the classroom to encourage a free exchange of ideas and saw schools as learning communities (Applebee, 1974; Hendley, 1986; Russell, 1991).

The scientific movement arose as a counterinfluence on schools during the progressive era. One of the early educational psychologists, Edward Thorndike, developed scientific theories that led to the development of objective measures of student achievement. These measures were used to sort students into ability groups so that teachers could provide instruction suited to particular needs. This movement came to exert the same control that the literary canon once had on curriculum and instruction in the form of skills instruction.

In the last forty years, our understanding of how students learn and our approach to studying reading and writing have changed rather dramatically as a result of two newer ways of thinking about teaching and learning: the cognitive revolution and the "social turn" (Geertz, 1983). These two perspectives, described more fully in the next section, are important because they prompted researchers and educators to consider reading and writing together, rather than separately. In addition, they are the basis for the interactive view described in this text. In describing these perspectives, we are greatly indebted to the thinking of Hiebert and Raphael (1996), McCarthey and Raphael (1992), and Englert and Palincsar (1991).

Cognitive Information-Processing Perspectives on Reading and Writing

During the World War II period, computer technology suggested new ways to model mental processes that influenced our views of learning. The new cognitive scientists viewed computers and the mind as similar: active, self-monitoring systems for processing information. Information-processing theories have been used to develop several models of both reading and writing processes (for example, Gough, 1972; Hayes & Flower, 1980; Kintsch & van Dijk, 1978; LaBerge & Samuels, 1974).

When an information-processing perspective is applied to reading and writing, three assumptions seem to operate: (1) reading and writing comprise a number of subprocesses used to perform specialized tasks; (2) readers and writers have limited capacity for attention so that trade-offs occur across the subprocesses; and (3) competence in reading and writing is determined by the degree of attention needed to operate subprocesses—i.e., the less memory needed, the more efficient the operation (McCarthey & Raphael, 1992).

Like the computer whose components perform specialized functions that interact to complete a task, information-processing models divide reading and writing processes into subprocesses, each with a different function. For example, Gough (1972) proposed a model of reading as a linear, hierarchical process. The reader works from the smallest units of analysis (letters) to the largest (text meaning), and each level of analysis triggers the next, with the sum of these analyses adding up to meaning.

In contrast, LaBerge and Samuels (1974) described reading in terms of the component processes that relate to the functions of different types of memory: visual, phonological, semantic, and episodic. At the heart of their model is attention, the process that allocates the reader's efforts to the subprocess or memory type needed for the task at hand. In this view, progress through the subprocesses may not be linear, because attention may be allocated to different memories in different patterns.

The information-processing perspective also includes interactive models (e.g., Rumelhart, 1977). Interactive models suggest that the processing of text is a flexible interaction among the different information sources available to the reader and that the information contained in "higher" stages of processing can influence, as well as be influenced by, the analysis that occurs at lower stages of analysis.

Information-processing models of writing are similar to those of reading. For example, Flower and Hayes (1981) described writing as consisting of three recursive phases: planning, in which writers set goals and make plans; translating, in which writers put ideas into written form; and reviewing, in which writers test the plans and translations. Similarly, Scardamalia, Bereiter, and Goelman (1982) distinguish between metacomponents, used to identify choices and make decisions, and performance components that allow writers to carry out their plans. Although these models differ in the division of tasks and specific definitions of the writing process, they share an emphasis on dividing the process into smaller components for analysis and description.

Information-processing theorists also use the computer metaphor to describe the limited capacity of readers and writers, who must often juggle several subprocesses at once (accessing background knowledge, organizing ideas, making decisions about relevant and redundant information, and monitoring). Just as the computer cannot attend to everything at once, humans also have limitations on their processing capacities. The cognitive juggling required for successful reading and writing performance is explained in terms of how much attention is actually necessary to engage in a given activity and how effectively individuals switch their attention to the process most useful for a particular task.

The term *automaticity* has been used to describe the way skilled readers' subprocesses operate as instinctive routines (LaBerge & Samuels, 1974). Initially, subprocesses such as decoding in reading and handwriting in composition demand so much of our attentional resources that higher-level processes cannot be employed. Eventually, however, lower-level subprocesses are mastered to the point of automaticity, and then new routines can be learned. Although not all subprocesses become automatic (comprehension and planning always involve some conscious attention), the more that do become automatic, the better able the reader or writer is to attend to more cognitively demanding activities.

Cognitive scientists investigating reading and writing can roughly be divided into those who adhere to an information-processing model of cognition and those adhering to the more recent constructivist model of cognition. The former conceptualize meaning as being transported from author to reader (e.g., Hiebert & Raphael, 1996); the latter (e.g., R. C. Anderson, 1977; Bransford, 1979; A. L. Brown, 1978) see meaning as being constructed by the reader based on information the reader already possesses (the reader's schema) and the information provided by the text. The constructivist view fits well with the social perspectives we are about to describe, and together they constitute what is known as a *sociocognitive view of reading and writing.*

Implications.   Information-processing models and research provide us with an increased understanding of reading and writing processes in terms of their components. These models, also provide a better understanding of the knowledge base of skilled readers and writers. However, most information-processing models do not account for the variability that occurs in reading and writing as a result of a host of contextual factors such as the nature of the task, goals, purposes, and instruction. They also tend to overlook or dismiss larger social and cultural factors that influence an individual's reading and writing performance.

There has been little effort to detail the specific links between reading and writing from within the information-processing perspective. Although there is some research from this perspective that deals with how reading and writing may be related (for example, Ehri, 1989; Shanahan & Lomax, 1986), information-processing theory sheds little light on how to encourage their development or on how less-successful or novice readers and writers become more skilled.

Social Perspectives on Reading and Writing

Recent social theories of language and learning suggest that meaning is not an individual construction, but a social negotiation that depends on supportive interaction and shared use of language. The assumptions underlying various social perspectives on reading and writing are quite different from those described above: (1) reading and writing are social and cultural phenomena; (2) knowledge is constructed through the individual's interaction with the sociocultural environment; and (3) cognitive processes related to reading and writing are acquired through contextualized activity and assisted learning (Englert & Palincsar, 1991; McCarthey & Raphael, 1992).

Sociocultural Nature of Reading and Writing.   The societies or cultures within which we live, learn, and work determine how reading and writing are defined, instructed, and evaluated. For example, at the district level, curriculum decisions such as the choice of guided reading approaches versus structured basal reading programs influence the instructional and assessment practices of teachers.

At the school level, the principal's and teachers' beliefs about learning and teaching have an effect on practices that determine, for example, the extent to which diverse groups of students are accorded equal opportunities to learn. Culture also manifests itself in classrooms in the form of patterns of social interactions and the sets of rules or routines that guide teachers' and students' social exchanges. These routines develop in the participants shared understandings about what it means to read and write, what "counts" as reading and writing, and appropriate uses of reading and writing (Dyson, 1999; Miller & Gadnow, 1995; Rogoff, 1990).

According to sociocultural theorists, the oral and written texts that students produce don't stand alone. Instead, they must be seen as related to all the activity and experience that have gone before with that teacher and classroom. Books have been read, ideas have been exchanged, and social interactions have occurred, all of which influence the types of oral and written exchanges that happen subsequently (Cole, 1990).

Viewing reading and writing in terms of cultural practices means that we must understand the political and social, as well as cognitive, dimensions of literacy. When the classroom is viewed as a culture, we must be concerned with teachers' and students' beliefs about reading and writing, and the patterns of interactions occurring among students and between teachers and students, rather than with discrete activities. We must consider factors such as the ways in which reading and writing are represented to students and the occasions students have to participate as readers and writers within the classroom culture.

Knowledge Construction through Interaction.   The social perspective on learning asserts that learning to think, read, and write are not individual, independent activities. Instead, the acquisition of such functions begins with the interactions of parent and child, among siblings and peers, or between teacher and students. The role of language and dialogue is critical, because it is through speech and social interaction that the learner acquires abilities such as reading and writing (Vygotsky, 1986).

Vygotsky (1978) proposed that from the early stages of development, people are involved in fundamentally social processes such as communication; later, in a schooling context, these processes are jointly performed and constructed by teachers and students as they cooperatively engage in dialogue. Processes that begin as social and shared become internalized in a second phase. In this phase, students' performance is assisted by their own vocalized self-talk; social speech becomes internalized as egocentric speech.

Finally, in a third phase, the self-directing speech of the learner goes underground as it becomes "inner speech." At this point, learners do not overtly vocalize or self-instruct, although self-talk may surface as the difficulty of the task increases. Learners do not simply take in information; they continually construct new, more complex meanings as they transform knowledge for application across a broad range of activities.

Contextualized Activity and Assisted Learning.   Vygotsky (1978) suggested that cognitive processes are best understood as context specific and learned through practical activity. This implies that reading and writing instruction must engage students at all ability levels as participants in contextualized, authentic, and holistic activities. Vygotsky (1978) proposed that the difference between what a child can do alone and what he or she can do with the assistance of a more capable other represents the "zone of proximal development" (ZPD) in which instruction should occur. The concept of the ZPD assumes that a deliberate transfer of control from the more knowledgeable to the less knowledgeable person takes place.

How the adult or more knowledgeable person assists the student in taking control of a process is integral to social views of learning. Assisted learning and instruction have been compared to a scaffold, in that it provides support but is also temporary and adjustable (Palincsar, 1984; Wood, Bruner, & Ross, 1976). This educational scaffolding involves structuring tasks through modeling, explaining, questioning, and feedback until the learner can operate independently and is essential to learning in a social view of reading and writing.

Implications. Social perspectives on reading and writing address a number of the weaknesses identified in cognitive models. Specifically, they account for variations among cultures in literacy practices and in the ways students learn to read and write in different settings. They highlight the role of social context and bring our attention to the need to be sensitive to the values and practices of different cultural groups in schools. In addition, the focus on language as a cultural tool helps us understand how new learning is acquired and how important it is in developing new instructional strategies (McCarthey & Raphael, 1992).

Social perspectives emphasize that reading and writing are connected through their uses within the culture and through the role dialogue plays in the development of literacy. Although there is research on issues related to the role of culture in literacy practices and in cognition, little research has been done on the connections between reading and writing from this perspective. Although variable within the range of social perspectives, some do offer insight into literacy development and instructional practices that support increased learning among less-skilled readers and writers.

An Interactive Perspective on Reading and Writing

The interactive perspective on reading and writing described in this book is an amalgam of the cognitive information-processing and social views. It rests on several assumptions: (1) reading and writing are processes of constructing meaning; (2) the construction of meaning results from an interaction between the reader/writer and the context of the reading/writing situation; and (3) the interaction is dynamic, or variable, as a function of numerous reader/writer and contextual factors (see Figure 1.1). Meaning, in the form of skilled reading and writing performance, is generated from the interaction between the learner and the reading/writing context, and there are many factors that influence learners' ability to comprehend and compose. A general discussion of this perspective is provided below.

Construction of Meaning in Reading and Writing. The interactive view acknowledges how development in reading and development in writing are interrelated. At both the word level (Bear & Templeton, 1998) and the discourse level (Tierney, 1992), writing informs reading and vice versa. An interactive perspective suggests that readers construct meaning when they comprehend in much the same way writers construct meaning when they compose. Meaning is created in the mind of the reader/writer as a function of the interplay between the cognitive information-processing abilities of individuals and the context of the reading and/or writing event. As with the sociocultural perspective, skilled performance is viewed as the ability to use reading and writing for personal, recreational, academic, and civic purposes.

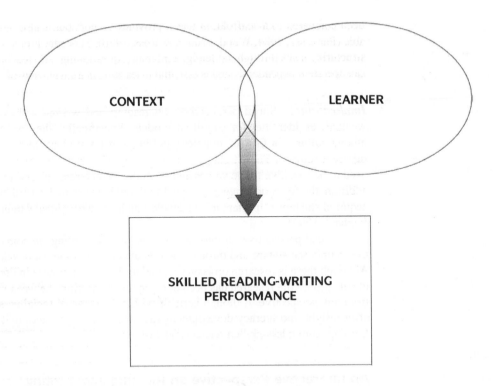

FIGURE 1.1   An Interactive View of Reading and Writing

Interactions.   The interactive view argues that *both* cognitive processes and socio-cultural aspects of context influence reading and writing processes and performance. Reader/writer factors that affect reading and writing performance and processes include prior knowledge of content, knowledge about reading and writing processes, and attitudes and motivation. Context factors include the setting for learning, the reading and writing curriculum, and the instructional methods, materials, and tasks employed. Each of these factors has been shown to affect how people approach reading and writing tasks and also how well they perform.

Dynamic Interactions.   The term *dynamic* is used to indicate that reading and writing are variable processes, adapting to the specific demands of each particular reading/writing experience. Reading and writing ability are relative properties, not stable, static constructs. Each person may have a range of reading and writing abilities, depending on texts, tasks, and contexts. For example, we may be very good at writing friendly letters but do poorly at writing research papers, or we may devour romance novels with good comprehension but shudder at the thought of reading a book about the latest breakthroughs in physics.

Implications.   An interactive perspective offers the most useful insights for educators working with less-skilled readers and writers. Indeed, Frankel, Pearson, and Nair (2011) have argued that it provides "the broadest possible framework for conceptualizing disability and pointing toward appropriate instructional interventions" (p. 222). From this perspective, the variability within and across individuals means that reading and writing performance is a function of what learners *can* and *will* do at any given moment. Appropriate instruction requires that we understand the variability that exists within and across individual learners. Issues of linguistic background, motivation, and/or cultural understanding and values are each as relevant as whether the learner can read sight words or understand punctuation. Instruction that takes these issues into account focuses on providing students with a rich and diverse selection of materials and opportunities for ample self-selection during both reading and writing. It also provides students opportunities to read and write for many different purposes.

UNDERSTANDING THE LEGAL AND POLITICAL ASPECTS OF READING AND WRITING

In this section, we turn away from theoretical perspectives and toward legal and political perspectives on the acquisition of literacy among students who are struggling. Reading has become a major topic of conversation and action in the political arena, with the initial emphasis on early reading expanding to an interest in adolescent literacy. The influence of policy on practice—at local, state, and national levels—has never been greater, and we examine here some of the activity surrounding these issues. In addition, because they influence literacy instruction so strongly, we consider the legal and social basis for present-day *special education* programs and describe the specific provisions for meeting existing legal requirements in that arena.

EDUCATIONAL REFORM, READING, AND LITERACY

Reading and literacy are at the heart of some of the most controversial debates about education. People care about how well students read and write. Some care about it because they are particularly concerned about reading and writing as the basis for most other learning. Others care about it because they view it as a general indicator of the health of public schools. Finally, some care about it because the methods of instruction may be emblematic of philosophical or personal orientations toward larger issues such as student-centered versus curriculum-centered learning.

We cannot, of course, take on all of these issues in this book. However, we cannot avoid them either. Many theoretical and pedagogical arguments are not new (see Lemann, 1997, and Mathews, 1966, for a discussion of the "reading wars"). Certainly, old arguments have been resurrected in the current debate. However, the contemporary version of the debate is also an argument about which knowledge counts (and to whom) and also about who will decide what counts.

To an extraordinary extent, the current debates are being conducted in state houses, legislative meeting rooms, and the halls of Congress. "This modern reform movement has been characterized by efforts to create new 'policy instruments' to elicit, encourage, or demand changes in teaching and learning" (Valencia & Wixson, 2000, p. 909). Whether by means of mandated assessments and standards, or teacher preparation requirements, teachers and teacher educators find their ability to make decisions influenced or constrained (see Lipson, Mosenthal, Daniels, & Woodside-Jiron, 2000; McGill-Franzen, 2000; Valencia & Wixson, 2004).

The attention given reading and writing policies and practices can have the positive effect of creating more-coherent programs, providing support for less-skilled and knowledgeable teachers, and helping everyone to gain clarity about a state or community's shared goals. Depending on how policy is developed and implemented, it can also have the less positive effect of creating divisions among educators, promoting cynicism and distrust among the public, and calling into question the motives of the participants.

If they did not know this before, most teachers now understand that policies and practices can make a very big difference in the choices they have available to them. Political forays might seem distant from the classroom and from our work with individual students who are having reading difficulties. However, they do affect instruction at all levels in significant ways. Under the No Child Left Behind Act (NCLB) of 2001, there is a mandate for all states to have aligned standards and tests. NCLB has also increased testing accountability by requiring states to administer annual reading and mathematics assessments in grades 3 through 8. State assessments are referred to as "high-stakes" tests because they have significant consequences for districts, schools, administrations, teachers, and students. Administrators and teachers can be rewarded or punished based on student performance on these tests, which can also be used to determine if students are retained or fail to graduate from high school. Many individuals and groups have expressed concerns about high-stakes testing, such as those in a position statement adopted by the Board of Directors of the International Reading Association (IRA, May 1999). The IRA position states a particular concern that "testing has become a means of controlling instruction as opposed to a way of gathering information to help students become better readers" and calls for "the evaluation of the impact of current types and levels of testing on teaching quality, student motivation, educational policy making, and the public's perception of the quality of schooling" (IRA, May 1999, p. 1).

NCLB has also influenced the nature of the programs or practices used to teach reading, primarily through its Reading First initiative. Commercial publishers shape their programs to accommodate both the intellectual and political debates. Teachers might find that they *must* use a particular program to teach a specifically mandated component of reading using a predetermined methodology similarly mandated. Tests that assess only limited aspects of reading competence encourage teachers to address a narrower range of reading behaviors.

In short, the policy perspective has moved into a central spot, governing (directly and indirectly) the decisions that teachers make every day. Debates continue about what types of text to use, whether students should be grouped or not, whether skills or literature should be taught, and whether to teach explicitly or implicitly. Over the years, these debates have triggered several significant attempts to specify the instructional imperatives for teaching reading. One of the earliest efforts in the recent past was initiated by the National Academy of Sciences, which created a Committee on the Prevention of Reading Difficulties and charged the committee to synthesize research on early reading and reading difficulties. In 1998, this prestigious group published *Preventing Reading Difficulties (PRD)* (Snow, Burns, & Griffin, 1998).

Shortly following the PRD report, Congress charged the director of the National Institute of Child Health and Human Development and the Secretary of Education to establish a panel of experts to synthesize and summarize the research-based knowledge related to teaching children to read. The charge was controversial, largely because it conceived of research so narrowly that it excluded a large amount of worthwhile literacy research and limited the usefulness of the findings for classroom teachers. The resulting document, *Teaching Children to Read: An Evidence-Based Assessment of Scientific Research and Its Implications for Reading Instruction* (National Reading Panel [NRP], 2000) was released amid significant debate (see, e.g., Garan, 2001; Shanahan, 2001). Despite the criticisms, the NRP report played a key role in federal reading policy and in establishing current reading standards and practices, primarily through the policies associated with the Reading First initiative (Wixson, Dutro, & Athan, 2004).

Following the attention to early reading came increased interest in reading comprehension and adolescent literacy. Attention to reading comprehension began with a research agenda-setting effort established by the U.S. Department of Education and managed by the RAND Corporation, which resulted in a volume entitled *Reading for Understanding: Toward an R&D Program in Reading Comprehension* (RAND, 2002), otherwise known as the RAND report. This report provided the impetus for the U.S. Department of Education's Office of Educational Research and Improvement (now the Institute for Educational Sciences, or IES) to create a new program of research on reading comprehension. Most recently, attention has moved toward comprehension in the middle and secondary schools, as reflected in the report entitled Reading Next (Biancarosa & Snow, 2004). The foreword to this report acknowledges that the country's attention to reading in the primary grades, described as "word recognition," has neglected "the core of reading: comprehension, learning while reading, reading in the content areas, and reading in the service of secondary or higher education. . . ." and that " . . . many excellent third-grade readers will falter or fail in later-grade academic tasks if the teaching of reading is neglected in the middle and secondary grades" (p. 1). This report delineates fifteen elements aimed at improving middle and high school literacy achievement, and calls on the funding, research, policy-making, and education communities to embrace "these recommendations in an effort to meet the needs of all students in our society, while also strengthening our understanding of exactly what works, when, and for whom. We will hereby strengthen the chances for striving readers to graduate from high school as strong, independent learners prepared to take on the multiple challenges of life in a global economy" (p. 5). Shortly following the release of Reading Next, the U.S. Department of Education announced its Striving Readers grant program, which made its first awards in 2006. The goals of this program are threefold: (1) to enhance the overall level of reading achievement in middle and high schools through improvements in the quality of literacy instruction across the curriculum, (2) to improve the literacy skills of struggling adolescent readers, and (3) to help build a strong scientific research base around specific strategies that improve adolescent literacy skills.

The most recent entry into the long line of reports and policy documents is the Common Core State Standards in English Language Arts (CCSS-ELA), released in June 2010 by the Council of Chief State School Officers (CCSSO) and the National Governors Association (NGA). Largely as a result of the tremendous variability across states with regard to standards, assessments, and proficiency criteria, there are renewed efforts to bring coherence to state standards and assessments in reading and mathematics. At this writing, forty-five states plus the District of Columbia have adopted the CCSS, and a similar number of states have joined together in two consortia to develop new state assessments aligned with the CCSS for implementation in 2014–2015.

Throughout this book we describe more fully our own interactive perspective, one that we believe successfully accounts for a wide array of research findings and provides a place in the dialogue for a perspective that honors both the findings of research and the diverse contexts of teaching and learning in U.S. schools.

LEGAL AND SOCIAL ROOTS OF SPECIAL EDUCATION

During the 1950s and 1960s, a combination of social and political factors combined to create an environment in which unusual and extensive attention was focused on students who were failing to learn easily and well in the public schools of the United States. National attention was captured by a series of legal battles initiated by a group of advocates who wanted to see that all students received appropriate public education.

One such legal battle was *PARC v. Commonwealth of Pennsylvania* (1971), in which the court concluded that students had been excluded or excused from attendance in public schools simply because they were disabled and ordered the state to support public education for such students. As a result, any school-age child, no matter how impaired, was eligible to receive a free, appropriate public education for the first time in history.

Access to public education was only one of the problems confronting the field at that time, however. The practices surrounding testing and labeling students were suspect for many reasons. For minority students, the problems of abuses and inadequate protections were particularly apparent. Two other cases were directly related to practices in these areas. The decisions handed down by the court in *Diana v. Board of Education* (1970) and *Larry P. v. Riles* (which started in 1971 and concluded in 1979) required that the state of California test students in their primary language, reevaluate students from minority groups (African Americans, Latinos, and Asians) currently in classes for the mentally retarded, and develop and standardize IQ tests appropriate for minority groups.

A final concern among advocates in the area of special education involved the treatment and instruction provided to handicapped individuals once they were placed in specialized institutional settings. In two cases, *Wyatt v. Stickney* and *New York ARC v. Rockefeller*, judges ruled that residents of such placements had the right to appropriate treatment, and in the *Wyatt* case, the judge specified that this treatment should occur in the least restrictive environment.

The active round of legal rulings prompted both attention and concern and provided the basis for the legislative initiatives to follow. Beginning in the early 1960s, laws were passed that established federal programs related to service, training, and research designed specifically for the handicapped. These legislative actions culminated with the passage of Section 504 of the Rehabilitation Act of 1973 and the Education for All Handicapped Act (PL 94-142) in 1975. Replaced by the Individuals with Disabilities Education Act (PL 101-476, or IDEA) in 1990, it was further amended in 1997 (PL 105-17) and again in 2004 (PL 108-446). Taken together, these legislative actions define disability; describe the identification of students and the planning of instructional programs; and guide decisions about procedures for identification of, placement of, and programs for students with special needs.

Although Section 504 was actually passed before the other legislation, the regulations came out several years later, and many schools were slow to adopt the provisions of Section 504. On the other hand, all schools are well aware of the provisions of IDEA, which mandates the following:

- The right to education—all handicapped children are to be provided with free, appropriate public education
- The right to nondiscriminatory evaluation
- The right to an IEP (Individualized Education Plan)—a clear statement of objectives for each child, along with documentation of the child's current and expected performance
- The right to education in the least restrictive environment
- The right to due process
- The right of parental participation (Gallagher, 1984)

Special Education Identification

The actual procedures for implementing the mandates of IDEA vary somewhat from community to community, but the process must include provisions for meeting each mandate. Practically speaking, a teacher, administrator, or parent may make an initial referral for the purposes of determining whether a student is entitled to special education services. Following this referral, the child's parents must be fully informed about the prospective assessment process and permission to proceed must be received from them. Only after these stages have been completed are assessment procedures initiated to determine whether the student meets federal and local guidelines for exceptionality. In addition, the assessment is usually designed to determine the category of handicap that will be used for purposes of classification. For students identified as having a specific learning disability, the primary determining factor has been a discrepancy between their measured achievement and intellectual ability.

IDEA 1997 clearly specifies procedures for the assessment phase. The procedures designed to address the mandate that students have "the right to nondiscriminatory evaluation" are as follows:

- Tests must be selected and administered so as to ensure that results "accurately reflect the child's aptitude and achievement . . . rather than reflecting the child's impaired sensory, manual, or speaking skills."

- No single testing procedure may be used for determining an appropriate educational program for the child.
- The evaluation must be conducted by a multidisciplinary team.
- The child must be assessed in all areas related to health, vision, hearing, social and emotional status, academic performance, communicative status, and motor abilities. (See IDEA 1997 Regulations, C.F.R. § 300.532.)

In addition, the law provides guidelines for the types of assessment instruments that may be used, stating that tests and other evaluation materials

- should be provided and administered in the child's native language;
- should have been validated for the specific purpose for which they are used;
- should be administered by trained personnel; and
- should include materials tailored to assess specific areas of educational need and not merely those that are designed to provide a single general intelligence quotient. (See IDEA 1997 Regulations, C.F.R. § 300.532.)

When the assessment phase is completed, IDEA 1997 states clearly that there will be a meeting to develop the child's individualized education plan (IEP). As was previously noted, the IEP is mandated by the federal government and requires a clear statement of objectives for each child, along with documentation of the child's current and expected performance. In addition, the IEP must contain a statement that specifies who will be responsible for each component of the plan and ensures periodic reevaluation of the child's status.

IDEA 1997 regulations require that the multidisciplinary team involved in developing the IEP must include a public education representative who is qualified to provide or supervise the provision of special education, a regular education teacher, the child's teacher, one or both of the child's parents, the child where applicable, and other individuals at the discretion of the parent or agency (see IDEA Regulations, C.F.R. § 300.344 [1977]).

The parent(s) must agree to the designation of the child under a particular handicapping condition and to the information provided in the IEP. If the parents do not agree with the recommendations of the team, a series of legal procedures are set in motion to settle the disagreement.

When IDEA was reauthorized in 2004, it included a new approach for determining eligibility for learning disability services. This law indicates that schools will not be required to take into consideration whether a student has a severe discrepancy between achievement and intellectual ability. Rather, they may use a process called response to intervention (RTI) that determines if the student responds to scientific, research-based interventions as part of the evaluation process. After receiving one or more such interventions, students who do not demonstrate adequate progress are then considered for an evaluation for a specific learning disability. According to a white paper by the National Association of State Directors of Special Education (NASDSE) and the Council of Administrators of Special Education (CASE), RTI builds on recommendations made by the President's Commission on Excellence in Special Education (2002) that children with disabilities should first be considered general education students and that special education should embrace a model of prevention as opposed to a model of failure (NASDSE/CASE, 2006).

Although some have been quick to instantiate the RTI concept with a particular, special education–oriented three-tier model, others have provided a broader perspective. For example, the NASDSE/CASE (2006) white paper stresses that, while RTI has been given a boost by IDEA 2004, "it is first and foremost, a strategy to be used in the general educational classroom" (p. 2). In addition, a paper on RTI by the National Joint Committee on Learning Disabilities (NJCLD), an organization representing eleven national and international organizations, emphasizes that there is no universally accepted model or approach to RTI and that many possible variations can be conceptualized (NJCLD, 2005). More recently, the International Reading Association's Commission on RTI published a set of Guiding Principles for educators (IRA, 2009), with a particular focus on issues for professionals in the areas related to language and literacy education. These principles characterize RTI as a comprehensive, systemic approach to teaching and learning designed to address learning problems for *all* students through increasingly differentiated and intensified assessment and instruction. These principles emphasize the need for highly qualified professionals with appropriate expertise to deliver instruction. From this perspective, RTI is a process that cuts across general, compensatory, and special education, and is not exclusively a general or special education initiative. Similarly, it is not simply a prereferral process that must be carried out before students are identified as learning disabled. Carefully selected assessment and differentiated instruction, quality professional development, and genuine collaboration across teachers, specialists, administrators, and parents are among the factors described as important for the success of RTI.

Students with Disabilities

According to IDEA, a student's eligibility for special education services is determined by the type and degree of deficit in a particular area, following the guidelines developed through legal and judicial channels. There are currently nine categories of special needs:

1. Mental impairment
2. Hearing impairment
3. Visual impairment
4. Speech impairment
5. Orthopedic impairment
6. Other health impairments (limited vitality, strength, or alertness due to chronic or acute health problems)
7. Multiply handicapped
8. Serious emotional impairment
9. Specific learning disability

In most respects, the procedures and practical implications for students and schools are the same across IDEA and Section 504. All students who are eligible for special services under IDEA are also eligible for the protections of Section 504. However, Section 504 has a broader definition for eligibility, and some students may be eligible under Section 504 who would not meet the criteria for services under IDEA. Any student whose disability "substantially limits a major life activity or is regarded as a handicap by others" may be eligible. Thus, students with certain medical conditions (e.g., asthma, allergies, communicable diseases) or students with attention deficit hyperactivity disorder, behavior problems, or drug or alcohol problems may require support under Section 504.

Eligibility for children in many categories is established early and unequivocally, because many handicapping conditions are apparent prior to a student's entrance into school. However, learning disability and the less-severe cases of mental and emotional impairment are often identified after a student has entered school and failed to meet certain academic expectations.

Reading and writing personnel are often involved with students who have been identified as having special needs in the area of learning disability, because the referral is frequently made on the basis of a student's academic performance in the area of reading and writing. "Over 75–80% of school-age students with mild disabilities (i.e., learning disabilities, mild mental retardation, emotional disturbance, and behavioral disorders) experience significant problems in basic language and reading skills (Ellis & Cramer, 1994)" (quoted in Gaffney & Anderson, 2000, p. 71). Learning-disabled students currently account for approximately half of the children served through special education programs (U.S. Department of Education, 2002).

Learning disability is defined by the federal government in the following manner:

> "Specific learning disability" means a disorder in one or more of the basic psychological processes involved in understanding or in using language, spoken or written, which may manifest itself in an imperfect ability to listen, think, speak, read, write, spell, or to do mathematical calculations. The term includes such conditions as perceptual handicaps, brain injury, minimal brain dysfunction, dyslexia, and developmental aphasia. The term does not include children who have learning problems which are primarily the result of visual, hearing, or motor handicaps, of mental retardation, of emotional disturbance, or of environmental, cultural, or economic disadvantage. (*Federal Register*, Dec. 29, 1977, p. 65083)

It is important to understand how learning disability is related to other controversial issues surrounding reading and writing disability. For example, the similarity between the definition of learning disability and that of dyslexia offered by the World Federation of Neurology has not been lost on most educators:

> [Dyslexia] is a disorder manifested by difficulty in learning to read despite conventional instruction, adequate intelligence, and sociocultural opportunity. It is dependent upon fundamental cognitive disabilities which are frequently of constitutional origin. (Critchley, 1975)

These definitions suggest that for all practical purposes *learning disability* and *dyslexia* are synonymous. What is most important is that both definitions clearly imply either a medical or nonspecified etiology within the learner. As Spear-Swerling and Sternberg (1998) note, this intrinsic perspective has dominated the field of reading and learning disability for many decades. In this view, the students' difficulties are seen as internal and intrinsic to the learner. The extrinsic perspective—drawing attention to the quality and nature of school experiences, poverty rate, or linguistic variations—has never taken root in the special education literature. The interactive view has only recently generated interest among educators and researchers in that field.

Impact on Practice

Although it may appear that special education determinations are straightforward, they are generally far from clear-cut. In addition, schools throughout the country are struggling to decide what programs to offer, who should deliver instruction, and who is eligible for various special programs. For reading and writing professionals and for students who need help in reading and writing, these issues can be troublesome. More than any other classification of handicap, that of learning disabilities has revived discussion about the source of disability. In the process, troubling sociological issues have been raised as well.

Initially, the "learning disability" category was most likely to be used in identifying affluent and middle-class students. As a result, these students received federally mandated support through special education. Disadvantaged students and those from diverse backgrounds were more likely to receive support (when they received any additional help at all) from the nonmandated compensatory education system.

The Elementary and Secondary Education Act (ESEA) was originally passed in 1965 and was conceived as a program to provide additional educational assistance (compensatory education) to schools with large numbers of low-income families. It has been revised and reauthorized several times since then, and continues to provide funding for services in eligible schools through Title I (originally Chapter I) programs. Title I services are available in many elementary schools in the country, serving approximately 25 percent of all primary-grade students (see McGill-Franzen, 2000). The most recent reauthorization of ESEA is the No Child Left Behind Act of 2001, which makes eligible for Title I services any schools in which at least 35 percent of enrolled students or students in the attendance area are from low-income families.

More recently, researchers and educational policy experts have found that students from diverse backgrounds are disproportionately represented among both the special education and remedial populations (Donovan & Cross, 2002; Patton, 1998). This and other evidence supports the view expressed by Harry and Klinger (2006) that the use of disability categories is reliant on a variety of factors, which are influenced by social and political agendas of various states, groups, and individuals. What is important to realize is that these decisions to label students or place them in remedial programs have specific and serious instructional consequences. According to Au (2000, p. 840), "Students of diverse backgrounds, who tend to be categorized as poor readers, are likely to spend more time working on skills in isolation and less time actually reading and writing."

Although several studies have challenged the efficacy of Title I programs (see Allington & McGill-Franzen, 1989; Puma et al., 1997), there is also evidence that Title I can have a positive effect on the reading performance of students in high-poverty areas. The implementation of a model that permits school-wide classroom improvement projects rather than individual remediation and professional development for systemic reform appears to be central to success. Drawing on national data from the National Assessment of Education Progress (NAEP, 1996), McGill-Franzen (2000, p. 893) notes that, although still wide, "the achievement gap between Whites and minorities was reduced by one third during the (past) two decades, a time of increasing poverty for many families. This phenomenon has been attributed in part to federal educational interventions like Title I."

Not surprisingly perhaps, students whose first language is not English also receive instruction within a confusing context of policy and practice. The first Bilingual Education Act (BEA) of 1968, which was originally Title VII of ESEA, initiated experimental demonstration projects for educating language minority students from low-income families. The reauthorization of the BEA in 1974 eliminated the requirement that students must be below the poverty level to qualify for services, and the 1978 reauthorization expanded services to include students with limited academic proficiency as well as those with Limited English Proficiency (LEP). Importantly, these early versions required schools to attend to students' native languages and cultures. Subsequent reauthorizations (1984, 1988, 1994) have not ensured that students receive appropriate instructional support and have directed resources increasingly toward English-only and/or transition programs. In the most recent reauthorization of ESEA, the NCLB Act of 2001, the BEA/Title VII was replaced by the English Language Acquisition Act under Title III of this legislation, which clearly stresses skills in English only.

Once again, the impact of these social and political influences on students' opportunities to learn is significant (Garcia, 2000). As summarized by Crawford (1997, p. 7), the problem is a serious one: "A substantial minority of LEP children—estimates range from 22 to 30 percent—receive no language assistance whatsoever (Crawford, 1997; Donly, Henderson, & Strang, 1995; Moss & Puma, 1995). That is, as many as 1.1 million children, depending on which estimate of the LEP population one uses may be receiving no (English language instruction)."

Research has consistently demonstrated that students benefit from receiving early reading instruction in their native language (August & Shanahan, 2006; Cummins, 2001; Snow, Burns, & Griffin, 1998), and the 1994 reauthorization of the BEA establishes "proficient bilingualism as a desirable goal, which can bring cognitive, academic, cultural, and economic benefits to individuals and to the nation" (Crawford, 1997, p. 1). However, strong opposition to bilingual education and a widespread advocacy for English-only schools has meant that "the political climate for bilingual education has never been chillier" (p. 2).

The existence of two or even three distinct systems for handling reading, writing, and language difficulties creates an environment in which cohesive planning and intervention are often impossible. In many schools today, there are both special education and literacy professionals (Title I or locally supported developmental-reading teachers) serving students with reading and writing problems. In addition, teachers of English as a Second Language (ESL) students and English Language Learners (ELLs) often encounter students with literacy difficulties, but these teachers rarely interact in coordinated ways with the other professionals.

Although special programs can bring badly needed resources to schools and classrooms, there are costs associated with the potential benefits. Too often, classroom teachers see children in terms of the classifications used to get them help. The funds that are used to provide compensatory education are associated with high-poverty students, who are not infrequently seen as "educationally deprived" or "without background knowledge." Similarly, ELLs have been viewed as "culturally deprived" or "linguistically deficient" (see Crawford, 1997). Finally, Coles (1978) argued many years ago that the "learning disabled" label is an example of "biologizing social problems." By positing biological bases for learning problems, the responsibility for failure is put "within the head of the child" rather than placed on the shoulders of schools, communities, and other institutions. "The classification plays its political role, moving the focus away from the general educational process, away from the need to change institutions, away from the need to appropriate more resources for social use toward the remedy of a purely medical problem" (p. 333).

In other words, the labels and classifications may encourage teachers to think that these students are no longer their primary responsibility. The cost to all of us may be greater than we realize. Allington (1994, pp. 104–105) suggests, "As schools have been expected to educate a greater proportion of children to increasingly higher standards of literacy, the regular education bureaucracy has put in place an increasing array of special programs and employed an expanding bevy of special personnel in attempts to minimize the roles and responsibilities of the regular education system in educating all children." He further argues that it is this sense of regular education's retreat from responsibility that has led the U.S. Department of Education to call for reducing exclusionary programs and set the stage for the current inclusionary education initiative for educating handicapped children (Will, 1986). This concern has also led to a shift in federal program guidelines indicating that the academic success of disadvantaged students is the responsibility of the whole school, not just the Title I program (LeTendre, 1991) or the bilingual program (August & Hakuta, 1994, 1997).

It is clear that the trend in the past ten to fifteen years has been to address the instructional needs of students with special needs within the mainstream classroom setting. Although the pace and the effort vary considerably, movements for *full inclusion* mean that many special education students now often receive their education in the mainstream setting (Smith, Polloway, Patton, & Dowdy, 1995; Villa & Thousand, 1995). In addition, criticisms of pullout programs in Title I (e.g., Allington & McGill-Franzen, 1989; Slavin, 1989) have led to initiatives such as school-wide programs, Reading First, and RTI.

Although there is little doubt that neurological or constitutional dysfunction plays a role in certain cases of reading and writing difficulties, the percentage of cases accounted for by identifiable neurological problems appears to be extremely small (Spear-Swerling & Sternberg, 1998; Vellutino, Scanlon & Sipay, 1997). In fact, it has become quite clear that effective instruction and intervention can significantly reduce the number of students who become learning disabled (Dorn & Schubert, 2008; Mathes et al., 2005; Scanlon et al., 2008). We believe that the majority of difficulties in reading and writing are more likely to result from a complex interaction between the learner and the reading and writing situation than from some form of pathology. It is this complex interaction to which we turn our attention for the remainder of the text.

Pulling It Together: RTI from an Interactive Perspective

There is no doubt that schools are serving an increasingly diverse student population with an increasingly diverse set of programs. This means that all teachers, whether "special," "regular," or "remedial," need to consider individual differences among students. In addition, they need the skills and knowledge to work in multiple settings with other professionals. For many this means new roles and responsibilities. It is this perspective that is embodied within the response to intervention (RTI) approach to identifying students with learning disabilities under IDEA 2004, and many hope that RTI will provide the leverage necessary for this perspective to take hold in all educational settings.

It is our contention that the most effective assessment and instruction practices derive from interactive perspectives such as the one described here. This is entirely consistent with the perspective on RTI put forward in this book and by the International Reading Association but is not necessarily embodied in every approach to RTI. It is important to note that there are a number of different approaches to RTI, and the legislation does not specify any particular model or approach. In fact, the federal government purposely provides few details for the development and implementation of RTI procedures, stating specifically that states and districts should have the flexibility to establish approaches that reflect each community's unique situation. This means that the most widely used models are neither mandated nor the only possible approaches to RTI.

RTI most frequently involves a multitiered approach to the implementation of instructional modifications. The number of tiers varies across approaches, but the most widely described models involve either three or four tiers. In the three-tiered approach, low-performing students are identified and monitored as they participate in their classroom, or Tier 1, core instruction. Core instruction involves some differentiation and is intended to accommodate at least 80 percent of the students in a given class, school, or district. Those who do not make sufficient progress in Tier 1 instruction receive a second, more targeted and intensive tier of instruction intended to accelerate their progress (Tier 2). This might be accomplished by providing more time in instruction, smaller instructional groupings, and/or alternative methods of instruction targeted to specific areas of students' needs. Tier 2 instruction is intended to be provided in *addition* to the Tier 1 instruction and might be provided by the classroom teacher or a specialist in a small-group context. Students' progress continues to be monitored, and an additional 15 percent of students are expected to succeed with this supplemental instruction/intervention. Those who do not demonstrate accelerated progress with Tier 2 intervention/s are considered for even more intensive and targeted intervention in Tier 3 and/or possible LD evaluation/classification.

Tiered models of RTI are frequently characterized in the literature as one of two types: standard protocol or problem solving. The standard protocol approach (Fuchs, Mock, Morgan, & Young, 2003) emphasizes standardized (often scripted) interventions used for a standard amount of time with teachers often monitored for "treatment fidelity" (Gresham, 2007). The problem-solving approach (Marston, Muyskens, Lau, & Canter, 2003) involves collaborative efforts on the part of several members of the school community, to identify and implement optimal instructional interventions for each student who appears to be at risk for learning difficulties. Within this approach, a team of professionals assembles and develops an instructional plan designed to be responsive to the needs of the individual student. The student's response to such interventions determines future intervention plans in an iterative manner.

Although differences are often noted between standard protocol and problem-solving approaches, many writers argue that these distinctions break down quickly and that "most RTI models described in the literature combine the two approaches... and probably function optimally when integrated into one three-tiered service delivery system" (Jimerson, Burns, & VanDerHeyden, 2007a, p. 4). Indeed, writing from a problem-solving perspective, Burns and Coolong-Chaffin (2006) observe that "most Tier 2 interventions have a standardized component" (p. 6) whether they are focused on the needs of individuals or groups of individuals.

There are also important differences among standard protocol and problem-solving approaches that are often ignored in the literature. For example, both Reading Recovery (RR) (http://ies.ed.gov/ncee/wwc/) and the Interactive Strategies Approach (ISA) (Scanlon & Vellutino, 1996; Scanlon, Vellutino, Small, Fanuele, & Sweeney, 2005) have been referred to as standard protocol programs and described as "scripted" because there are consistent lesson segments (Fuchs & Fuchs, 2006; Gresham, 2007). However, these approaches are standard only to the extent that the teachers who provide the interventions have been trained in the approaches and can therefore plan and deliver instruction responsive to students' needs by taking into account what students know and are able to do and considering the characteristics and expectations of the classroom curriculum. This is quite different from the highly prescriptive interventions typically used in most standard protocol approaches to RTI.

Johnston (2011) has proposed a way of thinking about existing approaches to RTI that captures the most important distinctions between them. He describes approaches in terms of their primary emphasis on either measurement or instruction, arguing that the basis for this distinction comes from the legislation itself. In particular, he notes that the RTI legislation has a dual focus that poses both a measurement problem (i.e., how to replace the IQ discrepancy identification strategy [300.307]) and an instructional problem (i.e., how to reduce the number of students who end up with serious learning difficulties, by guaranteeing "appropriate instruction" [300.309]).

When conceived as a strategy for accurately *identifying* students with disabilities, RTI is seen more as a measurement problem, emphasizing standardization—in timing, interventions, and assessments. Most standard protocol and problem-solving models can be characterized as measurement approaches. Proponents of this approach favor standard intervention packages, preferably scripted, to increase the standardization. This assumes that an intervention that is effective *on average* in one setting will be effective with *each* new student in any new setting if implemented with fidelity and increasing intensity. If the intervention is not successful, the student is the likely source of the problem (e.g., LD, treatment resister, chronic nonresponder), because research has already demonstrated that the instruction is "effective." This is the perspective described by many special educators and school psychologists (e.g., Fuchs & Fuchs, 2006).

When conceived as a strategy for *preventing* serious learning difficulties, RTI becomes an instructional problem, emphasizing optimal instruction for individual students and providing the means and context for improving teaching and teacher expertise. In this frame, assessment must be informative about the *qualities* of learning *and teaching*, giving direction to instruction. In other words, instruction is not "evidence based" unless assessment shows it is effective for the student in question. If intervention is not successful in such an approach, teachers would first look to the instruction as the source of difficulty, before the student. The attention given to RTI throughout this book should be understood within the context of this preventative perspective, which reflects the interactive view of reading and writing subscribed to here.

Using Johnston's reasoning, Reading Recovery (RR) and Interactive Strategies Approach (ISA) are instructional approaches as opposed to standard protocol or measurement approaches. Neither program is scripted, and neither would work if it was scripted (Clay, 2005; Vellutino & Scanlon, 2002). Suppose, for example, that during instruction a child reads a word incorrectly. A scripted program would prescribe the teacher's response. By contrast, in RR and ISA, the teacher's response would depend on, among other things, the text difficulty, the instructional opportunity offered by the word, the context of the error, and the child's current processing strategies. Monitoring the teacher for "treatment fidelity" would miss the adaptive teacher expertise taking place and risk discouraging the teacher from adapting instruction as needed. To be clear, however, interventions such as RR and ISA are not "anything goes." Instead, they focus on developing teacher expertise, because research indicates that specific programs may or may not work for individual students.

In a measurement frame, the focus is on the design and selection of tests and packaged programs rather than the teacher's ability to adapt instruction. Expertise is minimized by the selection of instructional packages, particularly scripted ones, and testing instruments that can be used by people with limited knowledge and/or experience. Consistent with Johnston's classification scheme, scholars who promote measurement approaches describe RTI intervention as a test of whether the student is LD (Fuchs & Fuchs, 2006), whereas those who promote instructional approaches describe intervention as a test of the appropriateness of the instruction (Scanlon, in press).

In short, RTI is not a model to be imposed on schools, but rather a framework to help schools and teachers identify and support students before the difficulties they encounter with language and literacy become more serious. According to the research, relatively few students who are having difficulty in language and literacy have specific learning disabilities (Vellutino, Scanlon, & Tanzman, 1998). Many other factors, including the nature of educational opportunities provided, impact students' academic and social growth. For example, teaching practices and assessment tools that are insensitive to cultural and linguistic differences can lead to ineffective instruction or misinterpretations in evaluation. It is the combination of an interactive perspective on reading and writing and the preventative perspective on RTI that is articulated throughout this book. An underlying assumption of these perspectives is that instruction/intervention can and will be effective for the overwhelming majority of students who are presently experiencing school/literacy difficulties.

CHAPTER SUMMARY

This chapter began with the idea that theories of reading and writing are important because they help us make decisions about assessment and instruction. We then suggested how reading and writing came to be treated separately in education and how the "cognitive revolution" and "social turn" have led to more-integrated views of reading and writing.

Cognitive information-processing perspectives on reading and writing were described as emphasizing subprocesses in reading and writing, readers and writers as limited-capacity processors, and speed of processing. This view has increased our understanding of reading and writing processes in terms of their components and the knowledge base of skilled readers and writers but cannot account for the variability in performance that occurs as a result of a host of social and cultural factors.

Social perspectives on reading and writing were described as emphasizing reading and writing as social and cultural phenomena, knowledge as constructed through the individual's interaction with the sociocultural environment, and the acquisition of cognitive processes as related to reading and writing through contextualized activity and assisted learning. Social perspectives were seen as addressing some of the weaknesses observed in information-processing views and as helpful in formulating pedagogical goals and strategies for reading and writing.

The interactive view of reading and writing that serves as the basis for this text was characterized as an amalgam of the information-processing and social views. This perspective suggests that reading and writing are processes of constructing meaning through a dynamic interaction between the reader/writer and the context of the reading/writing situation. This means that reading and writing are not static, but vary as a function of *contextual factors* such as setting, curriculum, and instructional conditions and *reader/writer factors* such as background knowledge, motivation, and interests. These interactions are described more fully in Chapter 2.

The second section of this chapter described the legal, social, and political influences on reading instruction and briefly discussed the contemporary issues related to reading instruction. We began this section with a discussion of the relations between education reform efforts and reading education that linked pivotal research syntheses and the interactive view put forward in this text. We then described the legislative and legal bases for programs designed for students with special needs, including compensatory education and special education (e.g., IDEA, Section 504, and ESEA/Title I). The provisions and protections in IDEA for the rights of all handicapped children were noted, and the procedures for implementing these provisions were discussed, including recent changes to the methods schools are permitted to use in identifying students with learning disabilities (RTI). We presented criticisms of these "entitlement" programs—special education, Title I, and bilingual education—as mechanisms for minimizing the roles and responsibilities of regular education in educating all children. Responses to these criticisms have led to reforms such as the inclusionary education movement in special education, the RTI approach to identifying students with learning disabilities, the move to school-wide programs in Title I, and the reauthorization of ESEA as the NCLB Act of 2001, which included Reading First as part of Title I. Although these reforms are not without their own critics, they have all come about as a means of better addressing concerns about poor reading achievement, especially among marginalized and underserved populations.

The chapter concludes with a discussion of different perspectives on RTI and their relation to the interactive view of reading and writing that is the basis for this book. Perspectives on RTI were characterized as predominantly focused on either measurement issues, which are important for the purpose of identifying students as learning disabled, or instructional issues, which are important for the purpose of preventing learning difficulties. It is the latter preventative perspective that is emphasized throughout this book as one instantiation of an interactive view of reading and writing.

MyEducationLab™

Go to the Topic, Reading and Writing in the MyEducationLab (www.myeducationlab.com) for your course, where you can:

- Find learning outcomes for Reading and Writing, along with the national standards that connect to these outcomes.
- Complete Assignments and Activities that can help you more deeply understand the chapter content.
- Apply and practice your understanding of the core teaching skills identified in the chapter using the Building Teaching Skills and Dispositions learning units.
- Examine challenging situations and cases presented in the IRIS Center Resources.
- Check your comprehension of the content covered in the chapter by going to the Study Plan in the Book Resources for your text. Here you will be able to take a chapter quiz, receive feedback on your answers, and then access Review, Practice, and Enrichment activities to enhance your understanding of chapter content.

A+RISE A+RISE® Standards2Strategy™ is an innovative and interactive online resource that offers new teachers in grades K-12 just in time, research-based instructional strategies that meet the linguistic needs of ELLs as they learn content, differentiate instruction for all grades and abilities, and are aligned to Common Core Elementary Language Arts standards (for the literacy strategies) and to English language proficiency standards in WIDA, Texas, California, and Florida.

CHAPTER 2

An Interactive View
of Reading and Writing

*T*he interactive view of reading and writing and "preventative" perspective on RTI described in the first chapter frame our thinking about the nature of reading and writing. In this chapter, we discuss skilled reading and writing and the factors that interact and influence performance in these areas. Throughout the chapter, we present evidence that even the most mechanical aspects of reading and writing are influenced by both contextual and learner factors.

As we examine the conventional components of reading and writing performance, we need to also consider how these learner and contextual factors interact to influence student performance. If a complex and dynamic view of reading and writing is not used during assessment, we run the risk of developing a distorted picture of the reading and writing processes. Inaccurate or incomplete conclusions may be drawn about students, and ineffective or harmful instruction may result.

UNDERSTANDING THE ELEMENTS
OF SKILLED PERFORMANCE

It is easy to lose sight of the target of skilled reading and writing when we are working with less-skilled readers and writers. Both assessment and instruction too often focus on isolated aspects of students' knowledge and skill. Although we consider component aspects of reading and writing in the chapters that follow, we should always start with, and return to, questions of how these relate to skilled and motivated comprehension and composition.

So what is desirable performance in reading and writing? First and foremost, readers and writers read and write. They *use* their knowledge and skill to accomplish personal, recreational, academic, and civic purposes. This also means that reading and writing should be defined more in terms of authentic, real-world materials and tasks than by classroom practices and texts. Readers and writers can and do apply their knowledge and skill in flexible ways to accomplish meaningful tasks, suggesting that both reading and writing are adaptive and intentional activities (Dole, Duffy, Roehler, & Pearson, 1991). In addition, readers and writers from diverse backgrounds need to be able to perform appropriately in a wide range of contexts.

> People generally associate literacy with the ability to read and write. This is the common dictionary definition, the mark of literacy in society at large, and the one generally thought of in regard to schooling. However, literacy can be viewed in a broader and educationally more productive way, as the ability to think and reason like a literate person, *within a particular society.* As Vygotsky (1978) suggested, because the practices of literacy and ways of understanding them depend upon the social conditions in which they are learned, the skills, concepts, and ways of thinking that an individual develops reflect the uses and approaches to literacy that permeate the particular society in which that person is a participant. (Langer, 1991, p. 11)

Over the past three decades we have come to know a great deal about the nature of skilled and motivated reading and writing performance, about learners, and about the contextual factors that influence performance (see Figure 2.1). These are the elements and factors that we must examine in the assessment and instruction of students who are experiencing problems in reading and writing. We discuss first the elements of skilled performance and then the factors that influence it.

There is some risk in pulling out elements of skilled performance for discussion. In doing so, we may lead some to believe that these are isolated or entirely separable components of reading and writing. However, as we have already discussed and will demonstrate

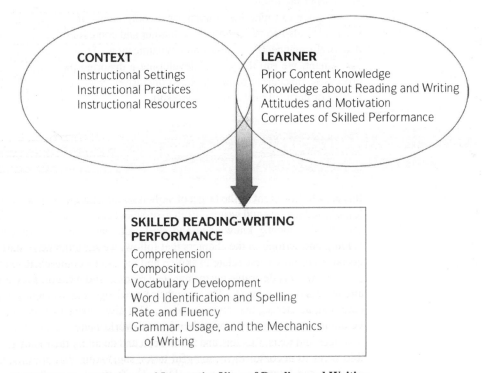

FIGURE 2.1   An Elaborated Interactive View of Reading and Writing

later on, each of these elements interacts with others and is influenced by contextual and learner factors. In short, the whole of skilled performance is variable and dynamic. As educators and specialists, though, we need to have some idea of the component elements so that we can consider which of these are targets for assessment and instruction. Skilled reading and writing performance comprises the following elements.

Comprehension

Comprehension is the ability to use previously acquired information to construct meaning for a given text (e.g., RAND Reading Study Group, 2002). The two aspects of comprehension considered here are reading for understanding and reading to learn and/or remember.

Reading for Understanding.   This area focuses primarily on readers' ability to reason their way through a text by integrating existing knowledge with new information, drawing inferences, and forming and testing hypotheses. The goal of comprehension is the construction of an integrated representation of the information suggested by a text that is appropriate for the reading purpose. Other activities that are critical to good comprehension include establishing purposes for reading, identifying important elements of information and their relationships within text, monitoring one's comprehension, and dealing with failures to comprehend (Baker & Brown, 1984).

The successful accomplishment of the activities that constitute good comprehension requires the use of a variety of strategies (Dole, Duffy, Roehler, & Pearson, 1991). Although there is no comprehensive list of such, we can identify a range of possible strategies that is appropriate given the developmental level of the readers and the reading activities in which they are engaged. As in the case of word analysis strategies, no single strategy is necessarily more or less important than the others. Rather, the appropriateness of a given strategy is determined by its utility in the interaction between a reader and a specific reading situation (Duffy, 1993). What matters most is how effective and efficient a strategy is for accomplishing a specific purpose.

Rather than focusing on the mastery of prerequisite skills, the interactive approach focuses assessment and instruction on the behaviors or activities that characterize good comprehension. Skills and strategies are the means to achieving the goal of good comprehension, not the end itself. It is important to keep this in mind, lest our old lists of skills be replaced by new lists of strategies and our assessment and comprehension instruction remain unchanged from past practices.

Reading to Remember/Learn.   Reading to learn and/or remember what has been comprehended or understood from text is often referred to as studying. Three primary activities are involved in effective studying. First, students must be able to preview text to familiarize themselves with its form and content and to make plans for reading. Second, students must be able to locate specific information within the text. Third, students must be able to identify the organization of information within the text.

As with comprehension, the successful accomplishment of studying activities requires the use of a variety of strategies. These may include outlining, note taking, summarizing, self-questioning, diagramming or mapping text, and underlining, as well as many of the strategies that are used in comprehending. What is most important is students' ability to select and apply these strategies in a manner that is appropriate to the study task at hand. It is not a question of which study strategies are best, but of how effective a selected strategy is in a given study situation.

Composition

Writing is essentially idea making. Writing is considered a skill, which is also a process dependent on a range of other skills; this interdependent skills set is continually shaped by the writer's changing purposes for writing (Dyson & Freedman, 2003). The writing process refers to a series of nonlinear compositional activities in which students engage to produce a finished piece of writing. These include prewriting, drafting, revising, editing, and publishing. To counteract the idea that these activities are discrete steps or stages, Pappas, Keifer, and Levstik (1999) refer to them as experiences of the composing process and provide descriptions of each of these writing experiences as follows.

Prewriting Experiences. Prewriting is generating and exploring ideas, recalling and rehearsing ideas, relating and probing ideas, planning, thinking, and deciding. Prewriting experiences occur when we talk, listen, read, research, observe, and so forth. They often include writing itself in forms such as notes, brainstorming, and outlines. Prewriting is an ongoing experience rather than a distinct period of writing and can interact with other writing experiences.

Drafting Experiences. Drafting involves attempts to get the ideas down and create a whole text. Writers try not to worry too much about spelling and punctuation during drafting, because they know that the text will be reconsidered, rearranged, and revised. Drafting can be interrupted by prewriting and can occur simultaneously with revising.

Revising Experiences. Revising has to do with attempts to rethink, review, remake, reconstruct, and reexamine the text. Revising is an ongoing activity that can occur during prewriting or during and after drafting. The writer becomes a reader when the text is reread and revised. This is also when other readers such as teachers and peers may interact with the text and provide feedback. Readers' responses to draft text may lead to more drafting as well as more prewriting.

Editing Experiences. Editing is intended to clean up text so that its message is communicated by using the most appropriate language. It involves changing words and sentences, changing, deleting, or rearranging them to make the message clearer. The tone or style of the text—as well as the spelling, punctuation, and grammar—is also checked during editing.

Publishing Experiences. Classroom publishing emphasizes sharing. The publishing of final drafts takes various forms in terms of the nature of the final product and how it is shared. Because publishing has to do with sharing in general, it can apply to any writing, not just final drafts. Publishing can also occur with a range of audiences within the classroom or beyond—in the school, community, or even state and national newspapers and magazines.

In summary, writing is a social and constructive meaning-making process representing a variety of genres. Both the text product and the process of constructing text are important.

Vocabulary Development

The importance of vocabulary development as a major contributor to reading comprehension has long been acknowledged and widely studied (Bauman & Kame'enui, 1991; Nagy & Scott, 2000; National Reading Panel, 2000). Skilled reading and writing require knowledge of the meanings of words and the ability to infer and learn the meanings of new words. Words are the labels for objects and ideas and provide an index of readers' and writers' prior knowledge. Readers and writers who do not have adequate knowledge of important words and concepts and/or are unable to determine word meanings will have difficulty successfully comprehending or composing texts.

The relationship between vocabulary development and reading extends beyond its significant impact on comprehension. According to Snow, Burns, and Griffin (1998, p. 47), for example, there is a "well-documented link between vocabulary size and early reading ability: the development of fine within-word discrimination ability (phonemic representations) may be contingent on vocabulary size rather than age or general developmental level." In addition, but perhaps not surprisingly, vocabulary has been identified as a critical factor in second-language students' reading abilities (Kim, 1995).

During the preschool years, children's vocabulary grows at an average of seven words per day, or 2,500 to 3,000 words a year (Nagy & Herman, 1987). However, Hart and Risley (1995) found that children whose parents receive welfare have been exposed to fewer than half the vocabulary words of children whose parents hold professional positions. In their study, a typical child in a household receiving welfare heard just 616 words per hour, less than half the number heard by a child in a working-class home (1,251 words per hour) and less than one-third of the words heard in a household headed by professionals (2,153 words per hour). Hart and Risley also found that low-income children add vocabulary words more slowly than do their cohorts from more-affluent families.

Vocabulary development is not, however, simply the number of dictionary definitions of words that students have acquired. The primary focus of this area is the depth, breadth, and organization of students' vocabulary knowledge, which seems to be much more complex and interconnected than was previously thought.

Although students' knowledge of specific vocabulary is important, we must also consider ability to infer and to learn the meanings of new words and concepts. Students are frequently confronted in their reading with new words for which they may not already have a concept. They need to develop strategies, such as different types of contextual and morphemic analysis, as described in the next section, for inferring the meanings of unfamiliar vocabulary and independently increasing their vocabulary learning. Indeed, humans appear to store and learn words using a highly elaborated mechanism for making connections. Word knowledge seems to grow because people establish relationships between new words and previously acquired words and concepts (Nagy & Scott, 2000). In addition, these newly acquired words change and influence the word meanings that were already stored in vocabulary.

Word Identification and Spelling

Rapid word identification is an essential component of skilled reading. Students must be able to recognize familiar words quickly and to decode unfamiliar words rapidly enough that the process of meaning construction is not unduly interrupted. As they read, people use a repertoire of word identification strategies and recruit a wide array of knowledge and skill. This information and these skills are related to each other but also make separate contributions to performance. That is, although readers and writers who are strong in one component area are generally strong in others, this can and does vary among individuals, and a disparity may produce difficulties in some readers or writers.

Sight Word Recognition.   The most efficient form of word identification occurs when students recognize words immediately on sight, without sounding them out or using any other strategy to help identify them. Words that can be recognized instantly are called *sight words* and are considered part of a student's *sight vocabulary.*

Sight words fall into several categories, especially in early reading. The first words that children can recognize in print are generally *high-potency* words (Hunt, n.d.), such as their own and other family members' names and words with heavy contextual support such as *McDonald's* (Hiebert, 1981). These words are relatively easy to remember because of their visual distinctiveness and/or because of the strong affect attached to them (Ashton-Warner, 1963).

A second type of sight words is the *high-frequency function* words (*the, of, but*) that appear over and over in written texts. These words are difficult to decode or figure out using word analysis strategies, because they are irregular and may not follow basic decoding rules. They are often more difficult to remember than other words, as many are similar in appearance (*where, there, here, when, then*). These words are usually learned as sight words when children are first learning how to read; however, many low-skilled readers have not mastered these words even by seventh or eighth grade. Limited recognition of these high-frequency sight words affects fluency and comprehension.

The last type of sight words includes all of the other words that students have learned to recognize instantly. Many of these are *content* words (*meal, bake, animal*) that are already part of a child's speaking or listening vocabularies. These words are often read initially through the application of various word analysis strategies and become sight words after repeated exposure through reading. Many poor readers simply do not read enough to acquire a sufficient number of these sight words. Others may rely too heavily on one or another of the word analysis strategies that are discussed in the next section. Either way, children who do not develop an adequate sight vocabulary are likely to have difficulty in all aspects of reading.

Word Analysis Strategies.   These strategies are used to identify printed words that we do not recognize immediately on sight. Unfortunately, word analysis has often been perceived as consisting only of (grapho)phonic analysis. Students may employ a variety of word analysis strategies, and no one strategy is necessarily any better or worse than another. However, children who rely too heavily on only one strategy often produce distorted reading and have limited comprehension.

Although it might seem that skilled readers move through text so quickly that they must be recognizing every word at sight, it is clear that they actually do speed their word recognition by using graphophonic (letter-sound correspondence) cue systems within our language and by making predictions about words based on the context (meaning and sentence structure). For example, it is the contextual cue system that enables us to predict that the missing word in the sentence "The window in the kitchen of our new _____ is beautiful" could be either *house*, *home*, or *apartment*. However, it is the graphophonic cue system that assists us in determining that the missing word in the sentence "Our new h _ r _ _ is beautiful" is *horse* instead of *house* or *home*.

The utility of a given strategy depends on its effectiveness in the situation in which it is being applied. Therefore, children need to have a repertoire of word analysis strategies that are available for use in a variety of reading situations. *Contextual analysis* and *morphemic analysis* are both meaning-based word identification strategies. *Phonic analysis* is a strategy based on sound-symbol correspondence that results in approximate pronunciation of individual words.

Contextual Analysis.   Probably the most common method of word identification is to use the context of the sentence in which the unknown word appears and/or the context that surrounds the sentence to determine what the word is most likely to be. Mature readers make use of two sorts of context during reading: general and local context (Durkin, 1983). General context is provided by the central topic and general organization of a text. For example, one would expect a story about the circus to include words such as *ringmaster*, *clown*, *acrobat*, *elephant*, and *trapeze*, or a chapter on heredity to include words such as *gene*, *meiosis*, and *chromosome*. Obviously, the use of general context requires prior knowledge about the topic of the text. Clues provided by the graphic aids in a text—such as charts, maps, illustrations, titles, and subtitles—are also likely to contribute to the general context of a text.

Readers who use local context take their cue from the phrases and sentences that surround an unknown word. For example, if you read, "Nora wished she had a _____ so _____ could listen to her favorite station," you would expect the first word to be *radio* or possibly *Walkman*, because these are what we use to listen to a station. The possible choices are constrained by the syntactic and semantic cues provided by the local context. Skilled readers use context to derive word *meanings*, but phonic analysis (see below) for word *recognition*.

Morphemic Analysis.   Morphemic analysis is a strategy in which the reader breaks down words into smaller meaning-bearing units as an aid to word identification and understanding. *Morpheme* is a linguistic term for the smallest unit of meaning in our language.

The meaning-bearing units used in morphemic analysis are root words, affixes, and inflections. For example, the word *returnables* can be divided into four meaningful parts: *re-*, *turn*, *-able*, and *-s*. The prefix *re-* and the suffix *-able* are affixes that change the function of the root word. The inflectional ending *-s* modulates the meaning of the root word without changing its function. Other common inflections signal possession (-*'s*), verb tense (-*ed*, -*ing*), or comparison (-*er*, -*est*). Finally, morphemic analysis can be used as an aid in the identification and understanding of compound words (for example, *fireman*, *breadbox*) and contractions (for example, *don't*, *he'll*).

Phonic Analysis.   The writing systems of some other languages are different, but English is an alphabetic language. Because it is, children must gain an understanding that what gets written (and read) is a representation of the sounds of the language. Specifically, they must learn which letters or letter combinations (graphemes) represent specific English sounds (phonemes). The ability to isolate *phonemes*—the linguistic term for the smallest unit of sound in our language—is central to successful application of phonic analysis. Words can be sounded out letter by letter or by using spelling patterns, letter clusters, or syllables that have predictable sounds.

This phonological knowledge is critical to skilled reading. As Barker, Torgesen, and Wagner (1992, p. 335) note,

> Skill at identifying words based on phonological information requires at least awareness of the phonological structure of words, knowledge of specific grapheme-phoneme correspondences, and skill in synthesizing the phonemes to produce a recognizable word. In many cases, phonological knowledge and skill can be used to identify words that have never before been encountered in print.

The specific graphophonic elements that are useful in phonic analysis are suggested by a framework for phonics instruction provided by Mason and Au (1990). These are consonant-sound relations in the initial, medial, and final positions in words; blends of two or three consonants in which each consonant retains its own sound (*spr, fl*); consonant digraphs, or combinations of two consonants that are pronounced as one sound (*ch, th*); and vowel–sound patterns represented by vowels followed by *r* or *l* (*ar*), as well as consonant-vowel-consonant (*sit*), consonant-vowel-consonant-silent *e* (*lake*), and consonant-vowel-vowel (*meal*).

The use of graphophonic information in longer words often requires *structural analysis*. In this analysis, readers must recognize and segment words by syllable boundaries (either through "rules" or by identifying recurrent spelling patterns) and then apply known graphophonic patterns to decode the segments (*seg/ment*) (see Figure 2.2).

Skilled readers most often decode unfamiliar words by comparing new, unknown words with known letter-sound combinations (Cunningham, 1975/1976; Ehri, 1994). Using knowledge of onsets and rimes and an analogy strategy is effective for readers with some knowledge of sound-symbol correspondence. However, some young children, especially those with very little phonological or letter knowledge, require specific instruction in individual phonemes and graphemes before they can use onsets and rimes for decoding (Gaskins et al., 1996/1997; Nation & Hulme, 1997, 2002; Vandervelden & Siegel, 1995).

Orthographic Processes and Spelling.   Most experts today agree that word identification in skilled readers involves two types of knowledge and skill: phonological and orthographic. Orthographic processes are linked to the appearance of specific

FIGURE 2.2 The Synchrony of Literacy Development

Layers of the Orthography

ALPHABET/SOUND
PATTERN
MEANING

Reading and Writing Stages:

Emergent	Beginning	Transitional	Intermediate	Advanced
Pretend read	Read aloud, word-by-word, finger-point reading.	Approaching fluency, phrasal, some expression in oral reading. "Wright brothers" of reading.	Read fluently, with expression. Develop a variety of reading styles. Vocabulary grows with experience reading.	
Pretend write	Word-by-word writing, writing moves from a few words to paragraph in length.	Approaching fluency, more organization, several paragraphs.	Fluent writing, build expression and voice, experience different writing styles and genres, writing shows personal problem solving and personal reflection.	

Spelling Stages:

Emergent →			Letter Name–Alphabetic →			Within-Word Pattern →			Syllables and Affixes →			Derivational Relations →		
Early	Middle	Late	Early	Middle	Late	Early	Middle	Late	Early	Middle	Late	Early	Middle	Late

Examples of spellings:

bed	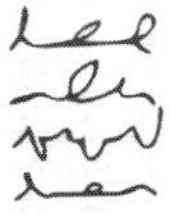	MST	E	bd				bed						
ship		TFP	S	sp	sep	shep		ship						
float		SMT	F	ft	fot	flot	flott	flowt	flowt	float				
train		FSMP	G	jn	jan tan	chran	tran	traen	traen	train				
bottle			B	bt	botl	bodol	botel	botel	bottel	bottle			
cellar			S	slr	salr	celr	celer	celer	seler	celler	cellar		
pleasure			P	pjr	plasr	plager plejer	plejer	pleser	pleser	plesher	pleser plesher	plesure	pleasure	
confident											confadent	confadent	confident confident confident	
opposition											opasishan	opasishan	opasishan opasishan	opposition

Source: From *Words Their Way,* 4th ed., by D. R. Bear, M. Invernizzi, S. Templeton, and F. Johnston, p. 19. Copyright © 2012, 2008, 1996 by Prentice-Hall, Inc. Reprinted by permission of Pearson Education, Inc., Upper Saddle River, NJ.

words. "Orthographic knowledge involves memory for specific visual/spelling patterns that identify individual words, or word parts, on the printed page. Orthographic knowledge . . . would seem to be acquired by repeated exposure to printed words until a stable visual representation of the whole word, or meaningful subword units, has been acquired" (Barker, Torgesen, & Wagner, 1992, p. 336).

Although there are relatively strong relationships between orthographic and phonological skills in most individuals, it is also quite clear that these two abilities make unique and separate contributions to reading and writing performance (Juel, Griffith, & Gough, 1986; Olson, Wise, Conners, Rack, & Fulker, 1989). For example, orthographic skills appear to make a bigger difference in the reading of connected text (versus isolated word recognition) and also seem more highly related to fluency in reading (see below). It also appears that the relationships between phonological and orthographic skills are developmental, with orthographic skill making a stronger contribution to word reading after first grade (that is, after the initial stages of reading acquisition).

What has become increasingly clear is the close relationship between early reading and spelling. (Templeton personal communication, September 20, 2001):

> Research strongly suggests that a common core of word knowledge underlies the process of word identification in reading and the process of spelling words in writing . . . in fact, what students learn about words in appropriate spelling activities helps the developing process of reading more than reading helps the development of spelling knowledge (Bosman & van Orden, 1997; Ellis & Cataldo, 1990). Spelling supports the ability to read words in two ways: First, the memory for each specific word and its structure is reinforced; second, common spelling patterns across words are discerned and abstracted; the construct of pattern in turn supports recognition and identification of words during the reading process.

In short, the orthographic knowledge that students build up by studying word spellings and examining spelling patterns is precisely what helps them to move from decoding individual letters and sounds to storing and retrieving larger chunks (see the discussion of fluency in the next subsection).

It is likely that word study is initially more useful to reading than to spelling, because the ability to spell appears to be a consequence of knowing about words in many ways—their visual or graphic characteristics, their phonological and structural properties, and their meanings. English does not have a one-to-one correspondence between graphemes (letters) and phonemes (sounds). The twenty-six letters of the alphabet represent approximately forty-four phonemes. To further complicate the situation, three letters—*c*, *q*, and *x*—do not represent unique phonemes, and there are anywhere between five hundred and two thousand spellings to represent the forty-four phonemes in English. The sheer number of spellings and the lack of fit between phonemes and graphemes suggest that children are unlikely to learn to spell simply through memorization or sounding out words.

Like learning to read and write, learning to spell is a developmental process. More than thirty years ago, the evidence began to show that young children, even preschoolers, use their knowledge of English phonology to invent spellings (Read, 1971, 1975, 1986). Since then, research has revealed that students move through stages in their spelling development and that these stages are marked by broad, qualitative shifts in the types of spelling errors children make (Bear, Invernizzi, Templeton, & Johnston, 2008). Students' knowledge and skill at each development stage are fairly predictable, although individual variation—the result of the sorts of interactions described earlier—is visible also (see Figure 2.2).

Not all children invent spellings in exactly the same way or at the same pace, but they do develop spelling strategies in roughly the same sequence (Henderson, 1980) and move through roughly the same stages to become conventional spellers (Gentry, 1981, 1982; Invernizzi, Abouzeid, & Gill, 1994). These stages are described more fully in Chapter 7. Generally, children move from early scribbles and letter-like forms to representing sounds without reference to conventional spelling combinations (semiphonetic and phonetic stages). Eventually, children stop relying only on phonological information and begin to use morphological (word parts) and visual information to spell many words correctly.

Researchers also study children's spelling development in later years (see Bear & Barone, 1998; Bear & Templeton, 1998; Bear et al., 2008). For example, Firth (1980) found that older students who are good readers and spellers make spelling errors that are characteristic of the within-word pattern or transitional stage, while students who are poor readers and spellers make errors that are characteristic of the semiphonetic and phonetic stages. Other studies indicate a developmental shift among better spellers from a reliance upon the phoneme-grapheme strategies used in the early school years toward a strategy of spelling words by analogy to other known words.

In summary, rapid and accurate word recognition is important to effective and efficient reading, and accurate spelling is important to effective communication in writing. A combination of strategies and abilities is useful, especially in the earliest stages of reading/writing acquisition. However, as quickly as possible, students need to acquire accurate and rapid word identification skills, which appear dependent on both good phonologic and orthographic skills.

Rate and Fluency

"Fluent readers can read text with speed, accuracy, and proper expression" (National Reading Panel, 2000, p. 3–1). Although accuracy and rate are related to fluency, they are not the same thing; oral fluency also involves readers' ability to group words into meaningful phrase units. Smoothness and the maintenance of comprehension are important as well (Rasinski, 2004, 2006).

Rate of reading refers to the speed of oral and/or silent reading as measured in words per minute. Proficient reading requires *automaticity*, or the ability to identify words rapidly enough that sufficient resources are available for attention to comprehension. Research suggests that beginning readers who develop automatic word identification skills are better able to comprehend text (Perfetti & Hogaboam, 1975; Torgesen et al., 2003). How fast is fast enough and how slow is too slow are questions that are still open for debate, however. Norms for reading rate vary widely, and research designed to improve comprehension by teaching rapid word identification has produced equivocal results. It appears that reading rate may be a necessary but insufficient condition for proficient reading and that decisions about the adequacy of a student's reading rate may need to be made on an individual basis.

Until fluency was made prominent by the National Reading Panel report in 2000 as a key area of reading instruction, it was often overlooked in assessment and instruction (Allington, 1983b, 2006). This is likely because, in the absence of evidence linking fluency to comprehension, it was mistakenly assumed to be merely a symptom of poor word identi-fication skills (Allington, 1983b; Rasinski, 2006). Research has now established that there is a strong relationship between fluency and comprehension, including evidence from two special studies related to the 1992 and 2002 National Assessment of Educational Progress (NAEP) reading assessments (Daane, Campbell, Grigg, Goodman, & Oranje, 2005; Pin-nell et al., 1995). There is also evidence that high levels of fluency are related to ample opportunities to practice reading (Rasinski, 2006; Snow, Burns, & Griffin, 1998). This, in turn, is likely related to the fact that the development of good orthographic knowledge and skill seems to make a strong contribution to both rate and fluency. Perhaps, as Barker, Torgesen, and Wagner (1992) note, orthographic skills allow readers to recognize whole words automatically, circumventing the need for deeper phonological analysis. This allows readers to focus more attention on the other aspects of reading text, most notably meaning.

Although fluency is now an important part of assessment and instruction, there is still a great deal of confusion about exactly what it is; there is no single definition. As Rasinski (2006) notes, to some it is primarily an act of oral reading—specifically the expressive-ness associated with the oral reading. To others, reading fluency has to do with accuracy and speed in word decoding. And to yet others it has largely to do with the comprehension that comes as a result of reading with appropriate expressiveness or decoding speed and accuracy. Depending on the definition, the method of assessment is likely to vary. Further clarification is needed of what it is, how it works, and what role it should play in assess-ment and instruction.

Grammar, Usage, and the Mechanics of Writing

Grammar is the description of the structure of a language, based on principles of word and sentence formation. In the case of oral language, students will need to learn about prag-matics, or the study of what is the appropriate language usage in varying social situations and contexts. In the case of written language, students will learn that most grammar and usage issues come into play during the revision and editing phases of the writing process. Through practice, students gradually become more and more familiar with the conventions of grammar and usage, but at some point the "rules" of grammar and usage may need to be addressed directly. However, to be helpful, they must be viewed as part of a real social context or of the revising and editing phases of writing.

Grammar.   Grammar can be defined as a system of rules by which words are arranged into meaningful units. Everyone who speaks and understands English knows the rules, even if they can't articulate them. For example, we know that *The dog chased the cat up the tree* is a grammatical sentence, while *Tree up cat dog the the chased the* is not, because it violates rules of English grammar. Because we are aware of the violations, we must, on some level, know the rules that have been violated, even if we can't state them clearly. Rules such as these are best characterized as *subconscious abstract concepts.*

In contrast, *explicit* rules have been created by individuals trying to describe English grammar as it is used. A perfect set of explicit rules would be one that described all of the sentences that most people would consider grammatical and excluded any that would not be considered grammatical. No one has ever developed a perfect set of rules, but linguists continue to try and in the process have developed different types of grammars. Elements of two kinds of grammar—structural and transformational—are most relevant to our concerns with grammar instruction and learning. These elements are: form classes or parts of speech, structures of common sentences, and transformation of sentences.

Structural grammar focuses on sentence patterns and the functions of words in sentences. It identifies four form classes resembling nouns, verbs, adjectives, and adverbs. All the words that can fill a particular slot in a sentence belong to the same class. Advocates of structural grammars describe patterns or basic sentence types. For example, Roberts (1962) developed a sequence of ten patterns that are frequently used in textbooks that use a structural approach (e.g., determiner-noun-verb [intransitive]-adverb).

Transformational grammar focuses on the process used to generate sentences and ideas. Using four or five basic sentence types (or kernels) as the starting point for making sentences, we add transformations to change our basic sentences into more-complex ones. Three kinds of sentence transformations are those that (1) change one type of sentence into another, such as questions, negatives, and passive sentences; (2) conjoin elements of several sentences into compounds; and (3) reduce some sentences into fragments and insert them into other sentences (Malmstrom, 1968).

Data from the National Assessment of Educational Progress (NAEP) writing assessments in 1998 and 2002 indicate that approximately 85 percent of students in grades 4 and 8, and 75 percent of students in grade 12 have achieved a basic level of proficiency in writing (U.S. Department of Education, 2003). Basic proficiency at grades 4 and 8 includes grammar, spelling, and capitalization accurate enough to communicate to a reader, although there may be mistakes that get in the way of meaning. At grade 12, the basic level requires that errors do not get in the way of meaning. So, it appears that nearly all students can use the basic sentence types in their writing but that instruction using such techniques as sentence combining can be beneficial to a broad range of students as their writing skills mature (Hillocks, 1986).

Usage. How language is used, or the pragmatics of language, differs quite a bit between daily life and school. Academic success requires that students master structures and conventions peculiar to academic discourse, and many students find it difficult to adjust to its constraints. Academic English uses features that are more common in written than in spoken language. It conforms to organizational patterns and genres tailored to content areas and is more common in some cultures than in others. Many English-language learners and students with language difficulties attain mastery only with expert instruction over many years (Snow, Griffin, & Burns, 2005).

Functional grammar provides a means of analyzing language in terms of what it enables us to do and to mean (Halliday, 1994; Schleppegrell, 2004). Citing Halliday (1994), Schleppegrell (2004) indicates that functional grammar provides a "principled" basis for describing how and why language varies in relation to both who is using it and the purposes for which it is used. A functional grammar is not just concerned with identifying grammatical elements (e.g., nouns, verbs, etc.) or with the role that different elements play within a sentence (e.g., subject, object, etc.). Rather, it is used to analyze the configurations of grammatical structures that are typical of or expected in different kinds of tasks and connects those linguistic choices with the social purposes and situations related to particular spoken or written texts. Functional grammar, then, can reveal how the context of schooling is realized in the language used in the texts and tasks that constitute classroom practices (Schleppegrell, 2004).

Mechanics of Writing.   The mechanics of writing include punctuation and capitalization. Punctuation and capitalization are important because they clarify meaning. During oral exchanges, listeners hear pauses, speech stops, and rising and falling intonation that help them construct meaning. Readers and writers replace these verbal signals with punctuation and capitalization.

Studies show that punctuation—particularly with commas and periods—is frequently a problem for elementary-age students (Porter, 1974). According to Snow and colleagues (2005), it appears that teaching punctuation rules or teaching a mechanical response, such as pausing whenever a comma is recognized, is not helpful. However, developing familiarity with grammatical structures more common in written language than spoken language may be helpful.

UNDERSTANDING CONTEXTUAL FACTORS THAT INFLUENCE PERFORMANCE

Contextual factors are the least likely to be considered in any discussion of reading and writing performance. Indeed, the importance of context has only recently been acknowledged. Most recently, the contextual factor of text complexity has taken a prominent role in the Common Core State Standards for English language arts. In the following sections, we describe briefly several aspects of context that have been shown to influence reading and writing: the settings in which reading and writing events occur, the reading and writing curricula, the instructional methods employed, the instructional materials and tasks associated with reading and writing, and the assessment practices relative to reading and writing instruction. This brief discussion serves only to introduce ideas that will be discussed at greater length in Chapters 5 and 6.

Settings

The community and culture of students exert central, often critical, influence on performance in reading and writing. It also appears that the willingness and ability of the school to respond to local and/or cultural characteristics has a powerful impact on reading and writing acquisition and performance and can determine the effectiveness of instruction and achievement (Gallego & Hollingsworth, 2000; Goldenberg & Gallimore, 1991). Home environments that are different from the dominant culture are not pathological. Students can be hopelessly handicapped, however, if the school expects and accepts only one type of entry experience from its students. For example, students of diverse backgrounds enter school with strengths in their home language, if not the standard language. However, it is not uncommon for schools to ignore these strengths through the exclusion or limited use of instruction in students' home language or through the low status accorded the home language. Research suggests that this can lead to poor literacy achievement and may cause students to lose confidence in their abilities as language and literacy learners (Au, 2006).

The settings in which reading and writing and their instruction take place affect reading and writing performance. Meaning making depends on the broader context in which a text is being written or read. For example, imagine that you are reading or writing a text on common antidotes to poisoning. Now imagine the effect that context would have in the following situations: the evening newspaper, a test of reading comprehension, at home after you believe your child has ingested some poisonous substance, and a first aid course. Similarly, researchers have found differences in students' performance on the same task, depending on subtle changes in the classroom context—that is, whether students were asked to do the task as part of an informal lesson or as part of a formal testing situation (Mosenthal & Na, 1980). Indeed, several aspects of classroom settings have been examined and found to contribute to students' reading and writing achievement. For example, grouping patterns influence both teachers and students. Reviews of ability grouping for reading instruction suggest that instructional and social reading experiences differ for students in high- and low-ability reading groups and that these differences influence students' learning (Allington, 1983a; Hiebert, 1983). Grouping practices may also communicate information to students about their relative ability and may eventually influences their learning (Opitz, 1998; Weinstein, 1976).

Instructional Practices

Standards and Curriculum.   The standards and curriculum in particular school settings have a critical influence on student performance, because they may influence access to instruction, dictate the type of instruction offered, and even determine what is counted as reading and writing performance. Teachers and schools decide what and how to teach by referring to the standards established by their district and/or state. Both the nature of these standards and the curricula that grow out of them have often been controversial. In some places, standards setting has been an inclusive matter, leading to strengthened instruction and enhanced learning. In other places, standards appear to have been imposed, and the quality is uneven. In either case, standards have the effect of making public what is valued in reading and writing (see Wixson & Dutro, 1999; Wixson, Dutro, & Athan, 2004).

As noted in Chapter 1, there is a new player in the standards arena—the Common Core State Standards for English Language Arts (CCSS-ELA). The CCSS-ELA provide an integrated view of the areas within the English language arts—reading, writing, speaking/ listening, and language. This integrated view further encompasses attention to literature and informational text reading and writing at K–5. The 6–12 standards are first organized by ELA and subject matter to distinguish which standards are the responsibility of the English language arts teacher and which are to be addressed by teachers of history/social studies and science/technical subjects.

The integrated view of ELA presented by the CCSS-ELA contrasts sharply with the heavy emphasis that has been placed on *reading* in recent years almost to the exclusion of other areas of the language arts and other subject areas in the K–12 curriculum. When reading is part of an integrated model, the emphasis changes dramatically from the "big 5" that have dominated curriculum and instruction for the last decade or more—phonemic awareness, phonics, fluency, vocabulary, and comprehension. Within the CCSS-ELA, phonemic awareness, phonics, and fluency are addressed primarily in the "foundational skills" addendum to the K–5 standards. Vocabulary is highlighted in the Language strand, and comprehension is emphasized throughout. Add to this the emphasis on reading and writing in the disciplines at 6–12, and these standards are likely to result in a major shift from an overemphasis on decoding to increased emphasis on comprehension of and learning with and from oral and written language.

For students who experience problems with reading and writing, the standards/curriculum issue is even more complicated. For decades, American education adopted the position that it was not fair to hold all students to the same standards and searched for the most appropriate techniques for differentiating instruction and for setting differential educational goals (Allington, 1991). Not until the 1970s and 1980s did anyone begin to suggest that what had been considered differentiation might actually be a form of discrimination (Carew & Lightfoot, 1979). It was observed that students with the least adaptive capacity were asked to make the greatest adjustments across the school day (Good, 1983), including exposure to multiple literacy curricula often representing divergent theories of reading and writing processes. Increasing evidence of the lack of efficacy of the "second system" programs that have evolved since the turn of the century (Allington, 1994) has resulted in the current movement toward establishing a common set of high-level curriculum standards for *all* students. Many believe that this is the only way to ensure that all students are provided equal opportunities to achieve.

The important point for this discussion is that reading and writing standards/curricula have a tremendous impact on student performance. Many local school districts have their own curriculum, as do many states, although the CCSS-ELA may alter this fact. Curricula that reflect a more skills-based perspective are likely to promote very different procedures for instruction and assessment than curricula that reflect a more interactive or sociocultural perspective. The nature of the curriculum cannot be underestimated as a factor in students' reading and writing performance.

Instructional Methods.   Teachers and the lay public both are aware that instructional methods make a difference in students' learning (see Wharton-McDonald, 2011). Differences in instructional methods that influence performance vary along a continuum from direct (or explicit) instruction to discovery (or implicit) learning. Direct instruction involves explaining or telling students the procedures involved in engaging in a particular reading or writing activity. Indirect methods instruct through repeated practice with activities that are examples of the desired reading behavior. Discovery methods emphasize placing students in a literate environment in which reading and writing will develop naturally.

Other aspects of instructional method that influence student performance include: the extent to which teachers support, or scaffold, students as they engage in reading and writing activities; the nature and content of instructional dialogue or discourse; and the level of instruction offered. In addition, students' motivation for reading and writing is affected by specific instructional methods. For example, there is evidence that instructional programs that focus on the processes of reading and writing have a powerful impact on students' *awareness* of what has been taught, awareness of comprehension and composing strategies, and performance on tasks that require strategic reading and writing (Duffy et al., 1986;

Paris, Cross, & Lipson, 1984). Attention to a strategic approach can enhance students' self-regulation and independence (Scanlon, Anderson, & Sweeney, 2010).

Morrison, Bachman, and Connor (2005) recently identified four critical dimensions of beginning reading instruction as follows: (1) explicit versus implicit, (2) code- versus meaning-focused, (3) teacher-managed versus child-managed, and (4) change in amount of instruction over time. Results of a study that examined the nature and impact of these instructional dimensions on decoding growth in first-grade students provided evidence that the effect of amount, type, and course of instruction depended on students' skills at the beginning of first grade (Connor, Morrison, & Katch, 2004). For example, children who started first grade with weak decoding and vocabulary skills achieved greater decoding skill growth when they were in classrooms where the teacher provided more time in teacher-managed explicit decoding activities, especially at the beginning of the year, and when the teacher started the year with smaller amounts of child-managed implicit instruction but increased the amount over the school year. In contrast, children who started first grade with strong vocabulary but weaker decoding skills experienced the greatest decoding skill growth when instruction consisted of high amounts of child-managed instruction along with high amounts of teacher-managed explicit instruction all year long. Similar interactions were found for reading comprehension growth with third-grade students. Results such as these demonstrate clearly the impact of instructional methods and how they interact with learner factors.

The tasks that students must complete in association with their reading and writing can also make a difference in performance. For example, questioning is probably the most frequently used task in reading instruction. The evidence suggests that the type of questions children are asked can influence their comprehension. It appears that implicit or inferential questions are more difficult for many children than explicit or literal questions (Pearson, Hansen, & Gordon, 1979). Furthermore, there is evidence that the type of questions asked influences the numbers and types of inferences students make. Specifically, questions with answers stated explicitly in the text result in fewer inferences, questions that require the integration of information in the text result in a larger number of text-based inferences, and questions that require students to draw heavily on their prior knowledge result in inferences that are more knowledge based (Wixson, 1983a). In sum, many dimensions of instructional methods are likely to have a major impact on reading and writing performance, including the motivation to read and write.

Instructional Activities and Routines.   The *instructional tasks* and *practice activities* that students perform define reading and writing for them. For example, in some classrooms students spend more time doing instructional tasks than they do actual reading and writing. It should be noted that these instructional tasks generally provide practice of separate component areas, not practice in the holistic act of reading or writing. This is especially true for students who are experiencing reading and writing difficulties (Allington, 1984; Vaughn, Levy, Coleman, & Bos, 2002).

Alternatively, many classrooms contain other types of materials and tasks, including large numbers of "little" books, or leveled readers, that are accompanied by instructional frameworks and suggestions for assessment. These program materials are often used by teachers who identify themselves as "literature based" or "balanced" and exert an influence on practice that is as substantial as basal programs. Similarly for writing, some programs are still defined by grammar books and teacher-assigned "creative writing" activities, and others involve writers' workshops, conferences, and self-selected topics. The students in these classrooms think about reading and writing differently than do students in classrooms where reading and writing are extensive and pervasive and where tasks are linked in authentic ways to the reading and writing products. These different tasks also produce different types of writers.

Assessment Practices.   One of the truisms of education is that you get what you assess. For a variety of reasons, teachers are likely to direct their instructional attention toward the types of performance that will be evaluated, especially if the evaluation is highly public or used for other high-stakes purposes. Most educators have concluded that the standardized tests that are currently used in U.S. schools fail to adequately assess either sophisticated literacy skills or real-world literacy abilities. On the other hand, the nature of many classroom-based assessment efforts is also inadequate, often failing to focus on important content, complex ideas, or high-level strategies. For example, there is evidence that classroom measures such as correct words per minute, which are commonly used as indicators of students' overall reading level, overestimate student's comprehension abilities (Carlisle, Cortina, Zerg, & Schilling, 2006).

With the adoption of the CCSS by most states, plans for new state assessments are under development. At the time of this writing, most states have joined one of two state consortia engaged in the development of new state assessments aligned with the CCSS, although there are still a handful of states that are not part of either consortia. The goal of both consortia is to create integrated assessment systems, which include a variety of assessments and resources designed to achieve a range of assessment purposes. The various measures and resources under development correspond roughly to the different assessment purposes described in this text (see Chapter 3) and include (1) measuring the level of performance of individuals and/or groups of students (screening), (2) monitoring student progress (interim or benchmark), and (3) evaluating overall achievement of individuals and groups (outcome).

Because assessment practices often exert a strong influence on instruction, they should be examined carefully. Teachers should be aware that the ways in which information is gathered and the specific abilities that are tested can both influence student performance and affect teacher appraisal of student competence (Valencia, 2004). For example, the form and content of external accountability measures can influence students' reading and writing performance. Specifically, student's performance is likely to suffer when the form and content of an external accountability measure is inconsistent with the form and content of classroom tasks. These types of inconsistencies can also confuse students about their learning goals.

It is important to be aware of what types of assessments are being used and for what purposes within specific instructional contexts. If the only form of assessment is testing that is focused on isolated skills, then students are likely to be attending to skill mastery at the expense of integrated skill performances. In contrast, if the only form of assessment is student self-reflection, then students are likely to become more responsible for their own learning but may miss some important skills and not progress as rapidly as needed to perform at desirable levels. Assessment practices can and do have a significant impact on student's reading and writing performance.

Instructional Resources

Students are presented with an enormous array of materials and tasks during their development as readers and writers. Prominent among these are commercial instructional programs, trade materials, tutoring programs, and computer technology. In many classrooms today, there is a combination of these resources available to students and teachers as part of reading and writing instruction. However, it is important to note that children who attend schools in disadvantaged districts have many fewer texts and technologies available than do children who attend schools in more-affluent areas (Duke, 2000), and that the availability of textual resources in homes and libraries varies similarly (Neuman, & Celano, 2001).

Core Instructional Programs. In many classrooms, students still work primarily from commercial, basal reading programs, and teachers are heavily influenced by the published materials that accompany these materials. Over half of the teachers and administrators surveyed in the late 1990s indicated that basal reading programs with trade-book supplements provided the foundation of their instruction (Baumann, Hoffman, Duffy-Hester, & Ro, 2000). A review of basal reading programs suggested that the curriculum presented by these programs changed during the 1990s (Hoffman et al., 1994). During the early 1990s, for example, the literature in anthologies was drawn from children's literature rather than contrived or commissioned pieces, the vocabulary was less stringently controlled, and there was a decreased focus on phonics and isolated skills instruction. Newer programs continue to emphasize good literature, while providing more-controlled vocabulary options for early reading practice. In addition, they are likely to include more-explicit phonics than was true previously.

Core instructional materials inevitably become a part of a teacher's instructional set and often determine both what is read and written and what instructional activities are employed, which in turn has an effect on student learning and achievement. For example, Wilson, Martens, and Arya (2005) found that the story retellings of second-grade students taught using basal programs emphasizing systematic, explicit phonics instruction were significantly less cohesive and included fewer inferences and connections than those of students taught using a literature-based approach to instruction. They concluded that the program of instruction affects students' strategy knowledge and use, as well as their comprehension abilities, and that it shapes the students' purposes or goals for reading.

Textbooks and Trade Materials. Students come into contact with a wide variety of trade materials in their daily lives as readers and writers: comic books, cereal boxes, assembly instructions, entry forms, Facebook pages, and so forth. It is possible, and perhaps even desirable, to consider any or all of these materials as having instructional potential. However, the range of materials used for instruction in most classrooms is more constrained than this, and the materials to which students are exposed during instruction often differ from those they encounter in other contexts (Wade & Moje, 2000).

In almost every classroom, students are asked to read various types of prose, or written, texts. Prose selections used for instructional purposes come from a variety of sources, including basal readers, trade books (children's fiction and nonfiction books), subject-area textbooks, magazines, reference materials, weekly news publications, and the students' own writing. Research consistently demonstrates that the printed materials students encounter in instructional contexts influence their reading and writing, and this awareness plays a prominent role in the attention to text complexity in the CCSS-ELA. In the past, one of the few text features that received a lot of attention was difficulty or readability, as measured by factors such as the number of syllables in the words and the number of words in the sentences. Current research has demonstrated that a number of other factors have a significant impact on both how much and what students understand and learn from a text. The presence or absence of these factors determines the extent to which a given text can be seen as "considerate" or "inconsiderate" (Armbruster, 1984).

Considerate texts are designed to enable the learner to gather appropriate information with minimal effort; *inconsiderate texts* require the learner to put forth extra effort to compensate for the inadequacies of the text. Inconsiderate texts are not necessarily incomprehensible, but they do require more effort, skill, and prior knowledge to comprehend. Two factors that determine the considerateness of a given text are its type and organization. For example, under certain circumstances students' oral reading and writing errors have been observed to vary according to the type of text they were reading or writing (stories versus informational articles, subject-area texts versus basal materials). Stories are more easily comprehended than informational texts for many students, and well-constructed stories are more easily comprehended than those less well organized (Brennan, Bridge, & Winograd, 1986; Olson, 1985). In addition, text structures differ among subject matter domains in ways that influence student performance (Snow et al., 2005).

The linguistic properties of texts including word usage, sentence structure, and sentence connectives constitute another factor influencing comprehensibility. These properties vary across different types of texts and influence performance on a variety of reading and writing tasks. For example, texts that include a large proportion of words that occur with high frequency in our language are more easily comprehended than are texts with a large proportion of low-frequency words (Ruddell, 1965; Wittrock, Marks, & Doctorow, 1975).

The comprehensibility or considerateness of a text is also influenced by its structural characteristics, including all the features of texts that authors and editors use to aid organization and understanding, such as headings, boldface type, illustrations, diagrams, and end-of-chapter questions and activities. For example, there is evidence that comprehension is enhanced when main-idea statements are highlighted through the use of italics or headings (Baumann, 1986). It also appears that students are actually led to attend to unimportant ideas when structural features focus on trivial information. For example, if questions that follow reading focus on insignificant details, children are more likely to learn this information than the more important ideas in the text (Wixson, 1984).

Electronic Texts.   Although access varies considerably by school and district, multimedia and computer activities are an important additional type of material. Careful examination of these programs is especially important for teachers who work with less-able readers and writers. There is continuing pressure to operate remedial settings through the use of diagnostic-prescriptive management systems that involve computer testing, computer-generated profiles of skill needs, and computer programs for remedial instruction. There are also many other types of computer programs intended for assessment and instruction in reading, and their role in instruction may have an important effect on students' reading and writing performance.

UNDERSTANDING LEARNER FACTORS THAT INFLUENCE PERFORMANCE

An interactive view of reading and writing suggests that a variety of learner factors influence reading and writing performance. These include prior content knowledge; knowledge about reading and writing, including both phonological and metacognitive awareness; attitudes and motivation; and the physical, cognitive, linguistic, and social-emotional correlates of reading and writing disability.

Prior Content Knowledge

It is difficult to overestimate the influence of children's prior knowledge and their experience. In their review of children's learning from text, Alexander and Jetton (2000, p. 291) conclude, "Of all the factors [involved in learning from text], none exerts more influence on what students understand and remember than the knowledge they possess."

Research findings have consistently demonstrated how prior knowledge and experience influence reading comprehension (Lipson, 1982, 1983). Simply put, the more accurate and elaborated knowledge readers have about the ideas, concepts, or events described in the text, the better they will understand. On the other hand, limited information and/or misconceptions create obstacles to comprehension.

Comprehension proceeds so smoothly under ordinary circumstances that most adults are unaware of the process of constructing a model or interpretation of a text that fits with their knowledge of the world. It is instructive to try to understand material for which meaning is not immediately apparent. For example, take a moment to read and try to understand the following paragraph in an exercise used in a classic study by Bransford and Johnson (1972, p. 722):

> The procedure is actually quite simple. First you arrange things into different groups. Of course, one pile may be sufficient depending on how much there is to do. If you have to go somewhere else due to lack of facilities that is the next step, otherwise you are pretty well set. It is important not to overdo things. That is, it is better to do too few things at once than too many. In the short run, this may not seem important, but complications can easily arise. A mistake can be expensive as well. At first the whole procedure will seem complicated. Soon, however, it will become just another facet of life. It is difficult to foresee any end to the necessity for this task in the immediate future, but then one never can tell. After the procedure is completed one arranges the materials into different groups again. Then they can be put into their appropriate places. Eventually they will be used once more and the whole cycle will then have to be repeated. However, that is part of life.

Were there any words you could not pronounce or for which you do not have some idea of the meaning? Is the syntax too complex? You probably did not have problems in either of these areas. Yet for most people this passage does not make much sense. However, it does become meaningful as soon as we use the title "Washing Clothes." Then the well-known concepts related to doing this job can be used to construct and assign meaning.

Learners also need to understand a great deal about social interactions and human relationships to connect ideas in texts. This type of prior knowledge seems to be especially important in inferential understanding (Lipson, Mosenthal, & Mekkelsen, 1999). Fragmented information and/or misconceptions can impede comprehension (Hynd & Alvermann, 1986; Lipson, 1982, 1983; Maria, 1986). This is especially troublesome when students attempt to learn from informational texts. People read unfamiliar text more slowly, they remember less, they construct meanings that are inconsistent with the author's intention, and they sometimes reject the text information outright. Misconceptions and limited information influence comprehension in a number of ways (see Guzzetti & Hynd, 1998). Of course, prior knowledge and text attributes interact. For example, the comprehension of students with low prior knowledge is significantly improved when they read "high-coherence" text, whereas students with high prior knowledge actually benefited from low-coherence text under some conditions. Presumably, with appropriate prior knowledge, they generated more inferences because the text provided less information (McNamara, 2001).

There are many times when a text written for an audience with certain background knowledge is given to an audience with different or limited knowledge of the topic. For example, certain learners will have difficulties trying to understand the materials in Figure 2.3, which were taken from newspapers in Vermont and Australia. Now suppose

NIGHT AUCTION

Thursday, Oct. 9th   7:30 PM

Located on the so-called Harry Domina farm on Route #118 between East Berkshire and Montgomery, Vt. Watch for Auction Signs at Route Jct. #105 & #118 in East Berkshire, Vt.

50 Holstein Heifers   50

22 of the heifers are fresh within the last ten days and are milking between 50 to 60 lbs. of weighted milk, balance are all springing, 5 of these heifers are registered with papers that will be handed out the same night. Heifers have good size and condition and are going to be sold for cash regardless of price. Heifers have all been T.B., blood tested and inoculated from shipping fever and I.B.R. Heifers are open for inspection anytime on site where auction is to be held. Trucking available.

Auctioneer: Ringman:
Tel: Berkshire, Vt.
Sales held inside tent   Tel:

Owners:
Berkshire, Vt. Tel.:

CRICKET MATCH
AUSTRALIA vs. ENGLAND

A hair-raising century by Australian opener Graeme Wood on Friday set England back on its heels in the third test at the Melbourne Cricket Ground. Unfortunately, living dangerously eventually cost the Australians the match. Wood was caught out of his crease on the first over after lunch. Within ten more overs, the Australians were dismissed. Four were dismissed by dangerous running between creases. Two were dismissed when the English bowlers lifted the balls from the batsmen's wickets. The three remaining batsmen were caught by English fieldsmen. One was caught as he tried for a six. When the innings were complete the Australians had fallen short of the runs scored by the English.

FIGURE 2.3   Text Taken from Newspapers in Vermont and Australia

you were asked to identify the main ideas of these texts. If you failed to complete this task successfully, would it mean that you do not know how to "get" a main idea? Obviously not; it simply means that you do not have sufficient background knowledge about the game of cricket, or about dairy cows, to be able to understand the most important points in these texts. This is why it is so important to consider students' prior knowledge when evaluating their performance on comprehension tasks.

Although there is little direct evidence regarding the role of prior knowledge as a factor in writing, common sense suggests that it would influence performance in analogous ways. Almost all views of the writing process, for example, involve a prewriting stage in which writers either activate existing topic knowledge or engage in experiences or information-gathering activities to expand knowledge. Authors can use only the voice they have or convey only the knowledge and experience they possess.

A basic fallacy of skills-based views of reading and writing is that skills are static across all reading and writing situations and that peoples' skill performance under one set of reading and writing conditions is indicative of their performance under all reading and writing conditions. Clearly, this is not the case for us or for our students. Children do not have the same experiential background as adults, and the meanings they construct for a given piece of text may be different from the meanings constructed by their adult teachers or authors of instructional materials.

Knowledge about Reading and Writing

There are two major types of knowledge that influence students' acquisition of and facility with reading and writing: *phonological awareness* and *metacognitive awareness*. Both of these factors are developmental; that is, in general, younger, less-experienced people have both quantitatively less and qualitatively different knowledge than older, more-experienced people. Both of these factors are also strongly implicated in the reading difficulties experienced by many students.

Metacognition.   This term was introduced by developmental psychologists to refer to individuals' knowledge about and control over their own learning and thinking activities (Flavell & Wellman, 1977; Paris, Wasik, & Van der Westhuizen, 1988).

Metacognition in reading and writing refers to one's understanding of reading and writing processes. This understanding is revealed in two ways. First, it involves the learner's knowledge of the nature of reading and writing; the purposes and goals of reading and writing; the various factors that influence reading and writing; and the what, how, when, and why of strategy usage in reading and writing. Second, learners' understanding is reflected in the control they have of their actions while reading and writing for different purposes. Active learners monitor their own state of learning, plan strategies, adjust efforts appropriately, and evaluate the success of their ongoing efforts (Brown, Armbruster, & Baker, 1986; Raphael, Kirschner, & Englert, 1988).

Research suggests that skilled learners know a great deal about reading and writing, and that this knowledge influences their ability to select and use appropriate strategies and skills in different reading and writing situations. It is becoming increasingly clear that learners need several types of knowledge in order to become proficient. First, they need to

[handwritten margin note: Students need to be aware of the different processes involved in writing so that they can think about it (meta?)]

understand that a skill or strategy exists and is available to be used for reading/writing. For example, writers need to be aware that they can edit or revise their writing when it does not communicate their meaning clearly. Many young and less-skilled writers seem unaware of this aspect of skilled writing. This type of knowledge is called *declarative knowledge* and requires only that the child know that a skill or strategy exists.

Knowing that a particular skill or tactic exists is not enough for successful performance, however. Learners also need to know how to perform the skill or strategy. To continue with our example, it is not sufficient to know that you can change your writing to clarify meaning; you must also understand how to go about editing and revising. This type of knowledge is called *procedural knowledge* because it refers to knowledge of the procedures necessary to execute and orchestrate the components of the reading process.

In the past, it was assumed that declarative and procedural knowledge would ensure application, that students who knew about the components and how to apply them would surely use this knowledge in the appropriate reading situations. Almost daily, however, teachers encounter students who appear to have mastered a skill or strategy sufficiently to employ it but fail to demonstrate any such competence during real reading or writing situations. These children often fail to apply their existing skills and strategies because they lack a third type of knowledge, *conditional knowledge* (Paris, Lipson, & Wixson 1983). Simply stated, conditional knowledge is knowledge about when and why to employ a known strategy or skill. For example, skimming is obviously not a universally helpful approach to reading. Readers need to know when and why it is appropriate to use skimming. Conditional knowledge is essential for students to be able to apply the strategies and skills learned during reading and writing instruction in other reading situations.

Skilled learners possess a wide range of knowledge related to reading and writing, including knowledge of purposes and goals, various text factors, task requirements, and skills and strategies used in reading and writing. For example, they know that the purpose of reading and writing is "to make meaning" rather than "to say all of the words right" or "to write neatly." Skilled learners also realize that reading and writing will be easier if they know a great deal about the topic of the text they are reading or writing and if they are interested in it. These examples may seem incredibly obvious, but there are many young and poor learners who do not have even these basic understandings about reading and writing.

Skilled learners also understand how various text factors can influence their reading and writing. Before we ever open a book or write the first words in a text, our knowledge of the type of text we are reading or writing influences the way we will read or write that text. We know about different kinds of texts such as encyclopedias, cookbooks, letters from friends, novels, newspapers, and so forth. We have expectations for how these texts are organized and for the types of information they contain, and this knowledge guides us in the selection of appropriate reading and writing strategies. For example, if you were reading or writing about a miracle cure for baldness from or for *Scientific American*, you would be likely to approach the task differently than if you were reading or writing about it from or for the *National Enquirer*.

Knowledge about the tasks that learners will be asked to complete in the course of reading and writing also affects strategy selection and usage. When we asked a group of fifth-grade students to tell us why they thought their teachers wanted them to work in their workbooks, one child responded indignantly, "Do you know what she [the teacher] did? She gave us a test on the workbook. You're not supposed to remember that stuff!" His response reflected his awareness that in many classrooms students need not remember the material in their workbooks; they must simply complete it and put it in the appropriate place.

Skilled learners also have knowledge about different skills and strategies for reading and writing and about how to use them (Paris, Wasik, & Turner, 1991). For example, they are aware of strategies for dealing with words and sentences they do not know (ask for help, use the dictionary, reread). They are also aware of the purposes for different strategies, such as planning or prewriting (it helps you get out all your ideas, you can see how your ideas go together). It is not sufficient to know what the strategies are and how to use them; learners must also know when and why to use them.

Skilled learners not only have a great deal of knowledge about reading and writing, but they can also apply that knowledge to monitor and regulate their reading and writing. There is evidence that they can adjust their strategies in response to different reading and writing situations (reading and writing for fun, reading and writing for specific ideas or for general impressions, studying) and that they use specific strategies to meet the demands of specific reading and writing situations (using different styles depending on their relationship to the intended audience of their writing). There is also a considerable body of knowledge that suggests that students with reading disabilities exhibit very little of these types of metacognitive abilities (Gersten, Fuchs, Williams, & Baker, 2002; Trainen & Swanson, 2005). In summary, students' knowledge and control of reading and writing processes play an important role in their reading and writing performance.

Phonological Awareness.   Over the course of their preschool years, most children become increasingly aware of the phonological structure of their language (see Chapter 7, "The Foundations of Literacy," for a more comprehensive discussion of this aspect of reading development). Phonological awareness refers to children's ability to divide sentences into words, break words into syllables, and identify common phonemes (e.g., recognize rhyming words). As we have already noted, in an alphabetic language such as English, it is essential to attend to the phonology of the language. Initially, children are likely to attend to word play, rhymes, and then syllables as units of sound. Eventually, however, children need to be able to isolate individual phonemes, the smallest distinguishable units of sound, within a word. This specialized aspect of phonological awareness is called *phonemic awareness* or *phonemic segmentation* (see Chapter 7). Because most children and adults attend primarily to meaning in spoken language, many young children do not acquire the idea that the sound structure is distinct from the meaning structure of the language until quite late in their preschool or their early school years. The majority of children do not acquire the ability to isolate (segment) phonemes until the age of 5 or 6 (Liberman & Shankweiler, 1979). There is additional research that suggests that phonological awareness, like other correlates, may be quite stable and linked to innate individual differences. A growing body of research has demonstrated that the vast majority of students who struggle in first and second grades can be taught to read with appropriate instruction (Dorn, 2011; McNamara, 2010; Scanlon, Anderson, & Sweeney, 2010; Vellutino, Scanlon, & Sipay, 1997). A very small number, however (called the "hardest to remediate" and totaling about 2 percent of all students), had a different profile of phonological awareness skills than other students. In particular, they were different in phoneme awareness and rapid naming tasks.

In their extensive review of research in this area, the Committee on the Prevention of Reading Difficulties in Young Children described the development of phonological abilities (Snow et al., 1998), concluding that phonological awareness is a strong predictor of subsequent reading achievement. They also conclude that early tests of phonological awareness may not always provide definitive information:

> Phonological awareness in kindergarten appears to have the tendency to be a more successful predictor of future *superior* reading than of future reading *problems*. That is, among children who have recently begun or will soon begin kindergarten, few of those with strong phonological awareness skills will stumble in learning to read, but many of those with weak phonological sensitivity will go on to become adequate readers [emphasis in the original]. (Snow et al., 1998, p. 112)

This is likely because researchers have also demonstrated that the relationship of phonological awareness to development is "bidirectional, involving reciprocal causation (Ehri, 1979, 1987; Perfetti et al., 1987)" (Snow et al., 1998, p. 56). That is, children with good phonological awareness abilities learn to read more easily and quickly. However, learning to read (experiencing instruction focused on reading and writing) results in improved phonological awareness. Thus, although very strongly related to reading ability (and to language development in general), good phonological awareness is not a prerequisite to reading and should not be used to limit students' access to good developmental instruction. On the other hand, there is also strong evidence to suggest that for students who need it, "instruction that heightens phonological awareness and that emphasizes the connections to the alphabetic code promotes greater skill in word recognition; a skill essential to becoming a proficient reader" (Blachman, 2000, p. 495).

Attitudes and Motivation

Whether children perform or learn in a particular situation depends on whether they can do what must be done and whether they choose to do it (Adelman & Taylor, 1977). Learning and performance require both *skill* and *will* (Paris, Lipson, & Wixson, 1983). Factors such as interest, the amount of time and effort required, willingness to take risks, or perceived competence can influence children's decisions of whether or not to use their skills.

The student's attitude toward reading and writing is a central factor affecting reading and writing performance. Positive attitudes and motivation can compensate for relatively weak skills, and negative attitudes can prevent a student from applying existing knowledge or from acquiring new information (Paris, Olson, & Stevenson, 1983). Motivation is an especially serious concern for middle and high school students (Van Ritzin, 2011). For example, only one in three students at age thirteen, and one in four at age seventeen, reports reading voluntarily (Snow et al., 2005). Students' motivation continues to decline throughout the middle and high school period.

Researchers have argued more recently that attitude is distinct from motivation, since students frequently report doing well on an academic task (e.g., reading) at the same time that they report disliking the activity (McKenna, Kear, & Ellsworth, 1995). These findings have resulted in a broader look at the purposes for which people engage in reading and writing activities. It is clear that some people have an intrinsic motivation to read for enjoyment. At the same time, other purposes prevail, including a "learning goal orientation" and a "performance or ego orientation" (Guthrie & Wigfield, 2000). Readers with a learning goal orientation want to improve their reading skills, whereas readers with a performance orientation have a competitive desire to do better than others. Still other readers have social motivation for reading. Young children, especially, might want to spend time with their peers and interact with them in a common experience. Clearly, different goals might result in varied levels of motivation, depending on the tasks and settings.

Although few educators would dispute the relationship between motivation and achievement, the research establishing these links is somewhat mixed, largely because of differences in definition, student population, and subject area. Recently, researchers have begun to think of motivation and student engagement as mediating factors in school success (Guthrie & Wigfield, 2000; Wigfield et al., 2006). They suggest that the individual classroom context factors might not influence performance directly. Instead, the instructional methods, materials, and tasks determine or affect student engagement, and it is this student engagement that directly impacts performance and achievement. According to Guthrie and Wigfield (2000), engagement is a combination of motivation, conceptual knowledge, social interaction, and strategy use.

Research indicates that positive self-perception (or self-efficacy) promotes achievement-oriented behavior, whereas low self-perception leads to decreased motivation. In addition, positive attitudes and self-perceptions are associated with a sense of control over reading and writing successes and failures. Perceived lack of control can grow out of repeated and prolonged failure experiences. This can have a debilitating effect, sometimes called *learned helplessness*, which in turn causes a general expectation that all events that happen to the person are uncontrollable. The end result can be passive behavior.

Butkowsky and Willows (1980) demonstrated this cyclic pattern. The poor learners in their study had significantly lower initial expectations for success than did average and good learners, and when confronted with failure, they persisted at the task for shorter periods of time. However, it also appears that children's beliefs about why they succeed or fail in reading and writing vary across reading and writing situations (Hiebert, Winograd, & Danner, 1984). Therefore, it is likely that learners' willingness to exert effort will also vary from situation to situation.

Correlates of Reading and Writing Performance

There are a number of learner factors related to successful learning and achievement. These factors are frequently referred to as *correlates* of reading and writing ability/disability, because strengths and weaknesses in any of these areas are often correlated with reading and/or writing performance. When one or more of these correlates is strongly present in a student or a student population, these students may be considered *at risk* for school failure (Vacca & Padak, 1990). It is important to understand, however, that a high correlation between some learner factor and performance in reading and writing does not ensure that this factor is the *cause* of the high or low performance. The research thus far has yielded only equivocal findings regarding the causal relationships between most correlates and reading and writing success.

Although correlates of reading and writing achievement certainly can and often do influence students' reading and writing, they may be much less critical than had previously been imagined. As Snow, Burns, and Griffin (1998, p. 24) explain:

> In all populations, reading ability occurs along a continuum, and biological factors are influenced by, and interact with, a reader's experiences. The findings of an anomalous brain system say little about the possibility for change, for remediation, or for response to treatment. It is well-known that, particularly in children, neural systems are plastic and responsive to changed input.

In the following sections, we briefly describe correlates of reading and writing performance in four major areas: social and emotional development, language development, physical development, and cognitive development.

Social and Emotional Development.   An area related to attitudes and motivation is students' social and emotional development. Students who have trouble adjusting to various social situations with peers and/or adults may experience academic difficulties. Students with emotional problems may also have difficulty concentrating in school, which often has a negative effect on their learning. However, it is frequently difficult to determine the extent to which emotional and social maladjustment are causes or results of reading and writing problems. Every poor learner is at risk for psychological disturbance, almost always because of but almost never as the cause of and often as a further contribution to poor reading and writing.

Research on the relationship between poor learners as a group and emotional or social difficulties is somewhat mixed, but it is certainly clear that individual students may exhibit reading and writing difficulties due largely to social or emotional problems (see Rock, Fessler, & Church, 1997). There are students for whom learning is made more difficult by family upheaval, by neglect, and by interpersonal problems in school. In addition, of course, physiologically based emotional problems (for example, from drug-related birth trauma) can lead to students who are easily discouraged or unable to relate to others, although it is increasingly clear that even students with these challenges can achieve high levels of success in literacy with the right instruction (Snow et al., 1998). At the same time, the research suggests that failure to learn to read may result in social-emotional difficulties (Arnold et al., 2005). Regardless of whether emotional or social problems are the cause or the result of reading and writing problems, if they are interfering with learning and performance, they must be considered in developing an instructional program.

Language Development.   The acquisition of language competence is a major factor influencing subsequent reading and writing achievement. Indeed, the researchers at the Center for the Improvement of Early Reading Achievement have affirmed that "oral language is the foundation on which reading is built, and it continues to serve this role as children develop as readers" (Hiebert et al., 1998, Topic 1, p. 1). As children learn language, they develop abilities in understanding and producing speech. This development involves learning how their language is structured, how humans use language to communicate, and the specific words and rules of their own language.

All languages have certain characteristics, described earlier in this chapter, that children must learn or acquire (see also Chapter 7). Humans use language for a variety of purposes, and understanding the functions embedded in language is critical to comprehending and composing messages. The communicative functions include regulating other people's behavior, expressing feelings, pretending and creating, conveying or obtaining information, and establishing and maintaining contact with others.

Children acquire language competence at varying rates and to varying degrees. With few exceptions, children will have mastered the language and communication patterns of their own families before entering first grade. Not all language and communication patterns are equally good matches with the demands of school settings, however. Children with delayed, underdeveloped, or merely different language skills are likely to have difficulty with conventional reading and writing. Indeed, one factor that is likely to place students at risk of school failure is limited English proficiency. Children's knowledge of the structure of language forms the foundation for learning to read. If the child's language differs significantly from the language he or she is encountering in books, the resulting mismatch will make initial learning difficult.

Although it seems obvious to point out that children will not easily learn to read a language they cannot speak, not all schools are equipped to provide the foundations in oral language that may be required for many students. Nor are many schools prepared to offer a rich multilingual experience that capitalizes on the knowledge and expertise of the larger community (Moll & González, 1994). Language and culture are strongly interrelated (Bernhardt, 2000; Ovando, 2005), which means that the aspects of context (culture, setting, etc.) influence learner factors as well as performance. The influence of context, in other words, can affect the learner directly or interact with learner factors (and other context factors) to influence performance. As Ruddell (1993, p. 325) has noted:

> Regardless of whether students are learning English as a second language or a third (or fourth) language, much of what they bring to school from their primary language is a part of the beliefs, attitudes, behaviors, and values of their primary culture as well. To teach bi- and multilingual students effectively, we need knowledge and understanding of their language and culture, and the relationships between the two.

These are particularly challenging concerns for two reasons. First, the proportion of language-minority children and youth speaking a language other than English at home has dramatically increased from 6 percent in 1979 to 14 percent in 1999 (August & Shanahan, 2006). Second, these students are far more likely to experience significant reading and learning difficulties, leading to gaps in school achievement. For example, "despite the group's progress in achievement over the past 15 to 20 years, [Hispanic] students are about twice as likely as non-Hispanic whites to be reading below average for their age" (Snow et al., 1998, p. 28). As described in August and Shanahan (2006), a survey of forty-one state agencies (Kindler, 2002) indicated that only 18.7 percent of the English language learners (ELLs) assessed scored above the state-established norms in English reading comprehension.

As young children are engaged in experiences with language, thought, and print, they gain an increasing awareness about what is required to accomplish literacy tasks.

Learning reading and writing, like most cognitive tasks, requires some degree of reflective ability, yet not all children have acquired appropriate abilities in this area. Some abilities, though potentially useful, are late in developing in all children (phonemic segmentation, for example). Because the assessment-instruction process needs to take these factors into account, we will return to the issue of language development in Chapter 7.

Physical Development.   Within the area of physical development, there are several factors that may influence reading and writing performance; hearing and vision are two of these.

Hearing.   There are several types of hearing loss. Some make it difficult for students to hear all sounds (measured by the intensity or loudness of sounds); others result in loss of hearing for particular sounds (or frequencies). Both of these types of hearing loss can occur in the same person, and hearing loss can occur in one or both ears. According to Richek, Caldwell, Jennings, and Lerner (2002, p. 347), "even a moderate loss in the ability to hear may substantially affect the ability to read." Generally speaking, the vowel sounds of English are low-frequency sounds, and the consonants are high-frequency sounds; impairments in either area might affect students' word recognition development.

An appropriate referral should be made if there is any evidence of impaired hearing, and if at all possible, the loss should be corrected before any further specialized instruction occurs. Hearing loss resulting from more-temporary physical conditions (for example, ear infections) can also interfere with learning and should prompt careful teachers to consider adapting their methods of instruction.

Vision.   There are several types of visual impairments we need to be concerned about. People who are farsighted have difficulty in seeing objects up close, as when reading or writing. Nearsightedness, on the other hand, results in difficulties seeing distant objects, such as the White board. Astigmatism results in distorted visual images, which could lead to problems such as keeping one's place while reading and writing. Other types of vision problems occur when the eye muscles do not work together in a smooth, coordinated fashion. These types of problems can result in fatigue and discomfort that interfere with reading and writing.

Research regarding the impact of these visual problems on reading and writing achievement appears to be equivocal. It seems that visual acuity and poor eye muscle coordination are "rarely the cause of poor reading" (Gunning, 2002, p. 52). In addition, visual problems that might make reading more difficult often go undetected, because the eye test that is commonly used in school screenings, the Snellen chart, is designed to detect only problems with far-point vision and not the near-point difficulties that might influence reading performance.

Cognitive Development.   As children grow and mature, they acquire an increasingly sophisticated repertoire of cognitive abilities, including the ability to read and write. Developmental stages or shifts in perspective are often used to capture this changing and increasing knowledge base (Bruner, 1964; Piaget, 1960; Vygotsky, 1978). Both Piaget and Bruner describe growth during the preschool and school years as a process during which children are moving toward the ability to transcend the present and think flexibly about the world. Teachers need to understand how their students think about their world so that they can provide experiences that are appropriate to children's cognitive functioning and that move them to expand and restructure their knowledge.

Cognitive factors include development in the areas of perception, attention, and memory, as well as encompassing traditional notions of intelligence and verbal ability. Although it is beyond the scope of this text to consider each of these aspects in detail, each will be discussed briefly below to provide an awareness of the scope of the cognitive-developmental factors that may influence reading and writing achievement.

Intelligence. Intelligence generally refers to overall mental ability. Included in the construct of intelligence are such indicators of ability as speed of learning, ability to solve problems, and ability to engage in high-level thinking tasks. Although overall cognitive-developmental ability certainly influences students' learning, the specific impact on the acquisition of literacy should not be overestimated. Snow, Burns, and Griffin (1998, p. 24) conclude, for example, that "the child's intelligence, as long as it is in the normal range, does not have much of an impact on the ease of learning to read" (Stanovich, Cunningham, & Cramer, 1984).

Given the importance of judgments about intelligence in school settings, several points need to be made here. First, intelligence is a construct. That is, the components of intelligence are not readily observable. Indeed, there is substantial disagreement about what the components are. Most psychological authorities note that intelligence is actually grounded in culture and that different societies value different sets of skills and define intelligence accordingly (Okagaki & Sternberg, 1991). Recent conceptualizations of intelligence involve a more expansive consideration of the components involved in cognitive activity. Gardner's (1983) set of multiple intelligences has been joined by others. Sternberg (1999), for example, suggests that intelligence involves five components: metacognitive skills, learning skills, thinking skills, knowledge (declarative and procedural), and motivation.

As Bransford, Goldman, and Nye (1991, p. 152) point out:

> A shift in the emphasis from academic intelligence to multiple intelligences carries with it the implication that intelligence is not a holistic trait that characterizes an individual. Thus, an individual might be relatively intelligent in school but relatively unintelligent in other contexts such as the auto repair shop and vice versa.

This supports the notion of an interactive view of learning and ability, rejecting the older view that intelligence was a relatively stable characteristic and, as such, was not susceptible to change via instruction.

On the other hand, certain abilities that are frequently measured on tests of intelligence but are not part of everyday definitions of intelligence may have significant implications for students' reading development. For example, many poor readers complete rapid automatized naming (RAN) tasks, which require the ability to quickly name random letters or numerals, more slowly than capable readers. Increasingly, it appears that speed of processing, especially speed and flexibility in manipulating the phonological aspects of language, may affect students' reading (Wagner et al., 1997).

Given this situation, caution needs to be exercised in attributing reading and writing problems to limited overall cognitive ability. In our multicultural society, it is possible for different types of behavior and knowledge to mean different things to different individuals. For example, some cultural groups take the aggressive display of information as totally inappropriate behavior—the mark of someone who is either not very smart or not very polite. Other groups teach children to provide creative, but not necessarily factual, answers to situational questions. Conclusions generated about intelligence in the absence of appropriate cultural context can be misleading.

Increasingly, it appears that intelligence can be influenced by certain experiences and instruction (Carnegie Corporation, 1994; Slavin, 1991). More important, there is an increased interest, not in static measures of intelligence as traditionally assessed, but in measures of potential to learn. The evidence to date suggests that measures of potential can contribute important information to the process of assessment and instruction, and we will return to these in Chapter 10.

Information-Processing Abilities. Student learning is also associated with the ability to process information in either written or spoken form. *Attention*, *perception*, and *memory* are all factors that influence learning and performance.

The ability and willingness to pay attention to important stimuli is a major factor in school success (Gage & Berliner, 1988). Human beings are surrounded by stimuli—that is, all aspects of the environment that are present to be learned, enjoyed, and noticed. Some students appear to have an exceptionally difficult time attending to school tasks and concentrating on print-related activities. Many of these students are being diagnosed with attention deficit disorder (ADD), sometimes also with hyperactivity (ADHD). The evidence regarding either the validity or the prevalence of ADD is controversial and inconclusive. The research does suggest that attention is very selective and is influenced by a number of other factors, including motivation, maturity, context, and instruction. For example, people focus more attention on unusual or unique stimuli (larger print, boldface, etc.). In other words, not all children who are inattentive have biologically based attention deficits. Clearly, whether because of biological disposition or for other reasons, if students cannot or do not attend to the parts of the environment that contain essential information, they cannot learn or retain new information and skills, and this issue should be examined during assessment.

The ability to impose order on sensory information is called *perception.* It too is central to student learning and performance in general. Perception, like attention and memory, is developmental. That is, important changes occur in this area during childhood and adolescence. Older children have more experience and knowledge, and this allows them to impose order on a greater array of stimuli, thus enhancing perception. Because reading is clearly a cognitive-perceptual process, many educators have assumed that reading difficulties arise from deficits in visual-perceptual processing. However, decades of research have demonstrated unequivocally that reading problems are *not* caused by such weaknesses. In reviewing the research in this area, Klenk and Kibby (2000, p. 671) concluded:

The validity of perceptual training programs as a method of improving reading has long been debunked . . . The conclusion from decades of research on this topic is abundantly clear: Perceptual training programs, although perhaps increasing perceptual ability, have no substantive affect on reading ability.

Finally, the development of memory is an important aspect of cognitive information-processing ability. *Memory* is the process of storing and retrieving information. "The ability to retain verbal information in working memory is essential for reading and learning" (Snow et al., 1998, p. 108). Indeed, recent research suggests that young children's ability to recall a short story that has been read aloud is more strongly related to their subsequent reading achievement than to scores on digit span, word span, or memory for pseudo-words (Scarborough, 1998).

As with all cognitive abilities, memory changes and develops over time. Older children are better at storing and retrieving information than are younger children, and adults tend to be better at this than children. Older children and adults clearly have better concept formation and a more elaborate network connecting concepts, which allows for better organization of new information. In addition, older children and adults tend to have better strategies for coping with information, and they are better at understanding what they need to do to remember information.

It is easy to see how individual differences in these areas of development can affect students' abilities to cope with school tasks. It is also becoming increasingly clear that these cognitive abilities are not static. Attention, perception, and memory operate in relation to *specific types of information*. It is misleading to talk of children's processing abilities without specifying exactly what it is they are trying to perceive and remember (Gage & Berliner, 1988). We see once again how culture, expectations, and experience can influence performance and potentially confound the measurement of these abilities.

CHAPTER SUMMARY

This chapter focused on the elements of skilled reading and writing performance, as well as the contextual and learner factors that influence performance. The first section of the chapter described skilled performance as the ability to use reading and writing effectively and creatively for personal, recreational, academic, and civic purposes. The elements of skilled performance were defined as comprehension; composition; vocabulary development; word identification and spelling; rate and fluency; and grammar, usage, and the mechanics of writing.

The second and third sections of the chapter identified and described the contextual and learner factors that influence performance. The contextual factors were grouped according to settings, instructional practices (standards and curriculum, methods, activities and routines, assessment practices), instructional resources (commercial programs, textbook and trade materials, and electronic texts). The learner factors were categorized as prior content knowledge, knowledge about reading and writing (metacognition and phonological awareness), attitudes and motivation, and correlates of skilled performance (social and emotional development, language development, physical development, and cognitive development, including the information-processing abilities of attention, perception, and memory). The correlates of performance were defined as those social, emotional, linguistic, cognitive, and physical factors that are related to, but do not necessarily cause, strengths and weaknesses in reading and writing.

Consideration of the conventional aspects of reading and writing performance must be constrained by concerns for the ways in which learner and contextual factors interact to influence performance. Unless this complex and dynamic view of reading and writing is employed during assessment, we run the risk of developing a distorted picture of reading and writing processes. This poses serious problems for assessment, but even more serious concerns about the quality and appropriateness of instruction.

MyEducationLab™

Go to the Topics, Phonemic Awareness and Phonics, Vocabulary, FLuency, Word Recognition, and Reading Comprehension in the MyEducationLab (www.myeducationlab.com) for your course, where you can:

- Find learning outcomes for Phonemic Awareness and Phonics, Vocabulary, FLuency, Word Recognition, and Reading Comprehension, along with the national standards that connect to these outcomes.
- Complete Assignments and Activities that can help you more deeply understand the chapter content.
- Apply and practice your understanding of the core teaching skills identified in the chapter using the Building Teaching Skills and Dispositions learning units.
- Examine challenging situations and cases presented in the IRIS Center Resources.
- Check your comprehension of the content covered in the chapter by going to the Study Plan in the Book Resources for your text. Here you will be able to take a chapter quiz, receive feedback on your answers, and then access Review, Practice, and Enrichment activities to enhance your understanding of chapter content.

A+RISE A+RISE® Standards2Strategy™ is an innovative and interactive online resource that offers new teachers in grades K-12 just in time, research-based instructional strategies that meet the linguistic needs of ELLs as they learn content, differentiate instruction for all grades and abilities, and are aligned to Common Core Elementary Language Arts standards (for the literacy strategies) and to English language proficiency standards in WIDA, Texas, California, and Florida.

2 Getting Started with the Assessment-Instruction Process

*I*n the first two chapters, we provided both a theoretical and a practical framework for thinking about assessment-instruction. The theoretical framework provides the rationale for much of the remainder of the text. Section Two is critical to understanding assessment more specifically and also understanding how the assessment-instruction process works in the practical context of schools. It is divided into two parts. The first, which comprises Chapter 3, is titled *Reading and Writing Ability and the Assessment-Instruction Process*. In that chapter, we discuss the different types and purposes for assessment and also demonstrate how an interactive model of reading and writing ability can and should be applied to reading and writing disability, using case study examples. This chapter also provides an overview of the assessment and instruction process that simultaneously describes the way literacy assessment and instruction typically progress, and provides a guided tour of the sequence of the chapters in this text. The steps of the assessment-instruction process detailed in Chapter 3 are used throughout the remainder of the book and highlighted in the introductory materials for each section.

Chapter 4, *Getting Started: Using Data to Understand Groups of Students and Identify Students for a Closer Look*, includes a discussion of tools and strategies for examining assessment data in order to make decisions about groups of students and to identify those students who might benefit from more-careful observation. This includes a section on using and interpreting standardized tests and strategies for making sense of the large amount of data that teachers and specialists often encounter in classrooms and schools.

CHAPTER 3

Reading and Writing Ability and the Assessment-Instruction Process

*C*hapters 1 and 2 focused on understanding reading and writing processes. In this chapter and in much of the remainder of the book, we focus on understanding the full spectrum of reading and writing abilities and applying this understanding to the assessment and instruction of reading and writing. A plan for the assessment-instruction process is presented, and we explain the reasons for using this plan, describing each of the following steps:

Steps in the Assessment-Instruction Process

Step 1	Getting Started: Using Data to Look at Groups of Students and Identify Students at Risk
Step 2	Evaluating the Context
Step 3	Evaluating the Learner: Looking More Closely
Step 4	Reflecting, Decision Making, and Planning
Step 5	Diagnostic Teaching and On-going Progress Monitoring

UNDERSTANDING AN INTERACTIVE VIEW OF READING AND WRITING ABILITY AND DISABILITY

In this text, we use contemporary views of reading and writing processes and the lessons of history to detail an interactive perspective on reading and writing ability and "disability." We are suggesting that an interactive view of reading and writing *ability* be adopted for both more- and less-skilled readers and writers. This means that reading and writing ability and disability are no longer viewed as absolute properties of the learner, but rather as relative properties of the interaction among specific learner and contextual factors (Lipson & Wixson, 1986).

An interactive view of reading and writing ability addresses several of the concerns we have about any theory of ability and/or disability. First, we believe that such a theory should respond to current conceptual and empirical evidence; it should account for the reading and writing behaviors of struggling students but should also suggest new areas of investigation. Second, we believe that theories of reading and writing ability/disability should lead to enhanced instruction. We now turn our attention to these issues.

A Theoretically Sound View of Ability and Disability

Current theory and research in reading and writing provide evidence that the ability to comprehend and/or compose varies for both more- and less-skilled learners, as a function of various interactions with different reading and writing situations. For example, there is evidence that young children of all ability levels are better able to recognize words that contain regular phonic patterns and that they are also more successful when reading high-frequency words than low-frequency words (Juel, 1988). The results of studies demonstrating this suggest that children's performance on measures of isolated word recognition can be expected to vary as a function of the particular words on a given test. Small samples of oral reading errors are often used to characterize a student's word recognition ability in all reading contexts. However, studies of oral reading errors suggest that children's word recognition ability is highly variable and is influenced by many factors. These factors include instructional method, type of prose being read, the student's prior knowledge of the materials being read, and the difficulty of the text (Wixson, 1979). This means that oral reading errors reflect particular strategies a learner employs in interaction with a particular reading activity. As such, they may or may not be representative of the strategies used by a particular learner in other reading situations.

Comprehension performance is also subject to variability for both more- and less-skilled learners. The two groups are similarly affected by differences in prior knowledge, text organization, and type of comprehension task. For example, Williams and her colleagues demonstrated in a number of studies that both skilled and less-skilled students in grades 3 through 7 were more successful at identifying main ideas in text when they were asked to select the best title than when they were asked to write a summary sentence (Williams, Taylor, & deCani, 1984).

There is also evidence that less-skilled learners perform like skilled learners under certain circumstances. For example, in an examination of the story comprehension patterns of sixth-grade learners, McConaughy (1985) found no differences between good and poor learners in either the quality or the accuracy of their recall summaries. Specifically, McConaughy reported that poor learners' story organization was as good as that of good learners of the same age when the structure of the text was explicit and learners were required to summarize what they thought was important rather than to recall as much as possible.

A related finding in the area of writing is that the relative difficulty of the expository text structures in writing tasks varies depending on the type of task that students are performing and the manner in which the writing is analyzed (Engelhard, Gordon, & Gabrielson, 1992).

If written productivity is evaluated, then an explanation text structure may be easier for students to produce than a comparison/contrast structure. If text organization is evaluated, then the comparison/contrast text structure might be easier for students to produce than the explanation text structure.

The foregoing suggests that the strategies students employ as they read and write should be expected to vary as a function of a number of factors. There is evidence that both the awareness and application of reading and writing strategies varies in relation to the difficulty of the text and task (Lipson, Mosenthal, & Mekkelsen, 1999). Evaluating strategic behavior in the absence of some consideration of potential sources of variability is problematic, because the cognitive processes in play vary according to the context of the reading and writing situation.

When reading and writing ability are viewed from an interactive perspective, it becomes clear how difficult, and probably fruitless, it is to search for a single causative factor within the learner for less-skilled performance. Yet this is the approach that often dominates the assessment and instruction of reading and writing ability. Despite the increased sophistication of perspectives on reading and writing ability, dominant views of reading and writing disability continue to be wedded to the historic "search for pathology" (Sarason & Doris, 1979).

Although written over two decades ago, an editorial in a research journal focused on learning disabilities is still fairly apt today: "Our entire field is DEFICIT DRIVEN; we spend millions of dollars and hours looking for deficits, defining them, perseverating on them, imagining that we are exorcizing them, and sometimes even inventing them to rationalize our activities" (Poplin, 1984, p. 133). Research has amply demonstrated that variability in performance is a normal part of reading and writing processes.

However, despite the increased use of approaches such as RTI, assessment and instruction for most struggling learners still often depend on the use of commercial, standardized test instruments that assume that reading and writing processes are static— that reading and writing ability can be measured at some point in time, using one set of materials and tasks to predict performance on other materials in other settings. This is especially problematic given the tasks included in existing reading and writing tests. Many current instruments are based on dated and incomplete notions about reading and writing. When a mismatch exists between the theories used to define reading and writing competence and those used to drive assessment and instruction, the assessment information is of little value (Valencia & Pearson, 1987; Valencia, Pearson, & Wixson, 2011). We discuss further the problems and advantages of standardized testing in Chapter 4.

The search for pathology as an explanation for reading difficulties has been further undermined in recent years by the "growing evidence [that] suggests that high-quality reading instruction can be a powerful lever for preventing reading problems, decreasing the number of students identified as learning disabled and significantly improving reading abilities of students who are low-performing ..." (Valencia, 2011, p. 25). As indicated in Chapter 1, it has become quite clear that effective instruction and intervention can significantly reduce the number of students who become learning disabled (Dorn & Schubert, 2008; Mathes et al., 2005; Scanlon et al., 2008).

An Instructionally Significant View of Reading and Writing Ability

An interactive view is well suited to the understanding of reading and writing abilities, because it predicts variability in performance within individuals across texts, tasks, and settings. This perspective moves discussions of reading and writing difficulties away from simply specifying deficits and toward the specification of the conditions under which a student can and will learn. In this view, a student's performance on various reading and writing measures is considered an indication of what he or she can and will do under a specific set of conditions rather than as a set of fixed abilities and disabilities (Wixson & Lipson, 1986). The necessity for identifying the disability is eliminated, and our attention is refocused on how each student performs under different conditions and which set of conditions is most likely to facilitate learning.

An interactive view of reading and writing abilities provides a unifying theoretical orientation for teachers and specialized support personnel. The clearest implication of such a reorientation is that the performance of both skilled and less-skilled students is subject to variability as a function of a variety of contextual factors. Although the factors that influence the reading and writing processes are the same for both populations of students, there continues to be a tremendous need for coordination of assessment and instruction between classrooms and specialized programs. If different views of reading and writing underlie the programs in these two settings, problems inevitably arise for students, and the prospects for potential transfer and learning are limited. Both classroom teachers and specialists need to recognize that the performance of the student who is experiencing difficulty in reading and writing represents only one of the salient factors in the reading and writing process.

An interactive view of reading and writing also provides a basis for communication between teachers and support staff. Personnel involved in the education of students with reading and writing problems can begin to talk about the specific contributions of the learner, the text, and the context as determiners of reading and writing performance. This is precisely the type of discussion envisioned by many proponents of RTI. All educators need to understand the importance of recognizing this so that we can begin to work together. Because learner performance is likely to be influenced by a wide array of factors, pullout programs are more effective when there is coordination between the classroom and the remedial setting (Harn, Chard, Biancarosa & Kame'enui, 2011; Wonder-McDowell, Reutzel & Smith, 2011). Teachers must provide opportunities for classroom practice and application of the skills and techniques developed in the remedial setting. Similarly, specialists can no longer ignore the content and context of classroom instruction, believing that remediation of some specific deficit will transfer to other settings.

Finally, an interactive view makes clear the important contribution of context. Both classroom teachers and specialists must be sensitive to the influences of their distinct environments on learner performance. Thoughtful teachers have always realized that information collected in one situation is not entirely helpful in another. Unfortunately, we have sometimes rejected information from various sources as unreliable because it did not coincide with our own. Such apparently contradictory information can be valuable in planning optimal student instruction. For example, it should no longer surprise us when a student performs differently as an individual, in small-group settings, and in large group settings. The documentation of these differences can provide the basis for genuinely collaborative professional relationships—relationships that will strengthen the prospects of learning for all students.

UNDERSTANDING THE ASSESSMENT-INSTRUCTION PROCESS

Few educators today would complain that there is too little assessment going on! In most schools and school districts, there are many tests, probes, and informal assessments conducted. That does not mean, however, that an effective assessment-instruction process is in place. Valencia (2011b) captures the situation well:

> . . . perhaps more than any previous time, the federal government and school systems are demanding more testing and assessment of students. Data-driven decision making is the new mantra, yet some have suggested that the result has been to leave educators data rich and information poor (Stringfield, Wayman, & Yakimowski-Srebnick, 2005); in other words, educators may be swimming in data, but the data may not be providing the sorts of information needed to improve teaching and learning. Equally worrisome is that some data may be misinterpreted or misused, leading to inappropriate teaching, learning, or inferences about schooling. (p. 379)

We have organized this book to acknowledge this conundrum and to focus squarely on an assessment-instruction process that ensures that appropriate attention is paid to the types of information needed to plan and replan instruction for students who are struggling in the areas of reading and writing.

Purposes and Types of Assessment

Good teaching relies heavily on good assessment. Effective schools have a comprehensive assessment system or plan that includes multiple types of assessment for diverse purposes (see Figure 3.1). No one assessment can meet all possible purposes. Common purposes in today's assessment systems include (1) measuring the level of performance of individuals and/or groups of students (screening), (2) monitoring student progress (interim or benchmark), and (3) evaluating overall achievement of individuals and groups (outcome). Although it is often the case that students are placed in intervention programs or settings based on information obtained from assessments used to screen, it is unlikely that the assessments used for this purpose provide the kind of information needed to plan effective instruction/intervention. Assessment systems need to include measures that address a broader range of purposes, including screening, diagnostics, formative progress monitoring, interim/benchmark progress monitoring, and outcomes (Wixson & Valencia, 2011; Lipson et al., 2011). The assessment-instruction process that is the focus of this book involves all of these assessment purposes, but because we are concerned with students who are struggling, there is a particular emphasis on *diagnostics* and *formative progress monitoring*.

FIGURE 3.1   Purposes and Types of Assessment

Purposes/Types
Screening—refers to the data gathered before instruction to determine which students may require further (diagnostic) assessment and to provide schools and teachers with aggregate data about the nature of student achievement overall.
Diagnostics—refers to data gathered on selected students to: (a) *inform instruction* (identify a student's specific areas of strengths/weakness and determine any difficulties s/he may have in learning to read or write and the potential source of such difficulties) or (b) *help to determine possible placement* decisions (instructional interventions and related special needs).
Formative progress monitoring—refers to data gathered *during* instruction (the original meaning of formative) to determine the appropriateness of instruction as evidenced by student progress and to help the teacher determine how to revise instruction.
Interim/Benchmark progress monitoring—refers to data gathered at predetermined times of the year (e.g. 3–4 times per year) to determine if students are making adequate progress in overall performance in relation to age/grade expectations or benchmarks; these measures serve as indicators of the general effectiveness of instruction.
Summative Outcome assessment—refers to data gathered at the end of the year (or term) to (a) *evaluate* whether or not students have achieved grade-level performance or improved their achievement; (b) hold schools and teachers *accountable*; and/or (c) to evaluate *program effectiveness*.

The problem of teaching and learning is the match between the student and the circumstances he or she encounters in the learning environment (Hunt, 1961). Assessment and instruction need to be focused on an evaluation of the existing match and the identification of the optimal match between a learner and the conditions of the reading and writing context. In many respects, this is what the RTI approach to identifying students with learning disabilities is all about. The idea behind RTI is to evaluate the effectiveness of one or more interventions appropriate for the individual student's strengths and weaknesses, to determine if the observed difficulties can be addressed without the need for special education services.

In this book, we focus on assessments that can help us find patterns of interactions—patterns that allow us to make relatively good decisions about instruction. Because few standardized tests provide this kind of information, and because these tests do not consider instructional context, we suggest a number of assessment strategies that are needed to supplement existing measures. We are not suggesting that current testing instruments be abandoned altogether, but rather that assessment move forward from a different perspective. Nor are we suggesting that the individual student is not an important factor in the assessment process. Rather, our view is that we must look to the individual in interaction with specific texts, tasks, and methods. In the past, such specification was incidental to the goal of identifying the learner's problem. This text is designed to help educators accomplish this in an intentional and thoughtful fashion, and in a manner that helps them apply a preventative perspective to RTI approaches (see Chapter 1) as a means of dealing with struggling readers and writers.

The long-range goal of the entire assessment and instruction process is to produce strategic, motivated, reflective readers and writers and to develop mature readers and writers who can and will apply their skills and strategies independently and in a flexible manner—not to identify causes or provide labels. To achieve an interactive approach to assessment and instruction, we need to gather information about the demands of the context (for example, what is required to read and write using various methods or materials) and explore how the context may influence a student's performance and learning. We also need to gather information about what the learner knows and how he or she behaves during reading and writing. We must additionally examine the interaction between these two components of the assessment-instruction process.

The best way to become proficient at the assessment and instruction of reading and writing is to learn as much as possible about learners, the contexts in which reading and writing occur, and how they interact to influence reading and writing performance.

A plan for proceeding with the process of assessment and instruction is described in the next sections of this chapter. This is a decision-making approach to assessment and instruction, much in the same vein as many RTI approaches to dealing with struggling learners. Throughout this text, we provide information about areas to be assessed and also describe in detail tools and strategies for gathering information. In addition, however, we need to make decisions at every stage of the process, because the complex of factors that interact is never quite the same for any two students. Effective decision making is dependent on knowing when and why we would engage in a particular activity, or use a particular test or instructional technique.

Implementing the Assessment-Instruction Process

The components of effective assessment and instruction are similar whether a classroom teacher or specialist conducts them in the classroom or in a remedial/support setting. However, the amount of attention devoted to each component and the procedures used to evaluate them are likely to be different. The classroom teacher has the benefit of daily contact with the student or students in question but limited time to spend with individual students. The specialist or clinician has the benefit of individual time with the student but limited knowledge about the student's daily interactions with reading and writing in the classroom.

It is important for classroom teachers to develop a repertoire of assessment techniques that can be incorporated easily into their daily instruction, and these will be discussed in the chapters that follow. Students who demonstrate difficulty on these assessments would then be seen individually or in smaller groups for further evaluation. The assessment of the methods and materials may be fairly straightforward for classroom teachers because of their daily access and repeated experience with them. Classroom teachers have the added benefit of being able to incorporate trial teaching procedures into the real context of their daily instruction.

In middle and high schools, the situation is more complex. Classroom teachers may see the student for relatively limited periods. In this case, the literacy specialist or special educator may actually have more-extensive knowledge of the individual student's needs and strengths.

The language arts specialist or clinician usually deals only with students who have already been identified by some means as having a problem. Specialists have the advantage of working closely in small settings with a handful of (or even individual) students. This may provide in-depth information unavailable to the classroom teacher. However, if specialists do not work in the classroom, evaluating the learner in interaction with the reading and writing context may be more difficult, because they do not have daily contact with the student(s) in question in the context in which the problem is occurring. They must rely on limited examinations of the materials, classroom observation, and interviews with the parents, the teacher, and the students for this evaluation. Furthermore, they must be aware of and sensitive to the teacher's style and the organization of the classroom to develop trial teaching procedures that would be appropriate for use in the student's classroom.

Specialists who are operating in pullout programs need to be especially aware of the potential difficulties in this situation. Too often, the students who are most in need of consistent, coherent reading and writing instruction are the ones who receive the most fragmented instruction. What is most important, however, is that students may be practicing and acquiring skills and abilities in one setting that are neither valued nor applied in another. Communication between classroom and clinical setting is of the utmost importance.

Increasingly, the advantages of these different settings are being tapped by innovative staffing configurations and stronger collaborations. Many schools have implemented student support teams composed of classroom teachers, special educators, and content specialists. The members of these teams confer about individual students and pool their insights, knowledge, and resources. Classroom teachers implement their own assessment and instruction strategies, and Title I or special education teachers may implement others. Any of these strategies may involve pulling the student out for individual assessment or instruction. In addition, special educators and general educators have been moving more strongly toward the increased role flexibility that may be offered by different service delivery models such as *co-teaching* (Murawski & Hughes, 2009; Villa & Thousand, 2008).

The remainder of this book is designed to provide information about the what, how, when, and why of the assessment-instruction process. The next section of this chapter provides a step-by-step plan for carrying out this process. The steps in this plan provide the framework for the subsequent sections of this book, and the procedures involved in each step are discussed in detail in at least one or more of the following chapters (see Figure 3.2). Within each chapter, the specific information needed to implement the assessment-instruction process is provided in as much detail as possible, including examples of what procedures to use and how to use them and explanations of when and why they are appropriate for use.

THE ASSESSMENT-INSTRUCTION PROCESS IN ACTION

In this section, we describe how the assessment-instruction process is likely to unfold in many situations. We further discuss the activities and thinking that occur during a series of steps. We use these steps to highlight the different types of information and decision making used over time as we focus on students who are struggling in the areas of reading and/or writing. In doing so, we do not mean to convey that there is a rigid or mechanistic

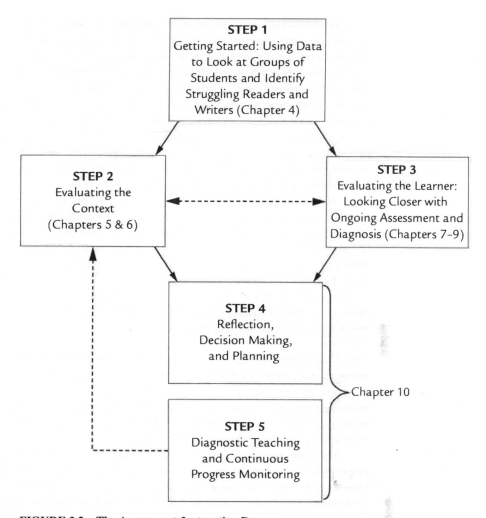

FIGURE 3.2   The Assessment-Instruction Process

set of activities that must occur. Indeed, things are rarely as neat and orderly as we might like. In the real worlds of schools and students, things often proceed in fits and starts. However, we use the steps as a means of making the process more evident.

Steps in the Assessment-Instruction Process

The foundation of the assessment-instruction process rests on an accurate assessment of the existing match between the learners and the context. Our first job is to determine which students are benefiting from current instruction and which are not. Once we have identified students who appear to be struggling, we need to look more closely to gain a better understanding of the students' strengths and areas of need and to explore the variation in student performance based on specific reading and writing conditions. Using this information, our next task is to generate hypotheses about the primary source of interference with learning or performance. It is critical that the hypotheses generated in this phase of the process focus on problems of major importance. All readers and writers have minor difficulties with certain aspects of literacy, but these problems are rarely a primary source of interference with learning or performance. To ensure that we are focusing on major problems, it is sometimes helpful to ask ourselves, "If I corrected this problem, would the individual in question be likely to demonstrate improved reading and writing learning or performance?" The steps focus on identifying the means by which learning or performance may be established or improved.

The steps of the assessment-instruction process are summarized below. We follow the case study of Jackson through all the steps, to provide an overview and to illustrate how the process was carried is with one student. However, this process can unfold in somewhat different ways for middle/high school students. Students who have not been identified as eligible for special education services, but who have been struggling, can really benefit from a close examination of their reading and writing performance during adolescence. Consequently, we have also provided the complete case example of Susie, a ninth-grade student (see Appendix B). Detailed information on how to proceed with each step is provided in subsequent chapters.

Step 1—Getting Started: Using Data to Understand Groups of Students and Identify Struggling Readers and Writers.
We start in the classroom (or school) by looking at groups of students. As teachers, our first goal is to provide effective instruction to all students based on state and local standards. The classroom- or grade-level data help teachers to know who is benefiting from the programs and approaches that are being used and who may need more support to be successful.

The first step in the process involves identifying students who are in need of a closer look. Some schools use every-pupil screening measures, and virtually all schools have student data from large-scale state assessments. As well, some schools have a comprehensive assessment process that involves multiple sources of data (see Chapter 4). It is important to have confidence in the data we are using, because we want to be sure that we actually identify all the students who may be at risk of failure and do not identify students who appear to be struggling but who are actually doing very well. We will take up these issues in later chapters, but for now it is important to be aware that we may need to reconsider decisions made at this stage. Some students who are identified will not really need intervention, and some students who did not appear to require attention will, upon further observation, be considered struggling.

Case Study.   Mrs. Hazlett teaches at Mason Elementary School. The teachers there have access to quite a lot of assessment data, including the results of statewide assessments and district-level reading tests. They use the Gates-MacGinitie Reading Tests to screen all students at the beginning of the year. As well, they administer structured inventories at the beginning and end of each year. Of course, Mrs. Hazlett also has data from her ongoing formative (classroom-based) assessments. Using this array of data, the teachers meet in

FIGURE 3.3   Data Team Record for Grade 3: Reading Performance

Grade 3 Teachers	Number of Students	Number Proficient	Number NOT Proficient	Close (to established benchmarks)	Far Away (from established benchmarks)	Intensive (significant gaps between established benchmarks and student knowledge/skill)
Hazlett	21	14	7	Adam, Carson	Melanie, Karl, Jackson	Isabelle, Jacob
Johnson	20	17	3	Micah		Lola, Mateo
Lesage	19	12	7	Madison Jakobi Hadley, Austin,	Ava	Darcy, Dylan
Mendenhall	22	17	5	Tristan, Kaylee	Emily, Brandon	Kaden
Quincy	22	15	7	Cassie Olivia	Caleb, Luke Mathew	Anastasia, Lejila
	104	75 (72% of total students)	29 (28% of total students)	11 (38% of not proficient)	9 (31%)	9 (31%)

data teams on a regular basis to identify students who are struggling and to collaborate on instruction and intervention.

As teachers consider their assessment data, they also note which students are already receiving specialized intervention services. The form in Figure 3.3 provides data teams in the school with a quick overview of the class and grade. It shows the type of format used by the data teams at each grade level. Using a "numbers into names" approach, the teachers meet to discuss who is struggling, what types of supports are being employed, and how instructional tactics might be deployed. During these meetings, teachers noted, where appropriate, what interventions or services are being provided for students who are "not proficient."

Mrs. Hazlett has a number of students who are performing below the grade-level expectations for the school. Isabelle and Jacob are already receiving specialized services from a special educator, and this specialist coordinates her instruction and support with Mrs. Hazlett. The specialist feels that Adam and Carson will be able to be successful in the classroom program, with differentiated instruction. She will keep an eye on them. Three children, however, require a closer look: Melanie, Karl, and Jackson. We will follow one of these students, Jackson, through the remaining process.

Case Discussion.   Jackson is not learning or performing as well as might be expected on the basis of his age, ability, and educational background. In this first step, we bring inquiry to existing data. The goal is to consider who is benefiting from existing instruction and who is not. Mrs. Hazlett summarized this information as follows:

1. On the reading portion of the statewide assessment, he was judged to be "partially proficient" (Level 2 of 4).

2. In addition, at the end of grade 2, his overall reading-level placement was several text levels lower than the benchmark target that had been established by the school. Notably, his oral reading accuracy and rate were extremely low.
3. The formative assessment data provided by last year's teacher indicate very slow performance and an increasingly negative attitude toward school.

Mrs. Hazlett and her colleagues consider other available information as they make decisions about how to proceed. In this earliest stage, that information may be limited to the student's school history, including any earlier assessment referrals, support services, or interventions that the student has experienced (see Step 2 below).

Step 2—Evaluating the Context.   Despite wide recognition that teachers and teaching methods contribute to academic success, academic assessments rarely include evaluations of these factors. If teachers and methods are rarely considered, the contribution of materials or setting factors are examined even less frequently, especially the nonschool literacy abilities that may accompany students from diverse backgrounds. Failure to even consider such factors leaves the learner as the sole source of difficulty and is something akin to blaming the victim in many cases (McDermott, Goldman, & Varenne, 2006; Stuckey, 1991). For educators using an RTI approach, this step is, of course, essential. Since the point of this approach is to inquire about whether a student is responding to instruction and intervention, it will be critical to know what the instruction and intervention are like.

A variety of procedures should be used to assess the learning context, including classroom observations, interviews, checklists, and visual inspection and analysis. Because most of these procedures are informal, care must be taken to examine this information systematically. Observation guidelines are helpful here, as are checklists. Important advances have also been made in the area of materials assessment, so a variety of procedures such as text analysis, comprehensibility checklists, and holistic scans have been added to traditional readability measures. Teachers, students, and parents can also provide invaluable information as they describe important aspects of the cultural and instructional setting for learning.

It is not always possible, or even desirable, to evaluate all possible contextual factors. However, it is imperative that the student's performance be examined from the perspective of the contexts in which he or she is expected to learn and perform. Not infrequently, students' reading or writing problems are exacerbated, if not actually caused, by contextual factors. In addition, we cannot make adjustments to the instructional context unless we know what the student has experienced and consider what might be changed to enhance performance and achievement.

Case Study.   Mason Elementary School has an elaborated EST (Educational Support Team) process. As teachers and specialists meet to discuss students about whom they are worried, they document the conversations. The process also involves making recommendations for changes in instruction that might improve students' learning. These EST notes and plans are maintained on the school's internal Web site, so, Mrs. Hazlett consulted these records first. Jackson's name had indeed been taken to the EST for discussion in both grade 1 and grade 2. In grade 1, he received some additional support from the classroom teacher, who met with him and another child several times a week. The teacher generally provided review and extra practice using the core program in the building. However, he exited grade 1 performing less well than his peers. In grade 2, he was identified for extra reading support. He saw the reading specialist all year, receiving 30 minutes of small-group instruction every day. His grade 2 teacher had also taken his name to EST, and the group entertained the possibility of referring him for special education. The records were very limited in their description of the instructional approach, texts, or tasks used with Jackson. At this point, Mrs. Hazlett was taking a graduate course and she enlisted a colleague to help her pursue this step of the process.

Mrs. Hazlett noted that Jackson seemed much "younger" than the other children in the class and that he sometimes asked questions or made comments that were "babyish." She indicated that Jackson asked for help frequently to get attention.

Additional information about the instructional context was gathered during a half-day classroom observation and interviews with Jackson's teachers. Jackson received instruction both in a regular classroom and outside the classroom in a Title I reading program. He was assigned to a regular reading group within the classroom, although he missed it when his reading support group conflicted, which was quite frequently. It appeared that he was rarely expected to read full-length texts in either setting. However, when longer selections were used, they were generally read aloud during a modified, guided reading group.

Although the classroom teacher read aloud as a daily part of the instructional program, Jackson went to his Title I reading class during much of this period. In the past, and contrary to federal guidelines, Jackson did not receive reading instruction in his regular classroom, but only in the Title I classroom. His reading instruction was focused largely on word analysis, and work was assigned from a program that emphasized visual and auditory perception of letter clusters in words. The method of instruction used by this particular program emphasized the analysis of words into their constituent parts rather than beginning with word parts and blending them together to form words. As a result of professional development and the expanded role of a reading specialist to work as a coach, the grade 3 teachers had all agreed to provide small-group instruction for all students (in addition to the pullout intervention that some students received).

Mrs. Hazlett indicated that Jackson was not able to complete the assigned work done by most students and that she had differentiated the independent work that students were assigned. The language arts, spelling, and social studies books used in Jackson's classroom, however, were standard third-grade texts with readability estimates ranging from a 2.5 to a 5.0 grade level. Jackson was expected to complete all classroom assignments before going to recess. The teacher reported that Jackson really liked recess and did not like to miss it, although he frequently did because his work was incomplete.

On the day we observed, Jackson's teacher was transitioning children from a painting project. Jackson was one of the first students done with his project. While the majority of the class continued to paint, he washed his hands and returned to work at his desk. After returning to his desk, Jackson looked up from his work only occasionally. Despite the noise level and the proximity of two groups of children chatting, Jackson seemed undistracted. However, he was very reliant on his teacher. He asked questions frequently, requiring her help on nearly every individual task on which the evaluator observed him working.

Jackson still had twelve math problems left to complete when recess time came. This would have been unremarkable if he had not demonstrated a high degree of competence earlier in the period. He repeatedly asked the teacher for help with his math problems—on every item, in fact. As we observed Jackson, we were able to determine that he had little idea about how to approach the math problems that were assigned. Each time Jackson approached the teacher for help, he was given information about how to do the specific problem he was working on, but he never received additional instruction targeted at his lack of understanding about how to do that *type* of problem. More troubling still was our observation that at least some of the assigned work was explained while Jackson was involved in reading instruction outside of the classroom. In this particular case, he had little recourse but to continue approaching the teacher for help. We did not see Jackson participate in small-group instruction in the classroom.

Discussion with Jackson provided additional information about his instructional context. After our visit to his classroom, we asked him about his favorite part of the day, and he noted that he really enjoyed the time when his teacher read to the class. Jackson had previously indicated that he enjoyed the period in the day when his teacher was reading *James and the Giant Peach.* During that earlier exchange, we had been concerned because, despite his obvious interest, he was unable to accomplish a coherent retelling of the story. This time, Jackson explained that he had to go to reading class during read-aloud time and was able to hear only the initial portion of each day's reading!

Our observation of the reading intervention also provided useful information. This instruction occurred in a small room that housed a desk and one of the reading specialists. She had a large array of leveled books, although many were old. Jackson's small group included four other boys. Although the period was scheduled for thirty minutes, actual instruction occurred for roughly twenty minutes because the group waited for two boys who were late arriving and then they discussed an incident on the playground for several more minutes. The teacher conducted a modified guided reading group that involved introducing the boys to a book through a picture walk and then a round-robin reading of the text, with each boy taking turns. Once this portion was completed, the boys played a sight-word game for the remainder of the period. As he had in the classroom, Jackson sought help when he perceived work to be too difficult for him, and in those situations he put forth little effort. When pressed, he would attempt difficult tasks, but if success was not immediate, he shrugged and said he could not do it.

Finally, Mrs. Hazlett spoke to Jackson's mother. Jackson lives in a trailer home on the edge of a midsized town with his mother and three younger siblings. His father lives in the same community and Jackson sees him frequently. Both parents work, and Jackson is expected to help out around the house as he is the oldest. The family responsibilities leave little time for other activities, and family life seems to revolve around the shared jobs. Jackson likes the outdoors, and the location of his trailer park on the banks of a small river provides him with many things to do. He and his friends ride bikes and fish. His mother indicates that there are not many books in the home and that she tried to read to Jackson when he was younger but he wasn't especially interested; then, when the other children came along, there just wasn't time. The mother reports that her husband struggled in school and did not complete high school. She did completed high school, and both parents work in the service industry. According to the mother, Jackson has struggled with reading since beginning school in kindergarten.

Case Discussion.   Our evaluation of the learning context revealed the following: classroom instructional materials written at a third-grade level and above; little evidence of materials that Jackson would be interested in and/or motivated to read; classroom assignments that emphasized task completion; limited individualization of classroom assignments; lack of direction and explanation for classroom assignments, caused in part by a pullout reading program; limited reading instruction in the regular classroom; Title I reading instruction focused on reading practice, with very little explicit instruction and little opportunity to read longer texts for meaning.

Step 3—Evaluating the Learner: Looking More Closely with Ongoing Assessment and Diagnosis.   As a practical matter, the assessment of student performance is cyclic and layered. We start with group data, information that is available on all or most students. When we have identified students who are struggling or who appear to be performing less well than their peers (or than we expect), there are several options. As noted previously, some educators suggest going directly from screening assessments (identifying the struggling students) to instruction/intervention. However, because we believe that an individual's abilities, skills, beliefs, interests, and instructional history influence reading and writing achievement, we recommend additional diagnostic assessment before proceeding to instruction/intervention.

The assessment-instruction process described here is not a standard set of tests and prescriptions to be used with all students. Rather, it is a dynamic process tailored to the needs of individual students that is continually evolving as each additional piece of information is uncovered. Individuals are identified, are referred for, or seek out help in reading and/or writing for a wide range of reasons. If there were only one or two possible sources of difficulty, our task would be relatively easy. But that is not the case. There are any number of factors that may converge to create reading and writing difficulties, and students may struggle with different aspects of reading and writing performance (see McGill-Franzen & Allington, 2011; Valencia & Buly, 2004).

Background information provided by the individual, parents, school records, interviews, and visitations can yield valuable insights into possible sources of difficulty. Information about both the learner and the context should be gathered. Trying to complete an assessment for an individual is rather like reading a good mystery. No clues should be ignored, no information overlooked in the early stages of the story. We cannot be sure at the beginning just what will turn out to be important, even when the evidence seems to lead to an obvious conclusion. The task in this first phase is not to arrive at conclusions, but rather to generate hunches that may be tested. In short, we try to avoid coming to any conclusions in the early stages and view our early findings as hypotheses to be tested against reality later on.

In the chapters to follow, we describe in detail the types of procedures that may be employed in evaluating the learner. Generally speaking, these procedures fall into three categories. First, we consider what is likely the best-known source of information about learners—*formal assessment* using standardized, norm-referenced tests (see Chapter 4). Although widely used, most formal tests have significant limitations in terms of the value of the diagnostic information they yield. However, they are often the starting point for a more in-depth understanding of an individual student's strengths and weaknesses. Second, we address *structured* assessments and inventories as a likely second layer of assessment in the process of identifying students' strengths and weaknesses (Chapters 7 & 8). Third, we describe more *diagnostic and formative assessment* instruments and techniques (Chapter 9). Both familiar and less-familiar strategies are presented. In Chapter 2, we outlined the components of reading and writing knowledge and skill that must be considered in any assessment. As in the evaluation of the context, a variety of sources should be used in evaluating the learner, because each source of information provides only a small part of the picture.

Case Study.   In addition to the standardized test information described in Step 1, Mason School conducts a fall assessment on all students, using a structured inventory (Fountas & Pinnell Benchmark Assessment System, 2010; see Chapter 8). Although all students take this test, Mrs. Hazlett examines Jackson's data more carefully. The results raise even more concerns. Jackson actually performed much less well in September than he had in the spring on the same assessment. The "summer loss" was quite dramatic for him. He is reading at a text level that is considerably below the target for students in grade 3. His teacher explored the patterns on performance on this test and found that he performed poorly on both word reading accuracy and comprehension. His rate was especially weak, suggesting that he has not yet become automatic in his word recognition abilities.

Formative and diagnostic assessments of several types were also employed with Jackson. Information was collected using tests of isolated word recognition and of word analysis skill. Formal diagnostic assessments, including norm-referenced tests of reading achievement and vocabulary knowledge, were administered to obtain estimates of Jackson's performance as compared to that of other children his age. The pattern of results indicated that, overall, Jackson's reading achievement was at least a year and a half below what we might reasonably expect given his age and school experience. His sight-word recognition was inadequate, and his word analysis skills were limited to the ineffective use of phonic analysis. Although his vocabulary knowledge was appropriate for his age, both his listening comprehension and reading comprehension were generally poor. In addition, his oral reading errors reflected little attention to meaning or contextual cues. However, in situations in which he had adequate background knowledge and sufficient interest, he was able to answer questions successfully, retell a story, and/or generate a main idea. Finally, early informal work samples suggested that he was almost entirely unable to produce a written product. Even with considerable support, his ideas were disjointed and his narratives were limited to three or four sentences.

As we began to plan for instruction, we conducted an interview with Jackson, who became animated in a discussion about animals and was genuinely enthusiastic when he talked about riding a four-wheeler with his father. Jackson said that he didn't like television very much, that he didn't like "being cooped up," and that he would rather play outside. Although he said he enjoyed stories, he reported that neither he nor his family read at home.

In response to questions focused on his knowledge about reading, Jackson could not give a reason why people read and said that he read because he wanted to be "smart." He appeared to believe that reading involved only accurate word recognition, naming only "sounding out" as a strategy for analyzing unknown words. Similarly, he used neatness as an indicator of "good writing" and seemed unaware of personal uses for writing. When asked what his teachers did to help him become a better reader and writer, he could think of nothing for writing but said that they helped him sound out the words in reading.

Case Discussion.   At this point in the assessment-instruction process, several specific areas of difficulty had been identified. Test results, Jackson's responses to interview questions, performance on other formative and diagnostic measures suggested that both his reading and writing knowledge and skill were limited. For example, although he believed that he usually understood what he read, he had difficulty retelling stories in a coherent fashion, could not write coherent texts, and could neither identify nor generate a main idea. Jackson did not appear to apply what skills and knowledge he had in a consistent way, so the products of his efforts were even less acceptable than might be expected. Although he was not actively resistant to reading or writing, Jackson did not appear to be motivated to read or write or to improve his skills; he greatly preferred to do other things. He worked hard when he experienced success, but application during difficult tasks was limited.

Step 4—Reflection, Decision Making, and Planning.   The fourth step involves evaluating the existing match between the student and the instructional context, to reflect on this evaluation and plan possible instruction and intervention opportunities. We ask: What is the primary source of interference with learning or performance? What variation do we see across texts, tasks, and contexts? Because an interactive view of reading and writing ability predicts variability, it becomes relatively easy to see why some students appear to thrive in the very environments that befuddle others. Our job in this stage of the assessment-instruction process is to pull together all that we know as the result of our professional efforts and experience and to evaluate how well existing demands, expectations, and supports of the context match the student's abilities, interests, knowledge, and level of independence.

Probably the most critical feature of skilled assessment is the ability to reflect on available data and realize what it means. Collecting information about learners is relatively easy compared to thinking about it and making sense of it. The assessment-instruction process must include sufficient time to reflect on information gathered. Indeed, the inexperienced evaluator may need to spend as much time reflecting on the information as has been spent gathering it. In later chapters, we provide guidelines and formats for summarizing and reflecting on available data.

Not all things are equally possible, given the realities of school life and the state of our current knowledge. Decision making is both a thoughtful consideration of instructional priorities (What does the student seem to need most?) and a consideration of the available resources and feasibility of change (How much control do we have over the mismatch?). At the same time, even after quite a lot of assessment, it may not be precisely clear what actions to take.

There is a temptation at this stage to begin mapping out a detailed instructional program. As we reflect on available information, new questions are often raised that need to be addressed through further evaluation. Therefore, the focus of this step is to identify possible solutions that can be tried out in some systematic way. This type of thinking can be especially productive when done with colleagues. Organizational frameworks such as professional learning communities (PLC) can be particularly effective in supporting teacher thinking and student achievement (DuFour, Eaker, 1998; DuRour, Eaker, & DuFour, 2008).

Case Study.   As we reached this point in the assessment-instruction process with Jackson, we began to see that the match between Jackson's abilities, interests, knowledge, and level of independence and the demands, expectations, and supports of his present placement was problematic in several ways. First, it appeared that his daily classroom assignments were mismatched with his knowledge and skills. The quantity of work was more than he could reasonably complete in the allotted time. In addition, the level of work was too difficult. He could not complete any of this work without additional help. This situation was aggravating his already-strong personal tendency toward dependency. Our assessment suggested that he was receiving no in-class support that might help to compensate for limited knowledge and skill.

Second, Jackson's interests lay outside the academic setting. He was not internally motivated to complete classwork in order to reap the rewards of school success. The content of the school's instructional materials and tasks was largely devoid of references to lifestyles or interests similar to Jackson's. His experiences were limited, and little prereading development was done to increase what appeared to be inadequate prior knowledge of school subjects.

The emphasis on reading practice and sight vocabulary in the pullout program appeared to represent a closer match to his existing needs and abilities; however, little attention was being given to his problems with comprehension, nor was any explicit instruction in decoding visible. Given his lack of self-regulation and initiative, it was worrying that there was little work on strategies for reading and writing. Finally, he was regularly denied access to the aspects of school life that he did enjoy—recess, book read-aloud time, and so on.

Case Discussion.   At this stage in the process, there were still many unanswered questions about the match between Jackson's specific problems and particular instructional approaches. Although our assessment of the learner had revealed a number of problem areas, these needed to be prioritized and the most effective instructional approaches identified. The issue of instruction was especially critical, as it appeared that the existing match was not ideal.

As we reflected on Jackson, we had several hunches about his strengths and weaknesses as a reader and the best use of our resources. First, his word identification skills were inadequate. His knowledge of sight words was far from automatic, and his decoding abilities were very undeveloped. The assessment results suggested that he had adequate phonological awareness and phonics knowledge. However, he was not using this knowledge automatically and frequently sought help from the teacher when he encountered unfamiliar words. He was uncertain about reading multisyllabic words. Even simple words with inflectional endings (such as *batting*) sometimes brought him to a halt. In addition, Jackson's comprehension problems were significant. He seemed unable to analyze stories at a global level, often failing to see connections between one event and another in a text. His retellings were typically fragmented, and he seemed unable to remedy the problems, even with discussion. Not surprisingly, during oral reading, Jackson was often content to leave nonsensical miscues uncorrected, suggesting that he was not attending to meaning.

Despite these serious difficulties, Jackson's strengths were notable. He had no difficulties in the areas of hearing or discriminating letter sounds. He both knew and regularly applied sound-symbol information for initial and final consonants. Jackson's overall reading behavior indicated that he was inattentive to meaning, but he did demonstrate ability in this area during isolated reading events. For example, while reading a selection about a boy's dog being hit by a car, Jackson's miscues were consistently meaningful, and his responses to subsequent questions indicated a strong ability to bring relevant prior knowledge to bear on the text.

We identified the primary source of interference with Jackson's learning or performance as inadequate word identification skills, compounded by limited background knowledge, interest, and motivation. Secondarily, we were concerned with his ability to read for meaning. Our best guess at this point was that Jackson needed an approach that would help encourage him to use a more strategic approach to word identification while attending to understanding what was being read. Given the range of his difficulties, we decided to try an approach that allowed for a focus on multiple outcomes and one that fit with the teacher and reading specialist's desire to have students reading text. The Interactive Strategies Approach (Scanlon & Anderson, 2011) is typically used with younger students, but it would allow his teachers to focus on his problems with word identification and comprehension while attending to background knowledge, interest, and motivation. However, we knew we would have to be selective, since he did not need all portions of this approach. In addition, we wanted to make sure that this approach would have the desired effect, so we planned a series of diagnostic teaching episodes, collecting data along the way to see if he was responding to the new strategy.

Step 5—Diagnostic Teaching and Continuous Progress Monitoring. The fifth step involves continued assessment based on the hypotheses and possible solutions generated in the previous step. The primary method of assessment used in this step is called *diagnostic teaching*. The two major purposes of diagnostic teaching are to provide additional diagnostic information about the interaction between the learner and the instructional context, and to identify instructional procedures that are likely to be effective in improving learning and performance. After an approach and focus have been derived from all of this (and previous) investigation, teachers continue to monitor the student's progress in order to make further decisions. These decisions, over time, will include: (a) continuation of intervention and instruction, (b) adaptations to interventions or instruction, (c) release of student from intervention services, and/or (d) referral of student for further assessment and placement.

Diagnostic teaching is a combination of assessment and instruction that provides information about how students perform under classroom-like conditions and how they might perform if we altered some aspects of the instructional setting. Diagnostic teaching usually involves systematically manipulating one or more components of reading and/or writing processes. Teachers are often gratified to know that there is a name for what might look like "messing around" or "trial and error." All instruction can be viewed as diagnostic teaching as long as it is thoughtfully planned using our best guesses about what may work for a given student and as long as we are prepared to monitor our work continually to see how adjustments have affected learning and performance.

The results of diagnostic teaching are used to plan an instructional program that is likely to respond to the most important needs of the individual student. There are times when instruction will proceed before assessment is completed. At other times the individual responsible for assessment will not deliver instruction. Wherever possible, of course, the preferred arrangement is for both assessment and instruction to be conducted by the same person.

In either case, initial instructional outcomes are established. Although attitude goals, content goals, and process goals may all be included in an individual's program, it is also possible that one or two of these will receive special emphasis. The information gathered in earlier portions of the process is used to inform decisions about what content to include and what delivery system to use. It is understood that these initial decisions may be changed or altered as further information is gathered.

Every instructional encounter with a particular reader is an opportunity for assessing and improving instruction. It is possible, and desirable, to continually monitor the effectiveness of the recommended instructional program and to make fine-tuning adjustments in the program as needed. Continuous monitoring of instructional progress is absolutely essential, and adaptive teaching involving modifications in texts, tasks, and materials is important. The full potential of this process can be realized only when it becomes part of daily practice.

Case Study.   Although we had a great deal of information about Jackson, we also had several questions and concerns that needed to be addressed in order to be able to identify a better match:

1. What approach to instruction should be employed with Jackson?
2. Would a more strategic approach help Jackson to become more actively engaged in his reading and writing?
3. Should the relative focus of instruction be placed on expanding Jackson's repertoire of word recognition skills, or could some generic instruction improve both word analysis and passage comprehension abilities?
4. Could reading and writing inform each other in Jackson's instructional program?

On the basis of our earlier reflections, we planned a series of diagnostic teaching episodes for Jackson. First, we introduced the Interactive Reading Strategies (see Chapter 10) to Jackson. We used a different interaction pattern than he was accustomed to, as Jackson read aloud. Our instructional moves were limited to encouraging Jackson to think about what he could do to solve the "puzzling" words he encountered (see Scanlon &

Anderson, 2011, for an elaborated explanation). We changed our own behaviors by waiting for him to make an attempt or to try a strategy. We collected data on Jackson's accuracy but also on his use of strategies. On the first day, Jackson seemed confused about the change of procedure and was not any more successful than he had been before. As a result, we introduced another dimension. First, we modeled for him the use of several strategies and then played the "Guess My Strategy" game. Jackson loved doing this. When it was his turn, we used colorful stones (available at many craft shops) to signal that he had used a particular strategy. The results were dramatic. Not only did Jackson engage in more self-correction and use of strategies, but his overall accuracy improved immediately. We did note, however, that his fluency diminished as he worked more strategically and that this would need to be added to his instructional program at some point.

The positive potential of this approach is that there are four code-based word identification strategies, but there are also four meaning-based strategies (such as "Think about what would make sense"). This attention to comprehension monitoring was likely to pay off in Jackson's comprehension as well. At the same time, he would need ample opportunity to participate in classroom read-alouds in order to develop age- and grade-appropriate concepts.

The reading specialist tried out an adaptation of the process writing approach used in Jackson's room to see if the adaptations had potential for use there. During the first phase, Jackson dictated a story. When he believed it to be complete, the tutor then rewrote the story so that it included an introduction, episode, and conclusion. This revised piece was discussed, with the emphasis placed on the components of a strong story. Finally, one component (the introduction, episode, or conclusion) was deleted, and Jackson was encouraged to write a replacement. This process was continued until Jackson had rewritten the entire piece. This practice proved especially helpful to Jackson and was later coupled with "story frames" (Fowler, 1982) to encourage Jackson to construct whole texts that contained important component pieces. In addition, contact between school and clinic was maintained to good effect.

Case Discussion.   After several manipulations such as those described above, we concluded that Jackson's program would need to contain significant amounts of work in both word recognition and comprehension, and these might need to be somewhat separate for the time being. Mrs. Hazlett changed her schedule slightly to ensure that Jackson could be present for the class read-aloud and the discussion that followed She incorporated the writing frames into her program for several other students as well. Similarly, she planned for a daily guided reading group for Jackson and used the same strategies to prompt other students during that period.

Although Jackson continued to receive reading support outside the classroom during the regularly scheduled reading instruction time, he no longer missed key components of the rest of the day. The support personnel in Jackson's school also agreed to incorporate several of the recommended instructional procedures.

It is especially important to recognize that only parts of Jackson's instructional program could really be accomplished outside of the classroom. Because some aspects of his progress in reading and writing were governed by the classroom and school settings, it was important to include teachers and specialists very early on in Jackson's instructional program. He clearly needed, and could benefit from, some individualized instruction. However, he also needed a total instructional program that was more responsive to his needs.

A Final Note.   When students receive classroom and supplemental instruction within a school setting, communication is generally very informal. Information about individual students can and should be collected in an ongoing way. However, there are times when this information must be summarized in written reports and/or oral conferences. This requires: a clear statement of the presenting problem(s); a description of the information collected in the evaluations of the learner, the learning context, and through diagnostic teaching; a synthesis of this information into a clear statement of the primary difficulty; and recommendations for future practice, including descriptions and examples of appropriate materials and methods.

Although procedures for writing and reporting vary, the reporting format should parallel as closely as possible the goals of the assessment-instruction process. For now, it is important only to arrive at a general appreciation of how important clear, concise communication can be for students.

Case Study.   We provide an example of a brief report that was written about Jackson (see Appendix A). His parents concluded that he did indeed need the help of special education placement and requested that he be evaluated for determination of eligibility. The school, in turn, used the information obtained from Jackson's assessment-instructional program as part of their special education process. Conferences were conducted with the Title I teacher and with the special educator, and the school effectively implemented the suggestions detailed in the final report. The special educator was especially interested in the mapping activities that had been done and incorporated these activities into Jackson's program. She also worked with the classroom teacher to find ways to provide prereading support activities for Jackson in social studies and science. It should be noted that if Jackson's school had been using a fully formed RTI process, the reading specialist and/or special educator might have continued with the interventions for some time, collecting progress monitoring data to see whether Jackson was responding to these new instructional adaptations. These data would have been used as part of the special education eligibility determination.

Jackson's fourth-grade classroom placement was made with an eye to teacher flexibility. In particular, the teacher's ability to both provide consistent and appropriate support and willingness to adapt and individualize instruction was considered. As a result, he was placed with a teacher who had demonstrated these abilities in the past and who was also capable of ensuring that Jackson took responsibility for his work. This fourth-grade classroom was shared by a classroom teacher and a special educator, who were co-teaching throughout the year, providing extra insurance that Jackson would receive the support he needed.

Case Discussion. Continuous assessment is critical, of course. In Jackson's case, this needed to be done by the special education team as they conducted their periodic reevaluation of Jackson's eligibility for their services. In addition, this would be done to make adjustments to the recommended program. It is likely that Jackson would need continued support for some time to come. Only ongoing assessment and adjustment would ensure his continued progress.

The case of ninth-grade Susie (see Appendix B) reveals a different profile entirely. Susie has good word recognition abilities but has both fluency and comprehension problems. In addition, it is clear that she is more successful when reading and writing narrative (versus expository) text. Like many adolescents, Susie is capable of managing the word-level aspects of reading but cannot orchestrate more-complex thinking and comprehending—especially in longer informational materials. Because she has not read a great deal, Susie's vocabulary and background knowledge are also somewhat suspect. Susie can be more successful than she is, but because she is in high school, many teachers will need to become involved if she is going to realize her potential.

CHAPTER SUMMARY

This chapter considered an interactive view of reading and writing ability and disability and its application to assessment and instruction. The first section of the chapter presented an interactive view of reading and writing ability and disability that is consistent with the interactive view of reading and writing processes presented previously in Chapter 1 and that provides the conceptual framework for this text. An interactive view of disability suggests that students' performance on various reading and writing tasks is an indication of what they can and will do under specified conditions, rather than a set of fixed abilities and disabilities. In other words, our attention is focused on how each student performs under different conditions and which conditions are most likely to facilitate learning rather than identifying the disability. The notion of the proper match between student and circumstance is what we must grasp if we are to be effective evaluators and instructors.

The second section of this chapter focused on an understanding of the assessment-instruction process described in this text. This process was characterized as an evaluation of the *existing* match and the identification of the *optimal* match between a learner and the conditions of the learning context, and as one that is similar to an RTI approach to the identification of learning disabilities. The long-range goal of the assessment-instruction process was described as the development of strategic, motivated, reflective learners who are able to apply their skills and strategies independently and in a flexible manner. Learning to read and write was characterized as a lifelong pursuit in which the knowledge gained from each reading/writing experience affects subsequent experiences. Because there are differences between instructional settings (classroom, resource room, clinic, etc.), different applications of the assessment-instruction process for these settings were discussed. Classroom teachers have the benefit of daily contact with students but limited time to spend with individual students. In contrast, the specialist or clinician has the benefit of individual time with the student but limited access to the student's daily interactions with reading and writing in the classroom. As a result, the amount of attention devoted to individual components and the procedures used to evaluate them are likely to vary.

In the final section of this chapter, we provided an elaborated example of how the assessment-instruction process might unfold in a typical school setting. The steps in the assessment-instruction process are guided by a series of questions. The steps in the assessment-instruction process are as follows:

Step 1   Getting Started: Using Data to Look at Groups of Students and Identify Struggling Readers and Writers

Step 2   Evaluating the Context

Step 3   Evaluating the Learner: Looking Closer with Ongoing Assessment and Diagnosis

Step 4   Reflection, Decision Making, and Planning

Step 5   Diagnostic Teaching and Continuous Progress Monitoring

MyEducationLab™

Go to the Topics, Reading Instruction, Reading Assessment, and Progress Monitoring, in the MyEducationLab (www.myeducationlab.com) for your course, where you can:

- Find learning outcomes for Reading Instruction, Reading Assessment, and Progress Monitoring, along with the national standards that connect to these outcomes.
- Complete Assignments and Activities that can help you more deeply understand the chapter content.
- Apply and practice your understanding of the core teaching skills identified in the chapter using the Building Teaching Skills and Dispositions learning units.
- Examine challenging situations and cases presented in the IRIS Center Resources.
- Check your comprehension of the content covered in the chapter by going to the Study Plan in the Book Resources for your text. Here you will be able to take a chapter quiz, receive feedback on your answers, and then access Review, Practice, and Enrichment activities to enhance your understanding of chapter content.

A+RISE A+RISE® Standards2Strategy™ is an innovative and interactive online resource that offers new teachers in grades K-12 just in time, research-based instructional strategies that meet the linguistic needs of ELLs as they learn content, differentiate instruction for all grades and abilities, and are aligned to Common Core Elementary Language Arts standards (for the literacy strategies) and to English language proficiency standards in WIDA, Texas, California, and Florida.

CHAPTER 4

Getting Started: Using Data to Understand Groups of Students and Identify Students for a Closer Look

*A*ssessments of student reading and writing ability must begin somewhere. In this chapter, we provide a road map for Step 1 in the assessment-instruction process: using data to look at the performance of all students.

This chapter begins with a brief discussion of the nature of assessment and some guidelines that are important for the entire assessment-instruction process. Then, we turn our attention to providing information about the properties of formal assessment because this type of assessment information is so often available to teachers; indeed, it may be the *only* information that teachers have about their students.

The first half of the chapter describes the aspects of standardized testing that are essential for evaluating formal tests, including issues of type and purpose, important statistical concepts, validity, reliability, the characteristics of norming populations, test fairness, and the interpretation of test scores. The second half of this chapter provides detailed examples of formal reading and writing that are commonly administered to groups of students.

We also discuss issues related to the management of assessment data and provide both low-tech and high-tech ways of keeping track of the data you collect on groups and individuals. Finally, we provide examples of how data are used to make decisions and identify students for further assessment.

UNDERSTANDING STUDENT ASSESSMENT AND ASSESSMENT DATA

Contexts for Assessment

Most students learn to read and write in *developmental* programs at the elementary and middle school levels. These programs are based on materials and tasks that have been developed so that they increase in difficulty and complexity across age and grade levels and are designed for use with large numbers of students. The assumption underlying developmental (sometimes called *core*) reading and writing programs is that the same, or very similar, base materials, content, instructional plans, delivery systems, and sequence are appropriate for all "normally developing" students. Consequently, everyone proceeds through the program in the same order and in the same way, although the pace may vary for some students. Indeed, models of RTI generally assume that this good "first" instruction will be successful in teaching 80 percent (or more) of students to learn to read and write.

In most classrooms, however, there is a wide range of student achievement in reading and writing. Many teachers accommodate individual differences in their classrooms by varying their instruction somewhat, within the parameters of the developmental program. In fact, this differentiation is typically considered to be a hallmark of the good core instructional program. When students fail to maintain the pace or make anticipated progress, they are generally referred for help. In a tiered model of RTI, this would likely involve Tier 2 or Tier 3 instruction, depending on whether the district is using a 3-tier or a 4-tier approach.

Specialized programs of all sorts exist to serve students who have not learned to read or write as well or as quickly as their peers or whose progress is slower than expected. Students may be referred to *intervention* programs, designed to identify struggling students at the very onset of school and provide them with frequent, fast-paced instruction, in order to prevent reading problems by accelerating their literacy development (Dorn & Schubert, 2008; Pikulski, 1998; Scanlon et al., 2005). Until quite recently, special programs almost invariably involved identifying students based on formal achievement/diagnostic tests and then removing them from their regular classroom for some period during the day/week so that they could work with a specialist in a remedial program. Most of the instruction for struggling students was delivered by someone other than the classroom teacher and in an area outside the regular classroom (often called the *pullout model*).

Although these configurations are still quite common, many schools and classrooms have moved toward a new generation of procedures and processes for working with students at risk for failure, because traditional reading programs and special education placements have not been very successful (Hiebert & Taylor, 2000). We now have evidence that intervention in both one-on-one and small-group situations can reduce dramatically the number of students who are struggling (Dorn & Schubert, 2008; Mathes et al., 2005; Scanlon et al., 2008). Even more interesting is the evidence that classroom teachers can generate results that are about as successful as what is produced by specialists if they receive appropriate professional development and systemic support (Dorn & Henderson, 2010; Scanlon, Anderson, & Sweeney, 2010).

These alternatives generally provide additional diagnostic flexibility and also focus more attention on the role of the classroom and the teacher. There is an increased awareness that assessment and evaluation should be located in the classroom and be conducted by the classroom teacher whenever possible (Chappuis, Commodore, & Stiggins, 2010). The vast majority of diagnostic information needed to plan and evaluate instruction can be gathered in the course of everyday literacy events, as long as the teacher is knowledgeable and skilled. At the same time, there has been a troubling move away from diagnosis and an impulse to provide standard interventions on the basis of screening data alone. In this chapter, we explore the problems associated with that practice and advocate that any screening or whole-group data be supplemented by appropriate diagnostic and/or ongoing assessment. The evolving procedures and practices of RTI reflect a growing commitment to early identification and ongoing monitoring of students at risk of failure in the areas of reading and writing.

Guidelines for Student Assessment

Assessment must reflect our best and most current understandings of reading and writing. Over the past twenty years, there has been a significant change in the amount and type of assessment in schools. Throughout the 1990s, states moved toward more-challenging and complex standards, and therefore assessment tasks changed. Outcome measures often reflect a view of literacy achievement that is very comprehensive. However, "since 2001, there has been a dramatic decrease in the use of performance assessments and open-ended responses, and a corresponding increase in multiple-choice tests, because more students must be tested and the cost of testing has skyrocketed (U.S. Government Accounting Office, 2009)" (Valencia, 2011b, p. 381). Thus, it is possible to have a great deal of assessment information and at the same time have insufficient evidence to plan appropriate instruction, much less to plan for student-tailored individual intervention.

The International Reading Association and the National Council of Teachers of English have jointly published a document detailing assessment standards, *Standards for the Assessment of Reading and Writing*, revised (IRA/NCTE, 2009). The eleven standards are summarized in Figure 4.1, and an expanded description of them is available at www.ncte.org/standards/assessmentstandards. We strongly recommend that you read them, since they

FIGURE 4.1 Standards for the Assessment of Reading and Writing

1. The interests of the student are paramount in assessment.
2. The teacher is the most important agent of assessment.
3. The primary purpose of assessment is to improve teaching and learning.
4. Assessment must reflect and allow for critical inquiry into curriculum and instruction.
5. Assessment must recognize and reflect the intellectually and socially complex nature of reading and writing and the important roles of school, home, and society in literacy development.
6. Assessment must be fair and equitable.
7. The consequences of an assessment procedure are the first and most important consideration in establishing the validity of the assessment.
8. The assessment process should involve multiple perspectives and sources of data.
9. Assessment must be based in the local school community, including active and essential participation of families and community members.
10. All stakeholders in the educational community—students, families, teachers, administrators, policymakers, and the public—must have an equal voice in the development, interpretation, and reporting of assessment information.
11. Families must be involved as active, essential participants in the assessment process.

Source: Figure from Task Force on Assessment. (2010). *Standards for the Assessment of Reading and Writing.* National Council of Teachers of English and International Reading Association. Reprinted with permission of the International Reading Association. All rights reserved.

provide a great deal of important information. The standards are both implicitly and explicitly visible in the recommended practices described throughout this text.

In addition to these standards, we offer several additional guidelines for assessment focused specifically on students who are struggling in the areas of reading or writing. For these students, it is essential that we directly assess the factors that are known to influence reading and writing, rather than ignoring them or attempting to create situations where they do not matter. What is needed is a structured approach to determine how an individual handles actual reading materials or writing tasks under conditions that simulate real reading and writing situations both in and out of the classroom. The following guidelines provide the basis for assessment practices that achieve these goals.

Assess Meaningful Activities in Appropriate Contexts.   To evaluate students' reading and writing abilities, we must assess students as they read and write real texts for real purposes. There are times when it may be reasonable to evaluate some component skill in isolation (for example, sight-word vocabulary). However, we should avoid generating conclusions about the contribution of any single skill to overall reading and writing ability until we have also observed the component in context.

In addition, we must consider how relevant the component abilities are for real, or *authentic*, reading and writing activities. Authenticity describes both tasks and materials (Valencia, 1998). There should be a purpose for reading or writing that transcends assessment or instruction. School tasks and texts in reading and writing should be similar to those used by people in nonschool settings. If they are not, questions of authenticity are raised.

Similarly, the most informative assessments are those that occur within the everyday instructional context rather than artificial testing contexts. There is evidence that people are aware of the differences among contexts and alter their performance accordingly (Adams, Smith, Pasupathi, & Vitolo, 2002; Spiro & Myers, 1984). Anyone who has ever puzzled over the discrepancy between students' performance in the classroom and their test performance is aware of this problem.

In general, students tend to consider formal testing situations to be more important than everyday classroom tasks. However, this perception can have very different effects on different students. Some students perform better in the formal testing situations because of increased motivation to do well; others perform less well because of the anxiety created by the pressure to do well. Therefore, we do not want to collect information that tells us only how students perform in formal testing situations. We want to be able to make some predictions about students' performance in everyday instructional contexts.

Match Assessment to Purpose and Instruction.   No single assessment tool or strategy can do everything. We must think carefully about what we want to know and why we are assessing. If we need comparative data on large numbers of students, then informal, classroom-based assessment probably is not practical. On the other hand, if we want information that will help us plan instruction for individuals or groups of students, then standardized, norm-referenced tests are not likely to be helpful.

We noted the multiple purposes for assessment in Chapter 3. Because tests can be such powerful influences on instruction, it is important to remember that decisions about instructional goals and outcomes should *precede* assessment decisions. Except in the circumstance where the only purpose for assessment is to determine eligibility for a special program, the test should be "instructionally illuminating" (Popham, 2001). At the very least, there should be good alignment between the assessment and the nature and goals of the instructional program (Valencia, 1998). Similarly, the ways in which students demonstrate competence should be similar across the assessment and instructional contexts.

Having a clear model of reading ability (and disability) and a strong curricular focus are extremely important, since assessment should follow *from* an articulated description of what we want students to know and learn. If tests are allowed to determine what is important, the consequences can be quite serious. High-stakes reading assessments are likely to become "curricular magnets" for both teachers and students, encouraging teachers to teach test content to the exclusion of all else (Popham, 1993, 2001).

Be Systematic.   Whether we use formal, standardized (norm-referenced or criterion) tests or formative, classroom-based procedures, our assessments must be dependable, or trustworthy. We use students' performance on one measure (a test, for example) to characterize their abilities more generally. The results of an assessment would have little meaning if they fluctuated wildly from one administration to the next (are not reliable). Similarly, if the content of the test was very different from what we teach and value, we would not be able to make valid inferences about what students know and can do in our classrooms and communities.

The reliability of formal test instruments typically is addressed through the standardization process and reported in the testing manual (see Appendix C). The trustworthiness of informal assessments depends on the extent to which we are systematic and consistent in our use of these techniques (Valencia & Calfee, 1991). In either case, we are concerned about the extent to which educators can have confidence in the decisions they make based on the data generated (Messick, 1989; Kame'enui et al., 2006).

When making comparisons among individuals, we must attempt to evaluate all of our students under the same conditions, with the same level of support. For example, we should attempt to formalize at least some of the probing questions asked during story retellings. If the student is given additional assistance, then it is important to record the information provided to clarify the conditions under which the performance occurred. Otherwise, the information will not be instructionally useful. At the same time, it is important to have a systematic way to capture information about students, because a comprehensive assessment system will inevitably include a wide range of measures with diverse purposes (see Kame'enui et al., 2006; Paris et al., 2005).

Use Multiple Assessments.   Multiple samples of students' performance are always preferable to a single sample. Not only does ongoing evaluation improve the reliability of the assessment, but it also permits us to observe the *patterns* of behavior that are most informative for assessment and instruction. In addition, ongoing data collection casts assessment and instruction in their proper roles—as interacting elements of teaching. Viewing every instructional interaction with a student as an assessment opportunity enhances our diagnostic powers.

We have found that continuous assessment helps us to view both our own teaching and the students' abilities in a different light. A student's failure to perform can be viewed as an opportunity to gather information rather than a reflection of some static and inherent ability (in either the teacher or the child). Teacher evaluations must be taken seriously. Indeed, the majority of assessments in reading and writing can and should be done continuously and in conjunction with the daily instructional program, as an aid to planning, adapting, and refining instruction.

Promote Reflection and Self-Assessment.   Most educators do not think of assessment as an opportunity to promote student independence and self-evaluation. Nor do most of us think of assessment as an opportunity to reflect on our own teaching practices and glean insights for self-improvement. Indeed, most of us think of assessment as something that is done *to* us. However, contemporary views of literacy assessment acknowledge an important truth: appropriate self-assessment and the ability to set appropriate goals lead to learning and improved performance—for both teachers and students.

As Valencia (1998, p. 20) has noted:

> Reflection grows naturally out of classroom assessment because instruction and assessment are integrated. Both teachers and students learn that people improve by judging their own performance against exemplars and clearly defined standards. In turn, they become more expert at understanding what good work looks like, more likely to be self-directed, and more invested in their own learning and progress—all of which leads to success.

Many, perhaps most, struggling readers and writers have ceded the responsibility for judgment to the teachers. They acquire a passive approach to learning that is harmful to their progress. Teachers and students alike need to acquire the skills related to self-reflection.

Teachers are increasingly aware of the importance of taking an inquiry approach to assessment information. "Interrogating the data" (Valencia, 2007) is critical to understanding and using the information we have—especially in the early stages of the assessment-instruction process, when we are often working with many different types of data and many different students. Asking questions such as who is doing well and who is not are the first steps in examining our practice and making a difference for students.

The Management of Assessment Information

Thoughtful reflection and good records are essential when a variety of standardized and informal procedures are used to plan instruction, evaluate progress, and communicate with parents and administrators. Although a small number of schools continue to employ physical or electronic portfolios as a way to support and promote the ongoing and multisource type of assessment, the assessment context has changed considerably in recent years. There is a focus on both standardized and more-formative assessments (Chappuis, Commodore, & Stiggins, 2010). Not surprisingly, there has also been a rapidly emerging use of online data management systems. Some of these capture only the assessment data from a specific test or set of tests (e.g., AIMSweb), some of are commercially available through publishers (e.g., Scholastic Achievement Manager [SAM]), and still others are designed so that states or districts can capture multiple types of assessment data, often aligned with standards (e.g., Strategic Teaching and Evaluation of Progress [STEP™] in Chicago or the Vermont Comprehensive Assessment Tool [VCAT]).

The point has been made that these online data management systems are not necessarily the same thing as an electronic *portfolio*, with its focus on depth, breadth and self-reflection. Indeed, Barrett and Carney (2005) have argued that these might actually constitute competing purposes, with portfolios focused more on student learning and managements systems focused on teacher accountability—what Chappuis, Commodore and Stiggins call "assessment *for* learning and assessment *of* learning." Most educators argue that there is a need for a balanced assessment system. Such an assessment system is designed to improve teacher decision making through more-comprehensive and representative assessment and to get a richer and more authentic view of the student's literacy knowledge and use in order to rethink and/or reshape instruction (Stiggins, 2008).

The system needs to address the various types of assessment purposes but also to encompass various sources of information, including artifacts and student work samples. In this way, it is similar to a portfolio—an *organized* and *intentional* collection. As we move through the assessment-instruction process, we need to include materials that exemplify the depth and breadth of a student's expertise. It is especially important that there be a variety of different types of information collected over time, as indicators of growth in reading and writing. This makes it easier for teachers, specialists, and students to plan the experiences that will encourage additional progress and make decisions about students' placement in more-progressively individualized and tailored interventions.

We recommend that the system be organized into several layers of information to address the diverse purposes and audiences for assessment information. These include the *classroom level of use*, where people make instructional decisions; the *program level of use*, where teachers, teams, and administrators examine the impact of instructional program(s) on students; and the *policy level of use*, where decisions are made about overall impact, resources, etc. (Stiggins, 2008). Recall that we discussed different purposes and types of assessment in Chapter 3. Here, we make the point that different types of assessment are often required at these different levels. In a *layered system* (Lipson, 2007),

- ✔ some assessment information is collected for all students;
- ✔ some data are collected only for certain grades or at specific times;
- ✔ some data are only for specific students or groups of students; and
- ✔ after looking at the data for groups of students, we identify students who require a closer look.

The advantage of this approach is that we can do somewhat less assessment on everyone in order to spend more time assessing students who need a more tailored approach. For these students, we use summary or profile sheets to help synthesize the information. Inclusion of the raw data enables us to examine students' actual work and progress notes, rather than relying simply on a number or grade. This can be especially important when working with data teams to problem solve for individual students.

The data that are collected will vary in relation to the particular program of assessment and instruction in effect and the age/grade of the student. The universal data collected on all students are likely to be primarily of the outcomes and screening (plus the periodic benchmarking sort), but some schools include formative assessment data also. For students who are struggling, the diagnostic information and periodic progress monitoring data might also include written responses to reading, reading logs, selected daily work, pieces of writing at various stages of completion, classroom tests, observational checklists, unit projects, audio or video tapes, as well as digital materials. An important addition to these suggestions, for those who follow the assessment-instruction process outlined in this book (or who are engaged in RTI processes), is the inclusion of measures designed to evaluate various aspects of the instructional context. "The key is to ensure a variety of types of indicators of learning so that teachers, parents, students, and administrators can build a complete picture of the student's development" (Valencia, 1990a, p. 339).

UNDERSTANDING FORMAL ASSESSMENT

In many districts, test batteries are administered that survey several subject areas. They are intended to measure student progress. Since 2001, when the No Child Left Behind Act was passed, virtually every district in the United States must annually assess reading and mathematics in grades 3 through 8. In addition, these subjects must be assessed at least once in high school. Most states also require some sort of large-scale assessment of all students at some point during the primary grades. And there have been a number of significant changes in school assessment. For classroom teachers and specialists, one of the biggest changes is the shift away from total reliance on norm-referenced test scores, with their focus on ranking, and a shift toward the use of standards-based assessments, with their focus on identifying students who have or have not met standards. Stiggins (2008) refers to

> . . . our slow but steady shift from almost total reliance on norm-referenced interpretation of test scores to criterion-referenced interpretation of results. This parallels the evolution of our collective thinking about the purposes of assessment. We have emerged from the era of assessing merely to rank students based on achievement to asking the key question: Who has and has not met standards? (p. 2)

As we write this text revision, the majority of states have adopted the Common Core State Standards (CCSS) and have joined one of two possible assessment consortia: (1) SMARTER/Balanced Assessment Consortium (SBAC) or (2) Partnership for the Assessment of Readiness for College and Career (PARCC). These organizations are charged with creating assessments that reflect the outcomes described by the CCSS. Although it is not clear at this time what the consequences will be of school/district failure to meet these goals, but the heightened focus on standards and student performance will not doubt continue.

Although state/regional assessments are generally used primarily to measure student outcomes for accountability purposes (i.e., to assess the degree of success of schools and districts), most schools also use the data to make judgments about subgroups and even individual students. When these types of tests are administered at the beginning of the year, they are often used to assist in placing students into groups or selecting them for materials and to screen for referral to special programs. When they are administered at the end of the school year, they may be used for decisions about promotion and retention and about placing students in summer programs or fall classes. Many districts also involve kindergarten and first-grade teachers in the administration of tests of readiness and emergent literacy for screening and program placement.

Reading specialists, special education personnel, or school psychologists often administer formal (norm-referenced) diagnostic and psychological tests. Although classroom teachers are unlikely to actually administer these types of tests, they generally do receive reports describing the test results. Because the classroom teacher often spends considerably more time with these students than does any specialist, the teacher shoulders a major portion of the responsibility for understanding the nature of the students' special needs and addressing them through classroom activities. This is why it is extremely important that classroom teachers be knowledgeable about the tests being administered to their students, so that they can follow up the results with informal measures in the classroom that will lead to appropriate classroom practice.

Specialists are more likely to have direct contact with diagnostic tests and with those focusing on other language arts and related areas than are classroom teachers. Resource personnel are most likely to use these tests to demonstrate program effectiveness with individual students, to identify specific strengths and weaknesses as an aid to program planning, and as an aid in the identification of students with special needs. Even when the limitations of formal tests in these areas are recognized, their administration is still necessary because of legislative mandates and the need to have common measures that cut across schools, districts, and states. School districts that elect to use RTI procedures may not rely so heavily on formal assessments to make eligibility determinations, but they are still likely to use some of these for screening, diagnosis, and/or monitoring.

Data-driven decision making is frequently cited as one of the major strategies for school improvement (McCrel, 2003). Although school practices vary widely across the United States, the fact is that most teachers have a great deal of data about students. This widespread availability of data does not necessarily mean that teachers have good *information* (Stringfield, Wayman, & Yakimowski, 2005; Valencia, 2011b; Yakimowski, 2005; Valencia, 2011). This makes it that much more important that the individuals who administer and interpret the tests have a clear understanding of what the tests can and cannot tell us. In the Getting Started phase of the assessment-instruction process, teachers and administrators need to be quite skilled in interpreting and managing data if it is going to yield useful information.

General Characteristics of Standardized Tests

Formal assessment devices typically are published tests that provide standardized methods of administration, scoring, and interpretation and are often at the heart of the procedures used in traditional diagnoses of reading and writing problems. When educators sit down to look at their assessment data and think about their whole class/grade/school, they must know about the properties of both norm-referenced and criterion-based (or standards-based) forms of assessment. In this section of the chapter, we describe key characteristics of these different types of assessment and describe concerns that should be well understood by test users. We also provide background for interpreting the results. This chapter is intended to provide teachers and specialists with information about the properties of formal instruments that are important for intelligently evaluating the usefulness of available tests in light of their purposes for assessment.

Test selection and evaluation begin with an understanding of the purpose for which a test is being given. Information relative to a particular test must always be examined in relation to the purpose(s) for which it is being used.

The title, author, publisher, and date of publication reveal information about a test's quality and the appropriateness of its purpose and content for different students or testing situations. For example, a test with the word *survey* in the title suggests that the test will provide general information about a student's achievement rather than specific information about strengths and weaknesses. Similarly, the reputation of the test author and/or publisher in reading, writing, or testing may suggest something about both the content and quality of the test. A recent date of publication or revision increases the likelihood that the test reflects the most recent theory and research and that any norms used for scoring are current.

Other general characteristics of a formal test that are important for determining its appropriateness for specific students or testing situations include the level of difficulty and type of administration. Some tests are intended for a wide range of age, grade, and ability levels; others are intended only for restricted levels. Still others have different forms for different levels. Therefore, it is important to determine that a test is appropriate for the age, grade, and ability of the student with whom it will be used.

The appropriateness of the test administration for specific students and purposes depends on factors such as whether the test is group or individually administered and whether it is timed or untimed. Group tests are efficient to administer but tend to provide more-general information than do individual tests, and do not allow for the variety of response formats (e.g., oral reading, extended writing activities) that are allowed by individual tests. Individual tests require significantly more time to administer than group tests but tend to provide more-specific information about the student. Timed or speed tests determine what a student can do under specified time constraints, whereas untimed or power tests evaluate a student's performance without any time constraints.

The two basic types of test interpretations that we discuss in this chapter are *norm-referenced* and *criterion-referenced* interpretations. As we noted above, criterion-referenced, or standards-based, interpretations are increasingly common in educational testing. Such tests are designed primarily to provide information about how well a person has learned a specific body of knowledge or acquired specific objectives. The emphasis is on describing the level of performance of individuals and groups on the behavior that a test is measuring. Propelled by federal legislation, most states developed standards-based assessments in (at least) reading.

> Reporting percentages of students meeting or exceeding performance standards was seen as preferable to reporting means or normative information because the standards were supposed to specify a level of performance that was judged to be good enough or exemplary without referring to the performance of other students. (Linn, 2006, p. 5)

Almost all states and/or districts have adopted content standards that specify what students should know and be able to do in various content domains. They (sometimes in conjunction with other states or publishers) have also adopted performance standards that specify how much of the content a student should know. Then the "standards-based score reports interpret test performance with reference to cut scores defining categories like 'below basic' or 'proficient' or [advanced]" (Haertel & Lorie, 2004, p. 5).

Norm-referenced interpretations examine a given student's performance in relation to the performance of a representative group. The emphasis in norm-referenced testing is on the individual's relative standing rather than on absolute mastery of content (Salvia, Ysseldyke, & Bolt, 2010). Although the term *standardized* is often used synonymously with tests emphasizing norm-referenced interpretations, tests that emphasize criterion-referenced interpretations can be, and often are, standardized. *Standardized* means only that all students perform the same tasks under uniform directions (Swanson & Watson, 1989).

The difficulty of test items and the manner in which items are selected also differ between tests emphasizing norm-referenced and criterion-referenced interpretations. Test items that produce a wide range of scores and discriminate well between high-scoring and low-scoring individuals are desirable for norm-referenced interpretations that determine an individual's relative position in comparison to a group of his or her peers. Therefore, the best norm-referenced items are those that 40 to 60 percent of the students answer correctly, because they produce the greatest variance in test scores. In well-constructed tests using norm-referenced interpretations, half of the population will score above the average, and half will fall below the average.

For standards-referenced (criterion-referenced) tests, however, the best items are those that accurately measure the content standards at a given age/grade level and that, taken together, result in an appropriate overall emphasis. In well-constructed tests using standards-based interpretations, distribution of students might occur in any combination of categories. The quality of the items depends on the extent to which they reflect the level of performance of the student population in relation to the standards.

Key Concepts

There are a number of key concepts important for literacy professionals to understand, no matter which type of assessment is being used. Those related to statistics and testing can be found in Appendix C. In this chapter, we begin with a discussion of validity, which is often considered together with other topics such as reliability and fairness. We have chosen to give it greater prominence here, because it is the concept that is at the heart of appropriate use and interpretation of assessment results.

Validity

"Validity is, hands down, the most significant concept in assessment" (Popham, 2002, p. 47). This broadly held sentiment is evident in the most recent volume of *Standards for Educational and Psychological Testing* (the *Standards*), which was published in 1999 by the American Educational Research Association (AERA), the American Psychological Association (APA), and the National Council on Measurement in Education (NCME). Professionals sometimes talk about a test as "being valid," suggesting that this is a "static property" of the test (Goodwin & Leech, 2003). However, that view of validity has been abandoned for many years. Instead, according the *Standards*, validity is defined in terms of the quality of the inferences that are made from assessment results. Validity is judged on the appropriateness, meaningfulness, and usefulness of the interpretations made by users of the assessment results, *not* on the assessment itself. Accordingly, the valid use of an assessment is the responsibility of both the developer and the user.

A major factor in the valid use of tests is the extent to which there is a match between the test's and the test user's conceptualization of the domain being measured. In our case, we would ask whether the test content and process matches our concepts of reading and writing so that we can make good inferences about students within a specific setting. Tests may be used and interpreted in a variety of ways, and evidence must be collected to support each interpretation and use. For example, standardized achievement tests are used both to provide accountability information to the public about schools and districts and to place students in particular classes and programs. Each of these purposes implies a different interpretation and use of test scores, which must be validated by accumulating appropriate evidence.

Caution must also be exercised, because inferences that are valid for the majority of students might not be valid for all. For example, Salvia and Ysseldyke (2001) point out that judgments about students who are not steeped in American culture based on their performance on tests written for a general U.S. audience may be unfounded (see section below on test fairness). Similarly, some tests assume that students have received certain instruction. If a student has not been given such instruction, inferences about that student's ability to learn the material may be invalid.

The 1999 assessment standards indicate that tests should include evidence of validity that specifies what inferences can reasonably be made. In addition, these documents argue that test consumers should be warned against making specific kinds of inferences if the evidence that these inferences are warranted is not available. Again, it is the range and accuracy of possible inferences to other real-world phenomena (other tests, classroom performance, future success, etc.) that constitute evidence for the validity of a particular interpretation or use of a test score.

Construct-Related Evidence of Validity.   In previous versions of the *Standards* (and, as a result, in the minds of many educators), three categories of evidence are considered in the process of test validation: content-, criterion-, and construct-related evidence of validity. These three categories of evidence are often treated separately, giving the false impression that they are alternatives or options. However, the 1999 *Standards* argue for a unitary view of validity, which integrates evidence across categories under the heading of construct validity.

> The term construct has an important meaning in educational testing because it emphasizes the fact that we are not measuring tangible attributes of students. Educational tests attempt to measure students' knowledge, skills, and abilities. Given this endeavor, it must be assumed that (a) such concepts exist within students and (b) they are measurable. Since we do not know for sure if such intangible student attributes or proficiencies really exist, we admit they are "constructs"; they are hypothesized attributes we believe exist within students. Hence, these attributes were "constructed" from educational and psychological theories, and they are subsequently operationally defined using test specifications and other elements of the testing process. (Sireci, 2004, p. 7)

In other words, we aren't actually measuring "reading ability" on any specific test. Instead, we are measuring something that is a stand-in for reading ability. The test has items and tasks that are meant to capture important aspects of this ability or, in the case of standards-based assessments, important aspects of the content standards that students are expected to know or be able to do.

Within a construct validity framework, the process of gathering validity evidence begins with a conceptual framework that describes the phenomena or construct/s that are being assessed (e.g., reading comprehension) and the purpose(s) for which the assessment has been developed and will be used (e.g., decisions about grade placement or high school graduation). From this framework, hypotheses about the relations among the construct(s) and assessment purposes are evaluated by gathering evidence of valid uses and interpretations of assessment results.

For the purposes of this book, we are concerned about the constructs of *reading* that underlie the assessments we describe. We have proposed a construct of reading and writing in the introductory chapters of this text. Test publishers, whether norm referenced or standards based, should be clear about the construct they are sampling. As noted previously, these constructs or definitions vary in relation to the purposes for which an assessment is designed and to the ages, grades, and skill levels of those from whom an assessment is intended.

Assessment validity can be threatened in a number of ways related to the underlying construct(s), including by construct underrepresentation. *Construct underrepresentation* refers to an assessment that is so narrow that it fails to capture important aspects of the construct being evaluated. For example, tests measuring the speed of reading are sometimes used as indicators of general reading achievement. Since these tests do not evaluate reading comprehension, the validity of these tests when used to evaluate general reading achievement is threatened by construct underrepresentation.

Validity can also be threatened by construct-irrelevant variability. This occurs when an assessment is so broad that it requires capabilities that are irrelevant or extraneous to the intent of the assessment. For example, the claim that an assessment measures reading comprehension may be threatened by the fact that performance on the assessment depends unduly on knowledge of a particular subject matter such as history or biology, which introduces variability into the scores that is irrelevant to the construct of reading.

Validity Evidence.   Decisions about test validity depend on gathering evidence. One source of validity evidence can be obtained from an analysis of an assessment's *content* or internal structure. The content of reading assessments refers to characteristics such as the reading selections; wording and format of the items, tasks, or questions; as well as the guidelines for administration and scoring. Content validation involves a careful examination of the content of an assessment in relation to the construct(s) it is intended to measure. Inferences about reading achievement may be unwarranted or invalid when test content is a poor reflection of reading processes as we understand them. For example, many believe that too many reading assessments distort the process by evaluating nothing more than isolated subskills or by requiring students to engage in contrived or highly constrained activities that are not representative of reading as it occurs in everyday contexts.

Another type of evidence can be gained by evaluating the *internal structure* of an assessment to determine whether the components of an assessment and their organization support or compromise validity, and to consider whether items or groups of items function as expected. For example, analyses may be conducted to determine whether items on an assessment are equally difficult for individuals of similar ability from different racial groups. If there are differences among these groups, the validity of the assessment as a means of assessing all students is called into question.

Validity evidence can also come from an examination of the *relations between an assessment and criterion measures* that extend beyond the assessment itself. For example, you might evaluate how well a test score for reading comprehension predicts performance on another test purporting to measure the same thing or in some everyday reading comprehension activity. Similarly, a test that claims to prepare students for the world of work should predict how students actually perform in the work world. In the case of standards-based assessments, most claim that the levels of proficiency actually describe the appropriate expectations for students of specific ages/grades and that this proficiency is measured on the test (Haertel & Lorie, 2004).

Consequential Validity. Perhaps the most controversial aspect of the 1999 *Standards* was their call for considering consequential (rather than evidential) evaluations of validity (Messick, 2004). The intended and unintended consequences of testing may be an important source of evidence for validity. According to VanLehn and Martin (1997):

> Consequential validity judges the *indirect* consequences of using the test on the overall educational system. For instance, schools and teachers often change their instruction in order to improve students' performance on standardized tests. This is not necessarily bad. However, if the test assesses a deep, complex competence (e.g., verbal reasoning skill) with superficial tasks (e.g., vocabulary tests) that were once correlated with the complex competence, then "teaching to the test" means teaching students the superficial tasks instead of the complex competence. Because one consequence of using the test would be "dumbing down" the curriculum, this test would have low consequential validity. On the other hand, if the assessment used tasks that really did tap the target competence, then teaching to the test would cause the assessment to have high consequential validity. (p. 180)

Concerns about the consequential validity of tests have been especially focused on high-stakes, large-scale assessment, where the consequences may be far-reaching. With regard to differential test performance among groups, "evidence about consequences may be directly relevant to validity when it can be traced to a source of invalidity such as construct under-representation or construct irrelevant components. Evidence about consequences that cannot be so traced—that in fact reflects valid differences in performance—is crucial in informing policy decisions but falls outside the technical purview of validity" (AERA, APA, & NCME, 1999, p. 16). More generally, if tests are administered to produce some benefit—for example, improved instruction or student motivation to learn—validation should consider whether the benefit is indeed likely to result.

Summing Up. The utility and value of tests rely on evidence of their validity. No matter what else is true, if the behavior or performance is not characteristic of the student in other related settings or tasks, then the scores are misleading. Validity involves an overall evaluative judgment. It requires an evaluation of the sufficiency of evidence that justifies the interpretations and uses of assessment results as well as the consequences of those interpretations and uses. Validity does not exist on an all-or-nothing basis. Rather, validity is the degree to which the assessment process leads to correct inferences about a specific group or person in a specific situation for a specific purpose. This means that inferences that are valid for the majority might not be valid for every individual. For example, judgments about individuals who are not native English speakers on a reading assessment written for a general U.S. population may be unfounded.

The 1999 *Standards* recommend that the available evidence from a variety of these sources be integrated to build a solid account of the extent to which the data support the proposed interpretations and specific uses of a test. As tests continue to be revised, it will be interesting to see how the validity arguments for formal tests of reading and writing accommodate changes in the concept of validity.

Reliability

After validity, reliability is the most important characteristic of assessment results. Reliability refers to the consistency or stability of assessment results from one administration to another. Consistency is essential, because it is important to be able to generalize assessment results obtained under one set of conditions to other occasions and circumstances. We would not administer a test if we knew that the student's score might be fifteen or twenty points higher or lower if the student were retested.

Reliability Evidence.   It is important to be able to generalize assessment results in three different ways. First, we would like to be able to assume that comparable but different assessment items or tasks would provide similar results. Imagine that a teacher wants a quick indicator of her students' ability to recognize high-frequency words (e.g., *that*, *is*, *when*, etc.) on sight. She would have to select a sample of the domain of these words for her assessment, because it would be impossible to assess the entire domain. She would like to assume that her students would earn about the same score whether they were assessed on the sample she selected, on the entire domain of sight words, or on any other sample of sight words. Evidence of this type of reliability is often gathered by comparing results on alternate or equivalent forms of an assessment, or on different subsets of items or tasks within a particular assessment. Evidence of consistency of performance under these different conditions indicates that assessment results are generalizable to different samples of items or tasks (often referred to as either *alternate-form* or *split-half reliability*).

Second, we would like to be able to assume that the results we obtain today would be similar to those we would obtain tomorrow or next week if the assessment were given again. Suppose our teacher evaluates students' high-frequency sight-word recognition on Tuesday at 10:00 a.m. She would like to assume that the students would earn the same scores if they were evaluated the following day in the afternoon—or on any other day or at any other time that week. A teacher would like to generalize the results found at one time to all possible times, or the total domain of times. This type of reliability evidence is often gathered by administering a given assessment a second time on another day and/or at another time (often referred to as *test-retest reliability*).

Third, we would like to be able to assume that the results would be the same if another equally qualified individual administered and/or scored the assessment. Our teacher would like to assume that any other teacher would score the students' responses in a similar way, leading to comparable results. This type of reliability evidence is often gathered by having different evaluators administer and score the assessment and compare their results (often referred to as *inter-rater reliability*).

We need to be confident that our results would be fairly similar if we administered an assessment under different conditions, including a different sample of items from the same domain, a different day/time, and a different administrator and/or scorer. Assessment results have limited utility if they fluctuate greatly from one occasion to the next. For an assessment to be useful, it must be reliable.

Measurement Error.   Differences between scores from one administration to another as a function of the sample of items or tasks, the day/time of administration, and/or the particular administrator or scorer can be characterized as measurement error. This is not the same as differences that are attributable to maturation or instructional intervention, which is often what we want to measure. Our previous example can be used to illustrate measurement error in our teacher's assessment of students' ability to read high-frequency sight words. A sample of these words consisting of *stop*, *big*, *run*, and *go* would probably provide a much easier test than a sample of words such as *where*, *when*, *which*, and *who*. Students would do better on the easier sample of words and worse on the sample of more-difficult sight words, which means that their performance on one of these samples would not generalize to their performance on the other sample. Similarly, if one administrator used flash cards to briefly show the words one at a time and another presented students with all the words in a long list and gave them unlimited time to respond, the results might be different for a particular student. The variability across the sample of items and the administration in this example introduce error into the students' scores and therefore affect the reliability and generalizability of the assessment results.

The reliability of an assessment is usually expressed as a correlation coefficient known as a *reliability coefficient*. A reliability coefficient indicates the degree of relationship between two sets of results (e.g., the relationship between results from assessment at two different times or the administration's alternate forms, etc.). A coefficient of 1.00 would indicate a perfect relationship with no measurement error, and a coefficient of 0.00 would indicate that the results were completely random—that there was no relationship between the two sets of results. The degree of reliability we demand in educational assessments depends largely on the decision(s) to be made from the assessment results. Miller, Linn, and Gronlund (2009) note that high reliability is demanded when the decision is important, is final, is irreversible, concerns individuals, and has lasting consequences. Lower reliability is tolerable when the decision is relatively minor, is reversible, is confirmable by other data, concerns groups, and has temporary effects.

Standard Error of Measurement (SEM).   One of the primary reasons for obtaining a reliability coefficient is to be able to estimate the amount of error associated with an individual's score. The *standard error of measurement (SEM)* permits the user of an assessment to do this. The SEM provides information about the certainty or confidence with which assessment results can be interpreted. When the SEM is relatively large, the uncertainty is great. When the SEM is relatively small, the uncertainty is minimized.

The SEM can be used to suggest the distance between an individual's "true" score, with all the sources of error removed, and his or her actual score. An individual's "true" score actually may either be above or below the obtained score. Using the SEM, we can define a range, or confidence interval, within which we can be relatively certain where the individual's true score lies.

Because the SEM is based on a normal distribution of scores, we can say that 68 percent of the time the individual's true score will fall within $+1$ or -1 SEM of his or her obtained score. Therefore, if an individual's obtained score is 60 and the SEM is 4, the person's true score is somewhere between 60 $+4$ or -4, or between 56 and 64. This means that an individual's score fluctuates within four points on either side of the true score 68 times out of 100. This also means that the obtained score is likely to either underestimate or overestimate the student's true score about 30 percent of the time. If we want a higher degree of confidence, we can expand the size of the interval. A 95 percent confidence band is represented by $+2$ or -2 SEM, which in the case of our example is $+8$ or -8 points and provides the interval within which an individual's true score will lie 95 out of 100 times.

It is important to realize what the SEM means for the interpretation of assessment results. When we say that someone's reading score corresponds to a grade equivalent of 4.5 (see the section on scores), it sounds very precise. But consider the SEM and the confidence intervals. If the SEM is .3, we are only 68 percent certain that the true score falls between 4.2 and 4.8 and 95 percent certain that it falls somewhere between 4.0 and 5.1—a range of over one year. A larger SEM would mean even larger intervals. This example illustrates clearly the importance of examining the evidence of reliability available for the assessment results we are interpreting.

In terms of the level of error that is acceptable, Salvia, Ysseldyke, and Bolt (2010) recommend three standards or cutoff points for reliability coefficients. If results are to be reported for groups rather than individuals and are to be used for general administrative purposes, a reliability coefficient above .60 is acceptable. If results are to be used to make decisions about individual students, the standard should be much higher. For important educational decisions, such as placing a student in a special class, a reliability coefficient of .90 should be considered minimum. For more-general purposes such as initial screening, a reliability of .80 is acceptable.

The importance of a particular source of error and other information about reliability depends on the specific use of the assessment. Estimates of the reliability of an assessment should consider not only the relevant sources of error, but also the types of decisions that are anticipated to be based on the scores and whether these decisions are made at the group level or disaggregated for subgroups and/or individuals. Assessment developers and publishers have primary responsibility for obtaining and reporting evidence concerning reliability and errors of measurement related to the intended uses. Although assessment users usually do not conduct separate reliability studies, they do have a responsibility to determine that the available information is relevant to their intended uses and interpretations. Information about the reliability of an assessment should be readily available to the user in either a technical manual or the manuals used for scoring.

Reliability and Validity.   An assessment that produces very inconsistent results (i.e., is not reliable) cannot possibly provide valid information. Conversely, evidence of highly consistent assessment results does not ensure that the assessment is measuring the right things or being used in appropriate ways. Reliability is a necessary, but not sufficient, condition for validity; it simply provides evidence of the consistency that makes validity possible. Therefore, it is important for authors and publishers to present sufficient information about reliability for the user to interpret assessment results accurately. Reliability information for each type of score should be reported for each age and grade.

Test Interpretation

The raw score, or the number of points received on a test, is usually the basic score in tests emphasizing either norm- or criterion-referenced/standards-based interpretations. These raw scores alone tell us very little, since we know neither how other individuals performed nor how many total points might be reasonable or possible on the test. However, raw scores become more meaningful when they are converted into either a description of how well a student or group of students performed in relation to an established performance standard (criterion-referenced interpretation) or some type of derived score (e.g., percentile ranks) that indicates a student's or group of students' relative standing in a clearly defined reference group (norm-referenced interpretation). Each of these modes of interpreting assessment results can be useful under various circumstances, and occasionally both are reasonable.

Criterion-Reference Interpretations. Criterion-referenced test interpretation permits us to describe an individual's test performance on some preestablished standard, or *criterion.* In this method, it is not necessary or even desirable to refer to the performance of others. Students' performance might be described in terms of the speed or precision with which a task is performed or the percentage of items correct on some clearly defined set of learning tasks.

Although percentage-correct scores are often used as the standard for judging whether a student has mastered each of the instructional objectives measured by a criterion-referenced test, there are many ways to report these scores. Swanson and Watson (1989, p. 58) present five measures, or *metrics*, that are commonly accepted as appropriate for criterion-referenced interpretation, several of which are basically raw scores:

1. A rate metric simply refers to the time it takes to complete the specified task.
2. A sign metric indicates the mastery or nonmastery of the task.
3. An accuracy metric gives the proportion of times the examinee is successful.
4. A proportion metric specifies the portion or percentage of the items in a domain on which the student performs accurately.
5. A scaling metric describes the point along a continuum at which the student's performance occurs.

Miller, Linn, and Gronlund (2009) point out that criterion-referenced interpretation of test results is most meaningful when the test has been designed to measure a specific set of clearly stated learning tasks. In addition, there should be sufficient coverage to make it possible to describe test performance in terms of a student's mastery or nonmastery of each task. The value of criterion test results is enhanced when the domain being measured is delimited and clearly specified and the test items are selected on the basis of their relevance to the domain being measured. Most schools, for example, test new kindergarten students to determine how many letters students can identify. The letters of the alphabet constitute a clearly delimited domain. There should be a sufficient number of test items to make dependable judgments concerning the types of tasks a student can and cannot perform. So, for example, schools might also screen kindergarten children for their ability to write some words, but they would not attempt to test all possible words.

Performance on the items on tests emphasizing criterion-referenced interpretations can range in difficulty from 0 to 100 percent accuracy, depending on the nature of the specific learning tasks to be measured. If the learning tasks are easy, the test items should be easy. Little attempt is made to modify item difficulty or to eliminate easy items from the test to obtain a range of test scores. On a test emphasizing criterion-referenced interpretations, we would expect all, or nearly all, students to obtain high scores when the instruction has been effective (Gronlund, 1985).

Over the past decade, teachers and schools have been held accountable for assessments that are aligned with state standards. Such tests are customized to states and school districts so that they measure state standards in order to influence effective instruction. In contrast to national achievement tests, which tend to be norm referenced, state standardized tests are usually criterion referenced, or standards referenced.

Unlike for a norm-referenced test, standards-based test results are based on a cut score that is determined for different levels of performance. There are no cut scores for norm-referenced tests; students do not fail the Gates-MacGinitie Reading Tests or the Peabody Picture Vocabulary tests, for example. Typically, four levels of performance are set (e.g., *above the standard*; *meets the standard* (or *proficient*); *approaching the standard*; and *below the standard*).

Schools receive summary data that is designed to communicate about the overall performance of students compared to that of other schools or to the data (see Figure 4.2). This group data is usually also disaggregated for key subgroups by gender, race/ethnicity, socioeconomic status, and/or status in specialized programs. Each student also receives a report of his/her performance against these standards, and teachers receive results for their grade and/or class, reporting on the proportion of students who have achieved at the various levels of proficiency.

Norm-Referenced Interpretations.   Norm-referenced interpretations indicate how an individual's performance compares to that of others who have taken the same test. The emphasis in norm-referenced assessment is on the individual's ranking relative to other students' performance rather than on mastery of content at a level specified by a set of performance standards as in criterion-referenced assessment.

According to Miller et al. (2009), the simplest type of comparison is to rank-order the raw scores from highest to lowest and to note where an individual's score falls. Noting whether a particular score is second from the top, about in the middle, or one of the lowest scores in relation to a particular reference group provides a meaningful report to both teachers and students. If a student's score is second from the top in a group of ten or more, it is a relatively high score whether it represents 95 percent or 60 percent of the items correct. The fact that a test is relatively easy or difficult for the students does not alter the interpretation of test scores in terms of relative performance.

Although the simple ranking of raw scores may be useful for reporting the results of a classroom test, it is of limited value beyond the immediate situation. To be useful, norm-referenced interpretations depend on a comparison of an individual's performance to that of others whose performance defines the normative scores. Norms are usually obtained by using a norming sample representative of the people for whom the assessment is designed. On the basis of the responses of this standardization, or normative sample, raw scores

FIGURE 4.2

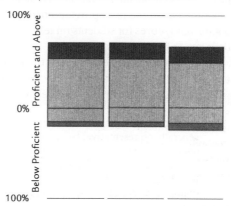

Assessment Report

Organization: Galleston Elementary School
Teaching Year: 2009–2010
Test/Subject: NECAP Reading Grades 3–8
Breakdown: Across all the grades tested, how did our students do?
Comparison: Compared to its District and State?

	School	LEA	State
	All Students	All Students	All Students
Number of Students Tested	387	387	37,804
Proficient with Distinction	20%	20%	20%
Proficient	58%	58%	53%
Partially Proficient	17%	17%	18%
Substantially Below Proficient	6%	6%	9%
Total Proficient and Above	77%	77%	73%
Total Below Proficient	23%	23%	27%

The NECAP Math, Reading, and Writing tests are administered in October and measure student achievement of Grade Expectations for previous school years. NECAP Science tests are administered in May and measure student achievement of Grade Expectations in current and previous school years. District assessment data are for the accountability LEA which is either the town or union school district.

obtained from any subsequent examinee can be converted into a measure of relative standing in comparison to the normative group.

There are two important points related to the fact that test scores are based on the performance of individuals in the normative sample. First, even the slightest variation of the administration procedures for norm-referenced tests from those used with the standardization sample will render the norms—and therefore the test scores—invalid. The second point is that norms are applicable only to individuals of the same age and/or grade as the students in the normative sample. This can be a major problem when testing students with serious academic difficulties. If a test at the student's age or grade level is administered, the norms are of questionable value because the student is at the extreme end of the distribution (not to mention the student's frustration at taking a test that is far too difficult). However, if a test designed for younger or lower-grade students is administered, the norms are inappropriate, because older students were not included in the normative sample. To get around this problem, some tests provide norms for out-of-level testing that make it possible to obtain valid scores for students on tests that approximate their skill level more closely than their age or grade level.

Norms are important because the normative sample may be used to obtain the various statistics on which the final selection of test items is based, and an individual's performance is evaluated in terms of the performance of the individuals in the normative sample:

> . . . in evaluating a test's norms, users should consider not only whether the norms are generally representative, but also the age of the norms (that is, Are the norms current?), the relevance of the norms (that is, Is it appropriate to compare the performance of a specific test taker with the performances represented by the norm sample?), and the appropriate use of the norms (that is, Are the inferences derived from the comparisons appropriate?). (Salvia & Ysseldyke, 2001, pp. 118–119)

An evaluation of representativeness requires particular attention to demographic variables. According to Salvia, Ysseldyke, and Bolt (2010), representativeness hinges on two questions: Does the norm sample contain individuals with the same characteristics as the population that the norms are intended to represent, and are the various kinds of people present in the sample in the same proportion as they are in the population represented by the norms? Among the factors that must be considered in answering these two questions are the age, grade, sex, acculturation of parents (SES and education), geographic factors, race, and intelligence of the individuals in the norm sample in relation to the characteristics of the population for whom the test is designed.

Another, often overlooked, consideration in ensuring representativeness is the date the norms were collected (Salvia, Ysseldyke, & Bolt, 2010). Ours is an age of rapidly expanding knowledge and communication of knowledge. Children of today know more than the children of the 1930s or the 1940s and probably less than the children of tomorrow. A norm sample must be representative of the current population. Finally, tests that are used to identify children with particular problems should include children with such problems in their standardization sample.

According to Salvia, Ysseldyke and Bolt (2010, p. 50), the number of subjects in a norm sample is important for several reasons. First, the sample "should be large enough to guarantee stability." If the size of the sample is small, the norms will be undependable because another group might produce significantly different results. The larger the sample, the more stable the norms. Second, the sample should be large enough that infrequent elements in the population can be represented. Third, the sample should be large enough to produce a full range of scores. As a rule of thumb, the norm sample should contain a minimum of one hundred subjects per age or grade, although in practice the sample should have more than one hundred cases.

A third factor related to the adequacy of norms is the extent to which individuals in the norm sample can provide relevant comparisons in terms of the purpose for which the test was administered. For some purposes, national norms are the most appropriate; in other circumstances, norms developed on a particular portion of the population may be more meaningful.

The appropriate use of norms requires that users ensure that the test taker can be compared to the test takers in the norm sample. For example, if a test manual contains tables for converting raw scores to percentile ranks based on both grade and age, the test administrator should use the grade table if the norm sample was selected on the basis of grade. Similarly, she should use the age table if the norm sample was selected on the basis of age. A final note concerns the ethical issues associated with reporting and using tests with inadequate norms. If the test publisher or author recognizes that the test norms are inadequate, the test user should be explicitly cautioned (AERA, APA NCME, 1999). However, even if the publisher acknowledges inadequacies, the problems remain. As Salvia, Ysseldyke, and Bolt (2010) note, "Test-based inferences can only be correct when a test is properly normed, yields reliable scores, and has evidence for its general validity. If evidence for any one of these elements is lacking, then the inferences cannot be trusted" (p. 165). Inadequate norms can lead to serious misinterpretation of test results.

Concerns

Important information can be obtained from formal tests of reading, writing, and related areas. Many of the most serious problems with formal testing involve test abuse—that is, people using test information inappropriately. It is absolutely essential that both teachers and resource personnel be critical consumers of formal tests, to ensure that they are used properly.

It is our belief that instructional decisions should never be made solely on the basis of formal assessment instruments. It is absolutely essential that formal tests be followed up with informal measures (formative assessments) that are more reflective of classroom demands before decisions are made about placement or about instructional programs.

The public appetite for numerical answers to literacy questions has been fed by the educational community and, more recently, by the federal government. Classroom teachers and clinic personnel are often caught in the middle, forced to teach content they do not believe is useful so that students can perform well on standardized tests. We need to help the public understand both the uses and limitations of test information. Educators need to be especially alert to the types of information that are *not* available from particular tests. Much of what we know to be important in reading and writing processes is not reflected in any one formal assessment. We know that reading and writing are holistic, constructive processes that vary as a function of the interaction between learner, text, and contextual factors (see Chapter 1). However, many existing formal instruments treat reading and writing as aggregates of isolated skills. More than two decades ago, the authors of *Becoming a Nation of Readers* (R. C. Anderson et al., 1985, p. 100) identified the types of problems that continue to plague us today:

> If schools are to be held accountable for performance for reading test scores, the tests must be broad-gauged measures that reflect the ultimate goals of instruction as closely as possible. Otherwise, the energies of teachers and students may be misdirected. They may concentrate

on peripheral skills that are easily tested and readily learned. Holding a reading teacher accountable for scores on a test of, say, dividing words into syllables is like holding a basketball coach accountable for the percentage of shots players make during the pre-game warm up.

Most existing formal reading and writing assessments also imply that reading and writing are static processes—that students can be evaluated under one set of conditions and that this performance will be representative of their performance under all conditions. For example, many formal tests evaluate students on passages that are much shorter than the ones they are expected to read in their classroom texts and on tasks that do not represent authentic activities. It is then assumed that the results will generalize to reading and writing both within and outside the classroom. Many tests do not take into account differences in genre or the purposes for the reading and writing activities. Nor do they consider how students' reading and writing performance is affected by their background knowledge or their attitudes and motivation toward reading and writing. Teachers need to be aware of the limitations and take them into account in interpreting the results of these tests.

The widespread use of formal reading and writing tests makes it important to understand a number of different aspects of standardized testing in order to become a critical consumer of these types of assessment devices. The information in this section of the chapter provides the basis for guidelines for test evaluation that are discussed in the second section of the chapter.

Test Fairness

Fairness is an imprecise concept that is best viewed as a marker for a set of conditions and situations in which assessment outcomes are thought to be inaccurate or disadvantageous (Salvia, Ysseldyke, & Bolt, 2010). Concerns about fairness focus primarily on issues of bias related to the status of the individual being assessed, with regard to factors such as ethnic and racial background, gender, disability, and/or socio-economic status. These factors are also related to other issues of fairness including lack of opportunity to learn and inappropriate comparisons.

Assessment Bias.   There has been increasing attention in recent years to issues of fairness in assessment, especially related to racial, ethnic, disability, and socioeconomic status. Concern with the fairness of assessment parallels the general public's concern with providing equal rights and opportunities to all citizens. Critics have charged that many assessments are biased and discriminatory and provide barriers to educational and occupational opportunities for individuals from nonmainstream backgrounds. With regard to struggling readers and writers, the issue of fairness is a critical one, because there has been an historic overrepresentation of linguistic and racial minorities in special education programs. Indeed, this problem of "disproportionality," which appears to have remained unchanged over the past forty years (Hosp, n.d.) is one of the concerns that RTI was meant to address. Although test bias alone may not account for this problem, the fact is that placement decisions have often been made on the basis of results from one or two standardized tests.

At the most fundamental level of discussion on this topic is the fact that assessments are, almost by definition, culture-bound. It is impossible to construct an assessment that is independent of cultural content, and assumptions that assessments can be made culture-free are erroneous. Standardized tests, in particular, have typically emphasized content and values that were more familiar to white, middle-class cultures than to the languages and cultures of racial or ethnic minorities and students of lower socioeconomic status (Miller, Linn, & Gronlund, 2009).

A related issue of fairness is equal opportunity to learn what is being assessed. When a student lacks information or skill because of restricted or different opportunities to learn, inferences about what that lack of demonstrated ability means must be made with great care. Lack of opportunity to learn results from a variety of situations including inadequate financial or human resources, inadequate instruction, and student issues such as chronic health problems, and many of these problems are more common in educational settings serving low-income, minority populations.

Issues of potential racial and ethnic bias are also related to assessment results derived from inappropriate comparisons. This concern extends as well to students with disabilities. For example, if a student identified as intellectually challenged does poorly on a reading assessment with scores derived from a norming sample of students of average intellectual ability, many would consider the results of this assessment to be unfair. Similarly, comparisons should take into account issues of cultural and linguistic diversity.

Dealing with Bias.   Special efforts are now being made to correct many of the problems related to issues of fairness. Publishers employ staff members representing racial and cultural minorities, and new assessments are routinely reviewed for content that might be biased or offensive to minorities. Statistical analyses are also used to detect and remove biased items. For many years, assessment developers frequently excluded individuals with disabilities and/or people of color from the comparison groups used to establish scores. Today, however, most assessment development includes individuals from all of the larger minority groups in the United States. Unfortunately, even assessment results that are based on more broadly representative samples may be inappropriate for use with students who are members of minority groups that are unlikely to be represented in the comparison group because they make up a very small proportion of the larger population.

In considering how to deal with issues of fairness in assessment, it is important, to distinguish between the performance the assessment is intended to measure and factors that may distort the results in a biased manner. As explained in the *Standards for Educational and Psychological Testing* (AERA, APA, & NCME, 1999, p. 74),

> The idea that fairness requires equality in overall passing rates for different groups has been almost entirely repudiated in the professional testing literature. A more widely accepted view would hold that examinees of *equal standing* [emphasis added] with respect to the construct the test is intended to measure should on average earn the same test score, irrespective of group. Unfortunately, because examinees' levels of the construct are measured imperfectly, the requirement is rarely amenable to direct examination.

There are also standards of fairness for the developers and users of assessment instruments such as the *Code of Fair Testing Practices in Education* (2004), which was prepared by a Joint Committee on Testing Practices representing several professional associations. These standards are intended to apply to a wide range of published assessments that may be developed and required by school districts or states but are not applicable for assessments developed by individual teachers for use in their classrooms. The *Code* (see www.apa.org/science/fairtestcode.html) provides guidelines in four critical areas: (1) developing and selecting appropriate tests; (2) administering and scoring tests; (3) reporting and interpreting test results; and (4) informing test takers. In addition, these guidelines are offered separately for test developers and test users (see Figure 4.3 for test-user directives).

FIGURE 4.3   Code of Fair Testing Practices for Test Users

A. Developing and Selecting Appropriate Tests

TEST USERS should select tests that meet the intended purpose and that are appropriate for the intended test takers.

A-1. Define the purpose for testing, the content and skills to be tested, and the intended test takers. Select and use the most appropriate test based on a thorough review of available information.
A-2. Review and select tests based on the appropriateness of test content, skills tested, and content coverage for the intended purpose of testing.
A-3. Review materials provided by test developers and select tests for which clear, accurate, and complete information is provided.
A-4. Select tests through a process that includes persons with appropriate knowledge, skills, and training.
A-5. Evaluate evidence of the technical quality of the test provided by the test developer and any independent reviewers.
A-6. Evaluate representative samples of test questions or practice tests, directions, answer sheets, manuals, and score reports before selecting a test.
A-7. Evaluate procedures and materials used by test developers, as well as the resulting test, to ensure that potentially offensive content or language is avoided.
A-8. Select tests with appropriately modified forms or administration procedures for test takers with disabilities who need special accommodations.
A-9. Evaluate the available evidence on the performance of test takers of diverse subgroups. Determine to the extent feasible which performance differences may have been caused by factors unrelated to the skills being assessed.

B. Administering and Scoring Tests

TEST USERS should administer and score tests correctly and fairly

B-1. Follow established procedures for administering tests in a standardized manner.
B-2. Provide and document appropriate procedures for test takers with disabilities who need special accommodations or those with diverse linguistic backgrounds. Some accommodations may be required by law or regulation.
B-3. Provide test takers with an opportunity to become familiar with test question formats and any materials or equipment that may be used during testing.
B-4. Protect the security of test materials, including respecting copyrights and eliminating opportunities for test takers to obtain scores by fraudulent means.
B-5. Provide procedures, materials and guidelines for scoring the tests, and for monitoring the accuracy of the scoring process. If scoring the test is the responsibility of the test developer, provide adequate training for scorers.
B-6. If test scoring is the responsibility of the test user, provide adequate training to scorers and ensure and monitor the accuracy of the scoring process.
B-7. Correct errors that affect the interpretation of the scores and communicate the corrected results promptly.
B-8. Develop and implement procedures for ensuring the confidentiality of scores.

FIGURE 4.3   (Continued)

C. Reporting and Interpreting Test Results

TEST USERS should report and interpret test results accurately and clearly.

C-1. Interpret the meaning of the test results, taking into account the nature of the content, norms or comparison groups, other technical evidence, and benefits and limitations of test results.

C-2. Interpret test results from modified test or test administration procedures in view of the impact those modifications may have had on test results.

C-3. Avoid using tests for purposes other than those recommended by the test developer unless there is evidence to support the intended use or

C-4. Review the procedures for setting performance standards or passing scores. Avoid using stigmatizing labels.

C-5. Avoid using a single test score as the sole determinant of decisions about test takers. Interpret test scores in conjunction with other information about individuals.

C-6. State the intended interpretation and use of test results for groups of test takers. Avoid grouping test results for purposes not specifically recommended by the test developer unless evidence is obtained to support the intended use. Report procedures that were followed in determining who were and who were not included in the groups being compared and describe factors that might influence the interpretation of results.

C-7. Communicate test results in a timely fashion and in a manner that is understood by the test taker.

C-8. Develop and implement procedures for monitoring test use, including consistency with the intended purposes of the test.

D. Informing Test Takers

Test developers or test users should inform test takers about the nature of the test, test taker rights and responsibilities, the appropriate use of scores, and procedures for resolving challenges to scores.

D-1. Inform test takers in advance of the test administration about the coverage of the test, the types of question formats, the directions, and appropriate test-taking strategies. Make such information available to all test takers.

D-2. When a test is optional, provide test takers or their parents/guardians with information to help them judge whether a test should be taken—including indications of any consequences that may result from not taking the test (e.g., not being eligible to compete for a particular scholarship)—and whether there is an available alternative to the test.

D-3. Provide test takers or their parents/guardians with information about rights test takers may have to obtain copies of tests and completed answer sheets, to retake tests, to have tests rescored, or to have scores declared invalid.

D-4. Provide test takers or their parents/guardians with information about responsibilities test takers have, such as being aware of the intended purpose and uses of the test, performing at capacity, following directions, and not disclosing test items or interfering with other test takers.

D-5. Inform test takers or their parents/guardians how long scores will be kept on file and indicate to whom, under what circumstances, and in what manner test scores and related information will or will not be released. Protect test scores from unauthorized release and access.

D-6. Describe procedures for investigating and resolving circumstances that might result in canceling or withholding scores, such as failure to adhere to specified testing procedures.

D-7. Describe procedures that test takers, parents/guardians, and other interested parties may use to obtain more information about the test, register complaints, and have problems resolved.

Source: Code of Fair Testing Practices in Education. (2004). Washington, DC: Joint Committee on Testing Practices. (Mailing Address: Joint Committee on Testing Practices, Science Directorate, American Psychological Association, 750 First Street, NE, Washington, DC 20002-4242; www.apa.org/science/jctpweb.html) Contact APA for additional copies.

Summing Up.   The most controversial problems concerning the fair use of assessments are encountered when these tests are used as a basis for "high-stakes" purposes such as educational and vocational selection or placement. Much of the difficulty lies in the definition of fair use. One view is that an assessment is fair or unbiased if it predicts as accurately for minority groups as it does for the majority group. Alternative definitions of fairness in assessment favor some type of adjustment for minority groups such as separate cutoff scores or bonus points. Although it is essential for anyone dealing with assessments and their results to be aware of these issues, it is not likely that they will be addressed to everyone's satisfaction in the near future.

Guidelines for Evaluating Standardized Tests

In the sections to follow, we consider a way to analyze formal assessment data and provide information about a variety of formal assessment tools that are often used in school and clinical settings. The quality and usefulness of these tools should be considered in terms of the information we have just presented. Informed educators need to be critical consumers of assessment information. To do so, they must consider a variety of test characteristics within the context of use and interpretation. Specifically, they must consider evidence of the validity and reliability of the assessment tools for the purposes for which they are used. In addition, they must consider the methods for reporting and interpreting test scores. Finally, concerned educators need to evaluate tests for potential sources of bias and exercise care in administering and interpreting results with special populations. The outline in Figure 4.4 can be used to guide the evaluation of formal assessment tools.

TOOLS AND STRATEGIES FOR LOOKING AT SCHOOL AND CLASSROOM DATA

Educators do not need to be experts on the technical or psychometric properties of formal tests, but they can and should be careful consumers of test information. They should be able to critically evaluate the information provided by the tests themselves and know where to find critical reviews if necessary. This portion of the text is divided into two sections. First, we describe several types of formal assessment tools in the area of language arts and provide detailed descriptions and evaluations of each. Second, we provide tools and strategies for organizing and analyzing data in school contexts. Finally, we show how the group data can be used to make decisions and to identify students who require a closer look.

Formal Assessment Tools

In this section, we describe several standardized assessments that are frequently used by educators and school psychologists. The use of specific assessments varies significantly from one region of the country to another. In this chapter, we have limited our discussion to those tools that might be used to collect data on groups of students, where results might be available for many or all of your students right at the beginning of the assessment-instruction process. Other standardized tools are explored later in the text because they are more appropriate for use with individual students, for taking a closer look.

**FIGURE 4.4
Guidelines for Test
Evaluation**

General Information

Name: _____   Publication date: _____

Authors: _____   Focus area(s): _____

Target ages: _____   Type of administration: _____

Scores: _____

Interpretation of results: (Criterion-referenced, norm-referenced, or both?)

Type and Purpose

Type: Note if a survey or diagnostic test and list subtest areas.
Purpose: What purposes are stated by the author(s)?

Validity

Content-related, criterion-related, and construct-related evidence of validity:
    Definition of domain assessed; Are items representative of defined domain?;
    concurrent and/or predictive evidence; evidence of support for testable
    hypotheses derived from defined domain

Reliability

Measurement: Are reliability coefficients, test-retest, and alternate-form data
    acceptable for intended use?
Standard error of measurement: Is this acceptable?
Other factors: Sufficient numbers of items to test-specific components, to determine
    a year's growth, etc.?

Norms and Scores

Norming: Consider whether the norms and norming procedures are acceptable and
    the norming sample comparable to your students.
Scores: Note the types of scores generated and interpretations provided.

Special Considerations

Test fairness: Consider both content and use in terms of examinee's background.
Provisions for students with special problems: Consider administration flexibility,
    content, and interpretation (e.g., provision for out-of-level testing).

General Evaluation

Special features/problems of this test: Consider length, novel formats, etc.
Appropriateness for purposes and students: Consider ease of administration, time to
    score/interpret, difficulty, etc.
What do others say about this test? If possible, consult specialized colleagues, written
    reviews, etc.

Recommendations

Would you use this test?
For what? With whom?
What cautions should be exercised?

Screening and Survey Tests

According to the NCLB legislation (Title I, Part B, Subpart 1, Sec. 1208, No. 7):

> The term screening reading assessment means an assessment that is—
>
> 1. valid, reliable, and based on scientifically based reading research; and
> 2. a brief procedure designed as a first step in identifying children who may be at a high risk for delayed development or academic failure and in need of further diagnosis of their need for special services or additional reading instruction.

This definition is not unlike that used to describe survey tests, which emphasize norm-referenced interpretations of global achievement in a variety of academic areas, including the language arts. Generally speaking, the purpose of survey tests is to compare the performance of students or groups of students. They are most commonly used to screen large numbers of students for approximate levels of achievement in specific academic areas and to identify those who may have serious problems.

Because of their general nature, survey tests often lack content depth; they evaluate language arts in a most cursory fashion, using limited samples of behaviors. Also, because survey tests are intended for large general populations, they tend to estimate more accurately the ability of average students than those who are either very skilled or very unskilled. The general scores do little to indicate specifically what a student knows or has trouble with. A low score indicates only that a difficulty exists but does not reveal the nature or degree of difficulty.

Survey tests are easy to administer and score and can be useful screening devices; not all screening tests are survey tests, however. Under the "encouragement" of NCLB, many districts are screening students, especially young ones, for specific component abilities in, for example, fluency, decoding, or vocabulary.

Group survey tests are also often used to make general judgments about program success. For example, many Title I programs use a global test of achievement in reading or mathematics for program evaluation purposes. Under these circumstances, educators should be especially concerned that the evidence of validity supports the use of a test for this purpose. Average scores on these tests should parallel acceptable performance on the tasks assigned or expected in that age bracket.

Group Screening and Survey Tests

Screening tools should be quick estimates of students' overall ability. They are intended for use in identifying students who may be at risk of reading difficulties and who might benefit from a closer look. Consequently, group survey tests can be very useful for this purpose.

Gates-MacGinitie Reading Tests.   One of the most commonly used group screening tests of reading is the Gates-MacGinitie Reading Tests (MacGinitie, MacGinitie, Maria, & Dreyer, 2000). Consistent with its purpose as a survey test, the authors indicate that the Gates-MacGinitie Reading Tests (GMRT) are useful to teachers and schools for determining the general level of reading achievement of individual students throughout their entire school careers.

The fourth edition of the GMRT is substantially revised and includes several new features. At test-level PR (prereading) the four subtests address literacy concepts, oral language concepts (phonological awareness), letters and letter–sound correspondences, and listening (story) comprehension. At test level BR (beginning reading) the four subtests consist of testing on initial consonants and consonant clusters, final consonants and consonant clusters, vowels, and basic story words. There are no time limits for either level PR or BR.

Levels 1 and 2 are designed to provide a general assessment of early independent reading achievement. Levels 1 and 2 contain word and comprehension decoding subtests, and the level 2 tests include a subtest of word knowledge as well. All subtests are timed, ranging from twenty to thirty-five minutes. In a significant departure from earlier editions, the fourth edition includes much longer texts, including both exposition and narrative. Students respond by choosing among three pictures depicting the content of each segment (see Figure 4.5).

At levels 3 through AR (adult reading) the test contains two subtests, on vocabulary and comprehension, designed to provide a general estimate of students' reading achievement. The vocabulary subtest measures students' ability to identify synonyms in a multiple-choice format, and the comprehension subtest requires students to read brief passages and answer multiple-choice questions.

There are two parallel forms for each level from 2 through 6, 7/9, 10/12, and AR. The administration at these levels is timed, with the vocabulary tests taking twenty minutes and the comprehension tests taking thirty-five minutes each. As with the earlier levels, these materials have been completely revised. Comprehension passages are longer and more coherent than in earlier versions and are taken from authentic trade books and text materials. Although still much shorter than the texts read by students in these grades, they are a significant improvement over most norm-referenced multiple-choice passages, permitting at least some degree of inferential assessment (see Figure 4.6).

The authors describe specific efforts to provide evidence of the content validity of the GMRT, including careful selection of vocabulary and balancing passage content across several disciplines by developmental level. They provide readable and reasonable arguments regarding the nature of reading and the way in which it changes over time. Data on construct-related validity describe selection procedures for word items, passages, and questions. However, they do not directly provide any criterion-related evidence of validity, although this may be forthcoming in the new technical report.

Evidence of the reliability of the GMRT suggests that it ranges from acceptable to very good. Measures of internal consistency were determined for each level and each subtest, yielding reliability coefficients above .90 for all subtests and totals. Alternate-form reliabilities are also excellent for the total scores, but somewhat less so for subtests and one grade level (grade 11).

Similarly, the norming procedures for this test are good. Norms were established for the GMRT during the 1998–1999 school year, using a national sampling procedure and data from more than 40,000 students. At grades K–6, approximately five thousand students per grade were assessed, and the norming sample includes a representative proportion of black

FIGURE 4.5
Sample Comprehen-
sion Passage (drawn
from field-test
materials), Level 2,
GMRT, 2001

The Newspaper

Jane used to deliver newspapers. She carried them on her bike and threw them onto people's porches.

One day, Mr. Ross went outside to get his paper, but he couldn't find it.

He called Jane. "Did you bring my paper today?" he asked.

"I'm sure I did," Jane answered. So Mr. Ross looked again. Where did he find it?

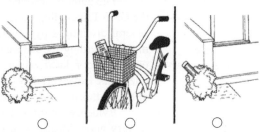

FIGURE 4.6
Sample Comprehen-
sion Passage (drawn
from field-test
materials), Level 3,
GMRT, 2001

On a tiny island in a vast blue sea, in a circle of stones, sits a little white egg. Pepe is born.

The first thing he sees is a pair of bright blue feet. His mama and papa are blue-footed boobies. They feed Pepe fish from the sea, and soon he is a little cloud of downy feathers.

There is danger in the sky. Big, hungry frigate birds and sharp-eyed hawks are watching. But Pepe is lucky. He and his world grow bigger.

Pepe looks up at the wide, blue sky and flaps his wings. But his feet will not leave the ground. Not yet.

Then one day he flaps his wings and this time they lift him high on the wind to join a flock of his kind.

10. What was Pepe's nest like?

O Hard

O Feathery

O Wet

O White

11. The cloud was really

O A white egg

O Blue feet

O Danger

O Pepe

O Wet White

12. What does the danger come from?

O Sharks

O Other birds

O The sun

O A strong wind.

13. Why don't Pepe's feet leave the ground at first?

O His world is too big

O He is tied down

O He is too young

O He looks up too quickly

Source: From *Linking Testing to Teaching*, pp. 15–16, by W. H. MacGinitie, R. K. MacGinitie, K. Maria, and L. Dreyer. Copyright © 2001. Reprinted by permission of Riverside Publishing, a Houghton Mifflin Company.

and Hispanic students. At grades 7 through 10, there were approximately three thousand students per grade level. The numbers for grades 11 and 12 were much smaller. Norms are available for all times of the year, and a broad range of out-of-level norms is also available. For example, for the grade 5 test level, norms are available for 3.1 through 12.9.

Finally, the GMRT authors have made extensive efforts to remove bias from the test items and from both the content and the scoring. During field testing, responses that favored one racial group over another were removed or revised. Similarly, gender-biased responses were eliminated or balanced with other items.

A feature new to the fourth edition of the GMRT is *Linking Testing to Teaching: A Classroom Resource for Reading Assessment and Instruction*, developed and written by the same authors. These exceptionally helpful manuals provide information about how to interpret the results of the GMRT; information about how to extend the assessment information through informal, classroom-based assessments such as retelling and think-aloud; and excellent instructional guidance focused on aspects of reading tapped by the GMRT. These materials increase the likelihood that teachers will use the test results in appropriate ways.

Nelson-Denny Reading Test, Forms G and H.   The Nelson-Denny Reading Test (Brown, Fishco, & Hanna, 1993) is a timed test designed to measure high school and college students' ability as regards vocabulary, reading comprehension, and reading rate. The test has been in use since 1929. The basic format has remained the same, but the test has been revised several times and is now available on CD-ROM. The latest revision, contained in Forms G and H, was completed in 1993 and attempts to reduce the time pressure students may feel as they complete the test. The test contains two sections: Vocabulary and Comprehension. The vocabulary section includes eighty items, and Comprehension consists of seven short reading passages and thirty-eight multiple-choice questions. To obtain a measure of reading rate, students are given one minute during which they begin reading the first passage in the comprehension section. They are asked to record the number of the line they are reading at the end of the minute. Students are given a total of thirty-five minutes to complete the entire test. The latest revision, however, also includes directions for administration and norms for students who are provided extended time (a total of fifty-six minutes) to complete the test. Test scores can be converted into percentiles, grade equivalents, standard scores, and stanines.

The selection of items and passages for the most recent form seems reasonable. The vocabulary words and passages in the comprehension section represent a range of difficulty and are taken from high school and college social studies, science, and humanities texts that were in use in the 1990s. Care was taken to support the assertion that the test does not systematically favor students of a particular racial group. However, the norms are perhaps biased. Middle-income students were overrepresented in the normative sample, so care should be taken in interpreting the norms of students from lower SES levels (Murray-Ward, 1998; Smith, 1998).

Beyond the ample description of test fairness, little evidence of validity is offered. The standard error of measurement and related reliability coefficients reported for Forms G and H appear adequate, as do the alternate-form reliabilities. Some estimates of reliability appear low, however. For example, the reliability of reading-rate scores obtained from students who took both Form G and H ($r = .68$) calls into question interpretation of these scores. This could very well be because the reading rate score does not take into account differences in purposes for reading and type and complexity of the text. Despite its age, the Nelson-Denny remains in use because it is one of the few tests that is designed for use with adolescents and young adults. Because of the several concerns already noted, the Nelson-Denny Reading Test is probably best used only for screening purposes.

The Learning and Study Strategies Inventory—2nd Edition (LASSI). This is a somewhat different type of screening instrument, developed originally by Weinstein and her colleagues and recently revised (Weinstein & Palmer, 2002). It is a thoughtfully conceived standardized test with national norms, designed to assess the metacognitive and study strategies of high school and college students.

The LASSI is a ten-scale, eighty-item assessment with subtests organized around several large component areas involving "skill, will, and self-regulation" designed to provide information about how students conceive of studying. This group-administered test asks students to report and evaluate their own behaviors, attitudes, and beliefs about learning and studying. The original form of the LASSI (Weinstein, Schulte & Palmer, 1987) consisted of seventy-seven items that are distributed among ten scales: (1) attitude, (2) motivation, (3) time management, (4) anxiety, (5) concentration, (6) information-processing, (7) selecting main idea, (8) study aids, (9) self-testing, and (10) test strategies. Students respond to each item on a five-point Likert scale ranging from "not at all typical of me" to "very typical of me."

Weinstein, Schulte, and Palmer (1987) reported internal consistency (coefficient alpha) for the scaled scores ranging from 0.68 to 0.86 and test-retest reliability coefficients ranging from 0.72 to 0.85 for the scaled scores. For the LASSI-2, items were updated and culled (with dated items removed). The authors report that they widened the scope of some scales and created an equal number of items for each scale. They also broadened their norming sample, which, nevertheless, remains small and limited to specific institutional types. For the LASSI-2, Weinstein, Schulte, and Palmer, report that the lowest coefficient is .73 and that most exceed .80. However, given the amount of research conducted using the LASSI, the technical information is somewhat sparse. Validity must be derived from theoretical studies supporting the uniqueness of the subtests. It is clear that only three large component areas can be distinguished for diagnostic purposes. Despite its limitations, most reviewers agree that this test is unique and offers important potential screening/diagnostic information (e.g., Prevat et al., 2006). Given the dearth of assessment tools focused on adolescents, we recommend the test because of its well-conceived theoretical and research base.

DIBELS. DIBELS assessments (Good & Kaminski, 2003) were developed to identify children in need of intervention and evaluate the effectiveness of intervention strategies (Good, Gruba, & Kaminski, 2002). These screening and monitoring functions make DIBELS a widely used assessment in Reading First programs and also in areas that have been implementing RTI. Perhaps no single test has caused more discussion and debate than this one. Because it is a mandated assessment in many states and/or federally-sponsored programs, schools and teachers have viewed it as a high-stakes program assessment. It is used for screening, monitoring, and program evaluation.

DIBELS is a set of timed, individually administered assessments that yield scores for sound fluency, letter-naming fluency, phoneme-segmentation fluency, nonsense-word fluency, and oral reading fluency. The entire test takes no longer than fifteen or twenty minutes to administer. Each subtest is administered in one to three minutes. Test materials are available at little cost (indeed, they can be downloaded for free from the Internet). DIBELS addresses:

- Phonemic awareness—subtests
- Early kindergarten (three minutes): Identify which picture begins with a particular sound
- Late kindergarten to grade 1 (two minutes): Phoneme segmentation
- Letter naming (one minute),
- Decoding skills (two minutes): Nonsense-word reading focused on VC and CVC spelling patterns
- Oral reading fluency (one minute): Read aloud brief passage for one minute—scored for speed and accuracy
- Reading comprehension (one minute): Recall what was read from the passage
- Vocabulary (one minute): Provide an oral sentence using specific words

Perhaps the most serious criticisms leveled at DIBELS involve the difficulty in accessing technical information about the validity and reliability of the test. It is possible to find some information, but it requires persistent efforts and the reading of multiple reports. There is no technical manual for the test, and its development is far from typical, leaving reliability measures, for example, somewhat meaningless. In his review of the DIBELS, Shanahan (2005) identifies alternate-form reliabilities from .64 to .97, depending on the subtest. However, these are difficult to interpret given the lack of data about what was being compared. A pervasive problem is the lack of coherent and consistent equating of texts and tasks. Much of the technical information that is available is based on teacher-reported data, a serious problem when considering the complex nature of the tasks.

The authors argue that these brief tests are excellent predictors of student performance on other, more authentic measures and also on subsequent student performance. According to Good, Gruba, and Kaminski (2002), "as early as fall of kindergarten, we are able to predict, with a high degree of accuracy, which children will have significant difficulty learning essential literacy skills" (p. 682). Unfortunately, there is considerable data to suggest either that these tests do not predict as well as the authors suggest or that significant caveats are necessary in using the results (see Goodman, 2006; Pressley, Hilden, & Shankland, 2005; Valencia, 2007; Valencia et al., 2004). For example, Hintze, Ryan, and Stoner (2003) concluded that, "analysis of decision accuracy [for the DIBELS] indicated that using the author-suggested cut scores resulted in extremely high sensitivity; however, this was at the expense of an inordinate number of false positives" (p. 541). Pressley (2006) draws the same conclusion.

Many authors conclude that there is interesting and useful information to be gleaned from the DIBELS (see, e.g., Shanahan, 2005). However, it is clear that this test is being used in ways that are problematic (see discussion of consequential validity above). Most seriously, the frequent administration and the instructional planning that is being done as a result leads educators to focus *solely* on speed, neglecting other important outcomes and abilities. Virtually every reviewer notes that there is no sensible measure of vocabulary or comprehension associated with this test. Though it is likely an adequate measure of speed at the letter, sound, and word levels, it should not be mistaken as a comprehensive measure of reading or as an adequate predictor of subsequent reading achievement.

Curriculum-Based Measures (AIMSweb).   The DIBELS tests just described are a form of standardized *curriculum-based measures (CBM)*. Perhaps the most widely used of this type of assessment today are the assessments posted on AIMSweb. We will discuss CBMs much more thoroughly in later chapters (see Chapters 8 and 9), because they are widely used for the purpose of progress monitoring—both benchmark and formative. However, AIMSweb is widely used for *every-pupil screening* as well, and it is important to acknowledge that some schools have this type of data on all students. Indeed, the example we share in the next section involves a school that uses CBM data. CBMs typically involve collecting oral reading accuracy data during very brief oral reading episodes (one-minute readings of texts, sometimes called "probles"). As a result, CBMs are also often called ORF tests (for oral reading fluency). The scores that result are numbers that indicate how many words a student read correctly in one minute (WCPM) (see Chapters 8 and 9). So, for example, a score of 68 means that the student read 68 words correctly in a one-minute period. There are a set of normative cut scores that inform the teacher about whether a student is considered at risk or not. Because it is quick and relatively easy, many educators find it useful as a screening device. Used *in combination with other assessments*, it can be helpful. For further information about collecting and interpreting oral reading accuracy and fluency we direct you to Chapters 8 and 9.

Group Diagnostic Tests

Diagnostic tests are designed to provide a profile of a student's relative strengths and weaknesses. Diagnostic tests differ from survey tests in a number of ways (see Linn & Miller, 2004). The number of subtest scores and the number of items are larger than for assessment tools, the items are devised to measure specific skills, and difficulty tends to be lower in order to provide adequate discrimination among students with problems. For example, rather than providing one or two general scores that represent a student's overall performance in reading, diagnostic tests break the domain of reading into various components such as knowledge of phonics, structural analysis, literal comprehension, inferential comprehension, and reading rate, and provide scores for each of these areas. The rationale underlying diagnostic tests is that instruction can be planned to help a student improve in areas where performance is low.

To have confidence in a diagnostic test, test users must satisfy their concerns for construct-related evidence of validity. It is entirely possible that a subtest is measuring nothing of consequence or that it measures something that does not lend itself to instruction. Ultimately, the utility of diagnostic tests relies entirely on the relationship between the subtests and the prevailing conceptions of what is important to learn in a particular area or discipline—both from the users' views and those of the school curriculum. Secondarily, these subtests should involve distinct component areas and not some global "reading" ability. When subtest scores are too highly correlated with the overall reading score, it may raise questions about the unique contribution of this diagnostic component.

Recently, specific reading programs have begun to publish their own diagnostic assessments. The *Word Identification and Spelling Test* (WIST) (Wilson & Felton, 2004), for example, is a norm-referenced diagnostic test of decoding and spelling that is tightly linked to specific instructional programs (the Wilson and Orton-Gillingham–based reading programs). Although the authors note that they intended to create a generally applicable diagnostic test of the key area of decoding and spelling, the test items are selected directly from the instructional program, calling into question the generalizability of the results. As always, multiple assessments (both formal and informal) of specific reading abilities are more likely to yield dependable and authentic results. Diagnostic tests can be individually or group administered and provide either norm- or criterion-referenced interpretations or both. Individual-administered assessments include the Woodcock Reading Mastery Test—Revised (Woodcock, 1987) and the Test of Written Language (TOWL-4; Hammil & Larsen, 2010). Others, such as the Gray Oral Reading Test—4 (Wiederholt & Bryant, 2001), have IRI-type oral reading tests. Finally, those that address important aspects of the foundations of literacy include the Test of Word Reading Efficiency, or TOWRE (Torgesen, Wagner, & Rashotte, 1999). Diagnostic tests will be discussed more fully in Chapter 8.

A Group-Administered Diagnostic Test: The Stanford Diagnostic Reading Test. The fourth edition of the Stanford Diagnostic Reading Test, or SDRT4 (Karlsen & Gardner, 1995) is the latest version of a widely used group diagnostic test. There are six test levels from first grade through junior college: Red, grades 1.5 and 2.5; Orange, grades 2.5 and 3.5; Green, grades 3.5 and 4.5; Purple, grades 4.5 to 6.5; Brown, grades 6.5 to 8.9; and Blue, grades 9 to 12.9. It is a multiple-choice test, with a single format for each of the first three levels and two alternate forms at each of the upper three levels.

The manual indicates that the SDRT4 views reading as a developmental process that encompasses four major components: decoding, vocabulary, comprehension, and scanning. The subtests of the SDRT4 reflect this view. For example, auditory vocabulary is assessed only at the lowest two levels and phonetic analysis at the lowest three levels. Reading vocabulary is measured at all levels but the lowest, and scanning is measured only at the top three levels. Reading comprehension is measured at all levels, although with some variations, such as the use of cloze in addition to comprehension questions at the lowest two levels.

The stated purpose of the SDRT4 is to diagnose students' strengths and weaknesses in the major components of the reading process. The SDRT4 results can be used to help teachers challenge students who are doing well and provide assistance for others who lack some of the essential reading skills. Although the manual suggests that this test is appropriate for evaluating program effectiveness, for measuring student gains, and for reporting to the community, we believe that most people prefer a more global test of reading behavior for these purposes.

The SDRT4 is a timed test, requiring from one and a half to two hours, depending on the level. Raw scores, for both subtests and total tests, are easily converted to percentile ranks and stanine scores. Schools may also choose scoring options that include scaled scores, grade equivalents, and normal curve equivalents (NCEs). In addition, criterion-referenced interpretation is offered.

Salvia, Ysseldyke, and Bolt (2010) conclude about the SDRT4 that is well standardized and is reliable enough to identify specific strengths and weaknesses in the reading domains that are represented. They also note that judgments of validity should be made based on the content that is tested and the construct of reading that is used by the local school or district.

The Group Reading Assessment and Diagnostic Evaluation (GRADE). Like the SDRT4, the GRADE (Williams, 2001) is a norm-referenced test of reading achievement. It can be group administered, is untimed, and takes from sixty to ninety minutes depending on age/grade. It is normed for students from preschool (age four) to twelfth grade (eighteen). There are two parallel forms at each grade level, covering five aspects of reading (depending on the test level): prereading, reading readiness, vocabulary, comprehension, and oral language. The test was normed on a large group of students that approximated U.S. census levels with respect to region, gender, community size and type, and socioeconomic status. However, the sample contained fewer low-income students and more high-income students than the overall population. As is often the case in achievement tests, the overall reliability of the test is excellent, but the reliability of data from some subtests is less so. The authors provide evidence of validity, primarily by providing correlations with other similar tests. Used as a global measure of students reading achievement and an indicator of general reading ability, this test is a good one, although it would be useful to examine the subtests and ensure that they reflect the reading process as it is conceived and taught in your district. For example, comprehension is assessed with very brief passages and multiple-choice questions. Students who perform well on the GRADE may not necessarily perform equally well on longer texts with different tasks.

Outcome Measures

Most schools and school districts do not use norm-referenced achievements as often as they did in the past. Instead, they rely heavily on state assessments that are typically standards (criterion) referenced. When teachers look at their classroom data, it will typically include the achievement level (usually 1–4, with 3 being proficient) for each student in the class. Many schools encourage all of the grade-level teachers to meet to examine the data by grade level for all students, to explore trends in student performance or examine disaggregated items.

For now, the important thing to recognize is that these state assessments may be dramatically different than the norm-referenced achievement tests just described. They are typically untimed and may be administered over a period of days. For reading, they often involve reading much longer texts, and students may be required to respond to both multiple-choice and constructed-response prompts (long and short written responses). In some places, students are asked to use evidence from the test and may be asked to compare and contrast two or more selections. Similarly, in writing, students may be asked to analyze the writing of others (with multiple-choice or constructed response) and are generally expected to write one or more pieces in response to a prompt. Figure 4.7, shows an excerpt from a folktale that is similar to the texts used on state assessments in the Northeast. After reading the passage, fourth graders are asked multiple-choice questions, but they must also answer "constructed response" questions such as: "What challenge does the tortoise make to the whale and the elephant?" and "Why did the tortoise make this challenge? Use details from the story." In writing at grade 5, students respond to a range of short answer items that test their ability

FIGURE 4.7

Excerpt from folk tale similar to the texts used on state assessments in the Northeast

THE TORTOISE AND THE ELEPHANT

I. THE TUG OF WAR

IN the long ago, the tortoise, the elephant, and the whale were good friends. In those days the whale often walked with his friends on the land.

One day the tortoise and the elephant were walking by the seashore.

"Friend Elephant," said the tortoise, "I can pull you into the water."

"No, you can't," replied the elephant, "you're not big enough."

"Yes, I can," was the answer. "Take hold of this rope and I'll show you."

The elephant was much amused at the little creature's challenge, but caught the end of the rope with his trunk to please him.

FIGURE 4.7
(Continued)

The tortoise picked up the other end and slipped into the water. There he met his friend, the whale.

"Friend Whale," said he, "I can pull you out of the water."

"No, you can't," replied the whale. "You're not strong enough."

"Let's try and see," said the tortoise. "Take this end of the rope."

The big whale laughingly caught the rope with his flippers and threw it over his head. Then the little tortoise swam back to land. The whale pulled and pulled with all his might.

"Brother Tortoise must be very strong," said he. "If I don't pull harder, he will soon have me out of the water."

The elephant pulled and tugged at the other end, but felt himself losing ground. Then he gave the rope a sudden jerk. Snap! it went in the middle, and the clumsy elephant rolled over and over on the sand. Splash! went the whale into the water, and there he has remained ever since.

to correct or enhance existing writing samples. For example, they might be asked, "Where should a comma be added to the sentence below: I turned five on September 4 2003, the same day school started." However, they must also write more-lengthy answers to prompts that include writing about their favorite foods, responding to a poem, and using information provided to write a report.

The results from these assessments are summarized in a number of ways. Schools get grade-by-grade data, including results for all students, and results for disaggregated groups of students (e.g., boys vs. girls and ELLs vs. non-ELLs, etc.). In this way, schools and teachers can examine overall performance. At the individual class level, teachers receive results for each student, indicating his or her achievement level and the overall score on the test.

USING FORMAL ASSESSMENT DATA TO IDENTIFY STRUGGLING READERS AND WRITERS

Data Analysis Guidelines

Data should invite action (White, 2005). Teachers and administrators should use data to help them decide what to do. If the data are not used or are not appropriate for the types of decisions to be made, then collecting the information is a waste of time and resources. Questions and actions such as the following are worth considering at the systems level (see NCREL, 2000; White, 2005):

- How do you use data to inform instruction and improve student achievement?
- How do you determine which data are the most important to use, analyze, or review?
- How do the various types of assessment data compare, or do they? And contrast?
- In the absence of data, what is used as a basis for instructional decisions?
- What does student achievement look like (in, e.g., reading and/or writing)?
- What variables that affect student achievement are within your control?
- Identify or look for patterns and trends. Can these be explained?
- Are the results what you expected?
- How do you currently explain your results in student achievement?
- Decide what actions are required.

After thinking globally about how data are used in your school or district, you can begin to look at the data you have. There are any number of ways to do this. Many people argue that having some sort of visual representation of the data is helpful. In looking at the overall picture, tables and graphs can be effective. Frost and Buhle (2009) suggest that the following questions should accompany an examination of the data:

- What do you notice?
- What percentage of our students are achieving at expected levels? Above expected levels? Below expected levels?
- What can we do to better meet the needs of our struggling students? Our students who are excelling?
- Where were we last year?

Using Data to Make Decisions

As we noted earlier, teachers may find themselves in the position of having a great deal of assessment data but very little information. Summary or profile sheets assist us in analyzing and synthesizing information in ways that help us make decisions and communicate with parents and administrators. This summary information includes forms and formats for looking at groups of students, and it also includes individual summary charts for students who we want to look at more closely. In this chapter, we are describing some of the tools and strategies for gathering information for Step 1 of the assessment-instruction process.

One format for beginning to look at groups of students in was introduced in Chapter 3 (see Figure 3.3). This type of data display moves the aggregated data to the level of specific students, who are judged to be at various levels of proficiency.

There are other ways to summarize and/or display group data. More or less simultaneously, several educator/researchers proposed variations on a technique that is. sometimes called an *assessment wall* (Dorn & Soffos, 2001; Kerbow, Gwynne, & Jacob, 1999) and sometimes called a *data wall* (Reeves, 2006), the techniques are different, but the intentions are similar. The work of Reeves and his colleagues involves more use of data for systemic purposes. Dorn and her colleagues have developed an elaborated set of procedures to help teachers and specialists examine data to monitor progress, plan instruction, and identify specific students for further assessment. According to Dorn & Soffos (2001), the purposes of the assessment wall are to:

- chart, monitor, and study students' progress over time.
- monitor the effectiveness of instruction.
- make data visible so that all those involved can see how every student in the school is progressing.
- allow for the study of certain groups of students and their performance.
- ensure that students who are performing below grade level standards level are receiving appropriate tiers of intervention. (p. 97)

An example of an assessment wall is presented in Figure 4.8. This one was developed by a school in Wisconsin and shows student performance for the whole school at two points in the year (Meyer & Reindl, 2010). As Meyer and Reindl explain,

> The four pocket charts divide our wall into four sections, one for each proficiency level. Moving left to right, the pocket charts are labeled as below, approaching, meeting, and exceeding. Down the left side of the wall we placed cards to label each row of the assessment wall, beginning with kindergarten reading. The second row is kindergarten writing, followed by first grade reading, first grade writing, etc. until we have rows for reading and writing all the way through fifth grade. (p. 124)

A simply glance at the wall can tell you that many more students were exceeding the standard at the end of the year. A closer examination of individual cards can provide information about specific children. Dorn and Soffos (2010) have produced a helpful video showing how to construct and use the assessment wall, and Frost, Buhle, and Blachowicz (2009) share a number of helpful forms and formats to support the use of an assessment wall. Basically, the wall is constructed of four large pocket charts that hang side by side and "represent categories of students who have been determined to be at a below basic, basic, proficient, or advanced level of literacy progress in reading and writing. Each student in the school is represented by a card placed in one of these categories on the assessment wall" (Dorn & Henderson, 2010, p. 109). The specific identity of each student is protected from public view by the use of a coding system. "For example, the code -2-03-15 represents a student in grade 2, assigned to teacher 3, with a corresponding student number of 15" (p. 109).

Both Dorn and Reeves emphasize the need to use multiple sources of data in drawing conclusions about students. Dorn and her colleagues, especially, emphasize the use on ongoing

FIGURE 4.8
Assessment Wall
at Two Points in the
Year

Beginning-of-Year Assessments

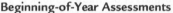
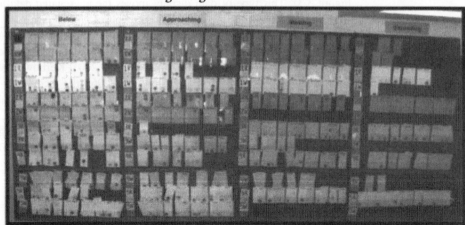

End-of-Year Assessment

Source: Meyer, K. E., & Reindle, B. L. (2010). Spotlight on the Comprehensive Intervention Model: The Case of Washington School for Comprehensive Literacy. In M. Lipson & K. Wixson (Eds.), *Successful approaches to RTI* (p. 125). Newark, DE: International Reading Association.

and formative assessments. Throughout this text, we demonstrate various types of assessment that can be included in what is called a "portfolio of assessments" (Meyer & Reindl, 2010). Even without a complex, school-wide system of assessment, however, there are ways to use data to identify students who deserve a closer look and/or a more differentiated instruction.

Using Data at the Classroom Level

In Figure 4.9, you can see a listing of the fall assessment results for the third-grade class-room of Mrs. Peters (pseudonym). These include results from the Gates MacGinitie Reading Tests (4th edition). As you have read above, these are norm-referenced timed tests of

FIGURE 4.9 Mrs. Peters's Classroom Assessment Data for Fall

Grade 3 Fall 2010 2011 Reading Assessment Data	Special Ed	ELL	FRL	Gates Vocab Fall	Gates Comp Fall	Gates Total Fall	AIMS CBM Fall	AIMS CBM Winter	NECAP FALL 2010 READING SCALED SCORE	NECAP FALL 2010 READING ACHIEVEMENT LEVEL
Milyne Bongwalanga		yes	F	63	37	5	101	98	353	3
Sudhamayi Bangalore		yes	F	54	23	4	82	105	353	3
Sadie Beltran				93	88	8		99	360	4
Tyler Bailey				51	56	6	188	160	364	4
Charlie Chase				60	47	5	40	69	337	2
Tabari Dodson			F	33			48	63	345	3
Arkin Ganiyev		yes		12	23	3	103	99	330	1
Michael Gage				25	71	5	110	105	347	3
Lesley Hawkins				91	97	9	133	151	373	4
Theo Morgan	yes			2	1	1	36	64	333	2
Sullivan O'Hare			F	76	82	7	117	156	353	3
Roan Perkins	yes			19	14	3	55	73	346	3
Ellie Reeves			F	Not Complete	26		54	93	353	3
Jaidyn Shelley				25	13	3	66	87	340	3
Oliver Stevens				47	68	6	88	121	346	3
Cody Stuart			F	38	42	5	88	96	355	3
Andrew Singer				63	63	6	112	140	355	3
Laila Ting				83	59	6	129	138	359	4
Anil Parajuli (NP)		yes	F	5	1	1	43	44	329	1
Keegan Walton				36	14	3	64	105	337	2
Mona Wilson				99	93	9	129	106	351	3

comprehension and vocabulary that result in standardized scores comparing each student with others in the same age/grade group (norming sample). Briefly, remember that:

■ Scores are distributed between the 1st percentile and the 99th percentile. The 50th percentile is considered average. A student whose score is in the 60th percentile is performing better than 59 percent of the norming sample.
■ Stanine scores range from 1 to 9, with 1 representing the lowest and 9 the highest. A score of 5 is the most common stanine because it falls directly on the mean, where most of the student scores are located. Each stanine encompasses a range of percentile scores.
■ The NCE (normal curve equivalent) is a standard score that has a fixed mean (average) score of 50. Students who have NCE scores above 50 are doing better than average.

Also in Figure 4.9, you can see the results of the AIMSweb subtest, the WCPM. As you may recall, this is a one-minute test of oral reading accuracy and automaticity. Finally, the fall results from the statewide standards-based assessment (NECAP) are available. In this school, teachers can see whether students have met the standards in reading and math (scores of 3 and 4), and they can also see the total score so that they can tell when students are very near the edge of a "cut score." When we look at the test results from Mrs. Peter's room, we can notice:

■ For total reading scores on the Gates MacGinitie, twelve of twenty-one students are at or above average (stanine 5 or higher).
■ Four of these students are well above average (stanines 7–9).
■ There are another two students who met the standard on the state test (with ambiguous Gates data).

There are other things to notice about these screening results. For example, students didn't always perform equally well on the vocabulary and comprehension subtests. For these students, the total score sometimes masks important information. Consider Sudhamayi Bangalore, for example. She scored at the stanine 5 for vocabulary (54th percentile) but stanine 3 for comprehension (23rd percentile). Her total score of stanine 4 masks this, although the added information from the NECAP and the AIMSweb suggests that she may be in better shape than the one subtest suggests.

Other screening data from AIMSweb suggest why some students may not have done well on the Gates-MacGinitie Test. Since it is timed, rate and fluency may affect some students. Tabari is an interesting example in this regard. His very low AIMSweb score of 48 WCPM likely accounts for the fact that he did not finish the comprehension subtest of the Gates. On the other hand, the NECAP, which is actually more demanding in terms of the types of comprehension tasks it employs, is not timed, and he was able to meet the standard on that test.

Mrs. Peters has her hands full with such a diverse class of students. There is not only a wide range of student abilities, but also several first languages. Milyne was born in the United States but speaks French and Lingala (a Congolese language) at home. Both

Sudhamayi and Anil are from India but speak different home languages. Arkin's family is from Uzbekistan. Looking at the multiple pieces of evidence available to her, the teacher could conclude that many are doing very well. That said, several students are clearly struggling. Mrs. Peters and her colleagues will discuss them and, in some cases, plan for further assessment. Among the students who definitely deserve attention are Arkin, Theo, Anil, Keegan, and Jaidyn.

Both Theo and Anil were tested using out-of-level testing procedures and both are already receiving attention (Theo on an IEP and Anil through ELL). Arkin too is receiving support, from the ELL teacher. All three of these students will require ongoing assessment to ensure that they are responding to instruction (see later chapters). Jaidyn performed poorly on the Gates and on the AIMSweb but *did* meet the standards on the NECAP. He, like Tabari (above), is likely to respond to instruction focused on building fluency. Keegan, however, is performing below expectations on all three assessments and is not currently receiving support or intervention from any source. Thus, Mrs. Peters decides that he deserves a closer look.

Once we have identified the student or students who we want to look at more closely, we have found it helpful to use a summary chart that we call the *thumbnail sketch* to facilitate and monitor decision making as we work through the steps of the assessment-instruction process (see Figure 4.10). This chart, or any form of written summary for that matter, forces us to think carefully about the important factors operating in individual cases. It can also identify areas about which we need more information. We will use the thumbnail-sketch format throughout the text as we follow two students who were identified during Step 1 as students who could benefit from a closer look.

GETTING STARTED WITH ASSESSMENT-INSTRUCTION

Finding the time to examine data and use it to make decisions, much less to conduct in-depth assessments on individual students, is problematic. One solution to the problem of achieving both in-depth and ongoing evaluation is to create strong collaborative working arrangements among classroom teachers and specialists or resource personnel. Classroom teachers can benefit from the assistance of specialists in obtaining more-detailed information about students and how they perform in a variety of settings. Support personnel can benefit from the assistance of classroom teachers in obtaining continuous assessments of students' knowledge, skills, and attitudes in various classroom contexts. This type of collaboration also allows teachers and specialists to coordinate their instructional efforts and evaluate the extent to which students are able to transfer their knowledge and skills from one setting to another. Schools are increasingly promoting teacher collaboratives (sometimes called professional learning communities or teacher learning communities), because these approaches have an impressive research base to support school change (see DuFour & Eaker, 1998; DuFour, DuFour, & Eaker, 2008; McLaughlin & Talbert, 2006).

Teacher reflection is a critical component of successful assessment. The Getting Started step requires using existing assessment data to make decisions. Some schools have more of this type of assessment information than do others, and this factor will influence

FIGURE 4.10 Thumbnail Sketch for Focus Students

Using Data to Understand Groups of Students and Identify Struggling Learners **(Step 1)** Chapter 4	Information About the Reading-Writing Context **(Step 2)** Chapters 5 & 6	Information About the Learner **(Step 3)** Chapters 7–9	Reflection, Decision Making, and Planning **(Step 4)** Chapter 10	Diagnostic Teaching and Continuous Progress Monitoring **(Step 5)** Chapter 10
Assessment Data: Reading: Writing: Other: **Focus Students** (list) who need further attention: **Progress Indicators:** Key Correlates: **Additional Data** about focus students or individual:				

FIGURE 4.11a
Tha'm's Thumbnail
Sketch: Getting
Started

Information about Tha'm gathered in the Getting Started step is summarized here. (Other information will be added later.)

Getting Started (Step 1)

About the Reading and Writing Context (Step 2)

Background

Name: Tha'm
Age: 10   Grade: 5
Key Correlates:

■ Average IQ

■ First Language: Vietnamese

■ Normal vision, hearing, and overall health

Whole-Class Data

Statewide Assessment:

■ Met the proficiency standard in reading for grades 3, 4, 5.

■ In reading at 5, she is just 1 point above the cut score.

■ In writing at grade 5, she is "partially proficient." ORF Data:

■ DIBELS results suggest "no risk" at end of grade 3.

Additional Data Available

■ ELL assessments show her to be reaching age-appropriate language proficiency in speaking, reading and writing.

■ Placed in grade-level core program.

■ Uneven classroom performance in grade 5.

what happens next for students who are identified for further assessment and/or more-focused instruction.

The Cases of Tha'm and Kyle

Information gleaned from various state, district, and school assessments should be summarized on the thumbnail sketch. Figure 4.11 gives two samples of what this looks like in the Getting Started step. The data reproduced here are summaries about Tha'm and about Kyle, who will be used frequently throughout the book to illustrate ongoing assessment.

Tha'm.   Tha'm was a fifth-grade student who was 10 years, 4 months old when her classroom teacher became concerned about her progress in reading and writing, which seemed to be "stalled" and "inconsistent." The teacher began to work with the reading specialist and an outside consultant (one of the authors) to determine whether she should be identified as a student who needed a closer look. The school used an array of assessment data to make decisions about students. The team looked first at the standards-based state-mandated test of reading and writing, administered in the fall of grade 5. Tha'm's score placed her in

**FIGURE 4.11b
Kyle's Thumbnail
Sketch: Getting
Started**

Getting Started (Step 1)	About the Reading and Writing Context (Step 2)
Background Name: Kyle Age: 6½ Grade: 1 Key Correlates: ■ Normal vision, hearing, and overall health/development ■ Difficult time "paying attention" **Whole-Class Data** Portfolio Review: Reading ■ Running records throughout grade 1 suggest that Kyle is making progress. ■ He does meet the benchmark for end of grade 1. Portfolio Review: Writing ■ He is able to reflect on his own writing and demonstrates an awareness of both craft and mechanics. ■ He takes risk in his writing, but spelling and volume are both less developed than for his peers. **Additional Data Available** ■ Says he doesn't really like to read—would rather play and build. ■ Cooperative and willing to work both in school and in extra sessions.	

the "proficient" range for reading, but just barely; indeed, her score was just 1 point above the cut score. In writing, that same test placed her at the very low end of "partially proficient." These results suggested that other existing data should be examined.

Tha'm had been in the same school since kindergarten, when she entered as a non-English-speaking student. Extensive and careful narrative records over the years of schooling were evident in her school records file. Tha'm's first language was Vietnamese and her family speaks only Vietnamese at home. Although she had entered school speaking no English, she had made steady progress in school. She was continuing to participate in an ESL/ELL pullout program designed to strengthen her English language abilities. Her school records contained the results of periodic ACCESS for ELLs English Proficiency Test, and her most recent evaluation suggested that she had achieved age-appropriate English (oral) language abilities in speaking, reading, and comprehension. This assessment also suggested that Tha'm might experience greater difficulties in writing and listening than in reading English, a finding consistent with the state assessment results.

School records also indicated that Tha'm had met the standards on the DIBELS assessments for the several years she was in primary school, suggesting that she had adequate word accuracy and fluency skills.

The specific areas of reading and writing difficulty suggested that Tha'm's background and prior knowledge may have contributed to her present performance. However, before we looked more closely, we felt that an investigation of the instructional context and her response to it was critical (see Chapters 5 and 6).

Kyle.   Kyle was just starting second grade in a multiage K–2 classroom. He had been with the same teacher, Ms. McIntyre, since kindergarten. Ms. McIntyre knew he had made progress, but he had struggled and she wanted to review and evaluate his literacy development to make the most of his last year with her, as well as to ask questions about possible referral for special services.

Like many schools, Kyle's school did not conduct every-pupil assessments before third grade. School records did include a literacy portfolio on each student. These included periodic running records, a reading log, and frequent self-reflections and written responses. A review of these formative assessments indicated that Kyle knew a great deal about his own emerging abilities (see Figure 4.12). These portfolios also supported the teacher's

FIGURE 4.12
Kyle's Reflections on Writing Progress

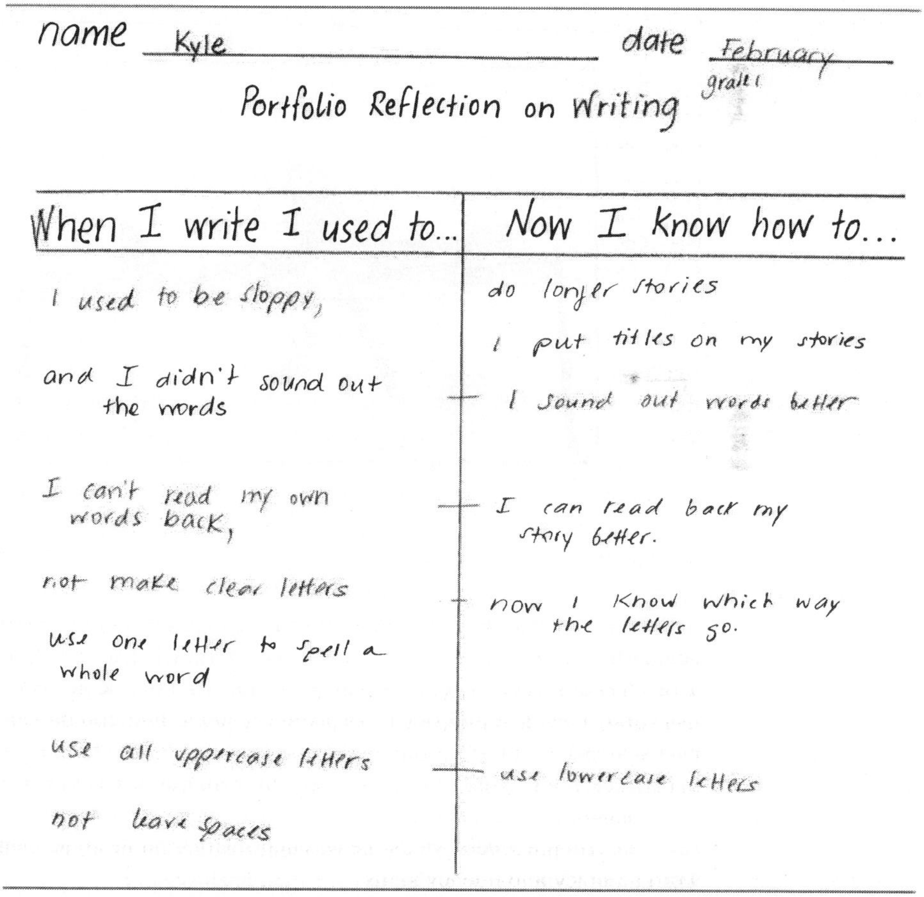

name   Kyle   date   February
                                                                      grade 1
                  Portfolio Reflection on Writing

When I write I used to...	Now I know how to...
I used to be sloppy,	do longer stories
	I put titles on my stories
and I didn't sound out the words	I sound out words better
I can't read my own words back,	I can read back my story better.
not make clear letters	now I know which way the letters go.
use one letter to spell a whole word	
use all uppercase letters	use lowercase letters
not leave spaces	

**FIGURE 4.13
Kyle's Preferences
for Tasks and
Projects**

name Kyle   date MAR 28

What have you enjoyed learning most this year? Why?

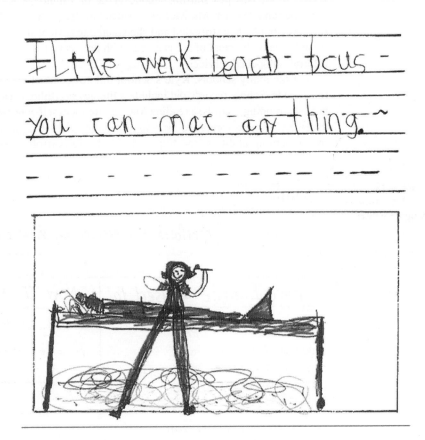

I Like werk bench bcus -
you can mac - any thing.

belief that Kyle had made progress. Writing samples from kindergarten and grade 1 clearly demonstrated his ability to apply his growing knowledge and skill (see Figures 4.13 and 4.14). These formative assessments also suggested that Kyle had not achieved the same level of literacy development as his age/grade peers. Because the school had little standardized assessment, we will return to the assessment data related to Kyle's reading and writing in Chapter 7. His instructional context and response instruction are discussed in the next two chapters.

As we move through the assessment-instruction process, further information about Tha'm and Kyle can be added to their thumbnail sketches.

FIGURE 4.14
Kyle's Reflections
Re: Paying Attention

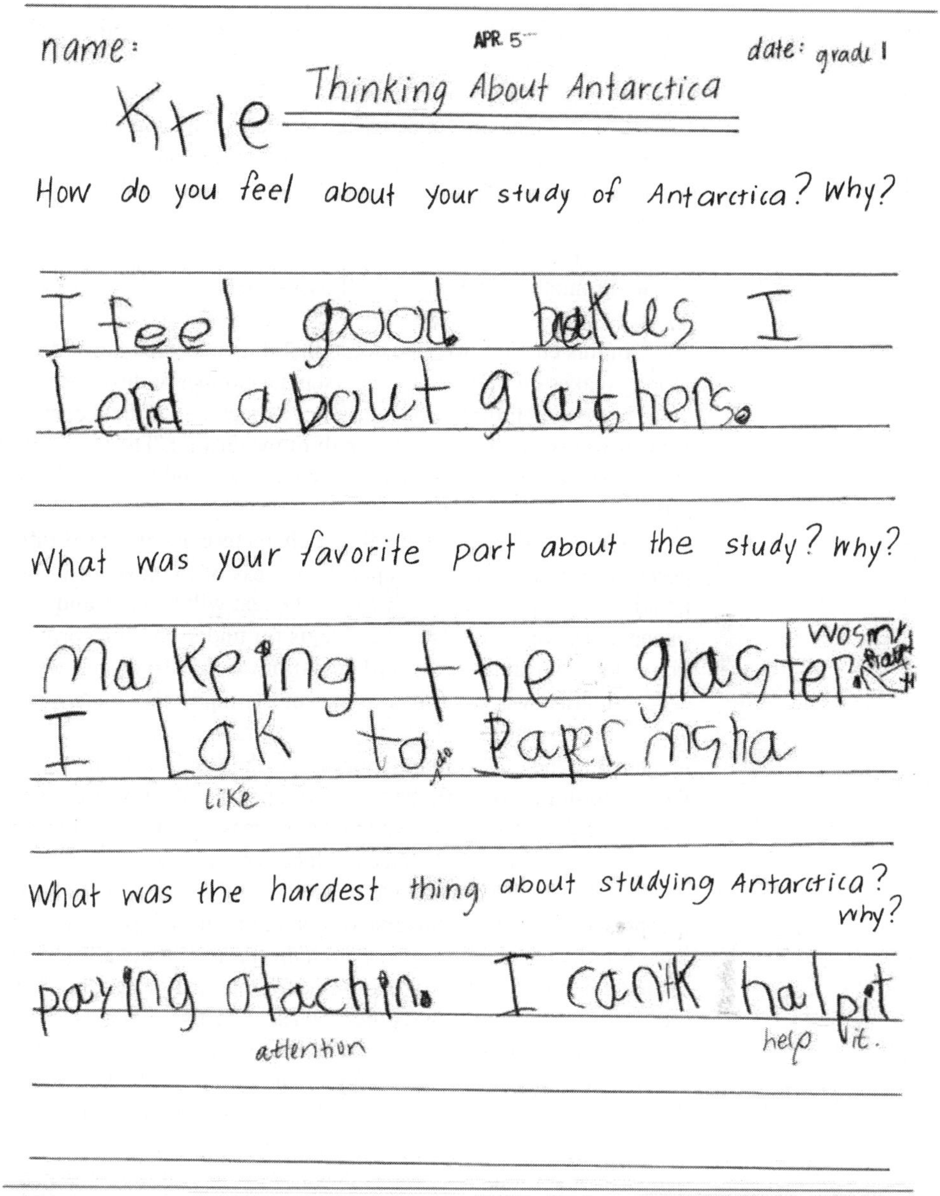

name:

APR. 5

date: grade 1

Kyle Thinking About Antarctica

How do you feel about your study of Antarctica? Why?

I feel good bekus I Lerd about glathers.

What was your favorite part about the study? Why?

Makeing the glagter wosmy fave
I lok to. paper mgha
like

What was the hardest thing about studying Antarctica? why?

paying otachin. I can't halpit
attention   help it.

CHAPTER SUMMARY

The purpose of this chapter was to assist the reader by providing the knowledge and techniques necessary for getting started using data to look at groups of students. We began with a set of guidelines that are important for the entire assessment-instruction process. These guidelines promote an approach to assessment that is contextualized, that examines how readers and writers perform in authentic classrooms or other real-world settings. They are as follows:

- Assess meaningful activities in appropriate contexts.
- Match assessment to purpose and instruction.
- Be systematic.
- Use multiple assessments.
- Assess continuously.
- Promote reflection and self-assessment.

In this chapter, we also noted that the widespread use of formal tests in reading and writing makes it important to understand a number of different aspects of standardized testing. The general information necessary to become a critical consumer of formal assessment devices was the focus of the first half of the chapter. The topics discussed were general test characteristics, important statistical concepts, validity, reliability, test interpretations, test scores, and test fairness.

The discussion of general test characteristics included information such as the importance of determining the appropriateness of the level of difficulty and type of administration for the students with whom the test will be used and the purposes for which it is intended. Important statistical concepts for understanding normal distribution and correlation (such as mean and standard deviation) were also discussed.

Validity was described as the most important concern in evaluating formal tests, as specified by the 1999 *Standards for Educational and Psychological Testing*. Validity is related to the claims made by users of the test information, and the valid use of tests is the responsibility of both the test developer and the test user. The three categories of evidence that should be considered in the process of test validation were described as content-, criterion-, and construct-related evidence of validity.

Content-related evidence of validity refers to the extent to which the test's content is representative of the universe of content being sampled by the test and requires that we have a precise definition of the domain the test items are intended to reflect. Criterion-related evidence of validity demonstrates that test scores should be systematically associated with one or more outcome criteria. The two types of criterion-related evidence of validity are concurrent and predictive. Concurrent evidence refers to the relationship between a person's score and an immediate criterion. Predictive evidence refers to the relationship between a person's score and performance on some measure at a later time.

Construct-related evidence of validity focuses on test scores as a measure of the psychological characteristic of interest. Most theorists now argue that all validity research should be conducted within a construct validity framework that requires an explicit conceptual framework, testable hypotheses deduced from it, and multiple lines of relevant evidence to test the hypotheses. Finally, consequential validity was discussed as we noted that it is essential for educators to consider the intended and unintended consequences of using a particular test.

Reliability was also described as a major criterion of test acceptability. Reliability refers to the consistency or stability of a test and involves the extent to which some attribute has been measured in a systematic and therefore repeatable way. The two types of reliability discussed here were test-retest and alternate form. The standard error of measurement (SEM) was also described as helpful to the test consumer in determining the confidence with which a test score can be interpreted.

Norm-referenced test interpretations were described in terms of the adequacy of the test norms. The size and representativeness of the norm sample are important, because an examinee's performance is evaluated in comparison to the performance of the individuals in the normative sample. On the basis of the responses of the normative sample, raw scores obtained from any subsequent examinee can be converted into a variety of derived scores designed to measure relative standing. For example, grade and age equivalents are derived from the average scores earned by students in the normative sample at a particular grade or age level. Other types of derived scores that were discussed include percentile ranks and standard scores.

Criterion-referenced (or standards-based) test interpretations were described as evaluating an individual's test performance on some preestablished standard or criterion. The issue of test fairness to racial and cultural minorities was discussed in terms of the possible presence of bias in the test content and the possible unfair use of test results. The first half of the chapter concluded with summary guidelines for evaluating formal assessment instruments.

The second half of the chapter described several types of formal assessment tools and provided detailed descriptions and evaluations of exemplars of tests designed for various purposes. The discussion focused on group-administered formal assessments for screening and diagnosis as well as on an examination of several standards-based assessments.

Next, we described techniques for using data to make decisions about which students might require a closer look. These included assessment walls and class-level summary data from a norm-referenced test. Finally, the chapter describes how to use a thumbnail sketch as a vehicle for summarizing information from the diagnostic portfolio. As we got started with assessment, Tha'm and Kyle were used as examples.

MyEducationLab™

Go to the Topic Reading Assessment, in the MyEducationLab (www.myeducationlab.com) for your course, where you can:

- Find learning outcomes for Reading Assessment, along with the national standards that connect to these outcomes.
- Complete Assignments and Activities that can help you more deeply understand the chapter content.
- Apply and practice your understanding of the core teaching skills identified in the chapter using the Building Teaching Skills and Dispositions learning units.
- Examine challenging situations and cases presented in the IRIS Center Resources.
- Check your comprehension of the content covered in the chapter by going to the Study Plan in the Book Resources for your text. Here you will be able to take a chapter quiz, receive feedback on your answers, and then access Review, Practice, and Enrichment activities to enhance your understanding of chapter content.

A+RISE A+RISE® Standards2Strategy™ is an innovative and interactive online resource that offers new teachers in grades K-12 just in time, research-based instructional strategies that meet the linguistic needs of ELLs as they learn content, differentiate instruction for all grades and abilities, and are aligned to Common Core Elementary Language Arts standards (for the literacy strategies) and to English language proficiency standards in WIDA, Texas, California, and Florida.

SECTION 3

Evaluating the Context

*T*he third part contains two chapters. The discussions in these two chapters provide the basis for carrying out Step 2 of the assessment-instruction process: Evaluating the Context. The chapters highlight the importance of determining what opportunities students have (or have had) to learn to read and write well. Although this type of close examination of classroom instruction has not been typical in the past, it can help us understand how and why students are performing they way they are in the area of literacy. Here, we describe more fully the contextual factors of setting, including both home and school; instructional environment, including methods and routines; and instructional resources, including texts and tasks. We discuss the contributions of these factors to reading and writing performance and describe ways in which these factors can be evaluated for individual students. The measures we suggest are designed to help summarize information about the setting, the specific instruction, the instructional materials, and the tasks students face in their literacy contexts. Each of these areas is considered in light of the most current research and also in terms of the desirable outcomes for reading and writing instruction.

CHAPTER 5

Evaluating the Instructional Environment/Context

*T*raditional assessment looks only to the student as the source of reading and writing difficulties. Clearly, students' knowledge, skill, and motivation are crucial factors in reading and writing achievement. However, a growing body of research demonstrates that instructional context and methods can support learning or contribute to disability. Assessment that is intended to inform instruction requires careful descriptions of how different aspects of the instructional environment influence learning in general and how they match the needs of particular students.

School success and failure result from a complex interaction of many factors (Fullan, 1999; Lipson, Mosenthal, Mekkelsen, & Russ, 2004; Preble & Taylor, 2008). Some factors that seem to negatively influence a particular student do not have the same effect on other students. Similarly, a program that has been successful in the past might not work for the student who is struggling now. The focus should be on assessing the context and method in terms of their likely impact on specific students' performance in reading and writing.

An analysis of fifty years of research suggests that "the different kinds of classroom instruction and climate had nearly as much impact on learning as the student aptitude categories" (Wang, Haertel, & Walberg, 1994, p. 74). Taken together, factors such as classroom management, climate, instruction, assessment, and social interaction influenced learning as much as the learner characteristics. In this and the next chapter, we discuss how different aspects of the instructional environment influence reading and writing performance and describe methods of evaluating these factors (see Figure 5.1).

This chapter begins with a discussion of the role of informal instructional settings—home and community contexts—in defining individuals' literacy practices and purposes. It continues on to describe how subtle interactions between home/community practices and the practices of formal, school instructional settings influence school achievement. Then we turn our attention to understanding and assessing the elements that make up formal instructional settings and practices, including classroom organization, instructional goals, methods, activities, and assessment practices.

FIGURE 5.1   Components of the Instructional Context

Home/Community Setting	Instructional Settings	Instructional Practices	Instructional Resources
Relations among home/community and school settings	Teacher beliefs and literate environment Classroom interaction Classroom organization Grouping Intervention programs Congruence among settings	Instructional goals Instructional methods Instructional activities Assessment practices	Commercial programs Trade materials Technology

UNDERSTANDING THE ROLE OF HOME AND COMMUNITY IN READING AND WRITING PERFORMANCE

Before turning our attention to the formal instructional settings of school, we consider the influence of home and community literacy environments as well as the relations among home/community and school settings. Young children are exposed to spoken language and print books and other texts in the home before they begin formal schooling. Many children participate in social groups devoted to story time or reading and writing in community settings such as day care, preschools, clubs, and church groups. Older children engage in out-of-school literacies in order to communicate with family and build relationships with friends as well as work and to pursue interests and entertainments. They often use information and communication technologies in their literacy practices. Across age groups, becoming literate occurs in social situations that shape purposes, conditions, constraints, audiences, standards, and motivation with regard to engaging in reading and writing activities (Paris & Wixson, 1987; Rueda, 2011).

Relations among Home/Community and School Settings: Early Language and Literacy Learning Practices

Every educator knows that literacy is not accomplished in schools alone. The children themselves contribute to learning and achievement, but so do parents, siblings, and the general community. Attributes that are important to consider regarding the larger literacy setting include the language(s) spoken in the home/community, the literacy status of the participants, the predominant socioeconomic status, and the relationships between the home/community and school. All of these factors affect individual and community literacy goals and practices.

Identifying attributes that affect school achievement should be a process of careful examination and description of the settings children encounter that can promote both understanding and adaptation. Poor instruction is a less prevalent problem than instruction that is unresponsive to the needs of individual students. The interactions among the features of home/community and school literacy settings can be both extremely subtle and profoundly important, affecting student learning and motivation. Teachers must consider the results of extensive research that offer insights into the ways in which home experiences can produce a mismatch between student/family and teacher expectations. The concept was initially highlighted in a groundbreaking study by Heath (1983).

Heath studied the patterns of language use in three communities in the southeastern United States and concluded that these patterns and social interaction differed strikingly among children in homes in these communities. In "Maintown," a middle-class, school-oriented community, the focus of literacy-related activities was on labeling, explaining, and learning appropriate interactional patterns of displaying knowledge. Children learned how to use language in literacy events and were socialized into the patterns of interaction that are central features of classroom lessons.

Families in "Roadville," a white working-class community, also focused on labeling and explanations; however, they did not link these ways of taking meaning from books to other aspects of their environment. Consequently, children from these homes were well prepared for the literate tasks of early reading instruction but not for reading assignments that call for reasoning and personal responses.

The third group of families lived in "Trackton," a black working-class community. The children in these homes were not taught labels or asked for explanations; rather, they were asked to provide reasons and express personal responses to events in their lives. As a consequence, these children were unprepared for the types of questions that are often used in beginning reading instruction and were unfamiliar with the interaction patterns used in reading lessons.

These differences in language use and interaction resulted in mismatches in the patterning of teacher-pupil interactions during reading and writing instruction (Heath, 1981). For example, a predominant characteristic of teachers' questions was (and still is) to ask students to name the attributes of objects or events in isolated contexts. Trackton parents did not ask children these kinds of questions, and their children had different techniques for responding to questions. Teachers reported that it was difficult to get responses from Trackton students; Trackton parents reported that teachers did not listen, noting that "we don't talk to our children the way you do"; and Trackton children reported that teachers asked "dumb" questions they already knew about.

To address the mismatch between home and school language use, Heath shared with the teachers examples of how Trackton children interacted at home. Then teachers incorporated into their instruction questions similar to those with which the children were familiar. As a result, the children participated much more frequently, and in time the teachers were able to involve them in more-traditional question answering as well. The point here is that children from these homes were initially viewed as disabled because they had not engaged in the type of interaction that is characteristic of classroom instruction. However, their disabilities were remedied by the social interaction they subsequently experienced with their teachers (Gavelek & Palincsar, 1988) or peers (Kliewer, 1998).

The findings of Heath, and the conclusion that disability can best be viewed from an interactive perspective, have been supported by a number of researchers (see, for example,

Au, 2000; Purcell-Gates, 1997; Spear-Swerling & Sternberg, 1998; Triplett, 2007). Differences among home/community and school literacy and language practices function in very subtle ways and may result in unintended consequences even when teachers employ generally well-accepted techniques. For example, many elementary classrooms are organized for collaborative work that would appear to be supportive of a wide range of students. However, research has demonstrated that students' literacy skill and/or social competence (i.e., ability to use the language appropriately and strategically) may keep some students from fully participating (Crago, Eriks-Brophy, Pesco, & McAlphine, 1997; Morrison & Cooney, 2002; Phillips, 1993). This is especially likely for English language learners and students with disabilities, who ". . . may not attain full citizenship with the literacy community of the classroom; rather, they may exist as squatters or aliens, relegated to remedial groups where little is expected" (Brinton & Fukiki, 2004, p. 144).

Because several researchers have observed such dramatic differences in students' engagement and performance across different contexts or with different curriculum practices, some educators are suggesting that the very idea of "struggling readers" should be reconceived (Alvermann, 2001b; McCarthey & Moje, 2002). Triplett (2007), for example, notes that students struggle in some circumstances and not in others. Her research invites several troubling conclusions. First, high-poverty students were much more likely to be labeled "struggling" than were more-affluent students. In fact, there were affluent students in her study who read less well than low-income students but who had not been referred for remedial reading. Because Triplett observed students in multiple settings, she was able to determine that students actually did behave differently in different contexts and that even though they were young (first and second graders), many could explain quite specifically why they did. A second conclusion was that students were more likely to struggle when their teachers were struggling—when they were not confident in their ability to teach reading, especially to students who needed additional help. Teachers in this study universally attributed students' difficulties to home environments. Whereas some teachers were sensitive to the interests and needs of diverse students and felt they knew how to teach reading, others blamed the families and were unaware of the ways that parents might have been trying to help. It is these complex social, cultural, and linguistic interactions that make the examination such a critical component of every student assessment.

Relations among Home/Community and School Settings: Later Literacy Learning Goals

Teachers and schools are often frustrated by the apparent lack of motivation and achievement among some students. Recent research and reflection have led to a more complex conclusion: all children are motivated to achieve, but they may direct their actions toward different goals, under different conditions, and for different reasons. It must be recognized that at least some children are motivated toward different goals than those emphasized by educators.

It is also important to realize the existence of different definitions of achievement and motivation. Students' achievement and motivation can be understood only in relation to the cultural contexts in which they live. Different cultures and different contexts dictate norms of behavior that vary. Individual behavior reflects, and is constrained by, these different norms. To the extent to which subcultures define achievement goals differently, differences in observed motivation to achieve those goals would be expected.

These differences have been captured by a number of researchers who have closely studied the highly motivated out-of-school literate behavior (vs. minimally motivated in-school literate behavior) of groups of middle school and high school students who are diverse with respect to language (Carbone & Orellana, 2010; Dorner, Orellana, & Li-Grining, 2007; Dorner, Orellana, & Jimenez, 2008; Orellana, Reynolds, Dorner, & Meza, 2003), race (Tatum, 2005, 2006), gender (Smith & Wilhem, 2002), and school achievement (Kajder, 2006). The studies revealed that many students who seem unmotivated in school and/or demonstrate limited achievement in academic reading and writing tasks are relatively skilled in the literacies required to function in their homes, communities, and peer groups. These literacies may not be valued by their teachers, nor recognized by the students themselves as worthwhile. However, as each of the researchers shows, out-of-school language and experience can be leveraged to develop in-school literacies. We feature here the work of Orellana and collaborators.

Orellana and colleagues (2003) have studied the children (aged 10–14) of Mexican immigrants living in large urban areas of the United States as they engaged in translating written texts in their homes for their families, a practice the researchers call "para-phrasing." In educational circles, children translating texts for their families is often referred to as "language brokering."

Data regarding students' in-home translation comes from the researchers' direct observations, audio recording, written surveys, interviews, and review of students' journals detailing their translation activities. (The same students have been followed over a number of years.) The data reveal the tremendous potential that students' translation experiences have to advance their literacy development. This potential, the researchers hypothesize, stems from the following features of para-phrasing: *variety and complexity* of texts, *meaningful purposes* for interacting with text, and *recognized and distributed expertise* in making sense of texts.

Children in immigrant families para-phrased, usually for their parents or other adult relatives, texts from a wide range of domains: commercial, community, educational, familial/recreational, financial, medical, legal/governmental, and religious. These texts, representing many different genres, can be demanding when they require that the reader deal with cultural references (advertisements, jokes), unfamiliar vocabulary (product labels, instruction manuals), the jargon of professional communities (letters from school, from insurers), and processes with which they have very little experience (jury summonses, job applications, IRS forms). The purposes for which children para-phrase these texts for adults are often a matter of immediate interest and concern to adults. The majority of para-phrases took place in parent-child dyads in which the child's expertise—the literacy skills already developed in English and perhaps familiarity with cultural practices observed at school—allowed the child to take a lead role. That role was often supported by parents in a distributed expertise model of learning. Parents added their own knowledge and experience of the events/topics of these texts to help the student figure out unfamiliar words or concepts.

It has long been hypothesized that the out-of-school literacy of language brokering is instrumental in developing children's linguistic and metalinguistic competence, as well as cognition and social-cultural aptitude. Such enriched speaking and listening, thinking, and social skills should support and enhance academic achievement. This hypothesis has been difficult to test. However, given the longitudinal nature of their data (following students over five years) and access to regular measures of academic achievement, the researchers were able to show that the literacy practice of para-phrasing may be instrumental in shaping thinking.

Students responded to a survey about their translation in the context of daily activities. On the basis of student responses to the survey, students were classified as "active," "partial," or "non-language brokers." Active translation was highly, positively related to achievement in reading and somewhat related to achievement in math, as measured by standardized tests of reading comprehension administered annually by the school district. That is, the home literacy practice of para-phrasing seemed to have educational benefits.

In subsequent work, Orellana and colleagues demonstrated that teachers could build on specific linguistic skills, developed in the practice of para-phrasing, to develop academic literacy. The researchers asked middle school students to write persuasive essays on a topic of high interest using different voices: an everyday voice appropriate for a familiar audience and a more academic voice for an unfamiliar audience (e.g., the president). In their analysis of these essays, researchers found clear evidence of both understanding of the language of argument as well as the language appropriate for addressing different audiences. They described how making transparent to the students the way they translate for different audiences in their essays, just as they translate for different audiences in real life, can serve as a tool for students in developing their academic writing. They state, "Valuing the competencies students brought with them was the first step in being able to leverage those competencies for academic purposes" (p. 311).

UNDERSTANDING THE ROLE OF INSTRUCTIONAL SETTINGS IN READING AND WRITING PERFORMANCE

In this section, we discuss how various aspects of instructional setting interact with cultural and home environments to influence students' learning. Setting factors do not operate in isolation from other aspects of the instructional environment; rather, they interact with each other and with other contextual factors. We have separated them somewhat for purposes of discussion and as a guide to the factors that must be considered in evaluating the instructional context. Wherever possible, however, we have tried to suggest the interrelationships between and among the elements of the instructional context.

Teacher Beliefs and the Literate Environment

Perhaps no single factor influences the instructional setting more than a teacher's knowledge and beliefs about teaching and learning. As we noted in Chapter 1, teachers are often unaware of the extent to which their views about learning and literacy influence and shape classroom instruction and the learning experiences offered to students.

According to DeFord (1986, p. 166), "beliefs will serve as a frame of reference for a teacher in selecting materials for instruction and for presenting and guiding the use of these instructional materials. These values will be communicated to the students, both verbally and nonverbally. Students will adhere to and improvise upon the contextual demands, or will find ways to change the nature of those demands through active, or passive, negotiation." As a result, students' behavior and the degree to which they participate in academic tasks are often determined by what others expect of them.

There is considerable evidence to show that teachers' beliefs about teaching and learning impact their instruction in many ways: shaping their selection of materials, determining how these materials are used, and guiding their assessment (DeFord, 1986; Lipson, Mosenthal, Daniels, & Woodside-Jiron, 2000). Teachers' expectations are also shaped by their beliefs about learning and literacy in general. In turn, these beliefs influence the type of classroom environment that is established (Lipson et al., 2000). The decisions teachers make about how to organize their classrooms, where to focus their instruction, and what materials to use are all influenced by their orientations or beliefs about teaching (Ares & Peercy, 2003; Lipson, Goldhaber, & Squires, 1993; Lipson et al., 2000). Students attend to these subtle and not-so-subtle clues as they determine how to behave and what to learn.

Evidence about how these beliefs and actions influence each other is provided by several intriguing studies. Even when teachers have been identified as "exemplary," their different orientations result in dramatically different classroom settings. Although the labels for different teaching practices vary across researchers and time periods, there does appear to be a small set of overarching orientations among teachers. For example, in one orientation, teachers tend to take a sort of organizational approach to teaching (see DeFord, 1986; Lipson et al., 2000). These teachers have a broad base to their literacy program, including both reading and writing, but it has a narrow focus. Lessons are thoroughly planned, allowing for a limited number of child-initiated decisions, and usually structured so that they can be completed in one work period. Reading groups are generally organized according to the core commercial program (or guided reading text), with "seatwork" consisting of workbook pages or other worksheets. For writing activity, the teacher typically assigns the topic, there is very little student-initiated writing, and teachers generally attend to the grammar and the mechanics of the writing. They create procedures for *managing* writing time and, if conferences are used during the writing process, they are teacher led. In their study of the relationship between teachers' beliefs and their instruction, Lipson et al. (2000) found that the children in these classrooms were generally responsible and cooperative. They participated actively in discussions *led by the teacher* and worked diligently to complete their assignments. Verbal interactions were most commonly teacher-child or teacher-group conversations. Although quiet child-child conversations are allowed during seatwork time to discuss assigned work, they are not collaborative discussions or peer-led conferences.

Different orientations produce different classrooms. Both DeFord and Lipson et al. describe a group of teachers whose orientation was more inquiry and process oriented (see also Fisher & Hiebert, 1990). In these classrooms, teacher goals and student goals tend to be negotiated to produce the curriculum and context in which children read more authentic literature and write a great deal of student-generated texts. Rules, which tend to be set by the teacher and children together, revolve around issues of productive work and social/child development. Reading and writing instruction tends to be handled individually or in small-group situations, with the teacher assessing and teaching on a daily basis from information gathered during the work period. For example, teachers may notice that one or more students could benefit from a mini-lesson in paragraph organization or more enticing leads. These students are called together for a quick lesson while others continue to work on reading or writing. The teachers of this orientation tend to structure open-ended activities and help students make decisions about personal outcomes. Children help each other and collaborate on projects. Child-child conversations and teacher-child conversations are most common here, with fewer teacher-group interactions.

These observational studies (DeFord, 1986; Lipson et al., 2000; Rueda & García, 1996) highlight the extent to which classroom organization, activities, and discourse may vary as a function of teacher beliefs about literacy and literacy education. Teachers' differing beliefs lead them to make different judgments about materials, tasks, assessment criteria, and interactional patterns. In turn, students have different experiences and construct the purposes and forms of literacy differently. In these ways, the unique attributes of classroom settings influence students' literacy learning. Although the research makes clear that teachers often negotiate "mandates" in light of their own beliefs about teaching and learning, it is important to note that individual teachers today may not have much say in how they orient themselves toward literacy. School policies and mandates can significantly impact the "belief" orientation that teachers espouse. In contemporary schools, the literate environment and beliefs are often imposed from above, but that does not mean that they are any less influential than the teacher's individual orientation in impacting the literacy context for students.

Classroom Interaction

Teachers rely on verbal interactions to make many educational decisions and judgments. According to Cazden (1986, p. 432), "spoken language is the medium by which . . . students demonstrate to teachers much of what they have learned. Spoken language is also an important part of the identities of all participants."

Variation in ways of speaking is a universal given. When the variation is significant, it can lead to mismatches for individual students or groups, and these mismatches can affect achievement (Cazden, 1986; Wilkinson & Silliman, 2000). Differences in how and when something is said may require only a temporary adjustment, or they can seriously impair effective teaching and accurate evaluation.

Linguistic and interaction patterns are important, because teachers make judgments about students' abilities and behavior based on them. For example, Michaels (1981) studied first-grade "sharing-time" experiences and found that when children's narrative styles were very different from the teacher's expectations, the event was generally unsuccessful. In addition, the teacher frequently made negative assessments of the students' ability and censured the students' performance. Similarly, Triplett's (2007) study of first-, second-, and third-grade "struggling" readers revealed that the classroom teachers and the reading teachers often had quite different appraisals of individual students' abilities and that these varying appraisals were based in part on the contexts and opportunities presented in the different settings. Thus, for example, the reading teacher had described a student as "engaged, thoughtful, and expressive," while the classroom teacher had described the same child as "off task," "not motivated," "stubborn," and "irresponsible" (Triplett, 2007, p. 110).

Teachers, like other groups of specialists, have unique ways of talking. Some of the more obvious features of teacher talk include asking known-answer questions and evaluating students' answers to the questions. Teacher talk is often characterized by its preoccupation with control of behavior and of talk itself. In order to be regarded as skilled in literacy activities in school, students must identify what reading means in their specific classroom, what is permitted in the way of interaction, and what is expected in response to reading (Alvermann, 2001b; Floriani, 1993). "The effects of students' not knowing these requirements are not limited to the obvious problem of unsuccessful communication with peers and teachers. If children do not understand the classroom and its unique communicative demands, they may learn little from classroom experiences. Accurate assessment of their achievement is unlikely, since access to their knowledge is predicated on optimal communicative performance" (Wilkinson & Silliman, 2001).

Studies of cultural differences also suggest that students would be better served if teachers took differences in prior experiences in the home community into account more than they now do (Au, 2000). Too often, teachers' responses to differences actually increase the gaps and inequalities among groups with different backgrounds and experiences (Cazden, 2001; Triplett, 2007). Research evidence suggests that some children come to school with an oral style of discourse that is incompatible with that of the teachers. These children often do not gain access to the kind of instruction and practice that are required to develop a more literate discourse style, and as a result they perform less well in school-based literacy activities.

Because interaction styles are so subtle and interwoven with individual identity, they can be difficult to assess. However, there is evidence that when instruction is shaped to respond to these differences, achievement and interaction improve. Research with native Hawaiians provides an example of the importance of cultural compatibility of communication styles in reading lessons.

Boggs (1985) learned that native Hawaiian adults rarely ask children questions for information, as white middle-class parents commonly do. Hawaiian parents use direct questions primarily when reprimanding their children. When telling a story, Hawaiians cooperate in taking turns to construct the story, with voices overlapping—an activity called "talk story." In addition, Hawaiians delegate household chores to an older child, who is responsible for making certain that the work is done. Apprenticeship and observation, rather than explanation or discussion, are used to teach children new skills.

Consistent with this knowledge about the interaction patterns of native Hawaiians, Au (1980) observed that Hawaiian children were more successful in reading lessons using the participation structures of the talk story than with the conventional recitation pattern commonly used in reading lessons with children from the mainstream culture. Teachers using these two participation structures clearly provided different kinds of social events, and Hawaiian students demonstrated much higher levels of achievement-related behavior in the lessons that incorporated the culturally compatible talk-story pattern. Since then, researchers have repeatedly demonstrated how even subtle mismatches can undermine achievement and small adaptations facilitate student learning (Cazden, 2001).

Classroom Organization

Over the past several years, research descriptions of classrooms have demonstrated what most classroom teachers know only too well: classrooms are busy places, and teachers are very active participants in classroom events. Because the classroom environment is busy and demanding, organization is a major factor in classroom teaching. According to Doyle (1986), activity is the basic unit of classroom organization. Activities take place in relatively short blocks of classroom time, during which students are arranged in a particular way. Labels for activities reflect either their organizational focus (e.g., seatwork, discussion) or their focal content (e.g., reading, journal writing). More than thirty separate activities occur each day in the average elementary school class.

Not surprisingly, Pressley, Wharton-McDonald, and Hampston (1998) found that the most effective primary-level teachers had "masterful" classroom management. However, the management of complex activities is challenging for some teachers, and there is evidence to suggest that teachers and students often reduce subject matter to a set of procedures to be followed in completing assignments, in order to satisfy management demands (Doyle, 1986). This disturbing finding is consistent with the evidence that, while in class, students often focus a significant part of their attention on information about how to do the work they are assigned as well as what behavior they are to display (Alvermann et al., 1996; Lehtinen et al., 1995). Clearly, the degree to which students have an opportunity to learn content or to practice significant literacy behaviors will depend, at least in part, on the types and quantity of classroom activity provided.

Teachers must also divide their attention among competing demands, and they vary considerably in how they do that. Importantly, differences in allocation of time and activity have an impact on reading achievement. For example, Taylor, Pearson, Clark, and Walpole (2000) found that the most effective teachers spent much more time instructing students in small groups and asking higher-order questions than did less-effective teachers. The most accomplished teachers spent forty-eight minutes per day in small-group instruction, whereas the least-accomplished teachers spent only twenty-five minutes a day. Similarly, among teachers in higher-performing schools, more than 90 percent engaged their students in challenging and interactive discussion. Among teachers in *less*-successful schools, fully 90 percent organized so that students did *not* work together. In fact, most of those teachers expected their students to engage in individual thinking.

Differences such as these among classrooms can and do account for differences in student performance and achievement (Au & Carrol, 1997; Mosenthal et al., 2001a, 2001b). Although classroom organization and management may vary within and among schools, the predominant pattern continues to be the teacher-directed classroom in which students are expected to work independently and to interact primarily with the teacher and the instructional materials. Increasingly, there are alternative classroom organizations in which teachers and students work more collaboratively, interact frequently about texts and tasks, and discuss reading and writing activities with peers in conferences and in literature groups (Guthrie, Wigfield, & Perencevich, 2004; Langer, 2001, 2004). Different patterns of organization affect particular students in unique ways. Some may find the open-ended, workshop-oriented classroom structure difficult; others may find the traditional patterns of organization problematic.

Researchers contend that families and cultures vary considerably in the extent to which they prepare children for various settings (Guthrie, Wigfield, & Perencevich, 2004; Langer, 2001, 2004). Children who are accustomed to assisting others in accomplishing tasks, collaborating on projects, and generally working together are at ease in the cooperative classrooms in which these activities are rewarded but uncomfortable in more-traditional classrooms. Hispanic homes have been characterized as fitting into the cooperative format (Madding, 2002), whereas Philips (1982), in a classic study of cultural effects on schooling, found that Native American children were accustomed to independent activities and were unaccustomed to the noise and competition that are characteristic of many classrooms. Differences between cultural values and classroom values were so extreme as to alienate the children from their teachers and their classmates. More-recent work confirms that students may experience "academic disorientation" as a result of these differences (e.g., Clay, 1998). The findings underscore the importance of examining the match between classroom organization and cultural or individual patterns of achievement. At the same time, caution needs to be exercised in generalizing within a cultural group. Although some cultural norms are likely to be characteristic of different racial or ethnic groups, there are still great differences among individuals within a group, and some apparent differences may actually be the result of other factors such as socioeconomic status and prior educational opportunity.

The Nature of Instructional Activities and Tasks.   Early research into the nature of teaching and learning concluded that classrooms ". . . can be described in terms of the recurrent activity structures teachers use. Activity structures such as reading circle or seatwork have different functions and possess rules and norms to guide the behaviour of individuals in the structure" (Berliner, 1983, p. 1). Interest in activities across various content areas persists, because it appears to capture important elements of the instructional content.

Activities and tasks consist of a goal and the set of cognitive operations required to meet the goal. They are defined by the products that students are required to create and the routes they can take to complete these products. Activities and tasks influence learners by directing their attention to particular aspects of content and promoting specific ways of processing information. They differ in both their content and their form—that is, in the procedures, social organization, and products they require. The elements of activities and tasks vary from simple to complex and combine in various ways to shape how students think and how they work, by determining how information is obtained, how it is processed, and how it is presented to the teacher for evaluation. Importantly, it appears that ". . . individual competence is an attribute of a person's participation in an activity system such as a classroom. In this perspective, what counts as "competent" gets constructed in particular classrooms and can therefore look very different from setting to setting" (Gresalfi, Martin, Hand, & Greeno, 2009, p. 49).

The *content* of an activity refers to its cognitive complexity and reflects the objectives students are expected to attain. Different learning objectives vary in difficulty for students, because they require different levels of cognitive processing and different prerequisite skills (Doyle, 1983). Variations in the difficulty of activity content affect student learning and behavior. For example, moderately difficult activities produce greater motivation than do "easy" ones (Clifford, 1991; Meece & Miller, 1999). The more difficult activities help learners calibrate their progress toward a goal by providing information about progress as well as concrete evidence of accomplishments (Schunk, 1989), and also because they generate greater effort (Newmann, Bryk, & Nagaoka, 2001; Miller & Meece, 1999). As a result, they enhance confidence and increase interest. Conversely, students may perceive minimally challenging situations or "safe" successes as evidence that others hold low expectations for them, which may reinforce a perception of their own low ability (Meece & Miller, 1999; Weiner, 1992).

The *form* of an activity also affects learning, irrespective of its content (Blumenfeld, Mergendoller, & Swarthout, 1987). As vehicles for the transmission of content, different forms vary in the extent to which learning objectives are evident to students. Forms differ in the obviousness of their purposes, the complexity of their procedures, the social organization in which they are carried out, and the products that result. For example, the purposes and procedures for completing worksheets are generally more straightforward than those surrounding a discussion.

When activities are procedurally complex, students may spend more time carrying out procedures than focusing on the content to be learned. In addition, tasks differ in the prerequisite skills they require. The more prerequisite knowledge and skill are required to accomplish the task, the more hesitant students may be to work at the activity (Blumenfeld et al., 1987). Finally, difficulty is determined by the nature of the product students must complete for evaluation and by the clarity of the evaluation criteria.

When the product can be evaluated according to numerous criteria, students—particularly younger ones—tend to focus on aspects that are more objective and easier to identify and define (e.g., neatness or length) at the expense of concentrating on content or richness of ideas, clarity of explanations, or complexity of analysis (Anderson, Brubaker, Alleman-Brooks, & Duffy, 1985). These tendencies are obviously strengthened when teachers' evaluative comments focus on neatness or effort. If teachers rely on assessment criteria that are ill matched to the original cognitive purpose of the activity, students will learn to process at the levels required by these criteria.

It is worth noting here the importance of employing authentic activities and tasks involving complex problems and projects. Newmann and his colleagues have engaged in a series of studies related to tasks and student performance (see Newmann & Wehlage, 1993; Newmann & Associates, 1996; Newmann, Bryk, & Nagaoka, 2001). These researchers use the word *authentic* to distinguish instruction and achievement that are significant and substantive from those that are trivial and meaningless. They use three criteria to define authenticity more precisely: "(1) students construct meaning and knowledge; (2) students use disciplined inquiry to construct meaning; and (3) students aim their work toward production of discourse, products, and performances that have value or meaning beyond success in school" (Newmann & Wehlage, 1993, p. 8).

A series of studies focused on high-poverty students and their teachers in Chicago schools highlighted two very important results: (1) when students were given challenging tasks, they were much more likely to produce authentic or high-quality responses (almost four times as likely), and (2) students who received the most challenging work showed significantly greater gains on norm-referenced tests of reading (Newmann, Bryk, & Nagaoka, 2001; Newmann, Lopez, & Bryk, 1998). Newmann and colleagues (2001) do caution that even activities that place students in the role of a more active, cooperative learner and that seem to respect student voices can be implemented in ways that do not produce authentic achievement. The challenge is not simply to adopt innovative teaching practices, but to work against two persistent problems that make conventional schooling inauthentic: the work students do often does not allow them to use their minds well, and the work frequently has no intrinsic meaning or value to students beyond achieving success in school.

Cumulative Effects.   Research suggests that students rely on prior experiences with lesson format and content as a guide to interpreting current activities. They construct knowledge, learning strategies, and representations of the subject itself according to their experience. The more frequent the experience of similar activities across subject matter, classrooms, and grades, the greater is the consistency with which students approach and think about their work. Even when conditions make such approaches inappropriate, students' approaches to activities are strongly influenced by their expectations about the form of the product and evaluative criteria to be used in assessment. If students are consistently exposed to activities with simple forms, they will have little practice in the form-related skills of planning, organizing, selecting among several alternative strategies, and monitoring their progress toward a goal. The result is limited opportunities to learn those self-regulation skills essential for accomplishing a variety of activities (Au, 1997; Bowles & Gintis, 2002; Corno & Mandinach, 1983; Darling-Hammond, 1995).

Generally speaking, students have to do two things as part of academic tasks: obtain information from reading/listening and show teachers that they understand the information by producing a product. In some cases, the form in which information is obtained is different from the form of the product required for evaluation. In some of these cases, students find it easier to obtain information than to display their knowledge or skill appropriately, because the performance task is more complex. Blumenfeld et al. (1987) note that it is possible for students to possess the cognitive skills necessary to achieve the content goal but to be unable to negotiate successfully the form in which they are required to display their knowledge. The actual problem may be failure to understand the form rather than an inability to comprehend the content.

The more complex the task form, the more important it is for teachers to provide clear and specific explanation and feedback during the lesson to distinguish between the content- and form-related aspects of the learning activity. Otherwise, students may spend considerable time on aspects of the activity that are irrelevant to the learning objective. In such cases, actual time on task may remain high, although much of it may be devoted to aspects of the activity that are irrelevant to the successful achievement of the objective.

Grouping

Although research suggests that whole-class instruction is the norm in many American classrooms (Vaughn, Hughes, Moody, & Elbaum, 2001), available evidence suggests that small-group instruction, in general, is more effective than whole-group instruction (Foorman & Torgesen, 2001; Paratore & Indrisano, 2003). However, teachers need to exercise caution if they group students for instruction, because such arrangements have implications for student motivation and achievement. As McCormack, Paratore, and Dahlene (2003) have noted, ability grouping in reading often results in a limiting of students' opportunities to acquire age- and grade-appropriate content and concepts. If the only instruction students receive is in small, guided reading groups that are organized by ability, the practice, ". . . will likely deny them an equal opportunity to acquire the knowledge they will need to continue to develop their cognitive and intellectual abilities, to succeed comprehending complex language and ideas, and to become proficient at writing and sharing complex language and ideas" (p. 130). Key components of the grouping structure in the classroom include the size and number of groups, the basis for grouping, consistency of groups across content areas, stability of groups over time, labeling of groups, mobility of individuals between groups, the number of groups functioning as groups at one time, and the amount of time spent in individual, group, or whole-class structure (Marshall & Weinstein, 1984).

Reviews of research on ability grouping for reading instruction suggest that instructional and social reading experiences differ for students in high- and low-ranked reading groups and that these differences influence student learning (e.g., Allington, 1983b; Hiebert, 1983; Gamoran, 2004). The social properties of ability groups are derived, at least in part, from the fact that students are grouped with those defined to be similar and separated from those defined to be different. Group placement is based on socially valued criteria, so that group membership immediately identifies some individuals as better than others. Therefore, high- and low-ranked reading groups are likely to form unique instructional-social contexts that influence the learning outcomes of the individuals within those groups (Cohen & Lotan, 1997).

As a consequence, students make judgments about their own and others' competence. Average- and low-achieving students who are in ability groups give lower self-evaluations than those who are not in ability groups. Research suggests that most groups that are based on homogeneous ability levels are relatively stable over time, with infrequent mobility of students from one group to another (Rosenbaum, 1980) and that membership in reading groups of different ability levels contributes significantly to the prediction of reading achievement beyond initial individual differences (Entwisle, 1995; Weinstein, 1976).

Student feelings of efficacy and motivation are affected by grouping decisions, but research suggests that students in different groups also receive distinctly different instruction. The research on ability-based instruction is somewhat dated, due partly to the decline in small-group instruction during the last fifteen years (and a concomitant increase in whole-group instruction). Especially in elementary grades, however, there is little reason to think that things have changed much. Students in low-ranked groups spend considerably less time in actual reading tasks than students in high-ranked groups do (McDermott, 1977). High-ability groups read silently more often than they read orally, whereas low-ability groups read orally much more frequently than silently (Allington, 1983b). In addition, teachers interrupt students following oral reading errors proportionally more often in low-ability groups than in high-ability groups and are more likely to emphasize word identification with low-ability groups and comprehension with high-ability groups (Allington, 1980; Greenwood, 1991).

The nature and extent of such differential treatment vary from teacher to teacher, and at least some of the variation can be seen as appropriate differential instruction (Gamoran, 2004; Haskins, Walden, & Ramey, 1983). Too often, however, low groups receive less-exciting instruction, less emphasis on meaning and conceptualization, and more rote-drill and practice activities (Gamoran, 1992; Good & Marshall, 1984). Differential treatment, coupled with the simple fact of group membership, provides students with additional messages about their potential for success in reading (Elbaum, Moody, & Schumm, 1999; Weinstein, 1986).

In sum, the evidence suggests that a low-group psychology develops wherever ability grouping is practiced, even in schools whose low-group students would be high-group students somewhere else (Good & Brophy, 2003). Such students may be prime candidates to become underachievers, because it may be easier for them to remain passive and to pretend indifference rather than risk failure by trying their best.

Writing instruction provides an interesting contrast. Teachers rarely group students by overall ability for writing. Instead, they are likely to form and disband small, flexible groups to address specific aspects of students' writing (Lipson et al., 2001). As a result, students who are poor readers may be relatively enthusiastic writers. If grammar, usage, and mechanics are not emphasized unduly, these students escape the negative consequences that result from grouping practices in reading.

It is important to note that other grouping patterns are quite prevalent today. Groups may be formed for reasons other than ability, such as for student interests or specific skill needs, promoting interaction among students of varying backgrounds, and fostering learning in all students. Over the past two decades, heterogeneous and/or cooperative groupings have become much more common (Vaughn, Hughes, Moody, & Elbaum, 2001). In contrast to stable and homogeneous groups, students have greater opportunity to work with more of their peers and to observe their own and others' strengths in a variety of areas when a flexible grouping strategy is used. Where external rewards are distributed, more children have the opportunity to receive recognition than where stable hierarchical grouping strategies result in the high-ability group consistently receiving more rewards and privileges. As Vaughn and colleagues note, more and more students with reading difficulties are receiving their instruction in the regular classroom, and it is critically important that they consider grouping practices in light of research about their impact on students' achievement and motivation.

The work of Connor and her colleagues sheds light directly on the impact of grouping and the ways in which different types and configurations of grouping result in different outcomes (Connor, Morrison, & Katch, 2004). These researchers examined the instructional contexts for students who came into grade 1 (and, later, grade 2) with different amounts and types of knowledge and skill. They identified different instructional contexts and coded them as: (1) *code-focused versus meaning-focused* and (2) *teacher-directed versus child-managed.*

The results are informative. A great deal of code-focused, teacher-directed instruction (in small groups) resulted in significant achievement gains in reading—*but only when* the students entered grade 1 with limited abilities in this area. Students who were more capable did less well with a strong code-focused, teacher-directed environment. These students were more successful when they had more meaning-focused, child-managed activity. In addition, the research suggests that the nature and amount of instruction needs to change over the course of the year for students to really make the strongest improvements in achievement. Thus, students who benefited from the code-focused, teacher-directed instruction in the fall required a decreasing amount of this and an increased amount of meaning-focused, child-managed activity later in the year. The more capable students benefited from a fairly stable amount of both throughout the year.

Clearly, grouping practices have an effect on student perceptions and performance. As a result, they need to be considered when evaluating the instructional setting in which a student performs.

Intervention Programs and Approaches

Intervention programs and settings are, by design, instructional contexts intended to influence students' reading and writing performance. Until recently, specialized reading instruction—sometimes called tutoring—generally meant "remedial instruction that is delivered by one teacher to one student, and this teacher is usually not the student's classroom teacher" (Shanahan, 1998, p. 218). In these remedial contexts, the instructor may be another teacher, a paraprofessional, a parent or other volunteer, or another student.

Research clearly supports the use of many forms of instructional support with a wide range of students. For example, drawing from eight literature reviews that summarize more than one hundred studies, Shanahan (1998) concluded that there is a consistent pattern of tutored students doing better than students who do not receive tutoring. What is more important, perhaps, is the fact that tutoring is not *always* effective and is more effective in some instances than in others. Circumstances that might outweigh the benefits of tutoring include the instructional time lost in moving between classroom and compensatory instruction, documented by Cunningham and Allington (2007). It may be difficult for tutoring, no matter how well designed and delivered, to compensate for the loss of ten to fifteen minutes of instructional time each day for movement from classroom to tutor and back again. The tutoring experience might also represent an incompatible change in the curriculum. Tutored students might receive instruction that contradicts what is offered in the regular classroom in ways that interfere with learning (see Wasik, 1998). Shanahan (1998) concluded that tutoring programs usually lead to at least small net gains in achievement beyond that accomplished through regular classroom instruction, but they in no way guarantee improved learning.

More recently, there has been a shift in perspective about instructional support for struggling readers and writers. Today, educators and researchers generally talk, not about remediation, but about *intervention*. The interventions have several characteristics that distinguish them from remedial programs. According to the Rhode Island Technical Assistance Center, interventions are enhancements of the instruction students receive in the general education curriculum. "The goal of the instructional modifications is to accelerate the children's rate of growth so that they will be able to meet grade-level expectations" (Scanlon & Sweeney, 2008, p. 17). They are focused on specific skills and abilities, and they are generally much shorter in duration. Whereas in the past the same student might remain in a remedial program for years, students' progress in response to an intervention is closely monitored and students are released from intervention as soon as they have closed the gap between their performance and that of their normally developing peers.

Marie Clay used the term *intervention* to describe her groundbreaking Reading Recovery (RR) approach to working with struggling readers. Reviews of research on Reading Recovery have consistently found that students who received RR instruction make sizable gains in reading achievement during the first-grade year. These gains compare favorably with those of higher-achieving first graders who receive only regular classroom instruction or such instruction along with compensatory support. (Schwartz, 2005; D'Agostino & Murphy, 2004). This one-on-one early intervention typically brings 80 to 85 percent of its students to grade-level proficiency in twelve to twenty weeks, making it one of the only early interventions to receive the highest ranking for evidence by the What Works Clearinghouse (2007).

Although Reading Recovery has an impressive, documented history of success, the good news is that it is not alone in its effectiveness. There are a number of options available today, and we can say with some assurance that appropriate early reading intervention can prevent long-term reading problems in the majority of students who experience early reading difficulties (Mathes et al., 2005; Scanlon, Vellutino, Small, Fanuele, & Sweeney, 2005; Torgesen et al., 2001; Vaughn, Linan-Thompson, & Hickman, 2003; Vellutino, Scanlon, Small, & Fanuele, 2006; Vellutino et al., 1996). Extending the good news is the fact that much of this research has also demonstrated that, for many children, classroom and small-group interventions can serve to accelerate the development of early reading skills, thereby reducing the number of children who need more-intensive one-to-one interventions (see, e.g., Mathes et al., 2005; Scanlon & Sweeney, 2009).

Despite the success of many early interventions and/or tutoring programs, research indicates that they may not always be effective with low-achieving readers. For example, although generally effective, Reading Recovery fails to help a significant number of students. Many students are dropped from the program because of poor attendance or mobility problems. In addition, a large number of referrals are made by RR to special education simply because the students fail to make adequate progress even with this intensive instruction, indicating the ineffectiveness of even this program with certain low-achieving students (Hiebert, 1994b). An important finding reported by Wanzek and Vaughn (2008) is that specific intervention may not be good for individual children, even when programs result in significant differences between the experimental group and the control group overall. These researchers used a standard protocol intervention focused primarily on word knowledge and reading speed and accuracy. Wanzek and Vaughn (2008) reported what other researchers often neglect: that although the intervention had a positive effect *on average*, many students did not improve. Indeed, 24 percent of the students who received a daily thirty-minute intervention actually deteriorated in word-attack abilities. We cannot take an intervention that worked on average with some students in one setting and expect it to work with each student in every setting, even if it is implemented with "fidelity."

The study by Wanzek and Vaughn revealed another important finding: that simply increasing the amount of time during which students receive instruction may not be appropriate. In addition to the standard intervention of thirty minutes a day, these authors also created a group that received sixty minutes a day (two thirty-minute interventions). Interestingly, the students who received the "double dose" did no better in word attack than the single-intervention students, less well in oral reading speed, and marginally worse than a control group focused on comprehension. Importantly, 35 percent of these students showed significant *deterioration* in their word-attack skills. The researchers indicated that the lack of academic progress from increased intensity was at least partly because "tutors reported difficulties throughout the 13-week intervention with student fatigue, group management, and increased problem behaviour during the second 30-minute session" (p. 139). This research suggests that when an intervention is not working for a student, simply increasing its intensity might not be the best course of action.

Taken together, the research and the syntheses indicate that it is better for teachers to adapt their instruction to the student rather than continuing to teach a program to ensure the fidelity of instruction, which minimizes the value of teacher expertise. Programs employing professional teachers as tutors produce more-substantial gains than do programs involving peer tutoring, parent tutoring, or various volunteer models, although these are also success-ful. For example, Pinnell, Lyons, DeFord, Bryck, and Selzer (1994) found that the reading achievement of students taught by RR trained teachers improved more than that of students in a RR-style tutoring program taught by teachers without this training. It is worth noting, however, that programs using teachers as tutors that provide far less training are less effec-tive than those providing more extensive training.

Although it appears that tutors with more training and experience do best, even pro-grams that employ less-knowledgeable tutors are sometimes effective (see Morris, 1999; Santa & Hoien, 1999). There is also evidence that tutor training might not be as necessary in situations in which tutors are carefully supervised and instructional decisions are made by knowledgeable professional teachers. In fact, professional development for classroom teachers can be as effective at reducing the number of students at risk as intervention provided by trained interventionists (Scanlon, Gelzheiser, Vellutino, Schatschneider, & Sweeney, 2008).

Congruence and Collaboration within and across Instructional Settings

As the preceding description of grouping options and intervention programs and approaches suggests, the school life of many poor readers involves several instructional contexts. Until the 1990s, most poor readers and writers received special instruction outside of the class-room (called pullout programs), a configuration that is still quite common. However, many less-skilled readers and writers now receive their instruction via *inclusion* programs—special instruction within the regular classroom. This instruction may still be planned and provided by a special teacher. In either arrangement, it is likely that students are experi-encing multiple settings, teachers, and program materials. Early research revealed that an astonishing 80 percent of classroom teachers did not know what instructional materials were being used for the remedial students in their room. The data also indicated that only 50 percent of the specialists could specify the reading book used by classroom teachers (Allington & Johnson, 1989; Johnston, Allington, & Afflerbach, 1985). If classroom and supplemental teachers do not know this general information, it is, of course, extremely unlikely that they have coordinated any other aspects of the students' reading and writing instruction.

More-recent research suggests that the situation has not changed much. According to Vaughn, Moody, and Schumm (1998), "students in pull-out reading programs (e.g., Title I and special education) often receive disjointed, inconsistent reading programs that are often not aligned with the reading program of the general education classroom" (p. 220). This means that the students who have the most difficulty integrating information and transferring learned skills to new situations are receiving the most fragmented, least unified instruction of all.

With the increased expectation that many schools will be using a response to in-tervention (RTI) system for determining both the type of instruction and the delivery for different students, the issue of communication, if not congruence, becomes especially im-portant. The "three-tier" approach described in Chapter 1 places the responsibility for core classroom instruction squarely on the shoulders of classroom teachers. For some students, additional instruction will be required. The expectation is that reading specialists will provide intervention instruction and monitor students' progress frequently. For students who do not make progress with Tier 1 or II instruction, special, more intensive instruction will be offered, typically by the special educator.

The coordination of efforts among classroom teachers, reading specialists, and special educators is essential if students are to benefit. It is crucial that educators communicate and collaborate so that they have shared goals and outcomes in mind for all students and so that the success of various instructional strategies can be assessed and students' progress can be monitored. There are some promising models. McCormack, Paratore, and Dahlene (2003) describe a model of intervention instruction that occurs within the classroom and has resulted in dramatic improvement in literacy. Their "pull aside" (instead of "pull out") program is designed to improve both basic reading abilities and also content knowledge:

> In the "pull-aside" model, the children would read the same text as their higher performing classroom peers; however, their instruction would be "beefed up" with more systematic and intensive instruction in word-study strategies, increased opportunities for repeated readings to build fluency, and more explicit and systematic instruction in comprehension monitoring strategies. (p. 122)

At the same time, there are models of pullout programs that insist on close coordination with classroom instruction. The Interactive Strategies Approach (ISA) developed by Vellutino and Scanlon and their colleagues is one such approach. Teachers and specialists use the same language, strategies, alphabet cues, etc., to ensure that vulnerable students do not have to navigate disparate instructional contexts (Scanlon et al., 2005; Vellutino et al., 1996). Clearly, congruence between instructional settings for remedial students is another aspect of the instructional context that affects student performance.

UNDERSTANDING THE ROLE OF INSTRUCTIONTIONAL PRACTICE IN READING AND WRITING PERFORMANCE

In this section of the chapter, we continue our examination of the instructional environment by focusing on the role of instructional practice in reading and writing performance. Specifically, we address the areas of instructional goals, instructional methods, reading and writing activities and tasks, and assessment practices.

Instructional Goals

Reading and writing goals should be as consistent as possible with our understanding of the reading and writing processes. Both instructional activities and student outcomes should emanate from a definition of skilled reading and writing (see Chapter 1). Reading and writing goals in the United States have too often focused on easily measured subskills with too little attention directed toward the acquisition of important overall ability (Newmann, Bryk, & Nagaoka, 2001). In a well-designed literacy program, mastering the parts is not the end in itself, but a means to an end, and there is a balance between practice of the parts and practice of the whole (Anderson, Hiebert, Scott, & Wilkinson, 1985; Snow et al., 1998).

In addition to overall curricular goals, effective teachers establish specific instructional objectives for individual lessons and students. Students who are made aware of goals and objectives before reading and writing are more successful than those who do not have this information. Despite this fact, many teachers are not clear about their goals, and many schools do not have well-considered program outcomes.

Evaluating the instructional context requires consideration of both *overall curricular goals* and *specific instructional objectives.* The fundamental questions to be asked regarding goals and objectives are "What is being taught?" and "Is the student likely to be a better reader and/or writer because she or he has achieved this goal or objective?" The answers to these questions are explored for general curricular goals in the next section and for instructional objectives in the following section.

Overall Curricular Goals and Standards.   Throughout the 1990s, there were many efforts to develop state and national content standards, an attempt to translate current theory and research into student outcomes (Pearson, 1993; Wixson, Dutro, & Athan, 2004). These efforts typically focused on reading, writing, listening, and speaking under the umbrella of English language arts. The outcomes or standards that were produced through these efforts were intended as guides for developing classroom or district curriculum and instruction.

The standards movement received a significant boost from the 2002 reauthorization of the federal elementary and secondary education act (ESEA)—often called the No Child Left Behind Act (P.L. 107–110), or NCLB, which was signed into law January 8, 2002 (see Chapter 1). Each state was required to establish measurable *grade-level expectations* (GLEs) for each grade from 3 to 8 and for one grade in high school. Most recently, efforts to develop K–12 state and national standards have culminated in the creation of standards, not only in the English language arts, but for a variety of content areas, with an eye to the competencies required for success in college and careers across disciplines (Common Core State Standards Initiative, 2011). At this writing, most states have adopted the Common Core State Standards (CCSS) for English language arts and literacy in history/social studies, science, and technical subjects.

Consistent with the notion that instructional activities and student outcomes should emanate from a definition of skilled reading and writing, rather than target subskills, the CCSS reflect an emphasis on the integration of the literate activities of reading, writing, listening, and speaking as learners "actively seek the wide, deep, and thoughtful engagement with high quality literary and informational texts that builds knowledge, enlarges experience, and broadens worldviews" (Common Core State Standards Initiative, 2011, introduction).

Of particular note as we consider instructional goals is the emphasis of the CCSS on text complexity. It is the premise of the authors of the standards that learners should be challenged by the texts they read, rather than offered a diet of "just right" texts that are relatively easy to read. Appendix A of the CCSS offers a general framework for evaluating text complexity (see Chapter 6). The CCSS also contains the caveat that beginning readers require materials "specifically written to correlate with their reading level and word knowledge." Shanahan (2011) agrees that the choice of materials for beginning readers should be ruled by the caution that, while there is evidence that students learn when challenged by demanding text, this evidence does not come from research with beginning readers. And we would note that the problem is similar for struggling readers.

For the purposes of this text, we have distilled current standards and outcomes into the goal of developing *knowledgeable*, *strategic*, *skilled*, and *motivated* readers and writers. Knowledgeable readers and writers have a grasp of the content of reading and writing (or knowledge of the "what" of text content), literary elements, genre, and the craft of written language for both literary and informational texts.

Strategic readers and writers use their knowledge and skills flexibly, adapting their approach for different purposes, tasks, and materials. They also develop and use their own standards to evaluate their reading and writing and the meanings they construct. They set personal goals for developing reading and writing abilities and for learning from reading and writing, and are aware of both their efforts and their accomplishments.

Motivated readers and writers are those who not only *can* read and write, but also *choose* to do so for a variety of recreational and functional purposes. They generally understand the various purposes of reading and writing and are reasonably skilled at using reading and writing to meet their needs. Not all motivated readers and writers enjoy and select the same types of reading and writing activities, but they do have one thing in common: they read and write voluntarily.

In developing knowledgeable, motivated, skilled, and strategic readers and writers, much of the traditional content of reading and writing instruction will continue to be important, but students and teachers must not focus on the acquisition of knowledge and skill as an end in itself. Instead, the goal is for students to use their knowledge and skill as they read and write widely. The total reading and writing curriculum across ages and grades must attend to the interplay among these outcomes. A program that does not balance these primary aspects of reading and writing may produce students who can but will not read or write, or students who enjoy books but cannot read them independently. Both breadth and depth are desirable in the developmental reading and writing program, but the relative attention to different aspects of the curriculum may vary across the developmental continuum.

Just as the emphasis on different outcomes may vary across the developmental continuum, it will also vary for individuals who are experiencing reading and writing difficulty. Some students will need to acquire knowledge about reading and writing, others will need ample opportunity to apply and adapt their reading and writing skills, and still others will need to develop an increased appreciation for the functional value of reading and writing practice. The issue here is a critical one: knowledge, skill, and motivation *are all factors in student achievement.*

Specific Instructional Objectives. General curricular goals provide guidance and direction for the identification of more-specific instructional objectives used for particular lessons and students at particular levels of development. It is important to understand that instructional objectives are not synonymous with activities (e.g., journal writing, dictating stories). When objectives are equated with activity completion, both teachers and students are likely to misconstrue the purpose of instruction. In addition, successful instruction is likely to be measured in terms of the number or levels of activities completed rather than the extent to which knowledge and/or competence has increased. This is an extremely important distinction that must be understood both to evaluate and to plan effective instructional programs.

The goal of developing knowledgeable, strategic, motivated readers and writers can be translated into three types of instructional objectives that relate to the outcomes required for students to become expert readers and writers (Duffy & Roehler, 1989). Sound instruction must contain provisions for each of the following types of objectives:

- *Attitude objectives:* Students need to develop the motivation and desire to read and write for a variety of purposes.
- *Content objectives:* Students need to learn the "what" of reading and writing and to understand the ideas they are reading and/or writing about.
- *Process objectives:* Students need to acquire skill in using reading and writing processes.

Until recently, the most neglected area in reading and writing instruction has been that reflected by attitude objectives. Attitude objectives are important, legitimate concerns for all teachers. The relationship between positive attitudes and achievement suggests that students' expectations and values have a significant effect on both their effort and their achievement (see Covington, 2000; or Wigfield et al., 2006). To become effective readers and writers, students must demonstrate both *skill and will* (Paris, Lipson, & Wixson, 1983). If they are not willing to engage in independent reading and writing, students will not have sufficient opportunity to practice acquired skills, nor will they develop the facility to read and write flexibly for their own purposes.

If attitude outcomes have been neglected in the past, the same cannot be said about process outcomes—especially those focused on strategy instruction. Many reading and literature lessons have focused almost exclusively on methods and techniques for helping students learn skills and strategies. Effective reading instruction must achieve the delicate balance between focusing on understanding content and developing the ability to process different types of materials for different purposes. Students must acquire the skills and strategies that will enable them to comprehend and *learn on their own*, and teachers need to think carefully about how they address these important process objectives. Similarly, effective writing instruction must balance attention to the content of writing with the skills and processes essential for effective writing in a variety of situations.

What we want to avoid is instruction that emphasizes process objectives at the expense of content objectives or vice versa. What is needed in both reading and writing instruction is a balance between attitude, content, and process objectives.

Instructional Methods

In this portion of the chapter, we summarize research on effective approaches to instructional practice. There are two ways in which this research can help in the assessment-instruction process. First, descriptions of effective instructional practice provide a framework for specifying the important attributes of the instructional context. Second, it is important to understand what characterizes good instruction, to evaluate its contribution to the reading and writing process for individual students.

The question of what constitutes effective instruction has prompted efforts to specify the attributes of successful schools, classrooms, and teachers. The important lessons from research are that students need to be actively engaged in order to learn and that initial learning requires teacher modeling and explanation. There is also support for the general conclusion that students need multiple opportunities to learn. These findings suggest that the effects of instructional method are intimately connected to the classroom management practices and teacher expectations described previously. Unfortunately, the evidence also suggests that teachers are spending too much time managing and assessing children by assigning them activities and asking questions and too little time teaching (Kane, 1994; Taylor el al., 2000). Existing methods often encourage teachers to view instruction as placement in a program rather than a series of decisions to be made about what content should be taught or what methods might work best.

It is important to emphasize that research on effective instruction in reading and writing is far from definitive. Indeed, the research in this area is so diverse that it is possible to find evidence supporting contradictory practices. Effective teaching can occur within the context of many programs and many materials, but no one set of materials nor any single program is likely to address the needs of every student (Lipson et al., 2004; Pressley et al., 2001). Our instructional guidelines are derived from two sources of information: (1) our conclusions about the best theoretical perspectives on the reading and writing process; and (2) our understanding of the best available research evidence regarding effective reading and writing practices, informed by several research syntheses (Bowman, Donovan, & Burns, 2000; Center for the Improvement of Early Reading Achievement, 2001; National Reading Panel, 2000; Snow et al., 1998).

Once important goals and objectives have been determined, attention can be directed to the best ways to help students meet these goals. This is the focus in the following sections, in which we move from *what* is being taught to the methods of instruction, or *how* it is taught. We begin by describing an effective model of instruction and proceed to a discussion of instructional activities and tasks that enhance reading and writing performance.

Creating Knowledgeable, Strategic, and Self-Controlled Readers and Writers. Good teaching must include instruction in how to read, write, remember, and think independently. This means both that students acquire reading and writing skill and that they are able to transfer this knowledge to a variety of reading and writing situations and tasks. The problem of how to maintain and transfer skilled and strategic behavior has been a major issue facing educators. The practice of teaching isolated component parts of reading and writing has proven less effective in improving reading and writing ability on transfer tests and on subsequent achievement tests than has instruction that is embedded in more-meaningful events (Denton, Vaughn, & Fletcher, 2003; Scanlon et al., 2005; Vaughn & Linan-Thompson, 2003). On the other hand, more-recent attempts to provide instruction through immersion-only approaches have often been disappointing, for somewhat different reasons. As Au (2000, p. 846) concluded, "Motivation is a necessary but not sufficient condition for students to develop higher level thinking about text. . . . Research on constructivist approaches shows that the teaching of literacy can and should be motivating and responsive to children's backgrounds and interests, while at the same time providing them with systematic instruction in needed skills and strategies."

It is possible to teach students how to be knowledgeable, strategic, motivated readers and writers (see Almasi, 2003). Extensive research over the past twenty-five years suggests a need for instruction based on the principle of gradually releasing responsibility for learning from the teacher to the student (Fisher & Frey, 2008; Pearson & Gallagher, 1983; Vygotsky, 1978) with a simultaneous focus on self-regulated learning (Paris & Paris, 2001). In the initial stages of acquisition, the teacher has primary responsibility for student learning. In the final stages of learning, the student has the primary responsibility for practicing, applying, and orchestrating what has been learned. What comes between is a form of guided instruction that represents joint responsibility between the teacher and the student. These features are discussed at some length below.

During the acquisition phase of the instructional process, the teacher has the primary responsibility for student learning. Reviews of research by the Center for the Improvement of Early Reading Achievement (2001) and the National Reading Panel (2000) confirm that we know a great deal about how to help children learn to read.

Teachers need to engage in both good explicit instruction and also active contextualized coaching. The attributes of teacher-based instruction that have demonstrably improved reading and writing performance include:

- Clear teacher presentations
- Good direct explanation
- Modeling and guided practice
- High levels of active student involvement
- Review and feedback

Using these techniques, researchers have demonstrated improvement in students' decoding abilities, vocabulary knowledge, and comprehension ability (see review by Foorman & Torgesen, 2001). At the same time, longitudinal observational studies of effective teachers reveal that they spend a great deal of time coaching students as they are engaged in active reading (Allington & Johnston, 2002; Langer, 2004; Pressley et al., 2001; Taylor et al., 2000). The instruction of accomplished teachers in successful schools consistently reflects the following:

- Collaborative construction of meaning
- Focus on higher-level questions and responses
- Movement beyond the basic to deep engagement with ideas
- Support for improved thinking through conversation and discussion

Although the relative contributions of each of these teaching practices have yet to be determined, it appears that clear, specific, teacher explanation with supportive discussion during reading and writing is particularly important to students' improvement. Clear explanations provide students with knowledge about how to accomplish various reading and writing tasks. However, having knowledge about *how* to perform a skill or strategy does not ensure that students will use that knowledge.

To increase the likelihood that students will use their skills, teachers must provide students with information about when and why to use the skills they are learning. Research suggests that this is a critical factor in students' ability to transfer the skills they have learned to other reading and writing contexts (Butler & Winne 1995; Paris, Lipson, & Wixson, 1983). Although it might seem obvious to teachers, students frequently do not understand how skills acquisition is related to real-life reading and writing. Effective reading and writing instruction must also involve feedback on the utility of the actions (Konold, Miller, & Konold, 2004; Lipson & Wickizer, 1989) and instruction in why, when, and where such activities should be applied (Paris, Cross, & Lipson, 1984).

Students need to read and write to become good readers and writers (Mosenthal et al., 2001a, 2001b). Simple workbook completion activities do not provide enough substantial practice and may actually contribute to students' lack of motivation for reading and writing authentic texts outside of school. The following sections discuss elements of practice related to the gradual-release model of learning and instruction: scaffolding, social interaction or dialogue, level of instruction, and reflection.

Scaffolding.   The hallmark of instruction involving the gradual release of responsibility is *scaffolding*. Scaffolding has been described as instructional assistance that enables someone to solve a problem, carry out a task, or achieve a goal that he or she could not accomplish without support (Wood, Bruner, & Ross, 1976). Wilkinson and Silliman (2000, p. 343) explain that a scaffold "is an external structure that braces another structure being built." The metaphor of a scaffold calls attention to a support system that is both temporary and adjustable. Teachers should expect students to need their support in moving from one level of competence to the next so that, in time, they will be able to apply problem-solving strategies independently and wisely (Paris et al., 1986).

Scaffolded instruction begins with selecting a learning task for the purpose of teaching a skill that is emerging in the learner's repertoire but is not yet fully developed. The task is evaluated to determine the difficulty it is likely to pose for the learner; the learner's attempts at the task are carefully observed to facilitate decision making about how to make the task simpler and the learner more successful (Rodgers & Rodgers, 2004). Modeling, questioning, and explanation are used during instruction to make the task explicit and to represent appropriate approaches to the task (Palincsar, 1986).

Students are engaged in learning activities in order to trigger the use of specific skills or strategies and also in order to evaluate student performance. This evaluation is conducted to determine the level of difficulty of the task, make appropriate adjustments in the level of instructional support, and provide the learner with information regarding his or her performance. The aim of scaffolded instruction is to support students as they develop independence in using the knowledge or skill in other, similar, contexts.

Such generalization is facilitated by the gradual withdrawal, or disassembly, of the scaffold as the learner demonstrates increased competence and no longer needs support (Palincsar, 1986; Stone, 1998).

Dialogue.   Instruction in the gradual-release model is also characterized by the ongoing interplay between teacher and learner in the joint completion of a task. These dialogues or conversations (see Goldenberg, 1993) are the means by which supports, or scaffolds, are provided and adjusted. When children engage in subsequent problem solving, they display the types of behaviors that are characteristic of dialogues they had when they were collaborating with a more expert individual. In a description of several dialogic approaches to constructing meaning with text, Palincsar (2003) suggests that such instructional support for reading comprehension is characterized by principles of teaching for self-regulation. That is, teachers:

- share with learners (rather than assume him/herself) the authority for deciding what information is worthy of attention and how it shall be interpreted. Teachers elicit student responses to text, support students to link their ideas to new information, and provide feedback to enable students to further develop their contributions to the dialogue.
- focus on the processes (rather than the products) of making sense of text by modeling, explicitly naming and describing "how he or she made decisions about the key points in the text, or by identifying what she or he regards as evidence for a particular interpretation of the text" (p. 100).
- teach learners to be strategic in their thinking, engaging with text ideas, facilitating and monitoring their own understanding, and correcting misunderstanding through the use of strategic behaviors such as self-questioning, predicting, paraphrasing, visualizing, and using text structure to organize information.

When this type of dialogue occurs with initial instruction, it "enables learners to participate in strategic activity even though they may not fully understand the activity and would most certainly not be able to exercise the strategy independently" (Palincsar, 1986, p. 75). The relationship between teacher and learner in this supportive dialogue is to be contrasted with that observed when students are left to discover or invent strategies independently or when students are passive observers who receive demonstrations and are "talked at" regarding strategy use. The available evidence suggests that teachers often conduct monologues, not dialogues, and rarely use student ideas as the basis for discussion and teaching. Teachers are taught to "tell" and are rarely provided with instruction or guidance in conducting effective dialogues with students. Wilkinson and Silliman (2000) refer to these formal patterns of social interaction between teacher and students as "directive scaffolds." Question-answer evaluation sequences, for example, do serve an instructional purpose but do not support the aim of student responsibility for learning as directly as do the dialogue patterns inherent in the supportive scaffolds described in the previous section.

Level of Instruction.   A gradual-release model of learning and instruction draws heavily on Vygotsky's (1978) view of the relationship between instruction and cognitive development. According to Vygotsky, instruction is best when it proceeds ahead of development and arouses those functions that are in the process of maturing. In other words, instruction leads development. Cognitive skills that are emerging but not yet fully mature are considered to lie within the zone of proximal or potential development. This zone is defined as the distance between the actual developmental level as determined by independent problem solving and the level of potential development as determined through problem solving under adult guidance or in collaboration with more-capable peers (Vygotsky, 1978). This means that instruction is likely to be most effective when teachers identify the zone or levels at which students can perform with some assistance and guide them to higher levels of performance and then to the point of independent learning (Wilkinson & Silliman, 2000).

A familiar example offered by Au and Kawakami (1986) may be helpful in describing what instruction within the zone of proximal development might look like. They observed skilled teachers conducting reading comprehension lessons and noted that these teachers consistently posed questions that they knew their students were likely to have difficulty answering. This, the authors argue, demonstrates how the students were being challenged to perform at higher levels than they were able to achieve independently. They also observed that the teachers responded to incorrect answers by helping the students work out a better answer, rather than just giving them a correct response. Students were given the opportunity to carry out rather advanced comprehension skills, if only with considerable assistance.

The appropriate level of instruction may also be influenced by other factors, such as the complexity of the materials that students are provided (see Chapter 6).

Reflection. Without reflection, neither knowledge nor the skills for applying knowledge are likely to be used thoughtfully (see Onosko & Newmann, 1994). Reflection encompasses a variety of traits, including: a persistent desire to understand the reasons for one's own and others' thoughts and actions, a tendency to take time to think problems through for oneself rather than acting impulsively or automatically accepting the views of others, a flexibility to entertain alternative and original thoughts and actions, the ability to recognize difficulties or dilemmas, and a habit of examining one's own thinking processes and establishing personal goals. It is important that teachers design instruction explicitly to help students become reflective readers and writers. Central to reflection is the ability to monitor and evaluate one's own literate activity (Paris & Paris, 2001). A common feature of students having trouble with reading and writing is their failure to monitor and self-correct. They look to others to see whether they are "doing it right." They do not feel able to evaluate their own performance.

Johnston (1992, 1997) describes a variety of practices that encourage self-evaluation. For example, it is important to recognize self-evaluation when it occurs. When a student becomes aware of a problem, we can say, "I like the way you noticed that yourself. That is a sign of a good writer/reader." The information conveyed is that self-evaluation is important to becoming a better reader/writer, not that they have performed as you wanted.

Other practices that promote self-evaluation include encouraging students to give it a try, anticipate, and check their predictions and attempts. It can also be encouraged by reflective responses that turn questions back to learners. For example, a question such as "How could we check whether that is correct?" might provide assistance, since it opens up one or more strategies for self-checking. The student's response is likely to give us information about the strategies the learner has available.

Paris and Paris (2001) note how important "collaborative reflection" is in helping students see other perspectives. Students need opportunities to share their work with their peers. Reflecting on their work with other students becomes a vehicle for students to discover important ideas, explore new concepts, think in new ways, and refine their methods of communicating to different audiences. Charts can be created and updated as a way to record student thoughts about reading and writing. Samples of student work can be used as examples of a certain feature that students think is important to emphasize. Charts developed from student input become the beginning of criteria for quality work that students recognize.

Once students have a variety of samples and have generated ideas about criteria for reading and writing, they are ready to start to apply their criteria to their own reading and writing. Student comments will not be as sophisticated as teachers' comments and may focus on features of reading and writing that are not that important at first, when students are just beginning to develop the tools necessary to think critically about themselves as readers and writers. As they become increasingly responsible for judging the quality of their own work, they are learning to take control of their own reading and writing.

Literacy portfolios, once promising classroom vehicles for ongoing assessment, were especially well suited to self-evaluation and reflection. Portfolios typically included entries selected by the students to represent their growth. Entries were often annotated with statements about why the work was important, what had been learned, and future goals. When portfolios were used for large-scale assessment, they were criticized for suspect reliability and generalizability. Because portfolio assessment is difficult to standardize, it proved almost impossible to use in the context of a high-stakes district or state assessment.

While these criticisms are valid, portfolios also provide the best vehicle for assessing performance aspects of literacy—authentic reading and writing in action. With the advent of a host of technological tools, students may now create electronic portfolios to document and share their own literate activities in ways that are engaging and convenient as well as reflective of the changing nature of literacy (Barrett, 2007; Fahey, Lawrence, & Paratore, 2007; Hicks, Russo, Autrey, Gardner, Kambodian, & Edington, 2007). Portfolios, whether in electronic or "hard copy" form, promote reflection in ways that very little else can do. Walters, Seidel, and Gardner (1994) observe that as students work on projects and collect artifacts for their portfolios, they can also be engaged in a continuing discussion of standards of quality. How does a student come to understand that one essay is more articulate than another? How do these judgments go beyond the issues of simple accuracy in spelling and grammar? Even very young students are quite capable of setting standards for themselves (see Higgins, Harris, & Kuehn, 1994). Setting standards is an important ability in continuing to learn outside of school. We need to spend a greater portion of our time as teachers helping students set their own standards instead of always establishing those standards independently of the students and in advance of their experience.

For students to become reflective self-evaluators, they must feel themselves to be able knowers and evaluators. Students need to have confidence and self-respect and to value their own knowledge to be self-critical and develop reflective commitment to their reading and writing. These conditions are most likely to occur when students feel that they have something to contribute. Students are made to feel this way when people actually listen to them and communicate that their ideas are not less valuable than those of the teacher or others. Whether reflection and self-assessment take place in the context of portfolios or simply in the course of ongoing teaching and learning, it is an important component of high-quality instruction.

Creating Motivated Readers and Writers. Reading and writing achievement are powerfully influenced by motivation and attitudes (see Chapter 1; Mallory, Marinak, & Gambrell, 2010). In the past, motivation was examined from the perspective of the individual. While many teachers believe that motivation is a relatively permanent feature of individual students' makeup, researchers have increasingly focused on the contextual impacts of motivation (Good & Brophy, 2003) or sociocultural (Rueda & Kim, 2001, 2011) views of motivation. Most current research suggests that the effort people are willing to expend on an activity is a product of the degree to which they expect to be able to perform the task successfully if they apply themselves and to which they value the rewards that successful performance will bring (Good & Brophy, 2003). This theory of motivation implies that teachers need both to help their students appreciate the value of school activities and to make certain that their students can achieve success in their school activities if they apply reasonable effort.

Good and Brophy (2003) argue that certain preconditions must be in place for motivational strategies to be effective: (1) the teacher must create a classroom atmosphere that is supportive of students' learning efforts, (2) students must be given tasks of an appropriate difficulty level, (3) activities must be selected with worthwhile academic objectives in mind, and (4) the teacher must show moderation and variation in using motivational strategies. Once these preconditions are established, there are several different types of motivational strategies that teachers use to promote students' expectations for success and value in learning.

Motivational Strategies.   Guthrie and his colleagues have studied the factors that foster reading engagement and motivation (Guthrie & McCann, 1998). Classrooms that improve engagement, and consequently achievement, have a number of features, including:

- A conceptual orientation
- Real-world instruction
- Interesting text
- Strategy instruction
- Collaboration
- Coherence
- Strong assessment

If students are to meet challenging goals, they must possess confidence and be willing to take risks; they must *expect* to be successful. Not surprisingly, the most basic technique for improving motivation and engagement involves assigning tasks on which students can succeed if they apply reasonable effort and instructing students thoroughly so that they know what to do and how to do it. An important, but sometimes overlooked, aspect of this is the importance of appropriately challenging tasks. When tasks are uninteresting or too easy, motivation wanes. Other techniques that enhance motivation include helping students to set appropriate goals; to commit themselves to these goals; to use appropriate standards for appraising their levels of success; to recognize the linkages between effort and outcome through modeling, socialization, and feedback; and to view effort as an investment rather than a risk.

Motivation is often influenced by students' expectations for success. Students' expectations are often related to their judgments about why they succeed or fail, which affect their willingness to try difficult tasks. These judgments are called *attributions*. Attributing success to ability and failure to lack of effort means that the person generally will expect to succeed and will be willing to try more-challenging tasks. In contrast, attributing success to a variable factor (such as task ease) and failure to lack of ability means that the person will not expect to succeed. In this condition, when the person fails, he or she will give up quickly, since extra effort will not overcome the person's perceived lack of ability (Wigfield et al., 2006).

Expectancy is not the only factor that influences student motivation. Remember that students must also value the activity. Good and Brophy (2003) suggest different strategies to address the *value* aspects of student motivation. These strategies emphasize motivation for *learning*, not merely performing. If students are motivated solely by grades or other extrinsic reward and punishment considerations, they are likely to adopt goals and associated strategies that concentrate on meeting minimum requirements that will entitle them to what they see as acceptable reward levels. They will do what they must to prepare for tests and then forget most of what they have learned (Good & Brophy, 2003). Strategies focused on learning, on the other hand, should motivate students to study and learn because they find the information or skill interesting, meaningful, or worthwhile.

Although the affective, emotional aspects of motivation are important, Good and Brophy (2000) argue that these will be insufficient for students in academic settings. Students should be focused on sense making and importance, not just enjoyment. This, they argue, will result in effective and motivated student effort. Teachers, especially teachers of older students, should attend to these distinctions.

Drawing from research by both Good and Brophy (2000) and Gambrell (1996; see also Marinak & Gambrell, 2008), we conclude that the general features of classroom learning environments that support the development of student motivation to learn are as follows:

- Modeling of the thinking and actions associated with motivation to learn
- Communicating expectations and attributions implying motivation to learn in students
- Creating a supportive environment for learning by minimizing the role of factors that produce performance anxiety and creating many opportunities for students to read
- Providing a book-rich classroom where teachers model reading and are familiar with many books
- Promoting social interactions about books

Voluntary Reading and Writing.   The cost of failing to address motivational issues is high. Too often, repeated experiences with failure or school experiences that do not make the value of reading and writing evident result in students with poor attitudes and limited willingness to attempt reading and writing tasks. Students with strong negative feelings about reading and writing are not likely to read or write voluntarily. These attitudes, in turn, influence performance.

There is a strong association between voluntary reading and writing and general reading and writing achievement (Greaney, 1980; McQuillan & Au, 2001; Stanovich, 1992). For example, children who demonstrate voluntary interest in books are rated significantly higher by teachers on school performance than are children with low interest in books (Morrow, 1986). They also score significantly higher on standardized tests and in work habits, social and emotional maturity, and language arts skills. Other evidence suggests that time spent in voluntary reading of books is the best predictor of reading achievement gains between second and fifth grade (Anderson, Wilson, & Fielding, 1988). Finally, research suggests that independent reading is one of the major determinants of vocabulary growth, especially among English language learners and students beyond third grade (McQuillan, 2006; Nagy & Anderson, 1984).

Relatively easy access to interesting books at appropriate reading levels exerts a strong influence on students' reading at all grade levels, right through high school. Morrow (1983, 1986) conducted a series of studies that examined instructional practice as well as its influence on students' motivation to read and its involvement in voluntary reading. Specifically, she examined the influence of classroom environment (e.g., library corners) and literary activities such as book talks on students' selection of reading as a voluntary activity.

The following practices appear to influence students' voluntary reading for primary-grade students (McQuillan & Au, 2001; Morrow, 1989):

- *Print-rich environment.* It appears that children need attractive and accessible libraries or other displays that provide a range of materials and levels of difficulty.
- *Active student involvement with reading.* These may include teacher-initiated activities and projects but also should encompass student-choice activities that feel authentic to the particular student population. In addition, ample practice time through recreational reading periods is essential.
- *Adult-child interactions focused on literature.* Teachers must invite students to interact with reading materials by reading aloud, telling stories, and/or engaging in discussion.

Intermediate students and adolescents in the middle and high school also need the opportunity to read widely (see Snow & Biancarose, 2004). Research by Guthrie (1997) and recommendations by Gay and Ivey (2006) highlight the importance of the following practices for early and late adolescents:

- *Diverse literature.* Students at these levels need a wide array of materials to read. Appropriate texts will include trade texts, newspapers and magazines, electronic texts, and a variety of primary sources. Students also need a variety of materials at different levels of difficulty.
- *Authentic opportunities* to examine and discuss texts from a variety of perspectives (student initiated, teacher supported).
- *Some degree of choice*, with easy access to materials.

These practices are not new, but their importance has been reaffirmed. Teachers need to model their love of reading and writing, but they also need to consider the nature of their planned instructional activities. At all grade levels and across all subject areas, teachers need to promote continued literacy development. A focus on personal engagement and meaning will look different in first grade than in tenth, but the idea is no less powerful. Reading and writing educators need to recognize how self-regard and motivation are influenced by instructional practices, in order to avoid the negative consequences of repeated failure.

Reading and Writing Activities and Tasks

Students are confronted with a wide variety of activities, tasks, and routines during the course of reading and writing instruction. In many classrooms, they are expected to answer questions, complete seatwork activities, read stories and books, produce book reports, write reports, keep a journal, engage in educational games, and complete projects. As we have already noted, activities and tasks influence how students interpret and experience the reading and writing curriculum and may be particularly powerful for students just beginning formal literacy instruction. They are the crucible in which student motivation, cognition, instruction, and learning fuse (Turner, 1995). The activities and tasks within a particular classroom define for students what literacy is, why it is important, and what it can do. They influence students' literacy learning in two ways: (1) by predisposing them to link literacy with specific cognitive strategies and (2) by focusing students on certain uses and purposes for literacy (Turner, 1995).

A study by Turner (1995) of twelve first-grade classrooms provides insight into the impact of literacy activities on students' voluntary strategy use, persistence, and attentional control during task completion. Literacy activities were classified as open (child-specified processes/goals, higher-order thinking required) or closed (other-designated processes/ goals, recognition/memory skills required). The results indicated that there were differences in both the types of literacy activities employed and the effects of open and closed literacy activities on student behavior.

Although student activities differed considerably between different types of classrooms, few classrooms were completely consistent in the use of activities reflecting a single type of instruction. Classrooms that relied on commercial reading programs tended also to rely more heavily on individual seatwork and teacher-directed reading groups. In these rooms, 77 percent of all activities observed were classified as closed, with work that was primarily, although not exclusively, of the practice type as exemplified by copying, workbook, and worksheet assignments.

In classrooms that were organized around more-holistic practices, structure consisted primarily of small groups. Activities were located at various centers in the classroom— such as the author's table, the library corner, and the listening center—and students were allowed some choice with regard to activities and order of completion. Within these classrooms, 73 percent of all the activities observed were classified as open.

An interesting finding of the Turner (1995) study was that the type of literacy task students received was a stronger predictor of behavior than was the type of classroom. Students used more strategies, persisted longer, and controlled their attention better during open than closed literacy tasks, regardless of the type of classroom in which these tasks occurred. The factors in open tasks that appear to influence students' motivated, strategic, reflective behavior are opportunities for challenge, personal control, satisfying interests, and collaboration (Turner & Paris, 1995).

In designing open tasks, teachers recast activities to emphasize the enjoyment and the value of literacy. They demonstrated to students the many ways in which a task can be done. Concrete examples of successful but different approaches to tasks are provided. Students are taught to assess the difficulty of a task and how to adjust their goals and strategies accordingly. Teachers emphasize the positive aspects of help seeking and help giving. They teach students how to give clues rather than answers, and group evaluation is a regular part of literacy instruction. These teachers help students see that real learning comes from error, since errors provide information about problems. By emphasizing the value of effort and refining strategies, they equip students to attempt increasingly difficult tasks and activities.

Turner (1995) notes that her study focused on average readers from white, middle-class populations and that her results may not apply to others outside this group. However, research by Newmann and his colleagues in urban, high-poverty schools in Chicago suggests the same conclusions (Newmann, Bryk, & Nagaoka, 2001; Newmann, Lopez, & Bryk, 1998). Students produce more high-level responses and are more engaged in learning when the tasks are authentic and demanding—no matter what the overall classroom orientation is.

Another example of this is evident in a study of students in a bilingual context. The study (Moll & Díaz, 1987) examined what happened when the literacy program shifted from word-by-word reading of English texts to discussion of story content, allowing students and teachers to switch to Spanish when needed to clarify the meaning of the text. By the third lesson, students were reading passages by themselves and answering comprehension questions at a level comparable to that of English monolingual readers at grade level. Similar results were reported in a case study of writing. It has also been demonstrated that integrating an activity such as teacher read-alouds and increasing teacher interaction on a regular basis can not only increase low-income students' engagement, but also their decoding and comprehending abilities (Feitelson, Kita, & Goldstein, 1986; Rosenhouse, Feitelson, Kita, & Goldstein, 1977). Increased participation of ESL students in reading trade books has resulted in reading and listening comprehension at twice the previous rate (Elley, 1991).

Hiebert (1994a) argues that open, or what she calls "authentic," literacy activities allow students without extensive literacy experiences to participate more fully in literacy events:

> Students who depend on schools to become literate are probably most in need of authentic literacy tasks. A regimen of skill and drill for these students fails to help them become readers and writers who engage in thoughtful, avid literacy as a lifelong pursuit (Commins & Miramontes, 1989; Moll & Diaz, 1987; Moll et al., 1980). The opposite of the skill-and-drill syndrome, however, is not the answer either. As part of authentic tasks, students benefit from modeling and discussions about features of written language, including the graphophonic system. (p. 405)

Although it may be tempting to view open tasks as always more preferable and closed structures as less preferable, the real issue is determining which activity structure(s) are most appropriate under different learning conditions. Because specific structures tend to promote or enhance some educational outcomes more than others, choice of literacy goals must drive instructional design. The situation is further complicated because the fit between activity and educational outcomes is not necessarily the same for students from different gender, racial, or sociocultural groups. For example, research suggests that combining both basic skills/strategy instruction and higher-order questioning leads to better comprehension among high-poverty students (Knapp, 1995; Puma et al., 1997).

We agree with Hiebert's (1994a) conclusion that many models of literacy activities are needed, especially ones that attend to students of different ages and prior literacy experiences. The one-size-fits-all assumption that underlies many current authentic literacy practices, with the same activities recommended for all students, requires careful examination for the instruction of students who vary in developmental levels and literacy backgrounds. This one-size-fits-all assumption suggests that the same activities will be effective for students who have had well over a thousand hours of literacy experiences before beginning kindergarten and those who enter first grade with the one hundred or so hours of kindergarten literacy instruction. Hiebert (1994a) indicates that this assumption is potentially damaging, "because it encourages teachers to suspect that there is something wrong with children and their parents when immersion in literacy does not produce fast results" (p. 107).

The following discussion highlights several different types of activity structures that are commonly used in classrooms today, including reading comprehension questions, writing process, reading-writing workshop, and discussion. Other activities, such as independent seatwork and guided reading, are addressed in Chapter 6.

Reading Comprehension Questions.   Many different types of questions are used in a variety of ways each day in virtually every classroom. Questions are an integral part of teacher presentations, discussions, seatwork, examinations, homework assignments, and remedial instruction. We have known for quite a long time that questioning strategies are associated with greater student growth, *especially* in the poorest schools. Three decades ago, Rosenshine (1983) found that teacher questions were related to student achievement. More recently, Taylor, Pearson, Clark, and Walpole, in their study of "beat the odds" schools (Taylor et al., 2000), found that teachers who had the highest levels of student achievement ("accomplished teachers") were much more likely to ask higher-level questions than were less-accomplished teachers. For example, 31 percent of the most accomplished teachers asked higher-order questions, whereas none of the least accomplished did. At the same time, accomplished teachers were also more likely to ask text-based questions. This suggests a generally more engaged and active teaching style for teachers whose students fare better.

A variety of question taxonomies have been used to classify various types of questions. Caution must be exercised in applying traditional question taxonomies; those that classify questions separately from the text or information being questioned (e.g., Barrett, 1976; Bloom, 1956; Huitt, 2004) are inadequate, given an interactive view of reading. Any interaction that occurs as a reader answers questions about a text will have a direct effect on comprehension and/or learning. Indeed, a large body of literature indicates that the type, content, and use of questions all influence student comprehension and learning.

A taxonomy of question-answer relations proposed by Pearson and Johnson (1978) provides one means for examining questions in a more interactive manner. Questions are classified in the context of, rather than apart from, the text or information being questioned. Pearson and Johnson identify three types of questions based on the probable source of the information the reader will use to answer the question. When the information needed is stated explicitly in the text, the question is textually explicit (TE). When the answer is implied rather than explicitly stated, the question is textually implicit (TI). Finally, there are some questions for which the appropriate answer is neither explicitly stated nor implied in the text but relies heavily on the background information or prior knowledge the reader brings to the text. Pearson and Johnson (1978) call these types of questions "scriptally implicit" (SI), using *script* as a synonym for *schema* or *knowledge structure*. Raphael has renamed these categories into student-friendly language that may be familiar to many teachers: TE questions are "Right There," TI questions are "Think and Search," and SI questions are of two sorts—"The Author and You" and "On Your Own" (Raphael, 1986; Raphael & Au, 2005).

Research by Wixson (1983a, 1983b, 1984) indicates that both the type and the content of questions promote different learning outcomes. Specifically, TE questions promote verbatim reproduction of the text, TI questions result in the generation of text-based inferences, and SI questions lead to the production of inferences based on prior knowledge. Furthermore, students learn and remember best the information they are questioned about, regardless of whether it is important or trivial to the important ideas in the text.

Indiscriminate use of questions can lead students away from, as well as toward, a desirable learning outcome. Questions should be used in a manner consistent with the goals and purposes of instruction. For example, in situations in which less-inferential processing is desirable—such as reading directions or conducting science experiments—explicit questions may be the most appropriate. When the integration of the ideas within a text is desirable, as is often the case in subject-area reading, textually implicit questions may be most helpful.

It is also important to remember that if we ask questions that focus on unimportant information, students are likely to learn this information at the expense of other, more important content. Furthermore, repeated use of similar types of questions shapes the way students approach their reading assignments. Students who received a steady diet of inferential and/or higher-order questions were able to answer those kinds of questions more easily than were students who had been asked only literal-level questions (Hansen, 1981). Indeed, many struggling students actually perform better when they receive instruction that sends them in this direction—perhaps because higher-level questions often focus on making either personal or real-world connections (Newmann, Lopez, & Bryk, 1998).

At different times throughout the history of reading and writing instruction, there has been a shift away from answering teacher-posed questions, with their implied "right" answers. Instead, teachers may be advised to solicit personal responses to reading (Parsons, 2001; Pritchard, 1993; Rosenblatt, 1978). Although the long-term effects of a heavy emphasis on personal response have yet to be determined, it is clear that both the tasks associated with response (e.g., oral or written) as well as the specific type of text influence the quality of students' responses (Guzniczak, 2004; Stotsky, 1995). In addition, we know that a steady diet of tasks of any sort—ones that permit only literal, "correct" responses or ones that ask only for a personal response without support or analysis—can have negative results. The tension between these two approaches permeates much of educational practice today, although it does appear that an emphasis on higher-order thinking promotes greater reading achievement over time than a focus on more-limited tasks (Taylor, Pearson, Peterson, & Rodríguez, 2003).

Writing Process.   Writing instruction today, like reading instruction, is in a state of flux. The widespread interest in the process of writing that dominated the 1990s is still very much alive in many parts of the country. Supporters of this approach argue that research demonstrates that writing is nonlinear, involving a recursive series of "stages" that include planning, drafting, editing, revising, and/or publishing written work. Opportunity to write is at the heart of process approaches to writing instruction. Advocates assert that students' writing improves by writing and by viewing and discussing good models of written work (Hillocks, 1986; Hillocks & Smith, 2003). Process approaches also include scaffolding during writing instruction. This support may take the form of conferences, modeling, and/or mini-lessons. Critics have charged that teachers sometimes focus on the process approach too rigidly, abandoning the role of teacher too completely. Graves (1994) remarks on the need for balance:

> We've learned much more about the essentials of teaching writing and how to use our time more effectively. Readers of my earlier book will find *A Fresh Look at Writing* more assertive: although listening to children is still the heart of the book, I think we now know better when to step in, when to teach, and when to expect more of our students. . . . We've learned that, right from the start, teachers need to teach more. (p. xvi)

Successful programs appear to have several common elements (Calkins, 1991; Graves, 1983, 1994; Lipson et al., 2000; Raphael, Englert, & Kirschner, 1989). First, the program provides for frequent, sustained time for writing that is both predictable and productive. Second, students write for real purposes and real audiences. Third, the environment is supportive, and students' are both challenged and encouraged. The environment is also organized so that students have access to materials and support. Finally, successful writing programs teach children the conventions of writing and are focused on improving students' writing abilities, not on the written product and/or the stages of the writing process (Graves, 1994; Lipson et al., 2000).

Although many classrooms across the country reflect this type of practice, others have turned the writing process into a mechanistic set of procedures. Students march through the "stages" of writing and teachers "correct" the work. As Lipson et al. (2000) have pointed out, the focus in these classrooms appears to be more on teaching students the stages or steps than it is on improving students' writing ability. In such classrooms, writing instruction involves little more than assigning students to produce a written product (while moving through the approved stages) and then evaluating it, with an emphasis on grammar, usage, and mechanics. This development prompted the National Council of Teachers of English to produce guidelines for the teaching of writing, to clarify the nature of high-quality writing instruction (NCTE, 2004). They argue:

> To say that writing is a process is decidedly not to say that it should—or can—be turned into a formulaic set of steps. Experienced writers shift between different operations according to tasks and circumstances. Second, writers do not accumulate process skills and strategies once and for all. They develop and refine writing skills throughout their writing lives. (p. 2)

Composition is much like comprehension in the sense that it is hard to pin down. Lipson (2006) has noted that comprehension is more like jazz improvisation than classical music. Successful composition ability results from years of practice during which writers acquire a "repertoire of routines" for writing and also procedures for managing writing challenges (how to get started, what to do when things don't go well, etc.) (NCTE, 2004). Like comprehension, composition instruction appears to be most effective for struggling learners when a combination of process approaches and strategic instruction are offered (De La Paz & Graham, 1997; Graham, Harris, & Larsen, 2001).

Process approaches to writing still flourish, but, despite the continuing research support for process writing as a vehicle for writing instruction (Gauvain, 2001; MacArthur et al., 1995), some schools and classrooms have responded to pressure from standards and/or high-stakes assessments by constraining the choices students make in writing to specific modes and genres and/or by returning to writing instruction that teaches more-discrete aspects of writing (e.g., grammar) in relative isolation from the longer discourse that is being produced (see, e.g., Strickland et al., 2001).

Clearly, reading and writing development and instruction are intimately related. What children read will affect what and how they write. Eckhoff (1983), for example, found that the features of the basal texts read by children were reflected in their own writing, whereas Aulls (2003) found that middle-grade students' knowledge of text structure strongly influenced their ability to write effective essays.

How children read may also affect their writing. Beal (1996), for example, found that students with poor comprehension monitoring ability were unsuccessful in revising their own writing. Importantly, training students in comprehension monitoring appears to help them in this area. Unfortunately, the writing instruction provided by teachers can be, and often is, distinct from the reading program, and this instructional program is likely to exert its own influence on students' writing performance. According to Raphael, Englert, and Kirschner (1989),

> The social context in which students engage in writing has a powerful impact on the type of writing they produce (DeFord, 1986). Key elements of successful writing programs include writing for a real purpose and a real audience in a supportive environment that provides frequent, if not daily, opportunities for sustained writing (Calkins, 1983; Graves, 1983). (p. 265)

What is very apparent is that writing performance, like reading, is influenced by the opportunities presented in the classroom and by the context for learning established at home and at school. Most significantly, children's understanding of what it means to write will be influenced by the types of writing that are promoted in the classroom and by the focus of the instruction (Lipson et al., 2000; Mabry, 1999).

Reading-Writing Workshop. The Reading-Writing Workshop represents a comprehensive approach to reading and writing instruction that has been formalized into an approach advocated by Nancie Atwell (1998) and Shelley Harwayne and Lucy Calkins (1987). It has subsequently been elaborated by others (see, e.g., Calkins, 1994; Fletcher & Portalupi, 2001; Ray & Laminack, 2001; Taberski, 2000). The tasks associated with this approach are designed to engage students in meaningful literacy activities and to develop strategic approaches to reading and writing. Two main ideas behind the Reading-Writing Workshop are that students own their own reading and writing and the teacher's role is that of expert reader-writer and guide rather than evaluator. Students are responsible for selecting their own reading material and their own topics for writing. Teachers read and write for their own purposes along with the students and share their experiences with students.

Although various authors emphasize slightly different aspects of the Reading-Writing Workshop, key elements common to all or most include:

- Time to read and write a variety of genres for many purposes
- Forums for response
- Conferences with the teacher
- Discussion with peers
- Mini-lessons (sometimes also called focus lessons)

Reading and writing workshops provide extended time for students to read and write. Atwell (1998) provides guidelines for student behaviors that help all members of the class to respect the reading and writing that are taking place and to keep reading and writing central to the activities in the classroom.

Guidelines for Reading Workshop time include: students are responsible for having a book in their possession at the beginning of the session; they must read a book for the entire period (no magazines or newspapers), preferably one that tells a story (no books of lists or facts for which readers can't sustain attention or build speed and accuracy); they cannot do homework or read material for another class; and they may not talk to or disturb others. Guidelines for Writing Workshop time include: students should write on one side of the paper only, to make it easier to cut and paste; they are not to erase but are to save a record of their thinking by simply drawing a line through text they wish to change; and they are to speak in quiet voices only, so that others who are thinking will not be interrupted.

Along with time to read and write, Reading-Writing Workshop also provides forums for responses to reading and writing. Responses can take both verbal and written forms. Verbal forms include literature response groups, peer conferencing, group sharing of writing, and conferencing with the teacher. Written forms include dialogue journals between teacher and student, as well as note writing between students about their reading.

Conferences between student and teacher that occur throughout the school year are the primary basis for evaluation in the Reading-Writing Workshop. Reading and writing conferences provide students with chances to review their progress toward old goals and to set new ones.

Teacher-student conferences can help students refine the focus on their piece, but they also provide an opportunity for teachers to identify students' needs, which often become the basis for a mini-lesson. Peer conferences provide students with feedback about their topic and also provide support for using checklists or monitoring guides. In the Reading Workshop, conferences have traditionally been a place where teachers evaluate students' progress and abilities. It is also, however, an opportunity for teachers to engage in quick, on-the-spot instruction and/or to encourage students to move in a different direction (e.g., attempt a new genre or author).

The final element of Reading-Writing Workshop is mini-lessons to assist students with their reading and writing. Mini-lessons can include a variety of activities, from reading of poetry and literature to short discussions of an author to the presentation of reading strategies. The teacher makes choices about which mini-lessons to present, based on students' dialogue journals and informal and formal conferencing. The key to mini-lessons is that they be relevant to students' actual reading or writing and that the topic can be addressed in a relatively timely way.

Evidence of the impact of Reading-Writing Workshop comes from several sources. Atwell (1987) presents numerous examples of students who started reading in Reading Workshop because that was the expectation and ended up reading because they enjoyed it. Others have found that Reading Workshop has a positive effect on the attitude and involvement with reading of learning-disabled students (Roller, 1996, 2002). There is evidence that combining a workshop approach with explicit strategy instruction has beneficial effects for struggling readers and writers (Katims & Harris, 1997).

Several issues have also been raised regarding Reading-Writing Workshop classrooms. Ash (1990) argues that although student ownership of reading is important, there is still an important role for whole-class or group readings of selected texts. Others point out that fiction and other narrative texts are privileged at the expense of great nonfiction with which students need to become familiar. It has also been suggested that such classrooms may actually limit students' engagement with diverse texts, since teachers tend to select mainstream literature (McCarthey, 1996). Similarly, there is some evidence that students may feel pressure to conform to certain content or modes of expression, thereby suppressing their engagement (see Finders, 1997; Moje, Willes, & Fassio, 2001).

Discussion. In a volume devoted to discussion as a means of promoting reading comprehension, Alvermann, Dillon, and O'Brien (1987) write that discussion is a curricular task selected by teachers for a variety of purposes. Some teachers may perceive discussion as a forum for raising important issues in relation to reading assignments. Others may see discussion as an opportunity for identifying and clarifying students' misconceptions. Still others may view discussion as a way of checking on whether students read assigned material. Alvermann et al. (1987) indicate that discussion is important both as a communication skill and as the foundation for developing higher-level reading skills. As a means of defining discussion, they propose three criteria:

> Discussants should put forth multiple points of view and stand ready to change their minds about the matter under discussion; students should interact with one another as well as with the teacher; and the interaction should exceed the typical two or three word phrase units common to recitation lessons. (p. 7)

Similarly, Goldenberg (1993) describes discussion as an interesting, engaging conversation that deals with an idea or a concept and has meaning and relevance for students. The focus remains discernible throughout, and there is a high level of participation without domination by any one person, especially the teacher. Teachers and students are responsive to what others say, so each statement builds on, challenges, or extends a previous one.

According to Goldenberg (1993), teachers or discussion leaders question, prod, challenge, coax, or remain silent. They clarify and instruct when necessary but without wasting time or words. They make certain that the discussion proceeds at an appropriate pace, knowing when to push to draw out an idea and when to ease up to allow for more thought and reflection. In essence, they are skilled at "weaving individual participants' comments into a larger tapestry of meaning" (p. 318).

On the basis of the experiences of practicing teachers, Goldenberg (1993) identifies the basic elements of discussion as instructional and conversational (see Figure 5.2). In one

FIGURE 5.2 Instructional Conversation Elements

Elements of the Instructional Conversation

Instructional Elements

1. *Thematic focus.* The teacher selects a theme or idea to serve as a starting point for forcusing the discussion and has a general plan for how the theme will unfold, including how to "chunk" the text to permit optimal exploration of the theme.
2. *Activation and use of background and relevant schemata.* The teacher either "hooks into" or provides students with pertinent background knowledge and relevant schemata necessary for understanding a text. Background knowledge and schemata are then woven into the discussion that follows.
3. *Direct teaching.* When necessary, the teacher provides direct teaching of a skill or concept.
4. *Promotion of more complex language and expression.* The teacher elicits more-extended student contributions by using a variety of elicitation techniques—invitations to expand (e.g., "Tell me more about that."), questions (e.g., "What do you mean?"), restatements (e.g., "In other words ..."), and pauses.
5. *Elicitation of bases for statements or positions.* The teacher promotes students' use of text, pictures, and reasoning to support an argument or position. Without overwhelming students, the teacher probes for the bases of students' statements—e.g., "How do you know?" "What makes you think that?" "Show us where it says _____."

Conversational Elements

6. *Fewer known-answer questions.* Much of the discussion centers on questions and answers for which there might be more than one correct answer.
7. *Responsivity to student contributions.* While having an initial plan and maintaining the focus and coherence of the discussion, the teacher is also responsive to students' statements and the opportunities they provide.
8. *Connected discourse.* The discussion is characterized by multiple, interactive, connected turns; succeeding utterances build upon and extend previous ones.
9. *A challenging, but nonthreatening, atmosphere.* The teacher creates a "zone of proximal development," where a challenging atmosphere is balanced by a positive affective climate. The teacher is more collaborator than evaluator and creates an atmosphere that challenges students and allows them to negotiate and construct the meaning of the text.
10. *General participation, including self-selected turns.* The teacher encourages general participation among students. The teacher does not hold exclusive right to determine who talks, and students are encouraged to volunteer or otherwise influence the selection of speaking turns.

Source: Goldenberg, C. (1993). Instructional conversations: Promoting comprehension through discussion. *The Reading Teacher, 46,* 316–326. Reprinted with permission of the International Reading Association.

sense, discussions are instructional because they are designed to promote learning. Teaching through discussion requires a deliberate and self-controlled agenda. In another sense, discussion is conversational in that it appears to be natural, spontaneous, and free from the didactic practices associated with formal teaching.

There is strong evidence that this type of discussion pattern is a more productive instructional approach for English language learners (ELL). In a follow-up study, Goldenberg and Patthey-Chavez (1995) found that ELL students both talked more and said more-significant things during instructional conversations than they did in the more didactic pattern in which a teacher asks a question, the student responds, and then the teacher evaluates the response before asking another question.

It is also important to be aware of factors that research indicates influence the effectiveness of discussion. For example, Evans, Alvermann, and Anders (1998) concluded that small groups can only work well when teachers have established a collaborative environment in the classroom. They focused, in particular, on the ways in which female students were "silenced" in small-group discussions unless clear guidelines had been established for participation. In the Evans (2002) study of fifth-grade students, she found that *both* male and female students preferred same-gender groups for discussions, because they felt less inhibited.

Many classroom teachers will recognize the challenges detailed by Villaume, Worder, Williams, Hopkins, and Rosenblatt (1994), who were engaged in an effort to improve discussion practices. These educators observed a great deal of inconsistency in students' movement beyond the role of answer giver in their early discussions. Some students assumed an active, responsible role naturally, while others appeared uncomfortable and uncertain and still others used the opportunity to be disruptive and silly. They determined that modeling was not sufficient, as only a few students had accepted their subtle invitation to engage in the behaviors modeled. They determined that instruction about discussion was needed and developed a series of strategies to teach their students about discussion.

Similarly, Maloch (2002) found that teachers needed to scaffold, or support, students' ideas and participation if they had not been engaged in discussion groups previously. According to Maloch, "when students move from a teacher-led format to a student-led one, they face multiple demands, including interpersonal, interactional, and response-related issues" (p. 109). Because this research suggests the potential for inequities in participation, it is especially important that teachers support struggling readers and writers in the early stages of discussion.

Discussions that are not well developed are likely to have a variety of unanticipated consequences for students, especially for those who are experiencing difficulty with reading and writing.

Assessment Practices

While this entire book deals with assessment, this section focuses specifically on assessment practices as a feature of instructional contexts that influence reading and writing performance. Within this context, we need to be concerned with at least two dimensions of classroom assessment: assessments required for external accountability purposes (which are examples of the summative, outcome assessment purposes described in Chapter 3) and assessments selected and/or created by the teacher for evaluation and to inform instruction (which relate primarily to the formative progress monitoring assessment purposes described in Chapter 3).

Assessments Required for External Accountability: Impact on Teaching and Learning.   Historically, both large-scale standardized tests as well as performance- and classroom-based assessments have had some accountability function, whether to audiences who are external to the classroom or to the teacher and/or students themselves. It is the accountability functions of tests and assessments, regardless of their form or frequency, that produce the greatest impact on teaching and learning. To the extent that performances of students and classrooms are made visible and have consequences ranging from prestige and shame to merit increases and management constraints, the nature of assessments tends to shape teachers' practice and therefore student learning and performance. In their discussion of the impact of assessment, Resnick and Resnick (1992) concluded:

> *You get what you assess*—Teachers will teach to the assessment if the tests matter in their own or their students' lives; and
> *You do not get what you do not assess*—What is not integral to classroom assessment tends to disappear from classrooms in time.

Others have made similar observations about large-scale assessments (e.g., Hillocks, 2002).

Given this conclusion, it is clear that the type and focus of assessment can make a big difference in students' school experience, opportunity to learn, and acquisition of knowledge and skill. There is extensive evidence to suggest that high-stakes assessments tend to focus teachers' attention on tested elements to the detriment of nontested content/processes (Guthrie, 2002; Linn, 2000). For example, because some standardized tests, and many computer-assisted assessments, still focus on isolated skills rather than on complex performances, they can and do drive instruction in the wrong direction. When tests are used as arbiters of many school decisions about placement, graduation, advancement, and so forth, they often exert great influence on what is taught, leading to a narrowed curriculum. Teachers are pressured to teach what is tested, and to teach these things in the particular forms and formats used on the tests. Indeed, Valencia (2007) notes that students and teachers "spend classroom time practicing on 'miniature' state tests and engaging in activities that may be counterproductive in producing real gains in students achievement (Linn, 2000)." This leads to an overemphasis on superficial content coverage and drills on discrete skills at the expense of in-depth projects and other complex tasks. It also leads to classwork in which students spend their time on test-like tasks, shallow learning, and work based on misperceptions of students' abilities.

This may have an even more insidious effect on nonmainstream students. First, these students are more likely to do less well on traditional assessments for a variety of reasons and are therefore more likely to be the recipients of test-like practice tasks. In addition, teachers in targeted schools are more likely to feel the pressure of raising test scores.

Several authors have noted that teachers may abandon rich literacy instruction involving, for example, discussion. Triplett (2006) cites several instances where teachers note that they are preparing for tests and are "much too busy to participate in discussions about stories" (p. 118). Yet there is evidence to suggest that discussion may be particularly helpful for struggling students (Moll & González, 1994; Triplett, 2007).

Assessments Required for External Accountability: Assumptions about Tests and Testing.   Resnick and Resnick (1992) point out that tests are the heritage of earlier psychological theories that promoted a concept of learning as the development of routinized skill. Most standardized tests were developed at this same time and reflect the same theories. Thus, for example, two key assumptions of standardized tests are *decomposability* and *decontextualization*. Because they influence our ideas about teaching as well as testing, these concepts are discussed next.

Earlier theories of learning suggested that reading and writing are *decomposable*— that is, they can be separated into discrete components and the parts would equal the whole. According to Resnick and Resnick (1992), built into the decomposability assumption is a metaphor that likens thought to a simple machine. A simple machine can be built by constructing each of the parts separately. When the parts are put together, if the design is good, the machine will run. It supports a notion of teaching and testing separate component skills, with the expectation that their composition into a complex performance will occur at some later time. This assumption has been seriously challenged by recent research that recognizes that complicated skills and competencies owe their complexity not just to the number of components they engage, but also to interactions among the components and strategies for calling upon them.

Complex competencies such as reading and writing cannot be defined just by listing all of their components. Efforts to assess reading and writing by identifying separate components of those abilities and testing them independently may interfere with effectively teaching such abilities. Assessing separate components encourages instructional activities in which isolated components are practiced. Because the components do not add up to reading and writing, students who practice only the components are unlikely to learn to do real reading and writing.

Even when contemporary standardized tests take a more complex view of the nature of complex learning, most still rest on a principle of *decontextualization* that asserts that each component of a complex skill is fixed and that it will take the same form no matter where it is used. This assumption suggests that if students know how to get a main idea, for example, they know how to do so under all conditions of text type, prior knowledge, and so forth. However, a great deal of research suggests that we cannot teach a skill component in one setting and expect it to be applied automatically in another. As a result, assessing students' competence in a context that is very different from the context in which it is practiced or used is likely to result in invalid conclusions.

There is widespread agreement among educators, researchers, and policy makers that most standardized tests currently used in American schools do not tap many of the skills and abilities that students need to develop to be successful in later life and schooling (Chudowsky & Pellegrino, 2003; Darling-Hammond, Ancess, & Falk, 1995). Consistent with the decomposability and decontextualization assumptions, the most frequent criticism of these tests is that they do not evaluate higher-order skills and students' abilities to perform real-world tasks.

> The decomposition of important knowledge and skill into disconnected bits and the decontextualization from meaningful situations of use that standardized tests impose virtually ensure their inability to validly assess complex capabilities in which knowledge and skill are combined to produce meaningful intellectual, artistic, or design products. (Resnick, 1994, p. 514)

A new effort is underway to develop, by 2015, assessments that will measure achievement with reference to the Common Core State Standards (CCSS). These measures are being developed by two different consortia of states. It appears that the measures will tacitly address some concerns (such as decomposability and decontextualization) typically associated with assessments that are used for accountability purposes. Rather than simply assess discrete skills, some test items will require students to engage in relatively complex, contextualized reading and writing tasks. For example, the English language arts assessment in one consortia requires that students work intertextually over a number of class sessions to locate information within a prescribed set of electronic resources, evaluate the quality/credibility of the source, and integrate information into an essay or research paper (ETS, 2010). While items like this essay resemble the authentic tasks of alternative, teacher-constructed assessment (see next section), the system of scoring the essays reminds us that the assessments for CCSS are designed as large-scale accountability measures; the plan is to score such essays using an automated (computer software) scoring system.

Although this discussion has focused primarily on standardized tests, it is worth noting that mandated assessments of all sorts—standardized measures to basal tests to teacher-made examination and questioning—can have the same unintended consequences. Valencia (2007) provides an extensive description of how informal, classroom-based assessments can become rigid and fragmented influences of teaching and learning, especially in the context of externally mandated policies. Importantly, these assessments can become decontextualized in the same way that standardized tests are: "selected by people outside the classroom to be used with all students, administered according to a fixed timetable . . . most of these assessments are selected without consideration of the particular curriculum in the classroom or specific needs of individual children" (p. 5).

Assessments Selected and/or Created by Teachers: Formative Assessments. In response to the concerns about standardized tests, many educators and researchers began developing alternative assessments throughout the 1990s. The idea was to examine students' work in context as a means of evaluating student performance. More recently, these assessments have been described under the label of formative assessments (see Chapters 3 and 4) and may take a variety of forms, including observation, portfolios, and performance tasks.

Formative assessments are designed to address several concerns about traditional testing (Black & Wiliam, 1998; Wiggins, 1991). First, they are designed to provide a more direct and nuanced assessment of a student. For example, students actually do writing—for real audiences—rather than taking spelling tests or answering questions about writing. The tasks are contextualized, complex intellectual challenges involving the student's own research or use of knowledge. In addition, they allow student learning styles, aptitudes, and interests to serve as a source for developing competence and for the identification of strengths that may have been hidden previously. This turns out to be especially important for struggling students and among culturally or linguistically diverse student populations (Laing & Kamhi, 2003; Wilkinson & Silliman, 2000).

Second, formative assessments are intended to create a more transparent and open system whereby well-articulated criteria are attached to well-identified types of performance. These are openly explained to students and others in the learning community, rather than kept "secure" in the tradition of tests. The argument has been that learning and performance are both supported when teachers and students know ahead of time what an assessment will evaluate. Performance-based criteria guide teaching, learning, and evaluation in ways that place teachers in the role of coach and students in the role of performers. Assessments that originate inside the classroom are meant to directly inform instruction—to educate, not audit (Black & Wiliam, 1998; Wiggins, 1998).

Third, formative assessments help students develop the capacity to evaluate their own work against public standards. These assessments promote students' ability to revise, modify, and redirect their energies, taking initiative to assess their own progress (Valencia, 1998; Valencia, 2007). The research evidence suggests that students who receive instruction in and support for self-assessment are likely to improve their overall achievement (Black & Wiliam, 1998; McDonald & Boud, 2003).

As educators and researchers have explored the dimensions and limitations of what was once called alternative assessment, new labels and concepts appear—including "assessment for learning" (Stiggins, 2001) and "inquiry assessment" (Valencia, 2007). According to Darling-Hammond (1995, 2004), because most traditional tests provide only a limited measure of a narrow aspect of learning or development, they are poor predictors of how students will perform in other settings. This promotes a view of students as having deficits that need to be corrected rather than as having individual differences, approaches to learning, and strengths that can be supported and developed. Neither do traditional tests reflect or capture the diversity of students' backgrounds and experiences (Figueroa & Garcia, 1994; Solano-Flores & Trumbull, 2003). They often contain assumptions and facts that are grounded in the context of the dominant culture and fail to include relevant forms of knowledge from other cultures. This places students from nondominant cultures at a disadvantage in demonstrating what they know and can do (Garcia & Pearson, 1994; Gopaul-McNicol & Armour-Thomas, 2002).

In contrast, formative assessments can, if properly designed, affect teaching and learning in more positive ways. Because students are involved in developing, exhibiting, and evaluating their own work, alternative assessments help them develop a sense of responsibility and ownership of their work and encourage them to regularly analyze and reflect on their progress. Effective assessments of this sort can encourage an intelligent, rich curriculum rather than the narrowed one fostered by teaching and coaching for tests. Of course, formative assessments are not immune to issues of cultural and linguistic diversity. If teachers create performance or classroom tasks that are alien to students, students' abilities can and will be misunderstood (Estrin, 1993). Joann Wilson-Keenan and her colleagues describe in superb detail how differences in background and experience can cause teachers to misunderstand and/or underestimate student performance—in this case, spontaneous language and written work in a first-and-second-grade classroom (Wilson-Keenan,

Solsken, & Willett, 2001). Because the "texts" that students produced were not recognizable within the teachers' framework, they evaluated some students as less capable. The researches conclude:

> Conventional expectations—including static conceptions of genre and cultural difference, familiarity with only white, middle-class community knowledges, practices and voices, and educational norms that shape our perceptions of student's abilities—act as barriers to recognizing and appreciating (student accomplishments). (p. 527)

The important point is that assessment practices can and do communicate to students what is important and also that they impact what aspects of student knowledge and skill teachers observe. As Valencia (2007) has noted, the amount of assessment, including classroom-based assessment, has increased enormously. This may have the unintended consequence of diminishing the amount of time and effort teachers devote to observing and noticing students' authentic efforts in context. This, in turn, will narrow the view that teachers have of students.

STRATEGIES AND TOOLS FOR ASSESSING THE INSTRUCTIONAL ENVIRONMENT

In this chapter, we are suggesting that it is important to observe the context for learning, not just the student in that context. Although this is important for understanding the performance of all students, it is essential for addressing the instructional needs of students who are struggling with reading and/or writing. Until recently, assessments of the instructional environment have been rare. Fortunately, there are now a sparse but growing number of strategies and tools for assessing instructional settings, methods, and materials.

Assessing Home and Community Influences and Perspectives

Understanding the nature of home and community literacy practices and their potentially profound influence on students' literacy learning is critical to making good decisions about assessment and instruction. Therefore, it is important to gather as much background information as possible from the home and the learner. Using several sources of information allows us to examine performance from several perspectives. This increases our confidence in the information and deepens our understanding of the student's reading and writing (Black & Wiliam, 1998).

Interviews.   The interactive perspective we adopt in this text requires that we examine the contextual influences on students' performance. Although interviews can be time-consuming to conduct, most professionals understand that they can provide information otherwise impossible to access and that they can enhance the diagnostic value of the overall assessment.

The strengths of interviews can also be a matter of some concern (see Afflerbach, 2000). For example, because interview information is *self-reported*, it can provide insight into the values and beliefs of those who are providing it. However, families might report information that is an inaccurate reflection of their true ideas, beliefs, or inclinations. In particular, it has been argued that students are likely to report what they think the teacher/ adult wants to hear.

A second concern is that individuals may find it difficult to talk about their ideas or abilities. This is a particular concern when students are very young, have speech/language differences or difficulties, or when English is not the primary language in the home. We must consider these potentially confounding factors and seek multiple indicators to confirm or validate the findings. However, it is also important to remember that research suggests that interviews and other types of self-report can provide both reliable and valid information that is difficult to glean otherwise (Cromley & Azevedo, 2007; Ericsson & Simon, 1980, 1993; Lipson, Irwin, & Poth, 1986).

Interviewing, like other assessment practices, requires a knowledgeable and skilled professional eye. It is important to structure interviews to gather information in systematic ways and record data in a consistent manner. Structured procedures, including tape recording, can increase the reliability of interview information and ensure that teachers interpret thoughtfully the results of such assessments. We turn our attention to strategies and questions designed to support a broad-based approach to diagnostic assessment.

Parent Interviews. Parents are particularly good sources of information about a student's background, because they have enduring contact with their child. They have information about the student's overall experiential background and developmental history that includes knowledge about physical, cultural, linguistic, affective, and cognitive factors. Parents are likely to have a somewhat different perspective about students than do school personnel. It is often more personal and more detailed, including critical cultural, motivational, and attitudinal information.

Parents also have a longer-range view of their child's school experience. They will remember and describe, for example, how first grade was such "a waste" because the teacher got sick in the middle of the year and they couldn't find a substitute teacher. Or they will know, even if the school records don't reveal it, that their daughter's problems in writing started in third grade, when the school started a new approach to writing. Although this information does not necessarily inform us about the specific difficulties that the student is experiencing right now, it can help our understanding of the overall context of the reading or writing problem.

Coming to understand how parents use reading and writing, what they believe about the value and nature of literacy, whether English is a primary language in the home, and how they try to teach knowledge and skills can be helpful in both assessment and instruction. An initial interview can provide information about the amount and type of reading and writing activity that takes place in the home and about how literacy and schooling are viewed there.

We prefer to elicit parents' ideas through in-person interviews (though phone interviews can work too) rather than use a written questionnaire, as the personal interaction can build a relationship, allows for follow-up questions that are responsive to parents' comments, allows us to read nonverbal signals, and avoids the possible scenario that that particular parent finds a written questionnaire intimidating or is unable to read it. We try to be informal, using a list of potential interview questions to remind us of important areas of discussion. Below, we have set forth sample questions that address these areas: eliciting parent concerns, understanding home literacy practices, learning of potentially contributing health and social factors, gaining a perspective on educational history, and discovering students' interests, experiences, and gifts.

Eliciting Concerns about Reading and Writing.   The question that we recommend to start an interview with a parent or caregiver of a student who appears to be struggling with reading or writing is:

- Tell me about any concerns you have with your child's reading or writing or learning.

This question is informed by the developmental pediatrics literature, particularly the work of Glascoe (2011). Glascoe found parents to be of tremendous help in accurately identifying and describing areas of concern in their children's development, when asked about their "concerns." Parents produced considerably less information in response to questions about "worries" and "problems," terms that proved to be negatively focused and off-putting. Also, Glascoe notes that parents' observations are seldom neatly packaged in terms of the subskills that professionals use to organize their observations; nor do parents use professional jargon to describe their observations.

Thus, it may be necessary to ask parents more in-depth questions to follow up on the concerns expressed, to do so in everyday language, and to ask for examples to make sure we are talking about the same construct. Depending on how parents respond spontaneously to the above starting question, we might ask questions that get at specific subskills and dispositions, such as:

- When you hear your child read aloud, do you have concerns about how correctly or how smoothly he reads the words? Can you give me an example of what you have observed?
- How well do you feel that your child understands when you read to him (when he reads on his own)? What does he do (say) that lets you know this?
- Tell me about your child's attitudes toward reading and writing. In what circumstances is he interested in reading (being read to) and writing?

Understanding Home Literacy Practices.   The interview provides an opportunity to understand some of the literacy practices of the student's home and community. (Recall the discussion at the outset of this chapter on how we can facilitate literacy learning when we understand home/community literacy practices.) Questions, such as those that ask how often students are read to or how much they read on their own and what are favorite books, provide valuable information, but they also suggest that what the interviewer values are literacy practices found in school. We recommend adding questions that go beyond asking how families "do school" to discover out-of-school literacies that provide real-world experiences with reading, writing, and using language to communicate. Examples of these questions include:

- What kinds of written words does your child notice in your home/community [and car!]? Besides words in books, magazines, and newspapers, this could refer to written words found in or on mail, hymnals and Bibles, sheet music, TV guide, recipes, maps, signs, directions and manuals, menus, sticky notes, bulletin or other boards, calendars, greeting cards, boxes or cans of food—to name a few. What does he do alone, or with other family members, with those written words?

- Does your child read words presented electronically? For example, does he use a home computer or other technology to read e-mail, access Web sites, download music, or play video games? Please give a few examples.
- What kind of writing does your child use to communicate at home? For example, does he write notes, draw pictures, send e-mail or text messages, or use other social media? What does his writing look like?
- Families' talk is very important in supporting reading and writing. Can you describe a few examples of the ways in which your child talks with others? For example, does he report what happened during the day, describe past interesting experiences, tell stories, joke, sing, engage others in conversation, or translate for family members who do not speak English fluently?

Learning about Potentially Contributing Health and Social Factors. Parents are also able to provide information about events that may contribute to reading and writing difficulty, though parents may not be aware of the significance of these events. For example, chronic ear infections can inhibit both language development and phonological awareness. Similarly, high parental expectations, competition with older, successful siblings, or early entrance into academic programs can cause students to avoid reading tasks. When parents appear to be uncomfortable sharing family information and health history, it is appropriate to explain very briefly that these may be factors in students' achievement, and then respect limits that parents set. Questions that may elicit this information include:

- Please tell me about any concerns that you or your child's doctor have, or have had, with your child's health? For example, has your child had frequent illnesses such as ear infections? Or did your child seem especially late in developing skills such as talking or walking? [Elicit description where clearly relevant.]
- Have other family members experienced health or learning problems? [Elicit description where clearly relevant.]
- Is there anything at home that may be a source of stress for your child (e.g., moving, new sibling, illness)? How does that seem to be affecting your child?

Gaining a Perspective on Educational History. Parents have had the opportunity to observe their child's academic progress in school as well as their affective responses to school. Research, again from pediatricians who depend on parent report (Glascoe, 2011), suggests that parents are more accurate reporters of current events than of past events. Even if parents' report of the previous years' schooling is colored by subsequent events, it is important to understand parents' impressions of their child's instructional experiences. Some parents attribute their child's difficulties in reading and writing development to poor teaching and schooling. Unsatisfactory initial instruction, poor classroom management, or simply lack of readiness for the program offered in the school can result in learning difficulties. It is possible to be an empathetic listener without fueling parents' discontent.

If schools or teachers appear to be a factor in the student's problem, we can respond to parents' concern or frustration by advocating tactfully for removing barriers to successful performance. Questions that can elicit parents' report of educational progress include:

- When did you first become concerned about your child's reading and writing?
- In what ways have your child's teachers helped him learn to read and write?
- How do you feel about the way that his educational needs have been handled?
- What can you tell me about your child's learning that will help me teach him [advise his teachers]?

Discovering Students' Interests, Experiences, and Gifts. The final topic to be considered is deliberately positioned at the end of the interview in order to wrap up conversations with family members on a high note and communicate to families our interest in their children. Fink (2006) and others provide convincing evidence that readers with learning difficulties thrive in instructional environments and with instructional materials that resonate with their own interests and experiences. Questions to family members might even be framed with this understanding:

- We know that a student's curiosity about something of great interest to him is very powerful in inspiring him to learn to read. Tell me, what do you observe your child to be curious about? What are some of the things that he is most interested in?
- Learners who have difficulty reading traditional print text often pursue their interests using other means: firsthand observation or hands-on exploration; accessing information using technology (e.g., Web sites); working with a mentor, friend, or expert. How has he pursued his interests so far?
- What would you say have been some of your child's favorite experiences?
- We also know that creative play helps children build their interests. How do you see your child using his imagination or being creative in play?
- Who is it within your family or outside of your family that takes special interest in your child's learning, reading, and writing? How do they do that?
- What are you most proud of about your child?

Additional Considerations. Cultural and linguistic differences between the interviewer and parents can certainly influence interviews. The interviewer will be able to interpret more accurately the information that parents provide if the interviewer develops sensitivity to parents' implicit rules for conversation and their perspective on authority figures as well as their expectations, which in some cases may differ considerably from those of native-born Americans (Civil, Bratton, & Quintos, 2005; Vang, 2005). Of course, when parents' primary language is not English, an interpreter will be required if the interviewer is not fluent in the parents' language.

Even if there are no apparent cultural or linguistic differences, parents are often confused and intimidated by professionals and their jargon. In addition, many parents of students with reading and writing difficulties are frightened and dismayed by their child's apparent inability to acquire these critical abilities. For many, this is interpreted to mean that their daughter or son is not very bright. Sometimes they are concerned that they have done or not done something that has caused the problem. It is important to be positive and supportive while working with parents, without raising any unrealistic hopes about magic remedies.

We have found the following guidelines helpful in conducting parent conferences or interviews (see also Friend & Bursuck, 2006; Spinelli, 2006):

- Meet in a private and confidential setting.
- Clarify the purpose of the meeting.
- Listen attentively, and avoid talking too much or using jargon.
- Keep note taking to a minimum; summarize major points at the end.
- When in doubt, clarify what was said, to avoid misunderstandings.
- Follow parents' cues regarding cultural expectations and rules for interaction.
- Be tactful; avoid making judgmental remarks.
- Encourage less-talkative people by asking open-ended questions.
- Do not be afraid of silences. They often elicit important information.
- Respond forthrightly to parents' anxiety; reassure without painting an overly optimistic picture.
- Remain relaxed, and avoid defensiveness and sarcasm at all costs.
- Assure parents that the information will be treated confidentially and then make sure that it is.

We suggest concluding the interview by gratefully acknowledging the expertise that parents are sharing, as the persons who know their child best, while simultaneously assuring parents of our interest in their child, by asking:

- Is there anything else that you would like to tell me that would help me teach your child?

Summarizing this information can be extremely useful in anticipating the "goodness of fit" between the student's home and community experiences and the expectations of the school.

Teachers and Students. In order to consider and facilitate interactions between home and school literacy learning contexts, it is necessary to understand how parent and teacher perspectives on a student's learning in school—her knowledge and skills, her responses to the instruction provided in school, and her teacher's perception of areas of strength and need—might be similar or contrast with those of the student herself. To that end, it would be appropriate to ask of teachers many of the same questions we recommended asking parents and students about concerns, educational history, and student interests and experiences in school. Here are examples of how some of those questions might be worded when posed to a teacher:

- What concerns, if any, do you have about the student's learning?
- Describe the student's literacy skills such as reading orally or silently, writing, expressing ideas by speaking, or listening to understand spoken information.

- Describe the student's interest and achievement in content areas such as math, science, and social studies.
- What methods and materials have been particularly effective with this student?
- What are the student's strengths, gifts, and interests, both academically and as a member of the classroom community?
- What are the student's needs, both academically and as a member of the classroom community?

School records can also suggest how well a student has functioned in an academic setting, what instructional materials have been used, and how far he or she has progressed in acquiring age-appropriate reading and writing knowledge and skill. School records can also help us avoid the duplication of assessment efforts. When available, recent test results and observational data may provide invaluable direction for preparing an assessment plan. In the best cases, information is obtained about what has worked instructionally and what has not.

Student information should be accessed and handled discretely. Schools are sometimes sensitive to the permanence of student records, which are always available to parents at their request. Students may view their own records at the age of majority (Family Educational Rights and Privacy Act/Buckley Amendment, or FERPA, 1974). If you are a teacher in the building, you may access and discuss any student information as long as you are planning instruction or making decisions. Schools are not permitted to distribute this information to any outside professionals without explicit parental consent, and most schools and school employees do not discuss individual students without parent consent either. If there is any question about whether a parent would be concerned about the assessment processes being used, it is a good idea to obtain written parental consent before reviewing student records.

Assessing Instructional Setting

In this section, we describe some techniques for examining and describing the general characteristics of instructional settings, to determine how they may be contributing to a particular student's struggles or successes.

Observation. Although some information may be collected by interviewing the teacher and/or the student and by examining materials and assignments (see also Chapter 6), reliable conclusions require some classroom observation. Observation, in the hands of an experienced evaluator, is one of the most powerful assessment tools a teacher or clinician can possess. Information about virtually every component of reading and writing can be collected by using observation. As Boyd-Batstone (2004) notes, "taking observational notes allows the teacher to record a wide range of authentic experiences and even unintended outcomes of literacy development" (p. 230). We have provided in-depth discussions of how to observe specific components in other portions of the book. In this section, we limit our discussion to general observational guidelines and try to capture the power of this tool as a rich source of information about the general instructional context.

Despite their value, questions are often raised about the reliability of observation data. When we say that a measure is reliable, we mean that the results we attain tomorrow using this tool would be roughly the same as those we achieved today. Reliability "depends, for all practical purposes, on the adequacy of the behavior sample on which the score is based, which, in turn, depends on the stability of the behavior being measured. Our experience indicates that a score based on a single visit to a classroom seldom has adequate reliability. . . . Since reliability is primarily a function of the adequacy of the sample of behavior observed, reliabilities can be raised by increasing the number of visits" (Medley, 1985, p. 101).

Because teachers have many opportunities to observe their classrooms, their observations are often quite trustworthy. External specialists who may observe a classroom only once or twice need to exercise caution in generalizing the results, for either student performance or classroom context. Other factors, such as observer (teacher) objectivity, may also influence the quality and reliability of observational information. Teachers must be aware that their observations are subject to personal bias. Like everyone else, teachers tend to see things from their own personal perspectives. Some teachers conclude that students are making satisfactory progress when they appear to be busy and attentive. Some teachers are prone to notice certain kinds of behavior and block out other kinds.

There are several ways to increase the reliability of observational data. First, teachers should determine exactly what will be noted before observing. Next, teachers should plan how, when, and where to observe (Borich, 2008). If these observation categories are important and well defined, then observation accuracy will increase. Finally, teachers should use some type of format or observation guide that helps to systematize the observation.

The ideas presented here are examples of the ways in which observations can be structured so that the information gathering is reasonably objective. Observing in a busy classroom requires fairly structured observations. This could involve making anecdotal records of what students say during different reading activities or during conversation, or making notations regarding the interactions in groups. "The important thing is that teachers think of observation as a form of problem solving; it is a selective search for knowledge to guide instruction" (Jaggar, 1985, p. 6).

As with all assessment instruments, the validity of observations is dependent on how carefully what is being assessed has been defined. Knowledge of the reading and writing processes is critical, since the validity of observation is related to what is worth noticing. In reading and writing, this means looking for authentic literacy behaviors where students are engaged in a variety of activities under a variety of conditions—engaged in independent seatwork, sustained silent reading, writing for a specified audience, cooperative work projects, teacher-guided lessons, and so forth.

Observation can be used as a tool in almost any phase of the assessment-instruction process. For example, observation can be used to get to know individual students, evaluate groups, assess progress, appraise teaching techniques, and identify problems. In this chapter, we provide specific and detailed ideas for evaluating the learning context, and observation plays a central role in these discussions. Generally, the goals are to gather information that helps us to interpret the interviews and work samples we are collecting at the same time, to gain insight into the school climate and culture, and to understand the organization and structure of the classroom.

Teacher and Classroom.   When students are struggling, it is critical to examine the context within which they function. Whether you are the student's classroom teacher responsible for the daily instructional setting or a support teacher responsible for planning and implementing a specialized program, it is important to understand what the student is expected to do and how. If you are observing in someone else's classroom, you should make it clear to the classroom teacher that your observation is intended to help you understand the student's instructional program and that the goal is to benefit the student. If you are the classroom teacher for the student, "observation" of your own classroom is, of course, impossible. However, you can take stock, using the questions and observation formats as guides for self-reflection.

If the student moves from one setting to another during the school day, your observations should include each one. Questions like the following can be used to organize your context assessment:

- What materials and tasks are used in teaching this student?
- What types of classroom organization, expectations, and interactions are apparent?
- What types of instructional groups does the student participate in?
- Does the instructional approach in each setting seem congruent with the others?

As any experienced teacher knows, each classroom has its own personality. The learning climate that teachers establish with their students can be an influential factor in students' learning and achievement. As described by Borich (2008), the *learning climate* is a combination of several factors: (1) the types of concerns that teachers have, (2) the amount of teacher control (high–low) and teacher warmth (high–low), and (3) the social environment. Teacher concerns can be thought to involve either themselves (How will my principal evaluate me?), their teaching (Is there a better way to do this?), or their students (Are my students learning what they need to?). Teachers also vary in their attitudes and expectations for student success, and they adopt varying beliefs about teaching and learning. They may vary in the extent to which they provide for student-centered activities, encourage a variety of responses, and engage students in active learning. Different behaviors result in different student outcomes.

The setting includes aspects of classroom management but also organizational issues related to grouping, access to literate activity, and integration of supportive instruction within the classroom context. Borich (2008) describes a complex of interacting features within the social environment, including organization, goals, physical setting, etc. However, he also notes that social dynamics such as group cohesiveness, diversity, and competitiveness impact students' learning. Teaching and learning benefit from safe, orderly environments. When teachers and students spend too much time in transitions, in managing unruly behavior, or in explanations of routine tasks, less time is available for teaching and learning. These management factors influence learning for all students, but for the student who is struggling, it is important to notice whether there are unique management issues operating. For example, these students are more likely to leave the room for instructional purposes. Is this time being used effectively? How much time is taken in transitions?

The instructional dimension, of course, is paramount. We return to this issue in Chapter 6. Issues that may be examined here could focus on the following:

- What types of assessments are done in this setting?
- How has the teacher used assessment information in planning the student's program?
- How does the teacher respond to individual differences in the classroom? (Is there evidence of accommodations, modifications, etc.?)

Different students interact with settings and materials differently. Observation of the student in the instructional setting provides the final, critical pieces of information as we get started.

There is considerable evidence that students from different cultures react differently to aspects of the learning climate, but it is also the case that teachers of students from diverse settings, especially those serving children of poverty, often provide the least warmth and the most controlling learning environments (see Allington, 1991a; Au, 2000; Slaughter-Defoe & Carlson, 1996).

Learner in Context.   Skilled teachers know that conclusions should not be drawn from one or even two instances of a particular behavior. Instead, when using observation, we are looking for *patterns of performance.* Patterns emerge when the same (or similar) behaviors are observed repeatedly over time. Alternatively, patterns can emerge that reveal the circumstances that influence reading and writing. You can see how the student performs *in interaction* with various texts and contexts (that is, subject-area texts, children's magazines, library research, reading groups, and so on), and you are watching for variability or stability. In this way, it is possible to determine what students can and will do under different conditions.

It should be easy to remember important events, but by the end of a busy day we frequently have forgotten what we meant to remember. Finding a convenient and accurate way to record information is important. Many teachers find it useful to keep sticky notes close at hand. Whenever you observe something of interest, jot down the time, date, and student information. Then, at your leisure, you can put these memos in a notebook or portfolio tabbed for each student.

Of course, there is merit to creating more-elaborated and ongoing systems for collecting anecdotal records. Boyd-Batstone (2004) offers several guidelines for making anecdotal records:

- Write observable data. Use the past tense and state specifically what students did. He recommends avoiding such vague terms as "few," "understood," or "can't."
- Develop a system of important abbreviations. Recommended samples are displayed in Figure 5.3.
- Link observations to standards. In this way, it is possible to assess students as they engage in tasks or texts that focus on a broad range of reading/writing outcomes—not just those that are represented on standardized tests.

FIGURE 5.3   Sample Abbreviations for Anecdotal Records

Abbreviation	Meaning	Example
ID	Identified	ID main idea
X	Times	Misspelled *tried* 3 × s
→	To or in relation to	Matched picture → words (see next example)
T	Teacher	Retold story → T
S(s)	Student(s)	Read to 4 Ss for 5 minutes
RA	Read alone	RA → 2 minutes
RT	Read with teacher	RT → 2 paragraphs
RS	Read with another student	RS entire book
SC	Self-corrected	Wrote *unitid* SC → *united*
WA	Wrote alone	WA 3 sentences
WT	Wrote with teacher	WT 4 paragraphs
WS	Wrote with another student	WS 7 sentences
def	Defined	def 6 terms correctly
Δ (delta sign)	Changed	Δ initial focus in writing
N or Ø (null sign)	Did not observe	Ø clarifying questions

Source: Boyd-Batsone, P. (2004). Focused anecdotal records assessment: A tool for standards-based authentic assessment. *The Reading Teacher, 58,* 234. © International Reading Association. Used with permission.

Many teachers use checklists such as the one in Figure 5.4 that provide a place to note students' overall interactions in the classroom. These should be created to facilitate observations of important classroom activities. The advantage here is that it focuses on multiple sources of information about students and can help us to establish patterns of behavior that can lead to fresh instructional approaches. Samples of the types of behavior we might want to look for to inform us about our students' behavior in the context of various reading and writing contexts are presented in Figure 5.4. More open-ended questions can be used to summarize our observations and are worth asking about all students:

- For what purposes does the student read/write: to accomplish classroom tasks or for pleasure?
- How does the student respond to different types of comprehension questions? Writing tasks?
- How does the student adjust his/her rate, strategy usage, and writing approach to meet the demands of different purposes, texts, and tasks?

As we have already discussed, students' attitudes can have a significant and cumulative effect on their achievement. Often, people do not like to read or write because they are not skilled at these tasks. However, it is also the case that skilled reading and writing require practice. Teachers and clinicians are obliged to help students find reading material and writing activities that respond to their individual interests and that help them to see the functional value of reading and writing.

One of the simplest and most effective ways of finding out students' interests is to watch their daily behavior and listen to their conversations (see Edmunds &

FIGURE 5.4   An Observation Guide for Reading and Writing

☐ Demonstrates flexibility in approach to reading tasks	☐ Uses different approaches to writing tasks
☐ Handles different genre with ease	☐ Writes different genre with ease
☐ Always seeks the same type of literature	☐ Always writes in the same modes and genre
☐ Reads about a range of topics	☐ Writes about a range of topics
☐ Adapts reading strategies to task demands	☐ Adapts strategies to demands of writing and written stage (i.e., has strategies for planning, revising, and editing)
☐ Selects books for recreation	
☐ Can use books to find information	☐ Writes for personal and recreational purposes
☐ Checks books out of library	☐ Uses writing to learn
☐ Discusses books with others	☐ Shares and discusses writing
☐ Uses literary references in informal conversation (e.g., "When I'm six, I'll fix Matthew.")	☐ Uses literary references in writing

Comments:

Bauserman, 2006; Lipson, 1995). The following are examples of the types of questions that can be used to guide these observations:

1. How do students approach reading and writing activities (active involvement or passive resistance)?
2. What types of reading and writing activities do students select during their spare time at school and at home?
3. Do students stick with reading and writing activities or give up easily?
4. Do students talk about reading? About writing? What is the content and tone of these remarks?

Gathering information in response to these questions will not provide a solution to the problems. It can, however, indicate whether a student understands and appreciates the value of reading or writing and is willing or able to use this knowledge to support the hard work of becoming a skilled reader and/or writer.

The Literate Environment and Teacher Beliefs.   The literate environment comprises the physical, social-emotional, and intellectual environments within a classroom, which often reflect teacher beliefs (Anders & Evans, 1994; Hoffman et al., 1998). We believe it is important to evaluate those aspects of the literate environment that directly influence the acquisition of reading and writing skills.

Wolfersberger, Reutzel, Sudweeks, and Fawson (2004) conducted an extensive review of research on print-rich environments and suggest that there are four components, including: (1) provisioning the classroom with literacy tools, (2) arranging the classroom space and literacy tools, (3) gaining students interest in literacy events, and (4) sustaining students' interactions with literacy tools (p. 90). The Classroom Literacy Environment Profile (CLEP) is an unusually well designed and carefully researched observation tool that was developed for use in grades K–6. For educators who work in middle and high schools, the text *Creating Literacy-Rich Schools* by Ivey and Fisher (2006) is invaluable. It contains a variety of tables and charts to focus attention on various aspects of literacy settings beyond the elementary years.

To begin evaluating the literate environment, an overall observation of the instructional setting can be helpful. The summary sheets in Figures 5.5 and 5.6 draw from a variety of sources and are designed to focus observation on the aspects of the instructional environment that are likely to influence reading and writing performance (Alvermann, 2001a; Hoffman, Roser, & Sailors, 2004; Ivey & Fisher, 2006; Roskos & Newman, 2011; Wolfersberger, Reutzel, Sudweeks, & Fawson, 2004).

The literate environment can communicate to students what their teacher values. Accessible (or inaccessible) reading and/or writing centers and inviting (or uninviting) activities and spaces affect students' understanding of the value and purposes for reading and writing. They also influence students' voluntary reading and writing. Similarly, seating arrangements can advance (or impede) the cooperative or verbal interaction patterns that are necessary for many students' literacy development.

Examinations of the literate environment also often reveal what teachers believe about teaching, learning, and literacy. While examining the environment, it would be useful to ask yourself: What does the teacher believe

- is the purpose of reading and reading instruction? of writing and writing instruction?
- is necessary for students to know and be able to do before they will become skilled readers and/or writers?
- are appropriate activities to promote reading and writing competence?
- are the most important priorities in literacy instruction?

It is helpful to follow up observation of the literate environment with a conversation with the teacher, who may not have enough distance from his own teaching to recognize that he is not providing for something that he believes is important. For example, most teachers believe that prior knowledge influences reading and that building background is important, but many teachers actually do not include these features in their instruction.

**FIGURE 5.5
Checklist for
Evaluating
the Literate
Environment of
Elementary
Classrooms**

Classroom Resources	Comments
Many different kinds of books and other print materials	
Many different types of writing materials and tools	
Students' work, messages, labels, and stories are displayed	
Messages and/or plans for the current day	
Print materials displayed near objects, pictures, and other center displays	
Books or print displays about community, culture, or language	
Print has functional use—sign-ups, charts, etc.	
Physical Arrangement	**Comments**
Library—well stocked, accessible, and comfortable	
Writing/publishing center—well stocked and accessible	
Listening/viewing areas	
Group meeting places	
Conference areas	
Places for sharing, performing, etc.	
Instructional Opportunities	**Comments**
Daily opportunities for sustained reading and sustained writing	
Students read and write for a variety of purposes	
Students write for real audiences and for a variety of authentic purposes	
Students have choices about what to read or write	
Students confer with teacher and other students about reading/writing	
Support (scaffold) students during reading and writing	
Teach the fundamentals of writing and reading (conduct mini-lessons, teach conventions, provide spelling instruction)	

**FIGURE 5.6
Checklist for
Evaluating the
Literate
Environment for
Adolescents**

Classroom Opportunity & Resources	Comments
Students have frequent opportunities for sustained reading and writing in all classes	
Students have access to diverse mix of textbooks, magazines, student-generated texts, hypermedia, etc.	
Many different types of writing materials and tools are available	
Students have access to texts with a range of difficulty	
Texts are available for diverse interests, cultures, and contemporary themes	
Students read and write for a variety of purposes	
Climate	**Comments**
Students have opportunities for social interaction (e.g. collaborating with peers, discussion)	
Teachers appear to care about their students at a personal level and promote student attachment to school	
A sense of community is evident in the school and classroom	
There are places for sharing, performing, etc.	
There are places for students to meet in small groups	
Teachers communicate high standards and expectations for all students	
Instructional Opportunities	**Comments**
Comprehensive, but flexible programs for literacy are available	
Focus on conceptual growth and knowledge	
Students have choices about what to read & write	
There is a coherent assessment system that includes student self-assessment	
Teachers focus on student self-efficacy and goal setting	
There is instruction and support for strategy use	
Differentiated instruction is available for students of varying abilities and needs	
Writing/publishing center—well stocked and accessible	
Attention to student engagement is evident in the planning and selection of materials and tasks	
There are authentic, student-initiated discussions about text	
Students use & create authentic texts and tasks, including digital and internet materials	

Recognizing mismatches between beliefs and practice helps teachers to more clearly identify what steps to take to help a student who is struggling to become literate.

A sound knowledge base and a commitment to literacy are extremely important, but teachers must also know how to maintain a functional learning environment for fairly large groups of children. The teacher's ability to organize the classroom and manage the daily routine influences the amount of time available for teaching and learning. Studies of successful schools suggest that effective teachers manage a variety of complex activity in their classrooms (Mosenthal et al., 2001b). Some key focus questions for assessing the management factors in classrooms are as follows:

- Do the routines help teachers address individual differences among students in the classroom? For example, are there multiple activities going on simultaneously?
- Are the practices designed to maximize students' engagement with authentic reading and writing tasks? For example, when children are not working with the teacher, are they engaged in sustained reading or writing?
- Do routines increase instructional time? For example, are there clearly understood classroom rules and routines and well-established procedures for seeking help and getting supplies?
- Are routine scheduling concerns handled smoothly and unobtrusively (e.g., movement by some students to special services or activities)?
- Are transitions between activities handled smoothly and quickly?

Any continuing factors or conditions that make it difficult to deliver instruction smoothly should also be identified. We are aware that there are a variety of constraints imposed on teachers that can influence the organization of their classrooms and their ability to make and execute good decisions. These should be identified and considered as the interactive case evaluation proceeds.

Classroom Organization, Interaction, and Grouping.   Other important aspects of the instructional setting are classroom organization, interaction, and grouping patterns. We are not only interested in the likely impact of these factors on reading and writing performance, but we also hope to gain insight into how they may influence a particular student's performance. According to Cambourne (2000) and Cambourne and Turbill (1994), teachers organize their reading and writing instruction in "episodes" consisting of various activities and routines such as sustained silent reading, teacher read-alouds, and reading-writing workshop. Within and across the instructional events or episodes that characterize a particular classroom or setting, we can examine both grouping and interaction patterns as well as the range of learning opportunities presented to individual students.

Classroom Organization.   Using the episodes of instruction as a unit of analysis can provide an overview of reading and writing instruction within a particular classroom or setting. Observational data can be gathered on the episodes of instruction that make up a typical class period, day, and/or week in a particular setting, along with information about the types of interactions and grouping they entail and the amount of time devoted to each (Good & Brophy, 2003). Completing a summary analysis such as the one provided in

FIGURE 5.7
Example of
Evaluating the
Instructional
Setting

Episode Setting	Time Frequency	Grouping	Interactive Patterns
Sustained silent reading (SSR)	15 min per day	Individual	None

Figure 5.7 will quickly reveal what types of instructional activities are used regularly and the concomitant interaction and grouping patterns.

This type of observational system can provide useful information, especially if distinctions are made in terms of the amounts of actual reading and writing that are done. For example, one study of this type reported that students in the remedial classes observed spent only 10 to 20 percent of their time actually reading and writing connected text, even when a single paragraph is considered connected text (Allington et al., 1986). Although these proportions may have changed somewhat in recent years, especially given the much stronger focus on leveled texts and repeated readings, our observations suggest that many struggling readers still read far too little connected text. After completing a summary analysis such as the one provided in Figure 5.7, examine the information to determine how much time and/or what proportion of time the students spend:

- Reading connected text
- Writing connected text
- Listening to connected text
- Interacting and working with other students, with or without the teacher, in whole- or small-group activities
- Interacting and working individually with the teacher
- Working individually/independently

Ultimately, it is the relationship between student performance and classroom activities that is important to ascertain. For example, some teachers actually evaluate students' reading competence not according to their ability to read and write connected text, but according to their ability to complete workbooks or other worksheets. There are other classrooms in which students are regularly engaged in fruitful reading and writing activity for extended periods of time. At the same time, there needs to be a clear and balanced focus on component aspects of literacy such as word identification, vocabulary, and fluency. To understand the experience of a particular student requires a clear description of the kinds of activities and tasks that are used and an examination of the proportion of time that is spent on different types of activities and tasks.

Interactions.   It is important to recognize how difficult it may be to describe the features of classroom interaction, much less assess its impact. However, it may be helpful to apply the following set of focus questions to characterize the general pattern of interaction in a classroom:

- What are the notable characteristics of the linguistic community of the students you are assessing?
- Who typically initiates language exchanges, decides on the form and content of written work, or directs discussions?
- How often do oral and written interactions serve the purpose of eliciting set or known responses, in contrast to open discussion or divergent responses?
- Do some students appear to have higher "status" in the classroom—socially or academically?
- Does this affect who participates?

The answers to these global questions can give a sense of the amount and type of verbal interaction that occurs in the classroom and the demands and opportunities likely to be present for individual students. In particular, this general observation can reveal unusual linguistic, cultural, or classroom characteristics. Research by Cohen (1994; Cohen & Lotan, 1977) has demonstrated that the more students are actively engaged in classroom talk and task, the more they learn. However, students who are social isolates or students who are seen as lacking academic skills often fail to participate and thus learn less than they would if they were more active in the groups.

Occasionally, a much closer examination is desirable or necessary to gather in-depth information about the interactions between the teacher and a particular child or group of children. In this case, careful and systematic classroom observation will be necessary. A procedure described by Page and Pinnell (1979) is useful in both classrooms and clinics. This procedure involves recording a conversation with the student and then using a checklist to evaluate the types of exchanges that occur. The oral interactions are evaluated to see which conversational partner:

- Asks and/or answers questions
- Gives personal information about self
- Gives information about something other than self
- Refers to past events
- Makes predictions
- Draws conclusions
- Makes evaluative statements
- Gives orders
- Makes requests

The authors report that teachers are often chagrined at the analyses that result, since the patterns are not always what they intended. Teachers working in our reading clinics often have similar reactions, finding that they do much more talking than they realized and are more likely to ask questions with discrete answers than they are to invite expansive discussion. When teachers use these initial results to shape subsequent interactions, there is often a dramatic increase in verbal *interaction* versus question-response patterns (Kucan, 2005).

Grouping.   As we discussed previously, grouping practices can exert a strong influence on student achievement and motivation. Consequently, effective assessment must include a consideration of school and classroom grouping practices. Teachers often use a variety of organizational patterns in their classrooms. It will be particularly important to identify the variety of patterns and their associated purposes.

Both observation and interviews may be necessary to get a clear picture of the complex ways in which students are organized. For example, it is important to determine what information teachers use to make their placement decisions. Although most teachers make careful and intentional grouping decisions using some systematic procedure, others generate groupings on the basis of untested assumptions (Good & Brophy, 2003). An example of an untested assumption might be something like "Her brother had trouble in reading and writing, so she will too." Placement decisions that are based on this type of reasoning are obviously problematic, especially because teacher judgment is often used to make other educational decisions as well.

The assessment of grouping practices should also examine the extent to which membership in a group for one purpose (e.g., a reading or writing group) defines *access* to other tasks, activities, and levels of achievement. This is a problem especially in middle and junior high schools, where scheduling is complicated and the need to receive specialized instruction in reading and writing, for example, may dictate the classes and sections for all other subjects. To gather this information, it may be necessary to observe or inquire about the grouping arrangements and grouping characteristics for subjects other than language arts.

As we have already seen, one of the reasons this information about grouping is so important is that it influences the patterns of interaction that occur among peers and between teachers and students. The quantity and quality of these interactions may profoundly affect both achievement and motivation.

Evaluating Intervention Programs and Approaches

As we have seen, although research suggests that tutoring programs are generally effective, their impact on individual students is likely to vary dramatically. Several authors have examined interventions and tutorial programs and it is now possible to detail a number of attributes of successful interventions. In this section, we draw from several of these key sources to create a plan for evaluating interventions (Denton & Vaughn, 2010; Scanlon & Sweeney, 2008; Walmsley & Allington, 2007; Wasik, 1998). Research indicates that the effectiveness of language arts tutoring programs depends on a knowledgeable person to provide a basic understanding of the reading and writing processes to tutors and also to give them feedback on their tutoring sessions. For younger students, outcomes are improved when intervention:

- Results in increased quantity of instruction (supplemental plus regular classroom reading instruction)

- Is provided in small-group or one-on-one formats
- Includes explicit, well-organized (systematic) instruction
- Provides opportunities to read connected texts
- Is engaging and interactive, often with manipulative
- Is provided for twenty to thirty minutes at least three to five times per week
- Addresses multiple instructional components
- Provides ample opportunities to practice and includes teacher feedback
- Includes continuous progress monitoring assessment
- Is coordinated with classroom instruction to the greatest extent possible

These attributes can be used as a checklist to begin the process of assessing your instruction and intervention programs (see Figure 5.8). This type of self-assessment is always more fruitful if all of the interested parties participate. Classroom teachers, specialists, and special educators as well as building leadership should be considering the extent to which interventions are similar to those that have a research base. It is essential that interventions be evaluated within the context of the overall literacy program. It is difficult to realize the most substantial improvements for vulnerable students if the good first instruction in the classroom is not good. Indeed, many experts believe that Reading Recovery results would be even more impressive if there were greater alignment between the general education classroom setting and the intervention principles. This led Linda Dorn and her colleagues to create the Comprehensive Intervention Model (CIM), which emphasizes the importance of the instruction across multiple "layers" (Dorn & Soffos, 2012). Their framework includes a combination of:

- High-quality, differentiated classroom instruction
- A portfolio of research-based interventions
- A seamless assessment system at an individual and systems level
- School-embedded professional learning for teachers

Finally, the nature of the instruction/intervention itself is exceedingly important. Intervention approaches with powerful research evidence often structure their lessons in

FIGURE 5.8   Steps in Improving Intervention Programs

1. Describe the current status
   a. Regular
   b. Support settings
2. Tasks
   a. Articulate program philosophy
   b. Articulate expectations for students
   c. Articulate expectations for regular and support programs
   d. Organization of instructional support services

Source: Adapted from Walmsley, S. A., & Allington, R. L. (2007). Redefining and reforming instructional support programs for at-risk students. In R. L. Allington & S. A. Walmsley (Eds.), *No quick fix: The RTI edition* (pp. 34–41). Newark, DE: IRA.

similar ways (see Scanlon, Anderson & Sweeney, 2010; Vaughn, Gersten, & Chard, 2000; Wasik, 1998). Common elements include:

- Reading of new materials by the student
- Reading (new) books in which either the words or the entire story are familiar to the student
- Or reading books that provide appropriate challenge for students to employ emerging strategies and skills
- An activity that emphasizes word analysis and letter-sound relationships
- Instruction focus on promoting metacognitive approaches so that children engage in problem solving during text reading
- A writing activity that emphasizes composing

Students are less successful in sessions in which the teacher/interventionist does most of the reading and writing activities than in those in which the student is a more active participant (Al Otaiba et al., 2009; Juel, 1996). Indeed, both RR and the Interactive Strategies Approach (ISA) (Scanlon, Anderson & Sweeney, 2010) are organized around helping students acquire a self-teaching mechanism—focusing on helping students to engage in strategic thinking and processing.

In general, successful interventions ensure adequate time on task for students, a high quality of instruction, and the appropriateness of curriculum (Shanahan, 1998). The ability of a program to deliver on these key elements is often a function of the knowledge and skill of the program coordinator and/or interventionist. Examinations of the role of a intervention program in a given student's reading and writing performance should emphasize these factors. Finally, the coordination between the intervention programs and classroom experiences is most likely to be helpful if both experiences are of high quality. Of course, one must also consider the effect of any inconsistency between the instruction in these two settings.

A word about interventions and tutoring programs for *older students* is in order. Generally speaking, there is much less information about these than there is about intervention/prevention programs for younger students (Kamil et al., 2008). However, educators and researchers are continuing to explore promising approaches, and some conclusions are possible. First, it is clear that older students present a diverse array of needs—from word-level difficulties to vocabulary and comprehension. Second, interventions designed for older students require more time. Most successful interventions have involved approximately fifty minutes daily with intervention extending over thirty weeks or more. Finally, caution needs to be exercised when planning interventions, to make sure that the types of instruction and intervention to be used have been demonstrated to work with struggling *older* students.

Edmonds et al. (2009) conducted a meta-analysis of research on interventions for older students that included twenty-nine studies. One of the encouraging conclusions they draw is that older students with reading difficulties/disabilities can improve their comprehension quite significantly *when* they are provided with appropriately targeted interventions. At the same time, these authors concluded that interventions focused on word-level aspects of reading had only a very small to moderate effect on reading achievement for older students. Importantly, they found a diminishing relationship between word-level components (word recognition accuracy and fluency) and comprehension with secondary students—such that increasing rate and fluency did not always improve comprehension. Finally, they concluded that interventions that have demonstrated efficacy for younger students do not necessarily reap the same rewards with older students. This is especially important to note since some schools and districts have attempted to implement the same types of interventions in middle and high school that they have used in the elementary school years.

Other critical features of instruction/intervention for older struggling readers should be evaluated also. Three are particularly critical. Motivation plays a pivotal role during the middle and high school years, so educators must consider ways to engage students—through inviting and interesting texts and tasks and by providing some degree of choice. Secondly, content become critically important, and at least one successful approach for older struggling students has created layered sets of reading that support both content and reading (Gelzheiser et al., in press). Finally, interventions for adolescents that focus on metacognitive strategy instruction are much more successful than those that focus on other components (Swanson, 1999).

Congruence among Settings.   Among the most critical aspects of an assessment of the instructional context will be the degree of congruence from one setting to another. In essence, it will be necessary to observe and collect information about multiple settings. A first step involves collecting information about the relationship between classroom instruction and any supplemental instruction. A simple form like the one in Figure 5.9 could be completed with relative ease by both the classroom teacher and specialists to summarize instruction across settings during the week. Each teacher writes a brief narrative for the day. A communication system such as this one makes it easy to assess the degree of congruence between instructional settings for students who are receiving special services.

Once the instructional context for a particular student has been described, the information needs to be analyzed and evaluated. In particular, teachers need to examine the degree of similarity between instruction for average and above-average students and that received by lower-achieving readers and writers. For example, teachers need to consider how much text students with differing skill levels are exposed to each day and/or week. In addition, it is important to consider similarities and differences in the approaches used to teach students with differing skill levels. If there are substantial and significant variations in the two programs of the sort described previously in this chapter, teachers and assessment personnel should examine the assumptions and rationale for these programs and procedures very carefully. Some students may require unusual programs; however, such decisions should be based on careful consideration, not unsupported assumptions.

Assessing Instructional Practice

In the following sections, we describe several ways to assess instructional goals, methods, and assessment practices.

Instructional Goals and Methods.   Most districts and/or schools now have published content standards and/or benchmarks for English language arts. Those that do not likely defer to the state's GLEs. While standards and benchmarks may be quite general, grade-level expectations likely are more specific. Schools or classroom teachers are expected

FIGURE 5.9   Communicating and Collaborating

Student _____   Week _____

	Location and Duration of Instruction	Goals/Objectives Addressed	Materials Used	Activities or Tasks
Classroom Teacher				
Specialist #1 (e.g., reading teacher)				
Specialist #2 (e.g., SLP)				

Notes:

to link GLEs with grade-level curricula. It is important to determine the role of standards in the schools and classrooms in which the students you are working with reside. This will help you know what is guiding the focus of instruction in the instructional environment.

It is also important to determine what role the instructional materials or mandated assessments play in determining the focus of instruction. Many schools and classroom teachers still rely heavily on commercially prepared material to define their instructional program. Schools receiving funds through Reading First were typically required to adopt and employ a "core" or commercial program. Wixson, Dutro, and Athan (2004) identify the potential difficulty with this situation: "With a few commercial programs determining the curriculum for a large number of districts, we wonder if federal mandates might bring us back full circle, with commercial programs again serving as the default curriculum" (Wixson, Dutro, & Athan, 2004, p. 100). If this is the case in the setting you are evaluating, it may be necessary to infer an instructional focus from the content of the materials being used (see Chapter 6). The following focus questions can be used to examine general aspects of instructional goals and methods.

- Is the general approach to reading and writing basal based? Literature based? Based on a subskills-mastery learning curriculum? Based on some combination of these?
- Does the teacher attempt to meet individual needs by grouping? Altering content? Changing the tasks? Providing different levels of support? Or does the teacher not appear to differentiate instruction in any way?
- Does the teacher define language arts instruction in terms of a specific published program? In terms of a specific approach (e.g., guided reading)?
- Does the teacher and/or school draw from a variety of sources and define the reading and writing curriculum in terms of clearly established outcomes?
- What is the relationship between the goals and methods in this classroom and those of other teachers in the building?

Asking yourself or the teacher these questions results in useful descriptions of the instructional goals and methods employed by the teacher. In some schools, these components of instructional goals and methods may be dictated by the administration of the school. In others, these are informally decreed between and among teachers, so that deviation from these practices may result in ostracism from the mainstream of professional contact.

Much has changed in education in recent years, and while teachers in many schools have a great deal of discretion about how they deliver instruction, others have found themselves marching to a highly prescribed and rigidly enforced curriculum (see MacGillivray, Ardell, Curwen, & Palma, 2001). It will be important to find out how much coherence exists within the school, but also how much autonomy teachers have to respond to the unique needs of their own students.

Increasingly, schools are using literacy coaches to help improve instruction, especially for the most struggling readers. Lyons and Pinnell (2001) have written a very useful book for educators who are involved in evaluating and supporting teachers. They suggest that coaches reflect before they make a classroom visit, asking questions such as these (Lyons & Pinnell, 2001, p. 249):

- What are your perceptions of the teacher's strengths?
- What are the differences between the way the teacher talks and what you observe in the classroom?
- What does the teacher say about children? To what degree does he or she describe children's behavior as evidence of learning?

Subsequently, they suggest using a structured observation device to look closely at teachers' instruction (see Figure 5.10). The tool they use is designed for observing student-teacher interactions and instruction within a guided reading format, but it is well suited to assessing any text-based reading experience.

Other general aspects of instructional method that are worthy of attention include the use of scaffolding, dialogue, and motivational activities to promote reading and writing performance.

Scaffolding and Dialogue.   It is difficult to evaluate the use of scaffolding and the quantity and quality of dialogue within a particular setting without close observation in the classroom. Although no good tools are available to evaluate these critical features, there are some specific teaching behaviors we can look for as we observe in the classroom. For example,

- Does the teacher encourage students' acquisition of new or difficult material?
- Does the teacher support learning by modeling and/or providing guidance?
- Does the teacher engage in dialogue with students (as opposed to lecturing)?
- Does the teacher support students' contributions to dialogue?
- Does dialogue have focus and direction?
- Does the teacher use student ideas and link those ideas to new information?
- Does the teacher use feedback constructively to help students improve their responses?

Few teachers have been well trained in these methods, but some have developed these skills to a high degree. The presence or absence of these methods will most likely influence the achievement or involvement of some less-skilled students.

Motivational Activities.   As we have seen, instructional techniques and student motivation for learning are strongly related. Student interviews can be exceptionally useful in assessing the relationship between instruction and motivation. Some of the interviews we have already suggested may provide information about the quality and appropriateness of the instructional program (see Chapters 4 and 10), although these should clearly be designed or adapted to gather information about specific aspects of the setting or instruction that may be influencing the student.

For example, interviews can be structured to collect information about the motivational impact of units of instruction. Rogers and Stevenson (1988) asked students questions such as the following:

- What went well for you?
- What did you enjoy most?
- Should the study of _____ be a part of everyone's education?

FIGURE 5.10
Observation
Summary Form

Observation of Guided Reading

Observer: _____ Teacher: _____ Date: _____

Grade: _____ Number of Children in Group: _____

Preparation	Independent Activities
Text selected:	Number: Engagement[1]: 1 **2 3 4**
Level:	Types represented:
Notes:	

Introduction of Text	**Engagement: 1 2 3 4**	**Start: End:**
Teacher's Language	*Children's Language*	*Other Observations*

Reading the Text	**Engagement: 1 2 3 4**	**Start: End:**
Teacher's Language	*Children's Language*	*Other Observations*

After Reading the Text	**Engagement: 1 2 3 4**	**Start: End:**
Teacher's Language	*Children's Language*	*Other Observations*
Word Work:		
Extension/Assignment:		

RUBRIC FOR ENGAGEMENT: 1 = Only a few children are on task and attending to instruction. There are many distractions, including noise and movement. Instruction is severely undermined. 2 = About half of the children are on task and attending to the instruction, but there are many distractions, including noise and movement. Instruction is undermined. 3 = Most of the children are on task and attending to the instruction. There are occasional distractions and some children are moving about. Instruction, in general, is being provided most of the time. 4 = Almost all children are on task and attending to the instruction. Instruction is being provided most of the time. There are only a few distractions.

Interestingly, the last of these questions often provoked the most honest assessment of interest *and* learning. Perhaps asking a question that is more distant and less personal encourages richer thinking.

The interview information will, of course, be supplemented with data generated through observation. The instructional context should be examined for evidence of the motivational practices we described earlier (see Figure 5.11). Although these strategies cannot be quantified easily, this is not necessary. A strongly negative profile of instructional factors linked to motivation can provide important information about the achievement and progress of specific students.

Assessment Practices.   According to the experts, assessment is more an attitude (Chittenden, 1991) or a habit of mind (Valencia, 2007) than it is a method. In his thoughtful work on authentic assessment, Chittenden observed four quite different attitudes or stances that teachers adopt with respect to monitoring and evaluating students' learning, which he refers to as *keeping track, checking up, finding out*, and *summing up*. These clearly parallel the larger purposes that society as a whole has assigned to assessment also.

A *keeping-track* stance is characterized by attention to what activities students have been involved in, such as what books a particular student has read or which students have not yet completed certain activities. Teachers devise many ways to make records to meet their keeping-track needs. For example, they create informal checklists and inventories and gather material from students' journal entries. Over the year, a fairly substantial record of activities and accomplishments is often compiled in the name of keeping track.

A *checking-up* stance is often approached both formally and informally. Informal checking up involves observing and asking students questions. Formal checking up is focused on testing, defined as any situation in which the student is asked a question to which the questioner or examiner knows the answer. Although a lot of this type of interrogation goes on in our schools, whether under the guise of classroom discussion or standardized tests, it is not characteristic of normal, everyday conversations and interactions.

The *finding-out* stance is focused on inquiry or figuring out what is going on. The teacher is attending to what a particular student response meant or what a student understood from a particular story. Teachers may be asking questions but clearly not with the intent of checking up. This is an attitude or habit of mind that Valencia (2007) believes is most critical to effective decision making and improved teaching and learning.

Finally, completing the picture is the *summing-up* stance. This stance directly addresses the needs of accountability through reporting to parents, districts, and students. Attention is focused on organizing information in ways that are meaningful outside the classroom.

The types of assessments used and the manner in which they are used are likely to vary according to these stances. In contexts in which all four stances are present, we would expect to see a full range of assessment instruments, including both tests and alternative assessments. These various assessments may complement each other in the sense that they reflect a consistent view of literacy learning. Alternatively, they may be in conflict in that some reflect a more traditional, isolated-skills approach to literacy learning and others reflect a more interactive, constructivist view of literacy learning. This situation can be confusing to students and lead to difficulties and/or mixed impressions related to reading and writing performance.

**FIGURE 5.11
Assessment of
Motivational
Strategies**

Motivational Analysis of Tasks and Activities

Use: Whenever particular classroom tasks or activities are observed
Purpose: To identify the motivational elements built into the task or activity

Check each of the motivational elements that was included in the observed task or activity.

A. Extrinsic motivational strategies

_____ 1. Offers rewards as incentives for good performance
_____ 2. Calls attention to the instrumental value of the knowledge or skills developed in the activity (applications to present or future life outside of school)
_____ 3. Structures individual or group competition for prizes or recognition

B. Intrinsic motivational features of the task or activity

_____ 1. Opportunities for active response (beyond just watching and listening)
_____ 2. Opportunities to answer divergent questions or work on higher-level objectives
_____ 3. Immediate feedback to students' responses (built into the task itself, rather than provided by the teacher as in C.8 below)
_____ 4. Gamelike features (the task is a game or contains gamelike features that make it more like a recreational activity than a typical academic activity)
_____ 5. Task completion involves creating a finished product for display or use
_____ 6. The task involves fantasy or simulation elements that engage students' emotions or allow them to experience events vicariously
_____ 7. The task provides opportunities for students to interact with their peers

C. Teacher's attempts to stimulate students' motivation to learn

_____ 1. Projects intensity (communicating that the material is important and deserves close attention)
_____ 2. Induces task interest or appreciation
_____ 3. Induces curiosity or suspense
_____ 4. Makes abstract content more personal, concrete, or familiar
_____ 5. Induces dissonance or cognitive conflict
_____ 6. Induces students to generate their own motivation to learn
_____ 7. States learning objectives or provides advance organizers
_____ 8. Provides opportunities for students to respond and get feedback (asks questions during group lessons, circulates to monitor performance during seatwork)
_____ 9. Models task-related thinking and problem solving ("thinks out loud" when working through examples)
_____ 10. Includes instruction or modeling designed to increase students' metacognitive awareness of their learning efforts in response to the task (includes information about mental preparation for learning, about the organization or structure built into the content, about how students can impose their own organizational structures on the content to help them remember it, or about how to monitor one's own comprehension and respond to confusion or mistakes)

Notes:

Source: From *Looking in Classrooms,* 4th ed., by Thomas L. Good and Jere E. Brophy. Copyright ©1987. Reprinted by permission of Allyn & Bacon.

Still other contexts may evidence heavy reliance on one or two stances. This situation is likely to direct curriculum and instruction in specific ways that may or may not support student literacy learning. For example, too much emphasis on checking up and/or summing up may lead to instructional practices that do not promote independence, motivation, and the problem-solving skills necessary for successful reading and writing performance. This, in fact, appears to be the danger inherent in the sorts of federally mandated assessments that are so common today (Shepard, 2001). Heavy dependence on these stances can also lead to misperceptions of students' abilities. Determining the extent to which these stances are present or absent within a particular instructional context and their potential impact on a student's reading and writing performance provides valuable information in the evaluation of the instructional context.

Instructional Behaviors.   There are relatively few tools for systematically assessing the impact of instruction on student performance. Ysseldyke and Christenson developed *The Instructional Environment Scale* (Ysseldyke & Christenson, 1987, 1993) because they believed, as we do, that student performance in school is a function of an interaction between the student and the instructional environment. Their concern lies with the "goodness of fit," or match, between the students and the instructional contexts they encounter each day. Most recently, these authors have developed the Functional Assessment of Academic Behavior (FAAB) (Ysseldyke & Christenson, 2002), which maintains a focus on identifying and coordinating instructional, home, and home-school supports for the student of interest, with the express purpose of designing feasible interventions to enhance academic success. The FAAB is a system designed to identify the presence or absence of environmental conditions that enhance a student's academic progress in school.

The authors describe four major purposes for the FAAB system: (a) gather information relevant to an individual student, (b) assess the instructional needs for the student, (c) assess supportive learning conditions, and (d) assist educators in designing instructional interventions. According to the authors, "FAAB is not to be used to evaluate or say what is wrong with the student, the classroom task, the teacher's instructional strategy, home support for learning, or the family-school relationship. It is designed to identify ways to change learning environments so that the student is responding to instruction more positively and to enhance a student's academic competence" (Ysseldyke & Christenson, 2002, p. 2).

FAAB consists of twenty-three "support for learning" components in three contexts: twelve classroom instruction components, five home components, and six home-school relationship components. These focus on alterable variables associated with positive academic performance. The twelve instructional components are grouped into the four areas of planning, managing, delivering, and evaluating instruction; they are defined in Figure 5.12.

The authors assume that careful, systematic gathering of data about the student's learning context will allow for accurate or relevant judgment about the student's highest-priority needs. In addition, they encourage individuals using this assessment system to maintain a focus on the individual student by addressing three questions: What does the student need to be successful on the task? What needs to be manipulated to produce a better student response? What resources do teachers and parents desire to assist the student?

The recommended steps for carrying out the portion of the FAAB that focuses on the assessment of the instructional environment are: (a) identify and clarify the concern,

FIGURE 5.12   FAAB Instructional Support Components

Instructional Planning: Decisions are made about what to teach and how to teach the student. Realistic expectations are communicated to the student.

➤ *Instructional Match:* The student's needs are assessed accurately, and instruction is matched appropriately to the results of the instructional diagnosis.

➤ *Instructional Expectations:* There are realistic, yet high, expectations for both the amount and accuracy of work to be completed by the student, and these are communicated clearly to the student.

Instructional Managing: Effective instruction requires managing the complex mix of instructional tasks and student behaviors that are part of every classroom interaction. This means making decisions that control and support the orderly flow of instruction. To do this, teachers make decisions about classroom rules and procedures, as well as how to handle disruptions, how to organize classroom time and space to be most productive, and how to keep classrooms warm, positive, and accepting places for the student with different learning preferences and performances.

➤ *Classroom Environment:* The classroom management techniques used are effective for the student; there is a positive, supportive classroom atmosphere; and, time is used productively.

Instructional Delivering: Decisions are made about how to present information, as well as how to monitor and adjust presentations to accommodate individual differences and enhance the learning of the student.

➤ *Instructional Presentation:* Instruction is presented in a clear and effective manner; the directions contain sufficient information for the student to understand the kinds of behaviors or skills that are to be demonstrated; and, the student's understanding is checked.

➤ *Cognitive Emphasis:* Thinking skills and learning strategies for completing assignments are communicated explicitly to the student.

➤ *Motivational Strategies:* Effective strategies for heightening student interest and effort are used with the student.

➤ *Relevant Practice:* The student is given adequate opportunity to practice with appropriate materials and a high success rate. Classroom tasks are clearly important to achieving instructional goals.

➤ *Informed Feedback:* The student receives relatively immediate and specific information on his/her performance or behavior, when the student makes mistakes, correction is provided.

Instructional Evaluating: Effective instruction requires evaluating. Some evaluation activities occur during the process of instruction (i.e., when teachers gather data during instruction and use those data to make instructional decisions). Other evaluation activities occur at the end of instruction (e.g., when the teacher administers a test to determine whether a student has met instructional goals).

➤ *Academic Engaged Time:* The student is actively engaged in responding to academic content; the teacher monitors the extent to which the student is actively engaged and redirects the student when the student is unengaged.

➤ *Adaptive Instruction:* The curriculum is modified within reason to accommodate the student's unique and specific instructional needs.

➤ *Progress Evaluation:* There is direct, frequent measurement of the student's progress toward completion of instructional objectives; data on the student's performance and progress are used to plan future instruction.

➤ *Student Understanding:* The student demonstrates an accurate understanding of what is to be done and how it is to be done in the classroom.

Source: Reprinted with permission from Sopris West Educational Services. From *Functional Assessment of Academic Behavior*, by James Ysseldyke, Ph.D, and Sandra Christenson, Ph.D. Newly revised copyright 2001.

(b) understand the student's instructional needs from the perspective of the teacher and the parents, and (c) collect data on the student's instructional environment. The FAAB system includes materials to assist in this process such as the Instructional Needs Checklist, which is designed to get information about the teacher's perspective of the student's instructional needs. The "Instructional Needs Checklist" asks for information in the following seven areas:

1. Referral concern
2. Instructional needs
3. Student responses to tasks
4. Instructional tasks and materials
5. Instructional modifications
6. If only two things could be done for this student, what would they be?
7. Other observations/relevant information

Areas two through five provide checklists with directions to the teacher for identifying any aspects in which a change may be needed to provide the student with an optimal learning environment.

The FAAB also provides "Instructional Environment Checklists" in both summary and annotated forms. These materials are designed to help identify the presence or absence of the components of the classroom, home, and home-school contexts that are likely to promote academic progress. The information needed to complete these checklists is intended to come from several sources, including classroom observation as well as student and parent interviews; additional materials are provided for data collection. The annotated Instructional Environment Checklist elaborates on the aspects of each of the twenty-three components that might be considered in determining if the component is one that might need some alteration. For example, the following items are listed under the "Cognitive Emphasis" component within the classroom/instructional context section of the inventory.

- The student understands the purpose of the lesson.
- The learning strategies that are used (e.g., memorizing, reasoning, concluding, and evaluating) are effective for the student.
- The student can explain the process used to solve problems or complete work.
- The student knows why and how his/her responses are correct/incorrect.

The FAAB and instruments like it are welcome additions to the repertoire of tools available for assessment, because they broaden the database upon which decisions about students are made. These types of materials are also likely to play an educative role for teachers, consultants, and parents in improving the instructional environment for all students.

Assessing Specific Activities and Episodes of Instruction

In addition to the assessment of general instructional goals, methods, and assessment practices, it is important to evaluate individual episodes of instruction to understand the

FIGURE 5.13
Evaluating
Instructional
Episodes

Objectives	Methods/Activities	Methods/Opportunities for Assessment
Content		
Process		
Attitude		

performance of particular students within and across specific instructional events. The evaluation of individual instructional episodes involves an examination of specific instructional objectives, the methods of instruction and/or activities used, and the methods and/or opportunities for assessing student performance.

The examination of instructional objectives involves identifying the content, process, and attitude objectives as articulated by either the teacher or the materials or as inferred by the observer. The evaluation of an instructional episode also involves an examination of what both the teacher and students do in the context of each instructional event, along with an assessment of the methods used for evaluating student performance or, alternatively, the opportunities that exist for assessing student performance. Figure 5.13 presents a simple chart for use in evaluating the objectives, instruction/activities, and methods/opportunities for assessment that characterize individual instructional episodes or events.

In evaluating the objectives for a particular instructional episode, it is important to remember that the overarching goal of reading and writing instruction should be the development of knowledgeable, strategic, and motivated readers and writers. To do this, teachers must provide instruction aimed at specific content, process, and attitudinal instructional objectives. Although there may be times when instruction needs to be focused heavily on just one of these three areas, it is always a good idea to consider the role that each of these areas plays in every instructional episode or event. In reflecting on the information gathered for the chart in Figure 5.11, it may be helpful to ask the following questions:

1. Do the objectives clearly identify the *content* to be addressed through this reading/writing episode, the reading and writing *process* skills to be learned or practiced in this episode, and how the instructional episode is intended to help develop positive *attitudes* toward reading, writing, and learning?
2. Does the episode provide opportunities to read and/or write about important ideas and/or persistent issues found in the content of the curriculum?
3. Does the episode focus on higher-level thinking and/or self-regulation of learning?

FIGURE 5.14
Research-Based
Standards for
Evaluating Quality
of Instruction

Standards for Evaluating Quality of Instruction			
Focus on higher-order thinking	1 ———▶	3 ———▶	5
Depth of knowledge	1 ———▶	3 ———▶	5
Connectedness to the world	1 ———▶	3 ———▶	5
Substantive conversation	1 ———▶	3 ———▶	5
Social support for learning	1 ———▶	3 ———▶	5

Source: Adapted from Newmann, F. M., & Wehlage, G. G. (February 1993). Five standards of authentic instruction. *Educational Leadership, 50*(7), 8–12, Figure 1. Reprinted with permission of the Association for Supervision and Curriculum Development. Copyright © 1993 by ASCD. All rights reserved.

4. Does the episode provide opportunities to learn important information about the reading and writing processes?
5. Does the episode encourage students to recognize patterns in their reading and writing so that they can apply these in other contexts?
6. Does the episode encourage students to immerse themselves in reading, writing, and/or responding?
7. Does the event encourage students to share what they have read and/or written?
8. Is the episode authentic and relevant to students' needs and interests?

In thinking about how to assess the instructional methods and activities described on the chart, it may be helpful to consider the set of broad-based standards developed by Newmann and Wehlage (1993) for defining "authentic" instruction that engages "students in using their minds well" (p. 8). The five standards developed by Newmann and Wehlage for evaluating the quality of instruction focus on higher-order thinking, depth of knowledge, connectedness to the world beyond the classroom, substantive conversation, and social support for student achievement. To evaluate these dimensions of instruction, Newmann and his colleagues (1996, 2001) developed a rating scale in which each standard is rated from 1 to 5 along a continuum from less to more (see Figure 5.14).

Scores on the higher-order thinking scale range from a 1, which represents lower-order thinking only, to a 5, which means that higher-order thinking is central to the instruction. A score of 3 means that students engage primarily in routine lower-order thinking, but there is at least one significant question or activity in which some students engage in some higher-order thinking. Lower-order thinking activities are defined as those that ask students to receive or recite factual information or to employ rules through repetitive routines. Students are in the role of information receivers and are asked to recall prespecified knowledge. In contrast, higher-order thinking activities require students to manipulate information and ideas in ways that transform their meaning and implications.

The "depth of knowledge" scale refers to the substantive character of the ideas in a lesson and to the level of understanding students demonstrate as they consider these ideas. Knowledge is thin or shallow when it does not deal with significant concepts and/or students have a trivial understanding of important concepts. Knowledge is deep or thick when it concerns important concepts and/or when students can make clear distinctions, develop arguments, solve problems, construct explanations, and otherwise work with relatively complex understandings. A score of 1 on this scale indicates that the student's knowledge is shallow, and a score of 5 indicates that the student's knowledge is deep. A score of 3 indicates that knowledge is treated unevenly during instruction; at least one significant idea may be presented in depth, but in general the focus is not sustained.

The third scale, concerning connectedness to the world, measures the extent to which instruction has value and meaning beyond the school setting. A score of 1 is given to instruction with little or no value beyond the school; students' work has no impact on others and serves only to certify student success in the instructional context. A score of 5 is given to instruction that is connected to the world outside of school and in which students address real-world problems and/or use personal experiences as a context for applying knowledge.

The fourth scale measures substantive conversation. A score of 1 indicates no substantive conversation, and a score of 5 indicates high-level substantive conversation. In classes with little or no conversation, interaction typically consists of teacher presentations that deviate little from a preplanned body of information and set of questions. The conversation is often choppy, rather than coherent, and there is often little or no discussion. High levels of substantive conversation are indicated by three features: considerable interaction about the ideas of a topic, sharing of ideas in exchanges that are not completely teacher directed, and cohesive dialogue that builds on participants' ideas.

The fifth and final scale, on social support for learning, involves high expectations, respect, and inclusion of all students in the learning process. Social support is low and earns a score of 1 when teacher or student behavior, comments, and actions tend to discourage effort or participation or when the overall atmosphere of the class is negative. Token acknowledgments of student actions or responses do not necessarily constitute evidence of social support. Social support is high and earns a score of 5 when the teacher conveys high expectations for all students, that it is necessary to take risks and try hard to master challenging work, that all members of the class can learn important knowledge and skills, and an understanding that a climate of mutual respect among all members of the class contributes to achievement by all.

The standards just described provide a framework through which to view instructional activities. In their extension of these ideas, Newmann and his colleagues have adapted the ideas to specific content areas. For example, in order to evaluate the challenge and authenticity of specific writing assignments, they use the following scoring rules:

4 = *Explicit call of generalization and support.* The assignment asks students, using narrative or expository writing, to draw conclusions or to make generalizations or arguments, and to substantiate them with examples, summaries, illustrations, or reasons.
3 = *Call for generalization or support.* The assignment asks students, using narrative or expository writing, either to draw conclusions or make generalizations or arguments, or to offer examples, summaries, illustrations, details, or reasons, but not both.
2 = *Short-answer exercises.* The assignment or its parts can be answered with only one or two sentences, clauses, or phrasal fragments that complete a thought.
1 = *Fill-in-the-blank or multiple-choice exercises.*

Numerical ratings alone cannot portray how lessons relate to one another or how multiple lessons might accumulate into experiences that are more complex than the sum of individual lessons. The relative importance of the different standards also remains open for discussion.

Previous research indicates that teaching for thinking, problem solving, and understanding often has more-positive effects on student performance than does traditional teaching. The effects of high levels of adherence to this specific set of standards are not well established. Many educators believe that there are appropriate times for traditional instructional practices such as memorizing, repetition, and quiet study without conversation. Clearly, the emphasis should be placed on moving instruction toward more-authentic achievements for individual students, however that might best be accomplished.

DIAGNOSTIC PORTFOLIO: THE INSTRUCTIONAL CONTEXT

In Chapter 4, we introduced the thumbnail sketch as a way to summarize information that is gathered throughout the assessment-instruction process. In these care studies, we examine community and school environments. Tha'm and Kyle live in very different communities and have substantially different home environments and experiential backgrounds. In the next chapter, we examine more-specific aspects of their school contexts, which also offer contrasts, and we update their thumbnail sketches (see Figures 6.14a and 6.14b).

Diagnostic Portfolio: The Cases of Tha'm and Kyle

Tha'm.   Tha'm lives in a densely populated urban community that was once a busy mill town. Although it is only three miles from a large and relatively affluent university city, it has a history of hard times. The median housing value is considerably lower than that of other communities in the county. The median income is among the lowest in the state, and the unemployment rate is considerably higher than the state or county average. More than 20 percent of the people in Tha'm's city meet the federal guidelines for poverty, and half of them are 50 percent below the poverty line. More than 80 percent of the students are eligible for free or reduced lunch (FRL). Twenty percent of the adult population has less than a high school education; fewer than half of the adults have any schooling beyond high school. Proportionately, it is one of the most diverse schools in the state, with more than twenty different languages spoken.

Tha'm has two much younger siblings, born in the United States, with the American names Tiffany and David. Although her parents do not speak English, they have been extremely supportive of the school and anxious to make sure that Tha'm has access to any of the services the school thinks are important. The school, in turn, has a well-developed system for communicating with parents through native-language liaisons. Tha'm's family is part of a relatively large group of Vietnamese people who came as refugees over the course of a ten-year period and has since formed community groups and started businesses. Like Tha'm's school, the town is very diverse linguistically. Children learn English as the common denominator. As a result, Tha'm's Vietnamese has gotten quite rusty and she is not literate in that language.

Franklin Roosevelt School has been involved in school reform efforts for the past ten years. When they began their work, student achievement was at the very bottom of the state. Today, it is ranked above the state average in percentage of students meeting or exceeding state standards. The teachers and the administration take their work seriously. They have been engaged in partnerships with an area university, and they received both Reading Excellence Act money and a Reading First grant. The faculty prize their professional development and their collaborative problem-solving orientation. They routinely examine their practice and attempt to do better.

During Tha'm's entire time at Roosevelt, her teachers have been examining and refining their practice. As a result of their work, Tha'm has participated in guided reading groups every day, using a core program, with supplemental reading exposure in leveled texts. All students are placed in ability groups. Every student is assessed after each unit or theme, using the materials provided by the publisher. In addition, teachers use other, locally developed, tools to monitor and assess their students regularly. This monitoring system has been in place for a decade (long before Reading First), and it involves the periodic release of faculty from their responsibilities to meet with the reading coordinator and review individuals and plan future instructional "moves." Tha'm's instruction has been carefully monitored for difficulty and also for breadth.

Teachers take care to provide instruction in word recognition, fluency, and comprehension. Their comprehensive program was heavily informed by their study-group reading of Harvey's *Strategies That Work* and Keene's *Mosaic of Thought*. All students are expected to write in strategy journals, and all participate daily in a teacher read-aloud that is linked to key comprehension strategies.

On the other hand, there is little evidence that Tha'm has had many opportunities to read lengthy texts (either narrative fiction or exposition), and her teachers have not engaged students in literature discussion outside the read-aloud time. Until recently, teachers had not examined the cognitive level of their questions, and attention to vocabulary is a new and recent consideration. Except for her work with the ELL teacher, Tha'm has not had an enriched exposure to vocabulary.

It is clear that Tha'm has had made excellent progress in large part because of the focused and intentional instruction she has received. Her school and her teachers have generally "beat the odds" in their attention to reading in the school. It is a matter of some concern that the writing program is much less well developed than the reading program. In addition, throughout Tha'm's school career, the school has placed content-area subject matter on the "back burner" as they focused on reading. There is virtually no social studies curriculum in the building and only recently a limited science curriculum. Given that the school is a primary source of content information for Tha'm, we suspected that her concept development might be somewhat weak.

Kyle.   Kyle lives in a middle- to upper-middle-class suburban community that is almost all white Caucasian. Fewer than 2 percent of the people in Kyle's town live in poverty, and more than 73 percent of the adult population has at least some college education. The median income for his community is among the highest in the state and almost twice that of Tha'm's town. Like the vast majority of his peers, English is Kyle's primary and only language. He lives at home with his parents and a sister. Both parents work, and his mother is deeply involved in school affairs.

Steven's Creek School has a reputation for excellence. Teachers there are well paid, and they pride themselves on their hard work and intelligent innovation. The school district has a well-articulated curriculum design. The outcomes clearly focus on students' literature-based reading and process writing.

Kyle is in a multiage K–2 classroom, one of many in his school. He had been with the same teacher, Ms. McIntyre, since kindergarten. His mother has volunteered in this room frequently. The literacy environment in the classroom is a rich one. As students enter each morning, they write their names in the sign-in book and also indicate with a check mark whether they want milk, hot lunch, or both. They sign up for their snack and make choices of activities each morning by moving their name tags to various activities being offered. There is a consistent message to students that they will read and they will write.

There are books of every sort. The library corner is attractive and accessible, teachers discuss books with children all the time, and book-dialogue journals start early. There are also small teacher-made booklets for special purposes, such as tiny alphabet books for the youngest students and small handwriting booklets for everyone who needs to practice. There are big books, there are books in the science area, there are counting books next to the basket of nuts, and so on. There are different shapes of paper and many types of writing utensils.

Ms. McIntyre believes in a child-centered classroom and expects that students will learn to read and write by reading and writing. Her job is to ask the right question at the right time or to provide the right prompt when things get stalled. No norm-referenced tests are used in this school, because it is a K–2 building (exempt from the federally mandated tests at grades 3–8). In order to provide appropriate instruction, Ms. McIntyre relies heavily on individual conference observations to alert her to next steps. For more-formal communication across teachers/grades, the teachers adopted a portfolio system and worked to put into place an assessment system that reflects and challenges their own instructional and curricular designs (see Chapters 8 and 9).

Ms. McIntyre can most often be found in corners and on the floor, having quiet but intense conversations with children about their work. Children interact with her and with each other continuously. The most frequent type of interactions involve discussions of ongoing work, activities, or personal responses. The children talk about their out-of-school experiences during share time and write about them in journals. The classroom is organized as a reading-writing workshop. There are no formal groupings of any sort, although Ms. McIntyre might call a group together to work on an area of interest or difficulty, and children frequently organize themselves into groups to accomplish tasks—to plan a puppet show, work on blocks, or read together, for example.

Kyle's classroom is one of many like it in his district. However, Ms. McIntyre is an unusually expert teacher. In her classroom, there are very few whole-group or even small-group lessons. Students do not receive direct instruction in skills except in response to their own reading and their own questions about print. Ms. McIntyre does discuss reading skills and strategies with individual children as they read and write. Conversations are explicit, and the feedback to students about strategies (e.g., using picture cues, thinking about the middle and endings of words) is very focused and direct.

At this point in the assessment-instruction process, Ms. McIntyre and Kyle's parents are asking many questions. Although they can see that he has made progress, they are worried about the slow rate and especially concerned that he will be going next year to a larger and less personal building for students in grades 3 to 5. So, the questions to be asked include these: (1) What types of books and materials have been used with Kyle? (2) Is the instruction he is receiving a good "fit" for his needs and strengths? (3) What can be done, additionally, to propel him forward?

CHAPTER SUMMARY

Most textbooks on reading and writing assessment do not examine the types of contextual factors discussed in this chapter. However, contextual factors clearly contribute to students' literacy development and can enhance learning or lead to difficulty.

The first major section of this chapter describes how standards of competent performance are determined by home, school, and community cultures and connections. Next, we discuss how the instructional setting can influence student performance. For example, differing teacher beliefs result in the creation of diverse learning environments that can result in problems for students whose expectations and beliefs may be at odds with those of the teachers. Similarly, the differential treatment teachers frequently offer to members of different ability groups can have a negative effect on student performance and perceptions. This section also explores the role of intervention programs and approaches.

The third major section addresses instructional goals, instructional methods, reading and writing activities and tasks, and assessment practices that are evident within a particular instructional environment. As a means of translating general curricular goals into instruction, three types of instructional objectives are described: content, attitude, and process.

Motivated readers and writers are those who choose to read and write for a variety of recreational and informational purposes. Strategic readers and writers use their knowledge and skills flexibly, adapting their approach for different purposes, tasks, and materials, evaluating their reading and writing along the way.

Creating knowledgeable, strategic readers and writers involves authentic, complex projects and instructional practices based on the principle of gradually releasing responsibility for learning from the teacher to the student. Three notable characteristics of the gradual-release model of learning and instruction are scaffolding, dialogue, and the level of difficulty.

Instructional practices that promote motivation are those that help students generate expectations for success and also help them focus on learning versus task completion as a valued endeavor. Key among these practices are activities that promote voluntary reading and writing.

Instructional methods also include classroom activities and tasks. Different types of tasks promote different student behaviors and need to be evaluated accordingly. Independent seatwork, reading comprehension questions, writing process, reading-writing workshop, and discussion are examined as examples of different types of literacy activities.

Finally, classroom assessment practices affect student performance because they so strongly influence the types of instruction offered to students—both by directing attention to what *will* be assessed and by limiting students' access to aspects of literacy that are *not* assessed.

The tools and strategies section of the chapter describes techniques for assessing the instructional setting, general instructional practice, and specific instructional activities. These techniques include questionnaires; interviews; and observational devices such as guiding questions, rating scales, and checklists. Most are informal and require some organization and reflection on the part of the person doing the evaluation. In addition, a relatively unique standardized instrument known as FAAB (Functional Assessment of Academic Behavior) is described and evaluated, with the conclusion that it adds an important tool to the repertoire of evaluation strategies for assessing context.

MyEducationLab™

Go to the Topics, Reading Difficulties & Intervention Strategies and Parents and Families, in the MyEducationLab (www.myeducationlab.com) for your course, where you can:

- Find learning outcomes for Reading Difficulties & Intervention Strategies and Parents and Families along with the national standards that connect to these outcomes.
- Complete Assignments and Activities that can help you more deeply understand the chapter content.
- Apply and practice your understanding of the core teaching skills identified in the chapter using the Building Teaching Skills and Dispositions learning units.
- Examine challenging situations and cases presented in the IRIS Center Resources.
- Check your comprehension of the content covered in the chapter by going to the Study Plan in the Book Resources for your text. Here you will be able to take a chapter quiz, receive feedback on your answers, and then access Review, Practice, and Enrichment activities to enhance your understanding of chapter content.

A+RISE A+RISE® Standards2Strategy™ is an innovative and interactive online resource that offers new teachers in grades K-12 just in time, research-based instructional strategies that meet the linguistic needs of ELLs as they learn content, differentiate instruction for all grades and abilities, and are aligned to Common Core Elementary Language Arts standards (for the literacy strategies) and to English language proficiency standards in WIDA, Texas, California, and Florida.

CHAPTER 6

Instructional Resources

*A*n increasing body of research suggests that the nature of the instructional materials used to teach reading and writing has a significant effect on students' performance. This realization has forced both educators and publishers to examine their assumptions about the sources of reading and writing difficulty and has encouraged teachers to promote "curriculum-based evaluations" (see Hall & Mengel, 2002; Howell & Nolet, 2000; Serafini, 2010) or "classroom-based assessments" (see Afflerbach, Reutschlin, & Russell, 2007). Curriculum- or classroom-based assessments evaluate performance using instructional resources and contexts typical of those regularly used in classroom instruction. For example, reading comprehension has been assessed using engaging narrative trade books (Roser, 2007) and informational trade books (Wood, Taylor, Drye, & Brigman, 2007), as well as advertisements (Afflerbach, Reutschlin, & Russell, 2007) in the context of the talking, writing, and drawing in response to those texts that is typical of the literacy practices of the classroom. A reading and writing assessment for any individual is incomplete until the characteristics of the materials used in the assessment have been described and the resources that are regularly used for instruction have been identified.

Resources specifically addressed in this chapter are commercial reading/language arts programs, textbooks and trade materials, and digital texts and technologies used in reading and writing instruction. The complexity of factors related to instructional environments makes assessment of instructional resources very difficult. We have attempted, however, to provide both quantitative and qualitative ways to evaluate the aspects of instructional resources that are known to influence reading and writing performance.

UNDERSTANDING THE ROLE OF INSTRUCTIONAL RESOURCES IN READING AND WRITING PERFORMANCE

A survey conducted in 2007 (Education Market Research, 2007, cited in Dewitz, Jones, & Leahey, 2009) revealed that 73 percent of U.S. schools surveyed use a commercially prepared basal program or use such a program "selectively." Mesmer (2006) conducted a national survey of teachers who were members of the International Reading Association and teaching in grades K–3. That survey sheds light on the "selective" use of commercial reading programs. It suggests that many teachers are incorporating a variety of resources and texts into their reading programs. In addition to core reading programs, teachers are using leveled texts and decodable texts as well as "trade books," or books published for wide sale rather than for instructional purposes, and also digital and multimedia resources (see also Labbo & Place, 2010; Martinez & McGee, 2000; Ranker 2010). Given the very rich array of resources that may be incorporated into reading and writing instruction, how do we consider the nature of the potential interactions of these texts with learners and instruction? Each of these resources has features or qualities that are unique. For example, core reading programs potentially provide a high level of support for teachers' instructional decisions; digital texts may be embedded with supports for learners' strategic thinking in making sense of text. All texts, however, can be examined in terms of their complexity and comprehensibility. The complexity of the language of a text is a major consideration in understanding how qualities of the text will interact with learner and instruction to affect reading and writing. So, we begin this chapter with a discussion of features that contribute to the complexity and comprehensibility of any text, and thus affect reading and writing ability. After this discussion of features common to all texts, we will examine specific features associated with particular types.

Features That Influence Text Complexity and Comprehensibility

The features of text that contribute to how well and how efficiently readers can make sense of it are discussed briefly in the sections that follow. These features include the genre and corresponding structure of the text, the language used to present ideas in prose, the knowledge and skills required to make sense of those ideas, graphic representations that complement prose, and typographic features that clarify the structure of the text.

Genre and Text Structure.   Genre refers to the language patterns that authors use to construct a written text in a manner that fits its particular purpose (Pappas & Pettegrew, 1998). Genres typically encountered in school include personal, factual, and analytical; these categories can be further refined by their purposes:

> *Personal genre:* includes *recount* (tells of events/personal experiences) or *narrative* (tells of an event with a problem or complication and focuses on the actions of participants in the event)
> *Factual genre:* includes *procedure* (provides directions or instructions, in sequence) or *report* (relates facts with supporting information)
> *Analytical genre:* includes *account* (describes why things happened in the way they did), *explanation* (interprets a phenomenon), or *exposition* (presents arguments in favor of a position) (Martin, 1989, cited in Scheleppegrel, 2004)

To the extent that texts conform to culturally established conventions for particular genres, readers who are familiar with those conventions can approach the text with expectations that will help them organize and make sense of the information they encounter.

They can expect particular subjects and treatment of those subjects, as well as certain qualities of information and purposes. The genre-specific conventions that authors adopt are often expressed in certain linguistic (language) choices, both at the microlevel of word choices and at the macrolevel of organization of ideas.

For example, in order to tell a story, authors choose words typical of the personal, narrative genre: particular nouns, or names, for specific people and places; verbs that emphasize characters' thoughts, feelings, and perceptions; words with poetic quality, to create an emotional tone critical to the story (Pappas & Pettegrew, 1998). Authors organize stories around the experiences of important characters in episodes of the form: setting → complication → resolution (Weaver & Kintsch, 1991).

On the other hand, in order to describe how things are done, authors write an account using language typical of the factual, procedural genre. Here, words include generic nouns for participants, classes of objects, and types of places; action verbs for processes, functions, and behaviors; and words selected for their usefulness in accurately presenting information on the topic (Pappas & Pettegrew, 1998). Authors organize procedural writing around the actions to be accomplished. Other factual writing might be structured around descriptions of categories, comparison and contrast, or illustrative examples (Weaver & Kintsch, 1991).

When we speak of the genre of texts that are used in reading instruction, we collapse the specific categories of genres described above into two broad classes: narrative (personal genre) and expository or informational texts (these terms are often used interchangeably for factual and analytical genres). Next, we look more closely at narrative and informational text, with respect to what research has to say about the effects of text genre on reading and writing performance.

Narrative Texts. A narrative tells a story about human events and actions. Researchers have concluded that narratives have identifiable structure. Narrative structures vary across cultures as well as across different types of stories such as fables, mysteries, and adventures. The story structure most familiar in mainstream culture in the United States is "story grammar" (see Duchene, 2004), which organizes stories around these common features: characters; setting or time placement; complications and major goals of main characters; plots and resolutions of complications; emotional patterns; and points, morals, and themes (Graesser, Golding, & Long, 1991; Graesser, Olde, & Klettke, 2002).

The principal aim of stories is often assumed to be entertainment, but "the range of purposes for telling a story is as varied as the motives that underlie human behavior. Thus, stories can be used to cause pain as well as pleasure (e.g., to embarrass, to humiliate, to parody, to flatter, to console, to teach, to arouse guilt, etc.)" (Stein & Policastro, 1984, p. 116). Readers and listeners use their knowledge of text purpose to anticipate text type and structure.

Individuals build internal story structures and use them to aid comprehension during reading. Text organization helps readers predict, focus attention on, and retain or recall content (Goldman & Rakestraw, 2000; McConaughy, 1982). Both children and adults comprehend better when story content is organized so that it conforms to expectations (Stein & Glenn, 1979; Stein & Nezworski, 1978). When stories present issues such as missing segments (e.g., initiating events) or altered sequence, readers comprehend and remember less (Lipson, Mosenthal, & Mekkelsen, 1999; Thorndyke, 1977).

Even very young children appear to have a rather well-developed sense of story. Evidence suggests that poor readers, at least by sixth grade, have as well developed a sense of story as do good readers and that they use it to enhance comprehension (Copmann & Griffith, 1994; McConaughy, 1985). It should also be noted that these internal story structures appear to develop as children listen to and read well-formed stories. Thus, it is extremely important that all readers are offered well-crafted stories containing strong story structures, so that they can develop this sense of story early and make the most efficient use of their knowledge.

Unfortunately, many of the materials used with struggling readers are poorly written. Analyses show that as texts become more decodable, they also became both less predictable and less engaging (Hoffman et al., 2002). Both of the "stories" in Figures 6.1a and 6.1b are typical selections encountered in the early years of school. Of course, these texts are not representative of the content or organization of *any* story. Neither segment in Figure 6.1 contains the expected story grammar element of conflict and it is difficult to imagine what would pull a reader through the text.

The text in Figure 6.1a is considered a "leveled" text because it is more predictable. Students are expected to pay attention to the "patterned-ness" of the text (in this case, the

**FIGURE 6.1a
Leveled Readers**

I open the drawer.
You close the drawer.

I open the box.
You close the box.

Source: Open and Close, Level C reader. Excerpt from Reading a–z, Leveled Readers. http://www.readinga-z.com/book.php?id=249

FIGURE 6.1b
Decodables

Pap gets a pan.
Pap gets in a pan.

Nan and Pap
are in a pan.

Source: Decodable reader excerpt from Reading a–z. www.readinga-z.com/book/decodable-books.php.

grammatical phrases where whole words are substituted). The pictures heavily support the meaning. On the other hand, the text in Figure 6.1b requires students to rely almost exclusively on their decoding ability and can, for students at a certain phase of development, provide useful practice in previously taught elements of phonics. However, exclusive reliance on this type of artificial text may actually make reading *more* difficult. Children find such texts uninteresting and difficult to comprehend, because they do not invite reader involvement (Bruce, 1984; Goldman & Rakestraw, 2000). Importantly, these texts also limit students' exposure to age-appropriate vocabulary and content (Biemiller, 2006) and provide no opportunity for comprehension instruction. In addition, they probably affect students' writing development. Children need good writing models if they are to improve their own writing. Hillocks (1986, 2003), who conducted an extensive review of research on writing, concluded that "research indicates that emphasis on the presentation of good pieces of writing as models is significantly more useful than the study of grammar" (1986, p. 249).

Informational Texts.   Five common structures are used repeatedly in writing informational texts, at least in the Western Hemisphere (Armbruster, 1984):

■ *Simple listing:* Information is presented in an unordered list that outlines broad concepts with specific facts.

- *Comparison/contrast:* Ideas are described in terms of their similarities and differences.
- *Temporal sequence:* Time order of ideas or events is used to organize the text chronologically.
- *Cause/effect:* The presentation of ideas or events focuses on the causal relationships between and among them.
- *Problem/solution:* Relationships between and among ideas or events are linked so that one represents a problem and another a solution to that problem.

Other structures include *description* (in which the author defines, labels, and characterizes phenomena) and *persuasion* (where the author makes an assertion and argues for that idea with supporting evidence).

Whereas even young children seem able to recognize and use *narrative or story structure*, it appears that many middle-grade students are either unaware of or unable to use *informational or expository text structure* to aid comprehension (Goldman & Rakestraw, 2000; Taylor & Samuels, 1983). Although the ability to use text organization to increase learning and promote comprehension improves with age, reading ability differences are also noted by the middle grades. In addition, struggling students are likely to be more affected by different genre structures than are good readers.

Expository text is often challenging, because both the content and structure are incongruent with students' skills and experiences. Elementary students generally have had limited exposure to expository text and the concepts represented in these texts. Expository texts place heavy demands on language skills and call for sophisticated new ways of thinking about text. All of these factors, detailed below, present challenges to comprehension even in typically achieving readers.

First, children may have less skill in reading expository text because they typically have much less experience reading this type of material. In elementary classrooms, narrative has historically been the primary, if not exclusive, genre of literacy instruction. At the turn of the 21st century, narratives still accounted for an overall estimated 90 percent of the materials and instruction in elementary classrooms (Dreher, 2003). The emphasis on stories has been particularly prevalent in the early grades. Duke (2000) found a scarcity of informational text in the libraries and print environments of first-grade classrooms. Students in these classrooms engaged with informational text for an average of 3.6 minutes per day—1.9 minutes per day in low-SES school districts. The scarcity of informational text among the "real books" and "real writing" of literacy instruction has been documented across the grades. Hiebert and Fisher (cited in Beck & McKeown, 1991) observed one hundred hours of literacy activities in second- through sixth-grade classrooms and found no instance in which expository text was the focus of instruction. Pappas (1991) described how a steady diet of narrative text becomes the only one considered for teaching reading and writing in the primary grades. In addition, differences between good and poor readers' ability to read exposition may be related to opportunity, because it appears that poor readers have even fewer opportunities to read informational text than good readers do, and this problem persists right through middle and high school (Clinton, 2002; Duke, 2000).

Second, limited opportunities to use informational text ensure that the text structures of this genre will be unfamiliar to readers. Informational text structures are also less predictable, because they do not resonate with daily life experiences. Kucan and Beck (1996) contrast narrative and expository text as follows: narrative texts are structured around goals; characters engage in a sequence of actions directed at solving problems and resolving conflicts. This overall framework can be used to organize what is read, because it is predictable. This pattern found in narrative text occurs consistently in children's everyday life experiences. Expository text, in contrast, does not have such a predominant, overall framework. It often alternates use of several different formats—descriptive, compare-and-contrast, and chronological sequences, for example—and therefore the patterns aren't clearly defined. The research in this area suggests that not all expository text patterns are equally easy for less-mature readers. For example, under some conditions, simple listing is more difficult than compare/contrast because it requires readers to impose an organization, often by inferring the relationships between and among listed items (Meyer & Freedle, 1984).

Without a tangible, familiar structure, students must depend upon knowledge of the topic to understand what is read. This presents the third challenge: the necessity of prior topic knowledge for comprehension of expository texts. It is the purpose of expository text to inform. Thus, the information presented is likely to be new and unpredictable; or it may be a familiar topic presented in a new or in-depth way. It is difficult for the reader to organize a new body of information with little background knowledge, or with naïve conceptions on a topic that are in error or in conflict with what he or she reads. In an analysis of social studies textbooks, Beck and McKeown (1991) concluded that "many ideas and events portrayed in the books were beyond a young student's grasp because the texts assumed unrealistic levels of knowledge" (p. 484).

Even when elementary students do have the opportunity to read expository text, they are often offered poor examples of exposition. Sometimes knowledgeable readers actually learn more from somewhat ambiguous text (McNamara, Kintsch, Songer, & Kintsch, 1996), but poorly written texts have a negative effect on comprehension for the vast majority of readers (see Graesser, Leon, & Otero, 2002; Shimmerlik, 1978). Studies designed to compare readers' comprehension of organized versus disorganized texts have consistently demonstrated that comprehension and recall are strongly affected by the organization of ideas in text. Well-organized text that highlights the overall structure and supports the relationships between ideas contributes to comprehension and enhances recall. Poor readers appear to be affected by these factors more seriously than are good readers (Alexander & Jetton, 2000).

Well-structured text promotes the integration of knowledge so that more-cognitive resources are available to process new, more-complex information. In turn, these more organized knowledge structures promote complex comprehension activities such as generating inferences, summarizing, and evaluating. Poorly written text is difficult even for proficient readers to comprehend and remember. Students, especially those with reading problems, need to read *good* informational texts (Goldman & Rakestraw, 2000).

Coherence Relations.   *Coherence* means "a sticking together" (Anderson & Armbruster, 1984a, p. 204). The ideas and concepts in texts are tied together by an underlying cohesive structure. According to Bateman and Rondhuis (1997), coherence establishes a meaning relationship between segments of a text that renders the segments "more than the sum of its parts" (p. 2). In coherent writing, the author moves smoothly from one idea to the next, making it easier for readers to understand the big ideas. The author clarifies facts and helps the reader to understand the significance of ideas or events.

Coherence exerts strong influence on comprehension and learning. When reading coherent (versus less coherent) text, readers take less time to read, they recall more, and the integration of ideas is improved (Gernsbacher, 1997; Goldman & Wiley, 2004). Readers are better able to build a model of the meaning of text when it has a strong, cohesive structure, which functions like a "roadmap to understanding" (Binkley, 1988, p. 104). For example, both reading time and recall are improved when authors repeatedly refer to key ideas (Goetz & Armbruster, 1980).

There are many ways in which authors tighten relationships and increase the flow of ideas (Goldman & Rakestraw, 2000; Halliday & Hasan, 1976). Authors can make effective use of *reference* by using pronouns to link previous or forthcoming events, people, and things. Similarly, authors use *lexical repetition* and *synonyms* to tie ideas together— for example, by repeating key words several times or using other words with the same meaning (e.g., *elephant* and *lumbering animal*). Coherent text also makes effective use of *intersentential connectives* such as *therefore* and *obviously* to tie ideas together.

Stories for young or less-able readers frequently have the effect of being "inconsiderate" of their audience due to attempts to control difficulty by using roundabout language or by omitting information completely. This can result in highly contrived and/or incomplete selections, such as the examples in Figure 6.1. Both able and less-able readers appear to take a very long time to recognize fully and use most cohesive ties in text (Bridge & Winograd, 1982; Singer & O'Connell, 2003). Connectives provide explicit cues to the type of relationship between ideas in a text, and thus increase text cohesion (Louwerse, 2001). Readers of all abilities benefit when text cohesion is explicitly flagged with language cues (Ozuru, Dempsey, & McNamara, 2009). However, some aspects of cohesion seem to pose special problems for less-able readers. For example, although the absence of explicitly stated connectives makes reading more difficult for all readers, the need to infer connectives is a much more serious problem for less-able readers (Marshall & Glock, 1978/1979). Importantly, thoughtful text cohesion can also help readers grapple with challenging ideas (Graesser, 2011).

Unity.   Although unity in text is closely related to coherence, they are not exactly the same thing. Unity refers to the degree to which the text addresses a single purpose. Distracting or irrelevant information can detract from the unity of a text (Anderson & Armbruster, 1984). The importance of unity can be seen quite clearly in the sample fifth-grade social studies text presented in Figure 6.2. Although this selection suffers from several problems, one of the greatest is its lack of unity. The reader is hard-pressed to know just what is important. Readers with little knowledge of the Civil War (most fifth-grade students) will have a difficult time forming an integrated picture of the information in this section of text, because the selection moves from topic to topic so quickly. Similarly, poor readers will have trouble because there is little opportunity to use prior knowledge (either preexisting or garnered from the text) as an aid to comprehension.

Sometimes authors include information that they think is interesting but not necessarily important. When readers pay too much attention to these interesting, but not very

FIGURE 6.2   Social Studies Text

The North and the South at War

In 1861 Lincoln became the President of a divided United States. He took the oath of office on a high platform in front of the capitol in Washington, D.C. He was dressed in a black suit, a stiff white shirt, and a high silk hat. He carried a cane with a gold handle.

Lincoln stepped forward and placed his left hand on a Bible. Raising his right hand, he promised to "preserve, protect, and defend the Constitution of the United States." People wondered how he would do this. Seven states had already left the United States. Would Lincoln try to punish them? What would he say about slavery?

Lincoln did not answer all of these questions in his Inaugural Address. He said that no state had the right to leave the United States. He warned that he would protect the forts and buildings which belonged to the United States government.

War broke out only a few weeks after Lincoln became President. It became known as the Civil War.

The war began at Fort Sumter in South Carolina. Fort Sumter was on a small island in Charleston harbor. Find it on the map. It belonged to the United States government. Union soldiers from the North held the fort. South Carolina, now a part of the Confederacy, ordered Fort Sumter to surrender. When the commander of the fort refused, the food supply was cut off.

Lincoln had food shipped to Fort Sumter. This made Confederate leaders angry. Southern soldiers fired on the fort. Northern soldiers fired back. A fierce battle took place. At last the Northern soldiers had to give up. This was the first battle of the Civil War.

Thousands offered to serve in the Union Army. Thousands rushed to join the Confederate forces, too. Everyone hoped the war would be over soon. But it wasn't. It dragged on for four years.

During the second year of the war, both sides ran short of troops. They then drafted, or ordered, people into the armies. This was the first time in United States history that soldiers were drafted.

Both sides needed money, supplies, and troops. Money-raising events were held in the Union and in the Confederacy. Groups were formed to help the families of soldiers.

Women who had never worked outside their homes went to work in offices and factories. Some women ran the family farms and businesses for the first time. Others knitted and sewed uniforms and made bandages to use in the hospitals.

Doctors and nurses went to serve on the battlefield. Mary Walker was one of the doctors. At first, she was allowed to work only as a nurse. Later, though, she became an Army officer and worked as a doctor.

Clara Barton was called the "Angel of the Battlefield." She was born on a Massachusetts farm on Christmas Day, 1821. For a while, she taught school near her home. Later she moved to Washington, D.C. She was a clerk in one of the government offices.

When the Civil War began, Clara Barton carried medicines and food to injured soldiers. The officers ordered her away. They said the battlefield was no place for a woman. But she did not give up. In fact, she got other women to join her. After a time, she ran a large hospital for wounded soldiers.

Clara Barton served suffering people the rest of her long life. She helped to find missing Union soldiers. She took care of the victims of wars in other parts of the world. She helped people who had lost homes in fires, floods, and storms. She founded the American Red Cross.

Dorothea Dix was another nurse during the Civil War. She had spent years trying to make life better for people in prisons and poorhouses. During the Civil War, though, she took time out from her work to care for wounded soldiers. She was in charge of all the nurses for the Union Army.

Source: From *Our Country,* by Gertrude S. Browns, Ernest W. Tiegs, and Fay Adams. Copyright © 1979 by Ginn and Company. Reprinted by permission of Pearson Education, Inc.

relevant, pieces of information, their comprehension suffers (Lehman et al., 2007; Silvia, 2006). Text unity is likely to have an especially strong effect on both less-knowledgeable and less-able readers. For comprehension to occur, readers need to integrate text information with prior knowledge and also integrate the information from one part of the text with information from earlier parts. If this does not happen, readers' memory for the text will be limited because they will be forced to recall isolated facts rather than organized sets of information (Anderson & Armbruster, 1984a; Cain, Oakhill, Barnes, & Bryant, 2001).

Conceptual and Knowledge Demands.   The understandings that learners develop in their interactions with text are highly dependent on the preexisting knowledge that they bring to the processes of making sense of text. "The contemporary view of learning is that people construct new knowledge and understandings based on what they already know and believe" (Bransford, 2000, p. 10). Thus, it is important to consider how appropriate both the content and structure of the materials are for those who are not yet expert in terms of either skill or knowledge. Teachers who are deciding if a text is suitable for their students must determine what knowledge the authors of the text assume that readers will have. It is also important to determine what preexisting naïve conceptions readers might hold and if the text confronts these beliefs in a way that persuades readers to consider a new way of thinking about previously held ideas. Hartley (2004) also recommends that teachers examine a text in relation to their teaching objectives and also consider whether the materials contain any outdated material, bias, or omissions.

Evaluating appropriateness of content can be extremely tricky for teachers, who have had many more experiences in the world than their students and are themselves often content experts. It is very clear that prior knowledge and expertise interact with structural cues in text, so more-knowledgeable readers can cope better with inferior texts than poor readers can (Goldman & Rakestraw, 2000). Because teachers are so familiar with the content they teach, they may underestimate the processing demands required to understand the vocabulary, concepts, inferences, and metaphors.

Even when materials are generally appropriate for the intended audience, however, mismatches can occur. This is where the knowledgeable and thoughtful teacher will need to exercise judgment. When working with special student populations or when the overall school curriculum does not support the content, we must make sure that we are judging the contribution of these materials to reader performance. Under some circumstances, failure to comprehend has very little to do with reading skill and everything to do with the texts that are being read.

Graphic and Typographic Features.   These adjunct aids are the structural features of texts that are intended to supplement or complement the information in the written text. Graphics, according to Carpenter and Just (1991), may be iconic (line drawings or photos, diagrams or maps, that resemble closely the structure of the objects they represent), schematic (e.g., graphic organizer charts, showing a functional rather than structural relationship), or graphs (tables and figures, which present information numerically). Typographic features include: variations in print font or characteristics (such as boldface or italics) that add emphasis; punctuation such as quotes, exclamation marks, or question marks that add nuance; and language-like symbols such as numbers and mathematical symbols, as well as musical notation. Adjunct aids also include organizational features such as headings and subheadings, introductions and summaries, and questions either within or at the end of a reading selection. These features are included specifically to focus and guide readers' understanding and are common in materials used for instructional purposes.

As with other features of the text, adjunct aids have an impact on students' comprehension and learning. For example, when topic sentences are clearly present, readers comprehend and recall text content better (Bridge, Belmore, Moskow, Cohen, & Matthews, 1984). Furthermore, comprehension of main ideas is enhanced when they are stated explicitly at the beginning of paragraphs or text sections (Baumann, 1986) or are highlighted in some way (Chambliss, 1995; Doctorow, Wittrock, & Marks, 1978). Complementary prose and graphics "provide different types of information about the same referent" (p. 648) for a deeper understanding; redundant prose and graphics provide multiple representations of the same ideas, to assist readers who do not efficiently process information from only prose or graphics (Hegarty, Carpenter, & Just, 1991).

The mere presence of such features does not ensure enhanced comprehension. Students must be aware of these features and understand how they contribute to understanding. For example, in spite of the potential benefits of linking prose and graphics, there is evidence that many novice readers fail to integrate graphics and prose and thus fail to learn optimally from text. Moore and Scevak (1997) found age-related differences in the degree to which readers integrated information from prose and graphics. While 48 percent of ninth graders studied reported how information in graphics facilitated their understanding of prose, fifth and seventh graders rarely did so. Dalton and Palincsar (2004) also found that fifth graders rarely spontaneously integrated information from graphics and prose. Readers who made the greatest gains in conceptual knowledge after reading an experimental text were those whose protocols showed the greatest evidence of prose-graphic integration. Struggling readers were less likely than typically achieving readers to integrate graphics and prose.

Many of the adjunct aids described above are unique to the materials used for instructional purposes, and students may need direct guidance and explanation from teachers to be able to take full advantage of these text features. Also, many graphic and typographic features as well as other adjunct aids are specific to the texts of particular domains (see next section for further explanation) and thus require significant domain knowledge to use productively.

Domain-Specific Features. The features described thus far that affect complexity of text come together in very particular ways in texts that might be characterized as *content-area texts*, or texts that address discipline-specific subject matter. Texts in academic disciplines such as social studies, science, literature, mathematics, or the fine arts make unique demands on readers who are novices to these disciplines. These texts present challenging ideas in specialized language reflecting thinking processes known only to the "insiders" (Buehl, 2011, p. 10) who created that knowledge. Shanahan and Shanahan (2008) provide more detail on how disciplinary texts challenge learners: concepts are abstract, ambiguous, unfamiliar, or at odds with understandings learners have developed through everyday experience. Language used to express those ideas includes (at a microlevel) specialized, technical vocabulary as well as sentence forms typical of the domain and (at a macrolevel) text structures that emphasize what is valued and how knowledge is organized in the discipline. Graphic and typographic resources include specialized notation or symbol systems and other visual or multimodal means of representing ideas.

On the basis of their observations of several experts in a variety of domains, Shanahan and Shanahan (2008) provide the following examples of how the features of texts in each discipline require that expert readers deploy different reading processes. The experts' different approaches to reading discipline-specific texts reflect what is valued and expected of those who contribute to knowledge in that discipline.

- Mathematicians read, and reread, with very close attention to each word, even function words such as *the* and *a*, which signal important nuances in mathematics but seldom carry exceptional significance in other domains. Mathematicians value accuracy and vigilance to ensure correctness.
- Chemists toggle back and forth between the prose and the array of "alternative representations" (p. 49) typical of chemistry texts, in their efforts to integrate descriptions in prose with the symbols and numbers found in formulas as well as graphics such as diagrams and graphs. Chemists produce knowledge through experiments; they value an understanding of the experimental procedure and the process revealed.
- Historians take a critical stance, evaluating the perspective, credentials, and credibility of the source in order to place the author's interpretation of historical events in the context of the author's own biases. Historians' scholarship consists of gathering a variety of documents and artifacts after an event has occurred. The historian values multiple perspectives in efforts to put historical events in context.

The demands of discipline-specific texts present considerable challenge to struggling readers who, as novices to the disciplines, do not have sufficient content knowledge, understanding of how experts think, or explicit instruction in how to approach disciplinary text to make sense of what they read (Lee & Spratley, 2010).

Now that we have considered some of the characteristics common across a variety of texts that affect text complexity and comprehensibility, we will look at characteristics unique to specific types of texts. These characteristics will also affect text complexity and, in turn, reading and writing performance.

Core Reading/Language Arts Programs

For a large number of teachers, commercial programs long known as *basal series*, now called *core programs*, provide the primary tools for reading/language arts instruction. Because they exert such strong influence, it is important to examine these materials to understand the nature of the instruction experienced by most students, including many who are struggling to learn to read and write. These materials have changed rather dramatically in recent years, and the impact of a core program may depend on which version is being used.

Until the early 1990s, commercial core programs reflected a skills-based approach to teaching reading/language arts, and the professional literature was critical of their use of contrived language, controlled vocabulary, and simplistic stories lacking in conflict, character development, and meaningful situations (Goodman, Shannon, Freeman, & Murphy, 1988). By 1989, skills-based approaches gave way to a more "literature-based" approach, with a heavy emphasis on strategic reading in the form of metacomprehension strategies such as generating questions, summarizing, paraphrasing, predicting, verifying, and thinking aloud (Wepner & Feeley, 1993). In the early 1990s, basal publishers moved toward literature-based programs that were more aligned with the dominant sociocognitive theories and research related to reading and writing.

At the outset of the twenty-first century, national concerns about levels of reading achievement and various state mandates resulted in yet another wave of basal program reform that reflected a better balance between the skills-based approaches of the 1970s and 1980s and the literature-based approaches of the early 1990s. At the same time, however, debates raged once again about the nature of early reading instruction, and beginning reading texts in particular became less "predictable" and more "decodable" with a more systematic emphasis on word-level features (Hoffman, Sailors, & Patterson, 2002; Menon & Hiebert, 2005). Now, following the close of the first decade of the twenty-first century, core reading programs continue to reflect trends, and debates, in educational research and practice as well as public policy. Core reading programs developed during the first decade of the current century, when response to intervention (RTI) became an established approach to supporting students who show signs of difficulty, provide materials corresponding to Tier 1, Tier 2, and Tier 3 instruction (Dewitz, 2009).

Recently, publishers have been called upon to include science and social studies content in core reading programs (Dewitz, 2009). The addition of this expository text is consistent with recent attention to the literacy needs of adolescents in mastering content areas (Carnegie Council on Advancing Adolescent Literacy, 2010; Moje, 2008) and the related concern about the dearth of informational text in the primary grades (Duke, 2000). The next iteration of core reading programs will need to attend to the Common Core State Standards (CCSS), a national framework for curriculum in reading/language arts (as well as social studies, science, and math), which states are just now in the process of adopting and studying for implementation. This brief overview of changes in basal programs over several decades suggests that the date of publication may be far more important to determining the nature of the instruction being provided than the publisher or the fact that it is a basal program. For example, Mesmer's (2006) study indicates that teachers who are using a basal program published prior to 2000 are significantly more likely to use predictable texts in their reading program than are teachers who are using a basal published after that date.

Despite changes in philosophy, the basic components of basal programs have remained fairly constant. These include a multilevel series of materials for both the student and the teacher. At each level, student materials consist of an *anthology of reading selections* of various types and a *collection of independent activities*. At each level, there is also a *teacher's guide* that includes detailed directions and suggestions for instruction. Most core/basal programs also include a wide array of supplemental materials that may include "little" and/or leveled books and/or decodable texts as part of instruction, as well as materials for independent seatwork. The next sections consider separately the main components of basal reading programs.

Basals.   The anthologies of reading material in core/basal programs contain a variety of different types of reading selections deemed appropriate for students at each grade or ability level. The quality and balance of these selections is highly variable and dramatically different over time. For example, older basal reading anthologies rarely include informational text, and when they do, the texts are not likely to represent the full range of informational materials students encounter in the real world of reading. For example, selections from subject-area textbooks were not (and still rarely are) included. Contemporary basal anthologies make much greater use of nonfiction material, often within mixed-genre themes. In addition, informational texts are often drawn from diverse sources, including news magazines and trade books.

Even when the quality of text in the anthologies is quite good, many students with reading and writing problems have only limited experience with the texts. Since they are likely to reflect the challenge appropriate for specific ages/grades, many struggling readers cannot read these texts. Consequently, the students may be diverted to texts of even less quality and variety. The nature and organization of selections to which students are exposed in these materials can have a major impact on their reading and writing performance. If core anthologies are the primary instructional material, students experience only the genre, authors, and topics included there. If they are reading only supplemental (controlled vocabulary) texts, the situation may be even more worrying.

Although teachers today are much more likely to use both basal texts and trade books in their reading programs, the vast majority of teachers still rely heavily on the core program (Bauman et al., 2000; Dewitz, 2010). In some cases, students actually have a greater range of reading experiences in an anthology, especially if their teacher or school does not have access to diverse texts. On the other hand, anthologies offer only relatively short stories. In the intermediate grades, almost all of the material is excerpted from longer texts, limiting students' opportunity to read complex materials over time. Students must have the opportunity to read many types of age-appropriate materials for a variety of purposes if they are to become competent readers and writers. More-specific features of narrative and informational text that influence comprehensibility are considered in the section on trade materials in this chapter.

Beginning Reading Materials.   Given our focus in this text on those students who are experiencing reading and writing difficulties, we want to pay special attention to the texts that are used to help students acquire reading skills. This will help us look at students' strengths and weaknesses in relation to the opportunities for learning. It will also help us understand some of our options in selecting materials that are likely to assist young students in becoming better readers.

Beginning reading texts have traditionally been "engineered" (Cunningham et al., 2005) to support students in the earliest stages of reading. These early reading materials are typically designed to focus on one of three elements: word frequency, word decodability, or predictability. Hiebert and her colleagues (Hiebert, 1999; Hiebert & Martin, 2000, 2002) have done extensive analyses of the early reading materials that have been most popular over time. They observed that older materials for beginning readers typically emphasize a particular feature of words and/or texts used to teach reading, often at the expense of other features. Specifically, the texts with copyrights before 1990 tend to emphasize either high-frequency words such as *boy*, *go*, and *look* or phonetically decodable words such as *can*, *ran*, and *pan*, but not both types of words. On the other hand, *little books* or *leveled books*, which gained popularity as a result of the Reading Recovery program in the 1980s (Clay, 1985), tended to focus on predictability. Little books became popular with teachers who were concerned about the quality of selections in older basal anthologies and the difficulty of selections in the literature-based anthologies, although many, if not most, of these texts could hardly be considered good literature (see the section on narrative text structure later in the chapter for more on this). In Mesmer's (2006) survey, more than half of the teachers reported using leveled texts five or more times a week in their instructional program. Little or leveled books have become so popular that most basal programs now include them as part of the program, often in addition to the student anthology, which may contain either decodable texts or unaltered literature.

As Hiebert and her colleagues have observed, phonics and high-frequency texts provide different opportunities to learn word recognition strategies that can be generalized to words outside the beginning reading materials. She argues that a relatively small number of high-frequency words should be used in beginning texts and advises focusing initially on the ten most frequently used words in written English (*the*, *of*, *and*, *a*, *to*, *in*, *is*, *you*, *that*, *it*). Although students need to acquire a cluster of sight words, many high-frequency words have irregular letter–sound relationships that do not reflect the common and consistent letter–sound patterns in English. A steady diet of texts consisting primarily of high-frequency words may make it difficult for beginning and poor readers to learn letter–sound principles that can be generalized to words not found in the beginning reading materials. On the other hand, a steady diet of phonics texts may lead beginning and poor readers to attempt to decode every word they encounter, which is likely to seriously impede fluency and attention to meaning.

As basal programs became more literature-based in the 1990s, so did beginning reading materials. Literature-based beginning reading materials emphasized the meaningfulness of the entire text, often in the form of "predictable" texts that repeat phrases and/or sentences. Over the course of the past two decades, beginning reading texts have taken on different emphases, shifting from highly controlled texts with low literary value to much more interesting, but also more challenging, texts with more unique words and fewer decodable words (Hiebert & Martin, 2000; Hoffman et al., 1994; Hoffman et al., 1998).

Textbook adoption standards in states such as Texas and California had a strong impact on the development of early reading materials in texts with copyrights beginning around 2000. These materials are more likely to attend to multiple criteria, including the proportion of high-frequency and decodable words in addition to the meaningfulness of the entire text. Hiebert and Martin (2000) used the dimensions of (1) the number of total and unique words; (2) the proportion of unique words that are phonetically regular, multisyllabic, and highly frequent; and (3) the "engagingness" to analyze these newer, "balanced" texts in comparison to those with earlier copyrights. The results of their analyses suggest that the newer texts may be more difficult on some dimensions and less difficult on others.

At present, the materials that are available for beginning readers vary considerably on the dimensions we know are likely to influence young readers' ability to access text. Available research indicates that these materials must be considered in relation to the program objectives and instructional orientation (Hiebert, 2006; Hoffman, Roser, &

Sailors, 2004; Scanlon, Anderson & Sweeney, 2011). Clearly, they have affected the ways in which teachers instruct. Mesmer (2006) found that teachers' instruction was related to the date of their basal materials. In addition, she found that state policy and mandates were strongly and significantly influencing the types of materials teachers used in their programs. One can certainly imagine that exposure only to materials that attend to a single dimension of words or text features could contribute to an individual student's early reading difficulties. Although many, if not most, students learn to read regardless of the types of materials used, others may struggle as a result of a particularly bad match between the materials used and their particular strengths and weaknesses. In addition, recent research suggests that students do better initially if the texts they read provide support and practice for taught skills. Furthermore, not all texts provide the same types of support, and not all texts are good for the same purposes. Understanding the types of texts students have used to learn reading may provide insight into their reading difficulties.

Independent Student Activities.   The independent student activities often found in journals or workbooks that are part of each level of a core/basal program also require careful examination. Widely published reports from the 1980s suggested that, on the average, elementary students spent fewer than ten minutes every school day reading connected text and between 40 and 70 percent of their reading time doing seatwork (Anderson, 1984; Anderson et al., 1985; Fisher et al., 1980). There is conflicting evidence about whether these estimates are still accurate today. Although some researchers argue that they are (Baker, 1999; Harman, Egelson, Hood, & O'Connell, 2002; Mulryan-Kyne, 2005), others report much less use of traditional seatwork. For example, 67 percent of the teachers in Memser's (2006) study reported that they did not use basal workbook materials at all. Mesmer does acknowledge that her sample of teachers (primary-grade teachers belonging to IRA) is not necessarily representative of all teachers.

In any event, because students do spend a great deal of time on independent work, close examination of both the content and use of these activities is essential. Educators have argued for decades that well-designed seatwork activities can facilitate the initial teaching of what is new and the maintenance of what has already been taught (Brophy, 2004; Osborn, 1984). In addition, there is growing evidence that collaborative and/or interactive group work improves students' engagement and their focus (Mulryan, 1995; Nystrand, 2006; Palincsar & Herrenkohl, 2002). On the other hand, poorly designed independent activities and practices waste countless hours on boring and sometimes confusing activities that do not promote reading and writing competence.

At this time, there are no recent reviews of the content of student workbook and skill-sheet materials. Earlier reviews suggested that many of these materials are unlikely to benefit students in any significant way (Osborn, 1984; R. C. Anderson et al., 1985; Scheu, Tanner, & Au, 1989). Because practice materials sometimes play such a prominent role in students' daily reading program, they should be examined with great care. Whether the practice materials are part of a commercial program or reproduced by teachers from various sources, our own observations suggest that too often they still involve very limited amounts of reading, focus on isolated drills of skills that are frequently only marginally useful in learning to read, involve little writing, and do not engage students in activities that promote comprehension.

Although newer core/basal programs are clearly intended to promote reading/language arts abilities and prepare students to read a wide range of authentic material (novels, reference books, content-area textbooks, and so on), it is doubtful that this can occur with the steady diet of contrived texts that even today may appear in workbooks. Extensive research suggests that the transfer of knowledge and skill from one context to another is far from automatic (see Hirsch, 2010/2011). This fact poses particular problems for teaching reading within the context of core programs. For example, Hare, Rabinowitz, and Schieble (1989) found that many students who could identify the main ideas in basal-skills texts were unable to construct main ideas in more-complex, naturally occurring paragraphs.

There are certainly better examples of seatwork in contemporary basal workbooks (see Figure 6.3) than in their earlier counterparts. Among the more promising features of some new core/basal worksheets is an inclination to activate and/or build students' prior knowledge and also to compare and contrast one text to another. In addition, many programs are now providing other practice materials in addition to traditional workbooks. Examples of these types of material include those for learning centers, such as manipulative letters and word cards, materials for word sorts, game pieces, digital texts, and such.

Although materials do exert a strong influence, it is clear that the way materials are embedded in instruction and the way they are used also has a profound effect on student learning. Bembry and her colleagues (1998) studied teachers from the same school district using a common curriculum. Despite the common core of materials, there were dramatic differences in student achievement across different teachers. Close examinations of teachers across primary classrooms reveals large differences in the use of methods and materials (L. M. Anderson et al., 1985; Mosenthal et al., 2004; Taylor et al., 2000). Anderson reported, for example, that the same form of assignment often was used two to five times a week, and in six of the eight classes observed, over half of the seatwork assignments were given to the whole class, despite the fact that students were assigned to different groups. Similarly, Barbara Taylor and her colleagues found that the least accomplished teachers were most likely to use whole-class, undifferentiated instruction (Taylor et al., 2000). Many researchers have found that teachers do not monitor seatwork closely enough or use it to inform their instruction. Teachers generally emphasize keeping busy and finishing assigned work, not understanding what is being taught.

The seatwork assignments that low achievers receive are often particularly inappropriate (Vaughn et al., 2002). In the study by Vaughn and colleagues, struggling students did poorly on their assignments and often derived answers by using strategies that enabled them to complete the assignments without understanding them. They spent a great deal of time waiting for help, because they could not accomplish the tasks themselves. These findings are compounded by the evidence that students assigned to lower-ability reading groups spend even more time on worksheet exercises and less time actually reading than students in higher-ability reading groups (Allington et al., 1986; Levy & Vaughn, 2002). It is not surprising that these students are especially likely to believe that reading is "finishing the workbook pages."

Contemporary studies of successful schools reinforce these ideas, suggesting that students in successful schools are much more likely than students in less-successful schools to be engaged in seatwork that involves sustained reading and writing and written responses to authentic texts (Lipson, Mosenthal, Mekkelsen, & Russ, 2004; Morrow,

FIGURE 6.3
Example of
Contemporary
Basal Workbook
Activity

Name _____

Growing and Changing

As you read each selection in this unit, Growing and Changing, fill in the boxes of the chart that apply to the selection.

	What kind of text is this? Is it a story about people or is it providing information?	What kinds of changes do you notice throughout the selection?
Christina Katerina and the Time She Quit the Family by Patricia Lee Gauch		
Monarch and Milkweed by Helen Frost and Leonid Gore		
Cactus Hotel by Brenda Z. Buiberson		
Best Friends for Francis by Lillian Hoban		

Tracey, Woo, & Pressley, 1999; Mosenthal et al., 2004; Taylor, Pearson, Clark, & Walpole, 2000). Effective teachers/schools are much more likely to use sustained reading as seatwork—a practice in sharp contrast to traditional workbook-type activities.

The consequences of poor-quality seatwork practices are likely to be significant. Some years ago, Anderson et al. (1985) suggested that poor seatwork habits developed in first grade may contribute to a subsequent passive learning style. Low achievers, who often work on assignments they do not understand, may come to believe that schoolwork does not have to make sense; therefore, it is not necessary to obtain additional information or assistance as an aid to understanding. In contrast, high-achieving students rarely have difficulty with seatwork, so that any problems they have are more likely to motivate them to seek help. Indeed, student engagement is highly related to motivation (Guthrie & Cox, 2001), and research indicates that students tend to be less engaged and focused during independent seatwork periods (Mulryan, 1995).

Effective teachers act as decision makers who consider both their students' needs as developing readers and writers and the qualities of the texts to be read. A good general model for developing seatwork includes the following elements (Levy & Vaughn, 2002; Scheu et al., 1989):

- Seatwork should be directly linked to current instruction. It should support students in reading specific texts or provide practice that leads to proficiency in specific areas of learning.
- Students' work should be corrected in the context of discussion about the assignment—not corrected by the teacher alone and then returned.
- Collaborative work and peer-assisted instruction should be encouraged in completing seatwork assignments.

The overwhelming consensus among experts has not fundamentally changed in twenty-five years: (1) children should spend less time completing workbooks and skills sheets, (2) they should spend more time in independent reading, and (3) students should spend more time writing (R. C. Anderson et al., 1985; Snow, Burns, & Griffin, 1998). "Real" reading and writing activities should be a part of each student's daily seatwork. Unlike the time spent on traditional worksheet activities, time spent reading and writing has been shown to contribute to growth in literacy ability (Mosenthal et al., 2004; Newmann, Byrk, & Nagaoka, 2001).

Teacher's Guides. The teacher's guides that accompany each level in a basal program are a significant feature of classroom practice that influences students' reading and writing performance. The instructional activities teachers choose are generally those described in the teacher's guides, although most teachers report adjusting the suggestions over time (Durkin, 1984; Kauffman, 2005). These guides provide a variety of information, including facsimiles of both the selections and the workbook pages that appear in the student materials, organizational procedures to follow in implementing the program, specific directions for presenting prescribed skills, suggested questions to ask when discussing selections with students, enrichment activities for use as follow-up or culminating activities, and assessments that can be used to evaluate student progress. Perhaps the most important feature of teacher's guides, however, is the lesson design provided for each reading selection throughout the series and the impact this has on the nature of instruction offered to students. The vast majority of (and especially novice) teachers report using the teacher's guides for at least some purposes (Grossman & Thompson, 2004; Kaufman, 2002). Indeed, many teachers—especially those who teach in schools under local, state, or federal sanctions—have been compelled to use these guides, sometimes quite rigidly (MacGillivray, Ardell, Curwen, & Palma, 2004). Although such curricular and instructional mandates exercise their own influence on instruction (see Chapter 5), it is certainly the case that the lesson plans and teacher's guide suggestions take on particular importance in such settings.

Directed Reading Activity.   The instructional design, or framework, that has traditionally been used in core/basal reading programs is known as the *directed reading activity* (DRA). The DRA was first introduced by Betts in 1946 to give teachers a basic format for systematic group instruction, improve students' word recognition and comprehension skills, and guide students through a reading selection. It has remained remarkably unchanged since that time. Wepner and Feeley (1993) found that all seven basal programs they reviewed used a DRA framework, and although Hoffman and colleagues (1994, 2002) reported some movement away from this model at the earliest levels, it is still a common feature of contemporary core programs.

In a DRA framework, instruction is organized around before-, during-, and after-reading activities for each selection in the anthology:

- *Prereading activities* often include providing relevant background, creating interest, introducing meanings and/or pronunciations for new vocabulary, and establishing purposes for reading.
- *During-reading activities* are intended to guide students' reading and often include silent reading focused on answering purpose-setting questions, oral reading and responding to questions dealing with short sections of the text, and/or oral rereading to clarify or verify a point.
- *Postreading activities* are of two types: activities focused on the reading selection, such as group discussion or end-of-selection questions, and activities focused on skill instruction and practice that may or may not be related to the reading selection.

The type of instruction that is typically associated with the traditional DRA promotes the role of the teacher as the presenter and the student as the receiver of information and encourages teacher-centered patterns of interaction (Ramirez, 2005). This high level of teacher support can be helpful to struggling readers, but teacher decision making is essential. Increasingly, some teacher guides are supporting scaffolded instruction involving the progression from teacher modeling and explanation to independent student practice and application and encouraging engagement in instructional dialogue (see Chapter 5). There are also other opportunities for student-initiated involvement in which students have opportunities to monitor and regulate their own reading. It is important to avoid what Pianta (2003) characterized as environments that are "socially positive but instructionally passive [where] children listen and watch [and] much time is spent on routines or management of materials" (p. 9). Although there is little direct evidence regarding the effects of different instructional frameworks on student learning, it seems safe to assume that a steady diet of teacher-centered exchange would provide different results than more-interactive patterns that scaffold student learning and place increased responsibility on the reader (see Nystrand, 2006; Palincsar & Brown, 1984; Rodgers, 2004/2005).

Instructional design in the core/basal programs of the 1990s reflected the general shift that occurred in reading instruction from skills-based to literature-based instruction. This shift is evident in the increased importance given to content goals associated with comprehending the reading selections. Lessons with post-1990 copyrights also include many instructional choices and multiple opportunities for student-initiated activity, and the tone of the teacher's guides has become less prescriptive, moving in the direction of a teacher-as-decision-maker model (Hoffman, et al., 1994). In addition, many programs have moved toward a shared reading model and away from the directed reading model of earlier years.

The core programs of the 2000s tend to be a hybrid of these earlier programs. Not only are the beginning reading materials much more controlled, the teachers' materials have tended to direct attention to word-level aspects of reading. They are not so much "scripted" as they are "ordered." Daily lesson plans are provided, with specific activities described for each day. The deep instructional directive is less visible, but a range of guidance for managing classrooms is more so. This may be the result, in part, of much more diverse materials. Teachers have the anthology, but there are also little books, phonics readers, and/or leveled texts to be used. Contemporary core programs have placed a much stronger emphasis on reading strategies, understanding authors and authors' craft, and analysis of literary features. Many also do a good job of activating and/or developing background knowledge for the specific texts being read. At the same time, there has been a resurgence of attention to skills—particularly phonemic awareness, phonics, and fluency. However, an examination of the most recent materials reveals that the teacher's guides "mention" the skills or strategy and then quickly move to brief examples available in application formats; these findings are very similar to Durkin's 1984 results.

While decodability dominated early reading materials at the beginning of the 2000s, concerns about vocabulary, oral language development, and background knowledge have rapidly become matters of great importance. Indications that existing reading practices in the primary grades do not improve oral language vocabulary (Biemiller, 2003) have led to a much greater concern for explicit and sustained vocabulary instruction in core programs. As a result, vocabulary instruction has changed dramatically in the past decade and is generally much more intentional and focused. For example, vocabulary is introduced more in the context of the story. This means that students are introduced to words in meaningful ways. According to Hiebert and her colleagues, however, this can lead to other, unintended difficulties including the fact that vocabulary instruction can be quite idiosyncratic—depending on the particular texts students read in the anthology (Hiebert & Cervetti, 2011).

At the same time, there is an ever-increasing press for more-leveled materials and a move away from whole-group to small-group instruction. Contemporary educators and basal publishers are much more aware that different texts are essential to accomplish different outcomes in a balanced and comprehensive literacy program. As we continue to learn more about teaching and learning, these programs will continue to change. A major concern, expressed by Hoffman and his colleagues (2002), is that the political context has exerted more influence in these changes than have data from research and practice. In this changeable and highly charged environment, teachers need to exercise good judgment, because texts are merely *mediating*, not defining, factors for instruction. As Menon and Hiebert (2005) note, "no text-based curriculum stands apart from its instructional usage" (p. 15).

Guided Reading.   A variant of the DRA that has garnered a lot of attention in recent years is known as *guided reading* (Fountas & Pinnell, 1996, 2001, 2006). Guided reading is a framework for the small-group instruction of students who read the same (leveled) text. The groups are temporary and are homogeneous in the sense that the students read at about the same level, demonstrate similar reading behaviors, and have similar instructional needs. The procedure begins with the introduction of a text that the teacher has selected for its design to support the students' reading of the text. Students then read the text silently and independently, although the teacher may ask individual students to read orally at regular intervals and talk with them individually about the book. Following reading, the teacher discusses the meaning of the text with the students and asks them to revisit the text to make connections, search for information, and/or find evidence to support their thinking. Finally, the teacher uses the just-completed reading experience as the basis for teaching processing strategies that can be applied to other fiction and/or nonfiction materials. Fountas and Pinnell also describe a guided writing procedure with a similar structure to that of guided reading.

Cooper and Kiger (2005) call this framework *observational guided reading* and distinguish it from *interactive guided reading*. "With interactive guided reading, the teacher carefully guides, directs, or coaches students through the silent reading of a meaningful chunk of text by asking them a question, giving prompts, or helping them formulate questions that they then try to answer as they read the designated section of text" (p. 32). Cooper and Kiger suggest using this much more participatory and supportive form of guided reading with students who need a great deal of support in comprehending the text. They note that interactive guided reading allows teachers flexibility in supporting students, because they can vary the type and amount of support offered to students before, during, and after reading.

At the same time, publishers are now producing packages of "guided reading materials," and these are almost always accompanied by instructional teacher's guides. While these are typically much less elaborate than the materials that accompany core/basal programs, they are no less prescriptive.

An important feature of guided reading is the almost-exclusive use of leveled texts. Although this was initially intended to closely match readers to texts at the beginning stages of learning to read, commercial publishers now make leveled texts for use right through the intermediate grades. The specific nature of these leveled texts (like the anthologies used in core programs) is critically important for teachers to consider. Until recently, the leveled texts were disproportionately narrative in genre. Now, however, publishers have added a great deal of attractive nonfiction. At least as important is the fact that commercially produced leveled texts constrain the length of text reading. At the earliest stages, this often means that students have the opportunity to read increasingly lengthy texts as they progress in their reading ability. However, at the older ages/grades, leveled texts are typically much shorter than traditional textbooks and provide limited opportunity to sample the wide range of informational texts that are appropriate for older readers.

Although many educators describe specific and highly prescribed practices for engaging in guided reading, as with the more traditional core/basal reading approach, teachers have adopted and adapted the practices over time. Ford and Optiz (2008) surveyed 1,500 K–2 teachers about their practices in the context of guided reading and found that there was a great deal of variability—including practices not generally associated with guided reading instruction. For example, there was inconsistent use of leveled texts and extensive use of seatwork.

To summarize, teachers need to examine very carefully the materials they use, to determine what contributions to reading performance they may be making (see Hoffman, 2001; Menon & Hiebert, 2005). Examining the content and method of instruction used to teach reading can provide insight into what a particular student has had the opportunity to learn with regard to reading and writing. Not infrequently, students who have difficulty reading specific texts or with certain reading skills simply have not had the instructional or practice opportunities necessary to become competent. An evaluation can also provide information about what has *not* proved helpful in teaching individual children to read. When an analysis of the instruction and the instructional materials suggests ample opportunity to learn, but the child has not benefited, further assessment and/or diagnostic teaching is needed (see Chapter 10).

Textbooks

Textbooks are resources specific to instructional content areas (e.g., social studies, math) and designed for use in educational settings. Historically, textbooks were the primary source of information for both teachers and students in subject-area classes (Kane, 2011). However, teachers have reported that although they use the textbook to guide their curriculum, they often do not require or expect students to read the textbook because of its difficulty. Factors that contribute to the difficulty of textbooks—essentially reference books—include the density of information, technical or unfamiliar nature of content, and complexity of language.

The term *considerate texts* was coined by Armbruster and T. Anderson to describe textbooks that enable readers to gather appropriate information with minimal effort, as opposed to "inconsiderate" textbooks that require readers to put forth extra effort in order to compensate for the inadequacies of the text (Armbruster, 1984; Anderson & Armbruster, 1984a). Researchers who study textbooks have often been critical of their inconsiderate nature. For example, Dornan, Rosen, and Wilson (1997) describe these features that contribute to the difficulty that students have had in learning with textbooks:

- A writing style without voice, "stiff and stripped of expression" (p. 79); the style neither inspires interest in the subject, nor enables the reader to identify what is most important
- Simplified explanations that, in an effort to make the text accessible to most students, fail to develop the background needed to consider complicated ideas in depth or in context
- Structures that seem to focus on factual details rather than conceptual underpinnings; information or application exercises may not be tied together in a coherent way

- Abridgements or excerpts, particularly in literature anthologies, that fail to convey the nuances of the original work
- Inaccurate assumptions about knowledge and experience that students bring from their own lives or from other texts

In response to these criticisms and to new understandings of reading processes, textbook manufacturers have been incorporating more-considerate features. Dornan, Rosen, and Wilson (1997) provide some examples of features that facilitate learners' making sense of textbooks:

- Introductory material designed to activate learners' own knowledge, spark interest, set goals for learning, and outline what is to come in a chapter or section of text
- Concluding material that summarizes key ideas, reviews important vocabulary, provides additional resources, and features opportunities for application
- Messages directly addressing the reader, engaging, encouraging, and coaching the reader to think in particular ways about the material
- Coherent frameworks in which details are explicitly connected to overarching important concepts; language that creates cohesion among ideas
- Rich graphics that complement the messages in the prose portions of the text.

Increasingly, teachers are balancing the broad and objective treatment of topics in textbooks with the in-depth and personal accounts of trade materials.

Trade Books

Trade books, intended for use by the general public, provide a vast number, and rich diversity, of print resources. Bowker's *Children's Books in Print* (2009) indexes more than 250,000 titles available from publishers in the United States. Trade books include many genres within the general classes of narrative and informational materials, as well as genres that seem to include both narrative and informational elements. More specifically, the designation "trade books" might include such diverse literature as biography, autobiography, or memoir; science fiction, historical fiction, or fantasy; poetry; picture books, graphic novels, and cartoons; and how-to and hands-on texts. Increasingly, trade books are incorporated into classroom instruction to supplement a core program in reading and language arts and to teach concepts in content-area classes. Kane (2008, 2011) offers rich resources for incorporating trade books into classroom instruction across content areas and these reasons that doing so is likely to facilitate learning (Kane, 2008):

- *Literature enhances the learning of content.* Research shows that difficult concepts can be more understandable when taught via trade books. Improved learning may be attributed to features including in-depth, detailed coverage of a narrow topic; elements of a story that make information more memorable; motivation of learners who choose their own topics and texts for inquiry; the high-quality artwork that makes usually invisible (e.g., scientific) phenomena accessible; and opportunities for reinforcing themes across multiple disciplines. These features of trade books prompt readers to engage in productive ways of thinking that suit the purposes of the texts with which they work. For example, a learner working intertextually may need to remember the details of a law and integrate those details with an understanding of the political climate that produced the law and the first-person accounts of those who were ill-treated by the law.

- *Literature creates opportunities for challenging discussions.* Authors of trade books often treat timely or sensitive topics, which may evoke strong personal responses to text. For readers who struggle when confronted with large amounts of dense text, picture books can provide access to these timely and important topics, engage their imagination, and generate a discussion that may not have taken place had students not had access to the ideas of the text.

- *Literature enables the teaching of content from multiple perspectives and sources.* Topics can be studied through multiple genres suited to offering the perspectives of different authors. For those trade books with relatively recent dates of publication, learners will likely be able to gather information about the author in order to better understand the author's perspective and the processes by which the author developed the ideas in the text. Topics can be studied through the lenses of different disciplines and through the words of experts and eyewitnesses, which may elicit strong emotional responses from the reader.

- *Literature stimulates interest and motivation to read.* Trade books treat an infinite variety of topics, at a wide range of reading levels, and thus enable learners to develop a passionate interest in a topic and simultaneously improve their reading skills. "The research evidence is overwhelming that students read better when they read more and they read more when they can choose from a wide range of reading material that are developmentally appropriate and engaging" (Farmer, 2003, cited in Kane, 2008). A critical component to support a struggling reader is to enable the student to develop a passion for a particular area of interest (Fink, 2006).

Electronic, Internet, and Multimedia Texts

The rapid growth in the use of personal computers for reading and writing instruction, and the impact of new technologies on the nature of literacy, demands that separate attention be paid to these materials. According to Coiro (2003), "electronic texts introduce new supports as well as new challenges that can have great impact on an individual's ability to comprehend what he or she reads" (p. 458). Text that is read in online environments, rather than offline in traditional print form, requires facility with specific reading processes, called "new literacies" (Mokhtari, Kymes, & Edwards, 2008):

> . . . online and offline reading comprehension are not the same . . . Online reading comprehension is almost always a problem-solving process with informational text. It begins with a question and takes place within a nearly limitless informational space where anyone may publish anything. It also takes place in a context where readers regularly communicate with others about the problem they're trying to understand. Each aspect alters traditional reading comprehension processing in important ways. (p. 354)

In this portion of the chapter, in which we consider instructional resources, we first provide an overview of some of the supports and challenges inherent in digital, or electronic, texts and the tools used to access those texts. Then, we will describe some of the reading processes, or new literacies, required to interact with texts via the Internet, so that we can appreciate the potential impact on struggling readers who must use these new literacies to learn and communicate. Consistent with the emphasis in this text on reading and writing authentic texts, we emphasize electronic texts that provide opportunities to read for real purposes and software that facilitates writing for real audiences.

Since the designs of digital texts and associated ICTs (information and communications technologies) are ever changing with innovation and our understandings of them are continually evolving with experience, it is appropriate to begin with definitions. Digital or electronic texts are those texts that people access via electronic means and usually read on some sort of screen or listen to from an electronic device. Included in this array are the following broad categories set forth by Dalton and Proctor (2008) (with our examples).

- Digital texts may look and function like traditional print texts. College students and their instructors who find journal articles via library databases or read supplemental textbook materials from a CD-ROM are using these sorts of "linear" texts.
- Digital texts may also be "nonlinear"; that is, they contain hyperlinks that take readers to other texts with related content. For example, in an online article entitled "What's next for NASA?" (NASA, 2011) are multiple hyperlinks (shown as words in blue print) that can take readers to more-detailed information as topics (e.g., Multi-Purpose Crew Vehicle, International Space Station) are introduced in the original article.
- Digital texts may also incorporate visual and auditory information. Again, in the NASA article, hyperlinks can take the reader to videos, for example, of a speech of the same title for the National Press Club or of the construction of a space exploration vehicle. Talking books are another form of auditory digital text.
- Some digital texts also offer the opportunity for readers to interact with the text; games are one type of interactive digital text. Both linear and nonlinear digital or electronic texts can offer a number of supportive features.

Importantly, publishers of core/basal programs are now making all of their conventional texts (from anthologies to leveled readers) available digitally. This is true as well for conventional science and social studies textbooks. Increasingly, publishers are embedding links to make these much more interactive. Thoughtful teaches will need to review these texts and proceed with caution, as there is virtually no research available to indicate what instructional impact these texts could have on students' reading development.

Supports and Challenges.   Electronic texts may be enhanced with affordances to facilitate learning with text for individuals who may not learn easily or effectively from traditional modes of reading and writing instruction. Such enhancements are made possible by the many functions and forms of computer output, including visual representations, print, and voice/communication capabilities (MacArthur, Ferretti, Okolo, & Cavalier, 2001). The use of such "supported e-texts" (Anderson-Inman & Horney, 2007) or "scaffolded hyper-texts" (Dalton & Strangman, 2006) is consistent with principles of the *universal design for learning* (UDL) philosophy. Proponents of UDL believe that "barriers to learning are not, in fact, inherent in the capabilities of learners but instead arise in learners' interactions with inflexible educational materials and methods" (Rose & Meyer, 2002). Technology provides opportunities to design materials and methods accessible and adjustable to all learners. In the paragraphs that follow, we describe affordances that *transform* and *augment* text, as well as *partner* with learners. While each of these types of affordances has proven valuable under some circumstances, they also present challenges.

Affordances That Transform. Supported electronic texts can be *transformed* into more accessible and understandable forms for learners with physical/sensory or learning challenges. For example, print and figures can be enlarged, text can be coupled with speech programs and read aloud, words can be translated into another language (e.g., American Sign Language, Braille), and unknown vocabulary can be linked to definitions. Texts that learners produce can also be transformed. Writers can hear—and monitor—their own text as it is typed, follow along as their own spoken words are transformed into written words, or choose from words offered by a word prediction program. In general, these transformations to text can facilitate reading and writing, where learners choose, or are guided, to use them.

Dalton and Proctor (2008) and Strangman and Dalton (2005) reviewed a number of studies and report improved comprehension among learners who used text-to-speech (TTS) programs to read challenging texts. Older students and those with relatively good oral language skills seem to benefit more from TTS than do younger students and those with language-learning difficulties. Students used TTS most productively when text was of high interest and highlighting guided them to follow along with print. The quality of TTS, while improving, remains mechanical and cannot supply the rate, stress, and inflection that human readers use to convey meaning. Thus, while TTS can give learners access to virtually any digital text, some learners choose not to use it.

Research also shows that learners who read digital texts with vocabulary support usually demonstrate improved vocabulary knowledge, though not necessarily independently. Proctor, Dalton, and Grisham (2007), working with English language learners and native English speakers, demonstrated increased use of vocabulary supports and a corresponding increase in vocabulary knowledge when learners were actively engaged before, during, and after reading in word-study activities including construction and study of glossary items.

MacArthur (1998) found that young students with learning disabilities who used a word-processing program with speech synthesis and word prediction demonstrated increased spelling accuracy and legibility. The review of existing research by Goldberg et al. (2003) indicates that most, but not all, students are likely to make more and better revisions while using word processing. Especially among struggling students, revisions might not automatically result from word processing. However, when revision prompts are added, word processing is also likely to result in more revision (MacArthur, 1996).

Affordances That Augment. Scaffolded hypertexts can be *augmented*, presenting supplementary information in multiple modes: auditory (e.g., speech, music, other sounds) and visual (e.g., static pictures, graphs, tables, drawings, animation or video), as well as print (word) forms. Sweller (2005) describes both challenges and affordances with multimodal forms of text. The (often) highly interdependent nature of complex ideas presented via these channels and the need to integrate the ideas with each other and with learners' background knowledge makes learning with multimedia text a challenging endeavor. On the other hand, processing information via two somewhat separate channels allows the learner to distribute the cognitive demands of complex text. For readers with language-based learning difficulties, information presented in multimedia may be more understandable than the same information presented in print alone (Rose & Meyer, 2002).

Scaffolded hypertexts with augmentative, multi-model resources are often nonlinear. That is, learners help determine the structure of the text (Eagleton & Dobler, 2007). Learners choose if and when to pursue a particular idea by viewing graphics or video, listening to audio, or selecting hyperlinked words or symbols. In order to direct their own path through a text in this manner, learners must be skilled in making intra- and intertextual connections, processes that place heavy demands on memory (Mayer, 2008). Nonlinear structures present opportunities for learners to be active, monitoring their understanding and deciding where to go next to facilitate their sense making. Compared to their typically reading peers, struggling readers may demonstrate poor monitoring of their own comprehension and limited knowledge of actions they can take to facilitate comprehension (Dickson, Collins, Simmons, & Kame'enui, 1998).

Affordances That Partner.   Supported digital texts can serve as "intellectual *partners*" (Pea, 1993, p. 75), offering guidance and tools that enable readers to learn in difficult-to-learn contexts. Such cognitive tools can be embedded in electronic text to enable readers to make the most efficient and effective use of their own cognitive resources. For example, a digital text could be designed to offer the reader guidance in the use of strategic activities for making sense of text.

McNamara and colleagues (McNamara et al., 2007) designed a Web-based program, i-START, to guide readers to facilitate their own comprehension via self-explanation. In this program, an animated agent initially models self-explanation (by paraphrasing, predicting, elaborating, and tying just-read information to previously read text) as a learner read segments of a challenging text. Gradually, the learner took over the process of creating self-explanation, and the agent evaluated the quality of the explanation. The program most successfully facilitated comprehension for readers with relatively little knowledge of the topic of the text and readers who were relatively less strategic in their spontaneous approaches to text.

Finally, readers might be provided with tools in the forms of "virtual realities," or visual models that can be manipulated so that they behave like real-world phenomena. When embedded in text, they offer rich opportunities to reason about scientific phenomena. Dalton and colleagues (Dalton et al., 2006) provided readers with manipulable graphics that readers used to engage in investigations of phenomena also described in the nearby prose (the behavior of light). The graphics had the effect of leveling the playing field; struggling readers made as much growth in their understanding of the phenomena under study as did typically achieving readers.

New Literacies and Reading Processes.   The Internet may pose particular challenges to students' literacy skills. Indeed, research suggests that different skills and strategies are required to read and learn from electronic and Internet texts. Members of the New Litera-cies Research Lab at the University of Connecticut have identified component processes of the new literacies needed to comprehend online text, such as the following: (1) generating a problem or question from one's social context, (2) locating information, (3) critically evaluating information, (4) synthesizing information from multiple sources, and (5) com-municating and exchanging information with others (Mokhtari, Kymes, & Edwards, 2008, p. 355).

As Coiro (2005) notes, "Reading online is a complex process that requires knowl-edge about how search engines work and how information is organized within Web sites—knowledge that many students lack" (p. 31). She notes also that students often need more-expansive monitoring abilities as well as more-sophisticated inferential reasoning skills to select, comprehend, and use Internet information. Students' purpose for interact-ing with information on the Web may be different than it is for conventional reading. In-deed, most experts refer to "searching" the Web, not "reading" it (see Henry, 2006).

Electronic and Internet texts do have one thing in common with traditional texts: students who have limited experience are likely to have trouble comprehending and using them. It appears that struggling readers, especially, may struggle with the new literacies. Sutherland-Smith (2002), for example, found that students may become easily frustrated when reading electronic texts. This causes some students to act impulsively, adopting a "snatch and grab" approach to finding answers. Similarly, Coiro & Dobler (2004) found that many less-skilled readers seemed less able to distinguish important from unimportant information and adopted a more passive approach when reading on the Internet. In other words, even though students may be more motivated to read materials online (see below), they may not be any more successful if they have not received good instruction in how to read and integrate alternative texts.

Collaboration.   Research suggests that the use of computers fosters interaction and col-laboration. For example, an early study of the writing program in a first-and-second-grade classroom showed that collaborative work at the computer created a new social organiza-tion that affected interaction patterns (Dickinson, 1986). During normal individual writing assignments, students rarely spoke to each other; however, during collaborative computer writing, students spoke to each other about plans, revisions, and issues of meaning and style. More-recent reviews of research indicate that children's writing and reading of digi-tal texts, including Internet searching, in classrooms is a social process characterized by face-to-face, child-initiated, collaborative verbal interactions around shared text, reflect-ing both the culture of the classroom and of student homes (Burnett, 2010; Goldberg, Russell, & Cook, 2003). Children also interact with each other over considerable distance to share experiences using tools such as blogs and podcasts, and to write collaboratively using tools such as Google Docs and wikis (Boling et al., 2008).

Other studies have found that the variety and complexity of language use increased during collaborative writing projects on the computer. For example, González-Edfelt's (1990) study of limited English speakers discovered that the quantity and quality of oral discourse increased during collaborative computer activities.

Research suggests that computer use has either enhanced or left unchanged the frequency and/or quality of teacher–student interactions. It appears that teacher–student writing conferences involve more-sophisticated interactions when a word processor is used, which may explain the enhanced writing of the word-processed compositions. Other studies have reported that the teacher's role and pattern of interaction with students undergo little change with the infusion of computers into their literacy practices once word-processing methods, programs, and instruction are introduced (Kamil & Intrator, 2000). On the other hand, it appears that increased use of other technologies such as multimedia, hypermedia, and Internet do shift teachers' roles so that they are more likely to act as a consultant and support and less likely to be the center of attention (Meskill & Mossop, 2000).

Most studies point to positive developments in the patterns of social interaction around writing with computers. However, several studies have highlighted ways in which collaborative work in technology environments occasionally results in interactions that do not approximate what is normally considered literate discourse (Kremers, 1990; Lanksheare & Knobel, 2003; Miller & Olson, 1995). As Snyder (1998) has noted, "the use and effect of a technology is closely tied to the social context in which it appears" (p. 140). In other words, teachers often use information and communications technology (ICT) in ways that are consistent with their preexisting orientations (Windschitl & Sahl, 2002).

Motivation. A consistent effect of the impact of computer technologies on students is an increase in motivation and closely related constructs such as interest and enjoyment of schoolwork, task involvement, persistence, time on task, and retention in school (Meyer & Rose, 1999). Lepper and his research group conducted the earliest and most complete series of investigations into the impact of computers on motivation (Lepper & Chabay, 1985; Lepper & Cordova, 1992). They concluded that computer-based educational activities can increase factors associated with the intrinsic motivation of students to the extent that they increase the opportunities to customize one's work and increase the control, curiosity, and challenge of the task. Specifically related to literacy development, computer use by children can increase their involvement in and enjoyment of writing and reading, thereby improving the quality of what they produce. For example, studies that compared word-processing revision versus handwritten revision commonly found that students were more highly motivated to revise, which led to more time spent on the revision process. Similarly, Goldberg, Russell, and Cook (2003) report that children persisted on tasks longer, produced longer texts, and engaged in more revision when using the computer, because it dispensed with recopying writings.

Researchers have been studying the effects of communication technology (Alfassi, 2000) and gaming on students' motivation and learning, as well as their use of Web-based and Internet applications of technology (Coiro, 2003; Gee, 2003). In both cases, it appears that at least some of the increases in motivation and performance occur because the technologies foster greater student discourse and an expanded social community.

ASSESSING INSTRUCTIONAL RESOURCES

Now that we have surveyed the range and characteristics of resources typically used in instruction, it is appropriate to consider how to evaluate these resources for these purposes: (1) to predict the likely impact of instructional resources on performance (that is, to assess the contributions of these resources to reading and writing ability) and (2) to gain insight regarding appropriate instructional materials (that is, to match the struggling reader and writer with materials that result in effective teaching and efficient learning).

Each of the resources surveyed—anthologies and/or sets of books, leveled texts and beginning reading materials of core reading programs, trade materials and text books, multimedia and digital texts—has unique features that demand particular analysis. For example, decodability and predictability are features of high interest for beginning reading materials, while intertextuality and nonlinearity are considerations in a hyperlinked electronic text. Thus, these resources each require very different questions to guide their analysis, and we will provide examples of such resource-specific questions for analysis later in this chapter. However, there are features common to *all* of the resources surveyed, which can be captured with the construct of "text difficulty" or text complexity. We begin with a review of tools for assessing text complexity and its effect on comprehensibility.

Evaluating Text Complexity and Comprehensibility

Despite the early recognition that determining text difficulty is extremely complex, the tools used to evaluate text have generally captured only limited aspects. For many years, educators have discussed and described text difficulty in terms of "readability." The earliest discussions of readability assumed that factors such as the physical appearance and format of the print, the style of written expression, the language usage, and the content of the text affected its difficulty (Gray & Leary, 1935). While readability formulas have been the subject of considerable criticism, they continue to exert a great deal of influence. These "text-based" methods for measuring text difficulty are only one type of tool available to us. We currently have other means of evaluating text and materials.

Hartley (2004) notes that another approach involves "expert-based" methods for estimating text difficulty. These methods involve making judgments about the quality of materials using some type of rating scale and/or features analysis. Checklists for estimating comprehensibility and contemporary text-leveling systems provide examples of this type of approach, and these will be described here also. Recently, the Common Core State Standards (Common Core State Standards Initiative, 2010) have provided a useful, recommended framework for evaluating text complexity using some dimensions of texts that can be measured quantitatively via text-based methods and other dimensions that can be described qualitatively using expert-based methods. Both quantitative and qualitative measures of dimensions are examined in light of what is known about the reader and the purpose for reading the text. We begin with a description of the Common Core State Standards framework for evaluating complexity of text, and then use that framework to organize our discussion of quantitative and qualitative tools for evaluating text complexity and comprehensibility.

Common Core State Standards (CCSS).   The CCSS framework for evaluating text complexity was developed in the context of concerns that K–12 students in the United States were neither sufficiently independent, nor sufficiently challenged, in reading texts that would prepare them for the literacy demands that they would encounter in their lives. Thus, the charge of the CCSS to educators is to both match the qualities of a text with the characteristics of the learner and challenge learners with increasingly complex texts. The CCSS measures text complexity via a three-part model of multiple dimensions of text that together help determine what makes a text challenging to read. The dimensions are: *quantitative*, *qualitative*, and *reader and task considerations.*

Quantitative dimensions are aspects of text—often linguistic features such as semantic (word meaning) and syntactic (sentence structure) difficulty—that can best be measured quantitatively, often more efficiently (especially for long texts) by means of computer software. The CCSS recommend using available quantitative measures of these dimensions, with the understanding that new tools may be developed. At this time, one might use such text-based methods as Lexile measures or readability formulas. These tools, which will be discussed further, use counts of word length and word frequency as well as sentence length to estimate text difficulty.

Coh-Metrics (Graesser, McNamara, & Kulikowich, 2011) is a new computer-based tool, currently used mostly in research contexts, that shows promise for producing additional, efficient, quantitative measures of text complexity. It measures important factors including the cohesiveness as well as the concreteness/abstractness of words, elements of narrative text structure, and dozens of other variables that affect complexity of text.

It is noteworthy that quantitative measures can capture only a portion of the dimensions of text that affect comprehensibility, and they capture some dimensions better than others. It is possible, for example, to find a text written with familiar words using relatively simple sentence structures and expressing complex ideas. Such a text would earn a score for text complexity that suggests that it is easy to read, when in fact it is not. Thus, it is important to balance and complement quantitative, often computer-generated, text-based methods of analysis with qualitative analyses conducted by well-informed human "experts."

Qualitative dimensions account for factors that contribute to text complexity but are not easily quantified; rather, they are best assessed by a knowledgeable person. The authors of the CCSS have recommended that the following four dimensions, which have been shown to affect comprehensibility of text, constitute an initial set of factors to be included in tools for qualitative analysis of text complexity:

- *Levels of meaning (literary text) or purpose (informational text):* Literary texts—such as fables, for example—may have at one level of meaning the events of a story and at another, less explicit level of meaning the author's underlying message. Informational texts may have implicit purposes as well.
- *Structure:* Texts that conform to readers' expectations of the genre—for example, literary texts in which the events of a story unfold in chronological order in an established setting—are less complex and easier to understand than texts that unpredictably flash forward or backward in time or space. Informational texts that are structured according to the ways in which knowledge is structured in a particular discipline are complex to the reader who is a novice in that discipline.
- *Language conventionality and clarity:* To the extent that the language of the text—word choices and sentence structures as well as register (e.g., academic, conversational)—is familiar to the learner, the text will be easier for the learner to understand.

Knowledge demands: Inherent in texts are authors' assumptions about the life experiences and knowledge that readers will bring to a text. When a high level of knowledge and experience is assumed, texts are more complex and may be harder to understand. Each of dimensions involved can be situated on a continuum (e.g., simple → complex, familiar → unfamiliar). See Figure 6.4 for a more complete overview of the CCSS-recommended qualitative dimensions and their associated continua. See Appendix A of the *Common Core State Standards for English Language Arts and Literacy in History/Social Studies, Science, and Technical Subjects* (http://www.corestandards.org) for some thorough examples of the application of these qualitative dimensions. Specific qualitative dimensions will be developed more fully below.

FIGURE 6.4
Qualitative Dimensions of Text Complexity from Common Core State Standards

Levels of Meaning (literary texts) of Purpose (informational texts)
- Single level of meaning → Multiple levels of meaning
- Explicitly stated purpose → Implicit purpose, may be hidden

Structure
- Simple → Complex
- Explicit → Implicit
- Conventional → Unconventional (chiefly literary texts)
- Events related in chronological order → Events related out of chronological order (chiefly literary texts)
- Traits of a common genre or subgenre → Traits specific to a particular discipline (chiefly informational text)
- Simple graphics → Sophisticated graphics
- Graphics unnecessary or merely supplementary to understanding the text → Graphics essential to understanding the text and may provide information not otherwise conveyed in the text

Language Conventionality and Clarity
- Literal → Figurative or ironic
- Clear → Ambiguous or purposefully misleading
- Conversational → General academic and domain-specific

Knowledge Demands: Life Experiences (literary texts)
- Simple theme → Complex or sophisticated themes
- Single themes → Multiple themes
- Common, everyday experiences or clearly fantastical situations → Experiences distinctly different from one's own
- Single perspective → Multiple perspectives
- Perspective(s) like one's own → Perspective(s) unlike or in opposition to one's own

Knowledge Demands: Cultural/Literary Knowledge (chiefly literary texts)
- Everyday knowledge and familiarity with genre conventions required → Cultural and literary knowledge useful
- Low intertextuality (few if any references/allusions to other texts) → High intertextuality (many references/allusions to other texts)

Knowledge Demands: Content/Discipline Knowledge (chiefly informational texts)
- Everyday knowledge and familiarity with genre conventions required → Extensive, perhaps specialized discipline-specific knowledge required
- Low intertextuality (few if any references to/citations of other texts) → High intertextuality (many references to/citations of other texts

Source: Common Core State Standards for English Language Arts and Literacy in History/Social Studies, Science, and Technical Subjects, 2011. Appendix A: Research Supporting Key Elements of the Standards and Glossary of Key Terms.

Dimensions of reader and task considerations including knowledge, experience, and interest of the reader, as well as the purpose of the instructional task in which the learner is engaged, constitute the context in which quantitative and qualitative dimensions of text are best viewed. This, of course, is the premise of the interactive model of reading set forth in this text: that reading and writing ability or *dis*ability can only be understood in the context of all factors—reader, text, and task variables—that interact in reading and writing tasks. In the following discussion, we set forth in more detail tools for evaluating dimensions of texts that can be measured quantitatively, with structured readability formulas, and systems used to "level" texts. Following that discussion is a description of possible ways to evaluate important dimensions of text that lend themselves to a somewhat more informal, qualitative analysis.

Quantitative Tools: Readability Formulas.   Readability formulas are quantitative procedures that have been developed to assess difficulty by counting some text feature that can be easily identified. According to Klare (1988), Lively and Pressey developed the first readability formula in 1923. Since that time, over fifty readability formulas have been developed (Schuyler, 1982). To understand the appropriate use and potential misuse of readability formulas, it is important to understand something about their development and notable features.

How Readability Formulas Are Used.   The greatest strength of readability formulas lies in their ease of use. However, they must be used cautiously. One of the easiest and most frequently used formulas today is the Fry Formula (Fry, 1968). It assesses syntactic and semantic difficulty using only counts of syllables and sentence length (see Figure 6.5). Although this obviously provides a limited view of readability, at least the formula was developed using trade books and other authentic reading material.

The use of rich-criterion passages makes readability formulas fairly reliable when used to rank real, noncontrived texts to be read by a general population (Klare, 1984). If materials are grossly unsuitable for use in a targeted grade, readability formulas can reveal this fact in a time-saving manner so that decisions about text appropriateness may be made more rapidly. However, as the Commission on Reading (R. C. Anderson et al., 1985) notes, "readability formulas are useful only as a rough check on the difficulty and appropriateness of books" (p. 81).

Estimates of text difficulty across different formulas can vary significantly (McConnell, 1982), especially in the upper ranges of the readability estimates (high school and college-level texts). Differences of two or more grade levels in the estimates generated are not unusual when several formulas are applied to the same piece of text. For placement purposes, the use of readability estimates alone clearly poses serious problems. When gross comparisons are needed, however, readability estimates can be helpful.

How Readability Formulas Are Developed.   General procedures used in development are quite similar for all readability formulas (see Conrad, 1984, for a complete discussion). Readability formulas are derived from detailed analyses of a small set of passages, called *criterion passages.* Since the difficulty of all other passages will be determined by comparison with these criterion passages and tasks, the selection and validation of the original

FIGURE 6.5
Fry Readability
Formula

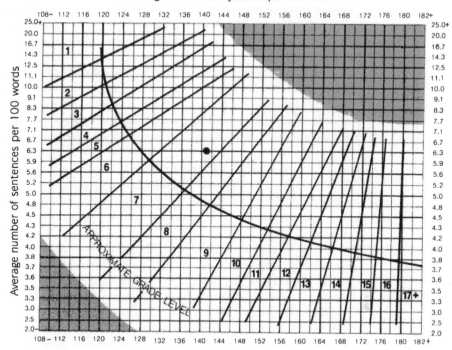

Average number of syllables per 100 words

Fry Readability Formula
(Description):
1. Select three 100-word selections from the beginning, middle, and end of the text. Don't count proper nouns.
2. Count the number of sentences in each selection. Estimate to the nearest tenth of a sentence.
3. Average the sentence count.
4. Count the number of syllables in each selection.
5. Average the syllable count.
6. Plot the two scores on the graph to get the grade level.

Source: From "A Readability Formula That Saves Time," by Edward Fry (1968, April). *Journal of Reading,* *11*(7), 513. Copyright © International Reading Association. Reprinted with permission. All rights reserved.

criterion passages is a critical first step. If the texts and tasks are not similar to those used by teachers or read by students, then the predictive power of the formula will be weak. Most of the existing readability formulas were validated by using extremely short criterion passages.

After the criterion passages are selected, they are examined for text elements that are likely to contribute to passage difficulty. Even the earliest readability researchers assumed that critical elements would include text features such as conceptual density and quality of writing. However, these abstract factors proved difficult to measure and were often either not selected for study or dropped because they could not be counted reliably.

The two elements that have proved to be the best predictors of text difficulty (at least using short criterion passages) are semantic difficulty and syntactic complexity of the sentences (Klare, 1984). Semantic difficulty is most often estimated using vocabulary, as measured by either frequency/familiarity or length of words; syntactic complexity is most often measured by sentence length.

Because different formulas have been developed using different criterion passages and different tasks, caution is needed in using any of the existing formulas. For example, the Spache Formula was developed so that it is appropriate only for primary-grade passages, while the Dale-Chall is applicable only to materials above the fourth-grade level. In addition, only some formulas examine elements that have theoretical or empirical support from current views of the reading process, and no formula provides a totally satisfactory assessment. Current iterations of these formulas in computer form have compounded the problem further, since not all computer languages have "translated" the formulas in the same way. This is a concern so serious that Hartley (2004) recommends always using the same computer and computer program to compute readability across texts!

Measuring Readability with Lexiles.   The Lexile system (see Stenner, Burdick, Sanford, & Burdick, 2006; Stenner & Wright, 2002) is a recent addition to the toolbox for the quantitative evaluation of text. Whereas traditional readability formulas did not take familiarity and prior knowledge into account, the Lexile system attempts to do so by including word frequency (Goldman & Wiley, 2004). The developers argue strongly that word frequency is an indicator of concept familiarity (individuals have more opportunity to acquire meanings for common, or familiar, words). In addition, they argue that using the same measure for both student ability and text difficulty allows teachers and researchers to evaluate comprehension more clearly. Students' results are reported in Lexile scores as opposed to reading levels or text levels. Text difficulty is also reported in Lexiles, with ranges for different grade levels; for BR (beginning reading) to Level 1500 at high school (see comparisons in Figure 6.6). On the other hand, Hiebert (2002) argues that the Lexile algebraic formula is quite similar to more-traditional readability formulas because it relies on relatively similar text features. She notes that Lexiles are "the most popular readability formula at this time." Widespread use of Lexile scores has been advanced by its sanctioned use by states and schools districts and also by the easy availability of information. A software program for measuring text readability is free and available online at the Lexile Web site—as is information about many book titles. No doubt the fact that the Common Core State Standards has embraced Lexiles will result in even greater reliance on this estimate.

Criticisms and Misuses of Readability Formulas.   Although formulas have proved quick and efficient, there are many concerns associated with them. Researchers have demonstrated what teachers have long known: that interest, motivation, and prior knowledge influence how readable a text will be. The research and commentary that flourished in the 1980s is now quite widely understood. Among the concerns and criticisms are the following:

- Many factors that have been shown to influence text difficulty are not accounted for by typical formulas (e.g., text structure, interest, motivation, and prior knowledge; see Entin & Klare, 1985; Fass & Schumacher, 1978).

FIGURE 6.6
Comparison Chart
of Text Levels

Guided Reading Level (A–Z)	Reading Recovery/ DRA	Lexile Reading Level (range 200–1700)	Estimated Grade Level
A–C	1–4	NA	Kindergarten
D–H	5–14	Up to 300	1
I–J	16–18	200–500	Late grade 1/early grade 2
K	21–22	350–500	2
L	24	350–500	2
M	26–28	350–500	2
N	30	500–700	3
O	34	500–700	3
P	38	500–700	3
Q	40	650–850	4
R		650–850	4
S		650–850	4
T		750–950	5
U		750–950	5
V		750–950	5
W		800–1050	6+
X		800–1050	6+
Y		950–1075	7+
Z		950–1075	7+
		1000–1150	7–9
		Up to 1700	10+

- Text that has short, choppy sentences can be difficult to read.
- The overall structure and relationships among ideas in text are not accounted for (Goldman & Wiley, 2004).
- Readability formulas do not take into account the order of the words and the sentences, nor do they assess the effects of other devices used to aid comprehension (e.g., typographical layout, tables, graphs, and illustrations; Hartley, 2004).
- Formulas ignore the readers' motivation, abilities, and prior knowledge.

One of the most serious concerns about readability formulas involves their misuse in rewriting existing materials, a practice that early formula developers promoted (Dale & Chall, 1948; Flesch, 1948). There has been an understandable temptation to revise text to make it easier and more accessible to readers. Recently, publishers and authors have tended to use other techniques (see decodability and predictability in the next section). However, many publishers, especially those publishing materials for struggling readers, have continued to use readability indicators, such as sentence length, to rewrite text. Unfortunately, this often has the unexpected result of making text more, rather than less, difficult (Davison, 1984; Davison & Kantor, 1982).

Text "simplifications" based on readability formulas can and do lead to incoherence and increased text difficulty (Goldman & Rakestraw, 2000). In addition, these alterations place a heavy burden on readers' prior knowledge, because the text provides fewer clues for constructing meaning. Indeed, it may actually be necessary to lengthen text through elaboration, paraphrase, and example to enhance readability when topics are complex or less familiar.

The benefits gained from using readability formulas need to be measured carefully against the potential dangers of their use. These concerns led IRA and NCTE to publish a joint statement providing guidance in the appropriate use of readability formulas (1984). Among other things, this joint statement urged educators to:

1. Evaluate texts based on teachers' knowledge of their own students' prior knowledge, experience, and interests
2. Observe student use of the materials in instructional settings to judge effectiveness
3. Use checklists and other methods to evaluate a comprehensive set of text features (including graphics, length, etc.).

Given the interactive model used in this textbook, it is easy to see how limited a readability estimate can be, as a text that may be difficult for one reader may be relatively easy for another of the same reading skill (see Alexander & Jetton, 2000; Goldman & Rakestraw, 2000). Users need to be particularly alert to possible mismatches between the reader and the text; readers from nontraditional backgrounds may be influenced by factors that are not measured in the formula. Each of these concerns, criticisms, and cautions has been leveled at the Lexile Framework also (see White & Clement, 2001). Fry (2002) provided an excellent summary of readability formulas and their various strengths and weaknesses, situating them in the context of other tools such as leveling systems. He concludes, as do we, that teachers need a repertoire of tools for selecting books for their students. We consider alternatives to readability estimates in the next section.

Text Leveling Systems: A Mix of Quantitative and Qualitative Approaches. Teachers need to consider the relative difficulty of the selections that students are reading. This has been especially important in the early grades, as "readability research has proven unable to account for the small gradations of difficulty that mark the typical sequencing or leveling of early reading materials" (Cunningham et al., 2005, p. 414). This fact means that educators who work with beginning (or very struggling) readers will continue to employ more-qualitative measures to evaluate text, even if Lexiles, for example, become more widely used at grades 3 and beyond.

There are a number of systems for "leveling" texts; the most commonly used were developed for Reading Recovery and subsequently applied to other texts and extended by Fountas and Pinnell (1996, 2001). It is important to evaluate texts leveled using this type of system, since "books originally leveled for use in Reading Recovery are now also widely used in regular and special education classrooms having no affiliation with Reading Recovery" (Cunningham et al., 2005, p. 415).

Texts are leveled using guidelines for creating what is called a *text gradient*, which can be used to classify selections "along a continuum based on the combination of variables that support and confirm readers' strategic actions and offer the problem-solving opportunities that build the reading process" (Fountas & Pinnell, 1996, p. 113). A significant advantage of these leveling systems over readability estimates is the fact that they include features other than sentence length and vocabulary.

This process can be used both to create a leveled set of materials and to evaluate existing sets of materials. In establishing a text gradient, the following factors should be considered:

- Length
- Size and layout of print
- Vocabulary and concepts
- Language structure
- Text structure and genre
- Predictability and pattern of language
- Illustration support

It is beyond the scope of this text to provide an extensive discussion of the criteria used by Fountas and Pinnell and others. A comparison of various systems for estimating text difficulty is presented in Figure 6.6. Although the Fountas and Pinnell system has the advantage of introducing important qualitative components to the estimates of text difficulty, there are concerns about its use. The most significant criticism of text leveling systems is their reliance on expert judgment and the very limited research evidence that supports the reliability of the gradient levels (see Hiebert & Mesmer, 2006). At the same time, text leveling systems, originally designed for use with beginning reading texts, may not provide appropriate degrees of direction about how to evaluate the elements that contribute to complexity at higher levels (Hiebert & Mesmer, 2006). We address qualitative elements in the next section.

Despite the problems associated with text levels, we have found that a set of "anchor" texts can improve the dependability of teachers' estimates of difficulty. These anchor texts are listed drawing from highly familiar and widely used books that have been leveled by using one system or another. For example, teachers who use the Pinnell and Fountas (2001) system would designate Brian Wildsmith's *The Cat on the Mat* at the very beginning level of first grade (Level B) and Frank Asch's *Just Like Daddy* at a level targeted for late first grade (Level F).

Similarly, books like *Leo the Late Bloomer* by Robert Kraus would provide an anchor for early grade 2 (Level I), while the *Cam Jensen* books by David Alder or James Marshall's *George and Martha* stories could help define reading performance at the end of that grade (Level L).

During grade 3, normally developing students would read books like *Freckle Juice* by Judy Blume (Level M) early in the year and *Ramona Quimby, Age 8*, by Beverly Clearly (Level O) by the year's close.

Teachers using these anchors can begin to internalize a system for evaluating increasingly difficult texts, since there is evidence that these text leveling systems are quite accurate (Hoffman et al., 2000). It is more important that everyone using a text leveling system agree on where to place the books than that everyone really like every decision. Educators should agree to use the commonly established levels for each text. In that way, when anyone refers to a particular level, everyone can agree about what texts would be read by students who had reached that level of proficiency.

Qualitative Dimensions: Genre and Text Structure.   Recall that genre is described earlier in this chapter as the patterns of language and conventions for organizing ideas that enable authors to design texts to meet particular purposes– and for readers to discover those purposes. It is important to examine texts to determine how they reflect conventions of genre. Struggling readers will need explicit instruction in how to use the conventions of genre to foster their own comprehension.

Evaluating Narrative Text.   Two major issues must be addressed in evaluating narratives for comprehensibility. First, the text must be examined to determine whether it is well structured, conforming to conventional expectations for story structure and language use. Structures and expectations will vary considerably, since the large class of narratives encompasses a wide range of genres, including realistic fiction, folktales, fables, fairy tales, myths, mystery, and science fiction (Buss & Karnowski, 2000).

However, all narratives have something in common, and that must be captured in their evaluation: they are meant to be interesting and enjoyable. When the characters and their relationships are well developed and their goals easily identifiable, children read with greater interest and understanding (Lipson, Mosenthal, & Mekkelsen, 1999; Sundbye, 1987). Because well-formed narratives are easier to read than more ambiguous ones, they should be evaluated for the common components of narrative texts (see also Chapter 9). The following set of questions adapted from Calfee (1987) might help to highlight these important, but more difficult to analyze, aspects of text:

- How does the story begin (setting, time)? How powerful, weak, or dull is the lead, or beginning, of the story?
- Who are the main characters? Who is telling the story (point of view)? How much do we learn about the characters? Will readers find them believable and be able to relate to them?
- What are the main problems or conflicts to be solved or resolved? Is the conflict interpersonal, with the environment, or internal to the character?
- How does the content of the story/plot teach a lesson or help readers learn about people, reasoning, problem solving, and so on?
- How does the story end (resolution)? Is the ending satisfying, interesting, and/or powerful?

In particular, the evaluation should identify the degree to which narratives have strong plots with well-defined characters whose motives and goals are clear. When these aspects of a narrative are obscure, poor readers have much more difficulty comprehending them.

Evaluating Informational Texts.   Informational texts include trade books that provide information about most any topic. Thus, a primary requirement of informational books is that they be accurate—though this was not always the case. "Today's nonfiction books for young readers are less likely to take liberties with the facts, and yet, because of their artistry, they retain enormous appeal" (Jacobs & Tunnel, 2004, p. 156). Because of this, informational books are assuming a more prominent, and trusted, role in classrooms. Some of the qualities to be considered when choosing informational texts for instructional use are the same as qualities considered in choosing textbooks, including: accuracy of content and trustworthiness of sources, nuance of word choice and clarity and economy of explanations, nature of illustrations and other graphic resources, and sufficiency of background information provided. Some other qualities that make informational trade books particularly appealing to students, as reported by Jacobs and Tunnel (2004), should be considered when evaluating the match between reader characteristics and features of text. These are qualities that make the text visually appealing, personal, novel—in a word, interesting. Figure 6.7 provides a checklist to be used in evaluating informational trade books.

Qualitative Dimensions: Coherence Relations. As we have seen, coherence relations represent a critical feature influencing students' reading performance. The CCSS has heightened attention to this aspect of text by encouraging the qualitative assessment of text complexity. Close reading of a text will reveal the extent to which the author has facilitated comprehension by providing "coherence markers"—linguistic devices that make ideas coherent—or to which text challenges the reader by requiring that the reader infer relations that are not explicitly stated. Graesser, McNamara, and Lowerse (2003) provide a comprehensive description of various coherence relations, which may be used in reading the text closely to see how demanding it will be for the reader. Look for examples of:

- *Coreference:* When the author uses multiple words to refer to the same person (president, commander in chief), event (disaster, flood), or object (it, baseball), is it clear that both words are referring to the same entity? Does each different word add useful detail?
- *Conjunctives:* When adjacent ideas are related, does the author explicitly signal the relations with a word that readers will understand? For example, does the author signal additive (in addition), temporal (later), causal (since), intentional (for the purpose of), adversative (by contrast), logical (thus) relations? If the relation is implicitly stated, does the author supply enough information that the readers can make the required inference?
- *Verb tense and chronology:* When there is a shift in time or when events are not reported chronologically (flashback), how does the author alert the readers? Is the description supplied adequate? Does verb tense make the time of events clear?
- *Scene change:* When the action or context of the story moves to a different place or space, does the author signal this explicitly (nearby, in the surrounding countryside . . .)?
- *Headers and highlighting:* Does the author supply tools that signal important information and direct readers to read purposefully (using bold font). Do these tools really make clear how information is organized, particularly in dense expository text?

Feature	Questions to Consider	Comments

Design	Is this Attractive?
	    Rich graphics?
	    Manageable amounts of print?
	    Interesting layout?	

Details	Is this Compelling?
	    Showing vs. telling?
	    Quotes?
	    1st person accounts? Anecdotes?
	    Prompt imagination?
	    Affective response?	

Background	Is it Considerate?
	    Invokes familiar experiences?
	    Relates new to familiar?	

Subject	Is it Interesting?
	    Unusual topic?
	    Unconventional point of view?	

Perspective	Is it Personal?
	    Author shares own point of view?
	    Talks to vs. at readers?	

Accuracy	Is it Accurate?
	    Sources provided?
	    Trustworthy?
	    Verifiable?	

Language	Is the Language Inviting and Appropriate?
	    Precise word choices convey nuance?
	    Language sparse, prompts inferences?	

Graphics	Complement ideas in print?	

Source: Adapted from Jacobs, J. S., & Tunnell, M. O. (2004). *Children's literature, briefly.* Upper Saddle River, NJ: Pearson.

- *Topic sentences:* Does the author alert readers to what they will be reading about by using the convention of beginning a paragraph with a topic sentence, particularly in conceptually demanding expository text?
- *Punctuation:* Does the author add nuance to the message with punctuation (using quotes to show exactly how someone expressed an idea)? Would this punctuation be meaningful to the readers?
- *Text structure signals:* When using a particular text structure, does the author supply words and phrases typical of that structure (number the steps of a procedure as step1, step 2 . . .)?

Qualitative Dimensions: Conceptual and Knowledge Demands. Each text presents a unique profile of demands that challenge readers' thinking and affordances that support readers for making sense of the text. This is particularly true with respect to the conceptual understandings of the text. In order to evaluate the conceptual and knowledge demands of a text, the teacher must read it very closely—more than once—and respond *as specifically as possible* to these questions:

- What are the important understandings that learners should develop in their interactions with this text?
- What are the conceptual challenges that are likely to limit readers' understanding? Are the understandings to be developed
  - ○ abstract or subtly nuanced?
  - ○ quite outside of readers' experience or perception?
  - ○ at odds with logic or with conceptions that readers may have already developed earlier, independently?
- How does the text address, or fail to address those conceptual challenges? Does the text
  - ○ offer alternative representations (graphic, multimedia) and sufficient explanation, including analogies to readers' own experiences, to enable the reader to identify subtleties and visualize the abstract?
  - ○ provide background information that is likely to be missing from readers' preexisting knowledge store?
  - ○ confront naïve, or logical but incorrect, conceptions and enable readers to hold these up against the correct conceptions?

Evaluating Core Reading/Language Arts Programs

Evaluating Anthologies and Sets of Books. As we have already noted, collections of stories, informational selections, poetry, and drama within a single volume or in a series of "little books" often provide students with the core of the material they will use in reading instruction. These anthologies and/or sets of books are often part of a larger set of instructional materials, but not always. For some students, these collections provide the only reading material they encounter, and the quality of their reading experience is determined by the content of these reading materials. For these reasons, such materials require careful evaluation (see Dewitz, Leahy, Jones, & Sullivan, 2010, for useful forms and suggestions).

The most recent versions of anthologies have additional material, however. They are not merely collections of text. First, there is generally an intentional grouping of several different *types* of texts, often organized around a central "theme" or "big idea." In addition, the new anthologies may include background materials designed to be used before reading the selection(s) and also prompts or questions designed to be used after reading. Finally, a few commercial programs are including "gloss"-like materials during reading—prompts, highlights, or callouts to encourage students to reflect on some aspect of the text or the reading process. The following questions should be asked in evaluating these collections:

- Are the selections likely to be enjoyable and interesting to students?
- Are the texts developmentally appropriate in terms of difficulty?
- Are they supported with effective instruction?

- Do the selections create a coherent theme that lends itself to comparing and contrasting texts, genres, or themes?
- Is there breadth and balance of type or genre?
- In mixed-genre themes, are the texts used for appropriate and authentic purposes?
- Is multicultural representation accurate and reflecting of an appropriate level of diversity?
- Is there adequate depth in the number of titles or selections at each level of difficulty?
- Are illustrations of high quality, and are they supportive of the text?
- Is the content, length, and format appropriate for the age and grade?
- Does the adjunct material make a substantive contribution to students' reading and learning?

Evaluating Leveled Texts.   Because so many struggling readers are assigned inappropriate, frustration-level materials, the assessment process should consider whether the books used by students are at an appropriate level of difficulty. This is the "third leg" of the text complexity framework. In addition, the assessment process should consider whether students have been making acceptable progress in applying their knowledge and skill to increasingly difficult texts.

The text leveling system described earlier can be and has been applied to trade texts (see https://leveledbooks.beaverton.k12.or.us/search.php or http://home.comcast.net/~ngiansante/ for a sample listings of books). However, the reality today is that schools and teachers often purchase whole sets of texts that are commercially available. Collections of "above" "at" and "below" leveled texts are typically available to supplement core/basal programs, and specialist teachers generally purchase sets of materials as well. In many areas, these collections of leveled texts have completely replaced core/basal programs and therefore represent the totality of texts many students read. When this is the case, the same features described above for anthology texts should be applied to leveled texts. When these features are examined, it is often the case that more narrative than informational text is available and there is a limited range of genre and text type.

Contemporary leveled texts have improved in these areas, but two areas that remain problematic, by definition, are length and content. At the earliest levels (e.g., Fountas & Pinnell, levels A–G), texts are often appropriate in length and content. Indeed, some leveled texts actually provide longer selections and more-interesting content than do core/basal program materials. A more in-depth discussion of some of these factors is provided in the next section, which focuses specifically on sets of books for beginning readers. However, by mid–grade 2 (approximately levels L–M), students can and should be able to read many available trade books and/or longer selections in anthologies. Students need a wide range of reading experiences in order to develop expertise.

There are some concerns that are unique to leveled text collections. As Szymusiak, Sibberson, and Koch (2008) note, "not all levelled texts are created equal." An evaluation of these materials should include both the elements described above and the following questions:

- What assurances are there that text leveling is reliable and accurate? Since the heart of guided reading and leveled text approaches is that students will have greater access to appropriately difficult texts, this is an important concern. In our experience, there can be considerable variation in a range of books labeled at a given level.

- Does the language structure flow and sound natural?
- Is vocabulary treated appropriately? When there is unfamiliar vocabulary, what supports are available? What vocabulary is repeated? What purpose does that serve?
- Is there a challenge in the reading—enough to build instruction around it?
- For predictable texts, does the pattern vary sufficiently to require students to "do some reading work?" (Szymusiak, Sibberson, & Koch, 2008, p. 25)

What is especially important to consider in evaluating leveled texts is "the issue of how the leveled texts reflect an underlying philosophical base and instructional plan for helping young readers become skillful readers" (Hoffman, Roser, & Sailor, p. 104). Simply using leveled texts without carefully considering the purposes and overall instructional design may be problematic. As Scanlon, Anderson and Sweeny (2010) note:

> There are multiple kinds of texts that might be used to promote the development of reading skill. The variety and types of texts that children encounter may play a substantial role in their approach to word solving. (p. 191)

In the next section, we turn our attention directly to the special case of beginning reading materials.

Evaluating Beginning Reading Books.   Evaluating the match between beginning reading books and the strengths and weaknesses of struggling readers is a task that has challenged educators for generations. Beginning reading materials represent a distinct type of instructional resource, representing as they do a type of "instructional scaffold" for novice readers (Hoffman, Roser, & Sailors, 2004; Mesmer, 2005). Over the past decade, there have been heated debates about the best type of beginning reading texts to use, reflecting different perspectives on early reading. Three distinct types of texts have been proposed and debated: leveled texts (see previous section), decodable texts, and predictable texts.

According to Mesmer (2001), there are two ways to measure the "decodability" of texts: (1) the proportion of phonically regular relationships between letters and sounds in the text and (2) the extent to which the letter–sound relationships represented in text match those that the reader has been taught. As a practical matter, publishers have adopted the latter tactic, and texts with high decodability are often those that use the same word or syllable rime repeatedly. As Mesmer notes, "the alteration of text that maintains high levels of regularity can render stories boring and nonsensical" (p. 125). It is not surprising in this context to find that, while decodability does appear to result in improved accuracy (at least in the early part of first grade), it has a negative effect on fluency (see Hoffman, Roser, & Sailors, 2004; Mesmer, 2005).

Predictability in a text is determined by a completely different set of features—by the language patterns and contextual supports offered in the text. Elements that increase predictability include rhyme, repetition, and pictures. Although the concept is simple, the ways of making texts predictable are numerous and complicated. As Hoffman and colleagues (2004) have noted, *both* decodability and predictability make positive contributions to beginning readers' word recognition. This has caused Hoffman and his colleagues to devise an evaluation scheme for beginning reading materials that is based on three major principles: engaging qualities, accessibility, and instructional design.

Both Hoffman et al, and Hiebert and her colleagues note that decodability is a word-level feature, whereas predictability supports attention to larger units such as sentence or text meaning. Hiebert and Raphael (1996) and Menon and Hiebert (2005) describe a wide range of features in early reading materials that influences beginning readers' access to the text: (1) predictability, (2) contextual support, (3) word density, (4) proportion of decodable words, and (5) proportion of core high-frequency words. The checklist in Figure 6.8 provides a means for evaluating beginning reading books in terms of the array of features suggested by these authors as well as others.

These various elements provide different types of support for beginning readers. For example, when texts have engaging qualities, they are more likely to be of interest to students who may use their familiarity with concepts and helpful illustrations in identifying key words. The content of books for beginning readers varies from a focus on familiar objects and actions, such as riding a bicycle, to objects and actions that are much less familiar, such as caring for exotic animals. Children's familiarity with a topic is clearly related to their abilities to decode unknown words related to the topic. Books in which illustrations support the identification of key words are also likely to be more accessible than those with illustrations unrelated to key words. Familiar concepts and supportive illustrations allow beginning readers to use what they already know about the world in combination with their emerging understanding of letter-sound correspondences to identify words.

According to Hiebert and Raphael (1998), children's success with an entire text depends on the number of words they find to be unique and their need to draw on word recognition strategies. Every time beginning readers encounter a new word in a book, they need to use their emerging repertoire of word recognition strategies. If there are many new words in a book, they may struggle and rely heavily on their ability to use contextual supports or on text predictability.

When at least some of the new words in a book contain common word patterns, or rimes, children have the opportunity to apply their emerging knowledge of letter-sound correspondences. However, selecting books that have some distinct words with common word patterns is quite different from selecting books in which words have almost perfect letter–sound relationships, such as *The Fat Cat* (Reading A–Z, http://www.readinga-z.com/book.php?id=337). Although consistency in the patterns of words in books read by beginning readers can be helpful, these types of materials will not help children generalize their knowledge of word patterns or develop an understanding of the variability of written English. Again, it is a matter of balance and of meeting the needs of particular students.

The books that are currently available for beginning readers vary considerably in both the presence and the progression of the features that are known to influence the accessibility of a text. Close examination of text features has begun to raise some provocative concerns. Cunningham and his colleagues, for example, closely examined books selected from the Reading Recovery leveled lists and found that these books avoided artificial language

FIGURE 6.8 Dimensions for Evaluating Beginning Reading Materials

Engagingness	Low 1	2	3	High 4
Content	Not interesting and/ or inaccurate; may interest only some students	Stories or information are of limited interest to beginning readers	Some elements of text are interesting	Interesting and appropriate characters, stories. and themes
Language	Language use is stilted as result of repetition and/or controlled use of phonic elements	Stilted use of language	Generally good use of language to interest and entice students to read and reread	Lively, clear, and interesting use of language
Format and design	Unattractive, cluttered, or difficult illustrations; text difficult to read	Adequate, but limited use of design and illustration	Attractive layout and illustration, but may not support text reading	Layout and illustrations contribute to comprehension and enjoyment
Decodability	**Easy 1**	**2**	**3**	**Most difficult 4**
	Consonant-vowel (me, go); consonant-vowel-consonant (cat, man)	Short-vowel words with blends and digraphs (trap, chip)	Long-vowel combinations (heat, rain)	Multisyllabic and compound words
Predictability	**None 1**	**2**	**3**	**Strong 4**
Predictable syntax and language features	N/A	Broad but not specific support, or picture support only	Has some predictable linguistic features	Rhyme, rhythm, or repeating phrases support word recognition
Story patterns	N/A	Weak story line with missing elements	Text and pictures tell a story, but little coherence or interest	Strong story structure using familiar frameworks
Instructional Design	**None 1**	**2**	**3**	**Strong 4**
Architecture of the text is clearly described	There is no explanation for how the books were created or how they should be used	There is some information available about text construction and/or use	Guidance is provided about when and how to use the texts, although information about sequencing, etc, may not be	The purpose and use of the materials is clearly articulated, and information about text features is obvious or available
Strong relationship between instruction and text design	There is no instruction	Weak relationship between instruction and texts	Good relationship between some elements of instruction and some elements of text	Comprehensive and clearly evident relationship between what is taught and the texts students read

Source: Adapted from several sources: (1) Hiebert, E. H., & Raphael, T. E. (1998). *Early literacy instruction.* Fort Worth: Harcourt Brace; Hiebert, E. H., & Martin, L. (2001). The texts of beginning reading instruction. In S. Neumann & D. K. Dickinson (Eds.), *Handbook of early literacy research* (pp. 361–376). New York: Guilford. (2) Menon, S., & Hiebert, E. H. (2005). A comparison of first-graders' reading with little books or literature-based basal anthologies. *Reading Research Quarterly,* 40.

and were typically interesting and attractive (Cunningham et al., 2005). However, they also concluded that they provided almost no systematic support for practicing onsets and rimes and did not provide enough print to reinforce high-frequency words.

The checklist in Figure 6.8 provides a means for attending to these features. It is important to remember that there is no such thing as the perfect set or sequence of books. Rather, books should be chosen in relation to the strengths and weaknesses of particular readers and for use in introducing particular strategies.

Evaluating Core Program Lesson Design.   In most commercial reading and language arts programs, the content, method, and tasks are dictated by the instructional framework used to teach the reading selections. Because core/basal reading programs provide so much more than specific plans for texts in the anthology, it is important to examine the entire set of materials. Guidelines for evaluating basal lesson frameworks and plans developed from a variety of critical reviews are provided in Figure 6.9.

It is especially important for teachers to evaluate the lesson frameworks and the content of commercially prepared lessons, because these materials have been shown to have a powerful influence on classroom reading instruction. Indeed, these materials have recently been placed on the frontlines of the "reading wars," with various political groups attempting to control both the content and the delivery of reading materials (see Chapter 1). Many states were required not only to adopt a core basal reading program, but to use a specific set of criteria to evaluate its adequacy. The guidelines developed by Simmons and Kame'enui (2003) are widely available and provide one such set of criteria. The overall framework they provide would be reasonably helpful for evaluating almost any core program, and it is not unlike the one provided in Figure 6.9. However, it also specifies the type of instruction that must be used to deliver content detailed for each grade K–3. This has caused some considerable controversy, privileging as it does a direct instruction model.

Dewitz, Jones, and Leahy (2009) analyzed the curriculum for comprehension strategy instruction for grades 3 to 5 in five popular core reading programs. Some of the questions that guided their work and their findings may be helpful in the evaluation of this aspect of core reading programs. They asked:

- *What skills and strategies are taught?* Does the curriculum address those skills and strategies (e.g., summarizing, predicting, questioning, using narrative and informational text structures) consistently reported in the literature? Dewitz et al. (2009) found that some popular core reading programs addressed a plethora of strategies; they often segmented a single construct (e.g., making inferences, elements of narrative structure) into multiple strategies that were taught separately, with little review or integration across lessons, placing the burden on the learner to create a coherent whole of the construct.
- *How are comprehension skills and strategies taught?* Does the curriculum support a full, direct explanation of each strategy, teacher modeling, guided practice, and independent practice sufficient to ensure mastery? Currently popular core reading programs have made some improvements in historical trends by providing relatively explicit explanations but maintain the problem of providing insufficient guided practice.

FIGURE 6.9   Evaluating Core Programs and Plans

The Overall Framework	Yes	No	Some
Scope of the Reading Program			
Evidence of goals and instruction for:			
Phonological Awareness (K–1)			
Phonics			
Fluency			
Vocabulary			
Comprehension			
Writing			
Genre and author's craft			
Text types and structures			
Thematic organization			
Opportunities for wide reading and discussion			
Developmental Progression of Skills and Strategies			
Coherent plan for developing phonics/decoding skills			
Instruction and examples provide for increasing challenge and depth			
Program highlights and prioritizes essential knowledge and skill			
Meaningful Relationship between Instruction, Text, and Practice			
Materials provide opportunities to practice taught skills/ strategies			
Vocabulary words receive multiple exposures			
Materials build conceptual knowledge			
Differentiation			
Resources provide for different texts, tasks, and assessments, depending on students' needs and interests			
Grouping patterns are flexible and provide for diverse needs			
Are there specific suggestions and provisions for ELL?			
Assessment			
Multiple types of assessment are evident			
Assessment information informs instruction			

FIGURE 6.9   (Continued)

Selection Lessons	Yes	No	Some
Prereading			
Evidence of process, content, attitude goals?			
Is background knowledge activated or developed?			
Does instruction inform students about the type of text they are asked to read, its properties, the purposes for which it might be read, and the strategies for reading it?			
Are there provisions for individual differences?			
Are there suggestions for different grouping or reading options?			
During Reading			
Do activities and questions help students achieve content, process, and attitude goals?			
Do instructional activities encourage students to become actively engaged in reading and to take responsibility for their reading?			
Is strategic, reading modeled throughout?			
Are there suggestions for assessment during reading?			
Are students encouraged to engage in self-evaluation?			
Is the focus on teaching students how to comprehend or merely on checking whether a student has comprehended?			
Postreading			
Does the text ask students for personal response to the literature?			
Do questions focus on major text concepts and elements?			
Do activities and questions focus on theme concepts?			
Are students asked to make intertextual connections (to think about this text in terms of previously read material)?			
Does skill instruction clearly relate to the literature?			
Are reading and writing connections made visible?			
Is there an integrated model of reading and language arts?			
Assessment			
Are there multiple types of assessment provided?			
Is assessment clearly linked to the instruction provided?			
Does assessment promote an appropriate view of reading and writing?			
Are students, as well as teachers, involved in assessment?			

■ *How do the pacing and timing of comprehension skills and strategy instruction in core programs compare with the instructional design of original research studies?* Does the curriculum guide teachers in the same instructional methods and the same frequency of lessons as used in research validating the use of skills and strategies? Dewitz et al. (2009) found that core reading programs did not take on the task of educating teachers by adopting important features of the instructional designs of original research studies.

Although the use of an evaluations framework such as the one in Figure 6.9 can be time consuming, "over time, these procedures are likely to become more a 'mind set' than a series of discrete steps" (Wixson & Peters, 1989, p. 60). In any event, the degree to which detailed evaluations suggest the need for extensive modification provides one estimate of the quality of the commercial plans.

Evaluating Textbooks

As it has become clear how strongly text features can influence text difficulty, a number of guidelines for evaluating textbooks have been generated. One of the most comprehensive of these, and one that has withstood the test of time, was developed by Irwin and Davis (1980) and is reproduced in Figure 6.10. An especially helpful feature of this checklist is that several dimensions of text difficulty are distinguished and evaluated separately. For example, learnability and understandability are evaluated separately. Consequently, teachers can evaluate the strengths and weaknesses of textbooks on the basis of the ways in which they wish to use them.

Expository text can be evaluated for understandability alone. However, when students are to be held accountable for learning and remembering information from textbooks, teachers need to evaluate texts somewhat differently. If students are having trouble learning information from text, an assessment of the textbook features may provide useful information about how to help them learn and remember more. Alternatively, an assessment may reveal the fact that the text obscures important or new information, making learning difficult.

Of course, it is important to remember that comprehension is the result of multiple factors. Recent research suggests that text structure and coherence may have a different effect on readers with high levels of knowledge versus those with low levels of knowledge (McNamara, 2001). In fact, there is some evidence that inconsiderate texts result in higher levels of learning for students who already know a great deal. Graesser, McNamara, & Louwerse (2003) suggest that it causes them to work harder at understanding and, since they have the requisite background, this increased effort and engagement leads to improved comprehension and learning. One technique for predicting whether your own students will understand text was suggested by Armbruster (1984), who suggests selecting a topic from a text and generating several questions that you would expect students to be able to answer after reading the text in question. Then read the selection and make sure that it is possible to answer these questions using *only* the textual information. When the text does not provide the information or makes it difficult to understand, teachers must either be prepared to compensate for the text's inadequacies or elect not to use it at all.

**FIGURE 6.10
Readability
Checklist**

This checklist is designed to help you evaluate the readability of your classroom texts. It can best be used if you rate your text while you are thinking of a specific class. Be sure to compare the textbook to a fictional idea rather than to another text. Your goal is to find out what aspects of the text are less than ideal. Finally, consider supplementary workbooks as part of the textbook and rate them together. Have fun!

Rate the questions below using the following rating system.

5	= Excellent
4	= Good
3	= Adequate
2	= Poor
1	= Unacceptable
N/A	= Not applicable

Further comments may be written in the space provided.

Textbook title:
Publisher:
Copyright:

Understandability

A. _____ Are the assumptions about students' vocabulary knowledge appropriate?

B. _____ Are the assumptions about students' prior knowledge of this content area appropriate?

C. _____ Are the assumptions about students' general experiential backgrounds appropriate?

D. _____ Does the teacher's manual provide the teacher with ways to develop and review the students' conceptual and experiential background?

E. _____ Are new concepts explicitly linked to the students' prior knowledge or to their experiential backgrounds?

F. _____ Does the text introduce abstract concepts by accompanying them with many concrete examples?

G. _____ Does the text introduce new concepts one at a time with a sufficient number of examples for each one?

H. _____ Are definitions understandable and at a lower level of abstraction than the concept being defined?

I. _____ Is the level of sentence complexity appropriate for the students?

J. _____ Are the main ideas of paragraphs, chapters, and subsections clearly stated?

K. _____ Does the text avoid irrelevant details?

L. _____ Does the text explicitly state important complex relationships (e.g., causality, conditionality, etc.) rather than always expecting the reader to infer them from the context?

M. _____ Does the teacher's manual provide lists of accessible resources containing alternative readings for the very poor or very advanced readers?

N. _____ Is the readability level appropriate (according to a readability formula)?

Learnability
Organization

A. _____ Is an introduction provided for each chapter?

B. _____ Is there a clear and simple organization pattern relating the chapters to each other?

C. _____ Does each chapter have a clear, explicit, and simple organizational structure?

D. _____ Does the text include resources such as an index, glossary, and table of contents?

E. _____ Do questions and activities draw attention to the organizational pattern of the material (e.g., chronological, cause and effect, spatial, topical, etc.)?

**FIGURE 6.10
(Continued)**

F. _____ Do consumable materials interrelate well with the textbook?

Reinforcement

A. _____ Does the text provide opportunities for students to practice using new concepts?

B. _____ Are there summaries at appropriate intervals in the text?

C. _____ Does the text provide adequate iconic aids such as maps, graphs, illustrations, etc., to reinforce concepts?

D. _____ Are there adequate suggestions for usable supplementary activities?

E. _____ Do these activities provide for a broad range of ability levels?

F. _____ Are there literal questions provided for the students' self-review?

G. _____ Do some of the questions encourage the students to draw inferences?

H. _____ Are there discussion questions that encourage creative thinking?

I. _____ Are questions clearly worded?

Motivation

A. _____ Does the teacher's manual provide introductory activities that will capture students' interests?

B. _____ Are chapter titles and subheadings concrete, meaningful, or interesting?

C. _____ Is the writing style of the text appealing to the students?

D. _____ Are the activities motivating? Will they make the student want to pursue the topic further?

E. _____ Does the book clearly show how the knowledge being learned might be used by the learner in the future?

F. _____ Does the text provide positive and motivating models for both sexes as well as for various racial, ethnic, and socioeconomic groups?

Readability Analysis

Weaknesses

1. On which items was the book rated lowest?
2. Did these items tend to fall in certain categories?
3. Summarize the weaknesses of this text.
4. What can you do in class to compensate for the weaknesses of this text?

Assets

1. On which items was the book rated the highest?
2. Did these items fall in certain categories?
3. Summarize the assets of this text.
4. What can you do in class to take advantage of the assets of this text?

Source: Chart from Irwin, J. W., & Davis, C. A. (1980, November). Assessing readability: The checklist approach. *Journal of Reading, 24*(2), 124–130. Reprinted with permission of the International Reading Association.

Careful examination of the text is absolutely essential. Checklists such as the one in Figure 6.10 can provide important guidance for evaluating texts with specific student populations in mind. A text that is appropriate for some students might not be appropriate for others. Some texts will be used as supplements, while others will be used by all students as the primary source of information about a discipline. The readability checklist permits a consideration of different responses given different purposes and different students.

Evaluating Trade Books

Many trade books used in classrooms can be evaluated using the guidelines supplied in the discussion above about narrative and informational text. However, there are a number of genres of trade books, as well as "hybrid" genres (e.g., expository fiction), multigenre formats (e.g., combinations drawing from a menu of genres such as diaries, letters, cartoons, newspaper articles), and "new" genres (e.g., graphic novels), whose unique qualities merit special consideration. Excellent sources for guidelines to be used in evaluating these texts include comprehensive textbooks on children's literature. For example Kieffer (2010) provides separate guidelines in print—with supplementary Web-based resources—for fiction, nonfiction, books for very young children, folktales, picture books, modern fantasy, poetry, contemporary realistic fiction, historical fiction, and biography. Books on issues and recent trends in children's literature (see Bedford & Albright, 2011; Fox & Short, 2003) provide additional nuances to be considered, such as cultural authenticity—an important consideration in choosing texts for English language learners.

Evaluating Electronic and Multimodal Texts and Web-Based Resources

Modern digital technologies, say Rose and Dalton (2009), "have the potential to radically transform the ecology of teaching and learning" (p. 74) in two ways. First, they are enabling us to understand how people learn and what factors contribute to individual variations in learning. Technologies such as functional magnetic resonance imaging (fMRI) enable us to see how the work of reading is distributed over different structures in the brains of typically achieving and struggling readers, in patterns that vary with individual, text, and task differences. Second, modern technologies are providing a means by which we might customize instructional approaches and resources to meet the needs of individuals. Text presented in digital media is flexible; it can provide readers with (1) multiple ways of representing information, (2) customized guidance in approaching text strategically, and (3) engaging opportunities for interaction. Multimodal representations (e.g., Braille, Spanish, audio, vocabulary defined) provide easier access and free up cognitive resources for making sense of text. Embedded models, prompts for guided practice, and feedback (available as needed) enable readers to develop strategic reading behaviors. The combination of multimedia, productive interactions with text, as well as choices that acknowledge individual differences are likely to be highly motivating.

The evaluation of electronic, multimodal, and Web-based texts should begin with these questions: How does the digital environment—software programs installed on computers and other information and communication technology (ICT) devices such as cellular phones and e-book readers or sites accessed via Internet—provide textual resources that can meet the needs of individual learners? How is the material consistent with current research on reading and writing processes, and does it match the philosophical and pedagogical frameworks of the larger reading and writing program? In this section, we provide guidelines for assessing electronic instructional resources and their potential to meet individual needs.

Pedagogical Considerations.   In addition to being consistent with instructional reading and language arts objectives, instructional resources should be pedagogically sound.

According to Ertmer, Gopalakrishnan, and Ross (2001), pedagogical beliefs and classroom practices strongly affect the way in which computer technology is integrated within the learning environment. It is important to understand the philosophical stances, purposes, and intended outcomes in a particular instructional environment (see Chapter 5) to evaluate the use of digital and multimodal texts and Web-based resources in that context. Coiro and Fogleman (2004) provide a framework for categorizing interactive, multimodal Web-based resources in terms of pedagogical support or support that reflects beliefs about effective teaching with technology and effective learning with content-specific digital texts. These categories include the following.

- *Level 1: Content-Specific Informational Web Sites* Information is presented in print and/or static picture and organized topically, looking and feeling much like a newspaper. Learners are expected to navigate and read independently, acquiring information without any instructional support from within the Web site.
- *Level 2: Content-Specific Informational Web Sites with Multimodal Interactive Features* Information is presented in multimodal forms. Learners may be able to manipulate objects or interact with hyperlinked information in other ways that allow them to build their own understandings. There is no support to coach the learner in how to use the opportunities for interaction, nor to coach the teacher in how to teach with the resources.
- *Level 3: Content-Specific Informational Web Sites with Multimodal Interactive and Pedagogical Features* Information is presented in multimodal forms with interactive features that are hyperlinked to separate (outside of the text) resources to support learning. Learners must chart their own routes through the available resources, deciding what hyperlinks to activate for what purpose.
- *Level 4: Content-Specific Informational Web Sites with Multimodal Interactive Features in a Pedagogical Interface* Information is presented in multimodal forms with interactive features that are all part of one cohesive instructional system that may be, for example, a simulation or virtual environment. Learners are guided to take more control as they demonstrate the thinking needed to do so successfully.

Digital and multimodal texts and Web-based resources should also be consistent with current research on reading and writing processes. As such, these programs and resources should have the following features:

- Include complete pieces of narrative or expository text that are meaningful and useful
- Provide well-organized and logically developed materials that actively engage readers
- Prompt reflection and responses that emphasize thinking rather than repetitive practice
- Provide skills practice in real content with real purpose that allow for rereading and editing
- Take advantage of relationships between reading and writing

In Figure 6.11, we provide guidelines for evaluating the pedagogical qualities of Web-based resources and other electronic texts. The educational issues surrounding the use of these materials should be paramount. The overall questions that you should explore as you use these guidelines include: What are the types/ranges of media, hyperlinked information, and interactive features? What is their potential to support learning?

Software Considerations.   While the Web-based resources described above engage students in working with authentic texts to explore ideas in content areas, other electronic resources target reading and writing skills more specifically to augment the reading and writing instruction of the classroom. A variety of software and Web-based resources are used to promote reading skills such as phonological awareness, fluency, vocabulary, and comprehension; they also support writing with aids such as concept mapping and presentation tools as well as spelling practice and illustration tools. The best programs encourage the exploration and construction of knowledge, the communication of ideas (such as collaboration, information access, and self-expression), the development of metacognitive strategies, and the performance of real-life applications (Grabe & Grabe, 1996). These software programs encourage students to manipulate text, explore ideas, and produce evidence of their thinking that can be shared with others.

Software programs for practicing word- and story-level comprehension provide opportunities for practicing phonemic elements, building vocabulary knowledge, and developing comprehension. Storybooks on CD-ROM are an example of software in this category. These are presented in a multimedia format. The speech capability of CD-ROM books allows students to choose to hear entire stories or only words that appear unfamiliar. Students can interact with any or all of the objects on each "page" of the story. These interactions may lead to developing conceptual knowledge about the story, exploring vocabulary meanings, examining story elements and characters, practicing phonic elements, and extending the reader's knowledge beyond the scope of the story.

As with any software or Web-based resource, decisions about appropriate use should be made cautiously. For example, some links in CD-ROM storybooks have little educational value. These links connect with information, sounds, or graphic movements for the sake of pure entertainment. Exploring all the links—especially in hypermedia and Web-based resources—may sidetrack students, causing them to forget their purposes. Students can become overwhelmed with all of the choices available to them. It is also important to be cautious about overassigning value to some of these computer-based activities. For instance, just because children can click on unfamiliar words in the CD-ROM storybooks does not necessarily mean that they will exhibit an increase in their ability to decode other unfamiliar words (Leu, 2000b). As with any instructional material, appropriate strategic behaviors need to be modeled and scaffolds provided for students' ongoing uses of the technology by helping them to set purposes, understand outcomes, and intentionally use metacognitive strategies (Labbo, 2000).

These software instructional resources should, above all, be *instructional*. That is, rather than duplicate the traditional print materials already available in the classroom or function simply as digital practice or electronic worksheets, they should take full advantage of their digital capacity to demonstrate reading-related skills, monitor progress, and provide feedback on how to correct incorrect responses. It should not be possible to, for

FIGURE 6.11 Pedagogical Considerations in the Evaluation of Electronic Texts/Web-Based Resources

How does electronic text/Web site reflect knowledge about:	Comments, Examples
Teaching, generally? Is content presented in a format that reflects understanding about the importance of	
■ setting a purpose?	
■ providing or activating sufficient background and interest?	
■ supporting integration of key concepts with own knowledge?	
■ applying new information to solve real problems?	
Domain/topic? Does the text/resource present information that is	
■ accurate?	
■ reflective of important concepts?	
■ typical of ways in which experts organize knowledge and communicate with each other?	
Teaching of reading strategies? Does text/resource include prompts that enable learners to engage in	
■ strategic thinking for facilitating their own comprehension?	
■ metacognitive processes for monitoring their own comprehension?	
New literacies of online reading? Does text/resource guide the reader to engage in processes required for learning with Web-based resources such as	
■ generating questions of appropriate scope and focus?	
■ locating and searching sites with key words?	
■ evaluating how useful and truthful resources are?	
■ working intertextually to integrate information across sites/texts?	
■ organizing and transforming information into products that can be used to communicate with others?	
Learning generally? Does text/resource gradually release responsibility to learner to construct own understanding by offering	
■ hierarchically ordered tasks of gradually increasing difficulty?	
■ just-in-time support that prompts learner decision making?	
■ multiple and varied opportunities to use newly learned skills?	
■ immediate feedback?	
Assessment and record keeping? Does text/resource	
■ adapt to learner, "branching" to additional supports or alternative paths?	
■ allow learner to stop at any point and save work?	
■ track learner's performance, summarize and display in easily understood form?	

Sources: The organization of this chart and the items in it were adapted and compiled from several sources: (1) Coiro, J. Critically evaluating educational technologies for literacy learning: Current trends and new paradigms. Accessed December 26, 2011, from U.S. (2) Lovell, M., & Phillips, L. (2009). Commercial software programs approved for teaching and reading in the primary grades: Another sobering reality. *Journal of Research on Technology in Education*, 42(2), 197–216. (3) Eagleton, M., & Dobler, E. (2007). *Reading the Web: Strategies for Internet inquiry.* New York: Guilford. (4) McVee, M. B., & Dickson, B. A. (2002). Creating a rubric to examine literacy software for the primary grades. *The Reading Teacher*, 55(7), 635–639.

example, use "uncontrolled continued clicking, which allows . . . games to be played without reading using the targeted skills until the only remaining option is the correct one" (Lovell & Phillips, 2009, p. 210). Writing software, to be instructional, should provide support for the entire writing process, rather than for an isolated aspect that then needs to be transferred to off-screen writing situations.

Multimedia Considerations.   To support a deeper exploration and richer representation of ideas requires software that allows students to add sounds, voice recordings, pictures, and video clips to their texts. However, it is important to remember that the addition to digital text of multiple static or animated visual images as well as auditory information does not necessarily enhance comprehension. In fact, it could have just the opposite effect. Mayer (2008), who has studied learners interacting with multimedia science text, offers principles for the design of multimedia texts. While Mayer's work was primarily with college students, some of his principles may provide a starting point in the evaluation of multimedia digital texts for younger students. In general, those principles are designed to reduce the cognitive demands on the learner so that the learner can devote his or her cognitive resources to processing the ideas of the text.

1. Do auditory, visual, and print messages work in concert to focus the learner on the important principles to be learned?
   a. Are multimedia explanations concise, without entertaining but nonessential graphics, video, and dramatic stories that will take the learner afield from the important message?
   b. Is essential information "signaled" or highlighted, supporting the reader with linguistic devices (e.g., topic sentences) and typographic features (e.g., font style, color)?
   c. Are printed words positioned advantageously right next to the relevant part of a graphic?
   d. Are spoken words (e.g., narration) coordinated—that is, are they produced simultaneously with a visual image?
   e. Does the text, when presenting graphic images with narration, avoid overloading the reader with presentation information in print form as well?
2. Are cognitively demanding ideas presented using materials and tasks designed in a manner that minimizes the demands on working memory?
   a. Are complex messages presented for processing in segments, preferably with the learner able to control the pace?
   b. Are complementary graphics and explanations presented in dual modes so as to distribute processing demands over visual (graphic) and auditory (spoken) channels?
3. Are spoken words presented in a manner that engages the learner in partnership with the computer—for example, using a conversational register and a standard-accented voice?

Technical Considerations.   It is difficult to assess important aspects of software and Web-based resources through program descriptions alone. Substantive evaluation of these materials requires a firsthand examination of the programs and resources, giving a variety of correct and incorrect responses. In this way, it is possible to analyze the feedback and support structures that are provided for the students. It may also be helpful to ask students for their opinions about content, delivery style, and perceived friendliness. Observing students' reactions and interactions with the material can also provide useful information.

Software programs and Web-based resources, like all educational material, should be accurate and free of errors. However, there are other technical factors, or factors related to interface design, to consider that are specific to software programs and Web resources. We have adapted from Lovell and Phillips (2007) a chart (Figure 6.12) that can be used to evaluate these factors.

FIGURE 6.12 Interface Design Considerations in the Evaluation of Electronic Texts/Web-Based Resources

Is the software/Web site media text, graphics, animation, video, sound:	Poor?	Fair?	Good?	Superb?	Comments, examples
High quality?					
Well organized?					
Integrally related to content?					
Modifiable by learner?					
Engaging, appealing?					
Does the software/Web site support learner by supplying instructions and function controls that are:	Poor?	Fair?	Good?	Superb?	Comments, examples
Easily located, clearly displayed?					
Informative, effective, consistent?					
Auditory as well as visual?					
Reviewable?					
Built on what learner already knows (e.g., icons are logical, familiar, or metaphors for real-world event)?					
To what extent does the software/Web site prompt learner interactions that are:	Poor?	Fair?	Good?	Superb?	Comments, examples
Consequential (make a difference in what program does, e.g., pace)?					
Frequent?					
Similar to real-world counterpart?					

Source: Adapted from Lovell, M., & Phillips, L. (2009). Commercial software programs approved for teaching and reading in the primary grades: Another sobering reality. *Journal of Research on Technology in Education, 42*(2), 197–216.

In summary, evaluating software and Web-based resources takes time and energy. For some struggling readers, technology may provide enough support and interest to encourage the persistence and effort that are needed to become more proficient. However, this is not likely to happen with repetitive, routinized activities that offer little after the initial novelty has worn off. In evaluating the resources that are at play in a particular instructional context, it is important to determine whether software programs and Web-based resources are providing the type of supportive and interactive setting within which students' reading and writing are likely to thrive. Using information from a variety of sources (Meyer & Rose, 1999; Michigan Reading Association, 1993; Patsula, 2002), we have created a set of guidelines in Figure 6.13 that may be used to evaluate the supportive and interactive nature of digital environments for reading, writing, and learning with text.

FIGURE 6.13   Guidelines for Evaluating Reading Software and Technology

Educational Soundness	Poor			Good	
Content consistent with curriculum and standards frameworks	1	2	3	4	5
Supports learning	1	2	3	4	5
Consistent with the instructional approaches being used in your classroom	1	2	3	4	5
Appropriate for classroom use and instructional activities	1	2	3	4	5
Appropriate to the level of intended learner(s)	1	2	3	4	5

Accuracy and Recency of Information	Poor			Good	
Regular updates available	1	2	3	4	5
Information is accurate and free of bias	1	2	3	4	5

Accessability and Useability	Poor			Good	
Easy to load or access	1	2	3	4	5
Clear directions	1	2	3	4	5
Flexible navigation options and easy cross-referencing	1	2	3	4	5
Varied search options (e.g., key word, topic, picture, search, etc.)	1	2	3	4	5
Options to quit and save at any time	1	2	3	4	5

Interactivity and presentation	Poor			Good	
Multiple presentation modes, including: text, graphics, sound, animated graphics, video	1	2	3	4	5

FIGURE 6.13 (Continued)

	Poor				Good
Opportunity for two or more learners to interact cooperatively	1	2	3	4	5
Clear, easy-to-read text	1	2	3	4	5
High-quality sound	1	2	3	4	5
Documentation and Support Features	**Poor**				**Good**
Clearly written user's materials	1	2	3	4	5
Teachers' supplements provide useful and appropriate information	1	2	3	4	5
Links are easy to find and use	1	2	3	4	5
Permits, supports, and/or provides high-quality feedback	1	2	3	4	5
Useful and efficient record-keeping capabilities, if appropriate	1	2	3	4	5
Classroom-management suggestions for using the program within the classroom	1	2	3	4	5
Motivation	**Poor**				**Good**
Program can be tailored to individual learning styles and actively responds to students' choices	1	2	3	4	5
Includes (or helps you develop) activities that engage students' existing interests	1	2	3	4	5
Varied media that provides choice and engagement	1	2	3	4	5
Flexibility	**Poor**				**Good**
Program can be tailored to individual needs	1	2	3	4	5
Can be adapted and modified by teachers and/or students	1	2	3	4	5
Contains or is open to a great variety of texts	1	2	3	4	5
Provides variable challenges and adjustable supports	1	2	3	4	5
Simulations and Problem-Solving Programs	**Poor**				**Good**
Realistic situations	1	2	3	4	5
Motivating designs	1	2	3	4	5
Helpful feedback regarding decisions	1	2	3	4	5
Links to other relevant information	1	2	3	4	5
Suggestions for integrating content within the curriculum	1	2	3	4	5

THE THUMBNAIL SKETCH: THE INSTRUCTIONAL CONTEXT

In Chapter 4, we introduced the thumbnail sketch as a way to summarize information that is gathered throughout the assessment-instruction process. Here we continue to add information gathered as we examine the contextual factors associated with literacy. This information is added to the initial information already collected about student achievement/performance. When we become aware that individual students are at risk of reading and/or writing difficulties, we want to identify information about their achievement in relation to that of their peers (see Chapter 4). However, it is also important (1) to examine the context to glean some initial information about the nature of instruction and intervention that students experience in their classroom and support settings and (2) to begin to evaluate the match between the students' experience, knowledge, and expectations and the school's resources, practices, and expectations. The thumbnail sketches for Tha'm and Kyle have been updated on the basis of our evaluation of the contextual factors described in Chapters 5 and 6 (see Figures 6.14a and 6.14b).

THE CASES OF THA'M AND KYLE

In Chapter 5, we summarized contextual information about the communities and families of Tha'm and Kyle. We also described key attributes of the overall instructional climate in their schools. Here, we examine the instructional materials and tasks that are characteristic of their two schools.

Tha'm

During Tha'm's entire time at Roosevelt School, her teachers have been examining and refining their practice. The school had traditionally used a somewhat dated basal program, which they used with rigid fidelity and close monitoring. About the time that Tha'm entered kindergarten, the school entered into a collaborative research and development project with an area university. The explicit agenda was twofold: (1) to improve students' performance on tests of reading and writing and (2) to accomplish that by improving teachers' knowledge and skill. As a result of their work, Tha'm presently participates in guided reading groups every day, using a new core program with supplemental reading exposure in leveled texts. She also participates in a whole-group teacher read-aloud with a mini-lesson focused on comprehension strategies, and she receives targeted skill instruction in an English language pullout program.

The core reading materials for Tha'm now include the basal reader anthology (a contemporary and broad-based mix of narrative and expository texts), leveled texts that accompany the core program for independent practice, and leveled texts that have been collected by the classroom teachers to supplement the program. Tha'm is expected to complete workbook pages and to give written responses in a strategy journal. In addition, she participates in a "Words Their Way" spelling group at her developmental level, generally

FIGURE 6.14a Tha'm's Thumbnail Sketch: Evaluating the Context

Step 1: Using Data to Understand Groups of Students and Identify Struggling Learners	**Step 2:** Information about the Reading-Writing Context
Information about Tha'm gathered in the Getting Started step is summarized here. (Other information will be added later.) **Getting Started (Step 1)** *Background* Name: Tha'm Age: 10 Grade: 5 Key Correlates: ■ Average IQ ■ First Language: Vietnamese ■ Normal vision, hearing, and overall health *Whole-Class Data* Statewide Assessment: ■ Met the proficiency standard in reading for grades 3, 4, 5. ■ In reading at 5, she is just 1 point above the cut score. ■ In writing at grade 5, she is "partially proficient." ORF Data: ■ DIBELS results suggest "no risk" at end of grade 3. *Additional Data Available* ■ ELL assessments show her to be reaching age-appropriate language proficiency in speaking, reading and writing. ■ Placed in grade-level core program. ■ Uneven classroom performance in grade 5.	*Home and Community Settings* ■ Vietnamese spoken at home ■ Few if any books ■ Does not visit public library because she has lost her card ■ Family is supportive and strongly attempting to assimilate ■ School sits in a diverse refugee resettlement community with more than 2 dozen different languages ■ Both longtime American citizens and refugees are hardworking, but the FRL rate is above 90% *Instructional Settings* ■ Small teacher–student ratio and extensive PD on the part of school and teachers ■ Pullout program for ELL since kindergarten ■ Classroom organization is structured with teacher-directed instruction ■ Literate environment is signaled by accessible texts, student writing, and engaging displays *Instructional Activities and Tasks* ■ Mostly closed tasks ■ Basal workbooks ■ Questions mostly explicit ■ Writing quantity and quality has varied from year to year ■ Limited student-initiated activity, goal setting, or inquiry ■ Little connection to outside-of-school texts or tasks *Instruction* ■ Small-group instruction by ability groups ■ Teacher-managed, code-focused instruction in primary grades ■ Student managed, meaning focused in intermediate grades ■ Content of instruction is balanced except for very limited vocabulary instruction ■ Limited reading outside of the basal program and small groups ■ Classroom teachers expected to provide differentiated instruction and extra support within the classroom *Methods* ■ Organized and focused instructional blocks ■ Modeling and explicit instruction in comprehension strategies ■ Limited cooperative book discussion or collaborative work ■ Ability groups

FIGURE 6.14a   (Continued)

	Assessment Practices ■ Close monitoring after each unit/theme in the core program ■ Student support team examines data to plan appropriate near-term interventions (at K–3) ■ State assessments annually from grade 3 on ■ At primary grades, teachers use an array of federally and state-mandated assessments generally focused on phonology, decoding, and fluency *Resources* ■ Contemporary core program ■ Broad collection of leveled texts (in primary grades) ■ Good school library, but limited access to it ■ Inadequate access to electronic media or digital texts

FIGURE 6.14b   Kyle's Thumbnail Sketch: Evaluating the Context
(1 reflects information from first and second grade)

Step 1: Using Data to Understand Groups of Students and Identify Struggling Learners	**Step 2:** Information about the Reading-Writing Context
Getting Started (Step 1) *Background* Name: Kyle Age: 6½ Grade: 1 Key Correlates: ■ Normal vision, hearing, and overall health/development ■ Difficult time "paying attention" *Whole-Class Data* Portfolio Review: Reading ■ Running records throughout grade 1 suggest that Kyle is making progress. ■ He does meet the benchmark for end of grade 1. Portfolio Review: Writing ■ He is able to reflect on his own writing and demonstrates an awareness of both Craft and mechanics. ■ He takes risk in his writing, but spelling and volume are both less developed than for, his peers. *Additional Data Available* ■ Says he doesn't really like to read—would rather play and build ■ Cooperative and willing to work both in school and in extra sessions.	*Home and Community Settings* ■ English only language spoken at home ■ Considerable home emphasis on reading and writing ■ Community is well educated and emphasizes academic achievement ■ Median income of school community well above average—FRL rate is above 15% *Instructional Settings* ■ Multiaged classrooms in a building that houses only K–2 ■ Child-centered classrooms ■ School and classroom environment is rich; exceptional access to texts, many opportunities to read and write ■ Support services are provided on a push-in basis and include reading, speech/language, and counseling *Instructional Activities and Tasks* ■ Many open tasks and significant student choice ■ Reading time spent in sustained reading of continuous texts ■ Students respond in multiple ways—writing, art, performance

FIGURE 6.14b   (Continued)

	■ Writing time spent writing original texts and revising for publication—in books, on walls, in class
	■ Additional writing in journals, theme booklets, and correspondences
	■ Students reflect on own work, select portfolio entries, and evaluate own learning
	Instruction
	■ Students confer with teacher and with each other
	■ Much student-managed, meaning-focused activity, although this shirts from kindergarten to grade 2
	■ Inquiry-based theme work and choice time each day
	■ Cooperative and collaborative groups
	■ Problem-solving focus
	Methods
	■ No commercial curriculum; students engage in self-selected reading and individual conferences
	■ Teacher identifies students to assess/instruct, and focus varies depending on student
	Assessment Practices
	■ Close monitoring on a daily basis
	■ Student work samples are organized, annotated, and dated
	■ Collections are organized in portfolios
	■ Student self-reflection is extensive
	■ Teachers collect weekly running records
	■ Other formative assessments daily and weekly during individual conferences
	Resources
	■ Beginning readers, little books, and own writing
	■ Emerging readers, commercially controlled vocabulary texts, and trade books (children's literature)
	■ Journals, portfolios, theme booklets
	■ Many read-alouds (children's literature)
	■ Excellent and accessible school library
	■ Limited access to electronic media or digital texts

doing word sorts several times a week. Her work is closely monitored and adjusted for "difficulty" (Bear, Invernizzi, Templeton, & Johnston, 2012).

The reading program is broad based and well articulated. It is also highly structured, and classroom management is a high priority. Teachers orchestrate a tightly timed series of small groups throughout the morning, and there are always multiple adults in the room, including volunteers, aides, and specialists. Students do very little self-selection, and their discussions are generally teacher led. Importantly, Tha'm gets a steady diet of lower-level questions and, although the core anthology has some higher-level questions, the teachers do not always use those.

Students do write every week, but the writing is quite "closed" and follows the state's recommendations for genre. Students have limited choice, and everyone is engaged in the same "phase" of writing at the same time.

Tha'm's program has been quite balanced (except for limited work in vocabulary), but she has few chances to make choices about what to read or write. The tasks, on the other hand, tend to demand at least some integrative thinking, and the state's high-stakes assessment requires that students be able to respond to their reading and justify answers with evidence from the text. In fact, Tha'm is fortunate that the state assessment is of relatively high quality, because test-like tasks are practiced often at this school.

In summary, the context in which Tha'm has learned to read and write has a great deal to recommend it. The strong focus on literacy has created many, and many varied, opportunities for reading. It should be noted that the program has included minimal amounts of informational reading, and both the science and social studies curriculum are very thin since teachers have focused a great deal of time on literacy and mathematics. Teachers have recently begun to introduce more expository texts, and they are using a contemporary basal that provides a reasonable balance of literature and explicit instruction. This has been supplemented through teacher-created lessons on comprehension strategies and read-alouds with mini-lessons. Student performance and achievement are both monitored closely, and instructional adjustments are made when necessary. As is the case in many intermediate classrooms, Tha'm's fifth-grade teacher engages in less assessment and more whole-class instruction than her primary teachers did. Importantly, the tasks they assign may not be demanding enough to ensure that Tha'm continues to make progress. Finally, there is virtually no evidence of an appropriate vocabulary program—for any students and none specifically designed for ELL students such as Tha'm.

Kyle

Ms. McIntyre believes in a child-centered classroom and expects that students will learn to read and write by reading and writing. Her job is to ask the right question at the right time or to provide the right prompt when things get stalled. The readers' and writers' workshop approach used in this classroom relies on student access to many books.

For reading, the youngest children read each other's writing and from a collection of early reading materials (predictable texts, picture-label books, etc.). Later, as they progress, they read from commercial easy-to-read controlled vocabulary books. There are also many children's literature trade books, and children read them as soon as they are able. By second grade, most children are choosing easy "chapter books" as well as more-challenging picture books. These texts may be self-selected, negotiated between teacher and child, or assigned. In early second grade, Kyle was reading from the easiest of the controlled vocabulary books (*Little Bear*, by Minarik, for example).

Kyle's classroom is one of many like it in his district. However, Ms. McIntyre is an unusually expert teacher. In her classroom, whole-group mini-lessons set the tone for the day, but most other instruction is done individually or in small, flexible groups. Students do not receive direct instruction in skills except in response to their own reading and their own questions about print. Ms. McIntyre does discuss reading skills and strategies with individual children as they read and write. Conversations are explicit, and the feedback to students about strategies (e.g., using picture cues, thinking about the middle and endings of words) is very focused and direct.

In addition, there are multiple types of formats for writing. The children in Ms. McIntyre's room write a great deal—in journals, in process writing folders, about their themes, to record their exploratory findings, and to communicate with each other.

Motivation to learn is shaped by the many activities and opportunities to explore personal issues. For example, Kyle wrote extensively throughout second grade about snakes; he conducted research, wrote a book, and made journal entries about snakes. In this classroom, there is a wide array of activities to engage students with different learning styles. Some will spend their time building with blocks during planning time, while others will work on a science experiment. However, everyone writes about what they have done when "choice time" is over.

Children expect to be successful because they see children of all ages around them being successful. Risk taking is supported through individual goal setting that Ms. McIntyre discusses with all students. In twice-daily class meetings, Ms. McIntyre models how to solve problems and how to establish goals and then encourages children to do the same. Older students frequently model by explaining how they think or what they learned or plan to do.

Ms. McIntyre is adept at providing scaffolding for students through the selection of predictable books, through shared and repeated readings, and in the instructional dialogue that she and others provide.

The use of scaffolding and dialogue is perhaps most visible in the dialogue journals used by Ms. McIntyre and her students. In Figure 6.15, Kyle and Ms. McIntyre have an exchange. Ms. McIntyre's response supports Kyle's ideas, provides him with correct spelling models, and challenges him to take on a new task.

There are no workbooks or worksheets in this classroom. The classroom is organized as a reading/writing workshop, and most tasks in Ms. McIntyre's room are open ones. Students are expected to make good decisions during planning time and to write about the work they did during that time. They also read books, discuss them with their teachers, write responses to their reading in response logs, keep track of what they read in reading logs, write letters to their teachers in their dialogue journals, and write about personal experiences in their journals. In their writing folders, they create drafts, keep notes, confer, and rework some pieces, and they also publish writing regularly in public displays and in bound books.

FIGURE 6.15
Kyle's Dialogue
Journal

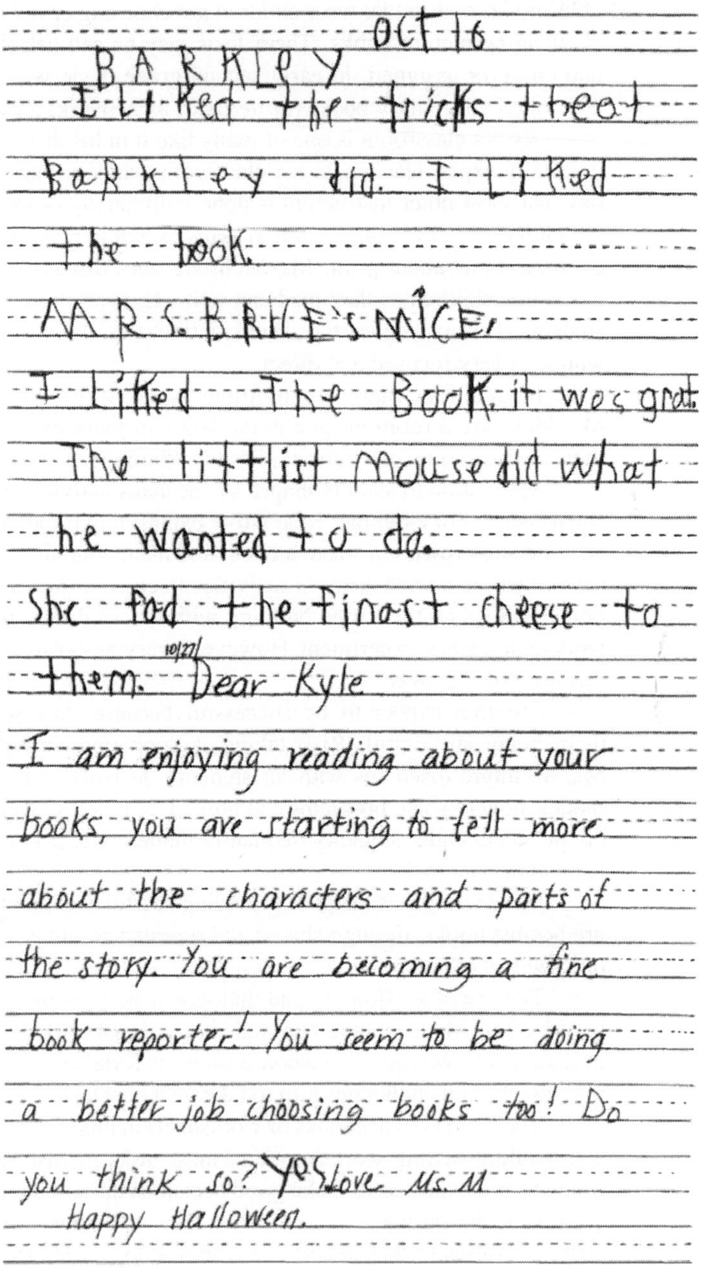

OCT 16

BARKLEY
I Liked the tricks theat
Barkley did. I Liked
the book.

MRS. BRICE'S MICE,
I liked The Book. it was grat
The littlist Mouse did what
he wanted to do.
She fed the finast cheese to
them. 10/27/ Dear Kyle
I am enjoying reading about your
books, you are starting to tell more
about the characters and parts of
the story. You are becoming a fine
book reporter! You seem to be doing
a better job choosing books too! Do
you think so? Yes Love Ms. M
Happy Halloween.

CHAPTER SUMMARY

The first half of this chapter addressed the role of instructional resources in reading and writing performance. We began with an examination of the features of texts (of all types) that affect complexity and, thus, comprehensibility. These features include genre and text structure, coherence and unity, conceptual and knowledge demands, graphics and typographics, as well as domain-specific features. Next, we examined the texts of commercial reading/language arts programs, including the reading anthologies, independent student activities, and teachers' guides, in order to understand how they are likely to influence reading and writing performance. We then considered how the features of textbooks make them "considerate"—that is, make reading easier or more difficult and learning more productive or more tedious. Trade books are increasingly being used to supplement textbooks; we reviewed the ways in which they offer a number of opportunities to facilitate learning. Finally, we discussed the role of electronic (or digital) and multimedia texts and Internet Web sites as resources. These texts offer a number of affordances that can transform and augment text as well as partner with learners to support their reading, writing, and thinking with text. However, there is a complex set of thinking skills, or "new literacies," needed to comprehend these online texts.

The second half of this chapter describes strategies and tools for assessing the instructional resources addressed in the first half of the chapter. The range of strategies and tools for assessing reading materials is captured in a framework recommended in the Common Core State Standards (CCSS), which includes both quantitatively and qualitatively measured dimensions of text. Traditional quantitative, text-based (often computer-based) measures consider difficulty of words and grammar, using structured readability formulas. Text leveling systems capture both quantitative and qualitative dimensions. Qualitative dimensions of text, which often need to be judged by human experts rather than computers, include characteristics such as genre and text structure, coherence, and knowledge demands, including knowledge specific to the domain of the topic of the text. We provide questions and informal checklists to use in the evaluation of these dimensions of text and refer to additional examples provided in CCSS. In addition, we provide guidelines for examining digital resources in terms of the new literacies that they require.

MyEducationLab™

Go to the Topic, Reading Difficulties & Intervention Strategies, in the MyEducationLab (www.myeducationlab.com) for your course, where you can:

- Find learning outcomes for Reading Difficulties & Intervention Strategies along with the national standards that connect to these outcomes.
- Complete Assignments and Activities that can help you more deeply understand the chapter content.
- Apply and practice your understanding of the core teaching skills identified in the chapter using the Building Teaching Skills and Dispositions learning units.

■ Examine challenging situations and cases presented in the IRIS Center Resources.
■ Check your comprehension of the content covered in the chapter by going to the Study Plan in the Book Resources for your text. Here you will be able to take a chapter quiz, receive feedback on your answers, and then access Review, Practice, and Enrichment activities to enhance your understanding of chapter content.

A+RISE A+RISE® Standards2Strategy™ is an innovative and interactive online resource that offers new teachers in grades K-12 just in time, research-based instructional strategies that meet the linguistic needs of ELLs as they learn content, differentiate instruction for all grades and abilities, and are aligned to Common Core Elementary Language Arts standards (for the literacy strategies) and to English language proficiency standards in WIDA, Texas, California, and Florida.

SECTION 4

Evaluating the Learner: Looking More Closely

*T*his fourth section of the book, Evaluating the Learner, contains three chapters. Of course, our discussion started back in Chapter 4 as we described the nature and type of information that most teachers have about groups of students. In this section, we turn our attention to the types of assessment that may *not* be used with all students. As we identify individual students who we want to look at more closely, the assessment process can become both broader and deeper. Each of the four chapters in this section contains information that will increase teachers' knowledge and understanding of reading and writing difficulties and provides descriptions of additional tools and strategies for assessment. These include standardized tests, traditional informal measures (i.e., informal reading inventories and formative tools and strategies). In Chapter 7, we examine the foundations of literacy, with a close look at language development and writing. In Chapters 8 and 9, we provide educators with an extensive array of tools for assessing students' reading and writing in classroom and specialized contexts. Using the strategies and approaches described in these chapters, teachers will be able to assess all major aspects of reading and writing performance.

7

Assessing Young Readers and Writers

A n understanding of the foundations of literacy is essential to the development of an appropriate program of assessment and instruction. A rich body of research produced over the last four decades has helped us understand the language basis for conventional literacy in reading and writing. Developments in the areas of psychology, linguistics, and emergent literacy provide teachers and specialists with information that can be used to develop more-effective assessment and instructional programs than have been possible with previous conceptualizations of literacy.

This chapter is divided into three major sections. The first section examines the knowledge and skills that underlie the development of literacy. It includes a discussion of early language development and the ways that early literacy experiences influence children's acquisition of the foundations of reading and writing. The second major section of this chapter describes strategies and tools for assessing the emergent abilities of young readers and writers. These include both standardized and less-formal assessment techniques. The latter are especially important for understanding very young students, since so many standardized assessments are not sufficiently sensitive to the underlying abilities so critical to reading and writing success. Then, in the final portion of this chapter, we apply the major concepts covered here to the ongoing assessment of Kyle (see Chapters 4–6).

UNDERSTANDING THE FOUNDATIONS OF LITERACY

Background

Over the previous century, educators have differed in their views of how children learn to read and write. The ideas and beliefs associated with various perspectives are still present in the thinking of many teachers and administrators and in instructional programs provided to young children. Early educators argued that children simply *grow into readiness*, much the way a tree or plant develops. Later, some teachers and theorists asserted that readiness is either caused or facilitated by the environment. During a period beginning in the 1920s and extending through the 1980s, there was a strongly held belief that "readiness" was biologically determined. Mental age, perceptual-motor development, social maturity, and general physical development were all considered critical aspects of reading readiness. Students' readiness would unfold in a predetermined way and time.

These ideas led, perhaps unwittingly, to an instructional mandate for inaction. The implications for educational practice seemed straightforward: instruction should be withheld until the child is "ready" (Teale & Sulzby, 1986). Today, some of these ideas seem almost quaint. It is hard to believe, given the increasingly strong academic focus in preschool and kindergarten, that educators once strongly argued that early print experiences in the kindergarten environment were inappropriate. At the same time, many scholars believe that contemporary early literacy instruction is focusing too narrowly on a subset of linguistic skills, thereby limiting children's development of more-general cognitive and social-interactive abilities.

Over the past three decades, researchers from several different disciplines have reconceived literacy. Educators no longer think in terms of student readiness, but rather in terms of *emergent literacy*. It is clear that children's written literacy skills gradually evolve in the context of general cognitive and oral language development (see Neuman & Dickinson, 2005, 2011). Educators and researchers who have studied young children's literacy development have come to understand that children begin to acquire literate knowledge, skills, and behaviors at home during their earliest years. From an emergent perspective, readiness is reconceptualized as the *process of becoming literate*, as opposed to a series of discrete, specifiable skills that must be developed before learning how to read. The available evidence certainly suggests that development, and therefore readiness for school tasks, is influenced by both experience and instruction.

In the sections that follow, we consider two important foundational aspects of literacy. First, we consider the nature of oral language development and how the acquisition of oral language competence prepares children for reading/writing tasks and vice versa. Second, we discuss the types of literacy experiences necessary for effective emergence into conventional reading and writing. We focus on the types of knowledge and insight that lay the foundation for subsequent success in reading and writing, including: developing print awareness, understanding the forms and functions of print, acquiring alphabet knowledge, and understanding the language and structure of stories. Finally, we explore the foundations and development of written language.

The Language Foundations of Literacy

It has become quite clear over the past three decades that the development of reading and writing relies on oral language processes and, additionally, that ". . . reading difficulties can follow from difficulties with speech processing (decoding problems) or from broader language processing impairments (comprehension problems)" (Snowling & Hulme, 2006, p. 63). In this section, we examine the progress of children's spoken language development.

Learning to Talk.   Learning to talk is one of the first productive cognitive tasks confronting young humans.

> There is much for children to learn: not just the words, but their pronunciation and the ways of combining them to express the relationships between the objects, attributes, and actions to which they refer. They also have to learn how the more subtle distinctions of intention

are expressed—indirect and direct requests; questions of various kinds, and expression of different attitudes, such as sympathy, anger, apology, and so on—through different selections and orderings of words and structures and the use of different patterns of intonation and facial and bodily gestures. (Wells, 1986, p. 39)

The ways in which children accomplish this task can tell us a great deal about how humans learn to acquire cognitive competence in general.

Learning to read and write is highly correlated with oral language competence. This relationship probably exists for a number of reasons. First, reading and writing are language-based, cognitive tasks. Second, both written language and spoken language are communicative processes. That is, reading, writing, and talking are used to exchange ideas, request information, demand and elicit help, share feelings, and so forth. Finally, both oral language communication and written communication are interactive, taking place in a context that influences the active search for meaning. By studying how children learn language, we can gain tremendous insight into the cognitive structures and strategies they will use in learning to read and write.

How oral lang correlates w. reading + writing

The connections here are reinforced in the findings from studies among English language learners (ELL) of learning to read and write. The research suggests that "knowledge acquired through the student's first language is not only useful but also crucial in the continuous cognitive development of the student in the second language . . . in fact, ample evidence suggests that cognitive and academic development in the first language can have a very positive effect on second language schooling" (Ovando, 2005, p. 294). In other words, ELL students who develop a strong base in their primary or first language tend to transfer those attitudes and skills to the other language and culture and are therefore more successful at learning to read and write in English than would otherwise be the case (Hudelson, 1987).

What Children Must Learn about Language. There are some features common to all languages that must be learned. "Language has many subsystems having to do with sound, grammar, meaning, vocabulary, and knowing the right way to say something on a particular occasion in order to accomplish a specific purpose. Knowing the language entails knowing its *phonology*, *morphology*, *syntax*, and *semantics*, as well as its social rules or *pragmatics*" [emphasis in the original] (Gleason, 1997, p. 20). Thus, one of the first tasks that confronts babies is to figure out that the auditory sounds of humans are meaningful. The sounds of a language provide only the starting point, however. Children must learn how to express their intentions by using language. To accomplish this, they must figure out *how* to name the objects and ideas in their language and mark subtle changes of meaning (tense, number, etc.) by using additional morphemes. In addition, they must figure out the *grammar* of their language. This grammar is composed of the rules for mapping meaning onto words. The grammar typically dictates that various meaning relationships are carried by particular word orders or syntactic structures (see Chapter 2). Not all languages have the same rules for mapping meaning on strings of words. For example, in most Romance languages (such as Spanish), adjectives usually follow the noun they are describing, whereas in English these modifiers are typically placed before the noun. Children must learn what word order is dictated by their particular grammar and the rules that tell them how to combine words.

These elements of language are addressed throughout this text, as they influence and are influenced by learning to read and write. In this section on the foundations of literacy, we focus on children's development of *phonology* and *vocabulary*, because each of these has been shown to be so centrally implicated in students' subsequent reading and writing success.

Phonology. All spoken languages have a phonological system comprised of discrete speech sounds, or phonemes. Different languages may contain different phonemes. In English there are forty-four or forty-five of these phonemes (depending on source and regional variations). Phonological knowledge and skill, like all other aspects of linguistic development, emerges over time and in response both to biological constraints (e.g., /th/ is more difficult to produce than /m/) and to experience (e.g., American children do not hear the click phonemes that are common in some African languages and therefore do not produce them once they begin to form words). "When [adults] know a language, they know what sounds their language uses, what sound distinctions signal meaning distinctions, and what sound sequences are possible" (Hoff, 2009, p. 97). Thus, for example, mature English speakers know that the /ng/ sound can occur at the end of words (*thing*) but never occurs at the beginning of words, something that does happen often in Kiswahili (as in *Ngorongoro*). Indeed, mature speakers know a whole variety of (tacit) phonological rules—about which they are generally unaware.

Individuals who study phonology and/or work with speech and language difficulties have elaborated ways of describing speech sounds. It is beyond the scope of this text to describe these fully, and we highly recommend that interested readers refer to one of the excellent language development texts available (see, e.g., Hoff, 2009). Some information about speech sounds can be very helpful, however, in both assessment and instruction work with very young and/or very delayed readers. There are two major classes of sounds: vowels and consonants. *Vowels* are sounds that are made with an unobstructed flow of air. Just open your mouth and say each of the sounds of the vowels and you will get the idea. *Consonants* are made with a more constricted vocal tract (see Menn & Stoel-Gammon, 2005). Simplifying the information considerably, it is useful to understand that consonant speech sounds are usually described in terms of

- *Voicing:* describes differences in speech sounds produced by vocal-cord vibration. Thus, the only difference in the sound at the end of the following words is voicing: *legs* (/z/) and *apes* (/s/)—the /z/ is voiced, the /s/ is not. Although we are so often unaware of voicing distinctions, young readers and writers who are isolating phonemes typically struggle to represent these differences.
- *Place of articulation:* refers to the location of the tongue, teeth, and lips as speech sounds are produced. You may want to say several words and attend to the location of production for the *initial* sound: *love, men, pit, zoo, church, fish,* etc.
- *Manner of articulation:* describes how the speech sound is produced. Here, linguistics uses descriptors such as *stops* (the difference between /b/ig and /p/ig), *fricatives* (difference between /f/at and /v/at), and other less frequent types such as *liquids* and *glides.*

Most linguists use a standard system called the International Phonetic Alphabet (IPA) to represent phonemes. We have elected here to use more-conventional symbols to represent phonemes, because we are more concerned in this text with the reading of words representing these sounds than we are with capturing children's oral productions (see Figure 7.1). The symbols, or graphemes, that are used to represent the sounds in English are also presented in Figure 7.1, and we will return to this issue shortly.

FIGURE 7.1
Phonics Content

Consonants are sounds that are produced when you stop or slow the breath coming through your mouth. There are roughly twenty-five consonant sounds (phonemes) in English.

Sound	Examples
/ b /	**b**all, sca**b**
/ d /	**d**og, ba**d**
/ f /	**f**og, gra**ph**, rou**gh**
/ g /	**g**ame, **gh**oul, fi**g**
/ h /	**h**at, **wh**o
/ hw /	**wh**ite
/ j /	**j**am, **g**em, wa**ge**, we**dge**
/ k /	**c**ar, **k**itten, ta**ke**, bla**ck**, anti**que**
/ l /	**l**ake, wa**ll**
/ m /	**m**onkey, sli**m**, ca**me**, li**mb**
/ n /	**n**ame, **pn**eumonia, **gn**at, fi**n**
/ p /	**p**ail, sa**p**
/ r /	**r**ain
/ s /	**s**un, **c**ereal, u**s**, ba**ss**, mi**ce**
/ t /	**t**ap, ca**t**, clapp**ed**
/ v /	**v**ote, li**ve**
/ w /	**w**ink
/ y /	**y**oke
/ z /	**z**oo, wa**s**, whi**z**, fi**zz**, ma**ze**
/ ch /	**ch**ain, mu**ch**, hu**tch**, lec**t**ure, ques**ti**on
/ sh /	**sh**eet, **s**ugar, **ch**aise, ma**sh**, fic**ti**on
/ th /	**th**imble, my**th**
/ *th* /	**th**em, la**the**
/ zh /	mea**s**ure
/ ng /	ri**ng**

Vowels are sounds that are produced when air flows in an unrestricted way through your throat and opened mouth. There are approximately sixteen vowel phonemes in English.

Sound	Examples
Long	
/ a /	m**a**ke, b**ai**t, fr**ay**, t**a**ble
/ e /	b**ee**t, s**ea**m, m**e**, pon**y**, k**ey**, rec**ei**ve
/ i /	b**i**ke, f**igh**t, tin**y**, l**ie**
/ o /	d**o**me, s**oa**p, n**o**, m**ow**, s**o**ld, tot**a**l
/ u /	f**u**se, p**u**ny

(Continued)

**FIGURE 7.1
(Continued)**

Short	
/ a /	cat
/ e /	bed, meadow
/ i /	fit
/ o /	top
/ u /	cup, come
r-controlled	
/ ar /	car
/ i r /	fir, her, fur
/ or /	for, more, pour, door
/ air /	hair, bare
/ eer /	fear, leer
Other vowels	
Schwa (ə)	button, about, model
/ oi /	foil, boy
/ ow /	owl, mouth
/ aw /	awful, taught, fall, balk, scoff
/ oo /	food, suit, flew, sue
/ oo /	book, should

Consonant digraphs and consonant blends require attention because they need to be visually identified by readers during words analysis, especially in more-advanced decoding.

Digraphs	Consonant digraphs are two consonants that work together to represent one sound (phoneme) (e.g., sh, ch, gh).
Blends	Consonant blends are two consonants that work together, but each continues to represent its original sound (e.g., br, fl, kw, scr, st, sp, ld).

Infants attend to speech sounds from the very beginning of life, begin babbling (exploring a wide range of phonemes) at about six months, and are able to distinguish among phonemes at about the same time. By age 7, most children sound like adults. However, some sounds are more difficult to acquire than others, and phonological development continues beyond the beginnings of formal schooling. When sounds are too difficult to produce, humans generally find "proxies" for the sounds—something close to the intended one. For example, many young children use *cluster reduction* in their pronunciation, reducing consonant clusters to a single phoneme. Thus, *school* becomes "cool" and *snow* becomes "no."

The development of phonology depends, of course, on the particular language that is being learned. Snow, Griffin, and Burns (2005) caution that teachers need to be especially sensitive to dialect differences among their students:

> . . . technically, everyone speaks a dialect. There is no dialect-free version of English or any other language. Some dialects are less noticeable than others, depending on the situation. . . . When members of an ethnic or social-class subgroup resettle in a different dialect region,

regional dialect features they use may become markers of ethnicity and social class in the new locales. Some dialect features . . . awaken attitude differences but are associated with no communicative or schooling difficulties. (pp. 65–66)

Indeed, they note that no dialect is an impediment to learning to read as long as teachers are aware of the students' language structure and variants. The danger lies in the possibility that teachers may misassess what they observe. "Without an adequate knowledge base about dialect variation, a teacher might think that the issue is sloppiness about [. . .pronunciation. . .] or about students' reluctance to use formal style" (p. 67).

Learning Words. Despite the significant importance of phonological development to children's subsequent success in learning to read, recent research suggests that it has relatively little impact on later reading comprehension (RAND, 2002; Torgesen et al., 1999). The aspect of language development that does predict comprehension is vocabulary (Senechal & LeFevre, 2002; Tabors, Snow, & Dickinson, 2001). Students' level of vocabulary development is significantly related to their reading comprehension at grade 4 (Senechal, Ouellette, & Rodney, 2005). In addition, it has now become clear that knowing more words has a significant impact on children's phonological awareness (Walley et al., 2003).

Children's first words are more about phonology than they are about semantics (or meaning). These "words" (sometimes called "protowords") generally appear first in early "babble." They contain phonemes that appear frequently in adults' language, and "they are either single syllables or reduplicated syllables, such as baba and dada" (Hoff, 2009, p. 127). Most children begin to understand individual words' meanings and to use words` in intentionally meaningful ways around ten months of age. However, their limited phonological abilities may make many of these words sound the same, and they may initially use the same (or a very similar) word to mean many different things. Linguists generally agree that very young children have "holistic" representations of these early words; that is, they have not identified individual sounds or syllables within these words. Importantly, they probably do not have adultlike concepts of word meanings, either. Most first words appear as context specific—as something you can say in *this* setting. First words are not all labels. Indeed, first words are as likely to be statements (*bye-bye*), directives (*more*), or sounds (*moo*), although about half of children's first fifty words are typically nouns (Caselli et al., 1995).

Interestingly, there are significant individual differences in children's vocabulary development, even at this early age and stage—differences both in rate and word types. For example, research suggests that some children initially learn and use words that label or refer to objects. These children have been called "referential" children (Nelson, 1973). Others tend to learn and use more personal or social words. Nelson called these children "expressive" children. Subsequent studies have supported this early research (see Goldfield & Snow, 2005, for a review). Children also vary enormously in the rate of their vocabulary acquisition (Fenson et al., 1994; Vasilyeva & Waterfall, 2011). Although there is very little definitive evidence to explain these differences, they appear to be related both to innate differences among individuals and to environmental or contextual differences.

Of course, the correlates described in Chapter 2, factors related to successful learning and achievement, are implicated (hearing and intelligence among the most significant). In addition, researchers have been able to link both personality and specific language learning skills as sources of difference. For example, it appears that children who are more outgoing (Slomkowski et al., 1992) and/or risk-taking in their orientation (see Goldfield & Snow, 2005) experience more-rapid language development. Phonological memory also plays a part in the acquisition of vocabulary. Children who are better at remembering sequences of sounds also remember newly presented words better (Gathercole, Willis, & Baddeley, 1992). On the other hand, more-recent research suggests a somewhat more complicated picture in which both lexical knowledge (vocabulary) and phonological short-term memory contribute to new-word learning (Gathercole, Hitch, Service, & Martin, 1997) (see next section).

Children begin to add vocabulary in earnest at around eighteen months. Once children acquire fifty words, many (but not all) experience a vocabulary "spurt," and the rate of acquisition speeds up even more. During this early word acquisition stage, children often demonstrate their general cognitive development in the use of language. Thus, many children engage in *overextension*—that is, applying a single term to more things than adults would—for example, using *dog* to refer both to dogs and to other animals. Children also reveal their emerging awareness of how words are generated by inventing words based on their knowledge of the language. Children might call someone a "cooker" (one who cooks) or talk about "airplaning to Florida" (à la *racing* to the door or *stitching* up a wound). What is clear during this period is that children understand a great deal more than they can produce. Children who can produce only twenty-five to fifty words can comprehend several hundred words (Pan, 2005).

By the time they are three years old, children in middle-class families have typically accumulated more than one thousand words (Hart & Risley, 1995). This rapid growth makes it increasingly difficult to assess children's vocabulary, but there are other problems with vocabulary assessment as well. As children's vocabulary (semantic knowledge) becomes more sophisticated, there are more ways to generate words. As Pan (2005) notes, questions quickly arise when thinking about how to count children's vocabulary (e.g., are *run* and *runs* two words?). She goes on to discuss how *semantic networks* appear to fuel children's vocabulary growth. These seem important both for understanding how children learn vocabulary and how we can estimate (or assess) the extent of their knowledge and skill:

> The words *walk, walks, walking,* and *walked* refer to similar actions that differ in tense or duration, while *eat* and *devour* refer to actions that differ in manner. *Compete, win,* and *lose* share some semantic components, but differ in the outcome each conveys. *Oak, spruce,* and *birch* are linked by virtue of their co-membership in the superordinate category of *tree.* (Pan, 2005, p. 131)

Clearly, children's vocabulary and more-general language development is related to ongoing cognitive development. This appears to be a reciprocal relationship in which language affects cognition and vice versa.

Attention to meaning is a striking feature of early language development. From the beginning, young children's utterances reflect semantic intent. Their productions reflect an awareness that the functional purpose of language is to create and communicate meaning. This is most evident at the two-word utterance stage, when children seem capable of producing only two-word constructions. During this stage, researchers have observed what is termed *telegraphic* speech, so called because children leave out the words that are left out in telegrams and retain only those most essential to convey meaning—for example, "baby ride" and "Mommy cookie." At very early ages, children come to recognize a range of *language functions.* Halliday (1975) and others have studied and categorized the functions of language. Language is learned to express certain intentions and to perform certain functions, such as expressing feelings (I scared), inform or communicate ideas (It's blue), regulate or control others (You do it), etc.

Oral Language and Its Relationship to Reading and Writing

The development of oral language abilities lays the foundation for successful acquisition of reading and writing competence (Snow, Burns, & Griffin, 1998). Taking all the evidence together, oral language competence is important to reading and writing for these reasons:

1. In learning to talk, children develop (or demonstrate) a number of general cognitive strategies for learning.
2. In learning to talk (and listen), children acquire much that they will use to aid them in bringing meaning to print: vocabulary, understanding of syntax, the ways in which meaning is carried in language structures, and alternative structures for communicating similar and dissimilar ideas.
3. An extensive vocabulary appears to promote phonological analysis in early reading and comprehension in later grades.
4. Children use known oral language structures in their writing.
5. Sophisticated vocabulary, syntax, phonological development, and word usage are all helpful in learning to read.

Analyzing Speech. Because the strategy of "pay attention to meaning" works so well for speech, young children seem not to be aware of the component pieces of language. Yet, in order to become successful readers and writers, children must acquire an awareness of language that is not required for speaking it (Bialystok & Ryan, 1985). The special requirements of reading or writing print are not obvious to the novice. Young children typically demonstrate limited awareness of language itself.

> Indeed, literacy growth, at every level, depends on learning to treat language as an object of thought, in and of itself (Halliday, 1982; Olson, 1995). *Metalinguistic* refers to language or thought about language: for example, noting that the word "snake" refers to a long skinny thing all in one piece but that the word itself is neither long nor skinny and has four parts when spoken and five parts when written. (Snow, Burns, & Griffin, 1998, p. 42)

This *metalinguistic awareness,* or conscious knowledge of the linguistic elements of language, continues to develop throughout the school years and appears to be especially critical in the development of comprehending abilities (Roth, Speece, & Cooper, 2002).

The Concept of Word.   Speech provides few cues to tell children about the word as a unit of analysis. Words that name objects are easily isolated, but in the flow of normal speech, individual words are not clearly marked. To be successful in reading and writing, though, children must acquire the ability to identify individual words in the context of other words—that is, they must acquire a *concept of word*, which is an "awareness of the match between the spoken word and the written word in the reading of text" (Morris, 1993).

The following example demonstrates how children who appear competent may have incorporated unanalyzed items into their language. A three-year-old sings, "Baa-baa, black sheep, *Have you any* wool? . . ." (a favorite song that she has sung for months). Then she asks, "Mom, what's 'pabuany'?" What has been understood by the informed listener (Mom) as "have you any" has actually been perceived and produced by the child as a single unit: "pabuany." However, the child's question does indicate her growing demand for clarity in language.

The first challenge that faces children as they take up the task of learning to read, is to learn what conventions are represented in print (Downing, 1978). For example, children must learn that words are bound configurations that are separated by white space in print and that the term *word* is used to refer to a specific aspect of language. The available evidence suggests that four- and five-year-old children have a difficult time selecting a word from among letters, numbers, phrases, and sentences (Ferreiro & Teberosky, 1979/1982; Reid, 1966). When asked, some identify whole sentences as words, some make only random guesses, and some say that words, phrases, and sentences are all words. Even when children are asked about reading and words with a book in front of them, many four- and five-year-olds demonstrate substantial confusion about what constitutes a word and what people look at when they read (Ehri & Sweet, 1991; Homer & Olson, 1999; Morris, 1993).

Children do not acquire the concept of word in one flash of insight. As with all such knowledge and skill, the concept develops over time. In a longitudinal study of thirty children between the ages of three and six, Ferreiro (1980) examined the development of children's hypotheses and strategies for reading and writing. Her findings demonstrate that children's early "guesses" about the nature of these processes are quite different from those of older children. For example, children at first thought that similarities and differences between words were determined by the characteristics of the referent items, not by any similarities in sound. Thus, more letters were needed to write the name of a large item than were needed to write the name of a small one. Ferreiro (1980) provides the following marvelous example from a child in this stage:

> Maria (age four) was asked how many letters it would take to write her name. She said four (as many years as she was old). When asked how many letters it would take to write her mother's name, she responded six. But, for her father (a large man), she responded: "As many as a thousand."

There was considerable agreement among children as they moved through several stages. For example, at some point all the children she studied clearly evolved a "syllabic hypothesis." During this stage, the children believed that each letter represented one syllable. Clearly, when children arrive at the syllabic hypothesis, they have begun to see the formal relationships between speech and print. And, although the timing varied, all the children eventually realized that words are written with strings of graphemes.

Many researchers have concluded that children learn about the concept of word *during* the process of learning to read and write (Ehri, 1987; Sulzby, 1986). For example, it appears that children are better able to identify specific words, or "voice-point," when they can identify the initial consonants in words (Ehri & Sweet, 1991; Morris, 1993). Finger-point reading (the ability to match spoken words to print in memorized text) appears to play a linchpin role, according to Morris (1993), but it in turn is dependent on knowledge of beginning consonants. The development of a concept of word is then used to develop and promote phoneme consciousness.

Many researchers agree that among infants and toddlers, vocabulary growth causes children to move toward more-segmental noticing: "Lexical development is the factor that pushes the child to a phonological analysis of his language and to the representation of a phonological system" (Hoff, 2009, p. 132). This interplay between phonology and vocabulary appears also to be implicated in children's later success or failure in learning to read. Snow, Burns, and Griffin (1998), for example, note that children with larger vocabularies appear to be more successful in phonemic awareness tasks, and they make greater gains in the development of phonemic awareness during their first year in school than do children with more-limited vocabulary (Senechal, Ouellette, & Rodney, 2006).

Phonological and Phonemic Awareness and Segmentation. The ability to "consciously recognize and manipulate units of the speech stream" is called *phonological awareness* (Pan, 2005, p. 134). This involves recognizing increasingly discrete aspects of the phonological system:

- *Syllables:* A syllable is a word part that contains a vowel or, in spoken language, a vowel sound (*e-nough, mis-hap*).
- *Onsets and rimes:* Syllables are comprised of an *onset*, the initial consonant or consonant combination and a *rime*, the vowel and what follows it (see Figure 7.2 for examples). Children can segment onset and rime during oral speech. When these onset and rime patterns are used for reading or writing, they are often referred to as *spelling patterns.*
- *Phonemes:* The smallest unit of sound within specific languages.

Researchers have demonstrated that syllables are the easiest units for children to segment, followed by onsets and rimes and then phonemes (Treiman & Zukowski, 1991).

The development of phonological awareness is particularly important in languages such as English because it is an *alphabetic language*. That is, the writing system

FIGURE 7.2
Examples of Onset and Rime in English

Word	Onset	Rime
sat	s-	-at
broil	br-	-oil
germ	g-	-erm
float	fl-	-oat
Other examples of spelling patterns, or rimes, include: -ake, -oat, -ile, -uke, -earn, -oat, -ork, -ail, -and, -oot		

is a representation of individual sounds, or phonemes. Some languages—Chinese, for example—are logographic languages; the writing system is not a representation of sounds, but rather ideas. Other languages, such as Cherokee, use a syllabic system in which the written symbols represent syllables, not individual sounds. Children who will read and write in English must gain insight into the phonological system. "When the insight includes an understanding that words can be divided into a sequence of phonemes, this finer-grained sensitivity is termed phonemic awareness" (Snow, Burns, & Griffin, 1998, p. 51). The ability to separate words into constituent sounds, or phonemic segmentation, is one ability that increasingly appears to distinguish children who have difficulty learning to read and write from those who make good progress (Juel, 1988; Nation & Hulme, 1997). For example, Juel's longitudinal study of a large group of at-risk children suggests that children who are poor readers in first grade remain poor readers in fourth grade. One hallmark of those poor first-grade readers was very limited phonemic awareness. Indeed, Juel's findings suggest that although poor readers' phonemic awareness grew steadily in first grade, they left first grade with a little less phonemic awareness than that possessed by other children upon entering first grade, who became average or good readers.

Clearly, children must be able to distinguish separate sound units in words before they will be able to identify letters in words that relate to these sounds. It is important to note that phonemic segmentation ability does not require that children know what letter stands for each sound they hear in a word. Phonemic segmentation is not the same as auditory discrimination, which refers to the ability to distinguish between two different sounds. Indeed, it appears that auditory discrimination tests are poor predictors of ability to segment speech (Yopp, 1988).

Research suggests that young children may take quite a long time to acquire phonemic awareness. Although very young children often demonstrate phonological *sensitivity* (Burgess, 2006), most will not be able to segment words into constituent phonemes until they are school age (Chaney, 1992). Early studies (see, e.g., Liberman & Shankweiler, 1979), reported results suggesting that hardly any four-year-old children were able to segment speech into constituent phonemes and syllables. In their study, only 20 percent of the five-year-old children were able to segment by phoneme and, even at age 6, only 70 percent were able to do so. Predicting students' abilities in this area is challenging because it is highly dependent on the experience of children. In particular, children are unlikely to develop the ability to segment words into separate phonemes on their own. We know this because, among readers in nonalphabetic languages, even capable adults are generally not at all phonemically aware (Read, Zhang, Nie, & Ding, 1986). So, simple biological development will not necessarily provide the opportunities for phonemic awareness. Because instruction in phonemic awareness provides a boost for even very young children, the type of preschool or school experiences that a child has impact his or her ability to segment by phoneme.

Whereas research suggests that there is a strong relationship between the rhyming abilities of children as young as three years old and their later success in reading (Bryant, MacLean, Bradley, & Crossland, 1990), more-recent findings point to the greater importance of phonemic segmentation over rhyming for subsequent reading achievement (Muter, Hulme, Snowling, & Taylor, 1997; Naslund & Schneider, 1996). Despite these strong correlations, phonological awareness and phonemic segmentation should not be viewed as *prerequisite* to reading *instruction*. Instead, many researchers argue that this relationship is due to differences in children's ability to detect individual phonemes. Other researchers argue convincingly that children learn these individual phonemes when they receive instruction in school reading programs (Bowey & Frances, 1991; Ehri, 1987; Torgesen, Wagner, & Rashotte, 1994). Ehri and Roberts (2006) conclude that, "the course of acquisition of phonemic awareness and reading proceeds reciprocally" (p. 127). In other words, although phonemic awareness influences reading acquisition, learning to read also impacts phonological awareness. Given the greater focus on phonological awareness and phonemic segmentation in most contemporary kindergartens, it is likely that these numbers would be higher today than those reported in earlier studies. However, it is clear that children who fail to acquire these critical abilities early in their school career are much more likely to experience reading difficulties (Ball, 1993; Troia, 2004/2006).

It is increasingly clear that there is a progression of phonological knowledge that children acquire in the preschool and kindergarten period. Yopp (1992) and others (see, e.g., Burgess, 2006) suggest the following "stages":

1. Rhyming
2. Blending (individual sounds to form words)
3. Counting (How many sounds do you hear in "man"?)
4. Segmenting (Tell me the sounds you hear in "man.")
5. Deleting (Say *man*, and now take the /m/ away—what is the word?)
6. Substituting (If I change the /m/ in *man* to /c/, what word do I have?)

Some early literacy programs still do not include instruction designed to help children segment words into either phonemes or onsets and rimes. Since the ability to segment speech into phonemic units appears to have strong predictive power, most researchers suggest that early instruction in this area is needed (Phillips & Torgesen, 2006; Snow et al., 1998; National Reading Panel, 2000). Indeed, recent research suggests that direct instruction in phonemic segmentation (Cunningham, 1990) or onset and rimes (Goswami, 1986) may be related to reading achievement at the beginning stages of reading development.

However, caution is needed in this area. Although the ability to segment sounds is clearly important, most researchers have also concluded that phonological sensitivity is necessary, but not sufficient by itself, for reading achievement (Phillips & Torgesen, 2006). Other aspects of language, including semantics and syntax, appear to contribute significantly to children's literate development also. In addition, for most children, good instruction in reading and writing leads to greater linguistic awareness. It is as though the child never thinks to analyze speech but, in learning to read and/or write, is forced to recognize units and subdivisions (Francis, 1973). Thus, early successful experiences with print can develop students' abilities in this critical area (see Ehri & Roberts, 2006; National Reading Panel, 2000; Pikulski, 1994b).

In her extensive review of research on the relationship between oral language and literacy development, Watson (2001) concluded that when oral language is acquired and used in highly literate environments, it appears to exert a broad-based influence on literacy acquisition. She speculates that this is because children learn how to select and use specific linguistic and pragmatic forms to communicate and comprehend. In other words, there might not be a simple one-to-one relationship between learning language and learning to read, but children who learn both more language and more-sophisticated language are better prepared for the types of literate skills they must acquire for learning to read and write in school settings. Over the past decade, other researchers have arrived at similar conclusions (see Neuman & Dickinson, 2005, 2011). In the next section, we take a closer look at how experience and opportunity impact children's language and literacy development.

The Contextual and Experiential Foundations of Literacy

How Language Is Learned.   Most humans appear to move toward oral language competence through a series of more or less similar stages. The presence of these developmental stages across cultural and linguistic boundaries provides strong evidence that humans have some biological basis for language production. It is clear that children learn to speak their language using differing types of information and interactive styles (see Gee, 2001), and an increasing body of research supports the idea that human babies have a biological predisposition toward learning language (Lidz & Gleitman, 2004). However, it should also be noted that this predisposition is played out in environments where others interact through language and encourage children to participate, and the result is considerable variability among groups and for individuals (Vasilyeva & Waterfall, 2011; Wells, 1986).

Many parents would assert that they "taught their children to talk" and that children learn language largely through imitation and reinforcement/feedback. However, the available research evidence suggests otherwise. The amount of information that children receive explicitly from adults varies enormously among human populations. Most children are not deliberately *taught* the language, and none learn to talk through imitation alone. Instead, it appears that children construct the grammar of their language through the internalization and generation of rules. What the child learns is not a set of utterances but a set of rules for processing speech. For example, young children frequently produce utterances such as "He *goed* to the store," "It's *darking* outside," or "I'm going to school today, *amn't* I?" These examples demonstrate how children produce speech that could not have been imitated, as no competent speaker of English produces them.

Children's mistakes reveal more about their knowledge than about their lack of knowledge. As children generate rules for the language they are learning, their speech reflects this growing knowledge. For example, when children come to know that nouns can be converted to verb forms (as in "That room is a mess" and "You're messing up my things"), they may create errors that are consistent with this knowledge, such as "We'll airplane to Florida" and "You're germing it all up." In these examples, we see that children search for regularities, create rules, simplify the task, and overgeneralize or extend the information they have to new situations. In short, they are engaged in the development of strategies.

Although it is clear that children are not taught language, they do not learn it without help. Children need to have language available to them so that they can work out the regularities and also identify the details of the specific language they are learning. In addition, they need responsive conversational partners who will help them to see how the language works and provide feedback on their efforts.

> Learning to talk should thus be thought of as the result of a partnership: a partnership in which parents and other members of the community provide the evidence and then encourage children to work it out for themselves. Andrew Lock sums it all up in a single phrase when he describes the process as "the guided reinvention of language." (Wells, 1986, p. 51)

Of course, this means that the concept of "literacy" is inextricably intertwined with the particular social and cultural contexts of the home and community. As Johnston and Rogers (2001) noted, "there is extraordinary variation in the languages and cultures that children bring to literacy learning and in the literacies into which they have been apprenticed prior to coming to school" (p. 386). Thus, children have different opportunities and different challenges in learning language. We have already seen how differences in context exert profound influences on students' learning. Nowhere is this more evident than in children's acquisition of the foundations of literacy.

Contextual Differences in Learning Language and Literacy. The intentions and purposes of language use are executed in the context of social interaction. It is our knowledge of language that allows us to translate the sounds speakers produce into a representation of the messages that they are trying to communicate. The end result of language learning is not simply mastering the language structures. Children master the forms of language to communicate. Mastery of vocabulary and word order results in nothing if the learner cannot use those forms for the purpose of producing and understanding thoughts, ideas, and feelings.

According to Ovando (2005), there are five culture-related domains involved in learning a language. These include (1) *discourse*, or knowledge of how to organize the language in longer chunks; (2) *appropriateness*, involving knowledge of what types of language to use in different settings (for example, with friends versus in school); (3) *paralinguistics*, which captures the nonverbal aspects of communication such as gesture and distance from speaker; (4) *pragmatics*, or knowledge of the implicit norms governing communication in social settings, such as when to speak, how to pace talk, and politeness rules; and (5) *cognitive-academic language proficiency*, which describes the language skills needed to learn specialized content. The complexity of this knowledge and the ways in which it interacts in different languages and cultures highlight how culture-specific language acquisition really is.

> By talking with grownups and capable peers as they go about doing the kinds of things literate people do, children are able to construct meanings for tasks that they could not understand on their own . . . Such instruction actually transforms the child's development so that tomorrow the child is able to independently do what he could do only with assistance today. (McGill-Franzen, 1992, p. 58)

Of course, the social conventions of language are an important determinant of school achievement (see Chapter 5). They dictate how we should speak to different individuals in different contexts. "Languages grow and develop as tools of communication within a given environment. In this sense, there is no such thing as 'right' or 'wrong' language, only language that is appropriate or inappropriate in a given context" (Ovando, 2005, p. 291). Mismatches between school conventions and the conventions that children have learned at home can lead to poor performance and wrong judgments about children's ability to learn in school.

The language that children hear is the language that they learn. Children raised in homes where family members speak only Spanish learn to speak Spanish; children raised in homes where family members say "pahk the cah" learn to say that; and children whose family members call a drinking fountain a "bubbler" or soft drinks "pop" call them that too.

Some differences in linguistic experience are easily accommodated, while others may have a significant impact on the foundations of literacy. Hart and Risley (1995) followed a group of children between the ages of ten months and three years, assessing their language development and examining the language used in the home. The forty-two families in this study in England were classified by the researchers as "professional" (college professors), working class, and "welfare support." Over time, the children in all families acquired the structures and phonology of language equally well. However, by age 3, the cumulative vocabulary differences across the three groups was startling. On average, children from professional families knew 1,100 words, children from working class families knew 750 words, and children from welfare families knew a bit more than 500 words (Hart & Risley, 1995). The relationships between parental speech and interaction patterns were highly correlated with children's vocabulary, and, using an extrapolation method, the researchers concluded that, "by age three, children from privileged families have heard 30 million more words than children from poor families. By kindergarten the gap is even greater. The consequences are catastrophic" (Hart & Risley, 2003). As Hoff (2006) noted, "children cannot learn words they do not hear" (p. 166).

Vocabulary has received recent attention because it has become clear how important vocabulary and conceptual development are for later success in school settings.

> Taken together, the findings . . . are consistent with previous findings showing that early vocabulary skills are indirectly associated with reading during the first years of instruction but that early vocabulary has a direct long-term relation to reading comprehension in grades 3 and 4. (Senechal, Ouellette, & Rodney, 2006, p. 180)

However, poverty has a dramatic impact on all aspects of children's language and literacy attainment (see Neuman, 2006; Vasilyeva & Waterfall, 2011). Virtually every measure of early literacy ability, including phonological awareness, letter recognition, and concepts of print are lower among high-poverty children.

It is important to note that virtually all of the research (including the Hart and Risley study) has also revealed that it is the *nature* of early interactions and experience, rather than the degree of poverty or sociocultural context, that exerts an impact. The *quality* of support for literacy in the home is a more important predictor of student success than family income or educational attainment (Wasik & Hendrickson, 2006). That said, the nature of the home experiences that support and promote literacy are extensive, and poverty may tend to deny children access to these experiences because families are more likely to have limited levels of education themselves and/or cannot afford to pay for opportunities available to high-SES children. Of course, high-quality preschool experiences can also support language and literacy development (Barnett & Frede, 2011; Dickinson, McCabe, & Clark-Chiarelli, 2004, 2006).

Literacy experiences that have been associated with early success in reading and writing include the following (Landry & Smith, 2006; Ollila & Mayfield, 1992; Vasilyeva & Waterfall, 2011; Wasik & Hendrickson, 2004, 2006):

- Families provide a variety of writing materials.
- Parents or others read to children.
- Children observe others reading and writing.
- Children are encouraged to experiment in writing.
- Parents read aloud to their children.
- Parents or others answer questions about reading and writing.
- There are books in the home and/or children are taken to the library.
- Adults interact with children—talking, singing, and playing rhyming games.

These experiences set the stage for learning to read and write but also promote the acquisition of specific knowledge and skill. They are important for developing print awareness, understanding the forms and functions of print, analyzing the task of reading, and gaining control of literacy behaviors/activities. Importantly, different types of home and preschool experiences influence different aspects of children's emerging literacy. For example, shared storybook reading does not appear to have a significant impact on phonological skills, although it does have an impact of consequence on children's oral language (vocabulary) development and comprehension (see Mol et al., 2008; Whitehurst & Lonigan, 2001). On the other hand, parental efforts to teach their children about print (during shared reading as well as at other times) are significantly related to children's alphabet knowledge, word reading, and invented spelling in kindergarten and first grade (Justice & Piasta, 2011; Senechal, LeFevre, Thomas, & Daley, 1998).

Although all parents want the very best for their children, not all engage in school-valued interactions. As Hannon (1998) has noted, "although almost all parents attempt to assist literacy development in some way, they do not all do it in the same way, to the same extent, with the same concept of literacy, or with the same resources" (p. 122). In some communities of low socioeconomic condition, for example, mothers and their children are very adept at reading and talking about newspaper ads, but they are not experienced in reading and talking about alphabet books (Pellegrini, 2001). Some ethnic groups are more inclined than others to ask children questions as they engage in storybook reading (Heath, 1983; Vernon-Feagans, 1996). At the same time, it is certainly true that many low-income parents have less time and fewer resources to devote to those things that are linked to early reading success (see above). Importantly, there are also wide variations *within* ethnic and SES groups in the types of activities that families use (Burchinal & Forestieri, 2011; Hammer, Scarpino, & Davison, 2011).

Children can and do learn to speak their first language with widely variant approaches. Children from very diverse backgrounds can and do learn to read and write. For us, the important matter is to recognize what types of knowledge and skill children have acquired prior to their entry into schools. If we assume that children *must* know certain things or that they *must* use language in specified ways, then some children are destined to fail. It is much more important for us to remember that it is the match between children's experiences and our expectations that must be included in the assessment. Pelligrini (2001) reminds us that ". . . the degree of similarity between home and school literacy events predicts success in school-based literacy" (p. 55).

Learning about the Forms and Functions of Print.   Children understand the functional value and significance of literacy when they experience it directly—as they "read" street signs and soup cans, through storybook reading with their parents, and as they send cards or help to write grocery lists. Although being able to read and write does have utilitarian value, it appears that many middle-class families actually stress the entertainment value of learning to read as they engage their children in book activities (Baker, Scher, & Mackler, 1997). At the same time, children in urban settings often live in neighborhoods that provide extraordinary amounts of environmental print, often within culturally rich contexts (Orellana & Hernández, 1999). As Purcell-Gates (1996) reminds us, "young children begin to learn about reading and writing initially in their homes and communities as they observe and participate in culturally situated literacy" (p. 406). Learning to read and write requires a responsive partner and a supportive environment, so children who grow up in contexts with limited print, with adults who do not engage in reading and writing activities, are less likely to understand the value and functions of print (Lipson, Biggam, & Wixson, 2006; Neuman & Roskos, 1993). Among all parents, however, there is much less attention to print knowledge than might be expected. Helping parents to make the most of storybook reading experiences is likely to have a positive effect on children from all backgrounds (Justice & Piasta, 2011).

Developing Print Awareness or Concepts of Print.   Children in our society are surrounded by print—on doors, cereal boxes, signs, television, even clothing. It appears that they acquire, at an early age, a fairly sophisticated understanding that these symbols convey meaning, although it may be that this understanding is not directly related to specific insights into the speech-print match. Over the years, researchers have begun to question the usefulness of this generalized awareness called "environmental print awareness" (for example, Ehri, 1987; Kassow, 2006), but it does seem that situational print awareness is part of a larger progression of acquired skill and knowledge for many children.

Just as children must come to understand the functional, meaningful nature of spoken language, they must also appreciate that print is communicative, functional, and meaningful. Available evidence suggests that most children in our society have a fairly well-developed "sense of print awareness in situational contexts" by the time they reach school age (Heath, 1983; Whitehurst & Lonigan, 2001). For example, Hiebert (1981) found that three-, four-, and five-year-old children were all sensitive to differences between print and drawing stimuli. In addition, when presented with words and letters in meaningful contexts, even very young children demonstrate competence in understanding concepts such as word and letter, provided they are not asked to use or understand specific terminology. Perhaps as a result of this early development, research suggests that *environmental* print awareness is not highly related to subsequent success in conventional reading (Kassow, 2006).

On the other hand, print awareness in the form of *concepts of print* has great importance for children's literacy development (Clay, 1979). The continuum of print awareness includes: knowing the difference between pictures and words, recognizing print in many forms and formats, understanding the difference between letters and words, understanding that print corresponds to speech, understanding the directionality of written language, and understanding that lines of text are read from top to bottom (Justice & Piasta, 2011; Lesiak, 1997; Whitehurst & Lonigan, 2001).

Some children copy from books or signs, others write notes or letters to friends and relatives. Many young children engage in "scribble writing" at a very early age and announce, as three-year-old Theo did, "Oh, I think I'll write in cursive." What is especially revealing is that children's early scribbles vary from culture to culture, reflecting the characteristics of adult writing in that system. So, for example, although young U.S. children and young Egyptian and Israeli children all scribble, the physical appearance of the scribbles are very different, though the purpose and intent are remarkably similar (Harste, Woodward, & Burke, 1984). As children develop, they acquire more and more specific ideas about how print is organized and why we read, gradually learning that (in English) graphemes represent phonemes and beginning to identify the specific graphemes used for specific phonemes.

Alphabet Knowledge.   Learning letter names and acquiring knowledge of the correspondences between letters and sounds is an important accomplishment in the development of both reading and writing ability. It is important to understand that alphabet knowledge is developed unevenly and is clearly not a prerequisite for launching reading and writing instruction. Treiman and Kessler (2003) reviewed research related to children's acquisition of letter-name knowledge and also their learning of letter-sound relationships, in both English and other languages. The review provides important insights into the normal course of development among English-speaking U.S. children. The researchers' first conclusion is that, in the United States, most children who are four years old know at least some letter names and sounds. Most teachers will not be surprised to learn that the reviewed the research indicates that young children learn uppercase letters before they learn lowercase letters, and that the most well-known letter for all children is the one that begins their own name! In addition, "among U.S. children, the ability to provide sounds for individual letters, which we refer to as letter-sound knowledge, lags behind the ability to provide the letters' names" (p. 110).

The Treiman and Kessler analysis provides other insights also. Some letters of the alphabet are recognized earlier and more frequently than others. In terms of *letter-name knowledge*, the visual appearance of the letters is a major determinant of performance. The most commonly recognized uppercase letters were A and O—both visually distinctive. In addition, children are much more likely to recognize lowercase letters when they are visually similar to the uppercase version of that letter (*o*, *s*, *w*, and *x*, for example). The lowercase letters that are most difficult for children to name appear to be those that are visually similar to other letters and are also different from their uppercase counterpart: *d*, *g*, *h*, *l*, and *q*.

In terms of letter-sound knowledge, there are also interesting differences. When the three- and four-year-olds the researchers examined were asked to provide the sounds of letters, the most commonly known correspondences were for *B*, *G*, *K*, *O*, *P*, *T*, and *Z*. Treiman and Kessler point out that children appear to find these easier because the phoneme represented by the letter—or a common sound for that letter—appears as the initial sound of the letter's name. In other words, children appear to use their knowledge of letter names to support the acquisition of sound-symbol knowledge: "'Children who know the names of letters can take advantage of certain relations between printed and spoken words . . . this helps children move from treating printed words as arbitrary visual patterns to treating them as maps of linguistic structure" (p. 133).

Of course, different children know different specific letter names and letter-sound relationships. Importantly, children whose first language (L1) is not English are very likely to draw on their knowledge of letter names in their first language, and, of course, their sound-symbol knowledge is likely to be affected by this prior knowledge. Letter-name knowledge would appear to be easy to assess, but some assessments do not take into account differences in upper and lower case, nor do they consider the font used in the assessment task. Treiman and Kessler also note that it is important to assess letter-sound knowledge using letters that students can name (and observe whether these are upper or lower case).

Understanding the Language of Books through Joint Book Reading.   Despite many commonalities, oral and written language are not identical, and young children need to learn the language of books. *Read-aloud transactions* or *shared book experiences* provide a pleasurable and supportive environment for this type of literacy learning. The Commission on Reading concluded in its 1985 report that "the single most important activity for building the knowledge required for eventual success in reading is reading aloud to children" (R. C. Anderson, Hiebert, Scott, & Wilkinson, 1985). Since then, educators and researchers have become even more united in their perception that joint book reading activities are critical for developing the foundations of literacy.

Perhaps because of this, storybook reading interactions have been well studied over the past two decades (Bus, 2001; Mol et al., 2011; van Kleeck, 2004/2006; Vernon-Feagans, Hammer, Miccio, & Manlove, 2001). The benefits of reading aloud to children and interacting with them about books are many: children's vocabularies are improved, they understand the language of books better, they acquire knowledge about literacy conventions, and it improves their metalinguistic awareness. Children also become familiar with the look of print, the direction of it, and the ways in which pages are turned to move through text (Clay, 1979; Karweit & Wasik, 1996), although the benefits to print knowledge vary depending on the degree to which adults draw children's attention to those elements (Justice & Piasta, 2011). This knowledge is as useful for writing as for reading. For example, one of the most important differences between spoken and written language is that written language is "decontextualized." This means that written language is produced so that it does not require the writer and the reader to share a physical context. To accomplish this, authors use a variety of cohesive devices to link information together in a meaningful whole. Children must learn to attend to the cues and referents that authors use, for sorting out events and motives and using them intentionally in their own writing for others to understand the messages they compose.

Increasingly, researchers are studying not only the specific knowledge gleaned during reading aloud, but also the lessons learned from the exchanges themselves. These events often provide opportunities for adults to model appropriate thinking and feeling responses. This active interaction with text is necessary, of course, if children are to become competent readers and skillful writers. In addition, these read-aloud transactions teach children to question the meaning of text and encourage them to begin to think and use language in ways that will later be critical for school success (Altwerger, Diehl-Faxon, & Dockstader-Anderson, 1985; Yaden et al., 2000).

Of course, the lessons learned are highly dependent on the specific interactional styles modeled, and there is considerable evidence to suggest differences among parents from diverse socioeconomic and ethnic groups (Heath, 1983; Pellegrini, Perlmutter, Galda, & Brody, 1990; Vernon-Feagans et al., 2001). Importantly, the quantity of storybook and shared reading varies enormously, and children from working-class homes engage in much less of this type of activity than do children from middle-class homes (Payne, Whitehurst, & Angell, 1994). Reese and Cox (1999) examined parents' reading styles and identified three distinct patterns (similar to those described by others):

- *Describer style:* The parent provides descriptive language and elicits labels.
- *Comprehender style:* The parent focuses on inferences, meaning, and predictions.
- *Performance style:* The parent reads through the story in a largely uninterrupted way, although conversation precedes and follows the reading.

In this study, the describer style was more likely to generate gains in vocabulary and print skills, but the results varied depending on the level of language development of the child. For example, children with strong vocabulary abilities tended to benefit from the performance style.

Not surprisingly, parents' own literacy experiences appeared to determine opportunities for young children to become involved in literacy-related interactions. Parents were more inclined to respond to their child's interest in books when they had a positive orientation toward literacy, which was manifested in mutually enjoyable book-reading sessions" (Bus, 2001, p. 186). The most experienced parents, regardless of socioeconomic or racial background, tended to shape the reading experience to their child's interests and abilities. Thus, with very young children, the book events tended to include a great deal of picture discussion and labeling, whereas more-experienced children and adults focused on comprehending the story, often with discussion throughout.

Because researchers have also observed systematic differences between parents from different backgrounds, it is important to be aware of differences that orient young children to one approach versus another. For example, Vernon-Feagans et al. (2001) observed that African American children have much less experience with question-and-answer formats than Caucasian children do. Importantly, however, the effects of joint book reading override any variations in approach—reading to children makes a difference across many settings and styles (Bus, vanIjzendoorn, & Pelligrini, 1995).

Understanding Narrative Story Structure.   Read-aloud transactions help children begin to internalize different structures for different types of text. Research suggests that young children need a well-developed sense of story to comprehend text fully. In addition, story sense appears helpful in generating predictions about upcoming text and also in remembering (or reconstructing) stories. As well, children's early oral narrative abilities often predict their later reading abilities (Dickinson & McCabe, 2001; Griffin, Hemphill, Camp, & Wolf, 2004; Hemphill & Snow, 1996; Roth, Speece, & Cooper, 2002).

Well-read-to youngsters generate a mental map for stories during the many interactions they have with storybook text (Mandler & Johnson, 1977; Stein & Glenn, 1979). These mental maps, or "story schema," are generalized structures that people use to comprehend and remember (Alexander & Jetton, 2000). Several types of story structures have been proposed. The stories children encounter in school settings typically contain the following elements:

Setting: generally the physical setting and characters

Initiating event: "It all started when . . ."

Internal response: how the main character reacts to the initiating event

Attempt: an action or series of actions by the character(s) to try to reach a goal or solve a problem

Consequence: what happens as a result of the attempt

Reaction: a final reaction or event that ties the rest of the story together (also called a resolution)

These features actually describe the elements present in stories that come from the European folk and fable tradition (Stein & Glenn, 1979). Other stories have different types of arrangements and are reflected in the stories children tell and in their comprehension of stories heard or read (Bloom et al., 2001; Gee, 1989; Minami & McCabe, 1991, 1995). Many experiences with different types of texts encourage children to see that stories have certain predictable features and that these can be relied upon to aid comprehension and memory.

Not surprisingly, children's ability to tell their own spontaneous narratives is also fueled by their language development and their experiences with stories—what Lee et al. (2004) call "narrative socialization." Recent research demonstrates that "the preferred way of telling stories varies from culture to culture . . . and children typically adopt the narrative style of their own community" (Gleason, 1997, p. 409). Students who have experienced stories that unfold in different ways or have symbols and meanings different from European folktales will have a different sense of story. They will have different mental maps available for comprehension. For example, Hispanic narratives revolve around personal and family relationships rather than events and what happened; indeed, they may combine things that happened at different times to different people (McCabe, 1992; McCabe & Bliss, 2003; Rodino et al., 1991). The story structure of narratives told by African American children (especially girls) tends to differ from that of white, middle-class children (Gee, 1989; Lee et al., 2004), and Japanese narratives are different yet (Minami, 2002).

Teachers and other professionals need to be aware of the ways in which children's narrative styles may vary from white, middle-class "norms" (Ely, 2005). As Klingner, Vaughn, and Boardman (2007) have noted, "unique cultural patterns affect students' understanding and recall of a story . . . as well as the type of information recalled" (p. 78). Importantly, failure to recognize these differences may cause teachers to misjudge children's competence during assessment, making them believe that students have poor narrative abilities when, in fact, they may be very competently reflecting the narrative structures and patterns they have learned.

Of course, children's primary language is also a factor in assessment. In order to appear competent, young English language learners must manage both a second language itself (forms, syntax, vocabulary, etc.) and also the narrative structures common to speakers of that language. Many very young L2 learners provide much more complete retellings if they are allowed to substitute their first language for key English vocabulary words they don't know or can't remember (García, 1991). This is likely to help educators separate out linguistic from cultural (and more general cognitive) differences. Our experience suggests that even native speakers may look different under different task conditions. In Figure 7.3, for example, you can see Ian's attempt at telling a story, which is weak and ill-formed. You can also see that when he is asked to tell a personal narrative ("tell a story about something that happened to you"), his knowledge and skill look far more impressive. Ian was a young, first-grade child from an isolated rural community. His experiences with literature and formal school tasks were very scant. However, his large, extended family obviously provided considerable experience in telling and retelling personal narratives.

The oral and written stories of less-skilled readers and writers are often less coherent and well developed than those told or written by their skilled classmates (Montague, Cleborne, Maddux, & Dereshiwsky, 1990). Research has consistently indicated that struggling readers produce poor narratives and have difficulty recalling narratives they have heard. In particular, they tend to delete causal and temporal connections from their stories (Dickinson & McCabe, 1991; Peterson, Jesso, & McCabe, 1999). Interestingly,

FIGURE 7.3
Ian's Storytelling and Personal Narrative

IAN, grade 2
I. Story Narrative: "Tell me a story"
Monster Meals. Monsters eat meals. Put some car doors, some old shoes, some nails. That's how monsters eat their meals. And I made that up.
II. Personal Narrative: "Sometimes people tell stories about a time when something exciting or sad happened, or about a good time with a friend. Did anything like that ever happen to you? Tell me a story about it."
When I was in kindergarten, my teacher told me to get off the ice. I didn't. I threw out a rock about this big and I went to go get it. I slipped and the rock landed on my thumb and I broke by thumb. And that hurt. (Pause.) They said my thumb was too small for a cast, so they said, "Gauze it up." So that's what my mom and dad put on it—gauze.
III. Retelling: "Now, tell *me* that story."
Dogger
There was this little boy that had a dog. He lost him. His parents and him were searching, but he didn't find him until they went to the fair and a little girl bought him. And he said, "Well," and his sister said, "Would you swap this teddy bear for my brother's dog back, please?" And she smiled. And then he said, "Did you like that teddy bear anyway?" She said, "No, I didn't like him because his eyes were too scary." And she said, "If I had another teddy in my bed, there wouldn't be room for me." They used to walk him like a real dog, and his mother showed him how to wash him. And sometimes he'd pull him in a wagon.

Gutiérrez-Clellen (2002) found that these students performed better on measures of recall and comprehension in the language used for classroom instruction, perhaps because the expectations of the assessment and the language of instruction are more closely aligned.

General literacy experiences such as read-aloud transactions provide children with the information they need to generate good hypotheses about conventional literacy. If children come to school without these experiences, the instructional program should build on the specific experiences children bring with them.

The Development of Written Language

In the same way that reading experiences promote phonemic awareness, writing appears to develop print-level awareness and skill. When very young children attempt to write, they manage the competing demands of meaning (the message they want to write) and form (mechanics). This often propels them forward in their metalinguistic understanding of the alphabetic principle. DeFord (1991) noted,

> When young children write, the reading/writing process is conveniently slowed down; to form messages and print, children must work on a variety of levels. They have to think about what they want to say, what they hear and how they represent it, what they expect to see if they can't hear it and it doesn't look right, where they are in their message, and how they can make their message clear to other readers . . . As young writers focus in on smaller or physical aspects of writing, they learn certain principles about print formation, letter-sound relationships, spelling patterns, and the meaning of certain morphological forms. (pp. 86, 88)

In the intervening years, researchers from a variety of philosophical perspectives have come to value the relationships between early reading and early writing (see below). As children increase their understanding of the requirements of reading and writing, they begin to acquire more cognitive control over their own literacy skills.

The Form and Function of Writing.   It seems clear that young children acquire writing competence by writing—in much the same way that they become competent in speech by talking. This does not, of course, happen without a supportive and responsive environment. When children see others around them using writing for functional purposes, they will model their own behavior accordingly, writing lists and messages and signs during play and to signal wants and needs. Of course, these notes and signs will reflect the child's knowledge and skill in writing.

The following stages are evident in the writing development of most children (DeFord, 1980; Sulzby, Teale, & Kambrelis, 1989).

- Scribbling
- Differentiation between drawing and writing
- Controlled scribbling; wavy and letter-like scribbles that are more carefully placed on the page, using left-to-right motion and top-to-bottom directionality
- Development of letters and letter-like shapes
- Combination of letters, possibly with spaces, indicating understanding of units (letters, words, sentences), but may not show letter-sound correspondence

- Writing known, isolated words; developing letter-sound correspondence
- Writing simple sentences with use of inventive spellings
- Combining two or more sentences to express complete thoughts
- Control of punctuation—periods, capitalization, use of upper- and lowercase letter
- Form of discourse—stories, information material, letters, and so on

Caution should be exercised in interpreting this information, because many of these characteristics will be evident simultaneously as children gain control over written forms.

Invented Spelling.   The term *invented spelling* is a considered one. It is used to refer to a consistent phenomenon observed in young emergent readers/writers: the ability to invent spellings on their own. It is increasingly clear that children's developing spelling abilities reflect their growing linguistic knowledge and control. As children acquire the conventions and patterns of a language, these appear in their own writing. "Invented spelling appears to be a vehicle through which children grapple with and begin to understand the alphabetic principle (that letters represent sounds)" (Whitehurst & Lonigan, 2001, p. 18). Thus, spelling "errors" across children are not random, as can be seen from the sample in Figure 7.4. This sample demonstrates how Kelly's writing reflects a rather considerable knowledge base; what appear to be mistakes are not. She can already isolate all initial and final consonants and represent them appropriately in print. Indeed, she can also represent most medial sounds.

**FIGURE 7.4
Writing Sample
(Age 6)**

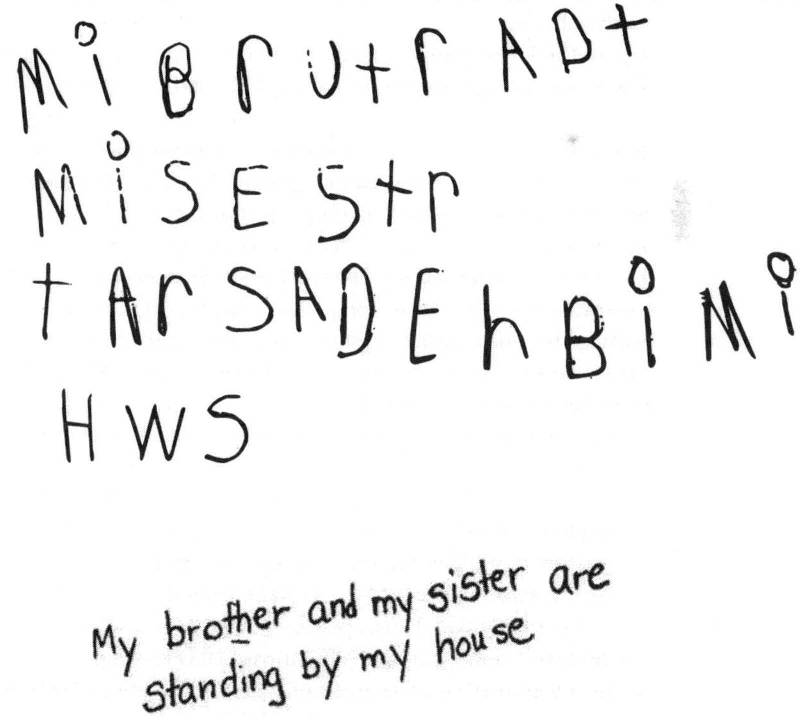

My brother and my sister are standing by my house

This ability to isolate and represent phonemes sets the stage for more-advanced decoding work. Torgesen and Davis (1996), for example, found that the best predictor of kindergarten children's success in a phonological training program was their pretest scores on a measure of invented spelling. Indeed, these authors have subsequently argued that a test of invented spelling is one of the very best ways to evaluate students' reading progress. At the same time, it appears that instructional programs that encourage young (grades K and 1) children to use invented spelling are likely to enhance students' reading development (Clarke, 1988; Torgesen & Burgess, 1996).

Emergent readers and writers proceed through distinctive developmental stages, moving from very immature spellings to those that approximate standard spellings (e.g., Gentry, 1982, 2000; Henderson, 1990; Templeton & Bear, 1992). Although there are some disputes about the content of each stage, the following distinctions are generally evident in the development of very young writers (see also Figure 2.2). Subsequent development of spelling knowledge and skill is discussed in Chapter 9.

Prephonemic Spelling.   Here, children use alphabetic symbols to "write" words, but these are generally unrelated to the target word. No sound-symbol relationship is present, and these are likely to reflect earlier notions about how the writing system works (see Ferreiro & Teberosky, 1979/1982).

Early Phonemic (or Semiphonemic) Spelling.   Children exhibit a clear awareness that there is a relationship between phonemes and print. However, children represent very little of the phonemic information in print—sometimes the initial, sometimes the final, graphemes. The letters that are used represent specific phonemes from the word, but not all the phonemes are represented. Example: DR GML 5—Dear Grandma.

Phonetic (and Letter Name) Spelling.   Children hear and produce sequences of sounds in words. At this stage, children may produce spellings that are quite readable ("wns" for *once* and "bik" for *bike*). However, children at this stage are also often using a strategy that results in rather strange productions. As they try to represent more and more sounds in words, they begin to use a *letter-name strategy* (Beers & Henderson, 1977). That is, they analyze the word they want to spell into its component sounds and then find a letter name to represent each sound. They then spell each sound by choosing the letter name that most closely resembles the sound they want to represent (Gillet & Temple, 1982). Thus, children in this stage also produce such words as "lavatr" for *elevator* (Morris, 1981). This approach causes problems in correct production of vowels and certain consonant combinations, in particular.

Transitional or Within-Word Pattern Spelling.   In this stage, children's spellings bear a much closer resemblance to standard spellings. They make use of visual as well as phonemic information (Gentry, 1982). Children generally represent short vowels appropriately in this stage and also mark long vowels, even though these often represent overgeneralizations of learned rules. Thus, spellings such as the following are typical of this stage: "dres" for *dress* and "rane" for *rain*. As Morris (1981) notes, "These transitional spellings, which begin to appear in late first grade or early second grade, are to be welcomed by the teacher, for they signal advancement in the child's understanding of English spelling. No longer does the child believe that spelling is a fixed, simple code in which letters map to sounds in a left-to-right, one-to-one fashion" (p. 664). As Templeton (1997) has noted, children in this phase understand the *patterns* that make up the letter-sound relationships.

Of course, the written productions of ELL children will look different. Importantly, however, there is evidence that children will use the same strategies in their invented spelling. Gort (2006), for example, reports that first graders whose L1 is Spanish employ their knowledge of Spanish sound-symbol relationships in English-language writing (e.g., "gat" for *got* and "tu" for *too*). Children's inventive spellings can provide a great deal of information about their emergent literacy skills. As Bear et al. (2012) have noted, there is a "synchrony of reading, writing, and spelling development" (p. 15). This means that development in one area is related to advances in the other areas. As children learn how written language works in English and how the sounds are represented in print, they use that knowledge in both writing and reading. Spelling continues to develop in a systematic way right through the early middle school years (see Chapter 9 for consideration of spelling development beyond the within-word phase).

STRATEGIES AND TOOLS FOR ASSESSING THE FOUNDATIONS OF LITERACY

Gathering dependable and useful information about the literacy abilities of young children can be a very tricky business. In this chapter, we describe a number of informal and standardized assessment strategies for observation, structured informal assessment, and diagnostic teaching. Before we turn our attention to these specific practices, however, it is important to consider the problems associated with the assessment of early literacy.

Assessment of Early Language and Literacy

With increased attention to RTI, screening and monitoring assessments of early literacy knowledge and skill will, no doubt, proliferate, and educators should consider their technical attributes very carefully.

Early literacy assessments generally share several significant problems. First, test results of very young children often do not predict future failure—they are typically better at predicting future success (Snow, Burns, & Griffin, 1998). They simply do not provide sufficient evidence of predictive validity to warrant making judgments about students' future performance. "Available tests for screening and identifying children with literacy problems have a 50% error rate according to data from the National Association for the Education of Young Children (1991); that is, they frequently over- or under-identify students in need of further services" (Roth, 2004/2006, p. 470).

This concern was articulated in a report on early childhood assessment. In 2006, Congress asked the National Research Council to study appropriate assessment for young children, and among the guidelines they proposed is a special alert related to screening: "screening assessment should be done only when the available instruments are informative and have good predictive validity" (Snow & Van Hemel, 2008, p. 8). They note that norming and validation studies for tests in early childhood are too often inadequate.

A second problem relates to the extent to which early literacy assessments are actually measures of students' opportunity to learn. Children from low-income families, minority children, and children from homes where English is not the first language often get lower scores because they have not acquired knowledge and skills that appear on school assessments. A final concern is also worth noting. Although we understand the foundations of literacy a great deal better today than we did two decades ago, the caution offered by Teale, Hiebert, and Chittenden in 1987 is still too often true: "Young children's reading and writing are being measured in ways that do not reflect an adequate conceptualization of early literacy development or sensitivity to the fact that children of age 4 or 5 have special social and developmental characteristics" (p. 773). Unusual or highly constrained tests are often so alien that young children don't recognize them as occasions for demonstrating what they know. The National Research Council guidelines are especially insistent that early childhood assessment be part of a larger systemic approach that includes standards and instruction, as well as socio-emotional considerations.

These concerns suggest that caution needs to be exercised in assessing young children. Ongoing and continuous assessment are especially important, because the literacy abilities of young children often change quite rapidly. Multiple types and forms of assessments increase the likelihood that children will show us all they know.

We have updated the list of attributes necessary for the assessment of children's early literacy abilities proposed in 1987, using recommendations proposed by Neisworth and Bagnato (2005) for the Division for Early Childhood of the Council of Exceptional Children and the National Research Council (Snow & Van Hemel, 2008). Early literacy assessment should:

1. Be useful (appropriate for the purpose and supportive of children's literacy development)
2. Occur as a part of instruction
3. Be authentic and varied (observe children during daily routines)
4. Have breadth (reflect the various dimensions of literacy)
5. Be sensitive and continuous (capture small increments and reflect varied contexts)
6. Be appropriate for children's developmental levels and cultural/linguistic background
7. Be acceptable (family and professionals agree beforehand to the assessment)
8. Be collaborative (parents and professionals make decisions together)
9. Attend to equity (individual differences are considered)
10. Assess the environments in which children are spending time for opportunities to learn

These characteristics are entirely consistent with our approach to *all* assessment, but they are critical in evaluating the knowledge and skill of very young children. Only a few formal assessments meet these standards, although a number of structured, developmental screening tools are available (see Meisels, Jablon, Diehtelmiller, Marsden, & Dorfman, 2001) that can be exceptionally helpful in assessing early literacy. The majority of early literacy assessment is conducted less formally, and, as a result, the need for organized means of managing data in the assessment of young, or very disabled, readers and writers is especially great (see Snow & Van Hemel, 2008).

Gathering dependable and useful information about the foundations of literacy requires continuous observation of children in actual literacy settings. As assessment is planned, it is helpful to reflect on the following questions:

- What do I already know about this child?
- How do I know that?

A summary form such as the one shown in Figure 7.5 should be used to organize information as it is gathered.

As we begin to look more closely at students who seem to be struggling, it can be particularly important to involve parents. Parents are particularly good sources of information about a student's background, because they have enduring contact with their child. They have information about the child's overall experiential background and developmental history that includes knowledge about physical, cultural, linguistic, affective, and cognitive factors (see Chapter 5 for further information about eliciting family history). Asking parents to complete a brief information sheet (or meeting briefly with parents to ask these questions in person) can provide important insights into the development and interests of specific students (see Figure 7.6).

In the following sections, we describe standardized assessments of key elements of emergent literacy as well as assessment strategies that can be conducted during everyday instructional exchanges. Classroom-based strategies, sometimes called curriculum-embedded performance assessments (Meisels, 1998) or formative assessments, involve both careful observation of children engaged in normal instructional events and observations of children in situations that have been structured by the teacher to assess specific components of literacy. Recommendations for early literacy instruction virtually always acknowledge the critical role of the less formal assessments and the need to employ multiple strategies, often captured in a literacy portfolio (see Jones, 2003; Neuman, Copple, & Bredekamp, 2000). In Figure 7.7, we have summarized most of the major component abilities relevant for examining emergent literacy and indicated the assessment strategies that can be used to capture that information. For each assessment technique described here, we indicate the types of information that can be gathered. Early literacy assessments can provide rich data about children, but it is important to guard against hasty judgments and assumptions. Conclusions *must* be documented and, given the rapid changes in learning that can occur in young children, it is important to gather multiple samples and observations. The strategies and forms provided below can help you bring an interpretive framework to these "raw data."

Observing Spontaneous Use of Knowledge and Skill

The procedures described in this section are especially central to early literacy assessment, because the knowledge and skill that very young students possess is more likely to be contextually bound and may be difficult to assess in contrived assessment contexts. Observations and interviews of students can provide good initial information about oral language development and concepts about print, but they are also useful in diagnosing specific difficulties and areas of strength.

FIGURE 7.5
Summary/Planning Form: Foundations of Literacy

Student: _____ Age: _____ Date: _____
Examiner: _____

I. Oral Language
    A. First language
    B. Phonological development
    C. Vocabulary
    D. Syntactic sophistication
    E. Pragmatics (functions and uses of language)

II. Literacy Knowledge/Experience
    A. Family/home print-literacy environment
    B. Print awareness (environmental)
    C. Book concepts (language, directionality, etc.)
    D. Concept of word (boundaries and linearity)
    E. Speech-to-print match
    F. Alphabet knowledge
        1. Uppercase
        2. Lowercase
        3. Letter-sound knowledge
    G. Phonological awareness
        1. Words
        2. Syllables
        3. Rhyming
        4. Phonemic segmentation
            A. blending
            B. segmenting
            C. deleting
            D. substituting

III. Sense of Story
    A. Retelling using narrative structure
    B. Comprehension
    C. Dictated stories
    D. Language use

IV. Writing
    A. Forms and functions of writing
    B. Invented spelling

V. Observations and Comments
    A. Checklists
    B. Observation notes
    C. Artifacts
    D. Environmental scan

FIGURE 7.6 Observation Guide for Parents (Early Literacy)

My Child as an Early Reader and Writer			
Name: _____ Date: _____			
Grade:_____			
Observe your child or think about the observations you've made in the past. Please comment as appropriate.			
	Yes	**No**	**Comments/Examples**
1. My child likes to listen to me read to him/her.	☐	☐	
2. My child likes to spend time looking at books.	☐	☐	
3. My child is interested in letters and words.	☐	☐	
4. My child likes to use crayons and pencils to "write" (this may include scribble writing).	☐	☐	
5. My child asks me how to spell some words.	☐	☐	
6. My child can recognize some familiar words (street or store signs, food names).	☐	☐	
7. My child can name some letters of the alphabet.	☐	☐	
8. My child tries to spell words using sounds and alphabet names.	☐	☐	
9. I can tell that my child understands stories when we read them together.	☐	☐	
10. My child is interested in learning to read and write.	☐	☐	

Questions for you:

1. Does your child have any books of her/his own? If so, how many?
2. Do you or someone else in the family go to the library to take out books?
3. Does your family have any children's magazine subscriptions?
4. Does someone in your family read to your child? If so, how often?
5. Does your child see anyone in the house reading or writing? Can you give examples?

FIGURE 7.7 Components of Emergent Literacy Assessment

Foundations of Literacy: Informal Techniques for Assessing Component Abilities

	Oral Language Competence	Print Awareness	Concepts of Book Print	Story Sense	Phonological and Phonemic Awareness	Speech-Print Match	Concept of Reading/ Writing
	Developmentally appropriate articulation and syntax Age-appropriate morphology Adequate vocabulary Elaborated use of language Wide range of language functions English language proficiency	Recognizes environmental print Recognizes various functions of print Print carries meaning	Parts of book (front, back, etc.) Directionality/orientation Language of book print (word/letter) Punctuation	Recognizes/recalls story elements Produces well-structured narratives Retains structure during recall	Word segmentation Syllable segmentation Onset-rime Phoneme segmentation • Identifies number of phonemes in word • Segments word into phonemes • Synthesizes and blends phonemes	Matches spoken word to print Recognizes some sight vocabulary Initial sound-symbol correspondence Naming speed	Alphabet knowledge Attempts reading/writing Knows letter names Uses some invented spelling
Assessment Strategy Informal observation	X XXXXX	XXX	X XXX	XXX	XXXXXXX	XXX	XXXX
Structured interview	X XXXXX	XXX	X XXX	XXX	XXXXXXX	XXXX	XXXX
Structured observation	X XXXXX	XXX	X XXX	XXX	XXXXXXX	XXXX	XXXX
Retailing guides	X XX X	X	XX	XXX		XXXX	
Dictated stories	X XXX X	X	XXXX	X		XXX	XX

	1	2	3	4	5	6	7
Writing samples	X	X X	X		X X X X X X X	X X X	X X X X
Joint-reading inventory	X X		X X X X	X		X X X	X X X
Standardized Assessment Tools							
TOLD, PPVT, etc.	X	X X					
Woodcock-Muñoz Language Survey – Revised-NU	X	X X	X				
IDEA Oral Language Proficiency Test (IPT I-English)	X	X X	X				
Test of Early Reading Ability-3		X	X X X			X X X	X X X
Phonological Awareness Literacy Screening (PALS)			X X X	X	X X X X	X X X	X X X
Early Reading Diagnostic Assessment (ERDA)				X	X X X X	X X X X	X X X

Teacher Rating of Oral Language and Literacy (TROLL).   This research-based assessment tool (see Dickinson, McCabe, & Sprague, 2003) was designed to provide a reliable and valid instrument for teachers to use in evaluating several critical aspects of students' early literacy development, including language, reading, and writing abilities. TROLL draws on benchmark abilities in speaking and listening that have been described for children of pre K to grade 3 (New Standards Project, Tucker & Codding, 1998). TROLL is designed for teacher use, with the expectation that teachers will track students' progress on a variety of language arts dimensions. Teachers rate students using a rubric related to specific abilities. Figure 7.8 presents a sample from TROLL.

In addition to language use in communicating personal experiences, as shown in Figure 7.8, TROLL items focus on other aspects of language use, vocabulary development, ability to engage in emergent reading and writing activities, and phonological segmentation abilities. These items yield various subtotals (writing, oral language, and reading) as well as a total TROLL score. The authors provide an extremely useful table that transforms the total TROLL scores into percentiles and provides recommendations/interpretations of these scores for children ages 3, 4, and 5. Because the tool is easily used by classroom teachers with no formal training, its authors hope that it will be used to flag struggling students so that appropriate instruction can be provided. In addition, it is available online at http://www.ciera.org/library/reports/inquiry-3/3-016/3-016.pdf.

Oral Language Checklists.   Teachers need to assess oral language competence to ensure that children can accomplish the tasks required in school settings (see Chapter 2). School tasks demand language use that is quite different from the language used in homes and among peers. Thus, even if children have language development appropriate to their home environment, they may not have acquired language appropriate for functioning in a school setting.

FIGURE 7.8 Sample Assessment from TROLL

Item 2 asks: "How well does the child *communicate personal experiences* in a clear and logical way?" Assign the score that best describes this child when he/she is attempting to tell an adult about events at home or some other place where you were not present.

1	2	3	4
Child is very tentative, only offers a few words, requires you to ask questions. Has difficulty responding to questions you ask.	Child offers some information, but additional information needed to really understand the event (e.g., where or when it happened, who was present, the sequence of what happened).	Child offers information and sometimes includes the necessary information to really understand the event.	Child freely offers information and tells experiences in a way that is nearly always complete, well sequenced, and comprehensible.

Source: Based on material from Dickinson, D. K., McCabe, A., & Sprague, K. (2001). *Teacher rating of oral language and literacy (TROLL): A research-based tool* (CIERA Report #3-016, p. 15). Ann Arbor, MI: Center for the Improvement of Early Reading Achievement.

Researchers and educators have come to realize that language is difficult to evaluate through short, controlled samples. Therefore, people who study language acquisition now frequently recommend evaluating language in naturalistic settings (see Lund & Duchan, 1988; MacSwan & Rolstad, 2006). This means talking and listening to children engaged in everyday school activities. However, if children's primary language differs in important ways from school English, observations may be conducted in other settings as well to distinguish generalized linguistic problems from issues of context and culture.

What is needed is an inclination to notice and a willingness to make narrative notes. A framework is helpful to focus the "noticing." Observations of children's functional use of language are relatively easy to make. For more-specific aspects of oral language, a diagnostic checklist can be useful in focusing attention. The one in Figure 7.9 was adapted from several sources (Rubin, 2000; O'Malley & Valdez Pierce, 1996; Valdez Pierce & O'Malley, 1992). As you observe the child, note the time, setting, materials, and activity, and also indicate which functions of language are being used. In addition, specific examples of language used should be noted next to each function; the child's actual word usage and syntax can be quite revealing. This approach works well in most classrooms for young children, because there may be times when children are in several centers around the room. Teachers can target one or several children for observation on a particular day. Many teachers find sticky-backed notepads useful.

English Language Learners. With students who are learning English as a second language, we need to be aware of the complex interplay between and among the language and

FIGURE 7.9 Oral Communication and Language Development Checklist

Checklist for Assessing Oral Communication and Language Development		
Student's Name:	Home Language:	
Grade:		
Teacher:		
Indicator	**Yes**	**No**
Oral Language Comprehension Understands normal classroom discussions/conversation without difficulty Repetition is sometimes necessary for understanding Has great difficulty following what is said Understands conversations with peers in social or family context		
Speech Articulation: The child's speech is Comprehensible Audible Fluent (versus halting and hesitant) Expressive Specific phonological difficulties:		

FIGURE 7.9 (Continued)

Pragmatics Facial expressions are appropriate for message Uses Hands effectively Controls body movements Maintains appropriate distance while speaking Uses appropriate touching		
Vocabulary Age-appropriate Rich Varied Accurate Local/home usage Context-appropriate		
Syntax Child uses age-appropriate construction of sentences Uses sentence fragments Uses complex sentences Uses standard English Uses regional variation or dialect English is not the dominant language for this child.		
Conversation and discourse Engages in conversation freely Respects other persons when speaking Can enter into class discussions Maintains topic Discourse is coherent Requires context to understand conversation and/or topic Flexible participation in varied settings with multiple partners		
Functions and uses of language. The child uses language to ■ explore the environment ■ acquire information ■ describe events or share information ■ role-play, imagine narrative, create drama, do puppetry, and engage in other creative purposes ■ gain and maintain attention ■ communicate feelings ■ make demands or meet needs ■ share thoughts and ideas Other:		

Source: Adapted from Rubin, D. (2000). *Teaching elementary language arts: A balanced approach* (6th ed., pp. 113–114). Copyright © 2000. Boston: Allyn & Bacon. Reprinted by permission.

literacy abilities. To the extent that it is available, we have embedded information about ELL students throughout the text. Clearly, these children, like all children, vary in their knowledge and skill about the foundations of literacy: "they are a diverse population that includes a wide range of languages, ethnicities, nationalities, and socioeconomic backgrounds" (Klingner, Soltero-González, & Lesaux, 2010, p. 134). These authors also make the point that one assessment cannot possibly capture all of the information that might be important to collect regarding the language and literacy development of ELL students. Even when the assessment is focused on language development, the multifaceted nature of language, and the fact that students tend to be stronger in some aspects of language than others, makes single assessments unhelpful or even dangerous. In the final section of this chapter, we review standardized tests of English language proficiency.

When using more-contextualized observations of students, the information in Figure 7.10 may be helpful in generating an initial assessment of second-language learners'

FIGURE 7.10
English Language Characteristics of Students Known As English Language Learners

Incipient Bilinguals	Ascendant Bilinguals	Fully functional Bilinguals
Comprehend very little oral English	Generally, comprehend oral English well. May have problems understanding teacher explanations on unknown topics.	Are native-like in their comprehension of oral English.
Comprehend very little written English	May have trouble comprehending written English in textbooks as well as other materials. Have limitations in academic and technical vocabulary.	When well prepared, have no problems in comprehending most written English materials. When at risk (like at-risk monolingual English speakers) and having trouble reading, have reading problems and not language problems.
Produce very little oral English	Produce English influenced by their first language. May sometimes be difficult to understand. May have trouble expressing opinions, explaining statements, or challenging others.	Produce oral English effortlessly. Can carry out presentations and work effectively in groups. Can challenge, contradict, explain, and so on. Traces of first language may be detected in their accent or word choice.
Produce very little written English	May produce writing that contains many "errors" that make it difficult for teachers to focus on their ideas. May take longer to complete written assignments and tests.	Depending on previous experience with writing, may produce writing that contains errors typical of monolingual basic readers. Disfluencies reflecting first-language influence may still be present.

Source: Darling-Hammond, L., Bransford, J., LePage, P., Hammerness, K., & Duffy, H. (2005). *Preparing teachers for a changing world: What teachers should learn and be able to do.* San Francisco, CA: Jossey-Bass.

English development. Many districts use a structured observation tool called the Student Oral Language Matrix (SOLOM). The SOLOM is a rating scale that is used to assess students' language use in multiple contexts. It evaluates students in five areas: listening comprehension, vocabulary, fluency, grammar, and pronunciation (See Figure 7.11) and also characterizes students' oral language development in five phases:

Phase 1: Scores 5–11 = Non–English proficient
Phase 2: Scores 12–18 = Limited English proficient
Phase 3: Scores 19–24 = Limited English Proficient
Phase 4: Score 25 = Fully English Proficient

Detailed directions for using the SOLOM, as well as other observational techniques, are provided in the classic and useful text *Reading, Writing, and Learning in ESL*, by Peregoy and Boyle (2008).

As with all good observational tools, the SOLOM takes advantage of the many opportunities teachers have to observe students in diverse settings and during day-to-day classroom instructional events. "As a result, your cumulative observations of student oral language will be much richer, more natural, and more educationally relevant than a standardized test" (Peregoy & Boyle, 2008, p. 138). As these authors note, the SOLOM permits in-the-moment assessments of language proficiency and is also a useful tool for tracking progress over time.

Joint Storybook Reading Inventories.   The *Adult/Child Interactive Reading Inventory* (ACIRI; DeBruin-Parecki, 2007) is an authentic tool that assesses interactions during shared storybook readings. The ACIRI was designed to be a culturally sensitive tool for observing the nature of adult/child interactions that surround a joint book experience. It is available in both English and Spanish and is intended to: (1) provide a tool for working with parents and caregivers to improve their storybook reading with young children, (2) serve as a program evaluation tool for preschool settings, and (3) provide guidelines for designing family literacy programs. The ACIRI helps teachers identify intervention goals and strategies. The following three literacy categories are rated for both child and adult and are to be used through observation:

- Enhancing attention to text
- Promoting interactive reading and supporting comprehension
- Using literacy strategies

In addition to assessing child-adult interactions, there are helpful ideas for parents and caregivers that are designed to promote literacy development. All of the materials for the assessment and the recommendations for activities (intervention) are provided in both English and Spanish.

A similar assessment tool was developed by Kaderavek and Sulzby (1998). The *Kaderavek-Sulzby Bookreading Observational Protocol* (KSBOP) was designed to observe joint reading behaviors of children and caregivers. The KSBOP assesses aspects of joint storybook reading very similar to those evaluated by the ACIRI, but has been primarily used in research and can be found only in the original publication. However, an especially

FIGURE 7.11 SOLOM Teacher Observations

Student Oral Language Observation Matrix

Student's name: _____

Grade: _____

Date: _____

Administered by (signature): _____

Language observed: _____

	1	2	3	4	5
A. Comprehension	Cannot be said to understand even simple conversation.	Has great difficulty following what is said. Can comprehend only social conversation spoken slowly and with frequent repetitions.	Understands most of what is said at slower-than-normal speed with repetitions.	Understands nearly everything at normal speed, although occasional repetition may be necessary.	Understands everyday conversation and normal, classroom discussions.
B. Fluency	Speech so halting and fragmentary as to make conversation virtually impossible.	Usually hesitant, often forced into silence by language limitations.	Speech in everyday conversation and classroom discussion frequently disrupted by the student's search for the correct manner of expression.	Speech in everyday conversation and classroom discussions generally fluent, with occasional lapses while the student searches for the correct manner of expression.	Speech in everyday conversation and classroom discussions fluent and effortless, approximating that of a native speaker.
C. Vocabulary	Vocabulary limitations so extreme as to make conversation virtually impossible.	Misuse of words and very limited vocabulary: comprehension quite difficult.	Student frequently uses wrong word; conversation somewhat limited because of inadequate vocabulary.	Student occasionally uses inappropriate terms and/or must rephrase ideas because of lexical inadequacies.	Use of vocabulary and idioms approximate that of a native speaker.
D. Pronunciation	Pronunciation problems so severe as to make speech virtually unintelligible	Very hard to understand because of pronunciation problems. Must frequently repeat in order to make him/herself understood.	Pronunciation problems necessitate concentration on the part of the listener and occasionally lead to misunderstanding.	Always intelligible, although the listener is conscious of a definite accent and occasional inappropriate intonation patterns.	Pronunciation and intonation approximate that of a native speaker.
E. Grammar	Errors in grammar and word order so severe as to make speech virtually unintelligible.	Grammar and word-order errors make comprehension difficult. Must often rephrase and/or restrict him/herself to basic patterns.	Makes frequent errors of grammar and word order that occasionally obscure meaning.	Occasionally makes grammatical and/or word-order errors that do not obscure meaning.	Grammar and word order approximate that of a native speaker.

Based on you observation of the student, indicate with an X across the category that best describes the student's abilities.

- The SOLOM should only be administered by persons who themselves score at level 4 or above in all categories in the language being assessed
- Students scoring at level 1 in all categories can be said to have no proficiency in the language.

339

helpful aspect of the KSBOP is its focus on assessing the (parent's) scaffolding behaviors used during the activity. The authors suggest asking whether the parent (or other adult):

- Labels or comments
- Explains or elaborates on the text (e.g., remarks how the character is similar to/different from the child)
- Pauses (allowing "room" for the child to respond)
- Recasts sentences (e.g., simplifies language or syntax)
- Uses tag questions ("He's really funny, isn't he?")
- Asks direct questions ("What did he do?")
- Elicits retelling

Writing Samples.   Student writing samples can provide information about several aspects of emergent literacy. They provide teachers with information about children's knowledge of the sound-symbol system and about their understanding of the functions of writing.

If the child's classroom includes many opportunities for writing, spontaneous samples of children's work can be gathered easily. This is desirable, because it permits an evaluation of not only what the child *can* do, but also of what he or she *does*. Not all young children come from homes where reading and writing are modeled. Those who don't will have a more limited understanding of conventions and possibilities. Bringing a diagnostic lens to evaluating students' written work is important, and there are a number of questions that can be helpful (see Figure 7.12).

FIGURE 7.12   Guidelines for Observing Early/Emergent Writing

When observing (watching, listening to, talking to children about) their writing, you might consider the following questions:

The Message
1. Does the child believe that he/she has written a message? If so,
2. Does the child know what the message is? That is, can he/she read it? If so,
3. Did the child freely formulate his/her own message? Or, did the child simply copy something? Or, was the message confined to a small set of words that the child could easily spell?
4. How long was the message?
   - one word or a list of unrelated words
   - a phrase
   - a sentence
5. How does the child's written message relate to other graphics on the page?

The Writing System
1. Can you read the child's message? If not,
2. Does there seem to be any system to how the child went from the formulated message to the print? For example, the child may have:
   - put down a certain number of letters per object
   - rearranged the letters in his/her name
   - written a certain number of letters per syllable

FIGURE 7.12 (Continued)

3. Does the child indicate an awareness of the conventions of print by:
   - using only letters or letter-like symbols (not numerals) in writing
   - using spacing or slash marks or dots to separate word boundaries
   - writing from left to right and top to bottom
   - order: Is there any order to the way the letters or words are arranged on the page? Or, does it appear that the child simply put letters where there was empty space?

4. If you can read the child's message, can you tell how the child wrote it? *For example, the child may have:
   - recalled the visual pattern (e.g., COOW—child intended to write moo)
   - based spelling on letter names (e.g., PT, which is read Petie)
   - requested spellings from peer or adult
   - based spelling on phonological analysis (e.g., APL, which is read apple)

Message Reading

1. Does the child appear to have written without any particular intended message? If so,
2. Did the child attempt to decode the written message?
3. If so, how did the child go from text to talk? The child may have:
   - relied on memory to recall intended message
   - requested that an adult read the unknown message (e.g., "What does this say?")
   - based the decoding on the perceived text segments (i.e., matched a number of oral syllables to the perceived number of segments in text)
   - used a letter-name strategy (i.e., "read" a word containing the name of a written letter, as in reading "Debbie" for PARA NB)
   - based decoding on visual recall of a word similar in appearance

Writing Purpose

Why did the child write? Possible reasons include:
   - Simply to write; no clearly identifiable purpose exists beyond this (e.g., "I'm gonna do it how my Mama does it.")
   - To create a message: the meaning of the message is unknown to the child (e.g., "Read this for me.")
   - To produce or to practice conventional symbols (e.g., the ABCs, displayed written language) without concern for a referent
   - To detail or accurately represent a drawn object (e.g., the S on Superman's shirt)
   - To label objects or people
   - To make a particular type of written object (e.g., a book, a list, a letter) without concern for a particular referent
   - To organize and record information (e.g., to write a list of friends)
   - To investigate the relationship between oral and written language without concern for a particular referent (e.g., "If I do (add) this letter, what does it say?")
   - To express directly feelings or experiences of oneself or others (i.e., direct quotations, as in writing the talk of a drawn character)
   - To communicate a particular message to a particular audience

Note: It may be that the child is using one of these methods, but you simply cannot read it. After asking the child to read the paper, you may be able to detect patterns in the child's encoding system.

Source: Adapted from *Language Assessment in the Early Years,* by C. Genishi and A. Haas Dyson. 1984. Ablex Publishing Corporation.

Some teachers and many parents mistakenly believe that only "correct" spelling and accurate reading are appropriate in the early stages of learning to read and write. Writing samples provided by Theo at the end of kindergarten and the end of first grade provide dramatic evidence of the difficulties that can develop because of classroom practice. Theo's work at the end of kindergarten is exemplified in Figure 7.13a. One year later, to the month, he was producing journal entries like those in Figure 7.13b. During a portfolio

**FIGURE 7.13a
Theo's Kinder-
garten Journal**

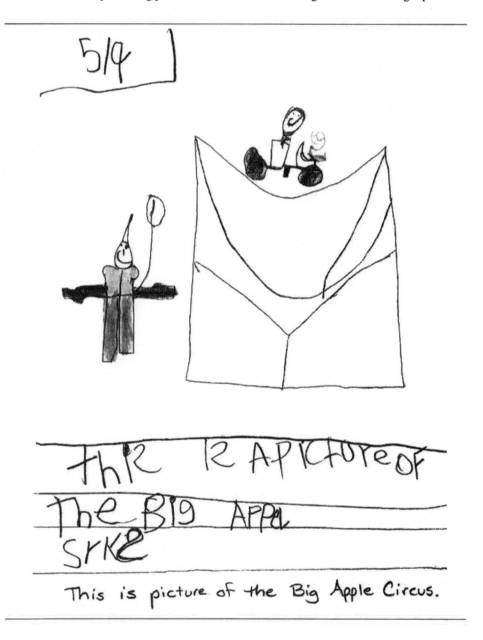

This is picture of the Big Apple Circus.

**FIGURE 7.13b
Theo: One Year
Later**

review, another teacher was struck by the fact that there was virtually no evidence of *writing* in the most recent samples, so she asked Theo to look at the two pieces and talk about them. He seemed impressed by his own production from kindergarten but did not offer an explanation as to the more recent samples. When the teacher remarked that he had done a lot of writing in kindergarten but there wasn't any in the first grade sample, Theo sighed and commented, "You always have to be so *neat*—and spell the words right too." He had actually stopped writing in order to avoid task expectations that he could not meet. Clearly, his writing samples were less representative of what he knew *how* to do than what he *chose* to do given the context.

Checklists for Concepts about Print.   Although there are several contrived ways to assess students' knowledge about the functions of literacy, evaluation in this area can be accomplished largely through observation. Many kindergarten and first-grade classrooms are print-rich environments. Print appears on labels, charts, schedules, and so on. In this type of environment, it is possible to observe how often and how well children employ print in their daily activities. As children use print to label, describe, and follow directions, teachers can document the growing competence of each child. For example, the teacher might watch children as they reread familiar books, charts, and papers. The following examples are suggestive of the types of events that are noteworthy:

> *Example A:* Four-and-a-half-year-old Nora picks up a newspaper and opens it appropriately, remarking, "Oh, here's some news."
> *Example B:* Five-year-old Joel works intently to make a label to describe his show-and-tell object so that people who see it on the science table "will know what it is."

These children clearly are acquiring a sense of the functional nature of print. Observations should focus on behaviors that demonstrate that children understand the various functions and conventions of literate behavior, not on accuracy (do they read/write correctly?).

As teachers watch for specific behaviors that will inform them about their students' emergent literacy, they should keep the following questions in mind:

- How well does the child distinguish print from pictures?
- How well does the child recognize the functions of print in the environment (signs, posted information, and so on)?
- How does the child reread familiar books (for example, does she or he "talk like a book," using the structure and vocabulary of book language)?
- What distinctions does the child make among pictures, scribbling, and print? In what ways does the child attempt to read familiar books, labels, charts, and so on?
- What distinctions can the child make among different forms of print (labels versus stories)?

Continuous observations of these types of behaviors yield a much richer picture of literacy knowledge than is permitted by formal measures alone. Despite the usefulness of observation, relying on spontaneous use of knowledge and skill cannot ensure that we have gathered information about all that students can do. Thus, systematic task structuring can be helpful.

Structured Interviews and Observations

In this section, we describe several techniques for conducting informal but structured interviews with very young children. We have used these techniques ourselves and found that they are manageable and also that they serve to differentiate among children who are more or less aware of the demands of beginning reading.

"Word" Reading.   Ferreiro (Ferreiro & Teberosky, 1979/1982) devised a number of ingenious tasks that are quite easy to administer and that yield a number of insights into children's understanding of the conventions of print. Yaden and Tardibuono (2004) have recently replicated these techniques and found that children today respond in very similar ways, providing support for the validity of the tools. The tasks are administered in a structured interview format that includes probing and discussing children's responses to elicit more information about their print concepts. The interviews are designed specifically to explore children's ideas about what is readable and what can be written.

The word-reading task involves sorting word cards. The stimulus cards should include letter strings, real words, "possible" words, repeated strings, and numbers. Some sample items include:

two   5   zzzz   me   n   iiio   PIE   jot   butterfly

To administer this task, simply ask the child:

1. Which are something to read?
2. Which are not something to read?
3. Can you read the cards that are "good for reading"?
4. What do they say?

The examiner should also probe to determine what criteria the child is using to classify the cards. In evaluating the child's responses, the following questions should be considered:

- Does the child distinguish between and among words, numerals, and letters?
- Does the child make judgments based on the length of the display?
- How sensitive is the child to repeated elements?
- How do uppercase and lowercase letters influence the child's decisions?

Patterns of response can indicate how aware the child is of the forms and conventions of written words.

Working with kindergarten children, we found that some children argue that all the cards are "good for reading." As we already noted, an interview of this type allows us to explore responses. In defending this response, two explanations are common. Some children assert that although *they* could not read the cards, other ("older" or "bigger") people could. Other children demonstrate that all the cards are "good for reading" by reading the letter names. Thus, the card *iiio* is read "i-i-i-o," and *jot* is read "j-o-t." In neither case do these children appear to follow conventional ideas about the forms and functions of reading and writing.

Finger-Point Reading.   There is considerable research to suggest that students' concept of word is a significant marker of their emerging literacy development. Ferreiro and others (Ehri & Sweet, 1991; Morris, 1993) developed an assessment strategy designed to assess students' developing concept of word. Finger-point reading can be used to answer the following:

- How well does the child appear to understand word boundaries?
- How well does the child understand the speech–print match?
- How well does the child appear to understand directionality?
- Is the child able to use initial or final consonants to mark word boundaries?

This assessment activity combines pictures and word reading. The examiner should prepare cards or book pages that contain pictures with strong action cues. Below the picture, write a sentence about the action (e.g., "The girl is walking in the rain" or "The boy eats"). The examiner/teacher engages in an open-ended dialogue with the child by asking the following questions:

1. Is there something to read on this card/page? (Have children point to it.)
2. What does it say? or What do you think it says?
3. Where does it say _____? (using a portion of the child's response)
4. Do you think it might say _____?

A fairly typical exchange between Nicole and her teacher took place when Nicole's teacher showed her a card with a picture of a dog chasing a cat up a tree. Also printed on the card was the sentence *The dog runs.*

TEACHER: Where is there something to read on this card?

NICOLE: *(Points to the words and runs her hands along the print.)*

TEACHER: What does it say?

NICOLE: I don't know.

TEACHER: What do you think it says?

NICOLE: The dog is chasing the cat.

TEACHER: Where does it say "The"?

NICOLE: *(Points to "The.")*

TEACHER: Where does it say "cat"?

NICOLE: *(Points to "dog.")*

TEACHER: Where does it say "dog"?

NICOLE: *(Points to "runs.")*

> **TEACHER:** Where does it say "chasing"?
>
> **NICOLE:** *(Laughs.)* There aren't any more of those . . . things.
>
> **TEACHER:** That's right. What do we call those "things"?
>
> **NICOLE:** Letters . . . or numbers.

This conversation reveals a great deal about six-year-old Nicole's concepts of print. We find out, for example, that she knows that the print is what is read. She also has a well-established sense of directionality. However, she clearly lacks a sense of speech–print match. She also lacks clarity about the terminology associated with reading instruction.

The purpose of these types of structured interviews is to delve into children's understanding and to gather instructionally useful information. Some of these same components are explored in the Concepts About Print test, discussed in the following section.

Structured Observations about Print Concepts. Some years ago, Clay (1985) created an informal test designed to assess young children's knowledge and use of print concepts. In its most recent form, the Concepts About Print (CAP) test is part of a diagnostic survey designed to detect reading difficulties among young children (Clay, 1985, 2006), which is also available in a Spanish-language version. In earlier editions, two books, *Sand* and *Stones*, were used to assess children's knowledge of print conventions. The new *Follow Me, Moon* (2000) offers a strong alternative, especially when used in conjunction with the revised *Observation Survey* (2006).

Using an interactive exchange, the examiner reads the book (*Follow Me, Moon*, or *Sand* or *Stones*), asking twenty-four questions along the way. The child is told to help read the book by pointing to features in the book. The questions are designed to provide assessment opportunities related to the following concepts: how to hold a book for reading; print orientation; print, not pictures, carries the message; uppercase and lowercase letters; punctuation marks; and directionality.

Reviews of the available research suggest that the CAP test is a valid measure of emergent literacy independent from intelligence (Denton, Ciancio, & Fletcher, 2006), especially for initial diagnostic and/or screening purposes. For the classroom teacher, the CAP has the advantage of structuring observations. It can provide teachers with a place to start, and it also increases reliability, since the same tasks and materials are used for each child. In general, it can provide you with a quick assessment of children's experiences with books.

Of course, teachers can obtain similar information in more-natural settings from regular picture books, and the CAP framework is so widely accepted that many professionals think of "concepts about print" assessment as a *process* rather than a specific assessment tool. Genishi and Dyson (1984) describe an adaptation that is quick and easy to use. Teachers select their own materials, including several different types of materials, for purposes of comparison. To implement this basic book-reading procedure, simply select a book and ask the child to do the following:

1. Show me the front of this book.
2. I'll read you this story. You help me. Show me where to start reading. Where do I begin to read?

FIGURE 7.14
Print Concepts
Checklist

	Yes	No	Some-times
Name: _____ Date: _____			
Directions: Using a book the child has never seen before, test the following concepts.			
1. Identifies front/back of book	☐	☐	☐
2. Can indicate title	☐	☐	☐
3. Identifies print as "what is read"	☐	☐	☐
4. Can indicate picture	☐	☐	☐
5. Knows where to start reading	☐	☐	☐
6. Shows correct direction of print display	☐	☐	☐
7. Indicates beginning of story on a page	☐	☐	☐
8. Can show return sweep for a line of print	☐	☐	☐
9. Indicates end of story	☐	☐	☐
10. Identifies bottom of page	☐	☐	☐
11. Identifies top of page	☐	☐	☐
12. Can locate a word (by cupping, etc.)	☐	☐	☐
13. Can locate two words that appear together	☐	☐	☐
14. Can locate the space between words	☐	☐	☐
15. Can locate a letter	☐	☐	☐
16. Can locate two consecutive letters	☐	☐	☐
17. Can indicate a period	☐	☐	☐
18. Can indicate a comma, question mark	☐	☐	☐

3. Show me where to start. Which way do I go? Where do I go after that?
4. Point to what I am reading. (Read slowly and fluently.)
5. Show me the first part of the story. Show me the last.
6. (On a page with print on both the left and right sides.) Where do I start reading?

Figure 7.14 provides a checklist of the concepts (distinctions between print and pictures, directionality, speech-to-print match) that can be used as a guide in evaluating the child's responses to these requests.

Recent reviews do suggest that the Text Reading and the Writing Vocabulary sub-tests of the CAP provide guidance for placing students for initial instructional texts as well as insights into students' early literacy knowledge and expertise. At the same time, Denton, Ciancio, and Fletcher (2006), note that the CAP does not provide sufficient diagnostic information about children's phonemic awareness, vocabulary, and comprehension. "Classroom teachers and reading interventionists must rely on their informal observations and judgments about these domains because they are not specifically assessed by the OS" (p. 31). We believe that these aspects can and should be addressed in systematic ways by means of both informal observation and more-structured surveys (see next).

Phonemic Awareness (PA) Tasks. Snow, Griffin, and Burns (2005) note that there are generally three types of phonemic awareness that are assessed and addressed in early literacy programs: identity, analysis, and synthesis. Teachers and clinicians can design informal assessments of PA that address students' emerging knowledge and skill. According to Snow, Griffin, and Burns (p. 69):

> *Identity:* Involves the recognition that phonemes can occur in different words and in different positions within a word. Identity tasks include asking students to listen to a string of words and identify the phoneme that is the same (or different). For example, children are expected to identify the phoneme /t/ if a teacher says *tin, tea, at, stamp.* Alternatively, the child might identify /p/ as the odd phoneme in an oral recitation of *pig, bell, bill.* Other tasks involve asking students to count how many times they hear a particular phoneme.

> *Analysis:* Most of the PA tasks in school require children to analyze words—to recognize that words are comprised of a sequence of specific phonemes. Assessment tasks include:

> - Identifying how many phonemes are in a word (two, for example, in the word *bow*)
> - Segmenting a word into phonemes (e.g., /k/ /a/ /t/ for example in cat or /m/ /a/ /k/ for make)
> - Deleting phonemes to create new words/syllables (e.g., *mat* becomes *at,* or *goats* becomes *oats*)

> *Synthesis:* Requires children to recognize individual phonemes and orally blend them together to create a word. For example, children might listen to the separate phonemes /s/ /ō/ /p/ and produce *soap.* Alternatively, the children may be asked to add a phoneme to another in a word (e.g., add /r/ to *ache* and the word becomes *rake*).

These types of tasks can provide valuable assessment information and can be easily incorporated into the ongoing instructional program.

Of course, teachers need to exercise extreme care when assessing the phonological awareness and phonemic segmentation abilities of young children, since kindergarten children are still developing their phonological abilities. In addition, as Snow, Burns, and Griffin (2005) note, regional dialects or other languages might influence children's performance.

Early and Emergent Reading Surveys. Recently, several educator-researchers have developed useful assessment tools for evaluating the early or emergent skills of young students. Two particularly useful tools are the Emerging Literacy Survey (ELS) (Pikulski, 1999) and the Early Reading Screening Instrument (ERSI) (Lombardino, Morris, Mercado, DeFillipo, & Sarisky, 1999; Morris, 1992, 1999). Each of these includes tasks that evaluate a more comprehensive range of early literacy abilities than most older tools do. The summary form for the ELS is shown in Figure 7.15, and it can be viewed online at: http://www.davis.k12.ut.us/district/curric/rt/files/EA76F324AF96458EA4F3B8EBE 5821FA1.pdf.

The Early Reading Screening Instrument (ERSI) is "a method for identifying at-risk beginning readers which is short, yet comprehensive, and allows for adaptations culturally"

**FIGURE 7.15
Emerging Literacy
Survey Summary
Form**

Child's Name _____ **Child's Date of Birth** _____

Examiner _____

Phonemic Awareness	Area Assessed	Assessment 1 Date _____	Assessment 2 Date _____	Assessment 3 Date _____
	Rhyme	_____/8	_____/8	_____/8
	Beginning Sounds	_____/8	_____/8	_____/8
	Blending Onsets and Rimes	_____/8	_____/8	_____/8
	Segmenting Onsets and Rimes	_____/8	_____/8	_____/8
	Phoneme Blending	_____/8	_____/8	_____/8
	Phoneme Segmentation	_____/8	_____/8	_____/8
Familiarity with Print	Concepts of Print	_____/8	_____/8	_____/8
	Letter Naming	_____/52	_____/52	_____/52
Beginning Reading & Writing	Word Recognition	_____/40	_____/40	_____/40
	Word Writing	_____ (words)	_____ (words)	_____ (words)
	Sentence Dictation	_____/67	_____/67	_____/67
	Comments			

(Lombardino et al., 1999). The ERSI assesses several components of students' emerging literacy ability:

- Letter knowledge
- Concept of word (using a finger-pointing task)
- Phonological awareness (using inventive spelling)
- Word recognition for decodable and high-frequency words

When the ESRI is administered in kindergarten, it is a good predictor of first-grade word recognition, word analysis, and comprehension; thus, it is an effective screening tool. The two best predictors of subsequent reading performance were the phonological awareness and word recognition components. A version of this tool is available online at http://www.uurc.utah.edu/Educators/Resources/UURC%20ERSI%20080214.pdf. Additional (abbreviated) directions for administrators are at: http://faculty.rcoe.appstate.edu/koppenhaverd/ERSI/tchrdirections1.pdf

Phonemic Segmentation. The phoneme segmentation component of the ERSI is especially interesting because it employs an inventive spelling task and involves a scoring system that could be adapted and used by most teachers. On the ERSI, children are asked to try to spell twelve words, each of which contains three or four phonemes. Then you award one point for each phoneme identified by the child.

> **RIDE:** (1 phoneme: R = 1 point, 2 phonemes: RD = 2 points, 3 phonemes: RID = 3 points)
> **MEAT:** (1 phoneme: M = 1 point, 2 phonemes: MT = 2 points, 3 phonemes: MET = 3 points)
> **CATS:** (1 phoneme: K OR C = 1 point, 2 phonemes: CS or CZ or KT, etc. = 2 points, 3 phonemes: CTZ or CAT, etc. = 3 points, 4 phonemes: CATS, CATZ, or KATZ, etc. = 4 points)
> **DUMP:** (1 phoneme: D or P = 1 point, 2 phonemes: DP, DM, etc. = 2 points, 3 phonemes: DUP, DOP, etc. = 3 points, 4 phonemes: DUMP, DAMP, etc. = 4 points)

It is important to recognize that kindergarten children are not likely to be able to complete all of these items with a full phonological analysis. In the validation study for the ESRI, for example, the average kindergarten child identified just over half of the phonemes. However, this type of assessment would provide excellent information for instructional purposes, especially when children do very poorly.

Another widely used assessment of phonemic segmentation is the Yopp-Singer Phoneme Segmentation test (Yopp; 1988; 1995). It is relatively easy, however, to devise your own informal assessment of phoneme knowledge. In Figure 7.16, we provide an example that includes both segmentation and blending for a more comprehensive picture.

In addition to these relatively informal (although systematic) assessments, there is a wide variety of more-formal measures being used to assess the phonological foundations of literacy. We examine several of these, including tests of phonic knowledge and skill, in Chapters 8 and 9.

Rapid Naming. The ability to quickly and fluently name (pictures, letters, etc.) predicts future reading ability. Rapid letter naming, in particular, has been associated with fluency in late second and third grades. In fact, early measures of rapid letter naming has sometimes predicted reading fluency more powerfully than has phonemic awareness (Phillips & Torgesen, 2006), which is probably not surprising given the fact that fluency relies more on orthography than on phonology. Rapid naming has gained attention in recent years as part of the "double deficit"—a hypothesized cause of reading difficulties.

> The claim is that serial naming (RAN) relies heavily on nonphonological processes for word recognition, including attention, visual recognition, and information processing speed. Children and adolescents with a "double-deficit" show reduced speed on naming task, which magnifies their word reading problems that arise from limited phonemic awareness. (Roth, 2004/2006, p. 464)

FIGURE 7.16
Phonemic
Segmentation
and Blending
Assessment

Student: _____ Age: _____ Date: _____
Examiner: _____ Number Correct: _____

Part I Phonemic Segmentation

Directions: We are going to listen for sounds in words. I am going to say a word and I want you to break the word apa t. You tell me each sound you hear in the word. For example, if I say "sat" you should say "/s/ /a/ /t/". Note: Be sure to say the *sounds* in the word, **not** the *letter names.* Let's **try** some first.

Practice Words (you can provide help if needed):
    me   mike   tan

Test Items: Record the students response on the line next to each item

1. tape	11. grab
2. moo	12. new
3. fog	13. tree
4. bed	14. path
5. go	15. ace
6. dine	16. shy
7. weave	17. teak
8. sit	18. mop
9. man	19. dye
10. bat	20. on

Part II Phoneme Blending

Directions: Let's **change the rules.** Now I'll say the sounds, and you tell me the word I am saying. I will say the word very slowly. You try to put the sounds together to make the word I am saying.

Practice Words:
/c/–/a/–/t/ - cat   /ch/—/i/—/p/ - chip   /f/ /a/ /t/ – fat

1. /f/-/i/-/g/ (fig)	6. /b/-/a/-/g/ (bag)
2. /p/-/e/-/t/ (pet)	7. /l/-/i/-/f/-/t/ (lift)
3. /s/-/oo/-/n/ (soon)	8. /n/-/i/-/t/ (night)
4. /o/-/p/-/e/-/n/ (open)	9. /u/-/p/ (up)
5. /sh/-/o/-/p/ (shop)	10. /f/-/l/-/a/-/m/ (flame)

According to some researchers, as many as a third of struggling readers have problems in both word recognition accuracy and sight-word recognition—a phenomena that could be as much effect as cause. Others question the utility of this construct, and the research is somewhat equivocal about the independence of RAN as a factor in reading success. Because it cannot be taught, it is more akin to intelligence and vision than it is to phonological awareness, which is highly responsive to instruction. Perhaps the most widely used test of rapid naming is the Rapid Letter Naming subtest of the DIBELS (Dynamic Indicators of Basic Early Literacy Success). This subtest consists of randomly selected upper- and lowercase letters presented on a page. It is administered individually, and students have one minute to name as many letters as possible in the order that they appear on the page. Similar assessments of letter-sound fluency and word recognition might also be administered to very young students. See Chapter 4 for a more complete discussion of DIBELS.

Word Recognition.   As we have seen, students' ability to recognize some words by the end of kindergarten is a good predictor of subsequent reading success. We would like to emphasize again that the particular words do not matter. Rather, it is important to know that students are at the stage at which they are sufficiently attentive to print that they have begun to recognize some words in print. Obviously, opportunity has a major impact on the specific words that children learn first. Therefore, it is important to examine what materials have been used with young children, especially if a particular list or structured inventory will be used to assess this ability. Both the ERSI and the Emerging Literacy Survey evaluate students' recognition of some high-frequency sight words (*the*, *and*, *is*, etc.), although only a few of the specific words are the same.

Both of these assessments (and many others) also evaluate students' word recognition of decodable words. The ERSI generally uses three-letter words that follow regular short-vowel rules (e.g., *cap*, *mop*, *dig*) to assess this ability. The Emerging Literacy Survey, in contrast, uses nonsense words that represent recurrent spelling patterns, with a greater range of samples (e.g., "zan" and "dit," but also "rame" and "strime"). We will return to the issue of assessing word recognition in Chapter 8. In terms of the assessment of early or emergent readers, it is important to keep in mind the impact of the assessment tools being used. In the very earliest stages of learning to read, when children know only eight to fifteen words, the particular words being tested can make a big difference in the conclusions drawn about students' abilities. We recommend exploring this ability broadly, and writing assessments can help.

Structured Writing Assessments

Dictated Stories.   Dictated stories are a rich source of information about oral language, print awareness, knowledge of the conventions of print, and story structure (Agnew, 1982; Ruan, 2004). Dictated writing samples are generally collected in one of two ways. In some classrooms, children produce journal entries several times a week. For very young children, this usually involves drawing a picture and "writing" any portion of the accompanying story that is possible. Then the child dictates the message to the teacher, who writes it down exactly as produced. Alternatively, the teacher may set a topic for a child (or group of children) and then proceed as above. Some children provide only a label, while others generate text-length stories, sometimes continuing their story for several days.

As children dictate and reread their stories, information about each component of emergent literacy can be gathered, using the type of form shown in Figure 7.17. After a

FIGURE 7.17
Dictated Story
Record Form

Dictated Experience Story Summary Form

Name: _____ Date: _____

Directions: Present topic, object, or experience for student to discuss or experience directly. Ask them to tell you something about it.

Dictated Story:

Assessment:

Language Development

- Does the child speak in sentences, in single words, or word clusters?
- Does the child use descriptive names for objects and events, or many ambiguous terms such as "it," "that," "this thing"?
- Does the child provide adequate information to reconstruct the experience?
- Does the child use appropriate grammatical structure?
- How does the child use language appropriate to the task?
- How easily and fluently does the child dictate?

Literacy Development

- Does the child speak clearly and pace the dictation to allow the teacher to record?
- What does the child do as the story is transcribed?
- Does the dictation have clarity and organization (does it make sense)?
- Does the child provide a title that reflects the major ideas or themes of the dictation?
- How does the child (attempt) to read back his or her dictation?

At the conclusion of a dictated story activity, it is helpful to reflect on the following:

- What evidence is there that the child understands the concepts of word, sentence, paragraph, and story?
- What aspects of the speech-to-print relationship does the child understand?
- In what ways does the child use memory for text as an aid to reading?
- What sight vocabulary does the child appear to have mastered?
- How does the child use graphophonic information to read?

Comments:

dictation is completed, it is possible to gather information about other aspects of emergent literacy (Agnew, 1982). Using the dictated story, simply ask the child to:

- Find a word (by circling or framing it)
- Match a story word on a card to the story itself
- Find a letter and/or a sentence
- Find a word that begins the same as another
- Point "to the letters you can name"
- Point "to the words you can read"
- "Reread" the story

At the same time, the quality of the story can be assessed for evidence of growing understanding of various genre attributes and narrative structures. Collected over time, these dictated stories and journal entries can provide strong evidence regarding children's growth in many areas of emergent literacy.

Prompted Writing Activities.   If spontaneous writing samples are not available, assessment information can be gathered by simply asking the child to write anything she or he knows how to write. It may be necessary to provide additional structure, because many young students balk at this. Two tasks that can be used to help generate writing samples are *all the words I know* and *supported writing.*

We have found that children often know how to write some words, even if they believe they are not yet writers. Thus, a paper headed "All the Words I Know" can sometimes produce results when the more generalized request to write has failed. Most children, for example, can write their own names, the names of some other people, and a few other high-potency words (Clay, 1985). To probe further, it also helps to ask the child to attempt to write specific words such as his or her mother's name, color names, the name of the month, the words on street signs or logos, and so forth. Such samples provide information about the child's word knowledge, phonemic awareness, and attention to recurring environmental print.

Eliciting writing samples of connected text is important for assessing the child's awareness of text organization, directionality, or concept of word boundaries. In addition, the connected writing sample generally permits observation of the child's strategy for spelling unknown words.

Children will often be able to write some connected discourse if they are provided with a little support. Supported writing can be done in several ways. For example, the child can be asked to draw a picture, then write about it. Alternatively, it is possible to brainstorm with the child, generating several possible topics.

An analysis of children's writing strategies can provide much information about the status of emergent literacy. Questions you might want to ask about the student's writing include the following:

- Does the child write from left to right?
- Does the child use letters to represent words?
- Does the child show an awareness of word boundaries and spacing?

- Is the child able to represent the phonemes in words?
- Does the child use punctuation (e.g., periods, capitals)?
- Is there a relationship between the print and the oral story that is "read"?

Students' development can be traced from scribbling through invented spelling to conventional orthography.

Using Stories to Assess Emergent Abilities

Because young children read or listen to many stories, it is relatively easy to embed this aspect of assessment into the regular instructional program.

Story Retelling Guides.   Story retelling can provide a wide range of assessment information. Because this assessment strategy is discussed at length elsewhere (see Chapters 8 and 9), the discussion in this chapter is limited to two aspects of emergent literacy that can be assessed using retelling procedures: sense of story and oral language development.

The ability to recognize and use story structure clearly aids in comprehension. As we assess children's retellings, we are looking for evidence that children have made use of the major components of stories to understand the text and to aid their recall. For young children, it is important to determine whether they have noted characters, events, and resolutions. In addition, the children should make at least some sequential and causal connections between events and resolutions explicit and clear.

To conduct a story retelling, simply ask the child to retell a story that he or she has just heard or read. Ask the child specifically to retell the entire story just the way the author did. When the retelling has stopped, ask the child whether there is anything else he or she can remember about the story. Record the child's retelling in writing and/or audio format.

The form presented in Figure 7.18 can be used as a guide for evaluating the retelling with regard to the child's language and sense of story structure. In addition, it may be helpful to collect retelling data from children on both familiar and unfamiliar stories. Repeated exposure to the same material should also permit the child to capture the language of the text. If the quality and quantity of the retelling do not improve with repeated exposures, it is likely that the child needs more story-reading opportunities or that oral language development (and experience) is not well matched to the text.

There are at least two more standardized, norm-referenced assessments of early narrative ability: the Strong Narrative Assessment Procedure, or SNAP (Strong, 1998), which uses wordless picture books to elicit and evaluate narratives, and the Test of Narrative Language (Gillam & Pearson, 2004). The latter assesses narrative comprehension, retelling, and generation with and without picture supports. For professionals engaged in formal evaluation of children's language, these may be helpful. However, ongoing informal assessment can generally provide all of the information teachers need to plan instruction.

When used over time, retellings can help us evaluate and document a child's growth in a number of areas, including language fluency, complexity, vocabulary, usage, and knowledge about story structures. Children who need greater support in comprehending stories may be evaluated on the Directed Listening Thinking Activity.

**FIGURE 7.18
Story Retelling
Form**

Child: _____ Date: _____ Story Title: _____

Language

	Yes	No	Some-times
1. A variety of sentence patterns to express ideas	☐	☐	☐
2. Complete sentences	☐	☐	☐
3. Grammar, conventions	☐	☐	☐
4. Precise, descriptive words	☐	☐	☐
5. Vocabulary is well developed	☐	☐	☐
6. Overall fluency	☐	☐	☐

Word count: _____

Story Structure

	Yes	No	Some-times
1. All basic structural elements present	☐	☐	☐
• Setting	☐	☐	☐
• Initiating event	☐	☐	☐
• The goal or problem	☐	☐	☐
• One or more attempts, or all major events	☐	☐	☐
• The resolution	☐	☐	☐
2. Oral retelling is accurately sequenced	☐	☐	☐
3. Student can recall the "big idea"	☐	☐	☐
4. Student can sustain a train of thought	☐	☐	☐

Comments

Directed Listening Thinking Activity (DLTA).   Throughout this section, we have encouraged a type of assessment that can be embedded in daily classroom exchanges. Indeed, most of these assessments can and should be done as a part of regular classroom routines. The Directed Listening Thinking Activity (DLTA) was developed by Stauffer (1980) as an instructional strategy, but it is easy to use on a continuous basis for assessment because it fits naturally in the classroom routine.

The strategy simply involves the teacher reading a well-crafted story aloud to children. Before the story is read, the teacher asks children to make predictions about what the story will be about—what will happen in the story. Then, as the read-aloud proceeds, the teacher stops periodically to solicit predictions. The children are also directed to monitor their predictions to see if they were correct. Retellings can also be incorporated into the DLTA. Throughout the activity, the teacher asks the children questions such as the following:

- What do you think this story will be about?
- What clues did you use to help you?
- Were your predictions right?
- What do you think will happen next?

To assess an individual child's participation in a DLTA, you should ask yourself the following types of questions:

- Can the child predict from the title, cover, pictures?
- Are these predictions plausible?
- Are these predictions based on prior knowledge?
- Are these predictions based on an understanding of story structure?
- Is the child able to monitor predictions?
- Is the text used to revise predictions?

Teachers can evaluate change in students' knowledge and ability to perform various types of school tasks if they use and summarize DLTA data regularly.

Standardized Tests of Early Language and Literacy

Up to this point, we have described the types of assessment that can be embedded quite seamlessly into the instructional context for young children. However, sometimes schools require more-standardized assessments that permit comparisons to standards or to other children. As well, sometimes teachers might conclude, based on these observations, work samples, and checklists, that they needed more-standardized data about individual children. We review here several widely used standardized tests of both language development and early literacy.

Diagnostic Language Tests.   In this section, we describe three individually administered diagnostic tests of language: the Test of Oral Language Development, Fourth Edition, Primary, or TOLD-4 Primary (Newcomer & Hammill, 2008); the Clinical Evaluation of

Language Fundamentals, Fourth Edition, or CELF-4 (Semel, Wiig, & Secord, 2003); and the Peabody Picture Vocabulary Test, Fourth Edition, or PPVT-4 (Dunn & Dunn, 2007). In addition, we have included a description of two tests designed for use with English Language Learners: IDEA Oral Language Proficiency Test (IPT I, 2006) and the Woodcock-Muñoz Language Survey-RNU (2010).

Test of Oral Language Development, Fourth Edition, Primary. The TOLD-4 Primary (Newcomer & Hammill, 2008) is an individually administered test designed for use with children ages 4.0 to 8.11. Norm-referenced interpretations are provided for scores on six core subtests and three supplemental subtests evaluating a student's skills in specific language areas. The semantic aspects of language are tested in the Picture Vocabulary, the Relational Vocabulary, and the Oral Vocabulary subtests; and the syntactic aspects of language are represented in the Grammatic Understanding, Sentence Imitation, and Grammatic Completion subtests. The Relational Vocabulary and Phonemic Analysis subtests are new with the fourth edition. The first was added to capture organizational ability and the second to measure awareness of phonemes. The phonological aspects of language are evaluated in the supplemental subtests: Word Articulation, Phonemic Analysis, and Word Discrimination. The TOLD-4 Primary is intended for use in identifying children whose language development is atypical, providing information about the strengths and weaknesses of individual children, documenting progress in specialized programs, and serving as a measure for research purposes. Administration time ranges from thirty minutes to an hour. Raw scores can be converted to percentile ranks, age equivalents, and standard scores for both subtests and composites.

The authors of the TOLD-4 provide criterion-related evidence of validity for their test, which includes moderate to high correlations between students' performance on the TOLD-4 and the Pragmatic Language Observation Scale (PLOS), as well as the Wechsler Intelligence Scale for Children-Fourth Edition (WISC-IV). In this most recent edition of the TOLD, the authors have provided additional validity evidence demonstrating both sensitivity and specificity. That is, the data show the ability of the TOLD-4 Primary to detect language problems of students assessed on other measures and also to specify aspects of language that were strong or weak (as identified by other indicators).

Content-related evidence of validity is presented in the form of expert judgment. This is a well-constructed test that contains tasks that are similar to those used on many formal tests of language. However, caution should still be exercised, since some experts have suggested that the test context does not really capture language use in the real world. Commenting on an earlier version of the TOLD, Westby (1988) concluded that the test should be used for screening only, supplementing it with language samples gathered in more-natural language contexts. The same suggestion may be made for use of the TOLD-4.

The authors provide a good discussion of reliability and provide coefficients that consistently exceed .80. Using a measure of internal consistency, the composites range from .89 to .96, with subtests somewhat lower. These results suggest that the test has adequate reliability at both the subtest and composite levels for screening purposes. Test-retest reliability information is limited to a small sample but appears adequate.

New norms were created for the fourth edition, and the norming procedures appear acceptable, with representative stratified sampling of acceptable numbers of students.

Earlier versions of the TOLD were criticized because the norms were based on speakers of mainstream English only. The authors assert that the issue has been addressed in the TOLD-4 and that it is not biased; however, there are some tests that demonstrate differential performance among subgroups in the population. The TOLD-4 is most likely to be useful in providing normative screening data to language arts professionals, especially when they are considering a referral to a language specialist. But test users should be especially careful about possible dialect usage and should also be alert to evidence of acceptable language use in normal daily discourse.

Clinical Evaluation of Language Fundamentals, Fourth Edition.   The CELF-4 (Semel et al., 2003) is intended to identify, diagnose, and further evaluate students aged 6 to 21 who have language skill deficits. The test contains eleven subtests that measure particular receptive and expressive language skills. There are eighteen subtests in the CELF-4. However, this completely revised test uses a new approach to assessment that involves a four-step process: (1) administer four core subtests to determine if there is a language problem; (2) determine the nature of the disorder; (3) evaluate underlying strengths and weaknesses by using composite scores in the areas of language structure, language content, language content and memory, and working memory, as well as supplementary subtests in such areas as phonological awareness, rapid naming, word associations, digit span, and others to determine underlying clinical problems; and (4) use the observational rating scales to describe/evaluate students' language performance at home and at school. The CELF-4 includes updated stimuli and new norms. There are also new subtests on the subjects of expressive vocabulary, word definitions, number repetition, and phonological awareness, and including a pragmatics profile and an observational rating scale. The new norms are based on a sample of English-dominant students who were demographically representative of the nation in 2002. Although the range of individuals includes those from ages 5 to 21, the numbers in the 17-to-21 age bracket are very small. In a change from earlier editions of the CELF, the sample now includes students from clinical populations, including students who had been diagnosed with a language difficulty. In addition, the authors have intentionally improved representation among diverse cultures.

As evidence of content-related validity, the authors explain that the language skills sampled are well documented in the literature on language and language disorders. In addition to traditional indicators of validity, the authors provide information about the "diagnostic validity" of the CELF-4 that involves assessments of sensitivity and specificity. In the first case, they examined the performance of students who had previously been identified as having a language disorder and tested the probability that these individuals would test positive for it based on the CELF-4. The diagnostic accuracy for these individuals was very high. The authors also explored the possibility that someone who *does not* have a language disorder would be appropriately assessed (i.e., their test results would be negative). Although the diagnostic accuracy for specificity was a bit lower, the overall validity of the test is quite good in this area also.

Criterion-related and concurrent validity is much less well demonstrated. Not surprisingly, the CELF-4 is highly correlated to the CELF-3, but the CELF-3 correlates only moderately with the Wechsler Intelligence Scale for Children, Third Edition ($r = .75$) and with the Peabody Picture Vocabulary test ($r = .37$ to $.79$, depending on age). Although test-retest reliability is good, tests of reliability also reveal that the subtest scores are less reliable than the composite scores and should be interpreted very cautiously, if at all. We agree with Gillam (1998, p. 262), who concludes: "Use of the CELF should be limited to contexts in which the examiner wishes only to determine a student's overall language ability with reference to a large sample of 'normal' children."

The CELF-4 is also available in a Spanish edition (2006), developed specifically for Spanish speakers in the United States. Although it mirrors the English version, it is not a translation of the English CELF-4 (Langdon, 2006). It assesses both basic communication skills and students' cognitive academic language skills (CALP). This test may be especially helpful for those contexts in which teachers are trying to distinguish a reading/language difficulty from an ELL situation.

In addition, the CELF-4 offers a screening test (2004). According to the authors, it provides a brief and easy-to-administer version of the "most discriminating" CELF-4 items. Of course, such a test would be quite useful in the context of RTI. Caution should be exercised, however, since shortening a test can affect its reliability. Perhaps because of this, the screening test reports scores only as criterion-referenced results.

Peabody Picture Vocabulary Test, Fourth Edition. The PPVT-4 (Dunn & Dunn, 2007) is an individually administered test of receptive vocabulary that provides norm-referenced interpretations of scores. It is designed for use with people aged two and a half to ninety years old and contains two parallel forms. Each form consists of 228 items arranged in increasing order of difficulty. The test is administered using an easel booklet (larger than in previous editions), which contains stimuli plates. Each plate page contains four pictures, one of which illustrates the meaning of the stimulus word that is read by the examiner. This latest edition contains larger, full-color illustrations with attention to gender and race/ethnicity. Students need only point or gesture toward the correct picture. Administration and scoring time is approximately twenty minutes.

Raw scores can be converted to standard scores (mean of 100, SD of 15), percentile ranks, stanines, normal curve equivalents, and age-equivalent scores. In addition, confidence bands for these derived scores are provided. The norming procedures for the PPVT-4 are good in terms of both representativeness and stratified sampling methods. Larger norm samples were used for the school-age group than for individuals in the youngest and oldest groups, making the test more reliable for students ages 4 to18. It is important to note, though, that the sample was restricted to individuals who were proficient in English.

The authors advise users of their test that people with uncorrected vision or hearing problems and those whose proficiency with English is limited were not included in the normative sample. The norms should not be considered valid for students with these characteristics. The fourth edition also contains the new Growth Scale Value (GSV), which is a non-normative transformation of the raw score that can be used to measure change over time in an individual's vocabulary performance.

Criterion-related evidence of validity consists of correlational studies of small groups of examinees' performance on the PPVT-III and four intelligence or language tests (including the CELF). Correlations were at least moderate and seem acceptable despite the small number tested.

As in past editions, the authors offered little information about content validity. Earlier concerns about the curricular relevance of the words used to test vocabulary (see Jongsma, 1982) are still appropriate. However, the PPVT-4 has "modernized" its core vocabulary, and the stimuli/word illustrations now appear reasonable. The lack of discussion of content validity does raise concerns about the appropriateness of using the GSV score, since the implication is that this score can be used as a progress monitoring measure. Without stronger content and/or curricular validity information (or strong developmental descriptions), the PPVT-4 should be used very cautiously for that purpose.

The manual reports reliability coefficients for internal consistency, test-retest, and alternate forms. All reported reliability measures were above .90, with the exception of the alternate form reliability, which ranged from .83 to .90. The test should provide reliable scores for screening purposes.

The PPVT-4 is a reliable test that is quick and easy to administer and score. The authors suggest that it serves as a measure of achievement when viewed as a test of receptive vocabulary and can also be considered to be a quick global measure of one aspect of verbal ability. Previous versions of this test resulted in so-called intelligence quotients, and the test was frequently—but wrongly—viewed as an IQ test. In this latest version, the authors are careful to characterize the test as a receptive vocabulary test only and to caution against using it as a comprehensive test of intelligence. Perhaps in order to reinforce this point, the PPVT-4 has been co-normed with the Expressive Vocabulary Tests, Second Edition.

Boehm Test of Basic Concepts, Third Edition.   Estimates of verbal and conceptual readiness are less controversial than estimates of physical and emotional development but no less difficult to evaluate in young children. One advantage to tests of basic concepts is that they are often simple to give and score. For example, the Boehm Test of Basic Concepts–3, or Boehm-3 (Boehm, 2001), is a group-administered test that takes only fifteen to twenty minutes to administer and provides normative data.

The Boehm-3 is designed to measure students' knowledge of concepts that are thought to be important for school achievement. According to the author, it can be used to identify children who are at risk for learning problems and children who have not mastered basic concepts, so that remedial instruction can be planned. The test evaluates students' understanding of fifty concepts representing various relationships (e.g., *next to*, *inside*, or *several*) by having them mark pictures that reflect concepts read by the teacher. The author provides documentation that these concepts are generally important to school settings. Alternate test forms are available for pretesting and posttesting. Pass-fail scores are generated for each item, and percentile ranks are available for total scores.

In comparison to its predecessor, the Boehm-R (Boehm, 1986), the Boehm-3 includes: a fourth response choice for each item; more-current and appealing illustrations; a parent report form; updated norms; a Spanish edition for which separate norms were developed; and an observation form, which is simply a checklist of concepts that teachers can observe throughout the day. The normative sample includes special education students who were mainstreamed in the tested classrooms, but the author does not report the number of such students. In addition, reliability coefficients are somewhat weak for test-retest estimates.

Woodcock-Muñoz Language Survey-RNU (WMLS-RNU)(2010).   The WMLS-RNU is an individually administered, norm-referenced test of reading, writing, listening, and comprehension. It is designed to establish language proficiency levels in English or Spanish and to ascertain students' cognitive-academic language proficiency. Two forms (A and B) are available in English and one form in Spanish, normed from two years to ninety-plus years. According to the manual, the total administration time is fifty-five minutes, although a screening measure can be used that takes about half that time. Like most language proficiency assessments, its purpose is to determine eligibility for ELL services and to evaluate program effectiveness. The authors also argue that the test can be used to monitor progress, plan instructional programs, and conduct research.

The WMLS-RNU contains a seven-test battery that includes the following subtests: picture vocabulary, verbal analogies, letter-word ID, dictation, understanding directions, story recall, and passage comprehension. These tests are designed to measure oral language, oral expression, reading and writing, and broad English proficiency. The items and subtests focus on academic language proficiency, assessing students' knowledge of school content such as letters and spellings as well as their linguistic knowledge for school-like tasks. In addition to the typical standard scores, the WMLS yields a CALP score—a measure of students' academic language proficiency in one of five levels from negligible to fluent.

The norms are newly updated in this edition (using 2000 census data released in 2005) and include a large sample population that reflects the general population and subgroups across the United States. The sample contains more school-aged subjects (than older or very young ones). However, for the purposes of this chapter, the numbers and distribution of young school-aged students is acceptable. Educators should be sure to use this latest edition, with its new norms, because of the shifting population demographics during the previous ten-year period. This is especially critical in several categories central to this test of oral language proficiency. For example, the test authors had previously used projected population totals to determine weightings. Between the projected-year census and the actual 2000 census statistics, the U.S. school-age population classified as Hispanic increased 3.8 percent. This changed the contribution of scores from this subgroup to the total norming population in a significant way. The authors also employed a new approach to creating a normal curve, which results in somewhat more-stable (reliable) derived scores. These are carefully detailed in a technical report on the norming procedures.

The other technical characteristics of this test rest on the development and standardization for the Woodcock-Muñoz-Revised (2005). Individuals are invited to find evidence for the validity of the WMLS-R by reviewing the content of each subtest. In addition, the authors demonstrate the validity by providing results of a series of validity studies (one each for preschool, school age, universal, and bilingual). Each of the validity studies compared the results of the WMLS-R with other tests of language or cognitive ability. For example, the school-age study involved a sample of 254 students from six years and two months to sixteen years and ten months. Students' performance on the WMLS-R was correlated with that on the Wechsler Intelligence Scale for Children (3rd edition). Correlations varied by subtest and ranged from .59 to .80, with most in the range of .65. Not surprisingly, the strongest correlate was between "Broad English Ability" and the verbal IQ score on the WISC-3. Importantly, the bilingual study examined the performance of subgroups of bilingual students (as measured by other tests of language proficiency) on the WMLS-R. These results demonstrate the specificity of the scores resulting from the WMLS-R. As expected, subjects with greater English language proficiency performed better on the WMLS-R and those with less proficiency performed less well. In addition, with a few exceptions, the correlations between and among tests of language proficiency and the WMLS-R were acceptable to good. Finally, the authors provide evidence of the correlations between the WMLS-R and school achievement, as measured by the Woodcock-Johnson III. The results suggest strong relationships between oral language and broad language clusters on the WMLS-R and school achievement. Importantly, the WMLS-R, like other tests of oral language proficiency, including the IDEA (see next), does not provide evidence of the relationship between tested proficiency and competence in other contexts (see Macswan & Rolstad, 2006). Given the nature of the validity evidence provided, users should be sure to collect multiple pieces of evidence about students' language proficiency (see SOLOM later in this chapter).

Evidence for the reliability of the WMLS-R is somewhat limited in that only internal consistency data were provided. These are generally good to very good. As might be expected, the reliabilities for clusters are stronger than for subtests; the median reliabilities for tests range from .76 to .97, and for clusters the range is .88 to .98. The authors do not provide any test-retest reliability data.

IDEA Oral Language Proficiency Test (IPT I-English). In the past decade, the federal government has moved to ensure effective assessment of oral language proficiency for ELL students. Title I, in §1111(b)(7), requires that students' English language proficiency be tested each year in the areas of oral language, reading, and writing skills (Ballard & Tighe, 2006).

The IDEA Oral Language Proficiency Test I-English (IPT I-Oral English) is a standardized, norm-referenced assessment of oral English language proficiency. It is designed to be individually administered to ELL students in grades kindergarten through 6. It assesses proficiency in four domains of oral English: vocabulary, comprehension, grammar/syntax, and verbal expression (including phonology). There are eighty-three items on this relatively short test, which is comprised of pictures, simple questions, prompts to repeat sentences, and prompts to describe the environment. The results are used to assess a skill area and yield a proficiency level from A through F (from "no English language ability" to "fluency").

The current version of the test was originally published in 2001 and then renormed in 2004. Unlike the WMLS (see above), the norming population for ITP I-English was normed with a majority (76%) of Hispanics, 67 percent of whom spoke Spanish as their primary language. In addition, the norming sample is not nationally representative; 93 percent of the students were from Texas, Colorado, and North Carolina, while the remainder came from California, Maryland, and Oregon. Although the sample is balanced for gender, there is no information provided by SES or student disability and/or linguistic status.

Reliability estimates are all very good, ranging from .83 to .91. There are two parallel forms of this assessment, and the alternate-form reliability is also acceptable (.89–.91). The IPT I manual establishes validity on the basis of correlations with teacher ratings of oral language proficiency. However, Lopez (2001) notes that no studies were conducted to investigate how test content relates to achievement, and this has been criticized by others as well. In particular, critics caution that this test underestimates students' competence, especially in relation to assessments of students' language in more-natural contexts (MacSwan & Rolstad, 2006).

The IPT I-English (and Spanish) are widely used in bilingual settings. Potential users should examine their own contexts carefully to determine whether the characteristics of the norming sample are sufficiently similar to warrant use of the interpretive scores. Of course, as always, educators should also combine the observations and conclusions drawn from this test with other available assessment data.

Diagnostic Early Literacy Assessments. In this section, we describe three individually administered diagnostic reading tests. Many other tests are either normed or have versions that make them appropriate for young school-aged students (ages 5–7). Most of these are reviewed in Chapter 9. For example, the Comprehensive Test of Phonological Processing (CTOPP) is an assessment that might be used in whole or in part with young children, but we discuss it with diagnostic assessments appropriate for other students as well. In this chapter, we limit our discussion to those tests that have special applicability for assessing early literacy development: (1) the Test of Early Reading Ability-3 (TERA-3), (2) the Phonological Awareness Literacy Screening (PALS), and (3) the Early Reading Diagnostic Assessment (ERDA). We include also a mention of one tool that we describe in more detail later (see Chapter 9): the Oral and Written Language Scales, Second Edition (OWLS-II).

Test of Early Reading Ability–3. The Test of Early Reading Ability–3, or TERA-3 (Reid, Hresko, & Hammill, 2001), is designed to identify students who are below average in reading development and to monitor progress in intervention programs. It is individually administered and takes fifteen to thirty minutes to complete. The TERA-3 test items relate to three component areas of early reading behavior: constructing meaning, alphabet knowledge, and conventions of print.

The original TERA, published in 1981, was "a significant departure from current readiness tests in that it provides a norm reference for the direct measurement of reading behaviors of preschool children" (S. E. Wixson, 1985, p. 544). The revised edition (TERA-3) has maintained the strong features of the previous-edition test, while remedying some of the problems. For example, illustrations in the students' picture book are now in color, and test administrators no longer have to prepare items. Current normative data were collected, and studies that search for gender, racial, and disability bias have been added. Because they are required in many jurisdictions, age- and grade-equivalent scores are now provided, and the authors wisely caution users against their misuse. In addition, standard scores, percentile ranks, and stanine scores are available.

Normative data from a large sample tested during 1999 and 2000 are provided in the manual and generally seem adequate. The TERA-3 has been improved by the addition of new items designed to capture the performance of students at the upper and lower ages covered. Also, the ages covered by the test have been reduced from 3.0 to 9.11 to 3.6 to 8.6. The reliability of this test is *supported* by using internal consistency coefficients for each of the three subtests at six age levels. The reliability coefficients are sufficiently high, except perhaps for the Conventions subtest at ages 3 and 8.

The item selection and test construction of the TERA-3 appear reasonable, but its validity really rests on its theoretical orientation. The TERA-3 is notable for its attempt to assess areas of emergent literacy that have been identified by research. The Meaning portion of the test contains items designed to assess environmental print awareness, knowledge of relationships among vocabulary words, print awareness in connected discourse, and the ability to anticipate written language (a cloze test). On the Alphabet portion, students are required to name letters, read orally, and determine the number of syllables in words. Conventions measure students' knowledge of left-to-right orientation, punctuation, spatial presentation of the story on a page, and general book-handling ability.

It is a matter of some concern that students may reach the ceiling on subtests before they ever get an opportunity to read connected text and answer comprehension questions. If the tasks themselves are at all unfamiliar to very young children, it is possible that the overall picture of students' competence would be distorted. The authors recommend using the TERA-3 as *part* of the overall picture of students' emergent literacy, and we strongly concur.

Students retell a story, choose correct answers, compare answers, fill in missing words, and find mistakes in printed material. The test manual suggests entry points for various ages of children and procedures for finding their basal and ceiling levels. Unfortunately, the score sheet does not permit notation regarding specific components of each item passed or failed. This limits the amount of diagnostic information that is targeted, and even a sophisticated examiner has no place to organize the data.

The TERA-3 assesses several traditional aspects of readiness (e.g., letter knowledge), as well as several aspects of metalinguistic awareness. The test is reliable, and young children seem to enjoy it and find the format nonthreatening. The TERA-3 has acceptable levels of reliability for testing concepts related to emergent reading.

The Phonological Awareness Literacy Screening (PALS).   PALS is one of the early literacy assessments that has gained traction over the past decade in the context of Reading First and other early literacy initiatives (Invernizzi, Juel, Swank, & Meier, 2004; Invernizzi, Meier, & Juel, 2005). Unlike the TERA-3, PALS is a set of criterion-referenced measures of young children's knowledge of literacy fundamentals. Despite its somewhat misleading name, the test includes assessments of not only phonological awareness but also alphabet knowledge, letter-sound knowledge, spelling, concept of word, word recognition in isolation, and oral reading. It is designed as both a screening and a diagnostic measure. Subtests on the PALS-K test assess rhyme and awareness of beginning sounds, alphabet recognition, letter-sound matching, concepts of word, and phonemic segmentation and developmental spelling abilities. The PALS for grades 1 to 3 includes continuation of the kindergarten assessment but also includes materials to assess word recognition, letter-sound blending, and oral reading in connected text (accuracy, fluency, and rate and comprehension). The purpose of PALS is to identify children who are behind their peers in their acquisition of fundamental literacy skills and to provide specific information about children's early literacy skills for instructional planning.

The content validity of the PALS rests on years of research studies with almost 300,000 students (Rathvon, 2004). The authors provide a conceptually strong rationale for the content of the test, which, because it is so similar to authentic school-based literacy tasks, is fairly transparent in any event. There is a wide sampling of tasks that can provide useful information to teachers and specialists, and several subtests are administered to whole groups of students, potentially reducing the amount of time needed to test. For example, in kindergarten, both rhyme awareness and beginning sound awareness can be assessed in groups (see Figure 7.19). Students look at the page shown in Figure 7.19, put their finger on the picture of the man, and then the teacher names all of the pictures. Students

FIGURE 7.19 PALS Kindergarten Reading Assessment: Rhyme Awareness

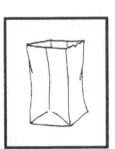   

  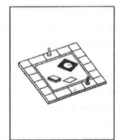 

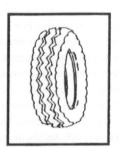   

mark the picture that shows the word that rhymes with *man* (*can*). Importantly, the PALS provides additional versions of these group tests so that teachers can assess individuals if needed. The criterion-related validity of the test is also strong. Correlations with the Qualitative Reading Inventory and the DRA range from .73 to .90. Correlations with the California Achievement Tests (CAT-5) are somewhat lower at .66 to .75. Finally, discriminant analyses demonstrate good diagnostic specificity. "Because PALS is designed to identify children who need additional interventions, items on each task should function differently for the two groups . . . Discriminant analyses at both levels have correctly classified 94–97% of students as Identified or Not Identified based on their subtask scores" (Rathvon, 2004, p. 258).

Finally, the authors provide three types of data regarding reliability: test-retest, internal consistency, and inter-rater reliability. The test-retest correlations range from .81 to .95, depending on the subtask and grade. Not surprisingly, the lowest correlation is for beginning sound awareness for the youngest students—a reminder that frequent informal assessment is necessary given the dynamic nature of learning in this age group. Inter-rater reliability was exceptionally high (.96–.99). Although the reliability samples were quite small (and nonrandom), the overall adequacy of the test construct and its iterative improvement over large numbers of administrations indicates that this is a reliable and valid test of early literacy.

The Early Reading Diagnostic Assessment (ERDA-2).   Like PALS, the ERDA-2 emerged in response to the increased attention to early assessment from the federal government. ERDA-2 is unique for its explicit positioning of itself as a *diagnostic* assessment. The test provides direct information about how it relates to a screening measure such as DIBELS (see Chapter 4) and argues that there is a need for more-comprehensive diagnostic information following from a screening outcome. Consequently, the authors also provide guidance for interpreting the results in relation to instruction. The ERDA is published separately for each grade K–3. We discuss only the K–1 materials and assessments in this chapter. The test assesses five component areas of literacy at each grade: phonological awareness, phonics, fluency, vocabulary, and comprehension. Appropriately, the amount of attention devoted to each component varies from grade to grade. For example, the Phonological Composite (several subtests having to do with phonological awareness, rhyming, etc.) is much more substantial in the kindergarten level than at any of the other levels. Students are assessed on letter recognition, ability to retell a story, rhyming ability, and phoneme deletion, as well as blending tasks. Both the advantage and the disadvantage of the ERDA-2 is its length. Given the breadth of the coverage, it is a relatively short assessment. Consequently, it samples many components but not completely. For example, although all lowercase letters are tested in Letter Identification, no uppercase letters are. As well, some aspects of early literacy are tested in ways that are not at all common. For example, the Concept of Print Observation Checklist-A is completed as students read the letter names on the letter identification test. Teachers are asked to note whether the "student read letter arrays from left to right" and from "top to bottom." Later, teachers are asked to note the same things as students read (assuming they can) a short sentence. Educators accustomed to a much richer conception of "concepts of print" will be disappointed by this assessment. Both "receptive" and "expressive" vocabulary are assessed using a format like that

**FIGURE 7.20
Picture Plate from
the ERDA-2**

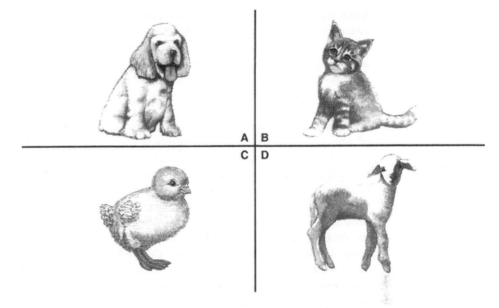

employed by the PPVT (see above). Children are shown a page with four pictures on it and asked to point to the "picture that goes with the word I say." The test has some ingenious items that provide insight into both oral vocabulary and concept development. For example, one item asks children to point to the picture "that shows the animal that has a *beak*" (see Figure 7.20). Unlike with the PPVT, children tested using the ERDA-2 are also assessed on their expressive vocabulary. This is done by showing the students a picture and then asking them to provide a word using a prompt. For example, children are shown a street corner where four streets meet at a stoplight. They are prompted to "Tell me the word that means 'the place where two roads cross.'" The answer is "intersection." These items are likely to provide some welcome information for teachers, especially since there are normative scores associated with the subtests. However, caution should be exercised, because there are very few items on the test (seven receptive vocabulary items and ten expressive items), and they get quite difficult quite quickly. This, no doubt, accounts for the unacceptably low reliability of these subtests at kindergarten. The authors acknowledge this and note that the tests "were not developed to measure the full range of skills, but rather to target problem areas" (ERDA-2 Technical Manual, p. 14). Presumably, if students do poorly on an ERDA-2 subtest, teachers or specialists could administer another, more reliable assessment.

The ERDA-2 was normed using appropriate standardization techniques, and the stratified sampling population reflects the population and demographic makeup of the United States in 2000. As well, students at all grade levels K–3 are equally well represented. That said, the total norming group is relatively small (only 800 students). The reliability coefficients for the ERDA-2 are generally very good (except for the vocabulary subtests, they range from .89 to .95). The validity evidence for the ERDA-2 is strong. The items themselves were constructed with reference to research, curriculum standards, and other, similar assessments. Although the content targets seem very good, the ways in which these are operationalized are sometimes problematic (see Concept of Print discussion above). In summary, the ERDA-2 may be used to enhance the diagnostic information available about young students. Particularly in school systems that rely heavily on a single, brief screening tool, these assessments should add useful additional information about young students' knowledge and skill. That said, much of what these tests capture can be collected using other devices.

Oral and Written Language Scales, Second Edition (OWLS-II). The OWLS-II is a norm-referenced test that has just been completely revised and expanded (Carrow-Woolfolk, in press). It is somewhat unique among early literacy assessments in that it addresses *both* oral language development and reading/writing ability. It contains four separate scales: Listening Comprehension (LC); Oral Express (OE); Written Expression (WE); and a newly added test, Reading Comprehension (RC). It was normed for ages 3 to 21; however, its real value lies in its extensive sampling of young children. Both the Listening Comprehension and the Oral Expression scales may provide useful information about the knowledge and skills of young students. The Listening Comprehension Scale, for example, is similar to the PPVT (see above) in that the child points to a picture that depicts the meaning of a word read by the examiner. In the second edition of this test, full color has been added to all items. On the Oral Expression Scale, children are asked to answer questions, finish sentences, and generate sentences in response to visual and oral prompts. These two subtests together take about thirty minutes to complete. We discuss the technical attributes of this assessment more thoroughly in Chapter 9. For now, however, it is useful to know that there is tool available that provides a more integrated view of students' language development and that it has been adequately normed with young children.

DIAGNOSTIC EVIDENCE OF EMERGENT LITERACY: THE CASE OF KYLE

In Step 3 of the assessment-instruction process (see Chapter 3), we look more closely at individual students, asking questions about the learner's knowledge of reading and writing, application of reading and writing skills, motivation, and independence or self-regulation. When assessing a student's emergence into conventional literacy, we need to remember that performance is dynamic: we get an ever-changing view of children's emerging knowledge, skill, and affect. As a result, educators need to focus on continuous assessment, authentic tasks, and student involvement.

A diagnostic portfolio is an especially good idea for young students. It should contain work samples and evidence that has been collected in the classroom, as well as more-traditional standardized assessments and structured inventories. The samples we use in this section come from a K–2 multiage classroom, which provides a good opportunity for looking at data over time. Kyle's teacher begins collecting information in kindergarten and continues to gather additional documentation and information for the three years that children are with her.

Ms. McIntyre began to dig a bit more deeply into Kyle's progress because she was concerned about his development. She sat down to have a one-to-one conversation with

Kyle and asked him about his favorite activities; this feedback provided insight into Kyle's motivation for reading and writing as well as his ownership of various activities. His self-knowledge was striking and powerful. This conversation clearly revealed that Kyle preferred action and choice to sitting and "paying attention." Not surprisingly, he readily noted in a casual conversation that he really didn't like to read. On the other hand, his book logs revealed the rather large amount of reading that he does do under the strong encouragement of Ms. McIntyre.

An interview with Kyle's mother supported Kyle's view of himself. She noted that he would prefer riding his bike to reading. She also said that although his overall development was normal, he was a "fast mover." He was running at nine months, and his verbal development was very quick—"above normal," according to her. Kyle's family was supportive of literacy. He had "always been surrounded by books; they've always been there," and he read in bed every night. He has a younger sister who is reading well above grade level already.

The rich portfolios that Ms. McIntyre and her class keep contain evidence and information about each aspect of the learner's development. You might remember that some of this information was used to "get started" with Kyle (see Chapter 4). For example, we noted that Kyle's self-evaluations (prompted by Ms. McIntyre's periodic requests for reflection) suggest that Kyle is a very active child who enjoys making things. In addition, he is aware that his writing is improving.

Samples of the extensive written work, including Kyle's self-selected "best pieces," also have gone into a diagnostic portfolio (see Figures 7.21 and 7.22). Although many other children in this classroom were writing more, and more skillfully, Kyle's progress from kindergarten to the end of grade 1 is obvious and clearly demonstrates his ability to apply his growing knowledge and skill.

In addition to these work samples, Ms. McIntyre summarized his progress using a "Stages of Spelling Development" form developed by teachers in her district. Throughout kindergarten, she noted his progress:

Observed Behavior	Date:
Pictures; no words	9/21 and 10/5
Scribble or imitative writing	10/29
Random letters to represent words	9/21; *throughout fall*
Initial consonants to represent words	11/29 "started making connection with teacher"
Initial/final consonants for each word	3/8 *jp* for *jump* 3/25 *dk* for *duck*
Initial, final, and medial consonants for each word	3/30 *sph dr* for *spider, smt* for *cement*
Vowels used as placeholders	
Approaching standard spelling	2/26 *my, dog, mom, me*

Taken together, the evidence in the portfolio suggests steady progress in the area of developmental spelling.

FIGURE 7.21
Kyle's Writing:
Kindergarten

KYLE   (K)

bY D)H5DAD
Me and my Mom and my sister and my friend
Brian are picking apples.

11/12

To summarize, at the end of kindergarten, Kyle was at the early phonemic stage of spelling development and had not yet begun to read conventionally. He was able to reread familiar books and could recognize many high-potency words from his environment (labels, planning-time choices, names, etc.). By the end of first grade, Kyle had begun to read and write. His spontaneous writing suggested that he had arrived at the phonetic stage of

FIGURE 7.22
Kyle's Writing:
Grade 1

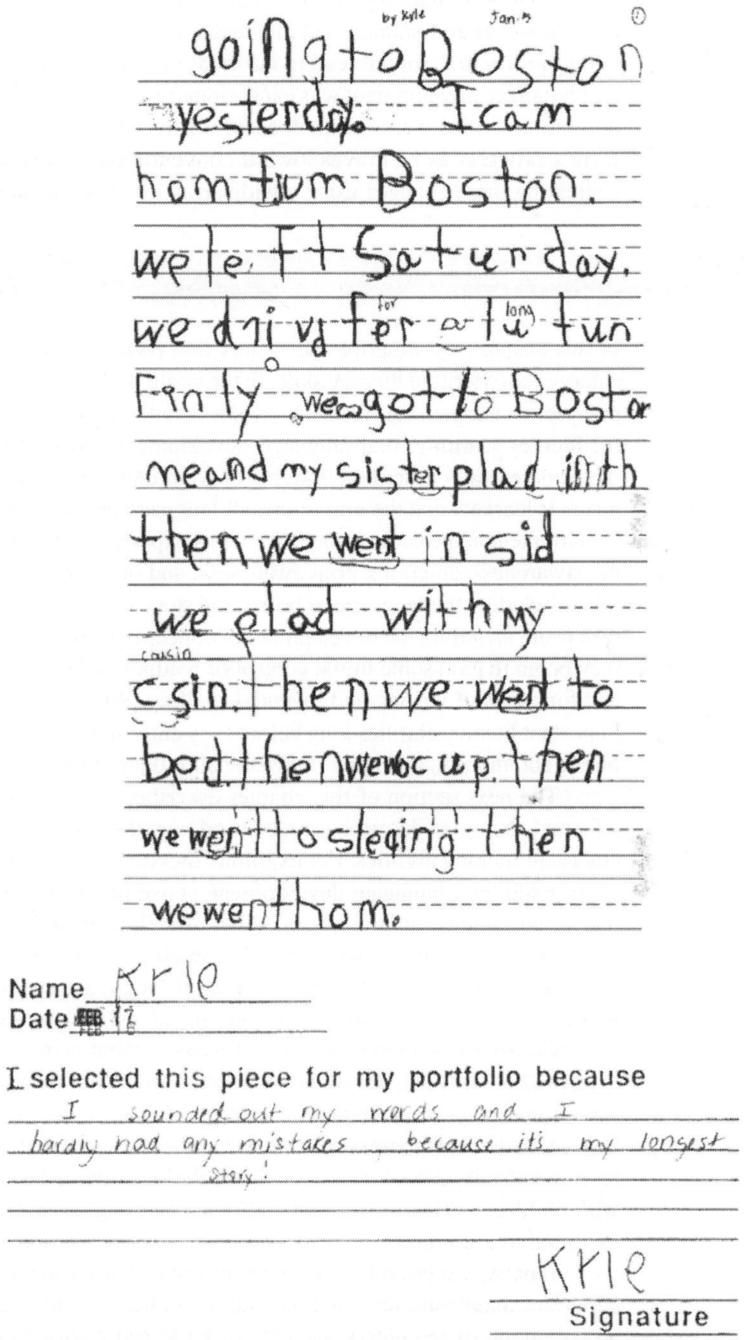

by kyle   Jan. 15

goiNg to Boston
yesterday. I cam
hom fum Boston.
we left Saturday.
we driv for a log tun
Fnly we got to Bostn
me and my sister plad inth
then we went insid
we plad with my
csin. then we went to
bed then wewoc up. then
we wen to sleaing then
we wenthom.

Name KYle
Date ___ 17

I selected this piece for my portfolio because
   I sounded out my words and I
harbly had any mistakes   because its my longest
      story!

KYle
_____
Signature

spelling development. Observations by the teacher indicate that he had made steady but slow progress in reading. He still read only a few familiar books, although his knowledge of sight words and phonics had increased. Although he was easily distracted, he had many opportunities to learn interesting information and to do projects, which he liked to do. His oral language development was exceptionally strong, and his retellings of both familiar and unfamiliar stories were detailed, accurate, and insightful. In the next chapters, we follow Kyle's progress as he moves toward conventional reading and writing, documenting and evaluating these changes using a wide array of tools and strategies.

CHAPTER SUMMARY

In this chapter, we describe the factors that form the foundations of literacy. The gradual emergence of written literacy skills in the context of oral language development provides the perspective adopted for this chapter. We detailed two major areas of competence necessary for literacy learning: oral language development and literacy experiences. Oral language development was described in terms of what children must learn about language, how language is learned, and the importance of language development in literacy learning. Literacy development in the earliest stages includes experiences that lead to phonological and phonemic awareness; emerging print awareness; and understanding of the forms and functions of print, including the language of books and story structure. In addition, children begin to analyze print, including the development of concept of a word and alphabet knowledge. Finally, they begin to gain some initial control of reading and writing processes, including the form and functions of writing and invented spelling. We noted that most children acquire many important literacy abilities long before they enter school and that the sociocultural context of home, community, and initial language all influence children's early development.

The next section of this chapter described a variety of assessment procedures. The informal strategies described can be used to gather information about a variety of different emergent literacy abilities. For example, dictated stories can be used to gather information about children's language development, sense of story, awareness of the speech-to-print match, and phonemic awareness. Other strategies include guidelines for using structured observations and interviews, checklists, retellings, and writing samples. We also described in some detail several standardized tests of language, including measures of English language proficiency and also three standardized tests of early literacy development.

Consistent with the guidelines for assessment provided in Chapter 4, the techniques described in this chapter allow for meaningful, unobtrusive, systematic, and continuous assessment of oral language and emergent literacy. Recognizing that readiness must be viewed within the context of the instructional program and tasks that children are going to encounter in school, many of the techniques described here are designed to be used with children during instruction and/or as they engage in tasks such as those they will be expected to accomplish.

Finally, we provided examples of student work and observational records that contribute to diagnostic information available about young students. The chapter ends with a description of the individual case of Kyle and details how the assessment information described in this chapter can inform our work with individual students.

MyEducationLab™

Go to the Topics, Reading Assessment, Oral Language, and Phonemic Awareness and Phonics, in the MyEducationLab (www.myeducationlab.com) for your course, where you can:

- Find learning outcomes for Reading Assessment, Oral Language, and Phonemic Awareness and Phonics along with the national standards that connect to these outcomes.
- Complete Assignments and Activities that can help you more deeply understand the chapter content.
- Apply and practice your understanding of the core teaching skills identified in the chapter using the Building Teaching Skills and Dispositions learning units.
- Examine challenging situations and cases presented in the IRIS Center Resources.
- Check your comprehension of the content covered in the chapter by going to the Study Plan in the Book Resources for your text. Here you will be able to take a chapter quiz, receive feedback on your answers, and then access Review, Practice, and Enrichment activities to enhance your understanding of chapter content.

A+RISE A+RISE® Standards2Strategy™ is an innovative and interactive online resource that offers new teachers in grades K-12 just in time, research-based instructional strategies that meet the linguistic needs of ELLs as they learn content, differentiate instruction for all grades and abilities, and are aligned to Common Core Elementary Language Arts standards (for the literacy strategies) and to English language proficiency standards in WIDA, Texas, California, and Florida.

CHAPTER 8

Structured Inventories and Benchmark and Progress Monitoring Assessments

*T*he information obtained through whole-class assessment provides the background for further evaluation of some students who require a closer look. Many schools and districts use a variety of structured inventories to expand the information they have about their learners. Some of these periodic or summative assessments can be used to determine if students are making adequate progress in overall performance in relation to age/grade expectations, as an indicator of the general effectiveness of instruction. We pursue the evaluation of the learner in this chapter, with a discussion of structured assessments—including informal reading inventories (IRIs), assessments of written language, word recognition tests, and school-based assessment "systems." In the hands of a skilled examiner, these structured assessments can yield exceptionally useful information about a student's knowledge and application of reading skills and strategies. Structured assessments generally capture the interactive nature of reading in ways that more formal tests cannot.

This chapter presents an overview of various structured procedures. The presentation of information about the IRI is extensive, since it represents the most commonly used structured, informal assessment. We discuss construction, administration, scoring, and interpretation of IRIs; identify some issues and problems with traditional IRIs; and describe contemporary innovations on the older tests. Other assessment tools and strategies include tests of phonics, word recognition, spelling, and writing.

UNDERSTANDING STRUCTURED INVENTORIES AND ASSESSMENTS

Structured inventories and other systematic assessments are used more frequently today than they were in the past. As part of an overall assessment system, these assessments are often used for interim, or benchmark, assessment—often administered two to four times per year. Within this type of framework, schools identify *benchmarks* for student progress and achievement across the school year. Benchmarks reflect the standard against which performance can be measured. In reading and writing, a benchmark helps teachers determine whether students are meeting, exceeding, approaching, or falling below the standards established for each grade level.

According to Valencia (in press), "There has been a dramatic increase in the use of interim reading assessments over the past 10 years (Olson, 2005; Perie et al., 2009; Stecher, 2008)" (p. 394). She notes that research indicates that more than 70 percent of district administrators report using some form of mandated or universal interim assessment. Although many of these are group-administered, paper-pencil tests, an increasing number of schools and districts are using individually administered inventories. Valencia further notes that these assessments may be intended to serve a number of purposes. These include *informing instruction*, using data to adjust or refine teaching; *prediction*, identifying students who are thought to be at risk and making intervention decisions about them; and *evaluation*, examining the effectiveness of various instruction and intervention settings.

Teachers whose work is supported by external sources (Title 1 and Special Education, for example) are generally required to collect and communicate information about the students they work with, based on systematic assessment practices. Until recently, most were required to use norm-referenced tests to gather this information. Now, however, a defensible system of standardized, but less formal, assessment is often acceptable and desirable. The tools and strategies that are used need to be carefully considered in order to ensure the interpretive accuracy of information gleaned during assessment.

The assessments described in this chapter share several common characteristics. They are *structured* approaches that contain the procedures and/or materials for creating *consistent*, *systematic* assessments that allow a student's performance to be compared across selections or to be compared to a commonly established standard or set of criteria. Thus, anyone using these tools can know that others are employing the same procedures, materials, or techniques for evaluating student performance.

The structured assessments described here are generally criterion referenced—that is, they are designed to evaluate a student's scores against some criteria for acceptable performance (e.g., 99 percent word recognition and 90 percent comprehension). See Chapter 4 for more information about criterion-referenced, or benchmark, assessments. The criteria for acceptable performance have been established independently of how any particular group of students might perform on the same test.

A key feature of all these structured assessments is their *authenticity*, the fact that the activities involved more closely approximate the activities found in daily classroom reading instruction than do many formal assessments. For this reason, the results that are obtained are more likely to be generalizable to classroom performance than results obtained from formal tests using activities that are farther removed from classroom practice. In addition, these are *informal* measures, because they can be used more flexibly than formal tests. Teachers have the latitude to modify a number of aspects of administration in order to glean as much information as possible about students' literacy skills under varied conditions. Of course, if the results are serving as benchmarks of student progress, care must be taken that everyone who is administering the assessments is using common procedures.

In short, these tools must create assessment conditions that are as trustworthy as possible, while still retaining an environment that permits more-frequent assessment of more-authentic literacy abilities. We start with the informal reading inventory because it is probably the most widely known form of systematic interim/periodic reading assessment.

STRATEGIES AND TOOLS FOR STRUCTURED ASSESSMENT

Informal Reading Inventories

Overview.   The most common type of structured assessment in reading is the *informal reading inventory* (IRI). An IRI is an individually administered reading assessment intended to help determine a student's reading instructional needs. These assessments yield various reading levels for individual children and were traditionally used for placement purposes, to decide what "group" a student would be placed in. Today, there are many different types of IRIs and differing purposes as well. Teachers still often use IRIs to make decisions about matching students to a specific level of difficulty (of text), but the inventories are often required by districts as part of a comprehensive assessment system and used for periodic progress monitoring (or benchmarking). As well, results are often used as indications of student *achievement*. This is especially true in schools that are no longer using norm-referenced achievement tests and that have also abandoned basal reading programs. Lacking easily available numeric indicators of students' reading levels, schools may use IRIs, or other benchmarking systems, to communicate with parents and with each other.

We spend quite a bit of time in this section describing the nature and issues related to IRIs, not only because they are still widely used, but also because many other assessments (not calling themselves IRIs) use the procedures, protocols and assumptions of IRIs. A firm understanding of this type of assessment provides teachers and specialists with useful tools for assessing students at all levels of proficiency and also provides a framework for evaluating other tools and tests that have been developed more recently.

An IRI (and many other benchmarking systems) is composed of a series of graded word lists and graded passages that the student reads aloud to an examiner. The examiner notes *oral reading* errors as the student reads and asks comprehension questions when the student has finished reading each passage. Most informal reading inventories also include *silent reading* passages, and some provide passages that are read to the student to determine a *listening comprehension* level; comprehension questions are used for each. When the student has finished, reading errors are analyzed and percentage scores are calculated for *word recognition* performance on the graded word lists and the oral reading passages. In addition, the examiner tallies performance on the comprehension questions for the various reading passages.

Betts (1946) and Kilgallon (1942) are frequently credited with the development of the IRI, although similar techniques were suggested by others even earlier (for example, Gray, 1920). As originally designed by Betts (1946), the IRI was to be constructed by the *teacher*, using reading materials in which the students might actually be placed and procedures for administration that were similar to those used in classroom reading instruction, such as silent reading followed by oral rereading. The intent was to evaluate students' reading performance under circumstances that were as similar to classroom reading conditions as possible.

Today, there are many types of IRIs and a variety of administration procedures. Many teachers now use one of the commercially available IRIs (see annotated list of commercially prepared IRIs in Appendix D). Alternatively, some use an IRI-like assessment that accompanies a particular core/basal reading series.

The two primary purposes for administering an IRI are (1) to place students in materials at the appropriate levels by establishing their *independent*, *instructional*, and *frustration* (or *hard*) reading levels and (2) to identify strengths and weaknesses in the areas of word recognition and comprehension by analyzing the amount and type of word recognition and comprehension errors. In this chapter, we will address the first of these purposes, saving the diagnostic discussions for the Chapter 9.

Four different levels of reading can be identified by applying established criteria to a student's word recognition and comprehension performance:

1. *Independent level:* This is the level at which students read fluently and make very few word recognition or comprehension errors. The reader can handle material at this level easily, without the assistance of the teacher. Free choice or recreational reading materials should be at this level, as should reading assignments such as homework, tests, and seatwork that the student is expected to complete independently.

2. *Instructional level:* At this level, the reader makes some errors; however, word recognition errors are not excessive, and comprehension is adequate. This is the level at which the student will benefit most from direct instruction. For each child, the materials used for direct instruction—such as basal readers, subject-area textbooks, and skill activities—should be at this level.

3. *Frustration (hard) level:* This is the level at which reading is often slow and halting, and the reader makes an excessive number of errors. Materials at this level are too difficult for the reader, even with assistance. Students should not be placed in materials at this level, because effective learning is unlikely to occur.

4. *Listening comprehension level:* This is the level at which the student can satisfactorily comprehend material that has been read aloud. This level provides a rough estimate of the student's receptive language comprehension and is often used as a measure of the student's potential reading level.

Many different procedures have developed since the IRI was first introduced. To help readers get a sense of IRIs, we present a description of various traditional IRI procedures in the next section.

Components of an IRI. The basic components of an informal reading inventory are graded word lists, graded reading passages, comprehension questions, and a summary/analysis sheet. To help illustrate some of these components, examples of an examiner's copy of graded word lists, a graded passage, and a summary sheet are presented (see summary sheet in Figure 8.1).

Graded Word Lists. Most IRIs begin with lists of words that have been graded to correspond with the grade levels in core reading materials. Although not originally included in the IRI, graded word lists have become a standard part of today's IRIs. Graded word lists are used to determine accuracy of word recognition in isolation and to assist the examiner in determining the level at which the student should begin reading the graded passages. Each graded word list typically contains between ten and twenty words (see Figure 8.2). Series-linked IRIs generally, but not always, contain selections from the anthologies at each level.

FIGURE 8.1
Sample IRI Components

Eighth Edition

BASIC READING INVENTORY PERFORMANCE BOOKLET

Jerry L. Johns, Ph.D.

B
Oral Reading

Student ______________________ Grade ________ Sex M F Date of Test ____________

School ______________________ Examiner ______________ Date of Birth ____________

Address ______________________ Current Book/Level ____________ Age ____________

SUMMARY OF STUDENT'S READING PERFORMANCE

Grade	Word Recognition						Comprehension			
	Isolation (Word Lists)				Context (Passages)		Oral Reading Form B		Silent Reading Form D	
	Sight	Analysis	Total	Level	Miscues	Level	Questions Missed	Level	Questions Missed	Level
PP										
P										
1										
2										
3										
4										
5										
6										
7										
8										
9										
10										
11										
12										

ESTIMATE OF READING LEVELS

Independent _____ Instructional _____ Frustration _____

LISTENING LEVEL

Grade	Form ____ Questions Missed	Level
PP		
P		
1		
2		
3		
4		
5		
6		
7		
8		

ESTIMATED LEVEL: ____

GENERAL OBSERVATIONS

INFORMAL MISCUE ANALYSIS SUMMARY

Types of Miscues	Frequency of Occurrence			General Impact of Miscues on Meaning		
	Seldom	Sometimes	Frequently	No Change	Little Change	Much Change
Substitutions						
Insertions						
Omissions						
Reversals						
Repetitions						

Source: From *Basic Reading Inventory: Pre-primer through Grade Twelve and Early Literacy Assessments,* Eighth Edition by Jerry Johns. Copyright © 2001 by Kendall/Hunt Publishing Company. Used with permission.

FIGURE 8.2   Sample IRI Component: Word List, QRI-5

Examiner Word Lists

Second	Identified Automatically	Identified	**Third**	Identified Automatically	Identified
1. morning	c		1. lunch	c	
2. tired	tried		2. celebrate	c	
3. shiny	c		3. believe	belief	
4. old	c		4. confused		c
5. trade	c		5. motion		c
6. promise		c	6. rough	rug	sc
7. pieces	c		7. engines	c	
8. suit	c		8. tongue		c
9. push	c		9. crowded	c	
10. though	through		10. wool	c	
11. begins	c		11. remōved		sc
12. food	c		12. curious		kircus
13. light	c		13. silver		c
14. visit	c		14. electric		c
15. clue	c		15. worried	wŏrry	
16. brĕathe			16. enemies	enemy	
17. insects		c	17. glowed		OK
18. weather		c	18. clothing		c
19. noticed	not īced	sc	19. interested		c
20. money	c		20. entrance	entray	

Second

Total Correct Automatic _13_ /20 = _65_ %

Total Correct Identified _4_ /20 = _20_ %

Total Number Correct _17_ /20 = _85_ %

Third

Total Correct Automatic _5_ /20 = _25_ %

Total Correct Identified _9_ /20 = _45_ %

Total Number Correct _14_ /20 = _70_ %

LEVELS		
Independent	**Instructional**	**Frustration**
18–20	14–17	below 14
90–100%	70–85%	below 70%

It is often unclear how the word lists have been generated for commercially prepared IRIs. The specific nature of these words varies considerably, and most authors do not specify exactly where or why they were selected (Nilsson, 2008). Some use only high-frequency sight words such as *the* or *want* at the lower grade levels—words that may or may not be easily decoded—drawing from previously published lists of graded words or word-frequency lists such as the *New Instant Word List* (Fry, 1980) or the Dolch list (Dolch, 1942). Two of the more recent IRIs draw all or some of the word-list words from the reading passages on the particular test used (Applegate et al., 2008; Leslie & Caldwell, 2011).

Graded (or Leveled) Reading Passages.   The graded word lists are followed by a series of graded/leveled reading passages. Most IRIs now have three to seven passages at each grade level, under the assumption that educators will want to make comparisons between oral, silent, and listening comprehension. Alternatively, the various forms for each level may be used to monitor progress (but see issues and concerns below). The graded reading passages are used for evaluating comprehension and for examining oral reading accuracy in context. Some contemporary IRIs also derive estimates of fluency using these leveled passages.

Graded/leveled reading passages range in length from 25 to 1,200 words. Typically, the length of the passages increases gradually, from the lowest to the highest grade levels, along the following lines: preprimer and primer, 25 to 60 words; grade 1, 75 to 100 words; grades 2 and 3, 75 to 350 words; grades 4, 5, and 6, 150 to 600 words; grades 7 through 10, 200 to 1,200 words. The authors of commercially prepared IRIs often construct their own passages or select excerpts from children's materials found in the library. When teachers or publishers construct IRIs to accompany a particular series, the passages are selected excerpts from the readers in the series.

Passage difficulty is determined by the level of the material from which it is taken and/or through the use of readability formulas or leveling systems (see Chapter 5 for a detailed explanation). Passages differ in other ways. For example, some IRIs contain illustrations along with their passages, some contain only expository text, and the length varies enormously within the IRIs, by grade level but also between IRIs. It is also accepted practice to vary the size of the print type in a manner that is consistent with the grade level of the passage.

Comprehension Questions.   The graded passages are accompanied by a series of open-ended comprehension questions. Most commercially prepared IRIs have between five and ten questions per passage. Most IRIs categorize the comprehension questions according to types. The most common system today involves variations on text-explicit and implicit distinctions (see Chapter 9). Some older IRIs continue to categorize their comprehension questions in terms such as *main idea, detail, literal, inferential, vocabulary, sequence*, and *cause-effect*, despite the fact, it must be emphasized, that these categories "have little or no empirical support" (Johns, 2005, p. 72). Although IRIs usually include a range of comprehension questions, few provide a rationale or framework for content.

Administering an IRI.   IRIs are administered individually and require 30 to 90 minutes for administration. Although IRIs are generally administered individually, the newest edition of one IRI (the QRI-5) provides guidance for administering it in a group setting, and the inventory's preliminary data indicate that this can be done successfully at grades 3 and above (Leslie & Caldwell, 2011, p. 30). IRIs can be administered in more than one session. It is usually a good idea to make an audio recording of the administration for later reference. As with all aspects of the IRI, there is no one right way to administer it. Decisions about how to administer the IRI must be based on the purpose for administration and the types of information desired. Before administering any IRI, it is important to get a firm grasp of the guidelines for that specific test. However, the general guidelines below are quite typical of most administration procedures.

Graded Word Lists. The word lists are introduced by saying something like, "I have some words I would like you to read for me today. Please read carefully, and if you come to a word you don't know, just try your best." The word lists are then presented, either as a whole or one word at a time. Administration of the word lists begins with the list that is at least two years below the student's grade placement. If the student misses any words in the first list, the examiner drops to lower lists until the student achieves an independent level of accuracy (usually 90%–100%). As the student reads, the examiner tallies all words read correctly and records exactly what the student says when a word is misread (see Figure 8.2). The student is encouraged to read words that are unfamiliar, and the administration of the word lists continues until the student makes a specified number of errors (for example, five errors in a list or three consecutive errors).

Some published IRIs have only a timed administration of the word lists, in which the student is given anywhere from two to ten seconds to respond. Some have only untimed presentations, in which the student is given unlimited time to respond. Still others have some combination of the two—for example, a timed administration followed by an untimed administration of the words that were missed the first time. The combined administration provides the greatest amount of information.

Oral Reading Passages. Administration of the oral reading passages (see, e.g., Figure 8.3) begins with the passage that is at the same level as the word list on which the student achieved some specified criterion (e.g., 90%–100%). If the student does poorly on the first passage, the examiner drops down one level at a time until performance is satisfactory. The examiner begins the administration by saying something like, "Now I have some passages I would like you to read out loud to me. Please read carefully, because I will ask you some questions when you are finished. If you come to a word you don't know, just try your best." Then the examiner reads the motivation statement, if there is one, and asks the student to begin reading. The examiner may also wish to begin timing the student's reading to calculate the oral reading rate.

As the student reads, the examiner uses a code to mark every deviation from the printed text on the teacher's response sheet. If the student stops reading at a difficult word, the examiner waits some specified amount of time (for example, five seconds) and then either pronounces the word or directs the student to skip it and continue. The administration of the oral reading passages is stopped when the student is visibly frustrated or is making excessive word recognition and comprehension errors. Because it is not always possible to score the test immediately, the decision to suspend testing is frequently based on the examiner's judgment.

FIGURE 8.3   Sample IRI Component: Reading Passage, QRI-5

Level: Two

Narrative

Concept Questions:

What is a repairman?

_____

_____ (3-2-1-0)

What is a treasure hunt?

_____

_____ (3-2-1-0)

What is it like inside a refrigerator?

_____

_____ (3-2-1-0)

Score: _____ /9 = _____ %

_____ FAM   _____ UNFAM

Prediction:

_____

_____

"Father's New Game"

It was a cold winter day. Too cold for Mary and Susan to go outside. They wanted something interesting to do. They went to their father and asked if he would take them to a movie. He said, "I'm sorry, girls. Someone is coming to see why the washer isn't working. If you'll play by yourselves for a while, I'll think of a new game for you. But you must promise to stay in your room until I call you." "Okay," said Mary and Susan.

Father wrote notes on pieces of paper and left them around the house. Each note gave a clue as to where to find the next note. Just as the person came to look at the washer, Father called to them. "Mary, Susan, you can come out now!" Then he went into the basement. Mary and Susan came out of their room. They didn't see anything to play with. They thought that their father had forgotten to think of a new game for them to play. Then Susan noticed a piece of paper on the floor. She picked it up and read it aloud. "I'm cold but I give off heat. I'm light when I'm open but dark when I'm closed. What am I? Open me and you'll find the next clue." The girls walked around their house thinking. They came into the kitchen and looked around. "That's it!" yelled Mary. "The refrigerator!" She opened the door and found the next clue taped to the inside of the door. The girls were off again in search for the next clue. After an hour they had found five clues. The person who had fixed the washer was just leaving as Susan found the last clue. It read, "Nice job, girls. Let's go to a movie!" (298 words)

The oral reading errors that are commonly coded include *omissions, insertions, substitutions, repetitions, hesitations, ignoring punctuation, prompts, reversals,* and *self-corrections.* The sample coding system presented in Figure 8.4 is just one of many that can be used. Which particular system is used is not as important as becoming familiar enough with one system so that it can be used quickly and consistently. It is important to code all deviations from the text so the student's performance can be reconstructed at a later time. Making an audio recording of the session helps with this, of course. The total number of

FIGURE 8.4   Recording Oral Reading Miscues

Type of Miscue	Sample Notation	Comments
Substitution— Mispronunciations or word replacements.	Write exactly what the student says over the text word(s) *cars dojs* I saw ~~cats~~ and ~~dogs~~.	May suggest difficulty in decoding/word recognition or language differences/dialect usage. Patterns of mispronunciation can provide good diagnostic information for planning instruction in phonics and/or structural analysis.
Insertion— Letters, syllables, or words that are added to the text.	Write exactly what the student has added and mark it with this symbol: ∧ *th* I saw ∧ cats and dogs.	These miscues often signal difficulties with high frequency sight words and/ or difficulties with syllables or morphemes. Wide range of qualitatively different miscues could be counted as "insertions" so a close analysis is needed.
Omissions—Letters, syllables, or words deleted from the text.	Circle the words or word parts that have been deleted: I saw cat(s) and dogs.	If meaning is maintained, these may not be serious. However, when students skip word parts in longer words, there may be need for word analysis instruction. Some omissions, particularly world endings, may signal oral language differences or difficulties.
Reversal—Letters, syllables, or words that are read out of order.	Mark the words or letter that have been reversed with this symbol: I saw cats and dogs.	This miscue can occur when students are anticipating upcoming text. If meaning is disrupted, it is often self-corrected. Unless this occurs frequently, it is typically not serious. A consistent pattern of letter/word reversal is common among very young readers and may signal very weak word recognition among older students.
Self-corrections—Spontaneous corrections of any miscues by the student.	Note the miscue using the notations above, but then mark it with a "C" or "SC": *S~~ears~~* **I saw cats and dogs.**	These miscues often indicate that the reader is attending to meaning and are often considered "good" miscues. However, students who must self-correct too frequently may not have acquired automatic word recognition skills. They may be overrelying on context. Some IRIs count self-corrects as errors in accuracy estimates and some do not. Whichever practice is used, it should be clear to all teachers and employed consistently.

(continued)

FIGURE 8.4   (Continued)

Type of Miscue	Sample Notation	Comments
***Repetition**—Words, word parts, or phrases that are read more than once.	Underline the repetition with a wavy line: I saw cats and dogs.	Repetitions often occur just before a challenging word and often indicate that the reader is trying to figure out a word or phrase. Sometimes repetitions are due to nervousness. Concerns are warranted when miscues lead to repetition, but not to self-correction. An overreliance on context may be indicated.
***Punctuation**—Student ignores (omits) punctuation.	Mark the omitted punctuation with an X: I saw cats and dogs×.	Miscues in this area are generally the result of poor attention to the meaning of the text. They typically contribute to poor fluency but may also result from too-rapid reading.

*Repetitions and omitted punctuation are not counted in scoring oral reading accuracy.

oral reading errors, or miscues (see Chapter 9), is recorded for accuracy, and most commercial IRIs provide organizers to make this relatively quick and easy (see Figure 8.5).

Silent Reading and Listening Passages.   In addition to oral reading passages, the examiner can administer silent and/or listening comprehension passages and may also want to time the silent reading to determine the student's silent reading rate. There are a number of

FIGURE 8.5
Recording Oral
Reading Accuracy:
Summary Form,
QRI-5 Grade 2

Number of Total Miscues
(Total Accuracy): _____

Number of Meaning-Change Miscues
(Total Acceptability): _____

Total Accuracy		**Total Acceptability**
0–7 miscues	___ Independent	___ 0–8 miscues
8–31 miscues	___ Instructional	___ 8–16 miscues
32+ miscues	___ Frustration	___ 17+ miscues

Rate: $298 \times 60 = 17{,}880$ / ___ seconds = ___ WPM

Correct WPM: $(298 - \underline{\quad} \text{ errors}) \times 60 =$
___ / ___ seconds = ____ CWPM

variations in the order of administration for oral, silent, and listening passages. Several of these variations are listed below:

1. Oral reading only
2. An oral reading passage followed by a silent reading, and possibly a listening comprehension passage, all at the same grade level before going on to higher levels
3. Oral reading passages until frustration level is achieved, followed by silent reading passages starting at that level or one level below until frustration level is achieved, which is then followed by listening comprehension passages
4. Silent reading followed by oral rereading of all or parts of the same passage

Many commercially prepared IRIs either disregard silent reading or make it optional, probably to shorten administration time.

Comprehension Questions.   After the student finishes reading (whether oral or silent), the passage is removed and the examiner says something like, "Now I am going to ask you some questions about the passage you just read." The examiner reads each question and provides ample time for the student to make a response. If the student does not respond or appears to have misunderstood a question, the question may be asked again or rephrased. Additional information may be elicited by neutral questions, such as "Can you tell me more?" However, leading questions that provide information related to the answer should be avoided.

Scoring an IRI.   Preliminary scoring occurs while the IRI is being taken, because scores are needed to make decisions about subsequent steps in administration. The final scoring is completed when the student has finished the IRI, and the scores are entered on a summary sheet. Most published IRIs provide a type of summary sheet for recording student performance on word lists, oral reading, and oral, silent, and listening comprehension at each grade level (see Figure 8.6). The scores are used to determine a student's independent, instructional, and frustration reading levels, which are recorded on the summary sheet. Many summary sheets also provide for recording the numbers and types of oral reading and comprehension errors made by the student. Increasingly, IRIs also provide guidance in scoring students' prior knowledge and fluency.

Graded Word Lists.   The examiner determines the percentage correct on each word list and enters the number and the placement level on the examiner's response sheets. Unfortunately, this is not quite as easy as it may at first appear. As soon as we attempt to score an IRI, we are confronted with the question "What is an error?" or, conversely, "What is an acceptable response?" Once again, there is no one correct way; it depends on the situation.

The biggest decisions that have to be made in scoring the word lists are how to handle self-corrections and the time factor. In other words, does a student know a word if it takes ten seconds to identify the word or if it is misread and then self-corrected? Some commercially prepared IRIs provide no guidelines for time limits or how to score self-corrections. Those that do recommend time limits for acceptable responses ranging from ten to fifteen seconds. Some IRIs suggest that all deviations, self-corrected or not,

FIGURE 8.6
Informal Reading Inventory, QRI Summary Form

Student Profile Sheet

Name _____ Kyle _____ Birthdate _3/27/94_ Grade _2→3_

Sex __M__ Date of Test _____ Examiner _____

Word Identification

Grade	1								
Level/% Automatic									
Level/% Total									

Oral Reading

	Bear/ Rabbit	Trip to Zoo	Wool Sheep to You	Johnny Appleseed	Amelia Earhart				
Passage Name									
Readability Level	1	3	3	4	4				
Passage Type	N	N	Exp	N	Exp				
Level/% Total Accuracy	94%	97%	95%	93%	95%				
Level/% Total Acceptability	100%	99%	98%	99%	92%	(skipped line)			
Familiar/Unfamiliar: %	80%	75%	66%	66%	33%				
Retelling: %									
# Explicit Correct	4/4	4/4	2/4	4/4	2/4				
# Implicit Correct	2/2	4/4	4/4	4/4	3/4				
Level/% Comprehension	IND	IND	INST	IND	INST				
# Explicit Correct: Look-backs									
# Implicit Correct: Look-backs									
Level/% Comprehension: Look-backs									
Rate									
Total Passage Level									

Silent Reading

	The Friend	Where Do People Live	Cahokia						
Passage Name									
Passage Section (High School)									
Readability Level	3	3	4						
Passage Type	N	Exp	Exp						
Familiar/Unfamiliar: %	80%	40%	25%						
Retelling: %									
# Correct Explicit	3/4	4/4	4/4						
# Correct Implicit	3/4	4/4	4/4						
Level/% Comprehension	INST	IND	IND						
# Correct Explicit: Look-backs									
# Correct Implicit: Look-backs									
Level/% Comprehension: Look-backs									
Rate									

count as errors, while others do not count self-corrections as errors. Clearly, when there are only ten to twenty words in a list, decisions about what constitutes an error are not trivial. Each error translates into a 5-to-10-percent difference in the scores, which can have a significant impact on decisions about placement levels and the entry level into the reading passages.

Oral Reading Passages.   The examiner counts the oral reading errors and determines the percentage of word recognition accuracy. This percentage can either be determined from a scoring guide or calculated by hand using the following procedure:

1. Subtract the number of errors from the total number of words in the passage to obtain the total number of words correct.
2. Divide the total number of words correct by the total number of words in the passage.
3. Multiply the result by 100 to convert to a percentage.

The percentage of word recognition accuracy and the placement level, if provided by a scoring guide, are entered on the summary sheet. In addition, the number of errors of each type is calculated and recorded on the summary sheet.

The question of what constitutes an error becomes even more complex in scoring the oral reading passages. Guidelines for scoring oral reading range from counting every deviation from the text as an error to the other extreme—counting only those deviations that alter the meaning of the text. Most scoring guidelines lie somewhere between these two extremes.

A review of the scoring guidelines of eleven commercially prepared IRIs indicates that the majority consider omissions, insertions, substitutions, reversals, prompts, and repetitions to be scorable errors. Self-corrections, hesitations, and punctuation are to be noted but not counted as errors (Jongsma & Jongsma, 1981). Most of these IRIs are still published today, and they have largely maintained these same scoring procedures. There is evidence that professionals are less reliable in identifying specific types of miscues than they are in establishing overall accuracy (Johns & L'Allier, 2004). Contemporary variations are evident. For example, the Qualitative Reading Inventory (QRI-5) recommends scoring oral reading in two ways: total accuracy and total acceptability (see further on). Carefully reading the administration procedures will clarify this type of test-specific variation.

Comprehension Questions.   The examiner determines whether the answers to each comprehension question are correct, incorrect, or partially correct, on the basis of the suggested answers and on an awareness of acceptable alternatives. The percentage comprehension score is calculated using a scoring guide or by dividing the number of questions that were answered correctly by the total number of questions and then multiplying by 100. The percentage comprehension score and the placement level, when provided by a scoring guide, are then recorded on the summary sheet. In addition, the number of each type of question missed is calculated and entered on the summary sheet. Because there are often as few as five comprehension questions per passage, scoring decisions have a major impact on the final results of the IRI.

Rate. The examiner determines the number of words read per minute for silent and/or oral reading, using the following procedure:

1. Convert the amount of time it took to read the passage to seconds.
2. Divide the number of seconds by the number of words in the passage.
3. Multiply the resulting number by 60 to reconvert it into words per minute.

When the rate in words per minute (WPM) has been calculated, it is entered on the examiner's response sheet, and the summary sheet when appropriate.

Some contemporary IRIs (e.g., QRI-5, 2011) have added another measure: the number of words *correct* per minute (WCPM), which provides a combined estimate of both speed and accuracy. We discuss this a bit later in the chapter.

Issues and Problems: Evaluating and Selecting IRIs. Whether teachers are constructing their own or using available commercial versions, serious attention must be given to the issues and problems surrounding the use of IRIs. The information gleaned from them can be useful, but because the decisions made about children can be quite serious, it is important to understand fully how to evaluate or construct IRIs for ethical use.

Construction. The major area of concern regarding the construction of IRIs focuses on the representativeness of the reading selections. When a passage is selected for use in an IRI, it is assumed to represent the materials the student will encounter during reading instruction. Alternatively, it is assumed that the passage is representative of other passages at a certain level of difficulty. This may have been an accurate assumption when IRIs were first suggested and the vocabulary and content of basal readers were more highly controlled than they are today. However, in today's core programs, passages taken from a single level may be highly variable. As commercial programs included more trade literature and introduced diverse texts, the range of difficulty increased. In addition, many teachers today do not use basal readers at all, choosing instead from a wide range of literature. Representing this literature can pose serious challenges.

A second problem related to the reading selections involves the comparability of alternate passages at each grade level. Although there is a clear advantage to having several alternate passages at each grade level, it is difficult to be certain that these passages are comparable. Some authors suggest creating different passages by using different portions of the same selection. However, there is also variability in readability within selections, although perhaps not as great as that within a book. When passages from the same selection are used, there is also the problem of accumulated prior knowledge affecting performance from one passage to the next. In a recent review of nine contemporary IRIs, Spector (2005) found that only four reported evidence that the alternate forms were equivalent and Nilsson (2008) reported even more limited evidence of comparability, with only the Qualitative Reading Inventory providing enough evidence to invoke confidence in the equivalence of the results from one passage to another within the inventory. Although a complete description of the Qualitative Reading Inventory-5 (QRI-5) is not possible here, the extensive research and development procedures used for each subsequent edition of the Qualitative Reading Inventory are impressive. We use it throughout this section to demonstrate how one contemporary IRI has responded to some of the concerns we are raising.

Most IRIs do not account for the fact that there are *many* text factors that are likely to influence a student's performance. For example, it has been found that the effects of interest are sufficiently strong to cause comprehension scores to vary between the frustration and instructional levels (Estes & Vaughan, 1973). Another finding is that the type and length of the passage influences the number and types of oral reading errors (see Deford et al., 2003; Wixson, 1979). Other factors, discussed in Chapters 5 and 6, include text organization and topic familiarity.

As we noted, the QRI-5 was designed and has been revised to respond to various criticisms of older IRIs. The first demonstration of this involves the types of text included in the inventory. The QRI-5 provides both narrative and expository texts at each level of difficulty. Both narrative and expository selections are intact texts, not excerpts, and are highly representative of the structure and topics of selections found in basal readers and subject-area texts. In the latest edition, there are three expository texts at grades 4 through high school that often contain tables or charts typical of authentic text materials. A significant improvement in the latest version of the QRI involves the use of pictures at the preprimer through second-grade levels and the inclusion of additional, easier, narrative passages for very beginning readers in kindergarten and grade 1. The authors have added more narrative passages at each level through grade 3 to permit periodic benchmarking as many as four times per year in the primary grades. One narrative and one exposition at each level contain supportive pictures so that the examiner can explore the impact of pictures on print reading and also so that teachers can assess students as they use more-authentic materials. In other words, it is possible for teachers to explore *how* the various text factors may influence a particular reader.

A third major area of concern in the construction of IRIs focuses on the nature of the comprehension questions. Peterson, Greenlaw, and Tierney (1978) constructed three sets of questions for a single IRI, according to a popular set of guidelines that called for one vocabulary, two literal, and two inferential questions. When these three sets of questions were used in testing, approximately 65 percent of students examined were assigned two different instructional levels, and 10 percent were assigned three instructional levels. This suggests that different questions for the same passages can produce different results. Great care should be taken to ensure that the comprehension questions capture the types of understanding that are expected in nonassessment settings. Finally, we must also be concerned with the degree to which comprehension questions are *passage dependent*. Questions that are passage dependent have answers that depend on information provided in the passage rather than on the reader's prior knowledge about the topic. To illustrate this problem, read and answer the following questions taken from Johns (1988):

1. Skyscrapers are different from other buildings because they are: a. bigger; b. higher; c. cleaner; d. prettier.
2. A person who "operates with a frying pan" uses the pan for: a. cutting fish; b. cooking fish; c. hitting fish; d. cleaning fish.

How did you do? Johns found that 134 of 160 fourth- and fifth-grade students answered the first item correctly, and 131 answered the second one right *without* reading the passages.

These questions were part of a study in which students scored significantly better than by chance when they answered the reading comprehension questions from a test *before* they read the passages.

Studies of IRI-type tests suggest that results may be influenced by questions that are passage independent. For example, an analysis of the comprehension questions on four IRI-type tests indicated that 23 to 31 percent of the questions were passage independent (Allington et al., 1977). In their study of IRIs in current use, Applegate, Quinn, and Applegate (2002) noted a similar concern. In addition, the analysis demonstrated that there was a large degree of variability in the number of passage-independent items from one passage to the next within each test. In other words, the results of these studies suggest that in some cases the variability in scores observed between passages may be attributable to differences in the comprehension questions, not to real differences in ability.

Of course, question dependency interacts with students' prior knowledge of the topics and genres. On the QRI-5, the passages were selected or created to provide intentional variation in familiarity, with some topics likely to be familiar to most students at that grade level and others likely to be unfamiliar. The QRI-5 provides two ways to assess a student's familiarity with passage content: each reading selection includes a conceptual questions task and a prediction activity that may be used to determine a student's familiarity with the topic of the selection. These tasks allow the examiner to identify each passage as either familiar or unfamiliar to each individual student. The use of passages that vary in familiarity enables the examiner to arrive at a more complete description of a student's reading ability. There are now a few additional IRIs that provide some means of determining whether students are familiar with content prior to reading, and examiners should be aware of the extent to which this type of variability in passages will influence results.

Administration.   The major issue in the administration of an IRI is the effect that different procedures might have on students' scores. For example, Brecht (1977) reports a study in which children were administered IRIs both with oral reading at sight and with silent reading followed by oral rereading. Only 20 percent of the students obtained the same instructional level under both types of administration. When the rereading format was used, 70 percent scored at least one grade level higher and 10 percent scored at least one grade level lower. Such findings raise further concerns about test reliability. If the IRI has not provided evidence that these two types of administration result in equivalent results, then the administration of the test should require providing evidence about both modes (see Spector, 2005).

Another factor in administration that may influence students' scores is the directions provided to both students and teachers. Some inventories clearly emphasize the importance of reading accurately and not making mistakes (Jongsma & Jongsma, 1981), while others provide additional support for comprehension (see Nilsson, 2008). Although this might seem trivial, the researchers point to evidence that directions can influence the number and type of oral reading errors, the degree of comprehension, and the rate of reading. One inventory actually directs the students to decrease their speed for subject-area material and to reread sections or words on which they made "careless mistakes." Two inventories direct the teacher to start all students, regardless of age or reading ability, at the lowest levels on both the word lists and passages. This practice could result in boredom and fatigue for both the student and the teacher.

A final issue to be considered in the administration of an IRI is the effect of different procedures for administering oral, silent, and listening passages. If passages are only administered orally, is it safe to assume that performance can be generalized to silent reading? Research has yet to provide a definitive answer to this question. However, an interactive view of reading suggests that there will be differences in performance under different reading conditions. This means that performance may vary when students are asked to read a passage orally, as opposed to silent reading followed by oral rereading. Therefore, caution is urged in generalizing from one reading situation to another. It may also be necessary to administer an IRI under various conditions that are representative of those the student encounters frequently in the classroom, to obtain a complete understanding of a student's reading abilities or to assess students on other types of texts and tasks—something that can be done if teachers are regularly monitoring students' reading performance (see also Chapter 9).

Scoring.   A major area of concern regarding the scoring of an IRI is that decisions about what gets counted as an error are going to make a difference in the scores used for determining placement levels. Early scholars (see, e.g., Betts, 1946) were not entirely clear about what constituted an error; however, an examination of the summary sheets he used suggests that all deviations from the text were counted as errors. Much of the controversy about scoring oral reading errors centers on so-called good errors—that is, errors that do not disrupt the meaning of the text and appear to arise from the reader's meaningful processing of the text rather than from some faulty skill or strategy. The degree of variation from one IRI to another and the potential this has for variation in students' estimated reading level is significant. In addition, even when an IRI specifies procedures for making these decisions, we find that teachers within a school may vary considerably in their application of the guidelines. It is less important what errors are counted than that everyone use the same scheme. Among the decisions to be made are the following.

- *Repetition errors.* Some argue that repetitions should not be counted as errors, because they represent the reader's attempt to preserve the meaning of the text (K. S. Goodman, 1973). Others argue that repetitions should be counted as errors, because failure to do so will result in readers becoming frustrated before they reach the percentage of errors normally recognized as the student's frustration level. For our part, it is difficult to make a single rule that accommodates all situations satisfactorily. In general, we do not consider repetitions, especially those that are accompanied by self-corrections, to be scorable errors. However, there are instances when repetitions are so disruptive that they are clearly interfering with effective reading. In these cases, repetitions should be taken into account in scoring.
- *Repeated miscue involving the same word.* The most common types of this error involve names (proper nouns) or specialized terms such as *sonar* that may be unfamiliar to students. Some inventories suggest counting each incidence of miscue individually, and others suggest counting the error only once no matter how may times it occurs. We do not think it makes sense to count each error of the same word separately, since it tends to underestimate the student's reading ability. On the other hand, counting it only once may overestimate it, as the accuracy percentage is then

based on an inflated number of words. We suggest counting the error once and then subtracting the other incidences from the total word count.

- *Aggregating different types of errors across passages.* This is generally done to look for patterns. Research has shown that the type of errors that readers make is directly related to the difficulty of the material. In fact, Kibby (1979) found that including frustration-level errors in an analysis can give a distorted view of the reader's skills and strategies and that students' strategic abilities function differently in frustration versus instructional text (Deford et al., 2003). Our position on this is that oral reading errors should not be aggregated across different levels of text. If some aggregation is necessary, then errors should be aggregated only for passages on which the student's performance was relatively comparable.

- *Data used in determining instructional level.* Too often, inventories suggest using only word recognition scores as the basis for determining instructional level. However, using both (and probably fluency as well for grades 2 and beyond) in combination is important. Exploring the relationship among these factors is important because oral reading accuracy affects various types of comprehension differently. Nicolsen, Pearson, and Dykstra (1979) report the results of research revealing that accurate word recognition is important for comprehension of specific information but relatively unimportant for global interpretation. Thus, projecting passage comprehension from oral reading errors might underestimate students' comprehension of the total text. They also found that meaningful sentence errors (for example, *giant* for *gorilla*) are more likely to disrupt comprehension of specific information than errors that clearly do not make sense (for example, *wall* for *gorilla*), because students are more likely to maintain a faulty interpretation that makes sense than one that is unreasonable. Finally, they found that students' ability to answer comprehension questions requiring the combination of ideas from two sentences is more affected by the word recognition error rate than by questions that require responses based primarily on prior knowledge. In other words (and not surprisingly), students' oral reading errors do not really impact their ability to comprehend material that is quite familiar. The important thing to remember, therefore, is that oral reading and comprehension errors should be examined in tandem to determine the abilities for a particular reader.

- *Placement and achievement.* The biggest problem confronting those who use IRIs for placement and related purposes is that there is no evidence that reading levels established through IRI testing actually correspond to classroom performance. The validity of IRI placement levels hinges entirely on readability estimates of the IRI passages and their relationship to classroom texts (see benchmarking systems later in the chapter). Needless to say, when the consequences of test results are significant, the reliability of the measures is critical too. The results of an IRI must be interpreted cautiously when placing a student in appropriate instructional materials, given the variability among commercially prepared IRIs (Jongsma & Jongsma, 1981; Spector, 2005). Of course, even more caution should be exercised if the uses extend to communicating outside the classroom.

Most IRIs, administered traditionally, simply are not constructed well enough to be used as indicators of overall student achievement in reading. Spector's (2005) analysis of the nine leading IRIs revealed that only one, the Qualitative Reading Inventory, had sufficient reliability for wide-ranging use. A few others (Bader Reading Inventory, Ekwall/ Shanker Reading Inventory, and Steiglitz Informal Inventory) demonstrated sufficient reliability to make informal classroom placement decisions—as long as teachers understand that the results must be monitored and errors in placement corrected if new information suggests the results are flawed. In addition, the issues described below raise serious concerns about the use of IRIs (alone) to communicate about *achievement*.

Even if IRI levels are indeed indicative of classroom performance, the next problem is to decide on the criteria for placement (achievement). The decision about which placement criteria to use seems not so much a question of which are best but rather which are most appropriate, given the administration procedures, criteria for scoring, and purposes for administering the IRI. Decisions about the appropriateness of placement criteria should not be made independently of decisions about administration and scoring. Variability in placement criteria *can* result in different placement levels. This is one reason why we are much less enthusiastic about using IRIs for placement than for the evaluative purposes discussed in the next section of the chapter.

A second area of concern is how well traditional error analysis reveals students' strengths and weaknesses in word recognition and comprehension. The major problem with these types of analyses is that they treat each error type as a separate entity, as though they occurred independently of each other. Research has demonstrated again and again that this is not the case; rather, error types are all interrelated and cannot be separated in this manner.

There are similar problems with using question types as a means of finding a student's relative strengths among an array of subskills (McKenna, 1983; Schell & Hanna, 1981), since we lack objective standards for classifying questions by subskill. In addition, IRIs have such a small number of questions per subskill that it is difficult to reliably classify a reader's comprehension problems by using these question types. Perhaps the most damaging of all is evidence that suggests that all questions are measuring the same skill (Drahozal & Hanna, 1978). Therefore, traditional analyses of oral reading and/or comprehension errors should not be relied on to produce a complete picture of a student's strengths and weaknesses in these areas.

Guidelines for Traditional Usage of IRIs.   The significant concerns that have been raised about the construction, administration, and scoring of IRIs indicate that caution needs to be exercised in developing, selecting, and/or using IRIs to place students in appropriate grade-level materials. The following guidelines are provided to assist those who choose and/or need to use IRIs for placement purposes. They are based on the information in this chapter and the recommendations of many scholars and educators (see Jongsma & Jongsma, 1981; McKenna, 1983; Pikulski & Shanahan, 1982; and Spector, 2005). For teachers and interventionists, it is important to "keep in mind that when using an IRI, as with any test, you're just sampling behavior. On another set of passages, given on another day, you might get different results" (Jongsma & Jongsma, 1981, p. 704).

1. Look for an inventory that corresponds to regularly used instructional materials with regard to content, difficulty, style, and length. Be alert to differences in the interest level of passages for different groups of students.

2. Stay alert to readability and leveling problems. Don't assume that texts are representative of classroom materials or that texts on alternate forms are comparable.

3. Consider the quality of the questions by field-testing them. Do not assume that questions on published instruments are passage dependent or that they capture high-quality thinking. Do not hesitate to replace some of them with your own.

4. Be wary of summary sheets that break down student responses into a large number of comprehension subskills, but do examine questions in terms of the demands they place on students' inferential thinking.

5. Determine procedures for administering and scoring and placement criteria within the context of the purpose(s) for using the IRI and across all individuals who will administer the inventory.

   a. Be sure that instructions for administering, scoring, and interpreting are clear and complete. Consider carefully what student directions communicate to the students.

   b. Carefully consider what constitutes an error on the word lists and oral reading passages.

   c. Consider which factors should be weighed most heavily in establishing placement levels, (i.e., word recognition, comprehension, and/or rate).

6. Examine the information provided about reliability in the manual, and avoid using IRIs that have no reliability information at all.

Interpreting Results from an IRI: Issues and an Example

Informal reading inventories, and their contemporary counterparts (e.g., benchmarking systems), have survived for decades because they can provide a great deal of information. The information on the summary sheet (see Figure 8.6) regarding the percentage of word recognition accuracy and comprehension at each level is evaluated to determine the student's independent, instructional, and frustration reading levels. In addition, the information on the summary sheet regarding different types of oral reading and comprehension errors is used to determine specific strengths and weaknesses. In this section, we describe how to interpret results form IRIs in general and we share specific examples from a well-constructed contemporary example, the Qualitative Reading Inventory-5 (QRI-5), written by Leslie and Caldwell (2011). The authors further note that the major strength of the QRI-5 is that it provides a profile of an individual reader's strengths and weaknesses across different types of text and in relation to the familiarity of the reading selections. These comparisons are facilitated by the inclusion of the Student Profile Sheet. Kyle's performance on the QRI (between grades 2 and 3) is summarized in Figure 8.6. The Student Profile Sheet is designed to provide the examiner with maximum flexibility in the amount of information to be recorded for a given student. Each of these scores provides good information about Kyle's reading abilities, and we discuss them below.

Placement/Achievement Levels. Determining the criteria for a student's overall independent, instructional, and frustration levels is a complex issue. It typically involves examining students' performance in oral reading accuracy and in comprehension. Although the original criteria, established by Betts (1946) are still the most widely accepted today,

**FIGURE 8.7
Powell's Placement
Criteria**

Reading Levels	Reading at Sight		Oral Rereading	
	Word		Word	
By Grade	Recognition	Comprehension	Recognition	Comprehension
Independent				
1–2	94% +	80% +	94% +	80% +
3–5	96% +	85% +	96% +	85% +
6+	97% +	90% +	97% +	90% +
Instructional				
1–2	88–94%	55–80%	92–94%	70–80%
3–5	92–96%	60–86%	95–96%	75–85%
6+	94–97%	65–90%	97–97%	80–90%
Frustration				
1–2	86% or less	55% or less	91% or less	70% or less
3–5	92% or less	60% or less	91% or less	75% or less
6+	94% or less	65% or less	96% or less	80% or less

problems associated with the use of these criteria have caused slight revisions. For example, most contemporary IRIs call for oral reading at sight rather than Betts's procedure of silent reading followed by oral rereading. In addition, research over the years has suggested that different benchmarks are appropriate for students at different ages or grades (Powell & Dunkeld, 1971).

The criteria presented in Figure 8.7 were suggested by Powell (1980) to account for both the grade level of the materials and two methods of administration: oral reading at sight and silent reading followed by oral rereading. The majority of commercially prepared IRIs have criteria that fall within a range (see Figure 8.8), which may be used as a guide for establishing reasonable placement criteria. Despite concerns about these criteria, there is evidence that many commercial IRIs provide a valid and reasonably reliable estimate of students' reading ability (Paris & Carpenter, 2003).

Oral reading accuracy is determined by finding the proportion of errors that students make during oral reading. Interpretation depends on using the designated "cut score" to assign a level of performance—independent, instructional, or frustrational. Kyle's oral

**FIGURE 8.8
Criteria Used by
Published IRIs**

	Word Recognition	Comprehension
Independent	96–99%	75–90%
Instructional	90–95%	60–75%
Frustration	90–92% or less	60–75% or less

reading accuracy is summarized in Figure 8.6. You can see that his highest accuracy score was 97 percent accuracy on the Level 3 narrative, "Trip to the Zoo." Using the Powell criteria for reading at sight, the data suggest that Kyle's oral reading accuracy on all passages was in the *instructional range* (93%–97%). Like some other contemporary IRIs, the QRI-5 includes materials that support alternative analyses of oral reading errors (see the discussion of miscue in Chapter 9).

Comprehension ability is judged on the basis of an analysis of errors on different types of comprehension questions. Students with a preponderance of errors on a particular type of comprehension question are believed to have difficulty with certain types of comprehension. Depending on the types of comprehension questions included on the IRI, these problems might include understanding literal ideas or factual information, drawing inferences, identifying main ideas, and so on. As we have already discussed, the classification systems for IRIs are based on such thin evidence that the data should be used quite cautiously. In any event, an examination of eight of the most widely used IRIs revealed that more than 91 percent of all the comprehension questions sampled were text based (Applegate, Quinn, & Applegate, 2002). In fact, two-thirds of the questions were simply literal-recall questions, requiring students to recall information they had read in the text. This study also demonstrated that there are significant differences between IRIs. For example, the proportion of questions that could be classified as requiring high levels of inference varied from less than 1 percent to almost 18 percent across IRIs. Needless to say, estimates of students' reading abilities are likely to vary considerably depending on the types of comprehension required, and, as a result, our assessment conclusions need to be considered in relation to the task demands.

Kyle's comprehension scores vary between independent and instructional, depending on the passage (see Figure 8.6). For example, on the grade 3 narrative fiction that he read with great accuracy, his comprehension was 8/8 correct questions, an independent score. On the two grade 4 passages (one familiar and one unfamiliar) he scored independent and instruction, respectively. It should be noted that the QRI-5, like many IRIs, guides teachers to examine both explicit- and implicit-question responses. Answers to explicit questions are directly stated in the text, and answers to implicit questions require the reader to make inferences from textual clues. Among IRIs, the QRI-5 has the largest proportion of high-level inferential questions (Applegate, Quinn, & Applegate, 2002). As you can see in Figure 8.6, Kyle actually performed better on the implicit than the explicit questions.

Additional Comprehension Information. Contemporary IRIs often include comprehension assessments based on retellings (in addition to or instead of questions), although this information is not generally included in the determination of placement/reading levels. The QRI-5 assesses comprehension using both questions and retellings. Each selection has an accompanying "text map" for recording and evaluating the student's unaided recall. A number of systems for scoring and interpreting passage recall have been proposed over the years. Most contemporary IRIs provide some sort of format for recording retellings. The QRI-5, for example, provides separate scoring forms for narrative and exposition. The narrative forms include details clustered on the superordinate elements of setting/background, goal, events, and resolution. The expository recording form is organized into a series of main idea and details. These can add excellent diagnostic information to the assessment but are rarely used for screening or progress monitoring purposes because they are time consuming to analyze.

FIGURE 8.9 Retelling Scoring Sheet for "Amelia Earhart" Level Four

Setting/Background

Recall Sequence	Recall	Importance Rating
	Amelia Earhart was an adventurer	1
	During World War I	2
1	she was a nurse	3
2	She cared for pilots	3
3	who had been hurt	3
	Earhart watched planes	1
	take off	3
	and land	3

Goal

	he knew	2
	that she must fly	2
	Earhart was the first woman	1
	to cross	1
4	the Atlantic	1
5	in a plane	1
	Someone else flew the plane	2
7	Earhart wanted to be more	2
8	than a passenger	2
9	She wanted	1
10	to fly	1
	across the ocean	1

She liked flying (handwritten)

Events

12	Earhart trained	1
13	to be a pilot	1
11	In 1932	2
	she flew	1
	alone	1

	across the Atlantic	1
6	to Ireland	3
16	Earhart faced dangers	1
	Airplanes were smaller	2
	Problems happened often	2
17	There were no computers	2
18	Earhart said	2
20	Women must try	2
19	to do things	2
21	as men have tried	2
	Earhart planned	1
14	to fly	1
15	around the world	1

Resolution

	Her plane disappeared	1
	over the ocean	2
	the Pacific Ocean	2
	People searched	2
	for a long time	2
	They gave up	2
23	Earhart	1
22	and her plane	1
24	were never found	1

Total number of units: 47
Number of units recalled: 24
Percentage recalled: 51%
Sequence evaluation: adequate
Percentage of important units recalled: 61%
Percentage of moderate units recalled: 39%
Percentage of unimportant units recalled: 50%

We include a more-comprehensive discussion of retellings in Chapter 9. For now, it is important to recognize how different tasks can yield different pictures of students' reading abilities, and we illustrate that by examining the combination of information for one student. A sample of Tha'm's recall of one grade 4 narrative is shown in Figure 8.9. You can see that Tha'm has recalled the text in reasonably good sequence, recalling a little more than 50 percent of the "ideas" suggested by the publishers. It is also important to note, however, that an examination of sequence reveals some faulty connections. For example, she adds the phrase "She liked flying" and then erroneously indicated that she had crossed the Atlantic in a plane to Ireland—linking material from two different parts of the text. You may also notice that Tha'm failed to recall important portions of the last part of the text. This failure to report crucial information about the resolution of the problem in relation to key information presented in the early part of the passage (e.g., that Earhart flew solo) is serious. In fact, after the retelling was over, Tha'm mused, "Do you think she must have been killed or disappeared? Maybe she just wanted to be alone."

Excellent diagnostic insights can be gained by comparing question responses to retellings. Tha'm missed four of eight questions posed to her after the recall (frustrational level). She could not recall how long it took Earhart to fly across the Atlantic and did not identify her goal (to fly around the world). Not surprisingly, she also could not speculate about why her plane was never found.

The QRI-5 also includes two other optional vehicles for evaluating students' comprehension: *look-backs* and *think-alouds*. At grades 3 through high school, teachers may add look-backs to the assessment, and for the new high school–level passages, examiners may ask students to think aloud while reading. When using look-backs, the examiner first scores the comprehension using the normal procedures, but then asks students to return to the text to correct or elaborate on their responses. According to Leslie and Caldwell (2011), look-backs allow the examiner to differentiate between comprehension during reading and memory after reading, and they note that "scoring comprehension without look-backs may underestimate a student's comprehension" (p. 79). Tha'm did not benefit very much from the use of the look-back. She was able to locate the information to answer the question about how long it took Amelia to fly but could not correct other question difficulties

During the think-aloud procedure, the reader is encouraged to stop at predetermined points and think aloud about what he or she is doing. Some of the expository text passages at sixth grade and beyond are formatted in two different ways so that the examiner can use them with or without think-alouds. The administrator's materials include a useful summary form on which the examiner can indicate whether the student's think-aloud statements fall into any of several defined categories that indicate understanding or lack of understanding of the text. As with other aspects of the QRI, this section is well documented and consistent with recent research. We discuss the diagnostic value of the think-aloud procedure more fully in Chapter 9.

Neither of the placement decisions about Kyle and Tha'm are straightforward. Kyle's results suggest generally very strong oral reading accuracy and good comprehension on all materials through grade 3. Familiarity does not appear to influence his comprehension. Kyle does show particularly strong comprehension abilities on exposition. His comprehension is really influenced only by oral reading accuracy (a tendency to skip lines in print). Using the results of the IRI, he appears capable of reading most grade 3 material with considerable accuracy and with good comprehension. Indeed, he is likely to be able to read more-challenging texts (grade 4 IRI) successfully too. Of course, these are relatively short texts (i.e., not chapter books or textbooks), so it is possible that Kyle would not fare so well on actual classroom material.

Tha'm, on the other hand, is struggling. Her IRI results suggest that she could read grade-level *narrative* texts, but her accuracy and comprehension both suffered while reading expository texts at grade 4 (a grade below her current placement). We now turn our attention to a more diagnostic use of the IRI data and provide further discussion of other assessment strategies in Chapter 9.

It is important to note that there is other information that can help to resolve some of the questions that arise from administering structured inventories. Although the QRI-5 does provide quantitative scores, they will vary for many students as a function of the type of text read, the familiarity of the passage content, and the manner in which comprehension is assessed. The interpretation of the scores must therefore be qualified by these factors. This is what sets the QRI-5 apart from other IRIs and the reason it has been called *qualitative.*

As the authors of the QRI-4 suggest (Leslie & Caldwell, 2011, p. 23):

> Although once common, it is now simplistic to talk about a single independent, instructional, or frustration level for an individual. The act of reading is highly complex and contextual.

The variety of passages on the QRI-5 allows the examiner to evaluate the effects of topic familiarity, text structure, and reading mode on the independent, instructional, and frustration levels of the student. "It is not inconceivable that a single reader may have different levels for familiar and unfamiliar text, for narrative and expository material, and for oral and silent reading modes" (Leslie & Caldwell, 2011, p. 24). We reconsider some of these issues in Chapter 9.

Rate.   Students' rate of reading is reported in terms of the number of words read per minute during oral and/or silent reading. Not all IRIs report rate. We return to a more extensive discussion of fluency later in the chapter. The point to be made here is that research suggests that it should be included in the estimates of reading placement levels (Rasinski, 1999; Rasinski & Padak, 1998; Valencia et al., 2007, 2010). A slow reading rate may indicate a reading problem, but an acceptable rate does not guarantee that the material is being comprehended at a satisfactory level. Desired silent reading rates are similar to oral reading rates at first- and second-grade instructional levels but begin to increase sharply at the third-grade instructional level when word identification becomes more automatic. It is also important to remember that reading rates will vary according to the conditions of the reading situation and that norms or standards are good only for the conditions under which they were obtained.

Contemporary Innovations on the IRI Format

We do not believe that the primary strength of IRIs and IRI-like measures lies in their use as placement procedures. If educators are using IRI-like procedures and tools for the purposes of benchmarking, special care needs to be taken. We caution against the use of a single (usually commercially prepared) IRI as the sole criterion for placement/achievement. Having said this, we also believe that the informal procedures embedded in IRIs, coupled with the addition of more-contemporary strategies such as retellings, can provide valuable diagnostic information (see Chapter 9).

Revisions to Traditional IRIs.   The close critical examination of IRIs that has occurred over the past several decades has resulted in changes. Several older IRIs have completed major revisions, and several new IRIs have appeared. In some cases, authors have addressed criticisms related to passage selection, scoring ambiguities, quality of comprehension items, and/or difficulties related to content. In other cases, authors have worked from an interactive, constructive perspective and have attempted to create inventories that reflect a contemporary model of reading. For example, the Analytical Reading Inventory, an IRI with considerable history, has added new dimensions in its most recent assessments (Woods & Moe, 2011). Thus, users can now evaluate comprehension questions in terms of "reader-text relationships," examining students' ability to retell explicitly stated facts, put information together, connect author and reader ("from head to text"), and evaluate and substantiate information with more individualized responses. Like the QRI-5, the Analytical Reading Inventory provides some tools for assessing prior knowledge, and the authors have added guidelines and materials to support the use of this tool for progress monitoring. As well, they offer a profile sheet of the sort that was pioneered by Leslie and Caldwell with the QRI.

Several older IRIs have also added early/emergent literacy assessments to their most recent revisions (Bader, 2009; Johns, 2008). These include assessments of concepts about print, interviews, and expanded phonemic awareness assessments with tests of blending and segmenting sounds in words. In addition, some inventories include screening assessments for English language learners. The Bader Reading and Language Inventory (BRLI, Bader & Pearce, 2009), for example, includes an "ESL checklist" that provides a way for teachers to informally assess students' English language development.

The Comprehensive Reading Inventory (Cooter, Flynt, & Cooter, 2007) is a recently expanded IRI. In addition to a comprehensive set of conventional IRI materials, it provides a complete set of parallel passages (four alternate forms) in Spanish. Interview materials and fluency assessment are also included. Since it includes both a small picture and a background-setting introduction, students who are younger and/or benefit from instructional support might do somewhat better on this IRI. The addition of impressive reliability and validity data also significantly improves the value of this IRI.

Other IRIs have included more exposition and texts appropriate for middle- and secondary-level students. The revised Classroom Reading Inventory (CRI) (Wheelock, Silveroli, & Campbell, 2008), for example, provides separate forms for elementary, junior high/middle school, and high school/adults. These additions are welcome, but until recently there were really no IRIs developed specifically for assessment in middle and high school. For an annotated listing of IRIs, see Appendix D. In the next section, we describe a relatively new option for teachers of adolescents.

Adolescent Literacy Inventory.   The recently published Adolescent Literacy Inventory, Grades 6–12, or ALI (Brozo & Afflerbach, 2011), was designed to be an IRI that "focuses on the specific academic literacy abilities of adolescents. . . . [through which] critical data related to decoding, fluency, vocabulary, and comprehension can be obtained" (p. xi). The authors indicate that the ALI can be used to identify students' reading levels, to gather diagnostic information to inform instruction, and to establish a baseline on students' academic performance.

The ALI is based on a comprehensive understanding of the factors that affect adolescents' literacy performance, including research on academic vocabulary, prior knowledge, reader engagement, and content variations. There are a number of innovative features to the ALI, including:

- ✔ Maze placement passages
- ✔ Variety of prereading options
- ✔ Assessment of metacognition
- ✔ Text passages in diverse content areas (language arts, science, social studies, and mathematics)
- ✔ Recommendations for instruction

The authors note that this inventory can be used by content teachers to make decisions about whether the reading abilities of particular students are appropriate for the textbook reading demands in their domain. However, it is more likely to be useful to reading specialists and other individuals as they assess the abilities of struggling students and plan instructional interventions for them. The advantages to this assessment are several, starting with the fact that the authors have been attentive to the selection of passages in order to have them be "representative of real reading in the middle and high school . . ." (p. 5). In addition, the ALI provides two distinct types of passages: high interest and textbook.

As with any IRI, the ALI provides the tools to assess students' reading fluency, oral reading accuracy, and comprehension. Importantly, the ALI provides assessment options that capture factors that are unique or especially important to understanding adolescent readers. Among these are:

1. *Assessments of academic vocabulary:* The test offers three possible ways to examine students' academic vocabulary: (a) prereading text impression activities; (b) prereading vocabulary self-awareness activities; and (c) maze placement passages requiring students to select the most appropriate words to complete short textbook excerpts.
2. *Interactive assessment option:* With this option, educators can mimic a textbook reading lesson, observe students' engagement and skills during authentic instructional exchanges, and examine what types of support might help students (see also Chapter 10).

With so many materials and options, the ALI can be a bit overwhelming, so the authors offer a helpful "decision tree." And, as a alternative to the graded word lists of more-conventional IRIs, the ALI uses *maze passages* to help the administrator make decisions about which levels of the passages to select for more complete assessment.

The maze passage is a variation on the cloze technique. Here, a passage of a known level is selected; then, words are systematically deleted from the passage—usually every fifth or eighth word. The student's job is to replace these words during reading. With the ALI maze passages, specific words have been removed that represent key vocabulary for those passages. Then, in place of the word, three choices are offered (see Figure 8.10). As you might imagine, the guidelines for scoring a cloze or maze are quite different from those of other comprehension/reading assessments.

**FIGURE 8.10
Sample Maze
Passage, ALI**

What Is Science?

INSTRUCTIONS   Read the story to yourself. When you come to a part where there are three underlined words in very dark print, choose the one word that makes sense in the sentence. Circle that word.

Suppose you could send a robot to another planet. What kinds of **(1) conduct, trials, experiments** would you **(2) list, program, code** the robot to carry out? Before you programmed the robot, you would need to figure out what **(3) information, order, rank** you wanted it to **(4) arrange, gather, group**. Scientists are currently **(5) emerging, mounting, developing** robots that they plan to send to Mars. These robots are being **(6) designed, deliberate, planned** to examine the **(7) atmosphere, ambiance, population,** rocks, gravity, and magnetic **(8) meadows, fields, turfs** of the planet.

Source: Brozo, W., & Afflerbach, P. (2010). *Adolescent literacy inventory, Grades 6–12.* NY: Allyn & Bacon, p. 23.

The vocabulary assessments are likely to be especially interesting for many teachers since there is so little of this type of assessment available for students at the intermediate levels and above. In Figures 8.11 and 8.12, you will find examples of the "Text Impressions" and "Vocabulary Self-Awareness" components of the ALI.

The authors of the ALI provide no information about reliability and very little about the development of the materials, assessments, or criteria for scoring. Consequently, teachers and interventionists are likely to find this tool most useful for formative, diagnostic purposes rather than benchmarking or progress monitoring (see later in this chapter).

Benchmark Assessment System.   The second edition of the Benchmark Assessment System-1 (Grades K–2) and Benchmark Assessment System-2 (Grades 3–8) (Fountas & Pinnell, 2010) are examples of contemporary assessments based on most of the principles of the original IRIs. The Developmental Reading Assessment (DRA) is another example that we discuss more fully near the end of this chapter (see page 438). The authors of the Fountas & Pinnell Benchmark Assessment System describe it as an ". . . assessment tool for teachers, literacy specialists, and clinicians to use in determining students' developmental reading levels for the purpose of informing instruction and documenting reading progress" ("Field Study of Reliability and Validity," n.d., p. 1).

Like an IRI, the Benchmark Assessment System (BAS or, as many call it, the F&P) is individually administered and students read increasingly difficult text in order for teachers to determine independent and instructional reading levels. Also like other IRIs, the Benchmark System makes these determinations based on students' oral reading and comprehension performance. Other scores that are computed include a self-correction rate and a fluency rate.

What is unique about the Benchmark System is that it is linked to the Fountas & Pinnell A–Z Text Gradient, rather than to a grade level. As well, students read full-length "little books" that tend to be much longer than is typical in more-traditional IRIs. For example, students in late grade 1 might read either the narrative fiction *The Best Cat*

FIGURE 8.11   Sample Text Impressions Task, ALI

Textbook Passage #1: *The Sound of Summer Running,*
by Ray Bradbury

Text Impressions

bleached	hard *sinews*	still *plenty* of
and *coiled* springs	you *dig* them	heavy *iron* shoes
soft *loam* of the	*peel* off the	big *chunks* of

DIRECTIONS   Read the above list of words and the *italicized* words in phrases taken from the passage you are about to read. In the space below, use all of the listed words to write a short description of what you believe the passage will be about.

_____

_____

_____

_____

_____

_____

_____

_____

_____

_____

_____

_____

_____

_____

_____

_____

_____

_____

_____

_____

_____

_____

_____

_____

_____

_____

_____

_____

_____

_____

_____

_____

Source: Brozo, W., & Afflerbach, P. (2010). *Adolescent literacy inventory, Grades 6–12.* NY: Allyn & Bacon, p. 72.

FIGURE 8.12   Sample ALI Vocabulary Self-Awareness Task

Textbook Passage #1: The *Sound of Summer Running*, by Ray Bradbury

Vocabulary Self-Awareness

PROCEDURES

1. Examine the list of words written in the first column.
2. Put a "+" next to each word you know well, and give an accurate example and definition of the word. Your definition and example must relate to the unit of study.
3. Place a "✓" next to any words for which you can write only a definition or an example, but not both.
4. Put a "–" next to words that are new to you.

Word	+	✓	–	Example	Definition
chunks					
plenty					
iron					
bleached					
sinews					
coiled					
loam					

Source: Brozo, W., & Afflerbach, P. (2010). *Adolescent literacy inventory, Grades 6–12.* NY: Allyn & Bacon, p. 73.

(334 running words) or the nonfiction text *All about Koalas* (217 running words). This contrasts with the longest QRI-5 narrative texts for grade 1 (around 264 words) or the nonfiction QRI passages, which range from 76 to 85 words. No other available IRI comes close in length to either of these two tools.

There are other differences as well. For example, the Benchmark System does not use a system of errors like that captured in Figure 8.4. Instead, it relies on a scoring system and coding scheme more associated with Reading Recovery (see discussion of miscue analysis in Chapter 9). Finally, in place of the traditional comprehension questions, the Benchmark System assesses students with a "comprehension conversation." The examiner uses one of the conversation starters ("Talk about what happened in this story" or "Talk about what you learned in this story." Once the student has begun the conversation, the teacher uses prompts such as the following to elicit more information: "Say more about that" or "What else?" As students provide information, teachers check off relevant areas of the scoring guide (see Figure 8.13).

The publisher has conducted considerable research related to the reliability and validity of the Benchmark System, available online from http://www.heinemann.com/fountasandpinnell/research/BASFieldStudyFullReport.pdf. Specifically, they provide evidence about the extent to which the test results in reliable estimates of students' reading ability, that the text levels actually represent the text gradients assigned, and that the texts within a gradient level are equivalent. The data and commentary provided suggest a rigorous developmental process, with data used to revise and refine both the text selections and the criteria employed. The results of the reliability study suggest that the test-retest reliability of the BAS is good to excellent. As well, the text levels are reasonably reflective of incremental changes in difficulty for fiction texts—and to a lesser degree for nonfiction texts—with some levels clearly more uneven than others. However, the fiction and nonfiction texts are much less equivalent, and schools who wish to use this assessment tool to measure progress would do well to insist on the use of only one type of text for benchmarking purposes. Not surprisingly, students were much more erratic and less successful in reading nonfiction than fiction texts at the same level of difficulty. This is particularly problematic given that there is only one fiction and one nonfiction at each text level.

During development of the BAS, the authors did conclude that the criteria for determining reading level (independent, instructional, and "hard") should differ between primary and intermediate grades, for oral reading accuracy only. This distinction seems a reasonable one and, given data reported in the BAS, we think the criteria are useful. These are provided in Figure 8.14. As you can see, the standards for oral reading accuracy are lower for the earlier levels than for the upper ones.

The validity evidence for the BAS is strong. The system itself represents an assessment of authentic reading content and tasks. As a result, students' performance is likely to be similar to their performance on classroom reading tasks. In addition, the authors compare students' results on the text leveling system with other measures of reading. Not surprisingly, it is highly correlated with the Reading Recovery text levels. This is important because the text reading levels of Reading Recovery have been demonstrated to be correlated with other measures of reading such as the Iowa Test of Basic Skills and the Gates-MacGinitie (Gomez-Bellenge, Rodgers, Wang, & Schulz, 2005; Gomez-Bellenge & Thompson, 2005). It is also moderately correlated with estimates of isolated word reading (Slosson) but much less so with the Degrees of Reading Power. In summary, the Fountas

FIGURE 8.13   Sample Comprehension Conversation, BAS

Part Two: Comprehension Conversation

Have a conversation with the student, noting the key understandings the student expresses. Use prompts as needed to stimulate discussion of understandings the student does not express. It is not necessary to use every prompt for each book. Score for evidence of all understandings expressed—with or without a prompt. Circle the number in the score column that reflects the level of understanding demonstrated.

Teacher: Talk about what happened in this story.

Comprehension Scoring Key

0 Reflects **unsatisfactory** understanding of the text. Either does not respond or talks off the topic.

1 Reflects **limited** understanding of the text. Mentions a few facts or ideas but does not express the important information or ideas.

2 Reflects **satisfactory** understanding of the text. Includes important information and ideas but neglects other key understandings.

3 Reflects **excellent** understanding of the text. Includes almost all important information and main ideas.

Key Understandings	Prompts	Score
Within the Text Spencer went to a farm to get a cat but he could not find one. Finally, he did find a cat. Recounts some essential information from the text, such as: the boy went to the farm to choose a cat; something was wrong with all the cats he saw; finally, a little cat chose him. *Note any additional understandings:*	What was the problem in the story? How was Spencer's problem solved? Tell what the boy did to find the best cat for him.	0 1 2 3
Beyond and About the Text Spencer really wanted a cat because (gives a plausible reason). Spencer was disappointed (or sad) when none of the cats at the farm were the right cat. The little cat wanted a home and the cat really chose the boy. Spencer was glad the cat chose him. You can tell Spencer really wanted a cat because it showed *really* in dark letters and he was thinking about a cat (or other feature of the text that the child has noticed). *Note any additional understandings:*	Tell why you think Spencer wanted a cat (or what kind of cat the boy really wanted). Tell how Spencer felt when he couldn't find a cat (or how he felt at the end). Why do you think the little cat was the best cat for Spencer? How did Spencer feel at the end? Look at page 3. How did the author and illustrator show you how much Spencer wanted a cat?	0 1 2 3

Guide to Total Score

6-7 Excellent Comprehension

5   Satisfactory Comprehension

4   Limited Comprehension

0-3 Unsatisfactory Comprehension

Subtotal Score: _____/6_____

Add 1 for any additional understandings: _____/1_____

Total Score: _____/7_____

**FIGURE 8.14
Oral Reading
Accuracy by Level
for the *BAS***

Levels A–K		Levels L–Z	
95%–100%	Independent	98%–100%	Independent
90%–94%	Instructional	95%–97%	Instructional
Below 90%	Hard	Below 95%	Hard

and Pinnell Benchmark Assessment System is sufficiently reliable and valid for use as a progress monitoring benchmark as long as educators take care to follow standardized procedures for administering the test. Schools/teachers who use the BAS (F&P) for periodic benchmark assessments would do well to recall that the text gradients represent smaller increments of change than the typical grade levels of IRIs and that therefore interpretation of results should probably be made across more than one text level.

Specialized Inventories: Using Structured Assessments of Study Skills/Strategies.
Although most high schools and colleges have some form of study-skills programs, there are only a few commercially available informal tools that assess study skills and habits. A recent addition to the choices for teachers in grades 4 to 8 is Science, Social Studies, and Mathematics Academic Reading Test (SSSMART) (Farr & Munroe, 2007), which comes in both diagnostic and survey test forms. As the title says, this test is intended to assess students' skills in reading-content materials in science, social studies, and mathematics. Each grade-level test has subtests related to academic vocabulary, comprehension, and CUES ("Concepts and Understanding of Essential Skills"). An additional skimming and scanning subtest spans all three subjects. This test has separate diagnostic tests for each of the three content areas and a shorter "survey" test that assesses students' general reading in the content areas. It is unique in its purpose and construction. The test items were developed using national and state content standards, content specialists, and reading experts. Reading tasks were developed that are representative of those typically found in content-area textbooks. The test booklets contain color graphics, photographs, and charts. This inventory was piloted in 115 schools in 29 states that were nationally representative. Reliability estimates for the composites in each content area are very good for a group-administered test (ranging from .89 to .92), and although the subtests for each content area (vocabulary, CUES, and comprehension) are not as reliable, the total for these subtests (across all content areas) is excellent. This test could provide exceptionally useful information to educators in the intermediate and middle grades who find their students performing less well in the content areas than they do in English language arts.

The Learning and Study Strategies Inventory—2nd Edition (LASSI).   This is a somewhat different type of diagnostic instrument, developed originally by Weinstein and her colleagues and recently revised (Weinstein & Palmer, 2002). It is a thoughtfully conceived standardized test with national norms, designed to assess the metacognitive and study strategies of high school and college students.

The LASSI is a ten-scale, eighty-item assessment with subtests organized around several large component areas involving "skill, will, and self-regulation"; it is designed to provide information about how students conceive of studying. This group-administered test asks students to report and evaluate their own behaviors, attitudes, and beliefs about learning and studying. The original form of the LASSI (Weinstein, Schulte, & Palmer, 1987) consisted of seventy-seven items that are distributed among ten scales: (1) Attitude, (2) Motivation, (3) Time Management, (4) Anxiety, (5) Concentration, (6) Information-processing, (7) Selecting Main Idea, (8) Study Aids, (9) Self-Testing, and (10) Test Strategies. Students respond to each item on a five-point Likert scale ranging from "not at all typical of me" to "very typical of me." Sample items include the following.

> Information Processing:
>> To help me remember new principles we are learning in class, I practice applying them.
>> I try to find relationships between what I am learning and what I already know.
> Motivation:
>> When work is difficult I either give up or study only the easy parts.
>> I set goals for the grades I want in my classes.
> Time Management:
>> I find it hard to stick to a study schedule.
>> I set aside more time to study the subjects that are difficult for me.

Weinstein, Schulte, and Palmer (1987) reported internal consistency (coefficient alpha) for the scaled scores ranging from 0.68 to 0.86 and test-retest reliability coefficients ranging from 0.72 to 0.85 for the scaled scores. For the LASSI-2, items were updated and culled (with dated items removed). The authors report that they widened the scope of some scales and created an equal number of items for each scale. They also broadened their norming sample, which nevertheless remains small and limited to specific institutional types. For the LASSI-2, Weinstein, Schulte, and Palmer report that the lowest coefficient is .73 and that most exceed .80. However, given the amount of research conducted using the LASSI, the technical information is somewhat sparse. Validity must be derived from theoretical studies supporting the uniqueness of the subtests. It is clear that only three large component areas can be distinguished for diagnostic purposes. Despite its limitations, most reviewers agree that this test is unique and offers important potential screening/diagnostic information (e.g., Prevat et al., 2006). Given the dearth of assessment tools focused on adolescents, we recommend the test because of its well-conceived theoretical and research base.

Of course, it would be helpful to know how students perform in their actual subject-matter study. To collect information about students' application of knowledge and skill, teachers will need to construct their own inventories.

Group Reading Inventory (GRI).   A GRI is designed for use in the classroom and is helpful for gathering information about how well students can read their textbooks (Rakes & Smith, 2001; Unrau, 2004). A GRI typically has two components: a book-handling component and a comprehension section. Both parts of the GRI are constructed by using the actual textbook employed in the classroom. Resource room teachers, of course, will need to construct an inventory that samples several types of texts.

**FIGURE 8.15
Excerpt from a
Group Reading
Inventory**

Using Book Parts

Introduction: These questions are designed to help you understand the organization of your text and to enable you to use it more effectively. You may use your text in answering the questions.

1. Where would you look to locate a short story in the text if you could not recall the title or the author?
   a. Glossary   **c.** Literary Terms and Techniques
   b. Table of Contents   **d.** Index of Authors and Titles

2. If you came across the word "demagoguery" in your reading in the text, where would you look *first* for a definition?
   a. Table of Contents   **c.** Glossary
   b. Literary Terms and Techniques   **d.** The Composition and Language Program

Source: From *Content Area Literacy: An Integrated Approach,* 7th ed., by John E. Readence, Thomas W. Beam, and R. Scott Baldwin. Copyright © 2001 by Kendall/Hunt Publishing Company. Used with permission.

Part I of the GRI is constructed by generating ten to twelve questions about the various parts of the text (see Figure 8.15). Part II of the GRI is akin to an IRI. A relatively short selection (about five hundred words) is drawn from a chapter in the text. Ten or fifteen questions are generated to test comprehension. Whereas students are directed to complete Part I of the GRI while using their textbook, the questions in Part II are to be answered without referring to the book. The information gleaned from this type of assessment can be used to complete an observation checklist like the one proposed in Chapter 9.

In summary, many of the commercial IRIs have recognized the variable nature of reading performance and have made some attempts to offer tools for collecting multiple samples under some varied conditions. The extent to which these are useful depends heavily on the orientation of the instructional program and the beliefs of the teacher. In the next sections, we describe various techniques designed to create a structured assessment for (1) analyzing oral reading miscues, (2) analyzing fluency, (3) analyzing comprehension, and (4) analyzing written language. When used in conjunction with each other, the procedures described form an assessment system that provides a great deal of information about the reader in a fairly economical fashion.

Gray Oral Reading Test, Fourth Edition.   First published in 1915 as the Gray Oral Reading Standardized Paragraphs, this test has been revised and published most recently as the Gray Oral Reading Test, Fourth Edition, or GORT-4 (Wiederholt & Bryant, 2001). Unlike any of the other assessments in this section, the GORT-4 is a norm-referenced test with two alternate equivalent forms. However, it is more like an IRI in its configuration than most tests and would most likely be used like one in terms of screening or periodic benchmark assessments. Each form contains fourteen passages of increasing difficulty, one more than was included in the previous edition, GORT-3 (Wiederholt & Bryant, 1992). Five comprehension questions follow each passage, and each passage is timed. The authors suggest four purposes for using the GORT-4, which involve identifying students with oral reading problems, evaluating the strengths and weaknesses of individual students, documenting progress in remedial programs, and measuring reading ability in research investigations.

Targeted for ages 7 to 18, the test is similar to an informal reading inventory in format and construction. However, norm-referenced interpretations of scores are available for reading rate, accuracy, a combination of rate and accuracy called the "passage score," and comprehension. Standard scores and percentile ranks are both reported. In addition, an oral reading quotient is generated that is a combination of the oral passage reading score and the comprehension score. Finally, guidelines and scoring aids are provided to conduct an error analysis of oral reading behaviors.

The three types of content-related evidence of validity provided for the GORT-4—a detailed rationale for the structure and content of the passages and comprehension questions, the procedures used to select items, and an analysis of comprehension item bias with respect to gender and race—appear reasonable. Criterion-related evidence of validity was not updated with the GORT-4. Correlation coefficients (median 5.64) from a series of smaller studies comparing GORT-3 (Wiederholt & Bryant, 1992) or its predecessor, GORT-R (Wiederholt & Bryant, 1986), with a variety of other assessment instruments are provided. Construct-related evidence of validity is supplied through a procedure that first identifies constructs that are presumed to account for test performance, then generates hypotheses based on these constructs, and finally tests these hypotheses either logically or empirically. An aspect of this test that concerns some is oral reading without any preparation or opportunity to read silently.

Norming procedures for the GORT-4 appear representative of the nation in 2000, although the number of individuals sampled at both ends of the age span is minimal. The evidence of reliability appears acceptable for the purposes for which the test is intended. Internal-consistency estimates of reliability, including subtest coefficients, are greater than .87. Alternate-form reliability coefficients for thirteen age levels range from .73 to .97; comprehension scores are lower than the others. The SEM at each age level is reported as 1 for subtest scores. Test-retest correlations, delayed alternate-form correlations, and inter-scorer correlations are also acceptable. Again, the correlations for the comprehension scores were the lowest.

The GORT-4 is relatively easy to administer and can provide guidance to a novice diagnostician, because the record form is quite comprehensive and helps to organize information. Although most of the information provided can also be obtained by using an IRI, the availability of normative data is desirable when the reporting of standardized scores is necessary.

Oral Reading Fluency

Most definitions of fluency include components of rate and accuracy but consider other dimensions as well: "Fluency is the ability to read with accuracy, expression/phrasing, appropriate rate, and comprehension" (Johns & Berglund, 2002, p. 5). There has been an increased interest in fluency among both educators and researchers, in part because there appears to be such a strong relationship between oral reading fluency and comprehension (Carnine, Silbert, & Kame'enui, 1997; Rasinski, Blachowicz, & Lems, 2006) and because diverse students require attention to fluency to reach high levels of reading achievement (Chard, Simmons, & Kame'enui, 1998).

In Chapter 9, we will address fluency assessment more broadly since there are many important diagnostic issues to be considered. Used diagnostically, fluency data can be enormously helpful in identifying key areas for struggling readers. However, many of these are more time consuming than is practicable for use with all or many students. So, for now, we consider the type of information that is likely to be gathered and recorded when structured inventories are used for benchmarking and/or preliminary diagnostic purposes.

Most, but not all, informal reading inventories now provide some guidance and resources for assessing oral reading fluency. Generally, this includes *measures of rate and accuracy*, and some provide additional materials such as fluency rubrics and/or checklists. Informal reading inventories typically suggest collecting data on rate, or the number of words read per minute (WPM). In order to find the students' rate, the teacher would:

1. Convert the amount of time it took to read the passage to seconds.
2. Count the number of words read during that time.
3. Divide the number words read by the total reading time,
4. Multiply the resulting number by 60 to reconvert it into words per minute.

More recently, researchers have argued that reading fluency (rate and accuracy) should be assessed using a slightly different approach. They advocate capturing the words read *correctly* per minute (WCPM), which provides a combined estimate of rate and accuracy (Kame'enui, Simmons, Good, & Horn, 2001). The following procedure is used to determine WCPM:

1. Convert the amount of time it took to read the passage to seconds.
2. Count the number of words read *correctly*.
3. Divide the number of words read *correctly* by the total reading time.
4. Multiply the resulting number by 60 to reconvert it into words per minute.

Determining the acceptable range for oral and silent reading rates is somewhat controversial. Traditionally, rate has been based on the number of words students read in a minute (WPM), and most IRIs report criteria for that. Guidelines provided by Powell (n.d.) for evaluating the oral and silent reading rates obtained on IRIs for students at different instructional levels are presented in Figure 8.16.

FIGURE 8.16
Reading Rate in Words per Minute

Instructional Reading Level	Oral Reading Rate at Sight	Silent Reading
Grade 1	45–65	45–65
Grade 2	70–100	70–100
Grade 3	105–125	120–140
Grade 4	125–145	130–180
Grade 5	135–155	165–205
Grade 6	140–160	190–220

FIGURE 8.17
QRI Rate Charts

Ranges of Oral Reading Rate and Correct Rate of Students Reading at Instructional Level

Level	Oral	
	Words per minute (WPM)	Correct Words per Minute (CWPM)
Pre-primer—P	23–59	13–55
Pre-primer—NP	22–64	11–59
Primer	28–66	10–52
First	37–77	20–68
Second	43–89	19–77
Third	56–104	53–101
Fourth	57–115	54–112
Fifth	65–121	62–118

Note: P = Pictured passages; NP = Non-pictured passages

Ranges of Silent Reading Rate of Students Reading at Instructional Level

Level	Silent
	Words per minute (WPM)
Fifth	73–175
Sixth	91–235
Upper Middle School	
Narrative	119–233
Expository	105–189
High School	65–334

Note: Figures based on means and standard deviations

Few IRIs address the issue of rate in relation to the specific demands of a specific test. However, the QRI-5 does offer rate ranges that were derived from students as they read the passages *on that specific test*. Using the means and standard deviations from their validation studies, the QRI-5 provides guidance for interpreting students' rates on the QRI-5 (see Figure 8.17). Tha'm's rate on the grade 4 passages ranged from 76 wpm (narrative) to 56 wmp (expository). Her words correct per minute rates (WCPM) were approximately the same. In other words, while she is accurate, she is reading very slowly.

Curriculum-Based Measures and Oral Reading Fluency. One commonly recommended approach for assessing fluency (rate and accuracy) is the *one-minute read*, in which students' oral reading accuracy is evaluated during one minute of reading. Students read unfamiliar text, and the number of words read correctly per minute is computed. Guidelines and norms for making judgments about students' oral reading have been developed by Hasbrouck and Tindal (2006) (see Figure 8.18).

FIGURE 8.18
Hasbrouck and
Tindal Rate
Guidelines for
Oral Reading

Grade	Percentile	Fall WCPM	Winter WCPM	Spring WCPM
		TABLE 1		
		Oral reading fluency norms, grades 1–8		
1	90		81	111
	75		47	82
	50		23	53
	25		12	28
	10		6	15
	SD		32	39
	Count		16,950	19,434
2	90	106	125	142
	75	79	100	117
	50	51	72	89
	25	25	42	61
	10	11	18	31
	SD	37	41	42
	Count	15,896	18,229	20,128
3	90	128	146	162
	75	99	120	137
	50	71	92	107
	25	44	62	78
	10	21	36	48
	SD	40	43	44
	Count	16,988	17,383	18,372
4	90	145	166	180
	75	119	139	152
	50	94	112	123
	25	68	87	98
	10	45	61	72
	SD	40	41	43
	Count	16,523	14,572	16,269
5	90	166	182	194
	75	139	156	168
	50	110	127	139
	25	85	99	109
	10	61	74	83
	SD	45	44	45
	Count	16,212	13,331	15,292
6	90	177	195	204
	75	153	167	177
	50	127	140	150
	25	98	111	122
	10	68	82	93
	SD	42	45	44
	Count	10,520	9,218	11,290

(continued)

**FIGURE 8.18
(Continued)**

Grade	Percentile	Fall WCPM	Winter WCPM	Spring WCPM
7	90	180	192	202
	75	156	165	177
	50	128	136	150
	25	102	109	123
	10	79	88	98
	SD	40	43	41
	Count	6,482	4,058	5,998
8	90	185,	199	199
	75	161	173	177
	50	133	146	151
	25	106	115	124
	10	77	84	97
	SD	43	45	41
	Count	5,546	3,496	5,335

WCPM: Words correct per minute
SD: Standard deviation
Count: Number of student scores

Source: Hasbrouck, J., & Tindal, G. A. (2006). Oral reading fluency norms: A valuable assessment tool for reading teachers. *The Reading Teacher, 59,* p. 639.

Hasbrouck and Tindal recommend using the fiftieth percentile as an appropriate standard for proficiency. Of course, rates are likely to vary considerably depending on the type and familiarity of text and the purpose for reading. As a result, Hasbrouck and Tindal (2006) conclude, "pushing every student to reach the ninetieth percentile or even the seventy-fifth percentile in their grade level is not a reasonable or appropriate goal for fluency instruction" (p. 642).

It should be noted that these norms were established using grade-level material only. That is, the fluency performance of all students, no matter their reading level, was estimated on texts appropriate for the grade level for each student. This raises issues when interpreting results for students who are well below grade level. As a practical matter, we suggest using the rates appropriate for the materials that the student is actually reading. For example, if a fifth-grade student is instructional at grade 3, then you would use the grade 3 proficiency levels. We must emphasize, however, that this will provide only some estimate for instructional purposes, since any normative information will be invalid given the changed conditions.

Adding data about rate and accuracy can create a more complete picture of students' performance on structured inventories. For example, Tha'm's rate varied somewhat from passage to passage, but her rate on the Level 4 (Tomie dePaola) passage of the QRI-5 yielded these results (during a spring administration):

WPM: 125 words per minute
WCPM: 89 correct words per minute

As you can see, it is useful to have both measures (see Chapter 9 for further discussion). Using the WPM rate, Tha'm would be judged to be at no risk in this area. However, using WCPM and the Hasbrouck and Tindal benchmarks, Tha'm is performing below the twenty-fifth percentile.

We are not aware of any IRI that factors rate/accuracy into its judgments of instructional reading level, although individual school districts could do this. On the other hand, an explosion of fluency resources and materials has appeared in recent years. Among the most common is the DIBELS (see Chapter 4). A number of schools engaged in federally supported programs and/or RTI development have also turned to AIMSweb, a Web-based software management system that provides passages for assessing students' accuracy and fluency using curriculum-based measurement techniques (CBM) and DIBELS (see Chapter 4). Of course, many educators are concerned about these procedures because they seem open to questions of both reliability and validity. The primary concern is that proponents suggest that the measures *alone* can be used to evaluate students' reading achievement, giving rise to questions about reliability. The rationale for using these measures rests largely with their predictive validity—the extent to which students' performance on, for example, a test of rapid reading of nonsense words predicts students' performance on other measures of reading. Valencia and colleagues (2010) also note that relying *only* on measures of WCPM can lead to both false positives (identifying students as at risk who actually read and comprehend well) and false negatives (failing to identify students who are at risk and are likely to fail). Others have also reported the under- and overidentification of students using the single fluency measure (see Pressley et al., 2006).

In Chapter 9 we address this issue more substantially. For now, it is important to note that questions remain about the best measures of fluency and their utility in predicting subsequent reading performance. Fuchs, Fuchs, and Compton (2004), for example, found that fluency assessments involving word recognition (real words) were a much better measure of progress than timed reading on nonsense words. In addition, students' performance on *word* recognition tasks was a stronger predictor of their reading comprehension *and* their ability to decode.

Tests of Word Recognition and Phonics Decoding

Word-level difficulties are very common among poor readers and writers. Indeed, most students who are identified as having reading or writing difficulties will have some weaknesses in the area of decoding, word identification, and/or spelling. Classroom teachers generally observe and assess students' performance informally and then bring their concerns to a staffing meeting or make a formal request for further evaluation. However, there are a number of structured evaluation tools that can be used to assess word-level skills and strategies. Many of these are structured, but informal assessments, but there is at least one widely used norm-referenced tool, the TOWRE, which we review here along with less-formal methods. In general, information is needed regarding three areas of word-level performance: *sight-word recognition*, *word analysis*, and *spelling*. The limitations of most structured word recognition tests is that they do not involve reading words in connected text. The results from these tests must, of course, be considered against information about students' word recognition performance *during reading* (see the discussions of running records and miscue analysis). Similarly, although spelling tests can and do provide important information, students' spelling should be examined during writing.

Test of Word Reading Efficiency (TOWRE).   The TOWRE (Torgesen, Wagner, & Rashotte, 1999) is a norm-referenced test of word reading accuracy and fluency that is often used to screen and monitor students' progress in these areas. The test has two alternative forms, each of which contains two subtests: Sight Word Efficiency and Phonetic Decoding Efficiency. Each is administered in forty-five seconds.

Both subtests are timed and require students to read from a list of printed words (or nonwords) as quickly as they can. The lists increase in difficulty. The Sight Word Efficiency subtest list consists of words selected primarily from *The Reading Teacher's Book of Lists* (Fry, Kress, & Fountoukidis, 1993), with the highest-frequency words at the beginning of the list and progressing to lower-frequency words at the end of the list. The Phonemic Decoding Efficiency Words (nonwords) test begins with words that contain two phoneme, both CV and VC. The test progresses in difficulty to multisyllabic words and includes the following elements and patterns: CCVCC, final *e* words, *r*-controlled, vowel digraphs. Students are instructed to use their finger to help keep their place if they wish. The words for each subtest and form are printed on separate cards. Scores for the Sight Word Efficiency subtest are the total number of words read correctly in forty-five seconds. For the Phonemic Decoding Efficiency subtest, the score is the total number of all nonwords pronounced correctly in forty-five seconds.

The TOWRE was normed on individuals between the ages of six and twenty-four years, using procedures that were both comprehensive and representative. Four types of reliability data are reported for the TOWRE: content sampling, alternate form, test-retest, and inter-scorer reliability. Coefficients on this short test range from .82 to .97, and the alternate-form reliability coefficients exceed .90, indicating acceptable reliability.

The authors use item analysis and differential item functioning analysis to demonstrate content validity. The authors do note that there are some items that reveal bias among subgroups, but it is difficult to determine what impact this would have on the validity of the test overall. The Woodcock Reading Mastery-R Word Attack and Word Identification subtests are used to establish concurrent validity. The correlations (between .86 and .94) reveal that the same construct is being assessed on both tests. Because the TOWRE is short and taps only one component area of reading ability, the predictive validity of the test is important. The authors have compared the TOWRE test scores with the Gray Oral Reading Test–3rd Edition and found acceptable correlations between the two.

As with other norm-referenced tests, the TOWRE provides percentiles, standard scores, and age/grade equivalents. The authors provide evidence of content, predictive, and construct validity. Test users should, however, be aware of the narrow construct tested by the TOWRE. The highly constrained time limits may very well mask students' word recognition abilities under untimed conditions. The authors make it clear that the TOWRE measures isolated specific reading skills that are *components* of reading. While rapid processing is predictive of other aspects of reading competence, these need to be examined separately in a comprehensive diagnostic examination.

Word Lists.   As we have already noted, it is generally wise to evaluate component skills in use, rather than in isolation. Clearly, using a word list to test word recognition skills is a very constraining procedure. However, one attribute of skilled reading is *automaticity* in word recognition. Good readers are able to recognize large numbers of words rapidly.

Allington and McGill-Franzen (1980) found that the scores generated by isolated word recognition tests were markedly different from those generated by in-context word recognition tests. The scores were especially divergent for less-able readers. It appears that context does facilitate word recognition, but it is used more heavily by poor readers than by able ones. Thus, students' ability to recognize high-frequency sight words should be evaluated both in isolation and in context.

There are many lists of high-frequency sight words. One of the most widely used is the Dolch Basic Sight Word Test (Dolch, 1942a). This test consists of 220 high-frequency sight words grouped into lists deemed appropriate from preprimer to third grade. The list has generated controversy, and many prefer to use one of the more recently created lists (for example, Fry, 1980; Johnson, 1971). The "New Instant Word List" (Fry, 1980) appears in Figure 8.19. Fry's analysis suggests that one-half of all written material comprises the first

**FIGURE 8.19
The Fry Instant
Word List**

First Hundred Instant Words				Second Hundred	
First 25 Group 1a	Second 25 Group 1b	Third 25 Group 1c	Fourth 25 Group 1d	First 25 Group 2a	Second 25 Group 2b
the	or	will	number	new	great
of	one	up	no	sound	where
and	had	other	way	take	help
a	by	about	could	only	through
to	word	out	people	little	much
in	but	many	my	work	before
is	not	then	than	know	line
you	what	them	first	place	right
that	all	these	water	year	too
it	were	so	been	live	mean
he	we	some	call	me	old
was	when	her	who	back	any
for	your	would	oil	give	same
on	can	make	now	most	tell
are	said	like	find	very	boy
as	there	him	long	after	follow
with	use	into	down	thing	came
his	an	time	day	our	want
they	each	has	did	just	show
I	which	look	get	name	also
at	she	two	come	good	around
be	do	more	made	sentence	form
this	how	write	may	man	three
have	their	go	part	think	small
from	if	see	over	say	set
Common suffixes: *s, ing, ed*				Common suffixes: *s, ing,*	

Source: Fry, E. B. (1980, December). The new instant word list. *The Reading Teacher, 34*(3), 284–289. Reprinted with permission of the International Reading Association. All rights reserved.

(continued)

**FIGURE 8.19
(Continued)**

Instant Words		Third Hundred Instant Words			
Third 25 Group 2c	Fourth 25 Group 2d	First 25 Group 3a	Second 25 Group 3b	Third 25 Group 3c	Fourth 25 Group 3d
put	kind	every	left	until	idea
end	hand	near	don't	children	enough
does	picture	add	few	side	eat
another	again	food	while	feet	face
well	change	between	along	car	watch
large	off	own	might	mile	far
must	play	below	close	night	Indian
big	spell	country	something	walk	real
even	air	plant	seem	white	almost
such	away	last	next	sea	let
because	animal	school	hard	began	above
turn	house	father	open	grow	girl
here	point	keep	example	took	sometimes
why	page	tree	begin	river	mountain
ask	letter	never	life	four	cut
went	mother	start	always	carry	young
men	answer	city	those	state	talk
read	found	earth	both	once	soon
need	study	eye	paper	book	list
land	still	light	together	hear	song
different	learn	thought	got	stop	leave
home	should	head	group	without	family
us	America	under	often	second	body
move	world	story	run	late	music
try	high	saw	important	miss	color
ed, er, ly, est		Common suffixes: *s, ing, ed, er, ly, est*			

one hundred of these instant words. The complete list of three hundred instant words makes up 65 percent of all written material, and studies by a variety of researchers have confirmed the utility of various high-frequency core words (Nation, 2001). Of course, if your school uses a core program and introduces high-frequency sight vocabulary as part of that core program, you would want to use a list that parallels the units of instruction. It is especially important to know whether very young readers (K–1) are learning what is being taught.

Assessment of sight-word skill is essential, since students will find fluent reading difficult if they do not master these words. Students can be expected, as a general rule, to have instant recognition of the entire list by the end of grade 3. Sight-word lists are generally administered on flash cards. The cards are used to control the rate of presentation, so that students' instant recognition can be evaluated. Most specialists suggest presenting cards or words at a rate of one second per word. After the initial presentation is completed (or stopped due to frustration), the words that were missed can be presented again to assess students' word *analysis* abilities.

The criterion level for isolated word recognition on word-list reading is often set at 70 percent (Botel, 1982; Roswell, Chall, Curtis, & Kearns, 2006). Because reading words in isolation is more difficult than reading words in context, the scoring procedure should be adjusted accordingly. In evaluating the student's responses to the word-list task, the following questions should be considered:

- Does there appear to be any consistent pattern to the errors?
- Is the pattern of these errors comparable at each level, or does it change with increasing difficulty?
- Does the student substitute initial consonants? Final consonants?
- Does the student attend to the medial portions of words?
- Does the student reverse letters or words?
- What is the student's overall level of mastery of high-frequency sight words in isolation?

Although some authors recommend equating the results from a sight-word list with reading-level ability, we caution against this practice. All that can reasonably be accomplished by administering a word list is an appraisal of the reader's instant recognition of words, without benefit of context. This can provide a quick, efficient clue as to the student's in-text reading and perhaps an idea of what may be impeding progress. Of course, it does not yield direct information about the student's word recognition during reading, nor does it indicate whether the student can manage both comprehension and word recognition simultaneously. Remember, children often misread different words in context and in isolation (Allington & McGill-Franzen, 1980).

An important next step, then, is to compare students' word recognition during reading to word recognition in isolation. Different patterns of response can be suggestive. For example, some children perform much better during reading than on isolated lists. This suggests good use of context and is frequently accompanied by better comprehension than word recognition. When there is a large discrepancy, it can be expected that students are actually *over*relying on context. The student who has not achieved automaticity in word recognition and reading may proceed very slowly.

Other children demonstrate exactly the opposite pattern. That is, they perform better on isolated word lists than they do in context. There may be several reasons for this, but often these students have too little experience with real reading. This limited reading experience often occurs in classrooms where students learn words in isolation (by completing workbook tasks, using flash cards, or playing games). Thus, these students have competence in recognizing words (or analyzing them; see below) but have not learned to transfer this skill to reading continuous text.

Of course, students' sight recognition of other words can be assessed as well. For example, word lists can be prepared from the instructional materials used in classroom or clinic. Lists created from basal readers or required trade books can be helpful in evaluating readiness to read specific materials and/or in assessing progress. If students are participating in a literature-based reading program, it may be advisable to examine high-frequency words derived from the literature commonly used in such programs. To this end, Eeds (1985) has analyzed four hundred books appropriate for grades K–3 and identified the high-frequency words in those books (see Figure 8.20). The 227 words listed account for 73 percent of all words in her sample of books. Specialists or other teachers assessing

**FIGURE 8.20
Bookwords High-
Frequency Sight
Words**

Final Core 227 Word List Based on 400 Storybooks for Beginning Readers							
the	1334	good	90	think	47	next	28
and	985	this	90	new	46	only	28
a	831	don't	89	know	46	am	27
I	757	little	89	help	46	began	27
to	746	if	87	grand	46	head	27
said	688	just	87	boy	46	keep	27
you	638	baby	86	take	45	teacher	27
he	488	way	85	eat	44	sure	27
it	345	there	83	body	43	says	27
in	311	every	83	school	43	ride	27
was	294	went	82	house	42	pet	27
she	250	farther	80	morning	42	hurry	26
for	235	had	79	yes	41	hand	26
that	232	see	79	after	41	hard	26
is	230	dog	78	never	41	push	26
his	226	home	77	or	40	out	26
but	224	down	76	self	40	their	26
they	218	got	73	try	40	watch	26
my	214	would	73	has	38	because	25
of	204	time	71	always	38	door	25
on	192	love	70	over	38	us	25
me	187	walk	70	again	37	should	25
all	179	came	69	side	37	room	25
be	176	were	68	thank	37	pull	25
go	171	ask	67	why	37	great	24
can	162	back	67	who	36	gave	24
with	158	now	66	saw	36	does	24
one	157	friend	65	mom	35	car	24
her	156	cry	64	kid	35	ball	24
what	152	oh	64	give	35	sat	24
we	151	Mr.	63	around	34	stay	24
him	144	bed	63	by	34	each	23
no	143	an	62	Mrs.	34	ever	23
so	141	every	62	off	33	until	23
out	140	where	60	sister	33	shout	23
up	137	play	59	find	32	mama	22
are	133	let	59	fun	32	use	22
will	127	long	58	more	32	turn	22
look	126	here	58	while	32	thought	22
some	123	how	57	tell	32	papa	22
day	123	make	57	sleep	32	lot	21
at	122	big	56	made	31	blue	21
have	121	from	55	first	31	bath	21
your	121	put	55	say	31	mean	21
mother	119	read	55	took	31	sit	21
come	118	them	55	dad	30	together	21
not	115	as	54	found	30	best	20
like	112	Miss	53	lady	30	brother	20
then	108	any	52	soon	30	feel	20
get	103	right	52	ran	30	floor	20
when	101	nice	50	dear	29	wait	20
thing	100	other	50	man	29	tomorrow	20
do	99	well	48	better	29	surprise	20
too	91	old	48	through	29	shop	20
want	91	night	48	stop	29	run	20
did	91	may	48	still	29	own	20
could	90	about	47	fast	28		

Source: Eeds, Maryann. (1985, January). Bookwords: Using a beginning word list of high-frequency words from children's literature K–3. The Reading Teacher, 38 (4), 418–423. Reprinted with permission of the International Reading Association. All rights reserved.

students who are learning to read in a literature-based classroom program should find this list helpful in evaluating sight-word knowledge.

Informal Tests of Phonics and Structural Analysis. Although we favor analyzing knowledge and application of phonics during the reading of actual text (see Chapter 9), most diagnostic batteries include some form of isolated assessment of phonics skill. Teachers sometimes find it helpful to use these commercial materials as they build their own knowledge base and increase their ability to reliably identify important phonic elements that may be influencing students' reading. Once information has been gathered about the student's knowledge and skill in phonics, it will be important to generate record-keeping forms that summarize the patterns of strength and weakness that were observed (see Figure 8.21). These may also be used to aid analysis of writing samples, which can provide powerful information about phonics skill (see below).

Both informal and formal tests of phonic and structural analysis typically contain lists of nonsense words that embody one or more of the sound-symbol patterns. A sample test might look something like the following:

1. fload
2. zam
3. drowt
4. dispount
5. strabble
6. mait
7. glavorful
8. kneef
9. jarf
10. bluther

The advantage of nonsense words is that it is possible to evaluate students' knowledge and application of word analysis strategies as they are used with totally unfamiliar "words." The disadvantage of this practice is that reading nonsense words is a more difficult task than reading real words in context (Harris & Sipay, 1990).

FIGURE 8.21 Summary Chart of Phonic and Structural Analysis

Directions: As the child reads, note how frequently she or he:	Always	Sometimes	Never
Recognizes major sounds of consonants	☐	☐	☐
Uses onsets and rimes (analogies)	☐	☐	☐
Uses major CVC vowel patterns	☐	☐	☐
Recognizes consonant influenced pattern	☐	☐	☐
Uses major CVVC clusters	☐	☐	☐
Uses other patterns (clusters/phonograms)	☐	☐	☐
Uses major syllable patterns	☐	☐	☐
Uses morphemic analysis	☐	☐	☐
Uses a combination of context/decoding	☐	☐	☐

FIGURE 8.22   Reordered Names Test

TABLE 3
Reordering of the augmented Names Test

1. Dee Conway	13. Ned Yale	25. Ginger Quincy
2. Cus Clark	14. Patrick Murphy	26. Dean Shepherd
3. Tim Brooks	15. Chester Skidmore	27. Troy Hoke
4. Fred Wright	16. Homer Sheldon	28. Zane Swain
5. Chuck Dale	17. Stanley Smitherman	29. Bertha Whitlock
6. Grace Wade	18. Flo Sherwood	30. Roberta Brewster
7. Jay Anderson	19. Jake Pendergraph	31. Thelma Middleton
8. Kimberly tweed	20. Shane Slade	32. Yolanda Rinehart
9. Wendy-Spencer	21. Glen Sampson	33. Bernard Cornell
10. Ron Blake	22. Floyd Shaw	34. Joan Thornton
11. Austin Westmoreland	23. Vance Fletcher	35. Gene Bateman
12. Neal Loomis	24. Cindy Preston	

Source: Mather, N., Sammons, J., & Schwartz, J. (2006). Adaptations of the Names Test: Easy-to-use phonics assessments. *The Reading Teacher, 60*, 116.

Cunningham (1990) devised a test that is designed to take advantage of the nonsense-word approach while tempering concerns about it. The original Names Test was comprised of a list of twenty-five names (first and last) that are "fully decodable given commonly taught vowel rules and/or analogy approaches to decoding" (Cunningham, 1990, p. 125). Subsequent revisions have been made by Duffelmeyer and colleagues (1994), who expanded the list of names by ten and most recently by Mather, Sammons, and Schwartz (2006). Mather and her colleagues were intent on adapting the Names Test for more-effective use with younger readers. Their work resulted in two changes. First, they reordered the original lists of names (shifting both order of presentation and the combinations of names) so that students would encounter easier names early on the list and so that an examiner could stop testing when students could not continue (see Figure 8.22). Second, they created an "Early Names Test" designed to include all letters of the alphabet as well as the most common rimes (see Figure 8.23). Readers are told that they represent the names of students in a fictitious class and are asked to pretend to be the teachers and to "take attendance." Students' attempts are counted as correct if they correctly decode all of the syllables, regardless of the stress or accent. For example, both "West-MORE-land" and "West-more-LAND" would be scored as correct.

Although this test is an improvement over a list of nonsense words, these words still appear in isolation, and it will be necessary to contrast performance on this type of test with performance during reading. This is especially important because some children (especially young ones) consistently attempt to make real words from nonsense words. Their attempts to make meaning override the visual display. Consequently, they may appear to have limited sound-symbol knowledge when in fact they regularly employ word analysis strategies during reading, in combination with their meaning-seeking strategies.

FIGURE 8.23   **Early Names Test**

```
                    FIGURE 1
                 Early Names Test

    Rob Hap              Jen Dut
    Jud Lem              Jake Bin
    Ray San              Sid Gold
    Pat Ling             Frank Lug
    Tim Bop              Grace Nup
    Brad Tash            Beck Daw
    Pam Rack             Dell Smush
    Trisn Mat            Gus Lang
    Fred Tig             Lex Yub
    Bab Fum              Ross Quest
    Kate Tide            Dane Wang
    Brent Lake           Torn Zall
    Flip Mar             Gail Vog
    Jet Mit              Rod Blade
    Rand Lun             Tag Shick
```

Source: Mather, N., Sammons, J., & Schwartz, J. (2006). Adaptations of the Names Test: Easy-to-use phonics assessments. *The Reading Teacher, 60,* 117.

Spelling Assessments

Virtually all experts in the area of English language arts agree that teachers should evaluate students' level of spelling and target instruction appropriately. To do that, of course, we need tools to help us. Although it is important for students to learn to spell high-frequency words, these don't really provide useful information about students' overall spelling development. Consequently, some authors suggest using any one of the available graded spelling lists from a commercial program to determine grade-level performance. Structured spelling tests can then created by selecting a sample of perhaps twenty-five words from each level. The word lists are administered to determine the level of difficulty at which students should be receiving instruction. Of course, these types of assessments are program specific and do not really provide information about students' spelling development.

Structured Inventories. Henderson (1992) suggested a different approach. He created a listing of words that reflected the recurrent spelling patterns of the English language. Building on this work, both Henderson and later Templeton (1995) argued that spelling knowledge proceeds through several developmental stages and effective assessment should be focused on determining which of these stages represents a student's present level of knowledge. Templeton (1995) describes a structured inventory for evaluating students' stage-level knowledge of spelling. The Qualitative Inventory of Spelling Knowledge (see Figure 8.24) is designed for individual administration. Students are asked to spell words as best they can. If a student spells the first ten words on a list correctly, testing moves to the next level. Teachers are advised to stop testing when a student misspells more than

**FIGURE 8.24
Qualitative
Inventory of
Spelling Knowledge**

Level I	Level II	Level III	Level IV	Level V	Level VI
bump	batted	find	square	enclosed	absence
not	such	paint	hockey	piece	civilize
with	once	crawl	helmet	novel	accomplish
trap	shop	dollar	allow	lecture	prohibition
chin	milk	knife	skipping	pillar	pledge
bell	funny	mouth	ugly	confession	sensibility
shade	start	fought	hurry	aware	official
pig	glasses	comb	bounce	loneliest	inspire
drum	hugging	useful	lodge	service	permission
hid	named	circle	fossil	loyal	irrelevant
father	pool	early	traced	expansion	conclusion
track	stick	letter	lumber	production	invisible
pink	when	weigh	middle	deposited	democratic
drip	easy	real	striped	revenge	responsible
brave	make	tight	bacon	awaiting	accidental
job	went	sock	capture	unskilled	composition
sister	shell	voice	damage	installment	relying
slide	pinned	campfire	nickel	horrible	changeable
box	class	keeper	barber	relate	amusement
white	boat	throat	curve	earl	conference
	story	waving	statement	uniform	advertise
	plain	carried	collar	rifle	opposition
	smoke	scratch	parading	correction	community
	size	tripping	sailor	discovering	advantage
	sleep	nurse	wrinkle	retirement	cooperation
			dinner	salute	spacious
			medal	treasure	carriage
			tanner	homemade	presumption
			dimmed	conviction	appearance
			careful	creature	description

Source: From *How to become a better reading teacher: Strategies for assessment and intervention* by Lillian R. Putnam. Copyright © 1996 by Prentice-Hall. Reprinted by permission of Pearson Education, Inc., Upper Saddle River, NJ.

60 percent of the words on a list. Templeton (1995, p. 322) suggests interpreting results about levels using the following guidelines:

- Independent Level: Over 90 percent of the words are spelled correctly
- Instructional Level: Between 40 percent and 90 percent of the words are spelled correctly
- Frustrational Level: Fewer than 40 percent of the words are spelled correctly

We discussed the earliest of these stages in Chapter 7. However, many students have difficulty in the next phases, which Templeton calls, respectively, "syllable juncture" and "derivational constancy." In the syllable-juncture phase, children make errors where syllables meet (for example, "hury" for *hurry* or "capcur" for *capture*). Some of students' spelling errors of this phase may include syllable junctures involving simple affixes such as -ing or -less. Students in the derivational constancy phase, however, understand these aspects of spelling and instead make errors involving more-advanced morphological processes, often including changes in pronunciation or involving an embedded base word (e.g., "compisition" for *composition*). Teachers can do a more qualitative analysis of the spelling errors to determine which aspects of spelling are controlled by the student and which are still problematic (see Figure 8.25).

The development of various inventories in recent years provides teachers with excellent new tools to evaluate and interpret students' spelling and phonics knowledge. Bear, Invernizzi, Templeton, and Johnston (2007), for example, provide several inventories in their excellent book *Words Their Way*. Different inventories focus specifically on early elementary grades, later elementary grades, upper-level spelling, and specialized vocabulary for content areas. Importantly, they provide examples of alternative spellings and detailed error analysis guides to aid in interpreting students' spelling productions.

Another excellent source of support for careful analysis of students' spelling is the Development Spelling Analysis (DSA) for grades 1 to 8 (Ganske, 1999, 2000). This screening inventory parallels the various phases of spelling development and permits teachers to examine students' knowledge of specific "features" of spelling within each stage. Students attempt to write a list of twenty-five words that are administered like a conventional spelling test. The twenty-five words represent particular features of English orthography. The teacher uses summary forms to locate the child's developmental stage. Armed with this information, teachers can provide differentiated instruction.

Test of Written Spelling, Fourth Edition.   The TWS-4 (Larsen, Hammill, & Moats, 1999) is a standardized measure for students ages 6 to 18. Unlike the TWS-3 (Larsen & Hammill, 1994), the TWS-4 contains two parallel forms to facilitate retesting after additional instruction has been given. The authors indicate that the TWS-4 may be used to identify students who might need interventions focused on spelling improvement, to document overall progress in spelling, and to provide a measure for. They say, however, that the measure is insufficient as the basis for instructional planning.

The TWS-4 uses a dictated word format, and results are reported as standard scores, percentile ranks, spelling ages, and grade equivalents. Content-related evidence of validity for the TWS-4 is derived from the content of the subtests and from the results of item analysis procedures used during item selection. Item development and selection seem adequate, and items do not seem biased toward students of a particular gender or race. On the basis of evidence of the equivalence of the 1976 and the 1999 TWS, criterion-related evidence of validity is provided from studies of performance on the 1976 TWS correlated with the spelling subtests of four other tests. Total score correlations range from .59 to .97, and most scores are .85 or above. A moderate correlation between teachers' 1998 ratings of eighty-two students' spelling ability and their scores on the TWS-4 provides more criterion-related evidence of validity.

Construct-related evidence of validity is provided through a procedure that first identifies constructs that are presumed to account for test performance, then generates hypotheses based on these constructs, and finally tests the hypotheses either logically or empirically. Given the constructs and hypotheses presented, the TWS-4 presents reasonable construct-related evidence of validity for use as indicated in the manual.

FIGURE 8.25   Qualitative Spelling Checklist

Student _____   Observer _____

Use this checklist to help you find what stages of spelling development your students are in. There are three gradations within each stage—early, middle, and late. The words in parentheses refer to spelling words on the first Qualitative Spelling Inventory.

This form can be used to follow students' progress. Check when certain features are observed in students' spelling. When a feature is always present check "Yes." The last place where you check "Often" corresponds to the student's stage of spelling development.

Date: _____ _____ _____

Emergent Stage
Early
- Does the child scribble on the page?   ☐ Yes   ☐ Often   ☐ No
- Do the scribbles follow the conventional direction? (*left to right in English*)   ☐ Yes   ☐ Often   ☐ No
Middle
- Are there letters and numbers used in pretend writing? (*4BT for ship*)   ☐ Yes   ☐ Often   ☐ No
Late
- Are key sounds used in syllabic writing? (*P for ship*)   ☐ Yes   ☐ Often   ☐ No

Letter Name—Alphabetic
Early
- Are beginning consonants included? (*B for bed, S for ship*)   ☐ Yes   ☐ Often   ☐ No
- Is there a vowel in each word?   ☐ Yes   ☐ Often   ☐ No
Middle
- Are some consonant blends and digraphs spelled correctly? (*ship, when, float*)   ☐ Yes   ☐ Often   ☐ No
Late
- Are short vowels spelled correctly? (*bed, ship, when, lump*)   ☐ Yes   ☐ Often   ☐ No
- Is the *m* included in front of other consonants? (*lump*)   ☐ Yes   ☐ Often   ☐ No

Within Word Pattern
Early
- Are long vowels in single-syllable words "used but confused"? (FLOTE for *float*, TRANE for *train*)   ☐ Yes   ☐ Often   ☐ No
Middle
- Are most long vowels in single-syllable words spelled correctly but some long vowel spelling and other vowel patterns "used but confused"? (SPOLE for *spoil*)   ☐ Yes   ☐ Often   ☐ No
- Are most consonant blends and digraphs spelled correctly?   ☐ Yes   ☐ Often   ☐ No
- Are most other vowel patterns spelled correctly? (*spoil, chewed, serving*)   ☐ Yes   ☐ Often   ☐ No

Syllables and Affixes
Early
- Are inflectional endings added correctly to base vowel patterns with short vowel patterns? (*shopping, carries*)   ☐ Yes   ☐ Often   ☐ No
- Are consonant doublets spelled correctly? (*cattle, cellar*)   ☐ Yes   ☐ Often   ☐ No

FIGURE 8.25 (Continued)

Syllables and Affixes (continued) *Middle* • Are inflectional endings added correctly to base words? (*chewed, marched, shower*)	☐ Yes	☐ Often	☐ No
Late • Are less frequent prefixes and suffixes spelled correctly? (*confident, favor, ripen, cellar, pleasure*)	☐ Yes	☐ Often	☐ No
Derivational Relations *Early* • Are most polysyllabic words spelled correctly? (*fortunate, confident*)	☐ Yes	☐ Often	☐ No
Middle • Are unaccented vowels in derived words spelled correctly? (*confident, civilize, opposition*)	☐ Yes	☐ Often	☐ No
Late • Are words from derived forms spelled correctly? (*pleasure, civilize*)	☐ Yes	☐ Often	☐ No

Source: From *Words Their Way*, 2nd edition, by D. R. Bear, M. Invernizzi, S. Templeton, and F. Johnston, p. 289. Copyright © 2000, 1996 by Prentice-Hall, Inc. Reprinted by permission of Pearson Education, Inc., Upper Saddle River, NJ.

The TWS-4 uses the same norms that were developed for the TWS-2 (Larsen & Hammill, 1986) and reinforced for the TWS-3 (Larsen & Hammill, 1994). Appropriate demographic characteristics of the sample were keyed to the 1990 census data. Reliability studies indicate that the TWS-4 is relatively free of error resulting from irrelevant or biased content, the passage of time, and differences in scorers, although it is unclear when and on whom these studies were conducted. The new alternate forms appear parallel: coefficients for each age level range from .86 to .98. The TWS-4 is easy to administer and interpret (see Figure 8.26). Also, the availability of normative data is helpful in evaluating students' general performance in the area of spelling.

Assessing Written Language

Traditionally, writing has been evaluated by examining written *products*, just as reading has traditionally been evaluated by examining the products of reading (for example, question responses). Product assessments have generally consisted of evaluating two aspects of written work: composition and mechanics (Cramer, 1982). Even though they were commenting on written composition among older students, in their position statement on writing assessment, the Conference on College Composition and Communication (2009), Committee on Assessment, highlighted critical issues for assessing writing at any age/grade:

> Assessments of written literacy should be designed and evaluated by well-informed current or future teachers of the students being assessed, for purposes clearly understood by all the participants; should elicit from student writers a variety of pieces, preferably over a substantial period of time; should encourage and reinforce good teaching practices; and should be solidly grounded in the latest research on language learning as well as accepted best assessment practices.

FIGURE 8.26 Summary and Response Form from *Test of Written Spelling, Fourth Edition* (TWS-4)

TWS-4

Test of Written Spelling

Fourth Edition

SUMMARY/RESPONSE FORM

Form A ☐

Form B ☐

Section I. Identifying Information

Name ______

Male ☐ Female ☐

School ______

Examiner's Name ______

Referred by ______

Reason for Referral ______

	Year	Month
Date Tested		
Date of Birth		
Age		

Section II. Record of TWS—4 Scores

Raw Score ______

Standard Score ______

Percentile ______

Spelling Age ______

Grade Equivalent ______

Section III. Other Test Scores

	Test Name	Date	Test Score	TWS-4 Score Equivalent
1.				
2.				
3.				
4.				

Section IV. Profile of Scores

Standard Score	TWS–4 Form A	TWS–4 Form B	Other Tests 1.	Other Tests 2.	Other Tests 3.	Other Tests 4.	Standard Score
150							150
145							145
140							140
135							135
130							130
125							125
120							120
115							115
110							110
105							105
100							100
95							95
90							90
85							85
80							80
75							75
70							70
65							65
60							60
55							55

Section V. Test Conditions

A. Testing Location ______

B. Environmental Characteristics

	Interfering	Noninterfering
Noise level		
Interruptions		
Distractions		
Lighting		
Temperature		
Other ______		

C. Notes and other considerations ______

Section VI. Comments and Recommendations

1 2 3 4 5 03 02 01 00 99

Source: Larsen, S., Hammill, D., & Moats, L. "Summary/Response Form" from *TWS-4 Test of Written Spelling,* 4th ed. Copyright © 1999, 1994, 1986, 1976 by PRO-ED, Inc. Reprinted by permission.

Unfortunately, many writing assessments do not capture the spirit, much less the letter, of this statement. Many are timed, constraining what students can write and how much they are likely to edit and/or reconsider their work. In addition, they rarely capture the various authentic purposes for which people write. In Chapter 9, we describe assessment strategies that can be used more formatively and diagnostically as teachers examine students' written engagement over time and in multiple settings. Here, we describe a sample of the more traditional tools used for periodic assessment. By far the most common of these are tests that states sponsor as a part of their comprehensive assessment systems—often assessing at grade intervals (e.g., grades 5, 8, and 11). However, writing tests are not required under federal education law, and some states have been tempted to turn away from their use. At the same time, most will respond to the more ambitious Common Core State Standards (CCSS) for writing. To be proficient, students and their teachers will need to be working toward "anchor standards" that include the following:

- Write arguments to support claims in an analysis of substantive topics or texts using valid reasoning and relevant and sufficient evidence.
- Write informative/explanatory texts to examine and convey complex ideas and information clearly and accurately through the effective selection, organization, and analysis of content.
- Write narratives to develop real or imagined experiences or events using effective technique, well-chosen details and well-structured event sequences.
- Produce clear and coherent writing in which the development, organization, and style are appropriate to task, purpose, and audience.
- Develop and strengthen writing as needed by planning, revising, editing, rewriting, or trying a new approach.
- Use technology, including the Internet, to produce and publish writing and to interact and collaborate with others.
- Write routinely over extended time frames (time for research, reflection, and revision) and shorter time frames (a single sitting or a day or two) for a range of tasks, purposes, and audiences. (CCSS, 2010, p. 18).

Needless to say, no single commercial test of writing comes close to assessing these standards. It remains to be seen what the state assessments will entail. We do know that the National Assessment of Educational Progress (NAEP) is rolling out a new writing assessment for 2011 (NAGB, 2007). The NAEP 2011 framework is a useful template for thinking about writing assessment. That assessment is designed around three communicative purposes and three writing features:

Communicative Purposes for Writing
- To persuade
- To explain
- To convey experience, real or imagined

Features of Writing
- Development of ideas
- Organization of ideas
- Language facility and conventions

As the NAEP Framework acknowledges, there are many other purposes for writing: for example, writing-to-learn activities and writing for personal purposes. As well, it is important to recognize that on the NAEP (and many state assessments), student performance in writing is assessed entirely through a collection of student essays in response to writing prompts. Students have approximately twenty-five minutes to respond to each prompt, and each student will be presented with two prompts.

Something that is likely to impact student performance and our decisions about students' writing abilities is the implementation of new technologies. The revised NAEP assessment will be the first completely computer-based assessment in the NAEP program. During the 2011 administration cycle, students in grades 8 and 12 will take the entire writing portion of the NAEP by computer. The plan is for computer-based NAEP assessment to be administered to grade 4 students in 2013. The NAEP developers acknowledge that:

> There are limitations to the range and scope of skills that NAEP can assess because, like most standardized assessments, NAEP is an "on-demand" assessment with limited time and resources. Therefore, the assessment results in 2011 and beyond should not be interpreted as a complete representation of student writing performance. (NAGB, 2007, p. 2)

For our purposes, it is important to realize that almost any single test of writing—used to identify students who require additional instructional support—will be an inadequate measure of the types and purposes for writing detailed in the CCSS. In this chapter, we discuss several of the commonly used structured and/or norm-referenced assessments, and then, in Chapter 9, we turn our attention to more-formative and diagnostic assessment strategies.

Test of Written Language, Fourth Edition.   The TOWL-4 (Hammill & Larsen, 2010) is a test of both receptive and expressive language designed for use with students ages 9-0 to 17-11. According to the authors, the TOWL is a diagnostic test that can be used to determine "students' particular strengths and weakness in writing abilities ... [and] document progress in special writing programs."

Students are asked to read, listen, and write in response to several stimuli. Both contrived and spontaneous writing formats are employed. With the exception of the fifteen minutes allocated to story writing, the TOWL-4 has no set time limits. It takes approximately an hour and a half to administer and score. Inexperienced examiners should allow considerable additional time for scoring. Although this test is typically administered individually, the authors do indicate that it can also be group administered.

The TOWL-4 has two alternate forms and includes seven subtests that can be reported as raw scores, percentiles, subtest and composite standard scores, written language quotients, and age and grade equivalents. Two of the subtest scores are generated by analyzing a spontaneous writing sample, a story that is written in response to a picture stimulus: Contextual Conventions and Story Composition. Extensive checklists are provided for this purpose.

The other five subtests involve contrived writing tasks. For example, subtest 4, Logical Sentences, requires students to rewrite sentences that have something wrong with them, so "that it makes perfect sense" (Hammill & Larsen, 1996, p. 20). Spelling and punctuation are both evaluated by using the same dictation task, and the vocabulary subtest requires students to write twenty-eight stimulus words in sentences.

The evidence of validity of the TOWL-4 is derived from the theoretical orientation of the test and from examination of the types of tasks generally required of students in school settings. Item development and selection seem adequate, and scores appear similar for male and female, white and nonwhite, and Hispanic and non-Hispanic students. Additional evidence of validity is offered using correlational data of students' performance on the TOWL-4 and a teacher rating scale, the Writing Scale of the Comprehensive Scales of Student Abilities (Hammill & Hresko, 1994, as cited in Hammill & Larsen, 1996). Correlations of averages of performance on both test forms and the Writing Scale yield coefficients for the subtests that range from .34 to .68. Many of these can be considered to be of only moderate size, as can the correlations with intelligence and other tests reported as evidence of construct validity. We believe that additional studies of the relationship of the TOWL-4 to other measures of writing ability are called for. Test-retest coefficients range from .72 to .94, with most in the high .80s. Inter-scorer reliabilities are reported, ranging from .83 to .97.

The norming procedures for the TOWL-4 are carefully described and appear acceptable. The normative data for the TOWL-4 is new. The stratified standardization sample included over 2,500 students, distributed in a representative fashion across geographic areas and other demographic factors based on 2005 population data. The authors provide reasonable evidence regarding the reliability of the TOWL-4. The overall reliability of the test, using inter-scorer reliability, content sampling, and time sampling, ranged from .82 to .95. The reliability of the composite scores is considerably stronger than for subtests. In addition, an examination of the correlations among the subtests suggests that the test as a whole is actually assessing one factor or ability. As Salvia, Yselldyke, and Bolt (2010) point out, the subtests may provide some information of interest, but they should not, by themselves, be used to make significant decisions about individual students.

This new edition of the TOWL includes other features that many will find attractive. The stimulus pictures are new and in color, and test items were evaluated to eliminate bias. The authors also provide information related to studies of sensitivity and include data related to false positives for screening purposes.

In general, the TOWL-4 is a reasonable standardized measure of writing. Teachers and students who are accustomed to a process writing approach, however, will find this a somewhat limited view of writing competence, given that students have the opportunity to write only one story, with no prewriting or editing allowed. Although the TOWL-4 does not really generate any information that could not be collected by a knowledgeable teacher during classroom instruction and observation, the standardized information can be used to document and substantiate students' weaknesses in written language.

CBMs in Writing.   Earlier in this book, we discussed CBM assessments of reading, using tools such as AIMSweb and DIBELS (see Chapter 4). Although not as widely used, there are CBM assessments like this for written language also. Indeed, AIMSweb contains a typical such assessment. Like the reading subtests, the written-expression CBM is time constrained. The instructions for this assessment include these specific directions:

1. Select an appropriate story starter (from a list provided).
2. Say: "You are going to write a story. First, I will read a sentence, and then you will write a story about what happens next. You will have 1 minute to think about what you will write and 3 minutes to write your story. Remember to do your best work. If you don't know how to spell a word, you should guess. Are there any questions? (Pause.) Put your pencils down and listen. For the next minute think about . . . (insert story starter)."
3. After reading the story starter, begin your stopwatch and allow 1 minute for students to "think." After 30 seconds say: "You should be thinking about . . . . (insert story starter)."
4. At the end of 1 minute say: "Now begin writing." Restart your stopwatch. (Powell-Smith & Shinn, AIMSweb Training Workshop, 2004).

Teachers are then directed to monitor and encourage their students during writing and then to stop them from writing after three minutes. Students can be allowed to finish their stories, but only if they do so on a separate piece of paper.

Using the three-minute writing samples, several scores can be generated:

- Teachers are informed that, after writing, the "most important task is to determine the number of total words written (TWW).
- Teachers may also elect to score the number of correct writing sequences (CWS). That is accomplished by locating the pairs of adjacent words that are spelled correctly and that include appropriate capitalization. In addition, these words must be semantically and syntactically correct (see Powell-Smith & Shinn, 2004, p. 11).
- A third option involves determining the words spelled correctly (WSC).

These scores are the most frequently referenced when CBM assessments of written language are discussed. Although earlier research on the reliability and validity of these measures suggested a significant correlation with other measures of writing (see Madden, Gardner, Rudman, Karlsen, & Merwin, 1978; Marston & Deno, 1981), more-recent research is quite mixed (Espin et al., 2000; Tindal & Parker, 1989). One of the most comprehensive examinations of the various types of measures revealed that there are significant variations in outcome depending on several context and student variables. Not surprisingly, the authors of this study (Jewell & Malecki, 2005) found that there were stronger relationships between other measures of writing ability (e.g., grades, untimed writing samples, etc.) and *untimed* CBM measures than between those other indicators and timed measures. In addition, the CBM measures were better predictors of *young* students' other writing results than they were for older students (e.g., grades 4 and 6). Clearly, as students get older, we expect that written language proficiency will be judged based on content, ideas, and textual coherence in addition to mechanics. In other words, assessments of quantity alone (TWW) or even words spelled correctly should be used with great caution in identifying students as at risk.

Periodic Benchmark Assessment

Teachers and schools have many more assessment options than they did a decade ago. Both the texts and the procedures among IRIs and other structured inventories has been vastly improved. Of course, most school districts know that they must have a coherent local assessment system to supplement mandated state and federal assessments. In addition, clearly identified, prescribed, and systematic procedures and policies are key ingredients for the success of RTI at the school level. Local assessment plans should include tools and data that can be used to inform instruction in the classroom, but also data that can be aggregated to report results to audiences *outside* of the classroom. Used wisely, the assessment tools described in this chapter may be used for both purposes. When teachers throughout a building/district use structured inventories, they must make sure that they and their colleagues are evaluating students in a comparable way, using agreed-upon materials and assessment tools. In this section, the overall system devised by one such school is described. Teachers there worked for two years to improve the consistency and trustworthiness of the information they pass along to colleagues and parents. We return to these issues after the next chapter.

The teachers in Kyle's school had agreed on a common assessment system, a set of common items that they would all document. Each teacher/child collected writing samples three times a year, collected continuous information about independent reading using a book log, evaluated students' word recognition using the Bookwords list (see Figure 8.20), and documented students' oral reading using running records (see Chapter 9) three times a year. Other schools make different decisions about what to include in their periodic assessments. Information from fluency assessments and developmental spelling assessments is most typical.

The teachers in this school felt strongly that they would like to have a means of evaluating students' growth in reading *in relation to* a set of increasingly difficult reading materials that were similar to those used in their literature-based reading program. Over time, they added expository texts to their collection too. These texts provide benchmarks for estimating the appropriateness of students' progress as compared with students that age and might also serve as a means of identifying students who were in difficulty. The benchmark system demonstrates how the basic strategies and frameworks of IRIs, miscue analysis, and retellings can be applied to everyday materials to create a structured assessment system for use at the school or district level.

The benchmark books provide a structured assessment system that yields useful information about students. Kyle's teacher evaluated him three times during the year, using the benchmark book system they had created. In November of grade 2, Kyle's word recognition accuracy was 99 percent on a leveled text designated for mid–first grade, so Ms. McIntyre had him read from a text designated for the end of grade 1. His accuracy score was 95 percent. Coupled with his good comprehension for the portion read, she judged this to be his instructional level. At the end of the year, Kyle was evaluated on one of the challenging texts designated for the last half of grade 2. Figure 8.27 contains a summary

FIGURE 8.27
Kyle's Results
on Benchmark
Assessment

Kyle—Spring, Grade 2

Christina Katarina, by P. Gauch

This delightful story tells the tale of a strong-willed girl, Christina, who, having become fed-up with her family (younger brother bothering her, mom and dad yelling at her) decides to "quit the family." She changes her name to Agnes, and with the tacit approval of her mother, occupies half of the house. At first Agnes enjoys her new-found freedom, but she quickly finds that being on her own means that there is no one to help with chores and small disasters. She also finds that she misses her family. In the end, mom "convinces" her that the rest of the family really cannot get along without her and Christina returns to the family.

Oral Reading Accuracy: 96% accuracy

Comprehension:

1. Would you like to read more stories about Christina? Is she anything like you? (personal response)
    Kyle: *No. I wouldn't want to quit the family. I wouldn't put things all over the place.*

2. Why did Christina quit her family? (text explicit)
    Kyle: *Because she didn't like how her mother nagged too much. Her brother followed her too much. She liked her dad, but he got angry at her too much.*

3. How could Christina quit the family and still stay in the house? (text implicit)
    Kyle: *She quit the family, not the house. Her mother wanted her to stay. They put places for her to be in the house and places for her not to be.*

4. Who is Agnes? (text implicit)
    Kyle: *Her, but she changed her name in the old part of the house.*

5. Name three things that Agnes did in the story. (text explicit)
    Kyle: *She marked her areas out. She started to get missing with her family. She ate underneath the table.*

6. Did she enjoy herself when she quit the family? (text explicit)
    Kyle: *In the beginning, yes. They didn't tell her what to do, she could do what she wanted.*

7. Was there any time in the story when being on her own was not a good idea? When? (text implicit)
    Kyle: *No, I guess not.*

8. What happens at the end of the story? (text implicit)
    Kyle: *She joined back the family because she missed getting helped tucked in.*

9. During the week that Christina quit the family, what did Christina learn? (theme)
    Kyle: *That you can't just do it all by yourself because you need other people.*

Total Comprehension: 8/9 (89%)

of Kyle's oral reading and comprehension at that level. His total accuracy was 96 percent, making this a comfortable instructional level for Kyle. He corrected two of six miscues, and two others were mispronunciations of proper nouns. In addition, his comprehension, as measured on the comprehension questions, was very strong, revealing his excellent verbal skills and response to literature.

Today, most schools elect to use one of the available benchmark assessment systems (e.g., Fountas and Pinnell discussed earlier). A credible leveling system and the lists of books provided can be used to accomplish this same end. In Chapter 6, we described and compared several of these. For example, in some of the schools we work with, teachers have identified common texts (at each level) that they use for interim progress monitoring. Alternatively, you might use an IRI or a set of commercially leveled assessment materials such as the Developmental Reading Assessment (DRA).

The DRA is a set of leveled stories of graduated difficulty appropriate for use in kindergarten through grade 3. From level A, 1 through 20, the materials closely parallel the difficulty levels of the Reading Recovery Program. From level B, 24 to 40, the stories become increasingly complex and much longer. Among the attractive features of this assessment system are the varying (and increasing) length of the texts, the "little books" design with full-color illustrations, and the fact that many (although not all) of the stories are engaging narratives much like those children would read in a literature-based program. We have done considerable research on these materials and have found the leveling system very reliable in terms of word recognition difficulty, though less so in terms of comprehensibility (see Lipson et al., 1999).

The DRA2 has been added for grades 4 to 8—with a "Bridge Pack" to create more options between levels 20 and 38, designed for grade 3 or struggling students in grades 4 and beyond (Beaver & Carter, 2003). Unfortunately, the procedures for using each of these iterations of the DRA are slightly different and require careful examination of the manual. There are several features of the DRA 4 to 8 that are attractive for teachers in the intermediate and middle grades. First, like the primary DRA, the reading materials are produced in little booklets with interesting photos and/or age-appropriate illustrations. They tend to be much longer than typical IRI selections and therefore provide a means for assessing students' stamina and ability to maintain comprehension and fluency in developmentally appropriate materials. Second, texts include both narrative and expository materials. Third, the student materials also include several tasks that mimic authentic classroom events. For example, before reading, students are asked to write a prediction and list several questions they think might be answered during reading. After reading, students write a summary, answer questions at varying levels of cognitive complexity, respond to and reflect on their reading, and engage in a task designed to capture their metacognitive strategies. The DRA has always had well-articulated word recognition criteria, and it has recently added a helpful comprehension rubric to aid in evaluating students' retelling.

In either case—whatever assessment tool is used—if these systems are to be used school-wide or for some other systematic assessment purpose, teachers will need to engage in careful consideration of the assessment tasks that accompany the text. What criteria will be used to evaluate accuracy? How will comprehension be assessed?

DIAGNOSTIC EVIDENCE FROM STRUCTURED INVENTORIES AND BENCHMARK ASSESSMENTS

Tha'm

Tha'm's performance on the informal reading inventory (QRI-4) suggested that her word recognition abilities were quite good on phonologically regular words. Her word recognition *acceptability* yielded an instructional level at grades 4 and 5, but her *accuracy* scores were frustrational on several of these passages. The results of structured inventories also suggested that her comprehension is somewhat weaker than her word recognition, although that also was below grade level. Tha'm's rate varied from passage to passage, but she generally maintained an appropriate pace. However, when accuracy and rate were examined together, her fluency suffers on more-difficult passages. She has likely not achieved full automaticity in her word identification abilities.

Tha'm's comprehension is stronger when reading familiar narrative, but even there she had a difficult time comprehending implicit main ideas and inferences in general, which posed particular problems. Tha'm really struggled while reading unfamiliar expository text. In addition, her ability to recall was less developed than her ability to answer questions. The analysis of her retelling indicated that she remembered less important information than would be expected of a good reader. Her writing was meager, and she was reluctant to participate. Tha'm has made some significant progress in literacy but is struggling to "stay abreast" of the demands of her grade-level content.

Kyle

Many primary-aged students such as Kyle do not have much standardized assessment information available until *after* they have been referred for an evaluation. However, the assessment system in Kyle's school generated good information. The results of a periodic benchmark assessment during fall and early winter of grade 2 suggested that Kyle was still struggling. However, his comprehension was often very good, and his word recognition abilities were growing. He had not yet acquired the more complex consonant-vowel patterns of the language.

Then, in late winter, Kyle began to show real progress. He had been reading voraciously during the past two months and was now tackling much more difficult and lengthy "chapter books" (e.g., *Ralph S. Mouse*, by Beverly Cleary). The end-of-the year benchmark book assessment indicated that Kyle's word recognition accuracy was instructional for easy grade 3 material, his ability to stay with a longer book had improved, and his comprehension was flourishing with the more complicated ideas in these new books. The Bookwords assessment revealed the same increasing abilities to recognize high-frequency words at sight. At the end of grade 2, Kyle missed only one word of 227 Bookwords.

At the end of the year, Kyle's teacher administered an IRI—required for all students (Spache, 1981). Both his word recognition accuracy and his comprehension were above grade level. Finally, Kyle's performance at the end of the university summer-school clinic was evaluated using the QRI-3. These results clearly showed that Kyle has become a strong and still-improving reader who can handle material at and above his grade placements. His written language abilities are more problematic. (Note: See Chapter 9 for the formative/diagnostic data that provided additional support between grade 2 and grade 3).

CHAPTER SUMMARY

This chapter focused on the types of structured inventories and norm-referenced assessments that might be used periodically to capture information about students' changing/emerging abilities in reading and writing. A major portion of the chapter was devoted to a discussion of the informal reading inventory (IRI), because it has exerted much influence on reading assessments generally. The IRI is an individually administered, informal reading test designed to place students in materials at the appropriate levels and to identify their strengths and weaknesses in the areas of word identification and comprehension. Traditionally, IRIs are used to identify students' independent, instructional, and frustration reading levels.

The components of an IRI include graded word lists, graded passages, comprehension questions, and separate materials for the student and the examiner. There are a variety of procedures that can be used for administering and scoring an IRI, and different procedures produce different test results. Similarly, the criteria used for interpreting students' placement levels can have a significant effect on the results of the IRI. We provide guidelines for using IRIs for placement purposes. These include looking for selections that correspond to regularly used instructional materials, evaluating the passage dependency of the comprehension questions, and determining administration and scoring procedures and placement criteria, together and within the context of the purpose for using the IRI.

In the next sections of this chapter, we described contemporary innovations on the IRI format, including assessments designed for use with older students and some that assess reading in the content areas and/or assess studying and motivation.

Finally, we described additional tools and strategies for assessing reading and writing. The techniques described in this section include the following:

1. Procedures for evaluating students' oral reading fluency
2. Informal but structured tools for evaluating sight-word and phonics knowledge
3. Procedures for assessing spelling and writing

IRIs and IRI-like procedures are potentially high-utility techniques for both classroom teachers and clinical personnel. For placement purposes, it is important that anyone using IRIs understand the issues associated with the representativeness of the reading selections to the materials in which a student is being placed. Although some might argue that IRIs should not be used for placement purposes, in reality there is no one measure that can serve this purpose adequately. The key to successful placement, both in the classroom and in the clinic, is the use of *multiple* indicators of performance on materials comparable to those in which the student is to be placed. This may include performance on an IRI but should not be limited to it.

Classroom teachers may not need or want to assess all their students using a traditional IRI. It is probably neither appropriate nor necessary. Teachers can screen their students by (1) observing their students as they engage in classroom-based assessment or (2) using a screening test to identify those students who need further diagnosis (see Chapter 9). Progress monitoring, using classroom materials and IRI-like techniques (as in benchmark books), can create the sort of structured assessment that can be useful for planning instruction and communicating with colleagues.

Whereas classroom teachers are likely to find procedures for ongoing assessment and instructional decision making most useful, clinical personnel and specialists are most likely to find these structured inventory procedures useful for making programmatic curricular and instructional decisions for a given student. Specialist teachers must be particularly sensitive to the potential abuses of IRIs and other structured assessments, given the limited amount of time that they are likely to come in contact with individual students. In particular, it may be difficult to predict a student's performance in the classroom from a small sample derived from administering just one IRI. However, in the hands of a skilled specialist, IRIs can provide a great deal of valuable information about the reader within a relatively short time period.

We concluded the chapter with a discussion of the diagnostic evidence accumulating for Tha'm and Kyle, based on their performance on various structured inventories and/or periodic assessments.

MyEducationLab™

Go to the Topic, Progress Monitoring, in the MyEducationLab (www.myeducationlab.com) for your course, where you can:

- Find learning outcomes for the Topic, Progress Monitoring along with the national standards that connect to these outcomes.

- Complete Assignments and Activities that can help you more deeply understand the chapter content.

- Apply and practice your understanding of the core teaching skills identified in the chapter using the Building Teaching Skills and Dispositions learning units.

- Examine challenging situations and cases presented in the IRIS Center Resources.

- Check your comprehension of the content covered in the chapter by going to the Study Plan in the Book Resources for your text. Here you will be able to take a chapter quiz, receive feedback on your answers, and then access Review, Practice, and Enrichment activities to enhance your understanding of chapter content.

A+RISE A+RISE® Standards2Strategy™ is an innovative and interactive online resource that offers new teachers in grades K–12 just in time, research-based instructional strategies that meet the linguistic needs of ELLs as they learn content, differentiate instruction for all grades and abilities, and are aligned to Common Core Elementary Language Arts standards (for the literacy strategies) and to English language proficiency standards in WIDA, Texas, California, and Florida.

9 Formative and Diagnostic Assessment

*T*he information obtained through whole-class and benchmark assessment provides the background for further evaluation of the learner, using formal and informal assessment instruments. The periodic or summative assessments discussed in the previous chapter can be used to determine if students are making adequate progress in overall performance in relation to age/grade expectations, as an indicator of the general effectiveness of instruction. Some assessments (IRIs, for example) can certainly be used to dig more deeply into students' reading abilities, but in practice they are not typically used that way. Other assessments, designed to identify struggling students, are usually quite general or sample only a snippet of skilled reading performance. They rarely provide the specific information needed to determine the most appropriate intervention or instruction. Too often educators have skipped over the critical contributions of good *diagnostic* assessment.

At the same time, there is an increasing awareness of the utility for ongoing *formative* assessment. Until recently, classroom assessment information has been used primarily to establish the need for referral for further assessment of struggling readers and writers. Now, however, there is a recognition of the importance of classroom-based assessment, in part because research findings indicate that when teachers engage in ongoing assessment, student achievement improves (Black & Wiliam, 1998; Black et al., 2004; Falk & Ort, 1998). We recognize that more-formative assessment can often provide powerful and flexible evaluation strategies: "If we wish to maximize student achievement in the U.S., we must pay far greater attention to the improvement of classroom assessment. Both assessment *of* learning and assessment *for* learning are essential" (Stiggins, 2004, p. 11).

This chapter focuses on assessment strategies that are selected and/or created by teachers and evaluators who are interested in gathering more-comprehensive and/or diagnostic information about one or more components of reading and writing. These tools are ideally suited to the monitoring and diagnosis aspects of RTI, because they permit continuous and/or periodic collection of information in authentic contexts. In addition, they often enlarge the picture we have of students' literate knowledge and skill, as the assessments can address complex and/or extended reading and writing events that are difficult to assess on large-scale norm-referenced or state-mandated tests.

After a brief discussion of the role of the teacher in assessing students' reading and writing, we identify some critical issues in the development and use of formative and diagnostic assessment strategies. Then, a wide range of strategies and tools are described for assessing component areas of literacy: phonics, word recognition, fluency, vocabulary, comprehension, studying, and writing. The assessment strategies described are almost exclusively *performance* measures. These are techniques for evaluating students' ability to *apply* their knowledge and skill. The variety of assessment strategies presented in this chapter are designed so that teachers can select from among a repertoire to examine some particular component area more closely and in an ongoing way. Many of these can (and should) be used as a routine part of the instructional program. Others may be designated for initial diagnostic purposes or as periodic assessments—for example, used for progress monitoring three to four times during the year.

Finally, we continue examining the diagnostic evidence that documents student progress and provides the basis for instructional decision making, using our ongoing case studies of Kyle and Tha'm.

UNDERSTANDING FORMATIVE AND DIAGNOSTIC ASSESSMENT

More often than not, teachers and specialists will need more information than can be provided by screening and benchmarking assessments in order to plan interventions and examine the impact of instruction. Whereas efficiency is a critical factor when assessing *all* students, depth and comprehensiveness are critical to diagnostic assessment of individual students. "Because the word "diagnosis" is so often associated with identifying disease or its symptoms, we want to be clear that we do *not* assume a medical model of reading difficulties. Instead, we want to promote the original meaning of the word diagnosis, from the Greek "to discern" the nature and cause of anything. According to Merriam Webster, a diagnosis is "an investigation or analysis of the cause or nature of a condition, situation or problem" (http://www.merriam-webster.com/dictionary/diagnosis). Without very good diagnostic information and/or a flexible formative assessment system our instructional programs and student performance will not improve and RTI will simply be an alternate route to special education placement or to permanent membership in Title I classrooms" (Lipson, Chomsky-Higgins, & Kanfer, 2011).

The assessment-instruction process described in this text relies very heavily on the knowledge and skill of the teacher/examiner. Extensive description of formal tests, the traditional heart of reading and writing "diagnosis," is not the centerpiece of the process. Instead, we acknowledge the complexity of the reading and writing processes and of learning to read and write. "Black and Wiliam (1998) define assessment broadly to include all activities that teachers and students undertake to get information that can be used diagnostically to alter teaching and learning. Under this definition, assessment encompasses teacher observation, classroom discussion, and analysis of student work, including homework and tests. Assessments become formative when the information is used to adapt teaching and learning to meet student needs" (Boston, 2002). The available evidence points to the conclusion that achievement gains are improved dramatically when teachers increase the accuracy of their classroom assessments and engage students in the process.

One of the most serious problems with traditional assessment practices is that they often lead teachers to believe that assessment and evaluation are someone else's job. When teachers rely too heavily on standardized test results, they may stop using their own good judgment (Valencia & Pearson, 1987; Valencia, 2007). Overreliance on formal tests may also cause teachers to discount or become inattentive to the high-quality information they themselves have. Teachers need the information they have before them, because it provides evidence about students' ability to perform the actual tasks required in their instructional settings.

By virtue of their daily contact with students in a variety of reading situations, classroom teachers are in a position to incorporate the assessment strategies described in this chapter directly into their regular reading instruction. Teachers can collect and interpret performance data—information about students' skills and strategies—as they read and respond to various school tasks. This frequent opportunity to observe students and interact with them about their reading and writing is probably the reason that Simmons and Resnick (1993) concluded that "the most authentic and reliable estimate of students' capabilities comes from work they do over extended periods of time under the guidance of teachers" (p. 11).

There has been a dramatic increase in the number of mandated standardized assessments in American schools. Many highly regarded educators and researchers have noted that this increase in "external" assessments has had the (unintended) consequence of reducing the commitment to classroom-based assessment (Black & Wiliam, 1998; Black et al., 2004; Valencia, 2011b). There are important, but distinctive, contributions of external and internal assessments (see Wixson, Valencia, & Lipson, 1994). The idea here is to honor both. According to Valencia (2007), classroom-based assessments have special value because they are:

- Tied to the curricular content and instructional strategies of the classroom
- More fine-grained than external assessments so that they help teachers plan specific lessons
- Focused on both the process and products of learning
- Timed to provide teachers and students with immediate feedback
- Designed to provide opportunities for teachers to interact with students and adapt assessment to their individual needs

Teachers gather information from multiple samples on a daily basis as a function of the different types of texts, tasks, and methods that are employed as a part of their regular reading activities. The opportunities are great but often go undetected. As Pinnell (1991, p. 81) has argued, "teachers need assessment tools that help them become 'noticing teachers.' " This chapter describes some tools and strategies that are more formal and standardized but also many that will help teachers to "notice" the information available to them on an ongoing basis.

Formative assessment is more a matter of knowing what to attend to than a one of having indefinite amounts of time to work one-on-one with students. For example, Lipson (1995) described ways in which conversations—even casual ones—with students can provide useful assessment information. "Noticing requires not only that teachers engage in careful observations of reading and writing as they occur in their own classrooms, but also that they assign importance or significance to what they note" (p. 167).

The strategies suggested in this chapter should probably become a part of the repertoire of all teachers. All formative assessments (and many diagnostic ones) allow us to examine students' performance using familiar text forms and tasks. Of course, the quality and nature of these in-school tasks need to be examined closely as well (see Chapters 5 and 6). However, researchers and educators generally agree that "the most productive and useful way to assess, or examine, rather than simply test what students understand, is to 'situate' assessment in the classroom, closest to the child and to instruction" (Valencia, 1997, p. 64).

Another advantage of formative assessment is that evaluations can be responsive to the specific cultural and/or linguistic characteristics of individual students. This is critical because standardized tests can distort information for some students, as they tend "to reflect the language, culture, or learning style of middle- to upper-middle-class" students (Neill & Median, 1989). To make good instructional decisions, teachers must come to trust that assessment is a continuous process that takes place within the instructional program. As Shea and colleagues (2005) note, "effective documentation of progress (however small the steps forward) requires a persistent focus on students as they go about learning" (p. 9). The goal of this type of assessment is to increase the goodness of the fit between each student and the materials and methods of instruction. Teachers in many school districts report that they are so busy collecting externally mandated tests that they have little time to reflect on other sorts of information. This can have the unintended consequence of diminishing teachers' sense of responsibility for engaging in ongoing assessment (Valencia, 2007). However, teacher prerogative and responsibility are at the heart of excellent assessment-instruction, and without them, teachers are less able to make decisions based on high-quality information.

Teachers can—indeed, they must—become expert evaluators. We have already noted one of the most important attributes of an expert evaluator: the ability to listen. Another important characteristic is the ability to recognize patterns. Expert evaluators are not concerned about an isolated event or behavior, but are able to connect pieces of information to create an integrated vision of the student's knowledge and skill. Informal, classroom-based assessment can provide exceptionally powerful and helpful information. Johnston (1997) reminds us that

> The concept behind a "good" reading assessment, whether it is a standardized test or alternative classroom assessment, is the same. First it should be authentic; it should assess what we have defined and value as real reading. Second, it should be trustworthy; it should have clearly established procedures for gathering information and for evaluating the quality of that information. (p. 60)

Formative and diagnostic assessment requires reflection and planning. Teachers should proceed cautiously. Formative assessments offer no guarantee of excellence. Many common informal assessment tools need to be considered carefully. For example, teacher questions are a common feature in many classrooms and are often used to judge students' comprehension, even when they may not have been generated with care and may not be used in the same way by other teachers.

To summarize, although less-formal tests can be a potent form of assessment, the techniques employed must be carefully examined for evidence that these capture what we know about skilled reading and writing. A serious problem in many existing tests, both formal and informal, is the lack of relationship between how reading and writing are measured and what we expect individuals to do during reading and writing. The truth is that we do *not* want students to know how to rapidly read isolated words or answer questions about fifty-word selections or correct the grammar and punctuation in a series of random sentences. Rather, we want them to be able to employ their skills during the reading and writing of real texts. In reviewing comments by the legendary educator Ralph Tyler, Horowitz (1995) noted that alternative assessment is not a panacea and that "all evaluation must be guided by a purpose and be sensitive to the uniqueness of the individual being assessed."

This means that we need to develop assessment procedures that evaluate more clearly the major goals of reading and writing instruction and use this information to promote learning. Valencia (2007) described an "inquiry-oriented approach" to assessment and instruction that requires teachers to collaborate with others and to collect evidence from multiple sources, to interpret the information based on knowledge about students and about literacy, and to use the information to guide teaching and learning. Using such an approach, educators can improve outcomes for all students.

Diagnostic assessment often involves just the sort of close examination of existing or ongoing information described above. Bringing an inquiry-oriented approach to existing data is essential, since many of the other assessment tools used mask important differences between and among students. A classic study by Valencia and Buly (2004) vividly demonstrates how diverse student needs might not be identified unless educators look more closely. The individuals in their study were a group of randomly selected fourth graders who had scored below the standard on the state assessment. None of these 108 randomly selected students was receiving specialized reading support of any kind. Intending to collect further diagnostic information, they administered a battery of assessments to these students. They explored students' accuracy, fluency, and comprehension. What they found was that although these students had all failed the state assessment and were similar in that way, they were extremely different in the particulars of their reading abilities. Indeed, Valencia and Buly identified six distinct clusters of students, each with a different profile. For example, some students were accurate and fluent but could not comprehend well. Others were accurate and could comprehend well, but they were extremely slow and disfluent. Needless to say, if these diverse students received the same instructional program, it would be unlikely to be helpful to all of them—perhaps to none—since it might not be focused sufficiently on their areas of strength and need.

In most cases, additional formative and/or diagnostic information will be necessary to make a significant difference in the literacy performance of struggling students. Research has consistently demonstrated that focus and tailored, responsive instruction can change the trajectory of students' achievement (Connor, Morrison, & Katch, 2004; Scanlon et al., 2005). In order to teach responsively and make individual adjustments, good, specific assessment information is required.

STRATEGIES AND TOOLS FOR FORMATIVE AND DIAGNOSTIC ASSESSMENT

In the remainder of this chapter, we describe specific techniques for evaluating the various components of reading and writing performance (see Figure 9.1). In using this organization, we do not mean to imply that these components operate independently of each other. Of course this is not the case. However, at this point in the assessment-instruction process, we will have quite a lot of information about individual students and it may be appropriate to explore specific aspects of reading and writing more deeply—more diagnostically. These techniques—some old, some newer—can provide the initial repertoire for both classroom teachers and specialists who want to expand their assessment practices.

Many of these strategies can be used to reexamine data that you have collected already. It is not always necessary to give *another* test or use new assessment materials. Often you can get exceptionally useful information by digging deeper with assessment information you already have or could collect quite quickly. Miscue analysis, for example, can be done using existing records of oral reading. Most of these strategies are also designed to provide for ongoing student assessment during instruction. Throughout, we also provide forms that can be used to summarize and display this information. These forms are useful whether you are engaged in further diagnostic analysis and interpretation, are using them for ongoing progress monitoring, or need them for examining students' response to instruction.

Evaluating Word Recognition and Decoding

Rapid, accurate, and automatic word recognition using a combination of strategies is a hallmark of skilled reading. Not surprisingly, many poor readers have a limited repertoire of word recognition and word analysis strategies (see Chapter 7 for assessments related to phonological awareness and early word recognition). Of course, the most effective way to assess students' word recognition and word analysis skills is to capture their reading behaviors as they read aloud. It is possible to achieve a very detailed picture of students' word recognition and monitoring abilities by using the procedures we describe below.

Records of Oral Reading and Running Records during Oral Reading.   In the previous chapter, we described how to mark students' reading behaviors during the administration of an IRI. This classic procedure is called a *record of oral reading*, because the teacher uses a copy of the student text to mark "errors" or deviations from the text.

A *running record* is a method of assessment that is ideally suited to continuous assessment. It is perfect for use in the classroom because "this task requires the teacher to observe and record the strategies the child uses 'on the run' while attempting to read a whole text" (Pinnell, 1985, p. 74). The technique was originally described by Clay (1979, 1985) and is based on the work of the Goodmans and their associates (K. S. Goodman & Goodman, 1977; Y. M. Goodman, Watson, & Burke, 1987).

Although the running record might seem complex at first, it is especially useful for classroom teachers because no special preparation is required ahead of time. It can be

FIGURE 9.1 Summary Chart of Formative and Diagnostic Assessments

Component and Strategy	Assessment Condition and Purpose(s)	Administration Notes	Age/Grade Level
Word Recognition			
Records of Oral Reading and Running Records	Individual (or individual within small-group setting). Formative and diagnostic purposes. Can also be used as a component in progress monitoring or screening (see Chapter 8).	Data gathered during any oral reading event. Advantage is on-the-spot performance data. Also, can capture students' performance on different types and difficulty of text.	Records of oral reading can be used at all levels. Running records are most appropriate for students reading at grade levels PP–grade 3.
Miscue Analysis Assessments	Individual (or individual within small-group setting). Formative and diagnostic assessment.	Uses data from running records or other records of oral reading	Any
Retrospective Miscue Assessment	Individual (or individual within small-group setting). Formative and diagnostic.	Data gathered during any oral reading event. Advantage: can be done with wide range of texts, including content-area reading assignments. Provides insights into *students*' thinking about word recognition.	Middle and secondary
Word Sorts	Individual or small group. Formative and diagnostic assessment.	Time varies. Students can complete independently if they record their sorts.	Any
Fluency			
Timed Reading (see Chapter 8)	Individual. Can be used for screening, progress monitoring, or formative assessment.	Continuous data collection using everyday reading texts. Quick and easy to collect.	Grade 1 & up
WPM and WCPM (see Chapter 8)	Individual. Can be used for screening, progress monitoring, formative or diagnostic assessment.	Continuous data collection using everyday reading texts. Relatively quick and easy to collect.	Grade 1 & up
Fluency Scales	Individual. Progress monitoring, formative and diagnostic assessment.	Provides multiple measures of fluency.	Grades 2 & up

Vocabulary

Word Sorts	Individual or small group. Formative and diagnostic.	Time varies. Students can complete independently if they record their sorts.	Any. Results may be confounded with decoding difficulties.
Self-Assessment and Yes/No	Individual or whole group. Formative and diagnostic.	Very little time. Students may over-estimate or underestimate their word knowledge.	Any
Free Recall	Individual or small group. Formative.	Very little time.	Young readers may find the unstructured tasks difficult.
Word Association	Individual or small group. Formative and diagnostic.	Teacher must select words ahead of time, but otherwise quick to administer.	Any, although less-verbal students may not fare well.
Structured Questions	Individual, small or large group. Formative and diagnostic.	Time consuming to prepare, although they yield good information.	Any
Recognition	Whole group. Formative and diagnostic.	Time consuming to prepare, although they yield good information,	Very effective for students with retrieval difficulties.
Unstructured Discussion	Individual, small or large group. Formative.	Yields least information, but easy to use.	Any
PReP	Individual, small or large group. Formative.	Used in conjunction with pre-reading preparation for reading. Some additional time needed to analyze responses.	Any

Comprehension

IRI Guides	Individual. Formative or diagnostic.	When coupled with importance ratings and sequence information, these can provide excellent diagnostic information and be used with both narrative and informational texts.	Most appropriate for grades 2 and up.
Story Maps	Can be used with whole groups (written retellings) or individuals (oral retellings). Formative and diagnostic.	Use with narrative text. Students can create maps, or their oral and written retelling is compared to the map.	Any age, although mapping longer or complex narratives for older children may be problematic.

(Continued)

449

FIGURE 9.1 (Continued)

Component and Strategy	Assessment Condition and Purpose(s)	Administration Notes	Age/Grade Level
Concept Maps	Can be used with whole groups (written retellings) or individuals (oral retellings). Formative and diagnostic.	Use with expository text. Students' oral and written retelling is compared to the map; or students create maps.	Most appropriate for grades 3 and up.
Retelling	Can be used with whole groups (written retellings) or individuals (oral retellings). Formative and diagnostic.	Use retellings *before* asking questions.	Any age, although summary is preferable for older readers.
Questioning	Groups or individuals. Depending on conditions, can be used for screening, progress monitoring, formative and diagnostic assessment.	Craft questions carefully so as to elicit the desired information	Any
Think-Aloud	Individual. Formative and diagnostic.	Focus is on *processes* versus content.	Any age, although most appropriate for grades 3 and up.
Study and Self-Regulation			
Observation	Individual. Formative or diagnostic assessment.	Use as student(s) is engaged in study activity.	Intermediate through secondary grades
Open-Book Reading Assessment (OBRA)	Individual or group. Could be used for screening, formative and/or diagnostic assessments.	Use as student(s) is engaged in study activity.	Intermediate through secondary
Self-Report Questionnaire	Survey (can be administered individually or in whole group). Screening and diagnosis.	Self-report of study strategies and self-regulatory abilities	Middle–high school students
Writing			
Holistic Scoring	Individual. All purposes, depending on conditions.	Use to analyze student's written work.	Any
Analytic Scoring	Individual. All purposes, depending on conditions.	Use to analyze student's written work.	Any
Observation Checklist	Individual. Formative and diagnostic.	Use as student(s) is engaged in writing activities.	Any
Self-Assessment Questionnaire	Individual. Formative and diagnostic.	Students reflect on their own writing abilities.	Any

created as long as the text being read by a student is visible to the teacher. Therefore, it is possible to collect data any time you are listening to a student read aloud. It does take time and practice to do running records accurately. But it is well worth the investment because of the wealth of assessment information they provide, especially for younger and/or disabled readers. In Figure 9.2, you will find a sample running record of Kyle's reading in grade 2, along with a key to the various markings.

After the record has been taken, the teacher uses it to analyze oral reading performance. Although a full miscue analysis is most useful for detailed diagnosis (see below), classroom teachers usually generate more-global, less-specific inferences about what the student is doing to construct meaning from text and which strategies seem to be used most often to accomplish this (Pinnell, 1987). A teacher's summary of the small sample you have examined in Figure 9.2 might read something like this:

> Kyle's most consistent miscues (oral reading "errors") are word substitutions. These substitutions are made using both language structure (syntax) and meaning (semantics) ("I tied it around a doorknob . . ."). Kyle also monitors quite effectively for problems caused by weak graphophonic skills (he tries, for example, to self-correct mispronunciations of the words *winced, shuddered, admired,* etc.). He regularly uses rereading when meaning seems distorted. What Kyle does not do is to make full and effective use of the graphophonic information available, nor does he appear to have mastered all high-frequency sight words. Miscues in this area ("emperted," "winkered") are tolerated even when they result in loss of meaning. Kyle often rereads, but his self-correction attempts too often fail due to lack of sound-symbol information and decoding skill. Although he generally seems to "read for meaning," his comprehension is affected by word recognition.

As with any "test," running records provide a *sample* of behavior that may or may not be representative of the way a student interacts with different types of texts under different reading conditions. Students' miscue patterns vary depending on a number of factors (Wixson, 1979). The best way to address the problem of variability in oral reading patterns is to obtain repeated samples of a particular reader's miscues under a variety of conditions. Detailed analyses of miscues are important in a complete assessment, and we discuss this next. However, running records provide classroom teachers with a practical assessment strategy and information about students' reading of multiple samples, since teachers can (and often do) collect information several times a week.

Because it can be a challenge to do running records, and because we feel so strongly that they are a useful classroom tool, a word about management is in order. We have found it useful to buy cheap spiral-bound notebooks in volume and use them for all running records. Each time we do a running record, we simply date the page, write the student's name on each new page, and note what text is being read (see Figure 9.3). Before starting, we take a minute to organize ourselves by writing the page numbers and numbering the lines for each page we are going to have the student read. That way, we can keep track of exactly what the student has read even if the student reads quickly or we get a bit lost along the way. Using this approach, we have all our running records in one place, and they are organized sequentially. This reduces the amount of paper shuffling and record keeping. If we want to focus on a particular student, we can always tear those pages out and put them in a file.

**FIGURE 9.2
Sample Running
Record for *Norman
Fools the Tooth
Fairy***

Norman was the only kid in his class who hadn't lost a baby tooth. One was sort of loose now. Instead of finishing his worksheet, Norman wiggled the tooth with his finger.

Later, while his teacher, Miss Harp, read them a story, Norman waggled the tooth with his tongue. How else was he going to get a tooth to put under his pillow for the tooth fairy?

His friends gave him lots of advice. "I tied a string around my loose tooth," said Toby. "Then I tied the other end to a doorknob, and my sister slammed the door." Norman winced.
"My dad pulled mine out," said Matt, "with his pliers."

Norman shuddered, but he admired the empty space between their teeth when they smiled. It showed that the tooth fairy had already paid them a visit.
"Try biting into an apple," said Sarah, "or eat lots of caramels."
Norman didn't have any caramels, but he did have a piece of licorice in his lunch bag.

Key for running record:
Accurate Reading   ✓ ✓ ✓
Substitution   <u>substitute</u>
                     text word

Appeal   <u>A</u>

Told   <u>T</u>

Self-Correction   <u>sc</u>

Omission   <u>text word</u>

Insertion   <u>inserted word</u>

Repetition   ✓R

Return & Repetition   ⌐✓✓✓R

FIGURE 9.2
(Continued)

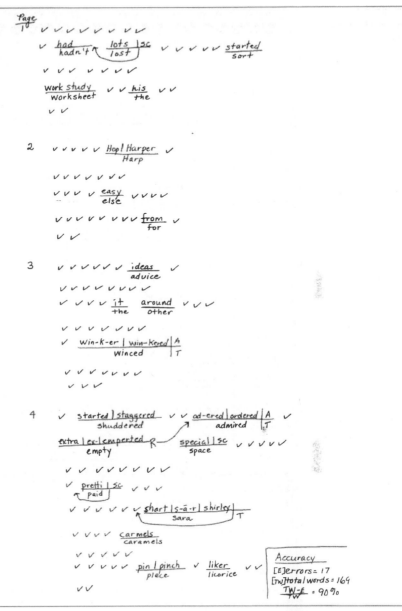

Source: Text from *Norman Fools the Tooth Fairy*, by Carol Carrick. Copyright © 1992 by Carol Carrick. Reprinted by permission of Scholastic, Inc.

Miscue Analysis.   Miscue analysis is an analytic procedure used to gain diagnostic insight into the ways that individual readers process print, by analyzing the oral reading errors made by students during reading. Although miscue analysis procedures are most often associated with Kenneth and Yetta Goodman (K. S. Goodman, 1969;

**FIGURE 9.3
Running Record
Notebook**

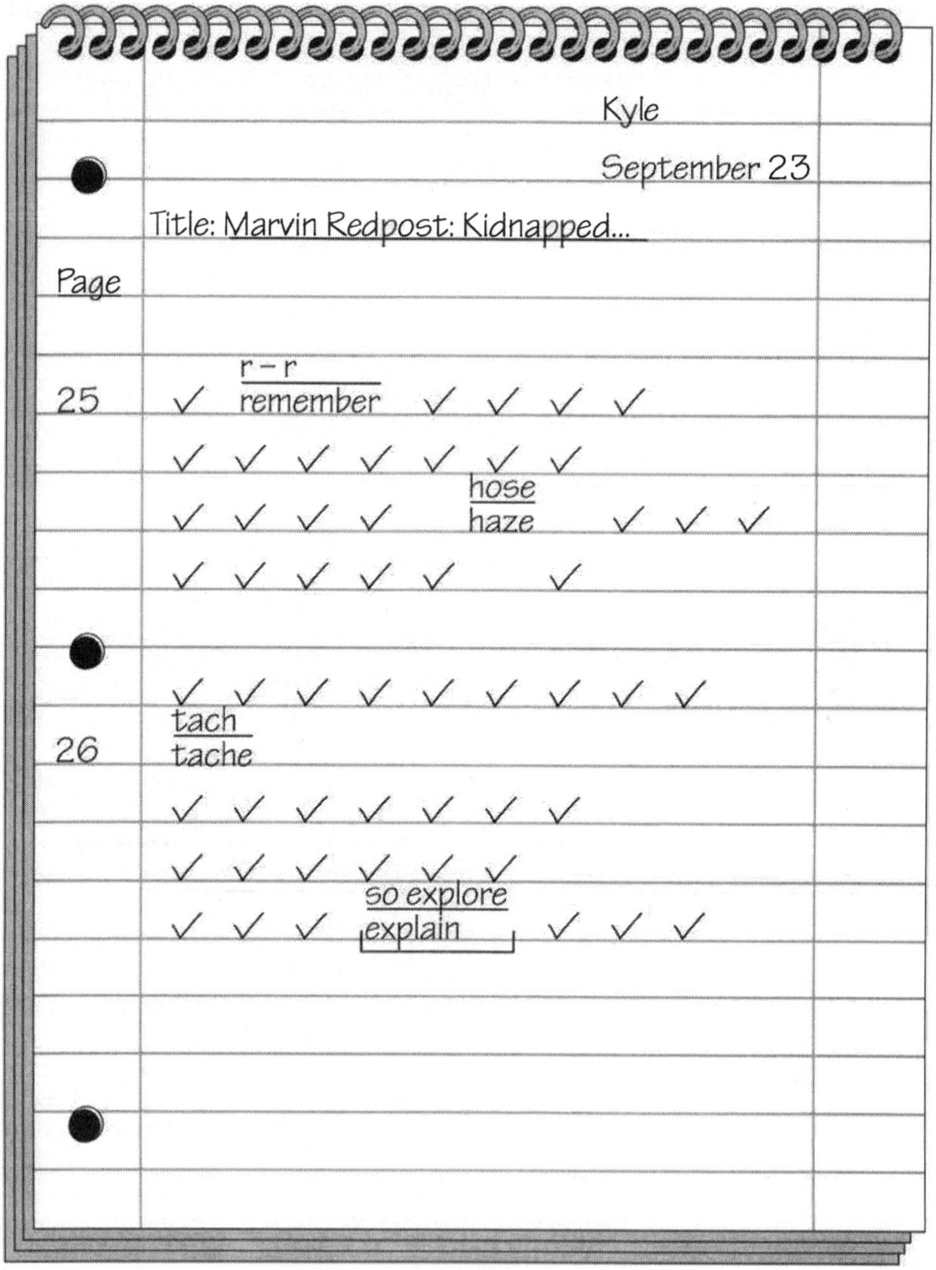

K. S. Goodman & Y. M. Goodman, 1977), interest in the ideas underlying miscue analysis dates back to Huey (1908/1968). The fundamental assumption underlying miscue analysis is the idea that readers use their knowledge of language to sample, predict, and confirm the meaning of a text. In addition, it is assumed that oral reading provides a means for examining readers' strategic use of the language systems during reading—*graphophonic, syntactic, and semantic cueing systems*. Although it appears that not each of these types of analyses are equally helpful, the fundamental idea that miscue analysis "provides specific information about a reader's strengths and weaknesses" (Y. Goodman, 1997, p. 534) continues to be as true today as it was when the Goodmans originally proposed the system.

Miscue analysis focuses special attention to times when students' oral reading deviates from the text—when the student says something other than what is printed in text. Oral reading "errors" have been renamed *miscues* because it is believed that they are not random errors but rather are mis-"cued" by the graphophonic, syntactic, and semantic systems the reader uses to process written material. Therefore, miscues are viewed as a "window on the reading process" (K. S. Goodman, 1973). The concept of miscues has become so popular that the term is commonly used when referring to oral reading errors, even when they are analyzed in a traditional manner. Despite some suggestion that miscue analysis should be used with caution (Mckenna & Picard, 2006), we find it extremely useful to do a careful examination of readers' oral reading behaviors.

Reading Miscue Inventory (RMI). The miscue analysis procedures developed by the Goodmans and their colleagues were simplified for research purposes and published as the *Reading Miscue Inventory* (Y. M. Goodman & Burke, 1972) and most recently revised in 2005 (Y. Goodman, Watson, & Burke). The RMI is designed specifically to identify and evaluate the strategies used by a particular reader to process written material. The following is a summary of the basic procedure:

1. A coherent reading passage is selected for the reader. The selection must be somewhat difficult and long enough to elicit a minimum of twenty-five miscues.
2. The reader is asked to read aloud and is informed that the reading will be unaided. A code sheet is marked as the selection is read. Audio of the reading is recorded for future reference.
3. The substitution miscues are coded.
4. Miscue patterns are studied, interpreted, and translated into instruction.

The reader is encouraged to guess after a thirty-second hesitation. If hesitations are continuous, the reader is told to continue reading even if it means skipping a word or phrase. The RMI procedures also include a retelling of the selection, which is scored subjectively by the examiner. More will be said about retellings in the next section.

Although all types of miscues are marked, only substitution (including mispronunciation) miscues are coded, according to RMI procedures. Each substitution miscue is coded on the basis of the answers to a specific set of nine questions.

- *Graphic similarity.* How much does the miscue look like what was expected?
- *Sound similarity.* How much does the miscue sound like what was expected?
- *Correction.* Is the miscue corrected?
- *Grammatical acceptability.* Does the miscue occur in a structure that is grammatically acceptable? Does intonation signal author's syntactic intent?

- *Semantic acceptability.* Does the miscue occur in a structure that is semantically acceptable? Does intonation signal author's semantic intent?
- *Meaning change.* Does the miscue result in a change of meaning? Is a dialect variation involved in the miscue? (Optional) *Grammatical function.* Is the grammatical function of the miscue the same as the grammatical function of the word in the text? (Y. M. Goodman et al., 1987)

There is also some variation in how these questions are used within each of the alternative procedures presented in the revised RMI.

The major advantage of miscue analysis over traditional analyses of oral reading errors is that it recognizes that some errors are better than others. Miscue analysis emphasizes the quality of errors as a reflection of the quality of strategies students are using to process text. Quality exists along a continuum from not-so-good to good, with a focus on how closely the miscues maintain meaning within the text.

Errors that focus on the meaning of the text are considered "better" than errors that focus on the letters and sounds, especially if the latter strategy results in nonsense-word substitution or substitutions that do not make sense within the context of the passage (Hood, 1978). Of course, the best errors are those that reveal attention to the multiple cueing systems; that is, they demonstrate that the reader is attending to the meaning of the *entire* passage and also to the print cues. For example, when reading aloud, good readers may substitute words that mean the same as the text, such as reading "frightened" for "afraid." In addition, they may omit unessential words—for example, by reading "told what he heard" instead of "told what he had heard." Words may be inserted, such as reading "the little old lady" for "the old lady." The writer's exact words may be read correctly but in a different order, such as reading "put the tent up" for "put up the tent." Unlike more-serious errors, which do not sound sensible, these specific examples are all good errors because they represent the same meaning as the words in the text. More important, they reflect the use of effective strategies to process the text.

There are no normative data to guide the interpretation of readers' miscue patterns. However, miscue analysis research does suggest the existence of several trends. A summary of these trends (Christie, 1981; Ferguson, Helmer & Suh, 2003; Wixson, 1979) includes the following:

1. Most readers, regardless of age or proficiency, produce a greater number of contextually acceptable miscues than graphophonically similar miscues.
2. As readers become more proficient, the proportion of graphophonically similar miscues stabilizes and the proportion of contextually acceptable miscues increases.
3. Less-proficient readers make fewer attempts to correct their miscues than more proficient readers do.
4. Less-proficient readers tend to correct acceptable and unacceptable miscues at almost an equal rate, whereas more proficient readers tend to correct unacceptable miscues at a higher rate than acceptable miscues.
5. Bilingual or non-native speakers of English make both quantitatively and qualitatively different miscues, particularly in the graphophonic cueing system.

Miscues should be interpreted with caution, however, because there is evidence that patterns vary as a result of the complex interaction among factors such as the instructional method; the reader's background, skills, and purpose for reading; and the specific nature of the written material. As with any test, miscue analysis provides a sample of behavior that may or may not be representative of the way a student interacts with different types of texts under different reading conditions. Miscue patterns are best regarded as a reflection of the particular strategies employed by a particular reader to satisfy his or her purpose for reading a particular passage.

The best way to address the problem of variability in miscue patterns is to obtain repeated samples of a particular reader's miscues under a variety of predetermined conditions. The nature and content of the reading selections should be varied with regard to each individual reader's skills and background, in an attempt to present the reader with a range of reading tasks and materials. An analysis of the miscues generated by a particular reader under a variety of conditions may reveal any pervasive problems the reader may have, as well as the particular conditions that present the reader with the greatest difficulty.

In addition to the problem of variability, the RMI often diverts attention away from a word-level analysis of miscues. Although the primary object of reading is, of course, comprehension and the maintenance of meaning, many struggling readers have decoding or word analysis difficulties, and an evaluation of miscues can provide valuable insight into readers' knowledge and skill in these areas. This is especially problematic because the RMI is designed to be used with materials that are at least one grade level above the student's reading placement level, and reading miscues may vary across texts of various levels of difficulty. Finally, the administration and scoring are too complex and time consuming to make them practical for either classroom or clinical use. Procedures that we advocate to simplify miscue analysis are provided in the next section.

Modified Miscue Analysis Procedures. The first step is to select text materials at what is believed to be the student's instructional level of difficulty so that information is being collected about the way the student is likely to perform during real classroom reading situations. Next, the substitution miscues are analyzed within the context of the following questions:

1. Does the miscue change the meaning of the sentence?
2. Is the miscue contextually acceptable within the context of the whole passage?
3. Was the miscue self-corrected?
4. Is the miscue graphophonically similar to the intended word?
5. If the miscue is graphically similar, does it reveal a pattern of difficulty in some component area?

In reflecting on the answers to these questions, we can begin to discover patterns of performance. In particular, we can begin to determine whether the student is attending to the meaningfulness of text (Are most of the miscues acceptable? Does the student self-correct most of those miscues that are not acceptable?).

The chart in Figure 9.4 illustrates Tha'm's miscues on several sentences from a level 4 selection on the Leslie and Caldwell *Qualitative Reading Inventory-4* (2006). One or two miscues of a particular type might not be significant. It is the *patterns* of performance that

FIGURE 9.4   Modified Miscue Analysis (Tha'm) Level 4 Narrative "Tomie DePaola" (familiar)

Subject _____ Level 4 _____ Level of Miscues ⟨Independent/Instructional⟩ Frustrational

Text	Tha'm	Meaning Change? [within sentence]	Contextually Acceptable? (whole passage)	Self-Corrected?	Graphophonic Similarity?	Component Difficulty?
1. *has*	had	no	yes	no	yes	High-frequency sight word
2. *read*	read	some	no [syntax]	no	yes	Verb tense; change on homonym
3. *interest*	interesting	yes	no (syntax/part of speech)	no	yes	Ending added
4. *there are*	they're	yes	no (syntax)	no	no	High-frequency sight words
5. *grew*	grow	no	No [syntax]	no	yes	Verb tense
6. *year*	years	no	yes	no	yes	Morpheme ending
7. *books*	his	yes	no	yes	some	High-frequency sight word
8. *he*	his	yes	no	no	yes	High-frequency sight word
9. *gifted*	gift	no	no	yes	yes	High-frequency sight word
10. *poems*	poem	yes	no	yes	yes	Morpheme ending
11. had	has	some	no	no	yes	Verb tense
12. arithmetic-er	arithmetic	Yes	no	No	Yes	Morpheme ending
–13.–	just	No	yes	No	NA	Insertion
14. suggested	suggest	Some	no	No	Yes	Morpheme ending
16. Fairmount	Fermont	No	yes	Yes	Yes	syllable juncture, vowel combination
17. walls	wall	Yes	no (syntax)	No	Yes	morpheme ending
18. drew	felt	yes	no	yes	no	
19. sheets	sheet	Yes	Yes	No	Yes	morpheme ending
20. stopped	stoped	No	No	No	yes	morpheme ending
21. writings	writing	No	No (syntax)	No	Yes	morpheme ending

FIGURE 9.4   (Continued)

22. children	child/ childrens	No	No	No	Yes	Irregular morpheme
23. children	childrens	no	No	No	yes	Irregular morpheme
24. children	childrens	no	No	No	Yes	Irregular morpheme
25. understanding	understand	yes	No	No	Yes	Morpheme ending
Accuracy: 92% Acceptability: 95–96% Comprehension: without look-backs: 5/8 = frustration Comprehension: with look-backs: 7/8 = instructional						

we are looking to reveal. One of the most important findings of miscue research focuses on the self-correction patterns of skilled and less-skilled readers. Skilled readers tend to self-correct miscues that are contextually unacceptable and to leave uncorrected errors that are contextually acceptable. As mentioned above, less-skilled readers are just as likely to correct acceptable as unacceptable miscues.

An examination of Tha'm's oral reading record reveals just this pattern. In this one grade 4 passage, there are nineteen contextually unacceptable errors—ones that we would expect a skilled reader (or native speaker) to correct (e.g., 2, 4, 5, 7, 9, and 10). Tha'm corrected only four of these (7, 9, 10, and 18), leaving the others uncorrected. This pattern is more like that of a less-skilled than a skilled reader.

Additional information can be obtained by examining the graphophonic similarity of the errors to the text word. All but one of Tha'm's nineteen miscues have at least some graphophonic similarity to the word in the text. This pattern, coupled with the fact that only six of her nineteen errors were contextually acceptable, suggests that Tha'm is relying heavily on the graphophonic cues in this text.

Finally, it is important to consider the effect of the errors on the meaning of the passage. In most cases, when an error is contextually acceptable, it will not change the meaning of the text, but when an error is contextually unacceptable, it will change the meaning of the text. However, occasionally, unacceptable errors do not change the meaning of the text, and acceptable errors do. This often happens with omissions and insertions. Although there were none of these in Tha'm's reading of the level 4 narrative (read at low instructional level), these errors became much more common when she read level 4 exposition (at frustration level).

Thus, on the passage, "Plant Structures for Survival," Tha'm read:

      adaption
This ~~adaptation~~ helps pine trees survive during the cold ~~winter months~~.

Neither the substitution of "adaption" for *adaptation* nor the omission of *winter* significantly affects the meaning of the passage—especially assuming that the word *adaptation* is not in her oral vocabulary.

The final column in Figure 9.4 is designed to provide further insights into readers' miscue patterns. In Tha'm's case, it provides exceptionally useful information. Almost every one of her meaning-changing errors reflects a morpheme shift. Across the board, Tha'm is making miscues of verb endings, plurals, possessives, and meaning-changing prefixes and suffixes. Most of these go uncorrected. Intermediate-grade students often make oral reading miscues on endings. Tha'm's miscues, however, are those common among ELL students: her errors are consistently located on verb forms and plurals. Native English speakers are more likely to make morphemic errors on suffixes such as *-ing*, *-ment*, etc. Once alerted to the pattern, it was possible to observe her oral language in a new light also. For example, when asked (as part of the QRI administration) to talk about an *adventurer*, she gave a plausible definition of *adventure*. When the ending was emphasized for her, she could not infer that it would mean "a person who goes on adventures"—although she did say that it was "...*familiar* to adventure." She likely meant to say that it was *similar* to adventure, or related to it. To the extent that the deletion of morphological endings reflects her oral language, some would argue that it should be treated more like a dialect miscue than a reading one. There is some evidence that the substitution of nonsense words for English words is much more common among ELL students (Valencia et al., 2007). This warrants examination for Tha'm. However, there is little doubt that the miscue analysis reveals diagnostically important information about Tha'm and her language development. Overall, Tha'm's oral reading accuracy is quite good (she achieved 93 percent of the fourth-grade narrative displayed in Figure 9.4). However, it is clear that the type of miscues she displays likely impacts her comprehension of the passage.

The QRI, administered to Kyle between grades 2 and 3 (see Chapter 8), provides support for summarizing and interpreting oral reading miscues. The summary form is presented in Figure 9.5 with Kyle's results from two instructional-level passages.

Unlike Tha'm's, Kyle's profile is more similar to that of a good reader than to a poor one. Sixteen of twenty-two miscues were semantically acceptable. Kyle attempted to self-correct four of the six remaining miscues. Only twice did Kyle leave uncorrected a miscue that was both syntactically and semantically unacceptable: substituting *then* for *when* and mispronouncing the word *formed*. In other words, Kyle is attending quite carefully to the semantic and syntactic cues in text. He also is making use of the graphophonic cues (only five of twenty-two miscues were not graphically similar). Kyle's miscues fall into two large categories: he frequently makes substitutions of high-frequency sight words (*the* for *it*, *there* for *where*, *to* for *of*), and he has problems with morphemes, frequently dropping or adding endings (*knit* for *knitted*, *dries* for *dry*, *class* for *classes*).

Before going on, it is important to remember that for both Kyle and Tha'm this is a very small sample of miscues taken from one or two texts. To make generalizations or predictions about Tha'm's reading in particular, we must examine a large number of miscues taken from a variety of texts under a variety of conditions. This issue will be considered further in Chapter 10 as we examine multiple samples of Tha'm's reading.

Rhodes and Shanklin (1990) devised a simplified assessment strategy for analyzing students' miscues in the classroom, and it serves as a useful companion to the running record. The Classroom Reading Miscue Assessment (CRMA) (see Figure 9.6) is used as students read a whole text. Rather than analyze each oral reading miscue, teachers get an overall picture of the student's reading proficiency. First, the teacher determines the

FIGURE 9.5
Miscue Analysis Worksheet (Kyle)

Subject ___Level 3___   Level of Miscues: (Independent/Instructional) Frustrational

Wool

Miscue	Text	Graphically Similar	Semantically Acceptable	Syntactically Acceptable	Self-Corrected	Word-Level Component
knit	knitted	yes	yes	no	—	word ending
clothes	clothing	yes	yes	yes	—	word ending
then	when	yes	no	no	—	high-frequency sight word
the	it	no	no	no	yes	sight word
looks	locks	yes	no	no	yes	vowel combination
dries	dry	yes	yes	no	—	word ending
com-bed	combed	yes	no	no	attempted, unsuccessful	silent letter
form-at	formed	yes	no	no	—	word ending
wove	woven	yes	yes	no	—	word ending
clothes	clothing	yes	yes	yes	—	word ending
hands	hand	yes	yes	yes	—	word ending
the	their	yes	yes	yes	—	sight word
class	classes	yes	yes	no	yes	word ending
Mar	Maria	yes	yes	yes	—	
Angelina	Angela	yes	yes	yes	—	
want	wanted	yes	yes	no	yes	word ending
the	one	no	yes	no	—	sight word
Lipoz	Lopez	yes	yes	yes	—	
there	where	partial	yes	yes	—	sight word
to	of	no	no	no	yes	sight word
Luzpa	Lopez	yes	yes	yes	—	
He	and	no	yes	yes	—	sight word
Column Total Total Miscues Column Total/Total Miscues = %		_____	_____	_____	_____	

300

FIGURE 9.6   Classroom Reading Miscue Assessment

Classroom Reading Miscue Assessment

Name: _____ Date: _____

Grade: _____ Teacher: _____

Text level read: _____

I. What percent of the sentences read make sense?

Sentence-by-sentence tally   Total

___ Number of semantically acceptable sentences

___ Number of semantically unacceptable sentences

___ % Comprehending score: $\dfrac{\text{Number of semantically acceptable sentences}}{\text{Total number of sentences read}} \times 100$ TOTAL _____

	Seldom	Sometimes	Often	Usually	Always
II. Constructive Meaning	1	2	3	4	5
Successful strategies for constructing meaning					
A. Monitors miscues and knows when meaning is disrupted					
B. Makes sensible substitutions					
C. Self-corrects miscues when meaning is disrupted					
D. Uses semantic cues (context, pictures, visuals, etc.) to support comprehension					
E. Uses rereading and predicting to enhance comprehension					
Reading behaviors that disrupt meaning					
A. Makes nonsense-word or other substitutions that distort comprehension					
B. Skips words or makes omissions that distort comprehension					
C. Relies too heavily on graphic cues					
III. Word Recognition					
Successful strategies for reading words					
A. Looks at the entire word and makes effective use of graphophonic information					
B. Attends to spelling patterns and to morphemes (endings, prefixes, etc.)					
C. Recognizes high-frequency sight words					
D. Can use syllabication for longer words					
E. Uses a decoding-by-analogy strategy					
F. Uses rereading to clarify and correct					
G. Monitors word recognition for meaning (see above)					
Less-successful strategies for reading words					
A. Uses only limited word features (e.g., initial or final consonants)					
B. Overrelies on context and pictures					
C. Skips words without rereading and/or makes refusal miscues					
D. Tries to use letter-sound decoding for all words, even high-frequency words					

Source: Adapted from Rhodes, L. K., Shanklin, N. L., & Valencia, S. W. (1990, November). Miscue analysis in the classroom. *The Reading Teacher*, 44(3), 252–254. Reprinted with permission of the International Reading Association. All rights reserved.

extent to which a reader is constructing meaning. To do this, each sentence in the text is considered separately. The teacher determines whether each sentence read by the student (after self-correction) is semantically acceptable or not. Then a percentage of semantically acceptable sentences is computed by dividing the total number of those sentences by the total number of sentences read. Teachers record their observations about reading behaviors using a five-point scale (see Figure 9.6).

Although the CRMA originally included a brief framework for evaluating retellings, we examine comprehension assessment in greater detail later in this chapter. We have adapted the strategy somewhat so that teachers can also make note of the word reading strategies used by students. In this way, teachers can focus first on student's attempts to construct meaning, but they can also examine word recognition and identification strategies during authentic reading.

Retrospective Miscue Analysis. The running record, while well suited for teachers and students in the primary grades, is not as useful with older students. Even students in the intermediate grades tend to read too quickly for this informal, "on the run" technique. In addition, students beyond the primary grades often have more-complex word identification difficulties. Informal reading inventories and more-comprehensive RMI procedures can be very helpful in assessing decoding or word identification. However, there is one technique, designed specifically for use with middle and high school students, that classroom teachers should consider adding to their repertoire. It is the retrospective miscue analysis (RMA) (Ebersole, 2005; Moore & Gilles, 2005). The technique was originally (and often still is) used as an instructional tool to encourage students to think about reading as a meaning-constructing process. But it also has excellent potential for examining students' orientation to their reading and gaining insights into their thinking. "Like other classroom-based procedures, one of its strengths is that it permits observation in authentic materials—often content area textbooks" (Ebersole, 2005).

The procedure is a simple one:

1. Students' reading is recorded.
2. They listen to the tape recording and discuss miscues using questions generated by the teacher.
3. These questions include prompts such as:
   Why did you say . . . ?
   Here you reread a part. Why did you do that?
   What were you thinking here?

This useful assessment technique can become the basis for instructional applications. Several authors have published excellent descriptions of approaches that promote comprehension among students, especially at the intermediate and middle grades (Bauman, Jones, & Seifert-Kessell, 1993; Kucan & Beck, 1997; Oster, 2001; Wilhelm, 2008).

Word Sorts. The word sort (Gillet & Temple, 1990; Invernizzi, Abouzeid, & Gill, 1994) is a flexible assessment strategy that can be used to assess a variety of word-level abilities. Gillet and Temple suggested using the word sort as a way to assess word recognition and/or word analysis, but we have also found it useful for evaluating vocabulary as well (see the next section), and many teachers are familiar with its use in word study or spelling (Bear et al., 2012). This technique capitalizes on the fact that words are organized in human memory by patterns or relationships.

There are two types of word sorts: *open* and *closed*. In an open sort, no criteria for sorting the words are provided. Because students must impose their own organization on the words, it is possible to observe the types of relationships available to them. In a closed sort, the teacher establishes in advance the criteria for sorting. Using word cards that are preprepared (or selected by students from their own word bank), the teacher asks the student to:

- Put the words that go together in the same pile (open sort)
- Put all the words together that have the same beginning letter and then name the group (closed sort)
- Put all the words together that have something the same and label the characteristic
- Put all the words together that have the same feature (for example, rhyme or spelling pattern)

As the student's performance is evaluated, it is helpful to consider the following questions:

- Does the student attend to meaning features or graphic features?
- Does the student recognize and use initial, medial, and final sounds?
- Does the student recognize and use structural cues (compounds, base words)?
- Can the student generate categories based on visual patterns (spelling patterns)?
- Does the student recognize multiple ways to represent sounds (the several ways to spell the short *e* sound)?
- Does the student use self-correcting strategies? Which?

Some teachers we have worked with keep a class summary chart of the ways students choose to sort the words they provide. This furnishes important information on students' growing knowledge and flexibility in using aspects of phonics, categorization, and/or content information.

Evaluating Oral Reading Fluency

In Chapter 8, we discussed fluency from the point of view of rate and accuracy (WPM and WCPM). Certainly, teachers and specialists will find it useful to consider rate and accuracy in their diagnostic and formative assessments of individual students, but this should be done within the context of a full understanding of the fluency component. For example, it is important to realize that differences in text can/do affect the results of assessments. Not surprisingly, the level of text difficulty affects students' rate, a fact that is critical in interpreting CBM data (see Chapter 8), since students are generally evaluated on *grade*-level text during CBM assessments. However, other text features also impact students' performance and assessment results. For example, emergent readers are likely to be more fluent when reading texts that have more high-frequency and decodable words

FIGURE 9.7 **Assessing/Monitoring Fluency**

Teacher: _____ Grade: _____			
Student	**Date (Fall)**	**Date (Winter)**	**Date (Spring)**	**Comments**
	Text: Level: WCPM:	Text: Level: WCPM:	Text: Level: WCPM:	
	Text: Level: WCPM:	Text: Level: WCPM:	Text: Level: WCPM:	
	Text: Level: WCPM:	Text: Level: WCPM:	Text: Level: WCPM:	
	Text: Level: WCPM:	Text: Level: WCPM:	Text: Level: WCPM:	

(Compton, Appleton, & Hosp, 2004; Hiebert & Fisher, 2002). Of course, this suggests that we need to be cautious in interpreting results. Although a number of rates have been suggested, none is sufficiently well developed to advocate as the benchmark for fluent reading, and most are very similar to the rate ranges described in Chapter 8 (see Figures 8.11 and 8.12). We suggest using those rates as a guideline for collecting data on students *over time* using *multiple* passages so that your estimates will have greater reliability. Because it is relatively easy to assess, and because it is possible to collect data from students as they read authentic and diverse texts, there is much to be learned by keeping track of students' fluency performance over time/texts (see Figure 9.7). Alternatively, Rasinski and Padak have produced sets of "three-minute reading assessments" that teachers have found easy and effective to use (Rasinski & Padak, 2005; Rasinski, Padak, & Davis-Swing, 2005). We recommend noting rate in terms of both WPM and WCPM *as well as* the level of text difficulty.

Various Components of Fluency. A study by Valencia and her colleagues (2010) demonstrates that caution must be exercised in assessing fluency. These researchers evaluated students in grades 2, 4, and 6 on multiple measures of fluency and in two different types of text (narrative and exposition). In addition, students' comprehension was measured on both specific passages and with a norm-referenced test. Their results demonstrate the need to evaluate each of these areas separately rather than combined as with WCPM, because "clearly wcpm scores do not provide the depth or breadth of information needed to make good instructional decisions or programmatic recommendations" (p. 288).

In this study by Valencia and her colleagues, measures of rate, accuracy, and expression contributed different amounts of information to the diagnostic picture for students.

Also, relationships among these elements were not necessarily the same across different developmental ages/grades. For example, WCPM tended to be a good predictor of word-list reading, but less good for predicting comprehension. Expression (see phrase-boundary measure below) tended to predict comprehension but was less good for predicting word-list reading. In addition, the relationships were different for different grades. Expression became more important across the grades. However, rate contributed less to reading performance (comprehension) between grades 2 and 4, while accuracy contributed less after grade 4. In other words, as students move through the grades, their performance becomes more dependent on a complex intersection of abilities.

Most experts consider fluency to be more than just accuracy and rate. Oral fluency also involves readers' ability to group words into meaningful phrase units. Smoothness and the maintenance of comprehension are important as well (Harris & Hodges, 1995). "Fluent readers can read text with speed, accuracy, and proper expression" (National Reading Panel, 2000, p. 3–1). We describe a procedure for capturing this additional information next.

The Fluency Rating Scale.   Originally used by the National Assessment of Educational Progress (NAEP), the oral reading fluency scale evaluates fluency by providing an estimate of whether or not a student consistently reads sentences predominantly word by word, in two-word groups with occasional word-by-word reading, in phrase groups with some two- or three-word groups, or in phrase groups (used by Valencia et al., 2010, as their measure of expression).

Selecting Materials.   Research with good and poor readers in grades 1 through 6, using a procedure similar to the one described here, suggests that word grouping strategies change as a function of the difficulty of the material, reading ability, and years of exposure to reading and reading instruction (see Aulls, 1982). Most good readers in grades 5 and 6 read consistently in phrase groups when reading instructional-level and even frustration-level material. However, good readers in grades 1 through 4 typically read material at the independent level with better word grouping strategies than they do material at the instructional or frustration level. What appears to be unique about poor readers at any grade level is that they group words in material at the independent and at the instructional level in the same fashion.

We recommend using material at the student's instructional level, since most instruction is carried out at the instructional level, and, because poor readers perform similarly at all levels, instructional-level materials seem acceptable. The materials should be no less than 250 words in length. The longer the text, the better the estimate. Texts of 500 to 1,000 words are equally appropriate and have the advantage of offering a highly confident estimate of the student's ability to consistently organize words into groups when reading texts of similar readability and text organization or type.

Scoring.   It is difficult to do a holistic scoring of fluency as you listen to students read. We recommend recording the oral reading sample that will be used for scoring. The Oral Reading Fluency Scale used by NAEP (Pinnell et al., 1995) is described in Figure 9.8. As the teacher listens to the oral reading sample, there are several key elements to consider. The first is *phrasing*. Phrasing patterns result from pitch sequences and pauses during oral reading. For the examiner, pauses provide the primary signal of the division of words into

**FIGURE 9.8
NAEP Fluency
Scale Levels**

NAEP's Integrated Reading Performance Record Oral Reading Fluency Scale
Level 4— Reads primarily in larger, meaningful phrase groups. Although some regressions, repetitions, and deviations from text may be present, these do not appear to detract from the overall structure of the story. Preservation of the author's syntax is consistent. Some or most of the story is read with expressive interpretation.
Level 3— Reads primarily in three- or four-word phrase groups. Some smaller groupings may be present. However, the majority of phrasing seems appropriate and preserves the syntax of the author. Little or no interpretation is present.
Level 2— Reads primarily in two-word phrases with some three- or four-word groupings. Some word-by-word reading may be present. Word groupings may seem awkward and unrelated to larger context of sentence or passage.
Level 1— Reads primarily word by word. Occasional two-word or three-word phrases may occur—but these are infrequent and/or they do not preserve meaningful syntax.

Source: Pinnel et al. (January, 1995). *Listening to children read aloud.* OERIA U.S. Dept. of Education, "Nation's Report Card." Report #23-FR-04. Washington, DC.

groups. Pitch provides a secondary signal of the meaning assigned to each group. Teachers who are assigning levels to fluency should also attend to how closely the reader *follows the author's syntax and/or sentence structure.* Stress placements and intonation can provide clues to guide the scoring. In addition, readers often insert pauses to signal meaning implied by the author. Finally, the fluency rating should consider the reader's *expressiveness* during reading. However, the degree of expressiveness expected will vary according to the age and/or grade of the reader. Only in the later elementary grades would we expect students to exhibit consistently good expressiveness during oral reading.

If a student rereads a phrase or sentence, the word grouping used in the first reading is scored. This provides the best estimate of how the student typically and spontaneously performs. Students can and do self-correct word groupings, but the intent is to characterize their spontaneous patterns for organizing text information fluently, not their self-corrections of disfluent reading.

To determine the fluency rating, you might wish to mark the phrase boundaries as students read. The following characterize different students' abilities to organize words into groups:

1. Word by word: *The/brown/pony/galloped/toward/the fence. /It/was. . .*
2. Beyond word-by-word reading, but not consistently in phrases: *The brown pony/ galloped/ toward/the fence. /It was/. . .*
3. Consistently in phrases: *The brown pony/galloped toward the fence./ It was/. . .*

In the first example, all words except two were read word by word. The words *the fence* were organized into a two-word group. Because the majority of words were read word

FIGURE 9.9   Sample Fluency Rating: Tha'm

"Tomie dePaola"

1. Tomie dePaola has illustrated /over/200 books./
2. He also has/has also authored/ over 100 of those he has illustrated./
3. Tomie was born in/1934/in/Connecticut,/one of four/children./
4. Tomie's mother read to him as a young boy/ and encouraged/his/early interest in art./
5. His father loved to take pictures and there are many/home movies of the dePaola family./
6. Tomie knew what he wanted to do when he grow (sic) up/ by the time (he was) five year (sic) old./
7. One day he came home (from) kindergarten (and) told his mother he was/ "going to draw pictures/ for books,/ sing and dance on stage,/ and paint all the scenery."/
8. In elementary school he was gift/gifted/ in his ability to learn songs after hearing them only once/and (to) memorize poems./
9. But he has (sic) a terrible time memorizing math facts./
10. He told his second-grade teacher he was not/going to be an/arithmetic (sic)./

Source: From p. 262, *Qualitative Reading Inventory-4*, by Lauren Leslie and Joanne Caldwell, 2006, Grade 4. Reprinted by permission of Pearson Education, Inc., Upper Saddle River, NJ.

by word, the student must be considered to be a word-by-word reader. In the second example, only two of seven words in the sentence were read word by word, and other words were grouped in two-word groups. In the third example, the entire text was read in phrase groups. Even if *galloped* had been read as part of the first word group (*The brown pony galloped/toward the fence*), it would still be an acceptable phrase group. The exact phrase grouping is not as important as the preservation of sensible word groupings.

To obtain an overall estimate of a student's word grouping during reading, the examiner considers the fluency across sentences and assigns a holistic score that captures reading for this student. A sample of Tha'm's fluency rating using this scoring procedure is provided in Figure 9.9. Tha'm reads many portions of the passage fluently (sentences 2, 6, and 8, for example). Overall, three- or four-word phrasings were Tha'm's most consistent pattern of grouping words. She is reading some sentences in complete phrases, but word-level challenges disrupt her reading. She does generally maintain the author's syntax or sentence structure. On the other hand, Tha'm does not read with much expression, and on occasion she reads past major sentence markers (e.g., periods). We would place Tha'm at a fluency level of 3.

Interpreting the Score.   In his groundbreaking work, Aulls (1982) suggested that students at different levels of fluency are characteristically different from one another. For example, he noted that all readers whose scores are not completely fluent (level 4) represent students who are acquiring word grouping strategies. A major distinction probably exists between levels 2 and 3. At levels 3 and 4, students seem to be able to give much more attention to the development of the more advanced strategies for processing sentence meaning.

Students at level 1 need to become more fluent before moving on. They might need to be provided with easier materials until they have learned to group words better. Those students at level 2 will be much more likely to be ready to refine the less complex sentence processing strategies involved in confirming word identification cues or integrating them.

Aulls suggests that once the student has attained a score at level 3, the teacher should begin stressing the development of more-sophisticated sentence-processing strategies.

Of course, it is important to interpret fluency in relation to text difficulty also. Aulls (1982) cautions:

> When a poor reader is an older, intermediate grade pupil who cannot read material beyond third-grade difficulty at the independent level, it is very likely that all or part of the reading problem is inability to read words in phrase groups and/or inadequately developed strategies, or the lack of use of them, for processing sentence meaning. A teacher who cannot or does not assess the sentence processing strategies of poor readers may incorrectly conclude that teaching word identification cues will be sufficient to enable a poor reader to become a fluent reader. (pp. 622–623)

Tha'm is reading beyond the third-grade level. Indeed, it appears that she is a reasonably fluent reader *in grade-level text* (she does even better in easier text). At the same time, she does demonstrate a willingness to sacrifice meaning for smooth and rapid oral reading. Valencia (2007) has noted that ELL students' overall reading ability may be masked when fluency alone is considered. In Tha'm's case, her word identification accuracy is reasonably good, and her fluency as measured by both speed and pausal prosody is also adequate. All of these scores are on the very low end of interpretive criteria, however, and they point to a troubling pattern of performance. There is no reason to think that she cannot make progress, but, as Aulls suggests, she needs to be working on more-sophisticated sentence-processing strategies that connect meaning across sentence boundaries.

The fluency rating scale just described is useful for screening and monitoring students' progress. Sometimes, however, teachers want a more multifaceted picture of students' fluency. The summary form in Figure 9.10 was designed to be used for continuous monitoring. This type of more-comprehensive picture of fluency appears to be essential, since both our own practical experience in working with struggling readers and recent research suggests a complicated picture.

Several comprehensive studies of component aspects of fluency and their impact on reading comprehension point to a complex set of relationships. Like Valencia et al. (2010), Schwanenflugel, Messinger, and Wisenbaker (2006) offer a compelling argument that these conflicting findings are the result of differences in the development of fluency and comprehension. Essentially, their findings indicate that fluency follows a "simple course" in its relationship to comprehension in younger students. That is, we may find out all we really need to know about students' fluency (and often their comprehension of texts read) by assessing only single-word aspects of fluency such as single-word naming accuracy and speed, reading rate, sight-word reading, and efficiency in using phonics. Importantly, the research by Schwanenflugel et al. (2006) "points to the diminishing role that automaticity plays in reading comprehension as children get older" (p. 519). On the other hand, among older readers (late grade 3 and up), *text reading fluency* (as opposed to single-word accuracy and rate) is a major (even primary) factor in reading comprehension (see Cain, Oakhill, & Bryant, 2004; Jenkins et al., 2003). In fact, Schwanenflugel and colleagues point out that their measures of text fluency and text comprehension may not have been complex enough (they used norm-referenced tests), and so even among young readers, the situation may not be as simple as they propose.

FIGURE 9.10   Fluency Summary: Tha'm

Student:	Tha'm		Date:	Winter of 5th grade

Text: _"Tomie dePaola"_ (Level 4, QRI-4)

	Level 1	**Level 2**	**Level 3**	**Level 4**
NAEP Fluency Rating	Reads primarily word by word. Occasional two-word or three-word phrases may occur, but these are infrequent and/or they do not preserve meaningful syntax.	Reads primarily in two-word phrases with some three- or four-word groupings. Some word-by-word reading may be present. Word groupings may seem awkward and unrelated to larger context of sentence or passage.	Reads primarily in three- or four-word phrase groups. Some smaller groupings may be present. However, the majority of phrasing seems appropriate and preserves the syntax of the author. Little or no interpretation is present.	Reads primarily in larger, meaningful phrase groups. Although some regressions, repetitions, and deviations from text may be present, these do not appear to detract from the overall structure of the story. Preservation of the author's syntax is consistent. Some or most of the story is read with expressive interpretation.
Rate WPM: 125 WCPM: 89	Rate is consistently low (across texts).	Reading rate' is below the 50th percentile in grade-level text OR varies considerably depending on the text. Rate while reading ability-appropriate text may be at or above the 50th percentile'	Rate, **while reading grade-level texts,** is at or above the 50th percentile.[2] Maintains this rate across diverse texts.	Rate, **while reading grade-level texts,** is at or above the 75th percentile.[3] Maintains this rate across diverse texts.
Automaticity (rapid, accurate word ID at the single-word level)	Single-word reading is labored—slow and/or inaccurate. May reflect some lack of knowledge/ skill in phonological awareness and/or phonics.	Appears to require time and/or effort to read individual, orthographically regular words. Phonics/decoding knowledge intact, but not automatic.	Reads individual, orthographically regular words accurately, but more slowly than optimal.	Reads individual, orthographically regular words quickly and accurately.
Summary and Comment	_Tha'm reads quite quickly and smoothly, typically maintaining good prosody, phrase boundaries, and expression. However, in text reading, she is not always accurate, resulting in a significant discrepancy between WPM and WCPM, which also vary considerably, depending on text type and familiarity. Word level tests of automaticity (DIBELS and TOWRE) indicate that she meets the standard for her age/grade._			

[1]Using the Hasbrouck and Tinsdale (2005) rates
[2]Using the Hasbrouck and Tinsdale (2005) rates
[3]Using the Hasbrouck and Tinsdale (2005) rates

The Fluency Summary of Tha'm's fluency ratings (in Figure 9.10) demonstrates how important it is to examine students' performance in multiple ways. Measures of word-level automaticity paint a positive picture of Tha'm's fluency abilities. However, during reading of continuous text, her rate and fluency are much more variable. Although she typically reads smoothly, maintaining phrase boundaries, the syntax difficulties revealed in the miscue analysis show up in a weak WCPM rate—and a very large discrepancy between the words-per-minute rate and the WCPM rate.

Despite the controversies surrounding fluency assessment, we recommend that teachers collect initial diagnostic information about students and that they continue to examine this issue whenever fluency appears to be implicated in students' reading difficulties.

Evaluating Vocabulary

Interest in assessing vocabulary knowledge has heightened dramatically over the past decade, yet surprisingly few assessment techniques have been suggested for validating individual differences in this area. Most diagnosticians employ one of the available standardized tests to estimate relative vocabulary strength, and we described several of these in Chapter 7. Most of them involve word-level assessments (finding definitions, picture associations, etc.).

One of the difficulties in assessing vocabulary is a lack of clarity about the purpose for doing so. Certainly, many teachers want to assess vocabulary in order to determine whether students have learned the specific (generally content-related) words that they have been teaching. However, that purpose is less relevant for us in this text, since we are interested in highlighting areas that either influence student performance or identify areas of strength and need. Thus, we might want to assess vocabulary in order to take this component into account as we evaluate students' performance on (e.g.) a measure of comprehension. That is exactly the tactic that is used when structured inventories such as the QRI assess students' prior knowledge of relevant words before reading a passage (see Chapter 8). Alternatively, we might want to know whether students' overall vocabulary was appropriately well developed (compared to other students) and was sufficient for the general demands of particular age/grade texts and tasks. In other words, we might want to know if students had an overall weakness in the area of vocabulary that might lead to comprehension difficulties. Either of these purposes can pose problems, but the latter is certainly more challenging than the former.

A word is a label for a concept or idea. It has been suggested that vocabulary words are important not because they are directly helpful in understanding text, but because the individual words reflect generalized knowledge about a topic and because a critical mass of vocabulary may trigger a student's metalinguistic analysis of words (Nagy & Scott, 2000; Whitehurst & Lonigan, 2001). When a reader knows a word, he or she probably knows many other related words. For example, a knowledgeable sailor generated in a few seconds the following words when asked what she thought of when she heard the word *spinnaker*:

> *spinnaker:* jib, fore, aft, mainsail, port, bow, sheets, heel, winch, cleat, starboard, heading, gaff, sloop, schooner, 12-meter, galley, tack

It should be apparent that simply learning a definition for the word spinnaker would not be as helpful as the knowledge base that results in knowing spinnaker but also knowing all those other words. As Nagy and Scott (2000) explain, word knowledge is extremely complex. In their review of research, they conclude that word knowledge has several characteristics that contribute to this complexity: (1) incrementality—"knowing a word is a matter of degrees, not all-or-nothing"; (2) polysemy—"words often have multiple meanings"; (3) interrelatedness—knowing a word often depends on our knowledge of other words; and (4) heterogeneity—"what we know about words often depends on the type of word" (Nagy & Scott, 2000, p. 270). Word meanings are related in such a way that they form concepts that are organized in a network of relationships. When asked to think about one word related to a concept, people generate many associated words.

Many experts have captured the incremental nature of vocabulary knowledge. Dale (1995) proposed the following stages:

- Stage 1: Never having seen the term before
- Stage 2: Knowing there is such a word, but not knowing what it means
- Stage 3: Having a context-bound and vague knowledge of the word meaning
- Stage 4: Knowing the word well and remembering it

The richness and flexibility of students' vocabulary is important to assess because vocabulary has such a strong impact on comprehension. When students learn about words, not only their meanings but how words are "built," they are in an excellent position to figure out the meanings of unfamiliar words and generate new vocabulary themselves. For example, students who begin to form and recognize words such as *new*, *newer*, *newness*, *renew*, *renewal*, and so on begin to see how word meanings are changed when morphemes are added. Similarly, students who know words such as *spectator* and *inspect* can begin to figure out the meanings of other words like *inspection*, *perspective*, *retrospective*, *spectacles*, or even *suspect*.

Because vocabulary is such a complex area, assessment of this component is also important. In a thoughtful essay about issues of vocabulary assessment, Pearson, Hiebert, and Kamil (2007) reviewed categorical schemes and highlighted the types of information each might provide. The important thing for us to remember here is that different assessments are likely to provide different information about individual students. Questions to ask about any vocabulary assessment include (see Read, 2000):

- Is vocabulary assessed separate from comprehension (as a discrete component), or embedded in the assessment of text understanding?
- How have the vocabulary words been selected? Are they representative enough for your purposes?
- How much context is provided (or needed)?
- What depth of knowledge is required for students to be successful?

Of course, it is important to make sure that students' word-level difficulties actually result from vocabulary problems, not decoding problems (Blachowicz & Fisher, 2010). Not infrequently, struggling readers demonstrate word-level difficulties and appear to have weak vocabulary knowledge when in fact they cannot decode or recognize target words. Needless to say, students who cannot identify the word will have difficulty assigning meaning! If you are at all concerned that decoding might be a factor in students' vocabulary scores, you should simply ask students to read the words aloud. You can provide any words that are mispronounced. Remember, the goal is to evaluate meaning vocabulary. If students still do not appear to comprehend the word, the problem is likely a vocabulary difficulty. Of course, many struggling readers exhibit *both* problems.

Word Sorts.   It is possible to get a general idea of the range and flexibility of students' vocabulary knowledge using word sorts. As the student's performance is evaluated, it is helpful to consider the following questions:

- Does the student attend to meaning features or graphic features?
- Can the student generate relational categories?
- Does the student recognize multiple meanings for words?
- Does the student recognize and use affixes?
- Does the student recognize and use morphological "family" information?
- Can the student generate superordinate categories?

Word sorts can easily be embedded in instruction and used repeatedly. This type of assessment strategy can be especially helpful if you are selecting content-area texts, are examining students' ability to understand basal texts, or want to compare your students' knowledge of some new theme or topic. In these cases, effective assessment can be done with word sorts using preselected words that capture the central ideas and key concepts of the new material and highlight the relationships between and among those concepts.

Multiple Measures of Prior (Vocabulary) Knowledge.   Although general measures of vocabulary knowledge can be helpful, teachers also need to know how vocabulary is interacting with specific reading demands. As we have seen, word knowledge is incremental. For assessment/instruction purposes, it is helpful to classify students' "levels" of knowledge. You may want to use the stages described above (Dale, 1995), or you could use the three-level classifications suggested by Beck, McKwon, and Omanson, 1987: unknown, acquainted, and established. Because prior knowledge can and does produce variation in reading performance, we suggest evaluating students' vocabulary within the context of specific texts. Concerns about vocabulary knowledge and development are especially critical for English language learners (ELL). These students might very well understand the concepts under consideration but not have the English vocabulary to understand the reading or to communicate their comprehension.

Because there are very few "standardized tests" of vocabulary for classroom use, our assessment should be varied, involving multiple measures. Dale Johnson (2001) suggests a variety of techniques. Using students' written work, teacher-made tests, cloze passages, and anecdotal records, teachers can ask students to

- read a word and circle a definition.
- read a word and circle a synonym.

- read a word and circle an antonym.
- read sentence and write the missing word.
- read a passage and fill in the missing blanks (a cloze passage).
- read a word and put it in a category.
- find the word in a category that doesn't belong.

Fortunately, vocabulary measures are relatively easy to incorporate into regular assessment-instruction efforts, and some recent evidence suggests that vocabulary is relatively easy to assess. For example, Biemiller and his colleagues (2005) have been using a technique they call the *"context sentence" approach*, a straightforward method that is done orally with young children and in writing with older students. Older students are informed that they can ask for any words or sentences to be read to them since it is not a reading test. Using this technique, students see or hear a sentence and are asked to tell what a highlighted (designated) word means in that sentence. For example:

"Donna had a new **dress** for the dance." In this sentence, what does **dress** mean?
"The **spectators** were excited by the action." In this sentence, what does **spectators** mean? Etc.

Students are told that they can use words, actions, or pointing to define the words. The challenge, of course, is to identify the appropriate words for testing. Sentences can be drawn from stories that students are about to read or that they have already experienced. For more-global measures of vocabulary, the challenge is greater. Researchers have recently made progress in determining a sequence of root-word meanings that could provide developmental benchmarks, but that work is incomplete at this time (Biemiller, 2005; Biemiller & Slonim, 2001; Hiebert, 2005).

Different assessment techniques may result in different estimates of students' prior knowledge/vocabulary. Holmes and Roser (1987) identify and compare five techniques that can be used during instruction and assessment: free recall, word association, structured questions, recognition, and unstructured discussion. The special value of the work of Holmes and Roser (1987) is that they have actually collected data to determine the utility and efficiency of these assessment strategies.

- *Free recall.* The teacher says to students, "Tell me everything you know about . . ." and records the responses. Free recall provides the most information in the least time, but can pose problems for young and/or disabled readers who have retrieval problems and/or disorganized information.
- *Word association.* This is much like the PreReading Plan (PReP) (see following discussion). Teachers select several key words and ask students what comes to mind when they hear each one. These are quick to prepare and administer and generally yield more information than free recall does.
- *Structured questions.* They are posed to determine what students know before reading. This technique is both the most effective and the most efficient, yielding by far the most information. However, the questions are time consuming to prepare.

- *Recognition.* This requires that the teacher prepare several statements or key terms beforehand. Then students select the words, phrases, or sentences they believe are related to the key terms or would be present in a particular selection. Recognition is second only to structured questions for efficiency and to free recall in effectiveness and is helpful for students who have trouble retrieving information in production tasks.
- *Unstructured discussion.* This is most like what is traditionally done in reading instruction, since students freely generate their own ideas about a topic, with no focusing from the teacher. However, this approach might not be worth the effort, as it is the least effective and efficient procedure of the five.

The five strategies are easily adaptable to any assessment or instructional setting. Each approach requires only an observant teacher who understands his or her purpose in gathering such information. Each of these techniques is designed to gather information that can be used to inform instruction and to provide quick, on-the-spot assessments of students' conceptual base regarding specific text information.

Self-Assessments.   Self-assessments can be useful, because they can provide information before, during, and after reading events. Shahl and Bravo (2010) provide detailed guidance for using several vocabulary assessments in the classroom (with a special focus on content learning). One of these is a technique developed for assessing vocabulary in an ELL population (Wesche & Parbakht, 1996), but it also provides a nice extension of a summary assessment we have suggested for years (see Figure 9.11). Interestingly, there is evidence that even a simple yes-no test (which could be done as a "thumbs up/thumbs down" activity for the whole class) is an effective way to assess students' vocabulary knowledge (White, Graves, & Slater, 1990).

**FIGURE 9.11
Self-Assessment of
Vocabulary about
Volcanoes**

Word	I have never heard this word.	I have heard this word and i know something about what it means.	I am very familiar with this word.
molten			
lava			
crater			
crust			
magma			
eruption			
plate			
composite			
extinct			
explosion			

PReP.   The PreReading Plan, or PReP, is a word association procedure designed to assess both the quality and quantity of students' prior knowledge. Developed by Langer (1982, 1984), it has been well researched and is especially appropriate for use with adolescents. PReP is a particularly effective strategy because it can be used for assessment purposes at the time of instruction. Indeed, there is some evidence that using this assessment technique with high school students in content-area reading actually improves students' acquisition of information over time (Molner, 1989).

To implement this procedure, preview the materials to be used and list two to four key concepts. The following questions are then used as the basis for a discussion:

> What comes to mind when you hear/read . . . ?
> What made you think of . . . ?
> Given our discussion, can you add any new ideas about . . . ?
> (Write the students' responses on the board.)

After the discussion, students' responses are evaluated by using the following classification scheme:

> *Much prior knowledge:* precise definitions, analogies, relational links among concepts
> *Some prior knowledge:* examples and characteristics, but no connections or relations
> *Little prior knowledge:* sound-alikes or look-alikes, associated experiences, little or no meaning relations

The technique can be used to generate diagnostic conclusions about how students' vocabulary (conceptual) knowledge is contributing to their reading difficulties, to make decisions about grouping and pacing, or to make decisions about appropriate instructional adaptations. If this information is needed for a group of students, Langer advocates creating a matrix. Students' names appear down one side, and the three categories (*Much, Some, Little*) appear across the top.

To summarize, vocabulary assessment can, and probably should, be done in association with the demands of reading selections. Teachers will obviously need to make decisions about which of these vocabulary assessment strategies is most effective for their purposes. However, because different procedures may actually provide different types of information, it is important to recognize the value of multiple measures of prior knowledge. This is obviously most easily accomplished by a skilled teacher during actual instruction.

Evaluating Comprehension with Retelling and Summary

The assessment of comprehension requires a dual focus. First, we are concerned with students' comprehension of a specific selection. Second, and more important, we need to assess students' growing comprehension *ability* (Johnston, 1985). In this section, we describe tools and strategies for assessing comprehension, designed to evaluate whether students have understood what they have just read and to reveal whether they are developing the abilities needed to understand other texts.

As we have already seen, a number of factors can influence reading performance. For example, students' ability to recall information and answer questions can be affected by the type and quality of the text (see Chapters 2 and 6). Therefore, it is important to assess students' comprehension of materials that are similar to those they are expected to read every day and/or that reflect the appropriate standards of performance for students of that age/grade. These are likely to be much longer, more complex selections than any that appear on most commercially available tests, although the forthcoming assessments attached to the Common Core State Standards are likely to change that. As well, remember that reader interest in or familiarity with passage content can affect understanding, memory, and recall. Familiarity appears to influence the content of recall, and both interest and familiarity seem to have an effect on the amount of inferential comprehension achieved during reading (Lipson, Mosenthal, & Mekkelsen, 1999).

Before making final judgments about a student's ability to comprehend/retell passages, it is important to be sure that samples of the student's best efforts have been gathered. To do this, the selections that are used should provide a good match for the student's interests, prior knowledge, and development ability. It is, of course, desirable to gather information regarding performance on materials that are routinely assigned to the reader in class (see the discussion of longer texts below). The point is that we are simply sampling the reader's abilities, not measuring them in some definitive way. The selections we make should reflect our assessment purposes.

Because reading materials can exert such a strong influence on comprehension performance, we suggest becoming somewhat adept at analyzing the selections to be used for assessment purposes). These analyses are likely to be different depending on the type of text. We make distinction below on the bases of length. Despite the fact that the passages on most commercially available texts are relatively short, students' performance on these measures can be examined for additional diagnostic needs. We turn our attention next to revisiting IRIs to mine them for additional assessment information.

Informal Reading Inventories: Selecting and Analyzing Short Passages. As we noted in Chapter 8, commercial IRIs generally assess comprehension with questioning techniques. However, many contemporary IRIs also provide some support for examining students' comprehension in other ways, notably through recalls or retellings. The coherence of a text can affect recall. Many IRI passages read more like fragments of text than intact stories or informational selections. This can hamper student recall, because it may be difficult for students to organize and retrieve the content presented.

A number of systems for scoring and interpreting passage recall have been proposed over the years. Most contemporary IRIs provide some sort of format for recording retellings. For example, the QRI provides clear organizational frameworks for examining student retellings of narrative texts as distinct from informational ones. The QRI-5, for example, provides separate scoring forms for narrative and exposition. The narrative forms include details clustered on the superordinate elements of setting/background, goal, events, and resolution. The expository recording form is organized into a series of main idea and details. A sample of Tha'm's recall of one grade 4 narrative was provided in Chapter 8 (see Figure 8.9)

One of the problems with such summaries, however, is that there is often little support for interpreting retellings. The authors of the QRI-5 suggest examining the retellings in light of the following questions:

1. Do the retellings of narrative material retain the basic structure of the narratives? Is the most important information included?
2. Do the retellings of expository material retain the main idea and supporting detail structure of the selection? Is the most important information included?
3. Are the retellings sequential?
4. Is the recall accurate?

We have found that it is useful to use an adaptation of a system designed specifically for use with IRIs by Clark (1982; also Clark, 1993—revised, personal correspondence). The steps in this procedure are as follows:

1. Use the scoring guides provided by the IRI (see Figure 8.9)
2. Number the list of the separate pausal units in the order in which they occur (or use the IRI form if it is already organized sequentially).
3. Rate the level of importance for each pausal unit by assigning a 1 to the most-important units, a 2 to the next-most-important units, and a 3 to the least-important units. To simplify this process, read through the units and assign a 1 to the major units, read through the units again and assign a 3 to the least-important information, and then assign a 2 to all remaining units. *Text events or statements that do not appear on this form are considered to be 3.*
4. Use a retelling form. We have created a retelling guide in Figure 9.12 that includes the ratings after each unit.
5. Record the order in which the idea units are recalled, by numbering them in the order in which they are retold. Give the student credit for responses that capture the gist of the unit.
6. Generate computer percentages for the various types of recall.

In Figure 9.12, we show how it might look to revise an IRI retelling form that reflects this rating information. Three types of information result from this technique: the amount recalled, the sequence of recall, and the level of recalled information. The assessment of sequence is purely subjective. A judgment should be made about whether the order of the retelling was reasonable. The amount recalled is determined by dividing the number of units recalled by the total number of units in the passage. The score is then converted to a percentage by multiplying by 100. There are no available guidelines to evaluate the amount recalled. Clark reports that generally acceptable levels will be below the 75-to-90-percent criterion level of the IRI, and numerous research studies have reported average recall levels ranging between 33 percent and 50 percent depending on the level of the students and the nature of the materials.

Finally, to get an indication of the level of information that was recalled, compute the percentage of ideas recalled for each level of importance. These are perhaps the most significant scores to result from the Free Recall procedure. To compute these scores, add

FIGURE 9.12 Adapted Retelling Scoring Sheet for "Amelia Earhart" (Level Four, QRI-4)

Setting/Background

Recall Sequence	Recall	Importance Rating
	Amelia Earhart was an adventurer	1
	During WWI	2
1	she was a nurse	3
2	She cared for pilots	3
3	who had been hurt	3
	Earhart watched planes	1
	take off	3
	and land	3

Goal

	She knew	2
	that she must fly	2
	Earhart was the first woman	1
	to cross	1
4	the Atlantic	1
5	in a plane	1
	Someone else flew the plane	2
7	Earhart wanted to be more	2
8	than a passenger	2
9	She wanted	1
10	to fly	1
	across the ocean	1

She liked flying [handwritten note]

Events

12	Earhart trained	1
13	to be a pilot	1
11	In 1932	2
	she flew	1

	alone	1
	across the Atlantic	1
6	to Ireland	3
16	Earhart faced dangers	1
	Airplanes were smaller	2
	Problems happened often	2
17	There were no computers	2
18	Earhart said	2
20	Women must try	2
19	to do things	2
21	as men have tried	2
	Earhart planned	1
14	to fly	1
15	around the world	1

Resolution

	Her plane disappeared	1
	over the ocean	2
	the Pacific Ocean	2
	People searched	2
	for a long time	2
	They gave up	2
23	Earhart	1
22	and her plane	1
24	were never found	1

Total number of units: 47
Number of units recalled: 24
Percentage recalled: 51%
Sequence evaluation: adequate
Percentage of important units recalled: 61%
Percentage of moderate units recalled: 39%
Percentage of unimportant units recalled: 50%

all the recalled units at a given importance value and divide by the total number of units *rated at that level.* The resulting average scores show if the most significant information (as judged by the examiner) has been remembered. For example, if a total of twenty idea units were rated as level 1 importance and the reader recalled ten of these, the percentage of recall would be 50 percent for level 1. The same method is used to determine percentages for levels 2 and 3. Of this earlier revision, Clark notes that an ideal recall would be, in effect, a summary of the most important information.

> As a summary, it should contain virtually all of the important level 1 idea units and none of the level 3 units. The percentages for level 1 should therefore approach 100, while the percentages for level 3 should approach zero. I have also found that the recalls which I subjectively feel are best contain approximately 50% of the material from level 2. The nature and length of the text, the background of the reader, and the purpose for the reading all affect this distribution. (Clark, 1993, personal communication)

Clark cautions that it is important to remember that there is a normal developmental tendency; older, better readers recall more information at higher levels of importance and in better sequence, so comparisons among individuals of different ages and abilities is inappropriate.

Interpreting Results from Short Passages.   The sample of Tha'm's retelling from Chapter 8 revealed that she recalled about fifty percent of all possible ideas identified by the publisher. However, a closer analysis, using importance ratings, provides even more information about Tha'm's comprehension (see Figure 9.12). For example, Tha'm has recalled 61 percent of the possible level 1 material, 39 percent of the level 2 information, and 50 percent of level 3 content. In addition, the mean importance level of units recalled (1.36) was good. Although she can recall a great deal of verbatim information (including quotes that were considered level 3 and not included on the record sheet), Tha'm appears to have trouble separating important from unimportant information and generating appropriate inferences about that information.

In addition, Tha'm failed to recall important portions of the last part of the text. Notice, for example, that she failed to recall that Earhart's plane disappeared during flight. This failure to report crucial information about the resolution of the problem in relation to key information presented in the early part of the passage (e.g., that Earhart flew solo) led to confusion about the outcome of this narrative.

Excellent diagnostic insights can be gained by comparing question responses to retellings. In this case, Tha'm missed four of eight questions posed to her after the recall (frustrational level). She could not recall how long it took Earhart to fly along across the Atlantic and did not identify her goal (to fly around the world). Not surprisingly, she also could not speculate about why her plane was never found. It certainly warrants further investigation with additional samples, using this and other procedures.

Although it would not be possible to conduct this type of in-depth analysis of comprehension for all students who take a periodic benchmark assessment, it is certainly appropriate to do so for the specific students for whom comprehension appears to be a problem and/or who are struggling with reading in many contexts.

Comprehension Materials: Selecting and Analyzing Long Passages.　　A point that is made repeatedly in the Common Core State Standards for English Language Arts is that the teacher must exercise his/her professional judgment and knowledge in determining whether a text is suitable for use (CCSS-ELA, 2010, Appendix A, p. 4). An important first step in developing comprehension measures is to identify what information, ideas, relationships, etc., must be understood in a particular text. Constructing maps for the reading selections is an excellent way to do this. The purpose of these maps is to identify important elements within each of the reading selections to ensure that test questions (or recall evaluations) are focused on important information. Stories and informational texts will, of course, differ. Students' recall should reflect an understanding of the relationships between and among key facts and ideas.

Story Maps: Analyzing Narrative Text.　　Story maps reveal the underlying relationships among characters, events, and settings in a given story. They create a visual representation of the elements of setting, problem, goal, events, and resolution (Beck & McKeown, 1981). As a result, they can provide the basis for assessment strategies that inform us about both the students' comprehension of a particular text and their literacy knowledge.

Story mapping generally begins with the identification of the problem, the attempt (or plan), and the resolution. The characters, events, and setting revolve around these elements. Sometimes, of course, these elements are especially important. For example, in many books by Ezra Jack Keats, the setting plays a central role (e.g., *Snowy Day, Evan's Corner*). Similarly, setting is often a critical element in science fiction books, as in Jeanne DuPrua's *City of Ember* and *People of Sparks*. Dymock (2007) actually suggests that students can be taught to analyze texts using a relatively simple "analysis of episodes" form like that in Figure 9.13. Once completed, the maps are used to generate assessment questions (see below) and/or to generate alternative assessment tasks. Given the types of close and analytic reading called for in the Common Core State Standards, teachers will need to be even more capable of analyzing texts than they have been in the past.

For *assessment* purposes, it is important to remember that the map should reveal the central ideas and should also capture the underlying relationships among events. To do this, teachers might need to use somewhat more elaborate maps. The more-complex maps reveal how events are organized and how they are related to each other. In Figure 9.14, the map of a fourth-grade basal reading reveals the story's problem-solution framework.

Although text mapping might seem time consuming, we have found that teachers (even preservice teachers) can learn to do this with just a little practice. Careful analysis of

FIGURE 9.13

Analysis of Episodes

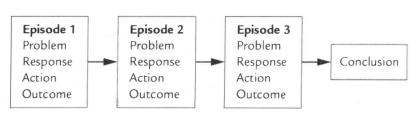

Source: From Calfee and Patrick (1995). Used by permission of R. Colfee.

FIGURE 9.14   Story Map for "The Sociable Seal"

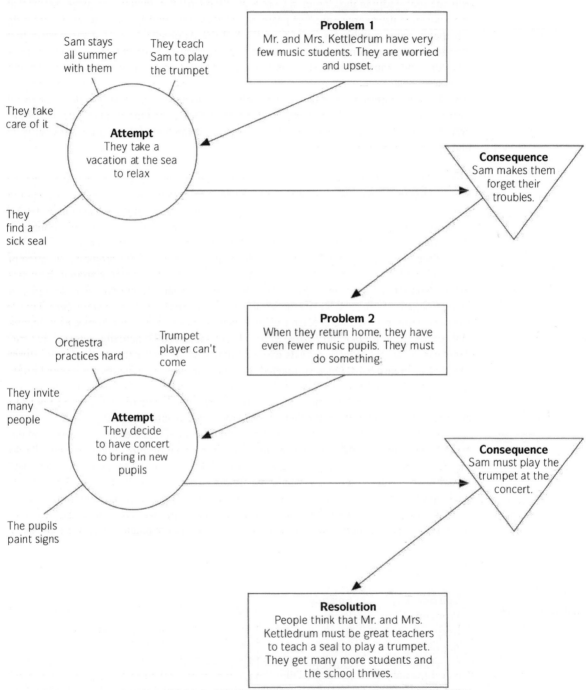

Source: From *Instructor's Resource Book to Accompany Reading Instruction for Today,* by J. M. Mason and K. H. Au. Copyright © 1986 Scott, Foresman and Company.

texts is likely to increase both the reliability and validity of informal assessments. Structuring our assessment tasks around carefully analyzed reading material is likely to increase the degree to which they provide us with trustworthy information. In addition, most teachers report that they begin to view comprehension differently when they analyze selections carefully. They are much less likely to ask trivial, detail questions and much more likely to pose thought-provoking, theme-related questions. We recommend that teachers choose some stories that they will use only for informal assessment. A small set of stories (one to three) from the current basal program, for example, could be analyzed and then used for assessment rather than instructional purposes. Certainly, a battery of such selection maps could be developed by a small group of teachers working together, or teachers could work together to evaluate a set of benchmark books for use in classroom assessment.

Conceptual Maps: Analyzing Expository Text.   Educators are increasingly concerned about students' ability to read informational texts (Duke, 2004; Purcell-Gates, Duke, & Martineau, 2001). In addition, many of the large-scale assessments have increased the amount of nonfiction material they include. Older students and adults read disproportionately more informational text than they do fictional material. Fortunately, there are more and better nonfiction texts available today than ever before. For the purposes of evaluating comprehension in general, and reading-to-learn in particular, it will be necessary to closely examine passages from authentic information materials (see Chapter 6).

A conceptual map is a way to analyze and represent informational texts (Hay, 2007; Novak, 1991; O'Donnell & Dansereau, 2002). When applied to text selections, we identify relationships in the same way that story maps do for narrative selections. Conceptual maps visually display important elements such as central purpose, main and supporting ideas, and text organization. In Figure 9.15, you will see a conceptual map of a nonfiction selection from a second-grade basal reader.

Wixson and Peters (1989, pp. 29–30) provide a functional description of the steps involved in creating a conceptual map:

> Concept mapping begins with the identification of major concepts within the text, through reading and an examination of important text features such as headings and photographs. These concepts are then arranged hierarchically to form the first two levels of the concept map—central purpose(s) and major ideas. Then the map is expanded to include a third level of information—supporting ideas. Relations between concepts are highlighted by adding relational links specifying how the concepts are connected. The more clearly organized the text, the more coherent the concept map. If the relation between two concepts is not clear, a link cannot be established.

It is important to identify any major organizational patterns and use these to guide your comprehension assessment.

The conceptual map in Figure 9.15 reveals a well-organized text. The ideas are linked together very clearly, and each concept is connected by a linking concept that appears in parentheses (for example, *first, types, steps*). The map also shows that the relationships among the levels of information in this selection are clearly hierarchical. The first level (central purpose) involves describing the daily routine of the sea otter. Then the second level (major ideas) describes the sequence of sea otter activity during one day (hunting,

FIGURE 9.15   Concept Map for "The Sea Otter"

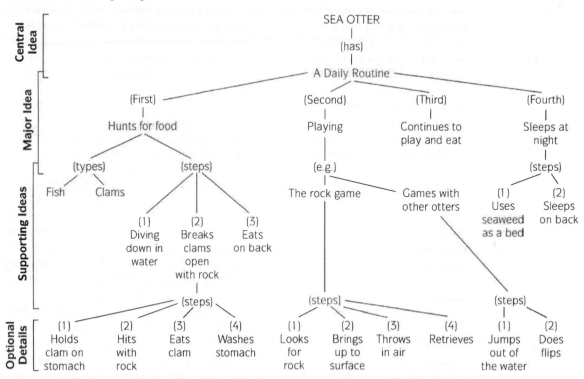

Source: Reprinted by permission of the publisher. Wixson, K. K., & Peters, C. W. (1989). Teaching the basal selection. In P. N. Winograd, K. K. Wixson, & M. Y. Lipson (Eds.), *Improving Basal Reading Instruction* (p. 306). New York, NY: Teachers College Press.

eating, playing, and sleeping). Finally, the third level (supporting ideas) details the steps or provides examples of these activities. Not all of the information provided in the text needs to be displayed in a concept map. But if it is not on the map, the implication is that it is not high in importance. Thus, although the text includes details about how the otter plays the rock game, these are considered insignificant to understanding the selection. Of course, this also signals the teacher to avoid asking questions about this information or to expect students to recall it. The organizational pattern should be visible to, and used to support, students' comprehension of the text. It will also be used to evaluate the retellings generated by students after they have read the selection.

Retellings.   Armed with a representation of the important elements of a particular text, it is possible to elicit recalls and assess lengthy selections with high levels of reliability. Readers' understanding of textual materials has traditionally been evaluated by using question-response scores. Indeed, the practice of answering questions is so pervasive that it is sometimes difficult for teachers to recognize that the ability to answer questions is not the same thing as understanding.

Retellings can add immeasurably to our understanding of readers' comprehension, because they allow us to get a view of the quantity, quality, and organization of information constructed during reading. Readers' initial responses to the material should involve free recall of the text, without the interference of the teacher. Text recall is natural for students and does not necessarily bias them to process text in a particular way, as questions do. Because it is important to influence student responses as little as possible, initial requests for retelling should be intentionally open-ended. The teacher can initiate the retelling of text with questions such as these:

- Tell *me* that story.
- Tell me what you have read, using your own words.
- What is the text about?
- Tell me as much information as you can about what you have just read.

Students should be allowed ample time to recall and relate information. This free recall can provide valuable insight into how the student processes text. Following the uninterrupted retelling, probing statements or questions can be used to elicit further information and to analyze readers' understanding of the text. Probes constructed by the teacher should be based directly on the students' retelling. An effective initial prompt is to say, "You said . . . ; tell me more about that."

Some young or less-skilled readers have had little experience in retelling. In fact, they may be surprised that you are not asking them questions. For them, the novelty of the task may influence results, and you might want to attempt another retelling shortly after an initial attempt.

In addition to free and probed retelling, teachers and specialists may also want to consider using structured questions. Then, teachers can distinguish among information generated freely, information elicited with minimal cueing, and information generated through direct cueing. The teacher should avoid their use until *after* students have provided all possible information during free and probed retelling, since structured questions impose someone else's view of what is important on an evaluation of text understanding.

Eliciting Narrative Recalls. For stories, it is often desirable to ask probe questions using elements of story grammar. Using specific prompts, teachers can gather information about a student's ability to recall and infer important story information. The following are examples of probe questions students might be asked for thematic stories (Lipson & Wixson, 1989):

- Where did . . . happen? (setting)
- How is the setting of the story important? (setting)
- What happens to get the story started? (initiating event)
- What did . . . do about . . . ? (attempt)
- What is the main problem the characters face? (problem)
- What makes it difficult for the characters to solve their problem? (conflict)
- How is the problem solved? (resolution)
- What lesson(s) are there in the story? (theme)
- What is the main thing that happens in the story? (theme)
- What do you learn about the main characters? (characterization)
- Which event is a turning point in the story? (events)

FIGURE 9.16   Reading Summary Record

Student _____ Date _____

Title/Type of Text _____

Task: (e.g., reading/listening; oral/written response; independent/scaffolded; easy/average/challenging text)

	Needs work	Developing	Well done
Synthesizes big ideas	No synthesis of big ideas	Partial synthesis of big ideas	Synthesizes critical content
Recalls important supporting information	Little, if any, key supporting information	Some key supporting information	Most key supporting information
Makes Inferences/Draws Conclusions	Only explicitly stated information	Some text-based inferences	Draws conclusions not explicitly in text
Coherence	Disconnected pieces of information	Somewhat coherent, but not complete	Coherent in ways that reflect essence of text

Source: Valencia, S. (2012).

Collecting and interpreting retelling information can be messy. Valencia suggests that teachers use a form to guide their thinking and to enhance their systematic evaluation of comprehension over time (see Figure 9.16). Classroom teachers might find it helpful to organize the retelling information with a checklist, which provides more-analytic information (see Figure 9.17).

Eliciting Informational Recalls.   Of course, the prompts for nonfiction, exposition text need to reflect the structure of those texts:

- What is the central idea (big idea) of this selection? (central purpose)
- Why do you think the author wrote this? (purpose)
- Using the headings to divide the text into sections, tell the main ideas in each smaller section. (major ideas)
- What details does the text provide to tell more about the important main ideas? (supporting details)
- How does the author organize the information to tell you about the central and major ideas? (structure)

FIGURE 9.17 Checklist Summary of Narrative Text

Key: 0   Not Yet
      ✓   Sometimes
      +   Under Control

Students' Names

Retelling Attributes														
Setting														
Characters														
Problem														
Character response														
Attempts														
Major Events														
Resolution														
Theme														
Maintains narrative organization														
Coherent														
Other														

Comments:

If concept maps were generated, they will be exceptionally helpful as you prompt students' recall and evaluate the quality of that recall.

Analyzing Recall Information.   Gathering retelling data is the easy part of this assessment strategy, resulting in a wealth of rich information about students' ability to comprehend and about what they choose to share. The problem is less in the gathering than in the interpretation. How to make sense of and evaluate this wealth of information is an altogether different (and more difficult) job. It may be helpful to reflect on the following:

- What does the student recall about this selection?
- How does this recall compare with the map of the text (quantity and quality)?
- How does the student organize the recall?
- How does the recall rate as a whole?

Of course, some system for analyzing and interpreting recall data is needed to answer questions like these. Both quantitative and qualitative systems are available—some easier to use than others.

The retelling guidelines suggested by Morrow (1989) involve a point system. The student's retelling is compared to an analysis of the original selection. To use this retelling procedure, point values are assigned to various aspects of the maps created earlier (setting, characters, problem statements, etc.). Then the student's recall is evaluated according to how well it reflected these major components. Each retelling yields a score, with the total possible equaling ten points.

Figure 9.18 shows the transcript of Tha'm's retelling of a full-length short story, *The Sociable Seal* (mapped in Figure 9.14). In Figure 9.19, you will find an analysis of this retelling using Morrow's (1989) system. Tha'm is able to identify the characters and focus on the central events of the story, and she finishes her retelling with an appropriate resolution.

It would be relatively easy to conclude that Tha'm has very good comprehension of this grade 4 story. However, there are indications of difficulty. For example, while she accurately recalls information from the text, Tha'm does not generally draw appropriate inferences. For example, the resolution in her retelling paraphrases the final lines from the story: "We must let Sam play his trumpets with the children again, dear." However, she misses the overall meaning. Similarly, when asked what the story was telling, Tha'm concluded, "That you can teach seals stuff," a theme that is not supported by the text analysis. Finally, there are several notable linguistic anomalies. Tha'm says that Sam "lagged" to go along—presumably meaning *begged*. More seriously, her response to question 8 is startling and, at first, difficult to decipher. She says that the Kettledrums are having problems with "puppets"—a word and concept that appears nowhere in the text. The word *pupils* does appear several times. Because Tha'm read this lengthy story silently, we can only infer the source of this confusion, but it seems likely that she misread the word *pupils* as "pup-ils" and then, since it was unfamiliar, could not recall it during the question period. Note that she says, ". . . puppets stands for students." Certainly, it appears that Tha'm can use context to infer word meanings, but she frequently fails to store the orthographic or phonological information clearly, and this leads to later confusions of meaning.

FIGURE 9.18
Sample Retelling

Tha'm's Retelling of "The Sociable Seal"

Mr. and Mrs. Kettledrum were spending the summer at the beach and they found a seal laying. . . . way back at the beach. So, they took the seal back to their summer home to take care of if. They were happy and they loved the seal so they named him Sam and they teached him how to play the trumpet because they have a musical school.

One day they led him to the beach to go back to where he belonged, but he didn't and then he wanted to go home with them . . . so he did. But . . . then winter was over until fall, so they had to go back to the musical school and they did. But Sam lagged to go along and they love him, but he had to sleep in the bathtub. So and they took a bath in morning and then Sam has the bathtub all to himself.

But then the music school is having a concert to get more students . . . 'cause some there were only five/four students. So they wanted to get more students so they made a concert. But one person who was playing the trumpet, he was missing, 'cause he was sick. So Sam had to go play and he played perfectly. The audience, "Wow" the teacher is SO great . . . to make a seal play the trumpet and then they signed up.

Mr. and Mrs. Kettledrum said we should let Sam play for the class. What our class needs is a seal to play with. And that's the end.

Probe Questions and Tha'm's Responses

1. Who found the seal? *Mr. and Mrs. Kettledrum*
2. What problem did the Kettledrums have? *Lots of students were little students and Sam wanted to go home with them and at the concert there was no one to play the trumpet.*
3. What was Sam like? *He was a funny little guy. He likes to be adored by people and he likes Mr. and Mrs. Kettledrum.*
4. Where did the story take place? *At the beach—and in the city.*
5. What do you think the story was telling you? *Even though there's a seal on the ground, you can teach him stuff.*
6. Why do you think they took Sam out to sea? *They thought Sam would be happier to go back to his family.*
7. Why did the Kettledrums go to the beach? *To relax and take all the troubles out.*
8. What kind of problems were they having? *They had puppets. And the students weren't being very good.*
9. Why do you think they had a musical? *Maybe they like music and a music school.*
10. Were they happy at the end? *Yes. Because lots of students signed up for the lessons.*

Story-Retelling Analysis

Student's Name: _____ *Tha'm* _____   Date: _____

Title of Story: _____ *The Sociable Seal* _____

General Directions: Place a 1 next to each element if the child includes it in his or her presentation. Credit gist as well as obvious recall.

Characters and Setting

A begins with introduction   1

Names main character(s)   1

Describes character traits   0

Includes statement about time and/or place   0

Theme

Refers to main character's primary goal or problem to be resolved   0

Plot Episodes

Recalls main events and episodes   1

Retells story in order and makes connections across text   1

Resolution

Names the problem-solution/goal attainment   1

Ends story   1

Response to Literature

Includes a personal or critical response to the literature   0

Highest Score Possible: (10)   **Student's Score:**   **6**

Comments:
Tha'm has an accurate but sparse retelling that leaves motivation and goal structures implicit. Although she is able to identify problems when prompted, she does not build this tension into the retelling. Importantly, even when prompted, she does not provide much character elaboration or internal response. Although Tha'm is able to retain a central narrative thread of events, the events appear more important than their causal relationship to each other.

The advantages to this type of system are that it is relatively easy to use and that it reduces large amounts of data into manageable and reportable pieces. The disadvantage to any quantitative system is that it is possible to miss the qualitative aspects of the retellings.

To extend the diagnostic value of a qualitative assessment, specific aspects of the retelling can be summarized and evaluated (see Figure 9.20). The qualitative analysis in Figure 9.20 clearly demonstrates that Tha'm was successful in summarizing text-based narrative information. However, she had difficulty generating inferences from text, especially with regard to major ideas and themes. Although Tha'm did recall detailed

FIGURE 9.20   Diagnostic Summary of Tha'm's Retelling

Directions: Indicate with a check mark the degree to which the reader's retelling includes the reader's comprehension in terms of the following criteria:

	None	Low Degree	Moderate Degree	High Degree
1. Retelling includes information directly stated in text.				✓
2. Retelling includes information inferred directly or indirectly from text.		✓		
3. Retelling includes what is important to remember from the text.			✓	
4. Retelling provides relevant content and concepts.			✓	
5. Retelling indicates reader's attempt to connect background knowledge to text information.		✓		
6. Retelling indicates reader's attempt to make summary statements or generalizations based on the text, which can be applied to the real world.		✓		
7. Retelling indicates highly individualistic and creative impressions of or reactions to the text.		✓		
8. Retelling indicates the reader's affective involvement with the text.			✓	
9. Retelling demonstrates appropriate reader's language fluency (vocabulary, sentence structure, language conventions, etc).		✓		
10. Retelling indicates reader's ability to organize or compose the retelling.			✓	
11. Retelling demonstrates the reader's sense of audience or purpose.				✓
12. Retelling indicates the reader's control of the mechanics of speaking or writing.			✓	

Interpretation: Items 1–4 indicate the reader's comprehension of textual information; items 5–8 indicate reader's response and involvement with text; items 9–12 indicate facility with language.

Source: Mitchell, J. N., & Irwin, P. A. (1988). The reader retelling profile: Using retellings to make instructional decisions. In S. M. Glazer, L. Searfoss, & L. M. Gentile (Eds.), *Reexamining reading diagnosis: New trends and procedures.* Copyright © 1988. Reprinted by permission of Dr. Pi A. Irwin.

information from text, she did not respond affectively to what she read—a likely result of her limited attention to the characters' motivations.

When teachers make judgments about students' responses, they must be guided by criteria, which are established before scoring begins. The tool that is used is called a *rubric.* A rubric is a scoring guide used to define the criteria that will be used to judge student performance. An effective rubric details the attributes or characteristics of different levels of performance—often in relation to established standards. It identifies the qualities one would expect to see in reading or in a written response at several points along a scale. Although they were initially used to assess written work and its relation to thinking, rubrics are now used to evaluate many aspects of literacy (see Arter & McTighe, 2001). Most rubrics use a three- or four-level scale (high, middle, low or 1–4, for example). These work especially well for discourse-level responses such as retellings. Irwin and Mitchell (1983) created a rubric for evaluating students' recall of *expository* text. This system attends to the "richness of retellings," assessing not only such features as the inclusion of major points and details, but also the degree to which students have gone beyond the text to generate cohesive generalizations and create a comprehensible whole. It was recently updated by Moss (2004).

The system employs a five-point scale. The criteria for assigning retellings to one of these levels are displayed in Figure 9.21. When the richness-of-retelling scoring system was applied to an earlier retelling that Tha'm had done (with an expository passage on the Venus Flytrap—see Figure 9.23 on page 498—we rated the richness of her retelling between a 2 and 3. Tha'm did include many major ideas and included appropriate supporting details. There is a cohesiveness and coherence to her recall. However, she also included some irrelevant details and, most importantly, misconstrued the major thesis (problem) of the selection. For example, Tha'm concluded her retelling with the following:

> So . . . it's a *killer* plant . . . I think all these/ I think the venomous (sic) flytrap, the killer plant/the other plant/the other plant that's waiting and setting up the trap is . . . actually taking orders from a bigger plant. A stronger, bigger plant. Like a queen or a leader.

FIGURE 9.21 Rubric for Evaluating Retellings of Information Text

Level	Criteria for Establishing Level
5	Student infers beyond the text; includes a summarizing statement of the major thesis or problem
	Includes all major ideas and supporting details, Uses text organization to generate cohesive and complete retelling Adds relevant supplementary detail, including opinions and questions
4	Student includes all major ideas and supporting maintains appropriate sequence and creates a coherent and complete retelling
3	Student includes major ideas and appropriate supporting details
	Sequence, coherence and completeness are adequate
2	Student includes a few major ideas and some supporting details
	May include irrelevant information or supplementary commentary
	Comprehensible, but incomplete retelling
1	Student provides details only, poor sequencing, irrelevant information or supplemental commentary; very incomplete or incomprehensible retelling

Source: Adapted from Irwin & Mitchell (1985) and Moss (2004).

Summarizing Information. The use of ongoing retellings in both narrative and expository text provides excellent information for classroom teachers about students' reading processes, but also about their conceptual development. In Tha'm's case, these retellings reveal that she is adept at locating the major or main ideas from text when they are explicitly stated. She can also infer some major events that are closely linked to these ideas, and she provides supporting details. However, she tends to generate misconceptions (the students were not behaving in the "Sociable Seal" or the idea that there was a "boss plant" that was setting a trap in the "The Deadly Trap"). These misconceptions sometimes seem to result from Tha'm's somewhat limited prior knowledge and background experience. At other times, they seem to result from a vivid imagination and a preference for narrative fiction. Whatever the cause, they do tend to drive her comprehension of the text, and although she seems troubled by some of the "gaps" in her comprehension, she cannot use the text or her understanding of the world to correct them.

With older students, written recalls may be employed. In either case, however, the task must be absolutely clear to students. As with all assessment procedures, task demands will most likely influence results. When written retellings are to be used, it is especially important that you differentiate a *retelling* from a *summary.* Although the evidence is slim, it does appear that written retellings are likely to generate more-limited productions than oral ones. On the other hand, written retellings are frequently more coherent and better organized. Using brief, written recalls that focus attention on important story components, we have arrived at high degrees of reliability between teachers using holistic ranking methods. When used over time, students' progress can be assessed and the effects of instruction can be demonstrated.

These techniques can be used to gather information about the student's ability to recall and infer important text information. In addition, affective responses to readings can be checked regularly with questions such as: Did you learn anything from reading this? Did you find this selection interesting? Did you enjoy reading this? Of course, close examination of the retelling itself can provide additional information about how students are understanding informational texts. As we just saw, for example, Tha'm tends to organize her retelling of an expository text in a distinctly story-like way. The following questions may focus ongoing evaluation:

- Is the student's personal interpretation evident from the retelling?
- Does the student make evaluative statements about the characters or events?
- Does the student attend to the language of the text, using it to support his or her interpretation?
- Does the student make explicit the various relationships between and among the events or ideas?
- Does the student make use of the text structure to support those relationships?

Before making final judgments about students' ability to retell passages, be sure that the samples gathered represent the students' best efforts. The selections used for assessment should provide a good match for the students' interests, prior knowledge, and developmental ability. Of course, teachers can decide to gather information regarding performance on materials that are routinely assigned to the reader, regardless of appropriateness. The point to remember is that these procedures are sampling the reader's abilities, not measuring them in some definitive way. The goal is to learn more about the reader, and the selections teachers make should reflect their assessment purpose(s).

Evaluating Comprehension with Questioning

Perhaps the most common form of formative/diagnostic reading assessment is questioning. Although we believe that retellings enrich the picture, careful questioning can reveal much about students' understanding of a particular selection and about their ability to comprehend in general.

The comprehension that is revealed through questioning is, at least in part, a function of the questions that are asked. Students' ability to answer questions is influenced by both the type and content of the questions they are asked (Applegate, Quinn, & Applegate, 2006; Pearson et al., 1979). In addition, both the type and content of questions influence what students recall and the types of inferences they make (Wixson, 1983a, 1984) (see Chapter 6).

Because structured questions impose someone else's view of what is important, they should be asked *after* students have provided all possible information during free and probed retelling. In this way distinctions can be made between the information generated freely, information elicited with minimal cueing, and information generated through direct probing.

Many commercially available assessments (such as those that accompany basal/core programs) use a classification scheme to label comprehension questions. These classification schemes are typically based on one of several well-known taxonomies (for example, Barrett, 1976; Bloom, 1956; Huitt, 2004). However, there is little evidence that these taxonomies represent real differences in comprehension skills or in the level of difficulty of different questions. As an alternative to these question taxonomies, Pearson and Johnson (1978) suggested that question types should be determined by the source of the answer. They originally devised a three-level taxonomy that captured the relationship between a question and its answer source: text-explicit questions, text-implicit questions, and scriptally implicit questions.

This taxonomy has been extended and used widely as an instructional tool by Raphael (1982, 1986). Her latest refinement of these *question-answer relationships* (QARs) are organized around two major types of questions: In the Text and In My Head (Raphael & Au, 2005; Raphael, Highfield, & Au, 2006).

I. *In the Text QARs:* The answer to the question (source of information) is in the book or article.
   A. *Right There QARs:* The answer is explicitly stated in the text, usually easy to find. The words used to make up the question and words used to answer the question are right there in the same sentence.
   B. *Think and Search QARs:* The answer can be inferred from text information. The answer is in the text, but you need to put together different parts to find it. Words for the question and words for the answer are not found in the same sentence.

II. *In My Head QARs:* These scriptally implicit questions (the question must be answered by referring to prior knowledge) have been divided into two types:
   A. *Author and You:* The answer is not in the text. You need to think about what you already know, what the author tells you in the text, and how it fits together.
   B. *On My Own:* The answer is not in the text. You can even answer the question without the text. You need to use your own experience and knowledge.

Distinguishing between questions on the basis of the source of the answer is extremely important in assessment. If we are not sure what is required to answer the questions we ask, then it will be difficult to make instructional decisions about comprehension. For example, if we think the answer is right there, when in fact the answer requires connecting text information through inference, then we may incorrectly assume that students cannot locate detail information in text, while the problem is actually related to inferential skills.

Other researchers have identified questions that are focused on eliciting personal or critical *response* (Langer, 1985; Ollmann, 1996). These questions require readers to engage in close reading, to discuss the underlying significance of the ideas in text, and, frequently, to defend their ideas using evidence from text or from their own experience. Because these varying questions elicit different insights into students' comprehension (see Chapter 6), the first task in assessing students' comprehension with questions is to determine the task demands of the questions themselves (Applegate, Quinn, & Applegate, 2002).

The placement of questions also affects students' performance and consequently our judgments about their abilities. Most teachers regularly ask questions after the selection has been read. Questions in this position place a premium on student recognition of important information. It is easy to underestimate students' comprehension, especially if the end-of-selection questions focus on details and text-explicit information. Therefore, teachers may want to ask questions before reading. This permits evaluation of students' ability to read for differing purposes and/or to locate key information.

Questions asked during reading can help to determine whether students are making connections and integrating relevant information. By refining the questioning strategies, important instructional information can be gathered.

Issues surrounding the quality and placement of questions in general are important, but so are concerns about the content and focus of questions. Maps or outlines like those we described earlier can serve as the basis for constructing comprehension questions. Teachers may find it useful to create a matrix like that in Figure 9.22. When the matrix is completed, an array of possible questions has been generated about important aspects of text (Wixson, Peters, Weber, & Roeber, 1987). In addition, teachers can check to make sure that they are assessing students' comprehension on a range of questions, including critical analysis or personal response.

Although these strategies may seem time consuming, the instructional value of assessment information is enhanced. Students do not have to be characterized simply as "good comprehenders" and "poor comprehenders." Instead, teachers can describe quite precisely what and how they understand.

FIGURE 9.22   Narrative Question Grid

Story Components	Text Explicit	Text Implicit	Author and You	Critical Response
Themes Main idea Level Abstract Level				
Plot Setting (Location and relation to theme)				
Characters (Traits and functions)				
Setting (Location and relation to theme)				
Problem				
Conflict				
Resolution				
Major Events				

Evaluating Comprehension Processes

We have described a variety of ways to gather information about the products of comprehension. Analyzing students' recall and question responses can provide information about *how* students comprehend, but this information is indirect; it must be inferred. Recently, educators have tried a number of newer assessment strategies designed to uncover the activity that goes on "inside the head."

Think-Alouds.   In a think-aloud procedure, readers are asked to stop at various points during their reading and "think aloud" about the processes and strategies they are using as they read. Wixson and Lipson (1986; see also Afflerbach, 2000, 2002; Loxterman, Beck, & McKeown, 1994) suggest that think-alouds can produce insights into readers' approaches to text processing. The following verbal report demonstrates this.

STACY: (reads title) "Spaceship Earth."

TUTOR: What were you thinking about when you read that title?

STACY: A space trip to earth. (reads first portion of text, haltingly and with many repetitions) Boy! I had a lot of trouble with that one.

TUTOR: What makes you think you had trouble with it?

> STACY: I kept messing up.
>
> TUTOR: What do you mean by "messing up"?
>
> STACY: I kept reading sentences twice.
>
> TUTOR: What do you think caused you to read sentences twice like that?
>
> STACY: Not understanding it.
>
> TUTOR: Okay, did any of the words give you trouble?
>
> STACY: No.

Stacy's verbal report reveals a view of reading that is governed by attempts to understand. "Although miscues were obvious during this segment, Stacy's 'fixup' strategy was driven by a desire not to sound good but to construct a sensible text representation" (Wixson & Lipson, 1986, p. 140).

Procedures for eliciting students' reports of mental activity generally include the following (Afflerbach, 2000; Lipson, Bigler, Poth, & Wickizer, 1987; Wade, 1990):

1. Teacher/evaluator selects a text (generally about two hundred words, but longer selections have been used).
2. The text is segmented and marked so that students will stop at predetermined spots.
3. The teacher/evaluator reminds students to think aloud about the text and/or their thoughts as they read the text.

Sometimes students are asked to provide *text-based think-alouds*. Wade (1990; Wade, Buxton, & Kelly, 1999), for example, designed a think-aloud procedure that requires students to generate hypotheses about the text as they read. Students are told to "tell what is happening," and they are then asked to detail the portions of text that led to their hypotheses. Student reports are analyzed in terms of the information they yield about the reader's ability to make hypotheses and integrate and revise information during reading.

On the other hand, Lipson and colleagues (1987) focused on readers' use of *cognitive processes*. Consequently, they asked students "to tell what you were *doing* and *thinking* as you read that part." Using this approach, students' verbal reports are analyzed for evidence that they employed various strategies known to enhance comprehension. (Paris (1991) describes a more prompted think-aloud that revolves around a specially created think-aloud passage, or TAP. We have used the TAP procedure for many years and find that information/expository texts work very well—especially if they contain some unusual or unexpected information.

In Figure 9.23, you see an example of a TAP that we have used to observe students' strategy use during comprehension. During a think-aloud assessment, it is useful to make observation notes using the form provided in Figure 8.18, which also provides an excellent summary of students' strategy use.

It is important to understand that verbal reports reflect what readers are doing as they read a specific text with specific task directions. There is good evidence that students' reading behaviors and verbal reports may vary as texts and tasks change (Afflerbach, 2000; Wade et al., 1999). Maria (1990) has pointed out that think-aloud assessment procedures are

FIGURE 9.23
Think-Aloud
Passage: The
Deadly Trap

The Deadly Trap •

There are many plant-eating animals. But did you know there are animal-eating plants? One of these is the Venus Flytrap. •

This rare plant has an amazing setup for capturing insects. Each leaf is divided into two parts. The parts are hinged together at the middle. These leaves are usually wide open. Strong "spines" point outward from their edges. There are three special hairs on the surface of each leaf part. Now and then, the plant's sweet juices attract an unsuspecting insect. If it brushes against one of the special hairs, the insect is in for a deadly surprise. In less than half a second, the two parts of the leaf snap shut. The unlucky insect finds himself a prisoner inside the leaf. The insect may be so large that the leaf cannot close completely. However, the spines act as prison bars. The insect cannot escape. •

As the insect is squeezed against the leaf, the plant's digestive juices go to work. The harder the insect struggles to free itself, the faster the juices are made. The plant takes nitrogen from the insect's body. The Venus Flytrap needs this chemical to grow. •

In eight to ten days, the insect is absorbed by the plant. Then the leaf opens again, and the plant waits for its next meal. After a leaf has claimed several victims, it dies. A new leaf soon takes its place. The new leaf carries on the work of the killer plant. •

---

very intrusive and require considerable teacher time. In addition, single think-aloud excerpts will not capture the variability we noted above. Both concerns can be addressed if teachers turn to careful observations of strategy use during normal instruction (see Figure 9.24).

Continuous Comprehension Assessment. The value of think-alouds can be improved significantly by specifying the factors related to text and varying them systematically. This generally requires regular, ongoing assessment of students as they read and interact with a variety of texts and tasks. Good assessment should capture the full range of students' comprehension ability, not just their best or worst efforts.

It is useful to create a comprehension profile for individual students, especially for those students who require a closer assessment (Applegate et al., 2006; McLaughlin & Allen, 2002; Wood, 1988). This can be done by creating a matrix to summarize the results gathered by the teacher/evaluator. The information is recorded as students read from their basal anthology, from their guided texts, and/or from their self-selected readings. For older students, information should be gathered from content-area readings also. The idea is to record observations that are made as students read under conditions that parallel the daily expectations in the classroom. Teachers/evaluators can enter columns for whatever conditions appear most important for their program and student(s).

We have used a variation on this procedure to create an individual reading record (see Figure 9.25). As students read, information relevant to their performance can be recorded. If students are thinking aloud (see above), for example, the information generated would probably be used to fill the "Process Knowledge/Strategy Use" column. The data recorded, coupled with specific information about the texts and tasks (see Chapters 5 and 6),

**FIGURE 9.24
Summarizing
Strategy Used in
Think-Aloud**

Name _____ Grade _____ Date _____		
Teacher _____ School _____		
Comprehension **Strategies**		
	Observed	**Comments/Notes**
Predict Uses title Uses pictures Uses prior knowledge Skims		
Infer Makes text-based inferences Makes personal connections (prior knowledge) Connects to other texts Connects to big ideas and themes		
Monitor Notices meaning disruptions Miscues retain meaning Uses rereading Skips and rereads		
Clarify Uses rereading and reading ahead Uses word recognition strategies Uses context and morphological analysis for meanings Uses text aids and illustrations		

Question
Generates text-based questions
  to clarify
Generates questions based on
  prior knowledge
Generates questions about purpose		

Summarize
Distinguish important versus unimpor-
  tant information
States mostly important information
Provides organized recall
Uses summarization to aid
  comprehension		

Evaluate Makes judgments and draws conclusions about significance Forms opinion		

FIGURE 9.25 Individual Reading Record

Name: _____

Grade: _____

Teacher: _____

School: _____

	Date	Text Description Genre, Level of Difficulty, Other	Topic Familiarity Topic, Structure, Genre, Domain	Attitudes and Interest	Reading Task(s) Complexity, Familiarity, Authenticity, Open or Closed, Solitary or Collaborative	Level and Type of Support Specific instructional techniques used before, during, after reading. Amount and location of scaffolding. Solitary or collaborative context.	Process Knowledge & Strategy Use Evidence of summarizing, inferring, predicting, connecting, evaluating, self-questioning, monitoring/regulating. Evidence of appropriate study/self-regulation abilities.	Reading Performance Accuracy, Fluency, Motivation
Text 1 (Title)								
Comments								
Text 2								
Comments								
Text 3								
Comments								

provide a very complete picture of a reader's knowledge, skills, and abilities, and how this varies across texts.

Evaluating Studying

Studying has traditionally been viewed as a specialized type of comprehension (Anderson & Armbruster, 1984b). In recent years, this view has been expanded somewhat, and many researchers distinguish between comprehension and metacognitive control of strategies for learning and remembering. For example, Peverly, Brobst, and Morris (2002), studied seventh- and eleventh-grade students, both average and above average. They assessed students' ability to comprehend as well as their metacognitive control of strategies (such as identifying important information or monitoring). Of course, many reading professionals would include these in a consideration of comprehension. The important insight from the work of Peverly, Brobst, and Morris (2002) is that metacognitive control increases in importance as students progress through the grades. Their research demonstrated that both ability to comprehend and metacognitive control contributed to successful recall for all students. However, metacognitive control was even more important for older students than younger ones. The authors suggest that good metacognitive skills may help students by "compensating for the cognitive strains of studying by more adequately monitoring their comprehension" (p. 204).

Studying involves intensive reading for specific purposes—typically to organize, retain, and retrieve information. Often, the purposes for reading have been imposed by others. However, many of the skills required for studying in the school context are also required in work settings. Even students who have a good foundation in the skills and strategies of reading through the elementary years may find the special demands of study and work reading difficult. We recommend assessing the study skills and habits of all students who have reached the sixth grade or beyond, since weaknesses in here often cause serious academic problems. Among the most useful of the commercially available assessments in this area is the LASSI, described in Chapter 8.

Although it is helpful and important to assess all components of reading ability in natural contexts, it is absolutely critical to do so when assessing study skills. If they are to provide any useful information, assessments of studying ability must be specific to the content to be learned and related to the materials to be studied (Rakes & Smith, 1986).

Assessment of students' studying abilities should move forward cautiously. Clearly, students may be aware of these skills and strategies but not use them during studying. In addition, many of these skills can be executed passively (for example, outlining by copying headings and subheadings). It should be apparent how important it is to determine what is really required to understand a particular text or accomplish a specific task.

In planning an assessment of study skills, Estes and Vaughan (1986) suggest the following steps:

1. Identify the study skills that students will need for success in their studying activities.
2. Construct a diagnostic checklist to record your assessments of students' studying abilities.
3. Prepare a student self-appraisal survey based on the study skills you consider important.

4. Construct informal activities to assess the study skills you have identified as critical.
5. Informally observe students' ability to use their study skills as they perform tasks during daily classroom activities.

Developing a Checklist of Critical Studying Skills and Strategies.   The specification of skills and strategies as reading-studying abilities is somewhat problematic, since many of these might arguably be considered generic comprehension skills. Rogers (1984, p. 346) has made a distinction between casual and study reading that is helpful: "Deliberate procedures for retaining or applying what is read are called study-reading skills. They permit people to complete tasks which they would not do as successfully if they read only casually." Long lists of study skills generally include specialized abilities such as alphabetizing, skimming, note taking, outlining, scanning, and reading maps, graphs, tables, and diagrams. Such lists are not entirely helpful, however, because the use of these studying skills does not ensure good comprehension, nor do all good readers use all of these skills (Armbruster & Anderson, 1981).

There are many checklists available to guide observations of students as they engage in studying activities. Rogers (1984) has collapsed the long lists of study-reading skills into three large categories: (1) special study-reading comprehension skills, (2) information location skills, and (3) study and retention strategies, and has designed a comprehensive checklist of discrete abilities (see Figure 9.26). As always, this checklist should be adapted to specific settings. As students are observed engaged in study activity, the teacher should consider the following questions:

- Does the student have an organized approach to the task?
- Does the student seem to know what to do and how to use the text to accomplish the task?
- Does the student exhibit enthusiasm and/or interest?
- Does the student appear to be using appropriate study skills and strategies?
- Does the student appear to read with a flexible rate?

Because metacognitive control and student beliefs (see below) are so strongly implicated in studying success, it is useful to ask students to engage in self-assessment. Teachers can devise their own set of questions (see e.g., Joseph, 2003) or use one like we provide in Figure 9.27. Joseph makes the important point that using the reading inventory improved her instruction because she was more aware of her students' approach to learning.

Contemporary concepts of studying, or deliberate learning, are likely to include assessment and instruction in the area of *motivation* and *self-regulation*. Among older students (high school and college), motivation for studying is often evaluated using the Motivated Strategies for Learning Questionnaire (MSLQ) (Pintrich, Smith, Garcia, & McKeachie, 1989; Pintrich, Smith, Garcia, & McKeachie, 1980, 1991). This tool has been widely used and determined to provide both valid and reliable information about students' motivation and value beliefs. This information can be used to adjust instruction and/or to

**FIGURE 9.26
Study-Reading
Skills Checklist**

Degree of Skill	Absent	Low	High
I. Specific study-reading comprehension skills			
A. Ability to interpret graphic arts			
Can the student interpret these graphic aids?			
1. maps			
2. globes			
3. graphs			
4. charts			
5. tables			
6. cartoons			
7. pictures			
8. diagrams			
9. other organizing or iconic aids			
B. Ability to follow directions			
Can the student follow . . .			
1. simple directions?			
2. a more complex set of directions?			
II. Information-location skills			
A. Ability to vary rate of reading			
Can the student do the following?			
1. scan			
2. skim			
3. read at slow rate for difficult materials			
4. read at average rate for reading level			
B. Ability to locate information by use of book parts			
Can the student use book parts to identify the following information?			
1. title			
2. author or editor			
3. publisher			
4. city of publication			
5. name of series			
6. edition			
7. copyright date			
8. date of publication			
Can the student quickly locate and understand the function of the following parts of a book?			
1. preface			
2. foreword			
3. introduction			
4. table of contents			
5. list of figures			
6. chapter headings			
7. subtitles			
8. footnotes			
9. bibliography			
10. glossary			
11. index			
12. appendix			

(Continued)

**FIGURE 9.26
(Continued)**

Degree of Skill	Absent	Low	High
C. Ability to locate information in reference works			
1. locate information in a dictionary			
a. using the guide words			
b. using a thumb index			
c. locating root word			
d. locating derivations of root word			
e. using the pronunciation key			
f. selecting word meaning appropriate to passage under study			
g. noting word origin			
2. locate information in an encyclopedia			
a. using information on spine to locate volume			
b. using guide words to locate section			
c. using index volume			
3. use other reference works such as:			
a. telephone directory			
b. newspapers			
c. magazines			
d. atlases			
e. television listings			
f. schedules			
g. various periodical literature indices			
h. others ( )			
D. Ability to locate information in the library			
Can the student do the following?			
1. locate material by using the card catalog			
a. by subject			
b. by author			
c. by title			
2. find the materials organized in the library			
a. fiction section			
b. reference section			
c. periodical section			
d. vertical file			
e. others ( )			
III. Study and retention strategies			
A. Ability to study information and remember it			
Can the student do the following?			
1. highlight important information			
2. underline important information			
3. use oral repetition to increase retention			
4. ask and answer questions to increase retention			
5. employ a systematic study procedure (such as SQ3R)			
6. demonstrate effective study habits			
a. set a regular study time			
b. leave adequate time for test or project preparation			

**FIGURE 9.26
(Continued)**

Degree of Skill	Absent	Low	High
c. recognize importance of self-motivation in learning			
B. Ability to organize information			
Can the student do the following?			
1. take notes			
2. note source of information			
3. write a summary for a paragraph			
4. write a summary for a short selection			
5. write a summary integrating information from more than one source			
6. write a summary for a longer selection			
7. make graphic aids to summarize information			
8. write an outline of a paragraph			
9. write an outline of a short selection			
10. write an outline for longer selections			
11. write an outline integrating information from more than one source			
12. use an outline to write a report or make an oral report			

Source: Chart from Rogers, D. B. (1984, January). Assessing study skills. *Journal of Reading*, *27*(4), 353–354. Reprinted with permission of the International Reading Association. All rights reserved.

promote self-assessment among learners. An abbreviated version of this tool is available online at http://www.ulc.arizona.edu/cgi-bin/MSLQ.exe?option=generatetest.

"Self-regulated learning is a process whereby learners set goals for their learning and then attempt to plan, monitor, regulate, and control their cognition, motivation, and behavior, guided and constrained by their goals and the contextual features in the environment" (Wolters, Pintrich, & Karabenick, 2005, p. 251). These types of self-regulation are, of course, essential for middle and high school students to acquire and are embedded in a set of phases that describe students' abilities:

Phase I involves *planning* and *goal setting*. It also involves examining task and context factors in relation to one's own knowledge, skill, and experience.

Phase II involves *monitoring*.

Phase III involves efforts to control and regulate different parts of the learning event, including one's own behavior (try harder, persist, seek help, etc.) and also the types of cognitive strategies to be used.

Phase IV involves *reactions* and *reflection* about the task, context, or self. (pp. 253–254)

The strategies-for-learning questionnaire that Wolters and colleagues (2005) developed provides excellent information about students' strategies for regulating their cognitive

**FIGURE 9.27
Thinking About
Reading**

Things That People Think	What I Think	
1. Good readers try to remember everything.	Yes	No
2. I read some things faster and some things slower.	Yes	No
3. Sometimes it helps to write things down as I read.	Yes	No
4. Good readers notice when they are not understanding something as they read.	Yes	No
5. When I am reading informational books or materials, I have a plan for finding and remembering information.	Yes	No
6. I never reread.	Yes	No
7. Only poor readers have to stop and think as they read.	Yes	No
8. It's a good thing to try to connect what you are reading with what you already know about a topic.	Yes	No
9. If I have to remember information, I read the whole text over and over.	Yes	No
10. I it is helpful to think about how the author has organized the ideas in an informational text.	Yes	No
11. I find some things easier to read than others.	Yes	No

strategy use, their academic motivation, and their studying efforts (see Figure 9.28) and can be enormously helpful in assessing adolescent readers and writers (see Appendix B).

Open-Book Reading Assessment. In the Open-Book Reading Assessment (OBRA) (Bader & Pearce, 2009), as its name suggests, students have access to the text throughout. According to the authors, there are several purposes for this type of assessment: (1) to obtain specific information on students' abilities to understand and use content-area, vocational, or daily-life reading materials; (2) to plan instruction; and (3) to confirm or supplement other diagnostic data (p. 140).

The OBRA is an especially useful assessment because it is responsive to some of the concerns raised by the Common Core State Standards (2010), in which text difficulty is considered quantitatively and qualitatively, but also in terms of the reader–text match. "Such assessments are best made by the *teachers* employing their professional judgment, experience, and knowledge of their students and the subject" (CCSS-ELA, Appendix A, p. 4). Using texts that students are actually expected to read, Bader and Pearce suggest creating items about such things as technical vocabulary, use of context clues, using charts,

FIGURE 9.28 Self-Regulation Questionnaire

Strategies for the Regulation of Academic Cognition

Rehearsal Strategies

When I study for this class, I practice saying the material to myself over and over.
When studying for this class, I read my class notes and the course readings over and over again.
I memorize key words to remind me of important concepts in this class.
I make lists of important terms for this course and memorize the lists.

Elaboration Strategies

When I study for this class, I pull together information from different sources, such as lectures, readings, and discussions.
I try to relate ideas in this subject to those in other courses whenever possible.
When reading for this class, I try to relate the material to what I already know.
When I study for this course, I write brief summaries of the main Ideas from the readings and the concepts from the lectures.
I try to understand the material in this class by making connections, between the readings and the concepts from the lectures.
I try to apply ideas from course readings in other class activities such as lecture and discussion.

Organization Strategies

When I study for the readings for this course, I outline the material to help me organize my thoughts.
When I study for this course, I go through the readings and my class notes and try to find the most important ideas.
I make simple charts, diagrams, or tables to help me organize course material.
When I study for this course, I go over my class notes and make an outline of important concepts.

Metacognitive Self-Regulation

During class time I often miss important points because I'm thinking of other things, (REVERSED)
When reading for this course, I make up questions to help focus my reading.
When I become confused about something I'm reading for this class. I go back and try to figure it out.
If course materials are difficult to understand, I change the way I read the material.
Before I study new course material thoroughly, I often skim it to see how it is organized.
I ask myself questions to make sure I understand the material I have been studying in this class.
I try to change the way I study in order to fit the course requirements and Instructor's teaching style.
I often find that I have been reading for class but don't know what it was all about. (REVERSED)
I try to think through a topic and decide what I am supposed to learn from it rather than just reading it over when studying.
When studying for this course, I try to determine which concepts I don't understand well.
When I study for this class, I set goals for myself in order to direct my activities in each study period.
If I get confused taking notes in class, I make sure I sort it out afterwards.

Strategies for the Regulation of Academic Motivation

Mastery Self-Talk

I tell myself that I should keep working just to learn as much as I can.
I persuade myself to keep at It just to see how much I can learn.

(Continued)

FIGURE 9.28   (Continued)

I challenge myself to complete the work and learn as much as possible.
I convince myself to work hard just for the sake of learning.
I tell myself that I should study just to learn as much as I can.
I think about trying to become good at what we are learning or doing.

Relevance Enhancement

I tell myself that it is important to learn the material because I will need it later in life.
I try to connect the material with something I like doing or find interesting.
I think up situations where it would be helpful for me to know the material or skills.
I try to make the material seem more useful by relating it to what I want to do in my life.
I try to make myself see how knowing the material is personally relevant.
I make an effort to relate what we're learning to my personal interests.

Situational Interest Enhancement

I make studying more enjoyable by turning it into a game.
I try to make a game out of learning the material or completing the assignment.
I try to get myself to see how doing the work can be fun.
I make doing the work enjoyable by focusing on something about it that is fun.
I think of a way to make the work seem enjoyable to complete.

Performance-Relative Ability Self-Talk

I think about doing better than other students in my class.
I tell myself that I should work at least as hard as other students.
I keep telling myself that I want to do better than others in my class.
I make myself work harder by comparing what I'm doing to what other students are doing,

Performance-Exercise Self-Talk

I remind myself about how important it is to get good grades.
I tell myself that I need to keep studying to do well in this course.
I convince myself to keep working by thinking about getting good grades.
I think about how my grade will be affected if I don't do my reading or studying.
I remind myself how important it is to do well on the tests and assignments in this course.

Self-Consequating

I promise myself I can do something I want later if I finish the assigned work now.
I make a deal with myself that if I get a certain amount of the work done I can do something fun afterwards.
I promise myself some kind of a reward if I get my readings or studying done.
I tell myself I can do something I like later if night now I do the work I have to get done.
I set a goal for how much I need to study and promise myself a reward If I reach that goal.

Environmental Structuring

I try to study at a time when I can be more focused.
I change my surroundings so that it is easy to concentrate on the work.
I make sure I have as few distractions as possible.
I try to get rid of any distractions that are around me.
I eat or drink something to make myself more awake and prepared to work.

FIGURE 9.28   (Continued)

Strategies for the Regulation of Academic Motivation

Effort Regulation

I often feel so lazy or bored when I study for this class that I quit before I finish what I planned to do. [REVERSED]

I work hard to do well in this class even if I don't like what we are doing.

When course work is difficult. I give up or only study the easy parts. (REVERSED)

Even when course materials are dull and uninteresting, I manage to keep working until I finish.

Regulating Time and Study Environment

I usually study in a place where I can concentrate on my course work.

I make good use of my study time for this course.

I find it hard to stick to a study schedule. (REVERSED)

I have a regular place set aside for studying.

I make sure I keep up with the weekly readings and assignments for this course.

I attend class regularly.

I often find that I don't spend very much time on this course because of other activities. (REVERSED)

I rarely find time to review my notes or readings before an exam. (REVERSED)

Source: Wolters, C., Pintrich, P. R., & Karabenick, S. A. (2003, April). Assessing academic self-regulated learning. Paper prepared for the Conference on Indicators of Positive Development. Sponsored by Childtrends, National Institutes of Health. Retrieved March 4, 2007, from http://www.childtrends.org/Files/Child_Trends-2003_03_12_ PD_PDConfWPK.pdf

and using book parts. In addition, they suggest testing students' ability to answer questions that require making inferences and interpreting text information.

To create an OBRA tailored for specific settings, examine the textbook carefully and consider the types of tasks generally expected of students (see Chapters 5 and 6). The OBRA is a very flexible assessment strategy, since it can accommodate almost any type of text-task context. Expository text chapters often contain features like the following:

- Chapter preview
- List of objectives
- Clearly labeled section headings (for example, 53.3, Fuel Flow System)
- Complex figures with detailed labeling
- A new terms section, with new vocabulary in boldface and brief definitions
- Marginalized concept notes
- Chapter review
- A section that discusses topics and activities

To create an OBRA, you ask conventional questions focused on content (e.g., "Circle the components of an airflow system") but also items that help you to see what students know about studying their specific content-area textbooks (e.g., "In my textbook, to find . . . I would turn to . . ., on page . . .").

FIGURE 9.29   Open-Book Reading Assessment Summary Form

| | Content Details | | | | | | | | | | | | Using Diagrams and Charts | | | | | | | | | | | | | | Using Book Parts | | | | | | | | | |
| | 1 | | | | | | | | | | | | 2 (Diagrams) | | | | | | 3 (Charts) | | | | | | | | | | | | | | | | | |
	a	b	c	d	e	f	g	h	i	j	k	l	a	b	c	d	e	f	a	b	c	d	e	f	g	h	4	5	6	7	8	9	10	11	12	13
Lorie				✓			✓						✓		✓																					
Jack				✓			✓																				✓	✓	✓							✓
Mark				✓			✓	✓																✓												
Judy				✓			✓									✓		✓																		
Shane				✓			✓	✓																✓												
Mike				✓			✓	✓																			✓		✓	✓		✓				
Greg		✓								✓				✓					✓																	
Jack R.						✓	✓																				✓		✓	✓		✓				
Keith				✓		✓	✓																				✓		✓							

Source: Adapted from Bader, L. A., & Pearce, D. L. (2009). *Bader reading and language inventory* (6th ed.). Upper Saddle River, NJ: Allyn & Bacon.

Source: Adapted from Bader, L. A., & Pearce, D. L. (2009). *Bader reading and language inventory* (6th ed.). Upper Saddle River, NJ: Allyn & Bacon.

After the students have completed the OBRA, the following questions should be considered in evaluating students' performance:

- Do the students recognize the parts of the text?
- Are students able to make use of graphic materials?
- When the text is available, can students locate specific information?
- Can students use the text to figure out unfamiliar, specialized vocabulary?
- Does the problem appear to be ability to use the text or ability to retain information?

This information is summarized and used to plan and adapt instruction using a chart to display the information for the class. The chart in Figure 9.29 was completed by a secondary vocational education teacher with students in an auto mechanics class. He learned, to his surprise, that most of his students were unable to make effective use of the diagrams and charts in their textbook. Similarly, few of them were adept at using the helpful features of the book to derive information. Whereas he had previously attributed the students' poor performance to lack of effort and/or motivation, he now realized that at least some students were unable to learn the information using the text. Instruction in textbook use and/or additional support for reading and studying would be needed.

Again, teachers may be concerned about the time-consuming nature of these assessment strategies. Although shortcuts are possible, the information gathered in this way will not be as useful. As Rogers (1984, p. 352) has noted, "students' use of study-reading can best be assessed by observing them while they are engaging in studying-reading for some personal interest or need. Contrived situations such as often occur when students are asked to complete worksheet pages from published materials are not as effective for assessing and teaching study-reading."

Writing

As we noted in Chapter 8, there are relatively few tests of writing outside the realm of state assessments, which generally assess primarily the products of writing. In today's classrooms, children write more than they ever have, and teachers have more information available to them about how to evaluate students' writing. As a result, teachers are likely to identify students as having difficulty in this component area during the course of their normal instructional interactions. That is a positive development, because educators and linguists are increasingly concerned with students' grasp of the writing *process* as well as the products of their efforts. Most experts suggest that the writing process involves several stages: a planning stage, for clarifying purpose and audience; a composing stage, which involves writing, reading, and attention to mechanics; and a revision stage, during which rereading and editing occur. Clearly both product and process assessment are likely to inform us about students' writing difficulties. We start with classroom writing products because they are so useful in examining the types of writing students can and do produce, and also because they can yield good evidence about the writing process.

Evaluating Written Samples. Folders, or portfolios, of ongoing and completed work are a normal part of classrooms where a process writing approach is used. Daily work samples, journal entries, and work from writers' workshop all provide rich information about students' developing knowledge, skill, and motivation.

One of the first strategies to use in assessing students' writing is to review the work they have already produced. When teachers and students collect writing over time, they can review the collections for evidence of growth and patterns of performance. In completing such a review, it may be helpful to reflect on the following:

- What types of writing is the student producing?
- What topics seem to fuel his/her writing?
- What new ideas are being generated?
- Is there evidence of topic or theme change/growth?
- What skills can and does this student employ?

These overall trends and patterns are very important, but teachers often need/want to evaluate students' individual writing samples more closely. Written work can be evaluated in several ways. Common approaches include both holistic scoring and analytic scoring. Using an analytic approach, specific aspects of the writing press are judged: syntax, vocabulary, and so on. Holistic scoring of written products is quite common both in classroom assessment and in large-scale assessment (even statewide assessment of writing). Using a holistic scoring system, you arrive at a rating that represents a global judgment about the overall quality of the written product.

Holistic Scoring. Holistic scoring of written products is quite common both in classroom assessment and in large-scale assessment (even statewide assessment of writing). Holistic scoring involves evaluating a composition as a whole piece of writing. Unlike analytic scores (see below), holistic scores produce a single score "based on an overall impression" (Arter & McTighe, 2001). Using a holistic scoring system, you arrive at a rating that represents a global judgment about the overall quality of the written product. Usually, the evaluator compares the writing to other pieces (called "anchors" or "benchmarks").

To do this, a teacher (or better yet a group of teachers) would collect a great deal of writing. For example, all fifth-grade teachers at a particular school might collect research papers for the whole year from all their students. They would then read them and agree on an exemplary paper or two—considered "high." Similarly, one or two very poor exemplars would be selected—considered "low." Finally, several papers considered to be "middle" would be identified. These pieces of writing become the "anchor" papers. Whenever a teacher evaluates a student's research paper in future, it is compared, holistically, to these anchors and classified in terms of its similarity to one or another of these types. Many states provide benchmark papers for this purpose (see e.g., Vermont Standards and Assessment Consortium, VTSAC, 2002).

Occasionally, holistic scoring proceeds using a scale to guide the evaluation. Arter and McTighe (2001, p. 19) provide the following example of a scale used in holistic scoring:

> Level 1: This score is given for work that "Does not achieve any requirements of the tasks . . ."
>
> Level 4: This score is given for papers that "substantially complete the requirements and show an understanding of the concepts and processes."
>
> Level 6: Work is given this score when it goes "beyond the requirements, showing . . . excellence and unusual insights. . . ."

It is essential that teachers have a clear sense of what constitutes a high-quality piece of writing if holistic scoring is to be useful. As Jenkins (1996, p. 23) so aptly notes, "when teachers are tossed into a sea of children's writing samples without a compass, they tend to bob aimlessly on the surface of children's work," often attending primarily to mechanics and little organization, genre attributes, or ability to communicate meaningfully.

An example of a rubric that is applied holistically to a specific type of writing is presented in Figure 9.30. Generally, these types of rubrics are task specific. That is, the performance assessment, or genre of writing, is clearly specified, and the attributes of excellent performance in that mode are identified. Other attributes are identified for other tasks.

Analytic Scoring.   Sometimes, teachers or other evaluators want to analyze writing in terms of its component parts. When using an analytic scoring approach, teachers attend to specific writing skills and/or features of written products (traits) and judge the whole piece in terms of the subcomponents. In this case, scores or points are generally assigned to the various component areas and then totaled to obtain a score or grade. From a diagnostic viewpoint, it can be helpful to analyze students' writing so that instruction can be tailored to the particular aspects that are causing a student difficulty. Written products are typically evaluated in four major areas—ideas, organization, style, and mechanics—and both large-scale and classroom assessments generally attend to these elements. In Figure 9.31,

**FIGURE 9.30
Sample Scoring
Rubric for Writing**

Writing to Inform	
4	These responses are well developed and have provided more than enough information to inform the reader about the topic. The information is extended and expanded through specific details. A. These responses contain numerous specific details that more than adequately explain the topic. B. The organizational plan is established and consistently maintained. C. The writer addresses the intended audience. D. The writer fluently uses language choices to enhance the text in a manner consistent with the purpose.
3	These responses are adequately developed and have provided enough information to inform the reader about the topic. The information is presented clearly, and irrelevant information does not interfere with clarity. A. These responses contain some specific details that adequately explain the topic, although some details may not contribute to the development of the explanation. B. An organizational plan is established and generally maintained. C. The writer addresses the intended audience. D. The writer uses language choices to enhance the text in a manner consistent with the purpose.
2	These responses contain little development and have a minimal amount of information. The information included does not clearly explain the topic, and irrelevant information interferes with clarity. A. These responses have details, but the details may be inaccurate or may not adequately explain the topic. B. An organizational plan is established and minimally maintained. C. The writer addresses the intended audience. D. The writer seldom uses language choices to enhance the text in a manner consistent with the purpose.
1	These responses provide sufficient evidence that the writer saw the prompt and attempted to respond to it. The responses lack development and have little information. The information included may be vague or inaccurate. A. These responses lack sufficient details to explain the topic. B. An organizational plan, if established, is not maintained. C. The writer may not address the intended audience. D. The writer does not use language choices to enhance the text in a manner consistent with the purpose.
NSR	A. Blank B. Off topic/off task C. Unscorable

Source: Prince George's County Scoring Guide for Reading/Writing/Language Usage (p. 54). Prepared by Rojulene Norris and Patricia Miller. Reprinted by permission of the authors.

FIGURE 9.31 Standards for Analytic Scoring: Narrative and Expository Writing

	Standards for Evaluating Composing Skills for Narrative Writing		
	Low	**Middle**	**High**
Story structure	No identifiable beginning, middle, or end. Story problem unclear. Action and characters not developed or related. Essential details missing or confusing. Story problem not solved, or resolution unrelated to events.	Beginning, middle, and end present, but not always identifiable. Story problem presented, but not completely developed. Some conversational or descriptive details included. End may not show logical resolution of problem.	Identifiable beginning, middle, and end. Characters introduced and problem presented. Characters and problem well developed with appropriate conversational or descriptive detail. Story ends with believable resolution of problem.
Story setting	Setting of the story not identifiable. Details inappropriate and confusing.	Time and place of story are hinted at but uncertain. Further references to setting may be inconsistent with original time or place.	Time and place of story clearly set. Specific details related to setting given in appropriate context. Setting consistent throughout.
Story characters	Characters not believable. Details related to character development are inconsistent, inappropriate, or missing. Difficult to distinguish one character from another. Action of characters unrelated to problem.	Characters somewhat believable. Some descriptive or conversational details given. Details may not develop character personality. Action of characters not always related to problem. Major and minor characters not clearly discernable.	Characters believable. Descriptive or conversational detail develops character personally. Action of characters relates to problem. Major characters more fully developed than minor ones.
Story conversation	Conversation among characters haphazard, incomplete, or muddled. Much of the conversation inappropriate to circumstances and to personality of story characters. Conversation seems unrelated to story being told.	Conversation sometimes appropriate to circumstances and to characters. Conversation may reveal character personality or relationships among characters. Conversation sometimes not clearly related to story.	Conversation appropriate to story circumstances and to personality of each character. Conversation used to reveal character and develop interrelationships among characters. Conversation clearly relates to story.
Story idea	Story idea is trite or otherwise uninteresting. Story lacks plot or plot is vague. Story ends abruptly or reaches no definite conclusion.	Story idea is interesting. Idea may lack freshness or imaginativeness. Story has a plot. Plot may not be well developed or entirely consistent. Story ending may not be satisfying or interesting.	Story idea is fresh or imaginative. Story plot is well developed, is consistent, and comes to a satisfying, surprising, or otherwise highly effective ending.

Standards for Evaluating Composing Skills for Expository Writing

	Low	Middle	High
Quality of ideas	Most ideas vague, incoherent, inaccurate, underdeveloped, or incomplete. Details often unrelated to topic. Nothing imaginative or thoughtful about the ideas.	Unevenness in completeness and development of ideas. Most ideas related to the topic; a few unrelated. Sound, but unimaginative ideas.	Ideas relevant to the topic, fully developed, rich in thought and imagination, and clearly presented.
Quality of organization	Introduction, development, and conclusion unclear. Emphasis of major and minor points indistinguishable. Sentences and paragraphs seldom related by transitions. Overall lack of coherence and foward movement.	Introduction, development, or conclusion not easily identified. Emphasis on major and minor points sometimes not well balanced. Transitions between sentences and paragraphs used, but without consistency. Foward movement variable.	Introduction, development, and conclusion well structured, complete, and easily identified. Emphasis of major and minor points well balanced. Sentences and paragraphs clearly related by transitions. Logical forward movement.
Selection of words	Word selection inexact, immature, and limited. Figurative language seldom used.	Word selection usually suitable and accurate. Overused words and clichés somewhat common. Figurative language may lack freshness, when used.	Facility and flair in word selection. Writer experiments with words in unusual and pleasing ways. Figurative language used, often in interesting and imaginative ways.
Structure of sentences	Not variety in sentence structure; often only simple sentences are used. Transitions limited to such words as **then**: conjunctions to **and**. Awkward and puzzling sentences common. Run-on sentences and fragments often appear.	Some variety in sentence length and structure. Transitions used when necessary. Few sentence constructions awkward and puzzling. Run-on sentences and sentence fragments appear, but do not predominate.	Sentence length and structure varied. Sentences consistently well formed. Smooth flow from sentence to sentence. Run-on sentences and sentence fragments rarely appear.
Structure of paragraph	Topic sentences seldom used. Irrelevancies common. Order of details haphazard. Little or no command of the four common paragraph types.	Topic sentences usually stated. Irrelevancies uncommon. Order of details usually suitable. Limited ability to use the four common types of paragraphs.	Topic sentences stated and supported with relevant details. Appropriate variety used in ordering details (chronological, logical, spatial, climatic). Four types of paragraphs used when appropriate (narrative, explanatory, descriptive, persuasive).

(Continued)

FIGURE 9.31 (Continued)

	Standards for Evaluating Mechanical Skills for Narrative or Expository Writing		
	Low	Middle	High
Grammar and usage	Frequent errors in the use of nouns, pronouns, modifiers, and verbs.	Grammatical conventions of inflections, functions, modifiers, nouns, pronouns, and verbs usually observed. Grammatical errors sometimes occur.	Grammatical conventions of inflections, functions, modifiers, nouns, pronouns, and verbs observed. Grammatical errors infrequent.
Punctuation	End punctuation often used incorrectly. Internal punctuation seldom used. Uncommon punctuation is almost never used correctly.	Sentences usually end with appropriate punctuation. Internal punctuation used, with occasional errors. Uncommon punctuation sometimes used, but often inaccurately.	Sentences consistently end with appropriate punctuation. Internal punctuation and other less common punctuation usually correctly used.
Capitalization	First word of sentence often not capitalized. Pronoun / often a small letter. Proper nouns seldom capitalized. Other capitalization rules usually ignored.	First word of sentences nearly always capitalized. I / always capitalized. Well-known proper nouns usually capitalized. Other capitalization rules used, but not consistently.	First word of a sentence and the pronoun / always capitalized. Well-known proper nouns nearly always capitalized. Good command of other capitalization rules regarding titles, languages, religions, and so on.
Spelling	Frequent spelling errors. Shows a frustration spelling level (less than 70%). Unable to improve spelling accuracy in edited work without help. Misspellings often difficult to recognize as English words.	Majority of words spelled correctly. Shows an instructional spelling level (70 to 80%). Approaches 90% accuracy in edited work. Misspellings approximate correct spellings.	Nearly all words spelled correctly. Shows an independent spelling level (90%). Approaches 100% accuracy in edited work. Misspellings close to correct spellings.
Handwriting/ neatness	Handwriting difficult or impossible to read. Letters and words crowded. Formation of letters inconsistent. Writing often illegible.	Handwriting usually readable, but some words and letters difficult to recognize. Some crowding of letters and words.	Handwriting clear, neat, and consistent. Forms all letters legibly with consistent spacing between letters and words.

Source: From Language Structure and Use. Teacher's Edition 8, by Ronald L. Cramer et al. Copyright © 1981 Scott, Foresman and Company.

you see a sample of an analytic scoring guide for narrative writing. As you can see, a composition is judged separately for narrative and exposition, whereas mechanical skills are judged together.

Many schools use an instructional approach to teaching writing that involves "6-trait writing" (Spandel, 2008) or, alternatively, 6+1 traits (Bellamy, 2005). Students' work is assessed using these six traits: idea/content, organization, word choice, sentence fluency, voice, and conventions (and maybe plus presentation). Rubrics for engaging in analytic scoring of each of these traits (and all grade levels) are easily available online from the Northwest Regional Laboratory (http://educationnorthwest.org/traits).

A related, but more theoretically refined, scoring procedure is called *primary trait scoring.* As described by Tompkins (2012, p. 94), primary trait scoring focuses on assessing compositions in relation to specific purposes or audiences so that students' work is "judged according to situation-specific criteria." Primary traits differ from one writing project to another, depending on the nature of the assignment. Thus, students would not be expected to be equally proficient writers in all settings on all modes of writing. One of the advantages of rubrics and other similar assessment strategies is that they "promote learning by offering clear performance targets to students for agreed-upon standards" (Marzano et al., 1993, p. 29). Students can use these or specially designed checklists to engage in more-effective self-evaluation. Valencia and her colleagues (see Valencia & Bradley, 1998) provide persuasive evidence of the potential benefits of developing students' self-reflection and self-evaluation abilities. For example, students are more likely to take charge of their own learning when they participate in self-assessment activities. Not surprisingly, they are also more likely to take responsibility for it and to set reasonable goals for themselves—at least in part because they have a better understanding of reading and writing processes. Teachers can convey to students important aspects of competent performance using well-defined self-assessments. Combs (2002) provides an example of an appropriate intermediate-grade rubric (see Figure 9.32). In this case, the five criteria are listed, and levels of competence are defined for each one. Everyone is a winner in this situation. Assessment is proceeding with authentic tasks, and the assessment criteria provide useful instructional targets and a focus for learning. In addition, these rubrics provide the systematic structure that allows teachers across classrooms to discuss and evaluate students' work with a common vision and a uniform set of standards.

Analytic or holistic evaluations of written products can certainly provide rich information about students' writing abilities. However, it is extremely difficult (perhaps impossible) to evaluate students' control of the writing process by considering only final products. Evaluation of student control over the process of writing requires that students be observed, over time, in a classroom that values process writing and encourages author development.

Observation Checklists. An effective observation framework should include examination of written work, but it should also provide for examining the writer at work. Using an observational checklist of behaviors can help teachers focus as they watch students write.

**FIGURE 9.32
Rubric for
Evaluating
Writing Traits**

Evaluating the Traits of My Writing

Ideas and Content

5 = I know a lot about my topic, my ideas are interesting, the main point of my paper is clear, and my topic is not too broad.

3 = The reader usually knows what I mean. Some parts will be better when I tell just a little more about what is important.

1 = When someone else reads my paper, it will be hard for them to understand what I mean or what it is all about.

Organization

5 = My beginning gets the reader's attention and make the reader want to find out what's coming next. Every detail adds a little more to the main idea. I ended at a good place and at just the right time.

3 = The details and order of my story/paper make sense most of the time. I have a beginning, but it may not really grab the reader. I have a conclusion, but it seems to sum up my paper in a ho-hum way.

1 = The ideas and details in my paper are sort of jumbled and confused. I don't really have a beginning or an end.

Voice

5 = My paper has lots of personality. It really sounds like me. People who know me will know it is my paper.

3 = Although readers will understand what I mean, they may not "feel" what I mean. My personality comes through sometimes. I probably need to know a little more about my topic to show, rather than tell, the reader about it.

1 = I can't really hear my voice in this paper. It was hard for me to write this paper. I really need to know much more about my topic or be more willing to take a risk about what I say.

Use of Language

5 = The sentences in my paper are clear and sound good when read aloud. Words fit just right.

3 = Some of my sentences are choppy or awkward, but most are clear. Some words are very general, but most readers will figure out what I mean.

1 = Even when I read this paper, I have to go back, stop, and read over, just to figure out the sentences. A lot of my sentences seem to be the same. The words I chose don't seem to be very interesting.

Use of Conventions

5 = There are very few errors in my paper; it wouldn't take long to get this ready to publish.

3 = My spelling is correct on simple words; most of my sentences begin with capital letters and end with the right punctuation.

1 = There are a lot of spelling and grammar errors in my paper. Punctuation and capital letters seem to be missing. My paragraphs are not indented.

Source: From *Developing Competent Readers and Writers in the Middle Grade*, by Martha Combs, p. 237. Copyright © 2002. Reprint by permission of Pearson Education, Inc. Upper Saddle River, NJ.

The results of these observations can be used to evaluate students' developmental progress and also to identify areas that might require instructional attention. The form that appears in Figure 9.33 parallels the major stages of writing, focusing on the student during planning, composing (drafting), and revision phases. In addition, this checklist addresses the critical affective outcomes addressed by creating good written products and provides for evaluation of student attitudes.

Teachers also need ways to summarize the information they have about students' writing. Teachers feel pressure to evaluate students' work in terms of mechanical proficiency. As teachers engage in retrospective analysis of their students' writing, they should also examine students' ability to write productively, their personal style, and whether they write for a range of purposes. A checklist devised by Temple and Gillet (1989) delineates the kinds of questions to ask during the evaluation of students' writing (see also Anderson, 2005). These include the following:

Functions of Writing
- What types of writing have been produced? (stories, expressive writing, descriptive writing, etc.)
- What topics have been selected by the writer? Who is the audience for this student's writing? (teacher, classmates, etc.)
- How sophisticated is the writer's awareness of audience?

Qualities of Writing Style
- Does the writing reflect good choices in language use?
- Does the writer make good use of descriptive language?
- Does the writer maintain a focus throughout the work?
- Are papers well organized, given the purpose of the work?
- Are the written products defined by effective openings and endings?
- Is the writer developing and maintaining a personal voice?

Mechanics of Writing
- How much control of standard English usage/grammar is reflected in the written works of this writer?
- What stage of spelling is reflected?
- Are complete idea units (sentences) used throughout?
- Are punctuation and capitalization used appropriately (for the age/grade)?

These examples demonstrate how teachers can focus on and gather evidence of the writer's reading interests, knowledge, and skill. It is possible to conduct much more extensive analyses of students' writing abilities; however, the important thing is to keep your purpose in mind. Anderson (2005) recommends using a simple T-chart. At the top of the first column is the question "What am I learning about this student as a writer?" At the top of the second column is this question: "What do I need to teach this student?"

FIGURE 9.33   Observation Checklist Focused on the Writing Process

Student: Teacher:	Date(s): Context(s):	
	Evidence of Independent Use and Control	**Comments**
Planning/Prewriting		
❏ Can generate and rehearse ideas		
❏ Uses some prewriting aids for planning (e.g. webs, brainstorms, notes, outlines)		
❏ Considers purpose		
Composing/Drafting		
❏ Can sustain writing activity		
❏ Can produce complete draft		
❏ Reads, reflects and reworks during production		
❏ Demonstrates risk-taking with topic, author's craft, and mechanics		
❏ Manages time well		
❏ Considers purpose and audience		
Revision		
❏ Engages in self-assessment of writing products		
❏ Seeks feedback and response from others		
❏ Responds to suggestions from others		
❏ Edits own writing (relative to developmental level)		
❏ Cultivates voice		
❏ Attends to mechanics		
Publication		
❏ Shares writing in formal and informal ways		
❏ Produces writing that is appropriate for the sharing context (and audience)		
❏ Is willing to re-work texts for sharing		
Additional Comments or Observations:		

Student Self-Evaluation

According to Valencia and her colleagues, assessment should be *collaborative*. "The essence of collaborative criterion lies in collaboration with students. When we work *with* students in developing assessments, we communicate our support of their learning process" (Valencia, McGinley, & Pearson, 1990). This means that students should share some responsibility for monitoring their own progress, but this also means that they must have access to information. They need to be clearly informed of the purposes for various work assignments, and important evaluative criteria will need to be shared with them as well. Collaboration necessarily involves at least some student self-evaluation. Indeed, the ability to evaluate one's own work should be viewed as an important goal in most literacy programs, since it is a necessary requirement of independence (Johnston, 1997). Importantly, effective use of student self-assessment can raise achievement (see Ross, 2006, for a review).

In writing, teachers use teacher-student and peer conferences to establish criteria for evaluating success and/or progress (see previous section). Then students are invited to contribute by evaluating their own efforts (see Figure 9.34). These self-evaluations must be taken seriously and must become part of the total assessment process.

**FIGURE 9.34
Self-Assessment
Questionnaire**

A Self-Assessment Questionnaire

Name: _____ Date: _____
Title: _____

As you publish your writing, reflect on your writing processes and this piece of writing. Please respond briefly to at least three questions in each section.

Part 1: Your writing processes
➤ What part of the writing process was most successful for you?
➤ What writing strategies did you use?
➤ What part of the writing process was least successful for you?
➤ What do you need help with?

Part 2: This piece of writing
➤ What pleases you most about this piece of writing?
➤ Are you comfortable with this topic and genre?
➤ How did you organize your writing?
➤ Does your lead grab your readers' attention?
➤ Which type of mechanical errors cause you the most trouble?

Source: Tompkins, G. E. (1992, November). Assessing the processes students use as writers. *Journal of Reading,* *36*(3), 244–246. Reprinted with permission of the International Reading Association. All rights reserved.

Starting in kindergarten and continuing through grade 2, Kyle's writing was collected and considered by both his teacher and by Kyle. His writing was filled with good ideas, but difficult to read. Over time, his purpose was generally clear, and the content was good, but the mechanics were weak. For example, in mid–grade 2, Kyle's writing folder contained the following story:

> Once there was a eagle. He was different than the others. Some of the others teased him. He didn't have any friends. But he had one. He was a hawk. His name was Eric. One day they went fishing. They saw some poachers. They flew back and warned the others. They all were saved! They were always kind from then on.

This captivating and well-structured story was difficult to read because Kyle's writing is large and ill formed and because his spelling is still at the phonetic level. On the other hand, sentences were marked by periods and some capitals. About the same time, Kyle reflected on his own writing. He noted that "I used to . . . *write one santins, only the bgining of werds, and no detal in pichers*" "But now I . . . *put mor santosis, sownd it out, and more dtal in pichers.*"

For our purposes, it is especially important to note the extent to which students' self-evaluations reflect their development and progress as writers. Comments such as the following reflect differences that are important to recognize: "I liked this story because it's long"; "I tried to make a good beginning to this story and I think I did"; "I was trying to make people understand how the boy in this story felt." We want to attend as well to changing self-evaluations. Students can help us understand their purposes in this way, but they also show us whether they have begun to take risks in writing or have internalized new standards for their work and can set their own goals.

Formal Diagnostic Tests of Reading

Standardized, norm-referenced diagnostic tests are designed to provide a profile of a student's relative strengths and weaknesses. Diagnostic tests differ from survey tests in a number of ways (see Miller, Linn, & Grunwald, 2009). Large-scale survey tests (like those discussed in Chapter 4) provide a more general measure of achievement, whereas diagnostic tests typically have distinct subtest scores and the number of items is larger in order to measure specific skills. In addition, the difficulty tends to be lower in order to provide adequate discrimination among students with problems. For example, rather than providing one or two general scores that represent a student's overall performance in reading, diagnostic tests break the domain of reading into various components such as knowledge of phonics, structural analysis, literal comprehension, inferential comprehension, and reading rate, providing scores for each of these areas. The rationale underlying diagnostic tests is that instruction can be planned to help a student improve in areas where performance is low.

A very large body of research is emerging to confirm what good teachers and specialists have always known: the underlying roots of students' reading difficulties are diverse (Aaron et al., 2008; Valencia & Buly, 2004). To have confidence in a diagnostic test, test users must satisfy their validity concern. It is entirely possible that a subtest is measuring nothing of consequence or that it measures something that does not lend itself to instruction. Ultimately, the utility of diagnostic tests relies entirely on the relationship between the subtests and the prevailing conceptions of what is important to learn in a particular area or discipline—both according to the users' views and those of the school curriculum. Secondarily, these subtests should involve distinct component areas and not some global "reading ability." When subtest scores are too highly correlated with the overall reading score, it may raise questions about the unique contribution of this diagnostic component. As always, results should be used cautiously and checked against the multiple indicators you have about students' performance and achievement.

In this section, we describe a number of commercially available norm-referenced diagnostic tests that are individually administered. Those described here are:

- *Oral and Written Language Scales, Second Edition* (OWLS-II, Carrow-Woolfolk, 2011)
- *Diagnostic Assessments of Reading* (DAR-2)
- *Woodcock Reading Mastery Test—Revised-Normative Update*, or WRMT-R/NU (Woodcock, 1987/1998)
- *Comprehensive Test of Phonological Processing*, or CTOPP
- *Test of Word Reading Efficiency*, or TOWRE (Torgesen, Wagner, & Rashotte, 1999)
- *Test of Reading Comprehension, Third edition*, or TORC-3 (Brown, Hammill, & Wiederholt, 1995)

Some of these are more-comprehensive diagnostic tests of reading performance that include several component areas (e.g., the Woodcock Reading Mastery Tests), while others assess only one component area (e.g., the Comprehensive Test of Phonological Processing).

Oral and Written Language Scales, Second Edition. The OWLS-II (Carrow-Woolfolk, 2011) is a norm-referenced test comprised of four scales: Listening Comprehension, Oral Expression, Reading Comprehension, and Written Expression. The OWLS is designed to be used in identifying students with learning disabilities, to plan instruction, and to monitor student progress. The reading comprehension scale is new to the second edition, and this edition also includes a new, parallel form to permit retesting of all scales. We discussed the oral language components of the OWLS-II in Chapter 7. The written language composite is comprised of Reading Comprehension (RC) and Written Expression (WE).

The RC scale has 140 items that require students to read a prompt and select the correct response from a series of four choices. The prompts include individual written words, sentences, or paragraphs (story, poem), and they are accompanied by a variety of tasks or questions. While the text length on the RC scale is much shorter than is typical for many tests of comprehension, the items are interesting and the linguistic analysis that accompanies them may be extremely helpful in identifying aspects of language and meaning that are barriers for individual students. For example, one item that requires understanding of meaning from context is:

> Select the most likely meaning for the following sentence: *When the highly paid baseball pitcher seemed to be complacent with a lackluster performance, the fans grumbled that he wasn't worth his salt.* (Carrow-Woolfolk, 2011, prepublication materials)

The longest items on the RC scale appear to be clustered under the heading of "Text Structure." At the time of this writing, the materials were not available, but the author indicates that these selections include a wide range of genre, including narrative fiction, exposition, and poetry. Multiple-choice items require students to identify main idea, select the appropriate mood, etc.

The WE scale contains a total of fifty items organized or clustered by age into sets of fourteen to eighteen items. According the the author,

> The WE scale comprises both direct and indirect items. The direct items present tasks such as retelling a story, completing a story, or interpreting a statement. These tasks provide an authentic and representative sample of the examinee's written expression skills. The indirect items present tasks such as copying words, writing dictated sentences, or combining sentences. These items are included because if only open-ended direct items were used, the test would not necessarily incorporate all the writing conventions and linguistic structures that should be addressed in a comprehensive writing assessment. (Carrow-Woolfolk, 2011, prepublication materials)

The second edition addresses several concerns expressed about the first edition, including improved normative data and updated color artwork. All of the norms were updated for the second edition using more than two thousand individuals ages 3 to 21, and the items were rescaled and supplemental items were added. The normative sample is concentrated in the younger ages, and the author explains that this was intentional because of the need to make smaller normative age groups during the period when language growth is the largest. Almost 70 percent of the norming population falls within ages 3 to 11. Educators using this assessment in the elementary grades can have confidence in the sampling process. However, it should be used cautiously with older students.

The author provides validity evidence that is good but is based on validation studies with relatively few students. The internal reliability estimates of all four scales is very high (ranging from .93 to .99 across all scales and all age groups). Test-retest reliability estimates are more variable, ranging from .73 to .95. The highest and most satisfactory reliabilities are, of course, associated with the composite scores. The weakest reliability is associated with the Listening Comprehension scale. It should also be noted that the reliability estimates between the two forms is acceptable, but a bit low; so comparing student progress over time should proceed with some caution.

The reading and the writing components (i.e., all four scales) were standardized with the same students so that educators may have some confidence that they can compare oral language, written language, and reading comprehension for individual students, to explore possible patterns or anomalies. As well, the expanded guidelines for interpreting results and the information about linguistic elements would be useful for closely examining the abilities of individual students. Three informative and comprehensive manuals describe the technical attributes, development, and interpretation of the OWLS-II.

The Diagnostic Assessments of Reading (DAR-2).   The DAR-2 (Roswell, Chall, Curtis, & Kearns, 2006) is a structured inventory that combines features of IRIs, fluency CBM techniques, and word recognition assessments. Especially when teachers want to assess all/most of their students, the DAR is a good option because it is relatively quick. It can provide additional diagnostic information that gives a degree of specificity beyond the screening tools they might use. The second edition of the DAR also contains two forms (A and B) that provide the user with more flexibility for testing again mid-year so that the instructional plan can be revised to reflect new needs resulting from the earlier instructional emphases. It contains these subtests: (1) Print Awareness, (2) Phonological Awareness, (3) Letters and Sounds, (4) Word Recognition, (5) Word Analysis, (6) Oral Reading, (7) Silent Reading Comprehension, (8) Spelling, and (9) Word Meaning. The interpretive profile provided organizes the useful summary information. However, more useful still are the many rubrics, checklists, and guidelines for managing the assessment. One of the most attractive features of this assessment is its range. For example, Word Analysis includes phonics assessments appropriate for early readers (e.g., consonant and short vowel sounds) but also includes solid assessments of multisyllabic words. The passages are short, but interesting, expository texts that may also provide useful supplementary information to some teachers. Of course, the convenience of this diagnostic inventory means that it is short, which may affect its reliability. Used cautiously and as an indicator that may point to areas requiring further exploration, this is a good assessment. Teachers and interventionists should also be aware that this assessment is coordinated with an unusual, and potentially very useful, resource called the Trial Teaching Strategies (TTS), which provide further diagnostic information about individual students and point to appropriate instruction and intervention.

Another test that has been used widely, especially for screening purposes, is the PALS-3 (*Phonological Awareness of Literacy Screening*, 2003). It includes measures of word recognition, spelling, oral reading in context, fluency, and phonological aspects of reading. It was reviewed more fully in Chapter 7.

Woodcock Reading Mastery Test—Revised Normative Update.   The WRMT-R/NU (Woodcock, 1987/1998) is a battery of individually administered tests designed to diagnose students' readiness for reading and assess their mastery of various components of the reading process. The six distinct subtests are grouped and reported as a readiness cluster, a basic skills cluster, and a comprehension cluster. There are two parallel forms of the WRMT-R/NU. Form G contains all three clusters, and Form H is used to measure basic skills and comprehension only (see Figure 9.35). Although the test itself is unchanged from the 1987 edition, the 1998 edition includes new norms and new components on several record forms. As Salvia and Ysseldyke (2007) note, "the difficulty with normative updates is that the content is unchanged . . . [and] normative updates will probably not fix problems associated with reliability and validity" (p. 114). This concern is applicable to the WRMT-R/NU.

FIGURE 9.35   Table of the WRMT-R Subtests and the Clusters

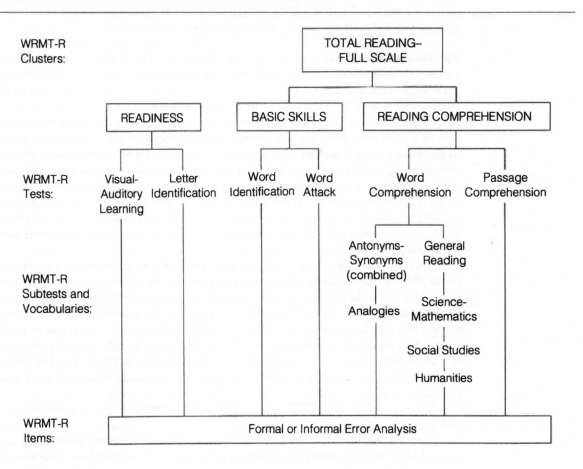

Test or Subtest

Readiness Cluster (Form G only)
Test 1: Visual-Auditory Learning
Test 2: Letter Identification

Supplementary Letter Checklist
Capital Letters
Lowercase Letters

Basic Skills Cluster
Test 3: Word Identification
Test 4: Word Attack

Reading Comprehension Cluster
Test 5: Word Comprehension

Subtests
Antonyms-Synonyms (combined)
Analogies

Vocabularies
General Reading
Science-Mathematics
Social Studies
Humanities

Test 6: Passage Comprehension

The WRMT-R/NU is untimed, requires between forty-five and ninety minutes to administer, and emphasizes norm-referenced interpretations. It is designed for use with students from kindergarten through college. This test provides several options for scoring and interpretation. Included among these are percentile ranks for total reading score and relative performance indices (RPIs) for subtests. RPIs indicate the individual student's percentage of mastery for tasks that the norming group performed with ease (90 percent mastery). With somewhat more effort, it is also possible to generate grade and age equivalents, a variety of standard scores, and confidence bands for the RPIs.

The test manual provides little documentation of validity, so it is left to users to decide whether reading has been appropriately tested by the subtests. The readiness cluster contains two subtests: Visual-Auditory Learning and Letter Identification, and Word Identification. The Visual-Auditory Learning subtest, taken from the *Woodcock-Johnson Psycho-Educational Battery* (Woodcock, 1978), requires students to learn rebus-like graphics for familiar words and use them for reading sentences. On the Letter Identification subtest, students are asked to name twenty-seven capital letters and thirty-six lowercase letters written in several different typefaces; this is the only criterion-referenced portion of the WRMT-R/NU.

The basic skills cluster also contains two subtests: Word Identification and Word Attack. The Word Identification subtest requires students to read real words in isolation. On the Word Attack subtest, students encounter forty-five nonsense words used to measure phonic and structural analysis skills. This subtest is among the most controversial, since many critics feel that reading nonsense words in isolation does not parallel normal reading. Clearly, the reader can neither check the approximation against known vocabulary words nor use the syntactic and semantic clues available in connected text. The WRMT-R/NU authors defend its use, however, arguing that this does approximate real-life decoding (Woodcock, 1987/1998, p. 6).

The comprehension cluster comprises word comprehension and passage comprehension. The Word Comprehension test has been expanded in this latest edition, and students are now required to display word knowledge by generating antonyms, synonyms, and analogies on three separate sections on the test. The Passage Comprehension subtest consists of sixty-eight sentences or short paragraphs, each containing a missing word (a modified cloze activity). Students are required to read each segment and supply the missing word.

Norming procedures for the WRMT-R/NU are reasonable. As compared to the previous normative group, the students studied for the 1998 edition whose performance was below average scored lower in most grades on most subjects. Generally speaking, this means that below-average scorers will earn higher percentile ranks and standard scores than they would under the norms of the past edition. Grade- and age-equivalent scores, however, will be very similar. None of the validity and reliability studies were revised with the normative update. Particularly given this fact, the manual reports somewhat dated information, asserting acceptable evidence of concurrent validity with unspecified editions of the *Iowa Test of Basic Skills*, PIAT reading subtest, and the WRAT reading subtest (see Woodcock, 1987/1998, p. 100). Internal consistency reliability coefficients are reported for all subtests and range from .34 on letter recognition to .98 on word identification. The reliabilities for all clusters are above .80, and most are above .90. No test-retest reliability data are provided.

The results of the WRMT-R/NU will be most helpful to teachers with a skills approach to teaching reading. In addition, general areas of difficulty can be highlighted by using the clusters, making it useful in identifying students for special and remedial services. However, we believe that this test should be used cautiously, recognizing that it provides little new information to those who have extensive diagnostic information from other sources.

Comprehensive Test of Phonological Processing.   The CTOPP (Wagner, Torgeson, & Rashotte, 1999) is designed for use in identifying individuals who are significantly below their peers in phonological abilities, determining their strengths and weaknesses, and documenting progress in the development of phonological processes.

There are two versions of the CTOPP, one for use with students ages 5 to 6 and one for use with individuals ages 7 to 24. Both versions contain three composite components:

> *Phonological Awareness Quotient* (PAQ) measures an individual's awareness and access to the phonological structure of oral language. Subtests: Elision (segmenting), Blending Words, Sound Matching

> *Phonological Memory Quotient* (PMQ) measures ability to code information phonologically for temporary storage in short-term memory. Related subtests: Memory for Digits and Nonword Repetition

> *Rapid Naming Quotient* (RNQ) measures ability to retrieve phonological information from long-term memory and ability to execute a sequence of operations quickly. Subtests: Rapid Color Naming, Rapid Object Naming

Both versions also have a supplemental subtest called "Blending Nonwords," and Version 2 contains additional supplemental composites and subtests for blending, segmenting, and rapid naming.

As evidence of content-related validity, the authors describe a theoretical framework for evaluating phonological processing and use the framework to provide a rationale for the three composites in each of the two versions. The authors also provide a discussion of relevant research that supports the inclusion of content for each subtest along with statistical data to support the appropriateness of items using an item analysis. Finally, they examine the relationship between content and external factors, specifically bias associated with particular groups, to demonstrate that the test items contain little or no bias. Items that appeared to be biased against one group were removed.

Evidence of criterion-related validity was provided for several indicators. Correlations between the CTOPP and the Woodcock Reading Mastery Tests—Revised (WRMT-R/NU) indicate the validity of the test with regard to decoding, word identification, and word analysis. There were also high correlations between the CTOPP and the Test of Word Reading Efficiency (see below) with regard to sight-word efficiency and phonetic decoding. Confirmatory factor analysis results support the construct validity of the CTOPP, although the correlations for some subtests are modest at best.

Memory for digits, for example, is consistently lower than most other subtests in its relation to other criteria.

The average reliability coefficient ranged from .77 to .90 on subtests and from .83 to .95 for the composites, suggesting acceptable levels of reliability for most purposes. However, subtest scores are less reliable than the composite scores and should be interpreted very cautiously, if at all. The authors caution users against using CTOPP results for individual instructional planning, suggesting instead that they be used as part of a more comprehensive assessment. Although the CTOPP was normed on a representative sample of more than 1,600 individuals ranging in age from five through twenty-four, more than half of the sample came from students in grades K–5, so it could be expected to be more reliable at those ages or grades.

Although the authors make a reasonable case for the assessment of phonological processing, they provide less-compelling evidence that such extensive consideration of phonological processing has validity for individuals beyond grade 3—even individuals with reading difficulty. The available research on phonological processes has been done almost exclusively with young children or early emergent readers. In short, there is little reason to believe that among older readers performance on this assessment will provide important distinctions among readers and reading abilities. For younger, struggling readers, this test is a welcome addition to the toolbox.

Test of Reading Comprehension, Third Edition.   The TORC-3 (Brown et al., 1995) is a silent reading test designed for use with students ages 7 to 17. The test should be administered individually, although group administration is possible. The four subtests of the TORC-3 are General Vocabulary, Syntactic Similarity, Paragraph Reading (which contains no nonfiction paragraphs), and Sentence Sequencing. Optional subject-area vocabulary subtests are available as well. Scores from required subtests are combined to determine a basic comprehension score, expressed as a reading comprehension quotient (RCQ). Raw scores can also be converted to standard scores, percentile ranks, and grade equivalents.

In addition to information about general reading comprehension ability, diagnostic information of a sort can be generated by comparing results from the various subtests. Other than Paragraph Reading, the subtests represent fairly unusual assessment formats and techniques. General Vocabulary, for example, requires students to read and consider three words that are related in some way by meaning. Then the students read four other words, selecting two of the four that are most closely related to the original three. The Syntactic Similarity test requires students to select two sentences that have the same meaning expressed with different syntactic structure, and the Sentence Sequencing test requires students to reorder randomly presented sentences into meaningful paragraphs.

Two types of content-related evidence of validity are provided for the TORC-3: a rationale for the content and format of the subtests as well as a rationale for the procedures used to select items. Criterion-related evidence of validity is provided in the form of correlation coefficients from six studies comparing the TORC-3 with other measures of reading comprehension. Median correlations for the subtests across measures range from .45 to .60. Construct-related evidence of validity is provided through a procedure that first identifies constructs that are presumed to account for test performance, then generates hypotheses based on these constructs, and finally tests these hypotheses either logically or empirically. Despite this evidence, some are still concerned that this test does not adequately represent the types of abilities necessary to read and understand connected text (see Perlman, 1998). Certainly, there is no doubt that the test formats are not a comprehensive representation of the types of texts and tasks that teachers would typically recognize as "comprehension"—a fact that the authors acknowledge.

All new normative data for the TORC-3 were collected in 1993 to 1994. The sample appears to be representative based on the 1990 census data and included students with disabilities who were enrolled in general classes. The reported reliability coefficients of the RCQ are above .90 for all age groups and range from .85 to .97 on the subtests. The test-retest reliability coefficients reported for a small sample of high school students are .85 for the RCQ and range from .79 to .88 on the subtests. The standard error of the means (SEM) is 1 for the subtests and 3 for the RCQ at every age level.

Given the evidence regarding reliability and our own assessment of the tasks on the TORC-3, it is likely that the test is more suitable for use with older than younger students in the seven-to-seventeen age range.

The TORC-3 provides reasonable evidence of the overall reading comprehension ability of individual students using the RCQ score. However, diagnostic information derived from subtest analysis is likely to be both less reliable and less valid. The information generated from the TORC will be most useful in meeting federal or state guidelines for screening purposes.

DIAGNOSTIC EVIDENCE FROM FORMATIVE AND DIAGNOSTIC ASSESSMENTS

Tha'm

Because Tha'm has been in the same school throughout her career, and because they engage in continuous monitoring practices, there are many indications of her reading and writing abilities. The end-of-theme tests from the core program reveal a student who is quite successful instructionally in grade-appropriate materials. The support of the reading group and the limited discourse are supportive of her reading development.

Formative classroom measures of fluency and running records of accuracy generally support the conclusion that Tha'm is a good reader. She can also locate details and often speaks quite knowledgeably about the text-explicit content of selections. In other words, she looks quite capable in both comprehension and word recognition.

However, a closer inspection using the diagnostic assessments described in this chapter raises some questions. They provide a more nuanced picture that places Tha'm at some risk. For example, the miscue analysis suggests that, despite good oral language skills, Tha'm is still not proficient in the morphological and syntactic structure of English. Even on the word lists that accompany the QRI, Tha'm made errors that reflect this difficulty (e.g., *illustrate* for *illustrated*; *guard* for *guarded*; and *adventure* for *adventurer*). The vast majority of her miscues occur at morphological word endings. Somewhat surprisingly, some measures of fluency reveal strength in this area. Tha'm consistently maintains good smoothness and prosody while reading connected text. During full-text reading, Tha'm sounds like a confident reader too, except that she regularly rushes past multisyllabic words, frequently substituting similar-sounding nonsense words ("callerpillar" for *caterpillar*, "finimans" for *victims*).

These miscues point to some vocabulary weakness that needs to be explored. Her discussions and retellings contain malapropisms, and she often substitutes more-general words "and stuff" for specific words and labels. Specialized (Tier 3) vocabulary poses special problems. Words like *nutritious* or *digestive* often get reduced to nonsense words ("nutrison" and "distat"). However, more-sophisticated everyday words are also absent from her oral vocabulary (recall *pupils/puppets*, "finimous"/*victims*).

Across many texts, Tha'm seems to struggle to identify the theme, major problems, or main idea. While she can recall a great deal of verbatim information, she is not adept at identifying key information and often does not generate the appropriate inferences required for deeper comprehension. Finally, Tha'm seems to have trouble generating cross-text inferences that go beyond the text. This is especially problematic because she does not typically reexamine conclusions, even when they are quite outrageous. Thus, she felt comfortable concluding that a "boss plant" was setting traps for insects in the Venus Flytrap. Similarly, her unscientific conclusion about the camels hump was that camels "save food at the lump, so when they're hungry they can take it out and eat." This concrete thinking is a matter of concern as Tha'm goes into middle school.

Kyle

In addition to the periodic benchmark progress monitoring used regularly in Kyle's school (see Chapter 8), Kyle's teacher used formative classroom assessment as part of her regular classroom practice. Running records had been collected on Kyle since late kindergarten. These revealed a struggling reader who nevertheless had gained considerable knowledge. By fall of second grade, Kyle was gaining ground on his age peers. As we have seen, he was still struggling with word-level skills, both graphophonic and sight. His comprehension was very good except when his serious word recognition difficulties limited his ability to use his excellent language and prior knowledge.

Over the course of three years, Kyle experienced very good classroom instruction, and both the periodic progress monitoring and the closer diagnostic assessments suggested that he was closing the gap between his knowledge/skill and that of his peers. However, both his teacher and his parents remained concerned, and he was referred to a university summer reading program. Between grades 2 and 3, Kyle participated in a summer reading program where they administered the QRI. The miscue analysis conducted at that time clearly revealed a dramatically increased ability to self-correct and an ability to read materials without benefit of picture cues. The only remaining difficulties in word recognition involved longer, multisyllabic words. In short, Kyle's word recognition abilities were reaching independence.

FIGURE 9.36a
Edited Writing:
Grade 2, Kyle

Dear Animals of the Earth

Kyle

May 10

Dear Animals of the Earth,

I give you your mountains. I give you your habitats. I am
your mother. I am the earth. I am just as small as you are in
this big universe of planets and galaxies. The people are your
brothers and sisters even though they pollute my skies and
oceans. I am working on a letter to the humans to tell them
that you are their brothers and sisters and the beauty they
are destroying and soon, I will be so sick. I will die and there
will be no more earth.

Love,
Mother Earth

Kyle's writing was a somewhat different story. While conceptually very interesting,
he had not yet reached the transitional stage of spelling development. In Kyle's diagnostic portfolio are two pieces of writing produced by Kyle in the same two-week period in
May that show this clearly. Kyle's earth letter (Figure 9.36a) is the result of a conference
and teacher-editorial support during the writing stage. It reflects his significant interest
in nonfiction topics and his willingness to stick with difficult writing tasks. Kyle's self-
initiated writing (see Figure 9.36b) reveals that he is still struggling with the mechanics
of writing.

At the end of the summer program, Kyle's performance was evaluated using the
QRI (see Chapter 8). Both his word recognition accuracy and his comprehension were
above grade level. These results clearly showed that Kyle had become a strong and still-
improving reader who could handle material at and above his grade placement. His written
language abilities remained problematic, requiring further attention over time.

FIGURE 9.36b
Self-Initiated
Writing:
Grade 2, Kyle

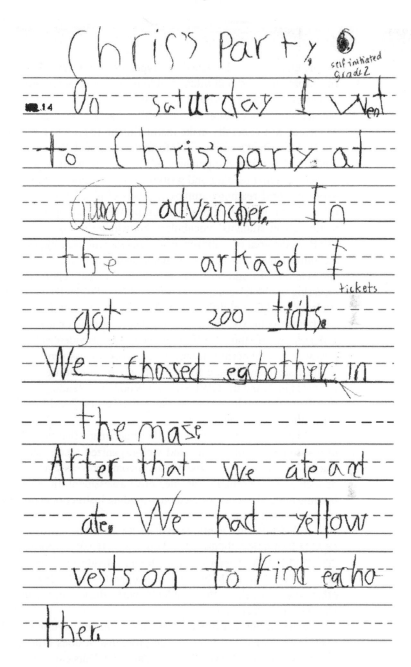

Chris's Party
On Saturday, I went to Chris's party at Jungle Adventure. In the arcade I got 200 tickets. We chased one another in the maze. After that we ate and ate. We had yellow vests on to find each other.

CHAPTER SUMMARY

In this chapter, we described the types of assessment that provide instructionally useful information for individual children. Although screening assessments and structured inventories—administered to all or most students—can provide very good data for making decisions about students' general status, a more elaborated assessment of strengths and needs will generally make instruction more effective for struggling readers and writers. We described a number of informal assessment strategies for evaluating specific components of reading competence. We suggested ways to gather information as students engage in actual reading and writing activities. For example, we described how existing data from oral reading samples can be examined using miscue analysis procedures to extend its utility and inform instruction. We also described methods for gathering information about students' vocabulary knowledge, using strategies such as free recall and PReP. In the area of comprehension assessment, we suggested techniques for enhancing the information that can be gathered using traditional techniques such as questioning and retelling. In addition, we described a verbal report, or think-aloud, procedure for assessing students' comprehension abilities. Strategies for gathering information about students' studying abilities were also discussed, stressing the need to assess this area in naturalistic contexts. Finally, several techniques for assessing writing were described, and a section of student self-assessment was provided as well. Finally, we identified and reviewed several norm-referenced diagnostic assessments that are likely to remain as part of the assessment picture for students at risk of reading and writing difficulty. The tests reviewed included the OWLS-II, the Woodcock Reading Mastery Tests, the Comprehensive Test of Phonological Processing, the Test of Word Reading Efficiency, and the Test of Reading Comprehension.

In each case, the assumption has been made that the information will become a part of a systematic, continuous, and well-organized assessment designed by well-informed teacher/evaluators. Assessment is an ongoing process. Each encounter with a student must be seen as an opportunity for interactive assessment. In this manner, teaching and testing become integral events focused on providing instructional programs that are responsive to the needs of all students.

Educators must continue to press for assessment instruments and methodologies that provide instructionally useful and contextually valid information. The assessment efforts described in this chapter can and should provide much more specific information about how and what to teach, but they are suggestive only. Ingenious teachers will find many other ways to evaluate their students' performance for the purpose of making placement and curricular decisions.

Most of the assessment strategies we have suggested can be easily incorporated in daily instructional and intervention programs. It does little good to evaluate component skills if we do not observe them in action. Students can, and often do, perform differently on tests of isolated skill or on tasks in constrained and artificial environments than they do in real classrooms accomplishing real assignments.

MyEducationLab™

Go to the Topics, Reading Assessment, Oral Language, Vocabulary, Fluency, Word Recognition, Reading Comprehension, and Reading and Writing, in the MyEducationLab (www.myeducationlab.com) for your course, where you can:

- Find learning outcomes for Reading Assessment, Oral Language, Vocabulary, Fluency, Word Recognition, Reading Comprehension, and Reading and Writing, along with the national standards that connect to these outcomes.

- Complete Assignments and Activities that can help you more deeply understand the chapter content.

- Apply and practice your understanding of the core teaching skills identified in the chapter using the Building Teaching Skills and Dispositions learning units.

- Examine challenging situations and cases presented in the IRIS Center Resources.

- Check your comprehension of the content covered in the chapter by going to the Study Plan in the Book Resources for your text. Here you will be able to take a chapter quiz, receive feedback on your answers, and then access Review, Practice, and Enrichment activities to enhance your understanding of chapter content.

A+RISE A+RISE® Standards2Strategy™ is an innovative and interactive online resource that offers new teachers in grades K-12 just in time, research-based instructional strategies that meet the linguistic needs of ELLs as they learn content, differentiate instruction for all grades and abilities, and are aligned to Common Core Elementary Language Arts standards (for the literacy strategies) and to English language proficiency standards in WIDA, Texas, California, and Florida.

5
Interactions:
Assessment As Inquiry

*T*his section is central to understanding the relationship between assessment and instruction. As we noted previously, the interactive nature of the assessment-instruction process requires careful observation of the ways in which the various factors may be influencing reading, writing, and learning in individual students. The chapter stands alone because it focuses exclusively on the relationship between assessment and instruction—on that moment in the assessment process when informed decision making is required of the teacher and when that teacher's expertise and knowledge will determine how the instructional planning to follow will proceed. Because reading and writing abilities are not viewed as static, teachers must be prepared to describe the variability observed within the individual student under different conditions and to engage in continued explorations of this variability through diagnostic teaching. This is also precisely the type of thinking and problem solving required to effectively implement a response to intervention (RTI) approach to identifying learning disabled students.

The steps of the assessment-instruction process that are addressed in this section are shaded in the figure that follows. They are: Step 4, Reflection, Decision Making, and Planning; and Step 5, Diagnostic Teaching and Continuous Progress Monitoring.

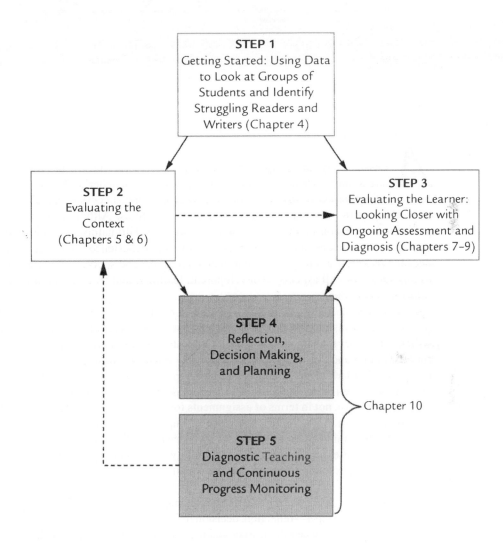

STEP 1
Getting Started: Using Data to Look at Groups of Students and Identify Struggling Readers and Writers (Chapter 4)

STEP 2
Evaluating the Context
(Chapters 5 & 6)

STEP 3
Evaluating the Learner: Looking Closer with Ongoing Assessment and Diagnosis (Chapters 7–9)

STEP 4
Reflection, Decision Making, and Planning

STEP 5
Diagnostic Teaching and Continuous Progress Monitoring

Chapter 10

CHAPTER *10*

Interactive Decision Making

*A*ssessment is not simply the gathering of information. The success of the assessment-instruction process depends on the teacher's ability to make informed, effective decisions. This too will determine the success of an RTI approach to working with students who have learning disabilities. Although we can provide guidance in decision making, we cannot prescribe it. Ultimately, the quality of decision making relies on the professional knowledge, experience, and judgment of the decision maker. Therefore, it is incumbent on teachers and specialists to learn as much as possible about all aspects of development, learning, and teaching in order to make informed decisions.

Informed decision making also requires a clear sense of the desired outcomes of the assessment-instruction process. We agree with Johnston (1987, p. 744) when he writes, "the most fundamental goal of all educational evaluation is optimal instruction for all children and evaluation practices are only legitimate to the extent that they serve this goal." Similarly, Duffy and Roehler (1989, p. 16) note that the first characteristic of teachers who are instructional decision makers is that they "think in terms of what students should learn, not in terms of assignments for students to complete." We would also like to emphasize the value of experience in implementing the assessment-instruction process for becoming an expert evaluator and decision maker. One of the most important characteristics of expert evaluators is their ability to recognize patterns. They know not only what patterns to look for, but also the conditions under which the patterns are most likely to occur.

This chapter addresses the understanding and implementation of two steps in the assessment process. Step 4—reflection, decision making, and planning—involves evaluating the existing match between the learner and the context. It also involves making decisions about what might improve the match as well as implementing an initial plan. We also address Step 5, diagnostic teaching and progress monitoring. The first half of the chapter addresses the understanding of the procedures involved in these two steps. The second half of the chapter illustrates the implementation of these steps through the use of several case studies.

UNDERSTANDING STEP 4: REFLECTION, DECISION MAKING, AND PLANNING

Evaluating the Match between Learner and Context

Using the information gathered in earlier stages of the assessment process, we evaluate the match between the knowledge, skills, and motivation of the learner and the instructional environments, settings, practices, and resources within the instructional context. We are working to answer the question "What is the current status of the interaction between the learner and the instructional context?" Our job in this stage of the assessment-instruction process is to pull together all that we know as the result of our professional efforts and experience and to evaluate how well existing demands, expectations, and supports of the context match the learner's abilities, interests, knowledge, and level of independence. Using our framework, Vogt and Shearer (2003) proposed what they call a contextualized assessment cycle. In their modified plan, they noted that professionals need to think of assessment as inquiry, asking questions such as:

- What do I know?
- What do I observe?
- What questions do I need to ask?
- What (additional) data do I need to collect?

As we examine the match between the learner and the instructional context, we are likely to find information about areas in which the fit is good—where the student is learning and improving. We are also likely to find areas where the match is weak—where the student is not making progress or closing the gap with peers. The information in this section comes both from an evaluation of interactions between learner and contextual factors and from an evaluation of how the student's performance varies under different conditions during assessment.

By the time we get to this step in the process, many of the successful and unsuccessful interactions will be obvious. If we are still uncertain about how the learner and the context interact in ways that either facilitate or inhibit learning and performance, we can examine the information in each of the categories of learner factors (background, knowledge about reading or writing, skills application, and attitudes and motivation) and ask ourselves how it fits with what we know about the contextual factors (settings, methods, and materials and tasks) and vice versa.

For example, the information about skills application might suggest that a particular reader does not fully analyze decodable words, failing to look through the entire word. As a result, she is not making use of orthographic patterns. The information about methods indicates that the reader's teacher focuses on helping students to acquire strategies and promote a decoding-by-analogy approach to word recognition. This is a good match, because this instruction is likely to meet the reader's need to develop her abilities to fully examine words in print and enhance fluency. Conversely, in the case of a particular writer, information about materials may suggest that writing instruction relies almost exclusively on drill sheets with brief sentences and that the writer performs better when producing stories to be shared with an audience. This is not a good match, because the writer needs different materials to facilitate learning. Other examples of poor matches that might be observed include the following:

- A third-grade student who has recently arrived in the United States, with limited English proficiency and limited native-language literacy, is placed in a program that addresses only English acquisition and vocabulary development, with no focus on building print skills in either language.
- An eighth-grade student who does not read independently in or out of school, whose sight vocabulary and word analysis skills are below grade level on tests of isolated skills but closer to grade level when reading coherent, full-length selections, is receiving isolated word analysis skill-drill and is not permitted to advance beyond these isolated practices because of his weak performance on criterion tests of those skills.
- A highly verbal first-grade student who does not have the concept of a word, nor can he voice-point, receives instruction that does not include writing with invented spelling or any explicit explanation about the conventions of print and the purposes of learning to read or write.

Although it will often be quite clear how effectively the instruction and the student's needs are matched, there are times when conclusions remain ambiguous. In these cases, we need to carry our questions and concerns into the next step. In other cases, we will have concluded that aspects of the match are clearly inappropriate, and in these cases, our questions and concerns will involve generating hypotheses about ways to remedy the mismatch. In either case, it is time to step back and really think about what we know or suspect and what can be done about it.

Generating Hypotheses

Once we have drawn some conclusions about the match between the learner and the context, we naturally ask questions such as: What does the learner need? What needs to be continued? What needs to be changed? This requires reflection—and, often, collaborative conversation with colleagues. It is at this stage that professional learning communities (PLCs) or data teams can be especially helpful. As professionals explore the data about individual students, different perspectives may emerge. It is helpful to have these different perspectives in generating hypotheses about what students need. This step will be absolutely essential in decisions about which interventions are appropriate in the implementation of an RTI approach with specific students. In an RTI approach, collaborative teams document and discuss the information about instruction and performance. At this point in the process, we already know a great deal about what the learner needs as a result of our previous analyses. Other things will still be unclear, however, and we need to begin to make some decisions about the relative importance of the various problems or needs we have identified.

Remember that we can always find a problem if we are looking for one but that not every problem is of equal importance to the student's progress. In evaluating the importance of the problem(s) we have identified, we should ask ourselves, "If I changed the source of interference, is this student likely to become a better reader or writer?" If the answer is no or we suspect that this intervention is unlikely to go very far in solving the problem, the problem we have identified is probably not a primary source of difficulty.

Another guide to determining what the learner needs is to reexamine the information gathered about the learner and the instructional context to determine whether any of the materials, methods, or settings were more effective than others. It is important to remember that we cannot decide what the learner needs without knowing the context in which the problem exists. Otherwise, we look only to the learner for the source of the problem, when in fact it is more often the interaction between learner and context.

For example, a writer with sufficient skill and major anxiety or attitude problems may display skill deficiencies but does not need more skill instruction. What is needed instead is instruction that supports and motivates the practice and application of known skills. Additional examples of this include instruction that capitalizes on strengths while attending to weaknesses; changes perceptions of the purposes and goals of reading and writing; or explains the how, when, and why of strategy usage rather than simply providing practice.

Generating hypotheses about students' needs is always a matter of informed decision making. It requires the use of all our knowledge and experience. Examples of specific student-needs hypotheses are as follows:

- A third-grade student with adequate word recognition skill and poor comprehension who is most often evaluated in terms of correct words per minute in oral reading may need instruction that promotes understanding of the goals of reading, the development of comprehension strategies, and/or vocabulary support.
- A student in kindergarten who does not understand print concepts but is receiving phonics instruction may need exposure to written language in a variety of contexts.
- An eighth-grade student with adequate reading skills who is uninterested and unmotivated to complete assigned reading activities and to read in or out of school may need instruction that interests and motivates him.
- A fourth-grade student who functions well at a second-grade level but is placed in a fourth-grade reader may need opportunities to read instructional-level materials.
- A first-grade student who overrelies on context but is placed primarily in predictable books may need materials that will facilitate/require greater attention to other word recognition/decoding strategies.
- A second-grade student whose cultural background promotes reticence in public interactions and who does not engage in challenging discussions of books in class may need models of how to reflect on familiar stories in nonthreatening ways—perhaps initially in a reading response log.

It is also important to recognize that many of these potential needs would never be identified if students were not examined within the instructional contexts in which their problems exist. Once hypotheses about learner needs have been generated and prioritized, we can begin planning the diagnostic teaching activities that will be used to evaluate the hypotheses.

UNDERSTANDING STEP 5: DIAGNOSTIC TEACHING AND PROGRESS MONITORING

Following Step 4, in which we reflected on the existing match and generated some preliminary hypotheses about what the learner needs, we need to address the question of what is most likely to (re)establish learning. At this point in the process, we are concerned with identifying a better or optimal match between the learner and the instructional context. To accomplish this goal, we rely primarily on the technique of *diagnostic teaching*. The following sections describe the purposes and procedures of diagnostic teaching. As well, this section addresses issues related to monitoring progress for individual students—an essential element of both successful diagnostic teaching and contemporary approaches to RTI.

Definition and Purposes of Diagnostic Teaching

The idea that we might use a student's response to instruction as a diagnostic procedure is not a new one. According to Harris and Sipay (1990), the procedure was developed first by Harris and Roswell in 1953. Current interest in interactive views of learning and in the value of diagnostic teaching as a tool within an RTI approach have resulted in significant advances in the development and implementation of these techniques. These types of procedures are referred to variously as *trial teaching* (Tzuriel, 2000), *dynamic assessment* (Feuerstein, Rand, & Hoffman, 1979; Lidz, 1991, 2001; Poehner, 2008), *intervention assessment* (Paratore & Indrisano, 1987), *contextualized assessment* (APA, n.d.), and *diagnostic teaching* (Harris, 1977; Wixson & Lipson, 1986). Although there are differences among these related procedures, they do share a critical feature: they are interactive assessments that provide for systematic modification of the instructional situation to observe what a student does under specified conditions.

Contemporary researchers have made the point that these approaches may be used in the context of different purposes—either to estimate the capacity of an individual student or to try out the efficacy of an intervention (Poehner, 2008). In the first case, the processes are usually employed only briefly as part of an ongoing assessment. In the latter case, the procedures may be used over a much longer period. We prefer the term *diagnostic teaching* because it reflects the dual purposes for which we use this procedure. First, the procedure is *diagnostic* because it allows us to collect additional information to clarify and test the hypotheses generated during the initial steps of the assessment-instruction process. Second, the procedure is *instructional* because it provides opportunities to try out methods that may be successful alternatives for working with a student. This last is a critical feature of diagnostic teaching because it allows us to explore a student's performance under circumstances that are more like those encountered in the classroom on a regular basis or that might represent small adjustments to classroom practice that could result in improved performance. In many respects, this is the logic behind the RTI approach to working with students who are struggling. By intervening in the classroom first, it is likely that some students' problems will be addressed satisfactorily, which then eliminates the need for a more comprehensive evaluation for the purpose of identifying a learning disability. Indeed, Fuchs and his colleagues (2011) have recently suggested that instruction (and students' response to it) should be viewed as the "test" in RTI.

Throughout this book, we have introduced numerous cautions, caveats, and concerns about traditional assessment practices. Diagnostic teaching procedures are flourishing, in part, as a response to these difficulties. The failure to test students under a range of conditions that represent authentic reading and writing events can result in both inaccurate diagnoses and erroneous conclusions about the focus for intervention.

Another reason why diagnostic teaching is enjoying such prominence is its utility in assessing students from linguistically and/or culturally diverse backgrounds (see Brice, 2002; O'Malley & Valdez-Pierce, 1996; Peña et al., 2006; Poehner, 2008). Problems with the static, product-oriented results of traditional assessments have raised serious questions about *equity* issues in assessment, particularly with the use of standardized tests of achievement and intelligence. For example, Campione and Brown (1987) note that although the scores individuals attain on static tests represent only estimates of competence, all too often the unwarranted inference is made that they are measures of ability level that are relatively permanent and resistant to change (see Sternberg, 1999, 2001). In many cases, particularly for children from culturally different backgrounds, these scores provide a dramatic underestimate of the potential level of performance under different circumstances. Clearly, most conventional assessments provide flawed information about bilingual students and others from diverse cultural communities, leading to a disproportionate representation of these students in special education (NASDSE, 1994a, 1994b). According to Wilson-Portuondo and Hardy (2001, p. 1), "It is important during the process of evaluation to understand and recognize normal difficulties resulting from the process of acculturation or to learning a second language from a disability." A significant body of evidence supports the conclusion that diagnostic teaching/dynamic assessment procedures provide better measures of learning potential by evaluating how a student can and will perform under different conditions (Day & Cordon, 1993; Lidz, 2001; Spector, 1992).

Finally, diagnostic teaching or interactive assessment techniques have gained traction because traditional assessments, focused on classifying or measuring students' abilities, do not typically provide much direction for instruction. As Haywood and Lidz (2006) point out,

> The role of dynamic assessment is to identify obstacles to more effective learning and performance, to find ways to overcome those obstacles, and to assess the effects of removal of obstacles on subsequent learning and performance effectiveness. By extension of that role, a goal is to suggest what can be done to defeat the pessimistic predictions that are often made on the basis of results of standardized, normative tests. . . . (p. 3)

The assessment procedures described in the preceding chapters are predicated on the assumption that we need to collect information about a range of learner and contextual factors. Until now, we have not really suggested gathering information specifically to confirm predictions about the nature of the problem and how to address it. However, diagnostic teaching is hypothesis driven. It assumes that teachers are intentionally setting out to examine more closely something that has come to their attention.

Most assessments can be modified to gather information about the impact of contextual factors, and a comprehensive assessment should include this information. Indeed, the American Psychological Association, in an advisory document (n.d.), recommended that any identification of a student for learning disability (LD) include "contextualized assessment . . . [to] reduce false positive and false negative diagnostic errors" (p. 4).

As well, most instruction can be modified to include diagnostic teaching, particularly if it is carefully planned using our best predictions about what may work for a given student and if we are prepared to monitor our work continually to see how adjustments have affected learning and performance. Diagnostic teaching permits the teacher to manipulate in a planned way any of the factors that are suspected to be contributing to or inhibiting reading and writing achievement. In addition, diagnostic teaching allows us to explore the "conditions that call forth learning" (Hunt, 1961).

Skilled teachers consistently engage in diagnostic teaching and recognize the value of the instructional information it yields. However, most teachers have undervalued the assessment information that is generated and failed to document the data gleaned during instructional exchanges. This is likely to change as more educators apply the technique to the real-world problems of identifying and classifying students and as more general education teachers become proficient using an RTI approach to working with students experiencing reading and writing problems (Haywood & Lidz, 2006). Without diagnostic teaching, we have few alternatives but to believe that all students with similar presenting problems will benefit from the same instructional program. Diagnostic teaching provides an opportunity for truly integrating instruction and assessment, and recent research suggests that there is value added by using dynamic assessment measures to the information available about students (Fuchs et al., 2011).

Diagnostic Teaching Procedures

The procedures used for diagnostic teaching vary considerably from situation to situation. Because each situation is unique, it is impossible to provide step-by-step procedures for conducting diagnostic teaching sessions. However, we can describe the process of diagnostic teaching, including its characteristics and tasks. The process we describe below involves three related tasks: planning, executing, and evaluating the diagnostic teaching effort(s).

Planning. Certainly, it is possible to engage in spontaneous diagnostic teaching; opportunistic adaptation in the face of student responses is exactly what many highly skilled and experienced teachers do on a regular basis. As part of a comprehensive assessment plan, however, planning is required. When we decide to use diagnostic teaching procedures, we focus our efforts on specific components, rather than continuing to gather more general information. We have noted elsewhere in this text that assessment should be continuous and that diagnostic information is available any time we work with a student. However, we are using diagnostic teaching here to describe specific, intentional activity rather than a general mind-set for observing instructional interactions. This perspective is also consistent with the initial interventions recommended as part of RTI.

It is important to keep in mind that we are attempting to verify hunches about both the source of the problem and the instructional manipulations that are most likely to call forth learning. Because of this dual focus, diagnostic teaching requires modification and manipulation of learners and instructional contexts. To identify a student's potential for learning under different instructional conditions or the factors and conditions that facilitate or inhibit learning, we need to view diagnostic teaching as "an interaction between an examiner-as-intervener and a learner-as-active-participant, which seeks to estimate the degree of modifiability of the learner and the means by which positive changes in cognitive functioning can be induced and maintained" (Lidz, 1987, p. 4).

During planning, we need to determine how we will focus the diagnostic teaching to address areas that need further exploration. As we have stated, the problems learners experience often lie in the interaction between the knowledge, skills, and motivation of the learner and the settings, methods, and materials of the instructional context. When it comes to diagnostic teaching, however, it is easier to think about the contextual factors that can and should be altered than about manipulating learner factors. We are focusing simultaneously on "what the *learner* needs" and on aspects of the instructional environments, settings, practices, and resources that are amenable to modification and manipulation (Campione & Brown, 1987; Paratore & Indrisano, 1987; Walker, 2007).

Changing the Setting. Using the elements of the context described in Chapters 5 and 6, the first area we might consider manipulating is the instructional setting. For example, we might consider modifications of the instructional setting as a means of altering the student's goals for literacy learning, which are often acquired from the instructional context. We might also consider altering the organization of instructional activities and groups (for example, from lecture to discussion or from a teacher-led group to a cooperative work group or individual instruction). Finally, we might consider altering the interaction patterns or "participation structures" used during instruction (e.g., from asking "known answer" questions to more student-centered open discussion or peer writing conferences).

Changing the Methods. The methods of instruction make up a second element of the instructional context we might consider manipulating. Within this area, we might consider altering what is being taught (focus) and/or how it is being taught (approach). For example, we might consider changing the focus of writing lessons from a heavy emphasis on individual skill instruction to the practice and application of skills in the service of writing for real audiences.

We might also wish to consider altering the methods of instruction being used to create motivated and/or strategic learning. For example, we might wish to change from extrinsic motivational techniques to those that are designed to enhance a student's desire to understand rather than simply comply with directions. We might also consider moving from methods that rely heavily on independent student practice to those that provide increased teacher support during the initial stages of learning. Some authors have suggested systematically varying the level of teacher support in the administration of traditional assessment procedures as a means of obtaining better instructional information. For example, Cioffi and Carney (1983) suggest a variety of modifications for administering an IRI, including eliminating time constraints, providing appropriate prereading instruction, observing miscues under prepared and unprepared conditions, and introducing instructional aids as needed. During each of these manipulations, the examiner takes careful note of the student's response.

Changing the Materials and Tasks.   The third area of the instructional context we might consider manipulating in diagnostic teaching consists of materials and tasks. The *characteristics of the texts* a student is reading can have a profound effect on learning and performance and are therefore serious candidates for manipulation. Those that are easily modified include:

- Text type (for example, various types of stories and/or informational materials)
- Text difficulty (length, readability, familiarity, etc.)
- Text structure and organization (temporal sequence, cause-effect), coherence/ unity, and structural characteristics (headings/subheadings, illustrations, charts, italics, etc.)

Similarly, the types of writing that students are asked to produce can be powerful predictors of success and should be considered possible candidates for alterations that would lead to improved performance.

It is also important to consider how the *task demands* that are being placed on the learner might be manipulated. Specifically, we might consider altering:

- the content (cognitive complexity) and/or
- the form (purpose and procedural complexity)

This might include alterations such as changing from recognition tasks to open-ended or discussion tasks; or from low- to high-level tasks; or altering factors such as the quantity and/or mode of presentation and response (oral, written), and/or the clarity of task directions.

Generally, we should anticipate using multiple setting, method, materials, and task options as we engage in diagnostic teaching. We are really attempting to set up the diagnostic teaching to represent or test certain interactions. However, not all interactions will be tested. It is important to recall that diagnostic teaching is hypothesis driven. Only those factors and influences that appear to be likely candidates for improving learning and performance need be attempted.

Investigating.   It is clear that there are many ways to proceed with diagnostic teaching. However, it is important to keep in mind that intentionally designing diagnostic teaching sessions that provide information about how a student performs under several different or contrasting conditions can help us clarify our hypotheses about what the student needs. The many options described above suggest a variety of ways that this might be accomplished. Among the many ways we can approach diagnostic teaching sessions, we discuss two here: (1) trying out several distinct alternatives to solving a particular problem and (2) introducing different levels of support to the learner in the context of our current instruction.

If our assessment of the match between the student and the instructional context suggests that we need to identify alternative instructional methods from those currently in use, then we would likely engage in diagnostic teaching sessions that try out different instructional procedures for teaching the same content or skill. For example, we might be working with a third-grade student who we have determined is experiencing serious word recognition problems and, in addition, seems to have difficulty learning either new words or the skills needed to learn new words. Therefore, our diagnostic teaching efforts might involve trying out several distinct instructional approaches such as phonics instruction that teaches him to break the whole into component parts, phonics instruction that teaches him to blend parts into wholes, and sight-word instruction.

One possible scenario is that the results of our diagnostic teaching sessions will reveal that the student learned equally well the words he was taught using each approach. However, he may have learned the new words in the part-to-whole phonics approach and the sight-word approach in a fraction of the time it took him to learn the words using the whole-to-part phonics approach. These results, combined with the student's perception that he had learned most easily in the part-to-whole method, might then lead to the recommendation that he be taught to recognize words using a part-to-whole phonics approach.

Although examining the impact of alternative instructional approaches is a technique that has been used for many years (Mills, 1956), current innovations in pedagogy have led to broader applications. For example, this approach was used in one of the authors' clinics with an articulate sixth grader who, despite excellent word recognition skills, was struggling with comprehension. His teachers were very worried that his increasingly negative attitude toward learning would hamper his success in middle school. The alternative approaches that were tried during diagnostic teaching included prereading discussion coupled with vocabulary instruction and an alternative questioning approach called Question the Author (QtA) (Beck, McKeown, & Kucan, 2002). As noted in the previous section, there are many aspects of instruction that can be altered as we investigate the instruction that best promotes student learning.

If after evaluating the match between learner and context we determine that the instructional approach is appropriate but learning isn't progressing sufficiently, we might want to design diagnostic teaching sessions that provide the student with different levels of support to identify an optimal level for facilitating student learning. This approach uses the instructional technique of scaffolding described in Chapter 5 as an assessment device. These diagnostic teaching sessions involve the teacher or specialist presenting the student with a reading or writing activity, observing the response, and then introducing modifications of the task. These modifications are really hypotheses about "the minimal instructional adjustments necessary for the child to succeed in materials at or near his or her grade placement" (Cioffi & Carney, 1983, p. 768).

The predominant form of these modifications is introduction of "layered" prompts, or increasingly explicit hints (Day & Cordon, 1993; Fuchs et al., 2011). The prompts continue until the student can perform the desired task and it becomes clear how much support is needed. Consider the case of a reader who is not able to answer questions about a grade-level passage even though word recognition is acceptable. We could plan an intervention that provided for activating background knowledge, preteaching vocabulary, focusing purpose setting, and guided reading questions. This type of instruction represents a heavy dependence on the teacher, however. As an alternative, we could teach a lesson providing only the one component of this instructional plan that we believe is crucial to improving the match so that the reader can perform effectively. For a very young or inexperienced student, this might involve just the preteaching of vocabulary. For another student who has limited stamina for long texts, it might involve providing only the guided reading questions.

The point is that we would start with one type of minimal support and increase it only as we see that the student requires it. We would prioritize, or layer, the prompts or supports so that we can clearly identify the intervention requiring least assistance. It is sometimes even possible to generate a highly specified set of ordered hints (Brown & Campione, 1986; Campione & Brown, 1987). These hints go from least support to most support and can be documented for assessment passages as we begin to use diagnostic teaching. Imagine, for example, that a student cannot edit her own writing for spelling and mechanical errors. We can add a sequence of ordered hints such as the ones in the following lists and record the point at which the student *can* answer the question(s).

For writing:
1. What could you do to make your story easier to read/understand?
2. Where is the part that you think needs work?
3. Can you figure it out?

If the student still cannot respond appropriately:

- Ask the student to reread his or her story to find any problems.
- If the student's response is inadequate, ask the student to reread a specific piece of the text to identify a problem (that is, misspelling, word left out, punctuation missing).
- Narrow the search to a sentence or two if necessary.
- Finally, provide direct feedback if that is required.

For reading:
1. Did that make sense?
2. Can you find the "puzzling" (difficult) part of this text?
3. What can you try/do to figure it out?
4. Reread that and think about ...
   (Then continue increasing the specificity of the prompts directing students at word-level or text-level elements.)

Diagnostic teaching sessions that explore the impact of alternative methods or of different levels of support are not mutually exclusive. In fact, these and other approaches to identifying the optimal match between the learner and instruction can be, and often are, apparent in combination within a diagnostic teaching session. An example of this comes, in one of the author's clinics, from a diagnostic teaching session for a fourth-grade student with poor vocabulary knowledge. The diagnostic teaching session employed vocabulary development activities both within and outside the context of reading connected text. In addition, the procedures that accompanied the text reading included the use of layered prompts to determine the level of support necessary to enable the student to identify, learn, and apply unknown words in the context of the student's reading.

Thus far, we have emphasized the intentional, well-planned nature of diagnostic teaching. Before leaving this section, it is important to understand that diagnostic teaching is also *opportunistic* and *flexible*. This means that a knowledgeable teacher who is able to set aside his or her own preconceived ideas about what will happen, and who can listen, is likely to gather a wealth of information from which to confirm hypotheses and plan instruction (Lipson, 1996). The following exchange occurred during a diagnostic teaching session in which the tutor was using a think-aloud procedure (see Chapter 9 to explore more carefully the tutor's hunch that Andrew did not have many comprehension strategies available for use during reading).

TEACHER: Tell me what you were doing and thinking as you read that part.

ANDREW: Not much.

TEACHER: Did that part make sense to you?

ANDREW: Not really.

TEACHER: Well, do you think it would be helpful to go back and reread that part to see if you can understand it?

ANDREW: I don't know. You tell me. You're the teacher!

This rather extraordinary, and unexpected, exchange demonstrates how much students can tell us about their reading and writing if we will listen. It is true that Andrew uses few comprehension strategies during reading, but his response demonstrates the more serious fact that he is willing to be compliant but not responsible for his behaviors during reading. It appears that he approaches reading and reading instruction passively rather than as an active participant (see Johnston & Winograd, 1985).

Good diagnostic teaching requires flexibility in order to take advantage of opportunities as they arise. Over time, we develop a repertoire of both assessment and instruction procedures, which can be used to respond to unexpected results or remarks. They will only be useful, however, to the extent that we recognize what is happening when it occurs and are prepared to revise our plans on the spot. This is opportunistic assessment-instruction. In the case we just described, the teacher decided to follow up on this exchange by asking Andrew what he thought it meant to be a good reader. She confirmed her new hypothesis: he believed good reading was flawless word calling, and he relied heavily on the teacher to set purposes and to monitor both word recognition and comprehension. Consequently, he paid no attention whatsoever to meaning and could not set purposes for reading. As Woolley (2011) notes:

> Disengaged individuals often wait for teacher direction, and do not know how to interact effectively with the text, or how to assimilate the text information with their existing background knowledge (Schunk, 2004; Stanovich & Cunningham, 1993; Zimmerman, 2002). (p. 150)

In subsequent sessions, Andrew's tutor pursued a line of diagnostic teaching aimed at discovering how he might learn to be a more active participant in generating meaning from text.

Evaluating.   The examples provided above suggest that diagnostic teaching is not usually a one-time event. Diagnostic teaching is cyclical and continuous. Generally, the results of diagnostic teaching will be used either to establish a new focus for diagnostic teaching or to plan an instructional program or sequence.

> Optimal methods of instruction and levels of difficulty suggested by trial teaching thus provide the initial approaches that teachers use in remediation. However, as students progress and their needs in reading change, additional tryouts of methods and materials occur. (Chall & Curtis, 1987, p. 786)

The thrust of the evaluation of the diagnostic teaching is to determine the impact of the manipulations on the student's learning, performance, attitude, motivation, and/or knowledge. When alternative methods have been used, this involves noting similarities and differences in a student's performance, motivation, and/or knowledge during and after the administration of the different interventions.

In the case of the third-grade student described above, this might mean several different types of evaluation. First, we would probably want to posttest his learning of new words under the different instructional methods, to compare the relative effectiveness of the different interventions. Second, we would want to observe the extent to which he participated actively in each of the interventions. Other things being equal, the extent to which he was willing to engage in the instructional activities—that is, the extent to which the techniques "made sense" to him—is perhaps the most important criterion for future success. No matter how good the instructional technique, it is unlikely to be successful if the learner resists rather than participates actively.

When the scaffolding approach has been used, the evaluation would focus on a comparison of the student's learning, performance, knowledge, and/or motivation at various levels of support, from unaided to the greatest amount of support provided. The purpose of this comparison is to find an optimal level of support—that is, the level at which the student is challenged enough to learn, but not so much that he or she gives up in frustration or so little that he or she does not have to become actively involved. Regardless of the nature of the diagnostic teaching, comparisons can and should be made with information about a student's performance, skill, and motivation obtained through the observations, interviews, and formal and informal measures used in Steps 1 to 3.

We should also not overlook the invaluable information that can be gained by interviewing the student during and/or after the intervention. We have found the following types of questions to be extremely useful indicators of student learning and knowledge:

1. What do you think we are trying to learn and why? Why am I asking you to do . . . ?
2. Tell me how you figured out . . .
3. What would you have done differently if you were (I asked you to) . . . ?
4. Which procedure/activity did you like best and why? Which did you think helped you the most and why?
5. What did you learn, how do you do it, and when would you use it/how would it help you to read better (to write better)?

These simple but powerful questions can reveal a great deal about students' understanding of how to use a new skill or strategy, as well as *their* attitudes and motivation for engaging in particular activities. These questions also serve an instructional purpose in that they convey to the student the need to consider when and why a skill would be used during other reading and writing events (Paris et al., 1983).

The need to accomplish both the implementation and evaluation of diagnostic teaching as efficiently as possible is obvious. The tremendous advantage to diagnostic teaching, as we have already noted, is that it melds assessment and instruction so that we need not take a great deal of time away from teaching. At the same time, it can save months that might otherwise be wasted implementing an instructional program that has little or no impact on the learner.

Progress Monitoring

Throughout this text, we have discussed and described specific assessments. In Chapter 3, we provided an overview of the assessment-instruction process, including the various types and purposes of assessment, and also provided an example of how this process worked with one student, Jackson. In Chapter 4, we noted that the process typically starts by understanding the performance of groups of students, using (generally) standardized data from summative and screening assessments to identify students who require a closer look. In Chapters 5 and 6, we examined the context for learning to assess its potential impact on student performance. Then, in Chapters 7, 8, and 9, we described student assessment strategies and tools designed to provide more and more specific diagnostic information. This chapter bridges the assessment-instruction divide, with diagnostic teaching serving both assessment and instructional purposes.

In addition, we emphasize progress monitoring as an essential element of an effective assessment-instruction system, particularly for monitoring the progress of specific students who are receiving more intentional and tailored instruction/intervention. Wixson and Valencia (2011, pp. 467–468) provide a useful scheme for categorizing progress monitoring:

> *Formative progress monitoring* refers to data gathered during instruction to determine the appropriateness of that instruction as evidenced by student progress and to help the teacher determine how to revise it.
>
> *Benchmark progress monitoring* refers to data gather at predetermined times of the year to ascertain if students are making adequate progress in overall performance in relation to age or grade expectations or benchmarks.

Because progress monitoring has become such a central feature of school assessment systems today, we recommend careful consideration of the types and forms of assessment used and suggest a close reading of Valencia's (2011b) excellent chapter delineating the various types of assessment, their utility, and the caveats associated with each.

For now, it is important to recognize that the two types of progress monitoring described above are often not distinguished, and schools/teachers may be unfamiliar with the uses (and possible misuses) of each. Formative progress monitoring, as it was originally conceived by researchers such as Black and Wiliam (1998), includes the following characteristics:

- Embedded in day-day instruction
- Used to provide feedback to students about their progress and performance
- Used by the teacher to inform and individualize instruction

A key feature, especially in light of our discussions in this chapter about diagnostic teaching, is that the assessment is integrated within the instructional/intervention program. According to Valencia (2011):

> Because the purpose of this assessment is to determine a student's learning in light of instructional goals that are specifically appropriate for him or her, formative assessment is associated with "the pedagogy of contingency" (Wiliam, 2006, p. 6). Simply put, this means that teaching should be contingent on, or responsive to, a student's responses during instruction. (p. 390)

Interim (benchmark) progress monitoring, on the other hand, occurs less frequently and is usually focused on more-general curricular goals. Although it may inform instruction, other purposes tend to be more central. For example, periodic benchmark progress monitoring is generally used to identify any (new) students who may be struggling (see Chapter 3) and/or to monitor the efficacy of a particular program or intervention. Earlier, we addressed many of the concerns about contemporary iterations of this type of progress monitoring (see Chapters 4 and 8). Importantly, it appears that interim assessments may be useful in identifying students who are struggling, but they are less useful in actually helping teachers modify and adapt instruction in ways that improve students' learning (see Valencia, 2011). It is precisely these conclusions that have lead many educators to take a closer look at dynamic assessment and diagnostic teaching.

IMPLEMENTING STEPS 4 AND 5 OF THE ASSESSMENT-INSTRUCTION PROCESS

Thumbnail Sketch

We introduced the thumbnail sketch in Chapter 4. It is a useful way to summarize information from the various steps of the assessment-instruction process. The first column summarizes the information gathered about groups of students and allows us to identify struggling learners as part of Step 1 (Chapter 4). The second column summarizes the information gathered about the context in Step 2 (Chapters 5 and 6). In the third column, we summarize information gathered about the learner in Step 3 (Chapters 7, 8, and 9).

Whenever possible, the information summarized in this part of the thumbnail sketch should describe the actual evidence rather than interpretations about the evidence. When generalizations or interpretations are necessary, it is helpful to indicate the sources of the information on which they are based. It should also be noted that it is not necessary to include every piece of evidence that has been gathered. It may already be clear that certain pieces of information are irrelevant and should be disregarded. However, if there is uncertainty as to the importance of the information, it is probably best to include it.

The procedures necessary for completing the fourth and fifth columns of thumbnail-sketch charts are described in this chapter. The fourth column summarizes the decisions made about the nature of the existing match and hypotheses about what the learner needs (Step 4). The fifth, and last, column summarizes information about the results of the diagnostic teaching used with the student and plans for continuous progress monitoring (Step 5).

The types of information provided in the last two columns of the chart are, of necessity, more interpretive than descriptive. However, whenever possible, it is still desirable to note the evidence leading to a particular conclusion. The remainder of this chapter is devoted to illustrating the implementation of Steps 4 and 5 and the thumbnail sketch, through the description of three case studies.

The Case Study of Tha'm

Figure 10.1 presents a summary of information gathered on the learner and contextual factors involved in Tha'm's case, most of which has been discussed extensively throughout the text. With this information in hand, we were ready to proceed with making some decisions about the appropriateness of the existing match, the nature of Tha'm's needs, how to change the match in ways that would lead to improvement in her learning and performance, and how to continue to monitor her progress. The first step in this process was evaluating the existing match between Tha'm's strengths and weaknesses as a learner and the characteristics of the settings, methods, and materials in which she was placed, for the purpose of generating hypotheses about the primary source(s) of interference with her learning and in order to plan for diagnostic teaching.

Reflection, Decision Making, and Planning (Step 4). Stopping to evaluate the existing match for Tha'm helped us to generate hypotheses about her major stumbling blocks and to establish some priorities. As we pursued the assessment-instruction cycle with Tha'm, several things had become quite clear. First, her instructional context had provided her with an excellent beginning. On most standardized measures of reading achievement, Tha'm was performing within the normal range. Measures of writing suggested greater difficulty. Since much of that can be attributed to limited instruction, we focused on diagnostic teaching in reading.

A summary of our evaluation of the existing match and of the hypotheses we generated about what Tha'm needed (Step 4) is provided in the left column of the thumbnail sketch presented in Figure 10.2. Recall that we said that one way to evaluate the existing match between a learner and the characteristics of her instructional/social context is to examine the information in each of the categories in the learner column and ask ourselves how it fits with what we know about the context and vice versa. Using this technique, we found more strengths than weaknesses in the existing match.

First, we noted that Tha'm's approximate *instructional* reading level (grades 4–5) was close to her grade placement level (grade 5). However, as her teacher had originally noted, her performance was inconsistent. Second, her knowledge about, and ability to use,

FIGURE 10.1   Thumbnail Sketch for Tha'm: Steps 1–3

Step 1: Getting Started: Using Data to Identify Struggling Learners	**Step 2:** Information about the Reading-Writing Context	**Step 3:** Information about the Learner
Focus Student Name: Tha'm Age: 10 Grade: 5 *Whole-Class Assessment Data* Statewide Assessment: ■ Met the proficiency standard for reading in grades 3, 4, 5 ■ In reading at grade 5, she was just 1 point above the cut score ■ In writing at grade 5, she is "partially proficient" ORF Data: ■ DIBELS results suggest "no risk" at end of grade 3 Additional Data Available: ■ ELL assessments show her to be reaching age-appropriate language proficiency in speaking, reading, writing ■ Placed in grade-level core ■ Uneven classroom performance in grade 5 *Key Correlates* ■ First language: Vietnamese ■ Vietnamese spoken in home ■ Average IQ ■ Normal vision, hearing, and overall health	*Home and Community Settings* ■ Vietnamese spoken at home ■ Few if any books ■ Does not visit public library because she has lost her card ■ Family is supportive and strongly attempting to assimilate ■ School sits in a diverse refugee resettlement community with more than 2 dozen different languages ■ Both long-time American citizens and refugees are hardworking but the FRL rate is above 90% *Instructional Settings* ■ Small teacher-student ratio and extensive PD on the part of school and teachers ■ Pullout program for ELL since kindergarten ■ Classroom organization is structured with teacher-directed instruction ■ Literate environment is signaled by accessible texts, student writing, and engaging displays *Instructional Activities and Tasks* ■ Mostly closed tasks ■ Basal workbooks ■ Questions mostly explicit ■ Writing quantity and quality has varied from year to year ■ Limited student-initiated activity, goal setting, or inquiry ■ Little connection to outside-of-school texts or tasks	*Knowledge about Reading and Writing* ■ Reports wide-ranging knowledge of authors and strategies ■ Reports using sounding it out and context as strategies for reading unfamiliar words ■ Good phonics knowledge and sight-word vocabulary ■ Limited awareness of expository text structures *Performance in Reading and Writing* ■ Oral language vocabulary, PR: 50, Stanine: 5 ■ Statewide achievement texts places her in the lowest end of "meeting the standard" in writing ■ Word recognition and fluency are both adequate through grade 4, variable at grade 5 ■ Comprehension is grade appropriate in familiar narratives ■ Comprehension is below grade level in unfamiliar narratives and most exposition ■ Oral and silent reading performance are comparable *Diagnostic Information* ■ Animated in discussion of texts ■ When reading in the "instructional comfort range" she comments freely and demonstrates interest ■ Uses prior knowledge to aid comprehension

FIGURE 10.1 (Continued)

Step 1: Getting Started: Using Data to Identify Struggling Learners	Step 2: Information about the Reading-Writing Context	Step 3: Information about the Learner
	Instruction ■ Small-group instruction by ability groups ■ Teacher-managed, code-focused instruction in primary grades ■ Student managed, meaning focused in intermediate grades ■ Content of instruction is balanced except for very limited vocabulary instruction ■ Limited reading outside of the basal program and small groups ■ Classroom teachers expected to provide differentiated Instruction and extra support within the classroom **Methods** ■ Organized and focused instructional blocks ■ Modeling and explicit instruction in comprehension strategies ■ Limited cooperative book discussion or collaborative work ■ Ability groups **Assessment Practices** ■ Close monitoring after each unit/theme in the core program ■ Student-support team examines data to plan appropriate near-term interventions (at K–3) ■ State assessments annually from grade 3+ ■ At primary grades teachers use an array of federally and state-mandated assessments generally focused on phonology, decoding, and fluency **Resources** ■ Contemporary core program ■ Broad collection of leveled texts (in primary grades) ■ Good shcool library, but limited access to it ■ Inadequate access to electronic media or digital texts	■ Does not monitor reading for misconceptions ■ Summarizes text-explicit text very well ■ Has difficulty generating inferences or drawing conclusions ■ Vocabulary knowledge poses problems in both reading and writing ■ Does not appear to use self-questioning or clarifying ■ In writing, little evidence of controlled use of strategics

FIGURE 10.2 Thumbnail Sketch for Tha'm (Steps 4–5)

Reflection, Decision Making, and Planning (Step 4)	Diagnostic Teaching and Continuous Progress Monitoring (Step 5)*

Summary of Key Information
What is the match between learner and literacy?
■ Reading performance below potential
■ Accuracy and fluency are adequate to good
■ Vocabulary, morphological knowledge/skill are weak
■ Has trouble comprehending long and/or complex and/or dense selections
■ Little experience reading long texts or engaging in tasks associated with learning content from text
■ Tends to use a narrative stance for all reading
 	
Reflection/Hypothesis
What does the reader need?
■ Prior knowledge is a matter of concern in two ways: (1) it is sometimes too limited and (2) inaccurate knowledge leads to misconceptions
■ Tha'm needs improved ability to read multisyllabic words
■ Improved ability to use morphology would help both comprehension and vocabulary development
■ Tha'm needs both experience and instruction in reading informational text—priority before next year in middle school.
 	
Planning
What is most likely to reestablish learning?
■ Engage in reading challenging texts with appropriate prereading assessment and a guided reading approach
■ Teach purposes and structure of expository text.
■ Evaluate level of instruction required for accurate reading of multi-syllabic and morphologically complex words
	Implementing and Assessing
	■ Two Actions
	  o Diagnostic teaching – use expository text and layered prompts
	  o Intervention – Classroom differentiation
	    ■ small-group, teacher-led guided reading of longer, complex texts
	    ■ small, flexible groups using spelling/meaning approach improve morphology
	
	Evaluating the Diagnostic Teaching Sessions
	■ Increased explicit instruction in reading expository text should improve comprehension
	■ Performs better with supported, guided discussion
	■ Can read and learn from age-appropriate expository texts – with support
	
	*__Note:__ See chapter discussion for details.

556

syllabication skills during reading, combined with her lack of familiarity and ability to read and use morphology, did not match well with the demands of reading at her grade level. Third, her problems comprehending complex texts and dealing with high-level comprehension tasks were not well matched to an instructional method that contained little opportunity for sustained reading or instruction with expository texts. In addition, our assessment data revealed that her hold on age/grade-appropriate abilities was tenuous. It seemed likely that she would struggle when she went into the middle school during the next school year. In particular, we were concerned about two things: (1) the discrepancy between her reading comprehension on narrative versus expository texts and (2) her weak morphological knowledge/skill. In short, these areas are ones where the match between learner and reading context might be improved in an effort to promote Tha'm's learning and performance in reading.

Diagnostic Teaching (Step 5). Once we had generated and prioritized our hypotheses, we were then ready to plan, implement, and evaluate the diagnostic teaching to be used to confirm or deny our hypotheses and identify a match that would promote Tha'm's learning and performance (see Figure 10.2).

Planning. Tha'm had a balanced reading ability through approximately grade 4. However, her performance in comprehension was not universally strong. In addition, her word recognition revealed troubling weaknesses also. These were two areas about which we thought that more information might be useful. As we reflected on Tha'm's needs and on what we could manipulate to "call forth learning," the following entered into our consideration.

What can/should be changed to improve the match for Tha'm?
1. Type of prereading instruction/support
   a. Vocabulary
   b. Concepts
2. Comprehension discussions that highlight and require engagement with complex syntax
3. Length of text and amount of reading
4. Knowledge about syllabication and morphology
5. Ability to infer main ideas

Not all of our conclusions about ways to improve Tha'm's performance needed to be pursued through diagnostic teaching. Although diagnostic teaching is an invaluable addition to our assessment-instruction repertoire, it is not required in all situations. For example, Tha'm's consistently poor performance in the area of word recognition was limited to morphological endings on longer words (see Chapter 8 and 9). There was no real reason to use diagnostic teaching to confirm that Tha'm lacked knowledge about the morphological structure and meaning of unfamiliar words, although we could have used diagnostic teaching to determine the best way to address this problem.

On the other hand, Tha'm's difficulties were most pronounced in dense expository text. We suspected that she could perform better if she were provided with more information before and during reading, since she seemed to make such good use of all available information in constructing meaning. At the same time, there was evidence that Tha'm had trouble generating inferences and that her unwillingness to reconsider the conclusions she did draw was posing problems for her in comprehension of informational texts.

Therefore, a diagnostic teaching session was planned that would involve the reading of lengthy expository text, with intentional probing by means of a supported think-aloud. *The Developmental Reading Assessment* (DRA) for grades 4 to 8 (Beaver & Carter, 2003) was used to explore Tha'm's comprehension of longer expository texts. The DRA was selected because it varies considerably in several important ways from other assessments, and we expected it to generate possible insights into Tha'm's performance. Not only are the DRA's texts relatively authentic, but they are longer than those in some other assessment materials and contain tasks that are similar to those expected of intermediate-grade students.

Tha'm had reached the frustration level on informational selections at grade 4, so level 40 was used in the diagnostic teaching episode. Tha'm was offered a choice of texts ("The Amazing Octopus" or "A Pack of Wolves"). She chose the selection on the octopus (see Figure 10.3). In its entirety, this text is eleven pages and approximately one thousand words long. It has labeled pictures, pictures with captions, and major headings (figures similar to Figure 10.4). There are no boldface words, maps, sidebar information, or supplemental

FIGURE 10.3   Excerpt from *DRA*, Used in Diagnostic Teaching

Meet the Octopus

Deep in the ocean lives a creature known for its tricks. It can get out of the tightest places. It can change its shape and its color in less than a second. This creature is coldblooded and is called an octopus. More than 150 kinds can be found around the world. The smallest is the size of a thumb. The biggest is more than 20 feet from arm tip to arm tip.

An octopus has no backbone. It has a body shaped like a balloon that is covered by a mantle. Each of the eight arms has rows of suckers. Most kinds of octopuses have about 2,000 suckers. These suckers help an octopus to pick up and eat food. They also help it to cling to a hiding place. Octopus arms are always busy. They use their arms to walk, crawl, dig, and eat.

An octopus has two eyes. It can turn its eyes in half circles without moving its head. Its eyesight is very sharp. An octopus uses gills and a funnel for breathing. Its funnel also helps the octopus move through water.

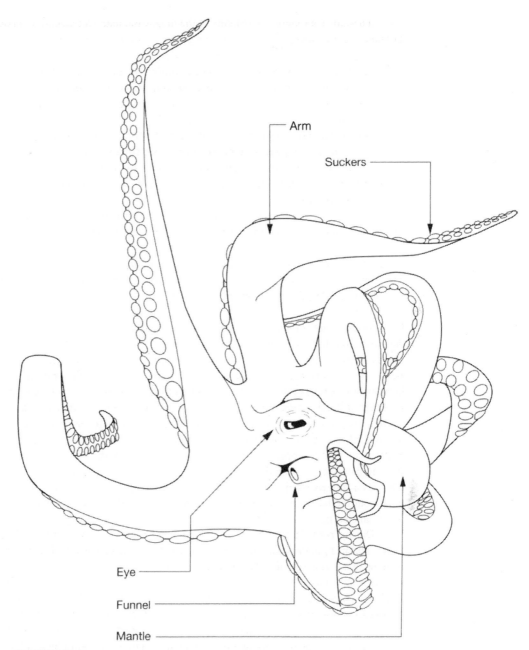

FIGURE 10.4

materials such as glossaries. Elements of the diagnostic teaching that we intended to pursue included the following.

1. *Tha'm's prior knowledge about the topic:* On earlier nonfiction texts, Tha'm had tended to let prior knowledge confound her acquisition of new information. A determination of her knowledge prior to reading would help us assess points of confusion.
2. *Ability to read multisyllabic words:* It was unclear from earlier assessments how much support Tha'm would require for more-accurate reading of multi-syllabic words. In this episode, we were testing a very low level of support by simply asking her to reread sentences with miscues in syllabication or morphology.
3. *Ability to use text to acquire new information or alter old ideas:* Through a modified think-aloud, we wanted to explore Tha'm's ongoing construction of knowledge and vocabulary.
4. *The appropriateness of guided reading in nonfiction text:* We were interested to see if guided reading enhanced Tha'm's ability to acquire information about expository texts and to comprehend and learn from it.

Description of the Diagnostic Teaching Session: Patterns and Variations.   We started the diagnostic teaching session by introducing some prereading probes. These revealed that Tha'm knew several things about octopuses: that they had eight legs, which she specified were called "tentacles," and that they used camouflage (no elaboration). Both of these ideas are important to the text she was about to read. However, she was unable to expand on either of these topics. Probes after the picture walk revealed that she also believed that the funnels (shown in a picture, see Figure 10.4) were used to shoot ink. Further, she noted that the ink contained poison to kill enemies (a fact that is refuted later in the text). As in the past, Tha'm's organization of information was weak, and her ability to expand on specific pieces of information was thin. Importantly, the background probe revealed that, while Tha'm possessed some accurate information, she also held at least one *misconception* about the topic and generated an erroneous conclusion during the examination of the initial labeled figure.

During reading, continued probing helped illuminate the complex interaction between Tha'm's background knowledge and the text comprehension. Tha'm was directed to read the first paragraph of "The Amazing Octopus." The examiner prompted her, "tell what you have learned." The results of this prompt confirmed what we had observed before: Tha'm is capable of acquiring a great deal of *explicitly* stated information. She recalled almost all of that level of information. Among the facts that she recalled was the statement that octopuses are "coldblooded." The examiner directed her attention to that sentence, and Tha'm interrupted to say that this meant that octopuses "don't have a heart." Startled, the examiner repeated this statement, and Tha'm said, "Well, they do, but they don't care about others." This provided the examiner with the opportunity she had been looking for to explicate the purpose and techniques for reading expository texts and also to encourage Tha'm to be careful about word meanings.

EXAMINER: Oh, in *stories* they sometimes say someone is "cold-*hearted.*" Cold-hearted means they don't care about others. But this is a nonfiction book. It's about real facts. Coldblooded means something else.

THA'M: mean, harsh

EXAMINER: If you think about an octopus, do they really have a personality, like a person?

THA'M: They don't have emotions.

EXAMINER: You're right! So do you think coldblooded means something a little more *scientific*? [The examiner defines coldblooded.] That's one of the things, Tha'm; when you're reading nonfiction texts, you really want to make sure that you understand all the things they are telling you. You're going to have to think in your brain, "Am I sure it means that?"

A second type of probe was focused on clarifying the type and intensity of instruction that would be needed to address her difficulties with syllabication and morphological analysis. We asked Tha'm to reread several sentences with miscues on multisyllabic words or morphological elements. For example, Tha'm read two sentences like this:

> the
> "By day, (the) octopus hunts by spreading its arms and body to create a web. When
> its   up   flo-er
> a meal comes along, (the) octopus floats down like an open flower and traps it."

She consistently deleted the article *the*, which, in the information material, designates a group or class of animal; she deletes the tense/number ending on three verbs (*hunts*, *comes*, *floats*); and she mispronounces the word *flower*. When directed to reread these two sentences, she self-corrected all of the miscues except the morphological verb endings. This pattern occurred several other times throughout the session. Tha'm was regularly able to self-correct multisyllabic words after she was asked to take a closer look. Slowing her reading just a bit improved her first attempts at these words also. Thus, it appears that she had both the knowledge and skill to read most multisyllable words (an exception may be the syllable patterns represented by *basic* and *cushion*).

Rereading did not result in self-corrections of the morphology, however. This suggests that Tha'm's miscues in these areas were actually the result of her existing language development. They should *not* be counted as miscues (this would change her accuracy estimates during oral reading of connected text), because they reflected her linguistic knowledge, not her reading skill.

With this information in hand, we were ready to make some decisions about the nature of Tha'm's needs and how to change the existing instructional match in ways that would lead to improvement in her learning and performance.

Evaluating. As we evaluated our diagnostic teaching efforts for Tha'm, we examined the impact of our manipulations on her performance. In the first instance, it was apparent that our instructional manipulation during the prereading phase had provided better assessment than instructional support. That is, it had produced good information about her prior knowledge, but it had not heightened her awareness of the topic. By itself, simply activating prior knowledge was not helpful to Tha'm, because she did not always monitor the relationship between her prior knowledge and textual information. Like many students, Tha'm used her own prior knowledge as a default when the text was confusing.

Our hypothesis that she could benefit from instruction in exposition—both its purposes and its organization—bore fruit. With just this little bit of encouragement, Tha'm seemed able to reorient herself to the text. She made a greater attempt to use specific vocabulary from the text in her discussion and attempted to discuss the factual content of the text. However, she was only able to take a refutation stance on information (that is, change her mind about a previously held belief) when she was explicitly guided to reconsider her preexisting ideas. Similarly, more instruction would be needed before she could generate superordinate organizing principles and concepts.

The diagnostic teaching sessions generated several instructional options. First, we determined that Tha'm could work, with support, in grade-level material and that these should be used whenever possible (this was a continuation of her existing program). Second, she needed to acquire much more automaticity in applying the word recognition and word analysis skills that she already possessed, to decode unfamiliar and/or multisyllabic words. Tha'm also needed additional knowledge and skill in word analysis, particularly in the area of structural and morphemic analysis. A vigorous vocabulary program, focusing on morphological transformations, needed to be started. Tha'm appeared to enjoy using specific vocabulary, but frequently falls back on fillers such as "stuff." With just a little support, she appeared capable of acquiring and using new, more sophisticated vocabulary. Finally, Tha'm needed to learn more about how complex expositions are organized and needs many instructional opportunities to read such materials with guidance and support. These two problems, weak knowledge about expository text and expertise in addressing more sophisticated words (decoding and meaning), converged in the need for Tha'm to acquire skill in reading the type of lengthy reading assignments often expected of middle-grade students.

Differentiated Instruction and Intervention with Progress Monitoring.   At the time of the original referral, Tha'm was placed in a regular classroom, receiving ELL support but no other support services in reading or writing. Her teacher referred her for assessment because of his concerns about her erratic academic performance. The assessment-instruction process was initiated by a literacy consultant who was working with the school, and, as a result, the assessments were executed outside the regular classroom setting by someone other than the teacher.

We recommended differentiated instruction in the classroom but also recommended that Tha'm receive intervention services in a *small-group* context, because she needed opportunities to discuss reading and writing in a socially supportive environment. She was herself a gregarious girl, and many of her interests revolved around people and social interaction. The focused instruction she had received had been helpful, but Tha'm needed more high-powered instruction and discussion in order to develop the sophisticated strategies and content knowledge she would need to be really successful in middle and high school.

In Tha'm's case, materials were chosen with two major criteria in mind. Only full-length stories or books were to be used, since this constituted an area of need for her. For narratives, these would involve fully developed, complex stories with a strong goal structure. For expository text, these would be article- or chapter-length materials. *The Story of Ember* (DuPrau, 2003) is a science fiction narrative involving both male and female characters and a strong adventure/suspense series of episodes. The narrative structure would support her comprehension, but the unusual and unexpected content would require her to make inferences and then really consider and reconsider them as the story unfolded. It required instructional support in the form of discussion and sustained her interest over several weeks. In addition, it provided a rich source of multisyllabic words from which to teach and practice structural and morphemic analysis.

For exposition, the booklets in *Houghton Mifflin Science Leveled Readers* (Fountas & Pinnell, 2006) materials are all fully developed, high-interest expository texts (roughly 16–25 pages long). Tha'm found these challenging, but she retained an interest in them. These expository texts were used for direct instruction to develop both vocabulary and comprehension. In later sessions, these selections provided excellent material for use with both text-mapping activities and a think-aloud strategy.

Tha'm continued to receive instruction in a supported context for the remainder of her fifth-grade year. She made steady progress, although her teachers were concerned about her ability to manage middle school texts and tasks. In the fall of grade 6, Tha'm took the challenging state-mandated reading assessment and again managed to meet the standard—a significant achievement and one that bodes well for her future academic success.

The Case Study of Kyle

The case of Kyle is unusual in the sense that we were able to follow his progress over a relatively long period of time because of the strong assessment system in place in his school and classroom. At many intervals along the way, his teacher, Ms. McIntyre, had made decisions about how and what to teach. The end of second grade was an important time to stop and take stock, because he was moving on to a different school for grade 3 and because he would be attending a university literacy clinic during the summer. The thumbnail sketch in Figure 10.5 summarizes the information that had been gathered about Kyle's reading and writing development. Using this summary of the information gathered in Steps 1 to 3, we turned our attention to the decision-making steps in the assessment-instruction process.

Reflection, Decision Making, and Planning (Step 4). A summary of the existing match and of the hypotheses we generated about Kyle's strengths and needs is provided in the excerpt of Kyle's thumbnail sketch (see Figure 10.6). First, we celebrated not only the fact that Kyle's reading performance had improved considerably, but also that both his word recognition and his comprehension were age and grade appropriate. Indeed, his reading comprehension was quite exceptional. The match between his rapidly changing (growing) abilities and the classroom had been an exceptionally good one. When Kyle's emerging abilities converged with the motivation to read a whole series of books, he had a teacher who was alert to the moment and waiting to make the most of it and a classroom structure that supported his exceptional growth during the last half of grade 2. In addition, Kyle's classroom had provided him with opportunities to be highly active and personally engaged in various literacy (and other) activities.

FIGURE 10.5   Thumbnail Sketch for Kyle: Steps 1–3 (Grade 2)

Step 1: Getting Started: Using Data to Identify Struggling Learners	**Step 2:** Information about the Reading-Writing Context	**Step 3:** Information about the Learner
Focus Student: Name: Kyle Age: 6.5–7.5 Grade: 1–2 **Whole-Class Assessment Data:** Portfolio Review-Reading: ■ Kyle has not met the benchmarks for reading at grade 1 ■ Running records throughout grade 1 suggest that Kyle is making progress Portfolio Review–Writing: ■ He is able to reflect on his own writing and demonstrates an awareness of both craft and mechanics ■ He takes risks in his writing, but spelling and volume are both less developed than for his peers Additional Data Available: ■ Reports that he does not like to read; would rather "play" and "build" ■ Cooperative and willing to work both in school and in extra sessions **Key Correlates:** ■ Normal vision, hearing, and overall health ■ Difficult time "paying attention"	***Home and Community Settings*** ■ English only language spoken at home ■ Considerable home emphasis on reading and writing ■ Community is well educated and emphasizes academic achievement ■ Median income of school community well above average – FRL rate is above 15% ***Instructional Settings*** ■ Multiaged classrooms in a building that houses only K–2 ■ Child-centered classrooms ■ School and classroom environment is rich; exceptional access to texts, many opportunities to read and write ■ Support services are provided on a push-in basis and include reading, speech-language, and counseling ***Instructional Activities and Tasks*** ■ Many open tasks and significant student choice ■ Reading time spent in sustained reading of continuous texts ■ Students respond in multiple ways – writing, art, performance ■ Writing time spent writing original texts and revising for publication – in books, on walls, in class ■ Additional writing in journals, theme booklets, and correspondences ■ Students reflect on own work, select portfolio entries, and evaluate own learning.	**Knowledge about Reading and Writing** ■ Reports that people read for enjoyment and to find out things ■ Can articulate ways to improve written work **Performance in Reading and Writing** ■ By end of grade 2, instructional reading level at grade 3 (Spache results; QRI, Benchmark books) ■ Ability to answer questions and recall passages better than word recognition, but gap closing ■ Excellent comprehension of complex stories and informational text ■ In writing, good control of topic, purpose, and voice ■ Spelling at phonemic level (approaching transitional) ■ Slow and illegible handwriting **Diagnostic Information** ■ Highly developed strategy use in reading; uses picture cues, context, and graphophonic information; uses prior knowledge, monitoring, and rereading ■ Enjoys writing about personal events and activities and also about science topics ■ In writing, strategies for managing lengthier texts and for revision are *not developed* ■ Exhibits exceptional self-evaluation and goal-setting behaviors ■ Provides specific information about task difficulty and can identify areas of growth

FIGURE 10.5   (Continued)

Step 1: Getting Started: Using Data to Identify Struggling Learners	Step 2: Information about the Reading-Writing Context	Step 3: Information about the Learner
	Instruction ■ Students confer with teacher and with each other ■ Much student-managed, meaning-focused activity, although this shifts from kindergarten to grade 2 ■ Inquiry-based theme work and choice time each day ■ Cooperative and collaborative groups ■ Problem-solving focus *Methods* ■ No commercial curriculum, students engage in self-selected reading and individual conferences ■ Teacher identifies students to assess/ instruct and focus varies depending on student *Assessment Practices* ■ Close monitoring on a daily basis ■ Student work samples are organized, annotated, and dated ■ Collections are organized in portfolios ■ Student self-reflection is extensive ■ Teachers collect weekly running records ■ Other formative assessments daily and weekly during individual conferences *Resources* ■ Beginning readers, little books, and own writing ■ Emerging readers, commercially controlled vocabulary texts, and trade books (children's literature) ■ Journals, portfolios, theme booklets ■ Many read-alouds (children's literature) ■ Excellent and accessible school library ■ Limited access to electronic media or digital texts	

FIGURE 10.6   Thumbnail Sketch for Kyle for the end of Grade 2 (Steps 4–5)

Reflection, Decision Making, and Planning (Step 4)	Diagnostic Teaching and Continuous Progress Monitoring (Step 5)*
Summary of Key Information What is the match between learner and literacy?<ul><li>Reading level is grade appropriate</li><li>Kyle is showing more interest in reading now that he can handle more-difficult and lengthy "chapter" books</li><li>In these books, however, he sometimes fails to monitor word recognition failures and has some word/sentence tracking problems</li><li>Has difficulty paying attention during more academic tasks; but his preference for action is addressed in his present classroom</li><li>Both his spelling and written language abilities overall are weak</li></ul>	**Implementing and Assessing** Intervention – Classroom differentiation<ul><li>Stages of spelling development</li><li>Small, flexible groups focused on written language</li></ul> **Evaluating the Diagnostic Teaching Sessions**
Reflection/Hypothesis What does the reader need?<ul><li>Continued support for self-selected high-interest reading materials</li><li>A literacy program that focuses on authentic reading and writing</li><li>Explicit instruction in spelling</li><li>Instruction in editing and revising his own written work</li><li>Some flexibility about activities; a real challenge as he moves to a more traditional school configuration next school year</li></ul>	*__Note:__ See chapter discussion for details.
Planning What is most likely to reestablish learning?<ul><li>Continued opportunities to engage in sustained reading and writing</li><li>Appropriate developmental reading program in grades 3 and beyond (including attention to fluency and instruction in multisyllabic word identification)</li><li>Specific, differentiated instruction in spelling and written language production</li></ul>	

The only area of significant need remained his weak skills in the conventions of writing and spelling. Kyle needed to acquire a better sense of conventional spelling and learn to manage, edit, and revise his own writing for better readability. In the normal course of Kyle's developmental reading program, he would also need instruction in some additional areas. For example, given the difficulty of the material he was now capable of reading, he needed better word analysis skills for longer and multisyllabic words. In addition, he needed instructional support for monitoring his reading of these more complex materials.

Diagnostic Teaching (Step 5). We noted earlier that diagnostic teaching is not required in all situations. We really did not need to use diagnostic teaching to confirm Kyle's areas of ongoing need or the type of instruction to which he would be responsive. For the most part, his remaining difficulties could and would be addressed in the course of a good, responsive literacy program. Both his teachers and his parents were aware that his placement for third grade could be critical. Kyle continued to require a flexible classroom context that encouraged self-control and focused on authentic reading and writing tasks. Self-selection and activity remained central to maintaining Kyle's motivation and momentum. Acting as advocates, Ms. McIntyre and Kyle's parents helped to place Kyle in a classroom where he would, in all likelihood, continue to flourish.

Over the summer, Kyle participated in a summer literacy clinic sponsored by the local university. The work there focused on adjusting the rate for text difficulty and on encouraging a self-control strategy for spelling and writing. With very little tutor support, Kyle was able to talk through some strategies for editing his written work. He generated the following description: "You write and check the spelling. You reread and see if it makes sense. Make sure it says what you want it to say." In spelling, his work focused on spelling patterns and an analogy strategy. Ms. McIntyre had provided all her students with self-addressed, stamped postcards so that they could write to her over the summer. At the end of August, Ms. McIntyre received a postcard from Kyle that said, "I am a reader!"

The Case Study of Yasmin

Yasmin moved to the United States from Mexico during the spring of kindergarten. Yasmin's first and dominant language is Spanish. Her parents speak only Spanish, and it is the only language spoken at home. Yasmin had not attended any school before her arrival in the United States and had extremely limited literacy experiences and knowledge. At the time of school entry, she recognized only eight letters out of fifty-two uppercase and lowercase letters combined and scored 3/24 on the *Concepts About Print* (CAP) assessment (Clay, 1993). Consequently, the school and her teachers were concerned from the very beginning and attended carefully to her development, although they did not at that time have an early intervention program in place (see ISA described later in this chapter).

During mid–second grade, her teachers determined that a closer examination of Yasmin's literacy development was appropriate. At that time, Yasmin was a 7-year-old who was reading at Reading Recovery level 20. She was making steady progress but was not meeting the benchmark standards established for her school district. A summary of the information gathered on the learner and contextual factors involved in Yasmin's case is presented in the thumbnail sketch in Figure 10.7.

The context for Yasmin's school achievement was complex. The majority (70 percent) of Yasmin's schoolmates spoke a language other than English—primarily Spanish or Haitian Creole. Hers was an urban school, with approximately nine hundred students, that had been targeted by the state because of its students' low performance in reading (scores on measures of writing were consistently higher). During Yasmin's first- and second-grade years, the school had received a large federal grant and was engaged in considerable professional development aimed at school improvement. Most of the teachers were highly committed and eager for students to do well.

FIGURE 10.7   Yasmin's Thumbnail Sketch, Steps 1–3

Step 1: Getting Started: Using Data	**Step 2:** Information about the Reading-Writing Context	**Step 3:** Information about the Learner
Assessment Data: Benchmark Level for Mid–grade 2: L22 *Focus Student:* Name: Yasmin Age: 7, Grade 2 **Progress Indicators:** ■ Knew few letters or sounds at school entry ■ Has made steady progress ■ Knows 17/20 sight words tested ■ Failed to meet Benchmark: scoring L20 ■ Oral language measure weak **Key Correlates:** ■ Spanish first language ■ Arrived in U.S. in kindergarten ■ Normal vision, hearing	**Home/Community Context** ■ Spanish only in the home ■ Extended family, interested in schooling ■ Limited educational experiences outside of school **Resources** ■ School has extensive book room and media center w/ multiple copies of leveled text along with quality children's literature ■ Use of running records and Lexile levels for matching text to readers ■ Shared reading texts (big books and charts) ■ Books on tape ■ Journals, portfolios ■ Classroom libraries ■ Computers with reading and writing software ■ Extensive teacher training in using assessment to plan instruction **Instruction** ■ Informed by assessment data ■ Whole group, small group ■ Includes guided instruction and modeling ■ Literacy learning centers ■ Individual practice **Settings/Approaches** ■ 1-hour reading block ■ 1-hour writing block ■ ESL class (pullout) ■ Class size 22:1	**Knowledge about Reading and Writing** ■ Understands the purpose of reading ■ Knows all letters and sounds ■ Hears discrete sounds in words, which she uses in both reading and writing ■ Knows reading should make sense ■ Has letter-sound knowledge in Spanish and English **Performance in Reading and Writing** ■ Running records indicate Level 20 ■ CAP: 22/24, but not able to change word and letter order ■ Gentry Spelling in context: 55/100 ■ Score of 4 (rubric possible 6 points) on county-wide writing prompt, first draft **Diagnostic Information** ■ Has overreliance on visual cueing system, using it in place of language structure and meaning (which is low as measured on the ROL) ■ Is inefficient, however, in using the visual system—does not read through words and search further for all visual information ■ Is beginning to develop rereading, self-correcting, and self-monitoring strategies ■ Has limited retelling ability (has increased with development of English-language competence) ■ Is not flexible in word analysis and does not use word families effectively ■ Developing greater fluency, but still slow ■ Needs to develop multiple strategies and cross-checking

Yasmin's teachers had taken their training seriously and developed classrooms that were rich in books, where student progress was carefully monitored. Her school and classroom teachers had been strongly influenced by the Reading Recovery program, shared reading (Holdaway, 1979), and guided reading (Fountas & Pinnell, 1996). Teachers used running records to track reading development and attended to students' strategy use as they reviewed these records. In addition, students were placed in increasingly difficult texts using leveled books. Less attention had been directed toward writing—in part because the performance of the school's ELL students had been stronger in writing than in reading. Yasmin's instructional program had not included much writing at all.

In terms of possible physical, linguistic, or cognitive correlates, Yasmin's status as an English language learner (ELL) was the major factor. She had attended an English-as-a-second-language class to promote English acquisition for her entire school experience. She received sixty minutes per day of instruction in this pullout program.

Yasmin's interviews and performance suggested that she had acquired considerable knowledge and understanding of initial reading and writing. Her performance on the *Concepts About Print* test, for example, placed her among the most capable students of her age (22/24) and indicated that she had developed significant print-related skills and abilities, although she was not able to change letter and word order. Similarly, she was able to read seventeen of twenty high-frequency sight words on the test administered in mid–second grade (*Ohio Word Test*). There were areas that concerned her teachers, however. First, she scored poorly on the school-administered *Record of Oral Language,* or ROL (a measure of the structure of the English language), and although she had acquired a corpus of sight words, her ability to decode using knowledge of word families was not strong. Indeed, a miscue analysis suggested that she relied too heavily on the visual cueing system and on meaning. For example, a running record taken early in grade 2 included miscues such as these:

> **TEXT:**   Deep in the jungle, alone in the river, swam a friendly crocodile.
>
> **YASMIN:**   Deep in the jungle a-a-an-al-alony in the r-i-v a friend crocodile . . .
>
> **TEXT:**   "Will you be my friend, Parrot?" smiled the friendly crocodile.
>
> **YASMIN:**   Will you be my friend? **Parrot**[R] swiled the friend crocodile.

Yasmin did demonstrate a positive attitude toward listening to stories and was cooperative during instruction. During the exploratory period, we discovered that although Yasmin's parents had limited formal education, they were very committed to her schooling, that they read to her often in Spanish, and that she had a well-developed sense of story.

Given this summary of the information gathered in Steps 1 through 3, we felt that diagnostic teaching procedures could provide additional insights to clarify the assessment picture and to guide instruction moving forward.

Reflection, Decision Making, and Planning (Step 4).   A summary of our evaluation of the existing match and of the hypotheses we generated about what Yasmin needed (Step 4) is provided in Figure 10.8. In Yasmin's case the match between her knowledge, skills, and attitudes and the settings, methods, and materials that confront her within the reading

FIGURE 10.8 Thumbnail Sketch for Yasmin (Steps 4–5)

Reflection, Decision Making, and Planning (Step 4)	Diagnostic Teaching and Continuous Progress Monitoring (Step 5)*

Summary of Key Information
What is the match between learner and literacy?
■ Reading level is within a second-grade range
■ Strong match between classroom structure and learning expectations, i.e., teacher modeling, small-group work determined by assessment information
■ Poor match between student choice of reading materials and student reading level
■ Writing, specifically spelling and content, not matched to reading level
Writing is much less developed, especially in areas of language structure, than reading
■ Flexibility in decoding similar words (decoding by analogy) does not match expectations
■ Strong knowledge of letter sounds and ability to hear sounds in words does not match application of visual cueing system. Can hear all sounds in words but does not search further in words (uses only first letter with unknown words) and does not stretch words when writing
 	
Reflection/Hypothesis
What does the reader need?
■ Support in self-selection of appropriate reading material
■ Own collection of books for reading practice
■ Continuing classroom support for explicit teaching of strategies through modeling, oral language practice, small-group work based on continuous formative assessment
■ Strong oral language models
■ Activities in making words, working with onsets and rimes to develop more flexibility and knowledge of word families and word endings
■ More writing instruction with emphasis on developing supporting details
■ Rereading own writing to begin knowledge of revising process
 	
Planning
What is most likely to reestablish learning?
Greater facility and fluency in word recognition. Diagnostic teaching plan to examine the effect of two decoding strategies on word identification:
■ Teaching making/breaking words using onsets and rimes
■ Teaching decoding by analogy
	Implementing and Assessing
	■ Two Actions
	  ○ Diagnostic teaching – testing two different approaches to word identification – **See chapter discussion**
	  ○ Intervention – Classroom
	    ■ small-group fluency practice
	    ■ whole-group explicit instruction on tracking through entire words to examine them for orthographic patterns.
	
	Evaluating the Diagnostic Teaching Sessions
	■ Word sorts are challenging for her but do encourage her to look through whole words and increase success
	■ Enjoyed and was successful with decoding by analogy
	■ Next steps: continue decoding by analogy and monitor progress
	
	*Note: See chapter discussion for details.

570

context was mixed. Generally, the organization, methods, and materials of her instruction appeared to be having a positive effect on both her general language development and her reading development. Her print-rich classroom environment, for example, had promoted and supported a love of books and improved vocabulary. Yasmin had developed good emergent skills and had proceeded through appropriately difficult texts.

It was clear, however, that the instructional program was not resulting in accelerated achievement. Her strong phonemic awareness ability had not developed into a strong use of the sound-symbol system or the orthographic spelling patterns of English. This weakness showed up in both her writing and her decoding of unknown words. She did not appear to be poised to read more fluently or write more extensively, because she was neither fully analyzing unknown words nor using her memory for word features to write longer pieces. In addition, there appeared to be too few opportunities to link reading and writing and not much authentic writing.

Our evaluation of the existing match provided us with the information necessary to generate hypotheses about what Yasmin needed to progress as a beginning reader and writer. Although there were many uncertainties still, it seemed likely that Yasmin needed two things. First, she needed instruction that encouraged her to examine all of the letters in a word. In the long term, she would also need to use writing to strengthen her print knowledge. The second thing Yasmin needed was to increase her flexibility in using her word knowledge to acquire a strategy for decoding unfamiliar words.

Diagnostic Teaching (Step 5). At this point in the process, we were ready to engage in diagnostic teaching as a means of confirming our hypotheses and identifying possible instructional interventions. A summary of Yasmin's diagnostic teaching and its results is presented in the thumbnail sketch in Figure 10.8.

Planning. In the planning phase of diagnostic teaching, we needed to determine the specific nature of the interventions that would address the needs identified in Step 4. To do this, as we noted previously, it is easiest to think in terms of the features of the settings, methods, and materials that can and should be modified and manipulated. In Yasmin's case, there was a genuine commitment on the part of the classroom teacher to improving Yasmin's instructional program and a willingness to try new things. The reading coach for Yasmin's classroom conducted the diagnostic teaching sessions, keeping in mind a variety of options that could be implemented in her everyday reading program.

The characteristics of the methods, materials, and tasks of Yasmin's instructional context offered several alternatives for diagnostic teaching. Specifically, the instructional method used for word work could be modified to include methods and tasks that focused her more clearly on the orthographic patterns of words. In addition, her reading materials could be altered to provide her with more-frequent opportunities for fluency practice.

After considering the various alternatives, the reading coach decided to try out two alternative approaches to word recognition instruction, one directing Yasmin's attention to onset and rime and the other to the application of this knowledge in decoding unknown words. These approaches are variations on the "making words" approach promoted by Cunningham (1995) and the "decoding by analogy" strategy described in the benchmark program (Gaskins, Ehri, Cress, O'Hara, & Donnelley, 1996/1997).

Investigating for Further Assessment.   The session began with a making-words lesson (*Systematic Sequential Phonics They Use*, by Patricia Cunningham). This technique was not being used by her second-grade teacher, but Yasmin was familiar with it because her first-grade teacher had used it occasionally. The steps used were as follows:

1. Using movable letters and a tray, Yasmin was directed to make *at*, *ate*, *rat*, *mat*, *mate*, *rate*, *rake*, *take*, and *make*, and the secret word was *market*.
2. Yasmin was then asked to sort the words that she made into rhyming words.
3. A series of layered prompts was used to help her accomplish the sorting task successfully.
   a. She said that she did not understand "sort," so the task was explained, and she began to sort by first letter.
   b. She was reminded to sort by rhyming families, and she put the *-ate* and *-ake* words together and the *-at* words in a separate pile.
   c. Then the words were displayed in columns sorted by ending. She was given two words, *date* and *cake*, and was asked to put them with the group that had the same ending.
4. The rhyming and sorting tasks were repeated to test for transfer.

During the making-words strategy, Yasmin was able to make the words but had some difficulty with the secret word (*market* in this case), which required putting all the letters together to make a word. She knew what the word was but did not know how to spell it (even with all the letters) until she was told to say the word slowly, listen to the sounds, and point to the letters.

Yasmin had significant difficulty sorting words using either rhyming or orthographic patterns. Even when reminded to sort by rhyming families, she still did not sort the words correctly. She was able to match words to correctly sorted lists, however. When this task was repeated with other words, Yasmin was unable to generate rhyming words, although she was capable of isolating individual vowel sounds.

Investigating Using Trial Teaching.   The next lesson involved a trial teaching session with decoding by analogy. Yasmin was taught to use a framing sentence: "If I know this word, _____, then it can help me read this word, _____." The lesson demonstrations used words she knew to help her decode unknown words. For example, the teacher used color words that she knew were very familiar to Yasmin and then showed her another much more difficult word with the same word part, such as *black* and *attack*. Yasmin caught on quickly and enjoyed the activity. After several attempts, Yasmin was able to read all the new words using the words she knew. She even remarked, "I think that I can use this when I read; its like finding little parts in big words!"

Evaluating.   In all examples, Yasmin had difficulty sorting by rhyming words and generating new rhyming words. The making-words strategy seemed to be a good one for encouraging Yasmin to move letters around and helping her become more flexible in transferring what she knew about some letters and words to other letters and words. The making-words tactic encouraged Yasmin to look at all the letters in words; and in creating the secret word, she had to stretch out the word and listen to the sounds—something she needed to do to move her toward more conventional (and less invented) spelling when writing. Although the making-words strategy was helpful, the difficulty she demonstrated suggested that she would need support to be successful.

On the other hand, during the decoding-by-analogy activity, Yasmin quickly began using the approach to read unknown words. In addition, she enjoyed the work and appeared to learn something about how to approach unknown words. In this case, the difficulty lies in Yasmin's inability to generate her own rhyming words. Thus, an approach that provided her with "key words" to use for making analogies would be important (see Gaskins et al., 1996/1997).

These sessions were evaluated by using an "All the Words I Know" task. In the past, Yasmin had demonstrated an inability to use orthographic spelling patterns to generate words. After these two thirty-minute sessions, Yasmin was given five minutes to write the words she knew. She still mostly wrote random sight words, but she did write two families of words: *may, lay, say* and *ring, sing*.

Differentiated Instruction and Intervention with Progress Monitoring. As a result of this diagnostic teaching experience, her classroom teacher, in consultation with the reading specialist, devised a support program based on explicit instruction in the close examination of entire words and the introduction of key vocabulary to use in decoding by analogy. Because the teacher noted that many of her ELL students were having the same types of difficulties that Yasmin was experiencing and because these activities had not been done in her grade 2 class, they were introduced to the whole class and used regularly throughout the week.

In addition, it was clear that Yasmin needed more print experience and practice reading easy books. Her teacher had already begun to provide some of this, but the reading coach also suggested an activity that would promote repeated readings. Finally, additional writing experience was introduced by the literacy coach and supported by the teacher.

For Yasmin, the benefits of diagnostic teaching were both immediate and long term. She was quickly engaged in an instructional program that held promise for addressing her needs. The faculty at Yasmin's school needed to continue to monitor her progress to ensure that she continued to close the gap between her performance and school expectations. One of the benefits of diagnostic teaching in Yasmin's case was that we were able to assure ourselves that Yasmin's problems appeared to be more likely the result of her non-English-speaking status at the start of school than to any significant learning disabilities.

Our first diagnostic teaching sessions do not always yield so rich a reward. One thing is abundantly clear, however. The quality of these sessions was directly related to two factors: the quality of the assessment information that was gathered before diagnostic teaching and the thoughtfulness of the planning that went into the diagnostic teaching segment.

Interventions and Continuous Progress Monitoring

The procedures we have recommended throughout this text, and particularly in this chapter, are designed to yield excellent diagnostic information about individual students who are struggling in the areas of reading and/or writing. The inquiry-focused assessment and diagnostic approach reveals insights that can help us to improve the match between learners and instructional contexts. Frequently, this inquiry leads to changes in the overall instructional context—as they did for Tha'm and Kyle. Differentiated practices in the classroom can and do make a critical difference for many students (see Connor et al., 2011; Coyne, Kame'enui, & Simmons, 2004).

Sometimes, however, students continue to struggle even when they have received very good classroom instruction. In these cases, thoughtful and well-informed intervention may be necessary. According to the Rhode Island RTI Technical Assistance Project, "interventions are enhancements of the general education curriculum." They are

- based on students' performance on a variety of assessment measures.
- targeted to a particular skill or set of skills to improve student outcomes.
- short-term, explicit instruction.
- monitored frequently to document progress.
- revised as necessary based on student performance.

(RITAP, http://www.ritap.org/rti/about/an-intervention-system.php)

Given this definition of interventions, we might think of interventions as a sustained version of diagnostic teaching (Fuchs et al., 2011).

Although it is beyond the scope of this text to take up an extensive discussion of intervention, it is important to understand that there are a number of promising practices—especially in the area of early intervention. We provide a supplemental reading list at the end of this chapter as a reference for further reading in this area. Whether the interventions are based in differentiated classroom practice or supplemental individual/small-group settings, progress monitoring is an essential component.

Formative progress monitoring informs us about the efficacy of our diagnostic teaching sessions in the context of a thorough literacy assessment. It is also an essential component of instruction in many interventions. For example, the interactive strategies approach (ISA) designed and tested by Donna Scanlon and her colleagues (Scanlon, Anderson, & Sweeney, 2010) is an early intervention with multiple goals. During ISA sessions, teachers are expected to shape their instruction as they observe and assess students' response. A detailed lesson-plan format is used to focus the intervention. One of the authors of this text (Lipson) has been working with a large elementary school to implement an early intervention/prevention system using ISA. We have adapted the Scanlon et al., lesson plan slightly to ensure that formative progress monitoring assessment data is gathered each day. Figure 10.9, for example, shows how the reading specialist, Jane Kanfer, keeps a running record for each student in a two-child, grade 1, small-group session—a type of formative assessment associated with improved student outcomes (Ross, 2004). Similarly, Figure 10.10 demonstrates how she engages in daily assessment of kindergarten students' letter and letter-sound knowledge. In this case, the teacher puts a dash before and after each letter she is teaching. As she works with students, she puts a check mark in front of the letter if the child knows the letter name. She puts a check after the letter if the child knows the letter sound. This ongoing and continuous assessment provides daily and weekly data for planning and revising instruction. Of course, it also provides evidence about whether the intervention is benefiting the students.

**FIGURE 10.9
Formative Progress
Monitoring
Example: Excerpt
from ISA lesson
plan, Grade 1**

Date: Wed. 4-13-11   **Group Time:** 12:05

St 1: Susanah   **St 2:** Peter

1. Read-Aloud/Shared Reading or Rereading

Title/Level: reread Ladybugs, Level F

Test Comprehension: Gen'l Under, Active Engagement, RETell, Pic Cues, Making CON

AE CON	AE CON

Word ID Strategies

Picture Clues	Picture Clues
Sounds	Sounds
Make Sense	Make Sense
Chunks/Families	Chunks/Families
Read Past	Read Past
Reread	Reread
Flex Sounds	Flex Sounds
Break Up Words	Break Up Words

Letter/Sound: REC, NAM, ID

Running Record

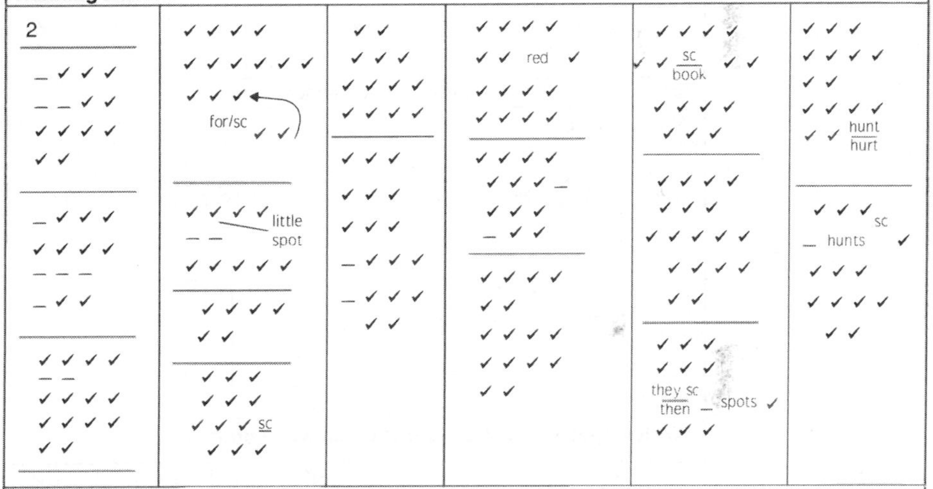

High-Frequency Words: REC, ID

Vocabulary

Comments/Notes

Source: Thanks to Jane Kanfer. Scanlon, D. M., Anderson, K. L., & Sweeney, J. M. (2010). *Early intervention for reading difficulties: The interactive strategies approach.* New York, NY: Guilford.

**FIGURE 10.10
Formative Progress
Monitoring
Example: Excerpt
from ISA lesson
plan, Grade K**

Date: Wed. 4-13-11   **Group Time:** 12:40–1:10

St 1: Malik   **St 2:** Ian

2. Phonological Awareness
Sound Sorting: Rhyme, Beg, End, Mid **Sound Blending:** Onset-Rime, **Single Phonemes** w/ Pix, w/o Pix?? **Sound Counting/Segmenting:** 2 Phonemes, 3 Phonemes Ending sound
Comments/Notes

St 1: Malik   **St 2:** Ian

3. Letter and Sounds, Alphabetic Mapping, Word Families, Decoding
Letter Names: Recognize, Name, Print: new letters: vowels **Letter Sounds: Letter/Sound Ass**, Consonant Sub (begin), Consonant Sub (end) **Other Decoding Elements:** Short Vowel, VCe, Digraph, Blend
Letter Symbol/Sound Identification playing Show Me!

St 1						St 2					
✓a✓	✓e✓	✓i✓	✓m✓	✓q✓	✓v✓	✓a✓	✓e?	✓i✓	✓m✓	✓q✓	✓v✓
✓b✓	✓f✓	✓j✓	✓n✓	✓r✓	✓w✓	✓b?	✓f✓	✓j✓	✓n✓	✓r✓	✓w✓
✓c✓	✓g✓	✓k✓	✓o✓	✓s✓	✓x✓	✓c✓	✓g✓	✓k✓	✓o✓	_s_	✓x✓
_d_	✓h✓	✓l✓	✓p✓	✓t✓	✓y✓	✓d✓	✓h✓	✓l✓	✓p✓	?t✓	✓y?
				✓u?	✓z✓					✓u✓	✓z✓

Extension Activity: Play Letter/Sound Memory Game
Word Building
Word Reading: Decode CVC words w/ pic support, using letter tiles

/u/	/b/ ⊕
	/e/
	/y/

Written Spelling—Letter Formation on white boards

a✓	e✓	i✓	m✓	q✓	u✓	y✓	a⑦	e✓	i✓	m✓	q✓	u✓	y✓
b✓	f✓	j✓	n✓	r⑦	v✓	z✓	b⑦	f✓	j✓	n✓	r✓	v✓	z✓
c✓	g✓	k✓	o✓	s_	w✓		c✓	g⑦	k✓	o✓	s✓	w✓	
d✓	h✓	l✓	p✓	t✓	x✓		d⑦	h✓	l✓	p✓	t✓	x✓	

Comments/Notes

Source: Thanks to Jane Kanfer. Forms adapted Scanlon, D. M., Anderson, K. L., & Sweeney, J. M. (2010). *Early intervention for reading difficulties:* The interactive strategies approach. New York, NY: Guilford.

Formative assessment can be equally important for work with older students. Gelzheiser, Scanlon, and Hallgren-Flynn (2010) have designed and tested a related intervention: Interactive Strategies Approach-Extended (ISA-X). Their Teacher Observation Checklist demonstrates how comprehensively teachers can capture students' emerging competence in key areas of literacy (see Figure 10.11).

FIGURE 10.11   Teacher Observation Checklist for Use with the ISA-X

Student: _____ *Teacher:* _____			
Motivation to Read and Write			
	Rarely	Sometimes	Regularly
Demonstrates motivation to read			
• Is eager to begin reading			
• Remains engaged while reading			
Demonstrates stamina for reading; able to read for long periods without needing a break			
Demonstrates interest in the content			
• Initiates conversations about content			
• Indicates that he or she thinks about the texts beyond the context of the lesson			
• Expresses interest in reading beyond the context of the lesson; asks to read the book at home			
Expresses book preferences (e.g., author, genre)			
Demonstrates interest in learning new words			
Strategic Word Identification			
	Support/Prompting Needed		
	Specific	Open-Ended	Without
Uses code-based strategies to identify unfamiliar words			
• Thinks about the sounds in the word			
• Looks for parts he or she knows			
• Tries different pronunciations			
• Breaks the word into smaller parts			
Uses meaning-based strategies to identify unfamiliar words			
• Checks the pictures			
• Thinks of words that might make sense			
• Reads past the puzzling word			
• Goes back to the beginning and starts again			

(Continued)

FIGURE 10.11   (Continued)

	Rarely	Sometimes	Regularly
Demonstrates appropriate use of 1- or 2-syllable words	◄		
Demonstrates appropriate use of 3–5-syllable words			
Integrates sources of information to cross-check identification of unfamiliar words			
Fluency			
	Rarely	Sometimes	Regularly
Reads text with fluency			
• Accuracy			
• Appropriate phrasing			
• Appropriate speed			
• Appropriate expression			

	Support/Prompting Needed		
Active Comprehension			
Within the Text			
	Specific	Open-Ended	Without
Notices, comments, and reacts to text			
• Details			
• Critical events, major ideas			
Monitors that what was read makes sense			
• Sentence level			
• Paragraph/page level			
• Chapter/text level			
Applies fix-up strategies			
• Rereads for accuracy, and information			
• Checks the illustrations			◄
• Checks the punctuation			
• Reads ahead for more information			
• Asks for assistance			
• Asks specific clarifying questions			
Uses story structure to support comprehension			
• Looks for character and setting at beginning			
• Attends to character motive and development over time			
• Attends to the problem and its resolution			
• Attends to point of view			

FIGURE 10.11 (Continued)

Uses text features to support comprehension			
• Illustrations			
• Headings			
• Captions and text inserts			
• Charts and maps			
• Timelines			
Beyond the Text			
Uses knowledge to support comprehension			
Sets purposes; asks questions for reading			
Seeks text information that addresses purposes and questions			
Makes personal connections with text			
Integrates text clues to make appropriate inferences			
Uses information in the text as the basis for predictions about what will happen next			
Attends to and reads with comprehension highly descriptive or inferential language			
Synthesizes information and attends to the big ideas and messages in the text			
About the Text			

	Support/Prompting Needed		
	Specific	Open-Ended	Without
Reads strategically, using the major features of genre to support comprehension			
• Informational text			
• Folktale			
• Historical fiction			
• Biography			
• Realistic fiction			
Considers the author's purpose and decision making while reading			

Vocabulary			
	Rarely	Sometimes	Regularly
Monitors whether he or she knows a word's meaning			

(Continued)

FIGURE 10.11   (Continued)

Uses resources to help determine meaning of unknown words			
• Context			
• Glossary			
• Teacher assistance			
Alphabetics			
	Knows Few	Knows Some	Knows All
Consonants			
• Consonant digraphs			
• Consonants that require flexibility			
Vowels			
• Long vowels			
• Short vowels			
• Combinations that make unique sounds			
• R-controlled vowels			
Common prefixes and suffixes			
	Rarely	Sometimes	Regularly
Applies knowledge when decoding			
• 1- or 2-syllable words			
• 3–5-syllable words			

Note. Knows Few = most exemplars are not automatic; Knows Some = some exemplars are automatic; Knows All = consistent and automatic with all exemplars.

Source: Successful Approaches to RTI: Collaborative Practices for Improving K–12, Literacy, edited by M. Y. Lipson and K. K. Wixson. Copyright 2010 International Reading Association. May be copied for classroom use.

Benchmark progress monitoring provides additional information about the progress of struggling readers and writers in relation to that of their peers. While formative progress monitoring can tell us if students are responding to specific instruction/interventions, benchmark progress monitoring helps us to see whether vulnerable students are closing the gap between their own performance and that of more normally developing peers. In the school described above, teachers and specialists have devised a comprehensive assessment system, with periodic benchmark assessments on all students three times a year. In grades K and 1, teachers have inserted an additional mid-fall assessment because they are aware that entry data on very young children can be unreliable. In this school, the data are entered into a data management system that allows many types of analyses for school and district use. However, specific students are monitored more closely.

Lionel is one such student. He entered grade 1 significantly behind his age peers in all areas of literacy. The end-of-kindergarten benchmark for this school is level B on the

Fountas and Pinnell Benchmark assessment. In addition, students are expected to know most letter names (upper and lower case) and the primary sound associated with each letter. They are also expected to be able to recognize eighteen high-frequency sight words and to read eight of ten decodable CVC words. This school has set a benchmark level for the beginning of grade 1 of "4/C" on the Fountas and Pinnell Benchmark Assessment System (BAS). Lionel read at level 1/A at both the end of kindergarten and the beginning of grade 1. Although he did meet the benchmark for letter recognition and phonological awareness, he did not for either letter-sound production or sight-word recognition. In addition, he could read only one CVC word (likely read at sight).

His reading teacher worked with him daily for thirty minutes using the ISA approach. She could see that he was making steady progress with this approach and kept daily/weekly records of his letter-sound knowledge, his sight-word recognition, and his progress in moving through increasingly difficult texts based on improving performance on running records. In November, grade 1 teachers assess all students using a common grade-level text (targeted for level 6/E) and a standardized administration procedure. At that time, it was clear that Lionel was responding to the intervention but that he was still lagging behind his age peers. Of course, while his normally developing peers had been expected to move from a level 4 to a level 6, Lionel had moved from a level 1 to a level 4; he was closing the gap. Lionel's progress for the year is graphed in Figure 10.12. By February, Lionel was reading at a level 12—more evidence that he was responding to instruction and intervention, and by the end of the year, Lionel met the ambitious benchmark set by that school: level 18.

When progress monitoring suggests that students are not responding to instruction or intervention, then further adjustments may be indicated. Simon is a good example of such a student. At the beginning of grade 1, he met the benchmarks established, but by February, it was clear that he was not responding to classroom instruction. Indeed, his

FIGURE 10.12   Benchmark Progress Monitoring for Lionel, Grade 1

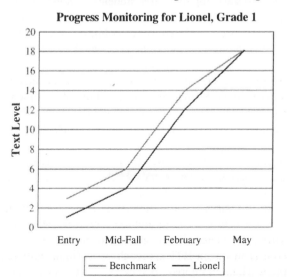

Progress Monitoring for Lionel, Grade 1

FIGURE 10.13   Progress Monitoring Graph for Simon, Grade 1–2

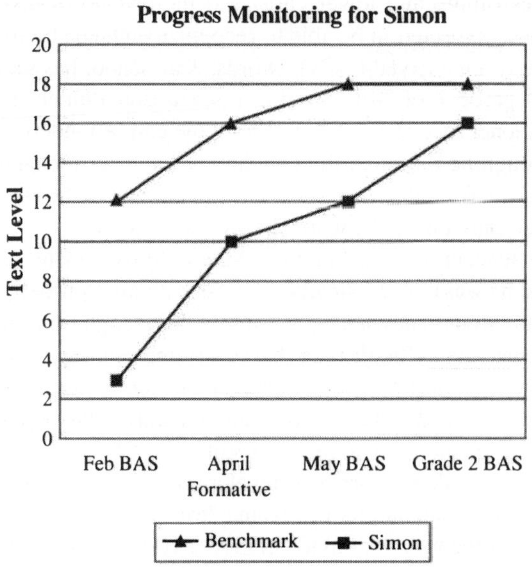

Progress Monitoring for Simon

mid-year assessment placed him at exactly the same text level at which he had begun the year (level 4/C). He began ISA intervention in late February, and his response was dramatic. Formative progress monitoring revealed that he was making excellent progress in word recognition accuracy and strategic word identification. As well, he was adding sight-word recognition, although more slowly. In May, Simon achieved a level 12 on the BAS. More impressively, he continued to close the gap, even with the summer break. Using the school policy of a "fast start" for vulnerable students, Simon was helped to continue steady progress in early grade 2. Despite these good indicators on the benchmark assessments, the formative assessment data offered were troubling. First, Simon's instant recognition of high-frequency words was not improving very rapidly. Second, although he was an accurate reader, he was extraordinarily slow. As a result, and in consultation with colleagues, Simon's grade 2 reading teacher introduced fluency components to his intervention (using diagnostic teaching tactics). Within two weeks, Simon had tripled his WCPM and consolidated some sight vocabulary. This provided good evidence that his adjusted program would continue to help him close the gap and sustain his progress (see Figure 10.13).

MAKING DIAGNOSTIC TEACHING WORK

Diagnostic teaching requires a solid knowledge base, a willingness to explore variation in student performance, a broad and deep knowledge of assessment, and a repertoire of activities and materials for creating instructional adaptations/interventions. Whether a school is using an RTI approach to working with struggling readers and writers or simply working to improve outcomes for all students in more-traditional contexts, expertise in these areas will make a difference. Decision making and diagnostic teaching require that classroom teachers, specialists, and special educators make their hunches (hypotheses) explicit, set priorities, and use them to plan and execute instructional adaptations. Maintaining careful assessment folders/files and reviewing the contents periodically can set the stage for this reflective teaching. When students' work and performance are reviewed over time and across multiple tasks and texts, it is often easier to inform instruction—to think about what might work or what should be attempted. As we have noted elsewhere in this text, data teams or other collegial groupings can make this process even more effective.

Good teaching requires that teachers establish and maintain their focus to accomplish assessment or instructional purposes. However, good teaching is also opportunistic and flexible. Interactive decision making during instruction is a hallmark of effective instruction (Coyne et al., 2011; Duffy & Roehler, 1989). This requires careful listening and refocusing—and a knowledgeable teacher.

To capitalize on the diagnostic teaching procedures we have described in this chapter, classroom teachers and clinicians will need to acknowledge the strengths and limitations of their own settings. In order to make diagnostic teaching more realistic for busy practitioners, we suggest two specific practices that may prove helpful, depending on the setting.

Target Selections for Diagnostic Teaching

Classroom teachers who are using a core reading system can designate specific selections at each level for use as diagnostic teaching selections. In this way, conditions can be set up that reflect the focus of classroom instruction. For example, predetermined selections can be used to:

1. Conduct an individual assessment that examines students' progress outside their usual group setting
2. Set up conditions that are analogous to classroom instruction and compare those to students' unaided reading of the selection
3. Manipulate aspects of the lesson that are critical for student(s) in a particular classroom
4. Select texts that make different demands as a means of exploring student flexibility

If selections are targeted periodically, it is possible to do more-elaborate assessment from time to time, rather than attempting it on a daily or even weekly basis.

Teachers who are using collections of leveled text can do the same thing. There are so many of these materials available, including online texts, that it should not be difficult to identify key texts at each level to use for diagnostic teaching. As we have seen, however, not all texts are created equal, so some care should be taken that the text affords the opportunities for observation and assessment that you want. Once these texts have been identified, they should be taken out of more-general instructional circulation so that they can be reserved for ongoing assessment.

You might use the form in Figure 10.14 to organize these diagnostic sessions. Over time, you will establish a collection of books and diagnostic assessment conditions that are especially effective for assessing one or another aspect of literacy. Some texts are superb

FIGURE 10.14
Diagnostic Teaching
Planning Guide

Focus for the Diagnostic Teaching:

Text(s):

Key Features of Text(s):

Possible Elements for Diagnostic Teaching	Notes

Prereading
• Introduce key vocabulary
• Build background
• Preview text
• Review strategy(ies)
• Structured overview
•
•
 	
During Reading
• Adjust level of support
  ○ Independent
  ○ Teacher guided
• Prompt for strategy use
  ○ Word identification
  ○ Comprehension Strategies
• Adjust Access
  ○ Teacher read-aloud
  ○ Taped read-along
  ○ Computer-assisted text
•
•
 	
After Reading (Adjust Task)
• Questions
• Retellings
• Story maps
• Structured overviews
• Discussion
• Performance
• Visual representation
Other Changes in Support or Tasks
• Story/text framework
• Repeated reading
• Length, size, etc.
•
•
 	
Change Text
• Quality of narrative
• Exposition
• Narrative vs exposition
• Interest
• Picture support
• Length	

for assessing narrative structure or inference or character development. Others provide effective opportunities to observe young students' development of early and emergent skills. Over the years, we have acquired a number of texts that are our favorites, but there are also many more commercially available texts for teachers. We have already noted how valuable we find the texts in the Developmental Reading Assessment (DRA). The DRA includes both narrative and expository texts that are long enough to provide interesting opportunities for manipulation. Similarly, several publishers have produced excellent sets of leveled guided reading materials—including materials in the content areas (see, e.g., *Houghton Mifflin Science Leveled Readers*, 2006). Using interesting and varied books for diagnostic teaching is especially important, because it allows us to examine students' affective responses along with the other aspects of reading.

A Collection of Diagnostic Teaching Selections

For both classroom teachers and specialists, the time and attention demands are so great that diagnostic teaching is more likely to be employed if the materials and tasks are readily available. Paratore and Indrisano (1987) have developed a set of materials they use for diagnostic teaching that include graded (or progressively more difficult) passages and a set of tasks and prompts to accompany these passages. These materials permit teachers to explore a range of student responses "on the spot." To be effective, a collection of diagnostic teaching selections must be organized and grouped for easy use and clearly labeled so that adjustments can be made during the assessment session. In addition, we recommend using a set of clearly tabbed task cards to facilitate administration. The following types of materials should be considered for inclusion in a diagnostic teaching collection.

- Selections ranked by difficulty or a list of books to be used for assessment purposes
- A listing of the types of tasks that can and should be used, and the order in which these will be presented
- A series of statements for each selection or book that could be expected in an adequate retelling of the text and a place to note these
- A summary sheet that includes key words to be used for assessment of vocabulary and/or word recognition
- A place to make notes about student comments

These ideas are, of course, only suggestions. Once started, a well-organized collection can and will grow. Furthermore, teachers who are committed to an ongoing formative assessment find this type of organization absolutely essential to effective assessment-instruction.

A Collection of Diagnostic Teaching Strategies

Although there is a temptation to "buy" instruction and intervention "off the shelf," there is very little evidence to support the efficacy of many of the available programs. Certainly, publishers can be helpful in providing and organizing materials, but the specific teaching tactics and approaches that result in significant changes for students rely heavily on teacher expertise. In this text, we have focused on understanding the reading process and on assessment practices that help us understand what individual students know and can do in the areas of reading and writing. It is difficult to make a difference for any student when you don't know how reading and writing work, and it is impossible to improve the performance of struggling students without a clear appreciation for what they know already and what is causing them difficulty.

There are many useful books on instruction and intervention available today. One useful compendium of instructional tactics that are embedded in a diagnostic teaching approach is the book by Barbara Walker, *Diagnostic Teaching of Reading: Techniques for Instruction and Assessment*, 7th ed. (Walker, 2011). A partial listing of other resources that we can recommend is available at the end of this chapter. We have limited our recommendations to those that have a significant body of evidence to support their use. Alternatively, there are several that provide excellent practical guidance based on practices that have proven to be successful. At the same time, assessment is a critical component of this success:

> Multiple ways of reading student progress, done over time and incorporated into the learning process, are essential for an accurate assessment of what students know and are able to do. (CLC, 2011, p. 1)

What is clear today is that almost every student can/should become literate. We have both the research to support specific practices and evidence of large-scale change in schools that are determined to do better.

CHAPTER SUMMARY

This chapter focused on the point in assessment when informed decision making is required to determine how instructional planning will proceed. Specifically, this chapter dealt with understanding and implementing the steps in the assessment-instruction process that involve evaluating the match between learner and context, reflection and generating hypotheses (Step 4), and diagnostic teaching (Step 5).

Step 4—reflection, decision making, and planning—involves using the information gathered in Steps 1 to 3 to determine the fit or match between the knowledge, skills and strategies, and motivation and reflectivity of the learner and the settings, instruction, resources, and tasks within the instructional context. We generated some preliminary hypotheses about what the learner needs. This step is designed to help us make decisions about the relative importance of the various problems/needs we have identified.

Once this has been accomplished, we need to identify a better or optimal match between the learner and the context in order to (re)establish learning and monitor progress on a continuous basis (Step 5). To accomplish this goal, we rely primarily on the technique of *diagnostic teaching*, which is characterized here as one type of an RTI intervention. This procedure is both diagnostic, because it allows for the collection of additional information in order to clarify and test hypotheses, and instructional, because it provides opportunities to try out methods that may be successful alternatives for working with a student.

The process of diagnostic teaching involves three related tasks: planning, executing, and evaluating. During planning, we need to determine how we will focus the diagnostic teaching to verify our hunches about both the source of the problem and the instructional interventions that are most likely to call forth learning. Executing involves administering diagnostic teaching sessions using either the alternative methods or scaffolding approach to gain information about how a student performs under several different or contrasting conditions. Successful execution also requires the flexibility necessary to be able to take advantage of opportunities as they arise.

The primary thrust of the evaluation of the diagnostic teaching is to determine the impact of the manipulations on the student's learning, performance, attitude, motivation, and/or knowledge. Diagnostic teaching activities can be facilitated in both the classroom and the clinic through procedures such as using targeted selections in basal reading programs or preselecting a collection of diagnostic teaching materials.

Diagnostic teaching episodes are generally planned for one or two sessions within an overall assessment. Based on the results, we make changes in the classroom instructional program and/or we plan for interventions. One of the most significant changes in recent years involves the expectation that classroom teachers and specialists will use ongoing *progress monitoring*. In this chapter, we discussed formative progress monitoring and periodic benchmark progress monitoring designed to: (1) inform and adapt our instruction and (2) determine whether the instruction and/or intervention is closing the gap between specific students and their more normally developing peers. This recursive process can and should be used at all levels of the educational enterprise in order to ensure that all students meet their educational potential.

MyEducationLab™

Go to the Topics, Reading Instruction, Reading Diagnosis, Progress Monitoring, and Struggling Readers and Intervention Strategies, in the MyEducationLab (www.myeducationlab .com) for your course, where you can:

- Find learning outcomes for Reading Instruction, Reading Diagnosis, Progress Monitoring, and Struggling Readers and Intervention Strategies, along with the national standards that connect to these outcomes.

- Complete Assignments and Activities that can help you more deeply understand the chapter content.

- Apply and practice your understanding of the core teaching skills identified in the chapter using the Building Teaching Skills and Dispositions learning units.

- Examine challenging situations and cases presented in the IRIS Center Resources.

- Check your comprehension of the content covered in the chapter by going to the Study Plan in the Book Resources for your text. Here you will be able to take a chapter quiz, receive feedback on your answers, and then access Review, Practice, and Enrichment activities to enhance your understanding of chapter content.

A+RISE A+RISE® Standards2Strategy™ is an innovative and interactive online resource that offers new teachers in grades K-12 just in time, research-based instructional strategies that meet the linguistic needs of ELLs as they learn content, differentiate instruction for all grades and abilities, and are aligned to Common Core Elementary Language Arts standards (for the literacy strategies) and to English language proficiency standards in WIDA, Texas, California, and Florida.

HIGH-UTILITY STRATEGIES FOR INSTRUCTION

Phonics/Decoding

Instructional Approaches

Chard, D. J., & Dickson, S. V. (1990). Phonological awareness instructional and assessment guidelines. *Intervention in School and Clinic, 34*, 261–270.

Hiebert, E. H., & Taylor, B. M. (2000). Beginning reading instruction: Research on early interventions. In R. Barr, M. L. Kamil, P. B. Mosenthal, & P. D. Pearson (Eds.), *Handbook of reading research* (Vol. 3, pp. 455–482). Mahwah, NJ: Erlbaum.

Metsala, J. L., & Ehri, L. C. (1998). *Word recognition in beginning reading literacy.* Mahwah, NJ: Erlbaum

Snow, C. E., Burns, M. S., & Griffin, P. (Eds.). (1998). *Preventing reading difficulties in young children.* Washington, DC: National Academy Press.

Stahl, S. A., Duffy-Hester, A. M., & Stahl, K. A. D. (1998). Everything you wanted to know about phonics (but were afraid to ask). *Reading Research Quarterly, 33*, 338–355.

Torgesen, J. K., Alexander, A. W., Wagner, R. K., Rashotte, C. A, Voeller, K., Conway, T., & Rose, E. (2001). Intensive remedial instruction for children with severe reading disabilities: Immediate and long-term outcomes from two instructional approaches. *Journal of Learning Disabilities, 34*, 33–58.

White, T. G. (2005). Effects of systematic and strategic analogy-based phonics on grade 2 students' word reading and reading comprehension. *Reading Research Quarterly, 40,* 234–255

Williams, J. P. (2006). Stories, studies, and suggestions about reading. *Scientific Studies of Reading, 10*, 121–142.

Strategic Word Identification

Gaskins, R. W., Gaskins, J. C., & Gaskins, I. W. (1992). Using what you know to figure out what you don't know. *Reading & Writing Quarterly, 8*, 197–221.

(See Scanlon et al. below.)

Schumaker, J. B., Deshler, D. D., Woodruff, S., Hock, M. F, Bulgren, J. A., & Lenz, B. K. (2006). Reading strategy interventions: Can literacy outcomes be enhanced for at-risk adolescents? *Teaching Exceptional Children, 38* (3), 64–69.

Sight Vocabulary

Chard, D. J., Pikulski, J. J., & McDonagh, S. H. (2006). Fluency: The link between decoding and comprehension for struggling readers. In K. Lems (Ed.), *Fluency instruction: Research-based best practices* (pp. 39–61).

Ehri, L. C. (1994). Development of the ability to read words: Update. In R. Ruddell, M. Ruddell, and H. Singer (Eds.), *Theoretical models and processes of reading* (4th ed., pp. 323–358). Hillsdale, NJ: Erlbaum.

Ehri, L. C. (2005). Learning to read words: Theory, findings, and issues. *Scientific Studies of Reading, 9*, 167–188.

See Hiebert, E. H., TextProject for lists of words and available texts for teaching sight words: http://textproject.org/teachers/word-lists/

McCormick, S., & Becker, E. Z. (1996). Word recognition and word identification: A review of research on effective practices with learning disabled students. *Reading Research and Instruction, 36*, 5–17.

Word Study

Bear, D. R., Invernizzi, M., Johnston, F., & Templeton, S. (2012). *Words Their way: Word study for phonics, vocabulary, and spelling instruction.* Upper Saddle River, NJ: Allyn & Bacon.

Fountas, I., & Pinnell, G. S. (2001). *Guiding readers and writers.* Portsmouth, NH: Heinemann.

Ganske, K. (2000). *Word journeys: Assessment-guided phonics, spelling, and vocabulary instruction.* New York, NY: Guilford.

Templeton, S. (1997). *Teaching the integrated language arts* (2nd ed.). Boston, MA: Houghton Mifflin.

Zutell, J. (April–June, 1998). Word sorting: A developmental spelling approach to word study for delayed readers [Special issue: Promoting word learning with delayed readers]. *Reading & Writing Quarterly; Overcoming Learning Difficulties, 14*(2), 219–238.

Fluency

Kuhn, M. R., & Stahl, S. A. (2003). Fluency: A review of developmental and remedial practices. *Journal of Educational Psychology, 95*(1), 3–21.

Rasinski, T. V. (2003). *The fluent reader: Oral reading strategies for building word recognition, fluency, and comprehension.* New York, NY: Scholastic.

Rasinski, T. V., & Hoffman, T. V. (2003). Theory and research into practice: Oral reading in the school literacy curriculum. *Reading Research Quarterly, 38*, 510–522.

Samuels, S. J., & Farstrup, A. (2006). *What research has to say about fluency instruction.* Newark, DE: International Reading Association.

Stahl, S. (1997). *Fluency-oriented reading instruction* (Reading Research Report No. 79). Athens, GA: National Reading Research Center.

Repeated Readings

Dowhower, S. L. (1987). Effects of repeated reading on second-grade transitional readers' fluency and comprehension. *Reading Research Quarterly, 22*, 389–406.

Herman, P. A. (1985). The effects of repeated readings on reading rate, speech pauses, and word recognition accuracy. *Reading Research Quarterly, 20,* 553–565.

Rashotte, C. A., & Torgesen, J. K. (1985). Repeated reading and reading fluency in learning disabled children. *Reading Research Quarterly, 20*, 180–188.

Comprehension

Reciprocal Teaching

Oczkus, L. (2003). *Reciprocal teaching at work: Strategies for improving reading comprehension.* Newark, DE: International Reading Association.

Palincsar, A. S., & Brown, A. L. (1984). Reciprocal teaching of comprehension-fostering and comprehension-monitoring activities. *Cognition and Instruction, 1*(2), 117–175.

Palincsar, A. S., & Brown, A. L. (1985). Reciprocal teaching: A means to a meaningful end. In J. Osborn, P.T. Wilson, & R. C. Anderson (Eds.), *Reading education: Foundations for a literate America* (pp. 229–310). Lexington, MA: D.C. Heath.

Palincsar, A. S., & Brown, A. L. (1986). Interactive teaching to promote independent learning from text. *The Reading Teacher, 39*, 771–777.

Rosenshine, B., & Meister, C. (1994). Reciprocal teaching: A review of the research. *Review of Educational Research, 64*, 479–530.

What Works Clearinghouse. http://ies.ed.gov/ncee/wwc/interventionreport.aspx?sid=434

Question-Answer Relationship

Raphael, T. E. (1982). Question-answering strategies for children. *The Reading Teacher, 36,* 186–190.

Raphael, T. E., & Au, K. H. (2005). QAR: Enhancing comprehension and test taking across grades and content areas. *The Reading Teacher, 59,* 206–221.

Raphael, T. E., Highfield, K., & Au, K. H. (2006). *QAR now: Question answer relationships.* New York, NY: Scholastic.

Questioning the Author (QtA)

Beck, I. L., Hamilton, R., McKeown, M. G., & Kucan, L. (1997). *Questioning the author: An approach for enhancing student engagement with text.* Newark, DE: International Reading Association.

Beck, I. L., & McKeown, M. G. (2006). *Improving comprehension with Questioning the Author: A fresh and expanded view of a powerful approach.* New York, NY: Scholastic.

Discussion

Applebee, A. N., Langer, J. A., Nystrand, M., & Gamoran, A. (2003). Discussion-based approaches to developing understanding: Classroom instruction and student performance in middle and high school English. *American Educational Research Journal, 40,* 685–730.

Fall, R., Webb, N. M., & Chudowsky, N. (2000). Group discussion and large-scale language arts assessment: Effects on students' comprehension. *American Educational Research Journal, 37,* 911–941.

Nystrand, M. (2006). Research on the role of classroom discourse as it affects reading comprehension. *Research in the Teaching of English, 40,* 392–412.

(See QtA above.)

Comprehension Strategies, General

Dole, J. A., Duffy, G., Roehler, L. R., & Pearson, P. D. P. (1991). Moving from the old to the new: Research on reading comprehension instruction. *Review of Educational Research, 61,* 239–264.

Harvey, S., & Goudvis, S. (2007). *Strategies that work: Teaching comprehension for understanding and engagement.* Stenhouse.

Harvey, S., Goudvis, A., & Wallis, J. (2010). *Comprehension intervention: Small-group lessons for the primary comprehension toolkit.* Portsmouth, NH: Heinemann.

Paris, S. G., Lipson, M. Y., & Wixson, K. K. (1983). Becoming a strategic reader. *Contemporary Educational Psychology, 8,* 293–316.

Informed Strategies for Learning (ISL)

Rottman, T. R., & Cross, D. (1990). Using informed strategies for learning to enhance the reading and thinking skills of children with learning disabilities. *Journal of Learning Disabilities, 23,* 270–278.

Paris, S. G., Cross, D. R., & Lipson, M. Y. (1984). Informed strategies for learning: A program to improve children's reading awareness and comprehension. *Journal of Educational Psychology, 76,* 1239–1252.

Vocabulary

Baumann, J. F., & Kame'enui, E. J. (2003). *Vocabulary instruction: Research to practice.* New York, NY: Guilford.

Beck, I. L., & McKeown, M. G. (2001). Text talk: Capturing the benefits of read-aloud experiences for young children. *The Reading Teacher, 55,* 10–20.

Beck, I. L., McKeown, M. G., & Kucan, L. (2002). *Bringing words to life: Robust vocabulary instruction.* New York, NY: Guilford.

Blachowicz, C. L. Z., & Fisher, P. J. (2009). *Teaching Vocabulary in All Classrooms* (4th ed.) Boston, MA: Allyn & Bacon.

Blachowicz, C. L. Z., & Fisher, P. J. (2011). Best practices in teaching vocabulary revisited. In L. Morrow & L. Gambrell (eds.), *Best practices in literacy instruction* (4th ed., pp. 224–249). New York, NY: Guilford.

Graves, M. F. (2006). *The vocabulary book: Learning and instruction.* New York, NY: Teachers College Press.

Hiebert, E. H., & Kamil, M. L. (2005). *Teaching and learning vocabulary: Bringing research to practice.* Mahwah, NJ: Lawrence Erlbaum Associates.

Stahl, S. A., & Kapinus, B. (2001). *Word power: What every educator needs to know about vocabulary.* Washington, DC: NEA Professional Library.

Writing

Gersten, R., & Baker, S. (2003). Teaching expressive writing to students with learning disabilities: A meta-analysis. *Elementary School Journal, 101,* 251–272.

Ray, K. W. (1999). *Wondrous words: Writers and writing in the elementary classroom.* Champagne: University of Illinois, NCTE.

Tompkins, E. (2012). *Teaching writing: Balancing process and product* (6th ed.). Boston, MA: Pearson.

Interactive Writing

Button, K., Johnson, M. J., & Purgerson, P. (1996). Interactive writing in a primary classroom. *The Reading Teacher, 49,* 446–454.

Lyons, C., & Pinnell, G. S. (2001). Systems for change in literacy education. Portsmouth, NH: Heinemann.

Interventions for Struggling Writers

Graham, S., MacArthur, C. A., & Fitzgerald, J. (2007). *Best practices in writing instruction.* New York, NY: Guilford.

Helsel, L., & Greenberg, D. (2007). Helping struggling writers succeed: A self-regulated strategy instruction program. *The Reading Teacher, 33,* 752–760.

Self-Regulated Strategy Development (SRSD)

Graham, S. (2006). Strategy instruction and the teaching of writing. A meta-analysis. In C. MacArthur, S. Graham, & J. Fitzgerald (Eds.), *Self-regulation of learning and performance* (pp. 203–228). Hillsdale, NJ: Erlbaum.

Graham, S., Harris, K. R., & Troia, G. A. (2000). Self-regulated strategy development revisited: Teaching writing strategies to struggling writers. *Topics in Language Disorders, 20*(4), 1–4.

Cognitive Strategy Development Instruction in Writing

Englert, C. S., & Mariage, T. V. (1991). Shared understandings: Structuring the writing experience through dialogue. *Journal of Learning Disabilities, 24*(6), 330–342.

Englert, C. S., Raphael, T. E., & Anderson, L. M. (1992). Socially mediated instruction: Improving students' knowledge and talk about writing. *Elementary School Journal, 92,* 411–449.

RESEARCH-BASED INTERVENTION APPROACHES

Overview of Successful Approaches to Intervention

Lipson, M. Y., & Wixson, K. K. (2010). *Successful approaches to RTI*. Newark, DE: International Reading Association.

Early Intervention in Reading (EIR)

Taylor, B. M., et al. (2006). *Reading Intervention for Early Success™*. Boston, MA: Houghton Mifflin.

Taylor, B. M., Hanson, E., Justice-Swanson, K., & Watts, S. W. (1997). Helping struggling readers: Linking small-group intervention with cross-age tutoring. *The Reading Teacher*, *51*, 196–209.

Taylor, B., Short, R., Frye, B., & Shearer, B. (1992). Classroom teachers prevent reading failure among low-achieving first-grade students. *The Reading Teacher*, *45*, 592–597.

Taylor, B. M., Strait, J., & Medo, M. A. (1994). Early intervention in reading: Supplementary instruction for groups of low achieving students provided by first grade teachers. In E. H. Hiebert & B. M. Taylor (Eds.), *Getting reading right from the start: Effective early literacy interventions*. Needham, MA: Allyn & Bacon.

What Works Clearinghouse, http://ies.ed.gov/ncee/wwc/InterventionReport.aspx?sid=156

Collaborative Strategic Reading

Klingner, J. K., & Vaughn, S. (1999). Promoting reading comprehension, content learning, and English acquisition through collaborative strategic reading (CSR). *The Reading Teacher*, *52*, 738–747.

Klingner, J. K., Vaughn, S., Argüelles, M. E., Hughes, M. T., & Ahwee, S. (2004). Collaborative strategic reading: "Real world" lessons from classroom teachers. *Remedial and Special Education*, *25*(5), 291–302.

Klingner, J. K., Vaughn, S., Dimino, J., Schumm, J. S., & Bryant, D. (2001). *From clunk to click: Collaborative strategic reading*. Longmont, CO: Sopris West.

Comprehensive Intervention Model (CIM)

Dorn, L. J., & Henderson, S. C. (2010). The comprehensive intervention model: A systems approach to RTI. In M. Y. Lipson & K. K. Wixson (Eds.), *Successful approaches to RTI: Collaborative practices for improving K–12 literacy* (pp. 88–120). Newark, DE: International Reading Association.

Dorn, L., & Schubert, B. (2008). A comprehensive intervention model for reversing reading failure: A response to intervention approach. *Journal of Reading Recovery*, *7*(2), 29–41.

Dorn, L. J., & Soffos, C. (2012). *Interventions that work: A comprehensive intervention model for preventing reading failure in grades K–3*. Boston, MA: Allyn & Bacon.

APPENDIX A

Sample Case Report: Jackson

	Date of Report: December, grade 3
Name: Jackson R.	*Grade:* 3
Address: North Westbury, Vermont	*Age:* 9 years, 11 months
Parent's/Guardian's Name: Mr. & Mrs. R.	*Phone:* 945-7324
School Name: Mason Elementary School	*Teacher:* Mrs. Hazlett

SUMMARY OF ASSESSMENT RESULTS

NECAP (State Assessment)	Partially Proficient (Level 2 of 4)		
Fall, Grade 3			
Gates-MacGinitie Reading Tests		**Percentile**	**Stanine**
Fall, Grade 3	Comprehension	38	
	Vocabulary	42	
	Total		4
Fountas & Pinnell Benchmark	Benchmark Target for Fall of Grade 3: 30/N		
Assessment	Instructional Text Level: 18/J		
Fall, Grade 3	Accuracy: 90%		
	Comprehension: 60%		
	Rate (WCPM): 43		
AIMSweb Oral Reading			
Fluency (ORF)	48 WCPM		
Fall, Grade 3			
Winter, Grade 3	63 WCPM		
Peabody Picture Vocabulary Test	Standard Score: 95		
(Form M)	Percentile Rank: 37		
Fall, Grade 3			
Sight-Word Recognition	Recognized 150/220		
Fall, Grade 3			
Woodcock Reading Mastery Tests-Revised	**Relative Mastery**		**Percentile Rank**
(Form G)			
Letter Identification	93%		58
Word Identification	27%		20
Word Attack	32%		9
Word Comprehension	65%		35
Passage Comprehension	29%		8

Specified areas of reading difficulty: Jackson is reading more than one year below grade expectations. Specific areas needing attention are high-frequency sight vocabulary, vowel teams, and fluency in oral reading. Miscue analysis suggests that Jackson has not mastered all consonant combinations and has difficulty blending. He also lacks age-appropriate comprehension strategies.

BACKGROUND INFORMATION

Reason for Initial Concern

Jackson finished grade 2 significantly below the benchmark for that grade and has been exhibiting an increasingly negative attitude toward school. Assessment results from early grade 3 indicate that he experienced some summer loss and that he is struggling in all areas of reading.

Home and Community Background

Although Jackson's family life does not allow much time for outside activities, he says that he likes to bike and fish with his friends in the trailer park where he lives. He does not have much interest in reading, however. As the oldest of four children, Jackson has responsibilities at home. His parents are separated, but his father lives nearby and spends time with Jackson on a regular basis. Jackson's home has few books, and Mrs. R says that her son has always struggled with reading in school. The father did not finish high school; both parents are employed in the service industry.

School History and Teacher Comments

The school records confirm Mrs. R's report that Jackson has struggled from the beginning of his schooling. Despite extra help with the school's core program after being identified in grade 1 as a student that was falling behind, Jackson was still behind his peers at the end of the year. He again received special help in grade 2, this time with a reading specialist in a small group over the entire year. Although the records are not specific as to the approaches and texts used with Jackson, they do show that Jackson was considered for special education.

SUMMARY OF ASSESSMENT RESULTS

Reader Factors

On the statewide assessment, the New England Consortium Assessment of Educational Progress, administered in the fall of third grade, Jackson scored at level 2, or partially proficient. His overall score on the school's screening assessment (the Gates-MacGinitie Reading Tests) places him in the fourth stanine, although his vocabulary results are lower than that. The fall benchmark assessment (BAS) results are even more worrisome, as Jackson scored at level 18, a result that is more typical of students entering grade 2. He also reads slowly, with oral reading fluency results that are well below grade-level expectations.

Given Jackson's history and the assessment results at the beginning of grade 3, the EST team decided to obtain additional diagnostic information. Jackson's standard score equivalent on the Peabody Picture Vocabulary Test-R (PPVT-R) was 95, placing him in the low-average to average range of ability on this test of receptive language.

Observations made by the examiner during the administration of the Fountas and Pinnell BAS indicate that Jackson only attempts to construct meaning from the text, but abandons that focus when he experiences word recognition difficulties.

Some miscues, however, do reflect an effort on Jackson's part to construct meaning from text. This was particularly evident on a passage about a boy who needs a haircut and gets one, with unintended results (*Edwin's Haircut*, Fountas & Pinnel, level K). Early in the text, Jackson misread "snag" for *shaggy* and "jocking" for *joking*. In addition, he consistently misread *snipped* as "snip-ped." On this selection, Jackson's miscues (twenty) rendered a score of frustrational level. However, his retelling of the text was reasonable, if brief. He offered that Edwin got a bad haircut and that he needed to wear a wig after that. On the other hand, Jackson made no reference at all to the initiating event in which Edwin's father was joking, and was unable to offer a resolution to the story—even when prompted to explain how the beginning and the end of the story are alike and/or different. Not surprisingly, Jackson did not appear to appreciate the humor in this story.

Despite Jackson's performance on this grade 2 (level K) passage, the examiner weighed the large number of miscues as well as his comprehension on a different second-grade passage that he read silently (42%) to determine this level as frustrational. Jackson's listening level was determined by weighing his answers to traditional postreading questions and the quality of his retellings. Jackson was tested at the third-grade level twice (levels M and N). In both cases, the percentage of questions answered correctly placed him at a level on the instructional/frustrational border. However, his retellings in both cases lacked organization and missed the main ideas. On the basis of this, the examiner determined Jackson's instructional listening level to be second grade.

Analysis of Jackson's miscues reveals strong attention to initial letters, such as *shaggy–snag* (the first word representing the actual text and the second, Jackson's rendering—here and following in this case report). Other miscues demonstrate use of both beginning and ending sounds (*joking–jocking, snipping–sniping, worse–wars*). Jackson also appears to rearrange letters in the medial portions of words to create new words (*instead–insaid*). Miscues on the Word Identification subtest of the Woodcock Reading Mastery Tests-Revised (WRMT-R) reflect these patterns as well (*grow–grew, happen–hope, heart–hurt*).

Except for the Letter Identification subtest, all of the other subtests of the WRMT-R indicate that Jackson is far below the norm in these tasks. His word comprehension score was relatively stronger and echoed the results on the Gates-MacGinitie Vocabulary subtest. Jackson's only errors before reaching a ceiling level involved analogies in which he could not read one or more of the words. For diagnostic purposes, the examiner gave Jackson those words. In all cases, Jackson was able to complete the analogies as long as the word was read aloud. The results of the Passage Comprehension subtest confirm observations made by the examiner during individual sessions. The cloze exercise requiring Jackson to use context to determine the meanings of words was especially difficult for him.

Word analysis skills were assessed with a miscue analysis (see above). The results of these analyses as well as those of the Word Attack subtest of the WRMT-R indicate difficulties in a number of decoding skills. The validity of tests requiring children to read nonsense words has been questioned; indeed, Jackson did miscall a number of the nonsense words as legitimate words. Despite the drawbacks of these kinds of tests, however, the skill difficulties that surfaced consistently are worth noting. Jackson consistently had difficulty with onset-rime blending, even when he was able to read the base phonogram in isolation. In addition, vowels, both long and short, surfaced as an area of weakness for Jackson on the Word Attack subtest of the WRMT-R. Other error patterns include adding an *m* before a final *p* (*shup–shump*), changing the initial sound entirely despite a correct pronunciation of it prior to word analysis (*quam–cume*), adding ending consonants (*blin–blant*), and separating the letters of blends (*plip–pilip*).

A second testing of the oral reading fluency, during early winter, suggests that Jackson continues to struggle with fluency/automaticity. His WCPM rate was below the target norms at both testings. Jackson lacks automaticity on many sight vocabulary words, something affecting his fluency.

In summary, Jackson's sight-word recognition is inadequate, and his word analysis skills are limited to the ineffective use of phonic analysis. Although his vocabulary knowledge is acceptable for his age, both his listening comprehension and reading comprehension are generally weak. However, in situations in which he has adequate background knowledge and sufficient interest, he is able to answer questions successfully, retell a story, and/or generate a main idea. Finally, early informal work samples suggested that he was almost entirely unable to produce a written product. Even with considerable support, his ideas were disjointed, and his narratives were limited to three or four sentences.

Instructional Factors

Jackson has received instruction both in a regular classroom and in a Title I reading program outside the classroom. Currently, Jackson receives daily supplemental reading instruction in a group of five boys. He is assigned to a regular reading group within the classroom, but it is unclear how often that group meets. In both contexts, relatively short, leveled texts are used. When longer selections are used, they are generally read aloud during a modified guided reading group in which students take turns reading aloud. Neither the observations nor the teacher reports suggest that there has been much explicit instruction of word identification or comprehension strategies.

Jackson is responsible for the same whole-group (independent) tasks assigned to all students during literacy time. The language arts, spelling, and social studies books used in Jackson's classroom are standard third-grade texts with readability estimates ranging from a 2.5 to a 5.0 grade level.

The examiner observed Jackson in his classroom for approximately one hour in late October. At the beginning of the observation, students were transitioning from art. Jackson completed his project, cleaned up, and returned to seatwork without prompting. Jackson worked diligently after returning to his desk. Despite the noise level and the proximity of two groups of children chatting, Jackson seemed undistracted. Although Jackson appears to work well independently, he is very reliant on his teacher. He asks questions frequently, requiring her help on nearly every individual task on which the examiner observed him working.

Jackson was also observed during reading intervention with a reading specialist. During that period, Jackson demonstrated some of the same behaviors. He sought help when tasks appeared to him to be difficult, and he demonstrated very little ability to regulate his own reading skills and strategies. The guided reading format of these sessions makes it difficult for the teacher to assess specific abilities for individual students or to modify and tailor instruction.

DIAGNOSTIC TEACHING

Given the information available, it appeared that Jackson would likely benefit from a comprehensive, but flexible and responsive, approach to instruction and intervention.

On the basis of our earlier reflections, we planned a series of diagnostic teaching episodes for Jackson. First, we introduced the **Interactive Word Identification Strategies** (see Figure A.1) to Jackson, noting that these strategies are useful whenever readers come to words that were unfamiliar or unknown. We also noted that we were aware that Jackson already employed some of these.

Using these strategies as the foundation, we introduced a different interaction pattern than he was accustomed to, as Jackson read aloud.

1. Our instructional efforts were limited to encouraging Jackson to think about what he could do to solve the "puzzling" words he encountered (see Scanlon & Anderson, 2011 for an elaborated explanation).
2. We changed our own behaviors by waiting for him to make an attempt or to try a strategy. If he did not, we simply asked him, "What can you try?"
3. We collected data on Jackson's accuracy, but also on his use of strategies. On the first day, Jackson seemed confused about the change of procedure and was not any more successful than he had been before. As a result, we introduced another dimension.
4. First, we modeled for him the use of several strategies and then played the "Guess My Strategy" game. In this "game," the tutor modeled a strategy when she came to "puzzling" words, and Jackson had to identify the strategy she used to figure out the word. Jackson loved doing this. When it was his turn, we used colorful stones (available at many craft shops) to signal that he had used a particular strategy.

The results were dramatic. Not only did Jackson engage in more self-correction and use of strategies, but his overall accuracy improved immediately. We did note, however, that his fluency suffered proportionately and that this would need to be added to his instructional program at some point.

FIGURE A.1
Interactive
Strategies Used in
Diagnostic Teaching

Identification Strategy List

To figure out a word:

Check the pictures.

fun

I think about the sounds in the word.

??

Think of words that might make sense.

sat

Look for word families or other parts
you know.

Read past the puzzling word.

Go back to the beginning of the sentence and
start again.

a e i o u

Try different pronunciations for some of the
letters, especially the vowel(s).

Look/ing

Break the word into smaller parts.

Source: Scanlon, D. M., & Anderson, K. L. (2010). Using the Interactive Strategies Approach to prevent reading difficulties in an RTI context. In M. Y. Lipson & K. K. Wixson (Eds.), *Successful approaches to RTI* (pp. 20–65). Newark, DE: International Reading Association.

The positive potential of this approach is that there are four "code-based" word identification strategies, but there are also four meaning-based strategies (such as "Think about what would make sense"). We expected that this attention to comprehension monitoring was likely to pay off in Jackson's comprehension as well.

DIAGNOSTIC STATEMENTS AND SUGGESTIONS FOR INSTRUCTION

Jackson is capable of becoming a much stronger reader (and writer) than he is at the moment. The results of the diagnostic teaching suggest that his word recognition and comprehension monitoring abilities can develop quite quickly in the context of a focused and tailored intervention. In addition, these same strategies, employed during classroom instruction, will accelerate his progress.

The advantage to the ISA approach is that Jackson should begin to demonstrate much more independence during reading. This is critical for a student in grade 3. Currently, Jackson is far too dependent on adults during almost all academic tasks, and during reading, he demonstrates very little ability to self-regulate. His persistence in the face of challenging text also needs to be strengthened, and again, the ISA should help cultivate that.

Jackson also needs continuing explicit instruction in many phonic elements. Because most of his peers have already mastered these basics, this should be done in his intervention program and reinforced in the classroom through multisyllabic word reading.

As the test results indicate, Jackson also needs to develop more-automatic recognition of high-frequency *sight vocabulary*. It is critical in this, and in all of Jackson's instruction, that a variety of techniques be employed. Initial presentation of each word should be in a variety of modes: Jackson should say the word, write it, hear it said and used in a sentence, and use it himself. Suggesting that he note configuration and providing opportunities for him to experience the word kinesthetically (such as tracing or building the word) would also be helpful.

Jackson must also improve his fluency. However, work on increasing his rate should be postponed until there is a stronger consolidation of his word recognition abilities. For now, rereading of familiar text could focus on improving his fluency and phrasing to enhance comprehension.

Jackson's miscues indicate that he lacks skill in *blending*. While teaching any of the skill areas, the teacher could include activities that provide practice in blending the sound taught to produce a word. Many enjoyable and productive oral activities can be employed to aid him in learning to blend all parts of a word. This should quickly develop into work on locating familiar word "parts."

A technique that might be of benefit to Jackson is that of using one book in all reading exercises in a given day. There is added power in doing this. It will be easier for him to operate within a familiar and consistent context, and to be working on varying skills toward one purpose—to complete and understand the story.

At the same time, Jackson needs ample opportunity to participate in classroom read-alouds in order to develop age- and grade-appropriate concepts. Full participation in these read-alouds and subsequent discussion is critical.

Finally, we recommend that the "intensity" of Jackson's intervention be increased significantly. He requires both more and more-focused opportunity to develop his abilities. Right now, Jackson is receiving supplemental instruction in a group of five struggling students. He could benefit from a much smaller group (perhaps 2:1). Careful progress monitoring should be employed to determine whether the focus and intensity of these interventions should be increased even further.

A word about writing is in order. Jackson is struggling with all aspects of written language. His compositions are very immature. The reading specialist who works with Jackson tried out an adaptation of the process writing approach used in Jackson's room, to see if it had potential for use there. During the first phase, Jackson dictated a story. When he believed it to be complete, the tutor then rewrote the story so that it included an introduction, episode, and conclusion. This revised piece was discussed, with the emphasis placed on the components of a strong story. Finally, one component (the introduction, episode, or conclusion) was deleted, and Jackson was encouraged to write a replacement. This process was continued until Jackson had rewritten the entire piece. This practice proved especially helpful to Jackson and was later coupled with "story frames" (Fowler, 1982) to encourage Jackson to construct whole texts that contained important component pieces. In addition, contact between school and clinic was maintained to good effect.

SUGGESTIONS AND RECOMMENDATIONS

The above are specific skill areas in which Jackson needs instruction. Other strategies can be employed both in school and at home to improve his reading.

1. The lack of self-reliance that Jackson demonstrated in the classroom indicates a need to provide assignments and tasks on which he can become self-directed. Jackson must fulfill the high standards set for him; however, he will benefit from a quantity of work that he can complete and a level of work at which he can succeed.
2. Goal setting is a technique that might be employed to encourage responsibility for himself and his work at both school and home. If Jackson is exhibiting difficulty in completing tasks, he can set a goal for himself (e.g., finishing a number of math problems before recess).
3. As was noted above, Jackson will benefit tremendously from using more-challenging texts, perhaps one book in all reading exercises in a given day.
4. Jackson needs help choosing books that are appropriate for his reading ability and interests.
5. Jackson needs more exposure to reading and language. At home, this could be accomplished by trips to the library, a family reading time, and a time during which Jackson is read to daily (or reads to a younger sibling). It is recommended that he be read to daily at school as well. Both his comprehending ability and his vocabulary will be improved by such practices.

Jackson brings to the reading process specific interests and a willingness to complete most tasks asked of him. The examiner believes that with opportunities to succeed, more exposure to literature that meets his interests, and, most importantly, a unified instruction plan across all of Jackson's instructional contexts, his reading will improve.

_____   _____
Title: Date

Confidential Diagnostic Report

Name: Susie*   *Date:* June 2007
Examiner:
Name of Parent/Guardian:
Address: *Birthdate:* October 16, 1992
School: Summerville High School *Age:* 14   *Grade:* 9

PREVIOUS TEST INFORMATION

Vermont Developmental Reading Assessment (VT-DRA)
Administered spring of grade 2

> Nearly achieved the standard—successfully read and comprehended texts at a late first to mid-second-grade level of difficulty (with at least 92% accuracy).

Stanford Achievement Test Series-9th Edition
Administered in grades 3, 5, and 7

Subtests and Totals	Grade 3 National PR-S	Grade 3 Levels	Grade 5 National PR-S	Grade 5 Levels	Grade 7 National PR-S	Grade 7 Levels
Total Reading	42-5	2	36-4	2	23-4	2
Vocabulary	47-5	3	43-5	2	68-6	3
Reading Comp.	40-5	2	34-4	2	9-2	1
Total Mathematics	51-5	2	17-3	1	16-3	1
Problem Solving	29-4	2	9-2	1	21-3	1
Procedures	85-7	3	33-4	1	13-3	1
Language	32-4	2	30-4	1	DNA	DNA
Lang. Mechanics	–	–	9-2	1	DNA	DNA
Lang. Expression	–	–	60-6	2	DNA	DNA
Open-Ended Reading	24-4	2	13-3	1	92-8	3
Open-Ended Mathematics	30-4	2	28-4	2	57-5	1
Composite Reading	36-4	2	33-4	2	7-2	2
Composite Mathematics	49-5	2	23-4	1	13-3	1

Levels
Level 1—indicates little or no mastery of fundamental knowledge and skills
Level 2—denotes partial mastery of the knowledge and skills that are fundamental for satisfactory work
Level 3—represents solid academic performance, indicating that students are prepared for the next grade
Level 4—signifies superior performance beyond grade-level mastery

*Susie selected her own pseudonym.

Woodcock-Johnson Tests of Achievement-Revised (WJ-R) (Administered in grade 6 by special educator)

Subtests	
Letter-Word Identification	Raw Score: 48
	Age Equiv: 13-7
	Standard Score: Not provided
	Percentile Rank: Not provided
Passage Comprehension	Raw Score: 25
	Age Equiv: 11-4
	Standard Score: Not provided
	Percentile Rank: Not provided

Math-Level Indicator (Administered in grade 6 by special educator)

Skills Cluster Summary			
Addition/Subtraction	9/9	Algebra	1/5
Multiplication/Division	6/8	Word Problems	9/13
Operations with Fractions	0/5	Concepts & Communication	7/13
Operations with Decimals	4/7		

Total Raw Score: 36/60
Percentile Rank: 52

Test of Written Language-2nd Edition (TOWL-2) (Administered grade 6 by special educator)
Spontaneous Writing Sample Only

Subtest	Raw Scores	Percentiles
Thematic Maturity	14	91
Contextual Vocabulary	18	75
Syntactic Maturity	169	91
Contextual Spelling	169	63
Contextual Style	14	75

New England Common Assessment Program (NECAP) (Administered fall, grade 8)

Content Area	Achievement Level	Scaled Score
Reading	Partially Proficient	838
Mathematics	Partially Proficient	837
Writing	Partially Proficient	831

Content Area/Subcategories	Possible Points	Student's Points
Reading		
Word ID/Vocabulary	10	6
Literary Text	22	11
Informational Text	20	12
Initial Understanding	18	11
Analysis and Application	24	12
Mathematics		
Numbers and Operations	13	5
Geometry and Measurement	16	4
Functions and Algebra	27	13
Data, Statistics, and Probability	10	5
Writing		
Language & Conventions	10	5
Short Responses	12	5
Extended Response	15	9

Comments about writing performance: Writing has a general purpose, with attempted focus and some supporting details. Appropriate word choice and some control of sentence structure.

SUMMARY OF ASSESSMENT RESULTS

Peabody Picture Vocabulary-4th Edition (PPVT-4) (Administered grade 9 by A. Backman, Literacy Specialist)

Standard Score: 83
Confidence Interval: 95%
Percentile: 13

Classification by Parts of Speech:

Totals	Noun	Verb	Attribute
# Taken	23	8	5
# Incorrect	7	1	2

Test of Reading Comprehension-3rd Edition (TORC-3) (Administered grade 9 by
   A. Backman, Literacy Specialist)

	Grade Equiv.	Percentile	Standard Score
General Vocabulary	7.4	37	9
Syntactic Similarities	4.2	9	6
Paragraph Reading	4.0	16	7
Sentence Sequencing	2.2	5	5
Total of Standard Scores	–	–	27
Reading Comprehension Quotient (RCQ)	–	7	78

Test of Written Language-3rd Edition (TOWL-3) (Administered grade 9 by A. Backman,
   Literacy Specialist)

Subtest	Percentile	Standard Score
Vocabulary	1	3
Spelling	25	8
Style	25	8
Logical Sentences	9	6
Sentence Combining	9	6
Contextual Conventions	16	7
Contextual Language	84	13
Story Construction	95	15

Composites	Sum of Standard Scores	Quotients	Percentile Rank
Contrived Writing	31	74	4
Spontaneous Writing	35	111	77
Overall Writing	66	88	21

Test of Word Reading Efficiency (TOWRE) (Administered grade 9 by A. Backman, Literacy
   Specialist)

Subtest	Age Equiv.	Grade Equiv.	Percentile	Standard Score
Sight-Word Efficiency	11-6	6.0	23	89
Phonemic Decoding Efficiency	13-3	7.6	39	96
Sum of Standard Scores				185
Total Reading Efficiency Standard Score				91
Total Reading Efficiency Percentile			27	

Gray Oral Reading Tests—4th Edition (GORT-4) (Administered grade 9 by A. Backman, Literacy Specialist)

	Rate Score	Accuracy Score	+ Fluency Score	=Comprehension Score
Standard Scores	9	7	8	8
Percentile	37	16	25	25
Grade Equivalent	8.7	6.7	7.4	7.4

Sum of Fluency and Comprehension Standard Scores: 16
Percentile: 21
Oral Reading Quotient (ORQ): 88

Development Spelling Assessment (Ganske) (Administered grade 9 by A. Backman, Literacy Specialist)

Syllable Juncture

Doubling & e-Drop with -ed & -ing	Other Syllable-Juncture Doubling	Long-Vowel Patterns (Stressed Syllable)	R-Controlled Vowels (Stressed Syllable)	Unstressed-Syllable Vowel Patterns	Stage Score
2	3	4	4	4	17

Derivational Constancy

Silent & Sounded Consonants	Consonant Changes	Vowel Changes	Latin-Derived Suffixes	Assimilated Prefixes	Stage Score
1	1	2	2	2	8

Qualitative Reading Inventory-4th Edition (QRI-4) (Administered grade 9 by A. Backman, Literacy Specialist)

Isolated Word Identification (Word Lists)

Grade	1	2	3	4	5	6	Upper Middle School	High School
Level/% Automatic	100	95	95	80	95	90	70	65
Level/% Total	100	100	95	95	95	100	90	75

Passage Reading

Passage Level and Type	Familiarity Concepts	% Oral Reading Word Recognition	Oral Comprehension
Sixth-Grade Expository *(Temperature & Humidity)*	17%	Total Accuracy: 98 Total Acceptability: 98 [Independent]	No. Explicit Correct: 0 No. Implicit Correct: 0 Level % Comprehension: 0 [Frustrational]
Sixth-Grade Narrative *(The Early Life of Lois Lowry)*	42%	Total Accuracy: 96 Total Acceptability: 97 [Independent]	No. Explicit Correct: 3 No. Implicit Correct: 2 Level % Comprehension: 63% [Frustrational]
Sixth-Grade Expository *(Lifeline of the Nile)*	16%	*Silent* Reading Comprehension No. Explicit Correct: 1 No. Implicit Correct: 1 No. Correct with Look-Backs: 5 Level % Comprehension: 13% (63% with Look-Backs) [Frustrational]	

Adolescent Motivation to Read Profile (Administered grade 9 by A. Backman, Literacy Specialist)

Self-Concept as Reader: 50%
Value of Reading: 53%
Full Survey: 51%

BACKGROUND INFORMATION

Reason for Referral

Susie is a freshman at Summerville High School, taking a full load of classes. Concerns about her reading and writing abilities, expressed by both school and parents, led to a referral for reading and writing assessments.

Observation and Interview Information

Susie lives at home with her mother, who works as an interventionist at a local elementary school, and her brothers Fred (age 18) and Patrick (age 11). Susie's father, who lives locally, was diagnosed with an illness this past year. The mother notes that Susie's younger brother has recently been diagnosed with Attention Deficit Hyperactivity Disorder (inattentive) this past year and struggles in the areas of reading and math. In addition, Susie has had stomach trouble since she was very small. Her mother also notes that the stress of Susie's father's illness has made her very emotional and has also triggered her stomach troubles recently.

In regards to reading, Susie's mother notes, "she likes true-life stories about kids and what they go through, but doesn't really care for it [reading] otherwise." Susie likes to write stories about things that have happened to her. Her mother says that she has "written some really great stuff." Although Susie seems to like going to school, her mom thinks she likes to go to see people. However, her mother does think that Susie has hopes of going to college.

When asked to reflect on reading and writing in general and her own abilities in particular, Susie varied on her responses. She feels that she is "a bad reader who is slow and doesn't understand what she reads." Although she had negative feelings about reading, when asked why people read, she noted, "to become smarter, better readers ... also because they like to or for amusement." With writing, she feels that she is "good at making things up." Susie notes that she doesn't really read, but if she does, it is usually a mystery book or true story. Although she initially said that she only writes when she has to, Susie also noted that she does write about her family. She also shared that she thought her brother was the best reader she knows and her grandmother the best writer. The most recent book that she has read is *Amy*, a story about a girl who meets someone over the computer who ends up attacking her. She found this book in the library and chose it because "it really happened and it has suspense." Susie also shared that she sometimes uses the computer "to instant message friends and to read about weather."

Susie likes going to the mall, hanging out with her dad, and bike riding with friends. She dances in a hip-hop class once a week and is going to start snowboarding this winter. Her mom notes, "she would like to work at the Humane Society because she loves animals." Her family has five animals because of her love of them.

School/Instructional History

Susie has attended school in Summerville since kindergarten. Her mother notes that struggles with reading started in about second grade. According to Susie's file, she was assessed by a special educator in sixth grade in the areas of reading, writing, and math. Since middle school, she has been on an educational support team plan with accommodations for classes; however, Susie's mother expressed that she feels that the teachers do not seem to know about these accommodations. She has made mention of wanting a full special education evaluation.

Susie took a full load of courses for her ninth-grade year, including English, World History, Earth and Physical Science, and Algebra I Part I. In addition, she had two study sessions per day. One was a smaller, supported study session where she received assistance with her work, and the other was a larger, traditional study session. Susie also participated in a team-taught English class with a certified English teacher and a special educator. On occasion, Susie received strategy instruction in English during her supported study session. However, since Susie was using this supported study session to try to get homework done in all of her subjects she was unable to spend time daily on English. Within the English classroom, strategy instruction was modeled in the areas of reading comprehension, writing, and vocabulary. Although direct strategy instruction was provided regularly in her English classroom, it is unknown whether it was provided in her other content-area classes.

SUMMARY OF ASSESSMENT RESULTS

In the spring of her second-grade year, Susie was administered the Vermont Developmental Reading Assessment (VT-DRA) and nearly met the standard. Most recently, she took the Stanford Achievement Test Series-9th Edition (STAT-9) in the spring of seventh grade.

In the area of reading, she scored at level 1, which indicates that she had little or no mastery of fundamental knowledge and skills. On Susie's previous STAT-9s, administered in the spring of third and fifth grades, she scored at level 2 in reading comprehension, which denoted partial mastery of knowledge and skills necessary for satisfactory work. During the fall of eighth grade, Susie was administered the New England Common Assessment Program (NECAP). At that time, she was partially proficient in the areas of reading. Although these are different assessments, it is important to note that Susie has consistently either nearly met the standard or been partially proficient in the areas of reading.

Susie's standard score equivalent on the Peabody Picture Vocabulary Test-4th Edition (PPVT-4) was 83. She scored at the thirteenth percentile. Her score places her in the low range of receptive language ability.

On the Test of Reading Comprehension-3rd Edition (TORC-3), Susie's overall reading comprehension quotient was 78. She scored in the seventh percentile rank. An analysis of the subtests reveals that she scored higher on the vocabulary section of the assessment, where she had to choose the word that is most like other words listed. This score is consistent with her levels 2 and 3 scores on the vocabulary section of the STAT-9. On the TORC-3, Susie struggled with the syntactic-similarities section, where she had to choose two sentences that mean almost the same thing, and the paragraph reading section, where she had to read short paragraphs and answer a series of comprehension questions. Out of all the tests administered, Susie had the most difficulty on the sentence-sequencing section, where she had to put a series of sentences in the correct order. Susie's difficulty with determining similarities between sentences and answering comprehension questions may have had an effect on her ability to answer test questions in content-area classes, where teachers sometimes tweak language slightly for questions and choice answers. In addition, in high school, paraphrasing and summarizing are two skills used often in academic classes to show that students understand material they are reading. If Susie is struggling with understanding material, it may be difficult for her to synthesize information into her own words to show her knowledge in an assessment situation.

Susie's performance on the Test of Written Language-3rd Edition (TOWL-3) varied. Although her overall writing quotient was 88, her quotient score for contrived writing was 74. Her spontaneous writing quotient was 111. Susie's strength is in the area of creating a story with relation to the elements of plot, prose, character development, and reader interest. This should benefit her when writing creatively for class; however, she struggles with contrived writing and is likely to have a more difficult time writing responses to questions or formulating structured essays within the academic classroom.

An analysis of various data related to fluency is revealing. Susie's total reading efficiency standard score on the Test of Word Reading Efficiency (TOWRE) is a 91. However, her scores vary on the two subtests. On the Sight Word Efficiency subtests, Susie's standard score was an 89, whereas her standard score on the Phonemic Decoding Efficiency was a 96. Observations made by the examiner during the administration of the TOWRE suggested that Susie read the words quickly and did not linger if she didn't know a word or pronounced it incorrectly. Results on the Gray Oral Reading Tests-4th Edition (GORT-4) are consistent with these findings; her overall oral reading quotient was an 88.

Across all oral reading tasks, the examiner made observational notes regarding the three areas of fluency: accuracy, automaticity, and prosody. Up until the seventh-grade material, Susie maintained consistent accuracy and automaticity with words. She read the material quickly and, for the most part, accurately. However, Susie did not adhere to the rules of prosody, including stopping for punctuation such as periods and commas or chunking meaningful pieces of text together. Struggles with fluency may affect Susie's ability to comprehend text. Because she often read through punctuation, she wasn't able to grasp some of the nuances of the passage. As the passages became harder, Susie struggled with all three areas, but most especially prosody. In addition, as Susie tried to read the material faster, she lost her place and on one passage missed an entire sentence, which affected her ability to answer the comprehension questions. Although Susie can read material quickly, her fluency may be affecting her comprehension, especially as material becomes more difficult.

Susie's word recognition (isolated) in the Qualitative Reading Inventory-4th Edition (QRI-4) varied across the grade levels. She scored at the independent level in all the grade levels from first through sixth grade for her "identified automatically", score, with the exception of scoring at the instructional level on the grade list. However, she did score at the independent level for total scores in all grades. She scored at the instructional level for the "identified automatically" score and at the independent level for a total score on the upper middle school word list. Susie scored at the frustration level for the "identified automatically" score on the high school word list and at the instructional level for the total score. For diagnostic purposes, the examiner assessed her at the grade 6 level for both narrative and expository text (see cover sheet). For oral reading, Susie scored at the independent level for total accuracy and total acceptability on the expository passage, and at the instructional level for the narrative passage.

Susie struggled to answer comprehension questions on all three of the QRI-4 passages she read. She scored at the frustration level for all three passages on comprehension, including the one on which she was allowed to use look-backs. Although Susie's word recognition was at the instructional or independent levels, she struggled with comprehension. (A discussion about how fluency can affect comprehension is mentioned in the next section.) However, her relatively low familiarity with these topics also likely impacted the results.

Finally, it appears that Susie's spelling knowledge and vocabulary are implicated in her reading difficulties. These abilities were explored in an administration of the Syllable Juncture and the Derivational Consistency components of the Developmental Spelling Assessment (DSA). As can be seen from her scores, in the syllable-juncture stage, she performed well in the areas of long-vowel patterns, *r*-controlled vowels, and unstressed-syllable vowel patterns (such as in *trample* or *fountain*). She struggled in the areas of doubling and e-drop with -ed and -ing endings, as well as with other syllable-juncture doubling (as in *minnow* or *baggage*). In derivational consistency, she struggled across the board. The words in this stage are related and derive from the same root. She performed very poorly on all aspects of word roots, prefixes, and suffixes—a fact that is probably related to limited instruction and reading experience. Her weak knowledge and skill in managing morphological roots may affect her understanding of the new words she encounters in her reading.

DIAGNOSTIC STATEMENTS AND SUGGESTIONS FOR INSTRUCTION

After analyzing Susie's assessments, evidence shows that fluency and comprehension are two areas that she may benefit from working on in regards to her reading. Understanding how to fluently read materials with attention to accuracy, automaticity, and prosody will be important for Susie so that she is able to comprehend materials. In addition, learning comprehension strategies for both narrative and expository text will be valuable for Susie in connection to reading in both academic classes and life skills.

As observations reveal, it will be important for Susie to work on prosody. An important start to this work will be to have a conversation about what prosody is and why it is important for understanding what we read. A good icebreaker would be to read the same sentence in a variety of different ways to Susie, to show that how we read a sentence directly relates to how we understand a sentence. In addition, it would be important to model how reading accurately and automatically doesn't always allow us to understand what we are reading. Modeling this concept might best be done by reading a short paragraph accurately and automatically but not stopping at all punctuation, then asking Susie to explain what it is about.

Once Susie is familiar with prosody, a technique that might help her work on it is "echo reading." In this exercise, the teacher would read one sentence of an appropriate text aloud, with appropriate intonation, expression, and phrasing. After the teacher has read it, Susie would then try to imitate the oral reading model. The exercise would continue until Susie could imitate more than one sentence at a time. This type of technique may be used with a wide range of materials, including her textbooks and novels.

Although working on prosody will be important in helping Susie increase her fluency and improve her concept of reading, it will hopefully also help her understand *what* she is reading. By chunking text appropriately, an author's ideas can better be understood by the reader.

To further expand instruction on comprehension, it will be important to model and teach Susie different strategies for comprehension that can be used for both expository and narrative text. Initially, it may be helpful to use a gradual-release-of-responsibility model (Pearson & Gallagher, 1983) in teaching her comprehension strategies (model strategy, guided practice, independent practice with feedback, then apply to other situations). This type of model is one that can be used in classrooms with groups of students or individuals. Susie may benefit from it in both settings.

The test results also indicate that Susie struggles with both implicit and explicit comprehension. To help her recognize the different types of questions, Susie may benefit from the strategy of question-answer relationship (QAR). QAR would allow Susie to understand that some questions are in the book questions that she can find in a specific location or in individual chapters. In addition, she would learn that some questions require information from both the author and her own knowledge or just from her own knowledge. Having Susie understand different types of questions will allow her to recognize them in the assignments teachers give and to build success in knowing how to answer them.

Of extreme importance for Susie is providing instruction that will teach her to think about what she is reading. By focusing on what she is reading, Susie is more likely to notice when she is not comprehending the text. There are metacognitive strategies that can help Susie improve her thinking and reading skills. Using Think-Aloud, a program that requires the reader to discuss what she or he is thinking about while reading, would be helpful in having Susie become more aware of herself as a reader. With Think-Aloud, Susie should work on comprehension monitoring by using fix-up strategies (i.e., reread, ask yourself a question, make an inference, stop and think about what you have already read, etc.) as part of the discussion. Once Susie is familiar with all the fix-up strategies, a bookmark listing them would be helpful in each book she has at school.

The last technique that would help Susie with reading is also one that will help her with her organized writing. With the amount of expository text that Susie encounters both at school and in life in general, it is important to be able to determine what is important in her reading. Using the SMART technique (Self-Monitoring Approach to Reading and Thinking) would connect the previous technique of comprehension monitoring with the skill of determining what is important. SMART is a technique that allows the student to focus on short pieces of a text and determine if they understand the key idea in each paragraph. A variation on this technique that would help Susie to remember what she is reading is to have her write the key idea on a sticky note for each paragraph. She would put a question mark if she didn't know the key idea of a paragraph. At the end, she would return to any paragraphs with question marks and use her list of fix-up strategies to help her understand what she has read.

Lastly, it will be important for Susie to continue to be able to summarize important information in expository texts, as well as to analyze and synthesize information for both paragraph and essay writing. For summarizing, the technique of "magnet summaries" would be helpful in organizing her information. If she uses the sticky notes to keep track of key ideas throughout a piece of text, she will be able to use those to help organize a summary as well. In addition, it will be important to work with her on translating her notes into a formal thesis statement with concrete supporting details through practice on authentic pieces. She will benefit from understanding the pieces of a structured essay, including the similar parts that make up both the introduction and concluding paragraphs (general statement, specific statement, thesis statement), as well as how to write strong supporting paragraphs.

Suggestions and Recommendations

Susie is a personable, hard-working, and caring young woman who will show progress in reading and writing if offered the opportunity. The following interventions are recommended.

1. Susie would benefit from both direct instruction and modeling of strategies in the areas of reading fluency and comprehension. In addition, it would be helpful to use frontloading strategies prior to having Susie read text, to engage her prior knowledge.
2. Some direct instruction and modeling would be beneficial for some of the reading comprehension strategies of question-answer relationship, SMART, and fix-up strategies. This direct instruction and modeling should be in a variety of different content areas so that Susie will learn to generalize the strategies across all settings.
3. Susie may benefit from direct instruction and modeling in the areas of structured writing, especially around constructing thesis statements and determining supporting details. This instruction would best be done in connection with authentic assignments in her classes.
4. Susie is a student who is interested in attending college. Many of the strategies mentioned in this report are ones that will help in her with reading in school and life. As someone who is social, Susie may benefit from learning strategies with other students she feels comfortable with, so that there are peer supports as well as adult supports for her within the school.

APPENDIX C

Key Background for Understanding Formal Assessment

Selection and evaluation of formal tests begins with an understanding of the purpose for which a test is being given. Information relative to a particular test must always be examined in relation to the purpose(s) for which it is being used.

The title, author, publisher, and date of publication reveal information about a test's quality and the appropriateness of its purpose and content for different students or testing situations. For example, a test with the word *survey* in the title suggests that the test will provide general information about a student's achievement rather than specific information about strengths and weaknesses. Similarly, the reputation of the test author and/or publisher in reading, writing, or testing may suggest something about both the content and quality of the test. A recent date of publication or revision increases the likelihood that the test reflects the most recent theory and research and that any norms used for scoring are current.

Other general characteristics of a formal test that are important for determining its appropriateness for specific students or testing situations include the level of difficulty and type of administration. Some tests are intended for a wide range of age, grade, and ability levels; others are intended only for restricted levels. Still others have different forms for different levels. Therefore, it is important to determine that a test is appropriate for the age, grade, and ability of the student with whom it will be used.

The appropriateness of the test administration for specific students and purposes depends on factors such as whether the test is group or individually administered and whether it is timed or untimed. Group tests are efficient to administer but tend to provide more-general information than do individual tests and do not allow for the variety of response formats (e.g., oral reading, extended writing activities) that are allowed by individual tests. Individual tests require significantly more time to administer than group tests but tend to provide more-specific information about the student. Timed or speed tests determine what a student can do under specified time constraints, whereas untimed or power tests evaluate a student's performance without any time constraints.

The two basic types of test interpretations that we discuss here are norm referenced and criterion referenced. Criterion-referenced interpretations are designed primarily to provide information about how well a person has learned a specific body of knowledge or acquired specific objectives. The emphasis is on describing the level of performance of individuals and groups on the behavior that a test is measuring. "A recent variation of criterion-referenced testing is 'standards-based testing' or 'standards-based assessment.' Many states and districts have adopted content standards that describe what students should know and be able to do in different subjects at various grade levels. They also have performance standards that define how much of the content standards students should know to reach the 'basic' or 'proficient' or 'advanced' level in that subject area ..." (Fair Test, n.d.).

Norm-referenced interpretations examine a given student's performance in relation to the performance of a representative group. The emphasis in norm-referenced testing is on the individual's relative standing rather than on absolute mastery of content (Salvia & Ysseldyke, 2007). Although the term *standardized* is often used synonymously with *norm-referenced* testing, tests that emphasize criterion-referenced interpretations can also be, and often are, standardized. *Standardized* means only that all students perform the same tasks under uniform directions (Swanson & Watson, 1989).

The difficulty of test items and the manner in which items are selected also differ between tests emphasizing norm-referenced and criterion-referenced interpretations. Test items that produce a wide range of scores and discriminate well between high-scoring and low-scoring individuals are desirable for norm-referenced interpretations that determine an individual's relative position in comparison to a group of his or her peers. Therefore, the best norm-referenced items are those that 40 to 60 percent of the students answer correctly, because they produce the greatest variance in test scores. In well-constructed tests using norm-referenced interpretations, half of the population will score above the average and half will fall below the average.

According to Swanson and Watson (1989), there is a shift in emphasis between criterion- and norm-referenced interpretations from items that best measure performance in a domain of knowledge to items that provide the greatest diversity in scores. They further note Popham's (1978, 2002) conclusion that the procedures used to construct tests emphasizing norm-referenced interpretations are likely to result in the exclusion of items that measure the major instructional emphases of the schools.

Important Statistical Concepts

Tests use statistics to describe and summarize data. As a result, there are several statistical concepts that must be understood to evaluate the utility of formal tests for specific purposes. In this section we briefly summarize several major statistical concepts: normal distribution, measures of variation and centrality known as the standard deviation and the mean, and a measure of relatedness known as correlation.

Normal Distribution. One way of summarizing test data is to describe the distribution of test scores. The two characteristics of a distribution that are most important for the interpretation of educational tests are the mean and the standard deviation. The mean is the arithmetic average of the scores and provides a central value or representative score to characterize the performance of the entire group. The standard deviation is a unit of measurement based on the degree to which the scores deviate from the mean. A large standard deviation indicates greater spread around the mean than does a smaller one. Test scores can be referred to in terms of the number of standard deviations they are above (+) or below (−) the mean, depending on whether the score is greater than or less than the mean.

A normal distribution of the behaviors or psychological characteristics we are interested in observing means that scores are distributed symmetrically around the mean. The normal curve is symmetrical and bell-shaped and has many useful mathematical properties. One of the most useful for test interpretation is that when it is divided into standard deviation

**FIGURE C.1   Normal
Distribution and
Sample Test Scores**

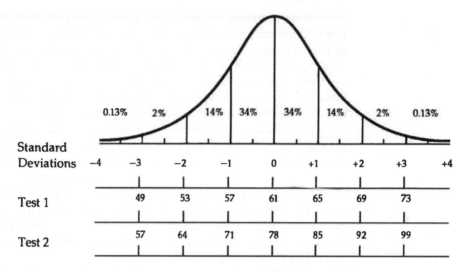

units, each unit under the curve contains a fixed percentage of cases (see Figure C.1). This means that in any normal distribution,

- Approximately 68 percent of the population will be between +1 and −1 standard deviations from the mean.
- Approximately 95 percent of the population will fall between +2 and −2 standard deviations from the mean.
- Approximately 99.7 percent of the population will fall between +3 and −3 standard deviations from the mean.

Raw scores from two different tests have been placed beneath the row marking the standard deviations in the figure, to illustrate how knowing the standard deviation and the mean contribute to the understanding of relative position within a group. Test 1 has a mean of 61 and a standard deviation of 4. Test 2 has a mean of 78 and a standard deviation of 7. Therefore, a score of 65 is equivalent to a standard deviation of 11 on test 1, and a score of 85 is equivalent to a standard deviation of 11 on test 2. Knowing the mean and standard deviation permits us to convert raw scores to a common scale that has equal units and can be interpreted readily in terms of the normal curve.

Correlation.   Another statistical concept that is important in the interpretation of test data is correlation. Whereas the mean and standard deviation describe a single distribution of scores, correlations describe the degree of association between two or more sets of scores. This measure is important in describing the relationship of test scores to other variables of interest and is critical to the evaluation of reliability and validity.

The strength of the correlation is expressed using a *correlation coefficient*. The values of correlation coefficients range from 11.00 to 0.00 to −1.00. A positive correlation (1) indicates that high scores on one variable are associated with high scores on the other variable. A negative correlation (−) indicates that high scores on one variable are associated with low scores on the other variable. A correlation coefficient of 0.00 between two variables means that there is no relationship between the variables—the variables are independent, and changes in one variable are not related to changes in the other variable. A correlation coefficient of either 11.00 or −1.00 indicates a perfect relationship between two variables (Salvia & Ysseldyke, 2007).

Measures of correlation provide useful information about the various components of tests and can also be used as an index of test validity and reliability (see below). However, educators must use correlational information sensibly, which means, in part, understanding that correlation is not the same as causation. Correlation is a necessary but insufficient condition for determining causality. The mere presence of a correlation between two variables does not imply that one causes the other. An extreme example of this principle is the likelihood that there is a positive correlation between the contents of a family's garbage can and their children's early reading success. It is well known that early success in reading is correlated with socioeconomic status, which will likely also result in differences in the contents of families' garbage cans. However, this does not mean that a certain type of trash causes success or failure in reading.

Salvia and Ysseldyke (2001, p. 80) point out that "for any correlation between two variables (A and B), there are four possible interpretations." The relationship could occur by chance, a third variable could cause both A and B, A could cause B, or B could cause A. Correlational data do not tell us which of these four possible interpretations are true; therefore we must never draw causal conclusions from such data. So, for example, the simple fact that there is a positive correlation between reading achievement and factors such as balance-beam walking or alphabet knowledge does not, by itself, mean that these factors cause skilled reading.

APPENDIX D

Annotated Bibliography of Informal Reading Inventories

Applegate, M. D., Quinn, K. B., & Applegate, A. J. (2008). *The Critical Reading Inventory-2.* Upper Saddle River, NJ: Pearson (Merrill Prentice Hall). Includes three passages for each level preprimer–grade 12. These include both narrative and expository passages. In addition to traditional graded passages and word lists, there are interviews for use with students, parents, and teachers, as well as an oral reading fluency rubric.

Bader, L. A. (2009). *Bader reading and language inventory* (6th ed.). Upper Saddle River, NJ: Prentice Hall. Includes passages for grades K–12. In addition to traditional graded passages and word lists, there are tests of emergent reading, word identification and phonics, spelling, writing, and oral language. A checklist to assess English language development is a new feature. The guide now includes revised comprehension questions as well as information about reliability and validity and information.

Brozo, B., & Afflerbach P. (2011). *Adolescent literacy inventory.* New York , NY: Pearson. Designed for use in grades 6–12. Reviewed extensively in chapter 8.

Burns, P. C., & Roe, B. D. (2011). *Informal reading inventory* (8th ed.). Belmont, CA: Wadsworth. Grades 1–12; two graded word lists and four sets of graded passages per grade level (preprimer–grade 12); eight questions at preprimer to grade 2 levels and ten at the other grade levels. Recent revisions include useful appendices, one including a list of leveled trade books for PreK–12 and the other about the construction of the test (but limited information about reliability and validity).

Cooter, R. B., Flynt, E. S., & Cooter, K. S. (2007). *Comprehensive reading inventory* (7th ed.). Columbus, OH: Pearson. Four forms include two sets each of narrative and expository passages for levels preprimer–9, with eight comprehension questions. The two narrative forms provide for early/emergent assessment using wordless picture-book tasks and an emergent reading checklist. There are also informal assessments of phonemic awareness, phonics, and alphabet knowledge. A complete set of comprehension passages and sentences are provided in Spanish.

Johns, J. J. (2012). *Basic reading inventory* (11th ed.). Dubuque, IA: Kendall/Hunt. Grades preprimer–12. Three forms consist of ten graded twenty-word lists and passages as well as two alternate forms for early literacy assessment. Three additional sets of passages contain both narrative and exposition. Four comprehension questions at preprimer level; ten at other grade levels. Spanish version available, K–4. CDs and other materials provide extensive examples of struggling students and include video clips that can be quite useful. No reliability data are reported.

Leslie, L., & Caldwell, J. (2011). *The qualitative reading inventory-5.* Boston, MA: Allyn & Bacon/Pearson. Reviewed extensively in chapter 8. Key features include multiple forms for assessing both narrative and expository comprehension. Assessments of prior knowledge and retelling. Thorough and comprehensive information about reliability and validity.

Shanker, J. L., & Cockrum, W. (2010). *Ekwall/Shanker reading inventory* (5th ed.). Boston, MA: Allyn & Bacon. Grades 1–9; each of four forms consists of eleven graded word lists (preprimer–grade 9); five comprehension questions at the preprimer level and ten at the other grade levels. Also contains tests of letter knowledge, basic sight words, the San Diego Quick Assessment (graded word list) and the El Pasco Phonics Survey, as well as tests of phonics and structural analysis in context.

Stieglitz, E. L. (2001). *The Stieglitz informal reading inventory* (3rd ed.). Boston, MA: Allyn & Bacon. The SIRI contains two alternate forms for both narrative (Forms B and D) and expository (Forms A and C) selections. In addition to offering comprehension questions, the author suggests using *free recall* as one means of evaluating comprehension. The test suggests analyzing comprehension difficulties using a unique system that distinguishes three types of difficulty: The SIRI also suggests evaluating both *familiarity* and *interest*. The prior-knowledge scale and the level-of-interest scale (ranging from 1 to 5) are self-reported measures that are administered *after* reading. The SIRI also offers tools for *evaluating emergent literacy* using a dictated story method and includes checklists for evaluating the abilities of early readers. Little information about validity; alternative-form validity is reported.

Temple, C. A., Crawford, A. N., & Gillet, J. A. (2009). *Developmental literacy inventory.* Boston, MA: Allyn & Bacon. The DLI is designed for use in grades K–12. It offers extensive resources at the earliest levels for use with young/emergent readers. As well, there are leveled passages that assess students comprehension for narrative, social studies, and science. Scores are reported as both grade equivalents and Lexiles©.

Wheelock, W. H., & Campbell, C. J. (2012). *Classroom reading inventory* (12th ed.). Monterey, CA: McGraw-Hill. Grade 1–adult. There is a "subskills" format (Form A, levels preprimer–8) and a Literature format (Form B, levels 1–5) for elementary-level passages. There are also separate forms (subskills format, levels 1–8) for use with junior high and with high school students–adults. Five comprehension questions on all forms but the Literature format, which uses a retelling to evaluate comprehension. No guidelines are provided for using the retelling rubric. New Web site provides downloadable forms and CDs. No reliability data are reported.

Woods, M. A., & Moe, A. J. (2010). *Analytical reading inventory* (9th ed.). Boston, MA: Allyn & Bacon. Grades 1–9. Each of three forms consists of seventeen graded twenty-word lists (primer–grade 6) and ten graded passages (primer–grade 9). Six comprehension questions for primer and grade 1; eight for the other grade levels. Two expository subtests consist of graded social studies and science passages. A separate booklet of reading passages enhances ease of administration, comprehensive summary forms provide for a thorough review of data, and the helpful DVD provides effective teacher support.

References

Aaron, J. E. (2007). *The little brown compact handbook*. New York, NY: Longman.

Adams, A., Carmine, D., & Gersten, R. (1982). Instructional strategies for studying content area texts in the intermediate grades. *Reading Research Quarterly, 18*, 27–55.

Adams, C., Smith, M. C., Pasupathi, M., & Vitolo, L. (2002). Social context effects on story recall in older and younger women. *Journals of Gerontology Series B: Psychological Sciences and Social Sciences, 57*, 28–40.

Adams, M. (2001). Alphabetic anxiety and explicit, systematic phonics instruction: A cognitive science perspective. In S. Neuman & D. Dickinson (Eds.), *Handbook of early literacy research*. New York, NY: Guilford Press.

Adams, M. J. (1990). *Beginning to read: Thinking and learning from print*. Cambridge, MA: MIT Press.

Adelman, H., & Taylor, L. (1977). Two steps toward improving learning for students with (and without) "learning problems." *Journal of Learning Disabilities, 10*, 455–461.

Afflerbach, P. (2000). Verbal reports and protocol analysis. In M. L. Kamil, P. B. Mosenthal, P. D. Pearson, & R. Barr (Eds.), *Handbook of reading research* (Vol. 3, pp. 163–180). Mahwah, NJ: Erlbaum.

Afflerbach, P. (2002). The use of think-aloud protocols and verbal reports as research methodology. In M. Kamil (Ed.), *Methods of literacy research* (pp. 87–103). Hillsdale, NJ: Erlbaum.

Afflerbach, P., Reutschlin, H., & Russell, S. (2007). Assessing strategic reading. In J. R. Paratore & R. L. McCormack (Eds.). *Classroom literacy assessment: Making sense of what students know and do*. New York, NY: Guilford Press.

Agnew, A. T. (1982). Using children's dictated stories to assess code consciousness. *The Reading Teacher, 35*, 450–454.

Alexander, L. (1964). *The book of three*. New York, NY: Holt.

Alamargot, D., & Chanquoy, L. (2001). *Through the models of writing*. New York, NY: Springer.

Alexander, P. A., Graham, S., & Harris, K. R. (1998). A perspective on strategy research: Progress and prospects. *Educational Psychology Review, 10*, 129–154.

Alexander, P. A., & Jetton, T. L. (2000). Learning from text: A multidimensional and developmental perspective. In M. L. Kamil, P. B. Mosenthal, P. D. Pearson, & R. Barr (Eds.), *Handbook of reading research* (Vol. 3, pp. 285–310). Mahwah, NJ: Erlbaum.

Alfassi, M. (2000). Using information and communication technology (ICT) to foster literacy and facilitate discourse within the classroom. *Education Media International, 37*, 137–148.

Allen, J. (2002). On the same page: Shared reading beyond the primary grades. Portland, ME: Stenhouse.

Allen, R. V. (1976). Language experience in communication. Boston, MA: Houghton Mifflin.

Allington, R. L. (1975). Sustained approaches to reading and writing. *Language Arts, 52*, 813–815.

Allington, R. L. (1977). If they don't read much how they ever gonna get good? *Journal of Reading, 21*, 57–61.

Allington, R. L. (1980). Teacher interruption behaviors during primary grade oral reading. *Journal of Educational Psychology, 72*, 371–377.

Allington, R. L. (1983a). Fluency: The neglected reading goal. *The Reading Teacher, 36*, 556–561.

Allington, R. L. (1983b). The reading instruction provided readers of differing reading abilities. *Elementary School Journal, 83*, 548–558.

Allington, R. L. (1984). Content coverage and contextual reading in reading groups. *Journal of Reading Behavior, 16*, 85–96.

Allington, R. L. (1991). The legacy of "slow it down and make it more concrete." In J. Zutell & S. McCormick (Eds.), *Learner factors/teacher factors: Issues in literacy research and instruction* (pp. 19–30). Chicago, IL: National Reading Conference.

Allington, R. L. (1994). Critical issues: What's special about special programs for children who find learning to read difficult? *Journal of Reading Behavior, 26*, 95–115.

Allington, R. L. (2006). Fluency: Still waiting after all these years. In S. J. Samuels & A. E. Farstrup (Eds.), *What research has to say about fluency instruction* (pp. 94–105). Newark, DE: International Reading Association.

Allington, R. L., Chodos, L., Domaracki, J., & Truex, S. (1977). Passage dependency: Four diagnostic oral reading tests. *The Reading Teacher, 30*, 369–375.

Allington, R. L., & Cunningham, P. M. (2002). *Schools that work: Where all children read and write* (2nd ed.). Boston, MA: Allyn & Bacon/Longman.

Allington, R. L., & Johnston, P. (1989). Coordination, collaboration, and consistency: The redesign of compensatory and special education intervention. In R. Slavin, M. Madden, & N. Karweit (Eds.), *Preventing school failure: Effective programs for students at risk* (pp. 320–354). Boston, MA: Allyn & Bacon.

Allington, R. L., & Johnston, P. H. (2002). *Reading to learn: Lessons from exemplary fourth-grade classrooms*. New York, NY: Guilford.

Allington, R. L., & McGill-Franzen, A. (1980). Word identification errors in isolation and in context: Apples vs. oranges. *The Reading Teacher, 33*, 795–800.

Allington, R. L., & McGill-Franzen, A. (1989). Different programs, indifferent instruction. In D. Lipsky & A. Gartner (Eds.), *Beyond separate education: Quality education for all* (pp. 75–98). Baltimore, MD: Brookes.

Allington, R. L., & Shake, M. C. (1986). Remedial reading: Achieving curricular congruence in classroom and clinic. *The Reading Teacher, 39*, 648–654.

Allington, R. L., Stuetzel, H., Shake, M., & Lamarche, S. (1986). What is remedial reading? A descriptive study. *Reading Research and Instruction, 26*, 15–30.

617

Almaguer, I. (2005). Effects of dyad reading instruction on the reading achievement of Hispanic third-grade English language learners. *Bilingual Research Journal, 29,* 509–526.

Almasi, J. F. (1995). The nature of fourth graders' sociocognitive conflicts in peer-led and teacher-led discussion of literature. *Reading Research Quarterly, 30,* 314–351.

Altwerger, B., Diehl-Faxon, J., & Dockstader-Anderson, K. (1985). Read-aloud events as meaning construction. *Language Arts, 62,* 476–484.

Alvermann, D. E. (1989). Creating the bridge to content-area reading. In P. Winograd, K. Wixson, & M. Y. Lipson (Eds.), *Improving basal reading instruction* (pp. 256–270). New York, NY: Teachers College Press.

Alvermann, D. E. (1991). The discussion web: A graphic aid for learning across the curriculum. *The Reading Teacher, 45*(2), 92–99.

Alvermann, D. E. (2001a). *Effective literacy instruction for adolescents.* Executive summary and paper commissioned by the National Reading Conference, Chicago, IL.

Alvermann, D. E. (2001b). Reading adolescents' reading identities: Looking back to see ahead. *Journal of Adolescent and Adult Literacy, 44,* 676–690.

Alvermann, D. E., Dillon, D. R., & O'Brien, D. G. (1987). Using discussion to promote reading comprehension. Newark, DE: International Reading Association.

Alvermann, D. E., Fitzgerald, J., & Simpson, M. (2006). Teaching and learning in reading. In P. Alexander & P. Winne (Eds.), *Handbook of educational psychology* (2nd ed., p. 427–455). Mahwah, NJ: Erlbaum.

Alvermann, D. E., & Phelps, S. F. (2002). *Content reading and literacy: Succeeding in today's diverse classrooms* (3rd ed.). Boston, MA: Allyn & Bacon.

Alvermann, D. E., Young, J. P., Weaver, D., Hinchman, K. A., Moore, D. W., Phelps, S. F., . . . Zalewski, P. (1996). Middle and high school students' perceptions of how they experience text-based discussions: A multicase study. *Reading Research Quarterly, 31,* 244–267.

American Educational Research Association (AERA) (1985). *Standards for educational and psychological testing.* Washington, DC: American Psychological Association.

American Educational Research Association, American Psychological Association, and National Council on Measurement in Education. (1999). *Standards for educational and psychological testing.* Washington, DC: American Educational Research Association.

Anders, P. L., & Bos, C. S. (1986). Semantic feature analysis: An interactive strategy for vocabulary development and text comprehension. *Journal of Reading, 29,* 610–616.

Anderson, B. (1981). The missing ingredient: Fluent oral reading. *Elementary School Journal, 81,* 173–177.

Anderson, L. M. (1984). The environment of instruction: The function of seatwork in effective commercially developed curriculum. In G. G. Duffy, L. R. Roehler, & J. Mason (Eds.), *Comprehension instruction: Perspectives and suggestions* (pp. 93–104). New York, NY: Longman.

Anderson, L. M., Brubaker, N. L., Alleman-Brooks, J., & Duffy, G. G. (1985). A qualitative study of seatwork in first-grade classrooms. *Elementary School Journal, 86,* 132–140.

Anderson, R. C. (1977). The notion of schemata and the educational enterprise. In R. C. Anderson, R. J. Spiro, & W. E. Montague (Eds.), *Schooling and the acquisition of knowledge* (pp. 415–431). Hillsdale, NJ: Erlbaum Associates.

Anderson, R. C., & Freebody, P. (1981). Vocabulary knowledge. In J. T. Guthrie (Ed.), *Comprehension and teaching: Research perspectives* (pp. 71–117). Newark, DE: International Reading Association.

Anderson, R. C., Hiebert, E. H., Scott, J. A., & Wilkinson, I. G. (1985). *Becoming a nation of readers: The report of the Commission on Reading.* Washington, DC: National Institute of Education.

Anderson, R. C., Wilson, P. T., & Fielding, L. G. (1988). Growth in reading and how children spend their time outside of school. *Reading Research Quarterly, 23,* 285–303.

Anderson, T. H., & Armbruster, B. B. (1984a). Content area textbooks. In R. C. Anderson, J. Osborn, & R. J. Tierney (Eds.), *Learning to read in American schools: Basal readers and content texts* (pp. 193–226). Hillsdale, NJ: Erlbaum.

Anderson, T. H., & Armbruster, B. B. (1984b). Studying. In P. D. Pearson, R. Barr, M. Kamil, & P. Mosenthal (Eds.), *Handbook of reading research* (pp. 657–679). New York, NY: Longman.

Anderson, V., Chan, C., & Henne, R. (1995). The effects of strategy instruction on the literacy models and performance of reading and writing delayed middle school students. In K. A. Hinchman, D. J. Leu, & C. K. Kinzer (Eds.), *Perspectives on literacy research and practice: Forty-fourth yearbook of the National Reading Conference* (pp.180–189). Chicago, IL: National Reading Conference.

Anthony, J., & Lonigan, C., (2004). The nature of phonological awareness: Converging evidence from four studies of preschool and early grade school children. *Journal of Educational Psychology, 96*(1), 43–55.

Anthony, R. J., Johnson, T. D., Mickelson, N. I., & Preece, A. (1991). Evaluating literacy: A perspective for change. Portsmouth, NH: Heinemann.

Applebee, A. (1974). Tradition and reform in the teaching of English: A history. Urbana, IL: National Council of Teachers of English.

Applebee, A. N., Langer, J. A., Nystrand, M., & Gamoran, A. (2003). Discussion-based approaches to developing understanding: Classroom instruction and student performance in middle and high school English. *American Education Research Journal, 40,* 685–730.

Applegate, M. D., Quinn, K. B., & Applegate, A. J. (2002). Levels of thinking required by comprehension questions in informal reading inventories. *The Reading Teacher, 56,* 174–10.

Applegate, M. D., Quinn, K. B., & Applegate, A. J. (2006). Profiles in comprehension. *The Reading Teacher, 60,* 48–57.

Ares, N. M., & Peercy, M. M. (2003). Constructing literacy: How goals, activity systems, and text shape classroom practices. *Journal of Literacy Research, 35,* 633–662.

Argiro, M. (1987). The development of written language awareness in black preschool children. *Journal of Reading Behavior, 19,* 49–67.

Armbruster, B. B. (1984). The problem of "inconsiderate text." In G. G. Duffy, L. R. Roehler, & J. Mason (Eds.), *Comprehension instruction* (pp. 202–217). New York, NY: Longman.

Armbruster, B. B., & Anderson, T. H. (1981). Research synthesis on study skills. *Educational Leadership, 39,* 154–156.

Armbruster, B. B., Anderson, T. H., & Ostertag, J. (1989). Teaching text structure to improve reading and writing. *The Reading Teacher, 43,* 130–137.

Armstrong, D. P., Patberg, J., & Dewitz, P. (1988). Reading guides: Helping students understand. *Journal of Reading, 31,* 532–541.

Arter, J. A., & McTighe, J. (2001). *Scoring rubrics in the classroom: Using performance criteria for assessing and improving student performance.* Thousand Oaks, CA: Sage Publications.

Asch, F. (1981). *Just like Daddy.* New York, NY: Simon and Schuster.

Ash, B. H. (1990). Reading assigned literature in a reading workshop. *English Journal, 79,* 77–79.

Ashton-Warner, S. (1963). *Teacher.* New York, NY: Simon & Schuster.

Atwell, N. (1998). *In the middle: New understandings about writing, reading, and learning* (2nd ed.). Portsmouth, NH: Boynton/Cook.

Au, K. H. (1979). Using the experience-text-relationship method with minority children. *The Reading Teacher, 32,* 677–679.

Au, K. H. (1980). Participation structures in a reading lesson with Hawaiian children: Analysis of a culturally appropriate instructional event. *Anthropology and Education Quarterly, 11,* 91–115.

Au, K. H. (1993). *Literacy instruction in multicultural settings.* Fort Worth, TX: Harcourt Brace.

Au, K. H. (1997). Ownership, literacy achievement, and students of diverse cultural backgrounds. In K. T. Guthrie & A. Wigfield (Eds.), *Reading engagement: Motivating readers through integrated instruction* (pp. 168–182). Newark, DE: International Reading Association.

Au, K. H. (1998). Social constructivism and the school literacy learning of students of diverse backgrounds. *Journal of Literacy Research, 20,* 297–319.

Au, K. H. (2000). A multicultural perspective on policies for improving literacy achievement: Equity and excellence. In M. L. Kamil, P. B. Mosenthal, P. D. Pearson, & R. Barr (Eds.), *Handbook of reading research* (Vol. 3, pp. 835–851). Mahwah, NJ: Erlbaum.

Au, K. H. (2006). *Multicultural issues and literacy achievement.* Mahwah, NJ: Erlbaum.

Au, K. H., & Carrol, J. H. (1996). Current research on classroom instruction: Goals, teachers' actions, and assessment. In D. Speece & B. Keogh (Eds.), *Research on classroom ecologies: Implications for inclusion of children with learning disabilities* (pp. 17–37). Mahwah, NJ: Erlbaum.

Au, K. H., & Carrol, J. H. (1997). Improving literacy achievement through a constructivist approach: The KEEP demonstration school project. *Elementary School Journal, 97,* 203–221.

Au, K. H., & Kawakami, A. J. (1986). The influence of the social organization of instruction on children's text comprehension ability: A Vygotskian perspective. In T. E. Raphael (Ed.), *The contexts of school-based literacy* (pp. 63–77). New York, NY: Random House.

Au, K. H., & Kawakami, A. J. (1994). Cultural congruence in instruction. In E. R. Hollins, J. E. King, & W. Hayman (Eds.), *Teaching diverse populations: Formulating a knowledge base* (pp. 5–23). Albany: State University of New York Press.

Au, K. H., Mason, J. M., & Scheu, J. A. (1995). *Literacy instruction for today.* New York, NY: HarperCollins.

August, D., & Hakuta, K. (1994, Fall). *For all students: Limited English proficient students and Goals 2000* (NCBE Focus, Occasional Papers in Bilingual Education, No. 10). Washington, DC: National Clearinghouse for Bilingual Education.

August, D., & Hakuta, K. (1997). *Improving schooling for language-minority children: A research agenda.* Washington, DC: National Academy Press.

August, D., & Shanahan, T. (Eds.) (2006). Developing literacy in second-language learners: Report of the National Literacy Panel on Language-Minority Children and Youth. Mahwah, NJ: Lawrence Erlbaum.

Aulls, M. W. (1982). *Developing readers in today's elementary school.* Boston, MA: Allyn & Bacon.

Aulls, M. W. (2003). The influence of reading and writing curriculum on transfer learning across subjects and grades. *Reading Psychology, 24,* 177–215.

Aulls, M. W., & Graves, M. S. (Eds.). (1985). *Electric butterfly and other stories* (Quest series). New York, NY: Scholastic.

Bader, L. A., & Pearce, D. L. (2009). *Bader reading and language inventory* 6th ed. Upper Saddle River, NJ: Allyn & Bacon.

Bailey, T. (2003). Shared reading in the upper grades? You bet! Whole-class shared reading of novels minimizes fear and maximizes motivation and learning. *Instructor* (March). Retrieved from http://www.thefreelibrary.com/Shared+reading+in+the+upper+Grades%3f+You+bet!+Whole+class+shared...-a098594731

Baker, J. A. (1999). Teacher-student interaction in urban at-risk classrooms: Differential behavior, relationship quality, and student satisfaction with school. *Elementary School Journal, 100,* 57–70.

Baker, L., & Brown, A. L. (1984). Metacognitive skills and reading. In P. D. Pearson, R. Barr, M. Kamil, & P. Mosenthal (Eds.), *Handbook of reading research* (pp. 353–394). New York, NY: Longman.

Baker, L., Scher, D., & Mackler, K. (1997). Home and family influences on motivations for reading. *Educational Psychologist, 32,* 69–82.

Balajthy, E. (1989). Computers and reading: Lessons from the past and the technologies of the future. Englewood Cliffs, NJ: Prentice Hall.

Ballard, R. (1978). *Talking dictionary.* Ann Arbor, MI: Ulrich's Books.

Balthazar, C. H. (2004, November). Classification accuracy of 31 articulation and language tests for children. Poster presented at the Annual Convention of the American Speech-Language-Hearing Association, Philadelphia, PA.

Bangert-Drowns, R. (1993). The word processor as an instructional tool: A meta-analysis of word processing in writing instruction. *Review of Educational Research, 63,* 69–93.

Bankson, N. W. (1990). *Bankson language test–2.* Austin, TX: PRO-ED.

Barker, T. A., Torgesen, J. K., & Wagner, R. K. (1992). The role of orthographic processing skills on five different tasks. *Reading Research Quarterly, 27,* 335–345.

Baron, J. (1977). Mechanisms for pronouncing printed words: Use and acquisition. In D. LaBerge & S. J. Samuels (Eds.), *Basic process in reading: Perception and comprehension* (pp. 175–216). Hillsdale, NJ: Erlbaum.

Barr, R., Blachowicz, C. L. Z., & Wogman-Sadow, M. (1995). *Reading diagnosis for teachers: An instructional approach.* New York, NY: Longman.

Barrett, T. C. (1976). Taxonomy of reading comprehension. In R. Smith & T. C. Barrett (Eds.), *Teaching reading in the middle grades* (pp. 53–58). Reading, MA: Addison Wesley.

Barron, R. (1969). The use of vocabulary as an advance organizer. In H. L. Herber & P. L. Sanders (Eds.), *Research in reading in the content areas: First report* (pp. 29–39). Syracuse, NY: Syracuse University Reading and Language Arts Center.

Bateman, J. A., & Rondhuis, J. K. (1997). Coherence relations: Towards a general specification. *Discourse Processes, 24,* 3–49.

Baumann, J. F. (1986). Effect of rewritten content textbook passages on middle grade students' comprehension of main ideas: Making the inconsiderate considerate. *Journal of Reading Behavior, 28,* 1–21.

Baumann, J. F. (1988). Reading assessment: An instructional decision-making perspective. Columbus, OH: Charles E. Merrill.

Baumann, J. F., Hoffman, J. V., Duffy-Hester, A. M., & Ro, J. M. (2000). "The first R" yesterday and today: U.S. elementary reading instruction practices reported by teachers and administrators. *Reading Research Quarterly, 35,* 338–377.

Baumann, J. F., & Kame'enui, E. J. (1991). Research on vocabulary instruction: Ode to Voltaire. In J. Flood, J. M. Jensen, D. Lapp, & J. R. Squire (Eds.), Handbook on research on teaching the English language arts (pp. 604–632). New York, NY: Macmillan.

Baumann, J. F., Ro, J. M., & Duff-Hester, A. M. (2000). Then and now: Perspectives on the status of elementary reading instruction by prominent reading educators. *Reading Research and Instruction, 39*, 236–264.

Baumann, J. F., Ware, D., & Edwards, E. (2007). Bumping into spicy, tasty words that catch your tongue: A formative experiment on vocabulary instruction. *The Reading Teacher, 61*, 108–122.

Beal, C. R. (1996). The role of comprehension monitoring in children's revision. *Educational Psychology Review, 8*, 219–238.

Bean, R. M. (2004). The reading specialist: Leadership for the classroom, school, and community. New York, NY: Guilford Press.

Bean, T. W., & Steenwyk, F. L. (1984). The effect of three forms of summarization instruction on sixth graders' summary writing and comprehension. *Journal of Reading Behavior, 16*, 297–306.

Bear, D. R., & Barone, D. (1998). Developing literacy: An integrated approach to assessment and instruction. Boston, MA: Houghton Mifflin.

Bear, D. R., Invernizzi, M., Johnston, F., & Templeton, S. (2012). *Words their way: Word study for phonics, vocabulary, and spelling instruction.* Upper Saddle River, NJ: Allyn & Bacon.

Bear, D. R., Invernizzi, M. Templeton, S., & Johnston, F. (2000) *Words their way: Word study for phonics, vocabulary, and spelling instruction.* Upper Saddle River, NJ: Prentice- Hall.

Bear, D. R., & Templeton, S. (1998). Explorations in developmental spelling: Foundations for learning and teaching phonics, spelling, and vocabulary. *The Reading Teacher, 52*, 222–242.

Beaver, J., & Carter, M. (2003). *Developmental reading assessment 4–8* (DRA-2). New York, NY: Celebration Press (Pearson).

Beck, I., & McKeown, M. (2001). Text talk: Capturing the benefits of read-aloud experiences for young children. *The Reading Teacher, 55*, 10–20.

Beck, I. L., & McKeown, M. G. (1981). Developing questions that promote comprehension: The story map. *Language Arts, 58*, 913–918.

Beck, I. L., & McKeown, M. G. (1983). Learning words well: A program to enhance vocabulary and comprehension. *The Reading Teacher, 36*, 622–625.

Beck, I. L., McKeown, M. G., & Kucan, L. (2002). Bringing words to life: Robust vocabulary instruction. New York, NY: Guilford.

Beck, I. L., McKeown, M. G., & McCaslin, E. S. (1981). Does reading make sense? Problems of early readers. *The Reading Teacher, 34*, 780–785.

Beck, I. L., McKeown, M. G., & McCaslin, E. S. (1983). Vocabulary development: All contexts are not created equal. *Elementary School Journal, 83*, 177–181.

Beck, I. L., McKeown, M. G., & Omanson, R. (1987). The effects and uses of diverse vocabulary instructional techniques. In M. G. McKeown & M. E. Curtis (Eds.), *The nature of vocabulary acquisition.* Mahwah, NJ: Erlbaum.

Beck, I. L., McKeown, M. G., Sandora, C., Kucan, L., & Worthy, J. (1996). Questioning the author: A year-long classroom implementation to engage students with text. *Elementary School Journal, 96*, 385–414.

Beers, J., & Henderson, E. H. (1977). A study of developing orthographic concepts among first graders. *Research in the Teaching of English, 11*, 133–148.

Beery, K. E. (1997). *The Beery-Buktenica developmental test of visual-motor integration.* Parsippany, NJ: Modern Curriculum Press.

Bellamy, P. (2005). *Seeing with new eyes* (6th ed.). Portland, OR: NWREL.

Bembry, K. L., Jordan, H. R., Gomez, E., Anderson, M. M., & Mendro, R. L. (1998, April). *Policy implications of long-term teacher effects on student achievement.* Paper presented at the Annual Meeting of the American Educational Research Association, San Diego, CA.

Bernard, R. M., & Naidu, S. (1992). Post-questioning, concept mapping, and feedback: A distance education field experiment. *British Journal of Educational Technology, 23*, 48–60.

Bernhardt, E. B. (2000). Second-language reading as a case study of reading scholarship in the 20th century. In M. L. Kamil, P. B. Mosenthal, P. D. Pearson, & R. Barr (Eds.), *Handbook of reading research* (Vol. 3, pp. 791–812). Mahwah, NJ: Erlbaum.

Betts, E. A. (1946). *Foundations of reading instruction.* New York, NY: American Books.

Bialystok, E., & Ryan, E. (1985). A metacognitive framework for the development of first and second language skills. In D. L. Forrest-Pressley, G. E. MacKinnon, & T. G. Waller (Eds.), *Metacognition, cognition, and human performance* (pp. 207–252). New York, NY: Academic Press.

Biancarosa, G., & Snow, C. E. (2004). *Reading next—A vision for action and research in middle and high school literacy: A report to Carnegie Corporation of New York.* Washington, DC: Alliance for Excellent Education.

Biemiller, A. (2003). Oral comprehension sets the ceiling on reading comprehension. *American Educator, 27*, 23.

Biemiller, A. (2005). Addressing developmental patterns in vocabulary: Implications for choosing words for primary grade vocabulary instruction. In E. H. Hiebert, & M. L. Kamil, (Eds.), *Teaching and learning vocabulary: Bringing research to practice* (pp. 243–263). Mahwah, NJ: Erlbaum.

Biemiller, A., (2005, November). *Vocabulary issues in measurement and effects across ages.* Paper presented at the International Dyslexia Association. Denver, CO.

Biemiller, A. (2006). Vocabulary development and instruction: A prerequisite for school learning. In D. K. Dickinson & S. B. Neuman (Eds.), *Handbook of early literacy research* (Vol. 2, pp. 41–51). New York, NY: Guilford Press.

Biemiller, A., & Slonim, N. (2001). Estimating root word vocabulary growth in normative and advantaged populations: Evidence for a common sequence of vocabulary acquisition. *Journal of Educational Psychology, 93*, 498–520.

Binkley, M. R. (1988). New ways of assessing text difficulty. In B. L. Zakaluk & S. J. Samuels (Eds.), *Readability: Its past, present, and future* (pp. 98–120). Newark, DE: International Reading Association.

Blachman, B. A. (2000). Phonological awareness. In M. L. Kamil, P. B. Mosenthal, P. D. Pearson, & R. Barr (Eds.), *Handbook of reading research* (Vol. 3, pp. 483–502). Mahwah, NJ: Erlbaum.

Blachowicz, C., & Ogle, D. (2001). *Reading comprehension: Strategies for independent learners.* New York, NY: Guilford Press.

Blachowicz, C, L. Z., & Fisher, P. (2010). *Teaching vocabulary in all classrooms* (4th ed.). Boston, MA: Allyn & Bacon.

Black, P., Harrison, C., Lee, C., Marshall, B., & Wiliam, D. (2004). Working inside the black box: Assessment for learning in the classroom. *Phi Delta Kappan, 86*, 8–21.

Black, P., & Wiliam, D. (1998). Inside the black box: Raising standards through classroom assessment. *Phi Delta Kappan, 80*, 139–148.

Block, C. C. (2000). *Teaching the language arts: Expanding thinking through student-centered instruction* (3rd ed.). Boston, MA: Allyn & Bacon.

Bloom, B. S. (Ed.). (1956). *Taxonomy of educational objectives. Handbook I: Cognitive domain.* New York, NY: David McKay.

Bloom, D., Champion, T., Katz, L., Morton, M. B., & Muldrow, R. (2001). Spoken and written narrative development: African American preschoolers as storytellers and storymakers. In J. L. Harris,

A. G. Kamhi, & K. E. Pollock (Eds.), *Literacy in African American communities* (pp. 45–76). Mahwah, NJ: Erlbaum.

Blumenfeld, P. C., Mergendoller, J. R., & Swarthout, S. W. (1987). Task as a heuristic for understanding student learning and motivation. *Journal of Curriculum Studies, 19*, 135–148.

Boehm, A. E. (1986). *Boehm Test of Basic Concepts* (Rev. ed.). San Antonio, TX: The Psychological Corporation.

Boehm, A. E. (2001). *Boehm Test of Basic Concepts* (3rd ed.). San Antonio, TX: The Psychological Corporation.

Boggs, S. T. (1985). *Speaking, relating and learning: A study of Hawaiian children at home and at school.* Norwood, NJ: Ablex.

Borich, G. D. (2008). *Observation skills for effective teaching* (5th ed.). New York, NY: Prentice Hall.

Bosman, A. M. T., & Van Orden, G. C. (1997). Why spelling is more difficult than reading. In C. A. Perfetti, L. Rieben, & M. Fayol (Eds.), *Learning to spell: Research, theory, and practice across languages* (pp. 173–194). Hillsdale, NJ: Erlbaum.

Boston, C. (2002). The concept of formative assessment. *Practical Assessment, Research & Evaluation, 8*(9). Retrieved April 25, 2011, from http://PAREonline.net/getvn.asp?v=8&n=9

Botel, M. (1982). New informal approaches to evaluating word recognition and comprehension. In J. J. Pikulski & T. Shanahan (Eds.), *Approaches to the informal evaluation of reading* (pp. 30–41). Newark, DE: International Reading Association.

Bowey, J. A., & Frances, J. (1991). Phonological analysis as a function of age and exposure to reading instruction. *Applied Psycholinguistics, 12*, 91–121.

Bowker. (2009). *Children's books in print.* New York, NY: R. R. Bowker.

Bowles, S., & Gintis, H. (2002). Schooling in capitalist America revisited. *Sociology of Education, 75*, 1–18.

Bowman, B. T., Donovan, M. S., & Burns, M. S. (2000). *Eager to learn: Educating our preschoolers.* Washington, DC: National Academy Press.

Boyd-Batsone, P. (2004). Focused anecdotal records assessment: A tool for standards-based authentic assessment. *The Reading Teacher, 58*, 230–239.

Bransford, J. (2000). *How people learn: Brain, mind, experience, and school.* Washington DC: National Academy Press.

Bransford, J. D. (1979). *Human cognition: Learning, understanding, remembering.* Belmont, CA: Wadsworth.

Bransford, J. D., Goldman, S. R., & Vye, N. J. (1991). Making a difference in people's abilities to think: Reflections on a decade of work and some hopes for the future. In L. Okagaki & R. J. Sternberg (Eds.), *Directors of development: Influences on the development of children's thinking* (pp. 147–180). Hillsdale, NJ: Erlbaum.

Bransford, J. D., & Johnson, M. K. (1972). Contextual prerequisites for understanding: Some investigations of comprehension and recall. *Journal of Verbal Learning and Verbal Behavior, 11*, 717–726.

Brecht, R. D. (1977). Testing format and instructional level with the informal reading inventory. *The Reading Teacher, 31*, 57–59.

Brennan, A. D., Bridge, C. A., & Winograd, P. N. (1986). The effects of structural variation on children's recall of basal reader stories. *Reading Research Quarterly, 21*, 91–104.

Bretzing, B. B., & Kulhavy, R. W. (1981). Note-taking and passage style. *Journal of Educational Psychology, 73*, 242–250.

Brice, A. (Ed.). (2002). *The Hispanic child: Speech, language, culture, and education.* Boston, MA: Allyn & Bacon.

Bridge, C., & Hiebert, E. H. (1985). A comparison of classroom writing practices, teachers' perceptions of their writing instruction, and textbook recommendations on writing practices. *Elementary School Journal, 86*, 155–172.

Bridge, C. A. (1989). Beyond the basal in beginning reading. In P. Winograd, K. Wixson, & M. Lipson (Eds.), *Improving basal reading instruction* (pp. 177–209). New York, NY: Teachers College Press.

Bridge, C. A., Belmore, S., Moskow, S., Cohen, S., & Matthews, P. (1984). Topicalization and memory for main ideas in prose. *Journal of Reading Behavior, 16*, 27–40.

Bridge, C. A., & Burton, B. (1982). Teaching sight vocabulary through patterned language materials. In J. A. Niles & L. A. Harris (Eds.), *New inquiries in reading research and instruction* (31st Yearbook of The National Reading Conference, pp. 119–123). Washington, DC: National Reading Conference.

Bridge, C. A., & Winograd, P. N. (1982). Readers' awareness of cohesive relationships during cloze comprehension. *Journal of Reading Behavior, 14*, 299–312.

Bridge, C. A., Winograd, P. N., & Haley, D. (1983). Using predictable materials vs. preprimers to teach beginning sight words. *The Reading Teacher, 36*, 884–891.

Brigance, A. H. (1981). *Inventory of essential skills.* North Billerica, MA: Curriculum Associates.

Brigance, A. H. (1984). *Assessment of basic skills* (Spanish ed.). North Billerica, MA: Curriculum Associates.

Brigance, A. H. (1991). *Inventory of Early Development* (Rev. ed.). North Billerica, MA: Curriculum Associates.

Brigance, A. H. (1994). Life Skills Inventory. North Billerica, MA: Curriculum Associates.

Brigance, A. H. (1995). *Employability skills inventory.* North Billerica, MA: Curriculum Associates.

Brigance, A. H. (2004). *Comprehensive inventory of basic skills* (Rev. ed.). North Billerica, MA: Curriculum Associates.

Brinton, B., & Fujiki, M. (2004). Social and affective factors in children with language impairment. In C. A. Stone, E. R. Silliman, B. J. Ehren, & K. Apel (Eds.), *Handbook of language and literacy* (pp. 130–153). New York, NY: Guilford Press.

Brophy, J. (Ed.). (1998). *Teachers' and students' expectations. Advances in research on teaching* (Vol. 7). St. Louis, MO: Elsevier.

Brophy, J. (2004). *Motivating students to learn* (2nd Ed.). Mahwah, NJ: Erlbaum.

Brophy, J. E. (1983). Conceptualizing student motivation. *Educational Psychologist, 18*, 200–215.

Brown, A. L. (1978). Knowing when, where, and how to remember: A problem of metacognition. In R. Glaser (Ed.), *Advances in instructional psychology* (Vol. 1, pp. 77–165). Hillsdale, NJ: Erlbaum Associates.

Brown, A. L., Armbruster, B. B., & Baker, L. (1986). The role of metacognition in reading and studying. In J. Orasanu (Ed.), *A decade of reading research: Implications for practice* (pp. 49–75). Hillsdale, NJ: Erlbaum.

Brown, A. L., & Campione, J. C. (1986). Psychological theory and the study of learning disabilities. *American Psychologist, 14*, 1059–1068.

Brown, A. L., Campione, J. C., & Day, J. D. (1981). Learning to learn: On training students to learn from texts. *Educational Researcher, 10*, 14–21.

Brown, J. I., Fishco, V. V., & Hanna, G. H. (1993). *Nelson-Denny reading test.* Itasca, IL: Riverside Publishing.

Brown, J. S., Collins, A., & Duguid, P. (1989). Situated cognition and the culture of learning. *Educational Researcher, 18*, 32–42.

Brown, V. L., Hammill, D. D., & Wiederholt, J. L. (1995). *Test of reading comprehension* (3rd ed.). Austin, TX: PRO-ED.

Brozo, W. G., & Simpson, M. L. (1999). *Readers, teachers, learners: Expanding literacy across the content areas* (3rd ed.). New York, NY: Prentice Hall.

Bruce, B. (1984). A new point of view on children's stories. In R. C. Anderson, J. Osborn, & R. J. Tierney (Eds.), *Learning to read in American schools: Basal readers and content texts* (pp. 153–174). Hillsdale, NJ: Erlbaum.

Bruner, J. S. (1964). The course of cognitive growth. *American Psychologist, 19,* 1–15.

Bryant, P. E., MacLean, M., Bradley, L. L., & Crossland, J. (1990). Rhyme and alliteration, phoneme detection, and learning to read. *Developmental Psychology, 26,* 429–438.

Budbill, D. (1978). *Bones of Black Spruce Mountain.* New York, NY: Dial Press.

Buehl, D. (2001). *Classroom strategies for interactive learning* (2nd ed.). Newark, DE: International Reading Association.

Buehl, D. (2011). *Developing readers in the academic disciplines.* Newark, DE: International Reading Association.

Burchinal, M., & Forestieri, N. (2011). Development of early literacy: Evidence from major U.S. longitudinal studies. In S. B. Nueman & D. K. Dickinson (Eds.), *Handbook of early literacy research* (3rd ed.) (pp. 85–96). New York, NY: Guilford.

Burgess, S. R. (2006). The development of phonological sensitivity. In D. K. Dickinson & S. B. Neuman (Eds.), *Handbook of early literacy research* (Vol. 2, pp. 90–100). New York, NY: Guilford Press.

Burnett, C. (2010). Technology and literacy in early childhood educational settings: A review of research. *Journal of Early Childhood Literacy, 10*(3), 247–270.

Burnette, J. (2000). *Assessment of culturally and linguistically diverse students for special education eligibility* (ERIC EC Digest E604). Arlington, VA: ERIC Clearinghouse on Disabilities and Gifted Education.

Burns, P. C., & Roe, B. D. (2002). Informal reading inventory (6th ed.). Boston, MA: Houghton Mifflin.

Bus, A. G. (2001). Joint caregiver-child storybook reading: A route to literacy development. In S. B. Neuman & D. K. Dickinson (Eds.), *Handbook of early literacy research* (pp. 179–191). New York, NY: Guilford Press.

Bus, A. G., vanIjzendoorn, M. H., & Pelligrini, A. D. (1995). Joint book reading makes for success in learning to read: A meta-analysis on intergenerational transmission of literacy. *Review of Educational Research, 65,* 1–21.

Buss, K., & Karnowski, L. (2000). Reading and writing literary genres. Newark, DE: International Reading Association.

Butkowsky, I. S., & Willows, D. M. (1980). Cognitive-motivational characteristics of children varying in reading ability: Evidence for learned helplessness in poor readers. *Journal of Educational Psychology, 72,* 408–422.

Butler, D. L., & Winner, P. H. (1995). Feedback and self-regulated learning: A theoretical synthesis. *Review of Educational Research, 65,* 245–281.

Button, K., Johnson, M. J., & Furgerson, P. (1996). Interactive writing in a primary classroom. *The Reading Teacher, 49,* 446–454.

Cain, K., Oakhill, J. V., Barnes, M. A., & Bryant, P. E. (2001). Comprehension skill, inference-making ability, and their relation to knowledge. *Memory & Cognition, 29,* 850–859.

Cain, K., Oakhill, J., & Bryant, P. (2004). Children's reading comprehension ability: Concurrent prediction by working memory, verbal ability, and component skills. *Journal of Educational Psychology, 94,* 31–42.

Calfee, R. C. (1987). The design of comprehensible text. In J. R. Squire (Ed.), *The dynamics of language learning.* Urbana, IL: ERIC Clearinghouse on Reading and Communication Skills and the National Conference on Research in English.

Calfee, R. C., & Patrick, C. L. (1995). *Teach our children well: Bringing K–12 education into the 21st century.* Stanford, CA: Stanford Alumni.

California Instructional Technology Clearinghouse. (1998–2000). Appendix C: Screening criteria for interactive technology resources [Online document]. Stanislaus County Office of Education, California. Available at www.clearinghouse.k12.ca.us/c/@B0DvQuqHKTomU/dev/appendc.htm

Calkins, L. (1991). *Living between the lines.* Portsmouth, NH: Heinemann.

Calkins, L. M. (1983). *Lessons from a child.* Exeter, NH: Heinemann.

Calkins, L. M. (1994). *The art of teaching writing.* Portsmouth, NH: Heinemann.

Cambourne, B., & Turbill, J. (1994). *Responsive evaluation.* Portsmouth, NH: Heinemann.

Cambourne, B. L. (2000). Conditions for literacy learning: Observing literacy learning in elementary classrooms: Nine years of classroom anthropology. *The Reading Teacher, 53,* 512–517.

Camilli, G., Vargas, S., & Yurecko, M. (2003) Teaching Children to Read: The fragile link between science and federal education policy. *Education Policy Analysis Archives, 11*(15). Retrieved June 8, 2007, from http://epaa.asu.edu/epaa/v11n15

Campione, J. C., & Brown, A. L. (1987). Linking dynamic assessment with school achievement. In C. S. Lidz (Ed.), *Dynamic assessment* (pp. 82–109). New York, NY: Guilford Press.

Campione, J. C., Brown, A. L., Ferrara, R. A., & Bryant, N. R. (1984). The zone of proximal development: Implications for individual differences and learning. In B. Rogoff & J. Wertsch (Eds.), *New directions for child development: Children's learning in the "zone of proximal development"* (Vol. 23, pp. 265–294). San Francisco, CA: Jossey-Bass.

Carew, J. V., & Lightfoot, S. L. (1979). *Beyond bias: Perspectives on classroom.* Cambridge, MA: Harvard University Press.

Carlisle, J. F., Cortina, K., Zeng, J., & Schilling, S. G. (2006). *Gains in reading achievement over two years in Michigan's Reading First schools.* (Technical Report 3.1, Evaluation of Reading First in Michigan). Ann Arbor: University of Michigan.

Carnegie Corporation. (1994). *Starting points: Meeting the needs of our youngest children.* New York, NY: Carnegie Corporation.

Carnegie Council on Advancing Adolescent Literacy. (2010). *Time to act: An agenda for advancing adolescent literacy for college and career success.* New York, NY: Carnegie Corporation of New York.

Carnine, D., Silbert, J., & Kame'enui, E. J. (1990). *Direct instruction reading* (2nd ed.). Columbus, OH: Charles E. Merrill.

Carnine, D. W., Kame'enui, E. J., & Coyle, G. (1984). Utilization of contextual information in determining the meaning of unfamiliar words. *Reading Research Quarterly, 19,* 188–204.

Carnine, D. W., Silbert, J., & Kame'enui, E. J. (1997). *Direct instruction reading* (3rd ed.). Upper Saddle River, NJ: Merrill/Prentice Hall.

Carr, E. (1985). The vocabulary overview guide: A metacognitive strategy to improve vocabulary and retention. *Journal of Reading, 28,* 684–689.

Carr, E., & Ogle, D. (1987). K-W-L Plus: A strategy for comprehension and summarization. *Journal of Reading, 30,* 626–631.

Carroll, J. M. (2004). Letter knowledge precipitates phoneme segmentation, but not phoneme invariance. *Journal of Research in Reading, 27,* 212–225.

Carrow-Woolfolk, E. (2011). *Oral and written language scales* (2nd ed.). Torrance, CA: Western Psychological Services.

Caselli, M. C., Bates, F., Casadio, P., Fenson, J., Fenson, L., Sanders, L., & Weir, J. (1995). A cross-linguistic study of early lexical development. *Cognitive Development, 10,* 159–199.

Castellani, J., & Jeffs, T. (2001). Emerging reading and writing strategies using technology. *Teaching Exceptional Children, 33*, 60–67.

Caswell, L. J., & Duke, N. K. (1998). Non-narrative as a catalyst for literacy development. *Language Arts, 75*, 108–117.

Cazden, C. (2001). *Classroom discourse: The language of teaching and learning* (2nd ed.). Portsmouth, NH: Heinemann.

Cazden, C. B. (1986). Classroom discourse. In M. C. Wittrock (Ed.), *Handbook of research on teaching* (3rd ed., pp. 432–463). New York, NY: Macmillan.

Cecil, N. L., & Gipe, J. P. (2003). *Literacy in the intermediate grades: Best practices for a comprehension program.* Scottsdale, AZ: Holcomb Hathaway Publishers.

Center for the Improvement of Early Reading Achievement. (2001). *Improving the reading achievement of America's children: 10 research-based principles.* Ann Arbor, MI: Author.

Center for the Improvement of Early Reading Achievement. (2002). Improving the reading comprehension of America's children: 10 Research-based principles [Online document]. Available at www.ciera.org/library/instresrc/compprinciples/index/html

Chall, J. S. (1984). Readability and prose comprehension: Continuities and discontinuities. In J. Flood (Ed.), *Understanding reading comprehension* (pp. 233–246). Newark, DE: International Reading Association.

Chall, J. S., & Curtis, M. E. (1987). What clinical diagnosis tells us about children's reading. *The Reading Teacher, 40*, 784–789.

Chambliss, M. J. (1995). Text cues and strategies successful readers to construct the gist of lengthy written arguments. *Reading Research Quarterly, 30*, 778–807.

Chamot, A. U., & O'Malley, J. M. (1994). Instructional approaches and teaching procedures. In S. Spangenberg-Urbschat & R. Pritchard (Eds.), *Kids come in all languages: Reading instruction for ESL students* (pp. 82–107). Newark, DE: International Reading Association.

Chaney, C. (1992). Language development, metalinguistic skills, and print awareness in 3-year-old children. *Applied Psycholinguistics, 13*, 485–514.

Chapman, J. W., & Tunmer, W. E. (2003). Reading difficulties, reading-related self-perceptions, and strategies for overcoming negative self-beliefs. *Reading & Writing Quarterly, 19*, 5–24.

Chappuis, S., Commodore, C., & Stiggins, R. (2010). *Assessment balance and quality: An action guide for school leaders.* Boston, MA: Pearson.

Chard, D. J., & Dickson, S. V. (1999). Phonological awareness Instructional and assessment guidelines. *Intervention in School and Clinic, 34*, 261–270.

Chard, D. J., Simmons, D. C., & Kame'enui, E. J. (1998). The primary role of word recognition in the reading process: Curricular and instructional implications. In D. C. Simmons & E. J. Kame'enui (Eds.), *What reading research tells us about children with diverse learning needs: The bases and the basics* (pp. 169–181). Mahwah, NJ: Erlbaum.

Chinn, C., Anderson, R. C., Waggoner, M. (2001). Patterns of discourse during two kinds of literature discussion. *Reading Research Quarterly, 36*, 378–411.

Chittenden, E. (1991). Authentic assessment, evaluation, and documentation of student performance. In V. Perrone (Ed.), *Expanding student assessment.* Alexandria, VA: Association for Supervision and Curriculum Development.

Chomsky, C. (1978). When you still can't read in third grade: After decoding, what? In S. J. Samuels (Ed.), *What research has to say about reading instruction* (pp. 13–30). Newark, DE: International Reading Association.

Christie, J. F. (1981). The effects of grade level and reading ability on children's miscue patterns. *Journal of Educational Research, 74*, 419–423.

Chudowsky, N., & Pellegrino, J. W. (2003). Large-scale assessments that support learning: What will it take? *Theory into Practice, 42*, 75–83.

Cioffi, G., & Carney, J. J. (1983). Dynamic assessment of reading disabilities. *The Reading Teacher, 36*, 764–768.

Civil, M., Planas, N., & Quintos, B. (2005). Immigrant parents' perspectives on their children's mathematics education. *ZDM, 37*, 81–89.

Cizek, G. J. (2001). Review of Brigance Diagnostic Comprehensive Inventory of Basic Skills, Revised. In B. S. Blake and J. C. Impara (Eds.), *Fourteenth mental measurements yearbook.* Lincoln, NE: Buros Institute of Mental Measurements.

Clark, C. H. (1982). Assessing free recall. *The Reading Teacher, 35*, 434–439.

Clark, C. H. (1993). Personal communication.

Clarke, L. K. (1988). Invented versus traditional spelling in first graders' writings: Effects on learning to spell and read. *Research in the Teaching of English, 22*, 281–309.

Clay, M. M. (1979). *Reading: The patterning of complex behavior* (2nd ed.). Auckland, New Zealand/Exeter, NH: Heinemann.

Clay, M. M. (1985). *The early detection of reading difficulties* (3rd ed.). Auckland, New Zealand: Heinemann.

Clay, M. M. (1993). *An observation survey (of early literacy achievement).* Portsmouth, NH: Heinemann.

Clay, M. M. (1998) *By different paths to different outcomes.* New York, NY: Stenhouse.

Clay, M. M. (2000). *Follow me, Moon: "Concepts about Print" tests.* Portsmouth, NH: Heinemann.

Clay, M. M. (2006). *An observation survey of early literacy achievement* (Rev. 2nd ed.). Portsmouth, NH: Heinemann.

Cleary, B. (1983). *Dear Mr. Henshaw.* New York, NY: Bantam Doubleday Dell Publishing.

Clifford, G. (1984). Buch und lesen: Historical perspectives on literacy and schooling. *Review of Educational Research, 54*, 472–500.

Clifford, M. M. (1991). Risk taking: Theoretical, empirical and educational considerations. *Educational Psychologist, 26*, 263–297.

Cline, R. L., & Kretke, G. L. (1980). An evaluation of long-term SSR in the junior high school. *Journal of Reading, 23*, 503–506.

Clinton, P. (2002, September/October). Literacy in America: The crisis you don't know about, and what we can do about it. *Book, 24*, 4–9.

Code of Fair Practices in Education. (2004). Washington, DC: Joint Committee on Testing Practices.

Cohen, E. G. (1994). *Designing groupwork: Strategies for the heterogeneous classroom.* New York, NY: Teachers College Press.

Cohen, E. G., & Lotan, R. (1997). *Working for equity in heterogeneous classrooms.* New York, NY: Teachers College Press.

Cohn, M., & D'Alessandro, C. (1978). When is a decoding error not a decoding error? *The Reading Teacher, 32*, 341–344.

Coiro, J. (2003). Reading comprehension on the Internet: Expanding our understanding of reading comprehension to encompass new literacies. *The Reading Teacher, 56*, 458–464.

Coiro, J. (2005). Making sense of online text. *Educational Leadership, 63*(2), 30–35.

Coiro, J., & Dobler, E. (2004). *Investigating how less-skilled and skilled readers use cognitive reading strategies while reading on the Internet.* Paper presented at the 54th annual meeting of the National Reading Conference, San Antonio, Texas.

Coiro, J., Karchmer, R., & Walpole, S. (2006). Critically evaluating educational technologies for literacy learning: Current trends and new paradigms. In M. McKenna, D. Reinking, L. B. Labbo, &

R. Kieffer (Eds.), *The handbook of literacy and technology* (2nd ed.). Mahwah, NJ: Erlbaum.

Cole, M. (1990). Cultural psychology: A once and future discipline? In J. Berman (Ed.), *Nebraska's symposium on motivation: Cross cultural perspectives* (p. 37). Lincoln: University of Nebraska Press.

Coleman, P. P. (1992/1993, Winter). Classroom observation checklist for literacy artifacts and events. *Clinical Connection, 12.*

Collins, James L. (1998). Strategies for struggling writers. New York, NY: Guilford Press.

Combs, M. (2002). *Developing competent readers and writers for middle grades* (2nd ed.). Upper Saddle River, NJ: Prentice Hall.

Commins, N. L., & Miramontes, O. B. (1989). A descriptive study of the linguistic abilities of a selected group of low achieving Hispanic bilingual students. *American Educational Research Journal, 26,* 443–472.

Common Core State Standards (CCSS) Initiative. (2010). *Common Core State Standards for English Language Arts & Literacy in History/Social Studies, Science, and Technical Subjects.* Washington, DC: National Governors Association Center for Best Practices and the Council of Chief State School Officers.

Compton, D. L., Appleton, A. C., & Hosp, M. K. (2004). Exploring the relationship between text-leveling systems and reading accuracy and fluency in second-grade students who are average and poor decoders. *Learning Disabilities Research and Practice, 19,* 176–184.

Conference on College Composition and Communication. (2009). *Writing assessment: A position statement.* Urbana, IL: National Council of Teachers of English. Retrieved November 7, 2011, from http://www.ncte.org/cccc/resources/positions/writingassessment

Connected Learning Coalition (CLC). (2011, November). Assessment: An essential component of learning. Retrieved from http://principlesforlearning.org/images/CLC_Assessment_paper.pdf

Connor, C. M., Morrison, F. J., & Katch, L. E. (2004). Beyond the reading wars: Exploring the effect of child-instruction interactions on growth in early reading. *Scientific Studies of Reading, 8*(4), 305–336. doi:10.1207/s1532799xssr0804_1

Connor, C. M., Morrison, F., & Katch, L. (2004). Beyond the reading wars: The effect of classroom instruction by child interactions on early reading. *Scientific Studies of Reading, 8,* 305–336.

Connor, C. M., Morrison, F. J., Schatschneider, C., Toste, J. R., Lundblom, E., Crowe, E. C., & Fishman, B. (2011). Effective classroom instruction: Implications of child characteristics by reading instruction interactions on first graders' word reading achievement. *Journal of Research on Educational Effectiveness, 4,* 173–207.

Conrad, S. S. (1984). *On readability and readability formula scores* (Ginn Occasional Papers No. 17). Columbus, OH: Ginn and Co.

Cooper, J. D., & Kiger, N. D. (2005). *Literacy: Helping children construct meaning* (6th ed.). Boston, MA: Houghton Mifflin.

Cooter, R. B., Flynt, E. S., & Cooter, K. S. (2007). *Comprehensive reading inventory.* Upper Saddle River, NJ: Prentice Hall.

Copmann, K., & Griffith, P. (1994). Event and story structure recall by children with specific learning disabilities, language impairment, and normally achieving children. *Journal of Psycholinguistic Research, 23,* 231–248.

Corno, L., & Mandinach, E. B. (1983). The role of cognitive engagement in classroom learning and motivation. *Educational Psychologist, 18,* 88–108.

Cotton, K. (1989). Classroom questioning. School Improvement Reading Series. NW Regional Laboratory. Retrieved August, 2003, from http://www.nwrel.org/scpd/sirs/3/cu5.html

Covington, M. V. (2000). Goal theory, motivation, and school achievement: An integrative review. *Annual Review of Psychology, 51,* 171–200.

Coyne, M. D., Kame'enui, E. J., & Simmons, D. C. (2001). Prevention and intervention in beginning reading: Two complex systems. *Learning Disabilities Research and Practice, 16,* 62–73.

Coyne, M. D., Kame'enui, E. J., & Simmons, D. C. (2004). Improving beginning reading instruction and intervention for students with LD: Reconciling "all" with "each." *Journal of Learning Disabilities, 37,* 231–239.

Crago, M., Eriks-Brophy, A., Pesco, D., & McAlpine, L. (1997). Culturally based miscommunication in classroom interaction. *Language, Speech, Hearing Services in the Schools, 28,* 245–254.

Craik, F., & Lockhart, R. (1972). Levels of processing: A framework for memory research. *Journal of Verbal Learning and Verbal Behavior, 11,* 671–684.

Cramer, R. L. (1982). Informal approaches to evaluating-children's writing. In J. J. Pikulski & T. Shanahan (Eds.), *Approaches to the informal evaluation of reading* (pp. 80–93). Newark, DE: International Reading Association.

Crawford, J. W. (1997). *Best evidence: Research on language-minority education.* Washington, DC: National Clearinghouse on Bilingual Education.

Cremin, L. (1989). *Popular education and its discontents.* New York, NY: Harper & Row.

Critchley, M. (1975). Specific developmental dyslexia. In E. H. Lenneberg & E. Lenneberg (Eds.), *Foundations of language development* (Vol. 2, pp. 361–366). New York, NY: Academic Press.

Cromey, A., & Hanson, M. (2000). An exploratory analysis of school-based student assessment systems. *Educational Policy.* Retrieved February 18, 2007, from http://www.ncrel.org/policy/pubs/html/data/index.html

Cromley, J. G., & Azevedo, R. (2007). Self-report of reading comprehension strategies: What are we measuring? *Metacognition and Learning, 1,* 229–247.

Cullinan, B., & Fitzgerald, S. (1984). *Statement on readability.* Joint statement by the Presidents of the International Reading Association and the National Council of Teachers of English.

Cummins, J. (2001). *Negotiating identities: Education for empowerment in a diverse society* (2nd ed.). Los Angeles: California Association for Bilingual Education.

Cunningham, A. E. (1990). Explicit vs. implicit instruction in phonemic awareness. *Journal of Experimental Child Psychology, 50,* 429–444.

Cunningham, A. E., & Stanovich K. E. (1998). What reading does for the mind. *American Educator, 22*(1&2), 8–15.

Cunningham, J. W., Spadorcia, S. A., Erickson, K. A., Koppenhaver, D. A., Sturm, J. M., & Yoder, D. E. (2005). Investigating the instructional supportiveness of leveled texts. *Reading Research Quarterly, 40,* 410–427.

Cunningham, P. (1995). *Phonics they use: Words for reading and writing* (2nd ed.). New York, NY: HarperCollins.

Cunningham, P. M. (1975–1976). Investigating a synthesized theory of mediated word identification. *Reading Research Quarterly, 11,* 127–143.

Cunningham, P. M. (1979). A compare/contrast theory of mediated word identification. *The Reading Teacher, 32,* 774–778.

Cunningham, P. M. (2004). *Phonics they use: Words for reading and writing* (4th ed.). New York, NY: Longman.

Cunningham, P. M., & Allington, R. L., (2007). *Classrooms that work: They can all read and write* (4th ed.) Boston, MA: Pearson.

Cutler, R. B., & Truss, C. V. (1989). Computer aided instruction as a reading motivator. *Reading Improvement, 26,* 103–109.

Daane, M. C., Campbell, J. R., Grigg, W. S., Goodman, M. J., & Oranje, A. (2005). Fourth-grade students reading aloud: NAEP 2002 special study of oral reading (NCES 2006–469). U.S. Department of Education, Institute of Education Sciences, National Center for Education Statistics. Washington, DC: Government Printing Office.

D'Agostino, J. V., & Murphy, J. A. (2004). A meta-analysis of Reading Recovery in United States schools. *Educational Evaluation and Policy Analysis, 26*, 23–38.

Daiute, C. (1986). Physical and cognitive factors in revising: Insights from studies with computers. *Research in the Teaching of English, 20*, 141–159.

Dale, E., & Chall, J. (1948). A formula for predicting readability. *Educational Research Bulletin, 27*, 11–20, 37–54.

Dalton, B., & Palincsar, A. S. (2004). *Investigating verbal protocols for what they reveal about upper elementary students' text processing across narrative and informational texts.* Paper presented at the National Reading Conference Annual Meeting, San Diego, CA.

Dalton, B., & Proctor, C. P. (2008). The changing landscape of text and comprehension in the age of new literacies. In J. Coiro, M. Knowbel, C. Lankshear, & D. J. Leu (Eds.), *Handbook of research on new literacies.* Mahwah, NJ: Erlbaum.

Dalton, B., Proctor, C. P., Palincsar, A. S., Mo, E., DeFrance, N., Robinson, K., ... Magnusson, S. (2006, November). *Reading to Learn: Investigating the effects of three versions of a digital reading environment featuring interactive diagrams and pedagogical agents.* Paper presented at the annual meeting of the National Reading Conference, Los Angeles, CA.

Dalton, B., & Strangman, N. (2006). Improving struggling readers' comprehension through scaffolded hypertexts and other computer-based literacy programs. In D. Reinking, M. C. McKenna, L. D. Labbo, & R. D. Keiffer, *Handbook of literacy and technology* (2nd edition, pp. 75–92). Mahwah, NJ: Erlbaum.

D'Amato, J. (1987). The belly of the beast: On cultural differences, castelike status, and the politics of school. *Anthropology and Education Quarterly, 18*, 357–361.

D'Amato, J. (1988). "Acting": Hawaiian children's resistance to teachers. *Elementary School Journal, 88*, 529–544.

Darling-Hammond, L. (1995). Inequality and access to knowledge. In J. A. Banks & C. A. M. Banks (Eds.), *Handbook of research on multicultural education* (pp. 465–483). New York, NY: Macmillan.

Darling-Hammond, L. (2004). Standards, accountability, and school reform. *Teachers College Record, 106*, 1047–1085.

Darling-Hammond, L., Ancess, J., & Falk, B. (1995). *Authentic assessment in action.* New York, NY: Teachers College Press.

Darling-Hammond, L., Bransford, J., LePage, P., Hammerness, K., & Duffy, H. (2005). *Preparing teachers for a changing world: What teachers should learn and be able to do.* San Francisco, CA: Jossey-Bass.

Davis, F. B. (1968). Research in comprehension in reading. *Reading Research Quarterly, 3*, 499–545.

Davison, A. (1984). Readability: Appraising text difficulty. In R. C. Anderson, J. Osborn, & R. T. Tierney (Eds.), *Learning to read in American schools: Basal readers and content texts* (pp. 121–140). Hillsdale, NJ: Erlbaum.

Davison, A., & Kantor, R. N. (1982). On the failure of readability formulas to define readable texts: A case study from adaptations. *Reading Research Quarterly, 17*, 187–209.

Day, J. D. (1992). *Population projections of the United States by age, sex, race, and Hispanic origin: 1992–2050.* Washington, DC: U.S. Bureau of the Census.

Day, J. D., & Cordon, L. A. (1993). Static and dynamic measures of ability: An experimental comparison. *Journal of Educational Psychology, 85*, 75–82.

De La Paz, S. (1999). Composing via dictation and speech recognition systems: Compensatory technology for students with learning disabilities. *Learning Disabilities Quarterly, 22*, 173–182.

De La Paz, S., & Graham, S. (1997). Strategy instruction in planning: Effects on the writing performance and behavior of students with learning difficulties. *Exceptional Children, 63*, 167–181.

De La Paz, S., & Graham, S. (2002). Explicitly teaching strategies, skills, and knowledge: Writing instruction in middle school classrooms. *Journal of Educational Psychology, 94*, 687–698.

De Temple, J., & Snow, C. E. (2003). Learning words from books. In A. van Kleeck, S. A. Stach, & E. B. Bauer (Eds.), *On reading books to children* (pp. 16–36). Mahwah, NJ: Erlbaum.

Debruin-Parecki, A. 2007). *Let's read together: Improving literacy outcomes with Adult-Child Interactive Reading Inventory ACIRI).* Baltimore, MD: Brookes.

DeFord, D. (1991). Using reading and writing to support the reader. In D. E. DeFord, C. A. Lyons, & G. S. Pinnell (Eds.), *Bridges to literacy* (pp. 77–95). Portsmouth, NH: Heinemann.

DeFord, D. E. (1980). Young children and their writing. *Theory into Practice, 19*, 157–162.

DeFord, D. E. (1986). Classroom contexts for literacy learning. In T. E. Raphael (Ed.), *The contexts of school-based literacy* (pp. 163–180). New York, NY: Longman.

DeFord, D., Morgan, D. N., Saylor-Crowder, K., Pae, T., Johnson, R., Stephens, D., ... Hamel, A. (2003). Changes in children's cue and strategy use during reading: Findings from the first year of professional development in the South Carolina Reading Initiative. Technical Report No. 002. University of South Carolina. ED478464.

Delpit, L. (1995). *Other people's children.* New York, NY: New Press.

Denton, C. A., Ciancio, D. J., & Fletcher, J. M. (2006). Validity, reliability, and utility of the Observation Survey of Early Literacy Achievement. *Reading Research Quarterly, 41*, 8–34.

Dewey, J. (1946). *The public and its problems.* Chicago, IL: Gateway.

Dewey, J. (1998). *How we think.* Boston, MA: Houghton Mifflin.

Dewitz, P., Carr, E. M., & Patberg, J. P. (1987). Effects of inference training on comprehension and comprehension monitoring. *Reading Research Quarterly, 22*, 542–546.

Dewitz, P., Jones, J., & Leahy, S. B. (2009). Comprehension strategy instruction in core reading programs. *Reading Research Quarterly, 44*, 2, 102–126.

Dewitz, P., Leahy, S. B., Jones, J., & Sullivan, P. M. (2010). *The essential guide to selecting and using core reading programs.* Newark, DE: IRA.

Dickinson, D., & McCabe, A. (1991). A social interactionist account of language and literacy development. In J. Kavanaugh (Ed.), *The language continuum.* Parkton, MD: York Press.

Dickinson, D. K., McCabe, A. 2001). Bringing it all together: The multiple origins, skills, and environmental supports of early literacy. *Learning Disabilities Research Practice,164*), 186–202.

Dickinson, D. K. (1986). Cooperation, collaboration, and a computer: Integrating a computer into a first–second grade writing program. *Research in the Teaching of English, 20*, 357–378.

Dickinson, D. K., McCabe, A., & Clark-Chiarelli, N. (2004). Preschool-based prevention of reading disability: Realities vs. possibilities. In C. A. Stone, E. R. Stillman, B. J. Ehren, & K. Apel (Eds.), *Handbook of language and literacy: Development and disorders* (pp. 209–227). New York, NY: Guilford Press.

Dickinson, D. K., McCabe, A., & Sprague, K. (2003). Teacher rating of oral language and literacy TROLL: Individualizing early literacy instruction with a standards-based rating tool. *The Reading Teacher, 566*), 554–564.

Dickson, S. V., Collins, V. L, Simmons, D. C., & Kame'enui, E. J. (1998). Metacognitive strategies: Instructional and curricular basics and implications. In E. C. Simmons & E. J. Kame'enui (Eds.), *What reading research tells us about children with diverse learning needs: Bases and basics*. Mahwah, NJ: L. Erlbaum Associates.

Diehl, H. L., (2005). Snapshots of our journey to thoughtful literacy. *The Reading Teacher, 59*, 56–69.

Doctorow, M., Wittrock, M. C., & Marks, C. (1978). Generative processes in reading comprehension. *Journal of Educational Psychology, 70*, 109–118.

Dodge, J. (1994). *The study skills handbook (Grades 4–8)*. New York, NY: Scholastic.

Dolch, E. W. (1942a). *Basic sight word test*. Champaign, IL: Garrard Press.

Dolch, E. W. (1942b). *Better spelling*. Champaign, IL: Garrard Press.

Dole, J. A., Duffy, G. G., Roehler, L. R., & Pearson, P. D. (1991). Moving from the old to the new: Research on reading comprehension instruction. *Review of Educational Research, 61*, 239–264.

Dombrowski, S. C. (2003). Norm-referenced versus curriculum-based assessment: A balanced perspective. *Communique, 31*(7): 16–20.

Donly, B., Henderson, A., & Strang, W. (1995). *Summary of bilingual education state education agency program survey of states' limited English proficiency persons and available educational services, 1993–1994*. Arlington, VA: Development Associates.

Donovan, H., & Ellis, M. (2005). Paired reading—More than an evening of entertainment. *The Reading Teacher, 59*, 174–182.

Donovan, M. S., Cross, C. T. (Eds.), & the Committee on Minority Representation in Special Education. (2002). *Minority students in special and gifted education*. Washington, DC: National Academy Press.

Dorn, L., & Schubert, B. (2008). A comprehensive intervention model for reversing reading failure: A Response to intervention approach. *Journal of Reading Recovery, 7*(2), 29–41.

Dorn, L. J., & Henderson, S. C. (2010). The comprehensive intervention model: A systems approach to RTI. In M. Y. Lipson & K. K. Wixson (Eds.), *Successful approaches to RTI: Collaborative practices for improving K–12 literacy* (pp. 88–120). Newark, DE: International Reading Association.

Dorn, L. J., & Soffos, C. (2012). *Interventions that work: A comprehensive intervention model for preventing reading failure in grades K–3*. Boston, MA: Allyn & Bacon.

Dornan, R., Rosen, L. M., & Wilson, M. (1997). *Multiple voices, multiple texts: Reading in the secondary content areas*. Portsmouth, NH: Heinemann.

Dorr, R. E. (2006). Something old is new again: Revisiting language experience. *The Reading Teacher, 60*, 138–146.

Downing, J. (1978). Linguistic awareness, English orthography and reading instruction. *Journal of Reading Behavior, 10*, 103–114.

Doyle, W. (1983). Academic work. *Review of Educational Research, 53*, 159–199.

Doyle, W. (1986). Classroom organization and management. In M. C. Wittrock (Ed.), *Handbook of research on teaching* (3rd ed., pp. 392–431). New York, NY: Macmillan.

Drahozal, E. C., & Hanna, G. S. (1978). Reading comprehension subscores: Pretty bottles for ordinary wine. *Journal of Reading, 21*, 416–420.

Dreeben, R. (1968). The contribution of schooling to the learning of norms. In *Socialization and schools* (Harvard Educational Review Reprint Series No. 1). Cambridge, MA: Harvard University Press.

Dreher, M. J. (2003). Motivating struggling readers by tapping the potential of informational books. *Reading & Writing Quarterly, 19*, 25–38.

Dressel, J. H. (1990). The effects of listening to and discussing different qualities of children's literature on the narrative writing of fifth graders. *Research in the Teaching of English, 24*, 397–444.

Duchene, J. F. (2004). The foundational role of schemas in children's language and literacy learning. In C. A. Stone, E. R. Silliman, B. J. Ehren, & K. Apel (Eds.), *Handbook of language and literacy: Development and disorders*. New York, NY: Guilford.

Duell, O. K. (1974). Effect of types of objective, level of test questions, and judged importance of texted materials upon posttest performance. *Journal of Educational Psychology, 66*, 225–232.

Dufflemeyer, F. A., Baum, D. D., & Merkley, D. J. (1987). Maximizing reader-text confrontation with an extended anticipation guide. *Journal of Reading, 31*, 146–150.

Duffelmeyer, F. A., Kruse, A. E., Merkley, D. J., & Fyfe, S. A. (1994). Further validation and enhancement of the Names Test. *The Reading Teacher, 48*, 118–128.

Duffy, G. G. (1993). Rethinking strategy instruction: Four teachers' development and their low achievers' understandings. *Elementary School Journal, 93*, 231–247.

Duffy, G. G., & Roehler, L. R. (1989). *Improving classroom reading instruction: A decision making approach* (2nd ed.). New York, NY: Random House.

Duffy, G. G., Roehler, L. R., Meloth, M. S., Vavrus, L. G., Book, C., Putnam, J., & Wesselman, R. (1986). The relationship between explicit verbal explanations during reading skills instruction and student awareness and achievement: A study of reading teacher effects. *Reading Research Quarterly, 21*, 237–252.

Duffy, T. M., & Cunningham, D. J. (Eds.). (1996). *Constructivism: Implications for the design and delivery of instruction*. New York, NY: Simon & Schuster Macmillan.

DuFour, R., DuFour, R., & Eaker, R. (2008). *Revisiting professional learning communities at work™: New insights for improving schools*. Bloomington, IN: Solution Tree.

DuFour, R., & Eaker, R. (1998). *Professional learning communities at work: Best practices for enhancing student achievement*. Bloomington, IN: Solution Tree formerly National Educational Service.

Duke, N., Bennett-Armistead, S., & Roberts, E. M. (2003). Filling the great void: Why we should bring nonfiction into the early-grade classroom. *American Educator* (Spring).

Duke, N. K. (2000). For the rich it's richer: Print environments and experiences offered to first-grade students in very low and very high SES school districts. *American Educational Research Journal, 37*, 441–478.

Duke, N. K. (2004). The case for informational text: Younger students need to expand their repertoire and build literacy skills with informational text. *Educational Leadership, 61*(6), 40–44.

Duke, N. K., & Pearson, P. D. (2002). Effective practices for developing reading comprehension. In A. E. Farstrup & S. J. Samuels (Eds.), *What research has to say about reading instruction* (pp. 205–242). Newark, DE: International Reading Association.

Dunn, L. M., & Dunn, L. M. (1981). *Peabody picture vocabulary test—Revised*. Circle Pines, MN: American Guidance Service.

Dunn, L. M., & Dunn, L. M. (2007). *Peabody picture vocabulary test* (3rd ed.). Circle Pines, MN: American Guidance Service.

DuPrau, J. (2003). *City of Ember*. New York, NY: Random House.

Durkin, D. (1978–1979). What classroom observations reveal about reading comprehension instruction. *Reading Research Quarterly, 14*, 481–533.

Durkin, D. (1983). *Teaching them to read* (4th ed.). Boston, MA: Allyn & Bacon.

Durkin, D. (1984). Is there a match between what elementary teachers do and what basal reader manuals recommend? *The Reading Teacher, 37*, 734–749.

Durkin, D. (1987). Testing in kindergarten. *The Reading Teacher, 40*, 766–770.

Dweck, C. S. (1975). The role of expectations and attributions in the alleviation of learned helplessness. *Journal of Personality and Social Psychology, 31*, 674–685.

Dymock, S. 2007). Comprehension strategy instruction: Teaching narrative text structure awareness. *The Reading Teacher, 61*, 161–167.

Dyson, A. H. (1999). Transforming transfer: Unruly children, contrary texts, and the persistence of the pedagogical order. In *Review of research in education* (Vol. 24, pp. 141–172). Washington, DC: American Educational Research Association.

Dyson, A. H., & Freedman, S. W. (2003). Writing. In J. Flood, D. Lapp, J. R. Squire, & J. M. Jensen (Eds.), *Handbook of research on teaching the English language arts* (2nd ed., pp. 967–992). Mahwah, NJ: Erlbaum.

Eagleton, M. B. & Dobler, E. (2007). *Reading the web: Strategies for Internet inquiry.* New York, NY: Guilford.

Ebersole, M. (2005). Reflecting on miscues in content area reading. *Academic Exchange Quarterly, 9*(2). Retrieved March 1, 2007, from www.rapidintellect.com/AEQweb/oct2750.htm

Eckhoff, B. (1983). How reading affects children's writing. *Language Arts, 60*, 607–616.

EdFormation, Inc. (2007). AIMSweb progress monitoring and response to intervention system. EdFormation. San Antonio, TX: Harcourt.

Edmonds, M. S., Vaughn, S., Wexler, J., Reutebuch, C., Cable, A., Klingler Tackett, K., & Schnakenberg, J. W. 2009). Synthesis of reading interventions and effects on reading comprehension outcomes for older struggling readers. *Review of Educational Research, 79*, 262–300.

Edmonds, R. (1980). *A discussion of the literature and issues related to effective schooling.* St. Louis, MO: Cemrel.

Edmunds, K. M., & Bauserman, K. L. (2006). What teachers can learn about reading motivation through conversations with children. *The Reading Teacher, 59*, 414–424.

Edwards, E. C., Font, G., Baumann, J. F., & Boland, E. (2004). Unlocking word meanings: Strategies and guidelines for teaching morphemic and contextual analysis. In J. F. Baumann & E. J. Kame'enui (Eds.), *Vocabulary instruction: Research to practice* (pp. 159–176). New York, NY: Guilford.

Eeds, M. (1985). Bookwords: Using a beginning word list of high frequency words from children's literature K–3. *The Reading Teacher, 38*, 418–423.

Ehri, L. (1979). Linguistic insight: Threshold of reading acquisition. In T. G. Waller & G. E. MacKinnon (Eds.), *Reading research: Advances in theory and practice* (Vol. 1, pp. 63–114). New York, NY: Academic Press.

Ehri, L. (1987). Learning to read and spell words. *Journal of Reading Behavior, 19*, 5–32.

Ehri, L. C. (1988). Movement into word reading and spelling: How spelling contributes to reading. In J. M. Mason (Ed.), *Reading and writing connections* (pp. 65–81). Needham Heights, MA: Allyn & Bacon.

Ehri, L. (1991). Development of the ability to read words. In R. Barr, M. Kamil, P. Mosenthal, & P. D. Pearson (Eds.), *Handbook of reading research* (Vol. 2, pp. 383–417). New York, NY: Longman.

Ehri, L. (1994). Development of the ability to read words: An update. In R. Ruddell, M. Ruddell, & H. Singer (Eds.), *Theoretical models and processes of reading.* Newark, DE: International Reading Association.

Ehri, L. (1995). Phases of development in learning to read words by sight. *Journal of Research in Reading, 18*, 116–125.

Ehri, L. C., Nunes, S. R., Stahl, S. A., & Willows, D. M. (2001). Systematic phonics instruction helps students learn to read: Evidence from the National Reading Panel's meta-analysis. *Review of Educational Research, 71*, 393–447.

Ehri, L., & Roberts, T. (2006). The roots of learning to read and write: Acquisition of letters and phonemic awareness. In D. K. Dickinson & S. B. Neuman (Eds.), *Handbook of early literacy research* (Vol. 2, pp. 113–134). New York, NY: Guilford Press.

Ehri, L., & Sweet, J. (1991). Fingerpoint-reading of memorized text: What enables beginning readers to process print? *Reading Research Quarterly, 26*, 442–462.

Ehri, L., & Wilce, L. S. (1980). Do beginners learn to read function words better in sentences or in lists? *Reading Research Quarterly, 15*, 451–476.

Ekwall, E. E., & Shanker, J. L. (1985). *Teaching reading in the elementary school.* Columbus, OH: Charles E. Merrill.

Ekwall, E. E., & Shanker, J. L. (2000). *Ekwall/Shanker reading inventory* (4th ed.). Boston, MA: Allyn & Bacon.

Elbaum, B., Moody, S. W., Schumm, J. S. (1999). Mixed-ability grouping for reading: What students think. *Learning Disabilities Research and Practice, 14*, 61–66.

Eldredge, J. L. (1990). Increasing the performance of poor readers in the third grade with a group-assisted strategy. *Journal of Educational Research, 84*, 69–77.

Elkins, J. (1986). Self-help for older writers with spelling and composing difficulties: Using the word processor and spelling checker. *Exceptional Child, 33*, 73–76.

Elkonin, D. E. (1963). The psychology of mastering the elements of reading. In B. Simon & J. Simon (Eds.), *Edu-ca-tional psychology in the U.S.S.R.* (pp. 165–179). London, UK: Routledge.

Elkonin, D. E. (1973). U.S.S.R. In J. Downing (Ed.), *Comparative reading: Cross-national studies of behavior and processes in reading and writing* (pp. 551–579). New York, NY: Macmillan.

Elley, W. B. (1989). Vocabulary acquisition from listening to stories. *Reading Research Quarterly, 24*, 174–187.

Ellis, N., & Cataldo, S. (1990). The role of spelling in learning to read. *Language and Education, 4*, 1–28.

Ellis, W., & Cramer, S. C. (1994). *Learning disabilities: A national responsibility* (Report of the Summit on Learning Disabilities in Washington, DC. September 20–21). New York, NY: National Center for Learning Disabilities.

Ely, R. (2005). Language and literacy in the school years. In J. B. Gleason (Ed.), *The development of language* (6th ed., pp. 395–443). Boston, MA: Pearson.

Engelhard, G., Gordon, B., & Gabrielson, S. (1992). The influences of mode of discourse, experiential demand, and gender on the quality of student writing. *Research in the Teaching of English, 26*, 315–336.

Englert, C. S. (1992). Writing instruction from a sociocultural perspective: The holistic, dialogic, and social enterprise of writing. *Journal of Learning Disabilities, 25*, 153–172.

Englert, C. S., Garmon, A., Mariage, T., Rozendal, M., Tarrant, K., & Urba, J. (1995). The early literacy project: Connecting across the literacy curriculum. *Learning Disability Quarterly, 18*, 253–275.

Englert, C. S., & Palincsar, A. S. (1991). Reconsidering instructional research in literacy from a sociocultural perspective. *Learning Disabilities Research and Practice, 6*, 225–229.

Englert, C. S., Wu, X., & Zhao, Y. (2005). Cognitive tools for writing: Scaffolding the performance of students through technology. *Learning Disabilities Research and Practice, 20*, 184–198.

Enright, B. E. (1991). *Brigance diagnostic inventory of early develop-ment—Revised technical report*. North Billerica, MA: Curriculum Associates.

Entin, E. B., & Klare, G. R. (1985). Relationships of measures of inter-est, prior knowledge, and readability to comprehension of exposi-tory passages. In B. Hutson (Ed.), *Advances in reading/language research* (Vol. 3, pp. 9–38). Greenwich, CT: JAI Press.

Entwisle, D. R. (1995). The role of schools in sustaining early childhood program benefits. *The Future of Children: Long-Term Outcomes of Early Childhood Programs, 5*(3), 133–144.

Erickson. F. (1993). Transformation and school success. In E. Jacob and C. Jordan (Eds.), *Minority education: Anthropological perspec-tives* (pp. 27–51). Norwood, NJ: Ablex.

Ericsson, K. A., & Simon, H. A, (1980/1993). *Protocol an analysis: Ver-bal reports as data* (Rev. ed.). Cambridge, MA: Bradford.

Ericsson, K. A., & Simon, H. A. (1998). How to study thinking in ev-eryday life: Contrasting think-aloud protocols with descriptions and explanations of thinking. *Mind, Culture, & Activity, 5*(3), 178–186.

Ertmer, P. A., Gopalakrishnan, S., & Ross, E. M. (2001). Technology-using teachers: Comparing perceptions of exemplary technology use to best practice. *Journal of Research on Technology in Educa-tion, 33*(5). [Online article]. Retrieved from http://www.iste.org/jrte/33/5/ertmer.html

Estes, T., & Vaughn, J. (1986). *Reading and reasoning beyond the pri-mary grades*. Boston, MA: Allyn and Bacon.

Estes, T. H., & Vaughan, J. L. (1973). Reading interest and comprehen-sion: Implications. *The Reading Teacher, 27*, 149–153.

Estrin, E. T. (1993). *Alternative assessment: Issues in language, culture, and equity*. (Knowledge Brief 11). San Francisco, CA: WestEd.

Evans, K. S. (2002). Fifth-grade students' perceptions of how they expe-rience literature discussion groups. *Reading Research Quarterly, 37*, 46–69.

Evans, K. S., Alvermann, D., & Anders, P. L. (1998). Literature discus-sion groups: An examination of gender roles. *Reading Research and Instruction, 37*, 107–122.

Fair Test. (n.d.). Criterion- and standards-referenced tests. Retrieved March 18, 2007, from http://www.fairtest.org/facts/csrtests.html

Falk, B., & Ort, S. (1998). Sitting down to score: Teacher learning through assessment. *Phi Delta Kappan, 80*, 59–64.

Fall, R., Webb, N. M., & Chudowsky, N. (2000). Group discussion and large-scale language arts assessment: Effects on students' compre-hension. *American Educational Research Journal, 37*, 911–941.

Farr, R., & Munroe, K. (2007). SSSMART: Reading in the content area—Academic reading text. Brewster, NY: Questar.

Fass, W., & Schumacher, G. M. (1978). Effects of motivation, subject activity, and readability on the retention of prose materials. *Jour-nal of Educational Psychology, 70*, 803–808.

Feitelson, D., Kita, B., & Goldstein, Z. (1986). Effects of listening to series stories on first graders' comprehension and use of language. *Research in the Teaching of English, 20*, 339–356.

Fenson, L., Dale, P., Reznick, J. S., Bates, E., Thal, D., Pethick, S. (1994). Variability in early communicative development. *Mono-graphs for the Society for Research in Child Development, 59*(5, Serial No. 242).

Ferguson, A., Helmer, K., & Suh, S. J. (2003). Miscue analysis of na-tive and non-native speakers. *Arizona Working Papers in SLAT, 10*, 51–67.

Ferreiro, E. (1980, May). *The relationship between oral and written language: The children's viewpoints*. Paper presented at the 25th Annual Conference of the International Reading Association, St. Louis, MO.

Ferreiro, E., & Teberosky, A. (1979/1982). *Literacy before schooling*. Exeter, NH: Heinemann.

Feuerstein, R., Rand, Y., & Hoffman, M. B. (1979). *The dynamic assess-ment of retarded performance*. Baltimore: University Park Press.

Fielding, L., & Pearson, P. D. (1994). Reading comprehension: What words? *Educational Leadership, 51*, 62–67.

Fielding, L. G., Wilson, P. T., & Anderson, R. C. (1986). A new focus on free reading: The role of trade books in reading instruction. In T. E. Raphael (Ed.), *The contexts of school-based literacy* (pp. 149–160). New York, NY: Random House.

Figueroa, R., & Garcia, E. (1994). Issues in testing students from cultur-ally and linguistically diverse backgrounds. *Multicultural Educa-tion, 2*(1), 10–23.

Finders, M. (1997). *Just girls*. New York, NY: Teachers College Press.

Fink, R. (2006). *Why Jane and Johnny couldn't read and how they learned: A new look at striving readers*. Newark, DE: Interna-tional Reading Association.

Firth, U. (1980). Unexpected spelling problems. In U. Firth (Ed.), *Cogni-tive processes in learning to spell*. London, UK: Academic Press.

Fisher, C. W., Berliner, D. C., Filby, N., Marliave, R., Cohen, L., Dishaw, M., & Moore, J. (1980). Teaching behaviors, academic learning time, and student achievement: An overview. In C. Denham & A. Lieberman (Eds.), *Time to learn* (pp. 7–32). Washington, DC: National Institute of Education.

Fisher, C. W., & Hiebert, E. H. (1990). Characteristics of tasks in two approaches to literacy instruction. *Elementary School Journal, 91*, 3–18.

Fisher, D., & Frey, N. (2008). *Better learning through structured teaching: A framework for the gradual release of responsibility*. Alexandria, VA: ASCD.

Fitzgerald, J., & Graves, M. F. (2004). *Scaffolding reading experiences for English-language learners*. Norwood, MA: Christopher-Gordon.

Fitzgerald, J., & Shanahan, T. (2000). Reading and writing relations and their development. *Educational Psychologist, 35*, 39–50.

Flavell, J. H., & Wellman, H. M. (1977). Metamemory. In R. Kail, Jr., & J. W. Hagen (Eds.), *Perspectives on the development of memory and cognition* (pp. 3–33). Hillsdale, NJ: Erlbaum.

Fleming, S. (1995). Whose stories are validated? *Language Arts, 72*, 500–596.

Flesch, R. (1948). A new readability yardstick. *Journal of Applied Psy-chology, 32*, 221–233.

Fletcher, R., & Portalupi, J. (2001). *Writing workshop: The essential guide*. Portsmouth, NH: Heinemann.

Flores, B., & Hernandez, E. (1988). A bilingual kindergartener's socio-psychogenesis of literacy and biliteracy. *Dialogue, 3*, 43–49.

Floriani, A. (1993). Negotiating what counts: Roles and relationships, content and meaning, texts and context. *Linguistics and Educa-tion, 5*, 241–274. Norwood, NJ: Ablex.

Florio-Ruane, S. (1991). Instructional conversations in learning to write and learning to teach. In L. Idol & B. F. Jones (Eds.), *Educa-tional values and cognitive instruction: Implications for reform* (pp. 365–386). Hillsdale, NJ: Erlbaum.

Flower, L., & Hayes, J. (1981). Plans that guide the composing process. In C. H. Frederiksen & J. Dominic (Eds.), *Writing: The nature, development, and teaching of written communication* (pp. 39–58). Hillsdale, NJ: Erlbaum.

Foorman, B. R., & Torgesen, J. (2001). Critical elements of classroom and small-group instruction promote reading success for all chil-dren. *Learning Disabilities Research and Practice, 16*, 203–212.

Ford, M. P., & Optiz, M. F. (2008). A national survey of guided read-ing practices: What we can learn form primary teachers. *Literacy Research and Instruction, 47*, 309–331.

Forget, M. A. (2004). MAX teaching with reading and writing: Using literacy skills to help students learn subject matter. Findlay, OH: MAX Teaching with Reading and Writing. Retrieved March 4, 2007, from http://missouricareereducation.org/pd/BBDoc/Presentations/BB05-Forget.pdf

Fountas, I., & Pinnell, G. S. (2005). *The Fountas & Pinnell leveled book list, K–8, 2006–2009.* Portsmouth, NH: Heinemann.

Fountas, I., & Pinnell, G. S. (2006). *Teaching for comprehending and fluency: Thinking, talking, and writing about reading, K–8.* Portsmouth, NH: Heinemann.

Fountas, I., & Pinnell, G. S. (2010). *Benchmark assessment system* (2nd ed.). Portsmouth, NH: Heinemann.

Fountas, I. C., & Pinnell, G. S. (1996). *Guided reading: Good first teacher for all children.* Portsmouth, NH: Heinemann.

Fountas, I. C., & Pinnell, G. S. (1999). *Matching books to readers (K–3).* Portsmouth, NH: Heinemann.

Fountas, I. C., & Pinnell, G. S. (2001). *Guiding readers and writers grades 3–6.* Portsmouth, NH: Heinemann.

Fountas & Pinnell Benchmark Assessment System. (2010). Field study of reliability and validity of the Fountas & Pinnell Benchmark Assessment Systems 1 and 2. Retrieved August 15, 2010, from http://www.heinemann.com/fountasandpinnell/researchBAS.aspx

Fowler, G. L. (1982). Developing comprehension skills in primary students through the use of story frames. *The Reading Teacher, 36,* 176–184.

Fox, D. L., & Short, K. G. (2003). *Stories matter: The complexity of cultural authenticity in children's literature.* Urbana, IL: National Council of Teachers of English.

Francis, H. (1973). Children's experience of reading and notions of units of language. *British Journal of Educational Psychology, 43,* 17–23.

Francis, N. (2004). Nonlinear processing as a comprehension strategy: A proposed typology for the study of bilingual children's self-corrections of oral reading miscues. *Language Awareness, 13,* 17–33.

Frankel, K. K., Pearson, P. D., & Nair, M. (2011). Reading comprehension and reading disability. In A. McGill-Franzen & R. L. Allington (Eds.), *Handbook of reading disability research* (pp. 219–231). New York, NY: Routledge.

Freebody, P., & Anderson, R. C. (1983). Effects on text comprehension of differing proportions and locations of difficult vocabulary. *Journal of Reading Behavior, 15,* 19–40.

Freeman, D., Freeman, Y., & Mercuri, S. (2004). *Dual language essentials for teachers and administrators.* Portsmouth, NH: Heinemann.

Freeman, D. E., & Freeman, Y. S. (2000). Teaching reading in multilingual classrooms. Portsmouth, NH: Heinemann.

Friend, M., & Bursuck, W. D. (2006). *Including students with special needs: A practice guide for classroom teachers* (4th ed.). Boston, MA: Pearson/Allyn & Bacon.

Fry, E. (1968). A readability formula that saves time. *Journal of Reading, 11,* 513–516, 578.

Fry, E. (1980). The new instant word list. *The Reading Teacher, 34,* 284–289.

Fry, E. (2002). Readability versus leveling. *The Reading Teacher, 56,* 286–291.

Fry, E. B., Kress, J. E., & Fountoukidis, D. L. (1993). *The reading teacher's book of lists* (3rd ed.). Englewood Cliffs, NJ: Prentice Hall.

Fuchs, D., Compton, D. L., Fuchs, L. S., Bouton, B., & Caffrey, E. (2011). The construct and predictive validity of a dynamic assessment of young children learning to read: Implications for RTI frameworks. *Journal of Learning Disabilities, 44*(4), 339–347.

Fuchs, D., Fuchs, L. S., & Compton, D. L. (2004). Identifying reading disabilities by responsiveness to instruction: Specifying measures and criteria. *Learning Disability Quarterly, 27*(4), 216–228.

Fuchs, L. S., Fuchs, D., Hosp, M. K., & Jenkins, J. R. (2001). Oral reading fluency as an indicator of reading competence: A theoretical, empirical, and historical analysis. *Scientific Studies of Reading, 5*(3), 239–25.

Fullan, M. (1999). *Change forces: The sequel.* Philadelphia, PA: Falmer Press.

Fulwiler, T. (1980). Journals across the disciplines. *English Journal, 69,* 14–19.

Fulwiler, T. (1982). The personal connection: Journal writing across the curriculum. In T. Fulwiler & A. Young (Eds.), *Language connections: Writing and reading across the curriculum* (pp. 15–32). Urbana, IL: National Council of Teachers of English.

Fulwiler, T. (Ed.). (1987a). *The journal book.* Portsmouth, NH: Boynton/Cook.

Fulwiler, T. (1987b). *Teaching with writing.* Portsmouth, NH: Boynton/Cook.

Gaffney, J. S., & Anderson, R. C. (2000). Trends in reading research in the United States: Changing intellectual currents over three decades. In M. L. Kamil, P. B. Mosenthal, P. D. Pearson, & R. Barr (Eds.), *Handbook of reading research* (Vol. 3, pp. 53–74). Mahwah, NJ: Lawrence Erlbaum.

Gage, N. L., & Berliner, D. C. (1988). *Educational psychology.* Boston, MA: Houghton Mifflin.

Galda, L. (1982). Assessment: Responses to literature. In A. Berger & H. A. Robinson (Eds.), *Secondary school reading: What research reveals for classroom practice* (pp. 111–125). Urbana, IL: National Council of Teachers of English and ERIC Clearinghouse on Reading and Communications Skills.

Galda, L., Ash, G. E., & Cullinan, B. E. (2000). Children's literature. In M. L. Kamil, P. B. Mosenthal, P. D. Pearson, & R. Barr (Eds.), *Handbook of reading research* (Vol. 3, pp. 361–379). Mahwah, NJ: Erlbaum.

Gallagher, J. (1984). Policy analysis and program implementation/PL 94–142. *Topics in Early Childhood Special Education, 4*(1), 43–53.

Gallego, M., & Hollingsworth, S. (2000). Research directions: Multiple literacies: Teachers' evolving perceptions. *Language Arts, 69,* 206–213.

Gallego, M. A., & Hollingsworth, S. (Eds.). (2000). *What counts as literacy: Challenging the school standard.* New York, NY: Teachers College Press.

Gamaron, A. (1992). Is ability grouping equitable? *Education Leadership, 50,* 11–17.

Gamaron, A. (2004). Classroom organization and instructional quality. In M. C. Wang & H. J. Walberg (Eds.), *Can unlike students learn together? Grade retention, tracking and grouping* (pp. 141–155). Greenwich, CT: Information Age Publishing.

Gamaron, A., Nystrand, M., Berends, M., & LePore, P. (1995). An organizational analysis of the effects of ability grouping. *American Educational Research Journal, 32,* 687–715.

Gambrell, L. B. (1978). Getting started with sustained silent reading and keeping it going. *The Reading Teacher, 32,* 328–331.

Gambrell, L. B. (1985). Dialogue journals: Reading-writing interaction. *The Reading Teacher, 38,* 512–515.

Gambrell, L. B. (1996). Creating classroom cultures that foster reading motivation. *The Reading Teacher, 50,* 14–25.

Gambrell, L. B., & Almasi, J. F. (1993). Fostering comprehension through discussion. In L. N. Morrow, J. K. Smith, & L. C.

Wilkinson (Eds.), *Integrated language arts: Controversy to consensus* (pp. 71–90). Boston, MA: Allyn & Bacon.

Gambrell, L. B., Palmer, B. M., Codling, R. M., & Mazzoni, S. A. (1996). Assessing motivation to read. *The Reading Teacher, 49,* 518–533.

Ganske, K. (1999). The developmental spelling analysis: A measure of orthographic knowledge. *Educational Assessment, 6*(1), 41–71.

Ganske, K. (2000). Word journeys: Assessment-guided phonics, spelling, and vocabulary instruction. New York, NY: Guilford Press.

Garan, E. M. (2001). What does the report of the National Reading Panel really tell us about teaching phonics? *Language Arts, 79,* 500–506.

García, G. E. (1991). Factors influencing the English reading test performance of Spanish-speaking Hispanic children. *Reading Research Quarterly, 26,* 371–392.

García, G. E. (1993). Spanish-English bilingual students' use of cognates in English reading. *Journal of Reading Behavior, 25,* 241–259.

García, G. E. (2000). Bilingual children's reading. In M. L. Kamil, P. B. Mosenthal, P. D. Pearson, & R. Barr (Eds.), *Handbook of reading research* (Vol. 3, pp. 813–834). Mahwah, NJ: Lawrence Erlbaum.

García, G. E., & Levin, M. (2001). Latino children in Head Start: Family characteristics, parent involvement, and satisfaction with the Head Start program. [Online]. Retrieved December 17, 2006, from http://www.acf.hhs.gov/programs/opre/hs/faces/pres_apers/latino_children/latino_children.pdf

García, G. E., & Pearson, P. D. (1994). Assessment and diversity. *Review of Research in Education, 20,* 337–393.

Garcia, M. W., & Verville, K. (1994). Redesigning teaching and learning: The Arizona state assessment program. In S. W. Valencia, F. Hiebert, & P. P. Afflerbach (Eds.), *Authentic reading assessment: Practices and possibilities* (pp. 228–246). Newark, DE: International Reading Association.

Gardner, E. F. (1978). Bias. *Measurement in Education, 9,* 1–4.

Gardner, H. (1983). *Frames of mind.* New York, NY: Basic Books.

Garner, R. (1990). When children and adults do not use learning strategies: Toward a theory of settings. *Reviews of Educational Research, 60,* 517–529.

Gaskins, I. W., Ehri, L. C., Cress, C., O'Hara, C., & Donnelly, K. (1996/1997). Procedures for word learning: Making discoveries about words. *The Reading Teacher, 50,* 312–327.

Gaskins, R. W., Gaskins, J. C., & Gaskins, I. (1992). Using what you know to figure out what you don't know. *Reading & Writing Quarterly, 8,* 197–221.

Gathercole, S. E., Hitch, G. J., Service, E., & Martin, A. J. (1997). Short-term memory and new word learning in children. *Developmental Psychology, 33,* 966–979.

Gathercole, S. E., Willis, C. S., & Baddeley, A. D. (1992). Phonological memory and vocabulary development during the early school years: A longitudinal study. *Developmental Psychology, 28,* 887–898.

Gauvain, M. (2001). The social context of cognitive development. In C. B. Kopp and S. R. Asher, (Eds.), *The Guilford series on social and emotional development.* New York, NY: Guilford.

Gavelek, J. R., & Palincsar, A. S. (1988). Contextualism as an alternative worldview of learning disabilities: A response to Swanson's "Toward a metatheory of learning disabilities." *Journal of Learning Disabilities, 21,* 278–281.

Gavelek, J. R., Raphael, T. E., Biondo, S. M., & Wang, D. (2000). Integrated literacy instruction. In M. L. Kamil, P. B. Mosenthal, P. D. Pearson, & R. Barr (Eds.), *Handbook of reading research* (Vol. 3, pp. 587–608). Mahwah, NJ: Erlbaum.

Gee, J. P. (1989). Commonalities and differences in narrative construction. *Discourse Processes, 12,* 287–307.

Gee, J. P. (2001). A sociocultural perspective on early literacy development. In S. B. Neuman & D. K. Dickinson (Eds.), *Handbook of early literacy research* (pp. 30–42). New York, NY: Guilford Press.

Gee, J. P. (2003). *What video games have to teach us about learning and literacy.* New York, NY: Macmillan.

Geertz, C. (1983). Blurred genres: The refiguration of social thought. In C. Geertz (Ed.), *Local knowledge: Further essays in interpretive anthropology.* New York, NY: Basic Books.

Gelzheiser, L. M., Scanlon, D., & Hallgren-Flynn, L. (2010). Spotlight on RTI for adolescents: An example of intensive middle school intervention using the Interactive Strategies Approach-Extended. In M. Y. Lipson & K. K. Wixson (Eds.), *Successful approaches to RTI.* Newark, DE: International Reading Association.

Gelzheiser, L. M., Scanlon, D., Vellutino, F., Hallgren-Flynn, L., & Schatschneider, C. (in press). Effects of the Interactive Strategies Approach-Extended: A responsive and comprehensive intervention for intermediate grade struggling readers. *Elementary School Journal, 111*(4),

Genishi, C., & Dyson, A. H. (1984). *Language assessment in the early years.* Norwood, NJ: Ablex.

Gentry, J. R. (1981). Learning to spell developmentally. *The Reading Teacher, 34,* 378–381.

Gentry, J. R. (1982). An analysis of developmental spelling in GYNS AT WORK. *The Reading Teacher, 36,* 192–200.

Gentry, J. R. (2000). Retrospective on invented spelling and a look forward. *The Reading Teacher, 54,* 318–332.

Gernsbacher, M. A. (1997). Two decades of structure building. *Discourse Processes, 23,* 265–304.

Gersten, R., & Baker, S. (2001). Teaching expressive writing to students with learning disabilities: A meta-analysis. *Elementary School Journal, 101,* 251–272.

Gersten, R., Baker, S., & Edwards, L. (1999). *Teaching expressive writing to students with learning disabilities.* (ERIC/OSEP Digest E590).

Gersten, R., Baker, S. K., Shanahan, T., Linan-Thompson, S., Collins, P., & Scarcella, R. (2007). *Effective literacy and English language instruction for English learners in the elementary grades: A practice guide* (NCEE 2007-4011). Washington, DC: Institute of Education Sciences US. Department of Education.

Gersten, R., Fuchs, L. S., Williams, J. P., & Baker, S. (2001). Teaching reading comprehension strategies to students with learning disabilities: A review of research. *Review of Educational Research, 71,* 279–320.

Gersten, R., Schiller, E. P., & Vaughn, S. (Eds.). (2000). *Contemporary special education research: Syntheses of the knowledge base on critical instructional issues.* Mahwah, NJ: Erlbaum.

Gillam, R. B. (1998). Review of the clinical evaluation of language fundamentals (3rd ed.). In J. C. Impara & B. S. Plake (Eds.), *Thirteenth mental measurements yearbook.* Lincoln, NE: Buros Institute of Mental Measurements.

Gillam, R. B., & Pearson, N. A. (2004). *Test of narrative language.* Austin, TX: Pro-Ed.

Gillet, J., & Temple, C. (1982). *Understanding reading problems.* Boston, MA: Little, Brown.

Gillet, J., & Temple, C. (1990). *Understanding reading problems* (3rd ed.). Glenview, IL: Scott Foresman.

Gipe, J. (1978–1979). Investigating techniques for teaching word meanings. *Reading Research Quarterly, 14,* 624–644.

Glascoe, F. P. (1999). CIBS-R standardization and validation manual. North Billerica, MA: Curriculum Associates.

Glass, G. G., & Burton, E. H. (1973). How do they decode? Verbalizations and observed behaviors of successful decoders. *Education, 94*, 58–64.

Glasswell, K., Parr, J. M., & McNaughton, S. (2003). Four ways to work against yourself when conferencing with struggling writers. *Language Arts, 80*, 291–299.

Gleason, J. B. (1997). *The development of language* (4th ed.). Boston, MA: Allyn & Bacon.

Goatley, V. J., Brock, C. H., & Raphael, T. E. (1995). Diverse learners participating in regular education "Book Clubs." *Reading Research Quarterly, 30*, 352–380.

Goertz, M. E., Olah, L. N., & Riggan, M. (2009, December). *Can interim assessments be used for instructional change?* CPRE Policy Briefs (RB-51). Philadelphia: University of Pennsylvania.

Goetz, E., & Armbruster, B. (1980). Psychological correlates of text structure. In R. J. Spiro, B. C. Bruce, & W. F. Brewer (Eds.), *Theoretical issues in reading comprehension* (pp. 201–220). Hillsdale, NJ: Lawrence Erlbaum.

Goldberg, A., Russell, M., & Cook, A. (2003). The effect of computers on student writing: A meta-analysis of studies from 1992 to 2002. *Journal of Technology, Learning, and Assessment, 2*(1). Retrieved May 28, 2006, from http://www.jtla.org

Goldenberg, C. (1993). Instructional conversations: Promoting comprehension through discussion. *The Reading Teacher, 46*, 316–326.

Goldenberg, C. (1994). Promoting early literacy development among Spanish-speaking children: Lessons from two studies. In E. H. Hiebert & B. M. Taylor (Eds.), *Getting reading right from the start* (pp. 171–199). Boston, MA: Allyn & Bacon.

Goldenberg, C., & Gallimore, R. (1991). Changing teaching takes more than a one-shot workshop. *Educational Leadership, 49*, 69–72.

Goldenberg, C., & Patthey-Chavez, G. (1995). Discourse processes in instructional conversations: Interactions between teacher and transition readers. *Discourse Processes, 19*, 57–73.

Goldfield, B. A., & Snow, C. E. (2005). Individual differences. In J. B. Gleason (Ed.), *The development of language* (6th ed.) (pp. 292–323). Boston, MA: Pearson.

Goldman, S. R., & Rakestraw, J. A. (2000). Structural aspects of constructing meaning from text. In M. L. Kamil, P. B. Mosenthal, P. D. Pearson, & R. Barr (Eds.), *Handbook of reading research* (Vol. 3, pp. 311–336). Mahwah, NJ: -Erlbaum.

Goldman, S. R., & Wiley, J. (2004). Discourse analysis: Written text. In N. K. Duke, & M. Mallette (Eds.), *Literacy research methodologies.* New York, NY: Guilford Press.

Goldstein, B. S. (1986). Looking at cartoons and comics in a new way. *Journal of Reading, 29*, 657–661.

González-Edfelt, N. (1990). Oral interaction and collaboration at the computer. *Computers in the Schools, 7*, 53–90.

Good, R., Gruba, J., & Kaminski, R. A. (2002). Best practices in early literacy assessment. In A. Thomas & J. Grimes (Eds.), *Best practices in school psychology IV* (pp. 679–700). National Association of School Psychology.

Good, R. H., & Kaminski, R. A. (1996). Assessment for instructional decisions: Toward a proactive/prevention model of decision making for early literacy skills. *School Psychology Quarterly, 11*, 326–336.

Good, R. H., & Kaminski, R. A. (2002). *DIBELS oral reading fluency passages for first through third grades.* (Technical Rep. No. 10). Eugene, OR: University of Oregon.

Good, R. H., & Kaminski, R. A., (2003). *Dynamic indicators of basic early literacy (DIBELS).* Eugene, OR: University of Oregon.

Good, T. (1983). Research on classroom teaching. In L. S. Shulman & G. Sykes (Eds.), *Handbook of teaching and policy* (pp. 42–80). New York, NY: Longman.

Good, T. L., & Brophy, J. E. (2003). *Looking in classrooms* (9th ed.). Boston, MA: Pearson.

Good, T. L., & Marshall, S. (1984). Do students learn more in heterogeneous or homogeneous achievement groups? In P. Peterson, L. Cherry-Wilkinson, & M. Hallinan (Eds.), *The social context for instruction* (pp. 15–38). New York, NY: Academic Press.

Goodman, K. S. (1969). Analysis of oral reading miscues: Applied psycholinguistics. *Reading Research Quarterly, 5*, 9–30.

Goodman, K. S. (1973). Miscues: Windows on the reading process. In K. S. Goodman (Ed.), *Miscue analysis: Applications to reading instruction* (pp. 3–14). Urbana, IL: ERIC Clearinghouse on Reading and Communication Skills and the National Council of Teachers of English.

Goodman, K. S. (1989). Whole language is whole: A response to Heymsfeld. *Educational Leadership, 46*(6), 69–70.

Goodman, K. S. (with others) (2006). *The truth about DIBELS.* Portsmouth, NH: Heinemann.

Goodman, K. S., & Goodman, Y. M. (1977). Learning about psycholinguistic processes by analyzing oral reading. *Harvard Educational Review, 47*, 317–333.

Goodman, K. S., Shannon, P., Freeman, Y. S., & Murphy, S. (1988). *Report card on basal readers.* New York, NY: Richard C. Owen.

Goodman, Y. (1997). Reading diagnosis – Qualitative or quantitative? *The Reading Teacher, 50*, 534–538.

Goodman, Y., & Goodman, K. S. (1994). To err is human: Learning about language processes by analyzing miscues. In R. B. Ruddell, M. R. Ruddell, & H. Singer (Eds.), *Theoretical models and processes of reading* (pp. 104–123). Newark, DE: International Reading Association.

Goodman, Y., & Marek, A. (1996). *Retrospective miscue analysis: Revaluing readers and reading.* NY: Richard C. Owen.

Goodman, Y., Watson, D., & Burke, C. (2005). *Reading miscue inventory: From evaluation to instruction.* Katonah, NY: Richard C. Owen.

Goodman, Y. M., & Burke, C. L. (1972). *Reading miscue inventory.* New York, NY: Richard C. Owen.

Goodman, Y. M., Watson, D. J., & Burke, C. L. (1987). *Reading miscue inventory: Alternative procedures.* New York, NY: Richard C. Owen.

Goodwin, L. D., & Leech, N. (2003). The meaning of validity in the new Standards for Educational and Psychological Testing: Implications for measurement courses. *Measurement and Evaluation in Counseling and Development, 36*, 181–191.

Gopaul-McNicol, S., & Armour-Thomas, E. (2002). *Assessment and culture: Psychological tests with minority populations.* San Diego, CA: Academic Press.

Gordon, C., & Pearson, P. D. (1983). *The effects of instruction in meta-comprehension and inferencing on children's comprehension abilities* (Technical Report 269). Urbana: University of Illinois, Center for the Study of Reading.

Gort, M. (2006). Strategic codeswitching, interliteracy, and other phenomena of emergent bilingual writing: Lessons from first grade dual language classrooms. *Journal of Early Childhood Literacy, 6*, 323–354.

Goswami, U. (1986). Children's use of analogy in learning to read: A developmental study. *Journal of Experimental Child Psychology, 42*, 73–83.

Goswami, U. (2000). Phonological and lexical processes. In M. L. Kamil, P. B. Mosenthal, P. D. Pearson, & R. Barr (Eds.), *Handbook of reading research* (Vol. 3, pp. 251–268). Mahwah, NJ: Erlbaum.

Gottfried, A. E. (1990). Academic intrinsic motivation in young elementary school children. *Journal of Educational Psychology, 82,* 525–538.

Gough, P. B. (1972). One second of reading. In J. F. Kavanagh I. G. Mattingly (Eds.), *Language by ear and by eye* (pp. 331–358). Cambridge, MA: MIT Press.

Grabe, M., & Grabe, C. (1996). *Integrating technology for meaningful learning.* Boston, MA: Houghton Mifflin.

Graesser, A. C., Golding, J. M., & Long, D. L. (1991). Narrative representation and comprehension. In R. Barr, M. L. Kamil, P. Mosenthal, & P. D. Pearson (Eds.), *Handbook of reading research* (Vol. 2, pp. 171–205). New York, NY: Longman.

Graesser, A. C., Leon, J. A., & Otero, J. (2002). Introduction to the psychology of science text comprehension. In J. Otero, J. A. Leon, & A. C. Graesser (Eds.), *The psychology of science text comprehension.* Mahwah, NJ: Erlbaum.

Graesser, A. C., McNamara, D. S., & Kulikowich, J. M. (2011). Coh-Metrix: Providing multilevel analyses of text characteristics. *Educational Research, 40,* 223–234.

Graesser, A. C., McNamara, D. S., & Louwerse, M. M. (2003). What do readers need to learn in order to process coherence relations in narrative and expository text? In A. P. Sweet, & C. E. Snow (Eds.), *Rethinking reading comprehension* (pp. 82–98). New York, NY: Guilford Press.

Graesser, A. C., Olde, B., & Klettke, B. (2002). How does the mind construct and represent stories? In M. C. Green, J. J. Strange, & T. C. Brock (Eds.), *Narrative impact: Social and cognitive foundations.* Mahwah, NJ: Erlbaum.

Graesser, A. C., & Riha, J. R. (1984). An application of multiple regression techniques to sentence reading times. In D. Kieras & M. Just (Eds.), *New methods in comprehension research* (pp. 183–218). Hillsdale, NJ: Erlbaum.

Graham, S. (2006). Strategy instruction and the teaching of writing: A meta-analysis. In C. MacArthur, S. Graham, & J. Fitzgerald (Eds.), *Handbook of writing research* (pp. 187–207). New York, NY: Guilford Press.

Graham, S., & Harris, K. R. (1994). The role and development of self-regulation in the writing process. In D. H. Schunk & B. J. Zimmerman (Eds.), *Self-regulation of learning and performance* (pp. 203–228). Hillsdale, NJ: Erlbaum.

Graham, S., & Harris, K. R. (2005). *Writing better: Effective strategies for teaching students with learning difficulties.* Baltimore, MD: Paul H. Brookes.

Graham, S., Harris, K. R., & Larsen, L. (2001). Prevention and intervention of writing difficulties for students with learning disabilities. *Learning Disabilities Research and Practice, 16*(2), 74–84.

Graham, S., Harris, K. R., & Troia, G. A. (2000). Self-regulated strategy development revisited: Teaching writing strategies to struggling writers. *Topics in Language Disorders, 20*(4), 1–4.

Graham, S., & Perin, D. (2007). *Writing next.* NY: Carnegie Corporation.

Graves, D. H. (1983). *Writing: Teachers and children at work.* Portsmouth, NH: Heinemann.

Graves, D. H. (1994). *A fresh look at writing.* Portsmouth, NH: Heinemann.

Graves, D. H., & Hansen, J. (1983). The author's chair. *Language Arts, 60,* 176–183.

Graves, M., & Graves, B. (1994). *Scaffolding reading experiences.* Norwood, MA: Christopher Gordon.

Graves, M. F. (2006). *The vocabulary book: Learning and instruction.* New York, NY: Teachers College Press.

Graves, M. F., Cooke, C. L., & LaBerge, M. J. (1983). Effects of previewing short stores. *Reading Research Quarterly, 18,* 262–276.

Graves, M. F., & Fitzgerald, J. (2006). Effective vocabulary instruction for English-language learners. In C. C. Block & J. N. Mangieri (Eds.). *The vocabulary-enriched classroom* (pp. 118–137). New York, NY: Scholastic.

Gray, W. S. (1920). The value of informal tests of reading achievement. *Journal of Educational Research, 1,* 103–111.

Gray, W. S., & Leary, B. E. (1935). *What makes a book readable?* Chicago, IL: University of Chicago Press.

Greaney, V. (1980). Factors related to amount and type of leisure reading. *Reading Research Quarterly, 15,* 337–357.

Green, G. (1984). On the appropriateness of adaptations in primary-level basal readers. In R. C. Anderson, J. Osborn, & R. J. Tierney (Eds.), *Learning to read in American schools: Basal readers and content texts* (pp. 175–191). Hillsdale, NJ: Erlbaum.

Green, J., & Bloome, D. (1983). Ethnography and reading: Issues, approaches, criteria, and findings. In *Searches for meaning in reading/language processing and instruction* (32nd Year-book of The National Reading Conference, pp. 6–30). New York, NY: National Reading Conference.

Greenwood, C. R. (1991). Longitudinal analysis of time, engagement, and achievement in at-risk versus non-risk students. *Exceptional Children, 57,* 521–535.

Griffin, T. M., Hemphill, L., Camp, L., & Wolf, D. P. (2004). Oral discourse in the preschool years and later literacy skills. *First Language, 2471,* 123–147.

Groff, P. (1986). The maturing of phonics instruction. *The Reading Teacher, 39,* 919–923.

Gronlund, N. E. (1985). *Measurement and evaluation in teaching* (5th ed.). New York, NY: Macmillan.

Gros, G. (2003). The impact of digital games in education. *First Monday, 8*(7). Retrieved May 28, 2006, from http://firstmonday.org/issues/issue8_7/gros/index.html

Grossman, P., & Thompson, C. (2004). *Curriculum materials: Scaffolds for new teacher learning?* (Research Report R-04-1). Seattle: Center for the Study of Teaching and Policy, University of Washington.

Gunning, T. G. (2002). *Assessing and correcting reading and writing difficulties* (2nd ed.). Boston, MA: Allyn & Bacon.

Gupta, A., & Oboler, E. (2001, September). Changing roles of Title I reading teachers in light of new provisions and team teaching models. *The Reading Matrix, 1*(2), 1–6.

Gurung, R. A. R. (2005). How do students really study (and does it matter)? *Teaching of Psychology, 32,* 367–372.

Guthrie, J. T. (1980). Research reviews: Time in reading programs. *The Reading Teacher, 33,* 500–502.

Guthrie, J. T. (1997). Engagement in reading for young adolescents. *Journal of Adolescent and Adult Literacy, 40,* 438–446.

Guthrie, J. T. (2002) Preparing students for high-stakes test taking in reading. In A. E. Farstrup & S. J. Samuels (Eds.), *What research has to say about reading instruction* (pp. 370–391). Newark DE: International Reading Association.

Guthrie, J. T., & Cox, K. E. (2001). Classroom conditions for motivation and engagement in reading. *Educational Psychology Review, 13,* 283–302.

Guthrie, J. T., & McCann, A. D. (1997). Characteristics of classrooms that promote motivations and strategies for learning. In J. T. Guthrie & A. Wigfield (Eds.), *Reading engagement: Motivating readers through integrated instruction* (pp. 128–148). Newark, DE: International Reading Association.

Guthrie, J. T., Schafer, W. D., Vaon Secker, C., & Alban, T. (2000). Contributions of integrated reading instruction and text resources to achievement and engagement in statewide school improvement program. *Journal of Educational Research, 93*, 211–226.

Guthrie, J. T., & Wigfield, A. (2000). Engagement and motivation in reading. In M. L. Kamil, P. B. Mosenthal, P. D. Pearson, & R. Barr (Eds.), *Handbook of reading research* (Vol. 3, pp. 403–422). Mahwah, NJ: Erlbaum.

Guthrie, J. T., Wigfield, A., Metsala, J. L., & Cox, K. E. (1999). Motivational and cognitive predictors of text comprehension and reading amount. *Scientific Studies of Reading, 3*, 231–256.

Guthrie, J. T., Wigfield, A., & Perencevich, K. C. (Eds.). (2004). *Motivating reading comprehension: Concept-oriented reading instruction.* Mahwah, NJ: Erlbaum.

Gutiérrez-Clellen, V. F., Peña, E., & Quinn, R. (1995). Accommodating cultural differences in narrative style: A multicultural perspective. *Topics in Language Disorders, 15*, 54–67.

Guzniczak, L. (2004). *Analysis of reader stance and efferent focus in eleven studies.* Unpublished paper. Oakland University, Oakland, MI.

Guzzetti, B., & Hynd, C. (Eds.). (1998). *Perspectives on conceptual change: Multiple ways to understand knowing and learning in a complex world.* Hillsdale, NJ: Erlbaum.

Haager, D., & Klingner, J. K. (2005). *Differentiating instruction in inclusive classrooms.* Boston, MA: Allyn & Bacon.

Hadwin, A. F., & Winne, P. H. (1996). Study strategies have meager support. *Journal of Higher Education, 67*, 692–715.

Hall, T., & Mengel, M. (2002). Curriculum-based evaluations. Wakefield, MA: National Center on Accessing the General Curriculum. Retrieved May 16, 2006, from http://www.cast.org/publications/ncac/ncac_curriculumbe.html

Halliday, M. A. K. (1975). *Learning how to mean: Explorations in the development of language.* New York, NY: Elsevier North Holland.

Halliday, M. A. K. (1994). *An introduction to functional grammar* (2nd ed.). London: Edward Arnold.

Halliday, M. A. K., & Hasan, R. (1976). *Cohesion in English.* London, UK: Longman.

Hammer, C. S., Scarpino, S., & Davison, M. D. (2011). Beginning with language: Spanish-English bilingual preschoolers' early literacy development. In S. B. Nueman & D. K. Dickinson (Eds.), *Handbook of early literacy research* (3rd ed.) (pp. 118–135). New York, NY: Guilford.

Hammill, D. D., & Hresko, W. P. (1994). *Comprehensive scales of student abilities.* Austin, TX: Pro-Ed.

Hammill, D. D., & Larsen, S. C. (1988). *Test of Written -Language–2.* Austin, TX: Pro-Ed. Hammill, D. D., & Larsen, S. C. (1996). *Test of Written Language–3.* Austin, TX: Pro-Ed.

Hannon, P. (1998). How can we foster children's literacy development through parent involvement? In *Children achieving: Best practices in early literacy.* Newark, DE: International Reading Association.

Hansen, J. (1981). The effects of inference training and practice on young children's reading comprehension. *Reading Research Quarterly, 16*, 391–417.

Hare, V. C. (1984). What's in a word? A review of young children's difficulties with the construct of "word." *The Reading Teacher, 37*, 360–364.

Hare, V. C., & Borchardt, K. (1984). Direct instruction of summarization skills. *Reading Research Quarterly, 20*, 62–78.

Hare, V. C., Rabinowitz, M., & Schieble, K. M. (1989). Text effects on main idea comprehension. *Reading Research Quarterly, 24*, 72–88.

Harman, P., Egelson, P., Hood, A., & O'Connell, D. (2002, April). *Observing life in small class-size classrooms.* Paper presented at the annual meeting of the American Educational Research Association. New Orleans, LA (April 3).

Harris, A. J. (1977). Ten years of progress in remedial reading. *The Reading Teacher, 31*, 29–35.

Harris, A. J., & Jacobson, M. D. (1972). *Basic elementary reading vocabularies: The first R series.* New York, NY: MacMillan.

Harris, A. J., & Sipay, E. R. (1990). *How to increase reading ability* (9th ed.). New York, NY: Longman.

Harris, K. R., Graham, S., Mason, L., & Saddler, B. (2002). Developing self-regulated writers. *Theory Into Practice, 41*, 110–115.

Harris, K. R., & Pressley, M. (1991). The nature of cognitive strategy instruction: Interactive strategy construction. *Exceptional Children, 57*, 392–404.

Harry, B., & Klingner, J. (2006). *Why are so many minority students in special education.* New York, NY: Teachers College Press.

Harste, J., Woodward, V. A., & Burke, C. (1984). *Language stories and literacy lessons.* Portsmouth, NH: Heinemann.

Hart, B., & Risley, T. R. (1995). *Meaningful differences in the everyday experience of young American children.* Baltimore, MD: Brookes.

Hart, B., & Risley, T. R. (2003). *The 30 million word disaster.* Washington, DC: American Federation of Teachers.

Hartley, J. (2004). Designing instructional and informational text. In D. H. Jonassen (Ed.), *Handbook of research in educational communications and technology* (2nd edition). Mahwah, NJ: Erlbaum.

Harvey, S. (1998). *Nonfiction matters: Reading, writing, and research in grades 3–8.* York, ME: Stenhouse.

Harvey, S., & Goudvis, A. (2007). *Strategies that work* (2nd ed.). York, ME: Stenhouse.

Harwayne, S., & Calkins, L. (1987). *The writing workshop: A world of difference.* Portsmouth, NH: Heinemann.

Hasbrouck, J., & Tindal, G. A. (2006). Oral reading fluency norms: A valuable assessment tool for reading teachers. *The Reading Teacher, 59*, 636–644.

Haskins, R., Walden, T., & Ramey, C. (1983). Teacher and student behavior in high- and low-ability groups. *Journal of Educational Psychology, 75*, 865–876.

Hasselbring, T. S., & Goin, L. I. (2004). Literacy instruction for older struggling readers: What is the role of technology? *Reading & Writing Quarterly, 20*, 123–144.

Hay, D. B. (2007). Using concept mapping to measure deep, surface, and non-learning outcomes. *Studies in Higher Education, 32*, 39–57.

Hayes, B., & Peters, C. W. (1989). The role of reading instruction in the social studies. In D. Lapp & J. Flood (Eds.), *Handbook of instructional theory and practice* (pp. 152–178). Englewood Cliffs, NJ: Prentice Hall.

Hayes, J. R., & Flower, L. S. (1980). Identifying the organization of writing processes. In L. W. Gregg & E. R. Steinberg (Eds.), *Cognitive processes in writing* (pp. 3–30). Hillsdale, NJ: Erlbaum.

Haywood, H. C., & Lidz, C. S. (2006). *Dynamic assessment in practice: Clinical and educational applications.* Cambridge: Cambridge University Press.

Heath, S. B. (1981). Questioning at home and at school: A comparative study. In G. Spindler (Ed.). *Doing ethnography: Educational anthropology in action* (pp. 102–131). New York, NY: Holt, Rinehart & Winston.

Heath, S. B. (1983). *Ways with words: Language, life, and work in communities and classrooms.* Cambridge, UK: Cambridge University Press.

Heath, S. B. (1991). The sense of being literate. In R. Barr, M. Kamil, P. Mosenthal, & P. D. Pearson (Eds.), *Handbook of reading research* (Vol. 2). White Plains, NY: Longman.

Heckleman, R. G. (1969). Neurological impress method of remedial reading instruction. *Academic Therapy Quarterly, 4,* 277–282.

Hegarty, M., Carpenter, P. A., & Just, A. (1991). Diagrams in the comprehension of scientific texts. In R. Barr, M. L. Kamil, P. B. Mosenthal, & P. D. Pearson, (Eds.) *Handbook of reading research* (Vol. 2). Mahwah, NJ: L. Erlbaum Associates.

Heinemann Publishers. (n.d.). *Field study of reliability and validity of the Fountas & Pinnell Benchmark Assessment Systems 1 and 2.* Retrieved from http://www.heinemann.com/fountasandpinnell/research/BASFieldStudyFullReport.pdf

Helfeldt, J. P., Henk, W. A. (1990). Reciprocal questioning: Answer relationship—An instructional technique for at-risk readers. *Journal of Reading, 33,* 509–514.

Helsel, L., & Greenberg, D. (2007). Helping struggling writers succeed: A self-regulated strategy instruction program. *The Reading Teacher, 60,* 752–760.

Henderson, E. H. (1980). Developmental concepts of word. In E. H. -Henderson & J. W. Beers (Eds.), *Developmental and cognitive aspects of learning to spell: A reflection of word knowledge* (pp. 1–14). Newark, DE: International Reading Association.

Henderson, E. H. (1990). *Teaching spelling* (2nd ed.). Boston, MA: Houghton Mifflin.

Henderson, E. H. (1992). *Teaching spelling* (2nd ed.). Boston, MA: Houghton Mifflin.

Hendley, B. (1986). *Dewey, Russell, Whitehead: Philosophers as educators.* Carbondale: Southern Illinois University Press.

Henkin, R. (1995). Insiders and outsiders in first-grade writing workshops: Gender and equity issues. *Language Arts, 72,* 429–434.

Henry, L. A. (2006). SEARCHing for an answer: The critical role of new literacies while reading on the Internet. *The Reading Teacher, 59,* 614–627.

Herber, H. L. (1970). *Teaching reading in the content areas.* Englewood Cliffs, NJ: Prentice Hall.

Herber, H. L. (1978). *Teaching reading in the content areas* (2nd ed.). Englewood Cliffs, NJ: Prentice Hall.

Herman, P. A., Anderson, R. C., Pearson, P. D., & Nagy, W. E. (1987). Incidental acquisition of word meaning from expositions with varied text features. *Reading Research Quarterly, 22,* 263–284.

Hiebert, E. H. (1981). Developmental patterns and interrelationships of preschool children's print awareness. *Reading Research Quarterly, 16,* 236–260.

Hiebert, E. H. (1983). An examination of ability grouping for reading instruction. *Reading Research Quarterly, 18,* 231–255.

Hiebert, E. H. (1994a). Becoming literate through authentic tasks: Evidence and adaptations. In R. R. Ruddell, M. R. Ruddell, & H. Singer (Eds.), *Theoretical models and processes of reading* (4th ed., pp. 391–413). Newark, DE: International Reading Association.

Hiebert, E. H. (1994b). Reading Recovery in the United States: What difference does it make to an age cohort? *Educational Researcher, 23,* 15–25.

Hiebert, E. H. (1999). Text matters in learning to read. *The Reading Teacher, 52*(6), 552–566.

Hiebert, E. H. (2002). Standards, assessment, and text difficulty. In A. E. Farstrup & S. J. Samuels (Eds.), *What research has to say about reading instruction* (3rd ed., pp. 337–369). Newark, DE: International Reading Association.

Hiebert, E. H. (2005). In pursuit of an effective, efficient vocabulary curriculum for elementary students. In E. H., Hiebert, & M. L. Kamil, (Eds.), *Teaching and learning vocabulary: Bringing research to practice* (pp. 243–263). Mahwah, NJ: Erlbaum.

Hiebert, E. H. (2006). Perspectives on the difficulty of beginning reading texts. In D. K. Dickinson & S. B. Neuman (Eds.), *Handbook of early literacy research* (Vol. 2, pp. 395–409). New York, NY: Guilford Press.

Hiebert, E. H., & Cervetti, G. N. (2011). *What differences in narrative and informational texts mean for the learning and instruction of vocabulary* (Reading Research Report No. 11.01). San Francisco, CA: TextProject, Inc.

Hiebert, E. H., Colt, J. M., Catto, S. L., & Gury, E. M. (1992). Reading and writing of grade 1 students in a restructured Chapter 1 program. *American Educational Research Journals, 29,* 545–572.

Hiebert, E. H. & Fisher, C. W. (April, 2002). *Text matters in developing fluent reading.* Paper presented at the Preconvention Institute, Tools for Global Understanding: Fluency, Comprehension, and Content Knowledge, at the annual meeting of the International Reading Association. San Francisco, CA.

Hiebert, E. H., & Kamil, M. L. (2005). *Teaching and learning vocabulary: Bringing research to practice.* Mahwah, NJ: Erlbaum.

Hiebert, E. H., & Martin, L. A. (2000). The texts of beginning reading instruction. In S. B. Neuman & D. K. Dickinson (Eds.), *Handbook of early literacy research* (pp. 361–376). New York, NY: Guilford Press.

Hiebert, E. H., & Martin, L. A. (2002). TExT (Text Elements by Task) software (3rd ed.). Santa Cruz, CA: TextProject.

Hiebert, E. H., & Mesmer, H. A. E. (2006). Perspectives on the difficulty of beginning texts. In S. B. Neuman & D. K. Dickinson (Eds.), *Handbook or early literacy research* (2nd ed., pp. 395–409). New York, NY: Guilford.

Hiebert, E. H., Pearson, P. D., Taylor, B. M., Richardson, V., & Paris, S. G. (Eds.). (1998). *Every child a reader: Applying reading research in the classroom.* Ann Arbor, MI: Center for the Improvement of Early Reading Achievement.

Hiebert, E. H., & Raphael, T. E. (1996). Psychological perspectives on literacy and extensions to educational practice. In D. C. Berliner & R. C. Calfee (Eds.), *Handbook of educational psychology* (pp. 550–602). New York, NY: Macmillan.

Hiebert, E. H., & Raphael, T. E. (1998). *Early literacy instruction.* Ft. Worth, TX: Harcourt Brace.

Hiebert, E. H., & Taylor, B. M. (2000). Beginning reading instruction: Research on early interventions. In R. Barr, M. L. Kamil, P. B. Mosenthal, & P. D. Pearson (Eds.), *Handbook of reading research* (Vol. 3, pp. 455–482). Mahwah, NJ: Erlbaum.

Hiebert, E. H., Winograd, P. N., & Danner, F. W. (1984). Children's attributions for failure and success in different aspects of reading. *Journal of Educational Psychology, 76,* 1139–1148.

Higgins, K. M., Harris, N. A., & Kuehn, L. L. (1994). Placing assessment into the hands of young children: A study of -student-generated criteria and self-assessment. *Educational Assessment, 2,* 309–324.

Hillocks, G. (1986). *Research on written composition: New directions for teaching.* Urbana, IL: National Conference on Research in English.

Hillocks, G., Jr. (2002). *The testing trap: How state writing assessments control learning.* New York, NY: Teachers College Press.

Hillocks, G. (2003). Reconceptualizing writing curricula: What we know and can use. http://www.ioe.ac.uk/schools/ecpe/ReconceptualisingWriting5-16/docs/hillocks.pdf

Hillocks, G., & Smith, M. W. (1991). In J. Flood, D. Lapp, & J. Squire (Eds.), *Handbook of research on teaching the English language arts* (pp. 591–603). New York, NY: Macmillan.

Hillocks, G., Jr., & Smith, M. W. (2003). Grammars and literacy learning. In J. Flood, D. Lapp, J. R. Squire, & J. M. Jensen (Eds.), *Handbook of research on teaching the English language arts* (2nd ed., pp. 721–737). Mahwah, NJ: Erlbaum.

Hine, M., Goldman, S. R., & Cosden, M. A. (1990). Error monitoring by learning handicapped students engaged in collaborative microcomputer-based writing. *Journal of Special Education, 23,* 407–422.

Hintze, J. M., Ryan, A. L., & Stoner, G. (2003). Concurrent validity and diagnostic accuracy of the dynamic indicators of basic early literacy skills and the comprehensive test of phonological processing. *School Psychology Review, 32,* 541–556.

Hoff, E. (2004). Poverty effects. In R. D. Kent (Ed.), *MIT encyclopedia of communication disorders* (pp. 369–371). Cambridge, MA: MIT Press.

Hoff, E. (2006). Environmental supports for language acquisition. In D. K. Dickinson & S. B. Neuman (Eds.), *Handbook of early literacy research* (Vol. 2, pp.163–172) New York, NY: Guilford Press.

Hoff, E. (2009). *Language development* (4th ed.). Belmont, CA: Wadsworth Cengage Learning.

Hoff, E., & Naigles, L. (2002). How children use input in acquiring a lexicon. *Child Development, 73,* 418–433.

Hoffman, J. (2001, December). *Words.* Review of research at the annual meeting of the National Reading Conference, Austin, TX.

Hoffman, J., Roser, N., Salas, R., Patterson, E., & Pennington, J. (2000). *Text leveling and little books in first grade reading* (No. CIERA-R-1-010). Ann Arbor, MI: CIERA.

Hoffman, J. V. (1987). Rethinking the role of oral reading. *Elementary School Journal, 87,* 367–373.

Hoffman, J. V., McCarthey, S. J., Abbott, J., Christian, C., Corman, L., Curry, C., . . . Stahle, D. (1994). So what's new in the new basals? A focus on first grade. *Journal of Reading Behavior, 26,* 47–73.

Hoffman, J. V., McCarthey, S. J., Elliott, B., Bayles, D. L., Price, D. P., Ferree, A., & Abbott, J. A. (1998). The literature-based basal in first grade classrooms: Savior, Satan, or same-old, same-old? *Reading Research Quarterly, 33,* 168–197.

Hoffman, J. V, Roser, N., & Sailors, M. (2004). Leveled texts for beginning readers: A primer, a test, and a quest. In J. V. Hoffman & D. L. Schallert (Eds.), *The texts in elementary classrooms* (pp. 113–124). Mahwah, NJ: Erlbaum.

Hoffman, J. V, Roser, N., Salas, R., Patterson, E. U., & Penington, J. (2001). Text leveling and little books in first grade. *Journal of Literacy Research, 33,* 507–528.

Hoffman, J. V, Sailors, M., & Patterson, E. U. (2002). Decodable texts for beginning reading instruction: The year 2000 basals. *Journal of Literacy Research, 34,* 269–298.

Hoge, R. D. (1999). *Assessing adolescents in educational, counseling, and other settings.* Mahwah, NJ: Erlbaum.

Holdaway, D. (1979). *Foundations of literacy.* Sydney, AU: Ashton Scholastic.

Holliday, W. G., Yore, L. D., & Alvermann, D. E. (1994). The reading-science-learning-writing connection: Breakthroughs, barriers, promises. *Journal of Research in Science Teaching, 31,* 877–894.

Holmes, B. C., & Roser, N. L. (1987). Five ways to assess readers' prior knowledge. *The Reading Teacher, 40,* 646–649.

Homer, B., & Olson, D. (1999). Literacy and children's conception of words. *Written Language and Literacy, 2,* 113–137.

Hong, L. K. (1981). Modifying SSR for beginning readers. *The Reading Teacher, 34,* 888–891.

Honig, B., Diamond, L., & Gutlohn, L. (2000). *Teaching reading sourcebook.* Novato, CA: Arena Press.

Hood, J. (1978). Is miscue analysis practical for teachers? *The Reading Teacher, 32,* 260–266.

Horowitz, R. (1995). A 75-year legacy on assessment: Reflections from an interview with Ralph W. Tyler. *Journal of Educational Research, 89*(2), 68–75.

Howell, K. W., & Nolet, V. (1999). *Curriculum-based education: Teaching and decision making.* Belmont, CA: Brooks/Cole Wadsworth.

Howell, K. W., & Nolet, V. (2000). *Curriculum-based evaluation: Teaching and decisions making* (3rd ed.). New York, NY: Wadsworth Publishing.

Hresko, W. P., Herron, S. R., & Peak, P. K. (1996). *Test of early written language* (2nd ed.). Austin, TX: Pro-Ed.

Hudelson, S. (1986). ESL children's writing: What we've learned, what we're learning. In P. Rigg & D. S. Enright (Eds.), *Children and ESL: Integrating perspectives* (pp. 23–54). Washington, DC: Teachers of English to Speakers of Other Languages.

Hudelson, S. (1987). The role of native language literacy in the education of language minority children. *Language Arts, 64,* 827–834.

Hudson, R. F., Lane, H. B., & Pullen, P. C. (2005). Reading fluency assessment and instruction: What, why, and how? *The Reading Teacher, 58,* 702–714.

Huey, E. B. (1908/1968). *The psychology and pedagogy of reading.* Cambridge, MA: MIT Press. (Republished: Cambridge, MA: MIT Press, 1968).

Hughes, S. (1989). *Dogger.* Boston, MA: Houghton Mifflin.

Huitt, W. (2004). Bloom et al.'s taxonomy of the cognitive domain. *Educational Psychology Interactive.* Valdosta, GA: Valdosta State University. Retrieved June 5, 2005, from http://chiron.valdosta.edu/whuitt/col/cogsys/bloom.html

Hunt, J. M. (1961). *Intelligence and experience.* New York, NY: Ronald.

Hunt, L. C. (n.d.). *Vocabulary development is a simple dumbbell operation.* Burlington: University of Vermont.

Hunt, L. C. (1970). Effect of self-selection, interest, and motivation upon independent, instructional, and frustrational levels. *The Reading Teacher, 24*(2), 146–151.

Hynd, C. R., & Alvermann, D. E. (1986). Prior knowledge activation in refutation and non-refutation text. In J. A. Niles & R. Lalik (Eds.), *Solving problems in literacy: Learners, teachers, and researchers* (35th Yearbook of The National Reading Conference, pp. 55–60). Rochester, NY: National Reading Conference.

International Reading Association (IRA). (1981, April). Misuse of grade equivalents. Resolution passed by the Delegates Assembly of the International Reading Association, April 1981. Published in *The Reading Teacher, 35,* 464.

International Reading Association (IRA). (1998). *Standards for reading professionals.* Newark, DE: Author.

International Reading Association (IRA). (1999, May). High stakes assessments in reading: A position statement of the International Reading Association. Adopted by the Board of Directors of the International Reading Association, May 1999. Newark, DE: International Reading Association.

International Reading Association (IRA). (2000). Teaching all children to read: The roles of specialists. *Journal of Adolescent and Adult Literacy, 44*(1), 99–104.

International Reading Association. (2002). Integrating literacy and technology in the curriculum (Position statement). Adopted by the

Board of Directors of the International Reading Association, September 2001. Newark, DE: Author.

International Reading Association. (2004). *The role and qualifications of the reading coach in the United States.* Newark, DE: Author.

International Reading Association. (2006). *Standards for middle and high school literacy coaches.* Newark, DE: Author.

International Reading Association Ad Hoc Committee on Response to Intervention (RTI). (2006). *New roles in response to intervention: Creating success for schools and children.* Washington, DC: Author.

International Reading Association & National Council of Teachers of English. (2010). *Standards for the assessment of reading and writing* Rev. ed.). Newark, DE: International Reading Association. Copublished with the National Council of Teachers of English.

Invernizzi, M., Abouzeid, M., & Gill, T. (1994). Using students' invented spelling as a guide for spelling instruction that emphasizes word study. *Elementary School Journal, 95* (2), 1655–1657.

Invernizzi, M., Juel, C., Swank, L., & Meier, J. (2004). *PALS-K: Phonological Awareness and Literacy Screening.* Charlottesville, VA: University Printing Services.

Invernizzi, M., Meier, J., & Juel, C. (2005). Phonological awareness literacy screening (PALS-1-3). Charlottesville, VA: University Printing Services.

Irvin, J. L. (1990). *Reading and the middle school student.* Boston, MA: Allyn & Bacon.

Irwin, J. W., & Davis, C. (1980). Assessing readability: The checklist approach. *Journal of Reading, 24,* 124–130.

Irwin, M., & Lipson, M. Y. (1985). Guidelines for evaluating reading. *Michigan Reading Journal, 18*(4), 23–26.

Irwin, P. A., & Mitchell, J. N. (1983). A procedure for assessing the richness of retellings. *Journal of Reading, 26,* 391–396.

Iverson, S., & Tunmer, W. (1993). Phonological processing skills and the Reading Recovery Program. *Journal of Educational Psychology, 85,* 112–126.

Ivey, G., & Fisher, D. (2006). *Creating literacy-rich schools for adolescents.* Alexandria, VA: ASCD.

Jacobs, J. S. & Tunnell, M. O. (2004) *Children's literature, briefly.* Upper Saddle River, NJ: Pearson.

Jaggar, A. (1985). On observing the language learner: Introduction and overview. In A. Jaggar & M. T. Smith-Burke (Eds.), *Observing the language learner* (pp. 1–7). Newark, DE: International Reading Association.

Jenkins, C. B. (1996). *Inside the writing portfolio: What we need to know to assess children's writing.* Portsmouth, NH: Heinemann.

Jenkins, J. R., Fuchs, L. S., VanDenBroek, P., Espin, C., & Deno, S. L. (2003). Sources of individual differences in reading comprehension and reading fluency. *Journal of Educational Psychology, 95,* 719–729.

Jewell, J., & Malecki, C. K. (2005). The utility of CBM written language indices: An investigation of production-dependent, production-independent, and accurate-production scores. *School Psychology Review, 34*(1), 27–44.

Jewell, M. C., & Zintz, M. V. (1990). *Learning to read and write naturally* (2nd ed.). Dubuque, IA: Kendall/Hunt.

Jiang, X., & Grabe, W. (2007). Graphic organizers in reading instruction: Research findings and issues. *Reading in a Foreign Language, 19,* 35–54.

Johns, J. J. (1988). *Basic reading inventory* (4th ed.). Dubuque, IA: Kendall/Hunt.

Johns, J. J. (2005). *Basic reading inventory* (9th ed.). Dubuque, IA: Kendall/Hunt.

Johns, J. L., & Berglund, R. L. (2002). *Fluency: Questions, answers, evidence-based strategies.* Dubuque, IA: Kendall/Hunt Publishing.

Johnson, D. D. (1971). A basic vocabulary for beginning reading. *Elementary School Journal, 72,* 29–34.

Johnson, D. D. (2001). *Vocabulary in the elementary and middle school.* Needham Heights, MA: Allyn & Bacon.

Johnson, D. D., & Baumann, J. F. (1984). Word identification. In P. D. Pearson, R. Barr, M. Kamil, & P. Mosenthal (Eds.), *Handbook of reading research* (Vol. 1, pp. 583–608). Mahwah, NJ: Erlbaum.

Johnson, D. D., & Pearson, P. D. (1984). *Teaching reading vocabulary* (2nd ed.). New York, NY: Holt, Rinehart & Winston.

Johnson, M. S., Kress, R. A., & Pikulski, J. J. (1987). *Informal reading inventories* (2nd ed.). Newark, DE: International Reading Association.

Johnston, P. H. (1985). Teaching students to apply strategies that improve reading comprehension. *Elementary School Journal, 85,* 635–645.

Johnston, P. H. (1987). Teachers as evaluation experts. *The Reading Teacher, 40,* 744–748.

Johnston, P. H. (1992). *Constructive evaluation of literate activity.* New York, NY: Longman.

Johnston, P. H. (1997). *Knowing literacy: Constructive literacy assessment.* York, ME: Stenhouse.

Johnston, P. H., Allington, R. L., & Afflerbach, P. (1985). The congruence of classroom and remedial reading instruction. *Elementary School Journal, 85,* 465–477.

Johnston, P. H., & Rogers, R. (2001). *Assessment of literacy development in early childhood: Handbook for early childhood practices.* New York, NY: Guilford Press.

Johnston, P. H., & Winograd, P. N. (1985). Passive failure in reading. *Journal of Reading, 17,* 279–301.

Joint Committee on Testing Practices. (2004). *Code of fair testing practices in education.* Washington, DC: Author.

Jones, B. F. (1983, April). *Integrating learning strategies and text research to teach higher order thinking skills in schools.* Paper presented at the Annual Meeting of the American Educational Research Association, Montreal, Canada.

Jones, J. (2003). *Early literacy assessment systems: Essential elements.* Princeton, NJ: ETS.

Jongsma, E. A. (1982). Test review: Peabody Picture Vocabulary Test—Revised (PPVT-R). *Journal of Reading, 20,* 360–364.

Jongsma, K. S., & Jongsma, E. A. (1981). Test review: Commercial informal reading inventories. *The Reading Teacher, 34,* 697–705.

Jordan, C. (1985). Translating culture: From ethnographic information to educational program. *Anthropology and Education Quarterly, 16,* 105–123.

Joseph, N. L. (2003, Winter). Metacognitive awareness: investigating theory and practice. *Academic Exchange Quarterly.* Retrieved from Find Articles.com, November 6, 2011. http://findarticles.com/p/articles/mi_hb3325/is_4_7/ai_n29059143/pg_5/

Juel, C. (1988). Learning to read and write: A longitudinal study of fifty-four children from first through fourth grade. *Journal of Educational Psychology, 80,* 437–447.

Juel, C. (1996). What makes literacy tutoring effective? *Reading Research Quarterly, 31,* 268–289.

Juel, C., Griffith, P. L., & Gough, P. B. (1986). Acquisition of literacy: A longitudinal study of children in first and second grade. *Journal of Educational Psychology, 78,* 243–255.

Juel, C., & Minden-Cupp, C. (1998). *Learning to read words: Linguistic units and strategies* (CIERA Report No. 1-008). Ann Arbor, MI: Center for the Improvement of Early Reading Achievement.

Juel, C., & Minden-Cupp, C. (2000). Learning to read words: Linguistic units and instructional strategies. *Reading Research Quarterly, 35*(4), 458–492.

Justice, L. M., & Piasta, S. (2011). Developing children's print knowledge through adult-child storybook reading interactions: Print referencing. In S. B. Nueman & D. K. Dickinson (Eds.), *Handbook of early literacy research* (3rd ed., pp. 200–213). New York, NY: Guilford.

Kaderavek, J. N., & Sulzby, E. (1998). Parent-child joint book reading: An observational protocol for young children. *American Journal of Speech-Language Pathology, 7*(1), 33–47.

Kame'enui, E. J., Fuchs, L., Francis, D. J., Good, R., O'Connor, R. E., Simmons, D. C., Tindal, G., & Torgesen, J. K. (2006). The adequacy of tools for assessing reading competence: A framework and review. *Educational Researcher, 35*(4), 3–11.

Kame'enui, E. J., Simmons, D. C., Good, R. H., & Harn, B. A. (2001). The use of fluency-based measures in early identification and evaluation of intervention efficacy in schools. In M. Wolf (Ed.), *Dyslexia, fluency and the brain* (pp. 307–331). MD: York Press.

Kamil, M. L., & Intrator, S. (2000). Technology and literacy. In M. L. Kamil, P. B. Mosenthal, P. D. Pearson, & R. Barr (Eds.), *Handbook of reading research* (Vol. 2, pp. 771–788). Mahwah, NJ: Erlbaum.

Kamil, M. L., Kim, H. S., & Lane, D. (2004). Electronic texts in the classroom. In J. V. Hoffman & D. L. Schallert (Eds.), *The texts in elementary classrooms* (pp. 157–176). Mahwah, NJ: Erlbaum.

Kamil, M. L., Mosenthal, P. H., Pearson, P. D., & Barr, R. (2000). *Handbook of reading research* (Vol. 3), Mahwah, NJ: Erlbaum.

Kamphaus, R. W. (2001). Review of the Metropolitan Readiness Tests, 6th ed. In B. S. Blake & J. C. Impara (Eds.), *Fourteenth mental measurements yearbook*. Lincoln, NE: Buros Institute of Mental Measurements.

Kane, C. (1994). *Prisoners of time research: What we know and what we need to know*. Washington, DC: National Education Commission on Time and Learning.

Kane, S. (2008). *Integrating literature in the content areas: Enhancing adolescent learning and literacy*. Scottsdale, AZ: Holcomb-Hathaway.

Kane, S. (2011). *Literacy learning in the content areas*. Scottsdale, AZ: Holcomb-Hathaway.

Karlsen, B., & Gardner, E. (1995). *Stanford Diagnostic Reading Test* (4th ed.). San Antonio, TX: Harcourt Brace.

Karweit, N., & Wasik, B. A. (1996). The effects of story reading programs on literacy and language development of disadvantaged preschoolers. *Journal of Education for Students Placed at Risk, 4*, 319–348.

Kassow, D. Z. (2006). Environmental print awareness in young children. *Talaris Research Institute, 1*(3). Retrieved January 18, 2007, from http://www.google.com/search?q=cache: AKEkrCNrOBcJ: www.talaris.org/pdf/research/EnviroPrintAwareness.pdf+%22environmental+print%22+%2B+research&hl=en&gl=us&ct=clnk&cd=4

Katims, D. S., & Harris, S. (1997). Improving the reading comprehension of middle school students in inclusive classrooms. *Journal of Adolescent and Adult Literacy, 41*, 116–123.

Katz, M. (1987). Reconstructing American education. Cambridge, MA: Harvard University Press.

Kauffman, D. (2002). *A search for support: Beginning elementary teachers' use of mathematics curriculum materials*. Unpublished Special Qualifying Paper, Graduate School of Education, Harvard University, Cambridge, MA.

Kauffman, D. (May, 2005). *Curriculum support and curriculum neglect: Second-year teachers' experiences*. NGT Working Paper. Cambridge,

MA: Project on the Next Generation of Teachers. Retrieved May 25, 2006, from http://www.gse.harvard.edu/ngt

Kearns, G., & Biemiller, A. (2010/2011). Two-question vocabulary assessment: Developing a new method for group testing in kindergarten through second grade. *Journal of Education, 190*(1/2), 31–41.

Keene, E., & Zimmerman, L. (1997). *Mosaic of thought*. Portsmouth, NH: Heinemann.

Kelley, M., & Clausen-Grace, N. (2006). R5: The sustained silent reading makeover that transformed readers. *The Reading Teacher, 60*, 148–156.

Kemp, M. (1987). *Watching children read and write*. Portsmouth, NH: Heinemann.

Kendall, J., & Mason, J. (1980). *Comprehension of polysemous words*. Paper presented at the Annual Meeting of the American Educational Research Association, Boston, MA.

Kenney, L. (1998). *Using data for school improvement: Report on the second practitioners' conference for Annenberg challenge sites*. Providence, RI: Annenberg Institute for School Reform at Brown University.

Kerbow, D., Gwynne, J., & Jacob, B. (1999). *Implementation of a balanced literacy framework and student learning: Implication for program development*. Paper presented at the American Education . . .

Kibby, M. W. (1979). Passage readability affects the oral reading strategies of disabled readers. *The Reading Teacher, 32*, 390–396.

Kieffer, B. Z. (2010). *Charlotte Huck's children's literature* (10th ed.). Boston, MA: McGraw-Hill.

Kilgallon, P. A. (1942). *The study of relationships among certain pupil adjustments in reading situations* (Unpublished doctoral dissertation). Pennsylvania State University, State College, PA.

Kim, S. A. (1995). Types and sources of problems in L2 reading: A qualitative analysis of the recall protocols of Korean high school EFL students. *Foreign Language Annuals, 28*(1), 49–70.

Kindler, A. L. (2002). *Survey of the states' limited English proficient students and available educational programs and services. 2000–2001 summary report*. Washington, DC: National Clearinghouse for English Acquisition.

King, A. (1991). Enhancing peer interaction and learning in the classroom through reciprocal questioning. *American Educational Research Journal, 27*, 664–687.

King, A. (2002). Structuring peer interaction to promote high-level cognitive processing. *Theory into Practice, 41*(1), 33–46.

Kintsch, W., & van Dijk, T. (1978). Toward a model of text comprehension and production. *Psychological Review, 85*, 363–394.

Klare, G. (1984). Readability. In P. D. Pearson (Ed.), *Handbook of reading research* (pp. 681–744). New York, NY: Longman.

Klare, G. (1988). The formative years. In B. L. Zakaluk & S. J. Samuels (Eds.), *Readability: Its past, present, and future* (pp. 14–34). Newark, DE: International Reading Association.

Klenk, L., & Kibby, M. W. (2000). Re-mediating reading difficulties: Appraising the past, reconciling the present, constructing the future. In M. L. Kamil, P. B. Mosenthal, P. D. Pearson, & R. Barr (Eds.), *Handbook of reading research* (Vol. 3, pp. 667–690). Mahwah, NJ: Erlbaum.

Kliewer, C. (1998). Citizenship in the literate community: An ethnography of children with Down syndrome and the written word. *Exceptional Children, 64*, 167–180.

Klingner, J., Vaughn, S., & Boardman, M. (2007). *Teaching reading comprehension to students with learning difficulties (What works for special-needs learners)*. New York, NY: Guilford.

Klingner, J. K., Soltero-Gonzalez, L., & Lesaux, N. (2010). RTI for English-language learners. In M. Y. Lipson & K. K. Wixson (Eds.), *Successful approaches to RTI: Collaborative practices for improving K–12 literacy* (pp. 134–162). Newark, DE: International Reading Association.

Knapp, M. S. (1995). Introduction: The teaching challenge in high-poverty classrooms. In M. S. Knapp (Ed.) Teaching for meaning in high-poverty classrooms (pp. 1–10). New York, NY: Teachers College Press.

Kong, A., & Pearson, P. D. (2003). The road to participation: The construction of a literacy practice in a learning community of linguistically diverse learners. *Research on the Teaching of English, 38*, 85–124.

Konold, K. E., Miller, S. P., & Konold, K. B. (2004). Using teacher feedback to enhance student learning. *Teaching Exceptional Children, 36*(6), 64–69.

Koretz, D. (2008). *Measuring up: What educational testing really tells us.* Boston, MA: Harvard University Press.

Koskinen, P. S., Blum, I. H., Bisson, S. A., Phillips, S. M., Creamer, T. S., & Baker, T. K. (2000). Book access, shared reading, and audio models: The effects of supporting the literacy learning of linguistically diverse students in school and at home. *Journal of Educational Psychology, 92*, 23–36.

Kremers, M. (1990). Sharing authority on a synchronous network: The case for riding the beast. *Computers and Composition, 7*, 69–77.

Krieger, V. K. (1981). Differences in poor readers' abilities to identify high-frequency words in isolation and context. *Reading World, 20*, 263–272.

Kucan, L. (2005, December). Mediating teachers' learning about discussion and comprehension through transcript analysis. Symposium presented at the annual meeting of the National Reading Conference. Miami, FL.

Kucan, L., & Beck, I. (1997). Thinking aloud and reading comprehension research: Inquiry, instruction, and interaction. *Review of Educational Research, 67*, 271–299.

Kucan, L., & Beck, I. L. (1996). Four fourth graders thinking aloud: An investigation of genre effects. *Journal of Literacy Research, 28*(2), 259–287.

Kucer, S. (1985). The making of meaning: Reading and writing as parallel processes. *Written Communication, 2*, 317–336.

Kuhn, M. R., Schwanenflugel, P. J., Morris, R. D., Morrow, L. M., Woom, D., Meisinger, E., . . . Stahl, S.A. (2006). Teaching children to become fluent and automatic readers. *Journal of Literacy Research, 38*, 357–387.

Kuhn, M. R., & Stahl, S. A. (2000). Fluency: A review of developmental and remedial practices (CIERA Report No. 2–008). Ann Arbor, MI: Center for the Improvement of Early Reading Achievement.

Kuiper, E., Volman, M., & Terwel, J. (2005). The Web as an information resource in K–12: Strategies for supporting students in searching and processing information. *Review of Educational Research, 75*, 285–328.

LaBerge, D., & Samuels, J. (1974). Toward a theory of automatic information processing in reading. *Cognitive Psychology, 6*, 293–323.

Labbo, L., & Place, K. (2010). Fresh perspectives on new literacies and technology integration. *Voices from the Middle, 17*(3), pp. 9–18.

Labbo, L. D. (2000). 12 things young children can do with a talking book in a classroom computer center. *The Reading Teacher, 53*(7), 542–546.

Ladson-Billings, G. (1994). *The dreamkeepers.* San Francisco: Jossey-Bass.

Laing, S. P., & Kamhi, A. (2003). Alternative assessment of language and literacy in culturally and linguistically diverse populations. *Language, Speech, and Hearing Services in Schools, 34*, 44–55.

Lancia, P. J. (1997). Literary borrowing: The effects of literature on children's writing. *The Reading Teacher, 50*, 470–475.

Landry, S. H., & Smith, K. E. (2006). The influence of parenting on emerging literacy skills. In D. K. Dickinson & S. B. Neuman (Eds.), *Handbook of early literacy research* (Vol. 2, pp.135–162). New York, NY: Guilford Press.

Langdon, H. W. (2006). What's new in the world of assessment materials in Spanish? *Bilingual Therapies.* Retrieved April 11, 2007, from http://www.bilingualtherapies.com/que_tal/past%20articles/mar_06.html

Langer, J. A. (1982). Facilitating text processing: The elaboration of prior knowledge. In J. Langer & M. T. Smith-Burke (Eds.), *Reader meets author/bridging the gap* (pp. 149–162). Newark, DE: International Reading Association.

Langer, J. A. (1984). Examining background knowledge and text comprehension. *Reading Research Quarterly, 19*, 468–481.

Langer, J. A. (1985). Levels of questioning: An alternative view. *Reading Research Quarterly, 20*(5), 586–601.

Langer, J. A. (1991). Literacy and schooling: A sociocognitive perspective. In E. H. Hiebert (Ed.), *Literacy for a diverse society* (pp. 9–27). New York, NY: Teachers College Press.

Langer, J. A. (2001). Beating the odds: Teaching middle and high school students to read and write well. *American Education Research Journal, 38*(4) 837–880.

Langer J. A. (2004). *Getting to excellent: How to create better schools.* New York, NY: Teachers College Press.

Lankshear, C., & Knobel, M. (2003). The new technologies in early childhood literacy research: A review of research. *Journal of Early Childhood Literacy, 3*(1), 59–82.

Lapp, D., & Flood, J. (2000). Reading comprehension instruction for at-risk students: Research-based practices that can make a difference. In D. W. Moore, D. E. Alvermann, & K. A. Hinchman (Eds.), *Struggling adolescent readers: A collection of strategies* (pp. 138–147). Newark, DE: International Reading Association.

Larsen, S. C., & Hammill, D. D. (1986). *Test of written spelling* (2nd ed.). Austin, TX: Pro-Ed.

Larsen, S. C., & Hammill, D. D. (1994). *Test of written spelling* (3rd ed.). Austin, TX: Pro-Ed.

Larsen, S. C., Hammill, D. D., & Moats, L. (1999). *Test of written spelling* (4th ed.). Austin, TX: Pro-Ed.

Lee, C. D., Rosenfeld, E., Mendenhall, R., Rivers, A., & Tynes, B. (2004). Cultural modeling as a frame for narrative analysis. In C. Daiute & C. Lightfoot (Eds.), *Narrative analysis: Studying the development of individuals in society* (pp. 39–61). Thousand Oaks, CA: Sage Publications.

Lee, C. D., & Spratley, A. (2010). *Reading in the disciplines: The challenges of adolescent literacy.* New York, NY: Carnegie Corporation of New York.

Lehman, S., Schraw, G., McCrudden, M. T., & Hartley, K. (2007). Processing and recall of seductive details in scientific text. *Contemporary Educational Psychology, 32*(4), 569– 587.

Lehtinen, E., Vauras, M., Salonen, P., Olkinuora, E., & Kinnunen, R. (1995). Long-term development of learning activity: Motivation, cognitive, and social interaction. *Educational Psychologist, 30*(1), 21–35.

Leinhardt, G., Zigmond, N., & Cooley, W. (1981). Reading instruction and its effects. *American Educational Research Journal, 18*, 171–177.

Lemann, N. (1997). The reading wars. *Atlantic Monthly, 280*(5), 128–134.

Lenz, B. K. & Deshler, D. D. (2003). *Teaching content to all: Evidence-based inclusive practices in middle and secondary schools.* Boston, MA: Allyn & Bacon.

Lepper, M., & Chabay, R. (1985). Intrinsic motivation and instruction: Conflicting views on the role of motivational processes in computer-based education. *Educational Psychologist, 20,* 217–230.

Lepper, M. R., & Cordova, D. I. (1992). A desire to be taught: Instructional consequences of intrinsic motivation. *Motivation and Emotion, 15,* 187–208.

Lesaux, N., & Geva, E. (2006). Synthesis: Development of literacy in language-minority students. In D. August & T. Shanahan (Eds.), *Developing literacy in second-language learners* (pp. 53–74). Mahwah, NJ: Erlbaum.

Lesaux, N., with Koda, K., Siegel, L., & Shanahan, T. (2006). Development of literacy. In D. August & T. Shanahan (Eds.), *Developing literacy in second-language learners* (pp. 75–122). Mahwah, NJ: Erlbaum.

Lesiak, J. L. (1997). Research based answers to questions about emergent literacy in kindergarten. *Psychology in the Schools, 34,* 143–160.

Leslie, L., & Caldwell, J. (2006). *Qualitative Reading Inventory–4.* Boston, MA: Allyn & Bacon.

LeTendre, M. (1991). The continuing evolution of a federal role in compensatory education. *Educational Evaluation and Policy Analysis, 13,* 328–334.

Leu, D., DeGroff, L. C., & Simons, H. D. (1986). Predictable texts and interactive-compensatory hypothesis: Evaluating individual differences in reading ability, context use, and comprehension. *Journal of Educational Psychology, 78,* 347–352.

Leu, D. J., Jr. (2000a). Literacy and technology: Deictic consequences for literacy education in an information age. In M. L. Kamil, P. B. Mosenthal, P. D. Pearson, & R. Barr (Eds.), *Handbook of reading research* (Vol. 2, pp. 743–770). Mahwah, NJ: Erlbaum.

Leu, D. J., Jr. (2000b). Our children's future: Changing the focus of literacy and literacy instruction. *The Reading Teacher, 53,* 424–431.

Leu, D. J., Karchmer, R. A., & Leu, D. D. (1999). The Miss Rumphius effect: Envisionments for literacy and learning that transform the Internet. *The Reading Teacher, 52,* 636–642.

Levy, S., & Vaughn, S. (2002). An observable study of teachers' instruction of students with emotional or behavioral disorders. *Behavioral Disorders, 27*(3), 215–23.

Liberman, I. Y., & Shankweiler, D. (1979). Speech, the alphabet, and teaching to read. In L. B. Resnick & P. A. Weaver (Eds.), *Theory and practice of early reading* (Vol. 2, pp. 109–134). Hillsdale, NJ: Erlbaum.

Lidz, C. S. (1987). Historical perspectives. In C. S. Lidz (Ed.), *Dynamic assessment* (pp. 3–34). New York, NY: Guilford Press.

Lidz, C. S. (1991). *Dynamic assessment.* New York, NY: Guilford Press.

Lidz, C. S. (Ed.) (2001). *Dynamic assessment: Prevailing models and applications (Advances in Cognition and Educational Practice).* JAI Press.

Lidz, J., & Gleitman, L. R. (2004). Argument structure and the child's contribution to language learning. *Trends in Cognitive Sciences, 8*(4), 157–161.

Lindamood, C., & Lindamood, P. (1998). *The Lindamood® phoneme sequencing program for reading, spelling, and speech.* Austin, TX: Pro-Ed.

Linn, R. (2000). Assessments and accountability. *Educational Researcher, 29,* 4–16.

Linn, R. (2006). *Educational accountability systems* (CSE Technical Report No. 687). University of Colorado at Boulder: CRESST.

Linn, R. L., & Gronlund, N. E. (2000). *Measurement and assessment in teaching* (8th ed.). Upper Saddle River, NJ: Merrill.

Lipson, M. Y. (1982). Learning new information from text: The role of prior knowledge and reading ability. *Journal of Reading Behavior, 14,* 243–262.

Lipson, M. Y. (1983). The influence of religious affiliation on children's memory for text information. *Reading Research Quarterly, 18,* 448–457.

Lipson, M. Y. (1995). Conversations with children and other classroom-based assessment strategies. In L. Putnam (Ed.), *How to become a better reading teacher: Strategies for diagnosis and remediation* (pp. 167–179). Columbus, OH: Merrill/Macmillan.

Lipson, M. Y. (2003). The challenge of comprehension instruction. *New England Reading Association Journal, 39*(2), 1–6.

Lipson, M. Y. (October, 2006). Comprehension and comprehension instruction as informed improvisation. Presentation at the New England Reading Association Annual Meeting. Sturbridge Village, MA.

Lipson, M. Y. (2007). *Teaching reading beyond the primary grades.* New York, NY: Scholastic.

Lipson, M. Y., Biggam, S. C., & Wixson, K. K. (November, 2006). *The challenges of multilingualism and instructional innovation in a world of limited print: The Ghana and Tanzania experiences.* Paper presented at the 56th Annual Meeting of the National Reading Conference. Los Angeles, CA.

Lipson, M. Y., Bigler, M., Poth, L., & Wickizer, B. (1987, December). *Instructional applications of a verbal report methodology.* Paper presented at the 37th Annual Meeting of the National Reading Conference, St. Petersburg, FL.

Lipson, M. Y., Chomsky-Higgins, P., & Kanfer, J. (2011). Diagnosis: The missing ingredient in RTI assessment. *The Reading Teacher, 65,* 204–208.

Lipson, M. Y., Goldhaber, J., & Squires, J. (1993). *Teacher beliefs and literacy practices in kindergarten: Competing interests and multiple practices.* 43rd Annual Meeting, National Reading Conference. Charleston, S.C., December, 1993.

Lipson, M. Y., Irwin, M., & Poth, E. (1986). The relationships between metacognitive self-reports and strategic reading behavior. In J. Niles & R. Lalik (Eds.), *Solving problems in literacy: Learners, teachers, and researchers* (35th Yearbook of the National Reading Conference, pp. 460–476). Rochester, NY: National Reading Conference.

Lipson, M. Y., Mosenthal, J. H., Daniels, P., & Woodside-Jiron, H. (2000). Process writing in the classrooms of eleven teachers with different orientations to teaching and learning. *Elementary School Journal, 101*(2), 209–231.

Lipson, M. Y., Mosenthal, J. H., & Mekkelsen, J. (1999). The nature of comprehension among grade 2 children: Variability in retellings as function of development, text, and task. In T. Shanahan & F. V. Rodriguez-Brown (Eds.), *Forty-eighth yearbook of the National Reading Conference* (pp. 104–119). Chicago, IL: National Reading Conference.

Lipson, M. Y., Mosenthal, J. H., Mekkelsen, J., & Russ, B. (2004). Building knowledge and fashioning success one school at a time. *The Reading Teacher, 57,* 534–542.

Lipson, M. Y., Valencia, S., Wixson, K. K., & Peters, C. (1993). Integration and thematic teaching: Integration to improve teaching and learning. *Language Arts, 70,* 252–263.

Lipson, M. Y., & Wickizer, E. (1989). Promoting reading independence through instructional dialogue. *Teaching Exceptional Children, 21*(2), 28–32.

Lipson, M. Y., & Wixson, K. K. (1986). Reading disability research: An interactionist perspective. *Review of Educational Research, 56*, 111–136.

Lipson, M. Y., & Wixson, K. K. (1989). Student evaluation and basal instruction. In P. Winograd, K. K. Wixson, & M. Y. Lipson (Eds.), *Improving basal reading instruction* (pp. 109–139). New York, NY: Teachers College Press.

Liu, M. (2004). Examining the performance and attitudes of sixth graders during their use of a problem-based hypermedia learning environment. *Computers in Human Behavior, 20*(3), 357–379.

Liu, M., & Reed, W. M. (1995). The effect of hypermedia assisted instruction on second language learning. *Journal of Educational Computing Research, 12*, 159–175.

Lomax, R. G., & McGee, L. M. (1987). Young children's concepts about print and reading: Toward a model of word reading acquisition. *Reading Research Quarterly, 22*, 237–256.

Lombardino, L. J., Morris, D., Mercado, L., DeFillipo, F., Sarisky, C., & Montgomery, A. (1999). The Early Reading Screening Instrument: A method for identifying kindergarteners at risk for learning to read. *International Journal of Language and Communication Disorders, 34*, 135–150.

Lorch, R. F., & Lorch, E. P. (1996). Effects of organizational signals on free recall of expository texts. *Journal of Educational Psychology, 88*, 38–48.

Lou, Y., Abrami, P. C., Spence, J. C., Poulsen, C., Chambers, B., & d'Appolonia, S. (1996). Within-class grouping: A meta-analysis. *Review of Educational Research, 66*, 423–458.

Louwerse, M. (2001). An analytic and cognitive parameterization of coherence relations. *Cognitive Linguistics, 12*, 291–315.

Lovell, M., & Phillips, L. (2009). Commercial software programs approved for teaching and reading in the primary grades: Another sobering reality. *Journal of Research on Technology in Education, 42*(2), 197–216.

Lovett, M., & Steinbach, K. (1997). The effectiveness of remedial programs for reading disabled children of different ages: Does the benefit decrease for older children? *Learning Disability Quarterly, 20*, 189–210.

Loxterman, J., Beck, I., & McKeown, M. (1994). The effects of thinking aloud during reading on students' comprehension of more or less coherent text. *Reading Research Quarterly, 29*(4), 352–367.

Lubliner, S., Smetana, L. (2005). Effects of comprehensive vocabulary instruction on students' metacognitive word-learning skills and reading comprehension. *Journal of Literacy Research, 37*, 163–200.

Lund, N. J., & Duchan, J. F. (1988). *Assessing children's language in naturalistic contexts.* Englewood Cliffs, NJ: Prentice Hall.

Lyons, C. A., & Pinnell, G. S. (2001). *Systems for change in literacy education.* Portsmouth, NH: Heinemann.

Mabry, L. (1999). Writing to the rubric: Lingering effects of traditional standardized testing on direct writing assessment. *Phi Delta Kappan, 80*, 673–679.

MacArthur, C. A. (1996). Using technology to enhance the writing processes of students with learning disabilities. *Journal of Learning Disabilities, 29*(4), 344–354.

MacArthur, C. A. (1998). Word processing with speech synthesis and word prediction: Effects on the dialogue journal writing of students with learning disabilities. *Learning Disability Quarterly, 21*, 151–166.

MacArthur, C. A. (1999). Word processing with speech synthesis and word prediction: Effects on the dialogue journal writing of students with learning disabilities. *Learning Disability Quarterly, 21*, 151–166.

MacArthur, C., Ferretti, R., Okolo, C., & Cavalier, A. (2001). Technology applications for students literacy problems: A critical review. *Elementary School Journal, 101*, 273–301.

MacArthur, C. A., Graham, S., Schwartz, S. S., & Schafer, W. D. (1995). Evaluation of a writing instruction model that integrated a process approach, strategy, instruction, and word processing. *Learning Disability Quarterly, 18*, 278–291.

MacDonald-Wharton, R., Pressley, M., & Hampston, J. M. (1998). Literacy instruction in nine first-grade classrooms: Teacher characteristics and student achievement. *Elementary School Journal, 99*, 101–128.

MacGillivray, L., Ardell, A. I., Curwen, M. S., & Palma, J. (2004). Colonized teachers: examining the implementation of a scripted reading program. *Teaching Education, 15*, 131–144.

MacGinitie, W. H., MacGinitie, R. K., Maris, K., & Dreyer, L. (2000). *The Gates-MacGinitie reading tests* (4th ed.). Itasca, IL: Riverside Publishing.

Madding, C. (2002). Socialization practices of Latinos. In A. E. Brice (Ed.), *The Hispanic child: Speech, language, culture and education* (pp. 68–84). Boston, MA: Allyn and Bacon.

Mahon, E. A. (2006). High-stakes testing and English language learners: Questions of validity. *Bilingual Research Journal, 30*, 479–497.

Maier, A. A. (1980). The effect of focusing on the cognitive processes of learning disabled children. *Journal of Learning Disabilities, 13*, 143–147.

Malmstrom, J. (1968). *Introduction to modern English grammar.* Rochelle Park, NJ: Hayden Press.

Maloch, B. (2002). Scaffolding student talk: One teacher's role in literature discussion groups. *Reading Research Quarterly, 37*, 94–111.

Mandler, J. M., & Johnson, N. S. (1977). Remembrance of things parsed: Story structure and recall. *Cognitive Psychology, 9*, 111–115.

Manzo, A. V. (1969). The request procedure. *Journal of Reading, 13*, 123–126.

Maria, K. (1986, December). *Refuting misconceptions: Its effect on middle grade children's comprehension.* Paper presented at the 35th Annual Meeting of the National Reading Conference. Austin, TX.

Maria, K. (1990). *Reading comprehension instruction: Issues and strategies.* Parkton, MD: York Press.

Marinak, B., & Gambrell, L. (2008). Intrinsic motivation and rewards: What sustains young children's engagement with text? *Literacy Research and Instruction. 47*(1), 9–26.

Markwardt, F. C. (1989). *Peabody Individual Achievement Battery—Revised.* Circle Pines, MN: American Guidance Service.

Marsh, G. P., Desberg, P., & Cooper, J. (1977). Developmental changes in reading strategies. *Journal of Reading Behavior, 9*, 391–394.

Marshall, H. H., & Weinstein, R. S. (1984). Classroom factors affecting students' self-evaluations: An interactional model. *Review of Educational Research, 54*, 301–325.

Marshall, N., & Glock, M. (1978–79). Comprehension of connected discourse: A study into the relationship between the structure of text and information recalled. *Reading Research Quarterly, 14*, 10–56.

Martens, P. (1998). Using retrospective miscue analysis to inquire: Learning from Michael. *The Reading Teacher, 52*(2), 176–180.

Martinez, M., & McGee, L. M. (2000). Children's literature and reading instruction: Past, present, and future. *Reading Research Quarterly, 35*, 154–179.

Martinez, M., & Roser, N. (1985). Read it again: The value of repeated readings during storytime. *The Reading Teacher, 38*, 782–786.

Martinez, M., Roser, N., & Strecker, S. (1999). I never thought I could be a star: A reader's theater ticket to fluency. *The Reading Teacher, 50*, 326–334.

Marzano, R. J., Pickering, D., & McTighe, J. (1993). *Assessing student outcomes.* Alexandria, VA: ASCD.

Mason, J. M., & Au, K. H. (1990). *Reading instruction for today* (2nd ed.). Glenview, IL: Scott, Foresman.

Mastropieri, M. A., & Scruggs, T. E. (1997). Best practices in promoting reading comprehension in students with learning disabilities: 1976–1996. *Remedial and Special Education, 18*, 197–214.

Mather, N., Sammons, J., & Schwartz, J. (2006). Adaptations of the Names Test: Easy-to-use phonics assessments. *The Reading Teacher, 60*, 114–122.

Mathes, P. G., Denton, C. A., Fletcher, J. M., Anthony, J. L., Francis, D. J., & Schatschneider, C. (2005). The effects of theoretically different instruction and student characteristics on the skills of struggling readers. *Reading Research Quarterly, 40*(2), 148–182.

Mathews, M. (1966). *Teaching to read: Historically considered.* Chicago, IL: University of Chicago Press.

May, F. (1990). *Reading as communication: An interactive approach.* Columbus, OH: Charles E. Merrill.

Mayer, R. E. (2008). Multimedia literacy. In J. Coiro, M. Knoobel, C. Lankshear, & D. Leu (Eds.), *Handbook of research on new literacies,* New York, NY: Erlbaum.

McCabe, A. (1992, December). *All kinds of good stories.* Paper presented at the 42nd Annual Meeting of the National Reading Conference, San Antonio, TX. ERIC document: ED355474.

McCarthey, S. (1996, December). *Learning the qualities of good writing: Literacy practices in elementary schools.* Paper presented at the annual meeting of the National Reading Conference, Charleston, SC.

McCarthy, S. J., & Moje, E. (2002). Conversations: Identity matters. *Reading Research Quarterly, 37*, 228–238.

McCarthy, S. J., & Raphael, T. E. (1992). Alternative perspectives of reading/writing connections. In J. W. Irwin & M. Doyle (Eds.), *Reading/writing connections: Learning from research* (pp. 2–30). Newark, DE: International Reading Association.

McConaughy, S. H. (1982). Developmental changes in story comprehension and levels of questioning. *Language Arts, 59*, 580–590, 600.

McConaughy, S. H. (1985). Good and poor readers' comprehension of story structure across different input and output modalities. *Reading Research Quarterly, 20*, 219–232.

McConnell, C. R. (1982). Readability formulae as applied to college economics textbooks. *Journal of Reading, 26*, 14–17.

McCormack, S. L., Paratore, J. R., & Dahlene, K. F. (2003). Establishing instructional congruence across learning settings: One path to success for struggling third-grade readers. In R. L. McCormack & J. R. Paratore (Eds.), *After early intervention, then what? Teaching struggling readers in grades 3 and beyond* (pp. 117–136). Newark, DE: IRA.

McCracken, R. A., & McCracken, M. (1971). Initiating sustained silent reading. *Journal of Reading, 14*, 521–524, 582–583.

McCracken, R. A., & McCracken, M. (1978). Modeling is the key to sustained reading. *The Reading Teacher, 31*, 406–408.

McDermott, R., Goldman, S., & Vareene, H. (2006). The cultural work of learning disabilities. *Educational Researcher, 35*(6), 12–17.

McDermott, R. P. (1977). The ethnography of speaking and reading. In R. W. Shuy (Ed.), *Linguistic theory: What can it say about reading?* (pp. 153–185). Newark, DE: International Reading Association.

McDonald, B., & Boud, D. (2003). The impact of self-assessment on achievement: the effects of self-assessment training on performance in external examinations. *Assessment in Education: Principles, Policy & Practice, 10*, 209–220.

McGill-Franzen, A. (1992). Early literacy: What does "developmentally appropriate" mean? *The Reading Teacher, 46*, 56–58.

McGill-Franzen, A. (1994). Compensatory and special education: Is there accountability for learning and belief in children's potential? In E. H. Hiebert & B. M. Taylor (Eds.), *Getting reading right from the start: Effective early literacy interventions* (pp. 13–35). Boston, MA: Allyn & Bacon.

McGill-Franzen, A. (2000). Policy and instruction: What is the relationship? In M. L. Kamil, P. B. Mosenthal, P. D. Pearson, & R. Barr (Eds.), *Handbook of reading research* (Vol. 3, pp. 889–908). Mahwah, NJ: Erlbaum.

McGill-Franzen, A., & Allington, R. L. (Eds.) (2011). *Handbook of reading disability research.* New York, NY: Routledge.

McKenna, M. C. (1983). Informal reading inventories: A review of the issues. *The Reading Teacher, 36*, 670–679.

McKenna, M. C. (1998). Electronic texts and the transformation of beginning reading. In D. Reinking, M. C. McKenna, L. D. Labbo, & R. D. Kieffer (Eds.), *Handbook of literacy and technology* (pp. 45–59). Mahwah, NJ: Erlbaum.

McKenna, M. C., Kear, D. J., & Ellsworth, R. A. (1995). Children's attitudes toward reading: A national survey. *Reading Research Quarterly, 30*, 934–956.

McKenna, M. C., & Picard, M. C. (2006). Assessment: Revisiting the role of miscue analysis in effective teaching. *The Reading Teacher, 60*, 376–380.

McLaughlin, M., & Allen, M. B. (2002). Guided comprehension: A teaching model for grades 3–8. Newark, DE: International Reading Association.

McLaughlin, M. W., & Talbert, J. E. (2006). *Building school-based teacher learning communities; Professional strategies to improve student achievement.* New York, NY: Teachers College Press.

McMillan, J. H. (2008). *Assessment essentials for standards-based education* (2nd ed.). Thousand Oaks, CA: Corwin.

McNamara, D., Kintsch, E., Songer, N. B., Kintsch, W. (1996). Are good texts always better? Interactions of text coherence, background knowledge, and levels of understanding in learning from text. *Cognition and Instruction, 14*, 1–43.

McNamara, D. S. (2001). Reading both high-coherence texts: Effects of text sequence and prior knowledge. *Canadian Journal of Experimental Psychology, 55*, 51–62.

McNamara, D. S. (2001). Reading both high-coherence and low-coherence texts: Effects of text sequence and prior knowledge. *Canadian Journal of Experimental Psychology, 55*, 51–62.

McNamara, D. S., O'Reilly, T., Rowe, M., Boonthum, C., & Levinstein, I. (2007). iStart: A Web-based tutor that teaches self-explanation and metacognitive reading strategies. In D. S. McNamara (Ed.), *Reading comprehension strategies: Theories, interventions, and technologies.* New York, NY: Erlbaum.

McNeil, J. D. (1992). *Reading comprehension: New directions for classroom practice* (3rd ed.). New York, NY: HarperCollins.

McQuillan, J. (2006). The effects of print access and print exposure on English vocabulary acquisition of language-minority students. *The Reading Matrix, 6*(1). Online. Retrieved July 24, 2006.

McQuillan, J., & Au, J. (2001). The effect of print access on reading frequency. *Reading Psychology, 22*, 225–248.

McREL. (2003). Data-driven decision making: Sustaining school improvement. Denver, CO: Author. Retrieved February 14, 2011, from http://www.mcrel.org/pdf/leadershiporganizationdevelopment/5031tg_datafolio.pdf

McVee, M. B., & Dickson, B. A. (2002). Creating a rubric to examine literacy software for the primary grades. *The Reading Teacher, 55*(7), 635–639.

McWilliams, L., & Rakes, T. A. (1979). *Content reading inventories: English, social studies, science.* Dubuque, IA: Kendall/Hunt.

Medley, D. M. (1985). Systematic observation schedules as measuring instruments. In R. A. Weinberg & F. H. Woods (Eds.), *Observation of pupils and teachers in mainstream and special education settings: Alternative strategies* (pp. 97–106). Minneapolis: University of Minnesota, Leadership and Training Institute/Special Education.

Meece, J. L., & Miller, S. D. (1999). Changes in elementary school children's achievement goals for reading and writing: Results of a longitudinal and an intervention study. *Scientific Studies of Reading, 3,* 207–229.

Meisels, S. J. (1998). *Assessing readiness* (CIERA Report No. 3–002). Ann Arbor, MI: Center for Improvement of Early Reading Achievement.

Meisels, S. J., & Piker, R. A. (2001). *An analysis of early literacy assessments used for instruction.* Ann Arbor, MI: The Center for the Improvement of Early Reading Achievement (CIERA).

Memory, D. M. (1986). Guiding students to independent decoding in content area classes. In E. K. Dishner, R. W. Bean, J. E. Readence, & D. W. Moore (Eds.), *Reading in content areas* (3rd ed., pp. 210–218). Dubuque, IA: Kendall/Hunt.

Menn, L., & Stoel-Gammon, C. (2005). Phonological development. In J. B. Gleason (Ed.), *The development of language* (6th ed.) (pp. 62–111). Boston, MA: Pearson.

Menon, S., & Hiebert, E. H. (2005). A comparison of first-graders' reading with little books or literature-based basal anthologies. *Reading Research Quarterly, 40,* 12–38.

Meskill, C. (2005) The language of learning: Using assistive technologies to support English language learners. *Threshold, Winter,* 22–25.

Meskill, C. , & Mossop, J. (2000). Electronic texts in ESOL classrooms. *TESOL Quarterly, 34*(3), 585–592.

Meskill, C., Mossop, J., & Bates, R. (1999). *Electronic texts and English as a second language environments.* Albany, NY: National Research Center on English Learning and Achievement (CELA).

Mesmer, H. A. (2001). Decodable text: A review of what we know. *Reading Research and Instruction, 40,* 121–141.

Mesmer, H. A. (2005). Text decodability and the first-grade reader. *Reading & Writing Quarterly, 21,* 61–86.

Mesmer, H. A. (2006). Beginning reading materials: A national survey of primary teachers' reported uses and beliefs. *Journal of Literacy Research, 38,* 389–425.

Messick, S. (1989). Validity. In R. L. Linn (Ed.), *Educational measurement* (3rd ed., pp. 13–103). New York, NY: Macmillan.

Messick, S. (2004). Test validity: A matter of consequence. *Social Indicators Research, 45,* 35–44.

Metsala, J. L., & Ehri, L. C. (1998). *Word recognition in beginning literacy.* Mahwah, NJ: Erlbaum.

Meyer, A., & Rose, D. H. (1999). *Learning to read in the computer age.* Cambridge, MA: Brookline Books.

Meyer, B. J., & Freedle, R. O. (1984). Effects of discourse type on recall. *American Educational Research Journal, 21,* 121–143.

Meyer, K. E., & Reindl, B. L. (2010). Spotlight on the Comprehensive Intervention Model: The case of Washington School for Comprehensive Literacy. In M. Y. Lipson & K. K. Wixson (Eds.),

Successful approaches to RTI: Collaborative practices for improving K–12 literacy (pp. 121–133). Newark, DE: International Reading Association.

Mezynski, K. (1983). Issues concerning acquisition of knowledge: Effects of vocabulary training on reading comprehension. *Review of Educational Research, 53,* 253–279.

Michaels, S. (1981). "Sharing time": Children's narrative styles and differential access to literacy. *Language in Society, 10,* 423–442.

Michaels, S. (1991). The dismantling of narrative. In A. McCabe & C. Peterson (Eds.), *Developing narrative structure* (pp. 303–351). Hillsdale, NJ: Erlbaum.

Michigan Reading Association. (1993). *Computers in the reading program* (2nd ed.). Grand Rapids, MI: Author.

Mikkelsen, N. (1990). Toward greater equity in literacy education: Storymaking and non-mainstream students. *Language Arts, 67,* 556–566.

Miller, D., Linn, R. L., & Gronlund, N. E. (2009). *Measurement and assessment in teaching* (10th ed.). New York, NY: Allyn & Bacon.

Miller, L., & Olson, J. (1995). How computers live in schools. *Educational Leadership, 53,* 74–77.

Miller, P., & Goodnow, J. J. (1995). Cultural practices: Toward an integration of culture and development. In J. J. Goodnow & F. Kessel (Eds.), *Cultural practices as contexts for development, No. 67: New directions in child development.* San Francisco, CA: Jossey-Bass.

Miller, P., & Mehler, R. (1994). The power of personal storytelling in families and kindergartens. In A. H. Dyson & C. Genishi (Eds.), *The need for story: Cultural diversity in classroom and community* (pp. 38–56). Urbana, IL: National Council of Teachers of English.

Miller, S. D., & Meece, J. L. (1999). Third graders' motivational preferences for reading and writing tasks. *Elementary School Journal, 100,* 19–35.

Mills, R. E. (1956). An evaluation of techniques for teaching word recognition. *Elementary School Journal, 56,* 221–225.

Minami, M., & McCabe, A. (1991). Haiku as a discourse regulation device: A stanza analysis of Japanese children's personal narratives. *Language in Society, 20*(4), 577–599.

Minami, M., & McCabe, A. (1995). Rice balls and bear hunts: Japanese and North American family narrative patter. ns. *Journal of Child Language, 22,* 423–445.

Mitchell, J. V. (1985). *Ninth mental measurements yearbook.* Lincoln, NE: Buros Institute of Mental Measurements.

Moje, E. B. (2006). Integrating literacy into the secondary school content areas: An enduring problem in enduring institutions. Retrieved July 4, 2006, from http://www.umich.edu/~govrel/adoles_lit/moje.pdf

Moje, E. B. (2008). Foregrounding the disciplines in secondary content teaching and learning: A call for change. *Journal of Adolescent and Adult Literacy, 52*(2), 96–107.

Moje, E. B., Willes, D. J., & Fassio, K. (2001). Constructing and negotiating literacy in a writer's workshop: Literacy teaching and learning in the seventh grade. In E. B. Moje & D. G. O'Brien (Eds.), *Constructions of literacy: Studies of teaching and learning in secondary classrooms and schools.* Mahwah, NJ: Erlbaum.

Mokhtari, K., Kymes, A., & Edwards, P. (2008). Assessing the new literacies of online reading comprehension: An informative interview with W. Ian O'Byrne, Lisa Zawilinski, J. Greg McVerry, and Donald J. Leu at the University of Connecticut. *The Reading Teacher, 62*(4), 354–357.

Mokhtari, K., & Reichard, C. A. (2002). Assessing students' metacognitive awareness of reading strategies. *Journal of Educational Psychology, 94,* 249–259.

Mol, S. E., Bu, A. G., deJong, M. T., & Smeets, D. J. H. (2008). Added value of dialogic parent-child book reading: A meta-analysis. *Early Education and Development, 19*(1), 7–26.

Moll, L. C., & Diaz, E. (1987). Change as the goal of educational research. *Anthropology and Education Quarterly, 18,* 300–311.

Moll, L. C., & Diaz, S. (1985). Ethnographic pedagogy: Promoting effective bilingual instruction. In E. Garcia & R. V. Padilla (Eds.), *Advances in bilingual education research* (pp. 127–149). Tucson: University of Arizona Press.

Moll, L. C., Estrada, E., Diaz, E., & Lopes, L. M. (1980). The organization of bilingual lessons: Implications for schooling. *Quarterly Newsletter of the Laboratory of Comparative Human Cognition, 2,* 53–58.

Moll, L. C., & González, N. (1994). Critical issues: Lessons from research with language-minority children. *Journal of Reading Behavior, 26,* 439–456.

Molner, L. A. (1989). *Developing background for expository text: PReP revisited.* Paper presented at the 39th annual meeting of the National Reading Conference. Austin, TX.

Monroe, B. W., & Troia, G. A. (2006). Teaching writing skills to middle school students with disabilities. *Journal of Educational Research, 100,* 21–33.

Montague, M., Cleborne, D., Maddux, D., & Dereshiwsky, M. I. (1990). Story grammar and comprehension and production of narrative prose by students with learning disabilities. *Journal of Learning Disabilities, 23,* 190–197.

Moore, P. J., & Scevak, J. J. (1997). Learning from texts and visual aids: a developmental perspective. *Journal of Research in Reading, 20,* 205–223.

Moore, R. A., & Aspegren, C. M. (2001). Reflective conversations between two learners: Retrospective miscue analysis. *Journal of Adolescent and Adult Literacy, 44,* 492–503.

Moore, R. A., & Gilles, C. (2005). *Reading conversations: Retrospective miscue analysis with struggling readers, grades 4–12.* Portsmouth, NH: Heinemann.

Mork, T. A. (1972). Sustained silent reading in the classroom. *The Reading Teacher, 25,* 438–441.

Morris, D. (1981). Concept of word: A developmental phenomenon in the beginning reading and writing processes. *Language Arts, 58,* 659–668.

Morris, D. (1992). What constitutes at-risk: Screening children for first-grade reading intervention. In W. A. Secord & J. S. Damico (Eds.), *Best practices in school speech language pathology* (pp. 43–51). Orlando, FL: Harcourt Brace & Jovanovich.

Morris, D. (1993). The relationship between children's concept of word in text and phoneme awareness in learning to read: A longitudinal study. *Research in the Teaching of English, 27,* 133–153.

Morris, D. (1999). *The Howard Street tutoring manual: Teaching at-risk readers in the primary grades.* New York, NY: Guilford Press.

Morrison, F. J., Bachman, H. J., & Connor, C. M. (2005). *Improving literacy in America: Guidelines from research.* New Haven, CT: Yale University Press.

Morrison, F. J., & Cooney, R. R. (2002). Parenting and academic achievement: Multiple paths to early literacy. In J. G. Borkowski, S. I. Ramey, & M. Bristol-Power (Eds.), *Parenting and the child's world: Influence on academic, intellectual, and social-emotional development* (pp. 141–160). Mahwah, NJ: Erlbaum.

Morrow, L. M. (1983). Home and school correlates of early interest in literature. *Journal of Educational Research, 76,* 221–230.

Morrow, L. M. (1986). Encouraging voluntary reading: The impact of a literature program on children's use of library centers. *Reading Research Quarterly, 21,* 330–346.

Morrow, L. M. (1987). Promoting voluntary reading: Activities represented in basal reader manuals. *Reading Research and Instruction, 26,* 189–202.

Morrow, L. M. (1989). Creating a bridge to children's literature. In P. Winograd, K. Wixson, & M. Lipson (Eds.), *Improving basal reading instruction* (pp. 210–230). New York, NY: Teachers College Press.

Morrow, L. M., Tracey, D. H., Woo, D. G., & Pressley, M. (1999). Characteristics of exemplary first-grade literacy instruction. *The Reading Teacher, 52,* 462–476.

Mosenthal, J. H., Lipson, M., Sortino, S., Russ, B., & Mekkelsen, J. (2001). Literacy in rural Vermont: Lessons from schools where children succeed. In B. Taylor & P. D. Pearson (Eds.), *Teaching reading: Effective schools and accomplished teachers.* Mahwah, NJ: Erlbaum.

Mosenthal, J. H., Lipson, M. Y., Toncello, S., Russ, B., & Mekkelsen, J. (2004). Contexts and practices of six schools successful in obtaining reading achievement. *Elementary School Journal, 104*(5), 343–367.

Mosenthal, P., & Na, T. (1980). Quality of children's recall under two classroom testing tasks: Towards a socio-psycholinguistic model of reading comprehension. *Reading Research Quarterly, 15,* 504–528.

Moss, B. (2004). Teaching expository text structures through information trade book retellings. *The Reading Teacher, 57*(8), 710–718.

Moss, M., & Puma, M. (1995). Prospects: The congressional mandated study of educational growth and opportunity. Cambridge, MA: ABT Associates. (Eric Document: ED 394334).

Moss, P. A. (1994). Validity. In R. J. Sternberg (Ed.), *Encyclopedia of human intelligence* (Vol. 2, pp. 1101–1106). New York, NY: Macmillan.

Mowat, F. (1985). *Lost in the barrens.* New York, NY: Bantam Books (paperback reissue, original copyright 1956).

Mulligan, J. (1974). Using language experience with potential high school dropouts. *Journal of Reading, 18,* 206–211.

Mulryan, C. (1995). Fifth and sixth graders' involvement and participation in cooperative small groups in mathematics. *Elementary School Journal, 95,* 297–310.

Mulryan-Kyne, C. (2005). The grouping practices of teachers in small two-teacher primary schools in the Republic of Ireland. *Journal of Rural Education, 20,* 1–14.

Murawski, W., & Hughes, C. (2009). Response to intervention, collaboration, and co-teaching: A logical combination for successful systemic change. *Preventing School Failure: Alternative Education for Children and Youth, 53*(4), 267–277.

Murphy, P. K., Wilkinson, I. A. G., Soter, A. O., Hennessey, M. N., Alexander, J. F. (2009). Examining the effects of classroom discussion on students' comprehension of text: A meta-analysis. *Journal of Educational Psychology, 101*(3), 740–764.

Murray, D. H. (1990). *Shoptalk: Learning to write with writers.* Portsmouth, NH: Heinemann.

Murray-Ward, M. (1998). Review of the Nelson-Denny Reading Test, Forms G and H. In J. C. Impara & B. S. Plake (Eds.), *Thirteenth mental measurements yearbook.* Lincoln, NE: Buros Institute of Mental Measurements.

Muter, W., Hulme, C., Snowling, M. J., & Taylor, S. (1997). Segmentation, not rhyming, predicts early progress in learning to read. *Journal of Experimental Child Psychology, 65,* 370–396.

Nagy, W. (2003). *Teaching vocabulary to improve reading comprehension.* Urbana, IL: National Council of Teachers of English.

Nagy, W. E. (1988). *Teaching vocabulary to improve reading comprehension.* Urbana, IL: ERIC Clearinghouse on Reading and Communication Skills and the National Council of Teachers of English.

Nagy, W. E., & Anderson, R. C. (1984). How many words are there in printed school English? *Reading Research Quarterly, 19,* 304–330.

Nagy, W. E., & Herman, P. (1987). Breadth and depth of vocabulary knowledge: Implications for acquisition and instruction. In M. G. McKeown & M. E. Curtis (Eds.), *The nature of vocabulary acquisition* (pp. 19–36). Hillsdale, NJ: Erlbaum.

Nagy, W. E., Herman, P. A., & Anderson, R. C. (1985). Learning words from context. *Reading Research Quarterly, 20,* 233–253.

Nagy, W. E., & Scott, J. A. (2000). Vocabulary processes. In M. L. Kamil, P. B. Mosenthal, P. D. Pearson, & R. Barr (Eds.), *Handbook of reading research* (Vol. 3, pp. 269–284). Mahwah, NJ: Erlbaum.

NASA. (2011, October). *What's next for NASA?* Retrieved December 14, 2011, from http://www.nasa.gov/about/whats_next.html

Naslund, J. C., & Schneider, W. (1996). Kindergarten letter knowledge, phonological skills, and memory processes: Relative effects on early literacy. *Journal of Experimental Child Psychology, 62,* 30–59.

Nation, I. S. P. (2001). *Learning vocabulary in another language.* Cambridge, UK: Cambridge University Press.

Nation, K., & Hulme, C. (1997). Phonemic segmentation, not onset-rime segmentation, predicts early reading and spelling skills. *Reading Research Quarterly, 32,* 154–167.

Nation, K., & Hulme, C. (2002). The limitations of orthographic analogy in early reading development: Performance on the clue-word task depends on phonological priming and elementary decoding skill, not the use of orthographic analogy. *Journal of Experimental Child Psychology, 80,* 75–94.

National Assessment Governing Board (NAGB). (1998). *Writing framework and specification for the 1998 National Assessment of Educational Progress.* Washington, DC: NAGB.

National Assessment Governing Board NAGB). 2007). *Writing framework for the 2011 National Assessment of Educational Progress.* Iowa City, IA: ACT.

National Assessment of Educational Progress (NAEP). (1996). *1994 reading report card for the nation and the states.* Washington, DC: U.S. Department of Education.

National Association of State Directors of Special Education (NASDSE). (1994a). *Disproportionate representation of culturally and linguistically diverse students in special education: A comprehensive examination.* Prepared by Project Forum. Alexandria, VA: Author (ED379812).

National Association of State Directors of Special Education (NASDSE). (1994b). *Disproportionate representation of students from minority ethnic/racial groups in special education: A policy forum to develop action plans for a high priority recommendation.* (Final Report, Project Forum). Proceedings of a Policy Forum in Disproportionate Representation (ED378716).

National Association of State Directors of Special Education (NASDSE) & Council of Administrators of Special Education (CASE). (2006, May). Response to intervention: NASDSE and CASE White Paper on RTI. Alexandria, VA: Authors.

National Council of Teachers of English Writing Study Group. (2004). *NCTE beliefs about the teaching of writing.* Urbana, IL: Author. Retrieved from http://www.ncte.org/about/over/positions/category/write/118876.htm?source=gs

National Institute for Literacy. (2001). *Put reading first.* Jessup, MD: Author.

National Joint Committee on Learning Disabilities (NJCLD). (2005, June). *Responsiveness to intervention and learning disabilities.* Rockville, MD.

National Reading Panel. (2000). *Teaching children to read: An evidence-based assessment of the scientific research -literature on reading and its implications for reading instruction.* Washington, DC: National Institute of Child Health and Human Development.

Neill, D. M., & Median, J. (1989). Standardized tests: Harmful to educational health. *Phi Delta Kappan, 70,* 688–697.

Neisworth, J. T., & Bagnato, S. J. (2005). DEC recommended practices: Assessment: Introduction. In S. Sandall, M. L. Hemmeter, B. J. Smith, & M. E. McLean (Eds.), *DEC recommended practices: A comprehensive guide for practical application in early intervention/early childhood special education* (pp. 45–46). Longmont, CO: Sopris West [Division for Early Childhood (DEC) of the Council for Exceptional Children (CEC)].

Nelson, K. (1973). Structure and strategy in learning to talk. *Monographs of the Society for Research in Child Development, 38*(1 and 2, Serial No. 149).

Nelson-Herber, J. (1986). Expanding and refining vocabulary in content areas. *Journal of Reading, 29,* 626–633.

Neufeld, P. (2005). Comprehension instruction in content area classes. *The Reading Teacher, 59,* 302–312.

Neuman, S. (2006). The knowledge gap: Implications for early education. In D. K. Dickinson & S. B. Neuman (Eds.), *Handbook of early literacy research* (Vol. 2, pp. 29–40). New York, NY: Guilford Press.

Neuman, S., & Roskos, K. (1993). Access to print for children of poverty: Differential effects of adult mediation and literacy-enriched play settings on environmental and functional print tasks. *American Educational Research Journal, 30,* 95–122.

Neuman, S., & Celano, D. (2001). Access to print in middle- and low-income communities: An ecological study of four neighborhoods. *Reading Research Quarterly, 36,* 468–475.

Neuman, S. B., Copple, C., & Bredekamp, S. (2000). *Learning to read and write: Developmentally appropriate practices for young children.* Washington, DC: National Association for the Education of Young Children.

Neuman, S. B., & Dickinson, D. K. Eds. (2005). *Handbook of early literacy research* 2nd ed. New York, NY: Guildford.

Neuman, S. B., & Dickinson, D. K. Eds. (2011). *Handbook of early literacy research* 3rd ed. New York, NY: Guildford.

Newcomer, P., & Hammill, D. D. (1997). *Test of oral language development—3 primary.* Austin, TX: Pro-Ed.

Newmann, F. M., & Associates. (1996). *Authentic achievement: Restructuring schools for intellectual quality.* San Francisco, CA: Jossey-Bass.

Newmann, F. M., Bryk, A. S., & Nagaoka, J. K. (January, 2001). *Authentic intellectual work and standardized tests: Conflict or coexistence?* Special Topics Report. Chicago, IL: Consortium on Chicago School Research.

Newmann, F. M., Lopez, G., & Bryk, A. S. (November, 1998). *The quality of intellectual work in Chicago Public Schools.* Special Topics Report. Chicago, IL: Consortium on Chicago School Research.

Newmann, F. M., & Wehlage, G. G. (1993). Five standards of authentic instruction. *Educational Leadership, 22*(2), 4–13, 22.

Newton, E. S. (1977). Andragogy: Understanding the adult as learner. *Journal of Reading, 20,* 361–363.

Nicolsen, T., Pearson, P. D., & Dykstra, R. (1979). Effects of embedded anomalies and oral reading errors on children's understanding of stories. *Journal of Reading Behavior, 11,* 339–354.

Nist, S. L., & Simpson, M. L. (2000). College studying. In M. L. Kamil, P. B. Mosenthal, P. D. Pearson, & R. Barr (Eds.), *Handbook of reading research* (Vol. 3, pp. 645–666). Mahwah, NJ: Erlbaum.

North Central Regional Educational Laboratory (NCREL). (2000). *Critical issue: Monitoring the School Literacy Program* (by D. Johnson & M. Foertsch). Boston, MA: Tufts University.

North, S. (1987). *The making of knowledge in composition*. Portsmouth, NH: Heinemann.

Novak, C. (2001). Review of the Metropolitan Readiness Tests (6th ed.). In B. S. Blake & J. C. Impara (Eds.), *Fourteenth mental measurements yearbook*. Lincoln, NE: Buros Institute of Mental Measurements.

Novak, J. D. (1991). Clarify with concept maps: A tool for students and teachers alike. *The Science Teacher, 58*, 45–49.

Nurss, J. R., & McGauvran, M. E. (1976/1986). *Metropolitan readiness tests (MRT)*. San Antonio, TX: The Psychological Corporation.

Nurss, J. R., & McGauvran, M. E. (1995). *Metropolitan readiness tests* (6th ed.). San Antonio, TX: The Psychological Corporation.

Nystrand, M. (1990). High school English students in low-achieving classes: What helps? *Newsletter: National Center for Effective Secondary Schools, 5*, 7–8, 11. Madison: Wisconsin Center for Education Research, School of Education, University of Wisconsin–Madison.

Nystrand, M. (2006). Research on the role of classroom discourse as it affects reading comprehension. *Research in the Teaching of English, 40*, 392–412.

Oakhill, J., Hartt, J., & Samols, D. (2006). *Reading and Writing, 18*, 657–686.

O'Connor, R. E., Jenkins, J., & Slocum, T. A. (1995). Transfer among phonological tasks in kindergarten: Essential instructional content. *Journal of Educational Psychology, 87*, 202–217.

Oczkus, L. (2003). *Reciprocal teaching at work*. Newark, DE: International Reading Association.

O'Donnell, A., Dansereau, D., & Hall, R. H. (2002). Knowledge maps as scaffolds for cognitive processing. *Educational Psychology Review, 14*, 71–86.

O'Flahavan, J. F., & Tierney, R. J. (1991). Reading, writing, and critical thinking. In L. Idol & B. F. Jones (Eds.), *Educational values and cognitive instruction: Implications for reform* (pp. 41–64). Hillsdale, NJ: Erlbaum.

Ogle, D. M. (1986). K-W-L: A teaching model that develops active reading of expository text. *The Reading Teacher, 39*, 564–570.

Ogle, D. M. (1989). The know, want to know, learn strategy. In K. D. Muth (Ed.), *Children's comprehension of text: Research into practice* (pp. 205–223). Newark, DE: International Reading Association.

Okagaki, L., & Sternberg, R. J. (1991). Cultural and parental influences on cognitive development. In L. Okagaki & R. J. Sternberg (Eds.), *Directors of development: Influences on the development of children's thinking* (pp. 101–120). Hillsdale, NJ: Erlbaum.

Oken-Wright, P. (1998). Transition to writing: Drawing as a scaffold for emergent writers. *Young Children, 53*, 76–81.

Ollila, L. O., & Mayfield, M.1. (1992). Home and school together: Helping beginning readers succeed. In J. Samuels & A. E. Farstrup (Eds.), *What research has to say about reading instruction* (pp. 17–45). Newark, DE: International Reading Association.

Ollmann, H. (1996). Creating higher level thinking with reading response. *Journal of Adolescent and Adult Literacy, 39*(7), 576–581.

Olshavsky, J. E. (1978). Comparison profiles of good and poor readers across materials of increasing difficulty. In P. D. Pearson & J. Hansen (Eds.), *Reading: Disciplined inquiry in process and practice* (27th Yearbook of The National Reading Conference, pp. 73–76). Washington, DC: National Reading Conference.

Olson, M. W. (1985). Text type and reader ability: The effects of paraphrase and text-based inference questions. *Journal of Reading Behavior, 17*, 199–214.

Olson, R. K., Wise, B., Connors, F., Rack, J., & Fulker, D. (1989). Specific deficits in component reading and language skills: Genetic and environmental influences. *Journal of Learning Disabilities, 22*, 339–348.

O'Malley, J. M., & Valdez-Pierce, L. V. (1996). *Authentic assessment for English language learners: Practical approaches for teachers*. White Plains, NY: Addison Wesley Longman.

Omanson, R. C., Beck, I. L., McKeown, M. G., & Perfetti, C. A. (1984). Comprehension of texts with unfamiliar versus recently taught words: An assessment of alternative models. *Journal of Educational Psychology, 76*, 1253–1268.

Onosko, J. J., & Newmann, F. M. (1994). Creating more thoughtful learning environments. In J. N. Mangieri & C. C. Block (Eds.), *Creating powerful thinking in teachers and students* (pp. 27–49). Fort Worth, TX: Harcourt Brace.

Opitz, M. (1998). *Flexible grouping in reading*. New York, NY: Scholastic Professional Books.

Orellana, M. F., & Hernandez, A. (1999). Talking the walk: Children reading urban environmental print. *The Reading Teacher, 52*, 612–619.

Osborn, J. H. (1984). The purposes, uses, and contents of workbooks and some guidelines for publishers. In R. C. Anderson, J. Osborn, & R. J. Tierney (Eds.), *Learning to read in American schools: Basal readers and content texts* (pp. 45–112). Hillsdale, NJ: Erlbaum.

Osborn, J. H. (1989). Summary: Improving basal reading programs. In P. Winograd, K. Wixson, & M. Y. Lipson (Eds.), *Improving basal reading instruction* (pp. 203–226). New York, NY: Teachers College Press.

Oster, L. (2001). Using the think-aloud for reading instruction. *The Reading Teacher, 55*, 64–69.

Otto, W., Wolf, A., & Eldridge, R. (1984). Managing instruction. In P. D. Pearson, R. Barr, M. Kamil, & P. Mosenthal (Eds.), *Handbook of reading research* (pp. 799–828). New York, NY: Longman.

Ovando, C., Collier, V., & Combs, V. (2006). *Bilingual and ESL classrooms: Teaching in multicultural contexts* (4th ed.). New York, NY: McGraw-Hill.

Ovando, C. J. (2005). Language diversity and education. In J. A. Banks & C. A. M. Banks (Eds.), *Multicultural education: Issues and perspectives* (5th ed., pp. 289–313). Hoboken, NJ: John Wiley and Sons.

Paas, F., Renkl, A., & Sweller, J. (2003). Cognitive load theory and instructional design: Recent developments. *Educational Psychologist, 38*(1), 1–4.

Page, W. D., & Pinnell, G. S. (1979). *Teaching reading comprehension: Theory and practice*. Urbana, IL: ERIC Clearinghouse on Reading and Communication Skills and the National Council of Teachers of English.

Palincsar, A. S. (1984). The quest for the meaning from expository text: A teacher-guided journey. In G. Duffy, L. Roehler, & J. Mason (Eds.), *Comprehension instruction: Perspectives and suggestions* (pp. 251–264). White Plains, NY: Longman.

Palincsar, A. S. (1986). The role of dialogue in providing scaffolded instruction. *Educational Psychologist, 21*, 73–98.

Palincsar, A. S. (2003). Collaborative approaches to comprehension instruction. In A. P. Sweet, & C. E. Snow, C. E. (Eds.), *Rethinking reading comprehension* (pp. 99–114). New York, NY: Guilford Press.

Palincsar, A. S., & Brown, A. L. (1984). Reciprocal teaching of comprehension-fostering and monitoring activities. *Cognition and Instruction, 1*, 117–175.

Palmatier, R. A. (1973). A notetaking system for learning. *Journal of Reading, 17*, 36–39.

Pan, B. A. (2005). Semantic development: Learning the meanings of words. In J. B. Gleason (Ed.), *The development of language* (6th ed., pp. 112–147). Boston, MA: Pearson.

Pappas, C. C. (1991). Fostering full access to Literacy by including information books. *Language Arts, 68*, 449–462.

Pappas, C. C., Kiefer, B. Z., & Levstik, L. S. (1999). *An integrated language perspective in the elementary school* (3rd ed.). New York, NY: Longman.

Pappas, C. C., & Pettegrew, B. S. (1998). The role of genre in the psychological guessing game of reading. *Language Arts, 75*(1), 36–44.

Paratore, J. R., & Indrisano, R. (1987). Intervention assessment of reading comprehension. *The Reading Teacher, 40*, 778–783.

Paratore, J. R., & Indrisano, R. (2003). Grouping for instruction in literacy. In J. Flood, D. Lapp, J. R. Squire, & J. M. Jensen (Eds.), *Handbook of research on teaching the English language arts* (2nd ed., pp. 566–572). Mahwah, NJ: Erlbaum.

Paris, S., & Carpenter, R. D. (2003). FAQs about IRIs. *The Reading Teacher, 56*, 578–580.

Paris, S. G. (1988). Models and metaphors of learning strategies. In C. Weinstein, E. T. Goetz, & P. A. Alexander (Eds.), *Learning and study strategies: Issues in assessment, instruction, and evaluation* (pp. 299–321). San Diego, CA: Academic Press.

Paris, S. G. (1991). Assessment and remediation of metacognitive aspects of children's reading comprehension. *Topics in Language Disorders, 12*, 32–50.

Paris, S. G., Cross, D. R., & Lipson, M. Y. (1984). Informed strategies for learning: A program to improve children's reading awareness and comprehension. *Journal of Educational Psychology, 76*, 1239–1252.

Paris, S. G., & Jacobs, J. (1984). The benefits of informed instruction for children's reading awareness and comprehension. *Journal of Educational Psychology, 76* 1239–1252.

Paris, S. G., Lipson, M. Y., & Wixson, K. K. (1983). Becoming a strategic reader. *Contemporary Educational Psychology, 8*, 293–316.

Paris, S. G., & Myers, M. (1981). Comprehension monitoring in good and poor readers. *Journal of Reading Behavior, 13*, 5–22.

Paris, S. G., Newman, R. S., & McVey, K. A. (1982). Learning the functional significance of mnemonic actions: A microgenetic study of strategy acquisition. *Journal of Experimental Child Psychology, 34*, 490–509.

Paris, S. G., Olson, G., & Stevenson, H. (Eds.). (1983). *Learning and motivation in the classroom.* Hillsdale, NJ: Erlbaum.

Paris, S. G., & Paris, A. H. (2001). Classroom applications for research on self-regulated learning. *Educational Psychologist, 36*, 89–101.

Paris, S. G., & Paris, A. H. (2003). Assessing narrative comprehension in young children. *Reading Research Quarterly, 38*, 36–76.

Paris, S. G., Wasik, B. A., & Turner, J. C. (1991). The development of strategic readers. In R. Barr, M. Kamil, P. Mosenthal, & P. D. Pearson (Eds.), *Handbook of reading research* (Vol. 2, pp. 609–640). New York, NY: Longman.

Paris, S. G., Wasik, B. A., & Van der Westhuizen, G. (1988). Metacognition: A review on research on metacognition and reading. In J. E. Readence & R. S. Baldwin (Eds.), *Dialogues in literacy research* (37th Yearbook of the National Reading Conference, pp. 143–181). Chicago, IL: NRC.

Paris, S. G., & Wixson, K. K. (1987). The development of literacy: Access, acquisition, and instruction. In D. D. Bloome (Ed.), *Literacy and schooling* (pp. 35–54). Norwood, NJ: Ablex.

Paris, S. G., Wixson, K. K., & Palincsar, A. S. (1986). Instructional approaches to reading comprehension. In E. Rothkopf (Ed.), *Review of research in education* (pp. 91–128). Washington, DC: American Educational Research Association.

Parr, J. M., & Maguiness, C. (2005). Removing the silent from SSR: Voluntary reading as social practice. *Journal of Adolescent and Adult Literacy, 49*, 98–107.

Parsons, L. (2001). *Response journals revisited.* Portland, ME: Stenhouse.

Patsula, P. J. (2002). Practical guidelines for selecting media: An international perspective. *The Usable Word Monitor*, February 1. Retrieved from http://patsula.com/usefo/usableword/report20020201_mediaselection_criteria.shtml

Patton, J. M. (1998). The disproportionate representation of African Americans in special education: Looking behind the curtain for understanding and solutions. *Journal of Special Education, 32*, 25–31.

Pauk, W. (1974). *How to study in college.* Boston, MA: Houghton Mifflin.

Payne, A. C., Whitehurst, G. J., & Angell, A. (1994). The role of the home literacy environment in the development of language ability in preschool children from low-income families. *Early Childhood Research Quarterly, 9*, 427–440.

Pea, R. D. (1993). Learning scientific concepts through material and social activities: Conversational analysis meets conceptual change. *Educational Psychologist, 28*(3), pp. 265–277.

Pearson, P. D. (1993). Standards for the English language arts: A policy perspective. *Journal of Reading Behavior, 25*, 457–475.

Pearson, P. D., & Fielding, L. (1991). Comprehension instruction. In R. Barr, M. Kamil, P. Mosenthal, & P. D. Pearson (Eds.), *Handbook of reading research* (Vol. 2, pp. 815–860). New York, NY: Longman.

Pearson, P. D., & Gallagher, M. (1983). The instruction of reading comprehension. *Contemporary Educational Psychology, 8*, 317–344.

Pearson, P. D., Hansen, J., & Gordon, C. (1979). The effect of background knowledge on young children's comprehension of explicit and implicit information. *Journal of Reading Behavior, 11*, 201–209.

Pearson, P. D., & Johnson, D. (1978). *Teaching reading comprehension.* New York, NY: Holt, Rinehart & Winston.

Pellegrini, A. D. (2001). Some theoretical and methodological considerations in studying literacy in social context. In S. Neuman & D. Dickinson (Eds.), *Handbook of early literacy research* (pp. 54–65). New York, NY: Guilford Press.

Pellegrini, A. D., Perlmutter, J., Galda, L., & Brody, G. (1990). Joint reading between black Head Start children and their mothers. *Child Development, 61*, 443–453.

Peña, E. D., Gillam, R. B., Malek, M., Ruiz-Felter, R., Resendiz, M., Fiestas, C., & Sabel, T. (2006). Dynamic assessment of school-age children's narrative ability: An experimental investigation of classification accuracy. *Journal of Speech, Language and Hearing Research, 49*, 1037–1057.

Perfetti, C. A., Beck, I., Bell, L., & Hughes, C. (1987). Phonemic knowledge and learning to read are reciprocal: A longitudinal study of first grade children. *Merrill-Palmer Quarterly, 33*, 283–319.

Perfetti, C. A., & Hogaboam, T. (1975). The relationship between single word decoding and reading comprehension skill. *Journal of Educational Psychology, 67*, 461–469.

Perlman, C. (1998). Review of the Test of Reading Comprehension, Third edition. In J. C. Impara & B. S. Plake (Eds.), *The thirteenth mental measurements yearbook.* Lincoln, NE: Buros Institute of Mental Measurements.

Persky, R., Daane, C., & Jin, Y. (2003). *The nation's report card: Writing 2002.* Washington, DC: U.S. Department of Education, National Center for Education Statistics.

Peters, C. W., & Wixson, K. K. (2003). Unifying the domain of K–12 English language arts curriculum. In D. Lapp. & J. Flood (Eds.), *Handbook of English language arts* (2nd ed., pp. 573–5589). Mahwah, NJ: Erlbaum.

Peterson, C., Jesso, B., & McCabe, A. (1999). Encouraging narratives in preschoolers: An intervention study. *Journal of Child Language, 26*, 49–67.

Peterson, C., Maier, S. F., & Seligman, M. E. P. (1993). *Learned helplessness*. Oxford, UK: Oxford University Press.

Peterson, C. L., Caverly, D. C., Nicholson, S. A., O'Neil, S., & Cusenbary, S. (2000). Strategies: Dictated stories/Language Experience Approach (LEA). In *Building reading proficiency at the secondary school level: A guide to resources* (pp. 83–85). Austin TX: Southwest Educational Development Laboratory. Retrieved April 20, 2006, from www.sedl.org/pubs/reading16/buidingreading.pdf

Peterson, J., Greenlaw, M. J., & Tierney, R. J. (1978). Assessing instructional placement with an IRI: The effectiveness of comprehension questions. *Journal of Educational Research, 17*, 247–250.

Peyton, J. K., & Staton, J. (1993). *Dialogue journals in the multilingual classroom: Building language fluency and writing skills through written interaction.* Norwood, NJ: Ablex.

Pflaum, S., & Pascarella, E. (1982). Attribution retraining for learning disabled children: Some thoughts on what the evidence suggests for practice. *Learning Disabilities Quarterly, 5*, 422–426.

Pflaum, S. W., & Pascarella, E. T. (1980). Interactive effects of prior reading achievement and training in context on the reading of learning-disabled children. *Reading Research Quarterly, 16*, 138–158.

Philips, S. U. (1983). *The invisible culture: Communication in classroom and community on the Warm Springs Indian Reservation.* New York, NY: Longman.

Philips, S. U. (reissued 1993). *The invisible culture: Communication in classroom and community on the Warm Springs Indian Reservation.* Prospect Heights, IL: Waveland Press.

Phillips, B. M., & Torgesen, J. K. (2006). Phonemic awareness and reading beyond the growth of initial reading accuracy. In D. K. Dickinson & S. B. Neuman (Eds.), *Handbook of early literacy research* (Vol. 2, pp. 101–112). New York, NY: Guilford Press.

Phonological awareness literacy screening (PALS). (2003). Charlottesville, VA: University of Virginia.

Piaget, J. (1960). *Language and thought of the child.* London, UK: Routledge & Kegan Paul.

Pianta, R. C., (2003). *Standardized classroom observations from pre-K to 3rd grade: A mechanism for improving classroom quality and practices, consistency of P-3 experiences, and child outcomes.* New York, NY: Foundation for Child Development. Retrieved July 27, 2006, from http://www.fcd-us.org/usr_doc/Standardized-ClassroomObservations.pdf

Pikulski, J. (1998). Preventing reading problems: Factors common to successful early intervention program. Available at http://www.Eduplace.com/rdg/res/prevent.html

Pikulski, J. J. (1994). Preventing reading failure: A review of five effective programs. *The Reading Teacher, 48*, 30–39.

Pikulski, J. J., (1999). *Emergent literacy survey.* Boston, MA: Houghton Mifflin.

Pikulski, J. J., & Chard, D. J. (2005). Fluency: Bridge between decoding and reading comprehension. *The Reading Teacher, 58*, 510.

Pikulski, J. J., & Shanahan, T. (1982). Informal reading inventories: A critical analysis. In J. J. Pikulski & T. Shanahan (Eds.), *Approaches to the informal evaluation of reading* (pp. 94–116). Newark, DE: International Reading Association.

Pinnell, G. S. (1985). Helping teachers help children at risk: Insights from the Reading Recovery Program. *Peabody Journal of Education, 62*, 70–85.

Pinnell, G. S. (1987). Helping teachers see how readers read: Staff development through observation. *Theory into Practice, 26*, 51–58.

Pinnell, G. S. (1991). Interactive assessment: Teachers and children as learners. In J. A. Roderick (Ed.), *Context-responsive approaches to assessing children's language* (pp. 79–96). Urbana, IL: National Conference on Research in English.

Pinnell, G. S., Lyons, C. A., DeFord, D. E., Bryck, A., & Selzer, M. (1994). Comparing instructional models for the literacy education of high-risk first graders. *Reading Research Quarterly, 29*, 8–39.

Pinnell, G. S., Pikulski, J. J., Wixson, K. K., Campbell, J. R., Gough, P. B., & Beatty, A. S. (1995). *Listening to children read aloud.* Washington, DC: U.S. Department of Education, National Center for Education Statistics.

Pintrich, P., Smith, D., & McKeachie, W. (1989, December) *Motivated strategies for learning questionnaire.* Ann Arbor, MI: National Center for Research to Improve Post Secondary Teaching and Learning.

Pintrich, P. R., Smith, D. A., Garcia, T. & McKeachie, W. J. (1991). *A manual for the use of the Motivated Strategies for Learning Questionnaire (MSLQ).* (Tech. Rep. No. 91-B-004). The Regents of The University of Michigan.

Pitcher, S. M., Albright, L. K., DeLaney, C. J., Walker, N. T., Seunarinesingh, K., Mogge, S., . . . Dunson, P. J. (2007). Assessing adolescents' motivation to read. *Journal of Adolescent and Adult Literacy, 50*, 378–399.

Plass, J. L., Chun, D. M., Mayer, R. E., & Leutner, D. (1998). Supporting visual and verbal learning preferences in a second-language multimedia learning environment. *Journal of Educational Psychology, 90*, 25–36.

Poehner, M. E. (2008). *Dynamic assessment: A Vygotskian approach to understanding and promoting second language development.* Berlin, DE: Springer Publishing.Palincsar, A. S., & Herrenkohl, L. R. (2002). Designing collaborative learning contexts. *Theory into Practice, 41*, 26-32.

Poncy, B. C., Skinner, C., & Axtell, P. K. (2005). An investigation of the reliability and standard error of measurement of words read correctly per minute using curriculum-based measurement. *Journal of Psychoeducational Assessment, 23*, 326–338.

Popham, W. J. (1978). *Criterion-referenced measurement.* Englewood Cliffs, NJ: Prentice Hall.

Popham, W. J. (1993). Circumventing the high costs of authentic assessment. *Phi Delta Kappan, February*, 470–473.

Popham, W. J. (2001). *The truth about testing: An educator's call to action.* Alexandria, VA: Association for Supervision and Curriculum Development.

Popham, W. J. (2002). *Classroom assessment: What teachers need to know.* Boston, Allyn & Bacon.

Popham, W. J. (2004). *Classroom assessment: What teachers need to know* (4th ed.). Boston, MA: Allyn and Bacon.

Poplin, M. (1984). Summary rationalizations, apologies and farewell: What we don't know about the learning disabled. *Learning Disabilities Quarterly, 7*, 130–134.

Porter, J. (1974). Research report. *Elementary English, 51*, 144–151.

Powell, W. R. (n.d.). *The finger count system for monitoring reading behavior.* Unpublished paper, University of Florida, Gainesville.

Powell, W. R. (1980). Measuring reading performance informally. *Journal of Children and Youth, 1*, 23–31.

Powell, W. R., & Dunkeld, C. G. (1971). The validity of IRI reading levels. *Elementary English, 48*, 637–642.

Powell-Smith, K. A., & Shinn, M. R. (2004). *Administration and scoring of written expression curriculum-based measurement (AIMSweb WE-CBM) for use in general outcome measurement.* Eden Prairie, MN: Edformation, Inc. *AIMSweb Training Workbook: Administration and scoring of written expression curriculum-based measurement* (WE-CBM) for use in general outcome measurement. http://www.aimsweb.com/uploads/pdfs/AdminAndScoringWe-CBM.pdf. Eden Prairie, MN: Edformation Inc.

Prensky, M. (2001). *Digital game-based learning.* New York, NY: McGraw-Hill.

President's Commission on Excellence in Special Education. (2002). *A new era: Revitalizing special education for children and their families.* Washington DC: U.S. Department of Education.

Pressley, M. (1995). Reading comprehension strategies. In M. Pressley & V. E. Woloshyn (Eds.), *Cognitive strategy instruction that really improves children's academic performance.* Cambridge, MA: Brookline Books.

Pressley, M. (2000). What should comprehension instruction be the instruction of? In M. L. Kamil, P. B. Mosenthal, P. D. Pearson, & R. Barr (Eds.), *Handbook of reading research* (Vol. 3, pp. 545–561). Mahwah, NJ: Erlbaum.

Pressley, M. (2006). *What the future of reading research could be.* Paper presented at the International Reading Association's Reading Research Conference. Chicago, IL., April 29, 2006.

Pressley, M., & Afflerbach, P. (1995). *Verbal protocols of reading: The nature of constructively responsive reading.* Hillsdale, NJ: Erlbaum.

Pressley, M., El-Dinary, P. B., Gaskins, I., Schuder, T., Bergman, J. L., Almasi, J., & Brown, R. (1992). Beyond direct explanation: Transactional instruction of reading comprehension strategies. *Elementary School Journal, 92,* 513–555.

Pressley, M., Gaskins, I. W., & Fingeret, L. (2006). Instruction and development of reading fluency in struggling readers. In Samuels, S. J. (Ed.), *What research has to say about fluency instruction* (pp. 47–69). Newark, DE: International Reading Association.

Pressley, M., & Ghatala, E. S. (1990). Self-regulated learning: Monitoring learning from text. *Educational Psychologist, 25,* 19–33.

Pressley, M., Hilden, K., & Shankland, R. (2005). An evaluation of end-grade-3 Dynamic Indicators of Basic Early Literacy Skills (DIBELS): Speed reading without comprehension, predicting little. Retrieved September, 28, 2006, from http://www.msularc.org

Pressley, M., Wharton-McDonald, R., Allington, R., Block C. C., Morrow, L., Tracey, D., . . . Woo, D. (2001). A study of effective first-grade literacy instruction. *Scientific Studies of Reading, 5,* 35–58.

Pressley, M., Wharton-McDonald, R., Hampson, J. M., & Echevarria, M. (1998). The nature of literacy instruction in ten grade-4/5 classrooms in upstate New York. *Scientific Studies of Reading, 2,* 159–194.

Prevat, F., Petscher, Y., Proctor, B. E., Hurst, A., & Adams, A. (2006). The revised learning and study strategies inventory. *Educational and Psychological Measurement, 66,* 448–458.

Preverly, S. T., Brobst, K. E., & Morris, K. S. (2002). The contribution of reading comprehension ability and meta-cognitive control to the development of studying in adolescence. *Journal of Research in Reading, 25,* 203–216.

Pritchard, R. J. (1993) Developing Writing prompts for reading response and analysis. *English Journal, 82*(3), 24–32.

Proctor, C. P., Dalton, B. & Grisham, D. L. (2007). Scaffolding English language learners and struggling readers in a universal literacy environment with embedded strategy instruction and vocabulary support. *Journal of Literacy Research, 39,* 71–93.

Puma, M. J., Karweit, N., Price, C., Ricciuiti, A., Thompson, W., & Vaden-Kiernan, M. (1997). *Prospects: Final report on student outcomes.* Washington, DC: U.S. Department of Education, Planning and Evaluation Services.

Purcell-Gates, V. (1996). Stories, coupons, and the "TV Guide": Relationships between home literacy experiences and emergent literacy knowledge. *Reading Research Quarterly, 31,* 406–428.

Purcell-Gates, V., Duke, N., & Martineau, J. A. (2001). Learning to read and write genre-specific text: Roles of authentic experience and explicit teaching. *Reading Research Quarterly, 42*(1), 8–45.

Rakes, T. A., & Smith, L. (1986). Assessing reading skills in the content areas. In E. K. Dishner, T. W. Bean, J. E. Readence, & D. W. Moore (Eds.), *Reading in the content areas: Improving classroom instruction* (2nd ed., pp. 145–159). Dubuque, IA: Kendall/Hunt.

Rakes, T. A., & Smith, L. (2001). Assessing reading skills in the content area. In J. Readance, T. Bean, & R. Baldwin (Eds.), *Content area literacy* (7th ed., pp. 399–413). Dubuque, IA: Kendall/Hunt.

Ramirez, R. (2005). *A case study inquiry into the relative impact of balanced reading instruction on Hispanic students in a highly culturally diverse elementary school* (Unpublished doctoral dissertation). Louisiana State University, Baton Rouge.

RAND Reading Study Group. (2002). *Reading for understanding: Toward an R&D program for reading comprehension.* Santa Monica, CA: RAND.

Ranker, J. (2010). The interactive potential of multiple media: A new look at inquiry projects. *Voices from the Middle, 17*(3), 36–42.

Raphael, T., Highfield, K., & Au, K. (2006) *QAR now: A powerful and practical framework that develops comprehension and higher-level thinking in all students.* New York, NY: Scholastic.

Raphael, T. E. (1982). Question-answering strategies for children. *The Reading Teacher, 36,* 186–190.

Raphael, T. E. (1986). Teaching question-answer relationships, revisited. *The Reading Teacher, 39,* 516–522.

Raphael, T. E. (1998). Balanced instruction and the role of classroom discourse. In J. Osborn & F. Lehr (Eds.), *Literacy for all* (pp. 134–169). New York, NY: Guilford Press.

Raphael, T. E., & Au, K. H. (2005). QAR: Enhancing comprehension and test taking across grades and content areas. *The Reading Teacher, 59,* 206–221.

Raphael, T. E., & Englert, C. S. (1989). Integrating writing and reading instruction. In P. Winograd, K. Wixson, & M. Lipson (Eds.), *Improving basal reading instruction* (pp. 231–255). New York, NY: Teachers College Press.

Raphael, T. E., & Englert, C. S. (1990). Writing and reading: Partners in constructing meaning. *The Reading Teacher, 43,* 388–400.

Raphael, T. E., Englert, C. S., & Kirschner, B. W. (1989). Acquisition of expository writing skills. In J. M. Mason (Ed.), *Reading and writing connections* (pp. 261–290). Boston, MA: Allyn & Bacon.

Raphael, T. E., & Hiebert, E. H. (1996). *Creating an integrated approach to literacy instruction.* Ft. Worth: Harcourt Brace.

Raphael, T. E., Highfield, K., & Au, K. H. (2006). *QAR now: Question answer relationships.* New York, NY: Scholastic.

Raphael, T. E., Kirschner, B. W., & Englert, C. S. (1988). Expository writing program: Making connections between reading and writing. *The Reading Teacher, 41,* 790–795.

Raphael, T. E., Winograd, P., & Pearson, P. D. (1980). Strategies children use in answering questions. In M. L. Kamil & A. J. Moe (Eds.), *Perspectives in reading research and instruction* (29th Yearbook of The National Reading Conference, pp. 56–63). Washington, DC: National Reading Conference.

Rasinski, T., Blachowicz, C., & Lems, K. (2006). *Fluency instruction: Research-based best practices.* NY: The Guilford Press.

Rasinski, T. V. (1986). Repeated readings—naturally. *The Reading Teacher, 39,* 244–245.

Rasinski, T. V. (1999). Exploring a method for estimating independent, instructional, and frustrational reading rates. *Reading Psychology: An International Journal, 20,* 61–69.

Rasinski, T. V. (2003). *The fluent reader: Oral reading strategies for building word recognition, fluency, and comprehension*. New York, NY: Scholastic.

Rasinski, T. V. (2004). *Assessing reading fluency*. Honolulu, HA: Pacific Resources for Education and Learning. Available at http://www.prel.org/products/re_/assessing-fluency.pdf

Rasinski, T. V. (2006). A brief history of reading fluency. In S. J. Samuels & A. E. Farstrup (Eds.), *What research has to say about fluency instruction* (pp. 4–23). Newark, DE: International Reading Association.

Rasinski, T. V., & Padak, N. (2005). *3-minute reading assessments, grades 1–4*. New York, NY: Scholastic.

Rasinski, T. V., Padak, N., & Davis-Swing, J. (2005). *3-minute reading assessments, grades 5–8*. New York, NY: Scholastic.

Rasinski, T. V., & Padak, N. D. (1998). How elementary students referred for compensatory reading instruction perform on school-based measures of word recognition, fluency, and comprehension. *Reading Psychology: An International Quarterly, 19*, 185–216.

Rathvon, N. (2004). *Early reading assessment: A handbook for practitioners*. New York, NY: Guilford.

Ray, K. W. (1999). *Wondrous words*. Urbana, IL: National Council of Teachers of English.

Ray, K. W. (2004). Why Cauley writes well: A close look at what a difference good teaching can make. *Language Arts, 82*, 100–109.

Ray, K. W., & Laminack, L. L. (2001). *The writing workshop: Working through the hard parts (and they're all hard parts)*. Washington, DC: NCTE .

Read, C. (1971). Preschool children's knowledge of English phonology. *Harvard Educational Review, 41*, 1–34.

Read, C. (1975). *Children's categorization of speech sounds in English*. Urbana, IL: National Council of Teachers of English.

Read, C. (1986). *Children's creative spelling*. London, UK: Routledge & Kegan Paul.

Read, J. (2000). *Assessing vocabulary*. Cambridge, UK: Cambridge University Press.

Readence, J. E., Bean, T. W., & Baldwin, R. S. (1985). *Content area reading: An integrated approach* (2nd ed.). Dubuque, IA: Kendall/Hunt.

Reese, E., & Cox, A. (1999). Quality of adult book reading affects children's emergent literacy. *Developmental Psychology, 35*, 20–28.

Reeves, D. B. (2006). *Guidelines for data walls or "The science fair for grownups." Center for Performance Assessment*. Retrieved October 13, 2010, from www.sde.ct.gov/sde/lib/sde/pdf/curriculum/cali/4fidtguidelinesdatawalls.pdf

Reid, D. K., Hresko, W. P., & Hammill, D. D. (2002). *The test of early reading ability—3 (TERA-3)*. Austin, TX: Pro-Ed.

Reid, J. F. (1966). Learning to think about reading. *Educational Research, 9*, 56–62.

Reid, L. (1997). Exploring the ways that dialogue journaling affects how and why students write: An action research project. *Teaching and Change, 5*(1), 50–57.

Resnick, L. (1994). Performance puzzles: Issues in measuring capabilities and certifying accomplishments. *American Journal of Education, 102*, 511–526.

Resnick, L. B., & Resnick, D. L. (1992). Assessing the thinking curriculum: New tools for educational reform. In B. R. Gifford & M. C. O'Connor (Eds.), *Future assessments: Changing views of aptitude, achievement, and instruction* (pp. 37–75). Boston, MA: Kluwer.

Reutzel, D. R. (1999). Organizing literacy instruction: Effective grouping strategies and organizational plans. In L. B. Gambrell, L. M. Morrow, S. B. Neuman, & M. Pressley (Eds.), *Best practices in literacy instruction*. New York, NY: Guilford Press.

Rey, H. A. (1941). *Curious George. Boston*. Boston, MA: Houghton Mifflin.

Reyes, M. L. (2001). Unleashing possibilities: Biliteracy in the primary grades. In M. L. Reyes & J. Halcón (Eds.), *The best for our children: Critical perspectives on literacy for Latino students* (pp. 96–121). New York, NY: Teachers College Press.

Rhode Island Technical Assistance Project (RITAP). *About interventions*. Retrieved May 10, 2009, from http://www.ritap.org/rti/about/an-intervention-system.php

Rhodes, L. K., & Shanklin, N. (1990). Miscue analysis in the classroom. *The Reading Teacher, 44*, 252–254.

Richek, M. A., Caldwell, J. S., Jennings, J. H., & Lerner, M. W. (2002). *Reading problems: Assessment and teaching strategies*. Boston, MA: Allyn & Bacon.

Ringler, L. H., & Weber, C. K. (1984). *A language-thinking approach to reading*. San Diego, CA: Harcourt Brace Jovanovich.

Roberts, P. (1962). *English sentences*. New York, NY: Harcourt Brace Jovanovich.

Robinson, F. (1946). *Effective study*. New York, NY: Harper Brothers.

Robinson, V. M. K. (1998). Methodology and the research—Practice gap. *Educational Researcher, 27*, 17–26.

Rock, E., Fessler, M., & Church, R. (1997). The concomitance of learning disabilities and emotional/behavioral disorders: A conceptual model. *Journal of Learning Disabilities, 30*, 245–263.

Rodgers, A., & Rodgers, E. M. (2004). *Scaffolding literacy instruction*. Portsmouth, NH: Heinemann.

Rodgers, E. M. (2004/05). Interactions that scaffold reading performance. *Journal of Literacy Research, 36*, 501–532.

Rodino, A. M., Gimbert, C., Perez, C., Craddock-Willis, K., & McCabe, A. (1991, October). *Getting your point across: Contrastive sequencing in low-income African American and Latino children's personal narratives*. Paper presented at the 16th annual Boston University Conference on Language Development, Boston, MA.

Roehler, L., & Duffy, G. (1984). Direct explanation of comprehension processes. In G. G. Duffy, L. R. Roehler, & J. Mason (Eds.), *Comprehension instruction: Perspectives and suggestions* (pp. 265–280). New York, NY: Longman.

Rogers, D. B. (1984). Assessing study skills. *Journal of Reading, 27*, 346–354.

Rogers, V. R., & Stevenson, C. (1988). How do we know what kids are learning in school? *Educational Leadership, 45*(5), 68–75.

Roller, C. (1996). *Variability not disability: Struggling readers in a workshop classroom*. Newark, DE: International Reading Association.

Roller, C. (2002a). Accommodating the variability in reading instruction. *Reading & Writing Quarterly, 18*, 17–18.

Roller, C. (2002b). *Comprehensive reading instruction across the grade levels*. Newark, DE: International Reading Association.

Rose, D., & Dalton, B. (2009). Learning to read in the digital age. *Mind, Brain, and Education, 3*(2), 74–83.

Rose, D. H., & Meyer, A. (2002). *Teaching every student in the digital age: Universal design for learning*. Alexandria, VA: Association for Supervision and Curriculum Development.

Rosenbaum, J. E. (1980). Social implications of educational grouping. In D. C. Berliner (Ed.), *Review of research in education* (Vol. 8, pp. 361–401). Washington, DC: American Educational Research Association.

Rosenblatt, L. (1978). *The reader, the text, and the poem: The transactional theory of literary work*. Carbondale: Southern Illinois University Press.

Rosenblatt, L. (1982). The literary transaction: Evocation and response. *Theory into Practice, 21*, 268–277.

Rosenhouse, J., Feitelson, D., Kita, B., & Goldstein, Z. (1997). Interactive reading aloud to Israeli first graders: Its contribution to literacy development. *Reading Research Quarterly, 32*, 168–183.

Rosenshine, B. (1983). Teaching functions in instructional programs. *Elementary School Journal, 83*, 335–351.

Rosenshine, B. V., & Stevens, R. (1984). Classroom instruction in reading. In P. D. Pearson, R. Barr, M. Kamil, & P. Mosenthal (Eds.), *Handbook of reading research* (pp. 745–798). New York, NY: Longman.

Rosenthal, R., & Jacobson, L. (1968). *Pygmalion in the classroom: Teacher expectation and pupils' intellectual development.* New York, NY: Holt, Rinehart & Winston.

Roser, N. (2007). Assessing literary understandings through book talk. In J. R. Paratore & R. L. McCormack (Eds.), *Classroom literacy assessment: Making sense of what students know and do.* New York, NY: Guilford Press.

Roser, N., Hoffman, J., & Carr, N.J. (2003). See it change: A primer on the basal reader. In L. M. Morrow, L. B. Gambrell, & M. Pressley (Eds.), *Best practices in literacy instruction.* New York, NY: Guilford Press.

Ross, J. A. (2004). Effects of running records assessment on early literacy achievement. *Journal of Educational Research, 97*(4), 186–195.

Ross, J. A. (2006). The reliability, validity, and utility of self-assessment. *Practical Assessment Research & Evaluation, 11*(10), 1–13.

Roswell, F. G., Chall J. S., Curtis, M. E., & Kearns, G. (2006). *Diagnostic assessment of reading (DAR-2)* (2nd ed.). Itasca, IL: Riverside.

Roth, F. P. (2004/2006). Word recognition assessment frameworks. In C. A. Stone, E. R. Silliman, B. J. Ehren, & K. Apel (Eds.), *Handbook of language & literacy* (pp. 461–480). NY: Guildford Press.

Roth, F. P., Speece, D. L., & Cooper, D. H. (2002). A longitudinal analysis of the connection between oral language and reading. *Journal of Educational Research, 95*, 259–272.a longitudinal analysis of the connection between oral language and early reading. *Journal of Educational Research, 95*, 259-272.

Rowe, M. B. (1974). Wait time and rewards as instructional variables, their influence on language, logic, and fate control: Part one—Wait time. *Journal of Research in Science Teaching, 11*, 81–94.

Ruan, J. (2004). Bilingual Chinese/English first-graders developing metacognition about writing. *Literacy, 38*, 106–112.

Rubin, D. (2000). Teaching elementary language arts: A balanced approach (6th ed.). Boston, MA: Allyn & Bacon.

Ruddell, M. R. (1993). Teaching content reading and writing. Boston, MA: Allyn & Bacon.

Ruddell, R. B. (1965). Effect of the similarity of oral and written language structure on reading comprehension. *Elementary English, 42*, 403–410.

Rudner, L. M. (1994). Questions to ask when evaluating tests. *Practical Assessment, Research & Evaluation, 4*(2). Retrieved March 18, 2007, from http://PAREonline.net/getvn.asp?v=4&n=2

Rueda, R., & Garcia, E. (1996). Teachers' perspectives on literacy assessment and instruction with language-minority students: A comparative study. *Elementary School Journal, 96*, 311–332.

Rueda, R., & Kim, S. (2001). Cultural and linguistic diversity as a theoretical framework for understanding multicultural learners with mild disabilities. In C. A. Utley & F. E. Obiaker (Eds.), *Special education, multicultural education, and school reform: Components of quality education for learners with mild disabilities* (pp. 74–89). Springfield, IL: Charles C. Thomas Pub.

Rumelhart, D. (1977). Toward an interactive model of reading. In S. Dornic (Ed.), *Attention and performance VI* (pp. 573–603). Hillsdale, NJ: Erlbaum.

Rupley, W. H. (1976). Effective reading program. *The Reading Teacher, 29*, 616–623.

Russell, D. (1991). *Writing in the academic disciplines, 1870–1990: A curricular history.* Carbondale: Southern Illinois University Press.

Ryder, R. J., & Graves, M. F. (1980). Secondary students' internalization of letter-sound correspondence. *Journal of Educational Research, 73*, 172–178.

Saddler, B., & Graham, S. (2007). The relationship between writing knowledge and writing performance among more and less skilled writers. *Reading & Writing Quarterly, 23*, 231–247.

Sadowski, M. (1980). Ten years of uninterrupted sustained silent reading. *Reading Improvement, 17*, 153–156.

Saenz, L. M., & Fuchs, L. S. (2002). Examining the reading difficulty of secondary students with learning disabilities: Expository versus narrative text. *Remedial and Special Education, 23*, 31–41.

Salinger, T. (1988). *Language arts and literacy for young children.* Columbus, OH: Charles E. Merrill.

Salvia, J., & Ysseldyke, J. E. (2001). *Assessment* (8th ed.). Boston, MA: Houghton Mifflin.

Salvia, J., Ysseldyke, J. E., & Bolt, S. (2010). *Assessment: In special and inclusive education* (11th ed.). Florence, KY: Wadsworth.

Samuels, S. J. (1979). The method of repeated readings. *The Reading Teacher, 32*, 403–408.

Samuels, S. J. (1988). Decoding and automaticity: Helping poor readers become automatic at word recognition. *The Reading Teacher, 41*, 755–760.

Sankofa, B. M., Hurley, E. A., Allen, B. A., & Boykin, A. W. (2005). Cultural expression and black students' attitudes toward high achievers. *Journal of Psychology, 139*, 247–259.

Santa, C., & Hoien, T. (1999). An assessment of Early Steps: A program for early intervention of reading problems. *Reading Research Quarterly, 34*, 54–79.

Sarason, S. B., & Doris, J. (1979). *Educational handicap, public policy, and social history.* New York, NY: Free Press.

Scanlon, D. M. (2011). Response to intervention as an assessment approach. In A. McGill Franzen & R. L. Allington (Eds.), *Handbook of reading disability research* (pp. 139–148). New York, NY: Routledge.

Scanlon, D. M., & Anderson, K. L. (2010). Using the interactive strategies approach to preventing reading difficulties in an RTI context. In M. Y. Lipson & K. K. Wixson (Eds.), *Successful approaches to RTI: Collaborative practices for improving K–12 literacy* (pp. 20–65). Newark, DE: International Reading Association.

Scanlon, D. M., Anderson, K. L., & Sweeney, J. M. (2010). *Early intervention for reading difficulties: The interactive strategies approach.* New York, NY: Guilford.

Scanlon, D. M., Gelzheiser, L. M., Vellutino, F. R., Schatschneider, C., & Sweeney, J. M. (2008). Reducing the incidence of early reading difficulties: Professional development for classroom teachers vs. direct interventions for children. *Learning and Individual Differences, 18*, 346–359.

Scanlon, D. M., Vellutino, F. R., Small, S. G., Fanuele, D. P. & Sweeney, J. M. (2005). Severe reading difficulties – Can they be prevented? A comparison of prevention and intervention approaches. *Exceptionality, 13*(4), 209–227.

Scarborough, H. S. (1998). Early identification of children at risk for reading disabilities: Phonological awareness and some other promising predictors. In B. K. Shapiro, P. J. Accardo, & A. J. Capute (Eds.), *Specific reading disability: A view of the spectrum* (pp. 77–121). Timomium, MD: York Press.

Scardamalia, M., Bereiter, C., & Goelman, H. (1982). The role of production factors in writing ability. In M. Nystrand (Ed.), *What writers know: The language process and structure of written discourse* (pp. 173–210). San Diego, CA: Academic Press.

Schell, L. M., & Hanna, G. S. (1981). Can informal reading inventories reveal strengths and weaknesses in comprehension subskills? *The Reading Teacher, 35,* 263–268.

Scheu, J. A., Tanner, D. K., & Au, K. H. (1989). Integrating seatwork with the basal lesson. In P. Winograd, K. K. Wixson, & M. Y. Lipson (Eds.), *Improving basal reading instruction* (pp. 58–73). New York, NY: Teachers College Press.

Schirmer, B. R., & Lockman, A. S. (2001). How do I find a book to read? Middle and high school students use a rubric for self-selecting material for independent reading. *Teaching Exceptional Children, 34*(1), 36–43.

Schlagal, R. (1995). Teaching disabled spellers. In R. Putnam (Ed.), *How to become a better reading teacher* (pp. 307–316). Englewood Cliffs, NJ: Merrill.

Schleppegrell, M. J. (2004). *The language of schooling: A functional linguistics perspective.* Mahwah, NJ: Erlbaum.

Schmar-Dobler, E. (2003). Reading on the Internet; The link between literacy and technology. *Journal of Adolescent and Adult Literacy,* 80–85.

Schmidt, W., Caul, J., Byers, J., & Buchman, M. (1984). Content of basal reading selections: Implications for comprehension instruction. In G. Duffy, L. R. Roehler, & J. Mason (Eds.), *Comprehension instruction* (pp. 144–162). New York, NY: Longman.

Schumaker, J. B., Deshler, D. D., Woodruff, S., Hock, M. F., Bulgren, J. A., & Lenz, B. K. (2006). Reading strategy interventions: Can literacy outcomes be enhanced for at-risk adolescents? *Teaching Exceptional Children, 38*(3), 64–69.

Schunk, D. H. (1989). Social cognitive theory and self-regulated learning. In B. J. Zimmerman & D. H. Schunk (Eds.), *Self-regulated learning and academic achievement* (pp. 83–110). New York, NY: Springer-Verlag.

Schuyler, M. R. (1982). A readability program for use on microcomputers. *Journal of Reading, 25,* 560–591.

Schwanenflugel, P. J., Messinger, E. B., & Wisenbaker, J. M. (2006). Becoming a fluent and automatic reader in the early elementary school years. *Reading Research Quarterly, 41,* 496–522.

Schwartz, R. M. (2005). Literacy learning of at-risk first-grade students in the Reading Recovery early intervention. *Journal of Educational Psychology, 97,* 257–267.

Scott, D., Kahlich, P., & Barker, J. (1994). Motivating at-risk students using a literature based writing unit with computers. *Journal of Computing in Childhood Education, 5,* 311–317.

Scribner, S., & Cole, M. (1981). *The psychology of literacy: A case study among the Vai.* Cambridge, MA: Harvard University Press.

Searfoss, L. W., & Readence, J. E. (1989). *Helping children learn to read* (2nd ed.). Englewood Cliffs, NJ: Prentice Hall.

Semel, E., Wiig, E. H., & Secord, W. A. (2003). *Clinical evaluation of language fundamentals* (4th ed.). San Antonio, TX: The Psychological Corporation.

Senechal, M., & LeFevre, J. (2002). Parental involvement in the development of children's reading skill: A 5-year longitudinal study. *Child Development, 73,* 445–460.

Senechal, M., LeFevre, J., Hudson, E., & Lawson, E. P. (1996). Knowledge of storybooks as a predictor of young children's vocabulary. *Journal of Educational Psychology, 88,* 520–536.

Senechal, M., LeFevre, J., Thomas, E. M., & Daley, K .E. (1998). Differential effects of home literacy experiences on the development of oral and written language. *Reading Research Quarterly, 13,* 96–116.

Senechal, M., Ouellette, G., Rodney, D. (2006). The misunderstood giant: On the predictive role of early vocabulary in future reading. In D. K. Dickinson & S. B. Neuman (Eds.), *Handbook of Early Literacy Research* (Vol. 2, pp. 173–184). New York, NY: Guilford Press.

Serafini, F. (2004). *Lessons in comprehension.* Portsmouth, NH: Heinemann.

Serafini, F. (2010). *Classroom reading assessment: More efficient ways to view and evaluate your readers.* Portsmouth, NH: Heinemann.

Shanahan, T. (1984). The reading-writing relation: An exploratory multivariate analysis. *Journal of Educational Psychology, 76,* 466–477.

Shanahan, T. (1998). Effectiveness and limitations of tutoring in reading. In P. D. Pearson & A. Iran-Nejad (Eds.), *Review of Research in Education* (Vol. 23, pp. 217–234). Washington, DC: American Educational Research Association.

Shanahan, T. (2001). A rebuttal to Garan: What does the report of the National Reading Panel really tell us about teaching phonics? *Language Arts, 79,* 500–506.

Shanahan, T. (2005). Review of the DIBELS: Dynamic Indicators of Basic Early Literacy Skills. In *The sixteenth mental measurements yearbook.* Lincoln, NE: Buros Institute of Mental Measurements.

Shanahan, T., & Barr, R. (1995). Reading Recovery: An independent evaluation of the effects of an early instructional intervention for at-risk learners. *Reading Research Quarterly, 30,* 958–997.

Shanahan, T., & Beck, I. L. (2006). Effective literacy teaching for English-language learners. In D. L. August & T. Shanahan (Eds.), *Developing literacy in a second language: Report of the National Literacy Panel.* Mahwah, NJ: Lawrence Erlbaum Associates.

Shanahan, T., & Lomax, R. (1986). An analysis and comparison of theoretical models of the reading-writing relationship. *Journal of Educational Psychology, 78,* 116–123.

Shanahan, T., & Shanahan, C. (2008). Teaching disciplinary literacy to adolescents. *Harvard Educational Review, 78*(1), 40–59.

Shankweiler, D., Lundquist, E., Dreyer, L. G., & Dickinson, C. C. (1996). Reading and spelling difficulties in high school students: Causes and consequences. *Reading and Writing: An Interdisciplinary Journal, 8,* 267–294.

Shapiro, E. S. (2009). *The two models of RTI: Standard protocol and problems solving.* Virginia Department of Education. Retrieved February 6, 2011, from http://www.doe.virginia.gov/instruction/response_intervention/guidance/two_models.pdf

Share, D., & Stanovich, K. E. (1995). Cognitive processes in early reading development: Accommodating individual differences into a mode of acquisition. *Issues in Education: Contributions for Educational Psychology, 1,* 1–57.

Sharp, S. J. (1990). Using content subject matter with LEA in middle school. *Journal of Reading, 33,* 108–112.

Shea, M., Murray, R., Harlin, R. (2005). Drowning in data. Portsmouth, NH: Heinemann.

Shefelbine, J., & Newman, K. K. (2001). *SIPPS: Systematic instruction in phoneme awareness, phonics, and sight words.* Oakland, CA: Developmental Studies Center and New York, NY: Scholastic.

Shefelbine, J. L. (1991). *Encouraging your junior high student to read.* Newark, DE: International Reading Association.

Shepard, L. (2001). The role of classroom assessment in teaching and learning. In V. K. Richardson (Ed.), *Handbook of research on teaching* (4th ed., pp. 1066–1101). Washington, DC: American Educational Research Association.

Shepard, L. A., & Smith, M. L. (1986). Synthesis of research on school readiness and kindergarten retention. *Educational Leadership, 20*, 78–86.

Shimmerlik, S. (1978). Organization theory and memory for prose: A review of the literature. *Review of Educational Research, 48*, 103–121.

Silva, C., & Martins, A. (2003). Relations between children's invented spelling and the development of phonological awareness. *Educational Psychology, 23*, 3–16.

Silvaroli, N. J., Kear, D. J., & McKenna, M. C. (1982). *A classroom guide to reading assessment and instruction.* Dubuque, IA: Kendall/Hunt.

Silvaroli, N. J., & Wheelock, W. H. (2003). *Classroom reading inventory* (10th ed.). Monterey, CA: McGraw-Hill.

Silver-Pacuilla, Ruedel, & Mistrett, S. (2004). *A review of technology-based approaches for reading instruction: Tools for researchers and vendors.* Washington, DC: National Center for Technology Innovation.

Silvia, P. J. (2006). *Exploring Psychology of Interest.* New York, NY: Oxford University Press.

Simmons, D. C., & Kame'enui, E. (2003). *The consumer's guide to evaluating a core reading program K–3: A critical elements analysis.* IDEA Institute for the Development of Educational Achievement. College of Education, University of Oregon.

Simmons, W., & Resnick, L. (1993). Assessment as a catalyst of school reform. *Educational Leadership, 50*, 11–15.

Singer, J., & Donlon, D. (1982). Active comprehension: Problem-solving schema with question generation for comprehension of complex short stories. *Reading Research Quarterly, 17*, 166–168.

Singer, M., & O'Connell, G. (2003). Robust inference processes in the comprehension of expository text. *European Journal of Cognitive Psychology, 15*, 607–631.

Sireci, S. G. (2004). *Validity issues in accommodating NAEP reading tests.* (Research Report No. 515). Amherst, MA: School of Education, University of Massachusetts Amherst.

Slaughter-Defoe, D. T., & Carlson, K. G. (1996). Young African American and Latino children in high-poverty urban schools: How they perceive school climate. *Journal of Negro Education, 65*, 60–70.

Slavin, R. E. (1989). Students at risk of school failure: The problem and its dimensions. In R. E. Slavin, N. L. Karweit, & N. A. Madden (Eds.), *Effective programs for students at risk* (pp. 3–19). Boston, MA: Allyn & Bacon.

Slavin, R. E. (1991). *Educational psychology.* Englewood Cliffs, NJ: Prentice Hall.

Slavin, R. E. (1992). When and why does cooperative learning increase achievement? Theoretical and empirical perspectives. In R. Hertz-Lazarowitz & N. Miller (Eds.), *Interaction in cooperative groups: The theoretical anatomy of group learning* (pp. 145–173). New York, NY: Cambridge University Press.

Slavin, R. E. (1995). *Cooperative learning: Theory, research, and practice* (2nd ed.). Boston, MA: Allyn & Bacon.

Slavin, R. E., & Cooper, R. (1999). Improving intergroup relations: Lessons learned from cooperative learning programs. *Journal of Social Issues, 55*, 647–664.

Slavin, R. E., Karweit, N. L., Wasik, B. A., Madden, N. A., & Dolan, L. J. (1994). Success for all: A comprehensive approach to prevention and early intervention. In R. E. Slavin, N. L. Karweit, & B. A. Wasik (Eds.), *Preventing early reading failure* (pp. 175–205). Boston, MA: Allyn & Bacon.

Slavin, R. E., Stevens, R. J., & Madden, N. A. (1988). Accommodating student diversity in reading and writing instruction: A cooperative learning approach. *Reading and Special Education, 9*, 60–66.

Slomkowski, D. L., Nelson, K., Dunn, J., & Plomin, R. (1992). Temperament and language: relations from toddlerhood to middle childhood. *Developmental Psychology, 28*, 1090–1095.

Smith, D. D. (1979). The improvement of children's oral reading though the use of teacher modeling. *Journal of Learning Disabilities, 12*, 39–42.

Smith, D. K. (1998). Review of the Nelson-Denny Reading Test, Forms G and H. In J. C. Impara & B. S. Plake (Eds.), *Thirteenth mental measurements yearbook.* Lincoln, NE: Buros Institute of Mental Measurements.

Smith, J. B., Lee, V. E., & Newmann, F. M. (January, 2001). *Instruction and achievement in Chicago elementary schools.* Special Topics Report. Chicago, IL: Consortium on Chicago School Research.

Smith, T. E. C., Polloway, E. A., Patton, J. R., & Dowdy, C. A. (1995). *Teaching students with special needs in inclusive settings* (5th ed.). Boston, MA: Allyn & Bacon.

Snider, V. E., & Tarver, S. G. (1987). The effect of early reading failure on acquisition of knowledge among students with learning disabilities. *Journal of Learning Disabilities, 20*, 351–356, 373.

Snow, C., & Tabors, P. (1996). Intergenerational transfer of literacy. In Benjamin, L. A., & J. Lord (Eds.), *Family literacy: Directions in research and implications for practice* (pp. 73–80). Washington, DC: U.S. Department of Education, Office of Educational Research and Improvement.

Snow, C. E., & Biancarosa, G. (2003). *Adolescent literacy and the achievement gap: What do we know and where do we go from here?* New York, NY: Carnegie Corporation of New York.

Snow, C. E., & Biancarosa, G. (2004). *Reading Next: A vision for action and research in middle and high school literacy.* New York, NY: Carnegie Carnegie Corporation of New York Adolescent Literacy Funders Meeting Report.

Snow, C. E., Burns, M. S., & Griffin, P. (Eds.). (1998). *Preventing reading difficulties in young children.* Washington, DC: National Academy Press.

Snow, C. E., Griffin, P., & Burns, M. S. (Eds.) (2005). *Knowledge to support the teaching of reading.* San Francisco, CA: Jossey-Bass.

Snow, C. E., & Kurland, B. (1996). Sticking to the point: Talk about magnets as a preparation for literacy. In D. Hicks (Ed.), *Child discourse and social learning: An interdisciplinary perspective* (pp. 189–220). New York, NY: Cambridge University Press.

Snow, C. E., & Van Hemel, S. B. (2008). *Early childhood assessment: Why, what, and how.* Washington, DC: National Research Council of the National Academies.

Snowling, M. J., & Hulme, C. (2006). Language skills, learning to read, and reading intervention. *London Review of Education, 4*, 63–76.

Snyder, I. (1998). *Page to screen: Taking literacy into the electronic era.* London, UK: Routledge.

Solano-Flores, G., & Trumbull, E. (2003). Examining language in context: The need for new research and practice paradigms in the testing of English-language learners. *Educational Researcher, 32*, 3–13.

Spache, G. D. (1981). *Diagnostic reading scales.* Monterey, CA: CTB/McGraw-Hill.

Spandel, V. (2008). *Creating writers through 6-trait writing assessment and instruction* (5th ed.). New York, NY: Ally & Bacon.

Spear-Swerling, L., & Sternberg, R. J. (1996). *Off track: When poor readers become "learning disabled."* Boulder, CO: Westview.

Spector, J. E. (1992). Predicting progress in beginning reading: Dynamic assessment of phonemic awareness. *Journal of Educational Psychology, 84*, 353–363.

Spector, J. E. (2005). How reliable are informal reading inventories? *Psychology in Schools, 46*(2), 593–603.

Spinelli, C. G. (2006). *Classroom assessment for students in special and general education* (2nd ed.). Upper Saddle River, NJ: Pearson.

Spiro, R., & Myers, A. (1984). Individual differences and underlying cognitive processes. In P. D. Pearson, R. Barr, M. Kamil, & P. Mosenthal (Eds.), *Handbook of reading research* (Vol. 1, pp. 471–504). New York, NY: Longman.

Squire, J. (1983). Composing and comprehending: Two sides of the same basic process. *Language Arts, 60*, 581–589.

Squire, J. (1991). The history of the profession. In J. Flood, J. Jensen, D. Lapp, & J. Squire (Eds.), *Handbook of research on teaching the English language arts.* New York, NY: MacMillan.

Stahl, K. A. D., & Bravo, M. A. (2010). Contemporary classroom vocabulary assessment for content areas. *The Reading Teacher, 63*, 566–578.

Stahl, S., & Kapinus, B. A. (2001). *Word power: What every educator needs to know about vocabulary.* Washington, DC: NEA Professional Library.

Stahl, S. A. (1986). Three principles of effective vocabulary instruction. *Journal of Reading, 29*, 662–668.

Stahl, S. A. (1999). *Vocabulary development.* Cambridge MA: Brookline Books.

Stahl, S. A., & Fairbanks, M. (1986). The effects of vocabulary instruction: A model-based meta-analysis. *Review of Educational Research, 56*, 72–110.

Stahl, S. A., Heubach, K. M. (2005). Fluency-oriented reading instruction. *Journal of Literacy Research, 37*, 25–60.

Stahl, S. A., & Murray, B. A. (1994). Defining phonological awareness and its relationship to early reading. *Journal of Educational Psychology, 86*, 221–234.

Stahl, S. A., & Murray, B. A. (1998). Issues involved in defining phonological awareness and its relation to early reading. In J. L. Metsala & L. C. Ehri (Eds.), *Word recognition in beginning reading* (pp. 65–87). Mahwah, NJ: Erlbaum.

Stanovich, K. E. (1986). Matthew effects in reading: Some consequences of individual differences in the acquisition of literacy. *Reading Research Quarterly, 21*, 360–406.

Stanovich, K. E. (1991). Word recognition: Changing perspectives. In R. Barr, M. L. Kamil, P. B. Mosenthal, & P. D. Pearson (Eds.), *Handbook of reading research* (Vol. 2, pp. 418–452). New York, NY: Longman.

Stanovich, K. E. (1992). Are we overselling literacy? In C. Temple & P. Collins (Eds.), *Stories and readers: New perspectives on literature in the elementary classroom* (pp. 209–231). Norwood, MA: Christopher-Gordon.

Stanovich, K. E., Cunningham, A. E., & Cramer, B. B. (1984). Assessing phonological awareness in kindergarten children: Issues of task comparability. *Journal of Experimental Child Psychology, 38*, 175–190.

Staton, J. (1987). The power of responding in dialogue journals. In T. Fulwiler (Ed.), *The journal book* (p. 63). Portsmouth, NH: Heinemann.

Stauffer, R. (1969). *Teaching reading as a thinking process.* New York, NY: Harper & Row.

Stauffer, R. (1980). *Directing the reading-thinking process.* New York, NY: Harper & Row.

Stecker, P. M., & Fuchs, L. S. (2000). Effecting superior achievement using curriculum-based measurement: The importance of individual progress monitoring. *Learning Disabilities Research and Practice, 15*, 128–134.

Stecker, P. M., Fuchs, L. S., & Fuchs, D. (2005). Using curriculum-based measurement to improve student achievement: Review of research. *Psychology in the Schools, 42*, 795–819.

Stein, N. L., & Glenn, C. G. (1979). An analysis of story comprehension in elementary school children. In R. O. Freedle (Ed.), *New directions in discourse processing* (Vol. 2, pp. 53–120). Norwood, NJ: Ablex.

Stein, N. L., & Nezworski, M. T. (1978). The effects of organization and instructional set on story memory. *Discourse Processes, 1*, 177–193.

Stein, N. L., & Policastro, M. (1984). The concept of a story: A comparison between children's and teachers' viewpoints. In H. Mandl, N. L. Stein, & T. Trabasso (Eds.), *Learning and comprehension of text* (pp. 113–158). Hillsdale, NJ: Erlbaum.

Stenner, A. J., Burdick, H., Sanford, E. E., & Burdick, D. S. (2006). How accurate are Lexile text measures? *Journal of Applied Measurement, 7*, 307–322.

Stenner, A. J., & Stone, M. H. (April, 2006). *Does the reader comprehend the text because the reader is able or because the text is easy?* Paper presented at the 13th annual International Objective Measurement Workshop. Berkeley, CA.

Stenner, A. J., & Wright, B. W. (2002, February). *Readability, reading ability, and comprehension.* Paper presented at the annual meeting of the Association of Test Publishers, San Diego, CA.

Sternberg, R. (2001). *Dynamic testing.* Cambridge, UK: Cambridge University Press.

Sternberg, R. J. (1999). Ability and expertise: It's time to replace the current model of intelligence. *American Educator, 23*, 1–30, 50.

Stevens, R. J., Madden, N. A., Slavin, R. E., & Farnish, A. M. (1987). Cooperative integrated reading and composition: Two field experiments. *Reading Research Quarterly, 23*, 433–454.

Stewig, J. W., & Nordberg, B. (1995). *Exploring language arts in the elementary classroom.* Belmont, CA: Wadsworth.

Stiggins, R. (2002). Assessment crisis: The absence of assessment for learning. Phi Delta Kappan, 83(10), 758–765.

Stiggins, R. (2004). *Student-involved assessment for learning* (4th ed.). Upper Saddle River, NJ: Prentice-Hall.

Stiggins, R. J. (2001). *Student-involved classroom assessment* (3rd ed.). Upper Saddle River, NJ: Merrill-Prentice-Hall.

Stotsky, S. (1983). Research on reading/writing relationship: A synthesis and suggested directions. *Language Arts, 60*, 627–642.

Stotsky, S. (1995). The uses and limitations of personal or personalized writing in writing theory, research, and instruction. *Reading Research Quarterly, 30*, 758–776.

Strangman, N., & Dalton, B. (2005). Using technology to support struggling readers: A review of the research. In D. Edyburn, K. Higgins, & R. Boone (Eds.) *Handbook of special education technology research and practice.* Whitefish Bay, WI: Knowledge by Design.

Strategic Teaching and Evaluation of Progress (STEP™). Available at http://uei.uchicago.edu/innovation/step/

Strickland, D. S., Bodino, A., Buchan, K., Jones, K. M., Nelson, A., & Rosen, M. (2001). Teaching writing in a time of reform. *Elementary School Journal, 101*, 385–397.

Stringfield, S., Wayman, J. C., & Yakimowski-Srebnick, M. E. (2005). Scaling up data use in classrooms, schools, and districts. In C. Dede, J. P. Honan, & L. C. Peters (Eds.), *Scaling up success: Lessons learned from technology-based educational improvement* (pp. 133–152). San Francisco, CA: Jossey-Bass.

Strong, C. J. (1998). *The Strong Narrative Assessment Procedure (SNAP) (1998).* Eau Claire, WI: Thinking Publications, division of McKinley Companies, Inc.

Stuckey, J. E. (1991). *The violence of literacy*. Portsmouth: Boynton/Cook Publishers.

Sulzby, E. (1986). Children's elicitation and use of metalinguistic knowledge about "word" during literacy interactions. In D. B. Yaden & S. Templeton (Eds.), *Metalinguistic awareness and beginning literacy* (pp. 219–234). Portsmouth, NH: Heinemann.

Sulzby, E., Teale, W. H., & Kamberelis, G. (1989). Emergent writing in the classroom: Home and school connections. In D. S. Strickland & L. M. Morrow (Eds.), *Emerging literacy: Young children learn to read and write* (pp.(63–79). Newark, DE: International Reading Association.

Sundbye, N. (1987). Text explicitness and inferential questioning: Effects on story understanding and recall. *Reading Research Quarterly, 22*, 82–98.

Sutherland-Smith, W. (2002). Weaving the literacy web; Changes in reading from page to screen. *The Reading Teacher, 55*, 662–668.

Swanson, H. L. (1999). Instructional components that predict treatment outcomes for students with learning disabilities: Support for a combined strategy and direct instruction model. *Learning Disabilities Research & Practice, 14*, 129–140.

Swanson, H. L., & Watson, B. L. (1989). *Educational and psychological assessment of exceptional children* (2nd ed.). Columbus, OH: Merrill Publishing Company.

Sweet, A. P., Guthrie, J. T., & Ng, M. (1998). Teachers' perceptions and students' reading motivations. *Journal of Educational Psychology, 90*, 210–223.

Sweet, A. P., & Snow, C. E. (Eds.) (2003). *Rethinking reading comprehension*. New York, NY: Guilford Press.

Sweller, J. (2005). Implications of cognitive load theory for multimedia learning. In R. E. Mayer (Ed.), *Cambridge handbook of multi-media learning* (pp. 19–30). New York, NY: Cambridge University Press.

Szymusiak, K., Sibberson, F., & Koch, L. (2008). *Beyond leveled books* 2nd ed. Portland, ME: Stenhouse.

Taba, H. (1967). *Teacher's handbook for elementary social studies*. Reading, MA: Addison Wesley.

Taberski, S. (2000). *On solid ground: Strategies for teaching reading K–3*. Portsmouth, NH: Heinemann.

Tabors, P. O., Snow, C. E., & Dickinson, D. K. (2001). Homes and schools together: Supporting language and literacy development. In D. K. Dickinson & P. O. Tabors, *Beginning literacy and language: Young children learning at home and school* (pp. 313–334). Baltimore, MD: Brookes Publishing.

Tait, H., Entwistle, N. J., & McCune, V. (1998). ASSIST: a reconceptualisation of the Approaches to Studying Inventory. In C. Rust (Ed.) *Improving students as learners*. Oxford, UK: Oxford Brookes University, The Oxford Centre for Staff and Learning Development.

Tancock, S. M. (1994). A literacy lesson framework for children with reading problems. *The Reading Teacher, 48*, 130–140.

Taylor, B., Harris, L. A., Pearson, P. D., & Garcia, G. (1995). *Reading difficulties: Instruction and assessment* (2nd ed.). New York, NY: McGraw-Hill.

Taylor, B. M. (1982). A summarizing strategy to improve middle grade students' reading and writing skills. *The Reading Teacher, 36*, 202–205.

Taylor, B. M. (1986). Teaching middle grade students to summarize content textbook material. In J. F. Baumann (Ed.), *Teaching main idea comprehension* (pp. 195–209). Newark, DE: International Reading Association.

Taylor, B. M., Harris, L. A., & Pearson, P. D. (1988). *Reading difficulties: Instruction and assessment*. New York, NY: Random House.

Taylor, B. M., Pearson, P. D., Clark, K. F., & Walpole, S. (2000). Effective schools and accomplished teachers: Lessons about primary-grade reading instruction in low-income schools. *Elementary School Journal, 101*(2), 121–165.

Taylor, B. M., Pearson, P. D., Peterson, D. S., & Rodriguez, . C. (2003). Reading growth in high-poverty classrooms: The influence of teacher practices that encourage cognitive engagement in literacy learning. *Elementary School Journal, 104*, 3–28.

Taylor, B. M., & Samuels, S. J. (1983). Children's use of text structure in the recall of expository material. *American Educational Research Journal, 20*, 234–237.

Taylor, B. M., Strait, J., & Medo, M. A. (1994). Early intervention in reading: Supplemental instructions for groups of low-achieving students provided by first-grade teachers. In E. H. Hiebert & B. M. Taylor (Eds.), *Getting reading right from the start* (pp. 107–121). Boston, MA: Allyn & Bacon.

Tchudi, S. (1994). *Integrated language arts in the elementary school*. Belmont, CA: Wadsworth.

Teale, W. H., Hiebert, E. H., & Chittenden, E. A. (1987). Assessing young children's literacy development. *The Reading Teacher, 40*, 772–777.

Teale, W. H., & Sulzby, E. (Eds.). (1986). *Emergent literacy: Writing and reading*. Norwood, NJ: Ablex.

Temple, C., & Gillet, J. W. (1989). *Language arts: Learning processes and teaching practices* (2nd ed.). Glenview, IL: Scott Foresman.

Temple, C., Nathan, R., Burris, N., & Temple, F. (1988). *The beginnings of writing*. Boston, MA: Allyn & Bacon.

Temple, C., Nathan, R., Temple, F., & Burris, N. A. (1993). *The beginnings of writing* (3rd ed.). Boston, MA: Allyn & Bacon.

Templeton, S. (1995). Spelling: The foundation of word knowledge for the less proficient reader. In M. L. Putnam (Ed.), *How to become a better reading teacher* (pp. 317–329). Englewood Cliffs, NJ: Merrill.

Templeton, S. (1997). *Teaching the integrated language arts*. Boston, MA: Houghton Mifflin.

Templeton, S., & Bear, D. (1992). *The development of orthographic knowledge and the foundations of literacy: A memorial Festschrift for Edmund H. Henderson*. Hillsdale, NJ: Erlbaum.

Templeton, S., & Morris, D. (2000). Spelling. In M. Kamil, P. Mosenthal, P. D. Pearson, & R. Barr (Eds.), *Handbook of reading research* (Vol. 3, pp. 525–543). Mahwah, NJ: Erlbaum.

Theurer, J. L. (2002). The power of retrospective miscue analysis: One preservice teacher's journey as she reconsiders the reading process. *The Reading Matrix, 2*(1). Retrieved March 1, 2007, from www.readingmatrix.com/articles/theurer/index.html

Thorndyke, P. W. (1977). Cognitive structures in comprehension and memory of narrative discourse. *Cognitive Psychology, 9*, 77–110.

Tienken, C. H., & Wilson, M. J. (n.d.). Technical characteristics of state assessments of skills and knowledge. Retrieved March 18, 2007, from http://www.fairtest.org/NJ%20Standardized%20Testing%20characteristics.pdf

Tierney, R., Readence, J. E., & Dishner, E. (1985). *Reading strategies and practices: A compendium* (2nd ed.). Boston, MA: Allyn & Bacon.

Tierney, R. J. (1992). Ongoing research and new directions. In J. W. Irwin & M. A. Doyle (Eds.), *Reading/writing connections: Learning from research* (pp. 247–259). Newark, DE: International Reading Association.

Tierney, R. J., Carter, M. A., & Desai, L. E. (1991). *Portfolio assessment in the reading-writing classroom*. Norwood, MA: Christopher-Gordon.

Tikunoff, W. J., & Ward, B. A. (1983). Collaborative research on teaching. *Elementary School Journal*, *83*, 453–468.

Toll, C. (2004). *The literacy coaches survival guide.* Newark, DE: International Reading Association.

Toll, C. (2007). Lenses on literacy coaching. Norwood, MA: Christopher Gordon.

Tompkins, G. E. (2012). *Teaching writing: Balancing process and product* (6th ed.). Boston, MA: Pearson.

Topping, K. (1987). Paired reading: A powerful technique for parent use. *The Reading Teacher*, *40*, 608–614.

Torgesen, J. (1990). The learning disabled child as an inactive learner. In P. Cole & L. Chan (Eds.), *Methods and strategies for special education.* Englewood Cliffs, NJ: Prentice Hall.

Torgesen, J., Wagner, R., & Rashotte, C. (1994). Longitudinal studies of phonological processing and reading. *Journal of Learning Disabilities*, *27*, 276–286.

Torgesen, J., Wagner, R., & Rashotte, C. (1999). *Test of word reading efficiency: Examiner's manual.* Austin, TX: Pro-Ed.

Torgesen, J., Wagner, R., Rashotte, C., Rose, E., Lindamood, P., Conway, T., & Gravan, C. (1999). Preventing reading failure in young children with phonological processing disabilities: Group and individual responses to instruction, *Journal of Educational Psychology*, *91*, 579–593.

Torgesen, J. K. (1977). The role of non-specific factors in the task performance of learning disabled children: A theoretical assessment. *Journal of Learning Disabilities*, *10*, 24–34.

Torgesen, J. K. (2002). The prevention of reading difficulties. *Journal of School Psychology*, *40*, 7–26.

Torgesen, J. K., Alexander, A. W., Wagner, R. K., Rashotte, C. A., Voeller, K., Conway, T., & Rose, E. (2001). Intensive remedial instruction for children with severe reading disabilities: Immediate and long-term outcomes from two instructional approaches. *Journal of Learning Disabilities*, *34*, 33–58.

Torgesen, J. K., & Bryant, B. R. (1994). *Test of phonological awareness.* Austin, TX: Pro-Ed.

Torgesen, J. K., & Burgess, S. R. (1996). Consistency of phonological processing throughout early childhood. In L. Metsala & L. Ehri Eds. *Word recognition in beginning literacy* pp. 294–311. Mahwah, NJ: Lawrence Erlbaum.

Torgesen, J. K., & Davis, C. (1996). Individual difference variables that predict response to training in phonological awareness. *Journal of Experimental Child Psychology*, *63*, 1–21.

Torgesen, J. K., & Hudson, R. (2006). Reading fluency: Critical issues for struggling readers. In S. J. Samuels & A. Farstrup (Eds.), *Reading fluency: The forgotten dimension* (pp. 2–17). Newark, DE: International Reading Association.

Torgesen, J. K., Rashotte, C. A., Alexander, A., Alexander, J., & McPhee, K. (2003). Progress toward understanding the instructional conditions necessary for remediating reading difficulties in older children. In B. Foorman (Ed.), *Preventing and remediating reading difficulties: Bringing science to scale* (pp. 275–298). Parkton, MD: York Press.

Tovay, D. R. (1980). Children's grasp of phonics terms vs. sound-symbol relationships. *The Reading Teacher*, *33*, 431–437.

Trainen, G., & Swanson, L. (2005). Cognition, metacognition and achievement of college students with learning disabilities. *Learning Disability Quarterly*, *28*, 261–272.

Treiman, R., & Kessler, B. (2003). The role of letter names in the acquisition of literacy. In R. Kail (Ed.), *Advances in child development and behavior* (Vol. 31, pp. 105–135). San Diego, CA: Academic Press.

Treiman, R., & Zukowski, A. (1991). Levels of phonological awareness. In S. Brady & D. Shankweiler (Eds.), *Phonological processes in literacy* (pp. 67–83). Hillsdale, NJ: Erlbaum.

Triplett, C. F. (2007). The social construction of 'struggle': Influences of school literacy contexts, curriculum, and relationships. *Journal of Literacy Research*, *39*, 95–126.

Troia, G. A. (n.d.). Teaching writing to diverse student populations. Access Center for Improving Outcomes for All Students K–8. Retrieved January 22, 2007, from http://www.k8accesscenter.org/riting/documents/TroiaWritingDocument.pdf

Troia, G. A. (2002). Teaching writing strategies to children with disabilities: Setting generalization as the goal. *Exceptionality*, *10*, 249–269.

Troia, G. A. (2004/2006). Phonological processing and its influence on literacy learning. In C. A. Stone, E. R. Silliman, B. J. Ehren, & K. Apel (Eds.), *Handbook of language & literacy* (pp. 271–301). New York, NY: Guildford Press.

Troia, G. A., & Graham, S. (2003). Effective writing instruction across the grades: What every educational consultant should know. *Journal of Educational and Psychological Consultation*, *14*, 75–89.

Tucker, M. S., & Codding, J. B. (1998). Standards for our schools: How to set them, measure them, and reach them. San Francisco, CA: Jossey-Bass.

Turner, J., & Paris, S. G. (1995). How literacy tasks influence children's motivation for literacy. *The Reading Teacher*, *48*, 662–673.

Turner, J. C. (1995). The influence of classroom contexts on young children's motivation for literacy. *Reading Research Quarterly*, *30*, 410–441.

Tzuriel, D. (2000). Dynamic assessment of young children: Educational intervention perspectives. *Educational Psychology Review*, *12*(4), 385–434.

Unrau, N. J. (2004). Content area reading and writing: Fostering literacy in middle and high school cultures. New York, NY: Pearson (Allyn & Bacon/Merrill).

U.S. Department of Education. (2002). To assure the free appropriate public education of all children with disabilities. (Twenty-fourth annual report to Congress on the implementation of the Individual with Disabilities Education Act). Washington, DC: U.S. Government Printing Office.

U.S. Department of Education. (2006). *Reading First implementation evaluation: Interim report.* Washington, DC: U.S. Government Printing Office.

U.S. Department of Education. Institute of Education Sciences. National Center for Education Statistics. (2003). *The Nation's Report Card: Writing 2002, NCES 2003-529*, by H. R. Persky, M.C. Daane, & Y. Jin. Washington, DC: U.S. Government Printing Office.

Vacca, R. T., & Padak, N. D. (1990). Who's at risk in reading? *Journal of Reading*, *33*, 486–488.

Vacca, R. T., & Vacca, J. L. (2004). *Content area reading* (8th ed.). Boston, MA: Allyn & Bacon.

Vadasy, P. F., Jenkins, J. R., & Pool, K. (2000). Effects of tutoring in phonological and early reading skills on students at-risk of reading disabilities. *Journal of Learning Disabilities*, *33*, 579–590.

Valdes, G. (1996). *Con respeto: Bridging the distances between culturally diverse families and schools.* New York, NY: Teachers College Press.

Valdez Pierce, L., & O'Malley, M. (1992). *Performance and portfolio assessment for language minority students.* NCBE Program Information Guide Series, 9. Washington, DC: National Clearinghouse for Bilingual Education.

Valencia, S., Stallman, A. C., Commeyras, M., Hartman, D. K., Pearson, P. D., & Greer, E. A. (1987, December). Three methods of assessing prior knowledge: A validation study. Paper presented at The National Reading Conference, St. Petersburg, FL.

Valencia, S. W. (1990). Portfolio assessment: Separating the wheat from the chaff. *The Reading Teacher, 44*, 60–61.

Valencia, S. W. (1997). Authentic classroom assessment of early reading: Alternatives to standardized tests. *Preventing School Failure, 41*(2), 63–70.

Valencia, S. W. (1998). *Literacy portfolios in action.* Fort Worth, TX: Harcourt Brace.

Valencia, S. W. (2007). Inquiry-oriented assessment. In J. R. Paratore & R. I. McCormack (Eds.), *Classroom literacy assessment: Making sense of what students know and do* (pp. 3–20). NY: Guilford Press.

Valencia, S. W. (2011a). Reader profiles and reading disabilities. In A. McGill Franzen & R. L. Allington (Eds.), *Handbook of reading disability research* (pp. 25–35). New York, NY: Routledge.

Valencia, S. W. (2011b). Using assessment to improve teaching and learning. In S. J. Samuels & A. E. Farstrup (Eds.), *What research has to say about reading instruction* (4th ed., pp. 379–405). Newark, DE: International Reading Association.

Valencia, S. W., & Bradley, S. (1998). Engaging students in self-reflection and self-evaluation. In S. W. Valencia (Ed.), *Literacy portfolios in action* (pp. 174–218). New York, NY: Harcourt.

Valencia, S. W., & Buly, M. R. (2004). Behind test scores: What struggling readers really need. *The Reading Teacher, 57*, 520–531.

Valencia, S. W., & Calfee, R. (1991). The development and use of literacy portfolios for students, classes, and teachers. *Applied Measurement in Education, 4*(4), 333–345.

Valencia, S. W., Hiebert, E., & Afflerbach, P. P. (Eds.). (1994). *Authentic reading assessment: Practices and possibilities.* Newark, DE: International Reading Association.

Valencia, S. W., McGinley, W., & Pearson, P. D. (1990). Assessing reading and writing: Building a more complete picture. In G. Duffy & P. Anders (Eds.), *Reading in the middle schools* (pp. 124–153). Newark, DE: International Reading Association.

Valencia, S. W., & Pearson, P. D. (1987). Reading assessment: Time for a change. *The Reading Teacher, 40*, 726–733.

Valencia, S. W., & Place, N. A. (1994). Literacy portfolios for teaching, learning, and accountability: The Bellevue literacy assessment project. In S. W. Valencia, E. H. Hiebert, & P. P. Afflerbach (Eds.), *Authentic reading assessment: Practices and possibilities* (pp. 134–166). Newark, DE: International Reading Association.

Valencia, S. W., Smith, A. T., Reece, A. M., Li, M., Wixson, K. K., & Newman, H. (2010). Oral reading fluency assessment: Issues of construct, criterion, and consequential validity. *Reading Research Quarterly, 45*(3), 270–29.

Valencia, S. W., & Wixson, K. K. (2000). Policy-oriented research on literacy standards and assessment. In M. L. Kamil, P. B. Mosenthal, P. D. Pearson, & R. Barr (Eds.), *Handbook of reading research* (Vol. 3, pp. 909–935). Mahwah, NJ: Erlbaum.

Valencia, S. W., & Wixson, K. K. (2004). Literacy policy and policy research that makes a difference. In R. Ruddell & N.J. Unrau, (Eds.), *Theoretical models and processes of reading* (5th ed., pp. 69–92). Newark, DE: International Reading Assoc.

van Kleek, A. (2004/2006). Fostering preliteracy development via storybook-sharing interactions: The cultural context of mainstream family practices. In C. A. Stone, E. R. Silliman, B. J. Ehren, & K. Apel (Eds.), *Handbook of language & literacy: Development and disorders* (pp. 175–208). New York, NY: Guildford Press.

VanDerHeyden, A. (Chair); Burns, M., Cash, G., Dawson, P., Gettinger, M. Jimerson, S., . . . Power, T. (2010). *Evidence-based guidelines for diagnosis of learning disabilities: Response to proposed DSM-5 criteria for learning disabilities.* Submitted on behalf of the School Psychology Division (16) of American Psychological Association and the National Association of School Psychologists.

Vandervelden, M. C., & Siegel, L. S. (1995). Phonological recoding and phoneme awareness in early literacy: A developmental approach. *Reading Research Quarterly, 30*, 854–875.

Vang, H., & Barrera, M. T. (2004–05). Hmong parents' perceptions on instructional strategies for educating their children with disabilities. *Hmong Studies Journal, 5*, 1–20. Retrieved March 10, 2007, from http://hmongstudies.com/VangandBarreraHSJ5.pdf

VanLehn, K., & Martin, J. (1997). Evaluation of an assessment system based on Bayesian student modeling. *International Journal of Artificial Intelligence in Education, 8*, 179–221.

Varaprasad, C. (2006). Reading strategies: Caught or taught? *Reflections on English Language Teaching, 5*, 63–86.

Vasilyeva, M., & Waterfall, H., (2011). Variability in language development: Relation to socioeconomic status. In S. B. Nueman & D. K. Dickinson (Eds.), *Handbook of early literacy research* (3rd ed., pp. 36–48). New York, NY: Guilford.

Vaughn, J., & Estes, T. (1986). *Reading and reasoning beyond the primary grades.* Boston, MA: Allyn and Bacon.

Vaughn, S., Gersten, R., & Chard, D. (2000). The underlying message in LD intervention research. *Exceptional Children, 67*, 99–114.

Vaughn, S., Hughes, M. T., Moody, S. W., & Elbaum, B. (2001). Instructional grouping for reading for students with LD: Implications for practice. *Intervention in School and Clinic, 36*, 131–137.

Vaughn, S., Levy, S., Coleman, M., Bos, C. (2002). Reading instruction for students with LD and EBD: A synthesis of observational studies. *Journal of Special Education, 1*, 2–13.

Vaughn, S., Moody, S., & Schumm, J. S. (1998). Broken promises: Reading instruction in the resource room. *Exceptional Children, 64*, 211–226.

Vellutino, F. R., Scanlon, D. M., & Sipay, E. R. (1997). Toward distinguishing between cognitive and experiential deficits as primary sources of difficulty in learning to read: The importance of early intervention in diagnosing specific reading disability. In B. A. Blachman (Ed.), *Foundations of reading acquisition and dyslexia: Implications for early intervention* (pp. 347–379). Mahwah, NJ: Erlbaum.

Vellutino, F. R., Scanlon, D. M., Sipay, E. R., Small, S. G., Pratt, A., Chen, R., & Denckla, M. B. (1996). Cognitive profiles of difficult-to-remediate and readily remediated poor readers: Early intervention as a vehicle for distinguishing between cognitive and experiential deficits as basic causes of special reading disability. *Journal of Educational Psychology, 88*(4), 601–638.

The Vermont Comprehensive Assessment Tool (VCAT). Retrieved from http://www.vcat.us/

Vermont Standards and Assessment Consortium (VTSAC). (2002). *A resource guide for teaching writing in grades K–4.* Montpelier, VT: VTSAC.

Vernon-Feagans, L. (1996). *Children's talk in communities and classrooms.* Cambridge, MA: Blackwell Publishers.

Vernon-Feagans, L., Hammer, C. S., Miccio, A., & Manlove, E. (2001). Early language and literacy skills in low-income African American and Hispanic children. In S. B. Neuman & D. K. Dickinson (Eds.), *Handbook of early literacy research* (pp. 192–210). New York, NY: Guilford Press.

The view from Washington, DC: The National Implementation of Reading First (July, 2006). 3rd Annual National Reading First Conference.

Villa, R., & Thousand, J. (2008). *A Guide to Co-Teaching: Practical Tips for Facilitating Student Learning.* Thousand Oaks: Corwin Press.

Villa, R. A., & Thousand, J. S. (Eds.). (1995). *Creating an inclusive school.* Alexandria, VA: ASCD.

Villaume, S. K., Worder, T., Williams, S., Hopkins, L., & Rosenblatt, C. (1994). Five teachers in search of a discussion. *The Reading Teacher, 47,* 480–487.

Vogt, M. E. (1999). *Read-2-Succeed: An intervention model for middle and high school students.* Paper presented at the Annual Meeting of the National Reading Conference, Orlando, FL.

Vogt, M. E., & Shearer, B.A. (2003). *Reading specialists in the real world: A sociocultural view.* Needham Heights, MA: Allyn & Bacon.

Vygotsky, L. S. (1962). *Thought and language.* Cambridge, MA: MIT Press.

Vygotsky, L. S. (1978). *Mind in society: The development of higher psychological process.* Cambridge, MA: Harvard University Press.

Vygotsky, L. S. (1986). *Thought and language.* Cambridge, MA: MIT Press.

Wade, S. E. (1990). Using think alouds to assess comprehension. *The Reading Teacher, 43,* 442–453.

Wade, S. E., Buxton, W. M., & Kelly, M. (1999). Using think-alouds to examine reader-text interest. *Reading Research Quarterly, 34*(2), 194–216.

Wade, S. E., & Moje, E. B. (2000). The role of text in classroom learning. In M. Kamil, P. Mosenthal, P. D. Pearson, & R. Barr (Eds.), *Handbook of reading research* (Vol. 3, pp. 609–627). Mahwah, NJ: Erlbaum.

Wagner, R. K., Torgeson, J. K., & Rashotte, C. A. (1999). *Comprehensive test of phonological processing.* Austin, TX: Pro-Ed.

Wagner, R. K., Torgeson, J. K., Rashotte, C. A., Hecht, S. A., Barker, T. A., Burgess, S. R., . . . Garon, T. (1997). Changing relations between phonological processing abilities and word-level reading as children develop from beginning to skilled readers: A 5-year longitudinal study. *Developmental Psychology, 33,* 468–479.

Walker, B. (2007). *Diagnostic teaching of reading* (6th ed.). Upper Saddle River, NJ: Prentice Hall.

Walker, B. (2011). *Diagnostic teaching of reading: Techniques for assessment and instruction* (7th ed.) Boston, MA: Allyn & Bacon.

Walmsley, S., & Allington, R. (1965). Redefining and reforming instructional support programs for at-risk readers. In R. Allington & S. Walmsley (Eds.), *No quick fix: Rethinking literacy programs in America's elementary schools* (pp. 19–44). Newark, DE: International Reading Association.

Walp, T. P., & Walmsley, S. A. (1989). Instructional and philosophical congruence: Neglected aspects of coordination. *The Reading Teacher, 42,* 364–368.

Walpole, S., & McKenna, M. C. (2004). *The literacy coach's handbook: A guide to research-based practice.* New York, NY: Guilford Press.

Walsh, S. B., & Betz, N. E. (2001). *Tests and assessment* (4th ed.). Upper Saddle River, NJ: Prentice Hall.

Walters, J., Seidel, S., & Gardner, H. (1994). Children as reflective practitioners. In J. N. Mangieri & C. C. Block (Eds.), *Creating powerful thinking in teachers and students* (pp. 289–303). Fort Worth, TX: Harcourt Brace.

Wang, M. C., Haertel, G. D., & Walberg, H. J. (1994). What helps students learn? *Educational Leadership, 51,* 74–79.

Wanzek, J., & Vaughn, S. (2008). Response to varying amounts of time in reading intervention for students demonstrating insufficient response to intervention. *Journal of Learning Disabilities, 42,* 126–142.

Warncke, E. W., & Shipman, D. A. (1984). *Group assessment in reading: Classroom teacher's handbook.* Englewood Cliffs, NJ: Prentice Hall.

Wasik, B. A. (1998). Volunteer tutoring programs in reading: A review. *Reading Research Quarterly, 33,* 266–292.

Wasik, B. H., & Hendrickson, J. S. (2006). Family literacy practices. In C. A. Stone, E. R. Silliman, B. J. Ehren, & K. Apel (Eds.), *Handbook of language and literacy* (pp. 154–174). New York, NY: Guilford Press.

Watson, R. (2001). Literacy and oral language: Implications for early literacy acquisition. In S. B. Neuman & D. K. Dickinson (Eds.), *Handbook of early literacy research* (pp. 43–53). New York, NY: Guilford Press.

Weaver, C. A., & Kintsch, W. (1991). Expository text. In R. Barr & M. L. Kamil, P. B. Mosenthal, & P. D. Pearson (Eds.), *Handbook of reading research* (Vol. 2, pp. 230–245). Hillsdale, NJ: Lawrence Erlbaum.

Weiner, B. (1992). *Human motivation: Metaphors, theories, and research.* Newbury Park, CA: Sage.

Weinstein C. E., & Palmer, D. R. (2002). *LASSI user's manual* (2nd ed.). Clearwater, FL: H&H Publishing.

Weinstein C. E., & Palmer, D. R. (2002). *Learning and study strategies inventory (LASSI)* (2nd ed.). Clearwater, FL: H&H Publishing.

Weinstein, C. E., Schulte, A. C., & Palmer, D. R. (1987). *Learning and study strategies inventory (LASSI).* Clearwater, FL: H&H Publishing.

Weinstein, R. S. (1976). Reading group membership in first grade: Teacher behaviors and pupil experience over time. *Journal of Educational Psychology, 68,* 103–116.

Weinstein, R. S. (1986). Teaching reading: Children's awareness of teacher expectations. In T. E. Raphael (Ed.), *The contexts of school-based literacy* (pp. 233–252). New York, NY: Random House.

Weinstein, R. S. (2002). *Reaching higher: The power of expectations in schooling.* Cambridge, MA: Harvard University Press.

Weir, C. (1998). Using embedded questions to jump-start metacognition in middle school remedial readers. *Journal of Adolescent and Adult Literacy, 41,* 458–468.

Weir, C. (2000). Using embedded questions to jump-start metacognition in middle school remedial readers. In D. W. Moore, D. E. Alvermann, & K. A. Hinchman (Eds.), *Struggling adolescent readers: A collection of strategies* (pp. 138–147). Newark, DE: International Reading Association.

Wells, G. (1986). *The meaning makers: Children learning language and using language to learn.* Portsmouth, NH: Heinemann.

Wenglinsky, H. (2003). Using large-scale research to gauge the impact of instructional practices on student reading comprehension: An exploratory study. *Educational Policy Analysis Archives, 11*(9). Retrieved September 15, 2007, from http://epaa.asu.edu/epaa/v11n19/

Wentzel, K. R., & Wigfield, A. (1998). Academic and social motivational influences on students' academic performance. *Educational Psychology Review, 10,* 155–175.

Wepner, S. B., & Feeley, J. T. (1993). *Moving forward with literature: Basals, books, and beyond.* New York, NY: Merrill.

Wesche, M., & Paribakht, T. S. (1996). Assessing second language vocabulary knowledge. Depth versus breadth. *Canadian Modern Language Review, 53,* 13–40.

West, R. F., & Stanovich, K. (1978). Automatic contextual facilitation in readers of three ages. *Child Development, 49,* 717–727.

Westby, C. (1988). Test review: Test of language development–2, Primary. *The Reading Teacher, 42,* 236–237.

Wharton-McDonald, R. (2011). Expert classroom instruction for students with reading disabilities. In A. McGill Franzen & R. L. Allington (Eds.), *Handbook of reading disability research* (pp. 265–272). New York, NY: Routledge.

What Works Clearinghouse. (2007). Effectiveness ratings for beginning reading programs in four domains. Retrieved August 25, 2010, from www.whatworks.ed.gov

White, T. G. (2005). Effects of systematic and strategic analogy-based phonics on grade 2 students' word reading and reading comprehension. *Reading Research Quarterly, 40,* 234–255.

White, T. G., Graves, M. F., & Slater, W. H. (1990). Growth in vocabulary in diverse elementary schools: Decoding and word meanings. *Journal of Educational Psychology, 82,* 281–290.

White, S. (2005). *Beyond the numbers: Making data work for teachers and school leaders.* Englewood, CO: Advanced Learning Press.

White, S., & Clement, J. (2001). *Assessing the Lexile Framework: Results of a panel meeting.* National Center for Education Statistics. Working Paper No. 2001-08. Washington, DC: U.S. Department of Education.

Whitehurst, G. J., & Lonigan, C. J. (2001). Emergent literacy: Development from prereaders to readers. In S. B. Neuman & D. K. Dickinson (Eds.), *Handbook of early literacy research* (pp. 11–29). New York, NY: Guilford Press.

Wiederholt, J. L., & Bryant, B. R. (1986). *Gray oral reading test–revised.* Austin, TX: Pro-Ed.

Wiederholt, J. L., & Bryant, B. R. (1992). *Gray Oral Reading Test–3.* Austin, TX: Pro-Ed.

Wiederholt, J. L., & Bryant, B. R. (2001). *Gray oral reading test–4.* Austin, TX: Pro-Ed.

Wiencek, J., & O'Flahavan, J. (1994). From teacher-led to peer discussions about literature: Suggestions for making the shift. *Language Arts, 71,* 488–497.

Wigfield, A., Eccles, J. S., Schiefele, U., Roeser, R., & David-Kean, P. (2006). Development of achievement motivation. In W. Damon (Series Ed.) & N. Eisenberg (Volume Ed.), *Handbook of child psychology, social, emotional, and personality development* (6th ed., Vol. 3, pp. 933–1002). New York, NY: John Wiley.

Wigfield, A., & Guthrie, J. T. (1997). Relations of children's motivation for reading to the amount and breadth of their reading. *Journal of Educational Psychology, 89,* 420–432.

Wiggins, G. (1989). Teaching to the (authentic) test. *Educational Leadership, 46,* 141–147.

Wiggins, G. (1991): Standards, not standardization evoking quality student work. *Educational Leadership, 48,* 18–25.

Wiggins, G. (1998). *Educative assessment.* San Francisco, CA: Jossey-Bass.

Wiggins, G., & McTighe, J. (2005). *Understanding by design* (2nd ed.). Alexandria, VA: Association for Supervision and Curriculum Development.

Wilhelm, J. (2001). *Improving comprehension with think-aloud strategies: Modeling what good readers do.* New York, NY: Scholastic.

Wilhelm, J. D. (2008). *Improving comprehension with think-aloud strategies.* New York, NY: Scholastic.

Wiliam, D. (2006, September). *Assessment for learning: Why, what and how.* Paper presented at the Cambridge Assessment Network conference, Cambridge, UK. Retrieved November 22, 2010, from web. me.com/dylanwiliam/Dylan_Wiliams_web- site/Papers_04-10.html

Wilkinson, G. S., & Robertson, G. J. (1993). *Wide range achievement test 3.* Wilmington, DE: Wide Range Inc.

Wilkinson, G. S., & Robertson, G. J. (2006). *Wide range achievement test 4.* Wilmington, DE: Wide Range Inc.

Wilkinson, L. C., & Silliman, E. R. (2000). Classroom language and literacy learning. In M. L. Kamil, P. B. Mosenthal, P. D. Pearson, & R. Barr (Eds.), *Handbook of reading research* (Vol. 3, pp. 337–359). Mahwah, NJ: Erlbaum.

Wilkinson, L. C., & Silliman, E. R. (2001, February). Classroom language and literacy learning. *Reading Online, 4*(7). Retrieved July 7, 2006, from http://www.readingonline.org/articles/art_index. asp?HREF=/articles/handbook/wilkinson/index.html

Will, M. (1986). *Educating students with learning problems: A shared responsibility.* Washington, DC: Office of Special Education and Rehabilitation Services, U.S. Department of Education.

Williams, J. P. (1980). Teaching decoding with an emphasis on phoneme analysis and phoneme blending. *Journal of Educational Psychology, 72,* 1–15.

Williams, J. P. (2006). Stories, studies, and suggestions about reading. *Scientific Studies of Reading, 10,* 121–142.

Williams, J. P., Taylor, M. B., & deCani, J. S. (1984). Constructing macrostructure for expository text. *Journal of Educational Psychology, 76,* 1065–1075.

Wilson, B. A., & Felton, R. (1973; 2004). *Word identification and spelling test (WIST).* Austin, TX: Pro-Ed.

Wilson, P., Martens, P., Arya, P. (2005). Accountability for reading and readers: What the numbers don't tell. *The Reading Teacher, 58,* 622–631.

Wilson, R. M., & Cleland, C. J. (1989). *Diagnostic and remedial reading for classroom and clinic.* Columbus, OH: Charles E. Merrill.

Wilson, R. M., & Hall, M. (1990). *Programmed word attack for teachers.* Columbus, OH: Charles E. Merrill.

Wilson-Keenan, J., Solsken, J., & Willett, J. (2001). Troubling stories: Valuing productive tensions in collaborating with families. *Language Arts, 78,* 520–528.

Wilson-Portuondo, M. L., & Hardy, P. R. (2001). *When is a language difficulty a disability? The assessment and evaluation process of English language learners.* New England Equity Assistance Center, Providence: Education Alliance, Brown University. [Online Document]. Available at www.alliance.brown.edu/eac/sped-MTSL101.shtml

Windschitl, M., & Sahl, K. (2002). Tracing teachers' use of technology in a laptop computer school: The interplay of teacher beliefs, social dynamics, and institutional culture. *AERJ, 39,* 165–205.

Winograd, P., Wixson, K. K., & Lipson, M. Y. (Eds.). (1989). *Improving basal reading instruction.* New York, NY: Teachers College Press.

Wittrock, M. C., Marks, C., & Doctorow, M. (1975). Reading as a generative process. *Journal of Educational Psychology, 67,* 484–489.

Wixson, K. K. (1979). Miscue analysis: A critical review. *Journal of Reading Behavior, 11,* 163–175.

Wixson, K. K. (1983a). Postreading question-answer interactions and children's learning from text. *Journal of Educational Psychology, 30,* 413–423.

Wixson, K. K. (1983b). Questions about a text: What you ask about is what children learn. *The Reading Teacher, 37,* 287–293.

Wixson, K. K. (1984). Level of importance of postquestions and children's learning from text. *American Educational Research Journal, 21,* 419–434.

Wixson, K. K., Bosky, A. B., Yochum, M. N., & Alvermann, D. E. (1984). An interview for assessing students' perceptions of classroom reading tasks. *The Reading Teacher, 37,* 354–359.

Wixson, K. K., & Dutro, E. (1999). Standards for primary-grade reading: An analysis of state frameworks. *Elementary School Journal, 100,* 89–110.

Wixson, K. K., Dutro, E., & Athan, R. G. (2004). The challenge of developing content standards. In R. E. Floden (Ed.), *Review of research in education* (Vol. 27, pp. 69–107). Washington, DC: American Educational Research Association.

Wixson, K. K., & Lipson, M. Y. (1986). Reading (dis)ability: An interactionist perspective. In T. E. Raphael (Ed.), *Contexts of school-based literacy* (pp. 131–148). New York, NY: Random House.

Wixson, K. K., & Peters, C. W. (1989). Teaching the basal selection. In P. Winograd, K. K. Wixson, & M. Y. Lipson (Eds.), *Improving basal reading instruction* (pp. 21–61). New York, NY: Teachers College Press.

Wixson, K. K., Peters, C. W., Weber, E. M., & Roeber, E. D. (1987). New directions in statewide reading assessment. *The Reading Teacher, 40,* 749–755.

Wixson, K. K., & Valencia, S. W. (2011). Assessment in RTI: What teachers and specialists need to know. *The Reading Teacher, 64,* 466–469.

Wixson, K. K., Valencia, S., & Lipson, M. Y. (1994). Critical issues in literacy assessment: Confronting the realities of external and internal assessment. *Journal of Reading Behavior, 26,* 315–337.

Wixson, S. E. (1985). Test review: The Test of Early Reading Ability (TERA). *The Reading Teacher, 38,* 544–547.

Wolfersberger, M. E., Reutzel, D. R., Sudweeks, R., & Fawson, P. C. (2004). Developing and validating the classroom literacy environmental profile (CLEP): A tool for examining the "print richness" of early childhood and elementary classrooms. *Journal of Literacy Research, 36,* 83–144.

Wolley, J. (2011). *Reading comprehension: Assisting children with learning difficulties.* Springer.

Wolters, C., Pintrich, P. R., & Karabenick, S. A. (2003, April). *Assessing academic self-regulated learning.* Paper prepared for the Conference on Indicators of Positive Development. Sponsored by Childtrends, National Institutes of Health. Retrieved March 4, 2007, from http://www.childtrends.org/Files/Child_Trends-2003_03_12_PD_PDConfWPK.pdf

Wolters, C., Pintrich, P. R., & Karabenick, S. A. (2005). Measuring academic self-regulated learning. In K. A. Moore & L. Lippman (Eds.), *Conceptualizing and measuring indictors of positive development: What do children need to flourish?* (pp. 251–270). New York, NY: Springer.

Wong, B. Y. L., Wong, R., & Blenkisop, J. (1989). Cognitive and metacognitive aspects of learning-disabled adolescents' composing problems. *Learning Disabilities Quarterly, 12,* 300–323.

Wong, F. L. (1991). Second-language learning in children: A model of language learning in social context. In E. Bialystok (Ed.), *Language processing in bilingual children* (pp. 49–69). Cambridge, UK: Cambridge University Press.

Wong, J., & Au, K. H. (1985). The concept-text-application approach: Helping elementary students comprehend expository text. *The Reading Teacher, 38,* 612–618.

Wood, D. J., Bruner, J. S., & Ross, G. (1976). The role of tutoring in problem solving. *Journal of Child Psychology and Psychiatry, 17,* 89–100.

Wood, K. D. (1987). Fostering cooperative learning in middle and secondary school classrooms. *Journal of Reading, 31,* 10–19.

Wood, K. D. (1988). Techniques for assessing students' potential for learning. *The Reading Teacher, 41,* 440–447.

Wood, K. D., Lapp, D., & Flood, J. (1992). *Guiding readers through text: A review of study guides.* Newark, DE: International Reading Association.

Wood, K. D., & Robinson, N. (1983). Vocabulary, language, and prediction: A prereading strategy. *The Reading Teacher, 36,* 392–395.

Wood, K. D., Taylor, D. B, Drye, B., & Brigman, M. J. (2007). Assessing students' understanding of informational text in intermediate- and middle-level classrooms. In J. R. Paratore & R. L. McCormack (Eds.), *Classroom literacy assessment: Making sense of what students know and do.* New York, NY: Guilford Press.

Woodcock, R. W. (1987/1998). *Woodcock reading mastery test—Revised.* Circle Pines, MN: American Guidance Service.

Woodley, J. W. (1985). *Retrospective miscue analysis as a tool in teacher preparation in reading.* Paper presented at the Annual Meeting of the National Council of Teachers of English (4th). Houston, TX. ERIC No. ED259324.

Woods, M. A., & Moe, A. J. (2007). *Analytical reading inventory* (8th ed.). Upper Saddle River, NJ: Prentice Hall.

Wylie, R. E., & Durrell, D. D. (1970). Teaching vowels through phonograms. *Elementary English, 47,* 787–791.

Yaden, D., Tam, A., Madrigal, P., Brassell, D., Massa, J. Altamirano, L. S., & Armandariz, J. (2000). Early literacy for inner-city children: The effects of reading and writing interventions in English and Spanish during the preschool years. *The Reading Teacher, 54*(2), 186–189.

Yaden, D. B., & Tardibuono, J. M. (2004). The emergent writing development of urban Latino preschoolers: Developmental perspectives and instructional environments for second-language learners. *Reading & Writing Quarterly, 20*(1), 29–61.

Ylimaki, R., & McClain-Ruelle, L. (2005). Instructional leadership at the crossroads: Unintended outcomes of current reading policies. *Leadership and Policy in Schools, 4,* 261–280.

Yopp, H. K. (1988). The validity and reliability of phonemic awareness tests. *Reading Research Quarterly, 23,* 159–177.

Yopp, H. K. (1992). Developing phonemic awareness in young children. *The Reading Teacher, 45,* 696–703.

Yopp, H. K. (1995). A test for assessing phonemic awareness in young children. *The Reading Teacher, 49,* 20–29.

Young, K. A. (2005). Direct from the source: the value of 'think aloud' data in understanding learning. *Journal of Educational Enquiry, 6*(1), 19–33.

Young, J. P., & Brozo, W. G. (2001). Conversations: Boys will be boys, or will they? *Reading Research Quarterly, 36*(3), 316–325.

Ysseldyke, J., & Christenson, S. (2002). *Functional assessment of academic behavior.* Longmont, CO: Sopris West.

Ysseldyke, J. E., & Christenson, S. L. (1987). *The instructional environment scale (TIES).* Austin, TX: Pro-Ed.

Ysseldyke, J. E., & Christenson, S. L. (1993). *TIES-II: The instructional environment system.* Longmont, CO: Sopris West.

Zakaluk, B. L., & Samuels, S. J. (1988). Toward a new approach to predicting text comprehensibility. In B. L. Zakaluk & S. J. Samuels (Eds.), *Readability: Its past, present, and future* (pp. 121–144). Newark, DE: International Reading Association.

Zaragoza, N., & Vaughn, S. (1992). The effects of process writing instruction on three 2nd-grade students with different achievement profiles. *Learning Disabilities Research and Practice, 7,* 184–193.

Zeno, S. M., Ivens, S. H., Millard, R. T., & Duvvuri, R. (1995). *The educator's word frequency guide.* Brewster, NY: Touchstone.

Zigmond, N., Vallecorsa, A., & Leinhardt, G. (1980). Reading instruction for students with learning disabilities. *Topics in Language Disorders, 1,* 89–98.

Zion, G. (1976). *Harry the dirty dog.* New York, NY: HarperCollins.

Zutell, J., & Rasinski, T. V. (1991). Training teachers to attend to their students' reading fluency. *Theory into Practice, 30,* 211–217.

Name Index

Burke, C.L., 319, 447, 455
Burnett, C., 257
Burns, M., 22
Burns, M.S., 13, 20, 31, 38, 39, 54, 57, 167,
    247, 306, 309, 311, 312, 327, 348, 349
Burns, P.C., 617
Bursuck, W.D., 195
Bus, A.G., 320, 321
Buss, K., 268
Butkowsky, I.S., 53
Butler, D.L., 169
Buxton, W.M., 497

Cain, K., 238, 469
Caldwell, J.S., 56, 382, 383, 396, 400–402,
    457, 468, 617
Calfee, R.C., 92, 268, 481
Calkins, L.M., 180–181
Cambourne, B.L., 205
Camp, 321
Campbell, C.J., 617
Campbell, J.R., 38, 402
Campione, J.C., 543, 545, 548
Canter, 22
Carbone, 149
Carew, J.V., 42
Carlisle, J.F., 44
Carlson, K.G., 199
Carney, J.J., 94, 545, 547
Carnine, D., 412
Carpenter, P.A., 238, 239
Carpenter, R.D., 397
Carrick, C., 453
Carrol, J.H., 154
Carrow-Woolfolk, E., 370, 523, 524
Carter, M., 437, 558
Caselli, M.C., 307
Cataldo, S., 36
Cavalier, A., 254
Cazden, C.B., 152–153
Celano, D., 45
Cervetti, G.N., 249
Chabay, R., 258
Chall, J., 265, 421, 525, 550
Chambliss, M.J., 239
Chaney, C., 312
Chappuis, S., 89, 93–94
Chard, D., 210
Chard, D.J., 66, 412
Chittenden, E.A., 216, 328
Chomsky-Higgins, P., 443
Christenson, S., 218, 219
Christie, J.F., 456
Chudowsky, N., 187
Church, R., 54
Ciancio, D.J., 347–348
Cioffi, G., 545, 547
Civil, M., 194
Clark, C.H., 478, 480
Clark, K.F., 154, 178, 247
Clark-Chiarelli, N., 316
Clarke, L.K., 326
Clay, M.M., 23, 155, 160, 243, 318, 320,
    347, 355, 447, 567

Cleary, B., 267, 438
Cleborne, D., 323
Clement, J., 266
Clifford, G., 4, 5
Clifford, M.M., 155
Clinton, P., 234
Cockrum, W., 617
Codding, J.B., 334
Cohen, E.G., 158, 207
Cohen, S., 239
Coiro, J., 253, 257, 258, 285
Cole, M., 8
Coleman, M., 43
Coles, G.S., 20
Collins, V.L., 256
Combs, M., 517, 518
Commins, N.L., 177
Commodore, C., 89, 93–94
Compton, D.L., 417, 465
Connor, C.M., 43, 159, 446, 574
Connors, F., 36
Conrad, S.S., 262
Cook, A., 257, 258
Coolong-Chaffin, 22
Cooney, R.R., 148
Cooper, 309, 321
Cooper, J.D., 246, 250, 350
Cooter, K.S., 402, 617
Cooter, R.B., 402, 617
Copmann, K., 232
Copple, C., 329
Cordon, L.A., 543, 547
Cordova, D.I., 258
Corno, L., 157
Cortina, K., 44
Covington, M.V., 166
Cox, A., 321
Cox, K.E., 247
Coyne, M.D., 574, 583
Crago, M., 148
Cramer, B.B., 57
Cramer, R.L., 429, 516
Cramer, S.C., 18
Crawford, A.N., 617
Crawford, J.W., 20
Cremin, L., 5
Cress, C., 571
Critchley, M., 18
Cromley, J.G., 191
Cross, C.T., 19
Cross, D.R., 43, 169
Crossland, J., 312
Cummins, J., 20
Cunningham, A.E., 57, 313, 424, 549
Cunningham, J.W., 242, 266, 276
Cunningham, P., 571
Cunningham, P.M., 34, 160
Curtis, M.E., 421, 550
Curwen, M.S., 213, 248

Daane, M.C., 38
D'Agostino, J.V., 160
Dahlene, K.F., 157, 163
Dale, 472, 473

Dale, E., 265
Daley, K.E., 317
Dalton, B., 239, 254–256, 282
Daniels, P., 12, 151
Danner, F.W., 53
Dansereau, D., 483
Darling-Hammond, L., 157, 187, 189, 337
Davis, C.A., 279, 281, 326
Davison, A., 266
Davison, M.D., 317
Davis-Swing, J., 465
Day, J.D., 543, 547
DeBruin-Parecki, A., 338
deCani, J.S., 64
DeFillipo, F., 349
Deno, 434
Denton, C.A., 167, 208, 347–348
Dereshiwsky, M.I., 323
Dewey, J., 3, 5
Dewitz, P., 229, 241, 242, 271,
    276, 279
Díaz, E., 177
Dickinson, D.K., 257, 275, 302, 307, 314,
    315, 321, 323, 334
Dickson, B.A., 285
Dickson, S.V., 256
Diehl-Faxon, J., 321
Diehtelmiller, 328
Dillon, D.R., 183
Ding, 312
Dobler, E., 256, 257, 285
Dockstader-Anderson, K., 321
Doctorow, M., 46, 239
Dolch, E.W., 382, 419
Dole, J.A., 27, 29
Donly, B., 20
Donovan, M.S., 19, 167
Dorfman, 328
Doris, J., 65
Dorn, L., 21, 51, 65, 89, 209
Dorn, L.J., 129–130, 209
Dornan, R., 251–252
Dorner, 149
Dowdy, C.A., 21
Downing, J., 310
Doyle, W., 154–155
Drahozal, E.C., 395
Dreher, M.J., 234
Dreyer, L.G., 116, 118–119
Drye, B., 229
Duchan, J.F., 335
Duchene, J.F., 231
Duffelmeyer, F.A., 424
Duffy, G.G., 27, 29, 42, 156, 166,
    538, 583
Duffy, H., 337
Duffy-Hester, A.M., 45
DuFour, 80, 133
Duke, N.K., 45, 234, 483
Dunkeld, C.G., 397
Dunn, J., 359, 361

Subject Index

Credits

Chapter 2

Figure 2.2: Bear; Invernizzi; Templeton; Johnston, *Words Their Way: Word Study, Phonics, Vocabulary & Spelling Instruction*, 2nd Ed., ©2000. Reprinted and Electronically reproduced by permission of Pearson Education, Inc., Upper Saddle River, New Jersey.

Chapter 4

Figure 4.1: *Standards for the Assessment of Reading and Writing* (Rev. ed.). (2010). Newark, DE: International Reading Association. Reprinted with permission.; **Figure 4.5:** Copyright © 2000 by The Riverside Publishing Company Gates-MacGinitie Reading Tests® (GMRT®), Fourth Edition reproduced with permission of the publisher. All rights reserved.; **Figure 4.6:** Copyright © 2000 by The Riverside Publishing Company. Gates-MacGinitie Reading Tests® (GMRT®) with permission of the publisher. All rights reserved.; **Figure 4.7:** Stanley, A. (1916). *Animal Folk Tales*. New York: American Book Company.; **Figure 4.8:** K.E. Meyers & B.L. Reindle. (2010) *Spotlight on the comprehensive intervention model: The case of Washington School for Comprehensive Literacy*. In M.Y. Lipson & K.K. Wixson (Eds.), Successful approaches to RTI: Collaborative practices for improving K-12 literacy. Newark, DE: International Reading Association. Reprinted with permission.

Chapter 5

Figure 5.2: Instruction conversations: Promoting comprehension through discussion. C. Goldenberg, © 1993 International Reading Association. Reproduced with permission of Wiley.; **Figure 5.3:** Focused anecdotal records assessment: A tool for standards-based authentic assessment, P. Boyd-Batsone, © 2004 International Reading Association. Reprinted with permission of Wiley.; **Figure 5.10:** Reprinted with permission from Systems for Change in Literacy Education: A Guide to Professional Development by Carol A. Lyons and Gay Su Pinnell. Copyright © 2001 by Carol A. Lyons and Gay Su Pinnell. Published by Heinemann, Portsmouth, NH. All rights reserved.; **Figure 5.11:** Good, Thomas L., *Looking in Classrooms*, 4th Ed., ©1987. Reprinted and Electronically reproduced by permission of Pearson Education, Inc., Upper Saddle River, NJ 07458.; **Figure 5.12:** "FAAB Instructional Support Components," in Functional Assessment of Academic Behavior. Sandra Christenson and James Yseeldyke. © 2001. Reprinted with permission, Cambium Education, Inc., Sopris Learning.; **Figure 5.14:** "Five Standards of Authentic Instruction," by Fred M. Newmann & Gary G. Wehlage, 1993 Educational Leadership, 50(7), pp 8–12. © 1993 ASCD. Reprinted with permission. Learn more about ASCD at www.ascd.org

Chapter 6

Figure 6.1: © LAZEL, Inc. All rights reserved.; **Figure 6.2:** From *Our Country* by Ernest W. Tiegs, Gertrude S. Browns, and Fay Adams. Copyright © 1979 by Ginn and Company. Reprinted by permission of Pearson Education, Inc. All Rights Reserved.; **Figure 6.5:** A Readability Formula That Saves Time, Edward Fry, © 1968 International Reading Association. Reprinted with permission of Wiley.; **Figure 6.8:** A comparison of first-graders' reading with little books or literature-based basal anthologies, S. Menon and E. H. Hiebert, © 2005 International Reading Association. Reprinted with permission of Wiley.; **Figure 6.10:** Assessing readability: The checklist approach. Judith Westphal Irwin and Carol A. Davis, © 1980 International Reading Association. Reprinted with permission of Wiley.

Chapter 7

Figure 7.9: Rubin, Dorothy, *Teaching Elementary Language Arts: A Balanced Approach*, 6th Ed., ©2000. Reprinted and Electronically reproduced by permission of Pearson Education, Inc., Upper Saddle River, NJ 07458.; **Figure 7.10:** *Preparing Teachers for a Changing World: What Teachers Should Learn and Be Able to Do.* Darling-Hammond, L., Bransford, J., LePage, P., Hammerness, K., & Duffy, H. Copyright © 2005 Jossey–Bass. Reproduced with permission of John Wiley & Sons Inc.; **Figure 7.19:** From the PALS Literacy Assessment series. www.palsmarketplace.com; **Figure 7.20:** Early Reading Diagnostic Assessment, Second Edition (ERDA-2). Copyright © 2003 NCS Pearson, Inc. Reproduced with permission. All rights reserved.

Chapter 8

Figure 8.10: Brozo, William G.; Afflerbach, Peter P., *Adolescent Literacy Inventory, Grades 6–12*, 1st Ed., ©2011. Reprinted and Electronically reproduced by permission of Pearson Education, Inc., Upper Saddle River, NJ 07458.; **Figure 8.11:** Brozo, William G.; Afflerbach, Peter P., *Adolescent Literacy Inventory, Grades 6–12*, 1st Ed., ©2011. Reprinted and Electronically reproduced by permission of Pearson Education, Inc., Upper Saddle River, NJ 07458.; **Figure 8.12:** Brozo, William G.; Afflerbach, Peter P., *Adolescent Literacy Inventory, Grades 6–12*, 1st Ed., ©2011. Reprinted and Electronically reproduced by permission of Pearson Education, Inc., Upper Saddle River, NJ 07458.; **Figure 8.13:** Reprinted with permission from Benchmark Assessment System 1 Assessment Forms by Irene Fountas and Gay Su Pinnell. Copyright © 2011, 2008 by Irene Fountas and Gay Su Pinnell. Published by Heinemann, Portsmouth, NH. All rights reserved.; **Figure 8.14:** Reprinted with permission from Field Study of Reliability and Validity of the Fountas and Pinnell Benchmark Assessment Systems 1 and 2 commissioned by Heinemann, 2006–2007: www.heinemann.com/fountasandpinnell/researchBAS.aspx; **Figure 8.18:** Oral reading fluency norms: A valuable assessment tool for reading teachers, J. Hasbrouck and G. A. Tindal, © 2006 International Reading Association. Reprinted with permission of Wiley.; **Figure 8.19:** The new instant word list, Edward B. Fry, © 1980 International Reading Association. Reprinted with permission of Wiley.; **Figure 8.20:** Bookwords: Using a beginning word list of high frequency words from children's literature K-3, Maryann Eeds, © 1985 International Reading Association. Reprinted with permission of Wiley.; **Figure 8.22:** Adaptations of the Names Test: Easy-to-use phonics assessments, N. Mather, J. Sammons, and J. Schwartz, © 2006 International Reading Association. Reprinted with permission of Wiley.; **Figure 8.23:** Adaptations of the Names Test: Easy-to-use phonics assessments, N. Mather, J. Sammons, and J. Schwartz, © 2006 International Reading Association. Reprinted with permission of Wiley.; **Figure 8.24:** Putnam, Lillian R., How to Become a Better Reading Teacher: Strategies for Assessment and Intervention, 1st Ed., ©1996. Reprinted and Electronically reproduced by permission of Pearson Education, Inc., Upper Saddle River, New Jersey.

Chapter 9

Figure 9.2: Illustrations copyright © 1992 by Lisa McCue from *Normal Fools the Tooth Fairy* by Carol Carricl. Reprinted by permission of Scholastic Inc.; **Figure 9.6:** Miscue analysis in the classroom, Lynn K. Rhodes, Nancy L. Shanklin, and Shelia Valencia, © 1990 International Reading Association. Reprinted with permission of Wiley.; **Figure 9.8:** U.S. Department of Education, Institute of Education Sciences, National Center for Education Statistics.; **Figure 9.13:** Calfee, Robert, and Cynthia Patrick. Teach your children well: bringing K-12 education into the 21st century. Stanford, CA: Stanford Alumni Association, 1995.; **Figure 9.15:** Reprinted by permission of the Publisher. From Peter N. Winograd, Karen K. Wixson, Marjorie Y. Lipson, Editors, Improving Basal Reading Instruction, New York: Teachers College Press. Copyright © 1989 by Teachers College, Columbia University. All rights reserved.; **Figure 9.26:** Assessing study skills, Douglas B. Rogers, © 1984 International Reading Association. Reprinted with permission of Wiley.; **Figure 9.29:** Bader, Lois A.; Pearce, Daniel L., *Bader Reading and Language Inventory*, 6th Ed., ©2009. Reprinted and Electronically reproduced by permission of Pearson Education, Inc., Upper Saddle River, NJ 07458.; **Figure 9.31:** From *Language Structure and Use* by Ronald L Cramer. Copyright © 1981 Pearson Education, Inc. or its affiliates. Used by permission. All Rights Reserved.; **Figure 9.32:** Combs, Martha, Readers and Writers in the Middle Grades, 2nd Ed., ©2003, p. 237. Reprinted and Electronically reproduced by permission of Pearson Education, Inc., Upper Saddle River, New Jersey.; **Figure 9.34:** Assessing the processes students use as writers, Gail E. Tompkins, © 1992 International Reading Association. Reprinted with permission of Wiley.; **Figure 9.35:** Woodcock Reading Mastery Test, Revised Edition (WRMT-R). Copyright © 1987 NCS Pearson, Inc. Reproduced with permission. All rights reserved.